EVIDENCE

EVIDENCE

by

SIR RUPERT CROSS, F.B.A., D.C.L.

Solicitor; Vinerian Professor of English Law
in the University of Oxford and Fellow
of All Souls College, Oxford

FOURTH EDITION

LONDON

BUTTERWORTHS

1974

ENGLAND:	BUTTERWORTH & CO. (PUBLISHERS) LTD.	
	LONDON: 88 KINGSWAY, WC2B 6AB	
AUSTRALIA:	BUTTERWORTHS PTY. LTD.	
	SYDNEY: 586 PACIFIC HIGHWAY, CHATSWOOD, NSW 2067	
	ALSO AT MELBOURNE, BRISBANE, ADELAIDE AND PERTH	
CANADA:	BUTTERWORTH & Co. (CANADA) LTD.	
	TORONTO: 2265 MIDLAND AVENUE, SCARBOROUGH, MIP 451	
NEW ZEALAND:	BUTTERWORTHS OF NEW ZEALAND LTD.	
	WELLINGTON: 26/28 WARING STREET, 1	
SOUTH AFRICA:	BUTTERWORTH & CO. (SOUTH AFRICA) (PTY.) LTD.	
	DURBAN: 152/154 GALE STREET	

First Edition	.. ..	*January 1958*
Second Edition	.. ..	*June 1963*
Third Edition	.. ..	*March 1967*
Reprinted	.. ..	*October 1969*
Second Reprint	.. ..	*December 1970*
Third Reprint	.. ..	*December 1972*
Fourth Reprint	.. ..	*August 1973*
Fourth Edition	.. ..	*October 1974*
Reprinted	.. ..	*November 1975*

BUTTERWORTH AND CO. (PUBLISHERS) LTD.

1974

ISBN—Casebound: 0 406 57002 7
Limp: 0 406 57003 5

PREFACE TO THE FOURTH EDITION

In preparing this edition my three principal objectives have been to incorporate most of the English decisions together with some Commonwealth decisions of general interest reported since the publication of the third edition early in 1967, to give reasonably full accounts of the Civil Evidence Acts of 1968 and 1972, and to comment on the major proposals of the 11th Report of the Criminal Law Revision Committee. I have made a few brief references to developments in the United States, especially when they differ from the course taken by English law, even though some of them took place before the appearance of the previous edition; but the aim and scope of the book as a whole continue to be as stated in the preface to the first edition.

The fulfilment of my principal objectives has, however, necessitated a great deal of rewriting and the following list only mentions the most extensive of the changes which have been made in this edition:

1. section 1 of chapter I on the development of the law of evidence is new;

2. section 1 of chapter IV on the different burdens has been rewritten;

3. there has been a good deal of rewriting in chapter IX on corroboration, and section 3 of that chapter is new;

4. the account of legal professional privilege in chapter XI has been rewritten;

5. section 1 of chapter XII on public policy has been rewritten;

6. section 2 of chapter XVI on convictions as evidence of the facts on which they were based is new;

7. the first four sections of chapter XVIII on hearsay in civil proceedings are new; and

8. the account of the admissibility of extrinsic evidence in aid of interpretation in chapter XXI has been rewritten.

The manuscript was delivered piecemeal between 1st February and 15th May of this year with the result that it has been possible to include some, but by no means all, of the English decisions reported since 1st February in the text or else in footnotes. I have, however, found it convenient to refer to some further recent English decisions in an addendum (see pp. ix-xii). In three instances (*R. v. Edwards, R. v. Boardman* and *R. v. Bishop*) I received copies of the judgments of the Court of Appeal, and I was thus able to mention points which were not included in the account of the cases in *The Times*.

Much of the thinking which has gone into this edition began at meetings of the Criminal Law Revision Committee at which its 11th Report was under consideration and at meetings of a subcommittee of the Law Reform Committee at which the 13th, 15th, 16th and 17th Reports of the main committee were under consideration. I would like to acknowledge my indebtedness to the other members of those committees. It is not for me to say whether the inclusion of academics in such bodies improves the quality of their recommendations, but I can vouch for the improving effect of extensive discussion of evidential problems with judges and practitioners on at least one academic.

I have very much enjoyed preparing this edition and greatly appreciate the co-operation of my publishers, but notes 2 and 3 on p. xii show that the authorship of legal textbooks has its tiresome aspects.

July 1974   RUPERT CROSS

EXTRACT FROM THE PREFACE TO THE FIRST EDITION

IN the preface to the first edition of his Law of Evidence, the late S. L. Phipson said that he had endeavoured to supply students and practitioners with a work which would take a middle place between "the admirable but extremely condensed Digest of Sir James Stephen, and that great repository of evidentiary law, Taylor on Evidence". Those words were written as long ago as 1892, and Phipson's book now has claims to be regarded as *the* great English repository of evidentiary law. I realise therefore that I am flying high when I say that I hope to have supplied students and practitioners with a work which will take a middle place between those of Stephen and Phipson. The needs of students and practitioners are not, of course, identical; but I have catered for the students by including a good deal more theoretical discussion in the text than is customary in the case of a book designed solely for the practitioner, and I have catered for the latter by including many more cases in the footnotes than any student could conceivably wish to consult. Nearly all the decisions that are really important from the student's point of view are mentioned in the text. Though I have primarily borne in mind the requirements of those who are working for a law degree, I trust that the book may not prove too long for those working for the professional examinations. The long book may often be tedious, but it is sometimes more digestible than the shorter one.

I have adopted the growing practice of citing a number of decisions of the courts of the Commonwealth. My citations are not intended to be exhaustive. I have, in the main, chosen those Commonwealth decisions in which English cases have been discussed or which provide a neat illustration of what is pretty clearly English law. Should a further edition be called for, it will not be difficult to keep the Commonwealth material up to date, but I am painfully conscious of the fact that I may have omitted important matter, and I would be most grateful to any reader who draws my attention to what he considers to be a serious omission.

I have laid myself open to the charge of having quoted at too great length from English judges and American writers. My answer is that I have endeavoured to meet the undoubted need of an up-to-date account of the theory of the subject—a need that is made plain by the fact that, in nine cases out of ten, any advocate can say whether evidence is admissible or inadmissible, but he is frequently at a loss to explain why this should be so. It is impossible to give a satisfactory account of the theory of our law of evidence without frequent reference to the *ipsissima verba* of the judges and the work of such great American exponents of the subject as Thayer, Wigmore, Morgan and Maguire.

RUPERT CROSS.

ADDENDUM

PAGE
85–90 In *R.* v. *Edwards* (*The Times*, 22nd May, 1974) the Court of
Appeal held that, although there is an exception to the rule that
the prosecution bears the legal burden of proving every element
of the offence charged limited to offences arising under enactments which prohibit the doing of an act, save in specified
circumstances, or by persons of specified classes, or with
specified qualifications, or with the licence or permission of
specified authorities, it is not dependent on the fact or presumption that the defendant has peculiar knowledge enabling him to
prove the positive of a negative averment. The exception was
said to be derived from the rules of pleading, and the decision
was that, on a charge of selling intoxicating liquor without a
licence, it is not incumbent on the prosecution to adduce any
evidence that the accused was not a licensee although it is
doubtful whether the defendant's possession of a licence can be
said to be a matter peculiarly within his knowledge as it could
be verified by inspection of the local Justices' register of licences.
The court held that, in cases coming within the exception, the
legal burden of proving licence etc. is borne by the defendant.

The judgment has the great merits of avoiding problems
about the nature of "peculiar knowledge" in this context (something which is not considered in any of the cases or textbooks),
and of simplifying the law. Decisions such as that in *R.* v.
Turner (1816), 5 M. and S. 206, the principle enunciated by
Lord MANSFIELD in *R.* v. *Jarvis* (1756), 1 Burr. 148, and the
Magistrates' Courts Act, 1952, s. 81 were, for instance, treated
as examples of a single exception to the rule concerning the
burden of proof. But it is difficult to reconcile the broad
formulation of the exception with *R.* v. *Curgerwen* (1865), L.R.
1 C.C.R. 1, and the conclusion that the legal burden is borne
by the accused will not be to everyone's taste. There is of
course no difficulty in treating s. 81 of the Magistrates' Courts
Act, 1952, as an exception to the rule in *Woolmington* v. *Director
of Public Prosecutions*, [1935] A.C. 462, indeed it would be
difficult not to do so, but can the same be said with equal
confidence of s. 160 (1) (a) of the Licensing Act, 1964, with
which *R.* v. *Edwards* was concerned? The question is a difficult
one because the distinction between the legal and evidential
burdens was not present to the minds of those who decided the
earlier cases about peculiar knowledge as it was present to the
minds of those who decided *Woolmington's Case* and *Mancini* v.
Director of Public Prosecutions, [1942] A.C. 1.

96 In *R.* v. *Gray* (1973), 58 Cr. App. Rep. 177, a summing-up in
which a reasonable doubt was described as "the sort of doubt

which might affect you in the conduct of your *everyday* affairs" was held to have been defective. *R.* v. *Walters*, [1969] 2 A.C. 26, was distinguished because the summing-up which was upheld by the Judicial Committee described a reasonable doubt as "that quality and kind of doubt which, when your are dealing with matters of *importance* in your own affairs, you allow to influence you one way or another." (The italics in the above passages have been supplied.)

146 (n. 1) The statute has been reintroduced and will no doubt become law if the present Parliament survives long enough.

155 In *R.* v. *Noble* (*The Times*, 14th May, 1974) the Court of Appeal held that a husband is a competent witness for the prosecution on a charge against his wife for forging his signature. The charge was not brought by the husband, and s. 30 (3) of the Theft Act, 1968, confers competency on him in the case of "any offence with reference to" him, or property belonging to him. The unsuccessful argument for the appellant was that the sub-section only applied to offences against the property or person of the accused's spouse because s. 30 (2), dealing with charges brought against the accused's spouse is worded differently: ". . . a person shall have the same right to bring proceedings against that person's wife or husband for any offence (whether under this Act or otherwise) as if they were not married, and a person bringing such proceedings shall be competent" etc.

175 In *R.* v. *Royce-Bentley*, [1974] 2 All E.R. 347, the Court of Appeal held that, where a prosecution witness who may be an accomplice gives evidence partly favourable and partly adverse to the defence, the question whether the accomplice warning should be given is a matter of discretion.

186–187 A point not mentioned in the report of *R.* v. *Boardman* in *The Times* of 15th May, 1974, is that, while not questioning the actual decision in *R.* v. *Baldwin*, *R.* v. *Chapman*, [1973] Q.B. 774, the Court of Appeal queried the generality of the proposition that the accused's lies in court could not corroborate evidence given against him.

332, 337 In *R.* v. *Boardman* (*The Times*, 15th May, 1974) the Court of Appeal held, on charges of buggery and incitement to commit buggery, relating to two youths, that the trial judge had rightly treated the fact that the accused had invited each of them in similar terms to play the active role constituted a sufficient nexus to render the evidence on the one count admissible on the other. The accused was the head of a language school attended by the youths, and his defence was that they were lying for various reasons. The court treated *Director of Public Prosecutions* v. *Kilbourne*, [1973] A.C. 729, as authority for the proposition that evidence of this nature is admissible because of its inherent probative value. *R.* v. *Chandor*, [1959] 1 Q. B. 545, was cited in the judgment, and the cases are no doubt distinguishable on the ground that the different acts alleged against Chandor had fewer significant features in common than those alleged against Boardman, although this does seem to involve taking judicial notice of the exceptional nature of the homosexual conduct alleged against Boardman.

R. v. *Boardman* may be contrasted with *R.* v. *Wilson* (1973), 58 Cr. App. Rep. 169, where it was held that there was not a sufficient nexus between the acts alleged against the accused on charges of rape and indecent assault on different women. The only significant common features were that the accused met each woman at a dance and took her for a drive in his car. In *R.* v. *Wilson* the question was left open whether, even where there is a sufficient nexus, two acts can be said to constitute evidence of system. In *R.* v. *Boardman* the Court of Appeal gave an affirmative answer. The fact that such a question could have been raised shows how great is the danger that the use of catch words may obscure the point that the question in all these cases is whether there is anything in the *modus operandi* of the accused rendering his conduct on other occasions more than ordinarily relevant. The House of Lords has given leave to appeal in *R.* v. *Boardman.*

359 The Rehabilitation of Offenders Bill at present before Parliament contains a provision that, although a previous conviction is "spent" within the meaning of the Bill, evidence may be given of it where, by virtue of any enactment or rule of court, such evidence is made admissible at the accused's trial or at committal proceedings. (But see p. xii.)

371, 374 In *R.* v. *Bishop* (*The Times*, 14th June, 1974), the accused, who was charged with burglary sought to explain the presence of his finger prints on various articles in the prosecutor's bedroom by alleging that he had a homosexual relationship with the prosecutor and had been in the bedroom on a number of occasions. The Court of Appeal held that the trial judge had rightly allowed cross-examination on previous convictions for dishonesty under s. 1 (f) (ii) of the Criminal Evidence Act, 1898, because the allegation constituted an imputation on the character of the prosecutor, notwithstanding that homosexual acts between consenting adults in private were now legal. The Court also held that, although the words of CHANNEL, J., quoted on p. 374 of this book, state the general principle on which such cross-examination may be justified, the cross-examination is permissible in spite of the absence of any intention to discredit the prosecutor's testimony, the accused's contention being that he had simply sought to explain the presence of his finger prints in the bedroom.

1st July, 1974.

NOTES ON ADDENDUM

1. *R.* v. *Edwards* is now reported in [1974] 2 All E. R. 1085; *R.* v. *Noble* is now reported in [1974] 2 All E. R. 811; and the decision of the Court of Appeal in *R.* v. *Boardman* is now reported in [1974] 2 All E. R. 958.

2. Boardman's appeal has been dismissed by the House of Lords (*The Times*, 31st July, 1974). Unfortunately it is not possible to defer publication until their Lordships' reasons are given because this may not occur until October or November.

3. The Rehabilitation of Offenders Bill has undergone a number of changes upon which it is impossible to comment because it is impossible to obtain up-to-dates copies of the Bill.

4. *R.* v. *Isequilla* (*The Times*, 30th July, 1974) is an important decision of the Court of Appeal on the admissibility of confessions. It confirms that, in order to render a confession involuntary, an inducement emanating from a person in authority must be improper, and the passage on the accused's mental state which now appears on p. 490 of this book is accepted as a summary of the present position in England.

31st July, 1974.

TABLE OF CONTENTS

TABLE OF STATUTES

References in this Table to *Statutes* are to Halsbury's Statutes 'of England (Third Edition) showing the volume and page at which the annotated text of the Act will be found.

TABLE OF CASES

In the following Table references are given to the English and Empire Digest and its Supplements where a digest of each case will be found

A

PAGE

D

T

LIST OF ABBREVIATIONS

C.L.J.   *Cambridge Law Journal.*
H.L.R.   *Harvard Law Review.*
L.Q.R.   *Law Quarterly Review.*
M.L.R.   *Modern Law Review.*
Wigmore   *A Treatise on the Anglo-American System of Evidence*
         (3rd edition, 1940).

CHAPTER I

INTRODUCTION

The evidence of a fact is that which tends to prove it—something which may satisfy an enquirer of the fact's existence. Courts of law usually have to find that certain facts exist before pronouncing on the rights, duties and liabilities of the parties, and such evidence as they will receive in furtherance of this task is described as "judicial evidence". The principal matters covered by that term are mentioned in section 2 because the chapter begins with a brief account of the development of the law of evidence; after the main classifications of judicial evidence have been discussed in section 3, the question whether any generalisations can usefully be made concerning the admissibility of evidence will be considered. The chief general rule is that of relevancy discussed in section 5; but the best evidence rule is first examined in section 4 because it was once believed to be fundamental.

SECTION 1. THE DEVELOPMENT OF THE
LAW OF EVIDENCE

Although some of the modern rules of evidence can be traced to the middle ages, the story of their development really begins with the decisions of the common law judges in the 17th and 18th centuries. Those decisions were responsible for a complex and now almost defunct body of law concerning the competency of witnesses together with other far from defunct rules such as the rule against hearsay with its numerous exceptions, the rule excluding evidence of opinion and the rudiments of the modern law of character evidence, although this is primarily the product of 19th and 20th century case-law. The 19th and 20th centuries have witnessed a number of statutory reforms, but it is the older decisions of the common law judges which dictate the form in which much of the law of evidence must be stated, for this law still consists to a large extent of exclusionary rules, rules declaring that certain matters which might well be accepted as evidence of a fact by other responsible inquirers will not be accepted by the courts, rules declaring, in other words, what is not judicial evidence.

For instance, a careful non-judicial inquirer into the question whether A. had been unfit through drink to drive a car on a particular occasion might well attach some importance to the following: (i) the fact that X., since deceased, told a police officer that he had seen A. consume 6 large whiskies before getting in to the car; (ii) the fact that Y., a publican who tells him hesitantly a year after the event that he served A. with 6 large whiskies, signed a statement to that effect the morning after the occasion in question; (iii) the fact that Z., a police officer, tells him that he spoke to A. immediately after he got out of the car and formed the opinion that he was unfit to drive through drink. Yet all three of the above items of evidence are inadmissible at common law and would therefore be inadmissible in a criminal case to-day.

Three factors that have contributed to the exclusionary nature of the law of evidence are the jury, the oath and the English adversary system of procedure. One reason why Z.'s evidence is excluded is the fear that a jury might treat his evidence as conclusive; one reason why Y.'s signed statement is excluded is that it was not made on oath; X.'s statement is excluded partly for this reason, partly because the jury might attach undue weight to it, but mainly because the statement has never been subject to cross-examination by A.'s counsel.[1]

Allowance must also be made for a deep seated fear that evidence will be manufactured by or on behalf of the parties.

> "The presumption . . . is that no man would declare anything against himself unless it were true, but that every man, if he was in a difficulty, or in view to any difficulty, would make declarations for himself."[2]

No doubt it was this fear which lay at the root of the extraordinary common law rule that the parties to litigation were incompetent to give evidence. It was abolished for civil cases by the Evidence Act, 1851, but it was not until the Criminal Evidence Act, 1898, came into force that the accused was allowed to give evidence on his own behalf in all criminal cases.

Changes such as those which have just been mentioned are climacteric, and they have a bearing on other rules of evidence. For example, the case for excluding the statement of X. deceased that he saw A. drink 6 large whiskies in the illustration given above is far stronger when A. is not allowed to give his version of the facts than when this is no longer so. One of the troubles about the law of evidence is that changes have been made piecemeal without any consideration of their repercussion on other branches of the subject. A policy of make do and mend is liable to have particularly unfortunate results in relation to a subject as highly integrated as this department of the law.

The persistent application of the policy led one commentator to speak of the law of evidence in the following terms:

> "Founded apparently on the propositions that all jurymen are deaf to reason, that all witnesses are presumptively liars and that all documents are presumptively forgeries, it has been added to, subtracted from and tinkered with for two centuries until it has become less of a structure than a pile of builders' debris."[3]

Yet it must not be supposed that all assessments of the modern law of evidence are equally critical. In *A.-G.* v. *Horner* (No. 2)[4] HAMILTON, L.J., consoled himself with the following reflections when holding that a map was inadmissible evidence of the extent of Spitalfields market in the 18th century:

> "Generally I quite agree that I should desire to know the historical evidence about Spitalfields which, for every purpose except that of deciding the issue as to property as between private persons, nobody would think of excluding; but I yield to authority on the law of evidence without reluctance, because I

---

[1] Although Y. could be cross-examined on his signed statement at the trial, a further reason for excluding it is that he was not subject to cross-examination when it was made.
[2] *Per* EYRE, C.J., in *R.* v. *Hardy* (1794), 24 St. Tr. 199, at pp. 1093-4.
[3] C. P. Harvey, *The Advocate's Devil* (1958 edition), p. 79.
[4] [1913] 2 Ch. 140, at p. 156.

am satisfied that in the main the English rules of evidence are just, and I am satisfied also that there is no portion of the English law which ought more rigidly to be upheld. My experience is that the public have in the result derived great benefit from their strict application."

Most lawyers would, however, probably have agreed that the time had come for a comprehensive survey of the whole field when, in September 1964, the Lord Chancellor and Home Secretary referred the law of evidence in civil and criminal cases respectively to the Law Reform Committee and the Criminal Law Revision Committee. The terms of reference were:

"To review the law of evidence in civil [criminal] cases and to consider whether any changes are desirable in the interests of the fair and efficient administration of justice, and in particular what provision should be made for modifying rules which have ceased to be appropriate in modern conditions."

The Law Reform Committee produced a series of reports which resulted in the Civil Evidence Acts of 1968 and 1972.[1] The Criminal Law Revision Committee made practically all its recommendations in one highly controversial report, the 11th Report, "Evidence (General)" published in June 1972.[2] This has not yet been acted upon, and it is unlikely that some of its more controversial recommendations will be adopted for a very long time, if at all. The result of the references of 1964 has therefore been to increase the pre-existing differences between the rules of evidence in civil and criminal cases. It is still formally true to say that, subject to exceptions, the rules of evidence are the same in each instance, but the number of the exceptions, coupled with the all important fact that the rules are applied with much greater rigour in criminal proceedings, renders the statement somewhat unreal.[3] It is not suggested that the increasing discrepancy is necessarily a bad thing. The common law rules of evidence were evolved for jury trial, a procedure which is obsolescent in civil cases although it is still the mode of trial for serious criminal charges and, even in the case of less serious ones, the fact that they are for the most part heard by lay magistrates may be thought to justify a greater restriction of the area of admissible evidence than is suitable in proceedings before a legally

---

[1] Hearsay Evidence in Civil Proceedings, Cmnd. 2964 (1966); The Rule in *Hollington* v. *Hewthorn*, Cmnd. 3391 (1967); Privilege in Civil Proceedings, Cmnd. 3472 (1967); Evidence of Opinion and Expert Evidence, Cmnd. 4489 (1970). The 19th report on the Interpretation of Wills, Cmnd. 5301 (1973) contains recommendations which are relevant to the law of evidence, but has not yet been acted on. Part I of the Act of 1968 and the equivalent part of the Act of 1972 have not yet been extended to magistrates' courts. This produces a further complexity in the current law of evidence which cannot be made fully plain in this book as there is no space to deal adequately with the Evidence Act, 1938, the predecessor of the Act of 1968.

[2] Cmnd. 4991. The 9th Report, Cmnd. 3145 (1966) contained recommendations on evidence now embodied in ss. 9–11 of the Criminal Justice Act, 1967. For comment on the 11th Report see Tapper, 35 M. L. R. 621, 36 M. L. R. 66 and 167; Zuckerman, 36 M. L. R. 609; MacKenna, [1972] Crim. L. R. 605; Williams, [1973] Crim. L. R. 76 and 139; Cross, [1973] Crim L. R. 329 and 400; Muir, [1973] Crim. L. R. 341; Miller, [1973] Crim L. R. 343. Memoranda on the Report submitted to the Home Office and separately published are also of great value, notably those of the Bar Council, Law Society, Magistrates' Association and Justice.

[3] On the theoretical similarity of the rules of evidence in civil and criminal cases and their practical differences see *R. v. Christie*, [1914] A. C. 545, at pp. 559 and 564, *per* Lords MOULTON and READING respectively. The following are the principal distinguishing features of criminal cases: the standard of proof is higher; the accused is only a competent witness for the defence; unsworn evidence may be given by the accused and young children; special rules govern the competence and compellability of the accused's spouse; corroboration is necessary in more cases; the reception of hearsay evidence is governed by the common law.

qualified judge sitting alone. Nevertheless, it is doubtful whether the total inapplicability of the Civil Evidence Acts of 1968 and 1972 to criminal cases can be justified.

Subject to the solution of the vexed problem of the right extent of the difference between the rules governing civil and criminal cases, the law of evidence is a fit subject for codification. If this task is ever undertaken in England, there will be some useful precedents which are mentioned from time to time in this book. There is the Indian Evidence Act, 1872, drafted by Sir James Stephen which still forms the basis of a number of Evidence Ordinances in the Commonwealth; then there are the Model Code of Evidence published by the American Law Institute in 1942, and the Uniform Rules of Evidence published by the American Commissioners on Uniform Laws in 1953.[1] Finally there are the Federal Rules for United States Courts and Magistrates, approved by a majority of the Supreme Court in 1972, although an Act of Congress has deferred the date on which they were to come into operation.

SECTION 2. PRINCIPAL ITEMS OF JUDICIAL EVIDENCE

Judicial evidence consists of the testimony, hearsay statements, documents, things and facts which a court will accept as evidence of the facts in issue in a given case. Something will be said about each of the five items of judicial evidence after the meaning of "facts in issue" has been illustrated.

A. FACTS IN ISSUE

(i) Main facts.—The main facts in issue are all those facts which the plaintiff [2] in a civil action, or the prosecutor in criminal proceedings, must prove in order to succeed, together with any further facts that the defendant or accused must prove in order to establish a defence. A few examples will show that the main facts in issue in a particular case can only be ascertained by reference to the substantive law and the pleadings.

Suppose the plaintiff is claiming damages for personal injuries which he alleges were caused by the negligent driving of a motor car by the defendant. The question whether the defendant owed a duty of care to the plaintiff is the concern of the law of tort; the respects in which the plaintiff contends that the duty was broken are to be gathered from the particulars of negligence set out in his statement of claim; and, if negligence is denied in the defendant's defence,[3] the law of evidence indicates how the plaintiff may substantiate, or the defendant disprove, the allegations of negligence. If negligence is not denied in the defence, and there is no plea of contributory negligence, the only issue between the parties will most probably concern the amount of damages to which the plaintiff is entitled; thus the sphere of the law of evidence may be restricted to one issue by the pleadings in a given case.

---

[1] See G. D. Nokes, 5 International and Comparative Law Quarterly 347 (1956).

[2] This term must be taken to include the applicant or petitioner where appropriate, and the word "defendant" must be taken to include the respondent.

[3] Under R.S.C., O. 18, r. 13(3), every allegation of fact made in a statement of claim or counterclaim which the party on whom it is served does not intend to admit, must be specifically traversed by him in his defence or defence to counterclaim, as the case may be; and a general denial of such allegations, or a general statement of non-admission of them, is not a sufficient traverse of them. Under r. 13(4) allegations as to damage are deemed to be traversed unless admitted.

Most cases involve more than one issue. Even the simplest claims for damages for assault or breach of contract normally give rise to disputes about the amount of damages to be awarded as well as the questions whether the defendant inflicted the blows, or made the agreement, as the plaintiff contends; while further issues may be raised by the defendant by means of such pleas as those of self defence, and contractual incapacity. In criminal cases:

> "whenever there is a plea of not guilty, everything is in issue, and the prosecution has to prove the whole of their case, including the identity of the accused, the nature of the act and the existence of any necessary knowledge or intent".[1]

As Thayer has shown,[2] failure to recognise the dependence of the law of evidence on the substantive law and rules of procedure has led to the inclusion in textbooks of much that is not comprised in the subject. For example, formal admissions, and some branches of estoppel belong to the heading of procedure, while other branches of estoppel and the rules governing the admissibility of evidence of character in civil cases are based on the substantive law. These matters are briefly discussed in this book for the sake of completeness and conformity with tradition, but every endeavour is made to avoid reference to decisions that turn exclusively on the substantive law or questions of pleading.

(ii) Subordinate or collateral facts.—Subordinate or collateral facts which may be in issue are those affecting the credibility of a witness and those affecting the admissibility of certain items of evidence; they may be in issue in a particular case on account of the law of evidence itself, and not on account of the substantive law or pleadings.

An illustration of a fact of the first kind is the existence of a relationship which would tend to make a witness biased in favour of a party calling him. The witness may be asked about the relationship in cross-examination and, if denied, the relationship may be proved by the opposite party.[3]

An illustration of a fact of the second kind is due search for the original of a lost document. The general rule is that a copy may only be produced to the court when the absence of the original has been satisfactorily explained.

B. TESTIMONY

To revert to the principal items of judicial evidence, "testimony" is the assertion of a witness in court offered as evidence of the truth of that which is asserted. Nothing more need be said about it at this stage, although it will be appreciated that many of the rules of evidence, such as those concerned with the oath, the competency of witnesses and their cross-examination, are designed to ensure that testimony shall be as reliable as possible. It should also be appreciated that there is a sense in which testimony is the only item of judicial evidence. A hearsay statement, if oral, has to be narrated to the court; if contained in a document, the document has usually, though not invariably, to be produced to the court and identified by a witness. The same is true of things, and the evidentiary facts mentioned under head F. below can usually only be proved by a witness. In all the above

---

[1] *Per* Lord GODDARD, C.J., in *R. v. Sims*, [1946] K. B. 531, at p. 539; [1946] 1 All E. R. 697, at p. 701.

[2] *Preliminary Treatise on Evidence at the Common Law*, passim.

[3] *Thomas v. David* (1836), 7 C. & P. 350.

cases, however, testimony is used for a widely different purpose from that of inducing the court to accept the witness's direct assertion concerning a fact in issue, and that is why hearsay statements, documents, things, and facts though normally proved by a witness,[1] may properly be regarded as separate items of judicial evidence.

C. HEARSAY

A litigant may endeavour to prove a fact in issue by direct testimony, that is by swearing to it himself, or calling a witness to swear to it, but it sometimes happens that the best he, or his witness, can do is to depose to what someone else was heard to say on the subject, and the rule against hearsay must then be borne in mind. In spite of the etymological ineptitude the rule applies to what people wrote as well as to what they were heard to say, and to what the witness himself said out of court as well as to what he proves to have been said by others whether they are or are not called as witnesses.

The following will suffice as a succinct statement of the rule: "a statement other than one made by a person while giving oral evidence in the proceedings is inadmissible *as evidence of any fact stated*". Examples of the exclusionary effect of the rule at a trial for driving when unfit through drink have already been given on p. 1. X. deceased's statement to the police officer that he had seen A. consume 6 large whiskies was not made by a person while giving oral evidence, and it would have been tendered as evidence of the fact stated—the consumption of the whisky. Y. would have been giving evidence at A.'s trial, but his signed statement to the effect that he served A. with 6 whiskies was not made while he was testifying, and it would have been rejected, although many people might think that it was more cogent evidence of the fact stated than Y.'s testimony given at the trial a year later. The words in italics in the above formulation of the hearsay rule are crucial. If the question had been whether the police officer had reason to believe that A. had drunk 6 whiskies X.'s statement would have been admissible because it would not have been tendered to prove the fact stated, but in order to justify the officer's belief. Similarly, if it were suggested to Y. when cross-examined on behalf of A. that his testimony was a recent invention, Y.'s signed statement could be proved in re-examination, not as evidence of the fact stated, but in order to rebut the suggestion of recent fabrication.

The rule against hearsay is not stated in any statute, and it has never been definitively formulated judicially; but the formulation in the last paragraph is in effect contained in s. 1 (1) of the Civil Evidence Act, 1968. It fuses two closely connected common law rules which are also fused in a number of other formulations of the hearsay rule.[2] Under the first of these rules, the previous statements of the witness who is testifying are inadmissible as evidence of the facts stated. If the statement is consistent with the maker's testimony, it is generally inadmissible, and, even when it is admissible, it is never admissible as evidence of those facts;[3] if the state-

---

[1] The only exception is a public document which proves itself, i.e. may simply be handed to the judge.

[2] Stephen, *Digest of the Law of Evidence*, art. 15; Cowen and Carter, *Essays on the Law of Evidence*, 1; Uniform Rules, r. 63.

[3] Statements admitted as part of the *res gestae* may be an exception.

ment is inconsistent with the maker's testimony, he may be asked in cross-examination whether he made it, and, if he denies having done so, it may be proved by another witness,[1] but, at common law, it is only admissible as evidence of the facts stated if the maker is a party to the proceedings; in all other cases it merely casts doubts on the credibility of the testimony. If a non-party witness swears in court that he saw A. on January 1st, and it is proved that he previously stated that he did not see A. on that day, the previous statement is inadmissible as evidence of the negative fact; it is merely something which would justify the conclusion that it would be unsafe to act on the positive assertion contained in the testimony.

The second common law rule embodied in the statement of the rule against hearsay adapted from the Civil Evidence Act, 1968, is what may be described as "the rule against hearsay in the strict sense". The rule is that statements by persons other than the witness who is testifying are inadmissible as evidence of the facts stated. To this rule there are many exceptions at common law. For example, A. is charged with the murder of X.; when on his deathbed X. said to Y. "I know there is no hope; A. shot me; see that he is caught." Y. will be allowed to prove X.'s statement at A.'s trial, as evidence of the fact that A. shot X. This is because dying declarations by the deceased are admissible in homicide cases as evidence of the cause of death under a well known common law exception to the hearsay rule in the strict sense.

Having formulated the rule against hearsay as the fusion of the two rules which have just been mentioned, the Civil Evidence Act, 1968, proceeds to provide (subject to conditions to be mentioned in chapter XVIII) for the admissibility, as evidence of the facts stated, of the previous statements of witnesses and of those who are not called as witnesses because they are unavailable through, for example, death or illness. The common law exceptions to the rule are abolished in civil cases by the express terms of the Act. These common law exceptions continue to apply in criminal cases and there are quite a lot of statutory exceptions applicable to criminal proceedings. There is thus a number of situations in which statements which are not made by a person while giving oral evidence in the proceedings are admissible as evidence of the facts stated. It seems proper to describe these statements as "admissible hearsay statements" and a hearsay statement may be defined as "a statement other than one made by a person while giving oral evidence in the proceedings tendered as evidence of the facts stated".

When a witness is asked to narrate another's statement for some purpose other than that of inducing the court to accept it as true, his evidence is said to be "original". Original evidence may therefore be defined as evidence of the fact that a statement was made, tendered without reference to the truth of anything alleged in the statement. Examples are afforded by a witness's testimony concerning the terms of an alleged libel, or his account of the words used when one party to a contract was making an offer to the other. These examples are simple enough, but it is not always easy to distinguish original evidence from hearsay. To do so with precision has even been said to be "the chief, if not the whole difficulty of the art of judicial evidence".[2] As is the case with so many other problems relating

---

[1] Criminal Procedure Act, 1865, ss. 3–5. These sections apply to civil as well as criminal cases.

[2] Gulson, *Philosophy of Proof* (2nd edition), 279.

to this subject, it is crucially important to have regard to the purpose for which the evidence is tendered to the court. It is also necessary to beware of the terminological difficulties which beset the exposition of the entire law of evidence,[1] for the word "hearsay" is occasionally used in a broad non-technical sense to denote all statements by a witness of that which he heard someone else say. From the etymological point of view, this usage is beyond criticism but it is confusing from the point of view of the lawyer because "hearsay" has acquired a technical meaning on account of the rule which bears its name, and this only prohibits its reception as evidence of the truth of that which was heard or recorded.

D. DOCUMENTS

The contents of a document may be incorporated in the evidence of a witness who swears, for instance, that he entered into a written contract, and the court may be referred to them because they contain admissible hearsay statements, as when an entry made by a registrar of births, deaths and marriages is produced to prove one of these occurrences. Strictly speaking, the contents of a document need not be treated as a separate item of judicial evidence, although it is convenient to do so because they are governed by special rules.

E. THINGS

Things are an independent species of evidence as their production calls upon the court to reach conclusions on the basis of its own perception, and not on that of witnesses directly or indirectly reported to it. If a witness swears that he saw a knife, and that it bore bloodstains, the court is asked to assume that both statements are true; but, if the witness swears that the bloodstained knife he produces is the one he saw on a particular occasion, only one assumption has to be made by the court in order to reach a conclusion as to the condition of the knife.

F. FACTS AS EVIDENCE OF OTHER FACTS

If the only evidence that could be given of facts in issue were testimony, admissible hearsay statements, documents and things, many claims would fail for want of adequate proof. The limited scope of the evidence provided by documents and things is obvious enough, and it is not often that every fact in issue was perceived, either by a witness, or else by the maker of an admissible hearsay statement. At some stage, resort almost always has to be had to "circumstantial evidence" which may be defined as any fact (sometimes called an "evidentiary fact", "*factum probans*" or "fact relevant to the issue") from the existence of which the judge or jury may infer the existence of a fact in issue (sometimes called a "principal fact" or "*factum probandum*"). A typical instance is afforded by the statement of a witness at a trial for murder that he saw the accused carrying a blood-stained knife at the door of the house in which the deceased was found mortally wounded. The prosecutor invites the jury first, to assume that the witness is speaking the truth, and secondly, to infer that the accused inflicted the mortal wound with the knife.

---

[1] "The law of evidence has suffered in its most vital parts from an ailment almost incurable,—that of confusion of nomenclature" (V *Wigmore*, p. 20).

Evidentiary facts may be proved by testimony, admissible hearsay, documents, things and other evidentiary facts. An example of the proof of one such fact by another is afforded by the statement of a witness at a trial for murder that he saw blood on the coat pocket in which the accused's knife was found. The jury is asked, first, to assume that the witness is telling the truth, secondly, to infer that the blood on the pocket came from the knife, and finally to infer that the blood was on the knife because the accused stabbed the deceased with that weapon. This process might be prolonged still further, but as the number of steps which have to be taken from the first evidentiary fact to the ultimate inference of a fact in issue increases, the weaker becomes the former as a means of proving the latter and the opportunities of adducing evidence in favour of a contrary conclusion are increased.[1]

SECTION 3. CLASSIFICATIONS OF JUDICIAL EVIDENCE

The main division of judicial evidence is into testimonial, circumstantial and real evidence. It will be convenient to deal with the last of these items at somewhat greater length than the others because the subject is not discussed elsewhere in this book; but the remaining matters can be disposed of very briefly. The rest of the section is concerned with subsidiary divisions. One of these is that into hearsay and original evidence, but there is no need to refer to it again at this stage.

A. TESTIMONIAL, CIRCUMSTANTIAL AND REAL EVIDENCE

(1) TESTIMONIAL EVIDENCE

"Testimonial evidence" is the assertion of a human being offered as proof of the truth of that which is asserted. It includes testimony and hearsay.

(2) CIRCUMSTANTIAL EVIDENCE

"Circumstantial evidence" has already been defined as a fact from which the judge or jury may infer the existence of a fact in issue. The evidentiary fact usually has to be proved by testimony, but it is an independent item of evidence because the witness's assertion may be perfectly true, and yet the inference from the fact asserted to the fact in issue may be incorrect. Circumstantial evidence is usually contrasted with "direct evidence"—a term which is employed in two senses.

(3) THE MEANING OF DIRECT EVIDENCE

In its first sense, "direct evidence" is testimony, as contrasted with hearsay, and may therefore be defined as an assertion made by a witness in court offered as proof of the truth of *any* fact asserted by him, including his own mental or physical state at a given time. In its second sense, "direct evidence" means a witness's statement that he perceived *a fact in issue* with one of his five senses, or was in a particular mental or physical state [2] if that is in issue; and the contrast is with circumstantial evidence.

---

[1] "Arguments upon evidence are generally arguments from effects to causes; and in proportion as the number of possible causes of a given effect increases, the force of the argument is diminished. It is impossible to fix the precise point at which the argument becomes so weak as not to be worth noticing" (Stephen, *General View of the Criminal Law*, 307).
[2] From time to time it has been suggested that a witness's evidence of his own mental state is inadmissible, but it is clearly admissible under the modern law (*R. v. Fitzpatrick*

When someone swears that he saw an alleged murderer carrying a blood-stained knife, his evidence is direct in the first sense, but not in the second.

No useful purpose is served by a comparison of the merits of direct and circumstantial evidence. Although, in legal parlance, circumstantial evidence does not mean a detailed account of what happened (as it formerly did in popular speech), the phrase retains an important element of its original meaning when used by lawyers because circumstantial evidence derives its main force from the fact that it usually consists of a number of items pointing to the same conclusion. The blood on the accused's knife may not be of much significance, but additional facts, such as the accused's animosity towards the deceased, benefits to be derived by the accused from the death of the deceased, and the accused's efforts to conceal the knife may give it a very damning complexion.[1]

(4) REAL EVIDENCE [2]

Although it was devised by Bentham and adopted by Best, "real evidence" is not a term which has received the blessing of common judicial usage. There is general agreement that it covers the production of material objects for inspection by the judge or jury in court, but it is debateable how much further the term should be extended.

(i) Material objects.—If the condition of a material object is among the facts in issue, as where it is alleged that a suit made by a tailor does not fit his customer,[3] or the defendant's dog is vicious,[4] the object may be produced to the judge and jury to enable them to form their own opinion on the matter. Indeed, failure to produce such an object may be the subject of observation by the judge,[5] and, if its value is in issue, a presumption adverse to his case operates against a party who fails to produce the thing.[6]

Real evidence may be used as a means of proving facts in issue, it may also be used in an endeavour to establish relevant facts, as when a knife found in the hands of a person accused of murder is produced in order to show the jury that it bears the stains of blood. But, although the production of exhibits is a common enough occurrence, the above example shows that real evidence is of little value unless accompanied by testimony identifying it as the object the qualities of which are in issue, or relevant to the issue. It is of great value so far as it goes, but it rarely goes very far.

(ii) Appearance of persons.—A person's physical characteristics

---

(1926), 19 Cr. App. Rep. 91; *Kelly* v. *Battershell*, [1949] 2 All E. R. 830, at p. 843; II *Wigmore*, para. 581). "Direct" evidence, as contrasted with circumstantial evidence, sometimes includes hearsay and real evidence about a fact in issue as well as testimony on the same subject.

[1] "It has been said that circumstantial evidence is to be considered as a chain, and each piece of evidence as a link in the chain, but that is not so, for then, if any one link break, the chain would fall. It is more like the case of a rope comprised of several cords. One strand of the cord might be insufficient to sustain the weight, but three stranded together may be quite of sufficient strength. Thus it may be in circumstantial evidence—there may be a combination of circumstances, no one of which would raise a reasonable conviction or more than a mere suspicion; but the three taken together may create a conclusion of guilt with as much certainty as human affairs can require or admit of" (*per* POLLOCK, C.B., in *R.* v. *Exall* (1866), 4 F. & F. 922, at p. 929). See also *Thomas* v. *R.*, [1972] N. Z. L. R. 34.

[2] On the whole subject, see an article by Nokes, 65 L. Q. R. 57 (1949), and Appendix A in Best, *Principles of the Law of Evidence* (12th edition), by Phipson.

[3] Thayer, *op. cit.* p. 263 (n).

[4] *Line* v. *Taylor* (1862), 3 F. & F. 731.

[5] *R.* v. *Francis* (1874), L. R. 2 C. C. R. 128, at p. 133, *per* Lord COLERIDGE, C.J.

[6] *Armory* v. *Delamirie* (1722), 1 Stra. 505.

are frequently included among the possible items of real evidence, and these may often serve as a valuable means of proof. For instance, the fact that the accused is left-handed, tall or short, strong or weak, may frequently render it more or less probable that he committed the crime charged; a physical deformity such as a rupture may lead almost inevitably to the conclusion that a man was not guilty of rape;[1] and the resemblance which a child produced to the court bears to its alleged father or mother may be some, though very weak, evidence of parentage.[2] If, at the hearing of a claim for damages for personal injuries, the court examines those injuries or their effects, it may be said to be receiving real evidence; but great caution is exercised in allowing wounds to be exhibited owing, no doubt, to the prejudice which might be excited.[3] Again, the court is acting on real evidence when it determines the age of a child by inspection.[4]

(iii) **Demeanour of witnesses.**—The late Professor Nokes included the demeanour of witnesses among the items of real evidence. If a witness gives his evidence in a forthright way, unperturbed by cross-examination, the court will no doubt be more disposed to believe him than would be the case with a halting and prevaricating witness. So far as its bearing on the facts in issue is concerned, this type of demeanour is analogous to the anwers given by a witness who is being cross-examined as to credit, and may rightly be regarded as evidence in the case.

When the court acts on the remarks or behaviour of a witness as constituting a contempt, it may be said to accept real evidence because it is not asked to do more than act on its powers of perception in determining the existence of a fact in issue—the contemptuous conduct.

(iv) **View.**—Doubts have been expressed about the true nature of the information derived from a view out of court.[5] It seems clear that when that which is shown at the view is something that might have been produced as an exhibit had it been convenient to do so, as when omnibuses are

---

[1] 1 Hale, P. C., pp. 635–636.

[2] *Burnaby* v. *Baillie* (1889), 42 Ch. D. 282; *Slingsby* v. *A.G.* (1916), 33 T. L. R. 120, at p. 122, where Lord LOREBURN regarded such evidence as of some weight, and Lord SHAW regarded it as worthless except where there was a difference in colour between the alleged parent and child; *Russell* v. *Russell and Mayer* (1923), 129 L. T. 151, at p. 153, where the evidence was admitted, but spoken of as unsafe and conjectural; *C.* v. *C. and C.*, [1972] 3 All E. R. 577 (photographic evidence of resemblance of child to alleged father admissible).

[3] See *Gray* v. *La Fleche, Saskatchewan Power Corporation* (1962), 31 D. L. R. (2d) 189, showing that the fact that liability is admitted makes a difference. In *Niznik* v. *Johnson* (1961), 28 D. L. R. (2d) 541 motion pictures were shown to the court in order to establish the fact that the plaintiff's manifestations of pain in court were faked. See also *Stevens* v. *William Nash, Ltd.*, [1966] 3 All E. R. 156 and *Draper* v. *Jacklyn* (1969), 9 D. L. R. (3d) 264.

[4] Children and Young Persons' Act, 1933, s. 99. In *R.* v. *Colgan*, [1959] S. R. (N. S. W.) 96, it was held that, subject to the judge's discretion, it was proper to allow the jury to see a girl alleged to be mentally defective with whom the accused was charged with having had intercourse, although the girl was not called as a witness.

[5] This matter is fully discussed in a case note on *Chambers* v. *Murphy*, [1953] 2 D. L. R. 705, in 31 Canadian Bar Review, 205. The actual decision in *Chambers* v. *Murphy* was disapproved in *Meyers* v. *Governments of Manitoba and Dobrowski* (1961), 26 D. L. R. (2d) 550, where the authorities are fully reviewed. Precautions must always be taken to ensure that both parties have an opportunity of being present, and that the tribunal does not act on information privately obtained. It is essential that the judge should be present when an occurrence is reconstructed by witnesses: *Tameshwar* v. *R.*, [1957] A. C. 476. [1957] 2 All E. R. 683. In *Salsbury* v. *Woodland*, [1970] 1 Q. B. 324; [1969] 3 All E. R. 863, it was held to be in order for the judge to go by himself to inspect a public place (the road on which an accident occurred) of which plans and photographs had been produced in court. The view is then a "visit" as distinct from a "demonstration". It is desirable for a judge to give notice of his intention to make a visit.

examined in the yard of the court,[1] or the tribunal visits the *locus in quo*
so that witnesses can show where they were standing at the material time,[2]
the court is being asked to act on real evidence; but what if the judge and
jury are taken to a factory where an accident occurred and the entire
happening is reconstructed? In *Goold* v. *Evans & Co.*,[3] DENNING, L.J.,
spoke of the view as real evidence, but HODSON, L.J., treated it as something
which enabled the court the better to understand the evidence which had
already has been given by witnesses, and this is the view taken by the High
Court of Australia.[4] In *Buckingham* v. *Daily News, Ltd.*,[5] the Court
of Appeal held that the trial judge had rightly taken into account his
opinion of the working of the machine formed at a view. PARKER, L.J.,
said that the occurrences at the view were part of the evidence; it was as if
the machine had been brought into the well of the court and the plaintiff
had there demonstrated what had occurred on the occasion under enquiry.
It is submitted that what takes place at a view is a species of real evidence.

(v) Tape-recordings.[6]—When a court permits a tape-recording to be
played over, it is acting on real evidence if it treats the intonation of the words
as relevant. If the court's attention is directed solely to the terms of the
recording, it may be considering whether to act on a hearsay statement,
as when a recorded conversation is received as evidence of an admission by
one of the parties, or the court may receive the recording as original evidence,
as when a recording of slanderous words is admitted in order to show that the
words were in fact spoken.

At a trial by jury the party relying on the tape-recording must satisfy
the judge that there is a prima facie case that it is the original, and it must
be sufficiently intelligible to be placed before the jury. The evidence must
define and describe the provenance and history of the recording up to the
moment of its production in court.[7] If a transcript of the recording is put
in evidence the court will of course have to be satisfied of its accuracy. It
has accordingly been held in Scotland that a typist who prepares a transcript after familiarising herself with the contents of a recording by playing
it over many times, may be treated as an expert for the particular occasion,
her evidence verifying the transcript as truly representing the contents of
the recording being evidence of expert opinion.[8]

---

[1] *London General Omnibus Co., Ltd.* v. *Lavell*, [1901] 1 Ch. 135, where, however,
the Court of Appeal regarded the evidence as insufficient; too much importance has been
attached to the *dicta* of Lord ALVERSTONE, C.J. in this case, see *R.* v. *De Grey, Ex parte
Fitzgerald* (1913), 109 L. T. 871. Where relevant, musical or dramatic performances may
be given in or out of court.

[2] *Karamat* v. *R.*, [1956] A. C. 256, [1956] 1 All E. R. 415, where the view was treated
as a substitute for, or supplementary to photographs and plans. See also *R.* v. *Martin*
(1872), L. R. 1 C. C. R. 378.

[3] [1951] 2 T. L. R. 1189.

[4] *Railways Commissioner* v. *Murphy* (1967), 41 A. L. J. R. 77.

[5] [1956] 2 Q. B. 534; [1956] 2 All E. R. 904; see also *Webster* v. *Burns*, [1964] N. Z. L. R.
749.

[6] See articles in [1954] Criminal Law Review 96, and [1961] Criminal Law Review 598.
Many of the relevant authorities are cited in *R.* v. *Maqsud Ali; R.* v. *Ashiq Hussain*, [1965]
2 All E. R. 464.

[7] *R.* v. *Robson and Harris*, [1972] 2 All E. R. 699, differing from *R.* v. *Stevenson*, [1971]
1 All E. R. 678 where it was suggested that the judge might have to be satisfied beyond
reasonable doubt that the recording was the original. See also *R.* v. *Matthews and Ford*,
[1972] V. R. 3, in which it was held that the rule requiring production of the original
writing did not apply to tape recordings which were treated as photographs or things as to
which secondary evidence could be received in the absence of an explanation of the nonproduction of the original.

[8] *Hopes and Lavery* v. *H.M. Advocate*, 1960 S. C. (J.) 104.

In *R.* v. *Senat* and *R.* v. *Sin*[1] tape-recordings of incriminating telephone conversations tapped on behalf of a party to divorce proceedings were held to have been rightly admitted at a criminal trial. If the tapping had been the work of the police acting without due authorisation, a problem relating to the admissibility of illegally obtained evidence might have been raised. The method by which a recording was obtained could give rise to a claim that the evidence concerning it should be excluded in the public interest,[2] or to a claim that the recording should be excluded as an improperly obtained confession.

In *The Statue of Liberty*[3] a shore radar station's cinematograph film strips and recordings of echoes of ships in the Thames were admitted as real evidence. The recording was not monitored, but "the law is bound these days to take cognisance of the fact that mechanical means must replace human effort."[4]

(vi) Documents.—A document may be put in evidence either as a chattel—a substance such as a paper or parchment bearing an inscription, or else as a statement—the inscription on the substance. When treated as a chattel, there is no doubt that it constitutes real evidence, as when a deed alleged to have been stolen is produced to the court in order to show that it bears the finger-prints of the accused. When treated as a statement, a document constitutes testimonial evidence in the vast majority of cases; but it may be used as circumstantial evidence, as when ancient leases are tendered to prove that the lessor, through whom the plaintiff claims a prescriptive title, was in possession of the *locus in quo*.

> "Ancient documents coming out of proper custody, and purporting on the face of them to show exercise of ownership, such as a lease or licence, may be given in evidence . . . as being in themselves acts of ownership and proof of possession."[5]

Although it is produced and identified by a witness, the document is not incorporated in his testimony as having been written or read by him, neither are its contents tendered as proof of anything they may assert. It is offered to the court as the kind of document which would only have been executed by someone in possession. In other words, its existence is a relevant fact proved by real evidence—the production of a material object for examination by the court.

Conclusion.—On the basis of the above discussion, the following would be a broad description of real evidence. "Real evidence is anything other than testimony, admissible hearsay or a document, the contents of which are offered as testimonial evidence, examined by the tribunal as a means of proof." It must be admitted, however, that most definitions or descriptions of real evidence are considerably narrower than this one.[6]

B. ORAL AND DOCUMENTARY EVIDENCE

Oral evidence consists of statements made in court by witnesses,

---

[1] (1968), 52 Cr. App. Rep. 282.
[2] *State* v. *Peake*, 1962 (3) S. A. 572.
[3] [1968] 2 All E. R. 195.
[4] Sir Jocelyn SIMON, P.
[5] *Malcolmson* v. *O'Dea* (1863), 10 H. L. Cas. 593, at p. 614, *per* WILLES, J.
[6] According to Phipson, "Real evidence" consists of "material objects other than documents produced for inspection of the court": *Law of Evidence*, (11th Edition), 3. Professor Nokes applies the term to "any thing other than a document which is examined by the tribunal as a means of proof": *Introduction to Evidence* (4th Edition), 452.

whether they are direct assertions of fact or narrated hearsay statements, and whatever category of admissible facts they may concern. Documentary evidence consists of documents produced for inspection by the judge and jury. Documents may be used as testimonial, circumstantial or real evidence, and, when used as testimonial evidence, their contents may be direct evidence, or hearsay. The distinction between oral and documentary evidence is important because special rules apply to the proof of the contents of documents, but it does not require detailed discussion.

C. PRIMARY AND SECONDARY EVIDENCE

"Primary evidence" is that which does not, by its very nature, suggest that better evidence may be available; "secondary evidence" is that which, by its very nature, does suggest that better evidence may be available. The original of a document is primary evidence, a copy secondary evidence, of its contents. The distinction is now mainly of importance in connection with documents, because their contents must, as a general rule, be proved by production of the original, but it used to be of much greater significance on account of the "best evidence" rule which occupied a prominent place in books on the law of evidence in the eighteenth and early nineteenth centuries.

SECTION 4. THE BEST EVIDENCE RULE [1]

The classic statement of the best evidence rule is that of Lord HARD-WICKE when he said that "the judges and sages of the law have laid it down that there is but one general rule of evidence, the best that the nature of the case will allow".[2] This comes from a judgment in which it was held that a Gentoo was a competent witness, although his evidence was not given on the Gospel, and it seems that Lord HARDWICKE was thinking of the rule as inclusionary as much as exclusionary. His view appears to have been that, where there was nothing better, recourse might be had to evidence which would be inadmissible in other cases; but the typical illustrations of the rule are provided by cases in which evidence is excluded because better was available.

Two such illustrations may be mentioned, although neither of them represents the modern law. In *Chenie* v. *Watson*,[3] oral evidence concerning a bushel measure was rejected because the measure ought to have been produced, and in *Williams* v. *East India Co.*[4] it was held that circumstantial evidence could not be given of a fact as to which direct evidence was available. The plaintiff claimed damages from the defendant for having caused the destruction of his ship by placing inflammable cargo on board without notice. The plaintiff could not call the ship's mate who received the goods because he was dead, but he adduced evidence which tended to show that notice had not been given. For example, he called the captain who swore that he would have been informed if the mate had been notified of the presence of inflammable material. The plaintiff was nonsuited because of his failure to call the officer of the defendant who put the goods on board.

---

[1] On the whole subject see Thayer, *A Preliminary Treatise on Evidence at the Common Law*, ch. 11.

[2] *Omychund* v. *Barker* (1745), 1 Atk. 21, at p. 49.

[3] (1797), Peake Add. Cas. 123.

[4] (1802), 3 East 192.

Phipson once said that "perhaps the most conspicuous feature of the modern law is its persistent recession from this once famous principle",[1] and he was justified whether the inclusionary or exclusionary aspect of the best evidence rule be under consideration.

(i) The inclusionary aspect.—If the only rule really were that a party must produce the best evidence of which the nature of the case will allow, hearsay ought to have been admitted at common law in many instances in which it was undoubtedly excluded. If A. sued B. on a deed, and B.'s defence was that the deed was improperly altered after execution by the attesting witness (since deceased), letters written by the attesting witness referring to the alteration were inadmissible on B's behalf, although they were the best evidence of which the nature of his case would allow because the witness was dead.[2] Again, if there were a rule to the effect that evidence is admissible if it is the best that a person can produce, the rules governing the competency of witnesses should be modified as the occasion demands; but there is no doubt that such rules as that which generally prohibits a prosecutor from calling the wife of the accused apply, even if no other evidence is available.[3]

(ii) The exclusionary aspect.—The doctrine of *Chenie* v. *Watson* was repudiated by the Court for Crown Cases Reserved in *R.* v. *Francis* [4] where it was held that the prosecutor was under no obligation to produce a ring by means of which the accused was alleged to have obtained money by false pretences, and *Williams* v. *East India Co.* is no longer law so far as the point turning on the admissibility of the circumstantial evidence is concerned.[5] A literal construction of Lord HARDWICKE's rule would also seem to require that hearsay should have been rejected, even in cases falling within one of the exceptions to the rule excluding it, if direct evidence was available; but a deceased mother's statement of the time of the birth of her child was received as evidence of that fact under a recognised exception to the rule against hearsay, although the child's father who might have been present at the birth was alive, and could have been called as a witness.[6]

(iii) The remains of the rule.—It is sometimes said that all that is left of the best evidence rule is the requirement that the original of a private document must be produced in order to prove its contents unless its absence can be explained;[7] apart from this, it is said that the rule is merely a counsel of prudence for the absence of the best evidence may always be the subject of adverse comment by the judge. There are, however, a few decisions which can be cited as isolated instances of the continued applica-

---

[1] *Law of Evidence* (11th edition), 61.

[2] *Stobart* v. *Dryden* (1836), 1 M. & W. 615. The letters would now be admissible under the Civil Evidence Act, 1968; if B. were being prosecuted for uttering a forged document, the letters would still be inadmissible as evidence of the forgery.

[3] Cf. *R.* v. *Algar*, [1954] 1 Q. B. 279; [1953] 2 All E. R. 1381.

[4] (1874), L. R. 2 C. C. R. 128, followed in *Hocking* v. *Ahlquist Brothers, Ltd.,* [1944] K. B. 120; [1943] 2 All E. R. 722. See also *R.* v. *Hunt* (1820), 3 B. & Ald. 566, and *Lucas* v. *Williams & Sons*, [1892] 2 Q. B. 113.

[5] Phipson, *Law of Evidence* (11th edition), 61; *Dowling* v. *Dowling* (1860), 10 I. C. L. R. 236.

[6] Baker, *The Hearsay Rule* 4, citing *R.* v. *Birmingham* (1829), 8 L. J. O. S. M. C. 41 from Hubbock's *Evidence of Succession.*

[7] *Garton* v. *Hunter*, Lord [1969] 1 All E. R. 451, at p. 453, *per* DENNING, M. R. This rule antedated the best evidence rule.

tion of the rule [1] although it has long since lost its title to be regarded as a general principle of the law of evidence. Thus, in *R. v. Quinn and Bloom*,[2] a film purporting to be a reconstruction of the strip-tease act on account of which the accused were charged with keeping a disorderly house was held to be inadmissible because it was not the best evidence. The case can only be distinguished from those in which a view has been allowed to take place at a factory in order to reconstruct an accident[3] on the ground that there was a far greater danger that the performance of the participants in the film (among whom a snake was included) would not have been an accurate reconstruction.

> "It would be almost impossible to analyse motion by motion these slight differences which may in the totality result in a scene of quite a different character than that performed on the night in question." [4]

R. v. Quinn and Bloom also shows that the distinction between the admissibility and weight of evidence, discussed in the next section, is not clear-cut because, in an extreme case, unreliable evidence may be inadmissible and weight may thus affect admissibility.

SECTION 5. RELEVANCE, ADMISSIBILITY AND WEIGHT OF EVIDENCE

The main general rule governing the entire subject is that all evidence which is sufficiently relevant to an issue before the court is admissible and all that is irrelevant, or insufficiently relevant, should be excluded.[5] The affirmative aspect of this rule (the exceptions to which constitute the bulk of the law of evidence) and its negative aspect (to which there are no exceptions) must be considered separately. When this has been done the distinction between the relevancy, admissibility and weight of evidence will be examined.

A. THE ADMISSIBILITY OF RELEVANT EVIDENCE

(1) DEFINITION OF RELEVANCE

It is difficult to improve upon Stephen's definition of relevance when he said that the word "relevant" means that:

> "any two facts to which it is applied are so related to each other that according to the common course of events one either taken by itself or in connection with other facts proves or renders probable the past, present, or future existence or non-existence of the other".[6]

Elsewhere the same writer suggested as a test for determining whether one fact should be regarded as evidence of, or relevant to another, that the

---

[1] *Morris* v. *Miller* (1767), 4 Burr. 2057, and *R.* v. *Christie*, [1914] A. C. 545 (so far as the admissibility of the evidence by the mother and policeman of the boy's act of identification was concerned); but see *R.* v. *Osborne* and *R.* v. *Virtue*, [1973] Q. B. 678; [1973] 1 All E. R. 649.

[2] [1962] 2 Q. B. 245; [1961] 3 All E. R. 88.

[3] *Goold* v. *Evans & Co.*, [1951] 2 T. L. R. 1189; *Buckingham* v. *Daily News, Ltd.*, [1956] 2 Q. B. 535; [1956] 2 All E. R. 904 (p. 12, *ante*).

[4] *Per* ASHWORTH, J. in *R.* v. *Quinn and Bloom*, *supra*.

[5] See *per* GODDARD, L.J. in *Hollington* v. *Hewthorn & Co., Ltd.*, [1943] K. B. 587 at p. 594; [1943] 2 All E. R. 35, at p. 39.

[6] *Digest of the Law of Evidence* (12th edition), art. 1.

matter under discussion should be cast into the form of a syllogism of which the alleged evidentiary fact constitutes the minor premise; it is then only necessary to consider whether the major premise is a proposition the truth of which is likely to be accepted by the person who has to draw the conclusion—in the case of a lawsuit, a reasonable man.[1] For example, suppose that goods were found in the possession of the accused shortly after they were missed, and he was unable or unwilling to give an adequate explanation of the manner in which he came by them. These would be relevant facts on a charge of stealing because, if the matter were cast into the form of a syllogism, it could be stated in the following way: men found in possession of goods which have recently been missed are frequently guilty of stealing them if they do not give an adequate explanation of their possession (major premise); the accused was found in possession of the goods in question shortly after they were missed, and he gave no adequate explanation of this fact (minor premise); therefore the accused may have been guilty of stealing the goods (conclusion). As the validity of the major premises on which courts are invited to act can usually be taken for granted, the deductive method outlined above is seldom used in practice, but the test of the syllogism may be found useful whenever there is any doubt about the relevance of evidence.

(2) EXCEPTIONS

This general rule that all relevant evidence is admissible is, however, subject to numerous exceptions because:

> " our law . . . undoubtedly excludes evidence of many matters which anyone in his own daily affairs of moment would regard as important in coming to a decision." [2]

The following four exceptions are frequently stressed, but there are many others.

(i) Hearsay.—Hearsay which is highly relevant on account of the contents of the statement and because the circumstances in which it was made greatly enhance the probability of its truth is often excluded, as when an attesting witness's death-bed confession of having altered a deed was rejected in an action on the document.[3]

(ii) Opinion.—Witnesses are generally not allowed to inform the court of the inferences they draw from facts perceived by them, but must confine their statements to an account of such facts.

> " It frequently happens that a bystander has a complete and full view of an accident. It is beyond question that, while he may inform the court of everything which he saw, he may not express an opinion on whether either or both of the parties were negligent." [4]

Opinion is often said to be excluded because it is irrelevant, but some-

---

[1] *General View of the Criminal Law*, 236.

[2] *Per* DARLING, J., in *R. v. Bond*, [1906] 2 K. B. 389, at p. 410. See also the remarks of HAMILTON, L.J., p. 2, *ante*.

[3] *Stobart v. Dryden* (1836), 1 M. & W. 615. The confession could now be proved under the Civil Evidence Act, 1968, but it would still be inadmissible as evidence that the deed was forged in a criminal case.

[4] *Per* GODDARD, L.J., in *Hollington v. F. Hewthorn & Co., Ltd.*, [1943] K. B. 587, at p. 595; [1943] 2 All E. R. 35, at p. 40.

thing more will have to be said on this subject in Chapter XVI; expert witnesses may testify to their opinion on matters involving their expertise.

(iii) Character.—An accused person's reputation among his neighbours as a man likely to have committed the offence charged is usually inadmissible evidence of his guilt, although it might be regarded as a relevant fact, and witnesses' opinions about a person's disposition to act in a particular way are generally excluded.

(iv) Conduct on other occasions.—It might be thought that the fact that someone behaved in a particular way on one occasion is relevant to the question whether he behaved in a similar fashion on the occasion which is being considered by the court, merely by reason of the general tendency of human behaviour to repeat itself. Nevertheless, evidence may generally not be given of a party's misconduct on other occasions if its sole purpose is to show that he is a person likely to have conducted himself in the manner alleged by his adversary on the occasion which is under enquiry.

"You must not prove, for example, that a particular engine driver is a careless man in order to prove that a particular accident was caused by his negligence."[1]

(3) MULTIPLE RELEVANCE AND ADMISSIBILITY

An item of evidence may be relevant for more than one reason. In other words, the major premise of a syllogism may be altered, although the minor premise and conclusion remain the same. To enlarge upon an example cited in an old case,[2] suppose that A is charged with stealing a shirt from B.'s house, that shortly before the alleged theft a shirt was stolen from C.'s house, and that C.'s shirt was found in B.'s house in circumstances suggesting that it had been inadvertently left there by the person who stole B.'s shirt. Evidence tending to show that A. stole C.'s shirt might be regarded as relevant on either of the following grounds: (i) people who steal one thing frequently steal another, A. stole C.'s shirt, therefore A. probably stole B.'s shirt; (ii) the man who stole B.'s shirt probably had C.'s shirt in his possession, A. stole C.'s shirt, therefore A. probably stole B.'s shirt. The first argument is of a general nature and is based on the tendency of thieves to repeat their conduct; the second is more specific and is based on the particular facts of the case. The evidence would be inadmissible on the first ground because it would merely show bad disposition, but it would be admissible on the second ground as tending to identify the thief of B.'s shirt.

If evidence is admissible for one purpose, it cannot be rejected on the ground that it is inadmissible for some other purpose. For instance, if a brother and sister are charged with incest, the brother's admission of intercourse may be proved by a prosecution witness as evidence against him of that fact since admissions may be proved against the accused who makes them under an exception to the rule against hearsay, but, because of

---

[1] *Per* STEPHEN, J., in *Brown* v. *Eastern and Midlands Rail. Co.* (1889), 22 Q. B. D. 391, at p. 393. The context makes it plain that STEPHEN, J., was concerned with conduct on other occasions as proof of disposition. See also *R.* v. *Westfield Freezing Co.*, [1951] N. Z. L. R. 456.

[2] *R.* v. *Whiley* (1804), 2 Leach 983, at p. 985. Cf. *R.* v. *O'Meally* (*No.* 2), [1953] V. L. R. 30 (proceeds of robberies left at scene of murder, accused's participation in the robberies could be proved); *R.* v. *Sims*, [1967] Qd. R. 432 (prison boot found near house broken into by escaped prisoner).

that rule, it is not evidence against the sister that she had intercourse with her brother.[1]

Wigmore described the principle involved as one of "multiple admissibility".[2] The term is not particularly well chosen, because it suggests that evidence may be admissible for more than one purpose. This is undoubtedly true, but the point of the rule under consideration is that evidence may be admissible for one purpose although it is inadmissible for another. It is, however, difficult to suggest anything better, and, although the term is not employed by English judges, the doctrine it embodies is mentioned in numerous dicta. The doctrine is fraught with danger, but the total exclusion of the evidence would be productive of even greater injustice.[3] The number of occasions on which it is necessary to act on the doctrine has been reduced by the provisions of the Civil Evidence Act, 1968, under which hearsay statements are admissible, and it would be still further reduced by their extension to criminal cases.

B. THE INADMISSIBILITY OF IRRELEVANT, AND INSUFFICIENTLY RELEVANT EVIDENCE

(1) ILLUSTRATIONS

A few illustrations may be given of the exclusion of evidence which is irrelevant, or insufficiently relevant, to any issue before the court.

(i) Remoteness.—In *Hart* v. *Lancashire and Yorkshire Rail. Co.*,[4] the fact that the defendant's method of changing the points was altered after an accident was held to be inadmissible as evidence that the accident was caused by the defendant's negligence. According to BRAMWELL, B.:

> "People do not furnish evidence against themselves simply by adopting a new plan in order to prevent the recurrence of an accident. Because the world gets wiser as it gets older, it was not therefore foolish before."

---

[1] *Rutherford* v. *Richardson*, [1923] A. C. 1; *Morton* v. *Morton*, [1937] P. 151, at pp. 154–155; [1937] 2 All E. R. 470, at p. 473. These were divorce cases founded on adultery; the admission of the one party would now be evidence against the other under the Civil Evidence Act, 1968.

[2] I *Wigmore*, para. 13.

[3] "No doubt it renders the administration of justice more difficult when evidence which is offered for one purpose or person, may incidentally apply to another; but that is an infirmity to which all evidence is subject, and exclusion on such a ground would manifestly occasion greater mischief than the reception of the evidence" (TINDALL, C.J., in *Willis* v. *Bernard* (1832), 8 Bing. 376, at p. 383). "It often happens, both in civil and criminal cases, that evidence is tendered on several alternative grounds, and yet it is never objected that if on any ground it is admissible, that ground must not prevail, because on some other ground it would be inadmissible and prejudicial." In such cases it is usual for the judge (not always very successfully) to caution the jury against being biased by treating the evidence in the objectionable sense" (*per* JELF, J., in *R.* v. *Bond*, [1906] 2 K. B. 389, at p. 411). There is, however, no rule of practice requiring such a warning to be given, the matter is entirely one for the judge's discretion (see *per* MURRAY, C.J., in *R.* v. *Kennewell*, [1927] S. A. S. R. 287, at p. 302).

[4] (1869), 21 L. T. 261. Cf. *State Electricity Commission of Victoria* v. *Gay*, [1951] V. L. R. 104, at p. 116 (change in lighting system after accident admissible to show warning could have been given before accident) and *Anderson* v. *Morris Wools Pty., Ltd.*, (1965) Qd. R. 65 (evidence of alteration of machine after accident admissible to show precaution which might have been taken). The U.S. Federal Rules, r. 407 reads: "When, after an event, measures are taken which, if taken previously, would have made the event less likely to occur, evidence of the subsequent measures is not admissible to prove negligence or culpable conduct in connection with the event. This rule does not require the exclusion of evidence of subsequent measures when offered for another purpose, such as proving ownership, control, or feasibility of precautionary measures, if controverted, or impeachment."

In *Hollingham* v. *Head*,[1] the defence to an action for the price of guano was that an express condition in the contract of sale provided that the goods should be equal to Peruvian guano. The defendant wished to call witnesses to swear that the plaintiff had entered into contracts with other customers containing a term similar to that for which he contended, but the Court of Common Pleas held that he was not entitled to do so.

> "It may be often difficult to decide upon the admissibility of evidence, where it is offered for the purpose of establishing probability, but to be admissible it must at least afford a reasonable inference as to the principal matter in dispute." [2]

In *Holcombe* v. *Hewson*,[3] a brewer claimed damages for breach of a publican's covenant to buy beer from him. The defence was that the plaintiff had supplied bad beer, and evidence to the effect that he had supplied other publicans with good beer was rejected. He "might deal well with one and not with the others".[4]

Relevancy is a matter of degree and it is as idle to enquire as it is impossible to say whether the evidence was rejected in the above two cases because it was altogether irrelevant, or merely because it was too remotely relevant; but there are decisions in which evidence has been held to be inadmissible on the score of insufficient relevancy when it would, by common consent, have been of considerable probative value if it had been easy to examine and adequately reliable, for two facts which may affect the relevance of evidence for the purpose of a legal enquiry are the danger that it will give rise to a multiplicity of issues, and the danger that it might have been manufactured.

(ii) Multiplicity of issues.—The judgment of WILLES, J., in *Hollingham* v. *Head* contains a timely reminder that litigants are mortal, and ROLFE, B., once pertinently observed that:

> "if we lived for a thousand years instead of about sixty or seventy, and every case was of sufficient importance, it might be possible, and perhaps proper . . . to raise every possible enquiry as to the truth of statements made. . . . In fact mankind finds it to be impossible." [5]

Evidence which might even be highly relevant in a protracted academic investigation is treated as too remote from the issue in a forensic enquiry because the body which has to come to the conclusion is controlled by the time factor, not to mention considerations such as the danger of distracting the jury,[6] and the undesirability of pronouncing upon matters which are not being litigated. Thus, in *Agassiz* v. *The London Tramway Co.*,[7] the plaintiff, a passenger on a tram, claimed damages for personal injuries caused by a collision which she contended was due to the negligence of the driver. She tendered the evidence that she heard a fellow passenger tell the conductor that the driver ought to be reported, only to be met by the disconcertingly frank reply "he has already been reported, for he has been

---

[1] (1858), 27 L. J. C. P. 241.
[2] *Per* WILLES, J., at p. 242.
[3] (1810), 2 Camp. 391. Cf. *R.* v. *Whitehead* (1848), 3 Car. & Kir. 202, where, on a charge of manslaughter against a doctor, evidence of his skilful treatment of other patients was excluded.
[4] *Per* Lord ELLENBOROUGH, C.J.
[5] *A.-G.* v. *Hitchcock* (1847), 1 Exch. 91, at p. 105.
[6] "The fewer and simpler the issues left to the jury, the less chance there is of a miscarriage of justice" (*per* BYRNE, J., in *R.* v. *Patel*, [1951] 2 All E. R. 29, at p. 30).
[7] (1872), 21 W. R. 199.

off the line five or six times today—he is a new driver". KELLY, C. B., rejected the evidence, not because it infringed the rule against hearsay, but because it would have given rise to many collateral issues as to whether the driver had been reported, and whether he had been off the points five or six times or was a new driver. Similar sentiments may account for the tendency to exclude expert evidence concerning the probable future decline in the value of money when damages for personal injuries are being assessed, although the basis of exclusion may be that there is a rule of substantive law against allowing for inflation in this context.[1]

The desire to avoid a multiplicity of issues accounts in whole or in part for several of the exclusionary rules of evidence,[2] and it explains the caution with which the courts approach arguments to the effect that A. caused B. because, whenever A. occurred, B. followed. FARWELL, J., considered that "the conclusion depends on the universality of the premise, and a negative instance unexplained breaks the chain". He added that the reception of evidence in support of such an argument "raises side issues upon which the court cannot decide without injustice to other parties".[3] In *Folkes* v. *Chadd*,[4] the question was whether an embankment erected by the plaintiff caused silting in the defendant's harbour. Mr. Smeaton, the distinguished engineer, testified to his opinion as an expert that the silting was not caused by the embankment, and the plaintiff sought to reinforce this opinion by showing that silting had occurred in other harbours on the same coast. The additional evidence was held to be admissible in so far as it concerned harbours in which there were no embankments, because it tended to confirm Mr. Smeaton's opinion that the silting arose from some other cause, but it was held to be inadmissible as to harbours in which there were embankments, since *"litem lite resolvit"*.[5] Lord O'HAGAN took this cryptic remark to mean that the existence of embankments "made the case in controversy and the case of illustration identical, proof as to the one could scarcely avail to explain, vary or confirm proof as to the other".

The last quotation is from the case of *Metropolitan Asylum District* v. *Hill*,[6] which was concerned with the effect of a smallpox hospital on the health of the inhabitants of the neighbourhood, and a majority of the House of Lords was disposed to hold that evidence of the effect of similar institutions on other localities was admissible, although the point was not finally decided. From time to time the courts have admitted evidence of particular instances to show that wherever A. has occurred B. has followed in support of an argument that A. caused B.[7] But an expert on the matter under consideration is often better equipped to adjudicate on the propriety of this inference, and evidence of opinion is usually taken in such cases. Particular instances may be put to the expert in cross-examination, and he can be contradicted by another expert; nevertheless, the court can

---

[1] *Mitchell* v. *Mulholland* (No. 2), [1972] 1 Q. B. 65; [1971] 2 All E. R. 1205.
[2] It accounts in whole for the rule that a witness's answers in cross-examination to credit are generally final, in part for the hearsay rule and the rules governing evidence of disposition.
[3] *A.-G.* v. *Nottingham Corporation*, [1904] 1 Ch. 673, at pp. 680 and 682-3.
[4] (1782), 3 Doug. K. B. 157.
[5] *Per* Lord MANSFIELD, C.J.
[6] (1882), 47 L. T. 29, at p. 32.
[7] *Hales* v. *Kerr*, [1908] 2 K. B. 601; *Akerele* v. *R.*, [1943] A. C. 255.

arrive at a decision more quickly and surely by this means than that of evidence concerning a multitude of isolated occasions.[1]

(iii) Danger of manufactured evidence.—The courts rightly take the view that the degree to which an item of evidence is relevant to an issue diminishes in proportion to the likelihood of its having been manufactured; but it is open to question whether people are as prone to manufacture evidence as some judgments suggest[2], and the bogey has led to certain exclusionary rules, the mechanical application of which may lead to the rejection of evidence of real probative value.

A case in point is the common law ban on the admissibility of the previous statements of witnesses of which a hypothetical example was given on p. 1 of the exclusion of the signed statement of the publican Y. who had seen A. drink 6 large whiskies. The rigour of the rule has been mitigated by the Civil Evidence Act, 1968, under which such statements are admissible evidence of the facts stated with the leave of the court in civil proceedings, but it is still applicable to criminal cases. The common law ban is part of the rule against hearsay as formulated on p. 6, and that rule is part of the general law of evidence, but the fear of fabrication may have led to special rules of evidence applicable only to particular types of case which are independent of the hearsay rule and may therefore be unaffected by the Civil Evidence Act.

For example in *Warren* v. *Gurney*,[3] it was held that statements made by a father (since deceased) after a transfer by him of shares into his son's name were inadmissible to rebut the presumption of advancement because of the ease with which they could have been manufactured. A living transferor can give evidence of the intention with which he purchased an estate[4] and, the case being one in which direct oral evidence by the father would have been admissible, *Warren* v. *Gurney* is apparently overruled by the Civil Evidence Act, 1968; but the advancement cases may be the subject of a special rule of evidence unaffected by the Act because it has been held that a father's subsequent acts are inadmissible to rebut the presumption of advancement in spite of the general rule, based on common sense, that subsequent acts can be examined as evidence of an earlier intention.[5] It was said that the father's subsequent acts "will not enable him to convert an advancement for his sons into a beneficial purchase for himself"; no one would deny the truth of this remark, but the court was concerned with the father's intention at the time of the purchase. However, it would be odd if subsequent acts were inadmissible as evidence of prior intent in an advancement case, although subsequent declarations were admissible.

(2) Alternative Statements of the Rule

It is sometimes contended that the rule governing the inadmissibility of irrelevant evidence should simply be stated to be that all irrelevant evidence is inadmissible without any reference to the exclusion of in-

---

[1] Cf. the exclusion of evidence of particular instances in *Boldron* v. *Widdows* (1824), 1 C. & P. 65.
[2] See the remarks of Eyre, C.J., p. 2, *ante*.
[3] [1944] 2 All E. R. 472.
[4] *Devoy* v. *Devoy* (1854), 3 Sm. & G. 403.
[5] *Murless* v. *Franklin* (1818), 1 Swan 13. See also *Finch* v. *Finch* (1808), 15 Ves. 43; *Crabb* v. *Crabb* (1834), 1 My. & K. 511; *Shephard* v. *Cartwright*, [1955] A. C. 431; [1954] 3 All E. R. 649.

sufficiently relevant evidence. On this view, the exclusion of evidence on the grounds of remoteness, tendency to produce a multiplicity of issues and ease of manufacture is due to special exclusionary rules, for that which is excluded often has a certain degree of relevance. The difference between the two approaches is, like the distinction sometimes drawn between logical relevancy and a higher degree of relevancy called "legal relevancy", devoid of practical importance. Whichever approach is adopted, allowance must be made for a considerable amount of judicial discretion with regard to the admissibility of evidence of low, though by no means insignificant probative value. On this last point, rule 403 of the United States Federal Rules of Evidence gets the best of both worlds by providing for both mandatory and discretionary exclusion:

> "(a) Although relevant, evidence is not admissible if its probative value is substantially outweighed by the danger of unfair prejudice, of the confusion of the issues, or of misleading the jury."
>
> "(b) Although relevant, evidence may be excluded, if its probative value is substantially outweighed by considerations of undue delay, waste of time, or needless presentation of cumulative evidence."[1]

(3) Apparent Exceptions

Three exceptions to the general prohibition on irrelevant evidence have been suggested, but it is submitted that all of them are unreal so far as English law is concerned.

(i) Facts affecting the admissibility of evidence.—Phipson said that Thayer was inaccurate when he asserted that "without any exception, nothing that is not logically relevant is admissible", because numerous facts are legally admissible although they have no logical bearing on the issue the court has to decide.[2] He referred to such facts as that a witness was not sworn in a particular way, that a hearsay declarant was dead at the date of the trial, and that due search had been made for a lost document. It seems, however, that the criticism is a purely verbal one, because it assumes that by "logically relevant" Thayer meant relevant to the main facts in issue. His statement might equally well be taken to mean that nothing is admissible which is not relevant, either to the main facts in issue, or else to such subordinate facts as those relating to the credibility and admissibility of evidence, in which case the relevance of the facts mentioned by Phipson is obvious enough.

(ii) Curative admissibility.[3]—It is sometimes said that, if irrelevant evidence is adduced by one party, his opponent may seek to dispel its effect by calling irrelevant evidence himself. Whatever the position may be in certain American jurisdictions, this principle (which Wigmore described as one of "curative admissibility") is not recognised by the English courts. Thus, in *R. v. Cargill*,[4] on a charge of unlawful intercourse with a girl between thirteen and sixteen, the prosecutrix swore that she had been chaste

---

[1] On the subject of relevance generally, see H. H. Glass, *Seminars on Evidence*, ch. 3; Eagleson, 4 University of Melbourne Law Review 180; Trautman, 4 Vanderbilt Law Review 395; James, 29 California Law Review 689.

[2] *Manual of Law of Evidence* (7th edition), 28; Thayer, *Preliminary Treatise on Evidence at the Common Law*, 266. The view taken in the text is followed by the present editor of Phipson's Manual (10th edition, p. 27). Contrast Nokes, *Introduction to Evidence* (4th edition), 6 and 86, notes 17, 18.

[3] 1 *Wigmore*, para. 15.

[4] [1913] 2 K. B. 271. See also *Ready v. Brown* (1968), 118 C. L. R. 165.

before the accused seduced her. This was irrelevant, because absence of consent and hence the girl's character, is immaterial in such a case, but it did not entitle the accused to call evidence concerning the girl's behaviour with other men because the court was not prepared to say that, if the prosecution introduced a matter irrelevant to the issue, the defence was entitled to call evidence with regard to that irrelevant issue.

(iii) Conditional admissibility.[1]—One fact may only be relevant to another if it is taken together with some further matter, and it may well be the case that this can only be proved by a witness who will be called after the one who testifies to the fact the relevancy of which is being considered. In such circumstances, the court allows the evidence to be given conditionally on its turning out to be relevant. If it proves to be irrelevant, the judge will tell the jury to disregard it. An excellent example is provided by the rules governing the admissibility of statements made in the presence of a party. These only have probative value in the light of the conduct of the person to whom they were made. If A. confronts B. and alleges that he has committed a crime against him, and B. is later tried for that offence, evidence of what A. said will usually only be relevant if B.'s conduct is something other than a stalwart denial of the charge; but there is no doubt that A.'s statement may always be proved in the first instance, although the judge may subsequently be obliged to tell the jury to disregard it altogether.[2] Such a state of affairs is better regarded as a concession to the fact that the evidence in a case often emerges slowly, and from the mouths of many witnesses, rather than an exception to the rule prohibiting the reception of irrelevant, or insufficiently relevant, matter.

C. RELEVANCE AND ADMISSIBILITY

Although there are no real exceptions to this rule, the existence of important exceptions to the rule that all sufficiently relevant evidence is admissible renders it essential to draw a sharp distinction between the relevancy and admissibility of evidence. The former is a concept arrived at inductively from experience, and its applicability can be tested deductively by the construction of a syllogism. It is not primarily dependent on rules of law.[3] The admissibility of evidence, on the other hand, depends first on the concept of relevancy of a sufficiently high degree, and secondly, on the fact that the evidence tendered does not infringe any of the exclusionary rules that may be applicable to it. To quote Wigmore:[4]

> "Admissibility signifies that the particular fact is relevant and something more,—that it has also satisfied all the auxiliary tests and extrinsic policies."

---

[1] I *Wigmore*, para. 14; Phipson, *Law of Evidence* (11th edition), 68, citing *Haigh* v. *Belcher* (1836), 7 C. & P. 389. The same notion is involved in the statement that evidence will be received *de bene esse* for the origin of which see F. D. M. in 62 L. Q. R. 38, and Plucknett, *ibid.*, 130.

[2] *R.* v. *Christie*, [1914] A. C. 545.

[3] Thayer sometimes wrote as though the doctrine of precedent was wholly inapplicable to questions of relevance (see 14 H. L. R. 139, answering Fox, *ibid.*, 39 (1900)). Wigmore, on the other hand, said "So long as courts continue to declare in judicial rulings what their notions of logic are, just so long must there be rules of law which must be observed" (I *Wigmore*, 298). For once the truth really does lie between the two views and Thayer conceded as much when he said decisions concerning relevance may "stand as a precedent to half settle other cases".

[4] I *Wigmore*, p. 300.

Although the distinction between relevancy and admissibility is expressly recognised in many English judgments, an oversimplification of Stephen's has exercised a somewhat baneful influence, and, by way of reaction perhaps, demands are sometimes made for the recognition of further basic concepts in the law of evidence.

(i) Stephen's terminology.—In his *Digest of the Law of Evidence* Stephen attempted to state the rules concerning the matters that may be proved in court wholly in terms of relevancy. The result was that he had to explain the rejection of hearsay on the ground that it was irrelevant or deemed to be irrelevant, while its reception under exceptions to the hearsay rule was based on the fact that it was relevant or deemed to be so. Other exclusionary rules were likewise said to involve the rejection of evidence which is irrelevant or deemed to be irrelevant. The objection to this mode of expression is that much of the evidence which English law rejects is highly relevant, and no one would now wish wholeheartedly to adhere to the terminology of the Digest, although its influence has been considerable.

(ii) The demand for more basic concepts.—It is sometimes said that, in addition to recognising the separate concepts of relevancy and admissibility, we should allow for the two further concepts of "materiality" and "receivability".[1] If this were done, "relevant" would imply that the evidence tendered tends to prove the fact it purports to establish, "materiality" would mean direct relevance to a fact in issue, "admissibility" would denote that the evidence did not infringe an exclusionary rule, while "receivability" would mean that the evidence was relevant, material and admissible. All that need be said here is that the additional concepts are not employed in practice, and it is by no means certain that their adoption would render the exposition of the law any clearer.

D. ADMISSIBILITY AND WEIGHT OF EVIDENCE

Questions concerning the admissibility of evidence must be distinguished from those relating to its weight. The former is a matter of law for the judge (although it may sometimes depend upon a preliminary finding of fact by him); the weight of evidence, on the other hand, is a question of fact, although, in cases tried with a jury, the summing-up frequently contains observations on the cogency of certain matters, and the judge can always withdraw an issue from the jury because the proponent has not adduced sufficient evidence in support of his claim. The distinction between admissibility and weight does not require further elaboration, but it is not clear-cut. The weight of evidence may affect its admissibility as this is to some extent dependent on the degree of relevancy of the matter under consideration.[2] The tendency of the modern law is in favour of a broad basis of admissibility.[3]

---

[1] Montrose, 70 L. Q. R. 527 (1954). The concept of materiality is employed by Wigmore, that of receivability is canvassed by Professor Montrose.

[2] *R. v. Quinn and Bloom*, [1962] 2 Q. B. 245; [1961] 3 All E. R. 88.

[3] "People were formerly frightened out of their wits about admitting evidence lest juries should go wrong. In modern times we admit the evidence and discuss its weight" (Cockburn, C.J., in *R. v. Birmingham Overseers* (1861), 1 B. & S. 763, at p. 767).

E. TERMINOLOGY

The fact that evidence may be of varying degrees of cogency gives rise to terminological difficulties which have not been solved.

(i) Insufficient evidence.—The lowest degree of cogency is where a party's evidence in support of an issue is so weak that no reasonable man could properly decide the issue in his favour. An example is afforded by *Hawkins* v. *Powells Tillery Steam Coal Co.*[1] where the Court of Appeal reversed the County Court judge's finding that a fatal attack of angina pectoris arose out of a workman's employment. The workman had been pushing trucks shortly before the attack occurred, but the disease was one of delayed action which might have been brought about by a great variety of causes such as the disordered state of the deceased's stomach, or a walk in windy weather. The claimant had failed to take the case out of the realm of conjecture, and, in such circumstances, the evidence in support of an issue is best described as "insufficient".

(ii) Prima facie evidence: first sense.—The next degree of cogency is where a party's evidence in support of an issue is sufficiently weighty to entitle a reasonable man to decide the issue in his favour, although, as a matter of common sense, he is not obliged to do so. An example is provided by *Smithwick* v. *The National Coal Board*[2] in which the Court of Appeal affirmed the trial judge's finding that a workman's death had been caused by the defendant's breach of statutory duty by failing to guard dangerous machinery on proof that the man's arm had been caught in the machine with fatal consequences. The catastrophe might have been due to a breach of statutory regulations on the part of the deceased, but the connection between his death and the unguarded machine was closer than that between the angina pectoris and the pushing of the trucks in the previous example. Accordingly, the evidence took the case out of the realm of conjecture into that of permissible inference.[3] In the words of DENNING, L.J.:

> "one often gets cases where the facts proved in evidence—the primary facts—are such that the tribunal of fact can legitimately draw from them an inference one way or the other, or, equally legitimately, refuse to draw any inference at all."[4]

When this is so, the evidence is most conveniently described as "*prima facie*", but there is no uniform usage with regard to the matter.

(iii) Prima facie evidence: second sense (presumptive evidence).—The next degree of cogency is where a party's evidence in support of an issue is so weighty that no reasonable man could help deciding the issue in his favour in the absence of further evidence. If a ship founders shortly after leaving port, and no further evidence appears in the case, the judge should direct the jury that they ought to infer unseaworthiness at the time

---

[1] [1911] 1 K. B. 988.   [2] [1950] 2 K. B. 335.

[3] "There can be no inference unless there are objective facts from which to infer the other facts which it is sought to establish. In some cases the other facts can be inferred with as much practical certainty as if they had actually been observed. In other cases the inference does not go beyond reasonable probability. But if there are no positive proved facts from which the inference can be made, the method of inference fails and what is left is mere speculation or conjecture" (Lord WRIGHT in *Caswell* v. *Powell Duffryn Associated Collieries, Ltd.*, [1940] A. C. 152, at p. 169; [1939] 3 All E. R. 722, at p. 733). See also *Kerr* v. *Ayr S.S. Co.*, [1915] A. C. 217, at p. 233, and *Jones* v. *Great Western Rail. Co.* (1930), 144 L. T. 194, at p. 202.

[4] [1950] 2 K. B. 335, at p. 352.

of departure.[1] If the jury were to find the contrary, "It would not be a finding against any principle of law, but it would be such a finding against the reasonable inference from the facts, that it would amount to a verdict against the evidence".[2] It would be convenient to describe evidence of this degree of cogency as "presumptive",[3] but it is usually said to be *prima facie*.

> "'*Prima facie* evidence' in its usual sense is used to mean *prima facie* proof of an issue, the burden of proving which is upon the party giving that evidence. In the absence of further evidence from the other side, the *prima facie* proof becomes conclusive proof and the party giving it discharges his onus." [4]

(iv) Conclusive evidence.—The evidence of a fact is sometimes said to be "conclusive" when the court must find that fact to be proved.

(v) Presumptions.—The word "presumption" is used in a variety of senses which are fully discussed in Chapter VI. Sometimes it merely means a permissible inference, as that someone who receives goods shortly after they have been stolen is aware of the theft, in which case it is said to be a "presumption of fact"; sometimes it means a conclusion which must be drawn as a matter of law unless and until evidence of the requisite degree of cogency is given to the contrary, as where, on proof of marriage, it must be assumed that husband and wife had access to each other so that any child born to the mother in wedlock is presumed to be legitimate. In such cases there is said to be a "rebuttable presumption of law". When a conclusion is necessitated by a rule of substantive law, whatever evidence there may be to the contrary, there is sometimes said to be an "irrebuttable presumption of law" to that effect. The rule that a child under ten cannot be convicted of crime is expressed in this way by section 50 of the Children and Young Persons Act, 1933, as amended by section 16 of the Children and Young Persons Act, 1963.

SECTION 6. JUDICIAL DISCRETION

There is an increasing recognition of a wide field of judicial discretion in relation to the admissibility of evidence. In 1790, GROSE, J. dreaded "that rules of evidence should ever depend upon the discretion of the judges;" he wished to find the rule laid down and to abide by it.[5] Lord HALSBURY expressed himself in similar vein as late as 1914,[6] but he was in a minority and it has since been recognised that:

> "In every criminal case the judge has a discretion to disallow the evidence even if in law relevant, and therefore, admissible if admissibility would operate unfairly against the defendant." [7]

---

[1] *Ajum Goolam Hossen & Co.* v. *Union Marine Insurance Co.*, [1901] A. C. 362, where there was much further evidence.
[2] *Per* BRETT, L. J. in *Pickup* v. *Thames and Mersey Marine Insurance Co.* (1878), 3 Q. B. D. 594, at p. 600.
[3] The terminology is suggested by Nigel Bridge in 12 M. L. R. at p. 277. He would designate as *prima facie* "That minimum of evidence which must be tendered before the issue can be submitted to the jury", and as "presumptive" "such evidence as shall, if believed, be legally conclusive in the absence of further evidence to rebut it".
[4] STRATFORD, J. A. in *R.* v. *Jacobson and Levy*, [1931] App. D. 466, at p. 478; *Lampard* v. *West*, [1926] S. A. S. R. 293. When used in statutes, *prima facie* evidence usually bears the meaning attributed to it by STRATFORD, J. A. see e.g. Partnership Act, 1890, s. 2 (3). See also the treatment of *May* v. *O'Sullivan* (1955), 92 C. L. R. 654 in *Campbell* v. *Inkley*, [1960] S. A. S. R. 273, and *R.* v. *Pace* (1967), 1 C. R. N. S. 45.
[5] *R.* v. *Inhabitants of Eriswell* (1790), 3 Term Rep. 707, at p. 711.
[6] *R.* v. *Christie* (1914), 10 Cr. App. Rep., at p. 149.
[7] *Per* Lord PARKER, C. J. in *Callis* v. *Gunn*, [1964] 1 Q. B. 495, at p. 501; [1963] 3 All E. R. 677, at p. 680.

The concept of fairness on which this exclusionary discretion is based will be briefly illustrated by reference to fairness before and at a criminal trial. After this has been done, the position in civil cases will be considered and the question of the existence of an inclusionary discretion will be mentioned.

(i) Unfairly obtained evidence in criminal cases.—The principal basis of the exclusionary discretion seems to be an offshoot of the privilege against self-incrimination discussed in Chapter XI. The underlying idea is that, in some circumstances, it is unfair to lead a man into supplying incriminating evidence against his will. In *Callis* v. *Gunn*,[1] the accused was asked by a police officer to allow his finger prints to be taken. No warning was given about the possible use of the prints as evidence, but it was held that the prints had been properly received in evidence against the accused. The Divisional Court seems, however, to have been of opinion that the case would have been one in which the trial court should have exercised its exclusionary discretion if the police officer had represented, contrary to the facts, that the accused was legally obliged to allow his finger prints to be taken.

In *R.* v. *Payne*,[2] the appellant had been convicted of driving a motor vehicle while unfit to do so through drink. He had been asked to submit himself to a medical examination stated to be for the sole purpose of ascertaining whether he was suffering from any illness at the material time. The doctor who conducted the examination gave evidence for the prosecution to the effect that the appellant had been unfit to drive through drink, and the Court of Criminal Appeal quashed the conviction because the appellant might have refused to undergo the examination if he had known that the doctor might give evidence concerning his fitness.

As Lord MACDERMOTT has said in a Northern Irish case in which self incriminating evidence was admitted although the police had, to some extent, acted as agents provocateurs:

> "Unfairness in this context cannot be closely defined. It must be judged in the light of all the material facts and findings and all the surrounding circumstances. The position of the accused, the nature of the investigation, and the gravity or otherwise of the suspected offence may all be relevant." [3]

In particular it seems that allowance must be made for the public's sense of propriety. Although, apart from those governing the admissibility of confessions, there are no legal rules prohibiting the reception of illegally obtained evidence, the court has a discretion to exclude it. In *King* v. *R.*[4] the Judicial Committee saw no reason why the discretion should have been exercised to exclude evidence obtained in consequence of a technically illegal search for drugs; but, speaking for the Committee, Lord HODSON said "This was not in their opinion a case in which evidence has been obtained by conduct of which the Crown ought not to take advantage. If they had thought otherwise they would have excluded the evidence even though tendered for the suppression of crime."[5] The desirability of avoiding the appearance of unfairness by allowing the Crown to take advantage of an official's wrong no doubt lies at the root of the discretion which the courts claim to exclude legally admissible confessions.

---

[1] [1964] 1 Q. B. 495; [1963] 3 All E. R. 677.
[2] [1963] 1 All E. R. 848.
[3] *R.* v. *Murphy*, [1965] N. I. 138, at p. 149.
[4] [1969] 1 A. C. 304.   [5] At p. 319.

(ii) Fairness at a criminal trial.—A type of unfairness against which the courts are particularly on their guard is the reception of evidence the prejudicial tendency of which outweighs its probative value in the sense that the jury may either attach undue weight to it or use it for inadmissible purposes. "A trial judge always has an overriding duty in every case to secure a fair trial."[1] These words were spoken by ROSKILL, J. in a case in which evidence of the accused's previous convictions was legally admissible in-chief under section 43 (1) of the Larceny Act, 1916.[2] Such evidence was admissible on charges of receiving stolen goods, but solely on the issue of guilty knowledge. It has been held that the judge should exercise his discretion to exclude the evidence when the live issue in the case is not the accused's knowledge that the goods or money in question were stolen, but whether he ever had possession of them.[3]

We shall see, in Chapter XIV, that, although evidence may generally not be given of a party's misconduct on other occasions if its sole purpose is to show that he is a person likely to have misconducted himself on the occasion in question, such evidence is admissible if relevant to an issue before the jury for some other reason.

> "In all such cases the judge ought to consider whether the evidence which it is proposed to adduce is sufficiently substantial, having regard to the purpose to which it is professedly directed, to make it desirable in the interests of justice that it should be admitted. If, so far as the purpose is concerned, it can in the circumstances of the case have only trifling weight, the judge will be right to exclude it. To say this is not to confuse weight with admissibility. The distinction is plain, but cases must occur in which it would be unjust to admit evidence of a character gravely prejudicial to the accused even though there may be some tenuous ground for holding it technically admissible. The decision must then be left to the discretion and sense of fairness of the judge." [4]

Further examples are provided by cases in which the evidence of misconduct on other occasions relates to something which occurred a long time ago,[5] or is of a tenuous nature.[6] Yet another example of the exercise of the exclusionary discretion under this head is provided by the power to exclude statements made in the presence of the accused on the ground that, when they consist of a charge which is denied, their evidential value is slight, whereas the effect on the minds of the jury of the accused's being publicly or repeatedly charged to his face might seriously prejudice the fairness of his trial.[7]

But the most controversial example of the courts' exclusionary discretion concerns section 1 (f) (ii) of the Criminal Evidence Act, 1898. The subsection permits cross-examination of the accused on his previous convictions if "the nature or conduct" of his defence is "such as to involve imputations upon the character of the prosecutor or the witnesses for the prosecution." The subsection would operate harshly on the accused with

---

[1] *R.* v. *List*, [1965] 3 All E. R. 710, at p. 711.
[2] Repealed by the Theft Act, 1968, and re-enacted with modifications by s. 27 (3) of that Act.
[3] *R.* v. *Herron*, [1966] 2 All E. R. 26.
[4] Lord DU PARQ in *Noor Mahomed* v. *R.*, [1949] A. C. 182, at p. 192, [1949] 1 All E. R. 365, at p. 370. See also Lord SIMON in *Harris* v. *Director of Public Prosecutions*, [1952] A. C. 694, at p. 707; [1952] 1 All E. R. 1044, at p. 1046.
[5] *R.* v. *Cole* (1941), 165 L. T. 125, at p. 128.
[6] *R.* v. *Doughty*, [1965] 1 All E. R. 540.
[7] *R.* v. *Christie*, [1914] A. C. 545, at pp. 560–564.

a criminal record if these words were literally construed without any allowance being made for the exercise of an exclusionary discretion, and the existence of such a discretion in favour of the accused at the expense of the prosecution was recognised by the House of Lords after full argument in *Selvey* v. *Director of Public Prosecutions.*[1] However, the House declined to hold that the discretion should always, or even generally, be exercised in favour of the accused when the imputations made by him were necessary for the proper development of his defence as when self-defence is pleaded, although it is arguable that such a conclusion was indicated by considerations of fairness to the accused. This is a difficult, if not impossible, basis for the exercise of an exclusionary discretion when persons jointly charged with the same offence give evidence against each other. The situation is contemplated by section 1 (f) (iii) of the Criminal Evidence Act, 1898, and it has been held by a majority of the House of Lords that there is no exclusionary discretion to be exercised in favour of one accused with a criminal record against the other accused jointly charged with the same offence.[2]

Although fairness to the accused is rightly treated as the primary consideration at a criminal trial, some allowance ought perhaps to be made in cases coming within section 1 (f) (ii) for the notion of fairness to the impugned witness for the prosecution. If he is subjected to infamous allegations by a man with a criminal record, perhaps it is fair to him and not unfair to the accused that the latter's record should be revealed, especially when the allegations were not necessary for the proper development of the defence. Fairness to the accused is a concept which must not be allowed to get out of hand. What the criminal courts seek to achieve is fairness "in the general circumstances of the administration of justice."[3]

The existence of a discretion to exclude evidence on the ground of an ill-defined notion of unfairness has the merit of avoiding technicalities such as those which have grown up around the rule of law that, in order to be admissible, a confession must be voluntary. It also has the merit of being able to cater for the unforeseen case. It was this latter consideration which led the Criminal Law Revision Committee to reject suggestions that the grounds upon which the discretion might be exercised should be specified in a statute. The rejection was of course without prejudice to any general principles which the courts may lay down.[4]

(iii) Civil cases.—It is in relation to claims to privilege from answering questions in cross-examination that the courts' exclusionary discretion has been invoked in civil cases. The basis on which the discretion has been exercised has been that of balancing the competing interests of disclosure in furtherance of the administration of justice between the parties and non-disclosure in the interest of confidentiality. It seems that the trial judge has a discretion to uphold a witness's claim to be privileged from answering certain questions although no privilege exists as a matter of law, and even though the questions are relevant and necessary for the purpose of the

---

[1] [1970] A. C. 304; [1968] 2 All E. R. 497 criticised in an article by B. Livesey in 26 C. L. J. 291 (1968).

[2] *Murdoch* v. *Taylor*, [1965] A. C. 574; [1965] 1 All E. R. 406.

[3] 11th Report of the Criminal Law Revision Committee, para. 27, citing *R.* v. *McGregor*, [1968] 1 Q. B. 371; [1967] 2 All E. R. 267.

[4] 11th Report, para. 278.

particular proceedings.[1] The only reported cases concern claims to privilege by doctors and priests and journalists; but, in the context of the exclusion of evidence in the public interest, it has been recognised that the public has an interest in the preservation of confidentiality which must be weighed against the private interest of the parties and the importance of the due administration of justice between them.[2]

There is no English authority suggesting that, in civil cases, the judge has a discretion to disallow improperly obtained admissions, or prejudicial evidence relating to misconduct on other occasions and, in each instance, there is Commonwealth authority to the contrary.[3]

(iv) No general inclusionary discretion.—In *Myers* v. *Director of Public Prosecutions*,[4] Lord REID said:

> "It is true that a judge has a discretion to exclude legally admissible evidence if justice so requires, but it is a very different thing to say that he has a discretion to admit legally inadmissible evidence."

It may therefore be assumed that, at common law, the judicial discretion with regard to the admissibility of evidence is entirely exclusionary, although the requirement of a fairly high degree of relevancy in order to render evidence admissible sometimes creates the appearance of the exercise of an inclusionary discretion. The terms of some statutes may be treated as conferring an inclusionary discretion as where section 8 of the Civil Evidence Act, 1968, and R. S. C. O. 38, r. 29 empower the court to admit hearsay statements although the conditions for their admissibility prescribed by the Act have not been fulfilled.[5]

---

[1] *A.-G.* v. *Mulholland*; *A.-G.* v. *Foster*, [1963] 2 Q. B. 477; [1963] 1 All E. R. 767.

[2] *Alfred Crompton Amusement Machines, Ltd.* v. *Commissioner of Customs and Excise* (No. 2), [1973] 2 All E. R. 1169; *Norwich Pharmacal Co.* v. *Customs and Excise Commissioners*, [1973] 2 All E. R. 943.

[3] *Ibrahim* v. *R.*, [1914] A. C. 599, at p. 610; *Manenti* v. *Melbourne Tramways*, [1954] V. L. R. 115, at p. 118.

[4] [1965] A. C. 1001, at p. 1024; [1964] 2 All E. R. 881, at p. 887.

[5] On the court's discretion with regard to affidavits see *Rossage* v. *Rossage*, [1960] 1 All E. R. 600, and Re *J.* (*an Infant*), [1960] 1 All E. R. 603.

CHAPTER II

EXAMPLES OF CIRCUMSTANTIAL EVIDENCE, EVIDENCE OF IDENTITY AND *RES INTER ALIOS ACTA*

The first section of this chapter illustrates one of the classifications of circumstantial evidence adopted by Wigmore.[1] His division of the subject into "prospectant", "concomitant" and "retrospectant" evidence involves the use of strange words, but it has the merit of stressing the main types of argument by which the relevance of one fact to another may be established. Evidence of identity is discussed in a separate section because the cases are concerned with direct as well as circumstantial evidence, and, as the chapter is largely introductory, the concluding section is the most suitable place for a general reference to the doctrine of *res inter alios acta*.

SECTION 1. EXAMPLES OF CIRCUMSTANTIAL EVIDENCE

When considering some of the illustrations given in the following paragraphs, the reader would do well to bear in mind that the number of witnesses allowed to give evidence was greatly restricted down to the middle of the nineteenth century. Those who had any interest in the outcome of the proceedings were generally unable to testify before the Evidence Act, 1843 came into force, parties in civil cases, and their spouses, were only made competent by the Evidence Acts of 1851 and 1853 respectively, and, as a general rule, the accused and his spouse were unable to give evidence at a criminal trial before the Criminal Evidence Act, 1898 came into force. The result was that circumstantial evidence was often all that was available on points upon which direct evidence would probably be given nowadays.

A. PROSPECTANT EVIDENCE

In its most general form, the argument for the reception of this kind of evidence is that the occurrence of an act, state of mind or state of affairs in the past justifies an inference that the act was done, or state of mind or affairs existed at the moment of time into which the court is enquiring.

(1) CONTINUANCE

If the speed at which someone was driving at a particular time is in issue, evidence of the rate at which he was travelling a few moments earlier is admissible;[2] in cases turning on the existence of a partnership, evidence of its existence at a time earlier than that with which the court is concerned is likewise admissible.[3] Evidence has been received of a person's theological opinions four years before the time at which their nature was in issue;[4] while the fact that someone was alive at an antecedent date

---

[1] I *Wigmore*, para. 43.
[2] *Beresford v. St. Albans JJ.* (1905), 22 T. L. R. 1.
[3] *Brown v. Wren Brothers*, [1895] 1 Q. B. 390.
[4] *A.-G. v. Bradlaugh* (1885), 14 Q. B. D. 667, at p. 711.

may support an inference that he was alive at a subsequent date.[1] Evidence of this sort is given so frequently that it is sometimes said that continuance in general, and the continuance of life in particular, is the subject of a rebuttable presumption of law; but the question is simply one of relevance, depending on the common experience of mankind, and it would be best to avoid the use of the word "presumption" altogether in this context, or, if that term must be employed, it should be qualified by the use of some such expression as a "presumption of fact" or a "provisional presumption".[2]

It is important to remember that there are degrees of relevancy when this kind of evidence is being considered. Proof of the theological beliefs entertained by a man thirty years earlier, would not support a reasonable inference concerning his beliefs at the time which the court was examining,[3] and neither law nor logic can specify the stage at which such evidence ceases to be of any weight—everything depends upon the facts of the particular case. If it were proved that a husband was in good health the day before his wife married someone else:

> "the inference would be strong, almost irresistible, that he was living on the latter day, and the jury would in all probability find that he was so. If, on the other hand, it were proved that he was then in a dying condition, and nothing else was proved, they would probably decline to draw the inference." [4]

(2) COURSE OF BUSINESS

To prove postage, evidence may be given that a letter was copied in an office letter book, and that, according to the practice of the office, all letters dealt with in this way were posted immediately.[5] Similarly, if delivery of a document to a particular individual must be proved, the jury may be invited to infer that it was handed to him by his servant on proof that it was delivered to the latter although he was not authorised to receive the document on behalf of his master.[6]

---

[1] In *MacDarmaid* v. *A.-G.*, [1950] P. 218; [1950] 1 All E. R. 497, HODSON, J., inferred the continuance of life of a healthy woman of 28 for a further three years; in *Re Peete, Peete* v. *Crompton*, [1952] 2 All E. R. 599, ROXBURGH, J., inferred the continuance of life of a healthy man for three years; in *Chard* v. *Chard*, [1956] P. 259; [1955] 3 All E. R. 721, SACHS, J., inferred the continuance of life of a woman of 26 for a further sixteen years. For a case in which death was inferred after a prolonged lapse of time see *Re Watkins, Watkins* v. *Watkins*, [1953] 2 All E. R. 1113. For other cases turning on the inference of continuance of life see *R.* v. *Inhabitants of Harborne* (1835), 2 Ad. & El. 540; *R.* v. *Lumley* (1869), L. R. 1 C. C. R. 196; *R.* v. *Willshire* (1881), 6 Q. B. D. 366, and *R.* v. *Jones* (1883), 11 Q. B. D. 118.

[2] "Nothing can be more absurd than the notion that there is to be any rigid presumption of law on such questions of fact, without reference to accompanying circumstances, such, for instance, as the age or health of the party. There can be no such strict presumption of law. I think that the only questions in such cases are, what evidence is admissible? and what inference may fairly be drawn from it?" (*per* DENMAN, C.J., in *R.* v. *Inhabitants of Harborne* (1835), 2 Ad. & El. 540, at pp. 544–5).

[3] *A.-G.* v. *Bradlaugh* (1885), 14 Q. B. D. 667, at p. 711.

[4] *Per* LUSH, J., in *R.* v. *Lumley* (1869), L. R. 1 C. C. R. 196, at p. 198.

[5] *Trotter* v. *McLean* (1879), 13 Ch. D. 574; cf. *Hetherington* v. *Kemp* (1815), 4 Camp. 193 (proof letter put on office table where letters for posting usually put insufficient). Proof of postage is evidence of delivery to addressee (*Watts* v. *Vickers* (1916), 86 L. J. K.B. 177). See Interpretation Act, 1889, s. 26 as to service by post.

[6] *McGregor* v. *Keily* (1849), 3 Exch. 794. Cf. *Tanham* v. *Nicholson* (1872), L. R. 5 H. L. 561, which turned on substantive law.

(3) HABIT

The fact that someone was in the habit of acting in a given way is relevant to the question whether he acted in that way on the occasion into which the court is enquiring. Thus, in *Joy* v. *Phillips, Mills & Co., Ltd.*,[1] a claim was made for workmen's compensation in respect of the death of a stable boy caused by a kick from a horse. The deceased was found near the horse, holding a halter which there was no occasion for him to use at that time of day. It was held that the defendant might call evidence of the boy's practice of teasing the horse as tending to negative the applicant's claim that the accident arose out of and in the course of the deceased's employment. PHILLIMORE, L.J., said:

> "wherever an enquiry has to be made into the cause of the death of a person and, there being no direct evidence, recourse must be had to circumstantial evidence, any evidence as to the habits and ordinary doings of the deceased which may contribute to the circumstances by throwing light upon the probable cause of death is admissible, even in the case of a prosecution for murder".[2]

There is no rule against the reception of relevant evidence prejudicial to the character of the deceased when his death, its cause, or the state of mind of the person who brought it about is in issue,[3] but, when the evidence of habit refers to the practice of a party to the dispute, the prohibition on evidence which merely goes to show that his disposition is that of a man likely to do the wrongful act in question must always be borne in mind.

(4) MOTIVE OR PLAN

Facts which supply a motive for a particular act, such as the impending discovery by the deceased that the man accused of his murder had procured loans from him by means of forged documents,[4] or the impecuniosity of an alleged forger,[5] are among the items of circumstantial evidence which are most often admitted. Further examples are afforded by more or less any murder trial at which proof is given of facts supplying a motive for revenge, financial or amatory[6] gain, or the removal of someone who was in a position to disclose unpleasant information concerning the accused.[7] Conversely, facts which tend to show a total absence of motive may be adduced, as where the lack of pecuniary embarrassment on his part is proved by someone accused of arson with intent to defraud an insurance company.[8] It is, however, easy to attach too much weight to evidence of motive.

> "Almost every child has something to gain by the death of his parents, but rarely on the death of a parent is parricide even suspected."[9]

---

[1] [1916] 1 K. B. 849; *Eichsteadt* v. *Lahrs*, [1960] S. R. Q. 487. It is not always easy to distinguish between the proof of isolated acts and of habit; the fact that the evidence amounted to no more than the former may have accounted for its exclusion in *Manenti* v. *Melbourne Tramways*, [1954] V. L. R. 115.

[2] At p. 854.

[3] The prosecution unsuccessfully contended that such a principle existed in *R.* v. *Hector*, [1953] V. L. R. 543. Cf. *R.* v. *Biggin*, [1920] 1 K. B. 213.

[4] *R.* v. *Palmer* (1856), Stephen, *History of Criminal Law*, III, p. 389.

[5] *Roupell* v. *Haws* (1863), 3 F. & F. 784.

[6] *Plomp* v. *R.* (1963), 110 C. L. R. 234, refuting the suggestion that evidence of motive is only relevant to *mens rea*.

[7] *R.* v. *Clewes* (1830), 4 C. & P. 221.

[8] *R.* v. *Grant* (1865), 4 F. & F. 322.

[9] Best, *Principles of the Law of Evidence* (12th edition), 384.

So far as lack of motive is concerned, "there is a great difference between absence of proved motive and proved absence of motive".[1]

Facts, such as the purchase of poison by someone who is accused of murder,[2] which suggest the existence of a plan or design, or preparation for a given course of action may always be proved, and this evidence is of considerable weight because it calls for an explanation of his conduct from the person against whom it is given. When it consists of declarations of an intention to act in a particular way, the hearsay rule has to be borne in mind. If the declarations are made by a party, they may often be brought within the category of admissions and thus be received under a well-recognised exception to the rule which applies to criminal cases by virtue of the common law and to civil cases by virtue of section 9 (1) of the Civil Evidence Act, 1968. Even if the declarations are not those of a party they are certainly admissible in civil cases under the Act of 1968, and probably in criminal cases under an ill-defined exception to the hearsay rule; but, assuming that such remarks are admissible, the judges seem to have taken different views about the relevance of the intention to the question whether an act said to have been intended was, in fact, performed. If the statement was that of the accused, and the conclusion that it was carried out would be favourable to his case, it may be excluded on account of the ease with which the evidence could have been manufactured;[3] but, even when there is no such obvious risk, some cases suggest that it is admissible as tending to establish the performance of the act said to have been intended,[4] while others appear to be against admitting the statement for this purpose.[5] The question whether evidence is sufficiently relevant to be admissible is pre-eminently one on which different views may be taken, and, assuming that a person's present declaration of his intention is admissible as evidence of that fact, it is probably best not to try to lay down any general principle on the subject of its relevance to the performance of a subsequent act by the declarant.[6]

---

[1] *Per* CHANNELL, J., in *R. v. Ellwood* (1908), 1 Cr. App. Rep. 181, at p. 182.

[2] *R. v. Palmer, supra.*

[3] *R. v. Petcherini* (1855), 7 Cox C. C. 79. For the court's attitude to evidence which can be easily manufactured, see p. 2, *ante*.

[4] *Johnson* v. *Lyford* (1868), L. R. 1 P. & D. 546 (declaration of intention to execute copy will evidence that will which was in fact executed was in terms of copy); *R. v. Buckley* (1873), 13 Cox C. C. 293 (declaration by police officer to superior that he would go in search of accused after dark admitted as evidence that he did so).

[5] *R. v. Wainwright* (1875), 13 Cox C. C. 171 (declaration by deceased that she was going to accused's premises inadmissible because intention might not have been carried out); *R. v. Thomson*, [1912] 3 K. B. 19 (declaration by deceased that she intended to perform illegal operation on herself inadmissible, but no attempt made by Court of Criminal Appeal to distinguish between these statements and statements that she had in fact operated on herself; both treated as inadmissible hearsay).

[6] A person's intention at a particular time may be in issue as when it is necessary to ascertain with what intention an act was done, and accompanying declarations are often tendered to establish this fact. It may also be relevant to the question of his intention at a later time on the principle of continuance.

There have been occasional suggestions that all declarations of intention which do not amount to admissions must be excluded as hearsay, but most difficulty has arisen on the score of relevancy when a declaration of intention has been tendered to prove the performance of the act said to have been intended. Similar problems have arisen in the United States, where the case of *Mutual Life Insurance* v. *Hillmon* (1892), 145 U. S. 284 in which a deceased's declarations of his intention to go on a journey were admitted as evidence that he went on it has attracted an extensive literature; see the citations in Morgan, Maguire & Weinstein, *Cases and Materials on Evidence*, 4th Edn., p. 668. For the position in Canada see *R. v. Workman and Huculak*, [1963] 1 Can. Crim. Cas. 297 affirmed on other grounds [1963] S. C. R. 267 and criticized in 3 Alberta Law Review 299.

(5) Knowledge or Capacity

Facts which tend to prove or negative a person's capacity to do an act into which the court is enquiring may be highly relevant. Thus, the accused's knowledge of the effects of certain drugs, his skill in their application, and his ability to procure them, would be admissible evidence at his trial for murder by means of their use, and the absence of any of these factors would likewise be admissible on his behalf. The most frequently cited case in which this type of evidence was discussed is, however, a civil suit. In *Dowling* v. *Dowling*[1] the plaintiff claimed repayment of money lent, and evidence of his consistent impecuniosity extending over a period of seven years up to the date of the alleged loan was received in support of the defendant's denial that it was ever made.

B. CONCOMITANT EVIDENCE

The general argument for the reception of evidence of this type is that circumstances existing contemporaneously with the transaction into which the court is enquiring render the facts alleged by one or other of the parties more or less probable. It is best illustrated by what is usually described as evidence of opportunity, but reference must also be made to the reception of evidence as part of the *res gestae* and the general question of the use of standards of comparison.

(1) Opportunity

The presence of the accused at the time and place of an alleged crime is something which must be proved by the prosecution on practically every criminal charge, and the establishment of an alibi is conclusive in favour of innocence. Any evidence which tends to prove either of the above facts is therefore admissible, and, if the defence consists of an allegation that other named persons committed the crime, their alibis in turn become relevant and admissible as part of the case for the prosecution.[2] The prosecution may be prejudiced by its inability to investigate an alibi of which it is made aware for the first time at the trial, and adjournments to enable an investigation to take place give rise to practical difficulties, especially at trials on indictment. Section 11 of the Criminal Justice Act, 1967, accordingly provides that, at such trials the defendant shall not, without the leave of the court, adduce evidence in support of an alibi, unless he has given notice of particulars of the alibi (including the names and addresses of witnesses thereto if known) not later than 7 days after the end of the proceedings before the examining justices.[3]

Opportunity is an important feature in many cases in which adultery is alleged. In *Woolf* v. *Woolf*[4] the Court of Appeal decided that the fact that a couple occupied the same bedroom must be treated as clear evidence of adultery in all but the most unusual circumstances. There is, however, no irrebuttable presumption of law to this effect, even if the evidence of

---

[1] (1860), 10 I. C. L. R. 236. For discussion see *Seminars on Evidence*, edited by H. H. Glass, Q.C., p. 83.

[2] *R.* v. *Dytche* (1890), 17 Cox C. C. 39.

[3] For cases on the construction of the section see *R.* v. *Hassan*, [1970] 1 Q. B. 423; [1970] 1 All E. R. 745; *R.* v. *Lewis*, [1969] 1 All E. R. 79; *R.* v. *Sullivan*, [1971] 1 Q. B. 253; [1970] 2 All E. R. 681.

[4] [1931] P. 134; but see *Ross* v. *Ross*, [1930] A. C. 1, as applied in *Webster* v. *Webster*, [1945] N. Z. L. R. 537.

opportunity is accompanied by evidence of inclination arising from the previous association of the parties.[1]

(2) Res Gestae

A fact may be relevant to a fact in issue because it throws light on it by reason of proximity in time, place or circumstance. This is frequently expressed by the statement that the relevant fact is part of the *res gestae*, although it is difficult not to sympathise with Sir Frederick Pollock when he described this as an unmeaning term which "merely fudges the truth that there is no universal formula for all the kinds of relevancy".[2] The doctrine is mainly concerned with the admissibility of statements made contemporaneously with the occurrence of some act or event into which the court is enquiring, and it is best discussed later, but this seems to be the proper place to illustrate the part which contemporaneity may play in the relevance of one fact to another. In *R. v. Moore*[3] the accused were charged with obtaining two pounds by false pretences in consequence of a card trick practised on the prosecutor in a railway train. As he alighted, the prosecutor said he would fetch the police, and he caused the accused to be arrested almost immediately. His evidence was that a total stranger handed him two pounds forthwith, and the Court of Criminal Appeal held that this fact was rightly admitted because "it related to part of the *res gestae* and an inference might fairly be drawn from it".[4] The fact's relevance to the issue is obvious enough. If someone is handed the exact sum of which he says he has been defrauded shortly after making a complaint to this effect, the two events are probably connected with each other. It is likely that the person who handed the money over was acting on behalf of the person against whom the complaint was made, and the payment suggests that the complaint was justified. If the prosecutor had received two pounds from an anonymous donor two days after his railway journey, that fact might still be regarded as relevant to the question whether he was defrauded in the train, but the relevance of such a payment would become more and more remote with the passage of time until it lapsed into insignificance so far as the guilt of the accused was concerned. It is questionable whether anything is gained by using such phrases as *"pars rei gestae"* to describe relevancy due to contemporaneity, but the terminology is in constant use in the courts.

(3) Standards of Comparison

Whenever it is necessary to determine whether someone's conduct complies with some objective standard, as where negligence is alleged, evidence is admissible to show how others might be expected to behave in similar circumstances. Thus, in *Chapman v. Walton*,[5] the plaintiff claimed

---

[1] *England v. England*, [1953] P. 16; [1952] 2 All E. R. 784.

[2] Pollock-Holmes, *Correspondence*, vol. 2, p. 285. Lord Tomlin suspected it of being "A phrase adopted to provide a respectable legal cloak for a variety of cases to which no formula of precision can be applied" (*Homes v. Newman*, [1931] 2 Ch. 112, at p. 120). "If you wish to tender inadmissible evidence, say it is part of the *res gestae*" (Lord Blackburn). Professor Julius Stone speaks of the law as to *res gestae* as "the lurking place of a motley crowd of conceptions in mutual conflict and reciprocating chaos" (55 L. Q. R. 66).

[3] (1914), 10 Cr. App. Rep. 54.

[4] At p. 56.

[5] (1833), 10 Bing. 57; followed in *Sulco, Ltd. v. E. S. Redit & Co., Ltd.*, [1959] N. Z. L. R. 45, where it was said that the evidence must be of a general practice, not what the witnesses would have done.

that brokers had been negligent in failing to take steps to have the terms upon which goods at sea were insured varied on receipt of a letter concerning their destination. The letter was not clearly expressed, and TINDALL, C.J., allowed the defendants to call other brokers to swear what they would have done in a similar situation, for:

> "if 9 brokers of experience out of 10 would have done the same as the defendants under the same circumstances, or even if as many out of a given number would have been of his opinion as against it, he who only stipulates to bring a reasonable degree of skill to the performance of his duty would be entitled to a verdict in his favour". [1]

When the issue concerns the practice of a particular trade, evidence of the practice which prevails with regard to the matter in dispute in a similar trade is likewise admissible. In *Noble* v. *Kennoway*, [2] the question was whether the underwriters were entitled to repudiate liability on an insurance of ship's cargo because of unreasonable delay in discharging it in Labrador, and the court held that evidence of a practice of delaying the discharge of cargo while ships were used for fishing in the Newfoundland trade was admissible in support of the plaintiff's contention that a similar practice prevailed in the Labrador trade. When speaking of the time of delay BULLER, J., said "If it can be shown that the time would have been reasonable in one place that is a degree of evidence to prove that it was so in another". [3] In *Fleet* v. *Murton*, [4] evidence of a practice under which brokers in the colonial fruit trade were personally liable on contracts into which they entered on behalf of undisclosed principals was admitted in support of the plaintiff's allegation that the same practice existed in the London fruit trade.

> "The evidence was relevant to this case and admissible, on the ground that, showing as it did, what was the custom in other trades, though not so analogous no doubt, to the trade in question, as was the trade in *Noble* v. *Kennoway*, it tended to show the probability, that in the fruit trade as well as in the colonial trade the broker did under given circumstances undertake a similar responsibility." [5]

No special rules apply to such cases beyond those which require the evidence tendered to be more than remotely relevant to the issue, and unlikely to raise a number of collateral questions. It is, however, essential that the point in dispute should concern some matter as to which the argument from analogous situations to the situation under enquiry is likely to be of real assistance to the court. For instance, if it becomes necessary to determine whether a book is obscene, *i.e.* whether it is likely to corrupt the morals of its readers, the court must answer this question by reading the book itself. It has been said that no useful purpose would be served by a perusal of other books in order to compare them with the one under consideration, and that if such other books are tendered in evidence, the evidence will be rejected because it is collateral, *i.e.* irrelevant, or insufficiently relevant to the issue. [6]

The courts are frequently asked to apply standards of comparison when

---

[1] At p. 63.   [2] (1780), 2 Doug. K. B. 510.
[3] At p. 513.
[4] (1871), L. R. 7 Q. B. 126.   [5] At p. 134, *per* MELLOR, J.
[6] *R.* v. *Reiter*, [1954] 2 Q. B. 16; [1954] 1 All E. R. 741; cf. *Dalton* v. *Higgins* (1964), 43 D. L. R. (2d) 574 (evidence of other provinces' fire prevention regulations excluded in action concerning a fire).

the identity of handwriting is in issue, but this question is best considered in connection with documentary evidence.

C. RETROSPECTANT EVIDENCE

(1) IN GENERAL

In its most general form, the argument for the reception of this kind of evidence is the converse of that which demonstrates the relevance of prospectant evidence: the subsequent occurrence of an act, state of mind or state of affairs justifies an inference that the act was done, or the state of mind or affairs existed, in the past. Thus, a driver's excessive speed may be proved to support the conclusion that he was going too fast a short distance further back.[1] Although proof that someone was alive on a particular day may warrant the conclusion that he was still living at a later date, a time must obviously come when, from the mere fact that he has not been heard of, it is reasonable to conclude that he has died, and this may be done without recourse to any rebuttable presumption of law such as the presumption of death discussed in Chapter VI.[2] A person's anterior intention may also be proved by his subsequent acts, although we have seen that this general principle of relevancy has had to give way to precedent based on the dread of manufactured evidence in the advancement cases.[3]

Similarly, the court may be invited to infer that an event occurred from subsequent events which followed it in the ordinary course of business, as when an endorsed cheque is produced by the drawer to show that a payment was made.[4] Servants usually claim arrears of salary shortly after their employer has defaulted, so failure to make such a claim is some evidence that no salary was due.[5] Quite apart from any question of the course of business, delay in taking action may always have to be explained in order to prevent the conclusion that the circumstances of which complaint is ultimately made did not justify such action.

(2) OMNIA PRAESUMUNTUR RITE ESSE ACTA

Proof that someone acted as holder of a public office is evidence of his title to do so.[6] On a charge of assaulting a police officer in the course of his duty, formal proof of his appointment is not essential as evidence that he acted as a police officer will suffice.[7] Similarly, if a solicitor claims damages for words spoken of him in the way of his profession, it is unnecessary for him to produce his practising certificate, or an extract from the roll of solicitors, provided there is evidence that he acted as a solicitor.[8] The principle applies to corporations, so proof that a company has acted as such

---

[1] *R.* v. *Dalloz* (1908), 1 Cr. App. Rep. 258. Cf. *Beresford* v. *St. Albans JJ.* (1905), 22 T. L. R. 1.
[2] *Re Watkins, Watkins* v. *Watkins*, [1953] 2 All E. R. 1113.
[3] p. 22, *ante*.
[4] *Egg* v. *Barnett* (1800), 3 Esp. 196.
[5] *Sellen* v. *Norman* (1829), 4 C. & P. 80.
[6] For a full citation of authorities see Phipson, *Law of Evidence* (11th edition), 146.
[7] *R.* v. *Gordon* (1789), 1 Leach 515.
[8] *Berryman* v. *Wise* (1791), 4 Term Rep. 366. See now Solicitors Act, 1957, s. 17 and s. 62 rendering the Law List admissible evidence.

is evidence that it was duly incorporated.[1] In short, there is a rebuttable presumption of law establishing due appointment and capacity to act— "*omnia praesumuntur rite ac solemniter esse acta*".[2]

So far as its application to the validity of appointments is concerned, the presumption is confined to those affecting the public at large. Although the fact that a man is a solicitor may be proved by his having acted in that capacity, retainer by a particular client cannot be proved in this way;[3] a letter in his handwriting relating to the client's affairs will not suffice, any more than the appointment of other private agents can be proved by the fact that they purported to act on behalf of named principals. On the other hand, if a statute provides that trustees of public property shall take an oath before acting, proof of their having acted as trustees dispenses with the necessity of showing compliance with this provision.[4] The distinction can be justified on the ground that absence of a right to act in a certain capacity is more likely to be discovered if the capacity is public than when it is private, but the matter has never been fully considered by the courts, and there is no doubt that private authorisation may sometimes be inferred from retrospectant circumstantial evidence. For example, if A. is injured by B.'s car, B.'s ownership of the car is some evidence that it was being driven by his servant or agent, and this is because those who drive other people's cars are, more often than not, authorised to do so.[5]

As has been truly said "The wheels of business will not go round unless it is assumed that that is in order which appears to be in order".[6] Much trouble and expense is saved when the courts act on this assumption, as when they hold that the fact that speed limit signs were erected is *prima facie* evidence that the local authority had carried out the duties imposed upon it by the Road Traffic Acts.[7] The maxim *omnia praesumuntur rite esse acta* must, however, be used with care in criminal cases. In the absence of evidence to the contrary, it may safely be assumed that a local authority has performed its statutory duties properly, but the presumption cannot be invoked to support the conclusion that a breathaliser was approved by the Secretary of State in accordance with statutory requirements from the mere fact that an instrument of that type was issued to the police.[8]

Those who are concerned to establish that things were done in the right order in the absence of affirmative evidence to that effect may be able to rely on an extension of the principle *ut res magis valeat quam pereat* even when it is clear that the maxim *omnia praesumuntur rite esse acta* is inapplicable because the evidence shows that at least one act was performed prematurely. Thus, in *Eaglehill, Ltd.* v. *J. Needham (Builders), Ltd.*,[9] a

[1] *R.* v. *Langton* (1876), 2 Q. B. D. 296. As to companies incorporated under the Companies Acts, see s. 15 of the Companies Act, 1948.

[2] The judgment of Lord ELLENBOROUGH in *R.* v. *Verelst* (1813), 3 Camp. 432 is strong authority for treating the presumption as a rebuttable presumption of law.

[3] *Bright* v. *Legerton* (1861), 2 De G. F. & J. 606. Such evidence might now be admissible to prove the relationship of solicitor and client under the Civil Evidence Act, 1968.

[4] *Pritchard* v. *Walker* (1827), 3 C. & P. 212.

[5] *Barnard* v. *Sully* (1931), 47 T. L. R. 557; *Manawatu County* v. *Rowe*, [1956] N. Z. L. R. 78.

[6] *Per* Lord SIMONDS in *Morris* v. *Kanssen*, [1946] A. C. 459, at p. 475; [1946] 1 All E. R. 586, at p. 592.

[7] *Gibbins* v. *Skinner*, [1951] 2 K. B. 379; [1951] 1 All E.R. 1049.

[8] *Scott* v. *Baker*, [1969] 1 Q. B. 659; [1968] 2 All E. R. 993; *R.* v. *Martin*, [1967] 2 N. S. W. R. 523.

[9] [1973] A. C. 992; [1972] 3 All E. R. 895.

notice of dishonour of a bill of exchange which plainly could not be met because it was drawn on a company which had since gone into liquidation was mistakenly posted on the 30th December, the day before, instead of the day after, the bill was presented. The notice was received on the 31st December and it was presumed that the bill had already been dishonoured on that day because, if two acts are done, one of which ought to be done after the other, it is presumed that they were done in the right order.

(3) MECHANICAL INSTRUMENTS

A presumption which serves the same purpose of saving the time and expense of calling evidence as that served by the maxim *omnia praesumuntur rite esse acta* is the presumption that mechanical instruments were in order when they were used. In the absence of evidence to the contrary, the courts will presume that stopwatches and speedometers[1] and traffic lights[2] were in order at the material time; but the instrument must be one of a kind as to which it is common knowledge that they are more often than not in working order.

(4) POSSESSION AS EVIDENCE OF OWNERSHIP

A further rebuttable presumption of law is that of lawful origin. It lies at the root of the substantive law of acquisitive prescription.

> "Modern possession and user, being *prima facie* evidence of property and right, the judges attached to them an artificial weight, and held that uninterrupted, uncontradicted, and unexplained, they constituted proof from which a jury ought to infer a prescriptive right, coaeval with the time of legal memory."[3]

Quite apart from any question of prescriptive right, possession is always treated as *prima facie* evidence of ownership of real[4] or personal[5] property. As Wills put it in a well-known passage:

> "The acts of enjoyment from which the ownership of real property may be inferred, are very various, as for instance, the cutting of timber, the repairing of fences or banks, the perambulation of boundaries of a manor or parish, the taking of wreck on the foreshore, and the granting to others of licences or leases under which possession is taken and held; also the receipt of rents from tenants of the property; for all these acts are fractions of that sum total of enjoyment which characterises dominium." [6]

Moreover, in disputes concerning the title to a small piece of land, the plaintiff's possession of other parts of the same property is admissible evidence of his right to possession of the strip in question, as in *Jones* v. *Williams*,[7] where the plaintiff claimed to be the owner of the entire bed of a river at a certain spot, and his possession of the bed lower down the river was admitted to rebut the presumption of law that the defendant, the owner of land on the bank opposite to the plaintiff's land, owned the bed up to the middle of the stream. In these cases there must be such a common characteristic of locality as would raise an inference that the place

---

[1] *Nicholas* v. *Penny*, [1950] 2 K. B. 466; [1950] 2 All E. R. 89; *Skalde* v. *Evans*, [1966] S. A. S. R. 176; *R.* v. *Amyot*, [1968] 2 O. R. 626.
[2] *Tingle Jacobs & Co.* v. *Kennedy*, [1964] 1 All E. R. 888n.
[3] Best, *Principles of the Law of Evidence* (12th edition), 322.
[4] *Doe* d. *Graham* v. *Penfold* (1838), 8 C. & P. 536.
[5] *Robertson* v. *French* (1803), 4 East 130.
[6] *Law of Evidence* (3rd edition), 62.
[7] (1837), 2 M. & W. 326; *Doe* d. *Barrett* v. *Kemp* (1835), 2 Bing. N. C. 102.

in dispute belonged to the plaintiff if the parts over which he is proved to have exercised possession belonged to him, and, in modern times, questions of the admissibility of such evidence will normally only arise where the title deeds are not clear. In most cases, the matter is, in the first instance, governed by some such rebuttable presumption of law as the right of riparian owners to the bed of a river up to midstream, or that, where two properties are separated by a hedge and ditch, the ditch is the boundary.

(5) Absence of an Explanation and Failure to Give Evidence

The evidence against a man may be greatly strengthened by his failure to give an explanation or the inadequacy of the explanation which he does give; these negative facts can therefore be regarded as a species of retrospectant evidence. It is of particular importance in relation to the inferences that may be drawn from the accused's possession of recently stolen goods, and this will be discussed before some more general illustrations are given, after which an attempt will be made to place the absence of an explanation and a party's failure to give evidence in their proper perspective.

(i) **Possession of recently stolen goods.**—If someone is found in possession of goods soon after they have been missed, and he fails to give a credible explanation of the manner in which he came by them, the jury are justified in inferring that he was either the thief or else guilty of dishonestly handling the goods, knowing or believing them to have been stolen, contrary to section 22 of the Theft Act, 1968. The absence of an explanation is equally significant whether the case is being considered as one of theft or handling, but it has come into particular prominence in connection with the latter because persons found in possession of stolen goods are apt to say that they acquired them innocently from someone else. Where the only evidence is that the defendant on a charge of handling was in possession of stolen goods, a jury may infer guilty knowledge or belief (*a*) if he offers no explanation to account for his possession, or (*b*) if the jury are satisfied that the explanation he does offer is untrue. If, however, the explanation offered is one which leaves the jury in doubt as to whether he knew or believed the goods were stolen, they should be told that the case has not been proved, and therefore the verdict should be not guilty.[1] It goes without saying that what constitutes recent possession within the meaning of the above doctrine is a question of fact depending on the circumstances of the particular case,[2] but it must be emphasized that, even if no explanation is given by the handler, "the jury are entitled, but not compelled to convict".[3] In the absence of further incriminating circumstances, an inference is not warranted that someone in possession of goods obtained by means of blackmail or deception[4] knew of the unlawful obtaining, even if no explanation is forthcoming. The inference

---

[1] *R. v. Aves*, [1950] 2 All E. R. 330, this is the effect of *R. v. Schama, R. v. Abramovitch* (1914), 84 L. J. K. B. 396 (the leading case); see also *R. v. Garth*, [1949] 1 All E. R. 773.
[2] *R. v. Marcus* (1923), 17 Cr. App. Rep. 191. The circumstances of the receipt may be relied on as proof that the goods were stolen (*R. v. Sbarra* (1918), 87 L. J. K. B. 1003; *R. v. Fuschillo* (1940), 27 Cr. App. Rep. 193; *R. v. Guidice*, [1964] W. A. R. 128). The accused's demonstrably false testimony is evidence to the same effect (*R. v. Young* (1952), 36 Cr. App. Rep. 200).
[3] *Per* Lord Goddard, C.J., in *R. v. Cohen*, [1951] 1 K. B. 505, at p. 508; [1951] 1 All E. R. 203, at p. 206.
[4] Theft Act, 1968, s. 24 (4).

of guilty knowledge is warranted in the case of recently stolen goods because theft is by far the most common means of unlawful acquisition.[1] Now that theft and handling, unlike the former larceny and receiving, are not mutually exclusive offences because most handlers by receiving become thieves through a later appropriation, it is probably safer to convict of theft, where both offences are charged and the evidence justifies the conclusion that one or other of them was committed.[2]

(ii) General illustrations.—The importance of a party's failure to give a credible explanation of apparently damning circumstances can be illustrated by numerous isolated instances throughout the whole law of evidence. If someone who is charged with burglary was found in the hall of a house without having been asked to come there, it is incumbent on him as a matter of common sense, though not as a matter of law, to give a satisfactory explanation of his presence, and, if this is not forthcoming, the jury will be justified in inferring the existence of the requisite guilty intent.[3] On a charge of theft, proof of the accused's possession of a cheque drawn by the receiver in respect of the goods in question, coupled with his failure to give evidence, will warrant a conviction.[4] In *R.* v. *Nash*,[5] the appellant was charged with the murder of her child whose body was found in a well. She had been seen near the well with the child for whom she could not find a home, and she also told lies concerning the child's whereabouts. When affirming the conviction Lord COLERIDGE, C.J., said, "the facts which are proved call for an explanation, and beyond the admittedly untrue statements, none was forthcoming".[6]

To turn to civil cases, at the hearing of a husband's petition for nullity on the ground of the respondent's impotence, her failure to comply with an order for medical inspection may be taken into account by the court.[7]

If two cars are involved in a collision, and a passenger in one of them claims damages from both drivers, it has been said that "proof of the collision is held to be sufficient to call on the two defendants for an answer".[8] The principle underlying the cases in which reliance has been placed on the maxim *res ipsa loquitur* is based on the importance of the absence of an explanation. In *Ellor* v. *Selfridge & Co.*, for instance, the plaintiffs were hit by a van which mounted the pavement, and SCRUTTON, L.J., said

---

[1] *Director of Public Prosecutions* v. *Nieser*, [1959] 1 Q. B. 254; [1958] 3 All E. R. 662, where it was said that one way of supporting an inference that the accused knew of the unlawful obtaining would be to prove an association with the obtainer showing that they were in each other's confidence.

[2] *Stapylton* v. *O'Callaghan*, [1973] 2 All E. R. 782.

[3] *R.* v. *Wood* (1911), 7 Cr. App. Rep. 56.

[4] *R.* v. *Kelson* (1909), 3 Cr. App. Rep. 230.

[5] (1911), 6 Cr. App. Rep. 225.

[6] At p. 228.

[7] *W.* v. *S.*, [1905] P. 231.

[8] *Baker* v. *Market Harborough Industrial Co-operative Society*, [1953] 1 W. L. R. 1472, at p. 1476, *per* DENNING, L.J. See also *Bray* v. *Palmer*, [1953] 2 All E. R. 1449, and *France* v. *Parkinson*, [1954] 1 All E. R. 739. The effect of these decisions is that if two cars are in collision on cross-roads of equal status, and there is no further evidence, the correct inference is that both parties were negligent. *Hummerstone* v. *Leary*, [1921] 2 K. B. 664, is a decision to the same effect; but it was pointed out in *Nesterczuk* v. *Mortimore* (1965), 115 C. L. R. 140 that all these decisions are explicable on narrower grounds and the High Court of Australia held that the trial judge had rightly dismissed both claim and counterclaim where one of the two cars involved in a collision must have swerved and there was no evidence which. An inference of joint negligence may not be justified where the collision was not head-on but between rear portions of two vehicles (*Wotta* v. *Haliburton Oil Well Cementing Co., Ltd.*, [1955] 2 D. L. R. 785).

"The fact that in the present case the van appeared upon the pavement, where it had no business to be, and injured the plaintiffs on the pavement, and *the further fact that the defendants offered no explanation why their van was there* seem to be more consistent with negligence than with the exercise of reasonable care".[1]

Further discussion of this matter must, however, be deferred to Chapter VI.

(iii) General effect.—The absence of an explanation of facts which tell against a party should only be treated as evidence against him when the facts in question constitute a *prima facie* case in the sense that they would justify, without in any way necessitating, a finding of liability.[2] Even then, the absence of an explanation is only significant when the party against whom the *prima facie* case is proved can reasonably be expected to give an innocent explanation if there is one. When these requirements are satisfied, the failure to give an explanation will support an inference against the party who does not produce one. In general the approach of the courts is in accordance with the above propositions of common sense, although there is a tendency to hint at what is suspiciously like a distinction without a difference by speaking of the failure to give an explanation as something which adds weight to the opponent's evidence rather than as a fact which constitutes a separate item of circumstantial evidence against the party failing to explain. Criminal cases give rise to special considerations calling for discussion in subsequent chapters.

(*a*) *Civil cases.*—In *McQueen* v. *Great Western Rail. Co.*,[3] the plaintiff claimed that his goods had been lost owing to the crime of one of the defendant's servants. All he could prove was that the goods were delivered to the company, and placed on a truck in a siding to which the public had access, after which they disappeared. It was held that the defendant's failure to explain the loss did not make the plaintiff's evidence sufficient to sustain his case. As Cockburn, C.J., said:

"If a *prima facie* case is made out, capable of being displaced, and if the party against whom it is established might by calling particular witnesses and producing particular evidence displace that *prima facie* case, and he omits to adduce that evidence, then the inference fairly arises, as a matter of inference for the jury and not a matter of legal presumption, that the absence of that evidence is to be accounted for by the fact that even if it were adduced it would not displace the *prima facie* case. But that always presupposes that a *prima facie* case has been established; and unless we can see our way clearly to the conclusion that a *prima facie* case has been established, the omission to call witnesses who might have been called on the part of the defendant amounts to nothing."[4]

Very soon after the parties were enabled to testify in most civil cases by the Evidence Act, 1851, Alderson, B., recognised that the failure of one of them to deny a fact which it is in his power to deny "gives colour to the evidence against him".[5] Almost a hundred years later the same point was made more forcefully by an Australian judge when he said:

"When circumstances are proved indicating a conclusion and the only party who can give direct evidence of the matter prefers the well of the court to the witness box, a court is entitled to be bold."[6]

---

[1] (1930), 46 T. L. R. 236, italics supplied.
[2] See the first sense of "*prima facie* evidence" mentioned on p. 26.
[3] (1875), L. R. 10 Q. B. 569.
[4] At p. 574.
[5] *Boyle* v. *Wiseman* (1855), 10 Exch. 647, at p. 651.
[6] Rich, J., in *Insurance Commissioner* v. *Joyce* (1948), 77 C. L. R. 39, at p. 49. See also *Black* v. *Tung*, [1953] V. L. R. 629, and *Albus* v. *Ryder*, [1956] V. L. R. 56.

Even more recently it has been held in England that the indication in an acknowledgement of service of an intention not to defend divorce proceedings founded on adultery might be treated as an admission;[1] but this may go too far,[2] and perhaps the indication is best regarded as something which can be taken into account together with the other evidence, although not in itself amounting to proof of adultery.[3]

(b) *Criminal Cases.*—As long ago as 1820 ABBOT, C.J., said:

> "No person is to be required to explain or contradict until enough has been proved to warrant a reasonable and just conclusion against him, in the absence of explanation or contradiction; but when such proof has been given, and the nature of the case is such as to admit of explanation or contradiction if the conclusion to which the *prima facie* case tends to be true, and the accused offers no explanation or contradiction, can human reason do otherwise than adopt the conclusion to which the proof tends?"[4]

In those days the accused was incompetent to give evidence on his own behalf, but the explanation might have been given by other witnesses, or it might have been advanced out of court. However, the passage of time has shown that there are difficulties in drawing inferences adverse to the accused from his failure to give an out of court explanation to a police officer inquiring into the questions whether and by whom an offence has been committed. Subject to a few statutory exceptions, no-one commits an offence by refusing to answer police questions, and once a police officer has reasonable grounds for suspecting that a person has committed an offence, he must caution him before asking further questions, the caution begins with a reminder of the suspect's common law right to silence by telling him that he is not obliged to say anything;[5] it would therefore be wrong to draw adverse inferences from his failure to speak. The relevant decisions are discussed in chapter XIX. The logical result of this line of reasoning would have been a refusal on the part of the courts to pay any attention to the fact that the explanation ultimately advanced by the accused was belated and there are *dicta* recommending judges to make no comment in such situations;[6] but in the main the courts have drawn a distinction of questionable validity which was expressed in the following terms by MELFORD STEVENSON, J., speaking for the Court of Appeal:

> "It is, we think, clear . . . that it is wrong to say to a jury 'Because the accused exercised what is undoubtedly his right, the privilege of remaining silent, you may draw an inference of guilt'; it is quite a different matter to say 'This accused, as he is entitled to do, has not advanced at an earlier stage the explanation that has been offered to you to-day; you, the jury, may take that into account when you are assessing the weight that you think it right to attribute to the explanation.'"[7]

Proviso (b) to section 1 of the Criminal Evidence Act, 1898, prohibits comment by the prosecution on the accused's failure to give evidence, but, almost immediately after the Act came into force, it was decided that the

---

[1] *Pidduck* v. *Pidduck and Limbrick*, [1961] 3 All E. R. 481.
[2] *Inglis* v. *Inglis and Baxter*, [1968] P. 639; [1967] 2 All E. R. 71.
[3] *Jenson* v. *Jenson and Howard*, [1964] 2 All E. R. 231.
[4] *R.* v. *Burdett* (1820), 4 B. & Ald. 95, at p. 120. See also *Purdie* v. *Maxwell*, [1960] N. Z. L. R. 599, and *Sanders* v. *Hill*, [1964] S. A. S. R. 327.
[5] Judges' Rules, 1964, r. ii; *Hall* v. *R.*, [1971] 1 All E. R. 322.
[6] *R.* v. *Lewis* (1973), 57 Cr. App. Rep. 860, citing HUMPHRIES, J., in *R.* v. *Tune* (1944), 29 Cr. App. Rep. 162.
[7] *R.* v. *Ryan* (1966), 50 Cr. App. Rep. 144, at p. 148.

judge may comment on this fact in his summing-up[1] and it has since been held that comment by or on behalf of a co-accused is permissible.[2] The nature and extent of the comment which is permissible varies from case to case and the matter is discussed in Chapter XV. The justification of the need for caution in this matter is the undesirability of suggesting to the jury that the exercise by the accused of his privilege not to testify is equivalent to an admission of any part of the prosecution's case;[3] but the result has been another questionable distinction, viz. that between treating the accused's failure to give evidence as something that diminishes the weight of any defence he may raise and as something which may support an indirect inference of guilt by suggesting that the defence is worthless.

(6) Finger-Prints, Blood Tests and Tracker Dogs

(i) Finger prints.—A witness informs the court, often with the aid of photographs, that he took the finger prints of the accused and found them to be identical with those on some object with which the case is concerned. This is very strong retrospectant circumstantial evidence, for the courts take judicial notice of the fact that no two people have identical finger prints, i.e. no proof is required of this fact. Convictions have been upheld when there was no other evidence of identity.[4]

No special rules apply to the admissibility of finger print evidence. We have seen that, in *Callis* v. *Gunn*, [5] such evidence was admitted although the accused had not been cautioned when asked by a police officer for his prints. The ordinary principles governing the judge's discretion to exclude evidence at a criminal trial would of course apply to such a case. A Magistrates' Court has power to order the finger prints or palm prints of anyone over fourteen charged with an offence to be taken.[6]

(ii) Blood tests.[7]—The development of the law on this subject has been influenced by the change of attitude towards evidence which might bastardise a child born in wedlock.[8] At common law no court has power to order adults to undergo a blood test.[9] This is not because such an order might result in a person's furnishing evidence against himself, but because its enforcement would constitute an infringement of personal liberty.[10] At common law, a blood test may be ordered in the case of a child, and, except when the court is exercising its custodial jurisdiction, the interest of the child is not necessarily paramount.[11] Such evidence can be of the greatest value

---

[1] *R.* v. *Rhodes*, [1899] 1 Q. B. 77.
[2] *R.* v. *Wickham* (1971), 55 Cr. App. Rep. 199.
[3] *Tumahole Bereng* v. *R.*, [1949] A. C. 253, at p. 280.
[4] *R.* v. *Castleton* (1909), 3 Cr. App. Rep. 74; cf. *R.* v. *Court* (1960), 44 Cr. App. Rep. 242 (finger-prints on car wind-screen insufficient evidence of possession on receiving charge).
[5] [1964] 1 Q. B. 495; [1963] 3 All E. R. 677; p. 28, *ante*.
[6] Magistrates' Courts Act, 1952, s. 40; Criminal Justice Act, 1967, s. 33.
[7] See *"The Nature and Use of Blood Group Evidence"* by H. J. Bartholomew, 24 M. L. R. 333 (1961), and Mary Hayes, *"The Use of Blood Tests in Pursuit of Truth"*, 87 L. Q. R. 85 (1971).
[8] "I know that it is a sad thing to bastardise a child but there are graver wrongs;" *per* Ormrod, J., *H.* v. *H.* (*H. by his guardian intervening*), [1966] 1 All E. R. 356, at p. 357.
[9] *W.* v. *W.* (No 4), [1964] P. 67; [1963] 2 All E. R. 386; affd. [1964] P. 67, at p. 72; [1963] 2 All E. R. 841; *S.* v. *S* and *W.* v. *Official Solicitor*, [1972] A. C. 24, at p. 43.
[10] *S.* v. *S.*, [1972] A. C. 24, at p. 43, per Lord Reid.
[11] *S.* v. *S.*, *supra*.

on issues concerning the paternity of a child, and it was acted on in a number of cases in which the adults consented to tests before this aspect of blood test evidence came to be controlled by the Family Law Reform Act, 1969.[1] The fact that the child's blood belongs to a certain group may exclude the possibility that a particular man is the father. Until judicial notice is taken of this exclusionary effect of a blood test, medical evidence will of course be required.

The effect of sections 18–24 of the Act of 1969 is that a court may direct any party to civil proceedings in which the paternity of any person falls to be determined to undergo a blood test. Persons over 16 must consent to the test, and, in the case of someone under 16, the consent of the person with care and control is to be obtained whenever possible. The court may draw such inferences as seem proper from a failure to obey the direction and, if the presumption of legitimacy operates in favour of a party claiming relief, who fails to obey the direction, the claim may be dismissed notwithstanding the absence of evidence rebutting the presumption. The result is that the courts are provided with an indirect means of obliging adults to submit to a blood test.

A similar technique is employed in section 7 of the Road Traffic Act, 1972, (re-enacting section 2 of the Road Traffic Act, 1962) under which, on charges of driving while unfit to do so through drink or drugs or of being in charge of a motor vehicle while unfit for these reasons, the court is directed to have regard to the presence of alcohol or drugs in the body of the accused as ascertained by an examination of samples of his blood or urine taken with his consent. It is expressly provided that the accused's refusal to supply the requisite specimens may, unless reasonable cause for not doing so be shown, be treated as supporting any evidence given on behalf of the prosecution, or as rebutting any evidence given on behalf of the defence with regard to the accused's condition.

(iii) Tracker dogs.—There does not appear to be any fully reported English case on the admissibility in evidence of the behaviour of tracker dogs. If, after being taken to the scene of a crime, a dog picks up a scent and leads those in charge of him to the accused, a useful piece of retrospectant circumstantial evidence may have been brought into existence. The South African Appellate Division regarded it as too unreliable to be received on account of the danger of misunderstanding the dog's behaviour.[2] Such evidence has, however, since been received in Scotland,[3] Northern Ireland[4] and New Zealand.[5] It would in every case be necessary for evidence to be received about the training, skill and habits of the particular dog and its handler, and evidence or judicial notice of the fact that each human being has a different scent which is liable to be picked up by a well-trained dog would be necessary. The person giving such evidence must not express his opinion about what the dog was thinking at the material time.[6]

---

[1] *H. v. H. (H. by his guardian intervening)*, [1966] 1 All E. R. 356; *B. v. A.-G. (B. intervening)*, [1966] 2 All E. R. 145.
[2] *R. v. Tupedo*, [1960] A. D. 58.
[3] *Patterson v. Nixon* 1960 S. C. (J) 42.
[4] *R. v. Montgomery*, [1966] N. I. 120.
[5] *R. v. Lindsay*, [1970] N. Z. L. R. 1002.
[6] *R. v. Te Whiu and Buckton*, [1964] N. Z. L. R. 748.

(7) Corpus Delicti [1]

Every contested criminal case raises two questions, although there may often be no dispute about the first. The questions are was the crime charged committed? and was it committed by the accused? The first is often said to be concerned with the "proof of the *corpus delicti*".

On a trial for murder, for example, the courts will be loath to convict unless someone deposes to the death of the deceased, or this fact is admitted by the accused who either denies malice aforethought [2] or withdraws his confession [3] at the trial. It was once thought that there could not be a conviction for murder or manslaughter in the absence of some direct proof of death. Great caution is obviously required before there can be a conviction for murder without a corpse but a person has been convicted of murder in the absence of such evidence,[4] when the facts were such as to render it highly probable that the accused killed the deceased and disposed of his body.

In *R.* v. *Burton* the accused was seen to come out of a warehouse with a quantity of pepper. As there was a great deal of pepper inside the warehouse, none was proved to be missing, but the accused was nevertheless convicted of stealing pepper. In fact he made statements amounting to confessions of guilt, but MAULE, J., said:

> "If a man go into the London docks sober, without means of getting drunk and come out of one of the cellars very drunk wherein are a million gallons of wine, I think that would be reasonable evidence that he had stolen some of the wine in the cellar though you could not prove that any wine was stolen, or any wine was missed." [5]

SECTION 2. EVIDENCE OF IDENTITY

Evidence of identity may be given in a great number of different cases, but, in each instance, the proposition in support of which it is tendered is the same, namely, that, contrary to the contention of one of the litigants, two persons or things are identical. The existence of a particular person or thing must be assumed before any such question can arise, and the court then has to determine which of two contentions is established: the contention that the person or thing to which reference is made by one of the parties is the same as the person or thing whose existence is assumed, or the contention that the two are different. The problem frequently arises in criminal cases where there may be no doubt that a crime has been committed, and the only issue is whether the accused was the criminal, but questions of identity may also be raised in civil cases as where each of the two claimants to an estate alleges that he is the only son of the deceased owner. Owing, perhaps, to the existence of several notorious instances of mistaken identity, a certain amount of case law has evolved on this subject,

---

[1] See Norval Morris in 68 L. Q. R. 391, and Delaney *ibid.*, 560 (Irish cases).

[2] As in *R.* v. *Camb* (1947), Notable British Trials (admission corpse pushed through porthole, though death alleged to have been accidental).

[3] As in *R.* v. *Davidson* (1934), 25 Cr. App. Rep. 21.

[4] *R.* v. *Onufrejczyk*, [1955] 1 Q. B. 388; [1955] 1 All E. R. 247. See also *R.* v. *Horry*, [1952] N. Z. L. R. 111, and case note by Northey, 15 M. L. R. 348.

[5] (1854), Dears. C. C. 282, at p. 284. See *R.* v. *Joiner* (1910), 4 Cr. App. Rep. 64, on the need for caution where the accused is in possession of goods in suspicious circumstances, but there is no evidence that they were stolen.

and it may be conveniently discussed under the heads of primary evidence of identification, secondary evidence of identification and circumstantial evidence of identity.

A. PRIMARY EVIDENCE OF IDENTIFICATION

It might be thought that in criminal cases there could not be better identification of the accused than that of a witness who goes into the box and swears that the man in the dock is the one he saw coming out of a house at a particular time, or the man who assaulted him. Nevertheless, such evidence is suspect where there has been no previous identification of the accused by the witness, and this is because its weight is reduced by the reflection that, if there is any degree of resemblance between the man in the dock and the person previously seen by the witness, the witness may very well think to himself that the police must have got hold of the right person, particularly if he has already described the latter to them, with the result that he will be inclined to swear positively to a fact of which he is by no means certain. It has therefore been held to be undesirable for the police to do nothing about the question of identification until the accused is brought before the magistrates, and then ask a witness for the prosecution some such question as "Is that the man?" [1] The correct procedure is for the police to hold an identification parade before the trial or preliminary examination, placing the accused with a sufficient number of other people, leaving the witness to pick him out if he can, without assistance. This latter requirement is most important, and the Court of Criminal Appeal may quash a conviction if the police have attempted to point the accused out beforehand to someone who is then asked to identify him.[2] These are essentially matters which go to the weight rather than the admissibility of evidence, and it has not been possible to lay down rules with regard to primary evidence of identification in civil cases. In suits for divorce it may, for instance, be necessary to call upon a witness to identify the co-respondent at the hearing, although he has not identified him previously. So far as criminal cases are concerned, several branches of the law of evidence are devoted to insuring the most scrupulously fair conduct on the part of the police, and this is why it is desirable to have something approximating to fixed rules on the subject of evidence of identification.

The courts insist on every precaution where photographs are employed as a means of identification before trial.

> "It is one thing for a police officer, who is doubtful upon the question who shall be arrested, to show a photograph to another person in order to obtain information or a clue upon that matter; it is another thing for a police officer dealing with witnesses who are afterwards to be called as identifying witnesses to show to those persons photographs of those whom they are about to be asked to identify beforehand. It is clearly illegitimate, it would be most improper, to inform a witness beforehand who is to be called as an identifying witness by the process of making the features of the accused familiar to him through a photograph. But even where the photographs are employed to obtain information on the question of arrest, it is fair that all proper precautions should be observed. . . . The fair thing is . . . to show a series of

---

[1] R. v. *Chapman* (1911), 7 Cr. App. Rep. 53; R. v. *Cartwright* (1914), 10 Cr. App. Rep. 219.
[2] R. v. *Dickman* (1910), 5 Cr. App. Rep. 135; R. v. *Bundy* (1910), 5 Cr. App. Rep. 270; R. v. *Varley* (1914), 10 Cr. App. Rep. 125.

photographs, and to see if the person who is expected to give information can pick out the prospective defendant." [1]

Even when this last method has been employed, it is desirable that every precaution should be taken against informing the jury that the witness's identification of the accused before trial had been made possible by means of a photograph in the possession of the police, for this would indicate that he had some kind of criminal record.

So great is the need for caution when identity is in issue that the Supreme Court of Eire has held that a cautionary warning must be given to the jury in all cases of visual identification of a stranger even when there is more than one witness,[2] a precaution which appears to have been held unnecessary by the English Court of Criminal Appeal even when there is only one witness.[3] In *Arthurs* v. *A.-G. for Northern Ireland,*[4] however, the House of Lords held that no special warning need be given where the identifying witness and the accused were previously acquainted with each other, leaving open for future consideration the necessity for a special direction where there was no such acquaintance. The Court of Appeal has since held that, even in such a case, the law does not require the judge to give a specific warning about the dangers of convicting on evidence of visual identification, still less is any particular form of words necessary.[5] The Court pointed out, however, that every summing-up must be fair and that it would be difficult for a summing-up to be fair in such a case unless it caused the jury to give careful consideration to the circumstances of identification.

The Criminal Law Revision Committee regarded mistaken identification as "by far the greatest cause of actual or possible wrong convictions", and, in addition to making various suggestions concerning police practice, the Committee recommended that, in all cases of disputed identification, the judge should warn the jury of the special need for caution before convicting.[6]

B. SECONDARY EVIDENCE OF IDENTIFICATION

As identification at the trial for the first time is liable to be suspect, there is no doubt that the identifying witness can swear that he identified the accused on a former occasion, and, in that event, another witness may be called to say that he saw him do so. In *R.* v. *Christie*[7] a doubt was expressed whether such evidence can be given when the witness who identifies the accused in the dock does not depose to having identified him on a former occasion. A little boy, who alleged that he was the victim of an indecent assault, identified Christie as his assailant at the trial, but did not state that he had identified him shortly after the events to which he had just deposed. Nevertheless, the boy's mother and a policeman were allowed to swear that they saw the boy approach Christie immediately after the episode of which he complained, touch him on the sleeve, say "That is the man", and give an account of what had

---

[1] *R.* v. *Dwyer*, [1925] 2 K. B. 799, at p. 802, *per* Lord HEWART, C.J. See also *R.* v. *Goss* (1923), 17 Cr. App. Rep. 196; *R.* v. *Haslam* (1925), 19 Cr. App. Rep. 59; *R.* v. *Hinds*, [1932] 2 K. B. 644; *R.* v. *Seiga* (1961), 45 Cr. App. Rep. 220. On identification parades generally see articles in [1955] Crim. L. R. 525 and [1963] Crim. L. R. 479 and 545.
[2] *People (A.-G.)* v. *Dominic Casey (No. 2)*, [1963] I. R. 33.
[3] *R.* v. *Williams*, [1956] Crim. L. R. 833.
[4] (1970), 55 Cr. App. Rep. 161.   [5] *R.* v. *Long* (1973), 57 Cr. App. Rep. 871.
[6] 11th Report, paras. 198–203.   [7] [1914] A. C. 545.

happened. The House of Lords held that this evidence was legally admissible as being concerned with statements made in the presence of the accused, but Lords ATKINSON and PARKER considered that the evidence was also admissible to show that the boy had previously identified Christie. They considered it quite as truly primary evidence of what took place as the boy's evidence would have been. Lord MOULTON, on the other hand, considered that the procedure adopted at the trial of asking the mother and policeman, but not the boy, about the latter's identification of Christie immediately after the event amounted to using secondary evidence where primary evidence was obtainable. In *R.* v. *Osborne* and *R.* v. *Virtue*[1] where one witness for the prosecution said that she did not recollect having pointed the accused out at an identification parade, and another prosecution witness said that she did not think that the man she pointed out was in court, it was held that the evidence of the police officer who conducted the parade that the witnesses did identify the accused had been rightly admitted at the trial. Accordingly, although they may have technically been in a minority, the views of Lords ATKINSON and PARKER may now be taken to represent the law.

C. CIRCUMSTANTIAL EVIDENCE OF IDENTITY

When there is no doubt that an act has been done, and the question is whether it was the act of a particular person, all relevant evidence is normally admissible in order to prove or disprove that fact. Obvious instances are afforded by cases in which the criminal has left traces behind him. The facts that the crime was probably committed by a left-handed man and that the accused was left-handed, or any other physical or mental peculiarity exhibited by the criminal may be shown to have been exhibited by the accused. This is, however, a branch of the law in which it is often necessary to have regard to the general prohibition on evidence which merely goes to show criminal tendencies, or a disposition to commit particular crimes on the part of the accused. From the point of view of relevancy, these should often be admissible because they go to show that the accused was a member of a comparatively small class of which the criminal was also a member, but the prejudicial nature of the evidence will render it inadmissible unless the tendency or disposition is of particular relevance to a matter in issue in the proceedings.

There is, of course, a variety of other factors which will go to prove membership of a restricted class. On a charge of bigamy, it is necessary for the prosecution to prove that the accused duly went through a ceremony of marriage with the first spouse. Since 1914, the latter has been a competent witness for the prosecution, and the necessary identification can often be accomplished by his or her direct evidence. But, where this is not forthcoming, and where there is no other direct proof of the first marriage, such as that of a witness who was present at its celebration, it may be established by circumstantial evidence of which a material item would be the identity of the accused's name with that of the person named in a marriage certificate produced by the prosecutor. Standing by itself it would probably be insufficient in any case, but a conviction for bigamy has been upheld by the Court of Criminal Appeal on such evidence coupled with the fact that the accused cohabited with a woman of the same name as the

---

[1] [1973] Q. B. 678; [1973] 1 All E. R. 649.

other person mentioned in the marriage certificate and referred to her as his wife.[1]

Personal identity may, of course, be established by many other factors than that of name, and obvious instances are provided by occupation, education, and mental or physical idiosyncrasies. In the *Lovat Peerage Case*,[2] it was held that the fact that an ancestor was reputed to have been guilty of manslaughter coupled with the fact that a similar tradition prevailed with regard to the lineage of one of the claimants was some evidence that the latter was the descendant of the former. The sole question with regard to the admissibility of circumstantial evidence of this nature is whether a particular characteristic is sufficiently rare, or a class sufficiently small, to make it worth while for the court to hear evidence tending to show possession of that characteristic, or membership of that class.[3]

SECTION 3. RES INTER ALIOS ACTA

The maxim *res inter alios acta alteri nocere non debet* (no one should be prejudiced by a transaction between strangers) used to be regarded as one of the principal rules governing the admissibility of evidence. It will therefore be convenient to conclude this chapter with a few observations on the subject, although the maxim does no more than indicate one among many other grounds for excluding certain items of circumstantial evidence on the score of irrelevancy, and one among many other grounds for excluding hearsay as evidence of the truth of that which was heard.

The maxim is, of course, invoked in controversies concerning the substantive law, as well as in those affecting the law of evidence, and Stephen pointed out that it fails as a statement of general principle:

"because it is not true that a man cannot be affected by transactions to which he is not a party. Illustrations to the contrary are obvious and innumerable; bankruptcy, marriage, indeed every transaction of life, would supply them."

To quote again from the same author:

"the application of the maxim to the law of evidence is obscure, because it does not show how unconnected transactions should be supposed to be relevant to each other". [4]

It is sometimes said to lie at the root of the exclusion of a party's misconduct on other occasions as evidence which merely shows disposition, but we shall see that such evidence is rejected, either on the ground that it is too

---

[1] *R. v. Birtles* (1911), 6 Cr. App. Rep. 177.   [2] (1885), 10 App. Cas. 763.
[3] "Where a certain circumstance, feature or mark may commonly be found associated with a large number of objects, the presence of that feature or mark in two supposed objects is little indication of their identity, because, on the general principle of relevancy, the other conceivable hypotheses are so numerous, *i.e.* the objects that possess that mark are numerous and therefore two of them possessing it may well be different. But where the objects possessing the mark are only one or a few, and the mark is found in two supposed instances, the chances of their being different are nil, or are comparatively small. . . . Suppose there existed a parent named John Smith whose heirs are sought; and there is also a claimant whose parent's name was John Smith. The name John Smith is associated with so many persons that the chances of two supposed persons of that name being different are too numerous to allow us to consider the common mark as having appreciable probative value. But the chances may be diminished by adding other common circumstances going to form the common mark. Add, for instance, another name-circumstance,—as that the name of each supposed person was John Barebones Bonaparte Smith; here the chances of there being two persons of that name in any district however large are instantly reduced to the minimum" (II *Wigmore*, p. 386).
[4] *Digest of the Law of Evidence* (12th edition), 189.

remotely relevant, or else because it is too highly prejudicial. The maxim can have no possible bearing on the latter reason for excluding such evidence, and, so far as the first is concerned, the real basis of exclusion is that an enquiry into other transactions would merely confuse the court by introducing a multiplicity of side issues. The maxim has been mentioned by the courts in a similar context. In *Holcombe* v. *Hewson*,[1] for instance, Lord ELLENBOROUGH spoke of the evidence tendered to show that the plaintiff had supplied other publicans with good beer as *res inter alios acta*, but he went on to say that he could not hear witnesses to the plaintiff's general character and habits as a brewer, and the evidence of the other publicans would probably have been admitted if it had concerned beer of the same brew as that of which complaint was made by the defendant.[2] If this is so, the case illustrates the unsatisfactory nature of the maxim as a test of relevancy. Transactions between strangers, or between one party to litigation and a stranger may be proved provided they have a real bearing on the issues in a given case.

A moment's reflection should suffice to show that much evidence which is regularly admitted would have to be excluded if the maxim were applied literally. On a charge of handling, it is essential to show that the goods were stolen or obtained by a deception, and, generally speaking, this fact could not be proved without reference to transactions to which the accused was not a party. On prosecutions for theft, evidence is constantly admitted to show how the prosecutor marked the goods or money in question, or put them in some place to which the accused had access; all evidence by which ownership of the *locus in quo* is proved by acts of possession over adjoining property, or by which custom and usage, or the qualifications of expert witnesses to speak on topics involving special knowledge is established, involves proof of *res inter alios acta*.

Reference is frequently made to the maxim in connection with the rule against hearsay, the theory being that a person ought not to be adversely affected by statements made, any more than by things done, behind his back. There is no doubt that in the days when parties were incompetent witnesses, the fact that statements tendered in evidence were made in their absence was stressed as a ground for excluding hearsay, but, in modern times, it is impossible to treat the maxim as the general ground for the exclusion of such evidence. The rule against hearsay applies as much to statements made in the presence of a party as to those made in his absence, and, in either event, they are inadmissible at common law to prove the truth of that which they assert unless they can be brought within one of the exceptions to the rule. Moreover, statements made in the absence of a party may sometimes be proved for a purpose which is nonetheless prejudicial to him although it is collateral to the main issues in the case, as where a complaint is admitted on a sexual charge, or proof is given of a previous inconsistent statement of a witness.

The maxim is also invoked as the ground for excluding judgments in former proceedings as evidence of the facts upon which they were based. No doubt it is a sound general principle that:

"a transaction between two parties, in judicial proceedings, ought not to be binding upon a third; for it would be unjust to bind any person who could

---

[1] (1810), 2 Camp. 391; p. 20, *supra*.
[2] *Manchester Brewery* v. *Coombs* (1900), 82 L.T. 347 at p. 349.

not be admitted to make a defence, or to examine witnesses, or to appeal from a judgment he might think erroneous"[1]

but it is difficult to see what force is added to the principle by referring to such a transaction as *res inter alios acta.*

No one would now treat the maxim as one of the fundamental rules of evidence, and it is best regarded as something which has contributed to the historical development of the modern law. The objection to all such broad statements is that they tend to draw attention away from the crucial question of the purpose for which evidence is tendered. If it be said that, as a general rule, evidence of things done and statements made behind a person's back is inadmissible, the result may be a mechanical approach to the question of admissibility which can lead to the exclusion of highly relevant evidence without any justification on the score of policy. This is well illustrated by the decision of the court of first instance in "*The Douglas*".[2] A ship had sunk in the Thames owing to the fault of its crew, and the mate communicated with the harbourmaster who told him that he would take steps to have the wreck lighted. This was not done, with the result that another vessel collided with the wreck. In the ensuing action for negligence brought against the owner of the wreck, the trial judge excluded evidence of the communications between the mate and the harbourmaster on the ground that they took place behind the back of the plaintiff, the owner of the other vessel. The Court of Appeal held that the evidence ought to have been received because "It was tendered as relating to an act done and tending to disprove negligence, a competent person having been sent to inform the harbourmaster". It seems almost incredible that such evidence should ever have been excluded, but this case is only one among several examples which could be given of the disastrous consequences of a slavish adherence to such statements as that evidence of what took place behind a person's back is usually inadmissible, and these statements are traceable to the application of the useless maxim *res inter alios acta alteri nocere non debet* to the law of evidence.

---

[1] *R.* v. *Duchess of Kingston* (1776), 20 Howell's State Trials 573, *per* DE GREY C.J.
[2] (1882), 7 P. D. 151.

CHAPTER III

THE FUNCTIONS OF THE JUDGE AND JURY

"Historically, the separation of the functions of the judge and jury has left
so deep a mark upon English jurisprudence that the rules and habits of
juristic thought, which it has engendered, are scarcely touched by the present
day decline of jury trial in civil matters. If jury trial is ever abolished, many
of these rules and conceptions will yet remain as long as the common law
system is in being. The judge sitting alone must constantly be aware of the line
which divides his two quite distinct functions. And the proper observation
of the distinction is by no means a mere academic matter, but of the highest
practical importance in its bearing on the exercise of appellate jurisdiction." [1]

A due appreciation of the respective functions of the judge and jury is
therefore essential to a proper understanding of the law of evidence, and
that is why a separate chapter has been allotted to them. The general rule
is discussed in the first section, and some of the more direct methods of
judicial control over the jury are considered in section 2.

Empirical research into the jury is beyond the scope of this book. It
must be admitted, however, that no discussion of the law of evidence in
criminal cases will ever be completely satisfactory until we have some idea
of the extent to which the average jury understands the directions which
the law requires the judge to give, and whether jurors are as comprehending,
uncomprehending or prejudiced as some of the rules of evidence suppose.
Is the statement that the extra-judicial admission of one of two accused is
only evidence against him although it also incriminates the other really
meaningful to the average jury? Is the distinction between treating the
accused's previous convictions of offences of the kind with which he is
charged as something which affects the credibility of his evidence (a permissible course) and treating them as something justifying an inference of
guilt (a prohibited course) really appreciated? These, and a number of
similar questions, could only be conclusively answered if there was a great
deal of random "bugging" of which juries were not apprised, but such a
procedure would, with some justice, excite hostility in some quarters. In
the meantime, other types of empirical research, though of great value,
can only be regarded as second best. [2]

SECTION 1. THE GENERAL RULE

The general rule is that questions of law must be determined by the
judge and questions of fact must be determined by the jury; but there are
some special cases as well as exceptions to the general rule.

---

[1] Nigel Bridge (now BRIDGE, J.), 12 M. L. R. 275. Many of the matters considered in
this chapter are discussed by Sir PATRICK DEVLIN (now Lord DEVLIN), in *Trial by Jury*
(The Hamlyn Lectures for 1956, revised in 1966). See also W. R. Cornish, *The Jury*, and
"English Jury and Law of Evidence", by G. D. Nokes, 31 Tulane Law Review 153.

[2] For examples, see Kalven and Zeisel, *The American Jury*; McCabe and Purves,
Bypassing the Jury, and *The Jury at Work* (occasional pamphlets published by Basil
Blackwell and Co. for the Oxford Penal Research Unit); W. F. Cornish and others,
"Juries and the Rules of Evidence", [1973] Crim L. R. 208; A. P. Sealey and W. R.
Cornish, "Jurors and Their Verdicts", 36 M. L. R. 496 (1973).

A. SOME SPECIAL CASES

(i) Construction.—In many cases, the actual words used by the parties may be a vital consideration, and, if there is any doubt concerning that which was in fact written or said, it must be determined by the jury in accordance with the general rule. The parties are presumed to have used words in their ordinary meaning in the absence of evidence to the contrary. The orthodox view is that the determination of the ordinary meaning of words comes within the province of the judge, although the jury must decide whether they were used in a peculiar sense or with reference to a particular surrounding circumstance. Accordingly it has been said to be the jury's duty to take the construction of words from the judge either:

> "absolutely, if there be no words to be construed as words of art or phrases used in commerce and no surrounding circumstances to be ascertained, or conditionally, when those words or circumstances are necessarily referred to them". [1]

In many cases the judge will no doubt deem it unnecessary to direct the jury with regard to the ordinary meaning of words, and the question whether a party's conduct or state of mind comes within the ordinary meaning has to be determined by the jury, as when they decide whether the accused appropriated property "dishonestly" within the meaning of section 1 of the Theft Act, 1968. [2] It is therefore only in a strictly limited sense that questions of construction constitute an exception to the general rule under consideration, if they can be said to do so at all.

(ii) Defamation.—Fox's Libel Act of 1792 provides that, in criminal prosecutions for libel, the jury shall, after direction by the judge on the law, give a general verdict upon the whole matter. In consequence of this statute, it has come to be the practice for the judge to determine whether the document in question is capable of bearing the meaning alleged by the prosecution, while the jury decides whether it does in fact amount to a criminal libel. This has been said to be because the intention of the parties is always a question for the jury, and the meaning of the document is part of that intention; [3] but the same procedure is adopted in civil cases where the intention of the parties is, to say the least, not so important as on a criminal charge. [4] It is therefore best to regard the established practice as a compromise. A literal adherence to the rule that the construction of documents and the ordinary meaning of words is a matter of law for the judge would mean that the jury simply determines whether the alleged libel was published, and whether the circumstances from which any suggested innuendo could be inferred existed. This was the usual practice before Fox's Libel Act, but it proved to be objectionable on political grounds, and because it contravened the jury's right to return a general verdict in criminal cases. [5]

(iii) Perjury.—Under s. 11 (6) of the Perjury Act, 1911, the question whether a statement on which perjury is assigned is material is one of law to be determined by the court of trial. In most cases the materiality of a

---

[1] *Neilson* v. *Harford* (1841), 8 M. & W. 806, at p. 823, *per* PARKE, B.
[2] *R.* v. *Feely*, [1973] Q. B. 530; [1973] 1 All E. R. 341.
[3] *Per* Lord ABINGER, C.J., in *Morrell* v. *Frith* (1838), 3 M. & W. 402, at pp. 404-5
[4] *Nevill* v. *Fine Arts and General Insurance Co.*, [1897] A. C. 68.
[5] Holdsworth, *History of English Law*, vol. 10, 688.

statement would naturally be treated as a question of fact, and there are some express statutory provisions to this effect,[1] but, in the case of perjury, it is probably convenient that the matter should be treated as one of law in the interests of certainty and uniformity.

B. EXCEPTIONS

(1) FOREIGN LAW

So far as the courts of England and Wales are concerned, the law of other countries, including Scotland, Eire[2] since 1921, and the British dominions and colonies, is a matter of fact to be determined on the evidence adduced in a particular case.[3] Thus, if the validity of a ceremony of marriage is among the facts in issue, proof of the ceremony will not be · sufficient, for it must usually be shown to have constituted a formally valid marriage according to the law of the place of celebration.

Down to 1920, the evidence relating to the foreign law was submitted to the jury, but s. 15 of the Administration of Justice Act of that year provided that, where for the purpose of disposing of any action or any other matter which is being tried by a judge with a jury in any court in England or Wales it is necessary to ascertain the law of any other country which is applicable to the facts of the case, any question as to the effect of the evidence given with respect to that law shall, instead of being submitted to the jury, be decided by the judge alone.[4] The difficulty of the points which may be involved is no doubt an ample justification for this provision which has been held to be wide enough to cover criminal proceedings.[5]

(2) REASONABLENESS

The reasonableness of a particular belief or course of conduct is essentially a question of fact, and, as such, it normally has to be determined by the jury, but, in certain civil cases, it must be decided by the judge, although he may leave subsidiary issues upon which the question of reasonableness ultimately depends to the jury. In an action for malicious prosecution, the question whether the defendant had reasonable and probable cause for initiating the criminal proceedings must be answered by the judge.[6] It is also the duty of the judge to determine whether the terms of a covenant in restraint of trade are reasonably necessary for the protection

---

[1] *E.g.*, Marine Insurance Act, 1906, s. 20 (7).

[2] See "Irish Law in English Courts" by G. D. Nokes 9 *International and Comparative Law Quarterly* 564 (1960). The Ireland Act, 1949 under which Eire is for many purposes not a foreign country, has not affected the position (*Todd* v. *Todd*, [1961] 2 All E. R. 881). So far as Northern Ireland is concerned the English Courts would probably take judicial notice of the common law of Northern Ireland, and of English statutes applying to Northern Ireland but not of statutes of the Northern Ireland Parliament. Under the Maintenance Orders Act, 1950, s. 32(2) judicial notice may be taken of the laws of all parts of the United Kingdom in maintenance proceedings.

[3] Except that the House of Lords takes cognisance of the law of Scotland, and the Privy Council takes cognisance of the law of the British Commonwealth (*Elliot* v. *Joicey*, [1935] A. C. 209, at pp. 213 and 236).

[4] S. 15 of the Administration of Justice Act, 1920, has been repealed so far as the High Court is concerned by the Judicature Act, 1925, but a similar provision is contained in s. 102 of that Act. See also s. 97 of the County Courts Act, 1959, as to County Courts.

[5] *R.* v. *Hammer*, [1923] 2 K. B. 786. For proof of foreign law see Chapter XXII.

[6] *Herniman* v. *Smith*, [1938] A. C. 305; [1938] 1 All E. R. 1. A similar rule applies in the case of false imprisonment.

of the covenantee;[1] but he may require the jury to find relevant facts concerning the information on which the defendant acted in the first case, and the nature of the covenantee's business in the second.

(3) Facts Affecting the Admissibility of Evidence [2]

"There are conditions precedent which are required to be fulfilled before evidence is admissible for the jury. Thus, an oath, or its equivalent, and competency, are conditions precedent to admitting *viva voce* evidence; and the apprehension of immediate death to admitting evidence of dying declarations;[3] a search to secondary evidence of lost writings; and stamps to certain written instruments;[4] and so is consanguinity or affinity in the declarant to declarations of deceased relatives.[5] The judge alone has to decide whether the condition has been fulfilled. If the proof is by witnesses, he must decide on their credibility. If counter-evidence is offered, he must receive it before he decides; and he has no right to ask the opinion of the jury on the fact of a condition precedent."[6]

Other examples of the application of the rule are afforded by cases in which the accused objects to the reception of a confession on the ground that it was not given voluntarily,[7] or a witness claims to be privileged from answering a particular question.[8] In all such instances, the judge, and not the jury, must determine disputed facts, and the entirely separate nature of these preliminary or incidental issues was emphasised by the old practice under which witnesses who deposed to them were required to take a different oath, known as the *"voir dire"* from that sworn by those giving evidence which was to be submitted to the jury. The trial of the incidental issues is often called "a trial within a trial".

It is probably true to say that the judge is not bound by all the exclusionary rules in determining what material to receive as proof of facts constituting a condition precedent to the admissibility of certain items of evidence, although he is generally as much bound by these rules when sitting alone as when there is a jury. An affidavit has been accepted in support of the contention that a witness was too ill to attend court, with the result that a deposition previously made by him could be read in evidence;[9] but it is impossible to speak with any certainty concerning the exact limits of this doctrine, because there is no modern English authority.[10]

---

[1] *Dowden and Pook, Ltd.* v. *Pook*, [1904] 1 K. B. 45.

[2] For thorough, if, from the English point of view, rather elaborate, discussions of this subject see Maguire and Epstein, *Preliminary Questions of Fact in Determining the Admissibility of Evidence*, 40 H. L. R. 392 (1926), and Morgan, *Functions of Judge and Jury in Determining Preliminary Questions of Fact*, 43 H. L. R. 165 (1929). See also Morgan, *Some Problems of Proof*, Chapter 3.

[3] Under an exception to the rule against hearsay as to the cause of death in prosecutions of homicide. For an early example of the exclusive control of the judge in such a case, see *R.* v. *Hucks* (1816), 1 Stark 521, N. P.

[4] For an example see *Bartlett* v. *Smith* (1843), 11 M. & W. 483.

[5] Admissible under a common law exception to the rule against hearsay on genealogical issues (now only applicable in criminal cases).

[6] *Doe* d. *Jenkins* v. *Davies* (1847), 10 Q. B. 314, at p. 323, *per* Lord Denman, C.J.

[7] *R.* v. *Chadwick* (1934), 24 Cr. App. Rep. 138.

[8] *Stace* v. *Griffith* (1869), L. R. 2 P. C. 420, at pp. 427–8.

[9] *Beaufort (Duke)* v. *Crawshay* (1866), L. R. 1 C. P. 699.

[10] In *R.* v. *Chadwick*, *supra*, it was held that the judge ought not to have referred to the depositions in order to decide whether a confession was voluntary. For early English cases and modern American authorities, see 36 Yale Law Journal 1141. Under r. 104 (a) of the United States Federal Rules the judge is not bound by the rules of evidence, except those concerning privileges, in determining preliminary questions with regard to the qualifications of a witness, matters of privilege or the admissibility of evidence.

It is often impossible to decide the question of admissibility without disclosing the evidence on which the dispute turns. If it is alleged that a confession was made under pressure, the question can often only be settled by considering the terms of the accused's statement, and the jury could scarcely help being influenced by them even if they were to conclude that the surrounding circumstances rendered the confession inadmissible.[1]

Although the validity of the reasons for the rule under consideration seems to be beyond dispute, its application has given rise to three practical difficulties—the question whether the evidence of facts constituting a condition precedent to admissibility should invariably be heard in the absence of the jury, the course which should be adopted when such facts are identical with the facts in issue and the distribution of the functions of judge and jury with regard to the admissibility of confessions.

(i) Absence of the jury.—Two settled rules in criminal cases are first, that the accused must be present throughout the entire trial of an indictable offence,[2] and secondly, that all the evidence should generally be given in the presence of the jury. Some qualifications are obviously necessary so far as the second of these rules is concerned, otherwise the accused might be prejudiced, and there is no doubt that the judge has power to dismiss the jury while hearing arguments on the admissibility of evidence or while holding a trial within a trial.

In *R.* v. *Dunne*,[3] however, the judge withdrew to his private room of his own motion in order to question a witness of tender years so as to ascertain whether she was competent to testify. In *R.* v. *Reynolds*,[4] the judge dismissed the jury while a similar question was considered. The ensuing convictions were quashed in both cases. The decision in *R.* v. *Dunne* is generally accepted as correct because the conduct of the trial infringed the first of the rules mentioned in the previous paragraph; but *R.* v. *Reynolds*, in which dicta in *R.* v. *Dunne* were applied, has been criticised on the ground that the question of a witness's competence ought to be disposed of in the absence of the jury. Against this it may be urged that the jury has to consider the weight of all the evidence concerning the facts in issue, and, although a schoolmaster testified concerning the competence of the witness in *R.* v. *Reynolds*, the judge usually deals with the matter by questioning the proposed witness himself. The answers to his questions may affect the weight of the witness's evidence when it comes to be given, and it is unlikely that the judge would put them to the witness again in the presence of the jury. Moreover, there is always the danger that the jury will think they are asked to withdraw because statements prejudicial to the accused are about to be made.[5] It is probably better that they should remain in court while evidence concerning facts constituting a condition precedent to admissibility is given, unless it is impossible to take such evidence without disclosing matters which the judge might ultimately hold to be inadmissible.[6]

---

[1] See *per* Lord GODDARD, C.J., in *R.* v. *Reynolds*, [1950] 1 K. B. 606, at p. 608; [1950] 1 All E. R. 335.

[2] *Lawrence* v. *R.*, [1933] A. C. 699, at p. 708. There are exceptions; for example in cases in which the accused renders his continued presence in Court impossible by his violence. See *R.* v. *Browne* (1906), 70 J. P. 472.

[3] (1929), 99 L. J. K. B. 117. Dicta in this case are criticised in 46 L. Q. R. 130.

[4] [1950] 1 K. B. 606; [1950] 1 All E. R. 335 (criticised 66 L. Q. R. 157).

[5] See *per* Lord HEWART, C.J., in *R.* v. *Anderson* (1929), 21 Cr. App. Rep. 178, at p. 183.

[6] R. 104 (c) of the United States Federal Rules reads: "Hearings on the admissibility of confessions shall in all cases be conducted out of the hearing of the jury. Hearings on other preliminary matters shall be so conducted when the interests of justice require."

(ii) Identity of preliminary fact with fact in issue.—In *Doe d. Jenkins* v. *Davies*,[1] the issue in an action of ejectment was whether one Elizabeth Stevens was legitimate. She was dead, and the defendant sought to call evidence of a declaration made by her to a solicitor when she handed him a certificate which apparently related to her parents' marriage. Statements by deceased persons as to pedigree are admissible at common law by way of exception to the rule against hearsay if they were made by legitimate members of the family in question. The plaintiff argued that the judge ought not to have received evidence on behalf of the defendant, tending to show that Elizabeth Stevens was legitimate, offered with a view to inducing him to admit her declaration. The answer given by Lord DENMAN, C.J.,[2] was that:

> "neither the admissibility nor the effect of the evidence is altered by the accident that the fact which is for the judge as a condition precedent is the same fact which is for the jury in the issue".

The Court of Exchequer accordingly held that, after deciding that Elizabeth Stevens was legitimate (presumably without relying on her declaration), the judge had rightly allowed this declaration to form part of the evidence to go to the jury on the issue of legitimacy.

The judge had heard evidence on the *voir dire* from both sides before deciding the preliminary question of legitimacy. This course has two disadvantages when the preliminary question of fact to be determined by the judge as a condition precedent to the admissibility of an item of evidence is identical with the issue which has ultimately to be decided by the jury. In the first place it means that the judge has to sum up to the jury on an issue which he has already decided; secondly, it may mean that all the evidence given on the *voir dire* will have to be given over again, and this will certainly be so when the trial within a trial is held in the absence of the jury. Considerations of this nature led Lord PENZANCE, in *Hitchins* v. *Eardley*,[3] a later case raising the same point as *Doe d. Jenkins* v. *Davies*, to reject evidence tendered on the *voir dire* by those denying legitimacy. He held that he ought to admit the declaration on being satisfied that those alleging legitimacy had adduced sufficient evidence of that fact to be left to the jury.

On practical grounds, the course taken by LORD PENZANCE may be preferable to that followed in *Doe d. Jenkins* v. *Davies*. However that may be, there are certainly cases involving the reception of documentary evidence in which all that the judge can require, as a condition precedent to the admissibility of a copy, is *prima facie* evidence of the existence of a genuine original. In *Stowe* v. *Querner*,[4] the plaintiff succeeded in a claim on an insurance policy which the defendant alleged had never been executed. The judge had allowed the plaintiff to give secondary evidence of the contents of the policy on the basis that the original had been lost and left the jury to decide the validity of the defendant's contention that the policy had never existed. It was held that the course followed by the judge was the right one for:

> "Where the objection to the reading of a copy concedes that there was primary evidence of some sort in existence . . . the judge must, before he admits the copy, hear and determine whether the objection is well founded. But where the

---

[1] (1847), 10 Q. B. 314.   [2] At pp. 323-4.
[3] (1871), L. R. 2 P. & D. 248.   [4] (1870), L. R. 5 Exch. 155.

objection goes to show that the very substratum and foundation of the cause of action is wanting, the judge must not decide upon the matter, but receive the copy and leave the main question to the jury." [1]

A similar situation would arise in a case in which the defendant contends that the document on which the plaintiff is relying as giving him a cause of action is forged.

Cases such as *Stowe* v. *Querner* must be carefully distinguished from those in which the preliminary issue is whether a document has been lost, or which of two originals is the proper one to place before the jury; [2] in such cases the question of fact to be decided by the judge is not the same as that which has to be decided by the jury. There is then no doubt that the judge must hear evidence on both sides on the *voir dire* and come to a definite decision on the preliminary issue instead of being content with *prima facie* evidence from the party arguing for admissibility.

The question whether the maker of a dying declaration was under a settled hopeless expectation of death, a condition precedent to its admissibility at a trial for homicide, should on principle be decided by the judge. [3] By way of contrast, the question whether a tape-recording was the original, being one which must ultimately be determined by the jury, the judge need do no more than decide whether there is sufficient evidence to leave the issue to it. [4]

(iii) Confessions.—The question whether a confession attributed to the accused in a criminal case was ever made by him is of the same type as the question whether a tape-recording is genuine, and it has accordingly been held that it is for the judge to decide whether there is *prima facie* evidence that the confession was made, leaving the jury to determine whether it was in fact made; [5] but the admissibility of confessions is governed by a special rule, and there has been a certain amount of case-law concerning the respective functions of the judge and jury in its administration.

The rule is fully considered in chapter XIX. It is now commonly stated as follows:

> "It is a fundamental condition of the admissibility in evidence against any person, equally of any oral answer given by that person to a question put by a police officer and of any statement made by that person, that it should have been voluntary, in the sense that it has not been obtained from him by fear of prejudice or hope of advantage, exercised or held out by a person in authority, or by oppression." [6]

The question whether a confession was voluntary is determined by the judge on the *voir dire* [7] when the accused may give evidence himself as well as call witnesses. [8] The truth of the confession is not directly relevant at this stage. It is of course the crucial question for the jury if the judge decides to admit the confession. The method by which a confession was

---

[1] At p. 158. [2] *Boyle* v. *Wiseman* (1855), 11 Exch. 360.

[3] But see *R.* v. *Christensen*, [1923] 2 D. L. R. 379; cf. *R.* v. *Donohoe*, [1963] S. R. N. S. W. 38, where the question was decided by the judge in accordance with English authorities.

[4] *R.* v. *Robson* and *R.* v. *Harris*, [1972] 2 All E. R. 699.

[5] *R.* v. *Roberts*, [1954] 2 Q. B. 329; [1953] 2 All E. R. 340; *R.* v. *Mulligan*, [1955] O. R. 240.

[6] Judges' Rules, 1964, principle (e), held to be an accurate statement of the law in *R.* v. *Harz and Power*, [1967] 1 A. C. 760 at p. 818 and p. 821.

[7] *R.* v. *Francis* (1959), 43 Cr. App. Rep. 174.

[8] *R.* v. *Cowell*, [1940] 2 K. B. 49; [1940] 2 All E. R. 599.

obtained may have an important bearing on the question of its truth, for a statement made in consequence of violence or some other powerful inducement is much less likely to be true than one which was given freely. Accordingly it was held in *R.* v. *Murray*,[1] that, at the trial proper before the jury, counsel for the defence has the right to cross-examine again the witnesses who have already given evidence on the *voir dire.*

The judge retains his control over the evidence ultimately to be submitted to the jury throughout the trial. Accordingly, if, having admitted a confession as voluntary on evidence given in the absence of the jury, the judge concludes, in the light of subsequent evidence, that the confession was not voluntary, he may either direct the jury to disregard it, or, where there is no other sufficient evidence against the accused, direct an acquittal, or, presumably, direct a new trial.[2] Subject to these possibilities, it ought to be open to the jury to act upon a confession which they believe to be true even though they may not consider it to have been voluntary within the meaning of the rule which has just been stated, while questions concerning the truth of the confession ought not to be raised on the *voir dire.* After a period of doubt engendered by *dicta* in *R.* v. *Bass*,[3] the first of these propositions has been accepted as English law; but the second is inconsistent with the decision of the Court of Criminal Appeal in *R.* v. *Hammond.*[4]

(a) *The rejected* dicta *in* R. v. Bass.—The *dicta* in *R.* v. *Bass* were capable of being construed to mean that, even if the judge holds that a confession is admissible after a trial within a trial, he should direct the jury to disregard it unless they are satisfied that it was made voluntarily. The objection to this course was that a confession might not be a voluntary one within the meaning of the exclusionary rule, although it might well be true, having been induced by some such minimal pressure as a statement by a police officer to a prevaricating suspect that he thought it would be better if the suspect made a statement.[5] This point was succinctly stated in the judgment of DIXON, C.J., in the High Court of Australia in which the *dicta* in *R.* v. *Bass* were disapproved:

> "A confessional statement may be voluntary and yet to act upon it might be quite unsafe; it may have no probative value. Or such a statement may be involuntary and yet carry with it the greatest assurance of its reliability or truth."[6]

The Australian case was followed by the Privy Council on an appeal from Hong Kong in a case in which the appellate court in that jurisdiction had said that the trial judge should have told the jury to disregard a confession if they thought that it had not been made voluntarily,[7] and the decision of the Privy Council has been followed on at least two occasions by the

---

[1] [1951] 1 K. B. 391; *Jackson* v. *R.* (1962), 108 C. L. R. 591; *People (A.-G.)* v. *Ainscough*, [1960] I. R. 136 (unrepresented accused, having cross-examined on the *voir dire*, must be told of his right to cross-examine again at the trial).

[2] Only the first two possibilities were mentioned by Lord MACDERMOTT in *R.* v. *Murphy*, [1965] N. I. 138, at p. 144.

[3] [1953] 1 Q. B. 680, at p. 684.

[4] [1941] 3 All E. R. 318

[5] *R.* v. *Richards*, [1967] 1 All E. R. 829.

[6] *Basto* v. *R.* (1954), 91 C. L. R. 628, at p. 640; *R.* v. *McAloon*, [1959] O. R. 441.

[7] *Chan Wei Keung* v. *R.*, [1967] 2 A. C. 160; [1967] 1 All E. R. 948.

English Court of Appeal.[1] The present law is summarised in the following statement by Lord PARKER, C.J.:

"The position now is that the admissibility [of a confession] is a matter for the judge; that it is thereafter unnecessary to leave the same matters to the jury; but that the jury should be told that what weight they attach to the confession depends upon all the circumstances in which it was taken, and that it is their right to give such weight to it as they think fit."[2]

Trials within the trial are time wasting in cases tried by jury and something of an unreality in cases tried before Magistrates because the question of admissibility has to be determined by the same tribunal as that which pronounces on liability. The procedure contemplated in *R. v. Bass* did nothing to eliminate the trial within a trial in cases in which the admissibility of a confession was in dispute; this object would be achieved if the following suggestion of the late Lord Justice General CLYDE were adopted:

"It would seem that there is much to be said for leaving the evidence once and for all before the jury. If the judge takes the view that the Crown has not led evidence that the confession was freely and voluntarily given, he can at the end of the day direct the jury to disregard the evidence on the confession, or, if the Crown case is otherwise insufficient, he may direct them to return a verdict of not guilty. But if he considers the confession was freely and voluntarily given, he leaves the matter to the jury."[3]

The adoption of the proposed course would, however, sometimes entail the disclosure to the jury of the terms of inadmissible confession; as it would be difficult for them to disregard those terms, it might too frequently be necessary for the judge to discharge the jury and order a new trial at which the confession would be inadmissible.[4]

(b) *R. v. Hammond*.—In *R. v. Hammond*[5] the accused was convicted of murder and the sole question before the Court of Criminal Appeal concerned the propriety of questions put to him by the prosecution on the *voir dire*. The accused had contended that a confession was inadmissible because it had been obtained in consequence of violence. He was asked whether the confession was true and admitted that it was. The judge held that the confession was voluntary[6] and the accused did not give evidence before the jury. The Court of Criminal Appeal held that the question concerning the truth of the confession was proper because it was relevant to the credibility of the accused's statements on the *voir dire* concerning the way in which the confession had been obtained.

"If a man says, 'I was forced to tell the story, I was made to swear this, that and the other', it must be relevant to know whether he was made to tell the truth or whether he was made to say a number of things which were untrue."[7]

---

[1] *R. v. Burgess*, [1968] 2 Q. B. 112; [1968] 2 All E. R. 54, n.; *R. v. Ovenell*, [1969] 1 Q. B. 17; [1968] 1 All E. R. 933.

[2] [1968] 2 Q. B. 112, at p. 117–18.

[3] *Thompson v. H. M. Advocate*, [1968] J. C. 61, at p. 66. For a discussion of the whole problem see Sir Bernard MacKenna, "The *Voir Dire* Revisited", [1967] Crim. L. R. 336. For similar problems in the United States see *Jackson v. Denno*, 389 U.S. 368 (1964).

[4] See the Northern Ireland Emergency Powers Act, 1973, s. 6.

[5] [1941] 3 All E. R. 318; 28 Cr. App. Rep. 84.

[6] He made it clear that, in coming to this conclusion, he had not been influenced by the fact that the accused had admitted the truth of the confession, and this fact was stressed by the Court of Criminal Appeal. It has, accordingly, been argued that the rest of the judgment of the Court of Criminal Appeal is obiter dictum (*R. v. Hnedish* (1958), 26 W. W. R. 685).

[7] (1941), 28 Cr. App. Rep. 84, at p. 87.

Against this it may be urged that the attitude of judge and counsel towards the conduct of the trial could hardly be unaffected by the accused's admission on the *voir dire* that he committed the crime charged. Considerations of this nature led the courts of some of the Canadian provinces[1] to decline to follow *R. v. Hammond*; but the decision has since been approved by a majority of the Supreme Court of Canada.[2]   If, in that case, the judge had held that the confession was inadmissible, and the accused had given evidence at the trial proper in which he denied committing the murder, could he have been cross-examined about the admission made by him on the *voir dire*?[3]

(iv) The burden and standard of proof at a trial within a trial.—We shall see in the next chapter that decisions on the question of which party bears the burden of establishing a particular issue are generally decisions on the substantive law.   Decisions as to which party bears the burden of establishing a fact constituting a condition precedent to the admissibility of an item of evidence belong to the law of evidence. However, there is very little authority on the subject, no doubt because, as a matter of common sense, the conditions of admissibility have to be established by those alleging that they exist.

It is settled that the burden of proving the facts constituting the condition precedent to the admissibility of confessions[4] and dying declarations[5] is borne by the person seeking to tender them in evidence. These items of evidence are admissible as exceptions to the rule against hearsay, and it is reasonable to suppose that the burden of establishing the facts rendering hearsay admissible is always borne by the party tendering the evidence.

In the days when interested witnesses were incompetent, it was held that the burden of establishing that incompetency rested on the party alleging it.[6] There does not appear to be any authority on the few remaining instances of incompetency under the modern law.   In the case of a claim to privilege by a witness, the burden of establishing the privilege would presumably be borne by the witness.

We shall see in Chapter V that there are two standards of proof according to which facts may have to be established, proof on a balance of probabilities, the standard appropriate to civil cases, and proof beyond reasonable doubt, the standard demanded of the prosecution in criminal cases.   Where the issue is one which must be decided once and for all by the judge, it would seem proper to hold that, in civil cases, the preliminary fact must be proved to the satisfaction of the judge on a preponderance of probability and that, in criminal cases, when the evidence is tendered by the prosecution, such fact

---

[1] *R. v. Weighill*, [1945] 2 D. L. R. 471 (British Columbia); *R. v. Hnedish* (1958), 26 W. W. R. 685 (Saskatchewan).

[2] *De Clerq v. R.* (1968), 70 D. L. R. (2d) 530.

[3] See the Common Calendar by Sir Fred. Pritchard pp. 88–89. See also F. M. Neasey, "Cross-examination of the Accused on the *voir dire*", 34 A. L. J. 110 (1960). The author mentions a Tasmanian case of *R. v. Monks* (1955) in which the accused's admission on the *voir dire* appears to have been proved against him by the clerk of the court at the trial. In *R. v. Gray*, [1965] Qd. R. 373 a statement made on the *voir dire* inconsistent with his testimony was proved against the accused on the issue of credibility. See also *R. v. Wright*, [1969] S. A. S. R. 256, and *R. v. Banner*, [1970] V. R. 240.

[4] *R. v. Thompson*, [1893] 2 Q. B. 12.

[5] *R. v. Jenkins* (1869), L. R. 1 C. C. R. 187, at p. 192.

[6] *Marsden v. Stansfield* (1828), 7 B. & C. 815.

must be proved beyond reasonable doubt.[1] The English authorities on confessions[2] and dying declarations[3] bear out the above views, at least so far as the standard of proof demanded of the prosecution on the *voir dire* is concerned. It has, however, been held in Australia with regard to both confessions[4] and dying declarations,[5] and in Canada with regard to confessions,[6] that the prosecution need only establish facts justifying admissibility on the balance of probabilities. The English view at least has the merit of ensuring that the utmost care is taken before a confession is placed before the jury, and this is particularly important because, in many cases, to admit a confession is virtually to ensure the conviction of the accused.[7]

Where the judge merely has to be satisfied that there is *prima facie* evidence, for example that a confession was made, or that a tape-recording was the original, he need theoretically, only hear evidence from the party tendering the confession or recording and it may always be sufficient if such evidence satisfies him on the balance of probabilities.[8]

SECTION 2. JUDICIAL CONTROL OF THE JURY

The exceptions to the general rule that questions of fact must be determined by the jury are one facet of the subject of judicial control of that body. Another facet of the same subject is illustrated by the rules governing rebuttable presumptions of law which restrict to some extent the jury's power of finding facts; but this section is concerned with more direct methods of control by means of withdrawing an issue from the consideration of the jury, the summing up and the setting aside of verdicts on appeal.

A. WITHDRAWAL OF AN ISSUE FROM THE JURY

Before an issue can be submitted to the jury, the judge must be satisfied that there is sufficient evidence in support of the proponent's contention for their consideration, and, if he is of opinion that the evidence is insufficient, he must decide the issue in favour of the opponent.[9]

> "It has always been considered a question of law to be determined by the judge, subject, of course, to review, whether there is evidence which, if it is believed, and the counter-evidence if any, not believed, would establish the

---

[1] If the evidence is tendered by the defence, the civil standard would seem appropriate, but there is no authority.

[2] *R. v. Sartori, Gavin and Phillips*, [1961] Crim. L. R. 397; *R. v. McLintock*, [1962] Crim. L. R. 549; *R. v. Cave*, [1963] Crim. L. R. 371. See an article by R. S. O'Regan in [1964] Crim. L. R. 287.

[3] *R. v. Jenkins* (1869), L. R. 1 C. C. R. 192; in *R. v. Booker* (1924), 88 J. P. 75, the words used were "If it appears to the satisfaction of the judge."

[4] *Wendo* v. *R.* (1963), 109 C. L. R. 559; *R. v. Saunders*, [1965] Qd. R. 409.

[5] *R. v. Donohoe*, [1963] S. R. (N. S. W.) 38.

[6] *R. v. Lee* (1952), 104 Can. Crim. Cas. 400.

[7] Proof beyond reasonable doubt is required of the prosecution in the case of a confession the admissibility of which is disputed by cl. 2 of the Draft Bill annexed to the 11th Report of the Criminal Law Revision Committee.

[8] *R. v. Robson* and *R. v. Harris*, [1972] 2 All E. R. 699; but see *R. v. Stevenson*, [1971] 2 All E. R. 678.

[9] The proponent is the party by whom the issue must be raised in the first instance. He is usually the plaintiff in a civil case, and the prosecutor on a criminal charge, but this is not necessarily so. To anticipate the terminology employed in the next chapter, the proponent bears the evidential burden in the first instance. He usually bears the legal burden also, but this is not always the case. Wigmore uses the term to describe the party bearing the legal burden of proof.

facts in controversy. It is for the jury to say whether and how far the evidence is to be believed. And if the facts, as to which evidence is given, are such that from them a farther inference of fact may legitimately be drawn, it is for the jury to say whether that inference is to be drawn or not. But it is for the judge to determine, subject to review, as a matter of law, whether from those facts that farther inference may legitimately be drawn."

These remarks were made in the case of *Metropolitan Rail. Co.* v. *Jackson*,[1] in which a passenger's thumb had been crushed by the slamming of the door of a railway carriage. There was evidence that the defendants had been guilty of negligence in allowing the carriage to become overcrowded, but there was no evidence that the overcrowding had caused the plaintiff's thumb to be where it was when the door was slammed, and the House of Lords held that the judge should have withdrawn the case from the jury for this reason.

When a judge comes to the conclusion that evidence in support of the contention of the proponent of an issue is insufficient, the course which he should adopt will vary from case to case. Sometimes he should discharge the jury and enter judgment for the opponent of the issue, as in a civil suit in which there is insufficient evidence in support of the plaintiff's allegation of negligence;[2] on other occasions, he will direct the jury to return a verdict in favour of the opponent, as in a criminal case where the prosecution's evidence is insufficient; while there may be other issues to be left to the jury, as on a criminal charge when the judge rules that there is insufficient evidence of insanity (an issue of which the accused is the proponent), and it is nonetheless necessary for the jury to decide whether the prosecution has established the accused's guilt in other respects. Whichever of these courses is adopted, the judge is obviously exercising considerable control over the jury, for he is either totally withdrawing facts from their consideration, or else directing them to come to a certain conclusion, whatever their own views may be.

The extent of this method of control increased during the nineteenth century, for, as WILLES, J., said in *Ryder* v. *Wombwell*:[3]

"It was formerly considered necessary in all cases to leave the question to the jury if there was any evidence, even a scintilla, in support of the case; but it is now settled that the question for the judge (subject of course to review) is, . . . not whether there is literally no evidence but whether there is none that ought reasonably to satisfy the jury that the fact sought to be proved is established."

The test to be applied by the judge in order to determine whether there is sufficient evidence in favour of the proponent of an issue, is for him to enquire whether there is evidence which, if uncontradicted, would justify men of ordinary reason and fairness in affirming the proposition which the proponent is bound to maintain, having regard to the degree of proof demanded by the law with regard to the particular issue.[4] This test is easy

---

[1] (1877), 3 App. Cas. 193, at p. 207, *per* Lord BLACKBURN. If substantially similar facts were to occur today, it is possible that the Law Reform (Contributory Negligence) Act, 1945, would be applied. This is also true of *Wakelin* v. *London and South Western Rail. Co.* (1886), 12 App. Cas. 41, another leading case on the subject under discussion.
[2] Even in this kind of case it may be desirable to have the damages assessed by the jury.
[3] (1868), L. R. 4 Exch. 32, at p. 39. In *Jones* v. *Great Western Rail. Co.* (1930), 144 L. T. 194, the trial judge referred to the scintilla rule in determining to leave the case to the jury.
[4] *Bridges* v. *North London Rail. Co.* (1874), L. R. 7 H. L. 213, at p. 233, *per* BRETT, J.

to apply when the evidence is direct, for the question whether witnesses are to be believed must be left to the jury, but it is necessarily somewhat vague when circumstantial evidence has to be considered. In that case, little more can be done than enquire whether the proponent's evidence warrants an inference of the facts in issue, or whether it merely leads to conjecture concerning them.[1]

Although the judge may withdraw an issue from the jury of his own motion, questions of the sufficiency of evidence are usually raised on a submission that there is no case to answer made by the opponent of the issue.[2] When ruling on such a submission, the judge assumes that the proponent's witnesses are telling the truth in cross-examination, as well as in their evidence-in-chief, and on matters which are unfavourable to the proponent, as well as those which are in his favour. He may rule in favour of the submission either because the proponent's evidence discloses no case as a matter of law or else because of the weakness of the proponent's evidence. If the judge rules against the submission, the issue must be determined by the jury, but, even when the opponent calls no evidence, their decision will not necessarily be in favour of the proponent. The jury may disbelieve the testimony given on his behalf, or, if they do accept it, they may not be prepared to draw the requisite inference.

There are certain practical differences in the procedure which ought to be followed by the judge according to the class of case which he is trying.

(i) Civil cases tried by a judge alone.—A submission that there is no case to answer may be made by one of the parties to proceedings before a judge alone, but, if this is done in a civil case, the judge must decline to rule on the submission unless the party making it elects not to call evidence.[3] At least two considerations justify this requirement. In the first place, the judge has to determine the facts as well as the law, and he ought not to be asked to express an opinion on the evidence until it is complete. No one would ask a jury at the end of a plaintiff's case to say what verdict they would be prepared to give if the defendant called no evidence.[4] Secondly, the parties might be put to extra expense if the judge ruled in favour of the submission before the evidence was complete, for, if the Court of Appeal were to decide against his ruling, a new trial would be necessary so that the party who made the submission could call his evidence.

(ii) Civil cases tried with a jury.—Neither of these considerations apply to civil cases tried with a jury. Accordingly, it has been held that the judge has a discretion in such cases, and he may rule on the submission without putting the party who makes it to his election whether to call

---

The last seventeen words which appeared in the first edition have been reinstated out of deference to a paper by Professor Eric Edwards in 9 Western Australian Law Review 169 (1970).

[1] See citations in n. 3, p. 26, *ante*.

[2] On the whole subject see articles by Glanville Williams in [1965] Crim. L. R. 343 and 410.

[3] *Alexander* v. *Rayson*, [1936] 1 K. B. 169. In matrimonial causes, the cases establish that the judge has a discretion whether to put a party to his election on a submission of no case although the party making the submission will normally be put to his or her election (*Yuill* v. *Yuill*, [1945] P. 15; [1945] 1 All E. R. 183; *Beal* v. *Beal*, [1953] 2 All E. R. 1228; *Gilbert* v. *Gilbert*, [1958] P. 131; [1957] 3 All E. R. 604; *Wilson* v. *Wilson*, [1958] 3 All E. R. 195; *Meyer* v. *Meyer*, [1959] 2 All E. R. 633; *Storey* v. *Storey*, [1961] P. 63; [1960] 3 All E. R. 270; *Holzer* v. *Holzer (Norley intervening)*, [1964] 3 All E. R. 989; *Inglis* v. *Inglis and Baxter*, [1968] P. 639; [1967] 2 All E. R. 71).

[4] *Per* ROMER, L.J., [1936] 1 K. B., at p. 178.

evidence.[1] If the judge decides in favour of the submission, there would have to be a new trial if his ruling is reversed on appeal, but this would also be the case if he deferred his ruling until the evidence was completed, for the verdict of the jury would have to be obtained in either event.

Whether a civil case is tried with a jury or not, it seems that, if a judge rules that there is a case to answer and the defendant gives evidence, the defendant's liability must be judged on the whole of the evidence and an appeal may be dismissed although the Court of Appeal is of opinion that the judge should have ruled in favour of the submission when it was made.[2]

(iii) Criminal cases tried with a jury.—In criminal cases tried with a jury, the accused is never put to his election whether to call evidence or not before a ruling is made on his submission that there is no case to answer. If the ruling is in favour of the submission the jury are directed to acquit. If the submission fails, the accused calls his evidence in the ordinary way. Contrary to what was once decided by the Court of Criminal Appeal,[3] it has been said that on an appeal against conviction, the Court of Criminal Appeal considers the evidence as a whole, and they can therefore dismiss the appeal although they may be of opinion that the judge ought to have ruled that there was no case to answer at the close of the prosecution's evidence if, as sometimes happens, the accused is incriminated by his own evidence.[4] But this does not apply to a case in which the Court of Criminal Appeal is of opinion that there was no case to answer and the trial judge only allowed the case to go the jury in fairness to a co-accused,[5] who incriminates the accused.

(iv) Magistrates.—A submission of no case may be made in proceedings before magistrates. If the proceedings are criminal, there is no question of the accused being put to his election. If the proceedings are civil, the party making the submission may be put to his election. If the magistrates rule against the submission, they should give the party making it a further opportunity to address them on the facts.[6] This is because a finding that there is a case to answer is not a decision of the whole case against the party making the submission. It is perfectly proper for magistrates to hold that there is a case to answer and decide the issue in favour of the party making the submission. They may come to the conclusion that the evidence of the opposite party is not to be believed.[7]

B. THE SUMMING UP

It is difficult to estimate the amount of control which a judge exercises over a jury by means of his summing up, for, quite apart from the legal rules that govern the matter, juries expect and receive considerable guidance from the judge with regard to the evidence submitted to them, and this guidance may be expressed in emphatic terms.[8] The legal rules on the sub-

---

[1] *Young* v. *Rank*, [1950] 2 K. B. 510; [1950] 2 All E. R. 166, where the authorities are reviewed by DEVLIN, J.   [2] *Payne* v. *Harrison*, [1961] 2 Q. B. 403; [1961] 2 All E. R. 873.
[3] *R.* v. *Joiner* (1910), 4 Cr. App. Rep. 64.   [4] *R.* v. *Power*, [1919] 1 K. B. 572.
[5] *R.* v. *Abbott*, [1955] 2 Q. B. 497; [1955] 2 All E. R. 899. See the discussion of the authorities by J. C. Wood, 77 L. Q. R. 491.
[6] *Disher* v. *Disher*, [1965] P. 31; [1963] 3 All E. R. 933; *Mayes* v. *Mayes*, [1971] 2 All E. R. 397.
[7] *De Filippo* v. *De Filippo* (1963), 108 Sol. Jo. 56.
[8] For general statements see *Clouston & Co., Ltd.* v. *Corry*, [1906] A. C. 122, at p. 130, *per* Lord JAMES OF HEREFORD, and *R.* v. *O'Donnell* (1917), 12 Cr. App. Rep. 219, at p. 221 *per* Lord READING, C.J. In the United States the judge's power to direct a verdict appears

ject have never been precisely formulated, but it seems that a judge must always put defences raised by the evidence to the jury [1] and he can never be justified in directing a jury that they must accept his view of disputed facts,[2] although he may, and sometimes should, tell them they ought to do so as reasonable men.[3]

Even when there is no apparent reason for rejecting it, the judge ought not to direct the jury that they must accept medical evidence[4] but it has been said that, very exceptionally, there may be criminal cases in which a judge can and should direct a jury that, on the evidence before them, an issue must be decided in a way adverse to the accused.[5] From the authorities mentioned by the Court of Criminal Appeal, it would appear that the court had in mind cases in which some or all of the facts were not disputed and it then became the duty of the judge to instruct the jury that a complete acquittal was out of the question, as in a murder case in which provocation is pleaded, when the judge tells the jury that their verdict must be either murder or manslaughter. Even in such cases Lord DEVLIN has questioned the propriety of an instruction to the jury to the effect that it is not legally possible for them to acquit because the determination of every fact is within their province.[6] The Court of Appeal has asserted on several occasions that where "the primary facts are undisputed," and the case can be decided on those facts alone, a directed verdict is justifiable, but their pronouncements on this subject are inconsistent.[7]

It is clearly the duty of the judge to instruct the jury on all matters of law, including the effect of any relevant presumption of law and the incidence of the onus of proof. This may oblige the judge to direct the jury that they must find one of the facts in issue to be proved if they are satisfied as to the existence of some other fact, for, when a rebuttable presumption of law applies to a case, proof of one fact is legally equivalent to proof of some other fact in the absence of further evidence. Thus, if the legitimacy of a child is among the facts in issue in civil proceedings, and the proponent adduces evidence to show that the child was born in wedlock, the judge must direct the jury to find in favour of the proponent if they accept this evidence, unless the opponent satisfies them on a balance of probabilities that there was no intercourse between the child's mother and her husband by which it could have been begotten. Similarly, if it becomes necessary to establish that a particular person is dead, the judge may have to tell a civil jury that they must find in favour of the proponent on being satisfied that the person in question had been absent for more than seven years, without having been heard of by those with whom he would most probably have communicated if he were alive.

In criminal cases, where the accused is the opponent, it is probably only

---

to be greater than in England, see Smith, *The Power of the Judge to Direct a Verdict*, 24 Columbia Law Review 111 (1924).

[1] *R. v. Keith Keba Badjam*, [1966] 50 Cr. App. Rep. 141.

[2] *Dublin Wicklow and Wexford Rail. Co. v. Slattery* (1878), 3 App. Cas. 1155, at p. 1186.

[3] See, for example, *Pickup v. Thames and Mersey Marine Insurance Co.* (1878), 3 Q. B. D. 594, at p. 600.

[4] *R. v. Lanfear*, [1968] 2 Q. B. 77; [1968] 1 All E. R. 683.

[5] *R. v. Healey*, [1965] 1 All E. R. 365, at p. 370, *per* ASHWORTH, J.

[6] *Trial by Jury* (1966 edition), Appendix 2, p. 188; Griew, [1972] Crim. L. R. 204; McConville, [1973] Crim. L. R. 164.

[7] *R. v. Martin* (1973), 57 Cr. App. Rep. 279; *R. v. Herd* (1973), 57 Cr. App. Rep. 560; *R. v. Bates*, [1973] 2 All E. R. 509.

necessary for him to adduce or elicit or point to evidence adduced or elicited by his adversary which is sufficient to raise a reasonable doubt.

When the judge directs the jury on the effect of a presumption of law, he is not telling them that they must accept his view of the facts. As a matter of ordinary reasoning, many people, including the judge, might not be prepared to infer legitimacy from birth in wedlock if there was evidence of prolonged intimacy between the child's mother and her paramour, any more than they would be prepared to infer death from seven years' absence if the person in question was young and healthy when he was last heard of. For a number of different reasons, the law attaches what may be an artificial probative value to certain facts, and the judge's direction in such a case informs the jury of the legal consequences which follow upon their finding these facts to exist.

C. APPEALS

(i) Criminal cases tried with a jury.—On the hearing of an appeal against conviction, the Court of Appeal (Criminal Division) may set aside the verdict of the jury on the ground that under the circumstances of the case it is unsafe or unsatisfactory.[1] The Court of Criminal Appeal quashed convictions under corresponding powers[2] but it naturally refrained from laying down any general rules. The evidence is considered together with the summing up, and the appeal may be allowed although the Court suspects that the conviction was right as a matter of conjecture, as opposed to inference from the evidence.[3] Conversely, the appeal may be dismissed if there was evidence to support the conviction, notwithstanding the trial judge's opinion that the verdict was unreasonable, for such an opinion is only one of the factors to be considered by the court.[4] If the court does set aside the verdict of the jury, the accused must normally be acquitted, but a verdict of guilty of some other offence may be substituted if it was one of which the accused could have been convicted on the indictment, and the court concludes that the jury must have been satisfied of facts which prove that he was guilty of such other offence.[5]

For the sake of completeness, it may be added that the court may allow an appeal on account of a wrong decision of any point of law, or because there was a material irregularity,[6] and these provisions are, of course, wide enough to cover any wrongful admission or rejection of evidence by the judge as well as an irregularity in his summing up. The court also has power to hear fresh evidence,[7] and, having done so, to order a new trial, but its entire jurisdiction is subject to the important proviso contained in section 2 (1) of the Criminal Appeal Act, 1968, under which an appeal may be dismissed if the court considers that no miscarriage of justice has actually occurred, notwithstanding its opinion that the point raised in the appeal might be decided in favour of the appellant. This proviso, like the cor-

---

[1] Criminal Appeal Act, 1968, s. 2 (1) (a).
[2] *R.* v. *Wallace* (1931), 23 Cr. App. Rep. 32; *R.* v. *Hyman Bookbinder* (1926), 19 Cr. App. Rep. 125; *R.* v. *Barnes* (1942), 28 Cr. App. Rep. 141; *R.* v. *Dent*, [1943] 2 All E. R. 596.
[3] *R.* v. *Bennett* (1912), 8 Cr. App. Rep. 10.
[4] *R.* v. *Perfect* (1917), 12 Cr. App. Rep. 273; *R.* v. *Moor* (1920), 15 Cr. App. Rep. 31; *R.* v. *Hopkins-Husson* (1949), 34 Cr. App. Rep. 47.
[5] Criminal Appeal Act, 1968, s. 3 (1).
[6] *Ibid.*, s. 2 (1) (b) and (c).
[7] *Ibid.*, s. 23.

responding rule in civil cases,[1] is of considerable significance in relation to the practical operation of the law of evidence, for it deters counsel on either side from taking frivolous technical objections at the original hearing with the result that an English trial bears little resemblance to that which occurs in many American films with constant interjections by the barristers on each side. The mere fact that an objection was overruled when an Appellate Court thinks it should have been sustained, or vice versa, does not mean that an appeal must succeed as it does in some American jurisdictions.[2]

(ii) Civil cases tried with a jury.—After a civil case has been tried with a jury, the party against whom their verdict has been given may apply to the Court of Appeal for an order for a new trial, and, if such an order is made, the verdict of the jury is set aside. A new trial may be sought on the ground that there was no evidence which ought properly to have been left to the jury in favour of the proponent of the issue in question, or because the verdict of the jury was against the weight of the evidence.[3] In order that a new trial should be granted on the latter ground:

> "it is not enough that the judge who tried the case might have come to a different conclusion on the evidence than the jury, or that the judges in the Court where the new trial is moved for might have come to a different conclusion, but there must be such a preponderance of evidence, assuming there is evidence on both sides to go to the jury, as to make it unreasonable, and almost perverse, that the jury when instructed and assisted properly by the judge should return such a verdict".[4]

If the Court of Appeal concludes that the judge ought not to have left an issue to the jury because there was insufficient evidence in support of the proponent's case, it will enter judgment for the opponent forthwith. It may also adopt this course where the evidence in support of the opponent's case was very strong, although there was some evidence favourable to the proponent, provided it is clear that no further material would be available at a second trial.[5] This is the result of the construction which has been placed on O. 59, r. 10 (3), of the Rules of the Supreme Court under which the Court of Appeal has power to draw inferences of fact and make any order which ought to have been made, but serious doubts have been expressed on the question whether it entitles the Court of Appeal to enter judgment for the proponent of an issue after setting aside a verdict for the opponent.[6]

---

[1] R.S.C., O. 59, r. 11 (2).

[2] I *Wigmore*, p. 271. On the proviso to the Act of 1907 see *Stirland* v. *Director of Public Prosecutions*, [1944] A. C. 315; [1944] 2 All E. R. 13, confirming *R.* v. *Haddy*, [1944] K. B. 442; [1944] 1 All E. R. 319, and rendering earlier authorities obsolete. See also *R.* v. *Farid* (1945), 30 Cr. App. Rep. 168; *R.* v. *Oster-Ritter* (1948), 32 Cr. App. Rep. 191; *R.* v. *Collins* (1950), 34 Cr. App. Rep. 146; *R.* v. *Whybrow* (1951), 35 Cr. App. Rep. 141 and *R.* v. *McVitie*, [1960] 2 Q. B. 483; [1960] 2 All E. R. 498. Although the beneficial character of the provisions mentioned can hardly be disputed they may have had a bad effect on the development of the law of evidence for they account, to some extent, for its being a body of rules which is nearly as much honoured in the breach as the observance.

[3] A new trial may be ordered on a number of other grounds conveniently discussed in Odgers on *Pleading and Practice* (20th edition), 373–8.

[4] *Per* Lord Selborne in *Metropolitan Rail. Co.* v. *Wright* (1886), 11 A. C. 152, at p. 153.

[5] See the judgment of Lord Atkin in *Mechanical and General Inventions Co. and Lehwess* v. *Austin and the Austin Motor Co.*, [1935] A. C. 346.

[6] *Ibid.*, at p. 369, and at p. 379, *per* Lord Wright, reiterating doubts of Lord Halsbury in *Toulmin* v. *Millar* (1887), 12 App. Cas. 746; but see *Croker* v. *Croker*, [1932] P. 173 and *Winterbotham Gurney & Co.* v. *Sibthorp and Cox*, [1918] 1 K. B. 625, at p. 634.

(iii) Civil cases tried by a judge alone.—For completeness it may be added that the appeal is a rehearing when a civil case has been tried by a judge alone, so the result is usually judgment for one of the parties rather than an order for a new trial. The Court of Appeal may hear fresh evidence, but only on special grounds, except on matters which have occurred after the decision from which the appeal is brought, and the case is usually dealt with on the basis of a transcript or note of the proceedings in the court below.[1] Appeals on matters of law may involve questions of the wrongful admission or rejection of evidence, and these are disposed of in the same way as appeals involving any other legal issue. The Court of Appeal will naturally be loth to disturb a finding of fact by the trial judge who has had the advantage of observing the demeanour of the witnesses, "their candour or their partisanship, and all the incidental elements so difficult to describe which make up the atmosphere of an actual trial".[2] Although the court occasionally takes the view that the judge was wrong to give credence to a particular witness,[3] it will be far more ready to reverse his decision in a case which depends on inferences from admitted or undisputed facts.[4]

Appeals lie from decisions of judges who have sat without a jury in civil cases tried in the County Court, and there may be appeals in matrimonial causes as well as criminal cases tried by the magistrates, but they do not call for separate discussion in a work of this nature.

---

[1] R.S.C., O. 59, r. 10(2). There is no distinction between cases tried with and without a jury so far as the hearing of fresh evidence is concerned (*Leeder* v. *Ellis*, [1953] A. C. 52; [1952] 2 All E. R. 814). On the refusal to hear fresh evidence, see *Ladd* v. *Marshall*, [1954] 3 All E. R. 745, and *House* v. *Haughton Brothers (Worcester), Ltd.*, [1967] 1 All E. R. 39, contrast *Skone* v. *Skone*, [1971] 2 All E. R. 582.

[2] *Per* Lord MACMILLAN in *Watt* v. *Thomas*, [1947] A. C. 484, at pp. 490–1; [1947] 1 All E. R. 582, at p. 590.

[3] E.g., *Coghlan* v. *Cumberland*, [1898] 1 Ch. 704, and *Yuill* v. *Yuill*, [1945] P. 15; [1945] 1 All E. R. 183.

[4] Cf. *Powell* v. *Streatham Manor Nursing Home*, [1935] A. C. 243 with *Flower* v. *Ebbw Vale Steel Co.*, [1936] A. C. 206, and see *Benmax* v. *Austin Motor Co., Ltd.*, [1955] A. C. 370; [1955] 1 All E. R. 326, together with an article by Goodhart in 71 L. Q. R. 402 (1955). See also the propositions of Lord THANKERTON in *Watt* v. *Thomas*, [1947] A. C. 484, at pp. 487–8; [1947] 1 All E. R. 582, at pp. 586–7.

CHAPTER IV

THE BURDEN OF PROOF

There are four occasions on which it is vitally important to know which of the two parties to litigation has the burden of proof on a given issue. These are when there is a dispute concerning the right to begin calling evidence—a procedural question which is mentioned in Chapter X, when there is a submission of no case to answer, when the tribunal of fact is left in doubt, and when an Appellate Court is considering the propriety of a judgment or summing up relating to the burden of proof. The term is used in different senses or, to be more precise, there are several different burdens, which are discussed in section 1, and the various tests which may help to determine the incidence of the two principal burdens are mentioned in section 2.

SECTION 1. THE DIFFERENT BURDENS

Writing at the end of the 19th century, the American scholar J. B. Thayer claimed that the phrase "burden of proof" is used in more than one sense. It is only necessary to discuss two of the three senses he mentioned because the third was said to be "an undiscriminated use of the phrase, perhaps more common than either of the other two, in which it may mean either or both of the others."[1]

Thayer's first sense of the term was:

> "The peculiar duty of him who has the risk of any given proposition on which parties are at issue—who will lose the case if he does not make this proposition out, when all has been said and done."[2]

This nearly corresponds to the legal burden, or burden of proof in the strict sense, which is discussed below. The correspondence is not complete because no allowance is made in the passage quoted for the fact that the burden in question is confined to particular issues. Most cases involve more than one issue, and the burden of proof upon the different issues may be variously distributed between the parties—a fact which can be readily appreciated by considering a claim in contract in which the terms of the agreement are in dispute and infancy is pleaded as a defence, a claim for damages for negligence in which the defendant raises the issue of contributory negligence, or a criminal charge on which insanity is pleaded. Owing to the possible multiplicity of issues, a party may have "the risk" of a given proposition and yet not lose the case if he fails to make the proposition out; an example would be a claim in contract in which the defendant pleaded both infancy and duress; the defendant would bear the

---

[1] *Preliminary Treatise on Evidence at the Common Law*, 355.
[2] *Ibid.*

burden of proof on each of these issues, but failure on one of them would not entail the loss of the case.

Thayer's second sense of the phrase "burden of proof" was:

> "The duty of going forward in argument or in producing evidence, whether at the beginning of a case, or at any later moment throughout the trial or discussion."[1]

This corresponds in part to the evidential burden discussed below, but it is a much broader concept because, in addition to embracing argument as well as the adduction of evidence, it covers not merely the obligation placed on a party by the law to be able to point to the existence of sufficient evidence to raise an issue before the tribunal of fact, but also the tactical obligation which may in fact be placed upon a party against whom evidence has been adduced on a given issue to adduce counter-evidence. To anticipate, Thayer's second sense of the term "burden of proof" conflates the evidential burden with what is sometimes called a "provisional" or "tactical" burden.

Thayer did not use any adjectives or descriptive phrases to distinguish the two burdens to which he referred, but these have been employed in profusion by his successors although there is nothing in the nature of a uniform terminology.[2] Another complicating factor is the metaphor, "now permanently embedded in the law", of speaking of proof as a burden that may be shifted in the course of a trial.[3] This metaphor is frequently employed by the judges, although, until recently, they have rarely used adjectives or descriptive phrases.[4]

---

[1] *Ibid.*

[2] In addition to Thayer, *op. cit.*, ch. 9 (1898), reference should be made to IX *Wigmore*, paras. 2485–9, Stone, 60 L. Q. R. 262 (1944), a commentary on *Joseph Constantine Steamship Line, Ltd.* v. *Imperial Smelting Corporation, Ltd.*, [1942] A. C. 154; [1941] 2 All E. R. 165, Lord DENNING, *Presumptions and Burdens*, 61 L. Q. R. 379 (1945), Rankin, *Presumptions and Burdens*, 62 L. Q. R. 135 (1946), discussing the application of Lord DENNING's distinctions to the Indian Evidence Act), Bridge, *Presumptions and Burdens*, 12 M. L. R. 273 (1949, a reply to Lord DENNING), Hanbury, *The Burden of Proof*, 61 Juridical Review 121 (1949), Glanville Williams, *Criminal Law, The General Part* (2nd edition), ch. 23, and Sir Francis Adams, *Onus of Proof in Criminal Cases*, in *Essays on Criminal Law in New Zealand*, edited by R. S. Clark, 67.

[3] Stephen, *Digest of the Law of Evidence* (12th edition), 214.

[4] There has always been an exception in the case of Lord DENNING whose views, stated in 61 L. Q. R. 379 are repeated in his judgments in the following cases—*Emanuel* v. *Emanuel*, [1946] P. 115; [1945] 2 All E. R. 494; *Dunn* v. *Dunn*, [1949] P. 98; [1948] 2 All E. R. 822; *Tilley* v. *Tilley*, [1949] P. 240; [1948] 2 All E. R. 1113; *Smithwick* v. *National Coal Board*, [1950] 2 K. B. 335; *Re Shephard, Shephard* v. *Cartwright*, [1953] Ch. 728; [1953] 2 All E. R. 608 (the decision was reversed by the House of Lords, [1955] A. C. 431; [1954] 3 All E. R. 649; but without reference to Lord Denning's views on presumptions and burdens); *Southport Corporation* v. *Esso Petroleum Co., Ltd.*, [1954] 2 Q. B. 182; [1954] 2 All E. R. 561 (the decision was reversed by the House of Lords, [1956] A. C. 218; [1955] 3 All E. R. 864, but without reference to Lord DENNING's views on presumptions and burdens); *Huyton-with-Robey Urban District Council* v. *Hunter*, [1955] 2 All E. R. 398; *Brown* v. *Rolls-Royce, Ltd.*, [1960] 1 All E. R. 577; *Bratty* v. *A.-G. for Northern Ireland*, [1963] A. C. 386, at p. 413; [1961] 3 All E. R. 523, at p. 535; *Panamanian Oriental Steamship Corporation* v. *Wright*, [1971] 2 All E. R. 1028. Professor Glanville Williams's distinction between the persuasive and evidential burdens was adopted in the judgment of the Court of Criminal Appeal delivered by Edmund DAVIES, J., in *R.* v. *Gill*, [1963] 2 All E. R. 688, and in *Henderson* v. *Jenkins & Sons and Evans*, [1970] A. C. 282, at p. 301, Lord PEARSON distinguished the "evidential burden of proof" from the "formal, or legal or technical burden of proof"; but he spoke of the evidential burden in terms of Lord DENNING's provisional burden and doubted the propriety of calling it a burden of proof. The distinction between the two principal burdens is frequently mentioned by Australian, Canadian and American judges.

A. THE TWO PRINCIPAL BURDENS

(1) THE LEGAL BURDEN, OR BURDEN OF PROOF SIMPLICITER

The legal burden of proof is the obligation of a party to meet the requirement of a rule of law that a fact in issue be proved [or disproved] either by a preponderance of the evidence or beyond reasonable doubt as the case may be. This definition is based on rule 1.04 of the American Uniform rules. The words in square brackets are intended to cover the case in which a party has to negative a particular fact if his opponent adduces sufficient evidence of its existence. An example would be provided by a murder trial at which self defence is pleaded; provided there is sufficient evidence to raise a reasonable doubt in the minds of a reasonable jury, it is incumbent on the prosecution to prove beyond reasonable doubt that the accused was not acting in self-defence.

The phrase "legal burden" is that of Lord DENNING and it is justified by the fact that its incidence is determined by the substantive law. Other English writers refer to it as "the burden of proof on the pleadings"[1] or "the fixed burden of proof";[2] but the pleadings do not always indicate which party bears the burden, and the answer to a somewhat controversial question is assumed if the burden is said to be "fixed", for this epithet is designed to emphasise the fact that the burden does not shift in the course of a trial—a matter of words about which there is room for two views in the case of issues to which certain rebuttable presumptions of law are applicable. Wigmore spoke of the "risk of non-persuasion" but this, like Professor Glanville Williams's "persuasive burden", is open to the objection that both parties may bear such a risk on the same issue; for instance, when self defence is pleaded on a charge of murder, the accused runs the risk of failing to induce a reasonable doubt in the minds of the jury although, provided the accused adduces sufficient evidence of self defence, it is ultimately incumbent on the prosecution to negative the plea. Some recent judgments in which the distinction between the two principal burdens is mentioned simply refer to this one as the "burden of proof",[3] and such a course may be justified by the fact that the discharge of the other principal burden, the evidential burden, proves nothing.[4]

(2) THE EVIDENTIAL BURDEN

The evidential burden is the obligation to show, if called upon to do so, that there is sufficient evidence to raise an issue as to the existence or non-existence of a fact in issue, due regard being had to the standard of proof demanded of the party under such obligation. The concluding clause is designed to meet the point that the amount of evidence required to induce a judge to leave an issue to the jury varies according to whether the case is civil or criminal, and whether the party bearing the burden is plaintiff, prosecutor, defendant or accused.

The phrase "evidential burden" is employed by Mr. (now Sir) Nigel Bridge and Professor Glanville Williams, while Phipson spoke with equal

---

[1] Phipson, *Law of Evidence* (11th edition), 40.
[2] Bridge, 12 M. L. R. 274.
[3] DEVLIN, J., in *Hill* v. *Baxter*, [1958] 1 Q. B. 277, at p. 284; *Bratty* v. *A.-G. for Northern Ireland*, [1963] A. C. 386, at p. 407 and p. 413; [1961] 3 All E. R. 523, at p. 530.
[4] *Jayasena* v. *R.*, [1970] A. C. 618; [1970] 1 All E. R. 219.

accuracy of the "burden of adducing evidence",[1] a phrase which is coming to be increasingly used by the English judges.

Wigmore described it as the duty "of passing the judge", and there is no doubt that the difference between the two principal burdens is best approached by considering the position of a plaintiff or prosecutor with regard to such issues which are about to be tried with a jury as negligence, or the doing of a criminal act by the accused. He has two hurdles to surmount. First, he must produce a sufficient quantity of evidence to prevent the judge from withdrawing the issue from the jury, and secondly he must convince that body. If he surmounts the first, he may yet fail at the second. This may be because the jury do not believe his witnesses, or will not draw the necessary inferences, or else because of the doubt raised by the counter evidence. To quote Wigmore:[2]

> "The important practical distinction between these two senses of 'burden of proof' is this: the risk of nonpersuasion operates when the case has come into the hands of the jury, while the duty of producing evidence implies a liability to a ruling by the judge disposing of the issue without leaving the issue open to the jury's deliberations."

Two further points must be stressed in connection with the definition of the evidential burden. In the first place, it caters for the abnormal situation where the party who starts with the legal burden of proof does not also bear the evidential burden, as well as for the normal situation where they are each borne by the same person in the first instance. To vary an illustration which has already been given with reference to self defence, on a prosecution for murder, for example, the Crown has the legal burden of negativing provocation, but questions of provocation do not have to be considered by the jury unless there is evidence on the subject, and it is up to the accused to produce this evidence, although he only has to raise a reasonable doubt in the minds of the jury as to whether his conduct was provoked or unprovoked.[3] Secondly, it must not be supposed that the production of evidence always involves the giving of testimony. This will be necessary in the vast majority of cases in which an evidential burden has to be discharged, but there are rare instances in which the evidence called on the other side is sufficiently equivocal to have this effect. On a prosecution for murder, the Crown witnesses might say enough in-chief about the provocation to make the judge feel obliged to raise the question in his summing-up, although the matter will usually be brought before the court in consequence of the cross-examination of the crown witnesses, reinforced by the accused's evidence-in-chief.

(3) Illustrations of Confusion

Failure to distinguish between the two principal burdens has produced mistakes which have had to be rectified on appeal, and it can render the formulation of the law unnecessarily difficult. These points may be exemplified by *Sutton* v. *Sadler* and *Redpath* v. *Redpath and Milligan* respectively.

---

[1] Phipson, *op. cit.*, 43.   [2] IX *Wigmore*, p. 284.
[3] *Mancini* v. *Director of Public Prosecutions*, [1942] A. C. 1; [1941] 3 All E. R. 272. See also *R.* v. *Lobell*, [1957] 1 Q. B. 547; [1957] 1 All E. R. 734 applying the same doctrine to self defence; *Bullard* v. *R.*, [1957] A. C. 635 at p. 642; *Rolle* v. *R.*, [1965] 3 All E. R. 582.

(i) Sutton v. Sadler.—In *Sutton* v. *Sadler*,[1] the heir at law claimed to be entitled to an estate as against a devisee on the ground that the testator was insane. The trial judge told the jury that, once the will was shown to have been duly executed, the burden of proving insanity shifted to the plaintiff who must accordingly fail if there was any doubt on the matter. This was held to be a misdirection in the full Court of Common Pleas where CRESS-WELL, J., said:

> "If, indeed, a will, not irrational on the face of it, is produced before a jury and the execution of it proved, and no other evidence offered, the jury would be properly told that they ought to find for the will, and, if the party opposing the will gives some evidence of incompetency, the jury may, nevertheless, if it does not disturb their belief in the competency of the testator, find in favour of the will and in each case the presumption in favour of competency would prevail. But that is not a mere presumption of law, and, when the whole matter is before the jury on evidence given on both sides, they ought not to affirm that a document is the will of a competent testator, unless they believe that it really is so." [2]

In other words, the defendant bore the legal burden of proving the testator's sanity, although the production of a rational will might be said to have shifted the evidential burden to the plaintiff, and the trial judge erred in suggesting to the jury that the presumption of testamentary capacity shifted the legal burden to the plaintiff in addition to the evidential burden.

Woolmington v. *Director of Public Prosecutions*[3] is in some ways the counterpart in the criminal law to *Sutton* v. *Sadler*. The accused was charged with murdering his wife from whom he was separated, and he gave evidence to the effect that he had shot and killed her accidentally while endeavouring to induce her to return to live with him by threatening to shoot himself. SWIFT, J.'s summing-up to the jury contained the following passage:

> "If the Crown satisfy you that this woman died at the prisoner's hands, then he has to show that there are circumstances to be found in the evidence which has been given from the witness box in this case which alleviate the crime, so that it is only manslaughter, or which excuse the homicide altogether by showing that it was a pure accident."

Woolmington was convicted, but his appeal was allowed when it reached the House of Lords because the jury had been misdirected.

The actual decision turned on the point that SWIFT, J.'s direction suggested that, the killing having been admitted, the legal burden of disproving malice aforethought shifted to the accused, but Lord SANKEY's speech in the House of Lords also shows that, even in cases in which the defence consists of something other than a denial of an essential element of the prosecution's case, a plea of provocation or self defence for instance, the accused does not, as was formerly believed, bear a legal as well as an evidential burden. The speech can be regarded either as marking a change in the law[4] or as an insistence on the distinction, ignored by the old

---

[1] (1857), 3 C. B. (N. S.) 87. See also *Purkess* v. *Crittenden* (1965), 114 C. L. R. 164.
[2] At p. 98. The word "mere" is equivalent to "pure". The presumption was treated as a mixed presumption of law and fact (whatever that may mean). If it had been one of law alone, it might have cast the legal burden on the plaintiff.
[3] [1935] A. C. 462.
[4] *Jayasena* v. *R.*, [1970] A. C. 618, at p. 625.

authorities, between the legal and evidential burdens.[1] Whichever be the correct view, there is no doubt that a number of appeals have been decided on the point that the judge wrongly instructed the jury that the accused bore the burden of proof on a particular issue whereas all that was borne by him was an evidential burden, a matter with which the jury has no concern.[2]

(ii) Redpath *v.* Redpath and Milligan.—In *Redpath* v. *Redpath and Milligan* [3] the wife's defence to a petition for divorce alleging adultery was that she had been raped. PILCHER, J., dismissed the petition although he did not consider that the respondent was a satisfactory witness, because he thought it was insufficient for the husband to prove an act of intercourse in such a case, leaving the wife to satisfy the court that the intercourse took place against her will. This judgment was reversed on appeal because it put an unnecessary burden on the husband, although BUCKNILL, L.J., added that, if at the end of a case there is a doubt in the judge's mind whether adultery has taken place or whether it is a case of rape, he should dismiss the petition. This seems to imply that the legal burden of proving that the intercourse was consensual rested on the husband, although it was incumbent upon the wife to adduce credible evidence of rape, and PILCHER, J., erred in holding that an evidential burden of negativing it had been cast on the husband in consequence of the unsatisfactory testimony of the respondent. But VAISEY, J., who was a member of the Court of Appeal, said that the judge should have asked himself whether he was satisfied that the admitted intercourse was involuntary, and this suggests that the wife bore a legal burden of negativing consent. It is therefore impossible to state the law on the incidence of the burden of proof where rape is pleaded as a defence to adultery with any certainty, and this is entirely due to the fact that the members of the Court of Appeal in *Redpath* v. *Redpath and Milligan* did not indicate what kind of a burden had been unnecessarily placed on the husband by PILCHER, J.

B. THE SHIFTING OF THE BURDEN

The practice of speaking of the shifting of the burden of proof is quite inveterate among both judges and writers, so all that can be done is to endeavour to ascertain the different situations to which the expression is usually applied.

It seems that there are three of these, namely, those in which the evidential burden on a particular issue is said to shift, those in which the legal burden on a particular issue may be said to shift, and those in which the burdens on the different issues in a given case are variously distributed between the parties.

---

[1] Sir Francis Adams in *Essays in New Zealand Criminal Law* (ed. Clark), 70–1.
[2] *Chan Kau* v. *R.*, [1955] A. C. 206; [1955] 1 All E. R. 266; *R.* v. *Lobell*, [1957] 1 Q. B. 547 [1957] 1 All E. R. 734; *R.* v. *Gill*, [1963] 2 All E. R. 688; *R.* v. *Wheeler*, [1967] 3 All E. R. 829; *R.* v. *Bone*, [1968] 2 All E. R. 644; *R.* v. *Moon*, [1969] 3 All E. R. 803; *R.* v. *Abraham*, [1973] 3 All E. R. 694. In Victoria it has been held that the legal burden of proving mistake as a defence to bigamy is borne by the accused (*R.* v. *Bonnor*, [1957] V. L. R. 227); see also *R.* v. *Reynhoudt* (1962), 107 C. L. R. 381, at p. 389 and p. 399; this is inconsistent with the speech of Lord DIPLOCK in *Sweet* v. *Parsley*, [1970] A. C. 132, at p. 164 and with *R.* v. *Strawbridge*, [1970] N. Z. L. R. 909; but see the speech of Lord Pearce in *Sweet's Case* at p. 157, which seems to have been cited in mistake for that of Lord DIPLOCK in *Strawbridge's Case*.
[3] [1950] 1 All E. R. 600.

It is a solecism for the writer to speak of the shifting of the evidential burden because that term has been defined as the obligation to point to the existence of sufficient evidence to raise an issue, and the cases about to be considered are ones in which a burden on an issue already before the jury is said to shift; but the point which is sought to be expressed is clear enough: a party against whom evidence on a particular issue has been given will often be well advised to adduce evidence on it in order to avoid defeat, or even be obliged to do so in consequence of a presumption of law.

(1) The Shifting of the Evidential Burden

(i) Tactical shifting.—Let us assume that the proponent of an issue discharges the evidential burden which rests on him by adducing evidence that is "*prima facie*" in the first sense explained on p. 26, *ante*. If the tribunal of fact believes his witnesses, the requisite inference may be drawn in his favour, and the chances of this happening will generally be increased by the opponent's failure to adduce evidence. Nevertheless, it is quite possible that the tribunal of fact will not draw the requisite inference, even if the opponent does not adduce any evidence. He merely runs a risk of losing the issue if he remains silent, and, in such a case, when it is said that the burden of proof has shifted from the proponent to the opponent, all that is meant is that the latter should adduce some evidence as a matter of common prudence. Examples are provided by any criminal case in which the prosecution has adduced sufficient evidence to warrant a finding of *mens rea* if its witnesses are believed. Lord Denning describes the burden of disproving the case made by the proponent on the issue in question as "a provisional burden".[1]

(ii) Legal shifting.—Now let us assume that the proponent of an issue discharges the evidential burden which rests upon him by adducing evidence which is "presumptive" or "*prima facie*" in the second sense explained on p. 26, *ante*. Provided his witnesses are believed, the tribunal of fact is bound to decide the issue in the proponent's favour if the opponent calls no evidence. In such a case, when it is said that the burden of proof has shifted from the proponent to the opponent, what is meant is that the latter must adduce evidence on the issue or lose. If the opponent does call evidence, and the jury are unable to come to a definite conclusion one way or the other, the proponent will lose if the legal burden rests on him. The effect of some presumptions of law is to produce such a situation. To appreciate this, it is only necessary to have recourse to a case to which the maxim "*omnia praesumuntur rite esse acta*" applies. As a matter of common sense, the mere erection of traffic signs might not be thought to amount to presumptive evidence of compliance with the relevant statutory provisions, but the legal force of the presumption is such that it casts the evidential burden of disproving compliance on the opponent of this fact.[2]

The effect of a presumption of law is governed by legal rules and, strictly speaking, it is only when such rules are applicable that the evidential burden can be said to have shifted for legal as opposed to tactical purposes; but the proponent's evidence in a civil case may be so weighty that the practical effect is the same as the application of a presumption of law. An example is provided by a case in which unseaworthiness is alleged, and it is proved that

---

[1] 61 L. Q. R. 380.
[2] Cf. *Gibbins* v. *Skinner*, [1951] 2 K. B. 379; [1951] 1 All E. R. 1049.

the ship foundered soon after she left port. If the opponent adduces no evidence, a verdict for the proponent would be necessitated by common sense, and a verdict to the contrary would be set aside by the Court of Appeal.[1] In criminal cases tried with a jury [2] the situation is complicated by the rules that there can generally be no directed verdict of guilty and that the Crown has no right of appeal; but, when the accused bears the evidential burden in the first instance, the judges sometimes speak of the shifting of that burden to the Crown in consequence of the weight of the evidence given on behalf of the accused.[3]

(2) The Shifting of the Legal Burden

The mere cogency of the evidence adduced by the party who bears the legal burden can never affect its incidence. As long as the matter is governed by the principles of ordinary reasoning, unaffected by rules of law, he who bears this burden on a particular issue continues to do so until the tribunal of fact has to come to a decision. Thus the Crown assumes the legal and evidential burdens of proving malice aforethought at the beginning of a murder trial. The evidential burden will be discharged by proof that the deceased met his death in consequence of the voluntary act of the accused, but:

> "if, at the end of and on the whole of the case, there is a reasonable doubt, created by the evidence given by either the prosecution or the prisoner, as to whether the prisoner killed the deceased with a malicious intention, the prosecution has not made out the case and the prisoner is entitled to an acquittal".[4]

Many writers strenuously contend that it is little less than a solecism to speak of the shifting of the legal burden in the course of a trial in any circumstances; but it is arguable that certain presumptions of law have this effect. In the case of some presumptions of law, the substantive law indicates the quantity of evidence required to rebut the presumption and this may amount to proof to the contrary on balance of probabilities. Where a child's legitimacy is in issue in civil proceedings, the jury must be told to find in favour of the party who bore the legal burden when he came into court if they accept his evidence that the child was born in wedlock, unless his adversary satisfies them on a balance of probabilities that the child's parents did not have intercourse by which it could have been begotten. One way of expressing this result is to say that the risk of nonpersuasion on the issue of legitimacy shifts when birth in wedlock is established. Those who maintain that the legal burden can never shift in the course of a trial argue that three issues are raised when legitimacy is disputed, namely, the validity of the marriage of the child's parents, the child's birth in wedlock, and access between its parents at the time of conception. This enables them to say that the legal burden of negativing access rests on the party denying legitimacy at the outset of the case; but it is not always easy to subdivide an issue in this way. For example, in *The Merchant*

---

[1] *Ajun Goolam Hossen & Co.* v. *Union Marine Insurance Co.*, [1901] A. C. 362; cf. *Pickup* v. *Thames and Mersey Marine Insurance Co.* (1878), 3 Q. B. D. 594.

[2] The Divisional Court frequently remits a case to the magistrates, on an appeal by the prosecutor, on the ground that the weight of his evidence was such that there was a case to answer.　　　　　　　　　　　[3] *R.* v. *Matherson*, [1958] 2 All E. R. 87.

[4] *Woolmington* v. *Director of Public Prosecutions*, [1935] A. C. 462, at p. 481, *per* Lord Sankey, L. C. See also *Dublin, Wicklow and Wexford Rail. Co.* v. *Slattery* (1878), 3 App. Cas. 1155.

Prince[1] the plaintiff claimed damages for negligence from the defendants whose ship collided with their vessel which was at anchor in a river while normal daytime weather conditions prevailed. The Court of Appeal held that, once these facts were established, it was incumbent on the defendants to show that the collision was the result of an inevitable accident. In other words, the legal burden of disproving negligence was cast on the defendants, and it is noteworthy that Lord DENNING, who maintained in 1945 that the legal burden on a particular issue never shifts spoke in 1954 of the shifting of that burden when discussing *The Merchant Prince*.[2]

Those who contend that the legal burden on a particular issue never shifts in the course of a case could urge that, on facts such as those of *The Merchant Prince*, there are three issues—the collision, the normality of the weather conditions and the question whether the collision was due to the defendant's negligence. They could say that the legal burden on the first two rests on the plaintiff from the outset, while the defendant bears the legal burden from the beginning so far as the third issue is concerned.

Perhaps those who contend that the legal burden on a particular issue never shifts have the better of this battle of words. They can say that, even in cases most favourable to the view that it may shift, such as those which have just been mentioned, the sounder analysis suggests that there is no shifting. The basic facts of the presumptions of legitimacy and negligence are either admitted on the pleadings or else in issue. If they are admitted, the legal burden of disproving legitimacy or negligence is fixed at the beginning of the trial by a rule of law, sometimes spoken of as a "rule of presumption". If the basic facts are not admitted, the party wishing to establish legitimacy or negligence bears the legal burden of establishing those facts. There is no means of knowing whether he has done so until the whole case is under consideration by the tribunal of fact, but, if that tribunal concludes that he has, the rule of presumption requires a finding of legitimacy or negligence unless the tribunal of fact is convinced to the contrary on the balance of probabilities.[3] The presumption simply discharges the burden of proof with a particular consequence defined by the rule of presumption. Unfortunately there is a tendency to speak of presumptions shifting burdens when what is meant is that they discharge them.

(3) DISTRIBUTION OF ISSUES

The fact that in some cases one party has the legal burden on one issue, while the opposite party has it on another issue has an important bearing on one of the senses in which the burden of proof is said to shift, for, if the issues are considered successively, it is possible to say that, if A. discharges the legal burden on the first issue, the onus of proof shifts to B. because he will lose the case unless he discharges his legal burden on the second issue. This is how the matter is occasionally stated by the judges, but it must be borne in mind that the burden which is then said to shift

---

[1] [1892] P. 179.

[2] Compare *Emanuel* v. *Emanuel*, [1946] P. 115, at p. 118; [1945] 2 All E. R. 494, at p. 496, with *Southport Corporation* v. *Esso Petroleum Co., Ltd.*, [1954] 2 Q. B. 182, at pp. 199–200; [1954] 2 All E. R. 561, at p. 571. Lord DENNING also spoke of the shifting of the legal burden in *Stupple* v. *Royal Insurance Co., Ltd.*, [1971] 1 Q. B. 50, at p. 72.

[3] This point is stated with great clarity on p. 216 in the 10th edition of Phipson's *Manual of Evidence*.

is not the burden of establishing a particular issue, nor the burden of adducing evidence with regard to it, but the burden on the ultimate issue that must arise in any litigation, namely, which party is entitled to judgment, or, as the late Ernest Cockle put it, "the burden of proof on the whole case". [1]

Some stress was laid on the shifting of the burden of proof in this sense in *Medawar* v. *Grand Hotel Co.*[2]—a case which turned on the substantive law governing the liability of innkeepers for the loss of their guests' goods. The innkeepers' liability was limited to £30 unless the loss was due to his negligence or that of his servants; but he escaped liability altogether if the loss was due to the guests' negligence. When going out for the day, the plaintiff negligently left a stand containing trinkets worth £140 in a hotel bedroom which the defendants' manager had permitted him to use for the purpose of washing and changing. In the evening, the defendants' servants removed the stand and negligently left it in the corridor. On the following day it was discovered that the trinkets had been stolen, but there was no evidence concerning the time at which the theft occurred. A majority of the Court of Appeal held that the relationship of innkeeper and guest existed between the parties with the result that, according to the substantive law, the defendants' liability was limited to £30 unless the plaintiff could prove that the trinkets were stolen in the corridor, while the defendants would escape liability altogether if they could prove that the theft took place in the room. The legal and evidential burdens of proving that the trinkets were stolen in consequence of the negligence of the defendants' servants rested on the plaintiff, and, as he was unable to establish that the theft occurred in the corridor, he failed on his claim for £140. But the defendants bore the legal and evidential burdens of proving that the trinkets were stolen in consequence of the plaintiff's negligence. They were unable to discharge these burdens because they could not show that the theft took place in the room. The defendants were therefore held liable to the extent of £30, BOWEN, L.J., observing that:

> "it is by no means a nonsensical or fanciful thing that a case of this kind should have to be decided by the shifting of the onus of proof". [3]

SECTION 2. THE INCIDENCE OF THE BURDEN OF PROOF

Various tests for determining the incidence of the burden of proof have been suggested, but they are deprived of much of their value by the fact that they do not indicate which burden is in contemplation. It is only possible to lay down a few vague general rules. After they have been stated, something will be said about the position when essential facts are peculiarly within the knowledge of one of the parties, the construction of typical statutes and the interpretation of typical contracts.

We are, of course, solely concerned with the evidential and legal burdens;

---

[1] *Cases and Statutes on Evidence* (8th edition), 127. Lord DENNING speaks of this burden as an "ultimate burden". That expression is however often used as a synonym for the legal burden on a particular issue.   [2] [1891] 2 Q. B. 11.
[3] At p. 23. The term "burden of proof" was used throughout this judgment without any qualifying adjective. See a similar reference to the shifting of the burden in *Coldman* v. *Hill*, [1919] 1 K. B. 443, at p. 452, *per* WARRINGTON, L.J. For a case of this type which was disposed of without any reference to the shifting of the burden of proof, see *Neal* v. *Fior*, [1968] 3 All E. R. 865.

the "provisional burden" and "burden of proof on the whole case" are products of the notion of the "shifting of the burden of proof" and are of no value from the point of view of the scientific exposition of the law of evidence because they are not the subject of legal rules.

A. THE GENERAL RULES

(1) THE EVIDENTIAL BURDEN

According to Taylor,[1] the right test for determining the incidence of the burden of proof is to consider first, which party would succeed if no evidence were given on either side, and secondly, what would be the effect of striking the allegation to be proved out of the record. The onus lies on whichever party would fail if either of these steps was taken. A moment's reflection should suffice to show that these tests are only applicable to the evidential burden; they cannot apply to the legal burden in all cases. Suppose, for example, that want of testamentary capacity is pleaded as a defence to a probate action. The defendant would fail on the issue if no evidence was given on either side, and the plaintiff would likewise succeed if the allegation was struck out of the record. Therefore, Taylor would have had to say that the burden of proof is on the defendant but the fact remains that the legal burden of establishing testamentary capacity is borne by the plaintiff.[2] Taylor's test is undoubtedly sound so far as the incidence of the evidential burden is concerned, although it has been said to be the statement of the effect of a rule, rather than the formulation of the principle underlying it.[3]

(2) THE LEGAL BURDEN

So far as the legal burden is concerned, Wigmore has truly said "There are merely specific rules for specific classes of case resting for their ultimate basis upon broad reasons of expedience and fairness";[4] but this does not often lead to difficulty in ascertaining the party upon whom the burden rests, for a fundamental requirement of any judicial system is that the person who desires the court to take action must prove his case to its satisfaction.[5] This means that, as a matter of common sense, the legal burden of proving all facts essential to their claims normally rests upon the plaintiff in a civil suit or the prosecutor in criminal proceedings.

The rule is sometimes expressed in terms of such maxims as "*omnia praesumuntur pro negante*", and "*ei incumbit probatio qui dicit, non qui negat*"; but this must not be taken to mean that the onus of proof cannot lie upon a party who makes a negative allegation. If this were so, the application of the rule could be made to depend upon the language in which a case happened to be pleaded. For instance, a claim for damages for breach of covenant to keep a house in repair may be stated by saying, either

---

[1] *A Treatise on the Law of Evidence* (12th edition), para. 365.
[2] *Sutton* v. *Sadler* (1857), 3 C. B. N. S. 87. Taylor's test was applied by FARWELL, L.J., in *Talbot* v. *Von Boris*, [1911] 1 K. B. 854, at p. 863, but the court was there concerned with the evidential burden (see *per* KENNEDY, L.J., at p. 866). The test is based on *Amos* v. *Hughes* (1835), 1 Mood. & R. 464, and is supported by BOWEN, L.J., in *Abrath* v. *North Eastern Rail. Co.* (1883), 11 Q. B. D. 440, at p. 457, where, however, the different burdens are not distinguished.
[3] Wills, *Law of Evidence* (3rd edition), 29.
[4] IX *Wigmore*, p. 278.
[5] *Dickinson* v. *Minister of Pensions*, [1953] 1 Q. B. 228 at p. 232; [1952] 2 All E. R. 1031, at p. 1033.

that the defendant did not repair the house, or else that he allowed it to become dilapidated, but the legal burden is borne by the plaintiff, however the claim is expressed.[1] It is probably true to say that a positive averment can always be converted into a negative statement by appropriate linguistic manipulation. However this may be, there are numerous instances in which a plaintiff or prosecutor assumes the legal burden of proving a negative.[2] Absence of consent must be established by the Crown on a charge of rape or assault,[3] and where lack of consent[4] or want of due notice of a particular fact[5] is alleged in a civil action, these matters must be proved by the plaintiff. As Bowen, L.J., said in the leading case of *Abrath* v. *North Eastern Rail. Co.*,[6] which decided that the legal burden of proving absence of reasonable and probable cause rests on the plaintiff in an action for malicious prosecution, "If the assertion of a negative is an essential part of the plaintiff's case, the proof of the assertion still rests upon the plaintiff".

(3) Some Precedents Affecting the Legal Burden

Difficulty may sometimes arise with regard to the question whether an assertion is essential to a party's case or that of his adversary. This is strikingly illustrated by *Joseph Constantine Steamship Line, Ltd.* v. *Imperial Smelting Corporation, Ltd.*[7] where the charterers of a ship claimed damages from the owners for failure to load. The owners pleaded that the contract had been frustrated by the destruction of the ship owing to an explosion, and the only question of fact was whether this had been caused by their fault. As the evidence was scanty, it became necessary to determine which of the parties bore the legal burden with regard to this matter. If the rule were that charterparties cease to be binding when the vessel, without default of either party, is disabled by an overpowering disaster, the negation of fault would be an essential of the defendant's case; on the other hand, proof of fault would be an essential of the plaintiff's case, if the rule were that charterparties cease to be binding when the vessel is disabled by an over-powering disaster, provided that disaster is not brought about by the fault of either party. The House of Lords decided that the latter was the correct formulation, and accordingly held that the plaintiff has the legal burden of proving fault when frustration is pleaded as a defence to an action on a contract. Their Lordships' speeches referred to principles, such as the difficulty of proving a negative and the presumption of innocence, but, as Professor Julius Stone has shown, general considerations of public policy probably

---

[1] *Soward* v. *Leggatt* (1836), 7 C. & P. 613.

[2] On the difficulties of proving a negative see Gulson, *Philosophy of Proof* (2nd edition), pp. 72–3, and *ibid.*, part I ch. 18. Generally speaking, negative facts are not observed to the same extent as positive ones—it is easier to find a witness to swear there was a clock in the room than to say that no clock was there. "Negative evidence, therefore, is always in some sort circumstantial or indirect, and the difficulty of proving the negative lies in discovering a fact or series of facts inconsistent with the fact which we are seeking to disprove, from which it may be possible to infer its absence with anything like an approach to certainty" (*ibid.*, p. 153). Though true of some of the instances in which the law requires a negative to be proved, *e.g.*, absence of fault, this is not true of all of them, *e.g.*, absence of consent.

[3] *R.* v. *Horn* (1912), 7 Cr. App. Rep. 200; *R.* v. *Donovan*, [1934] 2 K. B. 498.

[4] *Toleman* v. *Portbury* (1870), L. R. 5 Q. B. 288.

[5] *Williams* v. *East India Co.* (1802), 3 East 192.

[6] (1883), 11 Q. B. D. 440, at p. 457. This decision was affirmed by the House of Lords (1886) (11 App. Cas. 247).

[7] [1942] A. C. 154; [1941] 2 All E. R. 165.

constituted the decisive factor.[1] If such considerations are the guide where there is no governing precedent, it is obviously vain to seek for any set formula determining what facts are essential to a party's case and hence the incidence of the legal burden of proof can only be ascertained by consulting the precedents concerned with the various branches of the substantive law. In the case of bailment, for example, it is settled that the bailee has the onus of proving that the goods were lost without his fault,[2] and, at a criminal trial, the accused has the legal burden on a plea of insanity.[3] No *a priori* tests could have produced these results; it is pointless to collect numerous isolated precedents.

B. FACTS PECULIARLY WITHIN THE KNOWLEDGE OF ONE OF THE PARTIES[4]

The existence or non-existence of a fact in issue may be known for certain by one of the parties and this is often said to have an important bearing on the incidence of the burden of proof of that fact. It is only reasonable that the evidential burden should be affected in some cases. For example, in *R.* v. *Turner*,[5] the accused was prosecuted for having pheasants and hares in his possession without the necessary qualification or authorisation. Ten possible qualifications were mentioned in the relevant statute which has since been repealed, and the Court of King's Bench held that it was unnecessary for the Crown to prove that they did not apply to the case. Lord ELLENBOROUGH's judgment turned mainly on the construction of the particular statute with which the court was concerned, but we shall see that BAYLEY, J. made some observations which have come to be regarded as laying down a general rule for determining the incidence of the burden of proving the affirmative of certain negative averments. In the case of a statute containing a plurality of excuses it is not unreasonable to hold that the burden of adducing evidence with regard to any one of them should be borne in the first instance by the party seeking to rely on the excuse, and it may be that this was all that *Turner's* case decided.[6]

The fact that one party may be said to have peculiar means of knowledge of one of the matters in issue is sometimes said to affect the incidence of

---

[1] It seems to be the case that frustration occurs more often than not without fault on anyone's part, and absence of fault is undoubtedly difficult to prove. Hence "a rule requiring the defendant pleading frustration to negative fault will then *ex hypothesi* do injustice to the great majority of defendants. While, on the other hand, a rule requiring the plaintiff to prove fault will *ex hypothesi* do injustice to only a small minority of plaintiffs" (60 L. Q. R. 278).

[2] *Coldman* v. *Hill*, [1919] 1 K. B. 443 ; *Brook's Wharf and Bull Wharf, Ltd.* v. *Goodman Brothers*, [1937] 1 K. B. 534; [1936] 3 All E. R. 696, and cases there cited; *Hunt and Winterbotham (West of England) Ltd.* v. *B.R.S. (Parcels), Ltd.*, [1962] 1 Q. B. 617; [1962] 1 All E. R. 111; *Houghland* v. *R. R. Low (Luxury Coaches) Ltd.*, [1962] 1 Q. B. 694; [1962] 2 All E. R. 159.

[3] *M'Naghten's Case* (1843), 10 Cl. & Fin. 200; *R.* v. *Smith* (1910), 6 Cr. App. Rep. 19. For criticism see Glanville Williams, *Criminal Law (The General Part)* 2nd Edn., p. 516. Under s. 2 (2) of the Homicide Act, 1957, it is for the accused to prove diminished responsibility, see *R.* v. *Dunbar*, [1958] 1 Q. B. 1.

[4] On this subject as well as the construction of criminal statutes concerning the burden of proof see Sir F. B. Adams, *Criminal Onus and Exculpations* and Addendum, *ante.*

[5] (1816), 5 M. and S. 206.

[6] *Per* BOWEN, L.J., in *Abrath* v. *North Eastern Rail Co.* (1883), 11 Q. B. D. 440, at p. 457. See also *Graham* v. *Belfast and Northern Counties Rail Co.*,[1901] 2 I. R. 13, at p. 26, *per* PALLES, C.B.

even the legal burden of proof without having regard to the question whether the issue is affirmative or negative.

The existence of such a rule was, however, emphatically denied by the Court of Criminal Appeal in *R. v. Spurge*.[1] In that case it was argued that, where the defence to a charge of dangerous driving was that the accused's vehicle had a mechanical defect, the burden of establishing the defence rested on the accused on account of his peculiar means of knowledge. Although the court dismissed the accused's appeal because he had been negligent, they held that he did not bear the onus of proof. The court pointed out that, on a charge of murder, the facts relevant to self-defence or provocation are often peculiarly within the knowledge of the accused, yet, once there is evidence of these defences, the onus of disproving them rests upon the prosecution. The court concluded:

> "there is no rule of law that where the facts are peculiarly within the knowledge of the accused the burden of establishing any defence based on these facts shifts to the accused."[2]

All that can be said by way of generalisation with regard to the effect of peculiar knowledge is that it may mean that very little evidence is required to satisfy an evidential burden when borne by the party lacking such knowledge and that, subject to what is said in the Addendum, *ante*, where the affirmative of a negative averment is peculiarly within the knowledge of the opponent of that averment, he bears the evidential burden on the issue in the first instance.

(i) Discharge of the Evidential Burden

To quote Lord MANSFIELD:

> "It is certainly a maxim that all evidence is to be weighed according to the proof which it was in the power of one side to produce, and in the power of the other to have contradicted."[3]

The rule to be deduced from this and similar statements was formulated as follows by Stephen in his Digest:[4]

> "In considering the amount of evidence necessary to shift the burden of proof, the court has regard to the opportunities of knowledge with respect to the fact to be proved which may be possessed by the parties respectively."

This does not mean that the peculiar means of knowledge of one of the parties relieves the other of the burden of adducing some evidence with regard to the fact in question, although very slight evidence will often suffice.[5]

---

[1] [1961] 2 Q. B. 205; [1961] 2 All E. R. 688; *R. v. Mandry, R. v. Wooster*, [1973] 3 All E. R. 996.

[2] [1961] 2 Q. B., at p. 212. See also the very striking decisions on Ordinances based on s. 106 of the Indian Evidence Act: "When any fact is essentially within the knowledge of any person, the burden of proving that fact is upon him" (*Attygalle v. R.*, [1936] A. C. 338; [1936] 2 All E. R. 116; *Seneviratne v. R.*, [1936] 3 All E. R. 36; *Ng. v. R.*, [1958] A. C. 173).

[3] *Blatch v. Archer* (1774), 1 Cowp. 63, at p. 65.

[4] *Digest of the Law of Evidence*, 12th Edn., art. 104, applied in *R. v. Kakelo*, [1923] 2 K. B. 793, and *R. v. Cohen*, [1951] 1 K. B. 505; [1951] 1 All E. R. 203; see also *per* SARGANT, L.J. in *Stoney v. Eastbourne R.D.C.*, [1927] 1 Ch. 367, at p. 405. The judgment of Lord GODDARD in *R. v. Cohen* supports the view that the doctrine is only concerned with the evidential burden.

[5] *Elkin v. Janson* (1845), 13 M. & W. 655, at p. 662, *per* ALDERSON, B.; *Over v. Harwood*, [1900] 1 Q. B. 803.

(2) CASES IN WHICH THE AFFIRMATIVE OF NEGATIVE AVERMENTS IS PECULIARLY WITHIN THE KNOWLEDGE OF ONE OF THE PARTIES

In *R. v. Turner*,[1] BAYLEY, J., said that he had always regarded it as a general rule that:

> "If a negative averment be made by one party, which is peculiarly within the knowledge of the other, the party within whose knowledge it lies, and who asserts the affirmative, is to prove it, and not he who asserts the negative."

The principle embodied in this dictum has been discussed mainly in relation to criminal statutes which penalise the doing of certain acts without some special qualification.[2]

There is a line of cases in which the doctrine under consideration has been held to place the evidential burden in the first instance on the party against whom the negative averment is made with the result that his adversary need not adduce any evidence concerning an essential ingredient of the case. The prosecution has thus been relieved from showing that an apothecary charged with practising without a certificate did not possess one,[3] that a person charged with selling cocaine without a licence did not have a licence,[4] that a driver charged with infringing insurance regulations did not have a certificate of insurance,[5] that a sugar dealer charged with an offence against the Defence Regulations, 1939, had not been granted a licence to sell sugar,[6] that a motorist had not got a licence when he was charged with driving without one,[7] and that the accused was in possession of drugs without a prescription.[8]

Some of these cases have not gone uncriticised. This is partly due to the construction placed by the courts on the Regulations or Statute under which the accused were charged[9] and partly because the cases are considered to represent an unjustifiable extension of the decision in *R. v. Turner* from statutes containing a number of qualifications under which the acts charged would be lawful to issues concerning a single negative which would be as easy to prove by *prima facie* evidence as the affirmative. Suppose, for example, that a motorist is charged with driving without a licence. It would be as easy for the prosecution to provide *prima facie* evidence of guilt by calling a witness to say that the accused was asked to produce his licence and failed to do so[10] as it would be for the defendant to attend court and produce

---

[1] (1816), 5 M. & S., at p. 211.
[2] For a civil case in which the doctrine was applied, see *General Accident Fire and Life Insurance Corporation* v. *Robertson*, [1909] A. C. 404, especially at p. 413.
[3] *Apothecaries' Co.* v. *Bentley* (1824), 1 C. & P. 538.
[4] *R.* v. *Scott* (1921), 86 J. P. 69.
[5] *Williams* v. *Russell* (1933), 149 L. T. 190.
[6] *R.* v. *Oliver*, [1944] K. B. 68; [1943] 2 All E. R. 800.
[7] *John* v. *Humphreys*, [1955] 1 All E. R. 793; not followed in *McGowan* v. *Carville*, [1960] I. R. 330 where the matter is very fully considered. See also *A.-G. (Comer)* v. *Shorten*, [1961] I. R. 304 and contrast *R.* v. *O'Brien* (1965), 50 D. L. R. (2d) 92.
[8] *R.* v. *Ewens*, [1967] 1 Q. B. 322; [1966] 2 All E. R. 470.
[9] The absence of a licence was something which made a *prima facie* innocent act unlawful rather than a condition by virtue of which a *prima facie* unlawful act is innocent (see *per* GIBSON, J. in *Shehan* v. *Cork Justices*, [1908] 2 I. R. 1, at p. 11). But this distinction, though occasionally adopted (*R.* v. *Putland and Sorrell*, [1946] 1 All E. R. 85), is itself somewhat unreal. In *Everard* v. *Opperman*, [1958] V. L. R. 389 SHOLL, J. said that *John* v. *Humphreys* went further than Australian courts have gone and is irreconcilable with Australian cases.
[10] As in *Buchanan* v. *Moore*, [1963] N. I. 194.

his licence or explain its nonproduction. But *John* v. *Humphreys* [1] decides that this latter course must be adopted.

The most recent English judgment on this subject could be treated as authority for the view that the principle under consideration places the legal burden on an accused with "peculiar knowledge".[2] This is a very drastic consequence where there are no statutory words pointing expressly to such a result and, as the court did not refer to the distinction between the legal and evidential burdens, it may be wise to adhere to the following statement by a New Zealand judge:

> "If no evidence is given to prove the affirmative in respect of a negative averment which is peculiarly within the knowledge of the accused, then the finding ought to be against the accused on that fact. However, when the accused has produced evidence the question of the nature of the burden may require further consideration. Whether it is the same burden as that laid down for proof of insanity, or whether it is merely a burden of producing some evidence and thus throwing the burden back on the prosecution upon the principle of *Woolmington* v. *Director of Public Prosecutions* is a matter which does not arise for determination."[3]

C. STATUTES AFFECTING THE BURDEN OF PROOF

The doctrine stated by BAYLEY, J., in *R.* v. *Turner* is a principle of statutory interpretation, but there are two ways in which the incidence of the burden of proof may be more directly affected by a statute. In the first place, there may be some express provision covering the point, and secondly, the arrangement of the clauses may give an indication as to how the various burdens should be distributed on the different issues raised by the statute.

(1) EXPRESS STATUTORY PROVISIONS

It is not uncommon for statutes to provide that certain facts shall be deemed to exist until the contrary is proved. The precise words that are employed vary from statute to statute, and they could have a decisive effect. Typical provisions are section 30 (2) of the Bills of Exchange Act, 1882, and section 2 of the Prevention of Corruption Act, 1916.[4]

(i) Bills of Exchange Act, 1882, s. 30 (2).—Section 30 (2) of the Bills of Exchange Act, 1882, provides that every holder of a bill is *prima facie* deemed to be a holder in due course; but if in an action on a bill it is admitted or proved that the acceptance, issue, or subsequent negotiation of the bill is affected by fraud, duress, or force and fear, or illegality, the burden of proof is shifted, unless and until the holder proves that, subsequent to the alleged fraud or illegality, value has in good faith been given for the bill. In the light of cases decided before and after the Act came into force, when the subsection speaks of "proof" it is clear that all that is meant is "evidence upon which a jury would be entitled to base a verdict".[5]

---

[1] P. 87, *ante.*

[2] *R.* v. *Ewens, supra.* See an article by Michael Dean, [1966] Crim. L. R. 594.

[3] HENRY, J., in *Hall* v. *Dunlop*, [1959] N. Z. L. R. 1031, at p. 1036; see also *McBride* v. *Brown*, [1960] N. Z. L. R. 782 and Addendum, *ante.*

[4] For s. 30 of the Sexual Offences Act, 1956, see *R.* v. *Lawrence* (1963), 47 Crim. App. Rep. 42 and for s. 5 of the Road Traffic Act, 1960 (re-enacted by s. 5 (1) of the Road Traffic Act, 1972), see *Morton* v. *Confer*, [1963] 2 All E. R. 765.

[5] *Talbot* v. *Von Boris*, [1911] 1 K. B. 854, at p. 866 *per* KENNEDY, L.J.; *Hall* v. *Feather-stone* (1858), 3 H. & N. 284.

The result is that the holder has the legal burden of proving that he gave value for the bill in good faith, but he does not bear the evidential burden on the point until the defendant has made out a *prima facie* case that the bill was tainted with fraud, duress or illegality. No doubt this is commercially fair even if, from the point of view of literal interpretation, there is something to be said for a construction less favourable to the defendant.[1]

(ii) Prevention of Corruption Act, 1916, s. 2.—By section 2 of the Prevention of Corruption Act, 1916, on a charge under the Prevention of Corruption Act, 1906, a consideration is to be deemed to be given corruptly unless the contrary is proved. In *R. v. Evans-Jones and Jenkins*,[2] this was held to mean that, if the jury are in doubt as to whether they should accept the accused's explanation of a gift to a public officer, it is their duty to convict, and this construction was also adopted by the Court of Criminal Appeal in *R. v. Carr-Briant*,[3] where however, the conviction was quashed because the jury had been misdirected with regard to the standard of proof. HUMPHREYS, J. stated the judgment of the court in the following terms:

> "In any case where, either by statute or at common law, some matter is presumed 'unless the contrary is proved' the jury should be directed that it is for them to decide whether the contrary is proved, that the burden of proof required is less than that required at the hands of the prosecution in proving a case beyond reasonable doubt, and that the burden may be discharged by evidence satisfying the jury of the probability of that which the accused is called upon to establish."[4]

These observations were plainly intended to apply to all cases in which a criminal statute casts the burden of proof on the accused, and it seems that they will be applied to all such cases by the courts.[5]

(2) ARRANGEMENT OF CLAUSES

In *R. v. Jarvis*[6] Lord MANSFIELD said:

> "It is a known distinction that what comes by way of proviso in a statute must be insisted on by way of defence by the party accused; but, where exceptions are in the enacting part of a law, it must appear in the charge that the defendant does not fall within any of them."

The principle differs from that enunciated by BAYLEY, J., in *R. v. Turner*[7] because it is not confined to negative averments and says nothing about the defendant's means of knowledge; but it is confined to provisoes, while BAYLEY, J.'s dictum has been applied to exceptions "within the enacting part of a law".

Lord MANSFIELD's distinction has only been mentioned in connection with criminal statutes, although there is an analogy in the construction of contracts. It refers to matters of procedure rather than questions of evidence. Thus it has been held to justify the omission of various aver-

---

[1] Perhaps some significance should be attached to the word "alleged" as indicating a reference to the evidential burden alone. For the commercial justification of the law on this subject see ALDERSON, B. in *Elkin v. Janson* (1845), 13 M. & W. 655, at p. 664.

[2] (1923), 87 J. P. 115.

[3] [1943] K. B. 607; [1943] 2 All E. R. 156; followed in *Public Prosecutor v. Yuvaraj*, [1970] A. C. 913.

[4] [1943] K. B. 607, at p. 612; [1943] 2 All E. R. 156, at p. 158.

[5] *Jayasena v. R.*, [1970] A. C. 618; [1970] 1 All E. R. 219; *Mizel v. Warren*, [1973] 2 All E. R. 1149.

[6] (1756), 1 East 643, n.

[7] See p. 87, *ante*.

ments from an indictment, but it does have a bearing on the burden of proof because, if an allegation is left out of an indictment, the prosecution is relieved from calling evidence on the point.

Thus in *R.* v. *Audley*,[1] it was decided that an indictment for bigamy need not state that the accused was a British subject although the alleged second marriage took place abroad. The defence that would have been available to the accused was the consequence of words used in the proviso to the relevant statute but, although the decision makes it plain that the evidential burden was borne by the accused in the first instance, the position with regard to the legal burden is not so clear. So far as bigamy is concerned, it is settled that the Crown bears the legal burden of establishing that an accused whose spouse has been continually absent for seven years or more knew that he or she was still alive when the second ceremony was celebrated.[2] The accused bears the burden of adducing evidence on this matter as well as on the connected issue of the duration of the absence,[3] but it is not clear who bears the legal burden on this last point.[4]

Lord MANSFIELD'S doctrine finds its strongest expression in s. 81 of the Magistrates' Courts Act, 1952, which provides that, where the defendant to an information or complaint relies for his defence on any exception, proviso, excuse or qualification, the burden of proving it shall be on him. The section is confined to summary proceedings and reproduces the effect of s. 14 of the Summary Jurisdiction Act, 1848, and s. 39 (2) of the Summary Jurisdiction Act, 1879, which did not, however, employ the phrase "burden of proof". In this context "burden of proof" means the legal burden.[5]

Various tests have been suggested for determining when the section is applicable. It is doubtful whether any of them affords a helpful guide, but one of the best known is contained in the following words of an Irish judge speaking of a similar provision:

> "Does the section make the act described an offence subject to particular exceptions, qualifications, etc., which, where applicable, make the *prima facie* offence an innocent act, or does the statute make an act *prima facie* innocent an offence when done under certain conditions? In the former case the exception need not be negatived; in the latter words of exception may constitute the gist of the offence."[6]

D. THE PROPOSALS OF THE CRIMINAL LAW REVISION COMMITTEE

We have seen that it is difficult to believe that what may be called the "Carr-Briant" construction will not be applied by the courts to all

---

[1] [1907] 1 K. B. 383; *R.* v. *James*, [1902] 1 K. B. 540.
[2] *R.* v. *Curgerwen* (1865), L. R. 1 C. C. R. 1; the relevant statute is s. 57 of the Offences against the Person Act, 1861.
[3] *R.* v. *Jones* (1883), 11 Q. B. D. 118.
[4] The Australian authorities favour the view that the legal burden of proving the seven years' absence is borne by the accused (*R.* v. *Bonnor*, [1957] V. L. R. 227), but, on principle, there is much to be said for the dissenting judgments in this case, and it was not immediately concerned with the proviso concerning seven years' absence. The earlier case of *R.* v. *Broughton*, [1953] V. L. R. 572 (questioned by the majority in *Bonnor's* case) placed the legal burden on the Crown. See the discussion by Norval Morris, 18 M. L. R. 452 and McDougal, 21 *ibid*, p. 510.
[5] *Gatland* v. *Metropolitan Police Commissioner*, [1968] 2 Q. B. 279; [1968] 2 All E. R. 100; *Nimmo* v. *Alexander Cowan and Sons, Ltd.*, [1968] A. C. 107; [1967] 3 All E. R. 187; *Taylor* v. *Ellis*, [1956] V. L. R. 457; *Everard* v. *Opperman*, [1958] V. L. R. 389.
[6] GIBSON, J., in *Shehan* v. *Cork Justices*, [1908] 2 I. R. 1, at p. 11.

criminal statutes which expressly place the burden of proof on the accused, state that "proof" lies upon him or require him to "prove" something. It is in accordance with the ordinary principles of literal statutory construction that the burden imposed on the accused should be the legal burden; as has already been pointed out, the discharge of an evidential burden does not prove anything, and the construction of section 30 of the Bills of Exchange Act, 1882, can be explained on the footing that the section is a statement of the pre-existing common law.

Up to a point, the policy underlying statutes which place a burden upon the accused is justifiable because, in the absence of such a provision, a number of unmeritorious submissions of no case to answer, on account, for example, of the prosecutor's failure to give evidence of the lack of a lawful excuse, would have to be accepted. There is, however, an overwhelming objection to placing the legal burden on the accused in these cases, even after allowance has been made for the fact that the standard of proof would be that appropriate to civil proceedings; it means that the tribunal of fact may be obliged to convict a person of whose guilt they are so far from being sure as to regard the probabilities of the existence of a lawful excuse as equally balanced. The danger of unmeritorious submissions of no case can be met by placing an evidential burden with regard to lawful excuse, etc. on the accused. This is the recommendation of the 11th Report of the Criminal Law Revision Committee,[1] and it would apply to the common law burden of proving insanity placed upon the accused as well as to existing statutory burdens. The recommended clause[2] could of course be expressly excluded by subsequent legislation, and there is a necessary exception covering cases in which the accused may bring in a third party and is entitled to an acquittal on proof that his default was due to that of the third party; an example is provided by proceedings against a retailer under the food and drugs legislation who alleges that he was blameless and that the fault lay with the manufacturer.

The adoption of the Committee's recommendations would amount to a generalisation of section 25 (3) of the Theft Act, 1968, under which, on a charge of going equipped for stealing, proof that the accused had with him any article made or adapted for use in committing a burglary, theft or cheat shall be evidence that he had it with him for such use. The evidential, but not the legal burden, as to lawful user is thus placed upon the accused.[3]

E. THE INTERPRETATION OF AGREEMENTS AFFECTING THE BURDEN OF PROOF

The incidence of the burden of proof may be determined by the agreement of the parties in civil cases,[4] and, where there is such an agreement, there can be little doubt that the burden in question would generally be taken to be the legal one. This is also the burden which has been the subject of discussion in cases concerned with the construction of contracts for the carriage of goods by sea, and insurance against various types of loss.

---

[1] Paras. 137–42.

[2] Clause 9.

[3] Contrast s. 28 of the repealed Larcency Act, 1916, which was held, in *R. v. Paterson*, [1962] 2 Q. B. 429; [1962] 1 All E. R. 340, to place the legal burden of proving lawful excuse in such cases upon the accused.

[4] *Levy v. Assicurazioni Generali*, [1940] A. C. 791; [1940] 3 All E. R. 427.

(i) Perils of the sea—The Glendaroch.—If a plaintiff claims damages from shipowners for breach of contract to carry goods safely, and the defendants rely on a clause exempting them from loss or damage occasioned to the goods by a peril of the sea, they must prove that the latter occurred, and caused the damage in question; but, if the plaintiff relies upon a proviso to the exemption clause relating to negligence on the part of the defendants, the legal burden of proving negligence rests on him. These points were established in the leading case of *The Glendaroch* [1] where the ship on which the goods had been placed struck a rock, and Lord ESHER said:

> "The plaintiffs would have to prove the contract and the non-delivery. If they leave that in doubt, of course they fail. The defendants' answer is 'Yes; but the case was brought within the exception—within its ordinary meaning'. That lies upon them. Then the plaintiffs have a right to say there are exceptional circumstances, viz. that the damage was brought about by the negligence of the defendants' servants, and it seems to me that it is for the plaintiff to make out the second exception." [2]

(ii) Insurance exceptions.—This case was among those followed by BAILHACHE, J., in *Munro, Brice & Co.* v. *War Risks Association*,[3] which was concerned with an insurance policy covering the loss of a ship through perils of the sea, subject to an exception in respect of enemy action. He held that the defendants bore the legal burden of proving that the ship was lost in consequence of the latter with the result that the plaintiffs succeeded on their claim as the ship had not been heard of after she set sail, and there was no evidence of the cause of her disappearance. The law on this point cannot, however, be regarded as completely settled for, in the earlier case of *Hurst* v. *Evans*,[4] LUSH, J., had decided that, where an insurance policy against loss of jewellery contained an exception in respect of theft by the plaintiff's servants, it was incumbent on the plaintiff to negative loss from this cause. This is not the kind of problem that can be solved by logical argument, for there is no difference between a clause which is construed to read "The insurers shall be liable for loss except that which occurs in specified circumstances" and a rule which says "the insurers shall be liable for loss arising from all causes other than those specified",[5] but it is submitted that practical considerations as well as previous authority [6] are in favour of the view of BAILHACHE, J. He said that if he had been asked to advise on evidence in *Hurst* v. *Evans*, it would not have occurred to him to suggest that the plaintiff should call all his servants, one after the other to swear that they had not stolen the jewels. "The procession would be a long one if Messrs. Whiteley were the plaintiffs." [7]

---

[1] [1894] P. 226.
[2] At p. 231; contrast *Slattery* v. *Mance*, [1962] 1 Q. B. 676; [1962] 1 All E. R. 525. In the case of insurance of a ship against fire the insurer must establish scuttling on the balance of probabilities.
[3] [1918] 2 K. B. 78.
[4] [1917] 1 K. B. 352.
[5] Cf. the arguments of Professor Stone in 60 L. Q. R. 278 *et seq.*
[6] *Gorman* v. *Hand-in-Hand Insurance Co.* (1877), I. R. 11 C. L. 224.
[7] [1918] 2 K. B. at p. 86.

CHAPTER V

THE DEGREES OF PROOF

If the party who bears the legal burden of proof on a given issue is to succeed on that issue, the weight of the evidence adduced by him must be greater than that of the evidence adduced by his adversary. The legal requirements concerning the extent of the excess are discussed in this chapter. The cases show that there is a difference between the standards of proof in criminal and civil proceedings. This will be our main concern, but it will be necessary to refer to the standard of proof in matrimonial causes and some miscellaneous points.

A. CIVIL AND CRIMINAL CASES [1]

The question of the proper method of directing the jury concerning the standard of proof in criminal cases was brought to a head by the judgment of the Court of Criminal Appeal in *R.* v. *Summers*.[2] It will therefore be convenient to begin by considering the authorities before and after that decision.

(1) THE AUTHORITIES BEFORE R. *v.* SUMMERS

Several judgments delivered in the course of the second half of the nineteenth century indicate the existence of two standards of proof recognised by the law. They are proof on a preponderance of probabilities, the standard appropriate to civil cases and proof beyond reasonable doubt, the proper standard on a criminal charge. When giving the advice of the judges to the House of Lords in *Cooper* v. *Slade* [3] WILLES, J., said "In civil cases the preponderance of probability may constitute sufficient ground for a verdict"; but, in criminal proceedings which took place some seven years later, the jury were told that they must be satisfied of the accused's guilt beyond any reasonable doubt, "and this as a conviction created in their minds, and not merely as a matter of probability; and if it was only an impression from probability, their duty was to acquit".[4]

In the first half of the twentieth century, the House of Lords sanctioned a reference to proof beyond reasonable doubt by a judge when summing up in a criminal case,[5] and the distinction between the two standards was

---

[1] See further Cowen and Carter, *Essays on the Law of Evidence*, 242–249, and Glanville Williams, *The Direction to the Jury on the Burden of Proof* (Criminal Law Review, 1954, 464).
[2] [1952] 1 All E. R. 1059.
[3] (1858), 6 H. L. Cas. 746, at p. 772.
[4] *R.* v. *Winsor* (1865), 4 F. & F. 363.
[5] *Woolmington* v. *Director of Public Prosecutions*, [1935] A. C. 462, at p. 481; *Mancini* v. *Director of Public Prosecutions*, [1942] A. C. 1, at p. 11; [1941] 3 All E. R. 272, at p. 279. The question of the quantum, as opposed to the burden, of proof was not directly before the House in either case.

stated as clearly as it can be stated by DENNING, J., in *Miller* v. *Minister of Pensions*.[1] Speaking of the degree of cogency which the evidence on a criminal charge must reach before the accused can be convicted he said:

> "That degree is well settled. It need not reach certainty, but it must carry a high degree of probability. Proof beyond a reasonable doubt does not mean proof beyond the shadow of a doubt. The law would fail to protect the community if it admitted fanciful possibilities to deflect the course of justice. If the evidence is so strong against a man as to leave only a remote possibility in his favour, which can be dismissed with the sentence 'of course it is possible but not in the least probable' the case is proved beyond reasonable doubt, but nothing short of that will suffice."[2]

When speaking of the degree of cogency which evidence must reach in order that it may discharge the legal burden in a civil case, his lordship said:

> "That degree is well settled. It must carry a reasonable degree of probability, but not so high as is required in a criminal case. If the evidence is such that the tribunal can say: 'we think it more probable than not', the burden is discharged, but if the probabilities are equal it is not."

There were, however, at least two grounds for supposing that the law was not so clear and well settled as appeared to be the case. In the first place, suggestions were made that the onus borne by the plaintiff in civil litigation was the same as that undertaken by the prosecutor on a criminal charge.[3] Secondly, it seems to be fairly certain that confusion was sometimes occasioned by judicial endeavours to elucidate the nature of a reasonable doubt when directing juries in criminal cases. Lord GODDARD, C.J., went so far as to say that:

> "Once a judge begins to use the words 'reasonable doubt' and to try to explain what is a reasonable doubt and what is not, he is much more likely to confuse the jury than if he tells them in plain language, 'It is the duty of the prosecution to satisfy you of the prisoner's guilt'."[4]

(2) R. *v.* SUMMERS AND AFTER

Lord GODDARD returned to this theme in *R.* v. *Summers*,[5] but his words were much stronger as they amount to a prohibition on the use of the phrase "reasonable doubt" by trial judges when summing up in criminal cases. He said :

> "If the jury is told that it is their duty to regard the evidence and see that it satisfies them so that they can feel sure when they return a verdict of guilty, that is much better than using the expression 'reasonable doubt' and I hope in future that that will be done."

Lord GODDARD has since shown that his objection to the old formula is the difficulty of following explanations of what does, and does not, constitute a reasonable doubt. He thought that no real guidance is afforded by saying it must not be a fanciful doubt, and to say it must be such a doubt as would make jurymen hesitate in their own affairs does not

---

[1] [1947] 2 All E. R. 372, at p. 373–374.
[2] The propriety of summing up in terms of probability and possibility was questioned in *R.* v. *McKenna* (1964), 81 (Pt. 1) W. N. (N.S.W.) 330; but the reference to probabilities can be regarded as a direction to use commonsense (*R.* v. *Coe*, [1967] V. R. 712).
[3] *Munro Brice & Co.* v. *War Risks Association*, [1918] 2 K. B. 78, at p. 80, *per* BAILHACHE, J. *Flower* v. *Ebbw Vale Steel, Iron and Coal Co., Ltd.*, [1936] A. C. 206, at p. 221, *per* Lord ALNESS.
[4] *R.* v. *Kritz*, [1950] 1 K. B. 82, at p. 90; [1949] 2 All E. R. 406, at p. 410.
[5] [1952] 1 All E. R. 1059.

suggest any particular standard because one juryman might hesitate where another would not do so.[1] In another case Lord GODDARD said:

> "Let us leave out of account, if we can, any expression such as 'giving the prisoner the benefit of the doubt'. It is not a question of giving the benefit of a doubt; if the jury are left with any degree of doubt whether the prisoner is guilty, then the case has not been proved."[2]

An appeal founded on the ground that the trial judge had not told the jury to give the accused the benefit of the doubt was dismissed in *R. v. Blackburn* [3] where a direction which did no more than stress the point that the jury must be satisfied of the accused's guilt was approved. In *R. v. Murtagh and Kennedy*,[4] on the other hand, an appeal was allowed because the summing up had not made it sufficiently clear that the jury must acquit if they were left in doubt concerning the accused's explanation of the facts. In *R. v. Hepworth and Fearnley*[5] an appeal was allowed on the ground that a direction to the effect that the jury must be satisfied of the accused's guilt was inadequate when the charge was one of receiving. The judgment of the Court of Criminal Appeal was delivered by Lord GODDARD, C.J. After confessing that he had some difficulty in understanding how there can be two standards of proof, he continued:

> "One would be on safe ground if one said in a criminal case to a jury: 'you must be satisfied beyond reasonable doubt', and one could also say, 'you, the jury, must be completely satisfied', or better still, 'you must feel sure of the prisoner's guilt'."[6]

In spite of this approval of three possible formulations, including the reference to the time-honoured standard of proof beyond reasonable doubt, the Court of Criminal Appeal has expressed its disapproval of the trial judge's summing-up concerning the standard of proof in a number of subsequent cases,[7] and it is difficult not to feel considerable sympathy with the following words of the Chief Justice of Australia:

> "In my view it is a mistake to depart from the time-honoured formula. It is I think used by ordinary people and is understood well enough by the average man in the community. The attempts to substitute other expressions of which there have been many examples not only here but in England have never prospered. It is wise as well as proper to avoid such expressions."[8]

---

[1] *R. v. Hepworth and Fearnley*, [1955] 2 Q. B. 600, at p. 603; [1955] 2 All E. R. 918, at p. 919. For similar criticisms see *Brown* v. *R.* (1913), 17 C. L. R. 570. The idea of a doubt which would cause jurymen to hesitate in their own affairs is traceable to the summing-up of POLLOCK, C.B., in *R. v. Manning* (1849), 30 C. C. C. Sess. Pap. 654: "If the conclusion to which you are conducted be that there is that degree of certainty in the case which you would act upon in your own grave and important concerns, that is the degree of certainty which the law requires and which will justify you in returning a verdict of guilty."

[2] *R. v. Onufrejczyk*, [1955] 1 Q. B. 388, at p. 391; [1955] 1 All E. R. 247, at p. 249. The reference to giving the prisoner the benefit of the doubt has been traced back to the eighteenth century and appears to have the blessing of the House of Lords: *Woolmington* v. *Director of Public Prosecutions*, [1935] A. C. 462, at p. 481; *Mancini* v. *Director of Public Prosecutions*, [1942] A. C. 1, at p. 11; [1941] 3 All E. R. 272, at p. 279.

[3] (1955), 39 Cr. App. Rep. 84, n. The Attorney-General refused his fiat for an appeal to the House of Lords in this case, but it is difficult to say what is left of the decision after *R. v. Murtagh and Kennedy* and *R. v. Hepworth and Fearnley* (*infra*).

[4] (1955), 39 Cr. App. Rep. 72.   [5] [1955] 2 Q. B. 600; [1955] 2 All E. R. 918.

[6] At pp. 603, 920, respectively.

[7] Criminal Law Review (1961) 322; *ibid.*, 360 and 560; *ibid.* (1962) 52; *R. v. Head and Warren* (1961), 45 Cr. App. Rep. 225; *R. v. Attfield*, [1961] 3 All E. R. 243; *R. v. Stafford* and *R. v. Luvaglio*, [1968] 3 All E. R. 752, n. *Cf. R. v. Floyd*, [1972] 1 N. S. W. R. 373, at p. 382 and especially p. 390.

[8] *Dawson* v. *R.* (1961), 106 C. L. R. 1, at p. 18 (DIXON, C.J.). See also *Thomas* v. *R.* (1960), 33 A. L. J. R. 413 and the remarks of DIXON, C.J., in 31 Australian Law Journal,

In the words of Dixon, C.J.'s successor:

> "A reasonable doubt is a doubt which the particular jury entertain in the circumstances. Jurymen themselves set the standard of what is reasonable in the circumstances. It is that ability which is attributed to them which is one of the virtues of our mode of trial: to their task of deciding facts they bring to bear their experience and judgment."[1]

But the English courts[2] and the Judicial Committee of the Privy Council[3] are against any set form of words:

> "If the jury are made to understand that they have to be satisfied and must not return a verdict against the defendant unless they feel sure, and that the onus is all the time on the prosecution and not on the defence, then whether the judge uses one form of language or another is neither here nor there."[4]

It has from time to time been suggested that special instructions are required in criminal cases in which the evidence is purely circumstantial; but the English courts would no doubt follow the New Zealand Court of Appeal in rejecting the suggestion that the jury must be satisfied beyond reasonable doubt of the existence of each and every evidentiary fact, for different members of the jury may be convinced beyond reasonable doubt of the guilt of the accused by their acceptance of the existence of different facts.[5] The House of Lords has refused to lay down a rule that, in addition to directing the jury that the prosecution bears the burden of proving the accused's guilt beyond reasonable doubt, the judge must, where the evidence is circumstantial, direct them to acquit unless the facts are not only consistent with the accused's guilt, but also inconsistent with any other rational conclusion.[6] Such a requirement has been assumed to exist by the Canadian courts on the authority of *R.* v. *Hodge*.[7] In that case great stress was rightly placed on the destructive effect on the cumulative force of circumstantial evidence pointing to guilt of one rational hypothesis of innocence, but the direction to the jury was, rightly it is submitted, treated by the House of Lords as no more than a formula suitable in some cases, for instructing the jury that they must be satisfied of the accused's guilt beyond reasonable doubt.

(3) Conclusions

It remains to consider the authorities in favour of the view that there are at least two standards of proof in English law, and the nature of the distinction between proof on a preponderance of probability and proof beyond reasonable doubt.

(i) Cases showing there are two standards of proof.—Neither *R.* v. *Summers* nor any of the other decisions which have been mentioned has

---

at p. 269. For the dangers of a direction that it is for the jury to decide which side to believe without an indication that they must acquit if they do not know who to believe, see *R.* v. *Lapuse*, [1964] V. L. R. 43 and *R.* v. *Smith*, [1964] V. L. R. 217.

[1] Barwick, C. J., delivering the judgment of the High Court of Australia in *Green* v. *R.* (1972), 46 A. L. J. R. 545.

[2] *R.* v. *Allan*, [1969] 1 All E. R. 91.

[3] *Walters* v. *R.*, [1969] 2 A. C. 26; the direction upheld in this case is criticised in 32 M. L. R. 217. See Addendum, *ante*.

[4] Lord Diplock, [1969] 2 A. C., at p. 30.

[5] *Thomas* v. *R.*, [1972] N. Z. L. R. 34.

[6] *McGreevy* v. *Director of Public Prosecutions*, [1973] 1 All E. R. 503.

[7] (1838), 2 Lew. C. C. 227; for Australia see *Plomp* v. *R.* (1963), 110 C. L. R. 234.

affected *R.* v. *Carr-Briant*,[1] and we have already seen that the *ratio decidendi* of the Court of Criminal Appeal in that case was based on the existence of two standards of proof.[2] The conviction was quashed on the ground that the trial judge had not told the jury that it was only necessary for the accused's evidence to conform to the standard appropriate to the discharge of a legal burden in a civil suit when, by way of exception to the general rule, such burden is borne by the prisoner in criminal proceedings. To repeat the words of HUMPHREYS, J.:[3]

> "In any case where, either by statute or at common law, some matter is presumed against an accused person 'unless the contrary is proved', the jury should be directed that it is for them to decide whether the contrary is proved, that the burden of proof required is less than that required at the hands of the prosecution in proving the case beyond a reasonable doubt, and that the burden may be discharged by evidence satisfying the jury of that which the accused is called upon to establish."

This decision does not stand alone, for a similar doctrine was recognised by the Privy Council when insanity was raised as a defence to a criminal charge.[4] Moreover, the controversy concerning the standard of proof in matrimonial causes and the question of the appropriate measure to apply to an issue concerning the commission of a crime when it occurs in a civil suit could hardly have arisen were it not for the fact that the existence of two standards of proof is something which is firmly embedded in English law.[5] All that has happened is that a certain amount of judicial scepticism has sometimes been expressed on the subject.[6]

(ii) The nature of the distinction between proof on a preponderance of probabilities and beyond reasonable doubt.—It is difficult to go the whole way with the sceptics with regard to the distinction between the standard of proof appropriate to civil cases and the standard which has to be reached by the prosecution at a criminal trial. Once it is conceded that there are degrees of probability, the law can intelligibly require that a very high degree must be established by the prosecution, whereas a lower degree will suffice in civil proceedings. The distinction between "being satisfied on a balance of probability" or "reasonably satisfied" on the one hand, and being "sure", or "satisfied beyond reasonable doubt" on the other hand, is plain enough outside the law.

It is open to question whether any useful purpose is served by further analysis because there is no scale of differing percentages of certainty, and the suggestion that there is such a scale obscures the nature of the typical direction to juries in criminal cases. In effect, the jurors are told that, although they come to the conclusion, after considering all the evidence, that the prisoner probably committed the crime charged, they must not act

---

[1] [1943] K. B. 607; [1943] 2 All E. R. 156. Followed in *Public Prosecutor* v. *Yuvaroj*, [1970] A. C. 913.

[2] P. 89, *ante.*

[3] [1943] K. B. 607, at p. 612; [1943] 2 All E. R. 156, at p. 158.

[4] *Sodeman* v. *R.*, [1936] 2 All E. R. 1138.

[5] The war pension cases point to the same conclusion; see *Judd* v. *Minister of Pensions and National Insurance*, [1965] 3 All E. R. 642.

[6] See the remarks of Lord GODDARD, C.J., in *R.* v. *Hepworth and Fearnley*, [1955] 2 Q. B. 600, at p. 603; [1955] 2 All E. R. 918, at p. 920. The sceptics include HILBERY, J. "I personally have never seen the difference between the onus of proof in a civil and criminal case. If a thing is proved, it is proved, but I am not entitled to that view" (in the course of the argument in *R.* v. *Murtagh and Kennedy* as reported in *The Times* newspaper, 24 May, 1955).

on that conclusion by returning a verdict of guilty if they recognise that reasonable grounds exist for taking the contrary view. The essential difference between the two standards of proof consists in the effect which those who, *ex hypothesi*, believe in the probable existence of a certain state of affairs must give to their doubts on the subject. This point has been made with great clarity by Professor Coutts who says:

> "Normally, in a civil case, account must be taken of a doubt only if it results in a rational opinion that a fact in issue is less likely than not, whereas in a criminal case account must be taken of a doubt if it results in a rational opinion that the contradictory of the issue is more than a remote possibility".[1]

This brings us back to Lord DENNING's statement in *Miller* v. *Minister of Pensions*.[2] It will be recollected that he said:

> "If the evidence is so strong against a man as to leave only a *remote* possibility in his favour, which can be dismissed with the sentence 'of course it is possible but not in the least probable' the case is proved beyond reasonable doubt, but nothing short of that will suffice".

The word remote has been italicised because it has been suggested that Lord DENNING was defining a reasonable doubt in terms of the distinction between probabilities and possibilities, whereas a jury may have a reasonable doubt although that upon which they found their conclusion is only a reasonable possibility of innocence. "If they think there is that reasonable possibility, that it is one which arises from the evidence, or the absence of evidence, then I think it is one which to the jury would raise a reasonable doubt as to the guilt of the accused."[3] Perhaps it is impossible to improve upon Lord MAUGHAM's definition of a reasonable doubt as "the doubt which men of good sense may reasonably entertain, not the doubt of a fool or of a person of weakness of mind".[4]

Lord DENNING had more to say about standards of proof in the divorce case of *Bater* v. *Bater*,[5] and his words have frequently been quoted with approval by English judges :[6]

> "The difference of opinion which has been evoked about the standard of proof in recent cases may well turn out to be more a matter of words than anything else. It is of course true that by our law a higher standard of proof is required in criminal cases than in civil cases. But this is subject to the qualification that there is no absolute standard in either case. In criminal cases the charge must be proved beyond reasonable doubt, but there may be degrees of proof within that standard. ... So also in civil cases, the case may be proved by a preponderance of probability, but there may be degrees of probability within that standard. The degree depends on the subject-matter. A civil court, when considering a charge of fraud, will naturally require for itself a higher degree of probability than that which it would require when asking if negligence is established. It does not adopt so high a degree as a criminal court, even when it is considering a charge of a criminal nature; but still it does require a degree of probability which is commensurate with the occasion."

These words must not be taken to mean that there is an infinite variety of standards of proof according to the subject-matter with which the court is

---

[1] 14 M. L. R. 517 n. 35.
[2] See p. 94, *ante*.
[3] MACFARLAN, J. in *R.* v. *McKenna*, (1964) 81 (Pt. 1) W. N. (N.S.W.) 330, at p. 334. See n. 2, p. 94, *ante*.
[4] 17 Canadian Bar Review, 472.
[5] [1951] P. 35, at pp. 36-37; [1950] 2 All E. R. 458, at p. 459.
[6] For example by Lord PEARCE in *Blyth* v. *Blyth*, [1966] 1 All E. R. 524, at p. 539.

concerned, but rather that this latter factor may cause variations in the amount of evidence required to tilt the balance of probability or to establish a condition of satisfaction beyond reasonable doubt. As certain things are inherently improbable, prosecutors on the more serious criminal charges and plaintiffs in certain civil cases have more hurdles to surmount than those concerned with other allegations.

> "Though no court and no jury would give less careful attention to issues lacking gravity than to those marked by it, the very elements of gravity become a part of the whole range of circumstances which have to be weighed in the scale when deciding as to the balance of probabilities." [1]

Nor must Lord DENNING's reference to a matter of words be taken to imply that the distinction between the two standards of proof is no more than verbal. He was speaking on an appeal from a judge alone and alluding to the different ways in which judges had expressed themselves with regard to the degree of satisfaction required of them before giving relief in a divorce case. The same point as that made by Lord DENNING was made more recently by Lord PEARCE when he said:

> "Too close a judicial self analysis is not helpful in deciding the issue. When a judge begins to doubt whether or not he has reasonable doubt it obscures rather than clarifies his difficult task". [2]

No doubt the High Court of Australia had in mind each of the points which has just been made about Lord DENNING's judgment in *Bater* v. *Bater* when making the following observations in *Rejfek* v. *McElroy* : [3]

> "The standard of proof to be applied in a case and the relationship between the degree of persuasion of the mind according to the balance of probabilities and the gravity or otherwise of the fact of whose existence the mind is to be persuaded are not to be confused. The difference between the criminal standard of proof and the civil standard of proof is no mere matter of words: it is a matter of critical substance. No matter how grave the fact which is to be found in a civil case, the mind has only to be reasonably satisfied and has not with respect to any matter in issue in such a proceeding to attain that degree of certainty which is indispensable to the support of a conviction upon a criminal charge."

Granted that there are two clearly distinguishable standards of proof, the higher standard is applicable to criminal cases because, so long as the proportions do not become excessive, it is better that people who are probably guilty should go free than that those with regard to whom there is a reasonable possibility of innocence should be convicted. It is, however, by no means so clear why a plaintiff or petitioner in any civil case who establishes the probability of his contention should not be granted the appropriate relief. Very strong reason is required to justify the imposition of the standard of proof appropriate to a criminal charge in a civil case, and it is open to question whether that reason has ever been convincingly stated; but we shall see that the argument in favour of the application of the standard appropriate to crime has been urged in a number of civil cases.

---

[1] *Per* MORRIS, L. J. in *Hornal* v. *Neuberger Products, Ltd.*, [1957] 1 Q. B. 247, at p. 266; [1956] 3 All E. R. 970, at p. 978. This answers the observation of Sir Carleton Allen (Legal Duties 288) that it would startle the legal world and the public if, when trying an action for damages, the judge were to say to the jury, "You need not be as careful in arriving at your conclusions as if you were trying a criminal case".

[2] *Blyth* v. *Blyth*, [1966] 1 All E. R. 524, at p. 540.

[3] (1965), 39 A. L. J. R. 177, at p. 178.

B. THE STANDARD OF PROOF IN MATRIMONIAL CAUSES [1]

There has been a remarkable difference of opinion in the Courts of the British Commonwealth concerning the standard of proof in matrimonial causes. Must the petitioner establish his case beyond reasonable doubt, by a preponderance of probability or according to some other criterion? And does the standard vary with the nature of the relief sought or the grounds upon which it is claimed? Some authority can be found for affirmative and negative answers to all these questions. It will be convenient to begin with the decision of the English Court of Appeal in *Ginesi* v. *Ginesi* which was given in 1948, although, in so far as decisions preceding the Divorce Reform Act, 1969, are still relevant, the present law primarily depends on the interpretation to be placed upon the decisions of the House of Lords in *Preston-Jones* v. *Preston-Jones* and *Blyth* v. *Blyth*.

(1) GINESI *v.* GINESI AND PREVIOUS AUTHORITIES

In *Ginesi* v. *Ginesi* [2] the Court of Appeal decided that the standard of proof of adultery in a matrimonial suit was proof beyond reasonable doubt because:

> "Adultery was regarded by the ecclesiastical courts as a quasi-criminal offence, and it must be proved with the same strictness as is required in a criminal case." [3]

The previous English authorities consisted mainly, if not entirely of dicta [4] but ten years before *Ginesi* v. *Ginesi* was decided, the High Court of Australia had taken the contrary view in *Briginshaw* v. *Briginshaw*, [5] and it is unfortunate that this case was not cited to the Court of Appeal. It is even more regrettable that that court was not referred to *Mordaunt* v. *Moncreiffe* [6] in which the House of Lords decided that divorce suits in which adultery was alleged were civil proceedings, for this greatly detracts from the basis of the judgment of the Court of Appeal.

The quasi-criminal character of adultery in the past cannot possibly justify the imposition of the standard of proof appropriate to a criminal case in modern times when it may fairly be asked why there should be any distinction

---

[1] Cowen and Carter, *Essays on the Law of Evidence*, 249–268; Coutts, *The Standard of Proof of Adultery*, 65 L. Q. R. 220 (1949); Coutts, *The Standard of Proof in the Divorce Court*, 14 M. L. R. 417 (1951); Fridman, *Standards of Proof*, 33 Canadian Bar Review 665 (1955).

[2] [1948] P. 179; [1948] 1 All E. R. 373. The case concerned an application to discharge a maintenance order.

[3] *Per* TUCKER, L.J., at p. 181.

[4] *Loveden* v. *Loveden* (1810), 2 Hag. Con. 1, at p. 3 (circumstances must "lead the guarded discretion of a reasonable and just man to the conclusion") cf. *Rix* v. *Rix* (1777), 3 Hag. Ec., 74 where it was said that the proof must be "strict, satisfactory and conclusive"; *Wakeford* v. *Bishop of Lincoln*, [1921] 1 A. C. 813, at p. 822 (criminal standard in clergy discipline proceedings). In *Churchman* v. *Churchman*, [1945] P. 44, at p. 51; [1945] 2 All E. R. 190, at p. 195, Lord MERRIMAN, P., said, "The same strict proof is required in the case of a matrimonial offence as is required in connection with criminal offences properly so-called." *U.* v. *J.* (1867), L. R. 1 P. & D. 460, and *C.* v. *C.*, [1921] P. 399, support the view that the petitioner must prove his case beyond reasonable doubt in nullity founded on impotence. *Statham* v. *Statham*, [1929] P. 131 held that, when sodomy was the ground for divorce, the criminal standard applies. See also *D. B.* v. *W. B.*, [1935] P. 80 (strict standard of proof of unnatural practices in proceedings before magistrates), and *Lawson* v. *Lawson*, [1955] 1 All E. R. 341.

[5] (1938), 60 C. L. R. 336. The same rule was laid down for South Africa in *Gates* v. *Gates*, [1939] A. D. 150.

[6] (1874), L. R. 2 Sc. & Div. 374.

in this respect between the different bases on which it is alleged that a marriage has irretrievably broken down.

(2) From Ginesi to Preston-Jones v. Preston-Jones

Although the doctrine of *Ginesi* v. *Ginesi* was in effect followed by Lord Merriman, P. in *Fairman* v. *Fairman*,[1] considerations such as those which have just been mentioned led to criticism of *Ginesi* v. *Ginesi* in England,[2] the refusal by the High Court of Australia to alter its previous views,[3] and the reversal by the Supreme Court of New Zealand of its earlier decision based on *Ginesi* v. *Ginesi*.[4]

(3) Preston-Jones v. Preston-Jones and after

In *Preston-Jones* v. *Preston-Jones*[5] a husband petitioned for divorce on the ground of adultery and the only evidence in support of this allegation was the fact that his wife had given birth to a child three hundred and sixty days after he could have had such intercourse with her as might have resulted in the conception of the child. There was medical evidence to the effect that it was highly improbable that the child was the husband's, and the House of Lords decided by a majority of four to one that the petitioner had established his case beyond reasonable doubt—the test applied by the trial judge. In *Blyth* v. *Blyth*[6] Lord Pearce said that the real question in *Preston-Jones* v. *Preston-Jones* was whether on the assumption that proof beyond reasonable doubt was needed to establish adultery, such proof had been forthcoming on the evidence under review; but the case contains dicta, notably those of Lord Macdermott to be mentioned shortly, in favour of the view that the standard of proof with regard to all grounds of divorce was proof beyond reasonable doubt, as in a criminal case. This view was adopted on a considerable number of occasions in England between 1951 and 1966.[7]

During the same period, the High Court of Australia adhered to its previously expressed views that proof on a preponderance of probability suffices for adultery subject to the reservation, induced by the facts of *Preston-Jones* v. *Preston-Jones*, that a higher standard might be necessary where the practical effect of a finding of adultery is the bastardisation of a child.[8] Similar views, with or without the reservation, were taken in

---

[1] [1949] P. 341; [1949] 1 All E. R. 938.

[2] *Davis* v. *Davis*, [1950] P. 125; [1950] 1 All E. R. 40; *Gower* v. *Gower*, [1950] 1 All E. R. 804; see also *Bater* v. *Bater*, [1951] P. 35; [1950] 2 All E. R. 458.

[3] *Wright* v. *Wright* (1948), 77 C. L. R. 191.

[4] *Price* v. *Price*, [1951] N. Z. L. R. 1097, differing from *Andrews* v. *Andrews*, [1949] N. Z. L. R. 173. Proof on a preponderance of probability was also held enough in Ontario (*George* v. *George and Logie*, [1951] 1 D. L. R. 278.

[5] [1951] A. C. 391; [1951] 1 All E. R. 124. See case-note by G. H. Treitel in 14 M. L. R. 225.

[6] [1966] 1 All E. R. 524, at p. 539.

[7] *Galler* v. *Galler*, [1954] P. 252; [1954] 1 All E. R. 536; *Elphinstone* v. *Elphinstone* [1962] P. 203; [1962] 2 All E. R. 766; *Williams* v. *Williams*, [1964] A. C. 698 at p. 745 *Mulhouse (formerly Mulhausen)* v. *Mulhouse (formerly Mulhausen)*, [1964] 2 All E. R. 50; *Rudman* v. *Rudman and Lee* (Queen's Proctor showing cause), [1964] 2 All E. R. 102; *Senat* v. *Senat (K. H. and B. intervening)*, [1965] P. 172, at p. 174; *Inglis* v. *Inglis and Baxter*, [1968] P. 639; [1967] 2 All E. R. 72 (decided before *Blyth* v. *Blyth*, [1966] A. C. 643; [1966] 1 All E. R. 524).

[8] *Watts* v. *Watts* (1953), 89 C. L. R. 200. Many dicta stress the high standard required by the common law of evidence in rebuttal of the presumption of legitimacy, but, in Australia, the reservation so far as divorce is concerned, is no longer necessary because

Canada,[1] but, on the authority of *Preston-Jones* v. *Preston-Jones*, the New Zealand courts reverted, without reservation, to the view that adultery must be proved beyond reasonable doubt.[2]

In the course of his speech in *Preston-Jones* v. *Preston-Jones*[3] Lord MACDERMOTT said that the terms of the statute plainly recognised that "the marriage bond shall not be set aside lightly or without inquiry", and thought that it would be quite out of keeping with the anxious nature of the statutory provisions to hold that the court might be "satisfied" in respect of a ground for dissolution with something less than proof beyond reasonable doubt. He did not base this conclusion upon any analogy drawn from the criminal law because, since the decision in *Mordaunt* v. *Moncrieffe*,[4] it has been impossible to say that the two jurisdictions are other than distinct. The true reason "why both accept the same general standard—proof beyond reasonable doubt—lies not in any analogy, but in the gravity and public importance of the issues with which each is concerned."

The statute in question was section 4 (1) of the Matrimonial Causes Act 1950 (re-enacted by section 5 (3) of the Matrimonial Causes Act, 1965 but repealed by the Divorce Reform Act, 1969). It required that the court should, before pronouncing a decree of divorce, be "satisfied on the evidence" that the case for the petitioner has been proved, and that the petitioner has not been accessory to, connived at or condoned the alleged adultery. It is not clear what is meant by the "anxious nature of these provisions", and it is difficult to see how they point to one standard of proof rather than the other. It is true that judges have said that to be satisfied and, at the same time, to have a reasonable doubt, is an impossible state of mind,[5] but this carries with it the odd implication that something less than satisfaction will suffice to found a judgment for the plaintiff in an ordinary civil case in which it has hardly ever been suggested that satisfaction beyond reasonable doubt is required.

The word "satisfied" in the Matrimonial Causes Act refers to the incidence of the burden of proof rather than the standard of proof.[6]

Lord MACDERMOTT's justification for requiring the same strict proof in divorce as in crime is undoubtedly preferable to that of the quasi-criminal nature of adultery advanced in the earlier cases, but it is unconvincing. So far as the parties are concerned, the sanctity of marriage can hardly be fostered by finding a spouse who has probably committed adultery to be innocent of that act, for it can hardly be suggested that this will precipitate a reconciliation. No one would deny the gravity of all issues affecting status so far as the public is concerned, but what does the public gain by findings that those who have probably committed adultery have not done so, and that husbands are bound to maintain children of whom another man is probably the father?

"reasonable satisfaction" is the standard required in all cases by s. 96 of the Australian Commonwealth Matrimonial Causes Act, 1959.

[1] *Smith* v. *Smith*, [1952] 3 D. L. R. 449; *Boykowytch* v. *Boykowytch*, [1955] 2 D. L.R. 81; *May* v. *May*, [1952] 3 D. L. R. 725.

[2] *Macdonald* v. *Macdonald*, [1952] N. Z. L. R. 924; *Watkins* v. *Watkins*, [1956] N. Z. L. R. 754.

[3] [1951] A. C. 391, at p. 417.   [4] (1874) L. R. 2 Sc. & Div. 374.

[5] For example BUCKNILL, L. J. in *Bater* v. *Bater*, [1951] P. 35, at p. 36; [1950] 2 All E. R. 458.

[6] See *per* Lord DENNING in *Blyth* v. *Blyth*, [1966] 1 All E. R. 524, at p. 535.

(4) BLYTH v. BLYTH

The main issue in *Blyth* v. *Blyth* [1] concerned the standard by which condonation had to be disproved in proceedings for divorce founded on adultery. At the hearing of a husband's petition founded on adultery, the Commissioner said that he found, on a slender balance of probability, that the alleged adultery had not been condoned; but he dismissed the petition on the ground that the statutory provision permitting rebuttal of the presumption of condonation arising from intercourse was not retrospective. [2] The Court of Appeal and House of Lords held that the Commissioner's view that the relevant statutory provision did not operate retrospectively was wrong, but the Court of Appeal affirmed the dismissal of the petition because the requirement that the court should be "satisfied" that the adultery had not been condoned meant satisfaction beyond reasonable doubt. [3] By a majority of three to two, the House of Lords allowed the husband's appeal on the ground that condonation did not have to be disproved beyond reasonable doubt. The speech of Lord PEARSON who was one of the majority carefully went no further than the then bars to divorce, but Lord DENNING expressly applied his reasoning to the grounds for divorce and Lord PEARCE concurred in his speech although the conclusion of his own speech related solely to the bars to divorce.

Lord DENNING said:

> "So far as the grounds for divorce are concerned, the case, like any civil case, may be proved by a preponderance of probability but the degree of probability depends on the subject-matter. In proportion as the offence is grave, so ought the proof to be clear." [4]

Lord DENNING's view that in proportion as the offence is grave so ought the proof be clear was the ground upon which a majority of the Court of Appeal (WILMER and WINN, L.JJ.) allowed an appeal against a finding of adultery in *Bastable* v. *Bastable and Saunders*; [5] but Edmund DAVIES, L.J., while concurring in the result, preferred the statement of the High Court of Australia in *Rejfek* v. *McElroy* which has already been quoted: [6] "No matter how grave the fact which is to be found in a civil case, the mind has only to be reasonably satisfied. . . ."

The preceding account of the authorities shows that it would be rash to essay a general statement with regard to the standard of proof in matrimonial causes; but, assuming that there are only two standards known to English law, proof on a balance of probabilities and proof beyond reasonable doubt, there is no decision at the level of the House of Lords necessitating a conclusion in favour of the latter in the case of any matrimonial cause, and *Blyth* v. *Blyth* as interpreted in *Bastable* v. *Bastable and Saunders* supports the contrary view. The extent to which the courts will, when administering the new divorce law, regard themselves as bound by decisions on the old law based on the concept of a matrimonial offence remains to be seen; although the same word "satisfied" occurs in the new statute, the structure of the latter does not seem to point towards the need

---

[1] [1966] 1 All E. R. 524.
[2] Matrimonial Causes Act, 1963, s. 1.
[3] The relevant statutory provision has since been repealed.
[4] [1966] 1 All E. R. 524, at p. 536.
[5] [1968] 3 All E. R. 701.
[6] P. 99, *ante*.

for establishing beyond reasonable doubt that a case comes within any of its provisions.

C. THE QUESTION OF A THIRD STANDARD OF PROOF

Three standards of proof appear to be recognised in the United States, proof by "clear, strong and cogent" evidence lying midway between proof on a preponderance of probability and proof beyond reasonable doubt.[1] It is certainly not difficult to find support for the view that English law recognises standards other than those of proof beyond reasonable doubt and on a balance of probabilities. A claim for rectification must, it has been said, be established by "strong, irrefragable evidence",[2] and the Law Reform Committee, whilst conceding that the meaning, like the pronunciation of this expression is not beyond argument, consider it to be clear that a mere balance of probability is not enough.[3] A high standard has been called for in cases of alleged professional misconduct as the Judicial Committee could not envisage professional men condemning each other on a mere balance of probabilities.[4] The evidence in rebuttal of the presumption of the formal validity of a marriage must, it has been said, be "strong, distinct and satisfactory";[5] while an intention to change domicile must be "clearly and unequivocally proved".[6] Observations of this sort will no doubt continue to be cited by the courts, but they are far too imprecise to support the existence of a third standard of proof in English law. It is submitted that SCARMAN, J., put such observations in their right perspective when he said:

> "Danger lies in wait for those who would deduce legal principle from descriptive language. The powerful phrases of the cases are, in my opinion, a warning against reaching too facile a conclusion upon too superficial investigation or assessment of the facts of a particular case."[7]

In the same vein Lord TUCKER was, it is believed, expressing the commonly held opinion when he said:

> "I am quite unable to accede to the proposition that there is some intermediate onus between that which is required in criminal cases and the balance of probability which is sufficient in civil actions."[8]

We have already seen that, when the accused bears the burden of proof in a criminal case, he is only called upon to discharge it according to the civil standard.[9] It is now necessary to consider what standard is appropriate when the commission of a crime is alleged in civil proceedings.

---

[1] Morgan, *Problems of Proof in the Anglo-American System of Trials*, 82; Uniform Rules, 1.04.

[2] *Countess of Shelburne* v. *Earl of Inchiquin* (1781), 1 Bro. C. C. 338, at p. 341, *per* Lord THURLOW, L.C.

[3] 19th Report, para. 26.

[4] *Bhandari* v. *Advocates Committee*, [1956] 3 All E. R. 742.

[5] *Piers* v. *Piers* (1849), 2 H. L. Cas. 331, at pp. 380–1.

[6] *Moorhouse* v. *Lord* (1863), 10 H. L. Cas. 272, at p. 286.

[7] *In the Estate of Fuld, Hartley* v. *Fuld*, [1968] P. 675, at p. 685.

[8] *Dingwall* v. *J. Wharton (Shipping), Ltd.*, [1961] 2 Lloyds Rep. 213, at p. 216. See also the remarks of DIXON, C.J., in *Murray* v. *Murray* (1960), 33 A. L. J. R. 521, at p. 524.

[9] *R.* v. *Carr-Briant*, [1943] K. B. 607; [1943] 2 All E. R. 156; see also *Sodeman* v. *R.*, [1936] 2 All E. R. 1138 (insanity); *R.* v. *Dunbar*, [1958] 1 Q. B. 31; [1957] 2 All E. R. 737 (diminished responsibility); *R.* v. *Podola*, [1960] 1 Q. B. 325; [1959] 3 All E. R. 418 (fitness to plead). It is sometimes questioned whether, in a comparatively brief summing-up, it is possible to make the distinction clear to jurors.

D. CRIME ALLEGED IN CIVIL PROCEEDINGS

It is easy to think of any number of civil cases in which the question whether one of the parties has committed a crime may be raised. A. claims damages for a libel in which B. referred to him as a bigamist,[1] the insurer's defence to an action on a policy of fire insurance is that the assured was guilty of arson [2] or the plaintiff simply claims damages for a conspiracy to defraud. This is precisely what happened in *The People of the State of New York v. The Heirs of Phillips* [3] where the advice of the Judicial Committee of the Privy Council delivered by Lord ATKIN stated that the standard appropriate to criminal proceedings was the right one as "the proposition has been laid down time and again by the courts of this country and appears to be just".[4] If this remark was intended to apply to all civil cases in which criminal conduct is alleged, it must be admitted that observations which were capable of bearing a contrary meaning had previously been made in the House of Lords,[5] and, in *Doe d. Devine v. Wilson*,[6] the Judicial Committee had favoured the contrary view when holding that a party relying on a deed could discharge the legal burden of negativing its forgery on a preponderance of probability. *Doe v. Wilson* was preferred by the High Court of Australia in *Helton v. Allen*,[7] and again in *Rejfek v. McElroy*.[8] Similar views in favour of the civil standard have prevailed in New Zealand [9] and Canada.[10]

In *Hornal v. Neuberger Products, Ltd.*,[11] the Court of Appeal recognised that the earlier English cases conflicted, and concluded, in apparently general terms, that proof on a preponderance of probability will suffice when the commission of a crime is alleged in a civil action. The plaintiff claimed damages for breach of warranty and fraud on the ground that the defendant had falsely stated that a machine sold by him to the plaintiff had been reconditioned. So far as the alleged breach of warranty was concerned, the trial judge held that the words were spoken by the defendant, but the claim failed because he considered that the parties did not intend them to have contractual effect. The judge proceeded to award damages for fraud, although he said that he was merely satisfied on the balance of probability, and not beyond reasonable doubt, that the statement was made. If the statement had in fact been made, the defendant would have been guilty of obtaining money by false pretences, for it was beyond dis-

---

[1] *Willmett v. Harmer* (1839), 8 C. & P. 695 where the same strictness of proof was required in support of B.'s plea of justification as on a trial for bigamy. See also *Chalmers v. Shackell* (1834), 6 C. & P. 475.

[2] *Thurtell v. Beaumont* (1823), 1 Bing. 339 (jury should be as satisfied as in a criminal case); *Issaias v. Marine Insurance Co., Ltd.* (1923), 15 Lloyd L. R. 186, where the same view is taken by ATKIN, L.J., at p. 192. In *Slattery v. Mance*, [1962] 1 Q. B. 676; [1962] 1 All E. R. 525, it was decided that the insurer has the burden of proving that the assured set fire to the insured ship on balance of probability only.

[3] [1939] 3 All E. R. 952.

[4] At p. 954.

[5] *Lek v. Mathews* (1927), 29 Lloyd L. R. 141, at p. 164, *per* Lord SUMNER.

[6] (1855), 10 Moo. P. C. C. 502.

[7] (1940), 63 C. L. R. 691.

[8] [1965] 39 A. L. J. R. 177. There seems to be no point in referring to other Australian authorities.

[9] *Ellis v. Frape*, [1954] N. Z. L. R. 341. *Cheape v. New Zealand Law Society*, [1955] N. Z. L. R. 63; W. V. *Middleditch & Sons v. Hinds*, [1962] N. Z. L. R. 570.

[10] *Haynes v. Wawaneta Mutual Insurance Co.* (1963), 36 D. L. R. (2d) 718.

[11] [1957] 1 Q. B. 247; [1956] 3 All E. R. 970.

pute that he knew that the machine had not been reconditioned. The Court of Appeal dismissed the appeal mainly because:

> "it would bring the law into contempt if a judge were to say that on the issue of warranty he finds that the statement was made, and on the issue of fraud he finds it was not made".[1]

Yet this would have been the result of holding that the claim for damages for fraud had to be established beyond reasonable doubt.

Although there were several previous decisions which were not discussed by the Court of Appeal, *Hornal's* case may be taken to have settled the English law for the time being. An allegation of criminal conduct, even of murder,[2] need only be established on a preponderance of probability in a civil action. When the commission of a crime is alleged in civil proceedings, the stigma attaching to an affirmative finding might be thought to justify the imposition of a strict standard of proof; but the person against whom criminal conduct is alleged is adequately protected by the consideration that the antecedent improbability of his guilt is "a part of the whole range of circumstances which have to be weighed in the scale when deciding as to the balance of probabilities".[3]

E. POSSIBLE SURVIVING ANOMALIES

The legal writer is beset by the temptation to make the law appear tidier than it really is. The upshot of this chapter is that there are two standards of proof, the one appropriate to criminal, the other to civil, cases; that the civil standard is applied in a criminal case to issues on which the accused bears the legal burden; and that the criminal standard is always inappropriate in civil proceedings. The possibility of a third standard of proof has been acknowledged, as has the impossibility of speaking with any degree of certitude concerning the standard of proof in matrimonial causes. It remains to recognise that, read *au pied de la lettre*, there are at least two instances in which the authorities countenance a requirement of proof beyond reasonable doubt in civil proceedings, even though there is no question of an allegation of criminal conduct. These are claims for rectification,[4] and cases in which it is sought to rebut the presumption of the formal validity of a marriage.[5] No doubt further examples could be found, but it is submitted that those which have been mentioned and any others that may be discovered are anomalies which could be explained away by any court not minded to follow them.

---

[1] At pp. 258, 973, respectively, *per* DENNING, L.J. See also remarks of SCHOLL, J., [1951] V. L. R., at p. 166. Lord DENNING's remarks may be thought to conflict with his earlier observations in *Bater v. Bater* (p. 92, *ante*) where he said the Court will require a higher degree of probability for fraud than for negligence; but the ingredient of fraud which requires a high standard of probability is the defendant's knowledge of the falsity of his statement rather than the fact that he made it, and, if the statement was made, the defendant's knowledge of its falsity was beyond dispute in *Hornal's* case. On the question whether the statement was made there is no reason why the degree of probability for fraud and warranty should differ.

[2] *Re Dellow's Will Trusts, Lloyds Bank, Ltd. v. Institute of Cancer Research*, [1964] 1 All E. R. 771; *Nishina Trading Co., Ltd. v. Chiyoda Fire and Marine Insurance Co., Ltd.*, [1969] 2 Q. B. 449; [1969] 2 All E. R. 776 (theft proved on balance).

[3] *Per* MORRIS, L.J., see p. 92, *ante*.

[4] *Roberts & Co., Ltd. v. Leicestershire County Council*, [1961] Ch. 555; [1961] 2 All E. R. 545; cf. *Earl v. Hector Whaling, Ltd.*, [1961] 1 Lloyd's Rep. 459.

[5] *Mahadervan v. Mahadervan*, [1964] P. 233, at p. 236.

F. DISCHARGE OF THE EVIDENTIAL BURDEN[1]

No precise formulae have been laid down with regard to the standard of proof required for the discharge of an evidential burden and, as this is not a matter upon which it can ever be necessary for a judge to direct a jury, there is no reason why it should ever become the subject of formulae. It is, however, possible to distinguish between criminal cases in which the evidential burden on a particular issue such as provocation or automatism, is borne by the accused, and criminal cases in which the evidential burden is borne by the Crown.

When the accused bears the evidential burden, it is only necessary for there to be such evidence as would, if believed and uncontradicted, induce a reasonable doubt in the mind of a reasonable jury as to whether his version might not be true, for example as to whether he was provoked or in a state of automatism. In the words of Lord DEVLIN, the evidence must be enough to "suggest a reasonable possibility". When the evidential burden is borne by the Crown, it must be discharged, to quote the same judge, by "such evidence as, if believed, and if left uncontradicted and unexplained, could be accepted by the jury as proof".[2] "Proof" in this context must mean proof beyond reasonable doubt, and, in spite of occasional suggestions to the contrary,[3] the standard must, at least from the theoretical point of view, be higher than that required to discharge an evidential burden borne by a party to civil proceedings.

---

[1] See an article by Professor J. C. Wood, 77 L. Q. R. 491.
[2] *Jayasena* v. *R.*, [1970] A. C. 618, at p. 624.
[3] *R.* v. *Smith* (1865), 34 L. J. M. C. 153; *Wilson* v. *Buttery*, [1926] S. A. S. R. 150, at p. 154.

CHAPTER VI

PRESUMPTIONS

"Every writer of sufficient intelligence to appreciate the difficulties of the subject-matter has approached the topic of presumptions with a sense of hopelessness, and has left it with a feeling of despair."[1] This is an unduly pessimistic statement, but it has the merit of drawing attention to the extraordinary perplexity which has attended,[2] and still attends,[3] the extra-judicial discussion of presumptions. Two factors contributing to the difficulties of the subject are the terminological inexactitude which is a besetting sin of the whole law of evidence, and the tendency of writers to apply rigid scientific distinctions to somewhat unsuitable material. There is no need to enlarge upon the first, but the second should be stressed at the outset of our discussion. No doubt there is force in laments such as those of Lord DENNING, over the fact that presumptions "have been grouped into unscientific categories",[4] and all attempts to remedy this state of affairs must be beneficial to some extent; but the new classifications have to be applied to decided cases, and they will continue to wear a slightly unreal appearance so long as they are not employed by the judges by whom the cases are decided. Moreover, many of the problems that are rightly treated as fundamental in any thorough academic discussion, such as the correct formulation of the basic facts of some presumptions, and the precise effect which others may have upon the incidence of the burden of proof, have not been solved in practice for the simple reason that they have never been raised.

With these introductory warnings, it is proposed to discuss the meanings and classifications of presumptions in section 1, while section 2 will be devoted to a detailed consideration of a few of the more important examples.

SECTION 1. MEANINGS AND CLASSIFICATIONS OF PRESUMPTIONS [5]

A. THE TWO PRINCIPAL MEANINGS OF "PRESUMPTION"

There are two main senses in which the word "presumption" is used by lawyers, and the fact that they are closely connected with each other makes

---

[1] Morgan, 12 Washington Law Review 255, cited by S. J. Helman, 22 Canadian Bar Review, at p. 119.

[2] See the citation from Alciatus (d. c. 1550) in Thayer, *Preliminary Treatise on Evidence at Common Law*, 313.

[3] The subject provoked an acute difference of opinion among the draftsmen of the American Law Institute's Code of Evidence.

[4] 61 L. Q. R. 382.

[5] In addition to the citations in n. 4, p. 74 and n. 2, p. 74, *ante*, all of which have some bearing on the subject of presumptions, reference may be made to Thayer, *op. cit.*, ch. 8; IX *Wigmore*, paras. 2490–98; Morgan, *Foreword to American Law Institute's Code of Evidence*, 60 *et seq.*; *Some Observations Concerning Presumptions*, 44 H. L. R. 906 (1930); *Instructing the Jury on Presumptions and Burdens of Proof*, 47 H. L. R. 59 (1933); Helman, *Presumptions (A Review)*, 22 Canadian Bar Review 118 (1945).

it all the more desirable to distinguish carefully between them. In the first place, a presumption sometimes means nothing more than a conclusion which must be drawn until the contrary is proved; secondly, and more frequently, it denotes a conclusion that a fact (conveniently called the "presumed fact") exists which may, or must, be drawn if some other fact (conveniently called the "basic fact") is proved or admitted.[1] The difference between the two uses of the term thus depends on the presence or absence of a fact which can constitute the basis of the presumption in question.

(1) A Conclusion Until the Contrary is Proved
(Presumptions without Basic Facts)

In its first sense, the word presumption is simply employed as a means of stating the effect of the relevant rules with regard to the incidence of the legal and evidential burdens of proof. Typical examples are provided by the presumption of innocence, and the presumption of sanity in criminal cases.

(i) The presumption of innocence.[2]—When it is said that an accused person is presumed to be innocent, all that is meant is that the prosecution is obliged to prove the case against him beyond reasonable doubt. This is the fundamental rule of our criminal procedure, and it is expressed in terms of a presumption of innocence so frequently as to render criticism somewhat pointless; but this practice can lead to serious confusion of thought, as is shown by the much discussed decision of the American Supreme Court in *Coffin* v. *The United States.*[3] The accused had been convicted of misappropriating the funds of a bank after the jury had been told that they should acquit him unless satisfied of his guilt beyond reasonable doubt, and a new trial was ordered because the judge did not enumerate the presumption of innocence among the items of evidence favourable to the accused. In other words, the Supreme Court considered that the presumption was something different from the rule concerning the onus of proof on a criminal charge, for they regarded it as an instrument of proof —an item of evidence which had been withheld from the jury. This decision has been universally condemned, it could hardly have been pronounced if the court had not been misled by the verbal dissimilarity between the rule that the prosecution bears the legal burden of proof, and the presumption of innocence.

(ii) The presumption of sanity.—In criminal cases, the presumption of sanity is no more than a conclusion which must be drawn until the contrary is proved for the McNaghten Rules have decreed:

> "that the jurors ought to be told in all cases that every man is presumed to be sane and to possess a sufficient degree of reason to be responsible for his crimes until the contrary be proved to their satisfaction".

The McNaghten Rules apply to criminal charges, and the presumption of sanity which they entail must be distinguished from the same presumption in some other branches of the law. We have seen, for example, that, if a rational will is produced, and shown to have been duly executed, the jury

---

[1] The terms "presumed fact" and "basic fact" are taken from the American Law Institute's Code of Evidence, rule 701.
[2] Allen, *Legal Duties*, 253.
[3] (1895), 156 U.S. 432 discussed by Thayer *op. cit.*, appendix B.

ought to be told to find in favour of the testator's competence.[1] The legal burden rests on the party who propounds the will, but the rule that he does not have to adduce evidence of capacity in the first instance is sometimes said to raise a presumption of sanity in testamentary cases. This presumption is dependent on the proof of a basic fact—the execution of a rational will, therefore it is an illustration of the second principal meaning of the term.

Allowance must be made for a number of presumptions without basic facts, for example, Lord KILMUIR and Lord DENNING spoke of "the presumption of mental capacity" in *Bratty* v. *A.-G. for Northern Ireland*[2] simply as a compendious way of expressing the fact that the accused bears the evidential burden on the issue of non-insane automatism; and, although it is common enough to speak of a presumption that mechanical instruments were in working order when used as a means of indicating the fact that an evidential burden is borne by the party denying that this was the case,[3] it can hardly be said that any basic fact is involved.

(2) A Conclusion to be Drawn on Proof of a Basic Fact

Examples of the second sense in which the word presumption is used are the presumption of legitimacy under which a child must be held to be legitimate on proof of birth during its mother's wedlock, the presumption of the formal validity of a marriage which must be made on proof of the marriage ceremony, and the presumption of death arising from the fact that someone has not been heard of for seven years or more by those who would be likely to have heard of him. These are all conclusions which must be drawn in the absence of further evidence, but the dependence of each of them on proof of a basic fact distinguishes them from conclusions which are presumptions in the first sense.

B. THE CLASSIFICATIONS OF PRESUMPTIONS

The ensuing discussion is confined to presumptions in the second main sense of the term, for they play much the more important role in the law of evidence. We are concerned therefore with conclusions that a presumed fact exists which may, or must, be drawn on proof of a basic fact, and the words "may or must" give the clue to the orthodox classification of presumptions.

(1) The Orthodox Classification

This is largely the outcome of the deliberations of the civilians and canonists among whom the various types of presumption were much discussed. The division is into presumptions of fact (*praesumptiones hominis*) and presumptions of law which latter may be irrebuttable (*praesumptiones iuris et de iure*) or rebuttable (*praesumptiones iuris sed non de iure*).[4]

---

[1] P. 77, *ante.*
[2] [1963] A. C. 386, at p. 407 and p. 413 respectively.
[3] P. 41, *ante.*
[4] Reference is sometimes made to "mixed" presumptions of law and fact, but it is not clear what is intended by the expression.

(i) **Presumptions of fact.**—Presumptions of fact are merely frequently recurring examples of circumstantial evidence, and instances which have already been mentioned are the presumption of continuance,[1] the presumption of guilty knowledge arising from the possession of recently stolen goods [2] and the presumption of unseaworthiness in the case of a vessel which founders shortly after leaving port.[3] These are all inferences which *may* be drawn by the tribunal of fact. It is not obliged to draw them as a matter of law even if there is no further evidence, although there may be occasions on which a jury should be directed that they ought to draw the inference as reasonable men, and, in civil cases, a verdict, or even the decision of a judge sitting alone, might be set aside if the inference was not drawn. Further illustration would be pointless.[4]

(ii) **Irrebuttable presumptions of law.**—Irrebuttable presumptions of law are rules of substantive law or procedure expressed in presumptive form. For example, s. 50 of the Children and Young Persons Act, 1933, (as amended by s. 16 of the Children and Young Persons Act, 1963) says it shall be conclusively presumed that no child under ten can be guilty of any offence, and, under s. 137 (2) of the Bankruptcy Act, 1914, the production of a *London Gazette* containing any notice of a receiving order, or of an order adjudging a debtor bankrupt shall be conclusive evidence in all legal proceedings of the order having been duly made, and of its date. The common law rule that a boy under fourteen cannot be guilty of rape as a principal in the first degree is also sometimes stated as an irrebuttable presumption. In these, and all similar cases, there is a basic fact, and its establishment is legally equivalent to proof of the presumed fact. Another way of putting the same thing is to say that the conclusion that the presumed fact exists *must* be drawn,[5] and all rebutting evidence is inadmissible.

(iii) **Rebuttable presumptions of law.**—In the case of a rebuttable presumption of law, once the basic fact is established, the conclusion as to the existence of the presumed fact must be drawn in the absence of evidence to the contrary. Examples are provided by the presumption of death from seven years' absence unheard of, the presumption of sanity in testamentary cases and innumerable instances of the application of the maxim *omnia praesumuntur rite esse acta*.

Whenever reliance is placed on a rebuttable presumption of law, two legal rules are involved. First there is what may be termed the "rule of presumption" according to which the presumed fact *must* be found to exist until evidence tending to disprove it is adduced, and secondly there is the rule which prescribes the amount of rebutting evidence required.

The rule of presumption sometimes does little more than reflect the probative value of the basic fact. In the absence of further evidence, it would be highly unreasonable not to infer legitimacy from a child's birth in wedlock. On the other hand, a rule of presumption may have the effect of increasing the probative value of the basic fact where there is no evidence contradicting such inferences as might be drawn from it. In the

---

[1] P. 32, *ante.*   [2] P. 42, *ante.*   [3] P. 27, *ante.*
[4] For the presumption of intent, see Glanville Williams, *Criminal Law (The General Part)* paras 35 and 291.
[5] Thayer's oft-quoted and cryptic statement that the law has no *mandamus* to the logical faculty (*Preliminary Treatise on Evidence at Common Law*, 313–314, n. 1), is at best only a half truth. The law may order nobody to draw inferences, but it sometimes prohibits all rational investigation into the existence of a fact.

case of the presumption of death, for example, there is no particular magic in seven years' absence so far as the ordinary tests of probative value are concerned. Someone who has been absent unheard of by those who would be likely to hear from him for six and a half years is, for all practical purposes, just as likely to be dead as someone who has been absent in similar circumstances for seven years; but seven years' absence brings into play a rebuttable presumption of law, while absence for a shorter period merely gives rise to a more or less cogent presumption of fact that the person in question is dead. Reflections of this nature have led to the remark that:

> "presumptions of law are nothing else than natural inferences or presumptions of fact which the law invests with an artificial or preternatural weight."[1]

The artificial weight or enhanced probative value attached by the law to the basic fact of some presumptions is made plain by the rule concerning the amount of evidence required to rebut them. Judicial statements concerning the amount of rebutting evidence required vary from presumption to presumption, and they sometimes differ with regard to the same presumption. In certain cases it is said that the presumption stands until "some" evidence to the contrary is given. In other cases it is said that the rebutting evidence must be "clear", "strong" or even "conclusive". These variations suggest that it may be desirable to subdivide rebuttable presumptions of law according to the quantity of evidence required to rebut them, but they also suggest that it would be rash to expect anything in the nature of a precise classification.

(2) THE NEW CLASSIFICATIONS

Some presumptions of law have the effect of evidence which is *prima facie* in the second sense mentioned on p. 26. If the basic fact is found to exist, the presumed fact must likewise be found to exist unless sufficient evidence to the contrary is adduced; if such evidence is adduced, the legal burden comes into play and will be decisive of the issue of the existence or otherwise of the presumed fact. An example is provided by the ordinary application of the maxim *omnia praesumuntur rite esse acta*. If it becomes necessary to prove that a public officer was duly appointed, one way of achieving this result, in the absence of a statutory provision limiting the mode of proof, would be to show that the man in question had acted in the requisite capacity. If, however, the party denying due appointment were to adduce evidence fit to be left to a jury tending to negative the appointment, the party bearing the persuasive burden on the issue would lose unless the tribunal of fact was satisfied to the requisite degree of persuasion that the man was duly appointed. Further examples of this kind of presumption are afforded by the presumption of sanity in a testamentary case, and by the numerous statutes according to which fact A. is stated to be *prima facie* evidence of fact B.

Because the effect of such presumptions is to cast an evidential burden on the party against whom they operate, Professor Glanville Williams refers to them as "evidential" presumptions.[2]

---

[1] Gulson, *Philosophy of Proof*, 2nd Edn., p. 371.
[2] *Criminal Law (The General Part)*, (2nd Edn.) p. 877 *et seq.*

In the case of some presumptions of law, the evidence in rebuttal must be sufficiently cogent to persuade the tribunal of fact of the non-existence of the presumed fact on the balance of probability, or even beyond reasonable doubt. Instances are provided by the presumption of legitimacy and the presumption of the formal validity of a marriage. The effect of such presumptions is to place the legal or persuasive burden of disproving the presumed fact on the party against whom they operate, and Professor Glanville Williams speaks of them as "persuasive" presumptions.

Lord DENNING describes the last mentioned kind of presumption as "compelling";[1] he has no word for the other class of rebuttable presumption of law described by Professor Glanville Williams as "evidential", but Lord DENNING speaks of irrebuttable presumptions of law as "conclusive" and of presumptions of fact as "provisional". A presumption of fact is said by Lord DENNING to cast a provisional, or what is sometimes called the "tactical" burden of disproving the fact on the opponent of the issue.[2]

Occasional use is made of Professor Williams's terminology in the course of this chapter; but it should be borne in mind that the distinction between an evidential and a persuasive presumption is irrelevant in criminal cases and liable to be nebulous in civil proceedings. Proof of the basic facts of a common law presumption can cast no more than an evidential burden on to the accused and nothing less than a legal burden on to the prosecution. If someone charged with incest with his daughter contends that, though conceived and born in wedlock, she is the child of another man, it is difficult to believe that any court would hold it to be incumbent on him to do more than adduce such evidence as would suggest a reasonable possibility of illegitimacy. If, on the other hand, the prosecution were to contend that, though born during the accused's wife's marriage to another man, the girl was in reality the accused's daughter, the judge should withdraw the case from the jury if the prosecution could do no more by way of rebuttal of the presumption of legitimacy than prove statements by the accused to the effect that the girl was his child.[3]

Speaking of the persuasive presumption of legitimacy, now rebuttable in civil proceedings by evidence establishing illegitimacy on a balance of probabilities,[4] Lord REID said:

> "Once evidence has been led it must be weighed without using the presumption as a makeweight in the scale of legitimacy. So even weak evidence against legitimacy must prevail if there is not other evidence to counterbalance it. The presumption will only come in at the stage in the very rare case of the evidence being so evenly balanced that the court is unable to reach a decision on it."[5]

The only effect of the presumption is to require the party against whom it operates to adduce evidence which would, if believed and uncontradicted, justify a finding of illegitimacy. This may be contrasted with the effect, in a civil case, of the evidential presumption of death. The party against whom it operates must adduce such evidence as would, if believed and uncontradicted, justify either a finding that the person in question was alive, at the material time, or the inability of the tribunal of fact to come to

---

[1] 61 L. Q. R. 380. [2] See p. 79, *ante.*
[3] *R.* v. *Hemmings*, [1939] 1 All E. R. 417.
[4] Family Law Reform Act, 1969, s. 26.
[5] *S.* v. *S.*, [1972] A. C. 24, at p. 41.

a conclusion either way. Small wonder that the possibility of subdividing rebuttal presumptions of law has received more extra-judicial than judicial attention.

(3) A Note on Conflicting Presumptions

It has already been pointed out that the orthodox classification of presumptions is to some extent the outcome of discussions which took place among the civilians and canonists. These discussions were extremely minute, and they were much concerned with the relative strength of the various presumptions. To an English observer the conclusions at which the civilians arrived sometimes appear to have amounted to "the substitution of arithmetic for observation and reasoning when estimating the value of evidence",[1] and they were wholly unsuited to the atmosphere of a trial at common law. A pale replica of the civilians' discussions is to be found in an occasional allusion by English judges to the subject of conflicting presumptions; but they amount to nothing more than the recognition of the fact that, in certain situations, rebuttable presumptions of law cancel each other out.

In *Monckton* v. *Tarr*,[2] a woman claimed workmen's compensation in 1930 on the footing that she was the widow of a deceased workman. She had gone through a ceremony of marriage with him in 1913, but the employers contended that this marriage was void because the deceased was, at the time, a married man, having gone through a ceremony of marriage with A. J. in 1895. A. J. was alive at the date of the proceedings, but the applicant contended that the 1895 ceremony was void because A.J. was, at the time, a married woman, having gone through a ceremony of marriage with D.C. in 1882. D.C. deserted A.J. in 1887, and there was no direct evidence that he was alive at the time of the 1895 ceremony.

The County Court judge refused to infer, on the footing of the factual presumption of continuance, that D.C. was alive when A. J. married the deceased workman in 1895, and he accordingly dismissed the claim. His decision was affirmed by the Court of Appeal because the issue was simply one of fact—was D.C. alive at the time of the marriage of A.J. to the deceased? There was a rebuttable presumption of law that the 1913 ceremony was valid, but this was offset by the presumption of the validity of the 1895 ceremony. As Romer, L. J. put it:

> "Those two presumptions, one being on one side and one on the other, being considered of equal weight . . . we get rid of presumptions altogether".[3]

The situation with which *Monckton* v. *Tarr* was concerned was a complicated variant of a frequently recurring theme. In the earlier case of *R.* v. *Willshire*,[4] the accused had been convicted of bigamously marrying D. during the life of his wife C. He had married A. in 1864 and, in 1868, he was convicted of bigamously marrying B. in A.'s lifetime. The prosecution proved a formally valid marriage ceremony between the accused and C. in 1879, together with a further marriage ceremony with D. in 1880. The accused was therefore guilty of the offence charged in the indictment if he

---

[1] Best, cited Thayler, *op. cit.*, 343.
[2] (1930), 23 B. W. C. C. 504. For a thorough discussion of the problem see *Re Peatling*, [1969] V. R. 214.
[3] *Ibid.*, at p. 532.
[4] (1881), 6 Q. B. D. 366

was validly married to C., but his defence was that this was not the case because A., who was alive in 1868, was still alive when he married C. in 1879. The conviction was quashed because the jury had not been properly directed with regard to the burden of proof. To quote from the judgment of Lord COLERIDGE, C.J.:[1]

> "It is said, and I think rightly, that there is a presumption in favour of the validity of this latter marriage [the marriage to C.] but the prisoner showed that there was a valid marriage in 1864, and that the woman he then married was alive in 1868. . . . . The Common Serjeant did not leave the question to the jury . . . but held that the burden of proof was on the prisoner, who was bound to adduce other or further evidence of the existence of his wife in 1879; . . . I am clearly of opinion that in this the learned Common Serjeant went beyond the rules of law. The prisoner was only bound to set up the life; it was for the prosecution to prove his guilt."

At one stage Lord COLERIDGE, C.J. spoke of a conflict between the presumption of the validity of the 1879 ceremony and the presumption of continuance of A.'s life, but this is a presumption of fact, and it is preferable to regard *Willshire's* case as one in which the two rebuttable presumptions of law of the validity of the 1879 and 1864 ceremonies cancelled each other out. The incidence of the legal burden of proof is then decisive in the event of doubt.

Monckton v. *Tarr* [2] was not cited in *Taylor* v. *Taylor*,[3] a divorce case in which the issue concerned the validity of the petitioner's marriage to the respondent in 1942. The petitioner had married D. in 1928, and D. was alive at the time of the 1942 ceremony, but there was some admissible evidence, albeit of an inconclusive nature, that the 1928 ceremony was invalid because D. was, at the time, a married man. CAIRNS, J. held that the 1942 marriage was valid because "the existence of a doubtful earlier marriage is not sufficient to displace the presumption in favour of the petitioner's marriage to the respondent."[4] It is submitted that, on the reasoning adopted by the Court of Appeal in *Monckton* v. *Tarr*, the decision in *Taylor* v. *Taylor* should have been against the validity of the 1942 ceremony unless the petitioner were held to have discharged the legal burden of disproving the validity of the 1928 marriage. She bore the legal burden of proving the validity of the 1942 marriage, the presumption of law relating to that fact was cancelled out by the presumption in favour of the 1928 marriage, and the issue became one of fact unaffected by presumptions of law, the legal burden being decisive in the event of doubt.

SECTION 2. FOUR TYPICAL PRESUMPTIONS

It is now proposed to discuss the presumption of legitimacy, the presumption of marriage, the presumption of death and the presumption of negligence in cases to which the maxim *res ipsa loquitur* is applied. The collection and analysis of the other innumerable presumptions that are scattered throughout the length and breadth of the substantive law would be utterly beyond the compass of this work, and would, in any event, constitute what Thayer described as "an unprofitable and monstrous task".[5] These other presumptions are best considered under the particular rubrics

---

[1] *Ibid.*, at p. 369.   [2] (1930), 23 B. W. C. C. 504.
[3] [1965] 1 All E. R. 872.   [4] *Ibid.*, at p. 880.
[5] *Op. cit.*, 313.

of the substantive law to which they happen to belong. Those that are about to be discussed are of a more general nature, and another presumption of some generality, that based on the maxim *omnia praesumuntur rite esse acta*, has already been mentioned in Chapter II where references to some of the more common presumptions which are "presumptions of fact" within the orthodox classification will also be found.

A. THE PRESUMPTION OF LEGITIMACY [1]

(1) FORMULATION

Where a child is born or conceived in lawful wedlock, the husband not being separated from his wife by an order of the court, that child is presumed to be legitimate because:

> "Sexual intercourse is presumed to have taken place between the husband and his wife until that presumption is encountered by such evidence as proves, to the satisfaction of those who are to decide the question, that such sexual intercourse did not take place at any time, when by such intercourse, the husband could, according to the laws of nature, be the father of such child."

This statement of the presumption of legitimacy is a slightly modernised version of the answer given by Sir JAMES MANSFIELD, C.J., to one of the questions which the House of Lords put to the judges in the *Banbury Peerage Case*. At an earlier time it had been thought that the presumption was irrebuttable or, at least, that it could only be rebutted by evidence that the father was beyond the seas when the child must have been conceived. In fact the chief importance of the *Banbury Peerage Case* lies in the judges' insistence that the presumption can be rebutted by any evidence tending to show that the husband and wife did not have intercourse by which the child could have been begotten, although the standard of proof contemplated seems to have been a high one.

The different methods by which the basic facts of the child's birth and the marriage of its parents may be proved, if not admitted, are indicated in chapter XXII, while the unusual cases of the conception of the child before its mother's marriage, and its birth after the union has been terminated are best deferred until the question of the rebuttal of the presumption has been considered. The only other point in Sir JAMES MANSFIELD's statement of the basic facts which needs to be stressed is the requirement that the husband should not have been separated from the child's mother by an order of the court. While a decree of judicial separation, or magistrates' separation order is in force, the presumption is that the parties did not have sexual intercourse, so any child conceived by the mother during such a period is presumed to be illegitimate, although the presumption is rebuttable by evidence tending to show that the mother did have intercourse with her husband.[2] If the parties to a marriage are living apart under a separation agreement, or if there is a maintenance, as opposed

---

[1] The leading cases (all of which must now be read in the light of s. 26 of the Family Law Reform Act, 1969) are the *Banbury Peerage Case* (1811), 1 Sim. & St. 153; *Morris* v. *Davies* (1837), 5 Cl. & Fin. 163; *Cope* v. *Cope* (1833), 5 C. & P. 604; *Hawes* v. *Draeger* (1883), 23 Ch. D. 173; *Gordon* v. *Gordon*, [1903] P. 141. *Cox* v. *Juncken* (1947), 74 C. L. R. 277, contains a useful historical survey. For a discussion from the point of view of comparative law see Guttman, *Presumptions of Legitimacy and Paternity Arising out of Birth in Wedlock*, 5 International and Comparative Law Quarterly, 217 (1956).

[2] *Hetherington* v. *Hetherington* (1887), 12 P. D. 112.

to a separation, order in force against the husband, the ordinary presumption of legitimacy operates with regard to children conceived by the mother. These distinctions are undoubtedly somewhat artificial, but they appear to be perfectly well settled.[1]

(2) Rebutting the Presumption

The evidence required to rebut the presumption of legitimacy must go to show that the child's mother and her husband did not have intercourse by which the child could have been begotten. Proof that the mother committed adultery with any number of men will not, of itself, suffice, for *non constat* that she did not also have intercourse with her husband.[2] On the other hand it is not essential to show that there was no possibility of access between the child's mother and her husband at the time of the child's conception (though evidence of this nature, when the husband had gone abroad, is a common method of rebutting the presumption). Circumstantial evidence, such as the fact that the mother has been living with another man as his wife for a considerable time before the birth of the child,[3] the fact that the husband's opportunities of access to his wife were slight, while the circumstances were such as to render intercourse unlikely, and the conduct of the wife or her paramour with regard to the child may all be taken into account.[4] Proof of the husband's impotence is, of course, another method of rebutting the presumption.[5] The fact that intercourse between husband and wife took place about the time of the child's conception would not necessarily be fatal to the case of the party seeking to rebut the presumption if the intercourse was not such that the husband could "according to the laws of nature be the father of the child". Hence the presumption may be rebutted by blood group evidence [6] or, provided the court is satisfied with regard to their reliability, by evidence of the use of contraceptives.

The phraseology of Sir James Mansfield's advice shows that the legal burden of rebutting the presumption rests on those who wish to achieve this result, because their evidence must prove "to the satisfaction of those who are to decide the question" that sexual intercourse by which the child could have been begotten did not take place between the mother and her husband. The standard demanded by the common law of the evidence in rebuttal was absurdly high:

> "The presumption of law is not lightly to be repelled. It is not to be broken in upon or shaken by a mere balance of probability. The evidence for the purpose of repelling it must be strong, distinct, satisfactory and conclusive."[7]

In consequence of these rhetorical words of Lord Lyndhurst English judges were from time to time obliged to order a man to maintain a child

---

[1] *Ettenfield* v. *Ettenfield*, [1940] P. 96; [1940] 1 All E. R. 293 (separation agreement) where the authorities are reviewed. *Bowen* v. *Norman*, [1938] 1 K. B. 689; [1938] 2 All E. R. 776 (maintenance order).

[2] *R.* v. *Inhabitants of Mansfield* (1841), 1 Q. B. 444; *Gordon* v. *Gordon*, [1903] P. 141.

[3] *Cope* v. *Cope* (1833), 1 Mood. & R. 269; *Hawes* v. *Draeger* (1883), 23 Ch. D. 173; *Re Jenion, Jenion* v. *Wynne*, [1952] Ch. 454; [1952] 1 All E. R. 1228.

[4] *Morris* v. *Davies* (1837), 5 Cl. & Fin. 163; *Kanapathipillai* v. *Parpathy*, [1956] A. C. 580 (Citing *Head* v. *Head* (1823), Turn. & R. 138, at p. 140, *per* Lord Eldon); *Garfath* v. *Garfath*, [1959] S. R. (N. S. W.) 362.

[5] *Legge* v. *Edmonds* (1855), 25 L. J. Ch. 125.

[6] See p. 46, *ante.*

[7] *Morris* v. *Davies* (1837), 5 Cl. & Fin. 163, at p. 265.

of whom they thought thát he was probably not the father;[1] and a New
Zealand court, not without abetment from English *dicta*,[2] held that the
fact that the white wife of a white husband gave birth to a child of Mongol
stock, her paramour being Chinese, did not rebut the presumption of
legitimacy.[3]

Section 26 of the Family Law Reform Act, 1969, struck a blow for
common sense by providing that

> "Any presumption of law as to the legitimacy or illegitimacy of any person
> may in any civil proceedings be rebutted by evidence which shows that it is
> more probable than not that the person is illegitimate or legitimate as the case
> may be and it shall not be necessary to prove that fact beyond reasonable
> doubt in order to rebut the presumption."

We have already seen that Lord REID has said that this means that the
presumption will only apply in the very rare case of the evidence being so
evenly balanced that the court is unable to reach a decision on it.[4] His
Lordship was unable to recollect such a case, but there has already been at
least one decision in which the judgment in favour of legitimacy turned on
the onus of proof.[5]

So far as criminal cases are concerned, it has already been suggested
that it is necessary for the prosecution to rebut the presumption by evidence proving illegitimacy beyond reasonable doubt, while the accused
need only point to a reasonable possibility of illegitimacy.[6] This is the
outcome of the ordinary principles governing the burden and standard of
proof in criminal cases which would, it is assumed, be held to prevail over
rhetoric like that of Lord LYNDHURST.

(3) SOME UNUSUAL CASES

Presumptions are primarily meant to apply to situations which recur
with comparative frequency, and Thayer has aptly observed that the bringing forward of unusual facts often discharges the whole matter from the
operation of presumptions, and, like COKE's estoppel against estoppel,
"doth put the matter at large".[7] It seems, however, that there are at least
two unusual situations in which the presumption of legitimacy may
control the approach to the problems which they raise. These are cases of
premarital conception, and the birth of a child to a woman who marries
soon after the termination of a union during which the child might have
been conceived.

(i) Premarital conception.—It is settled that the presumption applies
in the case of a child born to a woman shortly after her marriage at such a
time that it must have been conceived before that event took place,[8] and
this situation is covered by Sir JAMES MANSFIELD's formulation of the presumption which has already been set out.

---

[1] *Watson* v. *Watson*, [1954] P. 48; [1953] 2 All E. R. 1013; *Cotton* v. *Cotton*, [1954]
P. 305; [1954] 2 All E. R. 105.

[2] 13 Jur. at 572.

[3] *Ah Chuk* v. *Needham*, [1933] N. Z. L. R. 559.

[4] P. 113, *ante*.

[5] *T.* (*H.*) v. *T.* (*E.*), [1971] 1 All E. R. 590.

[6] P. 113, *ante*.

[7] *Preliminary Treatise on Evidence at the Common Law*, 351.

[8] *The Poulett Peerage Case*, [1903] A. C. 395; *Cox* v. *Juncken* (1947), 74 C. L. R. 277; for
Scotland, see *Gardner* v. *Gardner* (1877), 2 App. Cas. 723.

(ii) Birth after termination of marriage.—The presumption applies, but may, of course, be rebutted, to children who, though conceived during wedlock, are born after the termination of their mother's marriage by divorce,[1] or the death of the husband.[2] In *Re Overbury, Sheppard* v. *Matthews*[3] the paternity of a woman who died intestate was in issue. Her mother's first husband died in January 1869. She married again in July of that year, and the intestate was born in September. It was held that she was the legitimate daughter of her mother's first husband, for such evidence as there was did not suffice to rebut the presumption. This decision is supported by the statement of a learned American judge in a case concerning the paternity of Frances M., born shortly after her mother's marriage to one Shuman when she might well have been conceived during her mother's previous marriage to one Ingle. He said:

"The rules of evidence by which it must be determined whether Frances M. is or is not the lawful issue of the marriage of her mother and Andrew Ingle, are unaffected by the fact that she was born after the marriage of her mother and Alexander Shuman. The last marriage may save Frances M. from being a bastard in case Andrew Ingle is not her father; but the same proof is required to demonstrate that he is not her father, as would be required had the last marriage not taken place."[4]

It is submitted that the principle underlying this statement will generally serve to solve all problems caused by the child's birth after the termination of the mother's marriage, but it would be of no avail in at least one case, supposed in the older books. If a widow marries so soon after the death of her first husband as to render it impossible to say during which union the child born during her second marriage was conceived, it is difficult to see how the child's paternity could be determined by presumption, but it is equally difficult to see what sort of proof is possible when there is, as might well be the case, no evidence either way. The problem is not one which can be solved on principle, and there is, as yet, no authority.

B. THE PRESUMPTION OF MARRIAGE

It is desirable to distinguish between three different bases on which a marriage may be presumed. In the case of the first two, the basic fact is the celebration of a marriage ceremony on the strength of which (i) its formal validity, and (ii) its essential validity are presumed. These are rebuttable presumptions of law. In addition, there is what also appears to be a rebuttable presumption of law under which, if it is proved that a couple cohabited as man and wife, enjoying that reputation in society, the antecedent celebration of a valid ceremony of marriage, or, where no ceremony is required by law, the exchange of the proper consents will be presumed. These presumptions are not always distinguished in the books and judgments, but it is desirable to distinguish between them, not only because the basic facts of the third differ from those of the other two, but also because the evidence required to rebut the presumption may differ in each instance.

---

[1] *Maturin* v. *A.-G.*, [1938] 2 All E. R. 214; *Re Leman's Will Trusts, Public Trustee* v. *Leman* (1945), 61 T. L. R. 566; *Knowles* v. *Knowles*, [1962] P. 161; [1962] 1 All E. R. 659, showing that the presumption applies where the issue is whether the child was conceived as the result of intercourse between husband and wife before or after decree absolute.

[2] *Re Heath, Stacey* v. *Bird*, [1945] Ch. 417.

[3] [1955] Ch. 122; [1954] 3 All E. R. 308.

[4] LYON, C.J., cited by Thayer, *op. cit.*, 350, n. 1.

(1) Formal Validity

Provided the ceremony is one which, on due compliance with the requisite formalities, is capable of producing a valid marriage according to the local law,[1] it is almost a judicial commonplace to say that:

> "Where there is evidence of a ceremony of marriage having been followed by cohabitation of the parties, the validity of the marriage will be presumed, in the absence of decisive evidence to the contrary."[2]

The leading case on the subject is *Piers* v. *Piers*[3] in which a marriage celebrated in a private house was upheld, although there was no evidence that the requisite special licence was ever granted. Lord CAMPBELL was of opinion that "A presumption of this sort, in favour of a marriage, can only be negatived by disproving every reasonable possibility . . . of any supposition that can be suggested to support the validity of the marriage", and he based his views as to the necessity of these strict requirements on the tremendous responsibility borne by the tribunal of fact with regard to the status of the woman and her children.[4] *Piers* v. *Piers* has been cited in several judgments upholding the formal validity of marriages in cases in which there was little or no evidence of a ceremony of any sort,[5] but the doctrine has also been applied to disputes which were solely concerned with the formal validity of a ceremony according to foreign law,[6] the question whether the necessary notices were given in the case of an English marriage[7] and the question whether the requirements of an Act of Barbados had been complied with in the case of a marriage celebrated in a clinic according to the rites of the Church of Scotland.[8] The rigorous requirements concerning the disproof of the formal validity of a marriage ceremony duly celebrated with the requisite intention on the part of all parties is analogous to the strict statutory provisions under which no evidence can be given of non-compliance with the conditions as to the residence of the parties once their marriage has been celebrated.[9]

In view of the manner in which this presumption is stated, there can be little doubt that, in a civil case, it casts a legal burden on the party against whom it operates. The words of Lord LYNDHURST concerning the standard to be reached by evidence in rebuttal of the presumption of legitimacy were, in fact, treated as applicable to the issue with which *Piers* v. *Piers* was concerned. This means that the rebutting evidence must be "strong, distinct, satisfactory and conclusive". The word "conclusive" is obviously an exaggeration, but Sir JOCELYN SIMON, P. has said that the presumption:

---

[1] *Kalinowska* v. *Kalinowski* (1964), 108 Sol. Jo. 260; it has been held in New South Wales that there is a presumption rebuttable by "reasonable" evidence to the contrary that the ceremony produces a monogamous union (*Ng Ping On* v. *Choy Fung Lam*, [1963] S. R. (N.S.W.) 782).

[2] *Russell* v. *A.-G.*, [1949] P. 391, at p. 394, *per* BARNARD, J.; applied in *Radwan* v. *Radwan (No. 2)*, [1973] Fam. 35; [1972] 3 All E. R. 1026.

[3] (1849), 2 H. L. Cas. 331.

[4] At pp. 380-1.

[5] E.g. *De Thoren* v. *A.-G.* (1876), 1 App. Cas. 686, and *Re Shephard, George* v. *Thyer*, [1904] 1 Ch. 456.

[6] *Spivack* v. *Spivack* (1930), 46 T. L. R. 243; *Mahadervan* v. *Mahadervan*, [1964] P. 233; [1962] 3 All E. R. 1108.

[7] *Russell* v. *A.-G.*, [1949] P. 391.

[8] *Hill* v. *Hill*, [1959] 1 All E. R. 281.

[9] Marriage Act, 1949, s. 24, s. 48 and s. 61 (re-enacting earlier provisions on which see *Bodman* v. *Bodman* (1913), 108 L. T. 383).

"Cannot be rebutted by evidence which merely goes to show on a balance of probabilities that there was no valid marriage: it must be evidence which satisfies beyond reasonable doubt that there was no valid marriage. In other words, the presumption in favour of marriage in such circumstances is of the same weight as the presumption of innocence in criminal and matrimonial causes".[1]

These words were spoken before the decision of the House of Lords in *Blyth* v. *Blyth*.[2] We have seen that this lends strong support to the view that the standard of proof in matrimonial causes is the civil standard. It is therefore possible that the standard by which the presumption of the formal validity of a marriage ceremony may be rebutted is not as high as was once supposed. Any question of status must of course be approached with caution, but it is open to question whether there is any compelling reason why a higher standard should be required in disproof of marriage in civil litigation than that required to prove murder.[3] There can be little doubt that the presumption of marriage would operate in the same way as it has been suggested that the presumption of legitimacy would operate.[4]

The reference to the cohabitation of the parties in most of the statements of the basic facts of the presumption may be explained by the fact that the presumption of formal validity and the presumption of an antecedent ceremony arising from cohabitation and repute are not always distinguished. The presumption of formal validity may, however, be applied to a deathbed marriage,[5] and the cohabitation of the parties ought not to be numbered among its basic facts.

(2) Essential Validity

The expression "essential validity" is intended to include questions concerning the parties' capacity to marry, and the reality of their consent. The presumption is generally stated in some such terms as the following— a marriage which is unexceptionable in point of form "remains a valid marriage until some evidence is adduced that the marriage was, in fact, a nullity".[6] Most of the cases concern second marriages of persons whose first spouse disappeared some time previously, and the judgments are often as much concerned with the presumption of death, or the inference of the continuance of life as with the presumption of the validity of the second union, but it seems that they are all susceptible of the following analysis which has already been illustrated in the discussion of conflicting

---

[1] *Mahadervan* v. *Mahadervan*, [1964] P. 233, at p. 246; [1962] 3 All E. R. 1108, at p. 1117.

[2] [1966] 1 All E. R. 524; see p. 103, *ante*.

[3] *Re Dellow's Will Trusts, Lloyd's Bank, Ltd.* v. *Institute of Cancer Research*, [1964] 1 All E. R. 771.

[4] P. 118, *supra*.

[5] The *Lauderdale Peerage Case* (1885), 10 App. Cas. 692; *Hill* v. *Hill, supra*.

[6] *Tweny* v. *Tweny*, [1946] P. 180, at p. 182; [1946] 1 All E. R. 564, at p. 565. Most of the following leading cases are also relevant to the presumption of death or the presumption of continuance of life: *R.* v. *Willshire* (1881), 6 Q. B. D. 366; *R.* v. *Morrison*, [1938] 3 All E. R. 787; *Ivett* v. *Ivett* (1930), 143 L. T. 680; *Monckton* v. *Tarr* (1930), 23 B. W. C. C. 504; *Hogton* v. *Hogton* (1933), 103 L. J. P. 17; *Chipchase* v. *Chipchase*, [1939] P. 391; [1939] 3 All E. R. 895; *Tweny* v. *Tweny (supra)*; *Gatty and Gatty* v. *A.-G.*, [1951] P. 444; *Re Peete, Peete* v. *Crompton*, [1952] 2 All E. R. 599; *Re Watkins, Watkins* v. *Watkins*, [1953] 2 All E. R. 1113; *Chard* v. *Chard*, [1956] P. 259; [1955] 3 All E. R. 721, and *Bradshaw* v. *Bradshaw*, [1956] P. 274, n, *Bullock* v. *Bullock*, [1960] 2 All E. R. 307; *Taylor* v. *Taylor* [1965] 1 All E.R. 872; *Axon* v. *Axon* (1937), 59 C. L. R. 395; *Jacombe* v. *Jacombe* (1961), 105 C. L. R. 355; *Danyluk* v. *Danyluk*, [1964] W. A. R. 124; *Re Peatling*, [1969] V. R. 214; *C.* v. *H.*, [1954] N. Z. L. R. 939; *Lewkowicz* v. *Korzewich*, [1956] 1 D. L. R. (2d) 369. For the possibility of a special rule governing cases within the bigamy statutes, see p. 128, *post*.

presumptions. The party who has the legal burden of establishing the validity of a marriage adduces evidence of a ceremony which must, for present purposes, be taken to be formally valid. This raises a presumption that the marriage is valid in other respects than that of form, and the presumption will prevail unless the party with the legal burden also gives evidence of a prior marriage without showing that it has been terminated,[1] or until the party against whom the presumption operates adduces evidence in rebuttal which is fit to be left to a jury. If the party with the legal burden does give evidence of a prior marriage which is not shown to have been terminated, or if the party against whom the presumption operates does adduce rebutting evidence fit to be left to a jury, the legal burden comes into play and the marriage will be held invalid if the tribunal of fact is not satisfied of its validity to the requisite degree of certainty.

The foregoing analysis assumes that less weighty evidence is required to rebut the presumption of essential validity than that required to rebut the presumption of formal validity. Such a conclusion is justified by the distinction between the typical descriptions of the rebutting evidence required in each instance. In the case of the presumption of formal validity what is said to be required is evidence which is "strong, distinct, satisfactory and conclusive" whereas "some" evidence will suffice in the case of the presumption of essential validity. It must be admitted, however, that very few cases stress this distinction,[2] and, in Australia, the presumption of essential validity (at least where a prior marriage is involved) appears to be considered to cast a legal burden on the party against whom the presumption operates.[3]

If there is a distinction between the two presumptions of formal and essential validity on account of the amount of rebutting evidence required, it can perhaps be justified by the fact that, although they are each instances of the application of the maxim *omnia praesumuntur rite esse acta*, that maxim applies with much more force in the case of formal validity than in that of essential validity for, in the case of essential validity, the registrar or celebrant of the marriage ceremony is often under no duty of inquiry, whereas, in the case of formal validity great care may be expected from the celebrant or registrar.

(3) COHABITATION AND REPUTE

The most frequently cited statement of the presumption of marriage arising from cohabitation is contained in the advice of the Privy Council

---

[1] As in *Ivett* v. *Ivett* (*supra*) and *Re Peete* (*supra*).

[2] But see the judgment of ROXBURGH, J., in *Re Peete* (*supra*).

[3] *Axon* v. *Axon* (1937), 59 C. L. R., especially at p. 407; *Jacombe* v. *Jacombe*, [1961] S. R. (N.S.W.) 735, especially at p. 745, *per* BRERETON, J. (affirmed 105 C. L. R. 355); but see *Re Peatling*, [1969] V. R. 214. There does not appear to be any English authority on the amount of evidence required to rebut the presumption of essential validity when age or reality of consent is in issue. In *Axon* v. *Axon* (1937), 59 C. L. R. at p. 404, DIXON, J. said: "The presumption in favour of a marriage duly celebrated casts upon those who deny it the burden of producing reasonable evidence of the fact which renders the marriage void, whether that fact is an impediment consisting in a prior marriage, or a prohibited degree of relationship or the failure to fulfil some condition indispensable to the efficacy of the ceremony." The last words might be thought to suggest that the presumption of formal as well as essential validity is evidential, but the case was concerned with a prior marriage and, at p. 407, DIXON, J. used words suggesting that the burden of establishing the continuance of the prior marriage rested on the party against whom the presumption of the validity of the second marriage operated.

in *Sastry Velaider Aronegary* v. *Sembecutty Vaigalie* [1] in the course of which it was said that:

> "Where a man and woman are proved to have lived together as man and wife, the law will presume, unless the contrary be clearly proved, that they were living together in consequence of a valid marriage, and not in a state of concubinage."

A ceremony had taken place in the particular case, and the Privy Council were of opinion that the trial judge had erred in supposing that it was incumbent on the plaintiff, who contended that she had been validly married according to Tamil customs, to prove either their nature or the fact that the ceremony complied with them. In the case of jurisdictions in which a marriage might be validly constituted by consent of the parties without a formal ceremony, the presumption under consideration has been invoked in favour of the giving of such consent, even when the parties began to cohabit in circumstances in which it could not be lawfully given.[2] In *Re Taplin, Watson* v. *Tate* [3] it was proved that a solicitor had lived with a woman as his wife in Rockhampton for nineteen years. The birth certificate of their children referred to a marriage in Victoria, a district in which the local law required marriages to be registered. No ceremony between the man and woman was registered in Victoria, but it was held that a valid marriage should be assumed because the presumption could only be rebutted by evidence of the most cogent kind.

In that case, as in the vast majority of instances in which reliance is placed on the presumption of marriage which arises from cohabitation, the parties were dead; but the presumption has been successfully invoked where one or both of them was alive. In *Elliott* v. *Totnes Union*,[4] a man contested a claim for maintenance of a child on the ground that he had never married its mother (since deceased), but his evidence was disbelieved and a marriage was presumed from cohabitation and repute although no ceremony was shown to have taken place. The legitimacy of a child was also in issue in *Re Shephard, George* v. *Thyer*,[5] and the marriage of its parents was presumed although they gave evidence to the effect that the only ceremony celebrated between them took place in France, and, according to expert opinion, that ceremony could not have constituted a valid marriage by French law. This is a strong case, because, if the evidence did not rebut the presumption, it is difficult to see what evidence would have that effect. It can only be supported on the footing that the judge did not accept the testimony of the parties which involved statements concerning events that occurred a long time before it was given.[6]

Is this aspect of the presumption of marriage a presumption of fact or a presumption of law? and, in the latter event, is it persuasive or evidential?

---

[1] (1881), 6 App. Cas. 364, at p. 371.

[2] *Breadalbane Case, Campbell* v. *Campbell* (1867), L. R. 1 Sc. & Div. 182; *De Thoren* v. *A.-G.* (1876), 1 App. Cas. 686; cf. *Lapsley* v. *Grierson* (1848), 1 H. L. Cas. 498.

[3] [1937] 3 All E. R. 105, see also *Re Taylor*, [1961] 1 All E. R. 55; cf. *Re Bradshaw, Blandy* v. *Willis*, [1938] 4 All E. R. 143 where the presumption was rebutted by proof of a ceremony in which the parties described themselves as "bachelor" and "spinster" after prolonged cohabitation as man and wife.

[4] (1892), 57 J. P. 151; *Goldstone* v. *Smith* (1922), 38 T. L. R. 403; *Doe* d. *Fleming* v. *Fleming* (1827), 4 Bing. 266.

[5] [1904] 1 Ch. 456.

[6] This explanation was put forward as a possibility in *Williamson* v. *Auckland Electric Tramways Co., Ltd.* (1911), 31 N. Z. L. R. 161. Another strong case is *Re Thompson, Langham* v. *Thompson* (1904), 91 L. T. 680.

On the English authorities,[1] there is no doubt that it is persuasive for a presumption that prevails "unless the contrary be clearly proved" must be taken to belong to this category. The precise manner in which the tribunal of fact should act when all the evidence leaves it in doubt concerning the existence of a valid marriage ceremony has, however, never been fully considered. It is usually said that the presumption of a valid marriage ceremony arising from cohabitation and repute must be rebutted by "clear proof", but there is no authority on the extent, if any, to which this differs from the "strong, distinct, satisfactory and conclusive" evidence said to be required to rebut the presumption of formal validity.

In *Morris* v. *Miller*[2] it was decided that the plaintiff's marriage could not be proved by cohabitation and repute in an action for criminal conversation. This was also said to be the case so far as a charge of bigamy is concerned, and, although the applicability of *Morris* v. *Miller* to bigamy was questioned by East, it is probably still true to say that, on a charge of bigamy the accused's first marriage cannot be proved by cohabitation and repute alone.[3]

C. THE PRESUMPTION OF DEATH [4]

Two seventeenth-century statutes deal, in varying phraseology, with the contingency of someone being absent and unheard-of for upwards of seven years. This was accordingly chosen as the basic period when the judges began to develop rules concerning a presumption of death in the nineteenth century.[5] These rules have never been formulated with precision. At first it was said that:

> "Where a person *goes abroad*, and is not heard of for seven years, the law presumes the fact that such person is dead, but not that he died at the beginning or the end of any particular period during those seven years."[6]

No one would now contend that absence abroad is essential to bring the presumption into play. More often than not, it is simply said that:

> "If a person has not been heard of for seven years, there is a presumption of law that he is dead: but at what time within that period he died is not a matter of presumption but of evidence and the onus of proving that the death took place at any particular time within the seven years lies upon the person who claims a right to the establishment of which that fact is essential."[7]

It will be convenient to begin with a more detailed statement of the basic facts, after which the limitations of the presumption and some relevant statutory provisions will be considered.

(1) FORMULATION OF THE COMMON LAW PRESUMPTION

SACHS, J., has said:

---

[1] In *Mulherne* v. *Clery*, [1930] I. R. 649 the presumption was treated as one of fact.

[2] (1767), 4 Burr. 2057.

[3] 1 East P.C. 470. It is difficult for there to be cohabitation and repute without an admission on the part of the accused, and an admission, together with the marriage certificate, has been held to be sufficient evidence of the first marriage (*R.* v. *Birtles* (1911), 6 Cr. App. Rep. 177). It is probably true to say that the presumption arising from cohabitation and repute cannot be relied on by the Crown in any criminal case, e.g. incest as well as bigamy (see *R.* v. *Umanski*, [1961] V. L. R. 242 where the previous authorities are fully considered). For proof of marriage generally, see Chapter XXII.

[4] See *The Presumption of Death* by G. H. Treitel, 17 M. L. R. 530 (1954). For some relevant cases not mentioned in the text see p. 121, n. 6, *ante*.

[5] The statutes were the Bigamy Act of 1603, and the *Cestui Que Vie* Act, 1666. For the historical development see Thayer, *Preliminary Treatise on Evidence at Common Law*, 319.

[6] *Nepean* v. *Doe* d. *Knight* (1837), 2 M. & W. 894, at p. 912 (italics supplied).

[7] *Lal Chand Marwari* v. *Mahant Ramrup Gir* (1925), 42 T. L. R. 159, at p. 160.

"Where as regards A. B. there is no acceptable affirmative evidence that he was alive at some time during a continuous period of seven years or more, then if it can be proved first, that there are persons who would be likely to have heard of him over that period, secondly, that those persons have not heard of him, and thirdly, that all due inquiries have been made appropriate to the circumstances, A. B. will be presumed to have died at some time within that period." [1]

Before referring to the question of the quantity of evidence required to rebut the presumption, something must be said about each of the basic facts mentioned by the learned judge.

(i) **Persons likely to have heard of the *propositus*.**—It is impossible to lay down any general rules concerning the category of those who would be likely to have heard of the person whose death is in question. They will usually have to be close relations, but some or all of these may be excluded by the fact that the absent party did not intend them to hear of him.[2] This means that there will be many instances in which there can be no question of applying the presumption of law to the issue of A. B.'s death for want of persons who would be likely to have heard of him over the prescribed period. For example, the case in which SACHS, J., formulated the common law presumption in the terms set out above was concerned with cross prayers for nullity of a marriage celebrated in 1933. The ground of each prayer was that the husband had previously married in 1909, and his first wife was alive in 1933. There was no evidence that she was alive after 1918, but there was also every reason why her husband should not have heard of her as he had been in prison more or less continuously. The first wife would only have been forty-three years old in 1933, and SACHS, J., who treated the question of survival as a matter of fact, unaffected by any legal presumption, inferred that she was still alive in 1933 with the result that each party was granted a decree of nullity.[3]

(ii) **Not hearing of the *propositus*.**—It seems that someone "hears" of the person whose death is in question within the meaning of the rule of presumption under consideration if reliable information is received to the effect that he is alive. In *Prudential Assurance Co. v. Edmonds*,[4] for instance, the defence to an action on a policy of life insurance was that the assured was not dead. Members of his family gave evidence of not having heard of him for more than seven years, subject to one point—they knew that his niece had written to her mother from Australia stating that she believed she had seen him in Melbourne, but he was lost in a crowd before she could speak to him. The niece gave evidence to this effect, and although the House of Lords was equally divided on the question whether the jury had been properly directed, no one doubted that the presumption would have been applicable if the niece's evidence was not accepted.

(iii) **Due inquiries.**—It is impossible to generalise on the question what will amount to appropriate inquiries, for everything depends on the circumstances and the failure to make inquiries may sometimes be justified.[5] ALDERSON, B., treated evidence of inquiries as an alternative to the testi-

---

[1] *Chard* v. *Chard*, [1956] P. 259, at p. 272; [1955] 3 All E. R. 721, at p. 728.
[2] *Watson* v. *England* (1844), 14 Sim. 29; *Bowden* v. *Henderson* (1854), 2 Sm. & G. 360; *Wills* v. *Palmer* (1904), 53 W. R. 169; *Re Lidderdale* (1912), 57 Sol. Jo. 3.
[3] Contrast *Re Watkins, Watkins* v. *Watkins*, [1953] 2 All E. R. 1113, where death was inferred as a matter of circumstantial evidence after an absence of twenty-five years. No proper inquiries concerning the person in question were made. See also *MacDarmaid* v. *A.-G.*, [1950] P. 218; [1950] 1 All E. R. 497.
[4] (1877), 2 App. Cas. 487.
[5] *Bullock* v. *Bullock*, [1960] 2 All E. R. 307 (failure to enforce maintenance order).

mony of someone who would be likely to have heard of the *propositus*,[1] and the two requirements may overlap because someone who makes prolonged and persistent inquiries about another person would be likely to have heard of him if he had been alive. There is no authority on the question when the inquiries must have been made if they are to rank as a basic fact of the presumption of death. Will it be sufficient if they take place shortly before the proceedings in which the presumption is invoked? Consistency with the rule that there is no presumption concerning the time of death suggests an affirmative answer, but the value of inquiries at some earlier period might well be greater as an item of circumstantial evidence because they would have been more fruitful at that time.

(iv) Effect of the common law presumption.—Death may be inferred as a matter of fact from an absence unheard-of for a period considerably less than seven years. Everything depends on the circumstances in which the person in question was last known to be alive, and the nature of inquiries concerning his whereabouts. Conversely, life may, as a matter of common sense, be taken to have continued for a much longer time. It follows that the presumption of death is a presumption of law, for:

> "there can hardly be a logical inference from any particular set of facts that a man had not died within two thousand five hundred and fifty-five days, but had died in two thousand five hundred and sixty".[2]

When the basic facts of presumption are established, the court must act on it in the absence of acceptable evidence to the contrary, but, if such evidence is given, the presumption is discharged for it is only evidential (i.e. it only casts a burden of adducing evidence on the party against whom it operates). This is borne out by *Prudential Assurance Co.* v. *Edmonds*[3] where all the members of the House of Lords appear to have agreed that the proper direction to the jury would have been to tell them to find that the assured was dead if they were satisfied that his niece was mistaken when she said she had seen him—an indication that the defendant should have the benefit of legitimate doubt on this matter because the legal burden of proving death rested throughout the case on the plaintiff.

(2) TIME OF DEATH

Practically all the statements of the rule of presumption suggest that it only applies to the fact of death. Let it be assumed that there is a continuous period of not less than seven years immediately preceding the litigation in which the presumption is invoked during which the *propositus* has not been heard of after due inquiry. In the absence of further evidence, the court must presume that he is dead. This will be sufficient for some purposes, such as a claim on a policy of life insurance, but there are many instances in which a finding of death at the commencement of the proceedings will not suffice because one of the parties must go further and prove that it occurred before or after a particular date. Passages in the

---

[1] *Doe d. France* v. *Andrews* (1850), 15 Q. B. 756. No inquiries were made in *Willyams* v. *Scottish Widows' Fund Life Assurance Society* (1889), 4 T. L. R. 489. Inquiries were treated as vital to the raising of the presumption in *Bradshaw* v. *Bradshaw*, [1956] P. 274, n., but see *Chipchase* v. *Chipchase*, [1939] P. 391; [1939] 3 All E. R. 895.

[2] *Per* SACHS, J., in *Chard* v. *Chard*, [1956] P. 259, at p. 272; [1955] 3 All E. R. 721, at p. 728.

[3] (1877), 2 App. Cas. 487, at p. 512. In *Chipchase* v. *Chipchase*, *supra*, it was said that very little evidence would rebut the presumption.

judgments in *Re Phené's Trusts*[1] show that the court will generally not make such an additional finding unless there is some evidence entitling it to do so. A testator died in January 1861, having bequeathed his residuary estate equally between his nephews and nieces. N., one of his nephews, was born in 1829, went to America in 1843, communicated with his family up to 1858, joined the American navy and was last heard of as a deserter in 1860. Advertisements for him were made in English and American newspapers in 1868, after which the plaintiffs obtained a grant of representation to his estate. It was held that their claim to his share of the testator's residue failed because the court was not prepared to infer that N. survived the testator, and, although he might be presumed dead in 1869, there was no presumption as to the time of his death.

In the course of the judgment it was said that:

"the law presumes a person who has not been heard of for over seven years to be dead, but in the absence of special circumstances it draws no presumption from the fact as to the particular period at which he died".[2]

If it is strictly construed, this rule deprives the presumption of much of its value in cases of succession and marriage—a fact which may account for the existence of some decisions which support a more lax construction of the rule. A brief reference may be made to these decisions, after which the effect of s. 184 of the Law of Property Act, 1925, must be considered.

(i) Decisions inconsistent with a strict interpretation of *Re Phené's Trusts*.—In *Re Westbrook's Trusts*[3] the property of someone who had disappeared without leaving a will behind him was divided among such of his next of kin as were alive seven years after his disappearance, to the exclusion of those who died before the expiration of that period. In *Chipchase* v. *Chipchase*[4] a woman who had married in 1915 and not heard of her husband since 1916, married the respondent in 1928. The validity of this second marriage was disputed when she applied to the magistrates for a maintenance order in 1939. The magistrates dismissed the application because there was no evidence that the man whom the appellant married in 1915 was dead in 1928, but the case was remitted to them by the Divisional Court on the ground that they should have considered whether there was evidence to rebut the presumption of death. *Re Phené's Trusts* was cited, but the judgment in that case, as strictly interpreted, notably by the Privy Council,[5] could only be authority for the proposition that the applicant's first husband was to be presumed dead in 1939. On the strict view, the period giving rise to the presumption is one continuous indivisible period of not less than seven years running back from the date of the proceedings. On the laxer view a continuous period of not less than seven

---

[1] (1870), 5 Ch. App. 139. In modern times N.'s life might be inferred to have continued. See *per* SACHS, J., [1955] 3 All E. R., at p. 727. See also *Re Wilson*, [1964] 1 All E. R. 196.

[2] At p. 144. There are passages in the judgment which could be cited in support of the laxer construction discussed below. See also *Re Lewes' Trusts* (1871), 6 Ch. App. 356, and the passages quoted above at p. 118. They are none of them quite as clearly in favour of the strict construction as is sometimes supposed.

[3] [1873] W. N. 167, criticised in *Re Rhodes, Rhodes* v. *Rhodes* (1887), 36 Ch. D. 586. See also *Re Aldersey, Gibson* v. *Hall*, [1905] 2 Ch. 181, perhaps the strongest authority in favour of the lax construction so far as the law of succession is concerned.

[4] [1939] P. 391; [1939] 3 All E. R. 895. This case can be explained on the basis of the special rule governing situations covered by the bigamy statutes mentioned by EVATT, J., in *Axon* v. *Axon* (1937), 59 C. L. R. 395, at p. 413.

[5] *Lal Chand Marwari* v. *Mahant Ramrup Gir* (1925), 42 T. L. R. 159.

years may be made to run back from any date chosen by the party relying on the presumption.

The laxer view is consistent with the actual decision in *Re Phené's Trusts* because, in that case, the nephew had not been unheard of for anything like seven years at the date of the testator's death. The laxer view is also supported inferentially by a number of matrimonial cases in which the facts are similar to those of *Chipchase* v. *Chipchase* and it was assumed that the presumption of death would have applied at the date of the second marriage had the basic facts been established.[1] It has, however, been suggested that these cases are governed by a special rule on account of the proviso to s. 57 of the Offences Against the Person Act, 1861, under which seven years absence is a defence to a charge of bigamy. For example, if W. married H.1 in 1950 and was deserted by him in 1952, she would have a defence to a charge of bigamy should she marry H.2 in 1962, if she had been unaware of the fact that H.1 was alive during the previous ten years. It is arguable that this would warrant a presumption that H.1 was dead at the time of the marriage to H.2.[2] The laxer view is so much the more convenient one that it may well come to be adopted for all purposes, but, so far as certain claims to property are concerned, s. 184 of the Law of Property Act, 1925, has solved the problem of the time of death in a somewhat different way.

(ii) The effect of s. 184 of the Law of Property Act, 1925, on *Re Phené's Trusts*.—According to s. 184 (1) of the Law of Property Act, 1925, where two or more persons have died in circumstances rendering it uncertain which of them survived the other, such deaths shall (subject to any order of the court), for all purposes affecting the title to property, be presumed to have occurred in order of seniority, and accordingly the younger shall be deemed to have survived the elder.[3] Contrary to what is sometimes supposed, this subsection is not limited to deaths occurring in a common calamity. It would apply where a husband went on a voyage and his ship disappeared in circumstances from which the fact, as opposed to the time, of his death could be inferred, while his wife died under an operation and there was no means of ascertaining which of them died first.[4] Is there any reason why it should not apply to a situation such as that which occurred in *Re Phené's Trusts*? N., who was last heard of in 1860, could be presumed dead in 1869, the date of the proceedings; the testator died in 1861; two people have died in circumstances rendering it uncertain which of them survived the other, therefore the deaths are presumed to have occurred in order of seniority. This reasoning has been adopted in Victoria.[5]

(3) Death Without Issue or Celibate

In some cases, notably those involving questions of succession, it will

---

[1] See the cases cited p. 121, n. 6, *ante*.

[2] See the judgment of EVATT, J., in *Axon* v. *Axon* (1937), 59 C. L. R. 395, at p. 413, citing *R.* v. *Lumley* (1869), L. R. 1 C. C. R. 196, at p. 199.

[3] There is no such presumption as between husband and wife on an intestacy (Intestates' Estates Act, 1952, s. 1 (4)) or in double death duty cases covered by the Finance Act, 1958. For the old law, which may still have to be applied in a case which does not involve the title to property, see *Wing* v. *Angrave* (1860), 8 H. L. Cas. 183. A preliminary question of the construction of the words used by the testator may arise in these cases even under the modern law. See *Re Pringle*, [1946] 1 All E. R. 88 and *Re Rowland Smith* v. *Russell*, [1963] Ch. 1; [1962] 2 All E. R. 837.

[4] *Hickman* v. *Peacey*, [1945] A. C. 304, at pp. 314–315; [1945] 2 All E. R. 215, at p. 218; *Re Brush*, [1962] V.L.R. 596.

[5] *Re Watkinson*, [1952] V. L. R. 123.

not be sufficient to establish the fact of death because the *propositus* must be shown to have died childless or celibate. It is said that these further matters must, like the time of death, be established by evidence and cannot be proved by presumption.[1] It seems clear, however, that the court will act on very little evidence in addition to that required to establish the presumption of death, so much so that we may be said to have reached the border line between proof by presumption and proof by evidence.[2] All that can be stated with certainty is that there must be some further element in the case than the basic facts of the presumption of death to induce the court to infer that someone died childless, or unmarried.

(4) Statutory Provisions

There are three statutory provisions, in addition to s. 184 of the Law of Property Act, 1925, which have a bearing on the presumption of death. They are the *Cestui Que Vie* Act, 1667, the second proviso to s. 57 of the Offences against the Person Act, 1861, and s. 19 of the Matrimonial Causes Act, 1973.

(i) The *Cestui Que Vie* Act, 1667.—The first of these statutes provides that if such persons on whose lives estates depend remain beyond the seas or elsewhere absent themselves in this realm for the space of seven years they shall be accounted as naturally dead. Nothing need be said about this provision beyond stressing the fact that cases turning upon it ought to be treated with caution when considering the precise basis of the common law presumption of death.[3] There is no authority covering the question whether a distinction must be drawn between cases in which someone has not been heard of by those likely to hear of him—the basis of the common law presumption, and cases in which someone has absented himself within the realm for the space of seven years—a requirement of the statute under consideration.

(ii) Proviso to s. 57 of the Offences against the Person Act, 1861.—After defining the offence of bigamy, s. 57 of the Offences against the Person Act, 1861, provides that nothing in the section shall extend to any person marrying a second time whose husband or wife shall have been continually absent from such person for the space of seven years last past, and shall not have been known by that person to have been living within that time. This does not expressly raise a presumption of death, for it provides a defence to a charge of bigamy which the jury need only consider when satisfied that the accused's first spouse was alive when the second ceremony was celebrated.

The distribution of the different burdens in proceedings under s. 57 of the Offences against the Person Act, 1861, is instructive, and the methods by which these burdens may be discharged are, to some extent, anomalous. Accordingly a brief reference may be made to the whole matter here, although it involves repeating some points that have already been

---

[1] *Re Jackson, Jackson* v. *Ward*, [1907] 2 Ch. 354.

[2] *Greaves* v. *Greenwood* (1877), 2 Ex. D. 289; see also as to death without issue *Rawlinson* v. *Miller* (1875), 1 Ch. D. 52; as to death unmarried, see *Dunn* v. *Snowden* (1862), 32 L. J. Ch. 104; *Re Westbrook's Trusts*, [1873] W. N. 167; and *Re Benjamin, Neville* v. *Benjamin*, [1902] 1 Ch. 723. See also *In the goods of Doherty*, [1961] I. R. 219 showing that the same advertisements which raise the presumption of death may support an inference of death without next of kin.

[3] See the caution of Sachs, J., in *Chard* v. *Chard*, [1956] P. 259, at p. 270; [1955] 3 All E. R. 721, at p. 727.

made. The prosecution bears the legal burden of proving the validity of the accused's first marriage. This burden probably cannot be discharged by proof of cohabitation and repute,[1] and the presumption of formal, as well as essential validity arising from proof of a marriage ceremony is probably only evidential.[2] The prosecution also bears the legal burden of proving that the accused went through a second ceremony when, to his knowledge, the first spouse was alive, but reliance may be placed in the first instance on the factual presumption of continuance with regard to both of these points.[3] Accordingly, if H. and W. are proved to have been living together in 1970, and H. goes through a ceremony of marriage in 1974, the jury are entitled to convict H. of bigamy in the absence of further evidence. The accused bears the evidential burden of rebutting the presumptions of formal and essential validity arising from proof of the first ceremony, but he may rely on cohabitation and repute to establish a prior marriage,[4] although this point is largely theoretical now that he can give evidence on his own behalf. The accused bears the burden of adducing evidence that his wife was continually absent from him for seven years and that he did not know her to be alive; it is clear that the legal burden rests on the prosecution so far as the second of these matters is concerned,[5] but there is no English authority with regard to the first.[6] There is likewise no English authority on the question whether the legal burdens of negativing the common law defence of mistake and the applicability of the other statutory provisoes also rest on the Crown,[7] although it must, of course, be incumbent on the accused to adduce evidence concerning these matters in the first instance.

(iii) Matrimonial Causes Act, 1973, s. 19.—S. 19 (1) of the Matrimonial Causes Act, 1973, enables any married person who alleges that reasonable grounds exist for supposing that the other spouse is dead to petition for a decree dissolving the marriage and presuming the death of such spouse. Under s. 19 (3), the fact that for a period of seven years or upwards the other party to the marriage has been continually absent from the petitioner and the petitioner has no reason to believe that the other party has been living within that time shall be evidence that he or she is dead until the contrary is proved. The onus cast on the petitioner in proceedings under the section is lighter than that borne by someone seeking to establish the common law presumption of death as formulated by SACHS, J. The petitioner simply has to prove that he has no reason to

---

[1] *Morris* v. *Miller* (1767), 4 Burr. 2057.

[2] *R.* v. *Kay* (1887), 16 Cox C. C. 292. In *R.* v. *Naguib*, [1917] 1 K. B. 359 and *R.* v. *Shaw* (1943), 60 T. L. R. 344, language was used which suggests that the legal burden of proving a prior marriage rested on the accused, but this is contrary to principle and the two burdens are not distinguished in the judgments.

[3] *R.* v. *Lumley* (1869), L. R. 1 C. C. R. 196; *R.* v. *Jones* (1883), 11 Q. B. D. 118.

[4] *R.* v. *Wilson* (1862), 3 F. & F. 119.

[5] *R.* v. *Curgerwen* (1865), L. R. 1 C. C. R. 1.

[6] Australian authority favours the view that the legal burden of proving absence is borne by the accused (*R.* v. *Bonnor*, [1957] V. L. R. 227).

[7] *R.* v. *Thomson* (1905), 70 J. P. 6; *R.* v. *Kircaldy* (1928), 167 L. T. Jo. 46. Language was again used suggesting that the legal burden is on the accused, but, as the legal and evidential burdens were not distinguished, these cases can hardly be regarded as decisions on the point. The Victorian case of *R.* v. *Bonnor* also favours the view that the legal burden of proving mistake is borne by the accused, but these decisions are hard to reconcile with Lord SANKEY's speech in *Woolmington* v. *Director of Public Prosecutions*, [1935] A. C. 462, and they are inconsistent with Lord DIPLOCK's speech in *Sweet* v. *Parsley*, [1970] A. C. 132; [1969] 1 All E. R. 347.

believe that the other spouse was alive during the material period; the fact that the other spouse would not have been likely to have communicated with the petitioner is immaterial.[1] S. 19 (3) has been construed to mean that the petitioner must have had no reason to believe that the other party to the marriage was alive by virtue of anything occurring within the preceding seven years. A husband whose wife leaves him on the 31st of December, 1964, has every reason to suppose she was alive in 1970, but he may nonetheless succeed on a petition filed on the 1st January 1972.[2]

(5) GENERAL OBSERVATIONS

The complexity of the law relating to the presumption of death has been attributed to an unresolved conflict of policies. On the one hand there is the court's dislike of being forced into conclusions of fact by rules of law, on the other hand, there is the binding necessity of giving some decision, even though the evidence is insufficient.[3] Perhaps the best criterion by which the existing law can be judged is its tendency to produce rules which can be clearly stated and easily applied. It would be idle to pretend that these tests are satisfied, and the time has certainly come for an authoritative formulation of the main presumption. It may well be the case that different rules should govern different situations, but what is lacking at present is a binding statement of the general rule.

D. THE PRESUMPTION OF NEGLIGENCE

The proof of negligence is most fully discussed in books on the law of tort. All that need be done in a work of this nature is to draw attention to three possible views concerning the cases to which the maxim *res ipsa loquitur* applies, and to endeavour to place them in the proper perspective of the proof of negligence generally.

(1) RES IPSA LOQUITUR [4]

Where the plaintiff suffers damage in consequence of one or more things which were under the exclusive control of the defendant or his servants getting out of control, reliance may be placed on the maxim *res ipsa loquitur* in lieu of further evidence of negligence. To quote from the leading judgment of ERLE, C.J., in *Scott* v. *The London Dock Co.*:[5]

"Where the thing is shown to be under the management of the defendant or his servants, and the accident is such as in the ordinary course of things does not happen if those who have the management use proper care, it affords reasonable evidence, in the absence of explanation by the defendants, that the accident arose from want of care."

Typical examples are provided by cases in which a barrel has fallen out

---

[1] *Parkinson* v. *Parkinson*, [1939] P. 346; [1939] 3 All E. R. 108.

[2] *Thompson* v. *Thompson*, [1956] 1 All E. R. 603, a decision on an identically worded provision of the Matrimonial Causes Act, 1937.

[3] 17 M. L. R. 430.

[4] The literature on this subject is strangely profuse; see in particular Paton, *Res Ipsa Loquitur*, 14 Canadian Bar Review 480; Baker, *Res Ipsa Loquitur*, 24 Australian Law Journal 194; Lewis, *A Ramble with Res Ipsa Loquitur*, 11 C. L. J. 78; O'Connell, *The Australasian Experience*, C. L. J. (1954) 118; Atiyah, 35 M. L. R. 337 and *Evidence Seminars*, edited by H. H. Glass, 49.

[5] (1865), 3 H. & C. 596, at p. 601.

of the window of premises occupied by the defendant,[1] a car has mounted the pavement,[2] a swab has been left in a patient's body after an operation [3] and two trains belonging to the same company have been in collision.[4] Many decisions turn on the question whether there was sufficient control by the defendant to bring the doctrine into play,[5] but, so far at any rate as the actual words used by the judges are concerned, the principal differences of opinion appear to turn on the incidence of the burden of proof in cases to which the maxim is applicable. The three views are (i) that nothing more than a provisional burden is cast upon the defendant, in other words such presumption as is involved is merely a presumption of fact (or a provisional presumption), (ii) that an evidential burden is cast upon the defendant as a matter of law, so that he will lose on the issue of negligence unless he adduces some evidence (on this view there is a presumption of law of the evidential variety), and (iii) that a legal burden of disproving negligence is cast upon the defendant, in which case *res ipsa loquitur* refers to the basic rule of a persuasive presumption of law.

(i) *Res ipsa loquitur* **as a presumption of fact.**—The clearest modern statement of the first view is that of GREER, L.J., in *Langham* v. *The Governors of Wellingborough School and Fryer*.[6] He thought the maxim was only a branch of a larger rule, namely:

> "where the proved facts render it reasonably probable, in the absence of explanation, that there was negligence on the part of the defendant, and that the damage was caused by that negligence, it is for the jury, the tribunal of fact, to say whether the case is or is not established".

A schoolboy had been injured while walking in a corridor by a golf ball struck by another boy in the playground with a stick, the ball having come through an open door. This is scarcely the kind of accident that does not happen without negligence in the ordinary course of things, and the real ground of decision was that the case was not one of *res ipsa loquitur* at all, but, on the view under consideration, the maxim merely alludes to a frequently recurring species of circumstantial evidence. Even if he does nothing, the defendant is not bound to lose as a matter of law, but it is rash to take refuge in silence in such a case.

(ii) *Res ipsa loquitur* **as an evidential presumption.**—There is thus no great practical difference between the first and second views of the incidence of the burden of proof in cases to which the maxim *res ipsa loquitur* applies. One of the clearest statements of the second view was that of LANGTON, J., in "*The Kite*".[7] A barge under the control of the defendants collided with a bridge and his lordship said:

---

[1] *Byrne* v. *Boadle* (1863), 2 H. & C. 722.

[2] *Ellor* v. *Selfridge & Co., Ltd.* (1930), 46 T. L. R. 236.

[3] *Mahon* v. *Osborne*, [1939] 2 K. B. 14; [1939] 1 All E. R. 535.

[4] *Skinner* v. *London, Brighton and South Coast Rail. Co.* (1850), 5 Exch. 787.

[5] *Easson* v. *London and North Eastern Rail. Co.*, [1944] K. B. 421; [1944] 2 All E. R. 425. This may account for the curious uncertainty surrounding the question whether the maxim applies to cases falling within the principle of *M'Alister (or Donoghue)* v. *Stevenson*, [1932] A. C. 562. See *Grant* v. *Australian Knitting Mills, Ltd.*, [1936] A. C. 85, at p. 101, and contrast *Daniels and Daniels* v. *White & Sons, Ltd. and Tarbard*, [1938] 4 All E. R. 258.

[6] (1932), 101 L. J. K. B. 513, at p. 518. Lord DENNING regards the presumption as provisional in *Emanuel* v. *Emanuel*, [1946] P. 115; [1945] 2 All E. R. 494 SACHS, J., speaks of it as a presumption of fact in *Chard* v. *Chard*, [1956] P. 259; [1955] 3 All E. R.721; see also GODDARD, L.J., in *Easson* v. *London and North Eastern Rail Co.*, *supra*.

[7] [1933] P. 154; *The Mulbera*, [1937] P. 82; *Ballard* v. *North British Rail. Co.*, [1923] S. C. (H. L.) 43; *Davis* v. *Bunn* (1936), 56 C. L. R. 246.

"What the defendants have to do here is not to prove that their negligence did not cause this accident. What they have to do is to give a reasonable explanation which, if it be accepted, is an explanation showing that it happened without their negligence. They need not even go so far as that, because, if they give a reasonable explanation which is equally consistent with the accident happening without their negligence, they have again shifted the burden of proof back to the plaintiffs to show, as they always have to show from the beginning, that it was the negligence of the defendants that caused the accident."

As the defendant gave such an explanation the action failed. On this view, though failure to adduce evidence is legally fatal to the defendant, the plaintiff must lose if the totality of the evidence is as consistent with the absence as with the presence of negligence because the persuasive burden of proving the latter rests upon him.

(iii) *Res ipsa loquitur* **as a persuasive presumption.**—The clearest statement of the third view is to be found in the judgment of ASQUITH, L.J., in *Barkway* v. *South Wales Transport Co., Ltd.*[1] in which case an omnibus had fallen over an embankment owing to a tyre burst, and the case was treated as one of *res ipsa loquitur* in the Court of Appeal. The House of Lords decided that the maxim does not apply where there is adequate evidence of the cause of the accident as there was in the present instance because the tyre burst had been shown to have been due to an impact fracture, and negligence was held to be proved against the defendants owing to the inadequacy of their system of tyre testing. ASQUITH, L.J., summarised the position with regard to the onus of proof in the following propositions:

"(1) If the defendants' omnibus leaves the road and falls down an embankment, and this without more is proved, then *res ipsa loquitur*, there is a presumption that the event is caused by negligence on the part of the defendants, and the plaintiff succeeds unless the defendants can rebut this presumption. (2) It is no rebuttal for the defendants to show, again without more, that the immediate cause of the omnibus leaving the road is a tyre-burst, since a tyre burst *per se* is a neutral event consistent and equally consistent, with negligence or due diligence on the part of the defendants. When a balance has been tilted one way, you cannot redress it by adding an equal weight to each scale. The depressed scale will remain down : *Laurie* v. *Raglan Building Co., Ltd.*[2] (3) To displace the presumption the defendants must go further and prove (or it must emerge from the evidence as a whole) either (a) that the burst itself was due to a specific cause which does not connote negligence on their part but points to its absence as more probable, or (b) if they can point to no such specific cause, that they used all reasonable care in and about the management of their tyres."

These propositions indicate that, once it has been decided that the case is one to which the maxim *res ipsa loquitur* is applicable, the legal burden of disproving negligence is cast on the defendant, and there are two ways in which it may be discharged.

(iv) **Conclusions.**—As there is no decision which turns on the question of how the tribunal of fact is to act in the event of its concluding that the evidence is evenly balanced in a *res ipsa loquitur* case, it is impossible to say with complete certainty which of the above views represents English law. For practical purposes, the choice lies between the second and third, as the distinction between the first and second is almost entirely theoretical because

---

[1] [1948] 2 All E. R. 460, at p. 471.
[2] [1942] 1 K. B. 152; [1941] 3 All E. R. 332. This case should be read in conjunction with *Richley* v. *Faull*, [1965] 3 All E. R. 109.

it can only have any meaning when the defendant does not adduce evidence. So far as the words used by the judges are concerned, the preponderance of modern English authority favours the third view,[1] but it is not clear whether the words used were intended to be of general application. In some cases it may be easier for the defendant to show that he was not negligent than to give an explanation of the accident which is as consistent with the absence as with the presence of negligence,[2] and facts giving rise to the application of the maxim point much more clearly to negligence in some cases than in others; but there may well be a limited number of situations in which it is sociologically desirable to hold the defendant liable for an unexplained accident. Everything depends on the answer to the question whether such accidents are, more often than not, the outcome of negligence. If the answer is in the affirmative, less injustice will be occasioned by placing the legal burden of disproving negligence upon the defendant than by leaving negligence to be proved by the plaintiff. Accordingly the third view may not be as anomalous as it is sometimes supposed to be.[3]

(2) PROOF OF NEGLIGENCE GENERALLY

It would, of course, be pointless to enumerate the different types of evidence, direct and circumstantial, by which negligence may be proved; but mention should be made of the existence of a large number of cases which are not strictly instances of *res ipsa loquitur* although it is held, as a matter of fact rather than law, that the defendant must fail if no explanation is forthcoming. Examples of such cases are provided by collisions between vehicles owned by different parties. Whenever there is virtually no evidence other than that of the collision, each driver will be held equally to blame [4]—a conclusion which is in accordance with the balance of probabilities and one to which particular effect can be given under the Law Reform (Contributory Negligence) Act, 1945. The court is not obliged to hold that neither party has discharged the onus of proving negligence and causation. As these issues are but rarely tried with a jury in modern times, the reported decisions of appellate tribunals on questions of fact tend to acquire the force of law.

---

[1] *Woods* v. *Duncan*, [1946] A. C. 401, at p. 419, *per* Lord SIMON, and at p. 439, *per* Lord SIMONDS, but Lord PORTER, at p. 434, favours the second view. *Turner* v. *National Coal Board* (1949), 65 T. L. R. 580; *Moore* v. *Fox*, [1956] 1 Q. B. 596; [1956] 1 All E. R. 182 expressly approving the views of ASQUITH, L.J., quoted in the text; *Walsh* v. *Holst & Co. Ltd.*, [1958] 3 All E. R. 33; *Swan* v. *Salisbury Construction Co.*, [1966] 2 All E. R. 138; *Henderson* v. *Jenkins & Sons and Evans*, [1970] A. C. 282; [1969] 3 All E. R. 756 (speeches of Lord REID and Lord DONOVAN, but contrast Lord PEARSON); *Colvilles* v. *Devine*, [1969] 2 All E. R. 53. Recent Australian authority favours the second or even the first view: *Nominal Defendant* v. *Haslbauer* (1967), 117 C. L. R. 448; *Piening* v. *Wanless* (1968), 117 C. L. R. 498; *Government Insurance Office of New South Wales* v. *Fredrichberg* (1968), 118 C. L. R. 403.

[2] *Woods* v. *Duncan* (*supra*) was such a case.

[3] Compare the argument of Professor Stone about the proof of fault in frustration cases cited, p. 85, n. 1, *ante.*

[4] The cases are cited n. 8, p. 43, *ante.*

CHAPTER VII

FACTS WHICH NEED NOT BE PROVED BY EVIDENCE—JUDICIAL NOTICE—FORMAL ADMISSIONS

The general rule is that all the facts in issue or relevant to the issue in a given case must be proved by evidence—testimony, hearsay statements, documents, things and relevant facts. If, in a moment of forgetfulness, the plaintiff or prosecutor fails to prove an essential fact, his opponent may succeed on a submission that there is no case to answer although the evidence was readily available, for the court has a discretion when deciding whether to allow a witness to be recalled.[1] There are two obvious exceptions to the general rule, for no evidence need be given of facts of which judicial notice is taken or of those that are formally admitted. It is often said that no proof is required of facts which are presumed, but the basic facts of every presumption have to be proved in the ordinary way and they are tendered as proof of the presumed fact. Evidence may also be said to be unnecessary in the case of an estoppel, but, so far as the party against whom it operates is concerned, estoppel is best regarded as an exclusionary rule rendering evidence of certain facts inadmissible and that is why it is discussed elsewhere in this book. The present chapter is therefore confined to judicial notice and formal admissions.

SECTION 1. JUDICIAL NOTICE [2]

When a court takes judicial notice of a fact, as it may in civil and criminal cases alike, it declares that it will find that the fact exists, or direct the jury to do so, although the existence of the fact has not been established by evidence. If, for instance, the date of Christmas should be in issue, or relevant to the issue, it will not be necessary for the party who desires to establish that fact to call a witness to swear that the birth of our Lord is celebrated on the 25th of December, because this is a matter of which judicial notice is taken. There are two classes of case in which the court will act in this way, for, to quote Lord SUMNER:

> "Judicial notice refers to facts which a judge can be called upon to receive and to act upon either from his general knowledge of them, or from inquiries to be made by himself for his own information from sources to which it is proper for him to refer."[3]

---

[1] *Middleton* v. *Rowlett*, [1954] 2 All E. R. 277 (prosecution failing to ask police witness at trial for motoring offence whether the driver of the car about which he testified was the accused, appeal against justice's refusal to allow case to be reopened failed).

[2] For theoretical discussion see Thayer, *Preliminary Treatise on Evidence at Common Law*, ch. 7; Morgan, *Some Problems of Proof Under the Anglo-American System of Litigation*, 36; Nokes, *The Limits of Judicial Notice*, 74 L. Q. R. 59 (1959); Schiff, 41 Can. Bar Rev. 335, at p. 344 *et seq.*

[3] *Commonwealth Shipping Representative* v. *P. and O. Branch Services*, [1923] A. C. 191, at p. 212. Morgan (*op. cit.*, p. 61) says the party who asks that judicial notice be taken of a fact "has the burden of convincing the judge (a) that the matter is so notorious as not to be the subject of dispute among reasonable men, or (b) the matter is capable of immediate accurate demonstration by resort to readily accessible sources of indisputable

From time to time statute has provided that judicial notice shall be taken of certain facts. It will therefore be convenient to illustrate the application of the doctrine by reference to facts which are judicially noticed without inquiry, facts judicially noticed after inquiry, and those of which notice must be taken under various statutory provisions. Certain theoretical questions are raised at the end of the section.

A. FACTS JUDICIALLY NOTICED WITHOUT INQUIRY

It would be pointless to endeavour to make a list of cases in which the courts have taken judicial notice of facts without inquiry. The justification for their acting in this way is that the fact in question is too notorious to be the subject of serious dispute. Familiar examples are provided by the rulings that it is unnecessary to call evidence to show that a fortnight is too short a period for human gestation,[1] that the advancement of learning is among the purposes for which the University of Oxford exists,[2] that cats are kept for domestic purposes,[3] that the streets of London are full of traffic[4] and that a boy riding a bicycle in them runs a risk of injury,[5] that young boys have playful habits,[6] that criminals have unhappy lives,[7] that the reception of television is a common feature of English domestic life enjoyed mainly for domestic purposes,[8] and that the Riding of York is coterminous with the city of that name.[9] The court may be taken to know the meaning of any ordinary expression in the English language,[10] and that the value of money has declined since 1189.[11] Judicial notice will also be taken of the fact that a post card is the kind of document which might be read by anyone,[12] but not that husbands read their wives' letters.[13] These conclusions have been reached without reference to any extraneous sources of information, but there is a number of cases in which judicial notice has only been taken after such reference has been made.

B. FACTS JUDICIALLY NOTICED AFTER INQUIRY

Foremost among these are cases in which the court acts on information supplied by a Secretary of State with regard to what may loosely be described as political matters; but other illustrations are provided by cases concerning inquiries into historical facts, questions concerning the existence of various customs and matters of professional practice. It is

accuracy''. Other classifications divide the subject into the law and practice of the courts, the government of the country and matters of common or certain knowledge (Wills), or else into cases in which judicial notice is required by statute, precedent or common sense (Thayer).

[1] *R. v. Luffe* (1807), 8 East 193.
[2] *Re Oxford Poor Rate Case* (1857), 8 E. & B. 184 (a decision that university premises came within special rating provisions).
[3] *Nye* v. *Niblett*, [1918] 1 K. B. 23 (cats protected by Malicious Damage Act, 1861).
[4] *Denis* v. *A. J. White and Co.*, [1916] 2 K. B. 1, at p. 6.
[5] *Ibid.*, [1917] A. C., at p. 492.
[6] *Clayton* v. *Hardwicke Colliery Company Ltd.*, (1915), 85 L. J. K. B. 292.
[7] *Burns* v. *Edman*, [1970] 2 Q. B. 541; [1970] 1 All E. R. 886.
[8] *Bridlington Relay, Ltd.* v. *Yorkshire Electricity Board*, [1965] Ch. 436; [1965] 1 All E. R. 264.
[9] *R. v. St. Maurice (Inhabitants)* (1851), 16 Q. B. 908.
[10] *Chapman* v. *Kirke*, [1948] 2 K. B. 450, at p. 454; [1948] 2 All E. R. 556, at p. 557.
[11] *Bryant* v. *Foot* (1868), L. R. 3 Q. B. 497. A South Australian court has taken judicial notice of a general increase in the cost of living, but not of particular statistics (*Re Richardson*, [1920] S. A. S. R. 25).
[12] *Huth* v. *Huth*, [1915] 3 K. B. 32.
[13] *Theaker* v. *Richardson*, [1962] 1 All E. R. 229.

sometimes said that the judges take judicial notice of the Common Law, but there is no need to deal separately with this aspect of the subject.

The sources consulted by the judge may include reports of previous cases, certificates from various officials, works of reference and oral statements of witnesses.

What was once a notorious fact to be noticed without further ado may become one of which notice will only be taken after the Court's memory has been refreshed. In *Hoare* v. *Silverlock*[1] for instance, the plaintiff had applied to a benevolent society for assistance, and she alleged that the defendant had defamed her by saying that her friends would realise the truth of the fable about the frozen snake. ERLE, J., said:

> "I may take judicial notice that the words 'frozen snake' have an application very generally known indeed, which application is likely to bring into contempt a person against whom it is directed."[2]

If such a point were to come before a jury to-day, they would require a good deal of instruction in the mysteries of Aesop's Fables.[3]

(i) Political matters.—In *Duff Development Co.* v. *Government of Kelantan*[4] the government of Kelantan applied for an order against the enforcement of an arbitration award on the ground that Kelantan was an independent sovereign state. The Secretary of State for the Colonies in reply to an inquiry from the Master wrote that Kelantan was a sovereign state and the Sultan ruler thereof. The House of Lords held that this concluded the matter because:

> "It has for some time been the practice of our courts, when such a question is raised, to take judicial notice of the sovereignty of a state, and for that purpose (in case of any uncertainty) to seek information from a Secretary of State; and when information is so obtained the court does not permit it to be questioned by the parties."[5]

The source of information to which the court resorts is treated as one of indisputable accuracy for reasons of public policy—the undesirability of a conflict between the courts and the executive. As in all cases in which the courts renounce their powers of determining facts on the basis of evidence, the practice may be represented as something like a submission to official dictatorship, but, in this instance, it is difficult to see how else a judge should act when confronted with such questions as the sovereignty of a foreign state, the membership of a diplomatic suite, the extent of our territorial waters or the existence of a state of war.[6] Moreover the courts form their own opinion of the effect of the Secretary of State's answer and they may differ *inter se* on this point.[7]

---

[1] (1848), 12 Q. B. 624.　　　　　　　　　　　　　[2] *Ibid.*, at p. 633.

[3] Nokes, *Introduction to Evidence* (4th edition), 54.

[4] [1924] A. C. 797. See also *Taylor* v. *Barclay* (1828), 2 Sim. 213 (judicial notice of non-recognition of South American republic after consultation with Secretary of State); "*The Fagernes*", [1927] P. 311 (Admiralty's statement of extent of territorial waters conclusive); *Engelke* v. *Musmann*, [1928] A. C. 433 (Secretary of State's letter as to membership of diplomatic suite conclusive); *R.* v. *Botrill, Ex parte Kuechenmeister*, [1947] K. B. 41; [1947] 2 All E. R. 434 (judicial notice of continuance of war with Germany after consultation with Secretary of State).

[5] *Per* Lord CAVE, [1924] A. C., at p. 805.

[6] See cases cited in n. 4 above and *Preston* v. *Preston*, [1963] P. 141, at p. 149; [1962] 3 All E. R. 1057, at p. 1060 *et seq.* Judicial notice will not be taken of a particular event in a modern war; *Commonwealth Shipping Representative* v. *P. & O. Branch Services*, [1923] A. C. 191.

[7] *Carl-Zeiss Stiftung* v. *Rayner and Keeler, Ltd.* (No. 2), [1967] 1 A. C. 853; [1966] 2 All E. R. 536.

(ii) Historical facts.—In *Read* v. *The Bishop of Lincoln*,[1] the question was whether the mixing of communion wine with water and various other practices were contrary to the law of the church. It was held, against an objection to their doing so, that the courts might consider historical and ritualistic works on the subject. In the course of his speech in the House of Lords Lord HALSBURY made it clear that the judge can rely on his own historical learning in such a case, although "where it is important to ascertain ancient facts of a public nature the law does permit historical facts to be referred to".[2] If questions concerning the tenets of a political creed were to arise, the English courts would no doubt do what Australian courts are prepared to do and consult the appropriate literature.[3] A similar practice would no doubt be adopted with regard to general scientific or aesthetic questions. The courts will also take notice of what people must have believed at a given time about such contemporary matters as the likelihood of a war.[4]

(iii) Custom.—As a general rule a court cannot treat a fact as proved on the basis of the evidence in a previous case;[5] but this rule does not apply to the proof of custom, for it has been recognised that a time must come when the courts, having had the question of the existence of a custom before them in other cases, are entitled to say that they will take judicial notice of it and will not require proof in each case.[6] This recognition was made by BRAY, J., in the Divisional Court when upholding a County Court Judge's right to take judicial notice of the custom whereby a domestic servant might terminate her employment within the first month of her engagement by less than a full month's notice but the doctrine he enunciated lies at the root of the court's recognition of a vast number of mercantile customs.[7] It is not always easy to say when a custom has been recognised with sufficient frequency to become the subject of judicial notice. Whereas the courts were not prepared to recognise that it was the usual practice of a hotel-keeper to be in possession of furniture under hire purchase agreements in 1875, they were prepared to do so in 1881.[8]

(iv) Professional practice.—In *Davey* v. *Harrow Corporation*,[9] Lord GODDARD, C.J., said:

> "Where a boundary hedge is delineated on an ordinance survey map by a line, that line indicates the centre of the existing hedge. That is in accordance with the practice of the ordinance survey and courts can take notice of that practice as at least *prima facie* evidence of what a line on the map indicates."

Judicial notice will likewise be taken of the practice of conveyancers.[10]

---

[1] [1892] A. C. 644.

[2] *Ibid.*, at p. 653; *Evans* v. *Getting* (1834), 6 C. & P. 586 (history of Breconshire not received on question of boundaries of Welsh parishes because of possible prejudice of author); *Darby* v. *Ouseley* (1856), 1 H. & N. 1.

[3] *Australian Communist Party* v. *Commonwealth* (1951), 83 C. L. R. 1.

[4] *Monarch S.S. Co., Ltd.,* v. *Karlshamns Oljefabriker (A.B.)*, [1949] A. C. 196, at p. 234; [1949] 1 All E. R. 1, at p. 20, *per* Lord DU PARCQ.

[5] *Roper* v. *Taylor's Central Garages (Exeter), Ltd.*, [1951] 2 T. L. R. 284.

[6] *George* v. *Davies*, [1911] 2 K. B. 445, at p. 448.

[7] *Brandao* v. *Barnett* (1846), 12 Cl. & Fin. 787.

[8] *Re Matthews, Ex parte Powell* (1875), 1 Ch. D. 501; *Crawcour* v. *Salter* (1881), 18 Ch. D. 30.

[9] [1958] 1 Q. B. 60, at p. 69.

[10] *Re Rosher* (1884), 26 Ch. D. 801.

C. STATUTORY PROVISIONS

The doctrine of judicial notice can be made to render assistance in connection with the proof of documents. We shall see in Chapter XXI that, subject to the presumption of due execution arising from the production of a document more than twenty years old from the proper custody, the due execution of a document, i.e. the fact that it was signed or sealed by the person by whom it purports to be signed or sealed, must be proved before the court will receive it in evidence. This would lead to endless trouble in the case of various documents in constant use, and there are numerous statutes which provide that judicial notice shall be taken of the signatures of various persons attached to official documents.[1] Difficulties formerly experienced with regard to the proof of statutes, i.e. showing that the document before the court corresponded with those of the Act duly passed by both Houses of Parliament, have been resolved by s. 9 of the Interpretation Act, 1889. It provides that every Act passed after 1850 shall be a public act and judicially noticed as such in the absence of an express provision to the contrary. Judicial notice has always been taken of a public act of Parliament, i.e. no evidence has ever been required concerning its passage through Parliament and its contents, but, before 1850, such evidence was required in the case of Private Acts unless, as was often the case, they contained some special provision about judicial notice. Even now, if reliance is placed upon a Private Act passed before 1850, it may be necessary to produce a Queen's Printer's copy of the statute.[2]

It is unfortunate that there is no express provision for the taking of judicial notice of statutory instruments because, even in modern times, the courts have varied in their insistence on the production of a Stationery Office copy [3] and it is not even clear that proof by this method is authorised in the case of all statutory instruments.[4]

D. THEORETICAL QUESTIONS

The principal theoretical questions raised by the practice of taking judicial notice concern its relationship to the reception of evidence, the use which a judge can make of his personal knowledge, the rationale of the practice and its scope.

(i) Judicial notice and the reception of evidence.—No problem arises with regard to the distinction between receiving evidence and taking judicial notice of a fact when the subject of judicial notice is a matter of common knowledge with regard to which no inquiry is made by the judge. In such a case the judge is acting on his own knowledge and that is a completely different procedure from the reception of evidence. The processes begin to approximate when the judge makes inquiries before deciding to take judicial notice. If learned treatises are consulted, it is not easy to say whether evidence is being received under an exception to the

---

[1] E.g., The Evidence Act, 1845, s. 2, and The Bankruptcy Act, 1914, s. 142.

[2] Evidence Act, 1845, s. 3. Before this statute it might have been necessary to call someone to prove that a Private Act was duly passed. Now it is sufficient that a copy of any such statute passed before 1850 should purport to be that of the printer to the King or Queen. By the Documentary Evidence Act, 1882, a Stationery Office copy is made equivalent to a Queen's Printer's copy.

[3] [1962] Crim. L. R. 334.

[4] But see *R. v. Clarke*, [1969] 2 Q. B. 91; [1969] 1 All E. R. 924.

rule against hearsay or whether the judge is equipping himself to take judicial notice.[1] When the certificate of a Minister is sought on the question of the sovereignty of a foreign state, law lords have said both that evidence is not being taken and that the best evidence is being received.[2] Speaking of the class of case in which assessors may be consulted under statutory powers, Lord DENNING said:

> "The court must possess itself of necessary information. Some judges may have it already because of their previous experience. Others may have to acquire it for the first time, but in either case the information they glean is not evidence strictly so-called. When an assessor explains the technicalities, he does not do it on oath, nor can he be cross-examined, and no one ever called the author of a dictionary to give evidence. All that happens is that the court is equipping itself for its task by taking judicial notice of all such things as it ought to know in order to do its work properly."[3]

The approximation of taking judicial notice to the reception of evidence is even more marked when sworn testimony is heard before judicial notice is taken. In *McQuaker* v. *Goddard*[4] the trial judge held that, in the absence of any evidence of scienter, those in control of a zoo had no case to answer when a claim for personal injuries was made in respect of a bite from a camel because camels are *mansuetae naturae*. The judge reached this conclusion after consulting books about camels and hearing witnesses, some of whom spoke to the wild habits of camels but the more expert of whom deposed to the tameness of these animals. The judge's decision was affirmed by the Court of Appeal, CLAUSON, L.J., being careful to point out that, when hearing the witnesses, the judge had not been taking evidence in the ordinary sense. The witnesses were simply assisting the judge in "forming his view as to what the ordinary course of nature in this regard in fact is, a matter of which he is supposed to have complete knowledge".[5] It seems that, even where the processes of taking judicial notice and receiving evidence approximate most closely, they remain essentially different, firstly, because, when the judge decides to take judicial notice of a fact after hearing witnesses, he may withdraw that fact from the jury although the witnesses do not speak with one voice.   Secondly, the judge's decision constitutes a precedent.

If the processes of taking judicial notice and receiving evidence of a fact are essentially different, no evidence should be admissible in rebuttal of a fact which is judicially noticed. It appears that this is the case in spite of occasional remarks suggesting that taking judicial notice is merely the equivalent of *prima facie* proof of a fact. These remarks turn on the extreme generality of the facts of which judicial notice may be taken. Judicial notice that the seal or signature on a document is that of a particular court or official merely means that the seal or signature is recognised as similar to that of the court or official, and evidence of forgery in a particular case, though plainly admissible, does not rebut the fact of which

---

[1] The distinction can only be of practical importance in a case tried with a jury. If evidence is being taken, the judge must place it before the jury.   If judicial notice is taken he can direct the jury to find the fact judicially noticed.

[2] Contrast Lord FINLAY and Lord SUMNER in *Duff Development Co.* v. *Government of Kelantan*, [1924] A. C. 797, at p. 813 and p. 824 respectively.

[3] *Baldwin and Francis Ltd.* v. *Patent Appeal Tribunal*, [1959] A. C. 663, at p. 691.

[4] [1940] 1 K. B. 687; [1940] 1 All E. R. 471; *cf. Turner* v. *Coates*, [1917] 1 K. B. 670. These cases were decided under the common law concerning liability for animals.

[5] [1940] 1 K. B. 687, at p. 700.

judicial notice is taken.[1] Similarly, evidence that a particular practice was not followed on a particular occasion would not rebut the existence of the practice of which judicial notice is taken, nor, strictly speaking, would evidence of a change of practice for judicial notice is simply taken of the current practice at a particular time. There are of course many cases of judicial notice in which there can be no question of evidence in rebuttal, as when judicial notice is taken of the facts stated in the certificate of a Government Department.

There is something to be said for a practice under which a judge could state that he proposed to take notice of the existence of certain facts within his personal knowledge, subject to anything urged upon him to the contrary,[2] but this raises the whole question of the extent to which a judge can make use of his personal knowledge.

(ii) Personal knowledge.—The general rule is that neither a judge nor a juror may act on his personal knowledge of facts.[3] This rule has reference to particular facts; when taking judicial notice a judge frequently makes use of his general knowledge, and justices can certainly make use of their knowledge of local conditions such as the extent of tidal waters.[4] The distinction is not always easy to draw. In *R. v. Field, JJ., Ex parte, White*,[5] for instance, the issue was whether cocoa must necessarily contain a quantity of foreign ingredients. This is not a matter of general notoriety or even something which can be put beyond dispute by reference to the appropriate sources of information. Nevertheless, some of the Justices had acquired knowledge of the subject in the navy, and the Divisional Court did not dispute the propriety of their making use of it. WILLS, J., said:

> "In the nature of things, no one in determining a case of this kind, can discard his own particular knowledge of a subject of this kind. I might as well be asked to decide a question as to the sufficiency of an alpine rope without bringing my personal knowledge into play".

In a later case in which the Court of Appeal held that the County Court Judge had gone too far in making use of his personal knowledge of the prospects of employment of a workman of a particular age and skill, Lord GREENE said:

> "The practice of County Court Judges of supplementing evidence by having recourse to their own local knowledge and experience has been criticised, praised as most beneficial, objected to and encouraged in different decisions." [6]

All that can be said is that, within reasonable and proper limits, a judge may make use of his personal knowledge of general matters, and that no formula has yet been evolved for describing those limits.

(iii) Rationale.—There are at least two reasons why we should have a

---

[1] *Holland v. Jones* (1917), 23 C. L. R. 149, at p. 154.

[2] Cf. *Thomas v. Thomas*, [1961] 1 All E. R. 19, where the Magistrates did not give the defendant an opportunity of urging them to take contrary action. Cf. Federal Rules 201 (e) reading in part as follows: "A party is entitled upon timely request to an opportunity to be heard as to the propriety of taking judicial notice and the tenor of the matter noticed."

[3] *R. v. Rosser* (1836), 7 C. and P. 648; *Manley v. Shaw* (1840), Car. & M. 361; *R. v. Antrim JJ.*, [1895] 2 I. R. 603; *Palmer v. Crone*, [1927] 1 K. B. 804.

[4] *Ingram v. Percival*, [1969] 1 Q. B. 548; [1968] 3 All E. R. 657. See also *Keane v. Mount Vernon Colliery Co., Ltd.*, [1933] A. C. 309.

[5] (1895), 64 L. J. M. C. 158; cf. *R. v. Tager*, [1944] A. D. 339.

[6] *Reynolds v. Llanelly Associated Tinplate Co.*, [1948] 1 All E. R. 140, at p. 142 where a number of the relevant authorities are cited.

doctrine of judicial notice. In the first place, it expedites the hearing of many cases. Much time would be wasted if every fact which was not admitted had to be the subject of evidence which would, in many instances, be costly and difficult to obtain. Secondly, the doctrine tends to produce uniformity of decision on matters of fact where a diversity of findings might sometimes be distinctly embarrassing. Thus, it has been said that the basic essential is that the fact judicially noticed should be of a class that is so generally known as to give rise to the presumption that all persons are aware of it.[1] No doubt this is the justification for taking judicial notice in the vast majority of cases, but it is not always so. It would be idle to pretend that the particulars with regard to the behaviour of camels of which the court heard evidence in *McQuaker* v. *Goddard* could be presumed to be generally known.[2]

(iv) Scope.—Thayer spoke of judicial notice as "an instrument of great capacity in the hands of a competent judge . . . not nearly as much used in the region of practice and evidence as it should be".[3] This is an exaggeration for there cannot be a much greater scope for the doctrine of judicial notice than there is at present, but perhaps the cases do indicate an excessive caution on the part of the courts. In *Brune* v. *Thompson*[4] the question was whether an undertaking to call evidence from London (made under the old procedure) had been satisfied by production of a document from the Tower, and the court refused to take judicial notice of the fact that that building is in London. Thayer pointed out that part of the tower is in Middlesex, as opposed to the County of London;[5] the apparent caution of the court was justified but the same can hardly be said of *Deybel's Case* [6] where the question was whether an arrest had been effected between Beachy Head and the North Foreland in Kent. The arrest took place eight leagues from Orford Ness in the county of Suffolk, but the court would not take judicial notice of the fact that this spot was outside the specified area because parts of Suffolk might have been in Kent. Lest it should be thought that such caution merely represents the timid approach of a past period, a further reference must be made to *Preston-Jones* v. *Preston-Jones.*[7] In that case the only fact of which the House of Lords would take judicial notice was that the duration of the normal period of

---

[1] *Holland* v. *Jones* (1917), 23 C. L. R. 149, at p. 153, *per* ISAACS, C.J.

[2] That they require help in the act of copulation.

[3] *Preliminary Treatise on Evidence at Common Law*, p. 309.

[4] (1842), 2 Q. B. 789.

[5] *Op. cit.*, pp. 310–311. *Cf.* the same author's explanation of *Kearney* v. *King* (1819), 2 B. & Ald. 301, sometimes erroneously cited for the proposition that judicial notice will not be taken of the fact that Dublin is in Ireland, when in fact it only decided that an allegation that a bill was drawn in Ireland was not proved by showing that it was drawn in Dublin for *non constat* that there was not a place called Dublin outside Ireland. See also *Thorne* v. *Jackson* (1846), 3 C. B. 661. *Collier* v. *Nokes* (1849), 2 Car. and Kir. 1012 is another example of a case in which the court's caution was apparent rather than real. The court would not take judicial notice that a distress took place after sunset when levied after 4 P.M. in November. There was an almanack showing that the sun did not set until after 4 P.M. on most of the days of the month. Canadian courts have taken judicial notice of the hours of darkness and there is no doubt that English courts would do likewise in appropriate cases (*Dugas* v. *Leclair* (1962), 32 D. L. R. 2d 459).

[6] (1821), 4 B. & Ald. 243. It has even been said that the Courts cannot take judicial notice of the relative distance of places (*per* WILDE, J. *arg.* in *Kirby* v. *Hickson* (1850), 14 Jur. 625). The question was whether Russell Square was within 20 miles of Grosvenor Square in London. A South Australian Court has taken judicial notice of the fact that a suburb of Adelaide is less than 100 miles away from that city (*Blatchford* v. *Dempsey*, [1956] S. A. S. R. 285).

[7] [1951] A. C. 391; [1951] 1 All E. R. 124, p. 101, *ante*.

gestation is about nine months. Only Lord MORTON OF HENRYTON was prepared to follow DENNING, L.J., in taking judicial notice of the fact that a child born to a woman 360 days after she last had intercourse with her husband could not be his child. As is so frequently the case, the problem is where to draw the line between the realm of facts which will be judicially noticed and those which must be proved by evidence. But there does not appear to be more enthusiasm for a bold application of the doctrine of judicial notice in the twentieth century than there was in the nineteenth.

(v) Tacit applications.—The tacit applications of the doctrine of judicial notice are more numerous and more important than the express ones. A great deal is taken for granted when any question of relevance is considered or assumed. For example, evidence is constantly given that persons accused of burglary were found in possession of jemmies or skeleton keys, that powder puffs and pots of vaseline were found on the premises of those charged with homosexuality, and that the accused became confused when charged; these facts are only relevant provided there is a common practice to use such things in the commission of the crime, or provided that guilty people tend more than innocent ones to become confused when charged, but no one ever thinks of calling evidence on such a subject.

SECTION 2. FORMAL ADMISSIONS

A party may admit facts for the purposes of the trial, thus saving his adversary the trouble and expense of proving them. In a civil case he may be induced to do this by the possibility that he will be made to bear the cost of proving such facts if he does not admit them. These formal admissions which cannot be contradicted by the person who makes them, and which are only binding for the purposes of the particular case in which they are made, must be distinguished from the informal admissions that are received under an exception to the rule against hearsay discussed in chapter XVIII. Unlike formal admissions, informal admissions are an item of evidence. Their maker may endeavour to explain them away at the trial at which they are proved.

Under section 10 of the Criminal Justice Act, 1967, a formal admission may be made by or on behalf of the prosecution or defendant before, or at any criminal proceedings, and may, with the leave of the court, be withdrawn.

The procedural details, with regard to formal admissions in civil and criminal cases are beyond the scope of this book.

CHAPTER VIII

THE COMPETENCE AND COMPELLABILITY OF WITNESSES

It is necessary to distinguish between three separate, though closely related, concepts—the competence, compellability and privilege of a witness. A witness is competent if he may lawfully be called to give evidence. Nowadays, most people are competent witnesses, but, under the law which applied to civil cases down to the middle of the nineteenth century, and to criminal trials until the end of that century, many of those who could give relevant evidence were not allowed to do so. The older books on evidence are largely concerned with the competence of witnesses, and it was not until Bentham had scathingly ridiculed the old law, that it was cast into a rational shape by statute.

A witness is compellable if he can lawfully be obliged to give evidence. The general rule is that all competent witnesses are compellable, but there are a few exceptions which will have to be mentioned in due course. If a compellable witness refuses to testify he may be sent to prison, and this is the sanction by which someone who has entered the witness box and been sworn is generally obliged to answer the questions that are put to him.

In a strictly limited number of situations, a witness who is both competent and compellable may refuse to answer certain questions, relying on a privilege conferred upon him by the law. The different privileges of witnesses are discussed in Chapter XI, while competence and compellability, are the subjects of s. 2 of this chapter. Section 1 is purely historical.

Generally speaking, the term "witness" must be taken to include parties to the proceedings. The latter expression comprises the parties to a civil action and the accused, but not the prosecutor, on a criminal charge. There are several respects in which the position of a party differs from that of an ordinary witness, and attention is drawn to them where it is necessary to do so, but subject to these points of difference, everything that is said in this book about witnesses applies to parties.

SECTION 1. HISTORICAL INTRODUCTION

Incompetence due to youth or defective intellect is perforce recognised under the modern law, but there were formerly five further classes of persons who were wholly or partially prohibited from testifying, namely, non-Christians, convicts, persons interested in the outcome of the proceedings, parties and their spouses. Something must be said about the way in which these people were rendered competent, by case-law and various Oaths Acts so far as the first class was concerned, and, with regard to the remaining four classes, by the Evidence Acts of 1843 and 1851, the Evidence Amendment Act, 1853, the Evidence Further Amendment Act, 1869, and the Criminal Evidence Act, 1898. These five statutes govern the modern law of competence and compellability. They could be consolidated with advantage.

A. NON-CHRISTIANS

Until the end of the seventeenth century the law was that evidence had to be given on oath and that oath had to be taken on the Gospel. If it could be shown that the proposed witness did not accept the authority of the Gospel, he would be held to be incompetent to give evidence. COKE included Jews as well as heathens in this class, and, although his views were not entirely shared by HALE,[1] it was only when Lord HARDWICKE sought the advice of the common law judges in *Omychund* v. *Barker* [2] in 1744 that the law on this subject was decisively modified. In that case, described by Wigmore as a great landmark of enlightened legal opinion,[3] it was held that the depositions of Gentoos should be received as they believed in a governor of the universe in whose name the depositions were sworn. PARKER, C.B., disposed of the old authorities by saying that they proved no more than that oaths are adapted to the natives of the kingdom,[4] while WILLES, C.J., founded his judgment on the fact that our Saviour and St. Peter have said God is no respecter of persons. "Lord Coke is a very great lawyer, but our Saviour and St. Peter are in this respect much better authorities than a person possessed with such narrow notions." [5]

WILLES, C.J., was, however, clearly of opinion that those who either did not believe in a God, or did not think that He would punish them in this world or the next, could not be witnesses in any case because "an oath cannot possibly be any tie or obligation upon them".[6] The law has been put on its modern basis by statute in the nineteenth century, although Quakers had previously been permitted to make a solemn affirmation. The present position is discussed in section 3 of this Chapter.

B. CONVICTS

Until the nineteenth century, if a person had once been convicted and sentenced for an infamous crime, he was incompetent as a witness for the rest of his life. A great deal of technicality was involved concerning the definition of an infamous crime which certainly included treason, felony and perjury, while an almost equal amount of learning was devoted to the effect of a pardon; but it is unnecessary to go into these matters any further because the incompetence of convicts to act as witnesses, incompetence through "infamy" as it used to be called, has been totally abolished. In 1828 the Civil Rights of Convicts Act rendered convicts capable of acting as witnesses after they had served their sentence, unless they had been found guilty of perjury. The Evidence Act, 1843, provided that no person should thereafter be excluded by reason of incapacity on account of a conviction from giving evidence in any proceedings. Under the present law, therefore, the fact that a witness has been convicted is a matter which concerns the cogency and not the competency of his testimony.

C. INTERESTED PERSONS

Until the nineteenth century, those who had a pecuniary or proprietary interest in the outcome of the proceedings were incompetent to act as

---

[1] 2 P. C. 279.
[2] (1745), 1 Atk. 21. A previous decision pointing in the same direction was *Robeley* v. *Langston* (1668), 2 Keb. 314.
[3] II *Wigmore*, p. 603, n. 1.   [4] 1 Atk. 40.   [5] *Ibid.*, 44.
[6] Willes, at p. 545.

witnesses in them. This is also a subject which attracted a considerable amount of learning, but, once again, it is unnecessary to go into detail because the Evidence Act, 1843, abolished incompetence through interest except in the case of the parties and their spouses. Interest is now something which only affects the weight of a person's evidence.

D. PARTIES

(1) CIVIL CASES

The parties to most civil proceedings were made competent and compellable witnesses by the Evidence Act, 1851. Section 4 contained an exception in respect of proceedings instituted in consequence of adultery and actions for breach of promise of marriage; it was repealed by the Evidence Further Amendment Act, 1869, and there is no doubt concerning the competence and compellability of parties at the present day;[1] this means that, should he be minded to do so a plaintiff can compel a defendant to testify.

(2) CRIMINAL CASES

A party's incompetence in a civil case was due to his interest in the proceedings, and the Act of 1851 was merely the corollary of that of 1843. The accused's interest in the outcome of the proceedings was one reason for his inability to give evidence at the hearing of a criminal charge against him; but there was a further reason based on what was largely an illogical application of the maxim "*Nemo tenetur prodere seipsum*"—no one should be obliged to give himself away. This lies at the root of the witness's privilege against self-incrimination discussed in Chapter XI. At first sight it may seem odd that a privilege against self-inculpation should be allowed to militate against self-exculpation by prohibiting all accused persons from giving sworn evidence on their own behalf; but there was an historical reason for this attitude. It had been the practice of the Star Chamber to oblige those who were brought before it to answer questions on oath, and the practice came to share the unpopularity of the tribunal by which it was instituted. To quote Professor Glanville Williams:[2]

> "The strong insistence, after the abolition of the Star Chamber, that the administration of an oath to a defendant was contrary to the law of God and the law of nature, was a race-memory from those evil days."

During the nineteenth century the accused came to be allowed to make an unsworn statement from the dock, a right preserved by the Act of 1898 and discussed in section 3 of this chapter.

The prohibition against the accused giving sworn evidence on his own behalf may have had its advantages if he was guilty, for the jury could be left with the impression that he had a complete defence to the charge but was unfortunately prevented from deposing to its exact nature,[3] but the situation could not be viewed with equanimity owing to the extreme hard-

---

[1] Theoretical doubts caused by the use of the word "competent" without "compellable" in the first limb of s. 3 (Carter and Cowen, *Essays in the Law of Evidence*, 220) are likely to be short-lived as it was included in the Statute Law (Repeals) Bill, 1973, which had its second reading before the dissolution of Parliament. Section 2 of the 1869 Act and section 43 (2) of the Matrimonial Causes Act, 1965, which raised similar doubts have already been repealed. See Addendum, *ante*.

[2] *The Proof of Guilt*, 3rd Edn., p. 41.

[3] It became so common for counsel for the defence to adopt this approach that judges used to remind them of the prisoner's right to make an unsworn statement.

ship that might be caused to an innocent accused. Accordingly, a number of statutes were passed between 1872 and 1898 under which the prisoner was made a competent witness in the case of specified charges such as those under the Criminal Law Amendment Act, 1885. It is unnecessary to refer to them in detail because, with one exception, they have been superceded by the Criminal Evidence Act, 1898, which provides in s. 1 that every person charged with an offence shall be a competent witness for the defence at every stage of the proceedings, whether he is charged solely or jointly with any other person.[1] The one exception is the Evidence Act, 1877, under which the defendant to any indictment or other proceeding for the non-repair of a public highway or bridge, or for a nuisance to a public highway, river or bridge, or any other indictment or proceeding instituted for the purpose of trying or enforcing a civil right only is an admissible witness and compellable to give evidence. Section 6 (1) of the Act of 1898 expressly preserves the effect of the Act of 1877, so that, in the exceptional class of case to which it refers, the accused is both competent and compellable.

E. SPOUSES OF THE PARTIES

(1) Extent of the Common Law Disability

Subject to comparatively unimportant exceptions which were confined to criminal cases, a party's spouse was incompetent as a witness for or against him at common law.[2] The incompetence extended to spouses of either sex and to testimony concerning events occurring before as well as during the marriage. In *Monroe* v. *Twistleton*[3] it was decided that the incompetence endured after the marriage had been dissolved by private Act of Parliament so far as transactions which occurred during its subsistence were concerned. Accordingly, the plaintiff in *assumpsit* could not call the divorced wife of the defendant to prove the contract as it was concluded during her marriage. This case was followed in *O'Connor* v. *Marjoribanks*[4] where personal representatives claimed damages for conversion of part of an estate from a bank, and it was held that the deceased's widow's evidence with regard to instructions received by her from her late husband concerning the disposal of his goods during his lifetime could not be received.

From time to time it has been suggested that, in addition to rendering the spouse of the parties incompetent, the common law prohibited the disclosure of marital communications by any witness, whether they passed between him and his spouse or were other people's marital communications overheard by him; but it has been authoritatively decided that the only relevant common law rule is that of incompetency.[5]

---

[1] The accused was allowed to give evidence on his own behalf a little earlier in parts of the Commonwealth.

[2] *Bentley* v. *Cooke* (1784), 3 Doug. K. B. 422; *Davis* v. *Dinwoody* (1792), 4 Term Rep. 678.

[3] (1802), Peake Add. Cas. 219.

[4] (1842), 4 Man. & G. 435. *Monroe* v. *Twistleton* was preferred to the contradictory decision in *Beveridge* v. *Minter* (1824), 1 C. & P. 364. See also *Doker* v. *Hasler* (1824), Ry. & M. 198.

[5] *Rumping* v. *Director of Public Prosecutions*, [1964] A. C. 814; [1962] 3 All E. R. 256; *Shenton* v. *Tyler*, [1939] Ch. 620; [1939] 1 All E. R. 827 criticised on historical grounds by Holdsworth in 56 L. Q. R. 137.

There was one clear exception to the common law rule and two further ones concerning which there is a high degree of uncertainty. The one clear exception was constituted by criminal charges involving personal violence by the accused against his or her spouse. To quote from one of the modern judgments on the subject:

> "There is no doubt that at common law the husband or wife was always a competent witness in such a case, and by the very nature of things it must have been so, for otherwise, where the assault was committed in secret by one spouse upon the other, there would be no means of proving it."[1]

The first of the uncertain exceptions is treason. If it exists it can be justified on the ground that the public interest in the safety of the state outweighs whatever public interests are promoted by preventing one spouse from testifying against the other.[2] The second uncertain exception relates to cases in which it has been held that on prosecutions under old statutes for abducting and marrying a girl against her will, she was a competent witness even if the marriage happened to be legally valid.[3] These may be accounted for on the ground that something in the nature of personal violence was involved.[4]

In *R.* v. *Sergeant*[5] it was said that a wife is in all cases a competent witness for her husband when admissible against him, and there is no reason to doubt that this doctrine applies to all the exceptions to the common law rule of the incompetency of spouses, and to husbands as well as wives. In the absence of some compelling reason to the contrary, what is sauce for the goose is sauce for the gander in the administration of justice no less than in other spheres of life.

(2) Statutes Affecting Civil Cases

The spouses of parties to litigation are now competent in all civil cases, and, subject to doubts that have been expressed in certain quarters with regard to proceedings instituted in consequence of adultery,[6] they are also compellable witnesses. Section 1 of the Evidence Amendment Act, 1853, provides that the husbands and wives of the parties should be both competent and compellable to give evidence except as thereinafter provided. The exception refers to s. 2 which reads as follows:

> "Nothing herein shall render any husband competent or compellable to give evidence for or against his wife, or any wife competent or compellable to give evidence for or against her husband in any criminal proceeding (or in any proceeding instituted in consequence of adultery)."

The words in brackets were repealed by the Evidence Further Amendment Act, 1869, but it is the terms of this latter statute which gave rise to the doubt that has been mentioned.

---

[1] *R.* v. *Lapworth*, [1931] 1 K. B. 117, at p. 121, *per* Avory, J. The exception goes back to the seventeenth century; see *Lord Audley's Case* (1631), 3 State Tr. 401.

[2] See *per* Lush, J., in *Director of Public Prosecutions* v. *Blady*, [1912] 2 K. B. 89, at p. 92. The other dicta for and against the competency of the accused's spouse in treason are collected in Cohen, *Spouse Witnesses*, 23.

[3] *R.* v. *Wakefield* (1827), 2 Lew. C. C. 279.

[4] See the judgment of Blackburn, J., in *Reeve* v. *Wood* (1864), 5 B. & S. 364.

[5] (1826), Ry. & M. 352.

[6] See p. 146, n. 1, *ante*.

(3) STATUTES AFFECTING CRIMINAL CASES

The main statutory alteration of the common law rule under which the accused's spouse was, generally speaking, neither a competent nor a compellable witness for the prosecution or defence is the Criminal Evidence Act, 1898. The general effect of the Act is that the accused's spouse is always a competent witness for the defence, although he or she will usually be incompetent for the prosecution, but there are several exceptional situations to be discussed in the next section.

SECTION 2. COMPETENCE AND COMPELLABILITY UNDER THE MODERN LAW

The general rule is that anyone is a competent and compellable witness in any case; but there are exceptions relating to children, persons of defective intellect, the accused and the accused's spouse.[1]

A. CHILDREN
(1) CIVIL CASES

The competency of a child to give evidence in a civil case is governed exclusively by the common law which was settled in *R. v. Brasier*.[2] The question whether a child under seven was competent to give evidence at a prosecution for an assault was reserved for the twelve judges who stated the law to be that no testimony whatever can be legally received except upon oath. They added that an infant, though under the age of seven years, may be sworn in a criminal prosecution, provided such infant appears, on strict examination by the court, to possess a sufficient knowledge of the nature and consequences of an oath.

> "There is no precise or fixed rule as to the time within which infants are excluded from giving evidence, but their admissibility depends upon the sense and reason they entertain of the danger and impiety of falsehood, which is to be collected from their answers to questions propounded by the court."

If the court comes to the conclusion that the child does not understand the nature and consequences of an oath, the evidence must be rejected, unless it is considered to be worth while to adjourn the case so as to instruct the proposed witness in these matters.

(2) CRIMINAL CASES

In criminal cases there is statutory power to accept the unsworn evidence of a child of tender years. This is now confirmed by section 38 of the Children and Young Persons Act, 1933,[3] the condition precedent to the reception of such evidence being that the child is possessed of sufficient intelligence to justify it, and understands the duty of speaking the truth. If the witness wilfully gives false evidence in such circumstances that, had

---

[1] *R. v. Webb* (1867), 11 Cox C. C. 133 decides that a person under sentence of death is incompetent because he would formerly have been an outlaw; but see the Abolition of Forfeitures Act, 1870.

[2] (1779), 1 Leach 199. Hale seems to have contemplated the possibility of unsworn evidence in the case of a very young child (1 P. C. 634). But nothing came of it so far as the Common Law was concerned.

[3] Replacing the Criminal Justice Administration Act, 1914, s. 28 (2) which generalised earlier enactments that only applied to specific charges.

his statements been made on oath, he would have been guilty of perjury, he is liable to punishment. The question whether a particular child is of tender years is best regarded as a matter for the good sense of the court.[1]

In Canada, children can give unsworn evidence in civil proceedings, and, at the very least, there seems to be no reason why section 38 of the English Act of 1933 should not be made applicable to such cases. In *Baker* v. *Rabetts*,[2] for instance, a girl of 12 was held incapable of giving unsworn evidence in affiliation proceedings which are civil.[3] She did not understand the nature of an oath, and the Divisional Court appears to have considered that the Magistrates might have adjourned the proceedings so that she could have been instructed; but, on a charge of unlawful intercourse, she would very probably have been allowed to give unsworn evidence in the absence of such instruction.

The above suggestion has been made as a minimal proposal because there is a lot to be said for adopting the recommendations of the Criminal Law Revision Committee[4] and making them applicable to civil as well as criminal proceedings. The recommendations are that all evidence by children under 14 should be unsworn and all evidence by children over 14 should be sworn. The condition precedent of the admissibility of the unsworn evidence would be that the court should be of opinion that the child is possessed of sufficient intelligence to justify the reception of his evidence and understands the importance of telling the truth in the particular proceedings. The present inquiry into the question whether the child understands the nature of an oath is thought to be unrealistic and even liable to be farcical; while the test under the Act of 1933 of the child's understanding of the duty of speaking the truth may be inadequate, because a child may appreciate that duty in a general way without appreciating its full importance in the particular proceedings. The proposals of course assume that, in general, evidence will continue to be given on oath, and, if there is to be a fixed age for doing so, different views may of course be taken on the question of what it should be.

B. PERSONS OF DEFECTIVE INTELLECT

At one time it appears to have been thought that lunatics so found were absolutely excluded from testifying, but *R.* v. *Hill*[5] decides that, in all cases where it is contended that the witness is of too weak an intellect to admit of his giving evidence, it is for the judge to decide whether he understands the nature of an oath and, if the judge answers this question in the affirmative, it is for the jury to say what degree of credit is to be given to the testimony. The inmate of an asylum whose only delusion was that spirits talked to him was accordingly allowed to give evidence at a prosecution for manslaughter. If it appears that, though duly sworn before the jury, the witness was in fact too weak-minded to testify or that, for some other reason, such as deafness or dumbness, the evidence cannot be taken, the judge may

---

[1] *R* v. *Campbell*, [1956] 2 Q. B. 432, at p. 436; [1956] 2 All E. R. 272 at p. 274. For a discussion of the examination by the judge of children of tender years see *R.* v. *Hampton* (1966), 55 W. W. R. 432.
[2] (1954), 118 J. P. N. 303; *Times*, April 30th 1954.
[3] *S.* v. *E.*, [1967] 1 Q. B. 367; [1967] 1 All E. R. 593.
[4] 11th Report, paras. 204–8.
[5] (1851), 2 Den. 254. See also *R.* v. *Dunning*, [1965] Crim. L. R. 372.

declare the witness to be incompetent.[1] Temporary incapacity, occasioned by illness or intoxication, would presumably lead to an adjournment in an appropriate case.

C. THE ACCUSED

(1) As a Witness for the Prosecution

The general rule is that the accused is not a competent witness for the prosecution in any criminal case. The rule is the result of the common law which, so far as this point is concerned, has not been modified by the Criminal Evidence Act, 1898. The effect of the rule is that one co-prisoner cannot be called by the prosecution to give evidence against another. Co-prisoners are persons who are being jointly tried when the question of competency has to be decided.[2] In *R. v. Grant*[3] and *R. v. Sharrock*[4] committals were quashed because one co-prisoner had been called on behalf of the prosecution at the preliminary examination. In so far as these cases decided that an indictment based on inadmissible evidence is necessarily bad, they have been overruled;[5] but they still serve as a warning to over-zealous prosecutors.

There are various devices by which the prosecution may render a co-prisoner competent and compellable on its behalf. Each of them has the effect of making the witness cease to be a co-prisoner within the above definition. A *nolle prosequi* may be filed with reference to his case, it may be stated that no evidence will be offered against him when he will be acquitted, an order for separate trials may be obtained or he may plead guilty. In this last event it is desirable that the witness should be sentenced before being called on behalf of the prosecution.[6] If the former co-prisoner was an accomplice, a warning against the danger of acting on his uncorroborated testimony will have to be given to the jury; this is discussed in the next chapter. Whether or not he was originally a co-prisoner, an accomplice against whom proceedings are pending must not, as a matter of practice, be called on behalf of the prosecution unless it is made plain that the proceedings will be discontinued.[7]

The only exception to the rule that an accused person is not a competent witness for the prosecution is constituted by the cases of public nuisance covered by the Evidence Act, 1877, and these are criminal in form only. In these cases the accused is both competent and compellable for the prosecution whether he is being tried alone or jointly with someone else.

(2) As a Witness for Himself

The effect of s. 1 of the Criminal Evidence Act, 1898, is that the accused

---

[1] *R. v. Whitehead* (1866), L. R. 1 C. C. R. 33; cf. *Jacobs v. Layborn* (1843), 11 M. & W. 685. It was held in *The People (A.-G.) v. Keating*, [1953] I. R. 200, that the judge must examine the witness although he has examined the same witness in a previous case; cf. as to children *R. v. Surgenor*, [1940] 2 All E. R. 249.
[2] *R. v. Payne* (1872), L. R. 1 C. C. R. 349; *R. v. Richardson* (1967), 51 Cr. App. Rep. 381. Reference should be made to R. M. Gooderson, "*The Evidence of Co-prisoners*", 11 C. L. J. 279 (1953). Much that is said on the subject of co-prisoners in this chapter is derived from that article.
[3] [1944] 2 All E. R. 311.
[4] [1948] 1 All E. R. 145.
[5] *R. v. Norfolk Quarter Sessions, Ex parte Brunson*, [1953] 1 Q. B. 503; [1953] 1 All E. R. 346.
[6] *R. v. Payne*, [1950] 1 All E. R. 102.
[7] *R. v. Pipe* (1966), 51 Cr. App. Rep. 17.

is a competent witness on his own behalf at every stage of a criminal trial.[1] The section contains important provisos concerning comment on the accused's failure to testify, marital communications and the cross-examination of the accused; they are discussed elsewhere in this book.[2]

Doubts have been raised whether that which an accused person says when testifying on his own behalf may be used against a co-prisoner whether the statement was made in chief or in cross-examination.

(i) Evidence in chief.—In *R.* v. *Rudd*,[3] the most recent case on the availability of a co-prisoner's testimony as evidence for the prosecution, the Court of Criminal Appeal held that the trial judge had rightly refrained from telling the jury to disregard the evidence implicating the appellant given by his co-prisoner. HUMPHREYS, J., said:

> "While a statement made in the absence of the accused person by one of his co-defendants cannot be evidence against him,[4] if the co-defendant goes into the witness box and gives evidence in the course of a joint trial, then what he says becomes evidence for all the purposes of the case including the purpose of being evidence against his co-defendant."

These remarks are well supported by authority, if not entirely to the extent suggested by HUMPHREYS, J.,[5] and it is submitted that they are sound on principle because it is the common lot of a party to litigation to have adverse as well as favourable testimony given by his own witnesses and, not infrequently, by himself. But even in modern times language is sometimes used which suggests that nothing said by one co-prisoner in the witness box is evidence against the other.[6] There was some authority in support of this view before the Act of 1898 when doubts were expressed whether the evidence of a prisoner who had been acquitted and testified for one of the two remaining co-accused was admissible against the other,[7] but it is submitted that this, and similar hesitancy, spring from a failure to distinguish between one co-prisoner's out-of-court testimonial assertions or unsworn statements in court which are certainly not evidence against the other, and his sworn evidence in court which is analogous to that of any other witness.

(ii) Evidence elicited in cross-examination.—On principle there can be no doubt that what a witness says in cross-examination may be relied on by the person responsible for the cross-examination as evidence in his favour. This would mean that anything that one co-prisoner says when he is being cross-examined by the prosecution may be treated as

---

[1] Even after a plea of guilty he may give evidence in mitigation of sentence (*R.* v. *Wheeler*, [1917] 1 K. B. 283). The accused may also give evidence on the *voir dire* (*R.* v. *Cowell*, [1940] 2 K. B. 49; [1940] 2 All E. R. 599.).

[2] See Chapter XV as to comment and cross-examination, and Chapter XI as to marital communications.

[3] (1948), 32 Cr. App. Rep. 138. To the same effect are *R.* v. *Hunting and Ward* (1908), 1 Cr. App. Rep. 177; *R.* v. *Paul*, [1920] 2 K. B. 183, and *R.* v. *Garland* (1941), 29 Cr. App. Rep. 46. See also *Young* v. *H.M. Advocate*, 1932 S. C. (J) 63 where the earlier English and Scottish authorities are reviewed.

[4] Because of the hearsay rule, but see *Mawaz Khan* v. *R.*, [1967] 1 A. C. 454; [1967] 1 All E. R. 80 where such a statement was original evidence.

[5] His Lordship said it had been the invariable rule to state the law in the same way (32 Cr. App. Rep., at p. 140).

[6] For a ruling that comes near to telling the jury to disregard the evidence of one co-prisoner when considering the case against the other see *R.* v. *Meredith* (1943), 29 Cr. App. Rep. 40. It was assumed that one co-prisoner's testimony was evidence against the other in *Rigby* v. *Woodward*, [1957] 1 All E. R. 391.

[7] *R.* v. *Burdett* (1855), Dears. C. C. 431.

evidence against the other; but principle sometimes has to give way to considerations of policy, and, if it is sound policy to prohibit the prosecution from calling co-prisoners to testify against each other, it is pertinent to remember that the policy is liable to be circumvented whenever the prosecution is allowed to rely on the statements of an accused person elicited in cross-examination as evidence against his co-accused. To some extent it is only proper that this permission should be accorded, but it is arguable that the court went too far in *R.* v. *Paul.*[1] Paul, Goldberg and others were jointly charged with an offence. Goldberg was told that he need not give evidence, but nonetheless went into the witness-box and declared that he was guilty. This was all he said in-chief, but the Court of Criminal Appeal held that the judge had rightly allowed the prosecution to cross-examine him on Paul's alibi—a subject on which his evidence assisted the Crown. This case was criticised by Lord Justice General CLYDE in *Young* v. *H.M. Advocate.*[2] The court has a discretion with regard to the cross-examination it will permit, and Lord CLYDE considered that this discretion should have been exercised in favour of Paul. It is, however possible to exaggerate the criticisms of *R.* v. *Paul* because, had the accused pleaded guilty in the first instance, his evidence would have been available for the prosecution, although it is true that the evidence could not then have been obtained by means of leading questions and the other forms of pressure permissible in cross-examination.

(3) As a Witness for a Co-prisoner

The general rule is that the accused is a competent but not a compellable witness for anyone being tried jointly with him. This is the effect of s. 1 of the Criminal Evidence Act, 1898.[3] It means that, if A. and B. are being tried together, B. may call upon A. to testify for him provided A. is willing to do so. A prisoner who has pleaded guilty is not a "person charged" within the meaning of the Criminal Evidence Act, 1898, because he is not concerned in any issue before the jury; he is therefore both competent and compellable for a co-accused.[4] He has ceased to be a co-prisoner within the definition of that term mentioned above. For the same reason someone who was originally jointly indicted with the accused but is subsequently being tried separately is both competent and compellable for the accused.[5]

An accused who gives evidence is liable to be cross-examined by his co-accused as well as by the prosecution even if his evidence was in no way adverse to the accused,[6] although he will enjoy the protection of section 1 (f) of the Criminal Evidence Act, 1898, against certain types of cross-examination if he does not give evidence against someone charged with the same offence.

The only case in which an accused may be compelled to testify by his co-accused is that of proceedings for public nuisance under the Evidence Act, 1877.

---

[1] [1920] 2 K. B. 183.
[2] 1932 S. C. (J) 63.
[3] See *R.* v. *Payne* (1872), L. R. 1 C. C. R. 349, as to incompetence before the Act.
[4] *R.* v. *Boal,* [1965] 1 Q. B. 402, at p. 414; [1964] 3 All E. R. 269, at p. 275.
[5] *R.* v. *Richardson* (1967), 51 Cr. App. Rep. 381.
[6] *R.* v. *Hilton,* [1972] 1 Q. B. 421; [1971] 3 All E. R. 541.

D. THE ACCUSED'S SPOUSE

(1) As a Witness for the Prosecution

The general rule is that the accused's spouse is an incompetent witness for the prosecution. It is subject to important exceptions under s. 4 (1) of the Criminal Evidence Act, 1898, s. 39 of the Sexual Offences Act, 1956 and s. 30 of the Theft Act, 1968; in these cases the accused's spouse is a competent though not a compellable witness for the prosecution. The general rule is also subject to exceptions under the Evidence Act, 1877, and the common law; in these cases the accused's spouse is both competent and compellable for the prosecution.

(i) The general rule of incompetence.—The general rule of incompetence results from the common law and is vividly illustrated by some modern decisions. For example, in *R.* v. *Mount*,[1] three men were convicted of shopbreaking. The wife of one of them had given evidence for the Crown, and this necessitated the quashing of all three convictions. Shopbreaking is not among the offences mentioned in the schedule to the Act of 1898, and it does not fall within any of the other exceptions to the rule. The general rule renders the accused's spouse incompetent to testify to matters occurring before as well as during the marriage, and to matters occurring after a judicial separation.[2]

(ii) Section 4 (1) of the Criminal Evidence Act, 1898, and s. 39 of the Sexual Offences Act, 1956.—Section 4 (1) of the Criminal Evidence Act, 1898, provides that the wife or husband of a person charged with an offence under any enactment mentioned in the schedule may be called as a witness either for the prosecution or for the defence and without the consent of the person charged.

Several later enactments have provided that s. 4 of the Act of 1898 shall have effect as though certain further offences were included and the following are the principal offences to which s. 4 now applies:

(i) neglect to maintain or desertion of wife or family;[3]
(ii) offences against and with reference to children under the Children and Young Persons Act, 1933[4] and the Indecency with Children Act, 1960;
(iii) child destruction;[5]
(iv) bigamy;[6]
(v) offences under the National Insurance Act and similar statutes.[7]

Sexual offences were originally included in the schedule to the Act of 1898, but they are now dealt with by s. 39 of the Sexual Offences Act, 1956, under which, subject to a very few exceptions,[8] the wife or husband

---

[1] (1934), 24 Cr. App. Rep. 135. See also *R.* v. *Boucher* (1952), 36 Cr. App. Rep. 152, and *R.* v. *Deacon*, [1973] 2 All E. R. 1145.
[2] *Moss* v. *Moss*, [1963] 2 Q. B. 799; [1963] 2 All E. R. 829.
[3] National Assistance Act, 1948, s. 51; National Assistance (Adaptation of Enactments) Regulations 1952, replacing Vagrancy Act, 1824.
[4] Children and Young Persons Act, 1933, s. 15, s. 26(5) and First Schedule.
[5] Infant Life Preservation Act, 1929, s. 2 (5).
[6] Criminal Justice Administration Act, 1914, s. 28 (3).
[7] National Insurance (Industrial Injuries) Act, 1946, s. 68 (5); National Insurance Act, 1946, s. 51 (5); Workmen's Compensation (Supplementation) Act, 1951, s. 4 (5); Pneumoconiosis and Byssinosis Benefit Act, 1951, s. 4.
[8] The section does not apply to buggery, indecent assault on a man and an assault with intent to commit buggery. Buggery and assault on a wife by her husband fall within the common law exception to incompetence and the wife is compellable in such cases.

of the accused is competent but not compellable to give evidence for the defence or prosecution at every stage of the proceedings and whether the accused is charged solely or jointly with another person.

As competence usually implies compellability, many people thought that s. 4 (1) of the Act of 1898 made the accused's spouse compellable for the prosecution in the specified cases, but, in *Leach* v. *R.*,[1] the House of Lords decided that this was not so. Leach was charged with incest with his daughter. His wife was called as a witness on behalf of the prosecution. She objected to giving evidence but was compelled to do so. Leach was convicted, and, after an unsuccessful appeal to the court of Criminal Appeal, he successfully appealed to the House of Lords. Lord ATKINSON summarised their lordships' answer to the argument that competence implies compellability when he said:

> "The principle that a wife is not to be compelled to give evidence against her husband is deep-seated in the common law of this country, and I think if it is to be overturned it must be overturned by a clear, definite and positive enactment, not by an ambiguous one such as the section relied upon in this case."[2]

(iii) Theft Act, 1968, s. 30.—Section 30 of the Theft Act, 1968, replaced the former legislation, traceable to the Married Women's Property Act, 1882, dealing with offences by one spouse against the other; but it is not confined to offences against property. The effect of section 30 (2) and section 30 (3) is that the victim of any offence alleged to have been committed by his or her spouse is a competent witness for the prosecution,[3] but only compellable when he or she would have been compellable at common law.

(iv) Evidence Act, 1877.—The wording of the Evidence Act, 1877, leaves no doubt that the defendant's spouse is both competent and compellable as a witness for the prosecution in the limited class of cases covered by the Statute. Its effect is expressly preserved by s. 6 of the Act of 1898.

(v) The common law exceptions.—So far as the common law exceptions are concerned, nothing more need be said about the cases of treason and forcible marriage [4] for the only clear exception to the general rule of incompetence at common law is an accusation of personal violence by one spouse against another. There is some uncertainty with regard to the extent of this exception. It certainly applies to assaults of all kinds, and it has been held to extend to the commission of an unnatural offence by a husband against his wife,[5] but, in *R.* v. *Yeo*,[6] a charge against a husband of writing a letter threatening to murder his wife contrary to s. 16 of the Offences against the Person Act, 1861 was held to fall outside the exception.

R. v. *Yeo* was not followed in *R.* v. *Verolla* [7] where a wife was held

---

[1] [1912] A. C. 305.   [2] *Ibid.*, at p. 311.   [3] See Addendum, *ante.*
[4] See p. 148, *ante.*   [5] *R.* v. *Blanchard*, [1952] 1 All E. R. 114.
[6] [1951] 1 All E. R. 864. The wife would now be a competent witness on such a charge under section 30 of the Theft Act, 1968.
[7] [1963] 1 Q. B. 285; [1962] 2 All E. R. 426. For further authorities on the common law exception see *Lord Audley's Case* (1631), 3 State Tr. 401 (husband accessory to rape on wife, wife competent); *Jagger* (1796), 1 East P. C. 455; *R.* v. *Pearce* (1840), 9 C. & P. 667; *Reeve* v. *Wood* (1864), 5 B. & S. 364 (wilful neglect to maintain); *Director of Public Prosecutions* v. *Blady*, [1912] 2 K. B. 89 (husband living on wife's immoral earnings incompetent but she would now be competent under the Sexual Offences Act, 1956).

competent to testify against her husband who was charged with attempting to murder her by putting poison in some milk. No violence was used, but there is much to be said for the view that the applicability of the exception depends on the nature of the charge rather than the supporting evidence. If, by definition, the crime involves injury to the spouse's person, or an infringement of his or her liberty, it should come within the exception.[1] On this basis it could be argued that there is no conflict between *R.* v. *Yeo* and *R.* v. *Verolla* for it is arguable that sending a letter threatening to murder is not, by definition, a crime of violence. But it is submitted that *R.* v. *Yeo* was wrongly decided. A threat to beat outrageously was mentioned in the old cases as amounting to an assault, and this warrants an extension of the common law exception to a threat to murder, even when made by letter.[2]

The cases in which the accused's spouse may be called as a witness without his consent at common law were preserved by the Act of 1898[3] and, in *R.* v. *Lapworth*,[4] the Court of Criminal Appeal concluded that these cases fell outside the observations of the House of Lords in *Leach* v. *R.* It was accordingly held that a wife could be compelled to give evidence against her husband when he was charged with causing her grievous bodily harm, and the decision may be taken as authority for the proposition that the accused's spouse is always compellable on charges of personal violence against that spouse. The doctrine of *R.* v. *Lapworth* is that, so far as the common law exception is concerned, competence implies compellability; accordingly, if treason does constitute an exception to the general common law rule of incompetence, the accused's spouse should be compellable in such a case.

R. v. *Deacon*[5] illustrates the dangers of a joinder of counts on which the accused's spouse is competent (or even compellable) and incompetent for the prosecution. Deacon was charged with murdering his brother-in-law in the presence of Mrs. Deacon, the accused's wife, by shooting him, and with the attempted murder of Mrs. Deacon by subsequently shooting at her. She gave evidence that she saw the shooting of the accused's brother-in-law, and Deacon was convicted of his murder; no verdict was taken on the charge of attempted murder. The conviction of murder was quashed by the Court of Appeal because Mrs. Deacon was not a competent witness for the prosecution on that count. Presumably the right course would have been for the prosecution to have applied for separate trials of the two counts, calling Mrs. Deacon at the trial for attempted murder.

(2) As a Witness for the Accused

The general rule is that the accused's spouse is competent but not compellable to testify on behalf of the accused. This is the effect of the

---

[1] See *Sharpe* v. *Rodwell*, [1947] V. L. R. 82. On the test of the nature of the injury as distinct from the supporting evidence a wife would be an incompetent witness for the prosecution at her husband's trial for dangerous driving even if she had sustained personal injuries; *cf. Parson* v. *Tomlin* (1956), 120 J. P. 129.

[2] See note by Olive Stone, 14 M. L. R. 341.

[3] Section 4 (2).

[4] [1931] 1 K. B. 117. In *Riddle* v. *R.*, (1911) 12 C. L. R. 620, the High Court of Australia expressed the opinion (*obiter*) that, at common law, a wife was competent but not compellable in these cases, but *R.* v. *Lapworth* has been followed in Victoria: *Sharpe* v. *Rodwell*, [1947] V. L. R. 82.

[5] [1973] 2 All E. R. 1145.

Criminal Evidence Act, 1898, and the decision in *Leach* v. *R.*[1] So far as sexual offences are concerned, the Sexual Offences Act, 1956 expressly provides that the accused's spouse is competent but not compellable on his behalf, and there is a similar provision in section 30 (3) of the Theft Act, 1968. The only exceptions to the general rule are cases in which the accused's spouse is not merely competent but also compellable. These are the cases of public nuisance covered by the Evidence Act, 1877, and the cases covered by the common law of personal violence by one spouse against the other together with the possible exception of treason.

(3) As a Witness for a Co-accused

At common law, if A. and B. were being tried together, not only was Mrs. A. incompetent to act as a witness for her husband, but she could not be called by B. with or without A.'s consent.[2] This was presumably subject to the exception that if A. and B. were jointly charged with violence against Mrs. A., she would have been a competent and compellable witness for B. as well as for the Crown. As a result of the Act of 1898, it is necessary to distinguish between cases in which the accused's spouse is competent with and without the consent of the accused. There are also the exceptional cases in which the accused's spouse is compellable for a co-accused.

(i) Competence with the consent of the accused.—The accused's spouse is a competent witness for a co-accused with the accused's consent in every criminal case. This is the effect of the Act of 1898 under which the accused's spouse is competent for the defence at every stage of the proceedings. The accused's consent is necessitated by proviso (c) to s. 1 according to which:

> "the wife or husband of the person charged shall not save as in this Act mentioned be called as a witness in pursuance of this Act except upon the application of the person so charged."

(ii) Competence without the consent of the accused.—The accused's spouse is competent for a co-accused without the accused's consent in the cases mentioned in the Schedule to the Act of 1898 as amended, and in those covered by section 30 of the Theft Act, 1968. The effect of *Leach* v. *R.* is that he or she is not compellable in these cases.

The position with regard to sexual offences is not altogether free from doubt. Section 39 (1) of the Sexual Offences Act, 1956, states that the accused's spouse shall be competent though not compellable for the defence. Had the section stopped there, sexual offences would have had to be numbered among the cases in which the accused's spouse is competent

---

[1] [1912] A. C. 305. The views in the following paragraphs are those of Cohen, *Spouse Witnesses*. There is no direct authority on several points. DARLING, J. evidently considered that there were cases in which the accused's spouse is not compellable on his behalf and he must have had in mind cases coming within s. 1 of the Act of 1898. See *R.* v. *Acaster* (1912), 7 Cr. App. Rep. 187, where DARLING, J. said that he would warn a wife that she could not be obliged to give evidence when called by her husband in any case in which she is not a compellable witness. It was assumed in *R.* v. *Boal*, [1965] 1 Q. B. 402, at p. 416; [1964] 3 All E. R. 269, at p. 275, that the accused's spouse is a competent but not a compellable witness for the defence. The Sexual Offences Act, 1956, s. 39, expressly states that the accused's spouse is competent but not compellable. An argument in favour of compellability for the defence on charges of personal violence against a spouse could be based on the principle of reciprocity mentioned in *R.* v. *Sergeant* (1826), Ry. & M. 352, p. 148, *ante.*

[2] *R.* v. *Thompson* (1872), L. R. 1 C. C. R. 377.

for a co-accused without the consent of the accused. There is no doubt that they belonged to this category before the Act of 1956 came into force as they were included in the Schedule to the Criminal Evidence Act, 1898, and, under s. 4 of that statute, the accused's spouse is declared to be competent for the defence without the consent of the accused in the scheduled cases. But s. 39 (3) of the Sexual Offences Act, 1956, provides that:

> "This section shall not affect section 1 of the Criminal Evidence Act, 1898 or any case where the wife or husband of the accused may at common law be called as a witness without the consent of the accused."

The subsection may well have been intended simply to make it clear that the provisos to s. 1 of the Act of 1898 which deal with the cross-examination of the accused and the giving of unsworn evidence by him apply to charges under the Sexual Offences Act, but it may also be taken to mean that s. 1 (c) of the Act of 1898 applies to these charges with the result that in cases coming within the Sexual Offences Act, 1956 the accused's spouse is only a competent witness for a co-accused with the consent of the accused.[1] In that event, the Act of 1956 had changed the law with regard to sexual offences. Against this view it may be argued that someone who is giving evidence under the Sexual Offences Act is outside s. 1 (c) of the Act of 1898 because that proviso only applies to someone called as a witness in pursuance of that Act.

(iii) Cases in which the accused's spouse is compellable for a co-accused.—The accused's spouse is compellable for a co-accused in cases of public nuisance falling within the Evidence Act, 1877. This is the effect of the wording of that statute. In the absence of authority on the subject it may be assumed that the accused's spouse is also compellable for a co-accused in the cases of personal violence against the spouse together, possibly, with treason. So far as sexual offences are concerned the common law is expressly preserved by section 39 (3), and proviso (a) to section 30 (3) of the Theft Act, 1968, is to the same effect. Accordingly if A. and B. are charged with robbing Mrs. A., she is a compellable witness for the prosecution, A. and B.

E. DIVORCED SPOUSE TESTIFYING TO MATTERS OCCURRING DURING THE MARRIAGE [2]

The position of a divorced spouse must be considered separately because it is difficult to fit *Monroe* v. *Twistleton*[3] into the modern law and not altogether easy to point to a statute which has overruled the effect of that decision. It will be recollected that the common law rule as to incompetency was held to apply to a divorced spouse testifying to matters occurring during the marriage, and it will now be convenient to consider criminal and civil cases separately.

(1) Criminal Cases

It seems that, in criminal cases, the law governing the competence and

---

[1] Nokes, *An Introduction to Evidence* (3rd edition), 388; but see 4th edition, 394.

[2] There is no authority in a civil or criminal case concerning the competency of a divorced spouse to testify to matters occurring before his or her marriage to a party to the litigation. But *Monroe* v. *Twistleton* (1802), Peak Add. Cas. 219 may be thought to imply that, so far as all matters preceding the divorce are concerned, a divorced spouse is in the same position with regard to competence as a party's present spouse who is incompetent to testify to matters occurring before the marriage when incompetent to testify to matters occurring after the marriage. [3] *Supra.*

compellability of the accused's divorced spouse to testify to matters occurring during the marriage is identical with the law governing the competence and compellability of his or her present spouse. It must be admitted, however, that this statement is wholly dependent on inferences from the judgment of the Court of Criminal Appeal in *R.* v. *Algar* ;[1] there is no more direct authority.

Mr. Algar was charged with having forged his wife's signature on cheques in 1947 and 1948. The bank on which the cheques were drawn was the party defrauded by this conduct as Mrs. Algar's account had to be reimbursed to the extent of the proceeds of the forged cheques. In 1949, the marriage between Mr. and Mrs. Algar was annulled on the ground that it had been rendered voidable by the husband's impotence. At the trial in 1953 Mrs. Algar was called as a witness by the Crown, and the former husband was convicted, but his conviction was quashed by the Court of Criminal Appeal because she was incompetent to testify to things occurring during their marriage. The decision was based on *Monroe* v. *Twistleton* [2] as the court was not prepared to distinguish between a decree annulling a voidable marriage and a divorce decree. The decision would have been different if the marriage had been void,[3] or, as the law then stood, if Mrs. Algar, and not the bank, had been the party defrauded, for, in that event, she would have been held to be a competent and probably also a compellable witness as the case would have come within the Married Women's Property Act, 1884.[4]

R. v. *Algar* has been criticised.[5] Undoubtedly it would have added greatly to the sense and simplicity of the law to have overruled *Monroe* v. *Twistleton.* The overruling would have had to be justified by the change of attitude towards marriage and divorce for it was said in *Monroe* v. *Twistleton* that the decision would apply to a criminal case, and there does not appear to be any statute earlier than the Evidence Act, 1877, which has altered its effect on criminal proceedings. The Evidence Act, 1843, which abolished incompetency through interest in civil and criminal proceedings can hardly have abolished the incompetency of a divorced spouse to testify to matters occurring during the marriage because such a spouse was not an interested person at the moment when the issue of his or her competency would have arisen.[6]

The construction of the relevant statutory provisions in the case of a divorced spouse presents a problem. In the limited class of proceedings for public nuisance covered by the Evidence Act, 1877, the "wife" or "husband" of the defendant is admissible and compellable to give evidence; under the Criminal Evidence Act, 1898, the "wife" or "husband" of the accused is made a competent witness for the defence, and the same words, "wife" or "husband" are used in section 39 of the Sexual Offences Act, 1956, and section 30 of the Theft Act, 1968. It is submitted that, in these statutory

---

[1] [1954] 1 Q. B. 279; [1953] 2 All E. R. 1381.
[2] Counsel for the Crown conceded the incompetence of a divorced wife to testify to matters occurring during the marriage in such cases and Lord GODDARD referred to *Monroe* v. *Twistleton* (*supra*) as a decision which has been followed again and again.
[3] *Wells* v. *Fisher* (1831), 1 Mood. & R. 99.
[4] Repealed by the Theft Act, 1968, under which she would now, on the facts supposed, be a competent witness for the prosecution.
[5] See [1959] Crim. L. R. 685.
[6] The second report of the Commissioners on Common Law Practice assumed that *Monroe* v. *Twistleton* was still law after the Act of 1843 had come into effect.

provisions, the expressions "husband" and "wife" may be taken to include a divorced husband or wife testifying to matters occurring during the marriage.

A possible argument against the above submission is that, in s. 1 (d) of the Criminal Evidence Act, 1898, the words "husband" and "wife" may have to be construed so as to exclude a divorced spouse. Under proviso (d):

> "no husband shall be compellable to disclose any communication made to him by his wife during the marriage, and no wife shall be compellable to disclose any communication made to her by her husband during the marriage."

The civil case of *Shenton* v. *Tyler*,[1] turning on the repealed but identically worded provision of the Evidence Amendment Act, 1853, decided that the words "husband" and "wife" did not include a widow or divorced person even when they are being questioned concerning matters occurring during the marriage. It is difficult to see why section 1 (d) of the Criminal Evidence Act, 1898, should be construed differently, and, if *Monroe* v. *Twistleton* must be fitted into the modern criminal law, it is necessary to hold that in the earlier parts of the Act of 1898, "husband" and "wife" include a divorced spouse testifying to matters occurring during the marriage.

(2) CIVIL CASES

It is generally assumed that *Monroe* v. *Twistleton* is no longer law so far as civil cases are concerned. It is certainly difficult to believe that a modern court would hold the divorced wife of a party incompetent to testify concerning a contract made by her former husband during his marriage to her; but how is such a result to be avoided? One view would be that it cannot be avoided because *Monroe* v. *Twistleton*, vested with the authority of the Court of Criminal Appeal, if not the House of Lords,[2] still governs the case; but the absurdity of a law of evidence according to which the present spouse of a party to civil proceedings is both competent and compellable while a divorced spouse is not even competent is sufficient to raise the gravest doubts concerning the soundness of this view. Assuming that the Evidence Act, 1843, did not overrule *Monroe* v. *Twistleton*,[3] the only alternative is to hold that, so far as civil cases are concerned, *Monroe* v. *Twistleton* has been overruled by the Evidence Amendment Act, 1853 s. 1. This rendered the "husbands" and "wives" of parties competent and compellable, and it is submitted that the words "husband" and "wife" must be given an extended meaning to cover a divorced spouse testifying to matters occurring during the marriage.[4]

Section 3 of the Act of 1853 conferred a privilege against the disclosure of marital communications in terms identical with those of proviso (d) to section 1 of the Criminal Evidence Act, 1898. In *Shenton* v. *Tyler*[5] it was

---

[1] [1939] Ch. 620. This aspect of the decision was neither approved nor disapproved by the House of Lords in *Rumping* v. *Director of Public Prosecutions*, [1964] A. C. 814; [1962] 3 All E. R. 256.

[2] The case was mentioned, although its present status was not considered, in *Rumping* v. *Director of Public Prosecutions, supra.*

[3] To hold that it did would entail the conclusion that *R.* v. *Algar* was wrongly decided.

[4] To obviate the effect of *O'Connor* v. *Marjoribanks* (1842), 4 Man. & G. 435, the words must also be taken to include a widow or widower testifying to matters occurring during the marriage when proceedings are brought against his or her deceased spouse's estate.

[5] [1939] Ch. 620.

held that a widow could be obliged to disclose a communication made to her by her husband during their marriage, and it was said that the disclosure of such a communication could also be compelled in the case of a divorced person. In civil no less than in criminal cases, it seems to be necessary to construe the words "husband" and "wife" in different senses in different parts of the same statute. In both instances the artificiality is due to the failure of the Court of Criminal Appeal to overrule *Monroe* v. *Twistleton* when the opportunity presented itself.

Lest the construction of section 1 of the Evidence Act, 1853, suggested above should prove to be unacceptable, a statutory provision placing the matter beyond doubt may be thought to be desirable. Subject to this relatively minor point, there is no case for any reform in the law relating to the competence and compellability of the parties' spouses in civil cases: but it would be a bold man who would say the same of the law governing the position of the accused's spouse in a criminal case.

F. THE NEED FOR REFORM OF THE LAW RELATING TO THE COMPETENCE AND COMPELLABILITY OF THE ACCUSED'S SPOUSE

A brief consideration of the reasons for the old common law disability of the spouses of the parties may serve as an introduction to this question.

One reason mentioned in the cases is the unity of husband and wife. All that need be said on this subject is that the doctrine can produce specimens of reasoning in the law of evidence which are as absurd as those produced by it in other branches of the law.[1] A second reason which was obviously relevant under the old law was that a party's spouse would usually be interested in the outcome of the proceedings, but this could not have been the sole ground of the disability. In *Stapleton* v. *Crofts*,[2] for instance, it was held that the abolition of incompetence through interest by the Evidence Act, 1843, and the extension of its provisions to the parties in civil cases by the Evidence Act, 1851, did not have the effect of rendering the spouse of a party a competent witness in a civil suit. Thirdly, there is the possibility that one spouse will be biassed in favour of the other,[3] but this is pre-eminently a matter which should concern the weight rather than the competence of testimony. Next there is the danger that marital peace and the confidential nature of the marriage relationship will be unduly disturbed if spouses are allowed to testify against each other. This is stressed in some of the old English judgments and, as recently as 1958, the United States Supreme Court held the accused's spouse to be an incompetent witness for the prosecution because "Adverse testimony given in criminal proceedings would . . . be likely to destroy any marriage."[4] Finally, there is the necessity of paying due regard to public opinion. It is most important that the rules of evidence should meet with general esteem, but, although public opinion might be horrified by the spectacle

---

[1] See for example *R.* v. *Neal and Taylor* (1835), 7 C. & P. 168. Holding that a wife cannot corroborate an accomplice because "the wife and accomplice must be taken as one for this purpose".

[2] (1852), 18 Q. B. 367.

[3] Mentioned in *Davis* v. *Dinwoody* (1792), 4 Term Rep. 678.

[4] *Hawkins* v. *U.S.*, 358 U.S. 74, at p. 87, *per* BLACK, J. Under r. 501 of the Federal Rules the accused has in general a privilege to prevent his spouse from testifying against him.

of one spouse being compelled to testify against the other, the number of objections to his or her being at liberty to do so would surely not be large.

It is in the light of the considerations mentioned in the last paragraph that the proposals with regard to spouse witnesses mentioned in the 11th Report of the Criminal Law Revision Committee[1] must be judged. Each of them is open to criticism, but it is submitted that they should all be adopted. The proposals are (i) that the accused's spouse should be a competent witness for the prosecution in all cases in which they are not jointly charged and compellable in cases of assault or threats of violence against the other spouse or against a member of the accused's household under 16 together with sexual offences against such a person; (ii) that the accused's spouse should be a compellable witness for him in all cases in which they are not jointly charged; (iii) that the accused's spouse should be competent, without the accused's consent, for a co-accused in all cases and compellable where he or she would be compellable for the prosecution; (iv) that a divorced spouse should be competent and compellable as if he or she had never been married to the accused.

The only valid criticism of the first proposal is that mentioned by the United States Supreme Court, but can it be seriously maintained that many marriages would be saved from destruction if persons who were willing and anxious to do so were restrained from testifying against their spouse? The extension of the present law of compellability is fairly minimal and surely in the best interests of the minors concerned. The only valid criticism of the second proposal is that it could lead to a spouse being confronted with the disagreeable choice between committing perjury and incriminating the accused; but this is more than outweighed by the sense of grievance which an accused must occasionally experience on account of his inability to compel his spouse to give evidence under the present law. As to the third proposal, it might be said that an accused who feared that his spouse might incriminate him while exculpating his co-accused should have the power to restrain him or her from giving evidence for the co-accused, but the right balance between this point and fairness to the co-accused seems to be struck by leaving the decision whether to testify to the accused's spouse. The only objection to making the divorced spouse of the accused competent and compellable on all matters for all parties is the possibility that untrue evidence would be given on behalf of of the prosecution out of spite towards the accused but this is a risk which is well worth taking for the sake of avoiding preposterous decisions such as that in *R.* v. *Algar*.[2]

G. OTHER RELATIONSHIPS

It is curious that there never seems to have been any pressure in this country for a change in the law under which parents and children are competent and compellable against each other; in Israel this is, generally speaking, not the case.[3]

H. THE SOVEREIGN AND DIPLOMATS

It goes without saying that the sovereign is not a compellable witness.

---

[1] Paras. 153–7.
[2] [1954] 1 Q. B. 279; [1953] 2 All E. R. 1381.
[3] Evidence Ordinance, 1971, clause 4.

The same applies to heads of other sovereign states, because they are not subject to legal process. Under various statutes diplomatic and consular officials, and officials of, and other persons connected with, certain international organisations, enjoy total or partial immunity from compellability to give evidence.[1]

J. BANKERS

Reference must finally be made to the limited immunity enjoyed by bankers under the Bankers Books Evidence Act, 1879. Section 6 provides that a banker or officer of a bank shall not, in any legal proceeding to which the bank is not a party, be compellable to produce any banker's book the contents of which can be proved under this Act, or to appear as a witness to prove the matters, transactions and accounts therein recorded, unless by order of a judge made for special cause. The object of this statute is to save the time of bankers and protect them and their customers from the inconvenience of producing the originals of their books. We shall see in Chapter XXI that, although it is sufficient to produce a copy of a public document to the court, the original of a private document has to be produced as a general rule. Banker's books, apart from those of the Bank of England, rank as private documents, but the Act of 1879 provides for their proof by means of a copy. There are various safeguards which it is not necessary to mention, beyond saying that the authenticity of the copy can usually be established by affidavit, thus sparing any bank official the necessity of attending court.

SECTION 3. OATH, AFFIRMATION AND UNSWORN EVIDENCE

We saw in section 1 that the law with regard to the swearing of witnesses developed from the notion that only those who were prepared to testify on oath on the Gospel were competent witnesses, but that other forms of oath and affirmation were gradually permitted. It is now necessary to say something more about each of these matters.

A. OATH AND AFFIRMATION

The Oaths Act, 1838, permits an oath to be administered in such form and with such ceremonies as the person taking it may declare to be binding upon him. The words to be used, and the procedure to be followed by the officer authorised to administer oaths are now prescribed by the Oaths Act, 1909. Under the Oaths Act, 1888, if someone objects to being sworn, and states as his ground for doing so either that he has no religious belief, or that the taking of an oath is contrary to his religious belief, he is permitted to make a solemn affirmation.

If a witness states that he is an agnostic and expresses a desire to affirm,

---

[1] See, in particular Diplomatic Privileges Act, 1964 (c. 81), s. 2 (1), Sch. 1, arts. 1, 31 (2), 37 (1), (2); Consular Relations Act, 1968 (c.18), s. 1 (1), Sch. 1, arts. 1 (1), 44, 58 (2); International Organisations Act, 1968 (c. 48); Diplomatic and Other Privileges Act, 1971 (c. 64), s. 4. I must acknowledge the assistance of G. V. Hart, late secretary of the Criminal Law Revision Committee, on this subject.

the judge ought not to refuse to allow him to do so on the ground that the witness expresses a belief in certain parts of the Gospel.[1]

If a witness affirms with wilful falsity, he is liable to be proceeded against and punished as if he had committed perjury. Once an oath has been duly administered, its validity is not affected by the fact that the person taking it had no religious belief. If the proposed witness has a religious belief which is not opposed to the taking of oaths but declines to say what form of oath binds him, he would still appear to be incompetent by virtue of the common law for no statute covers his case.[2] No doubt he would be guilty of contempt of court if his unco-operative attitude were prompted by a desire to avoid giving evidence, and, in an appropriate case, there might be an adjournment so that the witness could receive instruction with regard to the binding force of oaths. If a witness has a religious belief, but it is not reasonably practicable to swear him according to that belief because, for example, the book on which he wishes to be sworn is not available, the witness may be required to affirm.[3]

Although a majority of the Criminal Law Revision Committee advocated the abolition of the oath in favour of a declaration (subject of course to the same sanction in the event of falsity of that for perjury), no recommendation was made on account of the undesirability of a difference in this respect between civil and criminal proceedings. The Law Reform Committee was unwilling to report on the question of abolishing the oath in civil cases because they regarded the problem as a social one. There is the further point that oaths are used in many contexts other than that of litigation. The arguments for and against their employment in the latter are set out in paras. 279–81 of the 11th Report of the Criminal Law Revision Committee.

B. UNSWORN EVIDENCE

It is necessary to distinguish between the different classes of case in which unsworn evidence may be given.

(1) THE ACCUSED'S UNSWORN STATEMENT AT A CRIMINAL TRIAL [4]

The history of the accused's right to make an unsworn statement from the dock is connected with the history of his right to be represented by counsel. Representation by counsel was always permitted in the case of misdemeanours and, when the accused was so represented, he made answer to the charge through his counsel. Representation by counsel was not allowed in treason until 1695, and it was not allowed on a charge of felony until 1836. In these cases, as in the case of misdemeanours where he was unrepresented, the accused could answer the charge in his own words. He was allowed to do this at a trial for treason after 1695 even though he was represented by counsel. Immediately after 1836, a person charged with felony and represented by counsel was not allowed to make a statement himself,[5] but the practice varied and, before the Criminal

---

[1] *R.* v. *Clark*, [1962] 1 All E. R. 428.
[2] *Nash* v. *Ali Khan* (1892), 8 T. L. R. 444.
[3] Oaths Act, 1961, overruling the effect of *R.* v. *Pritam Singh*, [1958] 1 All E. R. 199; see also *R.* v. *Moore* (1892), 61 L. J. M. C. 80.
[4] Cowen and Carter. *Essays in the Law of Evidence*, Essay 7.
[5] See for example *R.* v. *Boucher*(1837), 8 C. & P. 141.

Evidence Act, 1898, came into force, it seems to have been customary to allow the accused to make an unsworn statement from the dock in all criminal cases whether or not he was represented by counsel.[1] This practice continued after the Act of 1898,[2] s. 1 (h) of which expressly provides that the right of the person charged to make a statement without being sworn shall not be affected. Anything that the accused has to say at the preliminary examination before a trial on indictment may be taken down and given in evidence at the trial,[3] and this is another way in which the accused's unsworn statement may be placed before the jury.

Both before and after the passing of the Act of 1898, different opinions have been expressed concerning the stage at which the accused's statement from the dock should be made.[4]

It is sometimes said that the accused's unsworn statement is not evidence in the case but something more like the arguments of counsel, the closest analogy being a speech in which it is suggested to the jury that certain things compatible with the accused's innocence might have happened.[5] It has, however, been held by the Court of Criminal Appeal that it is a misdirection to instruct the jury in these terms for, although the statement is clearly not evidence in the sense of sworn evidence that can be cross-examined, "it is evidence in the sense that the jury can give to it such weight as they think fit".[6] It is customary to remind the jury that they may take the statement into consideration when deciding whether they feel sure that the accused is guilty. If the statement were not evidence in the case, it could not serve to discharge an evidential burden resting on the accused but it has been suggested in a Tasmanian case[7] that it might, for example, constitute evidence of an accused's belief that a girl was above the age of sixteen. If the statement was not evidence in the case it would not necessarily be fatal to a conviction that the judge should have failed to put its contents to the jury or that it had not been included in the transcript of the proceedings, but these omissions have been held to be fatal to a conviction in an Irish case.[8]

---

[1] Stephen, *History of Criminal Law*, Vol. 1, p. 441.

[2] *R.* v. *Pope* (1902), 18 T. L. R. 717. See note by Sir Carleton Allen in 69 L. Q. R. 22 according to which it is common in summary cases for the accused to make an unsworn statement. Contrary to the English practice (for which see the contrast between Magistrates' Courts Rules, 1968, 13 (2) and 14 (2) stressed in *Aggas* v. *Aggas*, [1971] 2 All E. R. 1497) it has been held in South Australia that, when represented by counsel, the accused cannot make an unsworn statement in a summary case (*Lavender* v. *Peterick*, [1960] S. A. S. R. 108). Before the abolition of the right it has been held in New Zealand that the accused may make an unsworn statement although he calls witnesses (*R.* v. *Kerr*, [1953] N. Z. L. R. 75) although a contrary conclusion was reached in England before the Act of 1898 (*R.* v. *Millhouse* (1885), 15 Cox, C. C. 622).

[3] Criminal Justice Act, 1925, s. 12 (4).

[4] *R.* v. *Sheriff* (1903), 20 Cox 334 decides that the statement should be made before counsel for the prosecution sums up, and before the prisoner's counsel addresses the court. This may be taken to have settled the modern procedure. It has been held in South Australia that, though the statement may be read to the court by the accused, it may not be read for him by his counsel (*R* v. *Stuart*, [1959] S. A. S. R. 144). But see *R.* v. *Burles*, [1964] Tas. S. R. 256.

[5] *Shankley* v. *Hodgson*, [1962] Crim. L. R. 248; *R.* v. *Mackenna*, [1951] Q. S. R. 299; *R.* v. *Kerr*, [1953] N.Z.L.R. 75; but see *Peacock* v. *R.* (1911), 13 C. L. R. 619. The accused's unsworn statement is treated as evidence in South Africa: *R.* v. *Wooldridge*, 1956 (1) S. A. 5; *R.* v. *Cele*, 1959 (1) S. A. 245.

[6] *R.* v. *Frost; R.* v. *Hale* (1964), 48 Cr. App. Rep. 284. For the position before the Act of 1898 see *R.* v. *Shimmin* (1882), 15 Cox C. C. 122.

[7] *Masnec* v. *R.*, [1962] Tas. S. R. 254.

[8] *People (A. G.)* v. *Riordan*, [1948] I. R. 416. On the need for caution in directing the jury on the weight of the unsworn statement in a jurisdiction where judicial comment on the accused's failure to give evidence is prohibited see *Bridge* v. *R.* (1964), 38 A. L. J. R. 280.

The fact that the accused cannot be cross-examined on his unsworn statement means that it cannot be used as evidence against a co-prisoner for no statement made directly to the court can be evidence against a man unless he has an opportunity of cross-examining its maker.[1] The right to make an unsworn statement may be of some assistance to an accused with a record for it enables him to make animadversions on the witnesses for the prosecution without rendering himself liable to cross-examination on his previous convictions.[2] If the unsworn statement alludes to the accused's good character, the prosecution would presumably be allowed to give evidence of the accused's bad reputation in accordance with the principles discussed in Chapter XIV.

There remains the question whether, from the point of view of the proper administration of justice, any useful purpose is served by retaining the prisoner's right to make an unsworn statement. All that can be said is that it appears to be a harmless survival from a former age when it was a valuable concession. There are certainly more urgent cases for law reform than the repeal of s. 1 (h) of the Criminal Evidence Act, 1898. The question is linked with that of the extent to which pressure can properly be brought to bear on an accused against whom there is a case to answer to induce him to enter the witness box and that is considered in Chapter XV. The accused's right to make an unsworn statement has been abolished in New Zealand, and its abolition is recommended in the 11th Report of the Criminal Law Revision Committee.[3]

(2) Unsworn Evidence of Children

The unsworn evidence which children of tender years are allowed to give in criminal cases differs from the unsworn statement of the accused in two respects. In the first place the witness is liable to be prosecuted for giving wilfully false testimony, and secondly he is liable to be cross-examined. Furthermore there never has been any doubt that the child's testimony does constitute evidence in the case in which it is given although there is a statutory requirement that it should be corroborated in a material particular implicating the accused.

(3) Miscellaneous

The other cases in which a witness need not be sworn depend on the common law. Someone who simply produces a document pursuant to a *subpoena duces tecum* does not have to be sworn if there is another witness who can identify the document.[4] This means that the person producing it cannot be cross-examined. Another person who need not be sworn is the advocate giving evidence of the terms of a compromise reached between the parties to litigation in which he acted for one of them. It is customary for his statement to be made from the well of the court,[5] but the matter is dependent on convention and there is really no authority

---

[1] *Allen* v. *Allen*, [1894] P. 248; *R.* v. *Simpson*, [1956] V. L. R. 490.
[2] *Carroll* v. *R.*, [1964] Tas. S. R. 76 where, however, the imputations were made in counsel's speech.
[3] Paras. 102–6.
[4] *Perry* v. *Gibson* (1834), 1 Ad. & El. 48.
[5] *Hickman* v. *Berens*, [1895] 2 Ch. 638.   But see *Pioneer Concrete Gold Coast Pty., Ltd.* v. *Cassidy* (No. 2), [1969] Qd. R. 290.

on the question whether he can insist on his right not to take the oath.[1] Finally, it is said that if the sovereign were to give evidence she need not be sworn, but, in the absence of authority, there does not appear to be much point in making conjectures concerning the appropriate procedure in such a case.

---

[1] There are obvious objections to an advocate acting as a witness in a case in which he is professionally engaged (R. v. *Secretary of State for India, Ex parte Ezekiel*, [1941] 2 K. B. 169; [1941] 2 All E. R. 546); but it would probably be going too far to say that he is not a competent witness in such circumstances.

CHAPTER IX

CORROBORATION

The general rule of modern English law is that the court may act upon the uncorroborated testimony of one witness, and such requirements as there are concerning a plurality of witnesses, or some other confirmation of individual testimony are exceptional. This does not mean that the court must act upon the evidence of one witness, even if it is unshaken in cross-examination, and in no way discredited by the witness's demeanour. To quote Sir James Stephen:[1]

> "The circumstances may be such that there is no check on the witness and no power to obtain any further evidence on the subject. Under these circumstances juries may, and often do, acquit. They may very reasonably say we do not attach such credit to the oath of a single person of whom we know nothing, as to be willing to destroy another person on the strength of it. This case arises where the fact deposed to is a passing occurrence—such as a verbal confession or a sexual crime—leaving no trace behind it, except in the memory of an eye or ear-witness . . . The justification of this is, that the power of lying is unlimited, the causes of lying and delusion are numerous, and many of them are unknown, and the means of detection are limited."

It was to meet situations such as those which have just been mentioned that the judges developed rules of practice under which juries must be warned of the dangers of convicting on uncorroborated evidence. These rules are discussed in Section 1 together with the statutory provisions under which corroboration in some form or other is required as a matter of law. When corroboration is required as a matter of law, a conviction or finding of fact in its absence will necessarily be set aside by an appellate tribunal. On the other hand, when corroboration is required as a matter of practice, the greatest caution must be exercised in coming to a conclusion in its absence, but, provided due precautions have been taken, the conclusion cannot be assailed on legal grounds. Section 2 is concerned with the nature of corroboration—what does and does not constitute corroboration in the legal sense of the term.

The history of this subject is not without interest, for one of the great differences between the modern English law of evidence and that prescribed by the canon or civil law, which usually applied the maxim *testis unus testis nullus*, consists in the absence of any general requirement of a plurality of witnesses.[2] More than one oath helper was required when compurgation was among the standard methods of trial, so English law started with something like the requirements of a number of witnesses such as were demanded by the canon law under the influence of Roman law, although the compurgators were of course quite unlike the modern witness. The two systems diverged more or less completely when English jury trial

---

[1] *General view of the Criminal Law*, p. 249.
[2] There is a similar distinction between English and Scots law today.

began to assume its present form in the seventeenth century. Before that period, the jurors were themselves witnesses, rather than triers, of fact, so there was a sense in which it could be said that more than one witness was always necessary at a common law trial, and it is of some significance that Coke maintained that more than one witness was necessary in proceedings without a jury as where the validity of challenges fell to be determined. When the jurors ceased to resemble the modern witness, some efforts to impose rules requiring two or more witnesses were made by statute; but provisions of this nature were never generalised, and they are now of no importance.

The agreement of witnesses on matters of detail is often of the greatest significance, but, if it were invariably required, the testimony of one honourable man could not, as Napoleon observed, prove a single rascal guilty, though the testimony of two rascals could prove an honourable man guilty.[1] Rigid rules concerning the number of witnesses can hardly be justified as a matter of policy, although it is generally assumed there is a limited class of case in which some form of corroboration is desirable in the interests of justice. In all the situations which are about to be discussed, except the first, the required corroboration will not necessarily consist in the testimony of a second witness. It will often take this form, but an admission or letter will also suffice.

SECTION 1. WHEN CORROBORATION IS REQUIRED

A. STATUTORY PROVISIONS

(1) STATUTES REQUIRING TWO OR MORE WITNESSES

A few surviving criminal statutes provide that the accused can only be convicted on the oath of two or more credible witnesses. These include section 1 of the Treason Act, 1795, penalising the compassing of the death or restraint of the Queen, the Places of Religious Worship Act, 1812, dealing with the disturbance of religious meetings, and section 146 (5) of the Representation of the People Act, 1949 (replacing earlier legislation) dealing with impersonation at elections. These provisions are of no practical importance from the point of view of the general law of evidence, and their repeal is recommended in the 11th Report of the Criminal Law Revision Committee.

(2) SECTION 78A OF THE ROAD TRAFFIC REGULATIONS ACT, 1967

Under section 78A of the Road Traffic Regulations Act, 1967,[2] a person charged with the offence of driving a motor vehicle at a speed greater than the maximum allowed shall not be liable to be convicted solely on the evidence of one witness to the effect that in the opinion of the witness the person charged was driving the vehicle at such greater speed. The effect of this provision is that where the evidence is that of the opinion of witnesses concerning the speed at which the accused was travelling, there must be two or more of them, and it has been held that their opinion must concern the accused's speed over the same stretch of road at the same time. A.'s

---

[1] Cited IX *Wigmore*, p. 256, n. 3. The foregoing historical account is based on IX *Wigmore*, para. 2031.

[2] Inserted by section 203 of the Road Traffic Act, 1972, and re-enacting earlier legislation.

opinion that the accused was travelling at a particular speed in one place, and B.'s opinion that he was travelling at that speed a little further on will not suffice.[1] There may, however, be a conviction on the evidence of one witness if it amounts to something more than his opinion. In *Nicholas* v. *Penny*,[2] a police officer's evidence that he followed the accused in a police car and consulted its speedometer which showed an excessive speed was held to be sufficient. The speedometer reading is *prima facie* evidence of the speed recorded, although it is of course always open to the accused to raise a doubt whether the instrument was working properly. The reading is evidence of a fact, and not a statement of opinion. As a general rule the opinion of witnesses who are not experts is excluded, but we shall see in Chapter XVI that it is admissible in a number of cases in which its exclusion would be absurd. Estimates of the speed at which a vehicle was travelling are among these cases, but the fact that such estimates are more liable to be inaccurate than testimony concerning direct perception amply justifies the provisions of section 78A of the Road Traffic Regulations Act, 1967.

(3) PERJURY

Under s. 13 of the Perjury Act, 1911, a person shall not be liable to be convicted of any offence against this Act, or of any offence declared by any other Act to be perjury or subornation of perjury, or to be punishable as perjury or subornation of perjury solely upon the evidence of one witness as to the falsity of any statement alleged to be false. This confirmed the common law as settled in *R.* v. *Muscot*,[3] but the reason for the rule given in that case—"else there is only oath against oath"—is open to question because it would justify a requirement of corroboration in any number of situations in which it is not necessary as a matter of law or practice. There is an historical basis for the rule in the fact that perjury was originally punished in the Star Chamber—a court whose procedure was to some extent influenced by the civil law which, as we have seen, usually applied the principle that the testimony of one witness is insufficient. The require-ment of corroboration in the case of perjury and kindred offences may also be justified on the ground that nothing must be allowed to discourage witnesses from testifying, and the fact that a conviction for perjury might be secured on the oath of one witness could have this effect. A second witness to the falsity of the impugned statement is, however, not essential. A letter, the authenticity of which is duly proved or admitted, and which might be construed as a subornation to someone else to commit perjury in relation to the same matter will suffice.[4] If all that is proved is that the accused contradicted the impugned statement, there is not enough evidence to support a conviction for nothing more is established than that one of two allegations made by the accused is untrue. Additional evidence, such as the repetition of the contradiction of the impugned statement on a number of occasions to different people, will, however, be sufficient.[5]

According to para. 192 of the 11th Report of the Criminal Law Revision

---

[1] *Brighty* v. *Pearson*, [1938] 4 All E. R. 127.
[2] [1950] 2 K. B. 466; [1950] 2 All E. R. 89, where earlier decisions are reviewed.
[3] (1713), 10 Mod. Rep. 192.   [4] *R.* v. *Threlfall* (1914), 10 Cr. App. Rep. 112.
[5] *R.* v. *Hook* (1858), Dears. & B. 606. See also *R.* v. *Harris* (1822), 5 B. & Ald. 926; *R.* v. *Knill* (1822), 5 B. & Ald. 929, n.; *R.* v. *Yates* (1841), Car. & M. 132; *R.* v. *Parker* (1842), Car. & M. 639; *R.* v. *Wheatland* (1838), 8 C. & P. 238; *R.* v. *Mayhew* (1834), 6 C. & P. 315; and *R.* v. *Atkinson* (1934), 24 Cr. App. Rep. 123.

Committee, the provision in section 13 of the Act of 1911 that a person is not liable to conviction "solely upon the evidence of one witness as to the falsity of any statement alleged to be false" is treated, "rightly or wrongly", as requiring that a second witness should give evidence from his own knowledge of the falsity of the statement in question, at any rate where the falsity is not proved by the production of letters or repeated contradictions. Accordingly it is said not to be enough that a second witness should simply prove that the accused admitted the falsity of the statement. The Committee accordingly recommends an amendment of section 13 according to which the accused shall not be liable to be convicted on the evidence of one witness only as to the falsity of the statement in question "unless the evidence is corroborated in some material particular by other evidence". The Committee also recommends, as does the Law Commission, that the requirement of corroboration should be confined to perjury in judicial proceedings and should not, like the present law, apply to such other offences under the Act of 1911 as the making of false statutory declarations.[1] This is because the encouragement of people to testify without fear of too easy a prosecution is regarded as the justification of the requirement of corroboration.

(4) Procuration

Ss. 2–4 and 22 and 23 of the Sexual Offences Act, 1956,[2] which punish such offences as the procuration of girls for the purpose of prostitution, provide that no person shall be convicted of any offence under them upon the evidence of one witness, unless the witness be corroborated in some material particular by evidence implicating the accused. The requirement that the corroborating evidence must implicate the accused in a material particular is characteristic of several statutory provisions as well as the common law rules of practice on the subject. As will be explained more fully in the discussion of the evidence of accomplices, it is not enough that that which is relied on should confirm some part of the testimony of the witness to be corroborated, it must do so in relation to that part of the testimony which implicates the accused.[3] Procuration belongs to the class of charges which are easy to make and difficult to rebut. Moreover, the chief witness for the prosecution is usually the girl procured who cannot be numbered among the most reliable accusers, so the requirement of corroboration in this instance may be thought to be justified on the score of public policy.

(5) Unsworn Evidence of Children

We saw in the last chapter that a child is allowed to give unsworn evidence in criminal cases (and criminal cases only) provided it is of sufficient intelligence and understands the duty of speaking the truth. This is the effect of s. 38 of the Children and Young Persons Act, 1933. It is subject to the proviso that:

"where evidence admitted by virtue of this section is given on behalf of the prosecution the accused shall not be liable to be convicted of the offence unless

---

[1] 11th Report of the Criminal Law Revision Committee, para. 191.
[2] Re-enacting the Criminal Law Amendment Act, 1885, as subsequently amended.
[3] *R. v. Goldstein* (1914), 11 Cr. App. Rep. 27. Other cases on these sections are *R. v. Staub* (1909), 2 Cr. App. Rep. 6, and *R. v. Cohen* (1909), 3 Cr. App. Rep. 234.

that evidence is corroborated by some other material evidence in support thereof implicating him".

The unreliability of witnesses of tender years is the justification of this proviso; even if such a witness has a sufficient understanding of the nature of an oath to enable his or her evidence to be sworn, the jury must be warned of the danger of acting on it without corroboration.

The construction of the proviso to section 38 is not free from difficulty, but it has been clarified by the House of Lords in *Director of Public Prosecutions* v. *Hester*.[1] On a very literal construction the proviso could mean that, if a child gives unsworn uncorroborated evidence, there cannot be a conviction whatever the other evidence in the case may be. If this were the right view, a conviction of burglary based on the sworn evidence of two adults that they saw the accused enter a house empty handed and emerge therefrom carrying a bag full of silver, together with the uncorroborated evidence of an unsworn child that the accused made him a present of a silver spoon proved to belong to the householder, would have to be quashed; but, in the words of Lord DIPLOCK, "so preposterous an intention cannot reasonably be ascribed to Parliament".[2] On a broad construction, the proviso could mean that all that is required is corroboration of the evidence of the unsworn child by other material evidence from any source, including another unsworn child; but the House held that "other material evidence" means evidence admitted otherwise than by virtue of section 38. In the words of Viscount DILHORNE, "the effect of the proviso is to secure that no person is liable to be convicted solely on unsworn testimony."[3] The House thus confirmed a dictum in *R.* v. *Campbell*,[4] which had not gone unchallenged, to the effect that, as a matter of law, the unsworn evidence of one child might corroborate the sworn evidence of another, and *vice versa*. A particularly careful warning should, it was said in *R.* v. *Campbell* be given in such a case of the danger of acting on the evidence of children, and, on the particular facts of *Hester's Case*, the prosecution did not seek to uphold the conviction which had been quashed by the Court of Appeal.

The decision of the House of Lords is of some theoretical interest in relation to corroboration generally because it gets rid of a supposed ban on what had come to be called "mutual corroboration" on the strength of the following words of Lord HEWART, C.J., in *R.* v. *Manser*:[5]

> "Let it be granted that the evidence of Barbara [the elder child witness for the prosecution who was probably sworn] has to be corroborated: it is corroborated by the evidence of Doris [the younger child witness who was unsworn]. She, however, also needs to be corroborated. The answer is that she is corroborated by the evidence of Barbara, and that is called 'mutual corroboration'.
> "In truth and in fact the evidence of the girl Doris ought to have been obliterated altogether from the case, inasmuch as it was not corroborated."

This is an example of lawyers' pseudo-logic which unfortunately does not stand alone in the law of evidence; it is a pedantry so far as any layman is concerned and sheer nonsense to the reflective layman. If you believe what A. says but think, at the same time, that it would be dangerous to act on it without confirmation because the very young are inclined to be

---

[1] [1973] A. C. 296, at p. 303.　　　　　[2] At p. 323.
[3] At p. 318.　　　　[4] [1956] 2 Q. B. 432, at p. 438.
[5] (1934), 25 Cr. App. Rep. 18, at p. 20. The decision is overruled by *Hester's Case*.

inaccurate and over-imaginative, it is neither illogical nor nonsensical to treat the evidence of B. who is also very young but which you also believe as something which enables you to act on A.'s evidence with more confidence than would have been the case if such evidence had stood alone. Of course there can be no question of looking for corroboration of evidence which you don't believe or of finding corroboration in such evidence. To quote Lord MORRIS OF BORTH-Y-GEST:

> "The essence of corroborative evidence is that one creditworthy witness confirms what another creditworthy witness has said."[1]

This is not to deny the possibility, or even the desirability, of rules of law based on policy considerations according to which certain types of evidence which require corroboration, or are considered dangerous to act on in its absence, cannot corroborate evidence of a similar type. The House of Lords has, as we have just seen, construed the proviso to section 38 of the Children and Young Persons Act, 1933, as imposing such a rule in the case of the unsworn evidence of children of tender years, and we shall see that a similar rule still exists at common law with regard to the evidence of certain classes of accomplice.

(6) AFFILIATION

Under section 4 of the Affiliation Proceedings Act, 1957, as amended by the Affiliation Proceedings Amendment Act, 1972, the court shall not adjudge the defendant to be the putative father of the child in a case where evidence is given by the mother unless her evidence is corroborated in some material particular by other evidence to the court's satisfaction.[2] The fact that the charge is easy to make and difficult to refute is generally regarded as sufficient justification of the requirement as to corroboration.

It is difficult to say more by way of generalisation with regard to the nature of the corroboration required in affiliation proceedings than that it must implicate the alleged putative father in a material particular.[3] His admitted intercourse [4] or acts of familiarity [5] with the child's mother have been held to amount to corroboration although they took place some time before conception; the fact that he and the woman were intimately associated during the period in which conception must have occurred, being seen together in public houses and cinemas has likewise been held sufficient in the absence of any evidence of the mother's association with other men.[6] Attempts to suborn witnesses can amount to corroboration,[7] as may the making of false charges against the respondent of intercourse with other men.[8] False denials of significant incidents deposed to by the mother may, amount to corroboration of her testimony; a false denial of the opportunity of intercourse could, for instance, justify an inference that advantage was

---

[1] [1973] A. C. 296, at p. 315.
[2] See also Affiliation Proceedings Act, 1957, s. 8 (as amended by the Affiliation Proceedings Act, 1972) and *Whitton* v. *Garner*, [1965] 1 All E. R. 70 (corroboration unnecessary of allegation that complainant single).
[3] *Thomas* v. *Jones*, [1921] 1 K. B. 22, at pp. 44-45, *per* ATKIN, L.J.
[4] *Simpson* v. *Collinson*, [1964] 2 Q. B. 80; [1964] 1 All E. R. 262.
[5] *Cole* v. *Manning* (1877), 2 Q. B. D. 611.
[6] *Moore* v. *Hewitt*, [1947] K. B. 831; [1947] 2 All E. R. 270.
[7] *Mahoney* v. *Wright*, [1943] S. A. S. R. 61.
[8] *Mash* v. *Darley*, [1914] 3 K. B. 1226, described in *Cracknell* v. *Smith*, *infra*, as illustrating the high water mark of what can amount to corroboration.

in fact taken of that opportunity.[1] The mere fact of opportunity, as where the man and the mother were seen together in a barn to which they had to resort in the course of their employment as farm-hands will not suffice,[2] any more than the fact that the man allowed the mother, who was his housekeeper, to remain in his house for five weeks after the birth of the child,[3] or the fact that the man had falsely denied that he had had an interview with the mother some three months after the conception of the child. Neither the respondent's failure to give evidence nor the fact that his brother gave false evidence of intercourse with the mother corroborates her testimony;[4] nor do the mother's complaints to others about the conduct of the alleged putative father.[5]

At one time, difficulty was experienced with regard to letters from the alleged putative father to the mother. If they can fairly be treated as an admission of paternity, or even of intercourse, they are the best possible corroboration provided their authenticity is duly proved. This can be effected by evidence of handwriting and there is no difficulty when the writing is admitted by the respondent, or proved by some witness other than the applicant; but what if hers is the only testimony as to the respondent's handwriting? In *Moore* v. *Hewitt*[6] this was held not to constitute corroboration of the rest of her testimony although the contents of the letter compromised its author. This case was, however, overruled in *Jeffery* v. *Johnson*,[7] on the ground that, once the handwriting is proved, the contents of the letter prove themselves and amount to a separate item of evidence—an admission receivable under an exception to the rule against hearsay.

B. RULES OF PRACTICE

In the five cases mentioned below, the dangers of coming to a conclusion on uncorroborated evidence have been stressed by the judges. Where there is a jury, the judge must warn them of the danger of acting on uncorroborated evidence, and, where there is no jury the tribunal must warn itself of this danger. Subject to the requirement of a warning, both judge alone and jury are entitled to act on uncorroborated evidence.

(1) ACCOMPLICES

The desirability of some form of corroboration of the evidence of an accomplice of the accused has been stressed at criminal trials for a hundred years and more, but, down to 1954, the cases showed that two schools of thought existed on the subject. According to one school, it lay in the judge's discretion whether the jury were warned of the desirability of corroboration, while the other school insisted that the warning must be given. In

---

[1] *Corfield* v. *Hodgson*, [1966] 2 All E. R. 205; *Jones* v. *Thomas*, [1934] 1 K. B. 323; *Ridley* v. *Whipp* (1916), 22 C. L. R. 381; *Pitman* v. *Byrne*, [1926] S. A. S. R. 207; *Popovic* v. *Derks*, [1961] V. L. R. 413, where the authorities are exhaustively reviewed by SHOLL, J.
[2] *Burbury* v. *Jackson*, [1917] 1 K. B. 16; it might have been different if they had been seen together in a wood or some other dark place. *Cracknell* v. *Smith*, [1960] 3 All E. R. 569 (visits to girl's house and walks with her alone insufficient).
[3] *Thomas* v. *Jones*, [1921] 1 K. B. 22.
[4] *Cracknell* v. *Smith*, [1960] 3 All E. R. 569.
[5] *Luther* v. *Ryan* (1956), 3 D. L. R. (2d) 693.
[6] [1947] K. B. 831; [1947] 2 All E. R. 270.
[7] [1952] 2 Q. B. 8; [1952] 1 All E. R. 450.

Davies v. *The Director of Public Prosecutions* [1] the House of Lords settled this point in favour of what may be described as the "peremptory" school.

> "In a criminal trial where a person who is an accomplice gives evidence on behalf of the prosecution, it is the duty of the judge to warn the jury that, although they may convict upon his evidence, it is dangerous to do so unless it is corroborated. This rule, although a rule of practice, now has the force of a rule of law. Where the judge fails to warn the jury in accordance with this rule, the conviction will be quashed, even if, in fact, there be ample corroboration of the evidence of the accomplice, unless the Appellate Court can apply the proviso to s. 4 (1) of the Criminal Appeal Act, 1907." [2]

The danger that the accomplice will minimise his role in the crime and exaggerate that of the accused is the usual justification for the requirement of caution in such a case, although some writers consider that the requirement of the warning has become a mystique in the administration of justice and that the question whether the warning is given should depend on the facts of each case.[3] It will be observed that the passage which has just been quoted refers to an accomplice giving evidence on behalf of the prosecution. One of two co-prisoners may incriminate the other when giving evidence on his own behalf. On principle there does not appear to be any good reason for distinguishing the case in which an accomplice gives evidence on his own behalf from that in which he testifies on behalf of the prosecution. If there should, as a matter of law, be a warning of the dangers of acting on the uncorroborated evidence of the accomplice in the one case, it should be equally necessary in the other; but it is still treated merely as a matter of practice that it is desirable to warn the jury that, when an accused testifies in-chief or under cross-examination by the prosecution against a co-accused, he may well have an interest of his own to serve.[4]

It is now necessary to consider who is an accomplice for the purposes of the rule requiring a warning when the witness is called on behalf of the prosecution, the respective functions of the judge and jury in determining this question, and what constitutes corroboration of an accomplice's evidence.

(i) Who is an accomplice.[5]—In *Davies* v. *D.P.P.* it was recognised that the accomplice warning must be given with regard to the evidence of the following classes of witness when called by the Crown: (a) *participes criminis*, whether as principals and accessories before or after the fact in the case of felonies, or as persons committing, procuring, aiding or abetting a misdemeanour; (b) receivers giving evidence at the trial of those alleged to have stolen the goods received by them;[6] the crimes are intimately allied and the relationship is that of "one-sided dependence"—there could

---

[1] [1954] A. C. 378; [1954] 1 All E. R. 507, discussed by Edwards, *Accomplices in Crime*, Criminal Law Review (1954), 324. See Addendum, *ante*.

[2] At pp. 399, 513, respectively, *per* Lord SIMONDS, L.C.

[3] See article by Glanville Williams, Criminal Law Review (1962), p. 588. There is no corresponding requirement in the Model Code Uniform and Federal Rules; although there are stringent requirements with regard to corroboration under the laws of some States.

[4] *R.* v. *Prater*, [1960] 2 Q. B. 464; [1960] 1 All E. R. 298; *R.* v. *Stannard*, [1965] 2 Q. B. 1; [1964] 1 All E. R. 34; *R.* v. *Russell* (1968), 52 Cr. App. Rep. 147; *R.* v. *Carey* and *R.* v. *Williams* (1968), 52 Cr. App. Rep. 305. For earlier authorities see *R.* v. *Heathfield* (1923), 17 Cr. App. Rep. 80; *R.* v. *Barrow* (1934), 24 Cr. App. Rep. 141; *R.* v. *Rudd* (1948), 32 Cr. App. Rep. 138; *R.* v. *Barnes*, [1940] 2 All E. R. 229 (the strongest against the warning when the accomplice is a co-accused); *R.* v. *Teitler*, [1959] V. R. 321; *R.* v. *Anthony*, [1962] V. R. 440.

[5] The Anglo-American and Commonwealth authorities are helpfully reviewed in an article by Professor Heydon, [1973] Crim. L. R. 264.

[6] *R.* v. *Jennings* (1912), 7 Cr. App. Rep. 242; *R.* v. *Dixon* (1925), 19 Cr. App. Rep.

not be a receiver unless the goods had first been stolen; (c) the parties to other crimes alleged to have been committed by the accused, when evidence of such crimes is received on the ground that it is of particular relevance or that it tends to prove something more than mere criminal propensity.[1] Presumably, in spite of the abolition of the distinction between felonies and misdemeanours by section 1 of the Criminal Law Act, 1967, and the provision that the old law and practice with regard to misdemeanours should prevail, a corroboration warning is still necessary in the case of prosecution witnesses who have impeded the apprehension or trial of someone charged with an arrestable offence. This would seem to be required by Lord SIMONDS's speech, although the case for treating these witnesses, like that for treating the old accessory after the fact, as an accomplice, may be thought to be a weak one because it would so often be in their interest to give evidence tending to show that the principal offence had not been committed.[2]

Davies's case was treated as one in which there was no evidence that the witness was an accomplice, so an appeal which was primarily based on the absence of a warning against the danger of acting on his testimony without corroboration was dismissed. Davies was charged with murder by knifing the deceased. He and the witness were members of a gang who had assaulted the deceased—an offence for which the witness had been convicted, but the witness had desisted from the attack by the time the knife was used, and there was no evidence that he had previously been aware of Davies's possession of such a weapon. Although the judgment embodies the previous case law on the question of who is an accomplice, it is arguable that the principle which underlies the rule that the warning should be given covers all parties to the transaction in the course of which the crime is committed. In the words of an Australian judge (SHOLL, J.):

> "The temptation to exaggerate or make false accusations would appear to be much more related to the nature and possible punishment of the offence than to its technical identity with that alleged against the accused."

If SHOLL, J., had been free to do so, he would have held the true principle to be that:

> "that person is an accomplice within the common law rule who is charged in relation to the same events as those founding the charge against the accused with an offence (whether the same offence or not) of such a character, that he would be, if convicted thereof, liable to such punishment, as might possibly tempt that person to exaggerate or fabricate evidence as to the guilt of the accused".[3]

The mere fact that the witness has already been acquitted or convicted ought not to relieve the judge from the necessity of giving the warning because the witness's evidence at his trial may have been affected by the consideration mentioned by SHOLL, J., and it is likely that he would adhere to it on a subsequent occasion. *Davies* v. *D.P.P.* at least lends no countenance to the view that the fact that the witness has already been acquitted or convicted of the offence for which the prisoner is being tried can have any bearing on the question whether the warning should be given.

---

[1] *R.* v. *Farid* (1945), 30 Cr. App. Rep. 168.

[2] This point is stressed in *Khan* v. *R.*, [1971] W. A. R. 44, where the point is also made that Lord SIMONDS's definition of an accomplice may be too narrow because it does not cover the case of a witness liable to be convicted of a crime of which the accused could have been convicted on the particular indictment.

[3] *McNee* v. *Kay*, [1953] V. L. R. 520, at p. 530.

An agent provocateur or spy is not an accomplice,[1] however much his activities may be deplored. The youthful victim of a sexual offence is not an accomplice, nor is a woman on whose immoral earnings the accused is charged with having lived,[2] although a lot may depend upon the particular facts.

The terms of Lord SIMONDS's speech in *Davies's* case do not favour an extension of the meaning of "accomplice" in this context. It does not suggest that thieves are to be regarded as the accomplices of receivers to whom stolen goods are passed on, and there are undoubtedly cases in which it would be wrong to treat the thief as an accomplice. For example, if A. and B. steal something and C. is charged with receiving it from B., there may be good reason for treating B. as C.'s accomplice at C.'s trial, but there would be no reason for treating A. as C.'s accomplice.[3] But there seems to be every reason for treating the thief from whom the accused receives goods as an accomplice in all cases, and some recent judgments support this approach.[4]

(ii) Functions of judge and jury and direction of judge to jury.— It is at least arguable that it would be best if the question whether a witness is an accomplice were always to be decided by the judge, but such a view is untenable in the light of Lord SIMONDS's speech. It was said in *Davies's case* that the question whether a witness is an accomplice is often answered by his own confession or plea of guilty, or by the fact that he has been convicted of the crime under consideration, otherwise it is for the judge to rule whether there is evidence that the witness is an accomplice, while the jury must decide whether this is so in fact, the judge having warned them against the danger of convicting on the witness's uncorroborated evidence if they come to the conclusion that he was an accomplice.

It seems that there are three possible situations. In the first place there may be no sufficient evidence that the witness was an accomplice in which case the judge is not required to say anything to the jury with regard to corroboration, and this was held to be the position in *Davies's* case itself. In the second place, the question whether the witness was an accomplice may have to be left to the jury with a warning that, if they think he was, they should be cautious before convicting in the absence of corroboration. Finally, it may occasionally be the duty of the judge to direct the jury that a particular witness is an accomplice and, according to an Irish decision, this may be so in cases other than those mentioned above in which the question whether he is an accomplice has been answered by the witness

---

[1] *R. v. Mullins* (1848), 3 Cox C. C. 526; *R. v. Bickley* (1909), 2 Cr. App. Rep. 53; *Sneddon* v. *Stevenson*, [1967] 2 All E. R. 1277; *Dental Board* v. *O'Callaghan*, [1969] I. R. 181; *R. v. Phillips*, [1963] N. Z. L. R. 855.

[2] *R. v. Pitts* (1912), 8 Cr. App. Rep. 126 and *R. v. Tatam* (1921), 15 Cr. App. Rep. 132 (child victims of sexual offences), but see *Horsburgh* v. *R.*, [1967] S. C. R. 743; *R. v. Cratchley* (1913), 9 Cr. App. Rep. 232 (child not accomplice in stealing); *R. v. King* (1914), 10 Cr. App. Rep. 117 (woman not accomplice of man living on her immoral earnings. "On the other hand, the judge is justified in warning the jury against accepting the evidence of a girl who is leading such a life against a man, without corroboration. This is a matter for the discretion of the judge", *per* Lord READING, L.C.J.). See also *R. v. Bramhill* (1933), 24 Cr. App. Rep. 79.

[3] *Kenny's Outlines of Criminal Law* (17th Edn.), p. 483, n. 9. The position might be different if A knew that the goods would probably be passed on to C by B.

[4] *R. v. Vernon*, [1962] Crim. L. R. 35; *R. v. Hodgett*, [1957] N. I. 1; *R. v. Macdonald*, [1955] N. Z. L. R. 699. For earlier authority see *R. v. Crane* (1912), 7 Cr. App. Rep. 113; and *R. v. Reynolds* (1927), 20 Cr. App. Rep. 125.

himself.[1] There is a possible difficulty with regard to joint trials which has not yet been faced by the courts, for anything in the nature of a direction that a co-accused is an accomplice may be taken by the jury to be an indication of the judge's views concerning the guilt of the co-accused.

The danger of requirements such as that of the accomplice warning is that the courts will come to require something like a set form of words to be used, for example, that it must be specifically stated to the jury that it is "dangerous" to convict in the absence of corroboration; but the Court of Appeal has, in the main, very properly set its face against this, use frequently being made of some remarks of SALMON, L.J., in a case concerned with corroborative evidence of sexual offences.[2]

> "The rule that the jury must be warned does not mean that there has to be some legalistic ritual to be automatically recited by the judge, that some particular form of words or incantation must be used, and if not, the summing-up is faulty and the conviction must be quashed."

The fact that the word "corroboration" is not used is certainly not fatal for, as SALMON, L.J., went on to point out, that is not a word which the jury would understand without explanation. Nevertheless, it will generally not be enough to emphasise the need for care to be taken by the jury without inviting them to consider whether there is independent evidence implicating the accused in a material particular.[3]

(iii) Corroboration of an accomplice's evidence.—It was said in *R.* v. *Mullins* [4] that corroboration does not mean that there should be independent evidence of that which the accomplice relates, otherwise his testimony would be unnecessary, as it would merely be confirmatory of other independent testimony. In the leading case of *R.* v. *Baskerville* [5] Lord READING, L.C.J., said that what is required is some additional evidence rendering it probable that the story of the accomplice is true, and that it is reasonably safe to act upon his statement. This is a very general remark, but the judgment of Lord READING, L.C.J., is of the greatest importance because it settles a conflict between two views concerning the nature and extent of corroboration.

According to the first view, independent evidence tending to verify any part of the testimony of the accomplice would suffice, while the second required that the evidence should not only show that part of the accomplice's testimony is true, but it should also implicate the accused. The distinction may be illustrated by the facts of *R.* v. *Birkett*.[6] The accused was charged with sheep-stealing, and, after evidence of the theft, the accomplice repeated statements made by him to the police concerning the whereabouts of some of the sheep's skins. Another witness proved (a) that the skins were found where the accomplice said they would be discovered, and (b) that mutton corresponding to the carcases of the stolen sheep was found in the

---

[1] *People* v. *Carney*, [1955] I. R. 324, discussed by Professor Coutts in Journal of Criminal Law (1958), p. 61. In *R.* v. *Chrimes* (1959), 43 Cr. App. Rep. 149, the trial judge directed the jury that a witness who had not confessed or been convicted was an accomplice, although the Court of Criminal Appeal said that he need not have done so. In *R.* v. *Kay*, [1950] O. R. 235 it was held that the jury do not have to be satisfied beyond reasonable doubt that a witness was an accomplice.

[2] *R.* v. *O'Reilly*, [1967] 2 Q. B. 722, at p. 727.

[3] *R.* v. *Price*, [1969] 1 Q. B. 541; [1968] 2 All E. R. 282.

[4] (1848), 3 Cox C. C. 526, at p. 531.

[5] [1916] 2 K. B. 658.

[6] (1839), 8 C. & P. 732; *James* v. *R.* (1970), 55 Cr. App. Rep. 299 (sexual offence).

accused's house. On the first view of the nature of the required corroboration, item (a) would have been sufficient, but this would not have been so on the second view, although item (b) sufficed according to either view. The second view was favoured by the Court of Criminal Appeal in *R. v. Baskerville*, and it is unnecessary to go into the previous authorities. To quote Lord READING, L.C.J.:

> "Evidence in corroboration must be independent testimony which affects the accused by connecting or tending to connect him with the crime. . . . The test applicable to determine the nature and extent of the corroboration is thus the same, whether the case falls within the rule of practice at common law or within that class of offence for which corroboration is required by statute. The language of the statute, 'implicates the accused', compendiously incorporates the test applicable at common law in the rule of practice." [1]

The first view has been embodied in the ordinances applicable to British overseas territories since the judgment in *R. v. Baskerville* was delivered, but it is submitted that the decision in favour of the second view is sound on principle because "false evidence given by an accomplice is commonly regarded as more likely to take the form of incriminating the wrong person than of imagining the crime charged". [2]

Various decisions provide instances of corroboration similar to those which have been discussed in connection with the relevant statutory provisions. Compromising letters written by the accused to the accomplice will suffice, [3] as will any item of damning circumstantial evidence such as the discovery of the mutton in the accused's house in *R. v. Birkett*. The accused's silence when a reply was to be expected will also corroborate the testimony of an accomplice as in *R. v. Cramp* [4] where the evidence of a girl whose miscarriage the accused was alleged to have attempted was corroborated by his silence when her father came to him and said, "I have here those things which you gave my daughter to produce abortion".

There are some special points which should be noted with regard to the corroboration of an accomplice's evidence. An accomplice of the first class mentioned by Lord SIMONDS in *Davies v. Director of Public Prosecutions*[5] (a party to the crime including, it may be, someone who has impeded the apprehension or trial of a person charged with an arrestable offence) cannot corroborate another member of that class so that, if A., B. and C. are accomplices, B.'s evidence against C. is not corroborated by anything to which A. deposes. [6] Although it has been recognised by the House of Lords, [7] the merits of this rule have never been fully considered by an

---

[1] [1916] 2 K. B. 658, at p. 667.

[2] *Per* Lord MACDERMOTT in *Tumahole Bereng v. R.*, [1949] A. C. 253, at p. 265, commenting on the change of the doctrine of *R. v. Baskerville* in the Basutoland ordinances. The view that confirmation of any part of the witness's testimony will suffice is embodied in s. 157 of the Indian Evidence Act, 1872.

[3] As in *R. v. Baskerville (supra)*.

[4] (1880), 14 Cox C. C. 390.

[5] P. 175, *ante*.

[6] *R. v. Gay* (1909), 2 Cr. App. Rep. 327 ; *R. v. Prater*, [1960] 2 Q. B. 464, at p. 465; [1960] 1 All E. R. 298. Contrast the construction of the Swaziland Criminal Procedure and Evidence Proclamation, s. 231 in *Nkambule v. R.*, [1950] A. C. 379.

[7] *Director of Public Prosecutions v. Kilbourne*, [1973] A. C. 729, at p. 747, per Lord HAILSHAM, L. C., p. 751, per Lord REID, and p. 759 *per* Lord SIMON OF GLAISDALE. See also *Director of Public Prosecutions v. Hester*, [1973] A. C. 296, at p. 326, *per* Lord DIPLOCK, and p. 330, per Lord CROSS OF CHELSEA.

English court. It has been rejected after due consideration in South Africa,[1] and it is certainly difficult to justify on principle. If A.'s evidence standing alone is subject to a warning against the danger of acting on it in the absence of corroboration, sufficient to support a conviction, why should it not be sufficient to corroborate the evidence of A.'s accomplice B.? Assuming that the evidence of each witness implicates the accused in a material particular, and assuming that there is no question of a conspiracy between the witnesses, A.'s evidence adds considerably to the probability of the truth of B.'s and vice versa.

In *Director of Public Prosecutions* v. *Kilbourne*[2] the House of Lords held that the sworn evidence of young boys against whom the accused was alleged to have committed buggery or indecent assaults in 1971 could corroborate the sworn evidence of young boys against whom similar offences by the accused were alleged in 1970 and *vice versa*, the evidence being of particular relevance on account of the similarity of the conduct alleged against the accused on every occasion. A warning of the danger of acting on the uncorroborated sworn evidence of children is necessary, as it is on any sexual charge, and the boys may have been accomplices of the accused. However that may be, the importance of *Kilbourne's Case* is that it lays to rest the extraordinary notion, produced by earlier decisions, that evidence of the type in question is admissible because it may help the jury to decide whether the other evidence is true, although it cannot corroborate such evidence. This particular *bêtise* was the outcome of an undiscriminating adherence to the rule that the testimony of one accomplice cannot corroborate that of another accomplice. *Kilbourne's Case* decides that this is not so when the accomplice belongs to the third class mentioned by Lord SIMONDS in *Davies* v. *Director of Public Prosecutions*[3] (parties to other crimes alleged to have been committed by the accused when such evidence is admissible). Clearly there is far less danger of collaboration between accomplices called by the prosecution when they belong to different classes (one being a party to the crime charged and the other a party to a different crime) than when they are both alleged to be parties to the crime charged; but it is open to question whether this is something which ought to justify a rule of law that accomplices who are parties to the crime charged cannot corroborate each other. We have already seen that such a rule cannot be based upon the requirements of logic and the danger of collaboration between witnesses is something which naturally goes to the weight rather than the admissibility of their evidence.

The wife of an accomplice who is not called can corroborate one who does give evidence [4] and, after some uncertainty in the authorities, the Court of Criminal Appeal has decided that the wife of an accomplice who is called can corroborate his evidence, although her evidence naturally requires to be treated with caution.[5]

---

[1] *State* v. *Avon Bottle Store Pty, Ltd.*, 1963 (2) S. A. 389 (A. D.); *Nkambule* v. *R.*, [1950] A. C. 379 (construing the Swaziland Criminal Procedure Proclamation, s. 231).
[2] [1973] A. C. 729; [1973] 1 All E. R. 440.
[3] [1954] A. C. 378; [1954] 1 All E. R. 507.
[4] *R.* v. *Willis*, [1916] 1 K. B. 933.
[5] *R.* v. *Evans*, [1965] 2 Q.B. 295; [1964] 3 All E.R. 401. For earlier authorities see *R.* v. *Neal and Taylor* (1835), 7 C. & P. 168; *R.* v. *Payne* (1913), 8 Cr. App. Rep. 171; *R.* v. *Willis, supra*; *A. G.* v. *Durnan*, [1934] I. R. 308; *R.* v. *Ehberts* (1912), 7 D. L. R. 398; *R.* v. *Munevich*, [1942] 3 D. L. R. 482; *Tripodi* v. *R.*, [1961] A. L. R. 780.

Finally, where an accomplice gives evidence against two prisoners, the fact that there is corroboration so far as one of them is concerned does not corroborate his testimony against the other.[1]

The Criminal law Revision Committee[2] recommend the abolition of the requirement of the accomplice warning as a matter of law in the case of witnesses called by the prosecution. This is partly on account of the difficulty of stating who is an "accomplice" and partly on account of the fact that it is as safe to act on the uncorroborated evidence of some accomplices as it is dangerous to act on the uncorroborated evidence of many other witnesses of questionable character with regard to whom no warning is required as a matter of law. The Committee would also abolish the rule that one accomplice cannot corroborate another.

(iv) Extension to adultery.—In *Fairman* v. *Fairman*[3] it was held that caution should be exercised in finding that adultery had been committed when the only evidence to that effect was the uncorroborated testimony of one of the adulterers. A similar principle was stated and acted upon by the Court of Appeal in *Galler* v. *Galler*.[4] These decisions were based on the high standard of proof required for adultery but, even if the civil standard applies to adultery, there is a further ground upon which the decisions can be supported. The charge is easy to make and difficult to refute in a number of situations of which *Galler* v. *Galler* provides an example. The respondent, who was separated from his wife, had to employ a nurse to live in his house and look after his young children, and it was the nurse who gave uncorroborated evidence to the effect that he had committed adultery with her. Moreover, the charge of adultery could easily be concocted on account of hysterical or vindictive motives, and it seems reasonable enough to insist on the most careful consideration before uncorroborated evidence is acted upon.

(2) Sexual Offences

Considerations such as those mentioned in the last paragraph have led the courts to direct juries in the case of all charges of sexual offences that it is not safe to convict on the uncorroborated testimony of the complainant but that they may do so if satisfied of its truth.[5] This is best regarded as a peremptory requirement as appeals have been allowed because no such direction was given although there was abundant corroborative evidence,[6] but, as the Court of Criminal Appeal hinted in *R.* v. *Zielinski*,[7] allowance may have to be made for special facts, as when the age of the victim renders it improbable that the charge was promoted by hysteria or spite. This, if

---

[1] *R.* v. *Jenkins* (1845), 1 Cox C. C. 177, approved in *R.* v. *Baskerville*, [1916] 2 K. B. 658, at p. 670.

[2] 11th Report, paras. 183–5 and para. 194.

[3] [1949] P. 341; [1949] 1 All E. R. 938. Cf. *Robertson* v. *Robertson*, [1951] 1 D. L. R. 498 where objection is taken to the use of the word accomplice in this context. The precautionary rule of practice was not considered in *Morrow* v. *Morrow*, [1914] 2 I. R. 183 (criminal conversation).

[4] [1954] P. 252; [1954] 1 All E. R. 536.

[5] *R.* v. *Jones* (1925), 19 Cr. App. Rep. 40; *R.* v. *Freebody* (1935), 25 Cr. App. Rep. 69; *R.* v. *Winfield*, [1939] 4 All E. R. 164; *R.* v. *Burgess* (1956), 40 Cr. App. Rep. 144; *R.* v. *O'Reilly*, [1967] 2 Q. B. 722; [1967] 2 All E. R. 766; *R.* v. *Henry* and *R.* v. *Manning* (1968), 53 Cr. App. Rep. 150.

[6] *R.* v. *Trigg*, [1963] 1 All E. R. 490; *R.* v. *Midwinter* (1971), 55 Cr. App. Rep. 523; cf. *R.* v. *Rolfe* (1952), 36 Cr. App. Rep 4.

[7] [1950] 2 All E. R. 1114.

anything, is all that can still be meant by the suggestion, made as long ago as 1922, that it is safer to act on uncorroborated evidence in a sexual case than in that of an accomplice.[1]

According to a majority of the Court of Criminal Appeal, if evidence of an earlier indecent assault is admitted against the accused in order to negative his defence of accident in relation to the indecent assault with which he is charged, there need be no warning against accepting the earlier evidence if it is uncorroborated.[2]

The alleged corroborative evidence must implicate the accused in a material particular; accordingly, on a charge of rape, confirmation of the prosecutrix's evidence that someone had intercourse with her at the relevant time does not corroborate the case against the accused, for it neither negatives consent nor identifies him as the culprit.[3] In such a case evidence corroborating the prosecutrix's testimony that the intercourse was non-consensual could not amount to corroboration without more.

A majority of the Criminal Law Revision Committee was in favour of retaining a requirement of corroboration as a matter of law in the case of a sexual charge on which the complainant is under 14 (the age at which according to recommendations of the Committee already mentioned[4] sworn evidence can be given), and of providing that the jury must be directed that there is a special need for caution before convicting on the uncorroborated evidence of the complainant in every sexual case when he or she is 14 or over.[5]

Under the present law there could be several reasons why the same evidence should be received with caution if it is not corroborated for, in addition to coming under the present head, the evidence might be that of an accomplice, or it might be given by a person of tender years. In such a case each ground for the warning should be mentioned.[6]

(3) Sworn Evidence of Children

The sworn evidence of a child need not be corroborated as a matter of law, but a jury should be warned, not that they must find corroboration, but that there is a risk in acting on the uncorroborated evidence of young boys or girls though they may do so if convinced that the witness is telling the truth. This warning should also be given whether the witness of tender years is called to give sworn evidence in corroboration of the evidence (sworn or unsworn) of another child or the testimony of an adult.[7] It appears that the requirement of warning the jury of the danger of acting on the uncorroborated evidence of a young child is peremptory, and not a matter for the discretion of the particular judge.[8] Children may give sworn

---

[1] *R.* v. *Crocker* (1922), 92 L. J. K. B. 428.
[2] R. *v.* *Sanders* (1961), 46 Cr. App. Rep. 60.
[3] *James* v. *R.* (1971), 55 Cr. App. Rep. 299.
[4] P. 150, *ante.*
[5] 11th Report, paras. 186–8.
[6] *R.* v. *Gammon* (1959), 43 Cr. App. Rep. 155.
[7] *R.* v. *Campbell*, [1956] 2 Q. B. 432; [1956] 2 All E. R. 272.
[8] *R.* v. *Cleal*, [1942] 1 All E. R. 203, where Hilbery, J., delivering the judgment of the Court of Criminal Appeal, referred to it as a rule to be applied and observed in all cases. It is doubtful whether the distinction suggested in *R.* v. *Mitchell* (1952), 36 Cr. App. Rep. 79, between cases in which the child is and is not an accuser can be maintained either on principle or on authority. The warning must be given though the only issue is that of the identity of the perpetrator of a sexual crime against a child (*R.* v. *Sawyer* (1959), 43 Cr. App. Rep. 187).

evidence in civil and criminal cases, provided the judge is satisfied that they understand the nature of an oath. Great caution is required in accepting their evidence because, although children may be less likely to be acting from improper motives than adults, they are more susceptible to the influence of third persons, and may allow their imaginations to run away with them.[1] All the authorities on warning the jury in the terms indicated above are decisions in criminal cases, but the principle might well be applied in a civil suit for the justification of the rule is the tender years of the witness, rather than the nature of the case.

Director of Public Prosecutions v. *Hester*[2] decides that the sworn evidence of a child may be corroborated by the unsworn evidence of another child and *vice versa*.

(4) CLAIMS AGAINST THE ESTATES OF DECEASED PERSONS

A claim against the estate of a deceased person will not generally be allowed on the uncorroborated evidence of the claimant, but there is no rule of law against allowing it.[3] The absence through death of one of the parties to the transaction calls for caution in such a case, but claims have been allowed where there was no corroboration.

(5) MATRIMONIAL CAUSES

The rules governing the requirement of caution in the absence of corroboration in matrimonial causes were stated in the Divisional Court by Sir JOCELYN SIMON, P. in *Alli* v. *Alli*.[4] The rules are:

(*a*) Where a matrimonial offence is alleged, the court will look for corroboration.

(*b*) The court will normally, before finding a matrimonial offence proved, require such corroboration, if, on the face of the complainant's own evidence, it is available.

(*c*) These are not rules of law, but of practice only. They spring from the gravity of the consequences of proof of a matrimonial offence,[5] and because experience has shown the risk of a miscarriage of justice in acting on the uncorroborated testimony of a spouse in this class of case:

(*d*) It is nevertheless open to a court to act on the uncorroborated evidence of a spouse if it is in no doubt where the truth lies.[6]

(*e*) these statements are equally applicable to courts of summary jurisdiction.

Sir JOCELYN SIMON, P. also said that it is necessary to distinguish between cases in which the uncorroborated evidence relates to sexual misconduct[7] or is that of a willing participant in adultery[8] where an appellate court will intervene unless the trial court has expressly warned itself of the danger of

---

[1] *R.* v. *Dossi* (1918), 13 Cr. App. Rep. 158, at p. 161.
[2] [1973] A. C. 296; [1972] 3 All E. R. 1056.
[3] *Re Hodgson, Beckett* v. *Ramsdale* (1885), 31 Ch. D. 177; *Rawlinson* v. *Scholes* (1898), 15 T. L. R. 8; *Vavasseur* v. *Vavasseur* (1909), 25 T. L. R. 250; *Re Cummins, Cummins* v. *Thompson*, [1972] Ch. 62; [1971] 3 All E. R. 782; see note in 37 L. Q. R. 268.
[4] [1965] 3 All E. R. 480.
[5] Cf. *per* Lord PENZANCE in *U.* v. *J.* (1867), L. R. 1 P. & D. 460, at p. 461, speaking of nullity.
[6] For cases in which the court has acted without corroboration see *Curtis* v. *Curtis* (1905), 21 T. L. R. 676; *Riches* v. *Riches and Clinch* (1918), 35 T. L. R. 141 (adultery); *Getty* v. *Getty*, [1907] P. 334 (confession of adultery); *Kafton* v. *Kafton*, [1948] 1 All E. R. 435 (cruelty); *Hodgkins* v. *Hodgkins*, [1950] P. 183; [1950] 1 All E. R. 619 (nullity). As to desertion see *Barron* v. *Barron*, [1963] 1 All E. R. 215.
[7] *Statham* v. *Statham*, [1929] P. 131.
[8] *Galler* v. *Galler*, [1954] P. 252; [1954] 1 All E. R. 536.

acting on the evidence, and other cases in which the trial court's failure to warn itself will not necessarily lead to intervention by an appellate court, although it may have this effect, especially if the finding of the trial court is open to question on other ground.

(6) OTHER POSSIBLE CASES

In *People (A.-G.)* v. *Casey* (No. 2),[1] KINGSMILL-MOOR, J., speaking for the Supreme Court of Eire said:

> "The category of circumstances and special types of case which call for special directions and warnings from the trial judge cannot be considered as closed. Increased judicial experience, and, indeed, further psychological research, may extend it".

The case before the court concerned the reliability of evidence of visual identification and it was said that, in all such cases, whether or not there was a plurality of witnesses, the jury's attention should be drawn to the necessity of caution because there have been cases in the past in which responsible witnesses to identification have been subsequently proved to have been mistaken.

The words of KINGSMILL-MOOR, J., were repeated with approval by the Lord Chancellor in *Director of Public Prosecutions* v. *Kilbourne*;[2] but, as we have seen,[3] the House of Lords had already decided that, at any rate where the accused and the identifying witness were previously acquainted, there is no general rule that the judge must specially warn the jury on the danger of convicting on the visual identification of the accused by a single witness.[4] The Court of Appeal has since decided that, even when the accused and the identifying witness were not previously acquainted, no special warning is necessary.[5] In each case, however, the appellate court stressed the fact that the trial judge had emphasised the fallibility of the evidence of identification.

We have also seen that the risk of a wrongful conviction on account of mistaken identification was a matter of considerable concern to the Criminal Law Revision Committee who recommended that the judge should be obliged to warn the jury of the special need for caution in all cases of disputed identification.

SECTION 2. THE NATURE OF CORROBORATION

"Corroboration" is not a technical term, it simply means "confirmation" or "support".[6] But, in all cases in which it is required in law or practice, it must take the form of a separate item of evidence implicating the person against whom the testimony is given in relation to the matter concerning which corroboration is necessary.[7] This means that many things that show, or might be thought to show, that a witness is speaking

---

[1] [1963] I. R. 33, at p. 38.

[2] [1973] A. C. 729, at p. 740.

[3] P. 50, *ante.*

[4] *Arthurs* v. *A.-G. for Northern Ireland* (1970), 55 Cr. App. Rep. 171.

[5] *R.* v. *Long* (1973), 57 Cr. App. Rep. 871.

[6] *Director of Public Prosecutions* v. *Hester*, [1973] A. C. 296, at p. 325.

[7] In *Thomas* v. *Jones*, [1921] 1 K. B. 22, at pp. 44–45, the decision in *R.* v. *Baskerville*, [1916] 2 K. B. 658, was said to be of general application on the meaning of corroborative evidence. But see judgment of DENNING, L.J., in *Fromhold* v. *Fromhold*, [1952] 1 T. L. R. 1522 to the effect that any confirmatory evidence sufficed in divorce for cruelty.

the truth do not corroborate him in law. Examples of what does and does not amount to corroboration are scattered throughout the preceding paragraphs, but something further may be said on the subject under the headings of the conduct or condition of the witness whose testimony requires corroboration, the conduct of the party against whom corroboration is required, and the functions of the judge and jury.

A. CONDUCT OR CONDITION OF THE PERSON WHOSE TESTIMONY REQUIRES CORROBORATION

"In order that evidence may amount to corroboration it must be extraneous to the witness who is to be corroborated." This remark was made by Lord HEWART, C.J., in *R. v. Whitehead* [1] where the accused was charged with unlawful carnal knowledge of a girl under sixteen, and it was suggested that her testimony might have been corroborated by the fact that she spoke to her mother about her condition some time after the alleged intercourse, whereupon her mother laid an information against the accused. Lord HEWART demonstrated the absurdity of this contention when he said, "The girl cannot corroborate herself, otherwise it is only necessary for her to repeat her story some twenty-five times in order to get twenty-five corroborations of it." Another leading case which turned in part on the impossibility of self-corroboration is *R. v. Christie.* [2] The accused was charged with indecently assaulting a little boy who gave unsworn evidence. The boy's mother and a policeman testified to the terms in which the boy had described the assault shortly after it occurred when he also identified the accused; but the House of Lords held that these witnesses did not corroborate the boy's testimony and the conviction was quashed because the trial judge had suggested that it did have this effect.

We shall see in the next chapter that complaints by the victim of a sexual offence are admissible provided certain conditions are fulfilled but, even when they may be proved, either by the complainant or by the person to whom they were made, they do not corroborate the complainant's testimony. [3] We shall also see in chapter XVIII that a witness's previous statements may become admissible under various sections of the Civil Evidence Act, 1968, but section 6 (4) of that Act prohibits their use as corroboration of the maker's evidence.

Even if the statement is rendered admissible by virtue of a common law rule of evidence such as that relating to cross-examination on a diary or address book used to refresh memory discussed in the next chapter, it does not corroborate the evidence of the maker. [4]

The distressed condition of the complainant on a sexual charge can only amount to corroboration in exceptional circumstances, as when a bystander swears that the accused approached a child and that, shortly afterwards, they

---

[1] [1929] 1 K. B. 99, at p. 102.   [2] [1914] A. C. 545.
[3] *R. v. Evans* (1924), 18 Cr. App. Rep. 123; *R. v. Coulthread* (1933), 24 Cr. App. Rep. 44; *R. v. Coyle,* [1926] N. I. 208. The conversation between the girl and her mother in *R. v. Whitehead* would have been inadmissible as a complaint because it took place some months after the event of which complaint was made. The admissibility of the boy's statements as complaints was not argued in *R. v. Christie.* See also *Thomas v. R.,* [1952] 4 D. L. R. 306; *Eade v. R.* (1924), 34 C. L. R. 154.
[4] *Senat v. Senat (K., H. and B. intervening),* [1965] 2 All E. R. 405.

saw the child in a distressed condition.[1] If proved by the person to whom a complaint was made or by someone present on the occasion of the complaint, the distressed condition adds little, if anything, to the complainant's testimony and ought not to be left to the jury as corroboration.[2] The question whether the existence of physical injuries can amount to corroboration of the complainant's testimony concerning them implicating the person against whom the evidence is given is a question of fact varying from case to case.[3]

B. CONDUCT OF THE PARTY AGAINST WHOM CORROBORATION IS REQUIRED

Sometimes the conduct of the defendant or accused will be held to constitute corroboration of the evidence against him, and sometimes it will not have this effect. The matter is best considered under the heads of the evidence of the party against whom corroboration is required, the falsity of his evidence, his failure to give evidence, his false statements out of court, his silence when charged out of court and his conduct on an occasion previous to that with which the trial is concerned.

(1) EVIDENCE OF DEFENDANT OR ACCUSED

A person's statement in court may well be held to corroborate the case against him. In *R. v. Dossi*,[4] for instance, it was held that the accused's admission in evidence that he had platonically fondled the child who gave sworn testimony to the effect that he had indecently assaulted her could be treated as some corroboration of her statement. As ATKIN, L.J., said, "The question of corroboration often assumes an entirely different aspect after the accused person has gone into the witness box and has been cross-examined".[5] Whether anything that emerges in the course of the evidence of the defendant or accused does corroborate his opponent's witnesses in a material particular is of course a question of fact dependent on the circumstances of the particular case.

(2) FALSITY OF EVIDENCE

In *Tumahole Bereng* v. *R.*[6] Lord MACDERMOTT said that a prisoner does not corroborate an accomplice merely by giving evidence which is not accepted and must therefore be regarded as false.

> "Corroboration may well be found in the evidence of an accused person; but that is a different matter, for there confirmation comes, if at all, from what is said, and not from the falsity of what is said."

There is nothing in the context which suggests that this dictum is only applicable to the testimony of an accomplice, and there can be no doubt that it is generally true of all cases in which corroboration must be sought. In *R. v. Chapman* and *R. v. Baldwin*[7] the Court of Appeal held that the falsity of the evidence of the accused can never corroborate the evidence

---

[1] *R. v. Redpath* (1962), 46 Cr. App. Rep. 319; *Forgie v. Police*, [1969] N. Z. L. R. 101.
[2] *R. v. Knight*, [1966] 1 All E. R. 647; *R. v. Richards*, [1965] Qd. R. 354.
[3] *Fromhold* v. *Fromhold* (1952), 1 T. L. R. 1522; *R. v. Aubichon* (1964), 48 W. W. R. 529.
[4] (1918), 13 Cr. App. Rep. 158. *Goguen and Goguen* v. *Bourgeois and Bourgeois* (1957), 6 D. L. R. (2d) 19.
[5] At p. 162.   [6] [1949] A. C. 253, at p. 280.
[7] [1973] Q. B. 774; [1973] 2 All E. R. 624.

given against him, but the direction they held to be wrong had been couched in very general terms, and there is a good deal of authority in favour of the view that certain kinds of lie told in court can corroborate the evidence against the person telling them.[1] The lies must take the form of denials of specific allegations or the concoction of a particular story which can reasonably be construed as admissions of the truth of the case against the person who tells them. To quote from a South Australian judgment in affiliation proceedings,

"The court cannot, as is sometimes suggested, prefer the evidence of the mother to that of the defendant and then use its disbelief of his evidence as the basis of an inference to be used in corroboration of the mother's testimony."[2]

This is the type of error into which the trial judge seems to have fallen in *R.* v. *Chapman* and *R.* v. *Baldwin.*

In *Corfield* v. *Hodgson*,[3] on the other hand, a Divisional Court held in an affiliation case that the appellant's denial in-chief that he had taken the respondent home after a dance, admitted by him in cross-examination to have been false, could be treated as corroborative of the mother's evidence. The suggestion that the false denial of an opportunity to commit a crime may constitute evidence that advantage was taken of the opportunity is, after all, no more than a proposition of common sense, and we shall see that it has been acted on by the Divisional Court in a case concerned with lies to the police.[4] It is difficult to see why an English court should not follow a South African case on seduction,[5] and hold that the man's denial that he was alone with the girl in an empty house late at night, made in the course of his evidence, could corroborate the girl's evidence if the testimony of other witnesses that the couple were together in the house were accepted.

It is difficult to follow the rationale of the present law laid down by the Court of Appeal that his lies in court can never corroborate evidence against the liar. No doubt it is impossible to make a completely satisfactory generalisation concerning the requisite kind of lie, and it is a matter which calls for the most careful direction to a jury, but it is doubtful whether these considerations are sufficient to justify an absolute rule. Certainly it is not a matter on which it is proper to invoke logic. It is said that, if the question is whether A.'s evidence or B.'s evidence is true, the rejection of B.'s evidence does not mean that A.'s evidence must be accepted as true, for B. might have other reasons for lying. As a matter of logic, the rejection of B.'s evidence does mean that A.'s must be accepted if B.'s is its contradictory. On a charge of rape, the rejection of the man's assertion that the women consented entails acceptance of her assertion that she did not consent; but no one would contend that the false assertion of consent could, without more, be corroborative of the woman's evidence for the conclusion that it did have this effect would amount to holding mere disbelief in what the man said to be corroboration of the evidence against him. On the other hand, the accused's assertion of some such specific

[1] The authorities are exhaustively cited in an article by Professor Heydon in 89 L. Q. R. 552; and see *R.* v. *Boardman, Times,* 15th May, 1974, and Addendum, *ante.*
[2] NAPIER, J., in *Pitman* v. *Byrne,* [1926] S. A. S. R. 207, at p. 211.
[3] [1966] 2 All E. R. 205.
[4] *Credland* v. *Knowler* (1951), 35 Cr. App. Rep. 48.
[5] *Poggenpoel* v. *Morris,* [1938] C. P. D. 90.

incident as an invitation by the prosecutrix to take her home and make love to her there, alleged to be false by another witness, ought, on principle, to be corroborative of the complainant's testimony denying consent if the other witness is believed. The conclusion that the accused invented a particular falsity to support his allegation of consent is more than a mere utilisation of disbelief in that allegation as corroboration although, as a matter of logic, the rejection of this particular item of the accused's evidence does not entail acceptance of the prosecutrix's statement that the intercourse was nonconsensual.[1]

(3) Failure to give Evidence

In *R.* v. *Jackson*[2] Lord GODDARD, C. J., speaking for the Court of Criminal Appeal, said:

> "One cannot say that the fact that the prisoner had not gone into the witness box is of itself corroboration of accomplices' evidence. It is a matter which the jury very properly could, and very probably would, take into account, but it should be clearly understood that the direction [that failure to testify can amount to corroboration] is wrong in law."

The distinction between a matter which the jury can take into account and one which can amount to corroboration is perhaps, in this context, not as clear as it might be, and the Criminal Law Revision Committee recommend that the accused's failure to give evidence should, if the fact were such that an inference of guilt might properly be drawn therefrom, be treated as capable of amounting to corroboration of any evidence given by the prosecution;[3] but consideration of the merits of this proposal is best deferred until the merits of the proposal that such inferences as appear proper may be drawn from the accused's failure to give evidence are discussed in Chapter XV.

The rule that a party's failure to testify does not constitute corroboration of the evidence against him applies to affiliation proceedings. Thus, in *Cracknell* v. *Smith*[4] the applicant admitted to intercourse with the respondent's brother as well as the respondent on various occasions, but alleged that she had only had intercourse with the respondent during the month in which her child was conceived. The applicant's mother gave evidence of meetings between her daughter and the respondent, but the Divisional Court held that mere evidence of opportunity could not amount to corroboration. The Court came to a similar conclusion with regard to the fact that the respondent's brother gave what the magistrates considered to be false evidence concerning the periods at which he had had intercourse with the respondent, there being no evidence that he had been incited to do so by the respondent. The latter did not give evidence and, when allowing his appeal on the ground that this too did not corroborate the applicant's evidence, Lord PARKER, C.J., said:

> "If there is evidence and some corroborative evidence, it may be that the Justices are entitled to take into consideration the fact that he gave no evidence in considering the weight to be attached to the corroboration."

---

[1] See p. 172, *ante* for comments on lawyers as pseudo-logicians.
[2] [1953] 1 All E. R. 872.
[3] 11th Report, para. 111.
[4] [1960] 3 All E. R. 569.

The distinction between corroboration and a fact which, though not itself corroboration, adds weight to corroborative evidence is another one which is not altogether easy to grasp. In affiliation proceedings the respondent is a compellable witness for the applicant, but there would normally be no point in her calling him because a party cannot cross-examine his own witness. If the law were to be changed so as to allow the respondent's failure to give evidence to be capable of amounting to corroboration, it would in effect be placed on a par with that of some Commonwealth jurisdictions according to which corroboration is only required in affiliation proceedings if the respondent gives evidence.

It is scarcely necessary to add that failure to cross-examine is never in itself corroboration of the witness's evidence.[1]

(4) FALSE STATEMENTS OUT OF COURT

A false statement out of court will not necessarily constitute corroboration, but it may have this effect. Thus it was said in a Scottish case that the existence of an opportunity to do the act complained of, which would not amount to corroboration by itself, may have a complexion put upon it by a statement made by the defendant which is proved to be false.[2] It was on the strength of these remarks that the Divisional Court decided in *Credland* v. *Knowler*[3] that the fact that the accused had falsely, as he subsequently admitted, told the police that he had not left his house on a particular evening corroborated the unsworn evidence of two children that he had been guilty of an indecent assault a short distance away from his home. Similarly it has been held that false statements to the police and to the court concerning the manner in which the accused came by certain goods can sometimes be construed as an admission that the goods were stolen.[4] Lies may, however, be due to panic rather than a sense of guilt;[5] but this is a matter for the tribunal of fact. On principle, out of court lies of a certain type can corroborate evidence against the liar just as much as lies in court, and there is no authority to the contrary as there is in the latter case;[6] but they must be the concoctions of a guilty man.

(5) SILENCE WHEN CHARGED

There is a broad principle of common sense which was stated by CAVE, J., in the course of his judgment in *R.* v. *Mitchell*:[7]

> "Undoubtedly, when persons are speaking on even terms, and a charge is made, and the person charged says nothing, and expresses no indignation, and does nothing to repel the charge, that is some evidence to show that he admits the charge to be true."

---

[1] *Dingwall* v. *J. Wharton (Shipping), Ltd.*, [1961] 2 Lloyd's Reports 213, at p. 219.

[2] *Dawson* v. *McKenzie* (1908), 45 Sc. L. R. 473.

[3] (1951), 35 Cr. App. Rep. 48; *R.* v. *Vallance*, [1955] N. Z. L. R. 811; *White* v. *R.* (1956), 5 D. L. R. (2d) 328; *Lonergan* v. *R.*, [1963] Tas. S. R. 158; cf. *R.* v. *King*, [1967] 2 Q. B. 338, at pp. 349–350, where, however, the falsity of the denial of the opportunity was only proved by the witnesses whose evidence required corroboration.

[4] *R.* v. *Young*, [1953] 1 All E. R. 21 (no question of corroboration was involved in this case).

[5] *R.* v. *Clynes* (1960), 44 Cr. App. Rep. 158; for a full discussion of the situations in which lies may or may not amount to corroboration in affiliation proceedings, see *Popovic* v. *Derks*, [1961] V. L. R. 413.

[6] *R.* v. *Chapman* and *R.* v. *Baldwin*, [1973] Q. B. 774; [1973] 2 All E. R. 624.

[7] (1892), 17 Cox C. C. 503.

This principle was acted on in *R.* v. *Cramp*[1] in which the accused's failure to answer the observation of the girl's father about some pills was held to be capable of corroborating her evidence that the accused had attempted to procure her miscarriage. But what if the persons in question are not speaking on even terms?

In *R.* v. *Tate*[2] it was held that the accused's silence when arrested did not corroborate the evidence of an accomplice, and *R.* v. *Cramp* was distinguished on the ground that the statement might reasonably have been expected to call for a reply from an innocent person. In *R.* v. *Feigenbaum*,[3] however, the accused's failure to reply to a police officer who told him he was about to be arrested and charged as an accessory on account of statements made by the youthful principals was held to have been rightly treated as corroborative of their evidence; but this decision of the Court of Criminal Appeal was not followed in *R.* v. *Whitehead*[4] where the same court held that the appellant's statement that he did not wish to say anything when served with a summons charging him with unlawful intercourse with a girl under 16 did not corroborate her testimony. When delivering the judgment of the Court of Criminal Appeal in *R.* v. *Keeling*,[5] HALLETT, J., expressed a preference for *R.* v. *Whitehead* and the cases applying that decision. A similar preference was expressed by the Judicial Committee of the Privy Council in *Hall* v. *R.*,[6] when, in answer to a suggestion that *R.* v. *Feigenbaum* was distinguishable from the other cases because, in them, the accused had been expressly told that he need say nothing, Lord DIPLOCK said "the caution merely serves to remind the accused of a right which he already possesses at common law." It may therefore be assumed with a good deal of confidence that silence when charged by a police officer can never amount to corroboration of evidence against someone charged with a crime.

The effect of what is probably the most controversial recommendation of the Criminal Law Revision Committee would be to alter the law in this respect by providing that proper inferences drawn from the accused's failure, when charged, to mention facts subsequently relied on in his defence, can corroborate evidence against him if the fact is one which he could reasonably be expected to have mentioned; but full consideration of this proposal is best deferred to the discussion of the right to silence in chapter XIX.[7]

(6) CONDUCT ON PREVIOUS OCCASIONS

We shall see in Chapter XIV that facts tending to show that someone committed a crime or civil wrong, or conducted himself improperly on other occasions, may not be proved in order to establish his commission

---

[1] (1880), 14 Cox C. C. 390. See also *Bessela* v. *Stern* (1877), 2 C. P. D. 265, and contrast the position where the charge is made by letter when it would often, though not invariably, be wrong to draw an adverse inference from failure to reply (*Wiedemann* v. *Walpole*, [1891] 2 Q. B. 534).
[2] [1908] 2 K. B. 680.
[3] [1919] 1 K. B. 431.
[4] [1929] 1 K. B. 99; followed in *R. v. Charavanmuttu*, (1930), 22 Cr. App. Rep. 1, and *R. v. Naylor*, [1933] 1 K. B. 685. See also *R. v. Littleboy*, [1934] 2 K. B. 408, and *People (A.-G.)* v. *Quinn*, [1955] I. R. 57.
[5] [1942] 1 All E. R. 507.
[6] [1971] 1 All E. R. 322.
[7] See 11th Report of the Criminal Law Revision Committee, paras. 40–2.

of the crime or civil wrong into which the court is inquiring, if they are only relevant as showing a disposition to commit crimes or civil wrongs generally, or the kind of crime or civil wrong with which the court is concerned. This will often exclude the previous conduct of the party against whom corroboration is required, but such conduct is admissible if of particular relevance to a matter in issue. In two instances of this nature, such conduct may clearly corroborate the evidence against the accused. In the first place it may show a propensity which is more specific than that of committing a certain crime because it involves doing so in a particular way or with a particular person, and secondly it may corroborate a witness's story about statements made by the defendant or accused.

(i) **Previous conduct to show specific propensity.**—An example of the first kind of corroboration by previous conduct is provided by *R. v. Hartley*.[1] The accused was convicted of buggery with H. on a particular day. H. gave evidence of the commission of the offence on the day in question, and he also deposed to the fact that the accused had done the same thing to him on a previous occasion. There was no corroboration of H.'s evidence so far as the offence mentioned in the indictment was concerned, but his evidence with regard to the previous occasion was corroborated by another witness who saw the accused take H. to his office, lock the door and draw the blinds. It was held that H.'s evidence with regard to the previous occasion was admissible because, where a person alleges that an offence such as that with which the court was concerned has been committed against him, he is entitled to show that the offence was indulged in habitually. It was also held that the corroboration of H.'s testimony concerning the former crime constituted corroboration of his evidence with regard to the crime charged, and in this respect the case may be compared with those in which a man's conduct before the intercourse alleged has been held to corroborate the testimony of the claimant in proceedings for affiliation.[2]

An example of corroborative evidence supplied by the accused's *modus operandi* is provided by *Director of Public Prosecutions v. Kilbourne*.[3]

(ii) **Previous conduct to corroborate statement to witness.**— Evidence which tends to show that the accused incited a course of conduct resulting in the commission of the crime charged certainly implicates him in a material particular. Accordingly anything which confirms a witness's story with regard to such incitement will be held to constitute corroboration when this is required, and it sometimes happens that the alleged incitement takes the form of a reference to previous misconduct on the part of the accused. In *R. v. Mitchell*,[4] for instance, a man was charged with indecently assaulting a girl named Sheila, who gave sworn evidence against him. In addition to deposing to the assault upon her, Sheila said that the accused told her about his behaviour with a girl named Judy and it was held that this girl's testimony with regard to the accused's conduct corroborated the evidence of Sheila who could hardly have heard of Judy from anyone other than the accused as the two girls lived in different parts of the country.

---

[1] [1941] 1 K. B. 5; *R. v. Deen*, [1964] Qd. R. 569.
[2] *Cole v. Manning* (1877), 2 Q. B. D. 611; cf. *Wilcox v. Gotfrey* (1872), 26 L. T. 481.
[3] [1973] A. C. 729; [1973] 1 All E. R. 440, p. 180, *ante*; see also *R. v. Viljoen*, [1947] 2 S. A. 56.
[4] (1952), 36 Cr. App. Rep. 79.

C. FUNCTIONS OF JUDGE AND JURY

In a case in which there is no corroboration, the judge should direct an acquittal if corroboration is required as a matter of law. If the case is one in which corroboration is required as a matter of practice, and there is no corroboration, the judge may often have to warn the jury of this fact, in addition to warning them of the danger of acting on uncorroborated evidence. This is especially so where there is an item of evidence, such as a complaint, which the jury might mistakenly think to be corroborative, but, although there are decisions suggesting the contrary,[1] there does not appear to be any rule of law requiring a warning of the absence of corroboration.[2]

If he does direct them about corroboration, the judge must tell the jury what corroboration is—independent evidence of some material fact which implicates the accused person and tends to confirm that he is guilty of the offence.[3] The preponderance of authority favours the view that it is unnecessary for the judge to indicate which particular items of evidence could constitute corroboration;[4] but there should be a broad indication of the sort of evidence which a jury may treat as corroborative.[5] A conviction may be quashed if the judge refers to items of evidence as corroborative when they do not possess this quality.[6] Where there is corroboration so far as some counts are concerned, but not with regard to others this fact should be made plain to the jury.[7]

SECTION 3. THE QUESTION OF REFORM IN CRIMINAL CASES

Most of the recommendations of the Criminal Law Revision Committee with regard to corroboration have already been mentioned; but it will be convenient to restate the major proposals as the starting point of a brief discussion of other possibilities. The Committee's most important recommendations are (i) corroboration of the victim's evidence should be required as a matter of law in the case of sexual offences against children under 14; (ii) the jury should be warned of the special need for caution before convicting on the uncorroborated evidence of the victim in the case of sexual offences against persons of and above the age of 14; (iii) any rule of law or practice whereby in criminal proceedings the evidence of one witness is incapable of corroborating that of another witness should be abrogated; (iv) the court should warn the jury of the special need for caution when the evidence of identification is disputed.

One of several other plausible views is that no change is necessary. The rule of law requiring a warning of the danger of acting on the uncorroborated evidence of accomplices can never increase, and may decrease, the

---

[1] *R.* v. *Anslow,* [1962] Crim. L. R. 101.

[2] *R.* v. *Evans,* [1965] 2 Q. B. 295; [1964] 3 All E. R. 401.

[3] *R.* v. *Clynes* (1960), 44 Cr. App. Rep. 158.

[4] *R.* v. *Zielinski,* [1950] 2 All E. R. 1114; *R.* v. *Clynes* (*supra*); but a passage in *R.* v. *Sims,* [1946] K. B. 531, at p. 544 could be construed to mean that the judge must always point out to the jury what is capable of constituting corroboration; and see *R.* v. *Tragen,* [1956] Crim. L. R. 332.

[5] *R.* v. *Goddard,* [1962] 3 All E. R. 582. Such a direction is of course unnecessary where there is no corroboration (*R.* v. *Fisher,* [1965] 1 All E. R. 677).

[6] *R.* v. *Thomas* (1959), 43 Cr. App. Rep. 210.

[7] *The People* (*A.-G.*) v. *Shaw,* [1960] I. R. 168.

chances of a conviction of an innocent person; the same is true of the rule that accomplices who are parties to the crime charged cannot corroborate each other; and it is open to the courts to recognise new situations in which something like the corroboration warning is necessary.

On the other hand, it can be argued with equal plausibility that the proposals of the Criminal Law Revision Committee do not go far enough. At long last, it may be said, notice has been taken of the observations of Chief Baron JOY concerning accomplices made as long ago as 1836:

> "Why the case of an accomplice should require a particular rule for itself; why it should not, like that of every other witness of whose credit there is an impeachment, be left to the unfettered discretion of the judge, to deal with as the circumstances of each particular case may require, it seems difficult to explain." [1]

But why not apply the observations to sexual offences? Is the following statement in para. 186 of the 11th Report really convincing?

> "In sexual cases [the reason for a requirement of a warning about the danger of acting on uncorroborated evidence] is the danger that the complainant may have made a false accusation owing to sexual neurosis, jealousy, fantasy, spite or a girl's refusal to admit that she consented to an act of which she is now ashamed. In the case of an accomplice any special danger that there may be in relying on the witness's evidence is apparent from the fact that he is an accomplice or it can easily be made apparent by the defence. In the case of a sexual offence the danger may be hidden."

Those who take the view that the proposals of the Committee do not go far enough would applaud something like the following amended version of clause 20 (1) of the draft Bill attached to the 11th Report:

> "At a trial on indictment it shall be for the court to decide in its discretion, having regard to the evidence given, whether the jury should be given a direction about convicting the accused on uncorroborated evidence; and, accordingly, any rule of law or practice whereby at such a trial it is in certain circumstances obligatory for the court to give the jury such a direction is hereby abrogated."

References rendering the clause subject to the recommendations about sexual offences and the Perjury Act, 1911, have been omitted, and the word "direction" has been substituted for "warning" because it is assumed that proponents of the view under consideration would approve of the abolition of requirements of corroboration as a matter of law such as that which the Committee contemplates retaining in the case of sexual offences against children under 14.

The mention of trials on indictment in clause 20 (1) serves as a reminder that the requirement of warnings about the dangers of acting on uncorroborated evidence is unrealistic in the case of the vastly more numerous summary trials. The Criminal Law Revision Committee did about all that can be done by recommending the following clause:

> "At the summary trial of a person for an offence the court shall have regard to all such enactments as would or might in comparable circumstances at a trial on indictment require the court to warn the jury of a special need for caution before convicting the accused." [2]

---

[1] See para. 184 of the 11th Report.
[2] Clause 28.

But is it not somewhat odd to require a magistrate to reason as follows on a charge of indecent assault brought by a respectable middle-aged female: "I believe her evidence, but I must think twice before acting upon it because sex is a mysterious thing", whereas, on a charge of assault brought by a man with numerous convictions for violence, the magistrate can simply say to himself "I believe his evidence and I need not think twice about acting upon it because there is no particular danger that charges of violence will be made on account of neurosis, jealousy, fantasy or spite"?

Those who, in general, favour what may described as the "unfettered discretion" approach, can, with perfect consistency, approve of a requirement of some kind of cautionary direction, whether it is to be administered by a judge to a jury or a magistrate to himself, in cases of disputed identification because there is a consensus of opinion that it is in such cases that there is a specially grave risk of convicting an innocent man. The weakness of the present law and the recommendations of the Criminal Law Revision Committee is that they are based on assumptions which do not appear to be supported on a consensus of opinion, still less on anything that can be called "empirical evidence."

It is therefore submitted that, subject to reservations about cases of disputed identification, the unfettered discretion approach is the best answer that English law can give to the questions whether, when and to what extent corroboration should be required. The discretion would have to be subject to appellate control, and a possible argument against the commended approach is that it would lead to too many appeals; but this is exactly the same objection as that which is levelled against the present law. Such technical questions as "who is an accomplice"? "what is corroboration"? and "was the jury warned in the right terms"? are currently quite a fertile source of appeals. At least it would be an improvement to speak to juries in terms of a "special need for caution" rather than telling them that it is "dangerous" to act on "uncorroborated evidence" (whatever "corroboration" may mean) although they may do so if they believe the evidence, but something which enhances the credibility of the evidence is not necessarily corroborative of it.[1]

---

[1] I am fortified in my preference for the discretionary approach by the following remarks of Professor Heydon and Mr. C. E. Tapper respectively: "The Criminal Law Revision Committee's proposals [with regard to accomplices] appear to be the best solution yet offered" (Heydon in [1973] Crim. L. R. at p. 281). The proposals with regard to accomplices represent the discretionary approach, but Professor Heydon is not committed to it in any other respect. "It ought to be sufficient to warn the jury of the danger of convicting on the evidence of accomplices, children (sworn or unsworn), complainants in sexual cases or collaborators in concoction, the precise formulation of any such direction to vary with the facts of each case" (Tapper, 36 M. L. R. at p. 545). This does not preclude Mr. Tapper from advocating a fixed statutory list of cases in which such warnings should be given. I should add that, though in favour (not without some hesitancy) of the discretionary approach in the case of corroboration, I am less enamoured with it in relation to the admissibility of evidence, although I naturally recognise the need for some judicial discretion even in this latter context.

CHAPTER X

THE COURSE OF EVIDENCE

In this chapter an account is given of the principal rules governing the examination-in-chief, cross-examination and re-examination of witnesses. Such an account can hardly hope to be entirely satisfactory because it is concerned with regulations that are either matters of common knowledge or else can only be thoroughly mastered by experience; but the rules with which it deals are among the most characteristic of the English law of evidence. The elucidation of facts by means of questions put by parties or their representatives to witnesses summoned, for the most part,[1] by them, called mainly in the order of their choice,[2] before a judge, acting as umpire rather than inquisitor,[3] is the essential feature of the English "adversary" or "accusatorial" system of justice. Not only is an appreciation of this procedure desirable for its own sake, but it is necessary for a proper understanding of such matters as the law concerning the admissibility of the convictions and character of parties discussed in Chapter XIV, or the structure of s. 1 (f) of the Criminal Evidence Act, 1898, considered in Chapter XV.

The methods by which witnesses are brought before the court—subpoena, summons or voluntary attendance—are best studied in books on practice. This is also true of the ways in which evidence may be taken

---

[1] In civil cases the judge can only call a witness with the consent of the parties (*Re Enoch and Zaretsky, Bock & Co.*, [1910] 1 K. B. 327); but such consent is unnecessary on motions to commit for contempt (*Yianni* v. *Yianni*, [1966] 1 All E. R. 231). The judge's powers are wider in a criminal case, but he must have good reason for calling a witness after the defence is closed (*R.* v. *Harris*, [1927] 2 K. B. 587; *R.* v. *Cleghorn*, [1967] 2 Q. B. 584; [1967] 1 All E. R. 996; cf. *R.* v. *Tregear*, [1967] 2 Q. B. 574; [1967] 1 All E. R. 989); and neither he nor a party with his leave may call a witness after the jury has retired, even at the request of the jury (*R.* v. *Owen*, [1952] 2 Q. B. 362; [1952] 1 All E. R. 1040; *R.* v. *Wilson* (1957), 41 Crim. App. Rep. 226; *R.* v. *Gerring* (1965), 50 Crim. App. Rep. 18; *R.* v. *Lawrence*, [1968] 1 All E. R. 579; *R.* v. *Nixon* (1968), 2 All E. R. 33; as to proceedings before justices see *Webb* v. *Leadbetter*, [1966] 2 All E. R. 114 and *Phelan* v. *Back*, [1972] 1 All E. R. 901). The rule is too rigid and was not followed by the Supreme Court of Eire in *The People (A.-G.)* v. *O'Brien*, [1963] I. R. 65 where all the English authorities are reviewed; nor is the rule followed in Victoria (*R.* v. *Harrison*, [1966] V. R. 72 following *R.* v. *Hodgkinson*, [1954] V. L. R. 140. For a proposed relaxation of the English rule see 11th Report of the Criminal Law Revision Committee, paras. 213–216. In Australia the judge's powers calling a witness are more restricted, even in a criminal case (*Titheradge* v. *R.* (1918), 24 C. L. R. 107).

[2] *Briscoe* v. *Briscoe*, [1966] 1 All E. R. 465; but in a criminal case an accused who opts to give evidence must do so before his witnesses except where their evidence is formal or uncontroversial (*R.* v. *Smith*. [1968] 2 All E. R. 115; for a proposed relaxation of this rule see the 11th Report of the Criminal Law Revision Committee, para. 107). As to the obligation of the prosecution to have in court all witnesses named on the back of the indictment see *R.* v. *Oliva*, [1965] 3 All E. R. 116 where the authorities are reviewed. The prosecution has a large measure of discretion with regard to calling these witnesses or tendering them for examination. See also *R.* v. *Evans* [1964] V. R. 717.

[3] The judge may, of course, question the witnesses, but he must not descend into the arena (*Yuill* v. *Yuill*, [1945] P. 15; [1945] 1 All E. R. 183; *R.* v. *Clewer* (1953), 37 Cr. App. Rep. 37; *Jones* v. *National Coal Board*, [1957] 2 Q. B. 55; [1957] 2 All E. R. 155).

before trial, the right to begin and the order of the advocates' speeches; but, as reference is made to these matters during the exposition of other parts of the subject, they are discussed in the barest outline in section 1. Section 2 is concerned with the main rules governing examination-in-chief, while those that control cross-examination, re-examination and evidence in rebuttal are mentioned in section 3.

SECTION 1. MISCELLANEOUS PROCEDURAL MATTERS

A. EVIDENCE BEFORE TRIAL

(1) CIVIL CASES

In civil cases, all the evidence is normally given *viva voce* at the hearing; but it may be taken before trial and read at the trial when it is given by affidavit, on commission, under letters of request, in answer to interrogatories or by way of perpetuation of testimony.

(i) Affidavits.—In a number of cases, specially provided for by Rules of Court, evidence may be by affidavit. This is allowed in matters coming before the Chancery Division on originating summons or motion, and orders may be made for the proof of particular facts by affidavit on an interlocutory summons in any division of the High Court. The statements in the affidavit are, of course, not subject to cross-examination, and they may sometimes be based on the knowledge, information or belief of the deponent, but, in appropriate cases, he can be obliged to attend for cross-examination.

(ii) Commissions.—Under Order 39, rule 1, of the Rules of the Supreme Court, the court or a judge may, in any cause or matter where it shall appear necessary for the purposes of justice, make any order for the examination upon oath before the court or judge or any officer of the court, or any other person, and at any place, of any witness or person, and may empower any party to any such cause or matter to give such deposition in evidence therein, on such terms, if any, as the court or a judge may direct. The order is usually made when the witness is ill or abroad or is likely to be abroad at the time of the hearing. A practising lawyer, rather than an officer of the court, is usually named as examiner. The witnesses, parties and advocates attend before him, the witnesses are examined, cross-examined and re-examined. The examiner takes a note of any objection to the admissibility of evidence that may be raised. The judge will only allow the deposition to be read at the hearing, without the consent of the party against whom it is given if the maker is still unable to attend court.[1]

(iii) Letters of request.—Letters of request may be issued to a foreign, dominion or colonial court asking one of their judges to take the evidence of a specific person within the jurisdiction of the court. The depositions are remitted to the High Court, and may be read at the trial.[2]

(iv) Interrogatories.—If an order for interrogatories is made, they are answered on affidavit, and the affidavit may be read at the trial. An order

---

[1] Order 38, rule 9. The governing statute is the Evidence by Commission Act 1859. This permits the taking of evidence in England for the use of another British court. The taking of evidence in England for the use of a foreign court is governed by the Foreign Tribunals Evidence Act, 1856. See also R. S. C. order 70.

[2] Order 39, rule 2.

for interrogatories directs a party to answer written questions addressed to him by his adversary on oath. The procedure is designed to facilitate proof of the adversary's case and to save expense; but the court will not allow interrogatories of an oppressive nature.

(v) Perpetuation of testimony.—Under Order 39, rule 15, any person who would under the circumstances alleged by him to exist become entitled, upon the happening of any future event, to any honour, title, dignity, or office, or to any estate or interest in any property, real or personal, the right or claim to which cannot be brought to trial by him before the happening of such event, may commence an action to perpetuate any testimony, which may be material for establishing such right or claim. This procedure is rarely used, but it might have to be employed by someone who is contingently entitled to property if certain facts can be proved in the future when there is a danger that the evidence of these facts will not be available, and the court is unlikely to make a present declaration concerning future rights.

(2) Criminal Cases[1]

Written statements may be made for the purpose of committal proceedings against a person charged with an indictable offence in accordance with the provisions of section 2 of the Criminal Justice Act, 1967, and depositions may be taken at such proceedings. When the makers of the statements or depositions attend the trial, their testimony, and not the statements or depositions, constitutes the evidence in the case; but a limited provision is made for the use of the depositions and statements as evidence of the facts stated therein in the absence of the deponents. Similar use may also be made of depositions taken before a coroner, or under s. 41 of the Magistrates' Courts Act, 1952, and s. 6 of the Criminal Law Amendment Act, 1867, or under various other statutory provisions.

(i) Committal proceedings.—Some of the witnesses or makers of statements at the committal proceedings may be conditionally ordered to attend the trial, in which case their depositions or statements may be read as evidence if they have not been required to attend. This is the effect of section 13 (3) of the Criminal Justice Act, 1925, as amended by the Criminal Procedure (Attendance of Witnesses) Act, 1965, as applied to committals without consideration of the evidence by section 2 (7) of the Criminal Justice Act, 1967. The subsection also enables the deposition to be read if the maker is proved to be dead or insane, or so ill as not to be able to travel, or to be kept out of the way by means of the procurement of the accused.

(ii) Coroners.—When depositions are taken by a coroner, there does not appear to be any similar statutory provision for their being read at any trial that takes place on the coroner's inquisition; but in *R. v. Cowle*[2] it was held that the deposition of a dead deponent might be read if it was signed by him and the coroner, and the accused had an opportunity of cross-examination.

---

[1] According to Archbold (38th edition) § 460, commissions are not issued under the Evidence by Commission Act, 1859, in criminal cases. The Criminal Law Revision Committee recommended no change in the law or practice with regard to obtaining evidence from abroad (11th Report, para. 277).

[2] (1907), 71 J. P. 152, contra *R. v. Butcher* (1900), 64 J. P. 808; see also *R. v. Black* 1909), 74 J. P. 71 and *R. v. Marriott* (1911), 75 J. P. 288.

(iii) Section 41 of the Magistrates' Courts Act, 1952, and s. 6 of the Criminal Law Amendment Act, 1867.—Under s. 41 of the Magistrates' Courts Act, 1952, a deposition may be taken out of court by a magistrate from anyone who can give information with regard to an indictable offence if he is dangerously ill and it is impracticable to take the deposition in the ordinary way. The deposition may be read as evidence at the committal proceedings, but the provisions of section 6 of the Criminal Law Amendment Act, 1867, apply. This enables a justice of the peace to take a deposition from someone who is dangerously ill for use at the trial. Reasonable notice must have been given to the person against whom the deposition is to be read in evidence, and he must have had an opportunity of cross-examining the deponent.[1]

(iv) Miscellaneous statutory provisions.—Under s. 42 and s. 43 of the Children and Young Persons Act, 1933, the deposition of a child or young person may be taken out of court, and used at the preliminary examination or trial of a person for an offence under the Act. The conditions are that the child's attendance in court should cause serious danger to his life or health, and that the accused should have had an opportunity of cross-examining him.[2]

Under s. 691 of the Merchant Shipping Act, 1894, whenever, in the course of any legal proceedings instituted in any part of Her Majesty's dominions, the testimony of any witness is required, and he cannot be found within the United Kingdom if the proceedings are instituted there, any deposition that he may have previously made on oath in relation to the subject matter of the proceedings before any justice, magistrate or consular official, shall be admissible evidence. If the proceedings are criminal, the deposition must have been made in the presence of the accused.[3] Though they are ostensibly very wide, reliance cannot often be placed upon these provisions because it is not often that such a deposition as is contemplated by them was in fact made by a person who would, if he had been available, have been a useful witness.

B. THE RIGHT TO BEGIN

The plaintiff, prosecutor or their respective advocates open every case in the sense that they explain the issues to the court, but questions sometimes arise concerning the right to begin calling evidence. The Crown will almost always have the right to begin in criminal cases where there is a plea of not guilty,[4] because there will be some issue upon which the evidential if not the legal, burden will be borne by the prosecution; but, now that there can be formal admissions and agreed statements of fact under section 10 and section 9 of the Criminal Justice Act, 1967, respectively, it is theoretically possible to imagine a case, for example, a plea of

---

[1] The sections should be consulted for further procedural requirements.

[2] See also Children and Young Persons Act, 1963, as to committal proceedings in the case of sexual offences.

[3] The section applies in civil and criminal cases. It re-enacts earlier provisions, as to which see *R.* v. *Conning* (1868), 11 Cox C. C. 134; *R.* v. *Anderson* (1868), 11 Cox C. C. 154 and *R.* v. *Stewart* (1876), 13 Cox C. C. 296.

[4] Where a special plea is raised, such as *autrefois convict*, and there is a dispute of fact, the accused would begin. A plea of guilty does not admit everything on the depositions (*R.* v. *Riley*, [1896] 1 Q. B. 309, 318; *R.* v. *Maitland*, [1964] S. A. S. R. 332 according to which an accused pleading guilty should call evidence as to disputed facts).

insanity or diminished responsibility, in which the accused would have the right to begin. In civil cases, the plaintiff has the right to begin if he bears the evidential burden on any issue raised by the pleadings,[1] including the quantum of damages. This was established in *Mercer* v. *Whall*,[2] an action for wrongful dismissal in which the defendant admitted that he determined the plaintiff's contract of service prematurely, but alleged that he was justified in doing so. It was held that the plaintiff ought to begin calling evidence because the damages claimed by him were not agreed. If damages had not been in issue, the defendant would have had the right to begin, because there would have been no fact with regard to which the plaintiff bore the evidential burden.[3]

C. THE ADVOCATES' SPEECHES

The incidence of the right to begin may affect the order in which the advocates' speeches are made to the court. In civil cases, assuming that he has this right, the plaintiff opens the case to the court,[4] calls his witnesses and sums up if the defendant does not call witnesses. The defendant then replies and thus secures the last word. If the defendant calls witnesses, the plaintiff does not sum up at the conclusion of his case, but the defendant opens his case, calls his witnesses and sums up, leaving the plaintiff with the right of reply.[5] The foregoing procedure is reversed if the defendant has the right to begin calling evidence.[6]

In criminal cases tried on indictment, the prosecutor opens and calls his evidence. If the accused does not call evidence, the prosecutor sums up, leaving the accused with the right of reply. If the accused calls evidence, the prosecutor's closing speech is made after the close of the evidence for the defence with the result that the accused has the right of reply.[7]

In both civil and criminal cases, the above procedure may be interspersed with a submission that there is no case to answer, arguments about the admissibility of evidence,[8] or arguments on points of law.

SECTION 2. EXAMINATION-IN-CHIEF

The object of examination-in-chief is to obtain testimony in support of the version of the facts in issue or relevant to the issue for which the party

---

[1] *Pontifex* v. *Jolly* (1839), 9 C. & P. 202, showing that an amendment will not be allowed for the sole purpose of altering the right to begin. See *W. Lusty & Sons, Ltd.* v. *Morris Wilkinson & Co. (Nottingham), Ltd.*, [1954] 2 All E. R. 347, showing that, where a claim is admitted in court, the defendant may begin calling evidence on his counterclaim. See also *Seldon* v. *Davidson*, [1968] 2 All E. R. 755.

[2] (1845), 5 Q. B. 447.

[3] For the right to begin in matrimonial causes see *Arding* v. *Arding*, [1954] 2 All E. R. 671 and *Hewitt* v. *Hewitt*, [1948] P. 150; [1948] 1 All E. R. 242.

[4] He must not allude to facts with regard to which he cannot call evidence (*Faith* v. *M'Intyre* (1835), 7 C. & P. 44; *R.* v. *O'Neill* (1950), 34 Cr. App. Rep. 108).

[5] Even if the defendant merely puts documents to the plaintiff's witnesses in cross-examination so that the documents become exhibits he loses his right to the last word (*Weller* v. *O'Brien*, [1962] 3 All E. R. 65).

[6] This is laid down by Order 35, rule 7, for cases tried with a jury.

[7] Criminal Procedure (Right of Reply) Act, 1964. For summary trial see Magistrates' Courts Rules, 1968, rr.13 and 14.

[8] If, as will usually be the case, counsel knows that objection will be taken to an item of evidence, he should not refer to it in opening, and the objection should be raised when the evidence is about to be given (*R.* v. *Cole* (1941), 28 Cr. App. Rep. 43; *R.* v. *Zielinski*, [1950] 2 All E. R. 1114). This procedure can be applied to civil cases tried with a jury. The point is not so important when there is no jury.

calling the witness contends. The facts in issue and the concept of relevancy have already been discussed, while the various exclusionary rules which prohibit the proof of certain facts are considered elsewhere in this book. At present we are primarily concerned with the manner in which witnesses who can, *ex hypothesi*, give relevant and admissible evidence must be treated. Generally speaking they may not be asked leading questions, and, although a witness may refresh his memory by referring to documents previously prepared by him, he cannot usually be asked about his former statements with a view to their becoming evidence of the facts stated or in order to demonstrate his consistency. A party may call someone else to contradict his witness who has given unfavourable evidence with regard to a fact in issue or relevant to the issue, but he may only discredit his witness if the judge considers that witness to be hostile. We shall therefore be concerned with leading questions, refreshing memory, previous statements of witnesses consistent with their present testimony and unfavourable or hostile witnesses.

A. LEADING QUESTIONS

(i) Definition and illustration.—A leading question is one which either (a) suggests the answer desired, or (b) assumes the existence of disputed facts as to which the witness is to testify.[1] An example of the first type would be the following question put to one of the plaintiff's witnesses in a running-down case—"Did you seen another car coming very fast from the opposite direction?"[2] It should be split up into something like the following—"Did you notice any other traffic? Which direction was it coming from? Was it going fast or slow?" A typical example of the second type of leading question would be, "What did you do after Smith hit you?" put to the plaintiff in an action for assault before he had deposed to being hit by Smith.

Lord ELLENBOROUGH once said that if questions are asked to which the answer "yes" or "no" would be conclusive, they would certainly be objectionable;[3] but this is untenable as a test for determining whether a question is leading. The answer "yes" or "no" would be conclusive to such a question as "Did you notice any traffic?" but it would not if put to a witness who had just said that he was standing on the side of the road. Again, such a question as "Did you hear what A. said?" would be a leading question of the second type if the presence of A. in the witness's company, or the fact that A. said anything were in dispute, and as yet unproved by the witness, otherwise it would fall outside the definition of a leading question. As BEST said, "It should never be forgotten that 'leading' is a relative, not an absolute term";[4] everything depends on the context.

The answers to leading questions are not inadmissible in evidence although the method by which they were obtained may rob them of all or most of their significance.[5] Leading questions are objectionable because

---

[1] This is in effect the definition in Stephen's *Digest of the Law of Evidence* (12th edition), art. 140. The alternative is to describe questions of type (b) as improper rather than leading.

[2] Munkman, *Technique of Advocacy*, 42–43.

[3] *Nicholls* v. *Dowding and Kemp* (1815), 1 Stark. 81.

[4] *Law of Evidence* (12th edition), 562.

[5] *Moor* v. *Moor*, [1954] 2 All E. R. 458.

of the danger of collusion between the person asking them and the witness, or the impropriety of suggesting the existence of facts which are not in evidence. Account must also be taken of human laziness—it is easy to say "yes" or "no" on demand, and most leading questions can be answered in this way, even if the same is true of some questions that are not leading. There is, however, no doubt that leading questions save time, they are often an indispensable prelude to further interrogation, and a travesty could be made of any examination-in-chief by an over-emphatic insistence on the prohibition. There are, therefore, numerous recurring situations to which it does not apply.

(ii) Exceptions to the prohibition.—A witness may always be led on the formal introductory part of his testimony. The following is the beginning of almost any examination-in-chief—"Is your name John Smith?" "Are you a baker?" "Do you live at 1 Any Street, Anywhere?" Undisputed matters belong to the same category. In a divorce case in which the marriage was not denied by the respondent, the examination might well continue "Were you married at St. John's Church, Tooting?" "Did you live happily with the respondent until last June?"

It would often be impossible to persuade a witness to identify a person or thing in court without the aid of leading questions. Accordingly such questions as "Was he the man you saw?" or "Was that the book he lent you?" have to be allowed every day.[1]

Questions with regard to the identification of persons or things are, in fact, an example of a broader class of question rendered necessary in order to focus the witness's mind on a particular point. Someone is called to prove a partnership; in order to stimulate his memory, he may be asked whether named persons did, or did not, participate in the business.[2]

Lists are sometimes drawn up of the matters with regard to which leading questions are permissible. Introductory or undisputed matters, questions of identity and questions designed to bring the witness's mind to the point are among the items that commonly appear on such lists, but the subject does not lend itself to exhaustive treatment of this nature. There are bound to be cases which do not fall within any list. A witness is in court while a previous witness is giving evidence about the contents of a letter; when the time comes for the second witness to give his evidence-in-chief, he says that he read the letter; he can be asked whether it contained a particular passage.[3] A magistrate dies in the course of a case in which many witnesses have given evidence; provided there is an opportunity of cross-examination, each witness can be recalled before a new magistrate. After the witness has considered his deposition, he can be asked whether the document represents his evidence because long leading questions may be allowed, even in-chief, at the discretion of the judge.[4] No one would have dreamed of including these cases in any list before they were decided.

It is said on good authority[5] that leading questions may always be put in cross-examination. No doubt this is true so far as questions suggesting the desired answer are concerned; but those which suggest the existence of

---

[1] *R.* v. *Watson* (1817), 2 Stark. 116, at p. 128.
[2] *Acerro* v. *Petroni* (1815), 1 Stark. 100; *Nicholls* v. *Dowding and Kemp* (*supra*).
[3] *Courteen* v. *Touse* (1807), 1 Camp. 43.
[4] *Ex parte Bottomley*, [1909] 2 K. B. 14, at p. 21.
[5] *Parkin* v. *Moon* (1836), 7 C. & P. 408.

unproved facts might well be disallowed, even in cross-examination, and in *R. v. MacDonell*,[1] it was said that questions put to a prisoner in cross-examination ought to be put in an interrogative form; they should commence "did you?" and not "you did". The judge has a wide discretion in these matters, and it is difficult to say more than that leading questions will usually be disallowed in-chief, or in re-examination, although they will generally be permitted in cross-examination.

B. REFRESHING MEMORY

Perhaps the most important feature of an English trial, civil or criminal, is its "orality". Much greater weight is attached to the answers given by witnesses in court on oath or affirmation than to written statements previously made by them. We shall see that all previous statements of witnesses, whether made orally or in writing, are now admissible, with the leave of the court, as evidence of the facts stated in civil cases under the Civil Evidence Act 1968;[2] but the persistence of our faith in orality is shown by the fact that the Act renders the admissibility of a witness's previous written statement far less a matter of course than was the case under the Evidence Act, 1938. Under that statute, it was only necessary to call the maker of the statement, ask him whether the signature on it was his, and put the document in as of right without any examination-in-chief.[3] Such a course was frowned on and no doubt it was seldom adopted in practice, but it was undesirable as a possibility in any case in which the facts were seriously disputed because, contrary to what is commonly supposed by the laymen, the way in which a witness responds to examination-in-chief is often more informative with regard to his reliability than his reaction to cross-examination. Accordingly, in addition to requiring the leave of the court for the reception of the previous statement of a witness at the behest of the party calling him, section 2 (2) of the Act of 1968 stipulates that, in general, the statement shall not be admitted before the conclusion of the maker's examination-in-chief.

Yet, for all its apparent orality, an examination-in-chief is rarely conducted "out of the blue". The witness has usually given a statement (commonly called his "proof of evidence") to the solicitor for the party calling him or, if he is a prosecution witness in a criminal case, he will have made a statement to the police. It is on the basis of these statements that the questions put to the witness in-chief will be framed. The statement will frequently have been made a considerable time before the trial, and the witness may or may not have retained a copy of it. In these circumstances, it is inevitable as it is desirable that the witness should read his statement shortly before the hearing or even be taken through it by the person to whom it was made. If it were to transpire that there had been anything in the nature of "coaching" by such person, or some kind of pre-trial confabulation between witnesses, the judge would no doubt treat the evidence with the contempt it deserved. It was, however, once suggested that it is objectionable for prosecution witnesses to be provided with copies

---

[1] (1909), 2 Cr. App. Rep. 322
[2] Until Part I of the 1968 Act is applied to magistrates' courts, the Evidence Act, 1938 will continue to apply to civil proceedings in those courts.
[3] *Hilton v. Lancashire Dynamo Nevelin, Ltd.*, [1964] 2 All E. R. 769.

of their statements to the police to be read or gone through shortly before the trial;[1] but it would have been difficult to justify or enforce a special rule for this particular case, and, if the statement were an elaborate one, as even statements to the police sometimes are, the rule would have been absurd. The practice has since been held to be perfectly proper,[2] but the decision of the Court of Appeal to this effect has been strongly criticised[3] mainly on the ground that the witness's statement could not have been employed to refresh his memory while giving evidence in court because it was not made contemporaneously with the events to which it related. This is a rather technical point to take in relation to a general practice without which the ordinary trial process would be unworkable.

There is moreover, an important difference between the refreshment of a witness's memory in and out of court. The latter relates to the entirety of the witness's evidence whereas the former usually only relates to specific points, the date of a particular payment, or the words used at a particular interview for example. This will not be the case invariably because a witness may be called to prove a single point, whether a particular payment was made, for example. If a witness were to be called and simply say "I remember nothing about the events in question but I am prepared to swear that everything said in the proof I gave to Mr. Smith is true", the proof, if received by the court as evidence of the facts stated, would be a hearsay statement,[4] theoretically admissible with leave in a civil case,[5] and wholly inadmissible in a criminal case.[6] It would be no less a hearsay statement if the proof were read aloud to the court by the witness.

Judging by the reported cases, the English courts have not had to deal with the problem of the amnesiac or near amnesiac witness, and it is anybody's guess whether they would follow the practice adopted by a British Columbian court in *R. v. Pitt*.[7] On a charge of attempting to murder her husband, the accused, who was suffering from functional amnesia, said in court that she could remember little of what happened. Her counsel then applied for leave to have her hypnotised in court, a hypnotist having given evidence that her memory might be refreshed by an hypnotic trance. The application was granted, the wife giving her evidence after she had emerged from the trance. The decision was partly based on the analogy of refreshment of memory, but reference was also made to the unfairness of not allowing the accused the benefit of the latest medical techniques.

It will be convenient to enumerate the conditions on which a witness is allowed to refer to a document in order to refresh his memory while giving evidence, before distinguishing between the two types of case in which memory is said to be "refreshed" in court.

---

[1] *R. v. Yellow and Thay* (1932), J. P. 826.
[2] *R. v. Richardson*, [1971] 2 Q. B. 484; [1971] 2 All E. R. 773; see also *R. v. Mullins* (1848), 3 Cox C. C. 526; *Gleed v. Stroud*, [1962] Journal of Criminal Law 161; *Lau Pak Ngam v. R.*, [1966] Crim. L. R. 443; *R. v. Kerenko* (1964), 51 W. W. R. 53; *R. v. Musterer* (1967), 61 W. W. R. 63.
[3] M. N. Howard, *Refreshment of Memory Out of Court*, [1972] Crim. L. R. 351.
[4] P. 7, *ante*.
[5] Civil Evidence Act, 1968, s. 2.
[6] *R. v. McLean* (1968), 52 Cr. App. Rep. 80.
[7] (1968), 68 D. L. R. (2d) 513. The problem with which *R. v. Podola*, [1960] 1 Q. B. 325; [1959] 3 All E. R. 418 was concerned was of course quite different, the issue being whether amnesia affected fitness to plead not whether an amnesiac's memory can be refreshed.

(1) Conditions on which Memory may be Refreshed
by Reference to a Document

The document must have been made substantially at the same time as the occurrence of the events to which the witness is required to depose, it must have been made or read over by, or under the supervision of, the witness, it must be produced to the court or opposite party on demand, and, in one class of case, the document must be the original.

(i) Contemporaneity.—Contemporaneity is, as always, a question of fact. In *Jones* v. *Stroud* [1] it was held that a witness could not refresh his memory from a copy made six months after the original was brought into existence, but in *Burrough* v. *Martin* [2] a witness was allowed to refresh his memory with regard to a voyage by reference to the ship's log book, the entries in which were compiled after the events to which they related. In *R.* v. *Simmonds* [3] notes made by customs officers at the first convenient opportunity after returning to their office from lengthy interviews were held to comply with the condition of contemporaneity, and the officers were permitted to read them to the court. It was said [4] to be a course constantly adopted by police officers giving evidence of a long interview or series of interviews with suspects; our courts are not slaves to orality. [5]

There are cases suggesting that a witness may refresh his memory from depositions; but in one of them, a civil case, the deposition was said to have been signed at the time of the events to which it related, [6] in another the deposition was used in cross examination [7] and, in the third, the deposition may have been put to a hostile witness as a prelude to the use of leading questions. [8]

(ii) Documents supervised or read by witness.—*Burrough* v. *Martin* also shows that it is not essential that the document should have been made by the witness himself, for the compilation of the log-book was merely supervised by him. In *Dyer* v. *Best*, [9] a witness was allowed to refresh his memory concerning the day on which certain proceedings were brought by referring to an article in a newspaper which he had read at the time and then believed to be true. POLLOCK, C.B., said:

> "If a man at the time he has a recollection of certain facts reads a document containing a statement, which he knows to be true, of the facts, he may again refer to it to refresh his memory although, at the time he first read it, he made no memorandum." [10]

In *R.* v. *Mills*, [11] it was held that a police officer might refresh his memory

---

[1] (1825), 2 C. & P. 196.

[2] (1809), 2 Camp. 112; *R.* v. *Langton* (1876), 2 Q. B. D. 296.

[3] (1967), 51 Cr. App. Rep. 316.   [4] At p. 329.

[5] P. 202, *ante*.   [6] *Wood* v. *Cooper* (1845), 1 Car. & Kir. 645.

[7] *R.* v. *Edwards and Woodcock* (1837), 8 C. & P. 26.

[8] *R.* v. *Williams* (1853), 6 Cox C. C. 343. See also *R.* v. *Laurin* (1902), 6 Can. Crim. Cas. 138 and *R.* v. *Marshall* (1965), 51 W. W. R. 185. In *R.* v. *Woodcock*, [1963] Crim. L. R. 273, refreshing memory from depositions was not permitted.

[9] (1866), 4 H. & C. 189. See also Indian Evidence Act, 1872, s. 159. Conversely it has been held in South Africa that a witness may refresh his memory from a document dictated, but not read over by him at a time when the facts were fresh in his memory (*R.* v. *O'Linn*, [1960] 1 S. A. 545); but it is assumed that the English rule would not permit this (*R.* v. *McLean* (1968), 52 Cr. App. Rep. 80).

[10] 4 H. & C., p. 192.

[11] [1962] 3 All E. R. 298. There is no objection to police officers refreshing their memory from notebooks or statements prepared by them in collaboration (*R.* v. *Bass*, [1953] 1 Q. B. 681; *O'Sullivan* v. *Waterman*, [1965] S. A. S. R. 150).

by referring to a note which he had checked from tape recordings of conversations between accused persons. The officer had heard the conversations but confirmed and improved his note from the recording which was not put in evidence.

(iii) Production of the document.—The document must be handed to the opposite party or his advocate to enable him to inspect it and, if he so desires, to cross-examine the witness with regard to its contents.[1] The jury may also see the document as it may assist them in estimating the witness's credibility.[2]

(iv) The original.—So far as the requirement with regard to the production of the original is concerned, it was held in *Doe* d. *Church and Phillips* v. *Perkins*[3] that a witness may refresh his memory by any book or paper if he can afterwards swear to the fact from his own recollection, but, if he cannot swear to the fact from recollection any farther than saying that he will do so because he finds it in some book or paper, the original must be produced.

(2) Distinction Between Cases in which Memory is Not Refreshed and Those in which It is

At first sight it may seem strange that anyone should be prepared to swear positively to the truth of that which he does not remember, but a moment's reflection should suffice to show that there are many situations in which almost anybody would do this. If a man is asked whether he shaved himself a week ago last Monday, he will normally say "yes" without hesitation although he has no recollection of the fact, and the ground for his doing so is his confidence in the repetition of his daily practices. It is on this basis that witnesses who have had no recollection of receiving a payment or entering into an agreement have been allowed to swear that they did so because, on sight of a receipt or agreement in their handwriting, they are prepared to depose positively to the fact in question.[4] Indeed, this is such a common practice in cases concerned with refreshing a witness's memory that an Irish judge once said:

> "that is a very inaccurate expression; because in nine cases out of ten the witness's memory is not at all refreshed; he looks at it (the document) again and again; and he recollects nothing of the transaction; but, seeing that it is in his own handwriting, he gives credit to the truth and accuracy of his habits, and, though his memory is a perfect blank, he nevertheless undertakes to swear to the accuracy of his notes".[5]

The distinction between cases in which a past record is presently sworn to be accurate on the faith of a document and those in which present recollection is revived by the sight of such documents as notes and letters appears to be of importance in English law solely in connection with the question whether the original should be produced, the answer being

---

[1] *Beech* v. *Jones* (1848), 5 C. B. 696. See below as to the effect of cross-examination on the document.

[2] *R.* v. *Bass*, [1953] 1 Q. B. 680; [1953] 1 All E. R. 1064.

[3] (1790), 3 Term Rep. 749; *Howard* v. *Canfield* (1836), 1 Jur. 71; *R.* v. *Harvey* (1869), 11 Cox, C. C. 546; *Ames* v. *Nicholson*, [1921] S. A. S. R. 224; *Collaton* v. *Correl*, [1926] S. A. S. R. 87; *King* v. *Bryant*, (No. 2), [1956] S. R. Qd. 570.

[4] *Maugham* v. *Hubbard* (1828), 8 B. & C. 14; cf. *Birchall* v. *Bullough*, [1896] 1 Q. B. 325; and *R.* v. *St. Martin's, Leicester* (1834), 2 Ad. & El. 210.

[5] HAYES, J., in *Lord Talbot de Malahide* v. *Cussack* (1864), 17 I. C. L. R. 213, at p. 220. see also *R.* v. *Bryant* (1946), 31 Cr. App. Rep. 146.

in the affirmative in the first case (unless the original has been lost),[1] but not necessarily so in the second. Wigmore made it the basis of a much more systematic distinction which may well represent the law in other jurisdictions.[2] He argued that, in cases in which there is no revival of present recollection in consequence of the sight of the document, the latter is placed before the court as evidence of the facts recorded by it. This has been repudiated on several occasions in England. In *Maugham* v. *Hubbard*,[3] a witness was called to prove the receipt of money. Being unable to recollect this fact, he was shown an unstamped acknowledgement signed by himself, whereupon he said that he had no doubt that he received the sum specified in it, although he did not recall having done so. It was held that this was sufficient evidence of the payment in spite of the prohibition on the use of unstamped receipts in litigation.

> "The paper itself was not used as evidence of the receipt of the money, but only to enable the witness to refresh his memory; and when he said that he had no doubt that he had received the money there was sufficient parol evidence to prove the payment." [4]

Apart from questions connected with the Stamp Acts, there are at least two reasons why it is important to know whether a document duly authenticated by its author and before the court is evidence. In the first place, it may affect the order of counsel's speeches in civil cases, for putting a document in evidence is the equivalent to calling a witness. Hence, if the defendant does no more than ask one of the plaintiff's witnesses whether a letter is in his handwriting and proceeds to rely on various passages in it he forfeits his common law right to have the last word.[5]

Secondly, it is not until a letter is in evidence that it can lawfully be treated as having any probative value by the judge or jury. This is neatly illustrated by the Canadian case of *Young* v. *Denton* [6] in which the date of an accident was a material fact. The defendant was allowed to refresh his memory from a record made by him soon after the accident, and the judge treated this document as an item of evidence assisting him to decide in favour of the defendant's version of the facts. It was held that he was not justified in doing this because nothing had occurred to make it evidence in the case. The plaintiff had not used the document in cross-examination, and no exception to the common law rule, about to be discussed, that witnesses cannot be asked in-chief about their previous statements in order to prove their consistency applied to the case.

There is an old general rule, inadequately explored in the modern authorities, that, if a party calls for and inspects a document held by the other party,

---

[1] *Topham* v. *M'Gregor* (1844), 1 Car. & Kir. 320.

[2] II *Wigmore*, ch. 28. There is the further contention, hardly supported by the English cases, that, where present recollection is revived by the sight of the document, none of the conditions mentioned in the text need be fulfilled. Wigmore's statement has been acted on by the majority of the New Zealand Court of Appeal against the dissentient view that it was equivalent to applying the Evidence Act, 1938 (the provisions of which have in effect been extended and very considerably relaxed by the Civil Evidence Act, 1968), to criminal cases (*R.* v. *Caesar Naidanovici*, [1962] N. Z. L. R. 334).

[3] (1828), 8 B. & C. 14. *Birchall* v. *Bullough*, [1896] 1 Q. B. 325, is to the same effect, and even stronger because the statute with which it was concerned provided that an unstamped receipt should not be given in evidence or available for any purpose whatever. The decision can only be justified as a bold application of the *ejusdem generis* principle.

[4] Lord TENTERDEN, C.J.

[5] *Weller* v. *O'Brien*, [1962] 3 All E. R. 65.

[6] [1927] 1 D. L. R. 426.

he is bound to put it in evidence if required to do so.[1] But, "Where a document is used to refresh a witness's memory, cross-examining counsel may inspect that document in order to check it without making it evidence. Moreover he may cross-examine upon it without making it evidence provided that his cross-examination does not go further than the parts which are used for refreshing the memory of the witness."[2] If, therefore, a witness refreshes his memory concerning a date or an address by referring to a diary, he may be cross-examined about the form or terms of the entries used to refresh his memory without there being any question of the right of the party calling him to insist that the diary should become evidence in the case. On the other hand, if the witness is cross-examined about other parts of the diary, the party calling him may insist on its being treated as evidence in the case.

The major difficulty about the formulation of the general rule and the exception to it concerns the implication of such expressions as "making a document evidence". Presumably, once it has been "made evidence", the document becomes admissible as evidence of the truth of its contents by way of exception to the rule against hearsay; but there is no English authority on this point.

So far as civil cases are concerned, the matter is put beyond doubt by section 3 (2) of the Civil Evidence Act, 1968, which reads as follows:

> "Nothing in this Act shall affect any of the rules of law relating to the circumstances in which, where a person called as a witness in any civil proceedings is cross-examined on a document used by him to refresh his memory, that document may be made evidence in those proceedings; and Where a document or any part of a document is received in evidence in any such proceedings by virtue of any such rule of law, any statement made in that document or part by the person using the document to refresh his memory shall by virtue of this subsection be admissible as evidence of any fact stated therein of which direct oral evidence by him would be admissible."

Clause 33 (2) of the draft Bill annexed to the 11th Report of the Criminal Law Revision Committee is to the same effect. The subsection and the draft clause may well be declaratory of the existing law.

C. PREVIOUS CONSISTENT STATEMENTS

The general rule at common law is that a witness may not be asked in-chief whether he has formerly made a statement consistent with his present testimony. He cannot narrate such statement if it was oral or refer to it if it was in writing (save for the purpose of refreshing his memory), and other witnesses may not be called to prove it. Not only does the rule prohibit the reception of the statement as a hearsay statement,[3] but it also prohibits proof of the previous oral or written statements of the witness as evidence of his consistency. Thus, in *R v. Roberts*,[4] the accused was charged with murdering a girl by shooting her as she was letting him into

---

[1] *Wareham* v. *Routledge* (1805), 5 Esp. 235; *Calvert* v. *Flower* (1836), 7 C. & P. 386; *Palmer* v. *Maclear and M'Grath* (1858), 1 Sw. & Tr. 149; *Stroud* v. *Stroud*, [1963] 3 All E. R. 539.

[2] *Senat* v. *Senat*, [1965] P. 172, at p. 177; [1965] 2 All E. R. 505, at p. 512. This case probably does not, as the headnote suggests, conflict with *Stroud* v. *Stroud* (*supra*) where the documents called for and inspected were not used to refresh memory. See also *Gregory* v. *Tavernor* (1833), 6 C. & P. 280 and *Payne* v. *Ibbotson* (1858), 27 L. J. Ex. 341.

[3] P. 7, *ante*.

[4] [1942] 1 All E. R. 187.

her house. The defence was that the gun went off accidentally while the accused was trying to make up a quarrel with the girl. Two days later the accused told his father that the defence would be accident. The trial judge would not allow the accused to prove this conversation, and the Court of Criminal Appeal held that the judge had been right.

In this case, the reason given for the rule (sometimes loosely described as "the rule against narrative" or "the rule against self-corroboration") was the ease with which evidence of this nature can be manufactured.[1] But, generally speaking, this can only be apposite when the witness is a party and, in any event, the ease with which evidence can be fabricated is a matter which should affect its weight rather than its admissibility. A more convincing reason was given by Sir W. D. Evans in his notes to Pothier[2] when he said that in an ordinary case, the evidence would be at least superfluous, for the assertions of a witness are to be regarded in general as true, until there is some particular reason for impeaching them as false. The necessity of saving time by avoiding superfluous testimony and sparing the court a protracted inquiry into a multitude of collateral issues which might be raised about such matters as the precise terms of the previous statement is undoubtedly a sound basis for the general rule;[3] but the dangerous tendency towards inflexibility displayed by the common law of evidence may be illustrated by two civil cases which, though they would probably now be decided differently, thanks to the Civil Evidence Act, 1968, if their facts were to recur, would still be applicable in the contexts of criminal prosecutions for fraud and incest respectively.

In *Gillie* v. *Posho, Ltd.*,[4] the respondent company (plaintiff in the original action) claimed arrears of the purchase price of a farm in Kenya. The defendant counterclaimed for damages for fraud on the footing that he had been induced to enter into the contract of sale by a misrepresentation contained in an advertisement issued under the authority of the plaintiff's agent (the company's liquidator). The answer was that the defendant had agreed to buy the farm before the advertisement was published, and the liquidator gave evidence in support of this plea. He produced a letter written by him to the company's solicitor before the appearance of the advertisement, stating that the farm had been sold to the plaintiff, and the trial judge attached considerable importance to it; but the Judicial Committee of the Privy Council advised that there should be a new trial because the letter ought not to have been admitted in evidence.

In *Corke* v. *Corke and Cook*,[5] a husband petitioned for divorce on the ground of adultery. The wife had been in the co-respondent's bedroom, and, when challenged by the husband a few minutes later, both the wife

---

[1] At p. 191, *per* HUMPHREYS, J. See too *per* SWINFEN-EADY, L.J. in *Jones* v. *South Eastern and Chatham Rail. Co.'s Managing Committee* (1918), 87 L. J. K. B. 775, at p. 778.

[2] *Pothier on Obligations* (1806 edition), vol. 2, p. 289.

[3] Generally speaking, as is well known, such confirmatory evidence is not admissible, the reason presumably being that all trials, civil and criminal, must be conducted with an effort to concentrate evidence on what is capable of being cogent" (*per* Lord RADCLIFFE in *Fox* v. *General Medical Council*, [1960] 3 All E. R. 225, at p. 230.

[4] [1939] 2 All E. R. 196. The letter would be admissible with the leave of the court under the Civil Evidence Act, 1968.

[5] [1958] P. 93; [1958] 1 All E. R. 224. The conversation could now be proved with the leave of the court under the Civil Evidence Act, 1968, but, so long as that Act does not apply to magistrates' courts, the decision would govern summary proceedings based on adultery.

and the co-respondent denied adultery. Shortly after that, they phoned a doctor with a request that he should examine them in order to certify that recent intercourse had not taken place. The doctor declined to perform the examination because, in his view, it would have been useless. A majority of the Court of Appeal considered that evidence of the phone conversation ought not to have been admitted by the trial judge, and this was largely on the ground that the wife and co-respondent might have prepared themselves for the examination, or been aware of its inutility, with the result, in either case, that they would simply have been manufacturing evidence.

All previous consistent statements of witnesses are now admissible in civil cases with the leave of the court under the Civil Evidence Act, 1968. If admitted, they are evidence of the facts stated and there is thus no problem, as there is with the common law exceptions to the rule under consideration, of distinguishing between the admissibility of witnesses' statements as evidence of consistency and as evidence of the facts stated. The reception of statements under the Act of 1968 is further considered in chapter XVIII. At this stage it is proposed to consider three well recognised exceptions to the general common law prohibition of the proof of a witness's prior consistent statements—complaints in sexual cases, statements forming part of the same transaction as that to which they refer (admitted as part of the *res gestae*) and previous statements admitted to rebut the suggestion that the witness's testimony was an afterthought. The first may almost certainly be taken to be confined to criminal cases, but the second and third are still relevant to civil as well as criminal proceedings because the leave of the court is not required for the reception of statements to which they apply. There are in addition some further ill defined exceptions to the common law rule which probably only apply to criminal cases, and a word must be said in conclusion about the possibility of the reception of the statements made by a witness out of court under the influence of a truth drug.

(1) COMPLAINTS IN SEXUAL CASES

(i) Development of the law.

(*a*) *The fact of complaint.*—When absence of consent is among the facts in issue, as it is on charges of rape and sundry other sexual offences, it is relevant to consider whether a complaint was made by the person whose consent must be negatived. At the beginning of the eighteenth century HAWKINS referred to the strong presumption against the prosecutrix in a case of rape if she made no complaint within a reasonable time of the alleged outrage,[1] and a similar presumption may have existed in some other cases for, in *R.* v. *Wink*,[2] a policeman was allowed to prove the fact that the prosecutor had complained to him of the robbery with which the accused was charged.

In the Middle Ages, it was essential that the victim should have raised the hue and cry if an appeal of rape were to succeed. When criminal proceedings began to assume their modern form, the practice grew up of limiting the evidence of a complaint to the bare fact that it was made. Anything in the nature of a narrative of the words used by the prosecutrix was prohibited.

---

[1] 1 P. C. ch. 41, s. 9.　　　　　　[2] (1834), 8 C. & P. 397.

(b) *Terms of complaint.*—As HAWKINS, J., said when delivering the judgment of the Court for Crown Cases Reserved in *R.* v. *Lillyman*,[1] the disadvantage of the above practice was that it left the prosecutrix, or the
witness to whom the statement was made, to determine and report to the
jury whether her words amounted to a real complaint. He therefore allowed
the full terms of a complaint to be proved on a charge of attempted carnal
knowledge of a girl between the ages of thirteen and sixteen. HAWKINS, J.,
insisted that the judge must always impress upon the jury that they are
not entitled to make use of the complaint as evidence of the facts of which
complaint was made. There would be no danger of this happening in the
rare case in which the complaint is proved by the prosecutrix because the
facts complained of would be verified by her testimony,[2] but the danger is
present whenever, as is usually the case, the terms of the complaint are
narrated by another witness. This point can be seen most clearly by
imagining a case in which the complaint contained some detail to which no
reference had been made in the prosecutrix's testimony; if the jury were to
consider that the detail had been proved by the narration of the complaint,
they would be accepting hearsay as evidence of the truth of that which was
heard. HAWKINS, J., concluded that the complaint could only be used as
"evidence of the consistency of the conduct of the prosecutrix with the story
told by her in the witness box, and as being inconsistent with her consent to
that of which she complains".[3]

Consent was not relevant to the issue in *Lillyman's Case*,[4] but it
was denied by the prosecutrix, and the view has been expressed that the
terms of a complaint can only be proved when the question of consent is
raised;[5] but this is untenable in the light of the decision of the Court for
Crown Cases Reserved in *R.* v. *Osborne*,[6] where the charge was one
of indecent assault upon a girl of twelve, and the terms of her complaint
to another child were held to have been rightly received although
consent was neither legally nor factually in issue throughout the entire
proceedings.

(c) *Conditions of admissibility.*—*Osborne's Case* is also important because
it authoritatively lays down the conditions upon which evidence of the
terms of a complaint of a sexual offence may be admitted. These are that
it should not have been elicited by questions of a "leading and inducing
or intimidating character", and that it should have been made "at the first
opportunity after the offence which reasonably offers itself."[7]

---

[1] [1896] 2 Q. B. 167. The former practice was an excellent example of the ridiculous
results of the application of some such mechanical rule as that remarks made in the absence
of a party are generally inadmissible, though acts done in his absence may be admitted.
The practice was by no means uniform when *Lillyman's* case was decided.

[2] See *R.* v. *Duell*, [1964] Qd.R 451 (grandmother to whom complaint made too frightened
by alleged rapist to remember complaint); the decision to allow the prosecutrix to prove
the complaint was based in part on the reception of the first complaint in *R.* v. *Lee* (1911), 7
Cr. App. Rep. 31.

[3] At p. 170.

[4] Criminal Law Amendment Act, 1885, s. 5 (re-enacted by the Sexual Offences Act,
1956).

[5] *R.* v. *Rowland* (1898), 62 J. P. 459 (HAWKINS, J.); *R.* v. *Christie*, [1914] A. C. 545,
at p. 553 (Lord ATKINSON). The admissibility of the boy's statements as complaints was
not fully argued in *Christie's Case*. It was not then clear that the doctrine applied to offences
against males, and the report does not indicate how the boy was questioned by his mother
or the policeman.

[6] [1905] 1 K. B. 551.

[7] At p. 561, *per* RIDLEY, J.

So far as the first of these conditions is concerned, the court held that the complaint under consideration was not rendered inadmissible by the fact that it had been made in response to the question "Why are you going home? Why did you not wait until we came back?" put to the prosecutrix by her friend who had left her with the accused for a short time. RIDLEY, J., said that such questions as "What is the matter?" or "Why are you crying?" would not render the ensuing complaint inadmissible, whereas such questions as "Did so-and-so (naming the prisoner) assault you?", "did he do this and that to you?" would have that effect. He concluded that:

> "in each case the decision on the character of the question put, as well as other circumstances, such as the relationship of the questioner and the complainant, must be left to the discretion of the presiding judge. If the circumstances indicate that, but for the questioning, there probably would have been no voluntary complaint, the answer is inadmissible. If the question merely anticipates a statement which the complainant was about to make, it is not rendered inadmissible by the fact that the questioner happens to speak first."[1]

Clearly this is not a matter upon which a consideration of the reported cases is likely to be of much assistance.[2]

The same observation applies to the requirement that the complaint should have been made at the first reasonable opportunity that presents itself. Lord GODDARD, C.J., has stressed that this, too, is a matter concerning which the trial judge has a complete discretion provided he applies the principle that the complaint must be made as speedily as can reasonably be expected.[3] A complaint made as long as a week after the event in question has been admitted,[4] and it is settled that the mere fact that the complaint might have been made to others before it was made to the witness who narrates it in court does not prevent it from being received in evidence.[5]

(d) Extension to offences against males.—The only important development in this branch of the law since the decisions in *R. v. Lillyman* and *R. v. Osborne* was marked by *R. v. Camelleri,*[6] in which the Court of Criminal Appeal upheld the ruling of the trial judge that particulars of a complaint made by a boy of fifteen concerning an offence of gross indecency committed against him might be proved by his parents to show the consistency of the boy's conduct with his testimony in the box. Lord HEWART, C.J., recognised that little attention would or should be paid to a complaint by an abandoned male person of mature years, but he considered that this observation perhaps goes to the weight rather than the admissibility of the complaint.[7]

(e) The old cases.—According to Stephen's *Digest,*[8] it is difficult to suppose that in *R. v. Osborne* the court intended to interfere with:

---

[1] At p. 556.

[2] See, however, *R. v. Merry* (1900), 19 Cox C. C. 442; *R. v. Norcott,* [1917] 1 K. B. 347; *S. v. T.* 1963 (1) S. A. 484 (A.D.); *R. v. Adams and Ross,* [1965] Qd. R. 255.

[3] *R. v. Cummings,* [1948] 1 All E. R. 551; cf. *Bodechon v. R.* (1964), 50 M. P. R. 184.

[4] *R. v. Hedges* (1909), 3 Cr. App. Rep. 262.

[5] *R. v. Wilbourne* (1917), 12 Cr. App. Rep. 280.

[6] [1922] 2 K. B. 122.

[7] *R. v. Greenwood,* [1962] Tas. S. R. 319 raising the question whether some further limitation may not be necessary as a complaint is not to be expected in the case of an adult consenting male. See also *R. v. Hurst and Miller* (1966), 55 W.W.R. 358.

[8] 12th edition, 188.

"the established rule that evidence of the fact of the complaint having been
made (but not of its terms) is admissible in all cases, civil or criminal, involving
personal violence, whether sexual or not".

On the other hand, Phipson considered that the decisions on the admissibility of complaints in sexual charges had overruled *R.* v. *Wink* [1] and
Berry v. *Berry and Carpenter*,[2] cases of robbery and cruelty, in each of
which evidence of the fact that a complaint was made was admitted; [3]
while Wills says it is "doubtful" whether *R.* v. *Lillyman* and *R.* v.
Osborne have rendered such evidence inadmissible.[4]

In *Wink's Case* a policeman was asked whether the prosecutor complained to him of a robbery, and, when this question was answered in the
affirmative, counsel for the Crown was not allowed to ask whether the
prosecutor mentioned the name of the accused, although he was permitted
to inquire whether, in consequence of the complaint, the policeman
searched for Wink. This was rightly castigated in *R.* v. *Lillyman* as "an
objectionable mode of introducing evidence indirectly which if tendered
directly would be inadmissible", but *R.* v. *Wink* was not expressly overruled, and *Berry* v. *Berry and Carpenter* was not mentioned in the judgment.
Nevertheless, the reception of evidence of the bare fact that a complaint
was made is open to the same objection in all cases as that raised against
the previous practice on sexual charges in *R.* v. *Lillyman,* namely, that the
witness to whom the statement was made is left to decide whether it
amounted to a complaint. As *R.* v. *Wink* and *Berry* v. *Berry and Carpenter*
are isolated examples among reported decisions of courts of first instance,
it is submitted that Phipson's view that they have been overruled is correct
in the sense that they are inconsistent with the tenor of the judgments of
the Court for Crown Cases Reserved in *R.* v. *Lillyman* and *R.* v. *Osborne.*
There is no established rule that evidence of the fact that a complaint
was made is admissible in all cases of personal violence, although, as a
matter of practice, a party or prosecutor may no doubt be asked whether
he made a complaint in order to link his evidence up with that which is
about to be given by another witness such as a doctor consulted by him.
This might be allowed in any proceedings. In *O'H.* v. *O'H.*,[5] for instance,
counsel for a husband petitioner in a nullity case was permitted to ask his
client whether he consulted a doctor about his marital difficulties. Moreover,
evidence of a complaint may no doubt be given by the complainant on re-
examination, if the cross-examination has suggested that his or her story
is a recent concoction.

(ii) The present law

If what has been said above concerning the admissibility of complaints
in cases which do not involve a sexual charge is correct, the present law
can be summarised in the following propositions: (a) complaints may
only be proved as evidence-in-chief in criminal prosecutions for a sexual
offence; (b) the complaint must have been made voluntarily, and as speedily
as could reasonably be expected; (c) it makes no difference whether the
offence was committed against a male or female, and whether consent is,
or is not, an issue; (d) the particulars of the complaint may be proved, but

---

[1] (1834), 8 C. & P. 397.   [2] (1898), 78 L. T. 688.
[3] Phipson, *Law of Evidence* (11th edition), 158–9.
[4] *Law of Evidence* (3rd edition), 350.
[5] (1916), 33 T. L. R. 51.

(e) they are not evidence of the facts of which complaint was made, and must not be regarded as anything other than "corroborative of the complainant's credibility, and, where consent is in issue, of the absence of consent".[1]

It follows that, when consent is not in issue, the terms of a complaint are inadmissible if the victim does not give evidence. Thus, in *R. v. Wallwork*,[2] the accused was charged with incest with his daughter of five. Though called as a witness, she was too frightened to give evidence. Her grandmother was allowed to narrate the terms of a complaint made to her by the child. The accused was convicted and appealed to the Court of Criminal Appeal. Although they dismissed his appeal because there had been no substantial miscarriage of justice, the Court of Criminal Appeal held that the grandmother ought not to have been allowed to prove the terms of the complaint; but Lord GODDARD, C.J., went on to say that there would have been no objection to the grandmother saying "the little girl made a complaint to me", and she could have been asked "In consequence of that complaint what did you do?" and the answer would have been "I took her to the doctor and later to the police."

> "One realises that, although the terms of the child's statement must not be given, any jury could see at once that as a consequence of the complaint the grandmother took the child to the doctor and the police and that the terms of the complaint would mention her father."

It is submitted that these dicta ought not be be followed and that, in a case in which consent is not in issue, where the prosecutrix does not give evidence, no witness should be asked about the fact of a complaint having been made because the result of doing so is, in the words of HAWKINS, J., in *R. v. Lillyman*, "an objectionable mode of introducing evidence indirectly which, if tendered directly, would be inadmissible".

If consent is in issue, the proof of either the fact or terms of a complaint of a sexual assault would infringe the rule against hearsay if the evidence were tendered in order to establish positively the absence of consent. Expressly or by implication, a statement other than one made by a person while giving oral evidence would be received as of its truth. There is, however, much to be said for the view that complaints are not received as affirmative evidence of the absence of consent, but simply in order to rebut the factual presumption of consent which might otherwise arise. In the words of a Queensland court, "Failure to make fresh complaint is evidence of consent. The fact that fresh complaint was not made is not evidence of non-consent."[3] The question whether complaints can ever be received under an exception to the rule against hearsay as affirmative evidence of the the absence of consent to that of which complaint is made would best be

---

[1] *Per* RIDLEY, J., in *R. v. Osborne*, [1905] 1 K. B. 551, at p. 561. The word "corroborative" is used in a loose sense as a complaint is not corroboration for legal purposes (*R. v. Lovell* (1923), 17 Cr. App. Rep. 163).

[2] (1958), 42 Cr. App. Rep. 153; *R. v. Lambert*, [1919] V. L. R. 205. The dicta in *Wallwork's* case are more fully criticised in 74 L. Q. R. 352. See above *R. v. Burke* (1912), 47 I. L. T. 111 (complainant an imbecile).

[3] *R. v. Hinton*, [1961] Qd. R. 17, at p. 24. The first of the above two sentences is probably an overstatement, and the true view may be that taken by the High Court of Australia, viz., that the failure to make a complaint is relevant to the credibility of the whole of the prosecutrix's evidence, including that on the question of consent, but it is not an affirmative item of evidence in favour of the accused's contention of consent requiring a special direction to the jury (*Kilby v. R.* (1973), 47 A. L. J. R. 369.

tested by a case in which the victim of an alleged sexual assault was dead. If the only evidence of want of consent were her complaint, would there be a case to go to the jury? On this the English authorities are silent as the only reported cases of this nature antedate the development of the modern law concerning complaints.[1]

Two further observations are necessary. In the first place, although a complaint is received because it enhances the reliability of the prosecutrix's testimony, it does not constitute corroboration of her evidence when this is necessary, because corroboration must come from a source independent of the witness to be corroborated.[2] Secondly, words which amount to a complaint may sometimes be proved under a different rule of evidence from those which render them admissible to enhance the credibility of testimony on a sexual charge. In appropriate circumstances they may, for instance, be proved as statements made in the presence of a party whatever the nature of the proceedings may be; similarly, they may be proved as dying declarations on charges of murder or manslaughter, or they may be held to constitute part of the *res gestae*. In the first of these examples, the words are not received as evidence of their truth in the absence of something in the nature of an admission on the part of the person to whom they were spoken. On the other hand, dying declarations constitute an exception to the rule against hearsay, and, provided the requisite conditions are fulfilled, they are admissible as evidence of the truth of that which the deceased said with regard to the cause of his death. When an utterance is received as part of the *res gestae*, it may be used to enhance the credibility of testimony or, as we shall see in chapter XX, it may constitute an exception to the rule against hearsay in a criminal case.

So far as the merits of the present law are concerned, it may be said that complaints are admitted as an historical anomaly—a "perverted survival of the ancient requirement that a woman should make hue and cry as a preliminary to an appeal of rape".[3] On the other hand, it may be said that the procedure should not be limited to criminal prosecutions for sexual offences, because it ought at least to apply in all cases in which violence is alleged. There is some authority for this view,[4] but the preponderance of authority restricts the admissibility of complaints to prosecutions for a sexual offence.[5]

The effect of the recommendations of the 11th Report of the Criminal Law Revision Committee with regard to hearsay would, if they were adopted, be to abolish all special rules concerning complaints in sexual cases.

"Provided that the complainant gives evidence, they will be admissible as evidence of the fact complained of; and even if the complainant does not give

---

[1] *R. v. Megson Battye and Ellis*, (1840), 9 C. & P. 420; *R. v. Guttridge* (1840), 9 C. & P. 471; *R. v. Osborne* (1842), Car. & M. 622.
[2] *R. v. Lovell* (1923), 17 Cr. App. Rep. 163; *R. v. Evans* (1924), 18 Cr. App. Rep. 123, and see p. 185, *ante*: *Thomas v. R.*, [1952] 4 D. L. R. 306.
[3] HOLMES, J., in *Commonwealth v. Cleary* (1898), 172 Mass. 175, cited in *R. v. Osborne*, [1905] 1 K. B. 551.
[4] See *per* BANKES, L.J., in *Jones v. South Eastern and Chatham Rail. Co.'s Managing Committee* (1918), 87 L. J. K. B. 775, at p. 778. See also the discussion by R. N. Gooderson, [1968] C. L. J. 91–2 mentioning *inter alia R. v. Christensen*, [1923] 2 D. L. R. 379, raising the question whether complaints are admissible on behalf of the defence where provocation or self-defence is proved in answer to a charge of murder.
[5] See SWINFEN-EADY, L.J., in *Jones'* case, and *per* Lord PORTER in *Gillie v. Posho Ltd.*, [1939] 2 All E. R. 196, at p. 200; *Fromhold v. Fromhold*, [1952] 1 T. L. R. 1522.

evidence, they will still be admissible for this purpose provided that the appropriate conditions of admissibility [of hearsay evidence, such as the death of the complainant] are fulfilled."[1]

(2) Previous Consistent Statements Admitted as Part of the Res Gestae

The term *"res gestae"* is a blanket phrase when applied to the admissibility of statements, and may roughly be said to denote relevance through contemporaneity—part of the story.[2] The different types of statement that may be admitted under this head are considered later. At this stage it is only necessary to say that the credibility of a witness's testimony may be confirmed by the narration by himself or someone else of a statement to the same effect as his evidence if it can be said to form part of the transaction to which his evidence relates. In *Milne* v. *Leisler*,[3] for instance, the question was whether the plaintiff contracted to sell goods on the footing that A., to whom the goods were delivered, was the agent of B., or on the basis that A. was acting on his own behalf. On the first assumption, the defendant was liable in conversion, but not on the second. After the plaintiff had sworn that A. purported to contract as agent for B., he was allowed to put in evidence letters written by him to his firm's representative referring to the sale and asking for inquiries to be made concerning the solvency of B. Normally, letters by a party to his agent are excluded as irrelevant, or too remotely relevant, because of the facility with which a man can manufacture evidence for himself, but, in this instance, the letters were received, not as direct proof of the sale to B., but on account of their strong tendency to confirm the plaintiff's testimony. The crucial facts were that the letters could be regarded as part of the events to which the plaintiff was deposing. If a witness says that, in consequence of the naming of a referee, he made certain inquiries in order to determine whether a particular person should be a party to a contract of sale to which he also deposes, the letters containing those inquiries are better evidence than his testimony.

In *Spittle* v. *Spittle*,[4] on the other hand, a wife who had been negotiating a settlement of outstanding financial questions with her husband was not allowed to call her daughter to depose to the fact that, very soon after she received a cheque from her husband, she told her daughter that she had taken it on account. The statement could not, in any sense of the word, be said to have formed part of the settlement.

If the facts of *Milne* v. *Leisler* were to recur, the letter would be admissible with the leave of the court under the Civil Evidence Act, 1968, as direct evidence of the fact to which it referred, and not merely as evidence of consistency although, in the particular circumstances, this would be largely if not entirely a distinction without a difference because the plaintiff deposed to most if not all of the facts in question, but it seems that he would still be able to insist on the reception of the letter as evidence of consistency without the necessity of obtaining the leave of the court, for the Act of 1968 is solely concerned with the reception of statements as evidence of the facts stated. If the facts of *Spittle* v. *Spittle* were to recur,

---

[1] Para. 232.
[2] See note by F. P. in *Homes* v. *Newman*, [1931] 2 Ch. 112, at p. 120.
[3] (1862), 7 H. & N. 786.
[4] [1965] 3 All E. R. 451. The text at p. 205 of the second edition has been modified to meet the criticisms of Pennycuik, J.

the wife would, with the leave of the court, be able to prove what she said to her daughter and to call her daughter to do likewise under the Civil Evidence Act, 1968. The wife's remarks would be admitted as evidence that the cheque was taken on account although, as the greater includes the lesser, the remarks would also constitute evidence of consistency.

In *R.* v. *Fowkes*[1] a man commonly known as "the butcher" was charged with murder. The deceased's son gave evidence that he and a police officer were sitting in a room with his father when a face appeared at the window through which the fatal shot was then fired. At the trial he said that he thought the face was that of "the butcher". He was allowed to swear how he had shouted "There's Butcher" when the face appeared, and the police officer, who had not seen the face, was allowed to depose to the shouting of the name Butcher. Sir James Stephen commented on this case as follows:

> "It is . . . obvious that the fact that he said at the time 'There's Butcher' was far more likely to impress the jury than the fact that he was at the trial uncertain whether the person he saw was the butcher, though he was disposed to think so."

This meagrely reported decision is unaffected by any intervening legislation. Although there is really no authority on the point, it is certainly arguable that previous statements of witnesses constituting part of the *res gestae* are admissible as hearsay statements, and not merely as evidence of consistency.[2] If this is so, the conditions of admissibility are, in this very limited class of case, less restrictive in criminal than in civil proceedings, for the Civil Evidence Act, 1968, abolishes all common law exceptions to the hearsay rule in the case of the latter, and, on facts such as those of *R.* v. *Fowkes*, evidence of what the son said at the time of the shooting would be admissible under the Act with the leave of the court.[3]

(3) Previous Consistent Statements Admitted to Rebut Afterthought

When giving judgment in *R.* v. *Coll*,[4] Holmes, J., said:

> "It is I think clear that the evidence of a witness cannot be corroborated by proving statements to the same effect previously made by him; nor will the fact that his testimony is impeached in cross-examination render such evidence admissible. Even if the impeachment takes the form of showing a contradiction or inconsistency between the evidence given at the trial and something said by the witness on a former occasion it does not follow that the way is open for proof of other statements made by him for the purpose of sustaining his credit.[5] There must be something either in the nature of the inconsistent statement, or in the use made of it by the cross-examiner to enable such evidence to be given."

The fact that the whole of the witness's testimony is attacked will not bring the exception into play.[6] It has been said that the nature of the cross-examination must be such that it can be interpreted as containing the direct question "when did you first invent this story".[7]

---

[1] Stephen's *Digest of the Law of Evidence* (12th edition), 8.
[2] See R. M. Gooderson in [1957] C. L. J. 55, at p. 78.
[3] The distinction would probably be preserved by clause 37 of the draft Bill attached to the 11th Report of the Criminal Law Revision Committee.
[4] (1889), 25 L. R. Ir. 522, at p. 541.
[5] But see *Ahmed* v. *Brumfitt* (1967), 112, Sol. Jo. 32.
[6] *Fox* v. *General Medical Council*, [1960] 3 All E. R. 225.
[7] *Flanagan* v. *Fahy*, [1918] 2 I. R. 361.

If it is alleged that a prisoner's story is a recent concoction, a previous statement concerning the nature of his defence becomes admissible,[1] so too does a statement made by an accused's wife to a solicitor before she had seen her husband after his arrest if it is suggested in cross-examination that her evidence was the result of collusion with him,[2] and an allegation that a policeman is fabricating his testimony allows his notebook to be put in evidence.[3] Generally speaking the previous statement will be put to the witness in re-examination, but circumstances are conceivable in which he would be asked about it in-chief. This might be done when the cross-examination of a previous witness had contained a suggestion of fabrication by himself and the succeeding witness, or at a criminal trial when something of the sort had been suggested at the proceedings before the magistrates.

The question whether a situation has arisen in which a previous statement may be proved under this head is, both in civil and criminal cases, largely a matter for the judge's discretion. It is difficult to improve on the following observations of the Chief Justice of Australia:

> "In as much as the rule forms a definite exception to the general principle excluding statements made out of Court and admits a possibly self-serving statement made by the witness, great care is called for in applying it. The judge at the trial must determine for himself, upon the conduct of the trial before him, whether a case for applying the rule of evidence has arisen—and must exercise care in assuring himself not only that the account given by the witness in his testimony is attacked on the ground of recent invention or reconstruction or that a foundation for such an attack has been laid—but also that the contents of the statement are in fact to the like effect as his account given in his evidence and that having regard to the time and circumstances in which it was made it rationally tends to answer the attack."[4]

In *Ahmed* v. *Brumfitt*[5] DIPLOCK, L.J., said, with the concurrence of Lord DENNING, M.R., that:

> "It was clear law that when a witness in cross-examination had put to him a statement which was said to conflict with what he said in examination-in-chief, it was always admissible to put to him in re-examination an earlier statement consistent with what he said in examination-in-chief as rehabilitating his credit in respect of the evidence he had given."

The case is very briefly reported and the remarks of DIPLOCK, L.J., may not be inconsistent with any of the decisions cited above in which the suggestion made against the witness was concoction rather than inconsistency, but they are of course contradicted by the passage from the judgment of HOLMES, J., in *R.* v. *Coll*[6] with which this discussion began.

---

[1] *R.* v. *Roberts*, [1942] 1 All E. R. 187, at p. 191, *per* HUMPHREYS, J

[2] *R.* v. *Oyesiku* (1972), 56 Cr. App. Rep. 240.

[3] *R.* v. *Benjamin* (1913), 8 Cr. App. Rep. 146.

[4] DIXON, C.J., in *The Nominal Defendant* v. *Clements* (1961), 104 C. L. R. 476, at p. 479. This statement was cited in the Court of Appeal (Criminal Division) in *R.* v. *Oyesiku, supra.* Other important Australian authorities are *Woodward* v. *Shea*, [1952] V. L. R. 313; *Francombe* v. *Holloway*, [1957] V. L. R. 139; *Lavelle* v. *R.*, [1957] Tas. S. R, 162; *Transport and General Insurance Co., Ltd.* v. *Edmundson* (1961), 106 C. L. R. 23; *Wojcic* v. *Incorporated Nominal Defendant*, [1967] V. R. 263 leaving open, at p. 282, the question whether, if a party's testimony is contradicted in cross-examination by an admission, it is permissible for him to prove an earlier statement under the recent invention rule (this point was not mentioned on appeal in [1969] V. R. 323); *Damon* v. *Snyder*, [1970] V. R. 81. (Cross-examination on answers to interrogatories inconsistent with testimony held not to be within the recent invention rule.)

[5] (1967), 112 Sol. Jo. 32.

[6] P. 216, *ante.*

Section 3 (1) (b) of the Civil Evidence Act, 1968, provides that

> "Where in any civil proceedings . . . a previous statement made by a person
> called as [a witness] is proved for the purpose of rebutting a suggestion that
> his evidence has been fabricated, that statement shall by virtue of this section[1]
> be admissible as evidence of any fact stated therein of which direct oral
> evidence would be admissible."[2]

At common law, and therefore in criminal cases, the statement is simply
admissible as circumstantial evidence negativing the suggestion of afterthought or fabrication; but, in view of the requirement of close correspondence between the statement and the witness's testimony, the distinction is unimportant, if not non-existent.

(4) OTHER EXCEPTIONS

Although the existence of other common law exceptions to the general
prohibition of proof of a witness's prior consistent statements was recognised before 1968, it was not until the publication of an important article in
that year by Mr. R. N. Gooderson[3] that anything like a thorough account
was given of them. A brief reference must be made to three further
exceptions mentioned in that article, statements by the accused when
arrested, statements by the accused when incriminating articles are
recovered from his possession, and statements by witnesses when identifying the accused out of court.

(i) Statements on arrest.—Perhaps this exception would be better
described as "statements made by the accused to the police when taxed
with incriminating facts" for such statements are admissible whether or
not there is an arrest. If they are adverse to the accused they are, when
voluntary, admissible against him as confessions. If neutral, or favourable
to the accused, they are admissible for the reason that

> "A statement made voluntarily by an accused person to the police is evidence
> in the trial because of its vital relevance as showing the reaction of the accused
> when first taxed with incriminating facts."[4]

This means that such a statement is not, like a confession, received as
evidence of the facts stated; accordingly a judge does not have to take
those facts into account on the accused's submission that there is no case
to answer.[5] However, if the accused subsequently gives evidence of those
facts, his previous statement, made at a time before he had had time to
"think things out", may be of the utmost importance as proof of consistency.

(ii) Statements made on recovery of incriminating articles.—
We saw in chapter II that, if someone is found in possession of recently
stolen goods, there is a presumption of fact that he was either the thief or a
guilty handler of them. What he says by way of explanation is therefore
admissible on principles similar to those discussed in the last paragraph

---

[1] These words, which occur quite frequently in the Act, are necessitated by the fact
that, in consequence of the Act, hearsay statements are only admissible in civil cases by
virtue of a statutory provision or agreement.

[2] There is a similar provision in clause 33 of the draft Bill annexed to the 11th Report
of the Criminal Law Revision Committee.

[3] (1968), C. L. J. 64.

[4] *R.* v. *Storey* (1968), 52 Cr. App. Rep. 334, at p. 337.

[5] *R.* v. *Storey, supra.*

and, if he is subsequently charged, it may be valuable proof of consistency if he tells the same story in court.[1]

(iii) Previous identification of the accused.—To quote FERGUSSON, J., a judge of the Supreme Court of New South Wales, ". . . evidence has been admitted in criminal trials from time immemorial of the identification of the accused [by witnesses] out of court."[2] There can be no doubt that identification at the time of or soon after the offence will often strengthen the value of the witness's identification of the accused in court, and nothing more need be said in order to justify the reception of statements forming part of his act of identification.[3]

There is no suggestion in the cases that any of the three last mentioned exceptions to the rule prohibiting proof of prior consistent statements applies to civil proceedings, and, in view of the general admissibility of such statements under the Civil Evidence Act, 1968, as evidence of any fact of which direct oral evidence by the maker would be admissible, it is unlikely that there ever will be any authority dealing with the common law in these situations. The following would be a test case: A. is suing B. for negligence in a running down action; an hour after the accident, a police officer tells B. that A. has said that B. was driving with gross negligence, giving details. B. at once retorts that it was all A.'s fault, giving details in his turn. Assuming that B. were to give evidence, his statement would be admissible as proof of consistency at his trial for dangerous driving. B.'s statement would also be admissible with the leave of the court in the running down action under the Civil Evidence Act, 1968. But would it be admissible as of right at common law on the ground that it is sufficient to tender it as evidence of consistency and not as evidence of a fact of which B. could give oral evidence and has already done so? If such a distinction as the above, one well warranted by judicial statements, is tenable, the answer is "yes"; but is the distinction tenable? Surely a time comes when the distinction between admitting a witness's statement as evidence of a fact of which he can and does give oral evidence and as evidence of consistency ceases to exist.

(5) STATEMENTS MADE UNDER THE INFLUENCE OF A TRUTH DRUG

In *R.* v. *McKay*[4] the New Zealand Court of Appeal held that the trial judge had rightly rejected the evidence of a psychiatrist of statements made to him by the accused while under the influence of a truth drug. The statements were consistent with the accused's testimony, and reliance was placed by TURNER, J., on such cases as *Gillie* v. *Posho, Ltd.*[5] and *R.* v. *Roberts.*[6] Perhaps there is room for argument that this decision would be followed in England.

The psychiatrist was of the opinion that the accused's statements were

---

[1] Among the English authorities cited by Mr. Gooderson are *R.* v. *Abraham* (1848), 3 Cox C. C. 430; *R.* v. *Exall* (1866), 4 F. & F. 922; *R.* v. *Muller* (1865), 4 F. & F. 383 n, and 388–389 n. (a murder case); *R.* v. *Manzano* (1860), 2 F. & F. 64–65 n. See also *R.* v. *Graham* (1972), 7 C. C. C. (2d) 93.

[2] *R.* v. *Fannon* (1922), 22 S. R. (N.S.W.) 427, at p. 430.

[3] For the position where the maker of the statement gives no evidence of identification or gives hesitant evidence, see p. 50, *ante*, and p. 216, *ante*.

[4] [1967] N. Z. L. R. 139, citing *R.* v. *Barker*, [1954] Crim. L. R. 423, and a report in 98 Sol. Jo. 794. See also an article by Mathieson, [1967] Crim. L. R. 645.

[5] P. 208, *ante*.

[6] P. 207, *ante*.

true, but, to admit them as evidence of the facts stated would not only have been to admit hearsay evidence where no previous exception to the rule against hearsay existed; it would also have moved towards substituting trial by psychiatrist for trial by jury. On the other hand, there is the argument to which reference has already been made,[1] that the accused should be allowed the benefit of all the latest medical discoveries.

D. UNFAVOURABLE AND HOSTILE WITNESSES

A party calling a witness to prove certain facts may be disappointed by his failure to do so, and his difficulties may be increased by the witness's manifest antipathy to his cause. This lies at the root of the distinction between unfavourable and hostile witnesses. An unfavourable witness is one called by a party to prove a particular fact in issue or relevant to the issue who fails to prove such fact, or proves an opposite fact. A hostile witness is one who is not desirous of telling the truth at the instance of the party calling him.[2] It will be convenient to state the common law with regard to unfavourable and hostile witnesses separately, and then to mention the relevant statutory provisions—s. 3 of the Criminal Procedure Act, 1865, and the Civil Evidence Act, 1968; but something must first be said of the prohibition against a party impeaching his own witness.

(1) The Prohibition Against Impeaching a Party's Own Witness [3]

A party against whom a witness is called may impeach him in various ways. He may cross-examine him by means of leading questions, and ask him about his previous inconsistent statements and prove them if they are denied—a matter which is now covered by statute; he may cross-examine him with regard to his discreditable conduct in the past with a view to showing bad character, or he may ask the witness about his previous convictions or the existence of bias, and prove these two matters by other evidence if they are denied. Finally a party may call evidence to show that the opponent's witness is not to be believed on oath. The prohibition against a party impeaching his own witness means that there is a general rule preventing a litigant from taking any of the above steps with regard to witnesses called by him. Various reasons have been given for the rule. It is said that a party ought not to have the means of discrediting his witness, or that he guarantees the trustworthiness of the evidence he adduces, or that it would be unfair to subject the witness to two cross-examinations. Whatever its basis may be, the rule seems to work well enough in ordinary circumstances as applied to unfavourable witnesses, but it would be ludicrous to apply it to a hostile witness in its full rigour.[4]

(2) Unfavourable Witnesses

At common law a party was allowed to contradict his own witness by calling other evidence if he was unfavourable, but this did not amount to

---

[1] See *R. v. Pitt*, p. 203, *ante* and cf. *R. v. Lowry, post.*

[2] Stephen, *Digest of the Law of Evidence* (12th Edn.), art. 147.

[3] III *Wigmore*, para. 896 *et seq.*

[4] The rule is abrogated by r. 607 of the United States Federal Rules (following the Model Code and Uniform Rules); but the Criminal Law Revision Committee was in favour of its retention (11th Report, para. 162).

a modification of the prohibition against discrediting his witness because it did not involve resort to any of the methods mentioned at the beginning of the last paragraph. In *Ewer* v. *Ambrose* [1] someone whom the defendant called to prove a partnership proved the contrary, and it was held that the defendant could rely on the testimony of other witnesses in support of the existence of the partnership. In the words of HOLROYD, J.,

> " If a witness proves a case against the party calling him, the latter may show the truth by other witnesses. But it is undoubtedly true, that if a party calls a witness to prove a fact, he cannot, when he finds the witness proves the contrary, give general evidence to show that the witness is not to be believed on his oath, but he may show by other evidence that he is mistaken as to the fact which he is called to prove."

This last kind of evidence would necessarily concern the issue more directly than evidence with regard to the witness's credibility, and, in order to appreciate the enormity of the injustice which might be occasioned by rejecting it, a case may be supposed in which a party has four witnesses to support his version of the facts. If he happened to begin by calling a witness who disproved his case, he would be deprived of the testimony of the other three. If he called these before the one who disproved his case, it would have been a question for the jury upon the evidence whether they gave credit to the three or the one. The order in which the witnesses happen to be called ought not to make any difference. [2] Of course, there is a sense in which a man is being discredited if someone asks the court to believe what another man says in preference to his testimony concerning a fact in issue or relevant to the issue, but, although the question is one of degree, the discrediting is a great deal more obvious if one of the methods mentioned at the beginning of the last paragraph is adopted. When this is done, the whole of his testimony is impugned, but this is not necessarily the case when he is contradicted with regard to a particular fact. If a party contradicts part of the testimony of an unfavourable witness, he is not precluded from relying on the rest of that testimony.

(3) HOSTILE WITNESSES

The judge may allow the examination-in-chief of a hostile witness to be conducted in the manner of a cross-examination to the extent to which he considers it necessary for the purpose of doing justice. [3] The witness may be asked leading questions, challenged with regard to his means of

---

[1] (1825), 3 B. & C. 746.
[2] This is the basis of the judgment of LITTLEDALE, J., in *Ewer* v. *Ambrose*. See also *Bradley* v. *Ricardo* (1831), 8 Bing. 57. The much quoted statement of HAMILTON, J., in *Sumner and Leivesley* v. *John Brown & Co.* (1909), 25 T. L. R. 745, must be read with caution. He said, "If a party calls two equally credible witnesses who give evidence the tenor of which he might reasonably have expected, upon a major fact in issue, and such witnesses directly contradict each other, the party calling them is not entitled to accredit the one and discredit the other, and the testimony of both must be disregarded." The last eight words are inconsistent with the judgment of LITTLEDALE, J., in *Ewer* v. *Ambrose*. Neither witness can be discredited so long as they both are considered to be merely unfavourable, and it is not clear what is meant by "evidence the tenor of which might reasonably have been expected". No one calls witnesses whom he expects to contradict each other. HAMILTON, L.J.'s statement was disapproved in the light of the judgment in *Bradley* v. *Ricardo* and various Canadian authorities in *Cariboo Observer Ltd.*, v. *Carson Lines and Tyrell* (1962), 32 D. L. R. (2nd) 36.
[3] *Bastin* v. *Carew* (1824), Ry. & M. 127.

knowledge of the facts to which he is deposing or tested on such matters as the accuracy of his memory and perception; but the party by whom he is called cannot ask about his previous bad conduct and convictions, nor can he adduce evidence of the witness's doubtful veracity. This is the result of the common law, but it used not to be clear whether a statement inconsistent with his present testimony could be proved against a hostile witness —a matter that became increasingly important with the growth of the practice among attorneys of taking a proof of the evidence which a person was prepared to give. As ERLE, C.J., observed:[1]

> "There are treacherous witnesses who will hold out that they can prove facts on one side in a cause and then, for a bribe or for some other motive, make statements in support of the opposite interest. In such cases the law undoubtedly ought to permit the party calling the witness to question him as to the former statement, and ascertain, if possible, what induces him to change it."

In *R.* v. *Fraser and Warren*,[2] Lord GODDARD, C.J., said that if, in a criminal case, counsel for the prosecution has a statement contradicting a Crown witness who says, at the trial, that he is unable to identify the accused, he should at once show the statement to the judge and ask for leave to cross-examine the witness as a hostile witness; but it is doubtful whether the mere existence of an inconsistency between a witness's previous statement and his testimony at the trial will necessarily lead the judge to allow the witness to be treated as hostile. In a civil case, the mere fact that the witness is the other litigant does not mean that he may be treated as hostile.[3] Although the matter has been much more fully discussed in the Commonwealth than in this country, there seems to be no doubt that, in deciding whether to allow the witness to be treated as hostile, the judge may have regard to the witness's demeanour, the terms of any inconsistent statement and the circumstances in which it was made.[4] As the matter is dependent on judicial discretion, the judge's decision will seldom be reversed by an appellate tribunal.[5]

Although there does not appear to be a reported case on the point, it is believed that judges take different views on the question whether a party who has obtained leave to treat his witness as hostile has a right to re-examine him.

(4) STATUTORY PROVISIONS

(i) Criminal Procedure Act, 1865, s. 3.—Section 22 of the Common Law Procedure Act, 1854, was passed in order to settle the law with regard to proof of inconsistent statements by a party's own witness. As was pointed out five years later in *Greenough* v. *Eccles*,[6] the terms of the section

---

[1] *Melhuish* v. *Collier* (1850), 15 Q. B. 878, at p. 890.
[2] (1956), 40 Cr. App. Rep. 160.
[3] *Price* v. *Manning* (1889), 42 Ch. D. 372.
[4] *The People* v. *Hannigan*, [1941] I. R. 252; *R.* v. *Hunter*, [1956] V. L. R. 31 (citing *R.* v. *Harris* (1927), 20 Cr. App. Rep. 144, at p. 146 and doubting whether *Coles* v. *Coles and Brown* (1866), L. R. 1 P. & D. 70 supports the view that demeanour alone can be considered); *R.* v. *Hayden and Slattery*, [1959] V. L. R. 102; *McLellan* v. *Bowyer* (1962) 106 C. L. R. 94; *Wawanesa Mutual Insurance Company* v. *Hanes* (1961), 28 D. L. R. (2d) 386.
[5] *Rice* v. *Howard* (1886), 16 Q. B. D. 681. In a sufficiently strong case a new trial could be ordered by an appellate tribunal (see the review of the authorities by the High Court of Australia in *McLellan* v. *Bowyer, supra*).
[6] (1859), 5 C. B. N. S. 786.

were confusing so far as unfavourable witnesses were concerned, but they were re-enacted in s. 3 of the Criminal Procedure Act, 1865. This governs a party's right to impeach a hostile witness in civil and criminal cases alike at the present day and it reads as follows:

> "A party producing a witness shall not be allowed to impeach his credit by general evidence of bad character, but he may, in case the witness shall, in the opinion of the judge, prove adverse, contradict him by other evidence, or, by leave of the judge, prove that he has made at other times a statement inconsistent with his present testimony; but before such last-mentioned proof can be given the circumstances of the supposed statement, sufficient to designate the particular occasion, must be mentioned to the witness, and he must be asked whether or not he has made such statement."

The prohibition on general evidence of bad character applies to hostile and unfavourable witnesses alike. The section is declaratory of the common law and means that the witness cannot be asked about his bad conduct on former occasions or his previous convictions, in order that he may be discredited, while the party calling him cannot adduce evidence of his mendacious disposition. In *Greenough* v. *Eccles* it was decided that "adverse" means hostile, so the concluding portions of the sections are unambiguous so far as the proof of such a witness's previous statements is concerned. The section gives rise to two remaining questions—its effect on the old law concerning unfavourable witnesses and the evidential value of inconsistent statements that are proved or admitted under the Act.

(a) *Unfavourable witnesses.*—The words "he may, in case the witness shall, in the opinion of the judge, prove adverse, contradict him by other evidence" suggest that a party cannot do this when his witness is merely unfavourable and not, in the opinion of the judge, hostile. If this is so, the section has altered the common law as illustrated by cases such as *Ewer* v. *Ambrose*.[1] It appears to be universally agreed that this is not the effect of the section, and, as long ago as 1859, COCKBURN, C.J., said of the identical provision in the Common Law Procedure Act, 1854:

> "There has been a great blunder in the drawing of it, and on the part of those who adopted it. . . . Perhaps the better course is to consider the second part of the section as altogether superfluous and useless." [2]

The alternative, and probably the sounder method, of ignoring the implications of the section is that adopted by WILLIAMS and WILLES, JJ.:[3]

> "We think the preferable construction is, that in case the witness shall, in the opinion of the judge, prove 'hostile', the party producing him may not only contradict him by other witnesses, as he might heretofore have done, and may still do, if the witness is unfavourable, but may also, by leave of the judge, prove that he has made inconsistent statements."

Whatever means may be adopted in order to reach it, the conclusion is that an unfavourable witness can merely be contradicted with regard to facts in issue or relevant to the issue, he cannot be cross-examined or discredited in any other way; but a witness who is considered by the judge to be hostile may be contradicted on the issue by other witnesses and, in addition, cross-examined or even discredited, to the extent that his pre-

---

[1] (1825), 3 B. & C. 746.
[2] *Greenough* v. *Eccles* (1859), 5 C. B. N. S. 786, at p. 806.
[3] The quotation is from 28 L. J. C. P. 360.

vious statements inconsistent with his present testimony may be put in evidence by the party by whom he is called.

(*b*) *Evidential value of previous inconsistent statements.*—A question naturally arises concerning the use that may be made of these statements when they are admitted by, or proved against, the witness. Are they evidence of the facts stated, or do they merely constitute a ground for disbelieving the witness's testimony? As section 3 of the Act of 1865 only deals with procedure, the answer depends on the common law which still governs criminal cases on this point. Although judicial expression of the first view has not been wanting,[1] the common law is that statements of witnesses who are not parties put in evidence under section 3 of the Criminal Procedure Act, 1865 (and the same is true of those proved or admitted under section 4 and section 5, set out in the next section of this chapter), cannot be treated as proof of the facts stated.[2] When the witness is a party, his previous statement may be admissible as evidence of the facts stated because it is an admission.[3]

An illustration of the common law is provided by *R.* v. *White*. Several witnesses called by the prosecution had previously made statements to the police indicating that the accused had participated in a riot. At the trial these witnesses gave evidence in which they said that the accused did not participate in the riot. The previous statements were admitted, and the judge told the jury that they could choose between the witnesses' evidence at the trial and their statements to the police. The jury must have acted on the latter for they returned a verdict of guilty; but the conviction was quashed because:

> "quite obviously it is one thing to say that, in view of an earlier statement, the witness is not to be trusted: it is another thing to say that his present testimony is to be disbelieved and his earlier statement, which he now repudiates, is to be substituted for it".[4]

The deposition or statement for the purpose of committal proceedings of a witness who subsequently gives evidence at a criminal trial may be used to discredit his testimony if the judge allows him to be treated as hostile, but they cannot be substituted for his evidence at the trial.[5] Language is sometimes used which suggests that the jury is bound to disregard the entirety of the testimony of a witness who has previously made a contradictory statement, unless he can give a satisfactory explanation of his conduct, but it is doubtful whether this can be treated as a rule of law because everything depends upon the circumstances of the case;[6] and it has been held that a contradiction concerning a date did not obliterate testimony which

---

[1] See the judgment of POLLOCK, C. B., in *A.-G.* v. *Hitchcock* (1847), 16 L. J. Ex. 259, where he spoke of the jury being at liberty to believe either the one account or the other.

[2] *R.* v. *Dibble* (1908), 1 Cr. App. Rep. 155; *R.* v. *White* (1922), 17 Cr. App. Rep. 60; *R.* v. *Birch* (1924), 93 L. J. K. B. 385; *R.* v. *Harris* (1927), 20 Cr. App. Rep. 144; *R.* v. *Golder, Jones and Porritt*, [1960] 3 All E. R. 457; *R.* v. *Oliva*, [1965] 3 All E. R. 116; *R.* v. *Moore* (1957), 25 C. R. (Can.) 159.

[3] The witness is not likely to be a party in the case of statements admitted under s. 3, but might be in the case of those admitted under s. 4 and s. 5. A non-party witness may of course render his previous statement evidence of the facts stated by admitting its truth in cross-examination (*Birkett* v. *A. J. Little Ltd.*, [1962] N. S. W. R. 492).

[4] *Per* Lord HEWART, C.J., 17 Cr. App. Rep. 60, at p. 64.

[5] *R.* v. *Birch* (1924), 93 L. J. K. B. 385.

[6] See the comments on *R.* v. *Harris* in *Deacon* v. *R.*, [1947] 3 D. L. R. 772 in which earlier authorities are cited.

coincided with a deposition in all other respects, although the date was a very crucial one.[1]

The Court of Criminal Appeal has said:

> "when a witness is shown to have made previous statements inconsistent with the evidence given by that witness at the trial the jury should not merely be directed that the evidence given at the trial should be regarded as unreliable; they should also be directed that the previous statements whether sworn or unsworn do not constitute evidence upon which they can act."[2]

(ii) Civil Evidence Act, 1968.—Section 3 (1) (a) of the Civil Evidence Act, 1968, provides that:

> "Where in any civil proceedings—(a) a previous inconsistent or contradictory statement made by a person called as a witness in those proceedings is proved by virtue of section 3 of the Criminal Procedure Act, 1865, that statement shall, by virtue of this subsection be admissible as evidence of any fact stated therein of which direct oral evidence by him would be admissible."

There is thus a complete conflict between the civil and criminal law governing the evidential effect of the previous inconsistent statements of a hostile witness. If facts such as those of *R.* v. *White*[3] were to recur, the appeal would still have to be allowed if the judge suggested to the jury that they might choose to act on either of the two statements of the witness, his testimony or the statement which he made to the police. On the other hand, if the claim were a civil claim for damages caused by the riot, such a direction could well be held to have been proper. As there is a similar conflict with respect to the evidential effect of an inconsistent statement proved or admitted to have been made by any witness under cross-examination, it is worth while considering the merits of the conflict. Before doing so, however, it must be emphasised that the practical effect is likely to be negligible in the majority of cases, for the only safe course to adopt will be to ignore both the testimony and the inconsistent statement. The type of situation in which it is arguable that the tribunal of fact should be able to act on the statement rather than the testimony is that in which there is reason to suppose that the witness quarrelled with the party in whose favour the statement operates after it was made or was "got at" by the opposite party.

It is sometimes said that the approach of the common law under which the previous inconsistent statement merely neutralises the maker's testimony is the logical one, because rejection of the testimony does not entail acceptance of the statement; but this is simply another instance of the pseudo-logic occasionally indulged in by lawyers to which reference has already been made.[4] Everything depends upon the contents of the statement and testimony respectively. Of course the rejection of W.'s evidence that he was in Rome on May 1st because he had previously said that he was in Carthage throughout that day does not entail acceptance of this latter fact; but acceptance of W.'s previous statement that he was not in Rome on May 1st does entail rejection of his testimony that he was there during

---

[1] *R.* v. *Williams* (1913), 8 Cr. App. Rep. 133.
[2] *R.* v. *Golder, Jones and Porritt*, [1960] 3 All E. R. 457, at p. 459; the universality of the first part of this statement was questioned in *R.* v. *Jackson*, [1964] Qd. R. 26. See also *R.* v. *Oliva*, [1965] 3 All E. R. 116; *R.* v. *Pearson*, [1964] Qd. R. 471; *R.* v. *Schmahl*, [1965] V. R. 745.
[3] P. 224, *ante.*   [4] P. 172, *ante.*

that day. Statement and testimony usually cancel each other out because there is no particular reason why one should be preferred to the other. The testimony is on oath, but, in the absence of a convincing explanation of the inconsistency, it is the testimony of someone who has, or may have, lied on the same point on a previous occasion.

The common law approach, and hence that of the present criminal law, may, however, be justified by practical considerations. The earlier statement may have been put into the mouth of its maker by an over-enthusiastic police officer or solicitor, it will generally not have been made on oath, and the maker will generally not have been subject to cross-examination when it was made.[1] The solemnity of the occasion may lend support to the truth of the testimony and it will only be in rare cases that acceptable evidence tending to show that the statement rather than the testimony was true will be available.

(iii) Proposals of the Criminal Law Revision Committee.—Nonetheless, clause 33 of the draft Bill attached to the 11th Report of the Criminal Law Revision Committee contains a provision identical to section 3 (1) (a) of the Civil Evidence Act, 1968. The Report also recommends the adoption of a modernised version of section 3 of the Criminal Procedure Act, 1865, together with the retention of the prohibition on a party's impeaching his own witness by evidence of bad character; the new clause would make it plain that both unfavourable and hostile witnesses can be contradicted by other evidence without the leave of the court because it it does not refer to the point.[2]

SECTION 3. CROSS-EXAMINATION AND RE-EXAMINATION

The object of cross-examination is two-fold, first, to elicit information concerning facts in issue or relevant to the issue that is favourable to the party on whose behalf the cross-examination is conducted, and secondly to cast doubt upon the accuracy of the evidence-in-chief given against such party. So far as cross-examination to the issue is concerned, the ordinary rules with regard to the admissibility of evidence apply so that the prosecution cannot cross-examine the accused on the contents of an inadmissible confession,[3] and, in criminal cases, the rule against hearsay applies with as much force to the answers given by a witness in cross-examination as it does to those given by him in-chief. Thus, in *R. v. Thomson*,[4] it was held that a doctor charged with aborting a woman since deceased had been rightly refused permission to ask a prosecution witness in cross-examination whether the deceased had not told her that she intended to operate on herself and later that she had in fact done so. If the accused had called a witness to prove these statements, they would have been inadmissible hearsay and they would not have lost that character by being elicited in

---

[1] These objections do not apply to a deposition.

[2] The clause (clause 11) reads as follows: "In any [criminal] proceedings the party calling a witness shall in no circumstances be allowed to impeach his credibility as a witness by evidence tending to establish that he is a person of bad disposition or reputation; but, subject to that restriction, where in any [criminal] proceedings a party calls a witness who— (a) gives evidence adverse to that party; or (b) gives evidence which is inconsistent with a statement made by the witness on a previous occasion, that party may, with the leave of the court, cross-examine him as if he were a witness called by another party.

[3] *R. v. Treacey*, [1944] 2 All E. R. 229; cf. *R. v. Rice*, [1963] 1 Q. B. 857; [1963] 1 All E. R. 832.

[4] [1912] 3 K. B. 19.

cross-examination. There are decisions to the same effect in civil cases,[1] but it seems that, in civil proceedings, the court would now have a discretion to admit statements of deceased persons elicited from a witness under cross-examination as evidence of any fact of which the deceased could have given direct oral evidence.[2]

Any matter upon which it is proposed to contradict the evidence-in-chief given by the witness must normally be put to him so that he may have an opportunity of explaining the contradiction,[3] and failure to do this may be held to imply acceptance of the evidence-in-chief. Leading questions may be employed in cross-examination,[4] but, whether this is directed to the issue or the credit of the witness, the judge has a discretion under which he may disallow questions which he considers to be improper or oppressive.[5]

All witnesses are liable to be cross-examined except one who is called by the judge, one who is called for the sole purpose of producing a document and one who is not examined-in-chief because he had been called by mistake.[6] A witness who does not come within these excepted categories is liable to be cross-examined, not merely by the opponent of the party calling him, but also by all other parties.[7] All parties have the right to cross-examine witnesses not called by them, whether or not the witness is himself a party, whether or not the witness has given evidence against the party seeking to cross-examine him, and even though the witness is a co-accused.[8] Of course it would be wrong to allow a party to endeavour to discredit a witness who had not given evidence against him, but, so far as cross-examination to the issue is concerned, it is difficult to disagree with the following statement of a South African judge: "An accused ought, if a fair trial is what is aimed at, to be at liberty to cross-examine a co-accused or any witness not called by him who may not have inculpated him in any way in order to establish facts which might tend to support an alibi."[9] The absence of a right to discredit in such a situation led the other member of the court to prefer to speak of the accused having a right to put questions to rather than cross-examine his co-accused.

The matters that call for fuller treatment at this stage are the previous contradictory statements of witnesses under cross-examination (a subject

---

[1] *Beare* v. *Garrod* (1915), 85 L. J. K. B. 717; *Sharp* v. *Loddington Ironstone Co., Ltd.* (1924), 132 L. T. 229.

[2] Civil Evidence Act, 1968, s. 2, s. 8; R. S. C. O. 38, r. 29; it is assumed that a statement is "given in evidence" within the meaning of this rule if the statement is elicited in cross-examination.

[3] *Browne* v. *Dunn* (1869), 6 R. 67; *R.* v. *Hart* (1932), 23 Cr. App. Rep. 202; *Dayman* v. *Simpson*, [1935] S. A. S. R. 320; *R.* v. *Jawke*, 1957 (2) S. A. 182 (emphasising the absence of any absolute rule).

[4] *Parkin* v. *Moon* (1836), 7 C. & P. 408.

[5] See the statement of the Bar Council set out in Phipson, *Law of Evidence* (11th edition), 651–652. As a matter of law, a question concerning adultery is relevant to credibility (*Clifford* v. *Clifford*, [1961] 3 All E. R. 231, divorce on ground of cruelty to which respondents' adultery was irrelevant; cf. *Lewis* v. *Lewis*, [1958] P. 193; [1958] 1 All E. R. 859).

[6] *Wood* v. *Mackinson* (1840), 2 Mood. & R. 273.

[7] *Allen* v. *Allen*, [1894] P. 248, at p. 254; *Dryden* v. *Surrey County Council and Stewart*, [1936] 2 All E. R. 535 at pp. 537–538 (adversity of interest enough); *Re Baden's Deed Trusts, Baden* v. *Smith*, [1967] 3 All E. R. 159.

[8] *R.* v. *Hilton*, [1972] 1 Q. B. 421; [1971] 3 All E. R. 541; *Murdoch* v. *Taylor*, [1965] A. C. 574; expecially per Lord MORRIS at p. 584. *R.* v. *Hadwen*, [1902] 1 K. B. 882; *State* v. *Langa*, 1963 4 S. A. 941; *Nyense* v. *R.*, [1962] R. & N. 271; but see *Gemmel and McFadyen* v. *MacNiven* 1928 S. C. (J.) 5.

[9] HARCOURT, J. in *State* v. *Langa*, 1963 (4) S. A. 941, at p. 945. On the whole subject see an article by I. G. Carvell [1965], Crim. L. R. 419.

which may conveniently be followed by some general remarks concerning cross-examination on documents), the rule that the witness's answers to questions that are collateral to the issue must generally be treated as final and a party's right to call evidence impugning the credibility of his opponent's witness. When these matters have been considered, a few words will be added about re-examination and evidence in rebuttal.

A. PREVIOUS INCONSISTENT[1] STATEMENTS

The proof of previous statements of a witness under cross-examination that are inconsistent with his evidence-in-chief is governed by ss. 4 and 5 of the Criminal Procedure Act, 1865,[2] but their evidential effect is dependent on the common law and the Civil Evidence Act, 1968.

(1) CRIMINAL PROCEDURE ACT, 1865, S. 4

Under s. 4 of the Criminal Procedure Act, 1865,

> "If a witness, upon cross-examination as to a former statement made by him relative to the subject-matter of the indictment or proceeding, and inconsistent with his present testimony, does not distinctly admit that he has made such statement, proof may be given that he did in fact make it; but before such proof can be given, the circumstances of the supposed statement, sufficient to designate the particular occasion, must be mentioned to the witness, and he must be asked whether or not he has made such statement."

This is, almost, if not entirely, declaratory of the common law.[3] If a statement is admitted or proved under the section, it merely impugns the testimony of the witness under cross-examination (unless he happens to be a party when the statement may amount to an admission); it does not constitute evidence of the facts stated at common law. Under section 3 (1) (a) of the Civil Evidence Act, 1968, the statement is, however, also admissible in civil proceedings as evidence of any fact of which the maker could have given oral evidence.[4] The modern authorities on this point all turn on the previous inconsistent statements of hostile witnesses and they have already been discussed. There is no doubt about their applicability to the statements of a witness under cross-examination by the opponent of the party by whom he is called,[5] or by his co-defendant.

---

[1] There is no English authority on what constitutes an inconsistency for this purpose (see *Carbury* v. *Measures* (1904), 4 S. R. (N.S.W.) 569 and V *Wigmore*, para. 1040). There is a Victorian authority for the sound view that, if the statement is both consistent and inconsistent, the whole must go in (*R.* v. *Titijewski*, [1970] V. R. 371 citing *R.* v. *Riley* (1866), 4 F. & F. 964).

[2] These sections apply to civil as well as criminal cases (s. 1), and they re-enact ss. 23 and 24 of the Common Law Procedure Act, 1854.

[3] See the judgment of PARKE, B., in *Crowley* v. *Page* (1837), 7 C. & P. 789. The only doubtful point seems to have concerned the position when the witness did not clearly deny or admit the statement. See *R.* v. *Hart* (1957), 42 Cr. App. Rep. 47, at p. 50. This case confirms that the section is in no way confined to previous statements on oath.

[4] For a discussion of this conflict between civil and criminal proceedings see p. 225, *ante*. There is a provision corresponding to s. 4 of the Act of 1865 in clause 12 of the Bill annexed to the 11th Report of the Criminal Law Revision Committee, and under clause 33 the previous statement could constitute evidence of the facts stated.

[5] See the cases cited in n. 2, p. 224, *ante*. When speaking of a witness under cross-examination, Lord ESHER said "When a witness is asked as to what he said on a previous occasion, he is bound to answer the question; he cannot insist on seeing what he previously said before he answers it; he must answer. If his answer does not contradict what he said before, it is no use pursuing the topic further; he adopts his previous answer and it becomes part of his evidence; if he does not contradict it, he can be contradicted in turn by showing

(2) Criminal Procedure Act, 1865, s. 5

Section 5 of the Act of 1865 applies to cases in which the previous statement is in writing. Between 1820 and 1854, they had been complicated by the rule laid down by the judges when advising the House of Lords in relation to the divorce proceedings brought against Queen Caroline.[1] Wigmore referred to it as a rule which, "for unsoundness of principle, impropriety of policy, and practical inconvenience in trials, committed the most notable mistake that can be found among the rulings upon the present subject".[2] It required that, if a witness was to be cross-examined with regard to a previous statement made by him in writing, he must be shown the document before any questions were asked with regard to it. If he admitted that it was his statement, it could be read as the evidence of the cross-examining party, who was not obliged to inquire whether there was any explanation of the inconsistency. If the witness did not admit that the statement was his, it could be proved by another witness and read as part of the case of the cross-examining party. This procedure was attended by at least three disadvantages.

First, it was unfair to the cross-examiner because it deprived him of the invaluable weapon of surprise. In certain situations, the most effective procedure is to ask the witness whether he has ever said the contrary of what he now says on oath and only to show him the previous statement if he answers the question in the negative.

Secondly, the procedure under consideration was unfair to the cross-examiner by obliging him to read the statement as part of his evidence. This might affect the order of counsel's speeches, because even if the cross-examiner called no other witnesses, he had adduced evidence within the meaning of the common law rules concerning the order of speeches.[3] Those rules then applied at a criminal trial and the adduction of evidence by the accused gave the prosecution the last word. Moreover, there are certain situations in which the cross-examiner will not desire to put the witness's statement in evidence at all. In *R. v. Ford*,[4] for instance, counsel for the defence wanted to show a police officer called by the Crown his deposition in order to induce him to vary his answer to a question concerning a statement made by the prisoner. On the authority of *The Queen's Case* it was held that the correct course was to read the deposition to the witness. This would have had the disadvantage of showing the jury that the witness had, on many matters, told the same story as he told in court, and the reading of the deposition might have been more favourable to the Crown in some respects than the casting of doubt on one point of the witness's evidence would have been helpful to the accused. What counsel for the defence wants to do in such a case is to be able to ask the witness to read the deposition to himself, and then to inquire whether he adheres to the statement made in his evidence-in-chief. If the witness says "no",

---

him what he said before. That goes to his credit only, it proves nothing, it is only a contradiction" (*North Australian Territory Co., Ltd. v. Goldsborough, Mort & Co., Ltd.,* [1893] 2 Ch. 381, at p. 386). The actual decision in relation to which these remarks were made was to the effect that the party calling the witness could not see a copy of the particular statement from which he was cross-examined, but it was a deposition under the Companies Act, and the ruling, which depended on the terms of the statute, has no general application (see *Burnell v. British Transport Commission,* [1956] 1 Q. B. 187; [1955] 3 All E. R.822, *supra*).

[1] (1820), 2 Brod. & Bing. 286.   [2] III *Wigmore*, p. 497.
[3] See the judges' directions in 7 C. & P. 676.   [4] (1851), 5 Cox C. C. 184.

counsel for the defence has achieved his object; if the witness says "yes", then only should it be necessary for counsel for the defence to decide whether to use the deposition to contradict the witness; if he does so, the deposition then becomes evidence in the case.

Finally, the ruling in *The Queen's Case* could operate harshly from the point of view of the witness, because the cross-examiner was not obliged to give him an opportunity of explaining the inconsistency between his former statement and present testimony.

Section 5 of the Criminal Procedure Act, 1865, reads as follows:

> "A witness may be cross-examined as to previous statements made by him in writing or reduced into writing relative to the subject-matter of the indictment or proceeding, without such writing being shown to him; but if it is intended to contradict such witness by the writing, his attention must, before such contradictory proof can be given, be called to those parts of the writing which are to be used for the purpose of so contradicting him; provided always, that it shall be competent for the judge, at any time during the trial, to require the production of the writing for his inspection, and he may thereupon make such use of it for the purposes of the trial as he may think fit."

This appears to overcome all the disadvantages of the ruling in *The Queen's Case* to which reference has been made. The witness can be asked whether he made a statement and cross-examined on the general nature of its contents without being shown the document.[1] The cross-examiner is not obliged to put it in evidence, even if he shows it to the witness, but he must do so if he wishes to use the document as a contradictory statement made by the witness [2] and the latter must be given an opportunity of explaining the contradiction. The document is never evidence of the facts stated in it by virtue of s. 5 because the proviso with regard to the judge making such use of it as he may think fit does not extend to his directing the jury to choose between it and the testimony of the witness.[3]

A cross-examiner cannot make the contents of a document evidence in a case simply by requiring the person under cross-examination to read it aloud. Thus, in *R. v. Gillespie and Simpson*,[4] the manageress and cashier of a store were charged with theft and false accounting, the case against them being that they had accounted for sums less than those shown to have been received by documents prepared by sales' girls. Some of the girls gave evidence, but documents prepared by others were handed to the accused in cross-examination with a request, notwithstanding their dissent from what was said in the documents, to read them aloud. This was duly done and the judge referred to the documents in his summing-up. The procedure was held to have been improper by the Court of Appeal who quashed the convictions.

> "As it seems to this court, if a document is produced to a witness and the witness is asked: 'Do you see what that document purports to record?' The

---

[1] Wrottesley, *The Examination of Witnesses*, 2nd Edn., pp. 61 *et seq.* Cross-examining counsel must have the document with him even if he does not intend to contradict the witness with it. (*R. v. Yousry* (1914), 11 Cr. App. Rep. 13; *R. v. Anderson* (1929), 21 Cr. App. Rep. 178).

[2] *R. v. Riley* (1866), 4 F. & F. 964; *R. v. Wright* (1866) 4 F. & F. 967.

[3] *R. v. Birch* (1924), 18 Cr. App. Rep. 26. Clause 13 of the Bill attached to the 11th Report of the Criminal Law Revision Committee contains a provision similar to s. 5 of the Act of 1865; a statement admissible under that section is admissible as evidence of a fact stated in it under s. 3 (1) (a) of the Civil Evidence Act, 1968. It would be admissible as evidence of the facts stated in a criminal case if clause 33 of the draft Bill were also adopted.

[4] (1967), 51 Cr. App. Rep. 172.

witness may say 'I see it, I accept it as true' in which case the contents of the document become evidence: or he may say: 'I see what is there written, I do not accept it as true", whereupon that which is purported to be recorded in the document is not evidence against that person who has rejected the contents; it becomes what one might call non-evidence, the document itself being nothing but hearsay."[1]

B. CROSS-EXAMINATION ON DOCUMENTS GENERALLY[2]

But there are situations in which a document may become evidence of the facts stated in it by virtue of the common law rules concerning cross-examination. If, at the trial, a party calls for and inspects a document held by his adversary, he is bound to put it in evidence if required to do so, provided the document was not being used to refresh the memory of one of the adversary's witnesses. If the document was being used for this purpose, neither the inspection, nor cross-examination on such parts of the document as were used to refresh memory, makes it evidence in the case, though cross-examination on other parts will have this effect.

In *Stroud* v. *Stroud*,[3] a divorce case in which a doctor was giving evidence on behalf of the wife, the husband's counsel called for and inspected medical reports from other doctors which were in the hands of the doctor who was testifying although he was not referring to them for any purpose. Wrangham, J. held that the reports were thus made evidence in the case at the option of the wife. Unfortunately Wrangham, J. did not say, any more than do any of the older authorities on cross-examination on documents, whether or not they are used to refresh memory,[4] for what purpose the reports were made evidence in the case, but it is difficult to think of any purpose other than that of establishing the truth of the facts stated in the documents.

In Australia, it has been held that a document called for in cross-examination may become evidence of the facts stated in it at the option of the party thus obliged to produce it, although the rule against hearsay would have prevented him from relying on the document for this purpose in the first instance. Thus, in *Walker* v. *Walker* [5] a wife was applying for a maintenance order against her husband. She made a statement in-chief with regard to his income, and was cross-examined concerning her means of knowledge of this matter. She mentioned a letter received by her father from an accountant who had been making inquiries. Counsel for the husband called for the letter, and it was held that he had rightly been obliged to put it in evidence at the request of the wife's counsel. A majority of the High Court was also of opinion that the trial judge had been correct in treating the letter as some evidence of the husband's means.

---

[1] WINN, L.J.

[2] For a helpful set of notes see *Evidence Seminars*, edited by H. H. Glass, p. 136.

[3] [1963] 3 All E. R. 539. The headnote to *Senat* v. *Senat*, [1965] P. 172; [1965] 2 All E. R. 505 suggests that that case conflicts with *Stroud* v. *Stroud*, but this is doubtful because the diaries with which *Senat's* case were concerned were used to refresh memory.

[4] *Wareham* v. *Routledge* (1805), 5 Esp. 235; *Wilson* v. *Bowie* (1823), 1 C. & P. 8; *Calvert* v. *Flower* (1836), 7 C. & P. 386; *Palmer* v. *Maclear and M'Grath* (1858) 1 Sw. & Tr. 149.

[5] (1937), 57 C. L. R. 630. See also *Stunzi Sons Ltd.* v. *House of Youth Pty. Ltd.*, [1960] S. R. (N. S. W.) 220. In South Australia, *Palmer* v. *Maclear and M'Grath* has been held to authorise the treatment of an extra-judicial statement by the wife as evidence of the facts stated against the co-respondent because his counsel cross-examined the wife on the statement (*Whiting* v. *Whiting*, [1947] S. A. S. R. 363). For a consideration of the limits of the decision in *Walker* v. *Walker* see *O'Brien* v. *Clegg*, [1951] S. R. Q. 1.

The Criminal Law Revision Committee recommend the reversal of the effect of *Stroud* v. *Stroud* by a provision that, where a party calls for and inspects a document in the possession of an opposing party or of a witness called by such party, his doing so shall not of itself entitle the opposing party to make the document evidence in the proceedings.[1]   So far as civil cases are concerned, this result has been partially achieved by the Civil Evidence Act, 1968.   Section 1 provides that in any civil proceedings a statement other than one made by a person while giving oral evidence in those proceedings shall only be admissible as evidence of a fact stated to the extent permitted by the Act, or any other statutory provision, or by agreement.   The documents put in evidence in *Stroud* v. *Stroud* and *Walker* v. *Walker* were admitted by virtue of the common law;   under the Act of 1968, however, they would not be wholly inadmissible because the court would have a discretion to admit them as evidence of any fact of which the maker could have given direct oral evidence.[2]   Nothing has occurred to make the decisions irrelevant to English criminal cases since they were given.

C. FINALITY OF ANSWERS TO COLLATERAL QUESTIONS

(1) THE GENERAL RULE

There is a sound general rule, based on the desirability of avoiding a multiplicity of issues, that the answers given by a witness to questions put to him in cross-examination concerning collateral facts must be treated as final.   They may or may not be accepted by the jury, but the cross-examiner must take them for better or worse and cannot contradict them by other evidence.   A simple illustration of what has come to be known as the distinction between cross-examination to credit and cross-examination to the issue is provided by *Harris* v. *Tippett* [3] where the defendant's witness was asked in cross-examination whether he had attempted to dissuade one of the plaintiff's witnesses from attending the trial.   He demurred to this suggestion, and it was held that the plaintiff could not recall his witness to contradict him.   LAWRENCE, J., said he would permit questions to be put to a witness concerning any improper conduct of which he may have been guilty for the purpose of trying his credit:

> "but when these questions are irrelevant to the issue on the record, you cannot call other witnesses to contradict the answer he gives. No witness can be prepared to support his character as to particular facts, and such collateral inquiries would lead to endless confusion".

As relevance is a matter of degree, it is impossible to devise an exhaustive means of determining when a question is collateral for the purpose of the rule under consideration;   POLLOCK, C.B., said in the leading case of *A.-G.* v. *Hitchcock*:[4]

---

[1] 11th Report, para. 2231, draft Bill, clause 29.

[2] Civil Evidence Act, 1968, s. 8; R. S. C. O. 38, r. 29.

[3] (1811), 2 Camp. 637. The method of dissuasion is not stated in the report. If bribes were given and received, the decision would no longer represent the law because the witness would surely be held to be biased.

[4] (1847), 1 Exch. 91, at p. 99. POLLOCK, C.B., was really saying no more than that a witness may be contradicted on matters relevant to the issue (see *per* OGILVY-THOMPSON, J.A., in *S.* v. *Sinkankaka*, [1963] 2 S. A. 531, at p. 539. See also *Palmer* v. *Trower* (1852), 8 Exch. 247.

"The test whether a matter is collateral or not is this: if the answer of a witness is a matter which you would be allowed on your own part to prove in evidence —if it have such a connection with the issues, that you would be allowed to give it in evidence—then it is a matter on which you may contradict him."

The defendant was charged with using a cistern for making malt without complying with various statutory requirements. One Spooner gave evidence of the use of the cistern and was asked in cross-examination on behalf of the defendant whether he had not told Cook that the excise officers had offered him twenty pounds to say that the cistern had been used. Spooner denied that he had ever made such a statement, and it was held that the defendant could not ask Cook to narrate the alleged conversation. If Cook had been able to prove that Spooner had actually received a bribe from the excise officers, his testimony would have been admissible because it would have tended to show bias under an exception to the rule prohibiting contradictory evidence on collateral issues.

The effect of the judgments in *Hitchcock's Case* is aptly stated in the following passage from an American author:

"Independent evidence may be given to prove a self-contradictory statement by a primary witness only if (a) the statement contradicts testimony by the primary witness about a matter directly in issue in the litigation, or (b) the statement contradicts testimony by the primary witness as to "those matters which affect the motives, temper and character of the witness, . . . with reference to his feelings toward one party or the other.""[1]

But the rule concerning the finality of the witness's answers on collateral issues is not confined to self-contradictory statements, and a few more illustrations of its practical operation must be given.

Some of the clearest are provided by prosecutions for rape and kindred offences. The woman may be asked in cross-examination whether she has had intercourse with other men, but her answers are final.[2] On the other hand, she may be contradicted if she denies previous voluntary intercourse with the accused.[3] These decisions are consistent with the test for determining whether an issue is collateral suggested by Pollock, C.B., in *A.-G. v. Hitchcock*. Evidence of past intercourse with the accused would be admissible on behalf of the defence, even if the woman were not called as a witness, because it is highly relevant to the issue of consent as acts of voluntary intercourse between the same two people are liable to be repeated. Evidence of intercourse with others would generally not be admissible in-chief on behalf of the defence because it is insufficiently relevant to the issue of consent. Even if it tended to show promiscuity, its bearing on the question whether the woman had voluntary intercourse with the accused would be comparatively slight; but the distinction was questioned by Cardozo, J.,[4] and it has been held that the prosecutrix's denial that she is a prostitute may be contradicted by evidence of specific acts of prostitution.[5] Similarly, if the accused alleges that the prosecutrix to whose room he resorted after meeting her for the first time in a public house demanded money from him after consensual intercourse, he should be allowed to

---

[1] Maguire, *Evidence, Common Sense and Common Law*, 67. The subquotation is from the judgment of Pollock, C.B.
[2] *R. v. Holmes* (1871), L. R. 1 C. C. R. 334.
[3] *R. v. Riley* (1887), 18 Q. B. D. 481.   [4] *Nature of the Judicial Process*, p. 156.
[5] *R. v. Bashir* and *Manzur*, [1969] 3 All E. R. 692.

contradict her denial by calling a witness to depose to similar conduct on her part in his case.[1]

The Australian case of *Piddington* v. *Bennett and Wood Proprietary, Ltd.*[2] prompts speculation on the question whether POLLOCK, C.B.'s test can always be applied with satisfactory results. One of the plaintiff's witnesses in a running-down action was asked in cross-examination how he accounted for his presence at the scene of the accident, and he said that he had been to the bank on behalf of a named person. A new trial was ordered on the ground that the judge had wrongly allowed the bank manager to give evidence to the effect that no business was done on behalf of the man named by the witness on the day of the accident. No doubt a witness's evidence as to how he came to be at the place where the events of which he deposes occurred is collateral, and POLLOCK, C.B.'s test applies to the facts with which the court was concerned; but a question naturally arises with regard to the proper decision in such a case if the rebutting evidence goes to show that the witness was not present at the accident at all. It would be a perversion of language to describe such evidence as collateral to the issue, but, by its very nature, it could not be given in-chief.[3] Similar speculations are prompted by the Irish case of *R.* v. *Burke*[4] in which a witness was giving evidence through an interpreter. He was cross-examined about his knowledge of English, and it was held that evidence could not be given to contradict his statement that he was ignorant of the language. Once again it is difficult to deny the collateral nature of the question in the situation before the court, but it is easy to imagine circumstances in which a witness's linguistic ability would be directly relevant to the issue, as when it is crucial to know whether he understood what was said on the occasion about which he is deposing, and in such a case the test of POLLOCK, C.B., would prohibit the reception of evidence in rebuttal of the witness's denials. The decision of the House of Lords in *Toohey* v. *Commissioner of Metropolitan Police*[5] suggests that evidence may always be given of a witness's lack of opportunity or capacity to perceive the events about which he testifies and it is doubtful whether the Australian or even the Irish case to which reference has just been made would be followed in this country.

(2) EXCEPTIONS TO THE GENERAL RULE

The nature of the cross-examination will sometimes entitle the party calling the witness to call another one to testify to matters which could not have been deposed to in the absence of the cross-examination. For example, if the plaintiff in a running-down case is cross-examined in such a way as to suggest that he has suppressed information about a later accident in which he sustained injuries, his solicitor may be called to prove the prompt disclosure of those injuries. The point is directly relevant to the amount of damages claimed;[6] but cases of this sort do not constitute a real

---

[1] *R.* v. *Krausz* (1973), 57 Cr. App. Rep. 466.   [2] (1940), 63 C. L. R. 533.

[3] This has been held to go to the issue in Nova Scotia (*Tzagarakis* v. *Stevens* (1968), 69 D. L. R. (2d) 466, a decision which seems to follow from *Toohey* v. *Metropolitan Police Commissioners*, [1965] A. C. 595; [1965] 1 All E. R. 506).

[4] (1858), 8 Cox C. C. 44.

[5] [1965] A. C. 595; [1965] 1 All E. R. 506. See facts, p. 238 *infra*.

[6] *Drakos* v. *Smith*, [1958] V. L. R. 536; the solicitor's evidence was also admissible on the ground that it rebutted the cross-examiner's allegation of recent invention. Had the defendant been in a position to rebut the plaintiff's denials of his failure to disclose the later accident, no doubt he would have been allowed to call a witness to do so.

exception to the rule that a witness's answers to collateral questions or questions concerning credit only are final.

There are, however, four well-recognised exceptions—the fact that a witness has been convicted of a crime, the fact that he is biased in favour of the party calling him, the fact that he has previously made a statement inconsistent with his present testimony and the fact that the moral character or physical condition of the witness is such as to militate against his telling the truth. Nothing more need be said about the third exception and the fourth is mentioned later.

(i) **Previous convictions.**—The fact that a witness has suffered a criminal conviction may have a material bearing on his credibility, but, if the matter is considered on principle, the nature of the crime would appear to be most relevant. Little attention would normally be paid to the testimony of a confirmed perjurer, but the veracity of a reckless motorist concerning matters other than his own driving might be considered beyond reproach. Since 1854, the matter has, however, been covered by statute, and the provision which is now in force reads as follows:

"A witness may be questioned as to whether he has been convicted of any felony or misdemeanour, and upon being so questioned, if he either denies or does not admit the fact, or refuses to answer, it shall be lawful for the cross-examining party to prove such conviction."[1]

Although there is no direct authority on the point, the statute is usually taken to mean what it says, so that a witness may be asked about *any* conviction, whether it would ordinarily be thought relevant to credibility or not, and the conviction may be proved if it is not admitted.[2] The wisdom of such a broad provision is open to question, and the Criminal Law Revision Committee recommended that it should be made plain that the conviction must be relevant to the issue or to credibility;[3] but it is right that there should be an exception to the rule prohibiting evidence in rebuttal on collateral matters covering some types of conviction on account of the comparative ease with which these facts may be proved if they are denied.[4] The most important of the modifications of the law with regard to cross-examination that are made in the case of an accused person giving evidence on his own behalf consists of a restriction, discussed in Chapter XV, of the prosecution's power to question him about his previous convictions.

(ii) **Bias.**—It was recognised in *A.-G.* v. *Hitchcock* that the fact that a witness had given or received a bribe might be proved if it was denied by him because it tended to show bias in favour of one of the parties. This principle has been acted upon in a variety of situations both before and after *Hitchcock's Case* was decided. A witness may be asked about his relations with one of the parties or whether they have recently quarrelled,[5] and, if these matters are denied, evidence in rebuttal is admissible. In

---

[1] Criminal Procedure Act, 1865, s. 6. It applies to civil and criminal cases. On the position at common law see the judgment of DIXON, J., in *Bugg* v. *Day* (1949), 79 C. L. R. 442.

[2] *Clifford* v. *Clifford*, [1961] 3 All E. R. 231, at p. 232; *Ward* v. *Sinfield* (1880), 49 L. J. Q. B. 696; (deciding that a conviction for embezzlement may be proved against a witness in a commercial case, though going only to credibility).

[3] 11th Report, paras. 159–60.

[4] For proof of convictions generally see Chapter XXII, *post*.

[5] *Dunn* v. *Aslett* (1838), 2 Mood. & R. 122; *R.* v. *Shaw* (1888), 16 Cox C. C. 503.

Thomas v. *David*,[1] an action on a bill of exchange, one of the plaintiff's witnesses was asked whether she was his mistress, and it was held that the defendant might call witnesses to prove this fact after she had denied it. COLERIDGE, J., thought that, if the question had been whether the witness walked the streets as a common prostitute, it would have been collateral to the issue, and, had the witness denied such a charge, she could not have been contradicted; but the question was:

> "whether the witness had contracted such a relation with the plaintiff as might induce her the more readily to conspire with him to support a forgery, just in the same way as if she had been asked if she were the sister or daughter of the plaintiff, and had denied that".

It will be recollected that, in *A.-G.* v. *Hitchcock*,[2] a witness's denial of the fact that he had said that he had been offered a bribe by the excise officers could not be contradicted. In *R.* v. *Phillips*,[3] the accused's daughters gave evidence against him on a charge of incest. In cross-examination they denied that they had ever been "schooled" by their mother, or that she had told them what to say in previous proceedings against their father. The accused wished to call two women to swear that his daughters had made statements to that effect, but the judge would not allow him to do so on the ground that the cross-examination of the daughters merely went to their credit, so their denials were final. The conviction was quashed because the Court of Criminal Appeal was of opinion that the accused should have been allowed to call the women as their evidence went to the foundation of his defence. This decision can be distinguished from *A.-G.* v. *Hitchcock* because the daughters were asked whether they had in fact been suborned, not merely whether they had ever said that this was the case; but the judgments in *Hitchcock's Case* merely consider the effect of such remarks as "I have been offered a bribe" or "I have received a bribe" from the point of view of the maker's credibility as a witness, whereas proof that a bribe was in fact offered would have had a direct bearing on the innocence of the defendant, as it would have suggested that the excise officers were aware of the weakness of their case.[4]

The English courts have not had to consider the question whether an admission of bias for one reason lets in evidence of bias for another reason; a Victorian court has held that it does not.[5]

(3) THE DISTINCTION BETWEEN CROSS-EXAMINATION TO THE ISSUE AND CROSS-EXAMINATION TO CREDIT GENERALLY[6]

The distinction between cross-examination to the issue and cross-examination to credit is important because the only inference that can be drawn from the latter affects the question whether the witness is to be believed on oath. No inference may be drawn with regard to a fact in issue.

---

[1] (1836), 7 C. & P. 350; *cf. R.* v. *Finnessey* (1906), 11 O. L. R. 338.

[2] (1847), 1 Exch. 91. [3] (1936), 26 Cr. App. Rep. 17.

[4] Cf. *Moriarty* v. *London, Chatham and Dover Rail. Co.* (1870), L. R. 5 Q. B. 314.

[5] *Bakopoulos* v. *General Motors Holdens, Ltd.*, [1972] V. R. 732.

[6] See *Wren* v. *Emmetts Contractors Pty., Ltd.* (1969), 43 A. L. J. R. 213 holding that a question implying that a witness intended to rely, somewhat dishonourably, on his legal rights did not go to credit and ought to have been disallowed, and containing a valuable discussion of cross-examination to credit generally.

"If by cross-examination as to credit you prove that a man's oath cannot be relied on, and he has sworn he did not go to Rome on May 1st, you do not, therefore, prove that he did go to Rome on May 1st; there is simply no evidence on the subject." [1]

It is, however, equally important not to overemphasise the significance of the distinction when the witness is a party to the proceedings. We shall see in Chapter XV that, in cases in which the accused may be cross-examined on his previous convictions, attempts are sometimes made to distinguish between utilising the convictions as evidence of guilt, and utilising them as something affecting the credibility of the accused. The argument is that no direct inference may be made from the fact that the accused has a criminal record to the fact that he committed the crime charged, and we shall see in Chapter XIV that inferences of this sort are generally prohibited. But this does not render it possible to say that the convictions are being used for a wholly different purpose when the credibility of the accused is under consideration. The line of argument in the latter case is that the accused is not to be believed when he swears that he is innocent because he has a criminal record. Therefore he is guilty. For practical purposes there is no distinction between the two cases. The correct conclusion appears to be that, although the difference between the effects of cross-examination to credit and cross-examination to the issue is crucial when questions concerning the finality of the witness's denials, or the existence of any evidence of a fact in issue, are under consideration, it is not one that can be usefully applied to the answers given by an accused person who is being cross-examined on his testimony in which he has asserted his innocence; attempts to utilise it in this connection are in the nature of an unduly subtle refinement.

D. EVIDENCE IMPUGNING THE CREDIBILITY OF AN OPPONENT'S WITNESS

(1) EVIDENCE OF BAD REPUTATION OR OPINION AS TO VERACITY

In *R.* v. *Brown and Hedley*,[2] the Court for Crown Cases Reserved considered that a litigant's right to call a witness to swear that he would not believe the opposite party's witness on oath was too clear for argument. The following is a brief summary of the development of the law on this subject. In *Mawson* v. *Hartsink*,[3] it was held that the witness may be asked whether he is aware of the impugned witness's reputation for veracity and whether, from such knowledge, he would believe the impugned witness on oath. In *R.* v. *Watson*,[4] however, it was held that the witness might simply state whether he would believe the oath of the person about whom he was asked, and although *R.* v. *Rowton* [5] decides that, when asked about a prisoner's character, the witness must speak to the accused's general reputation and not give his personal opinion of the accused's disposition, *R.* v. *Brown* sanctions the form of question approved in *R.* v. *Watson*. The witness may not give his reasons for disbelieving the oath of the opposite party's witness when he is being examined in-chief, but he may

---

[1] *Per* SCRUTTON, L.J., in *Hobbs* v. *Tinling*, [1929] 2 K. B. 1, at p. 21.
[2] (1867), L. R. 1 C. C. R. 70.
[3] (1802), 4 Esp. 102.
[4] (1817), 2 Stark. 116, at p. 152.
[5] (1865), Le. & Ca. 520.

be cross-examined about them. In *R.* v. *Richardson and Longman,*[1] a doctor called for the defence was asked whether he would believe one of the prosecution witnesses on oath. He said she could be believed in certain particulars, and it was held that the judge was wrong in refusing to allow a further question to be put, namely, whether from his personal knowledge the doctor would believe the witness on oath; but the Court of Appeal doubted whether the doctor could have been allowed to say that the witness was not to be believed when frightened because that would come near to giving reasons for his opinion. It has been said to be neither very logical nor very useful to admit this kind of evidence of reputation which must necessarily be based on hearsay, but the rule is sacrosanct.[2] In theory, it could lead to an infinite regress because a further witness might be called to impugn the reputation for veracity of the impugning witness, and so on.

(2) EVIDENCE OF PHYSICAL OR MENTAL CONDITION TENDING TO UNRELIABILITY

A witness may be called to give evidence that the physical condition of one of the opponent's witnesses is such as to militate against his veracity. An obvious instance would be the calling of a witness to swear that one of the opponent's witnesses who had testified to events occurring at some distance from him only has limited vision.

In *Toohey* v. *Commissioner of Metropolitan Police,*[3] the accused were charged with assaulting a boy of sixteen with intent to rob him. The boy's case was that the accused had demanded money and cigarettes, taken him up an alley and assaulted him in the course of searching him. The accuseds' defence was that they had found him in a state of hysteria exacerbated by drink and were helping him home. The accused were not allowed to call a police surgeon to testify to the fact that the boy was in an hysterical condition when brought to the police station, that he smelt of drink, and that drink was liable to exacerbate hysteria. The accused were convicted and the conviction was affirmed by the Court of Criminal Appeal. It was, however, quashed by the House of Lords. The surgeon's evidence was relevant to the issue because it assisted in the resolution of the question whether the alleged assault accounted for the hysteria, or whether the hysteria accounted for the allegation of assault, but the primary importance of the decision of the House of Lords is that it sanctions the calling of a witness to impugn the reliability of an opponent's witness on medical grounds.

E. RE-EXAMINATION

The subject of re-examination can be disposed of briefly. Leading questions may not be put, any more than they may be put in-chief; previous consistent statements can only be put to the witness if rendered admissible by the terms of the cross-examination, or, with the leave of the Court, under the Civil Evidence Act, 1968, section 2. The most important rule is that the re-examination must be confined to matters arising out of the cross-examination, and new matter may only be introduced with the leave of the

---

[1] [1969] 1 Q. B. 299; [1968] 2 All E. R. 761.
[2] *Toohey* v. *Commissioner of Metropolitan Police,* [1965] A. C. at p. 606, per Lord PEARCE
[3] [1965] A. C. 595; [1965] 1 All E. R. 506. For an account of the impact of this decision on the previous law see an article by J. A. Andrews, [1965] Crim. L. R. 461.

judge. Thus, in *Prince* v. *Samo*,[1] an action for malicious arrest arising out of the non-payment of a loan alleged by the plaintiff to be a gift, the plaintiff had given evidence at the trial of one of the defendant's witnesses for perjury. The plaintiff's attorney was present at that trial, and he was called as a witness on behalf of his client in the present proceedings. The attorney could not be asked in-chief about statements made by the plaintiff at the earlier trial on account of the rule against hearsay, and the prohibition on evidence of a witness's prior consistent statements; but he was asked in cross-examination whether the plaintiff had not said, in the course of his evidence in the previous proceedings, that he had repeatedly been insolvent. It was held that he could not be asked in re-examination about other portions of the plaintiff's earlier evidence which had no connection with the statement concerning his insolvency. The rule is sound on principle because it prevents the reception of inadmissible evidence in re-examination, under the guise of dealing with points emerging from the cross-examination, and any hardship that the rule may occasion can be mitigated by the judge.

The terms of the cross-examination may, however, let significant and prejudicial evidence in through the re-examination although such evidence would not be admissible in-chief. Perhaps the most striking examples are provided by cases in which adverse insinuations to the effect that he is an agent provocateur are made in the cross-examination of a police witness. He may then be asked in re-examination about his reasons for approaching the accused, and the jury may thus be provided with information about suspicions entertained by the police concerning the accused.[2]

SECTION 4. EVIDENCE IN REBUTTAL

"There is a general principle of practice, although no rule of law, requiring that all evidential matter that the Crown intends to rely upon as probative of the guilt of the defendant . . . should be adduced before the close of the prosecution's case if it be then available."[3]   It follows that the power to allow further evidence to be called by a party after he has closed his case is exercised very sparingly. We have seen that evidence in rebuttal of that which a witness for a defendant says in cross-examination to credit is occasionally allowed as a matter of right, but, in most cases, the reception of evidence in rebuttal is a matter of discretion. The principal illustrations are provided by criminal cases in which the prosecution wishes to call rebutting evidence. When the evidence relates to a material, as opposed to a purely formal, point, the judge will only give leave to call it if it relates to a matter which the prosecutor was unable to foresee. It has even been said that the matter must be one which no human ingenuity could have foreseen.[4]

In *R.* v. *Day*,[5] for instance, the trial judge allowed the prosecution in a

---

[1] (1838), 7 Ad. & El. 627.
[2] *R* v. *Nation*, [1954] S. A. S. R. 189. See also *Wojcic* v. *Incorporated Nominal Defendant*, [1969] V. R. 323, where the cross-examination let in a crucial report to the defendant from his agent.
[3] *R.* v. *Rice*, [1963] 1 Q. B. 857, at p. 860, [1963] 1 All E. R. 832, at p. 839, per WINN, J. Although there does not appear to be any authority on the point, the practice no doubt applies in civil cases.
[4] This strict way of formulating the rule is due to TINDAL, C. J. in *R.* v. *Frost* (1839), 4 State Tr. N. S. 86. at p. 386 and not approved in the High court of Australia in *Shaw* v. *R.* (1952), 85 C. L. R. 365.
[5] [1940] 1 All E. R. 402. Lord GODDARD, C.J., considered TINDALL, C.J.'s statement to be too wide in *R.* v. *Owen*, [1952] 2 Q. B. 362, at p. 367; see also *R.* v. *Milliken* (1969),

case of forgery to call a handwriting expert after the case for the prosecution had been closed. The accused was convicted, but his conviction was quashed by the Court of Criminal Appeal because the evidence was of a kind the necessity of which should have been foreseen from the outset.

In *R.* v. *Milliken*,[1] on the other hand, the Court of Appeal held that the trial judge had rightly allowed the prosecution to adduce evidence in rebuttal of an allegation of a police "frame-up" made by the accused for the first time at the trial.

An example of a purely formal omission which the court will usually allow to be remedied, even after the close of the case for the prosecution, would be a case in which the Crown had failed to prove that the leave of the Director of Public Prosecutions had been obtained, when such leave is necessary, before the prosecution was begun.[2] The discretion in favour of allowing evidence in rebuttal is more likely to be exercised when the evidence sought to be tendered would only have been marginally, doubtfully or minimally relevant in-chief than when it would have been clearly relevant.[3]

---

53 Cr. App. Rep. 330. For a proposed statutory provision giving the court a complete discretion, see 11th Report of the Criminal Law Revision Committee, para. 212.

[1] *Supra.*

[2] *Price* v. *Humphries*, [1958] 2 Q.B. 353; [1958] 2 All E. R. 725. For the rigid rule that no further evidence is permissible once the jury has retired see cases cited n. 1 p. 195, *ante.*

[3] *R.* v. *Levy and Tait* (1966), 50 Cr. App. Rep. 198.

CHAPTER XI

PRIVILEGE

It is in relation to the law of privilege that the enactment by the Civil Evidence Act, 1968, of the recommendations of the Law Reform Committee[1] and the failure to enact the corresponding recommendations of the Criminal Law Revision Committee[2] make the rules of evidence appear most irrational. Several obsolete privileges were abolished by the Act of 1968, but they still apply to criminal proceedings. It must be admitted, however, that the irrationality is unimportant because the privileges are unimportant.

It will be convenient to deal in separate sections with the privilege against self-incrimination, legal professional privilege (both of which apply, with minor modifications to civil and criminal cases), privileges now solely applicable to criminal proceedings, and privileges solely applicable to civil proceedings. A few preliminary observations are also necessary.

In the first place, as the privilege is that of a particular person or class, matters covered by it may always be proved by the evidence of other witnesses. PARKE, B., once said:

> "Where an attorney entrusted confidentially with a document communicates the contents, or suffers another to take a copy, surely the secondary evidence so obtained may be produced. Suppose the instrument were even stolen, and a correct copy taken, would it not be reasonable to admit it?"[3]

and it was on the authority of this remark that the Court of Appeal allowed copies of proofs of witnesses with notes on the evidence in a former action brought by the plaintiff's predecessor in title to be put in by the defendant in *Calcraft* v. *Guest*,[4] the originals having been handed over by the defendant's solicitor to the plaintiff to whom they belonged. Similarly, if someone obtains possession of a confidential letter written by a husband to his wife it may be proved against the husband although, had it been received by her, the wife could not have been compelled to disclose it.[5] The Law Reform Committee considered that, at any rate where a document had been obtained as a result of a crime or deliberate tort, the party concerned should not thereby be deprived of his privilege; but, as the point forms part of the larger problem of illegally obtained evidence, they preferred to await the views of the Criminal Law Revision Committee. The latter body made no recommendations on this subject and we shall see in the next chapter that, in general, subject to the judge's exclusionary discretion, evidence is admissible in England although it was obtained

---

[1] 16th Report, 1967, Cmnd. 3472.
[2] 11th Report, paras. 169–173.
[3] *Lloyd* v. *Mostyn* (1842), 10 M. & W. 478, at pp. 481–482 in the course of argument.
[4] [1898] 1 Q. B. 759, *quaere* whether this decision has not overruled *R.* v. *Leverson* (1868), 11 Cox C. C. 152.
[5] *Rumping* v. *Director of Public Prosecutions*, [1964] A. C. 814; [1962] 3 All E. R. 256 where the relevant authorities are reviewed.

illegally, while the "fruits of the poisoned tree" are generally inadmissible in the United States.[1]

Secondly, the personal nature of the privilege means that a party will not necessarily be entitled to succeed on an appeal, or obtain an order for a new trial when the claim to privilege of his own, or his opponent's, witness has been wrongly rejected or accepted in the court below. There is express authority for this view in a case in which the witness had invoked the privilege against self-incrimination,[2] and practically all the decisions of Appellate Courts in which the judge's ruling on a question of privilege has been varied or reversed relate to issues in which the person claiming the privilege was a party to, and not merely a witness in, the proceedings. Many of them are concerned with the discovery of documents, or the propriety of interrogatories for, as often as not, the issue of privilege is raised in interlocutory proceedings before the actual trial of a civil action.

Thirdly, according to English law, no adverse inference should be made from the fact that the privilege is claimed.[3]

The last general observation concerns the effect of upholding a claim to privilege. This involves withholding important information from the court at the expense of what may be abstract justice to one of the parties. It follows that there should be good cause, plainly shown, for the existence of any privilege,[4] and it remains for us to consider whether this is so in the case of all the privileges discussed in this chapter. The crucial question is whether there is some interest protected by the privilege which is at least as significant as the proper administration of justice. It is, of course, important not to exclude the possibility that the law is defective on account of its failure to recognise certain legitimate claims to privilege, and not merely because of its protection of interests which do not merit such solicitude. The influence of public opinion must never be ignored. The proper administration of justice mentioned above includes the notion of the rejection of relevant evidence because its reception would be unduly offensive to contemporary public opinion. It follows that that which was the subject of privilege in one generation should not necessarily be privileged in the next and vice versa.

SECTION 1. THE PRIVILEGE AGAINST SELF-INCRIMINATION [5]

A. STATEMENT, HISTORY AND RATIONALE OF THE RULE

(1) STATEMENT OF THE RULE

"The rule is that no one is bound to answer any question if the answer thereto

---

[1] 16th Report of the Law Reform Committee, para. 32. The Report refers to rule 26 of the Uniform Rules which confers a very wide protection on the holder of the privilege; there is no equivalent in the Federal Rules.

[2] *R.* v. *Kinglake* (1870), 22 L. T. 335.

[3] *Wentworth* v. *Lloyd* (1864), 10 H. L. Cas. 589, at pp. 590–592. The contrast with Rule 233 of the Model Code is striking: "if a privilege to refuse to disclose, or a privilege to prevent another from disclosing, matter is claimed and allowed, the judge and counsel may comment thereon, and the trier of fact may draw all reasonable inferences therefrom"; but this rule was not adopted by the Uniform Law Commissioners (see Uniform Rules, r. 39) or the authors of the Federal Rules (r. 513).

[4] VIII *Wigmore*, p. 67.

[5] VIII *Wigmore* (McNaughton Revision), paras. 2250–2251 contains a classic history of the rule. See also an article by Edmund Morgan in 34 Minnesota Law Review 1.

would, in the opinion of the judge, have a tendency to expose the deponent to any criminal charge, penalty or [in a criminal case] forfeiture which the judge regards as reasonably likely to be preferred or sued for."[1]

The privilege extends to documents, and, subject to the unimportant modification in square brackets, it applies to civil and criminal cases alike. In the United States it appears that the privilege does not permit samples of "body fluids or substances" to be withheld.[2] We have seen that, at any rate as far as blood tests are concerned, the provision of samples of this nature may not be ordered at common law, although this is the outcome of the protection of personal liberty rather than the privilege against self-incrimination.[3]

A witness cannot claim to be privileged from answering questions on the ground that the answers will expose him to civil liability either at the suit of the Crown or of any other person.[4] It will be convenient to say something about the history and rationale of the rule before mentioning some miscellaneous points and considering various statutory provisions some of which constitute exceptions to the rule.

(2) HISTORY OF THE RULE

Three types of answer are contemplated as the possible subject-matter of a claim to privilege in the above statement—those which expose the deponent to the risk of a criminal charge, those which put him in danger of a penalty, and those which might lead to a forfeiture. It used to be customary to include within the rule answers which would tend to show that the deponent had committed adultery. Each of these matters has a different history, the result of which is that the so-called privilege against self-incrimination covers a wider ground than the liability to criminal punishment.

(i) Liability to a criminal charge.—We have seen that the privilege against self-incrimination in the narrow sense of the word originated in the unpopularity of the procedure in the Star Chamber under which those who were charged with an offence were interrogated on oath.[5] This contributed to the rule that the accused could not testify in a criminal case, and the idea that no one could be obliged to jeopardise his life or liberty by answering questions on oath came to be applied to all witnesses in all proceedings in the course of the seventeenth century. The rule extends beyond answers that would directly criminate the witness to those which might be used as a step towards obtaining evidence against him. In *R.* v. *Slaney*,[6] for instance, a witness who was giving evidence at a prosecution for a criminal libel contained in an advertisement in a newspaper was asked whether he knew who wrote to the proprietors with the advertisement,

---

[1] *Per* GODDARD, L. J., in *Blunt* v. *Park Lane Hotel, Ltd.*, [1942] 2 K. B. 253, at p. 257; [1942] 2 All E. R. 187, at p. 189.
[2] Uniform Rules 25 (c); *Schmerber* v. *California* (1966), 384 U.S. 757. The Uniform Rules and the decision in *Schmerber's Case* confine the privilege, even in the case of an accused, to evidence of a testimonial or communicative nature, but this is, of course, subject to the rights accorded to an accused by the constitutional proviso against unreasonable searches.
[3] P. 46, *ante.*
[4] Witnesses' Act, 1806.
[5] P. 146, *ante.*
[6] (1832), 5 C. & P. 213. See also *Short* v. *Mercier* (1851), 3 Mac. & G. 205, at p. 217, *per* Lord TRURO.

and, after he had answered in the affirmative, Lord TENTERDEN, C.J., upheld his objection to stating the name of the writer of the letter.

"You cannot only not compel a witness to answer that which will criminate him, but that which tends to criminate him: and the reason is this, that the party would go from one question to another, and though no question might be asked, the answer of which would directly criminate the witness, yet they would get enough from him whereon to found a charge against him."

At one time it was thought that it would be sufficient to establish the claim to privilege if the witness swore that his answer would tend to criminate him, but we shall see that it is now clear that the Court must examine the matter a little more closely.

(ii) Liability to a penalty.—The rule that a witness cannot be obliged to answer a question if the answer would expose him to the risk of a penalty seems to have originated in the doctrine that equity would not assist a common informer by making an order for discovery in his favour. This rule survived the Judicature Acts;[1] proceedings for penalties, as opposed to compensation,[2] are now virtually obsolete, but the Law Reform Committee considered that the privilege should continue so long as penalties are recoverable in some civil proceedings.[3]

(iii) Liability to forfeiture.—The inclusion of answers tending to establish liability to a forfeiture within this privilege is attributable to the rule that equity would not grant discovery or order interrogatories in aid of a forfeiture of property. This, too, survived the Judicature Acts, and, when declining to grant discovery in an action for the forfeiture of a lease in *Earl of Mexborough* v. *Whitwood U.D.C.*,[4] Lord ESHER referred to the equitable rule against assisting common informers or aiding a forfeiture of property, saying:

"The rule by which a witness is protected from being called on to answer questions which may tend to criminate himself is often referred to in connection with this subject, but it has really nothing to do with the two rules to which I have referred."

The Law Reform Committee could see no reason for the continued existence of this branch of the privilege against self-incrimination now that the courts possess wide powers of relief against forfeiture, and it was accordingly abolished, so far as civil cases are concerned, by section 16 (1) (a) of the Civil Evidence Act, 1968.[5]

(iv) Liability to a finding of adultery.—There can be little doubt that answers which might be used to establish the witness's adultery were once thought to be included in the common law privilege against self-incrimination. As recently as 1891, BOWEN, L.J., said in *Redfern* v. *Redfern*:[6]

"It is one of the inveterate principles of English law that a party cannot be compelled to discover that which, if answered, would tend to subject him to any punishment, penalty, forfeiture or ecclesiastical censure. In these days, when the thunders of the Church have become less formidable, the rule, so

---

[1] *Hunnings* v. *Williamson* (1883), 10 Q. B. D. 459; *Martin* v. *Treacher* (1886), 16 Q. B. D. 507. [2] *Adams* v. *Batley* (1887). 18 Q. B. D. 625.
[3] 16th Report, para. 13.
[4] [1897] 2 Q. B. 111, at p. 115; *Seddon* v. *Commercial Salt Co., Ltd.*, [1925] Ch. 187.
[5] There is a corresponding provision in clause 16 (1) (a) of the draft Bill annexed to the 11th Report of the Criminal Law Revision Committee.
[6] [1891] P. 139, at p. 147.

far as it relates to ecclesiastical censure, seems to wear an archaic form; but adultery is a charge of such gravity as to render it not unnatural that we should find the doctrine still applicable to it that no one is bound to criminate himself."

Redfern v. *Redfern* was in part concerned with the privilege conferred by the proviso to section 3 of the Evidence Further Amendment Act, 1869,[1] on parties to and witnesses in proceedings instituted in consequence of adultery against answering questions tending to show their adultery, but the above dictum was rendered obsolete by the decision of the Court of Appeal in *Blunt* v. *Park Lane Hotel, Ltd.*[2] That was an action for slander based on an allegation that the plaintiff had been guilty of adultery. She objected to answering interrogatories which the defendants wished to administer in support of their plea of justification, but the Court held that formal ecclesiastical censure of laymen for adultery was obsolete, and described the plaintiff's plea that her answers might expose her to the risk of not being allowed to partake of the sacrament as "fanciful". GODDARD, L.J., stated the rule in the terms quoted at the beginning of this section, and it will be seen that he adopted the words of BOWEN, L.J., in *Redfern* v. *Redfern* except that he made no allusion to the possibility of ecclesiastical censure.

(3) RATIONALE OF THE MAIN BRANCH OF THE RULE

Turning to the question of the rationale of the main head of the privilege, the idea that a man should be compelled to give answers exposing himself to the risk of criminal punishment is probably still repellent to public opinion, although it is no longer based on the unpopularity of the Star Chamber. There is the additional consideration that people must be encouraged to testify freely, and they might not be prepared to come forward as witnesses in the absence of some kind of privilege against incrimination. Although reliance on the privilege will sometimes obstruct the course of justice in the case in which it is claimed, and may militate against the discovery of crimes which ought to be traced in the public interest, there is probably sufficient justification for protecting a witness from exposing himself to the peril of criminal proceedings. Reference is sometimes made to the privilege in relation to the interrogation of suspects and the testimony of the accused, matters which are considered elsewhere in this book.

B. MISCELLANEOUS POINTS

There are three further points to be considered so far as the common law on this subject is concerned—the question whether the privilege extends to answers which would criminate the witness's spouse, the question whether the privilege extends to answers which would criminate the witness under foreign law and the part played by the judge in determining the criminating tendencies of a question to which the witness objects.

---

[1] Repealed by the Civil Evidence Act, 1968, s. 16 (5) on the effect of which see *Nast* v. *Nast and Walker*, [1972] Fam. 142; [1972] 1 All E. R. 1171.

[2] [1942] 2 K. B. 253; [1942] 2 All E. R. 187. See also *Evans* v. *Evans and Blyth*, [1904] P. 378, and *Elliott* v. *Albert*, [1934] 1 K. B. 650.

(1) Incrimination of Spouse

There is no direct authority on the first point, but dicta suggest that the privilege does extend to answers tending to criminate the witness's spouse.[1] The policy considerations underlying the existence of the privilege—conformity with public opinion and the encouragement of testimony appear to apply to such a case, but the line must be drawn somewhere and it is hardly surprising that it should have been decided that a witness cannot object to answering questions on the ground that his answers would incriminate strangers.[2] In the absence of any suggestion to the contrary, it may be assumed that there is no privilege against giving answers which might criminate members of the witness's family other than his spouse.

To make assurance doubly sure with regard to the incrimination of the witness's spouse, section 14 (1) (b) of the Civil Evidence Act, 1968 expressly extends the privilege to questions tending to have that effect.[3]

(2) Incrimination Under Foreign Law

In the *King of the Two Sicilies* v. *Willcox*,[4] it appears to have been decided that the privilege does not extend to answers that might incriminate the witness under foreign law because the judge ought to be able to determine the question whether disclosure would entail penal consequences as a matter of law. In the *United States of America* v. *McRae*,[5] on the other hand it was decided that, where the provisions of the foreign law were admitted on the pleadings, there could be no order for discovery if the production of documents might have penal consequences thereunder. In the circumstances it is impossible to state the common law on this matter with any certitude. Section 14 (1) (a) of the Civil Evidence Act, 1968, expressly confines the privilege to answers tending to criminate according to the law of any part of the United Kingdom.[6]

(3) The Role of the Judge

The judge will often warn a witness that he is not obliged to answer criminating questions, but there is no rule of law to this effect, and the fact that the witness was ignorant of his rights does not prevent the court from utilising his evidence in the case in which it was given, or in subsequent criminal proceedings brought against him.[7] The practice to be followed when someone objects to answering a question because he might be incriminated if he were to do so was laid down in *R*. v. *Boyes*.[8] The witness's mere statement that his answer might have this effect is not sufficient, although it is on oath and even if there is no doubt concerning his *bona fides*.

---

[1] *R*. v. *All Saints, Worcester* (1817), 6 M. & S. 194, at p. 201, *per* BAYLEY, J.

[2] *R*. v. *Minihane* (1921), 16 Cr. App. Rep. 38.

[3] There is a corresponding provision in clause 15 (1) (b) of the draft Bill attached to the 11th Report of the Criminal Law Revision Committee; perhaps it is merely declaratory of the common law.

[4] (1851), 1 Sim. N. S. 301. To the same effect are dicta in *Re Atherton*, [1912] 2 K. B. 251, at p. 255.

[5] (1868), L. R. 3 Ch. App. 79.

[6] There is a corresponding provision in clause 15 (1) (a) of the draft Bill attached to the 11th Report of the Criminal Law Revision Committee. It is not without interest that the United States Supreme Court appears to have approved the application of the privilege to incrimination under foreign law generally in *Murphy* v. *Waterfront Commission of New York Harbour*, (1964), 378 U.S. 52, although the actual case was concerned with incrimination under State law.

[7] *R*. v. *Coote* (1873), L. R. 4 P. C. 599. Cf. *S*. v. *Lwane*, 1966 (2) S. A. 433.

[8] (1861), 1 B. & S. 311; *Re Reynolds, Ex parte Reynolds* (1882), 20 Ch. D. 294.

The court must see, from the circumstances of the case and the nature of the evidence which the witness is called to give, that there is reasonable ground to apprehend danger to him from his answer. The judge must come to the conclusion that such danger is real and appreciable with reference to the ordinary operation of law in the ordinary course of things, not a danger of an imaginary and unsubstantial character, having reference to some extraordinary and barely possible contingency so improbable that no reasonable man would suffer it to influence his conduct. Accordingly in *Boyes's Case*, a witness who had been handed a pardon under the Great Seal was obliged to answer a question with reference to its subject matter although he might still have been impeached for the offence according to strict legal theory because a pardon cannot be pleaded in answer to an impeachment. If a witness has already made himself liable to a criminal prosecution by an admission, his refusal to answer may be held not to be *bona fide*.[1] The fact that an offence was of a trifling nature or committed many years ago, might likewise preclude the court from allowing the plea of privilege to succeed, but it was held in *Triplex Safety Glass Co., Ltd.* v. *Lancegaye Safety Glass (1934), Ltd.*,[2] that the mere fact that prosecutions for criminal libel are rare does not have this effect.

In order to satisfy the court that there are reasonable grounds for his fears, a witness may have to disclose some matter of a damning nature, but the danger that the secret must be told in order that the court may see whether it ought to be kept [3] is inevitably present when a claim to privilege is made if the worse evil of allowing the matter to depend exclusively on the claimant's word is to be avoided. If difficulties were to arise in this regard, they could no doubt be surmounted by allowing the witness to make his submission wholly or partially *in camera*, or under the protection of an undertaking that no use would be made of his statements outside the proceedings in which they were given. In any event, it is settled that anything that a person is wrongly compelled to say after he has claimed his privilege will be treated as having been said involuntarily, with the result that it will be inadmissible in subsequent criminal proceedings brought against him.[4]

C. STATUTORY PROVISIONS

Section 1 (e) of the Criminal Evidence Act, 1898, provides that the accused may be asked any question in cross-examination notwithstanding that it would tend to incriminate him as to the offence charged. This is an essential corollary to the main provision of the Act enabling the accused to give evidence on his own behalf. His position with regard to questions which might tend to show that he had committed other offences is

---

[1] *Brebner* v. *Perry*, [1961] S. A. S. R. 177, where various English authorities are mentioned.

[2] [1939] 2 K. B. 395; [1939] 2 All E. R. 613; *Lamb* v. *Munster* (1882), 10 Q. B. D. 110 decided that the privilege could be raised in a libel action against an individual. For the stage in the proceedings at which the objection should be taken, see *Spokes* v. *Grosvenor Hotel Co.*, [1897] 2 Q. B. 124.

[3] See *per* STEPHEN, J., in *R.* v. *Cox and Railton* (1884), 14 Q. B. D. 153, at p. 175.

[4] *R.* v. *Garbett* (1847), 1 Den. 236. Cf. *R.* v. *Noel*, [1914] 3 K. B. 848, leaving open the question whether a disclosure after an unsuccessful objection based on the privilege against self-incrimination would be made under a "compulsory process" within s. 85 of the Larceny Act, 1861.

governed by special provisions in s. 1 (f), considered in detail in Chapter XV.

Several statutes dealing with insolvency and liquidation are designed to give creditors the maximum chance of acquiring information concerning the assets out of which their debts may be paid by restricting the right of the debtor, or other person under examination, to claim privilege against self-incrimination, while protecting him against the use of his answers for the purpose of bringing criminal proceedings against him. A debtor cannot refuse to answer questions at his public examination under s. 15 of the Bankruptcy Act, 1914, on the ground that he might be incriminated by doing so,[1] but a statement or admission made by any person in any compulsory examination or deposition before any court on the hearing of any matter in bankruptcy shall not be admissible as evidence against that person in any proceedings for an offence under the Theft Act, 1968.[2]

The effect of section 31 of that Act is that the privilege against self-incrimination is abolished in the case of questions put to witnesses in proceedings for the recovery or administration of any property, for the execution of any trust or for an account of any property or dealings with property; but no statement is admissible against the witness or his spouse (unless they were married after the statement was made) in proceedings for any offence against the Act. The principle underlying this and similar statutes, of which there is a fairly large number,[3] is that the chances of persons entitled to property or payment would be greatly reduced if reliance could be placed on the privilege against self-incrimination, and it is therefore desirable to encourage full disclosure by the prohibition of the use of the statement in subsequent criminal proceedings. Whether there is a sound empirical basis for the principle is anybody's guess.

It seems that, if information has been lawfully obtained pursuant to statutory provisions and there is no express restriction on the use which can be made of the information, the person giving it cannot object to its being used in evidence against him either on the ground that such use would infringe his privilege against self-incrimination or because the information would not have been given voluntarily.[4]

SECTION 2. LEGAL PROFESSIONAL PRIVILEGE

A. STATEMENT AND RATIONALE OF THE RULE[5]

In civil and criminal cases, communications passing between a client and his legal adviser together, in some cases, with communications passing between these persons and third parties may not be given in evidence without the consent of the client if they were made either (1) to enable

---

[1] *Re Paget, Ex parte Official Receiver*, [1927] 2 Ch. 85.

[2] Bankruptcy Act, 1914, s. 166, as amended by Theft Act, 1968. The protection extends to the debtor's spouse unless the marriage took place after the statement or admission was made.

[3] For a full discussion and criticism of their construction see an article by Professor Heydon in 87 L. Q. R. 214.

[4] *R. v. Scott* (1856), Dears. & B. 47; *R. v. Coote* (1873), L. R. 4 P. C. 599; *Customs and Excise Commissioners* v. *Harz and Power*, [1967] 1 A. C. 760 (in the Court of Appeal; the appeal to the House of Lords was confined to oral statements).

[5] The rule stated below applies to communications with a foreign legal adviser and to cases in which the litigation contemplated is foreign (*Re Duncan, Garfield* v. *Fay*, [1968] P. 306; [1968] 2 All E. R. 395).

the client to obtain, or the adviser to give, legal advice; or (2) with reference to litigation that is actually taking place or was in the contemplation of the client.

It is pointed out in para. 17 of the 16th Report of the Law Reform Committee that the privilege covers three kinds of communication:

(a) "communications between the client or his agents and the client's professional legal advisers;"

(b) "communications between the client's professional legal advisers and third parties, if made for the purpose of pending or contemplated litigation;"

(c) "communications between the client or his agent and third parties, if made for the purpose of obtaining information to be submitted to the client's professional legal advisers for the purpose of obtaining advice upon pending or contemplated litigation."

In the following discussion, communications under heads (b) and (c) may be taken together, and the term "legal adviser" simply includes a solicitor and a barrister. Counsel's opinion taken by a solicitor is privileged under all three heads of the rule either because counsel counts as the client's legal adviser, or else because he is the *alter ego* of the solicitor.[1]

(1) Communications between Client and Legal Adviser

The first head of legal professional privilege was the last to gain full recognition by the courts for it was not until *Greenough* v. *Gaskell* was decided in 1833[2] that it was clear that the privilege attaches to communications between client and legal adviser, even though no litigation was contemplated by the client. In that case Lord Brougham said:[3]

> "If the privilege was confined to communications connected with suits begun, or intended or expected or apprehended, no-one could safely adopt such precautions as might eventually render any proceedings successful, or all proceedings superfluous."

This gives the clue to the rationale of the head of legal professional privilege under consideration. It is not the protection of confidentiality as such, but the additional fact that legal advice is exclusively concerned "with rights and liabilities enforceable in law, i.e. in the ultimate resort by litigation in the courts or in some administrative tribunal."[4] Litigation may not be contemplated by the client when the advice is sought and given, but the advice inevitably takes the form of "If you do so and so, it could lead to litigation with the following results."

The fact that there is no privilege protecting confidentiality as such does not mean that it is wholly disregarded by the law. There are many situations in which an injunction may be obtained against the publication of information given in confidence, and, although secondary evidence is, as we have seen, admissible of a privileged document in spite of the fact that such evidence was improperly obtained,[5] an injunction in unrestricted terms may be granted against the publication of copies of such documents. In

---

[1] *Bristol Corporation* v. *Cox* (1884), 26 Ch. D. 678.

[2] 1 My. and K. 98; some would say not until the judgment of Lord Selbourne in *Minet* v. *Morgan* (1873), 8 Ch. App. 361.

[3] At p. 103.

[4] 16th Report of the Law Reform Committee, para. 19.

[5] *Calcraft* v. *Guest*, p. 241, *ante*.

Lord Ashburton v. *Pape*,[1] Pape, a bankrupt, obtained possession of correspondence passing between Lord Ashburton and his solicitor, taking copies before returning it. In the court of first instance the injunction against publication excluded publication for the purpose of Pape's pending bankruptcy proceedings; but this restriction was removed by the Court of Appeal. The case was distinguished in *Butler* v. *The Board of Trade*[2] where a copy of the letter from the plaintiff's solicitor to the plaintiff warning him that persistence in certain conduct could lead to his prosecution was accidentally included in papers handed over to the official receiver who was inquiring into the plaintiff's conduct of the affairs of a company. The Board of Trade wished to put the copy in evidence at the prosecution of the plaintiff, and an injunction against their doing so was refused because a department of the Crown was seeking to use the copy in furtherance of a public prosecution. Although the privilege under consideration applies to communications made with the object of retaining a solicitor's services even if they are not in fact retained, the relationship of solicitor and client must at least be contemplated and the communications must be fairly referable to that relationship. "The mere fact that the person speaking is a solicitor and the person to whom he speaks is his client affords no protection."[3]

The privilege extends to communications by the client's agent to the clerk or other subordinate of the adviser and vice versa; but there is an important distinction between the head of legal professional privilege under consideration and that which will be discussed shortly arising from the fact that, when litigation is not contemplated, communications between the adviser and third parties to enable him to obtain information before giving his opinion are not always privileged. This was decided in the leading case of *Wheeler* v. *le Marchant*,[4] where the defendant was obliged to produce reports made to his solicitor by a surveyor with regard to property that became the subject of litigation, the litigation not having been contemplated when the reports were made. COTTON, L.J., observed that documents such as those with which the case was concerned had hitherto only been protected when made in contemplation of some litigation, and he did not consider that all communications between a solicitor and a third person in the course of advising his clients ought to be protected.

This head of privilege can of course be abrogated by statute, although statutes having such an effect are rare,[5] and it may also have to give way to the rule that, at a criminal trial, no-one should be able to refuse to produce documents which might establish the innocence of the accused. In *R.* v. *Barton*[6] the accused, a legal executive, was charged with the fraudulent conversion of the assets of an estate. He served a solicitor, who was in fact

---

[1] [1913] 2 Ch. 469.
[2] [1971] 1 Ch. 680; [1970] 3 All E. R. 593; see note by C. Tapper in 35 M. L. R. 83.
[3] *Minter* v. *Priest*, [1930] A. C. 558, at p. 568, *per* Lord BUCKMASTER; *Wilson* v. *Rastall* (1792), 4 Term Rep. 753; *Greenlaw* v. *King* (1838), 1 Beav. 137; *Smith* v. *Daniell* (1874), L. R. 18 Eq. 649. The mere fact that a solicitor advising trustees is himself a trustee does not exclude the privilege (*O'Rourke* v. *Darbishire*, [1920] A. C. 581). For the position where a solicitor acts for two parties see *Baugh* v. *Cradocke* (1832), 1 Mood. & R. 182; *Perry* v. *Smith* (1842), 9 M. & W. 681; *Warde* v. *Warde* (1851), 3 Mac. & G. 365; *Harris* v. *Harris*, [1931] P. 10.
[4] (1881), 17 Ch. D. 675.
[5] But see *Parry-Jones* v. *Law Society*, [1969] 1 Ch. 1; [1968] 1 All E. R. 177, where, however, the proceedings in which the privilege was inapplicable were not judicial. See also Civil Evidence Act, 1972, s. 2 (3).
[6] [1972] 2 All E. R. 1192.

a Crown witness, with a subpoena incorporating a notice to produce documents relating to the estate which he claimed would tend to establish his innocence. Although it was not clear whether the documents had been brought into existence in connection with advice tendered by the solicitor to his client or for the purpose of litigation contemplated by the client, there seems to have been no doubt that they were privileged. Nevertheless, CAULFIELD, J., ordered the solicitor to produce them and made the following observations when doing so:

> "If there are documents in the possession or control of a solicitor which, on production, help to further the defence of an accused man, then in my judgment no privilege attaches. I cannot conceive that our law would permit a solicitor or other person to screen from a jury information which, if disclosed to the jury, would perhaps enable a man either to establish his innocence or to resist an allegation made by the Crown."

We shall refer again in the next chapter to the doctrine that rules under which evidence may be inadmissible in the public interest must yield in situations in which it is reasonable to suppose that reception of the evidence might have the effects mentioned by CAULFIELD, J. The merits of the doctrine are obvious, but its precise implications and limitations, if any, have not been worked out.

(2) COMMUNICATIONS WITH THIRD PARTIES FOR THE PURPOSE OF PENDING OR CONTEMPLATED LITIGATION[1]

In order that communications between the client or his legal adviser and third parties should be privileged, there must be a definite prospect of litigation in contemplation by the client, and not a mere vague anticipation of it;[2] but it is not necessary that a cause of action should have arisen;[3] nor is it essential that the third party should anticipate litigation.[4] The communication must have been made, or the document brought into existence, for the purpose of enabling the legal adviser to advise or act with regard to the litigation. In the ordinary case this requirement gives rise to no particular difficulty. Communications with and proofs of witnesses are clearly privileged, and a mere request for information, unaccompanied by any suggestion that it was required for legal advice, is equally clearly not privileged, however probable the litigation may have been at the time the request was made.[5] There is, however, a number of difficult border line cases in which the communication was made for more than one purpose, and it is difficult to say much more with regard to the decisions in these cases than that they show that the utilisation of the communication in litigation must be one of its main purposes, even though the client may have intended to settle the claim without litigation if he could.[6]

---

[1] The privilege extends to communications passing between the members of a business organisation or government department and its salaried permanent legal advisers (*Alfred Crompton Amusement Machines, Ltd.* v. *Customs and Excise Commissioners* (No. 2), [1972] 2 Q. B. 102; [1972] 2 All E. R. 353, C. A., the point was not argued before the House of Lords), and there can be little doubt that this would be true of confidential communications in order to obtain legal advice *simpliciter*.

[2] Bray on *Discovery*, cited by Lord DENNING, M.R., in *Alfred Crompton Amusement Machines, Ltd.* v. *Customs and Excise Commissioners* (No. 2), *supra*, at p. 377.

[3] *Bristol Corporation* v. *Cox* (1884), 26 Ch. D. 678.

[4] *Di Pietrantono* v. *Austin Hospital (Heidelberg)*, [1958] V. R. 325.

[5] *Anderson* v. *Bank of British Columbia* (1876), 2 Ch. D. 644.

[6] *Ogden* v. *London Electric Rail. Co.* (1933), 149 L. T. 476.

Examples of material which has been held not to be privileged are reports to the directors of a railway company made simply for the purpose of conveying information, even if litigation is contemplated,[1] information supplied by a member of a trade union to officials of the union to enable them to decide whether to refer his claim for wrongful dismissal to the union's solicitors for legal action,[2] and the report of a private inquiry into an accident aimed primarily at preventing the recurrence of such an event.[3] Examples falling on the other side of the line are reports of an accident made to the directors of a company to be placed before the company's solicitors,[4] and correspondence by the Transport Commission with its servants concerning the cause of an accident intended to be placed before the Commission's solicitors.[5]

All the relevant decisions are probably reconcilable on their facts, but there is an undoubted cleavage in the authorities on the question of how detailed the claim to privilege should be when made, as it usually is, in an affidavit of documents.[6] The contemporary trend is strongly in favour of a detailed claim and, in cases in which there is any doubt, the exercise by the judge in interlocutory proceedings of his power to inspect documents in respect of which privilege is claimed.[7]

In *Alfred Crompton Amusement Machines, Ltd.* v. *Commissioners of Customs and Excise*[8] the company notified the Commissioners in 1967 that they were dissatisfied with the agreed formula under which they had been paying purchase tax. The prescribed procedure in the event of disagreement was that the Commissioners should state their opinion concerning the basis on which purchase tax was payable and, if this was not accepted, the taxpayer could proceed to arbitration. The Commissioners expressed their opinion in 1968 and the parties proceeded to arbitration. Both the Court of Appeal and House of Lords took the view that the Commissioners had reasonably anticipated arbitration since the receipt of the company's notification of dissatisfaction with the agreement in 1967. The Commissioners claimed legal professional privilege in respect of (1) communications with their salaried legal advisers in order to obtain advice, (2) communications with their legal advisers in order to obtain evidence for the anticipated arbitration, (3) internal communications with their officers and agents concerning the proper assessment of the purchase tax payable by the company, and (4) documents received in confidence from third parties concerning the market value of machines sold by the company. There was no argument in the House of Lords with regard to the first set of communications, so the decision of the Court of Appeal that they were privileged stands; the House held that privilege attached to the second set,

---

[1] *Woolley* v. *North London Rail. Co.* (1869), L. R. 4 C. P. 602.

[2] *Jones* v. *Great Central Rail. Co.*, [1910] A. C. 4.

[3] *Longthorn* v. *British Transport Commission*, [1959] 2 All E. R. 32; *Warner* v. *Women's Hospital*, [1954] V. L. R. 410.

[4] *Southwark Water Co.* v. *Quick* (1878), 3 Q. B. D. 315; *Ankin* v. *London and North Eastern Rail. Co.*, [1930] 1 K. B. 527.

[5] *Seabrook* v. *British Transport Commission*, [1959] 2 All E. R. 15; *Britten* v. *Pilcher & Sons*, [1969] 1 All E. R. 491.

[6] Contrast the judgments of BUCKLEY and HAMILTON, L. JJ., in *Birmingham and Midland Motor Omnibus Co., Ltd.* v. *London and North Western Rail. Co.*, [1913] 3 K. B. 851.

[7] 16th Report of the Law Reform Committee, para. 29; and see the speech of Lord KILBRANDON in *Alfred Crompton Amusement Machines, Ltd.* v. *Customs and Excise Commissioners*, [1973] 2 All E. R. 1169.

[8] *Supra.*

even if it were assumed that litigation had to be anticipated to found it; but the majority of the House held that the third and fourth sets were not subject to legal professional privilege because they came into existence for one single purpose—to assist the Commissioners to form an opinion about the basis on which purchase tax should be paid by the company, and not for the dual purpose of enabling an opinion to be formed and resisting the company's contentions in the arbitration. The House held that the third and fourth sets of communications ought not to be disclosed in the public interest, a matter which is considered in the next chapter.

The rationale of the head of legal professional privilege under consideration was succinctly stated by the Law Reform Committee to be "to facilitate the obtaining and preparation of evidence by a party to an action in support of his case."[1] The privilege is essential to the adversary system of procedure which would be unworkable if parties were obliged to disclose communications with prospective witnesses.

3. GENERAL

Legal professional privilege in both of its aspects is that of the client.[2] It enures for the benefit of his successors in title with regard, for instance, to documents handed over by him,[3] and the Court of Appeal accordingly held that the original of the proofs and notes on evidence with which the case of *Calcraft* v. *Guest*[4] were concerned were privileged from production. The fact that they had been brought into existence for the purposes of a particular action which had been concluded was treated as immaterial. LINDLEY, M.R., stated his conclusion in terms of a general rule—"once privileged, always privileged"; but it is important to remember that this simply means that, once a particular client's privilege has attached to a document, it remains for his benefit and that of his successors in title. It may well be the case that the maker of the document enjoys no privilege. In *Schneider* v. *Leigh*,[5] for instance, the plaintiff had claimed damages for personal injuries against a company, whose solicitor obtained the usual medical report—a document in relation to which the company enjoyed the ordinary litigant's privilege. The report was made by the defendant and the plaintiff contended that it libelled him. It was held that the defendant could claim no privilege with regard to his report. This case illustrates what Lord ATKIN once described as the "double nature" which problems relating to professional privilege may assume. First, there is the question whether the document or statement need be put in evidence —a general question of adjective law; and, secondly, there is the question whether the occasion on which the statement (*ex hypothesi* before the court) was published is an occasion of absolute or qualified privilege— a question with which the substantive law of defamation is concerned.[6] On facts such as those of *Schneider* v. *Leigh*, a plea of qualified privilege might ultimately succeed although the plea of professional privilege failed.

If a lawyer swears that a question cannot be answered without disclosing communications made to him professionally by his client his oath is

---

[1] 16th Report, para. 20.   [2] *Wilson* v. *Rastall* (1792), 4 Term Rep. 753.
[3] *Minet* v. *Morgan* (1873), 8 Ch. App. 361; followed in *Crescent Farm (Sidcup) Sports Ltd.* v. *Sterling Offices, Ltd. and Another*, [1972] Ch. 553; [1971] 3 All E. R. 1192.
[4] [1898] 1 Q. B. 759, *supra*.
[5] [1955] 2 Q. B. 195; [1955] 2 All E. R. 173.
[6] *Minter* v. *Priest*, [1930] A. C. 558, at p. 579.

conclusive unless it appears from the nature of the question that the privilege cannot be applicable.[1]

B. EXCEPTIONS TO THE RULE

Legal professional privilege may always be waived by the client, although a waiver with regard to conversations does not entail a waiver with regard to documents such as proofs and briefs brought into existence for the purpose of the litigation in which the privilege is claimed;[2] nor is a waiver of the privilege attaching to medical reports to be inferred from the acceptance of the opposite party's unconditional production of his medical report.[3] In addition to the possibility of waiver there are two exceptions to the rule which must be considered in turn[4]—communications made in order to facilitate the perpetration of a crime or fraud, and facts discovered in the course of the relationship.

(1) COMMUNICATIONS TO FACILITATE CRIME OR FRAUD

In the leading case of *R.* v. *Cox and Railton*,[5] the Court for Crown Cases Reserved decided that, if a client applies to a lawyer for advice intended to guide him in the commission of a crime or fraud, the legal adviser being ignorant of the purpose for which his advice is wanted, the communication between the two is not privileged. Accordingly a solicitor was compelled to disclose what passed between the prisoners and himself when they consulted him with reference to drawing up a bill of sale that was alleged to be fraudulent. As STEPHEN, J., pointed out when delivering the judgment of the Court, if the law were otherwise, a man intending to commit treason or murder might safely take legal advice for the purpose of enabling himself to do so with impunity, and the solicitor to whom the application was made would not be at liberty to give information against his client in order to frustrate his criminal purpose.[6] If the lawyer participates in the criminal purpose he ceases to act as a lawyer. STEPHEN, J. concluded that the Court must judge whether the evidence is admissible on the special facts of each particular case, and every precaution should be taken against compelling unnecessary disclosures. The doctrine of *R.* v. *Cox and Railton* has been applied to a civil case[7] in which fraud was alleged and it has since been stressed that there should be *prima facie* evidence that it was the client's intention to obtain advice in furtherance of his criminal or fraudulent purpose before the court will consider whether the situation comes within the exception to the rule relating to professional privilege.[8] "Fraud" in this context does not extend to every act or scheme which is unlawful such, for example, as an inducement of breach of contract;[9] and a letter from a solicitor to his client advising him that certain conduct could lead to his being prosecuted is outside the principle of *R.* v. *Cox and Railton*.[10]

---

[1] *Morgan* v. *Shaw* (1819), 4 Madd. 54.

[2] *George Doland, Ltd.* v. *Blackburn, Robson, Coates & Co.*,[1972] 3 All E. R. 959.

[3] *Causton* v. *Mann Egerton (Johnsons), Ltd.*, [1974] 1 All E. R. 453. Cf. Civil Evidence Act, 1972, s. 2 (3).

[4] For a possible statutory exception see s. 16 (7) of the Finance Act, 1962, discussed in an article by J. A. Speed 28 M. L. R. 18 at p. 25.

[5] (1884), 14 Q. B. D. 153.   [6] Cf. *R.* v. *Smith* (1915), 11 Cr. App. Rep. 229.

[7] *Williams* v. *Quebrada Railway, Land and Copper Co.*, [1895] 2 Ch. 751.

[8] *O'Rourke* v. *Darbishire*, [1920] A. C. 581; *Bullivant* v. *A.-G. for Victoria*, [1901] A. C. 196.

[9] *Crescent Farm (Sidcup) Sports, Ltd.* v. *Sterling Offices, Ltd.*, [1972] Ch. 553; [1971] 3 All E. R. 1192.

[10] *Butler* v. *Board of Trade*, [1971] 1 Ch. 680; [1970] 3 All E. R. 593.

(2) FACTS DISCOVERED IN THE COURSE OF THE RELATIONSHIP

The privilege only applies to communications; a solicitor can be obliged to disclose the identity of his client [1] and the privilege does not prevent the disclosure of facts observed by either party in the course of their relationship as client and legal adviser. In *Brown* v. *Foster*,[2] for instance, it was held that a barrister who saw a book produced at the trial of his client could testify, without the client's consent, in subsequent proceedings on the question whether it contained a particular entry when he previously saw it at the preliminary examination. Similarly, in *Dwyer* v. *Collins*,[3] it was held that the plaintiff's attorney must say whether he had a particular document in court with him although he could not be obliged to produce it. We shall see in Chapter XII, when dealing with illegally obtained evidence, that the distinction between communications and other facts is not always easy to draw but it does not appear to have given much trouble in the context which is under consideration. Some may think that *Conlon* v. *Conlons, Ltd.*,[4] comes near to the border-line, although it is not suggested that the case was wrongly decided. The defence to a claim for damages for personal injury alleged that the plaintiff had agreed to accept a sum in full settlement. In his reply, the plaintiff denied that his solicitor had been authorised to settle the claim and it was held that he could be obliged to answer an interrogatory as to whether he had authorised his solicitor to negotiate a settlement. If settlements made before the issue of a writ are to be binding, the client's instructions to his solicitor in this regard ought to be held to be outside the rule relating to legal professional privilege, for a solicitor has no implied authority to conclude negotiations at that stage, although he may bind his client by doing so later.

C. THE CLAIMS OF OTHER RELATIONSHIPS

Let it be granted that the rationale of legal professional privilege is a sound one, the question naturally arises as to whether a similar privilege ought not to be accorded to other relationships. It is hardly surprising that privilege should, at different times, have been claimed for confidential communications between friends,[5] the source of a journalist's information,[6] documents in the possession of an accountant relating to his client's affairs,[7] disclosures made to priests and doctors and even for information supplied to a pursuivant of the Royal College of Heralds.[8] All these claims have been unsuccessful, although a child care officer's notes made under

---

[1] *Bursill* v. *Tarner* (1885), 16 Q. B. D. 1.
[2] (1857), 1 H. & N. 736; *Re Cathcart, Ex Parte Campbell* (1870), 5 Ch. App. 703.
[3] (1852), 7 Exch. 639.   [4] [1952] 2 All E. R. 462.
[5] *Duchess of Kingston's Case* (1776), 20 State Trials 355.
[6] *A.-G.* v. *Clough*, [1963] 1 All E. R. 420; *A.-G.* v. *Mulholland*, [1963] 2 Q. B. 477; [1963] 1 All E. R. 767; *McGuiness* v. *A.-G. of Victoria* (1940), 63 C. L. R. 73; *Re Buchanan*, [1965] S. R. (N.S.W.) 9.   There is a prohibition on interrogatories concerning the source of the defendant's information where qualified privilege or fair comment is pleaded in actions for defamation (R.S.C. Order 82, r. 6).
[7] *Chantrey Martin & Co.* v. *Martin*, [1953] 2 Q. B. 286; [1953] 2 All E. R. 691. It would be different if the documents were the property of the client.
[8] *Slade* v. *Tucker* (1880), 14 Ch. D. 824. See also *Jones* v. *Great Central Rail. Co.*, [1910] A. C. 4 (trade union official). So far as bankers are concerned, their contractual duty is not to disclose the state of their customer's account without his consent except under order of the court or pursuant to a public duty (*Tournier* v. *National Provincial and Union Bank of England*, [1924] 1 K. B. 461). See also *R.* v. *Daye*, [1908] 2 K. B. 333.

the Boarding Out of Children Regulations, 1955, have been held to be privileged in wardship proceedings.[1]

It is only necessary to add a few remarks on the subject of the relationship between priest and penitent, and physician and patient. There are, however, two points that should be stressed before this is done. In the first place, the court has a discretion to disallow questions unless they are relevant and necessary, or such as to serve a useful purpose in relation to the proceedings in hand;[2] secondly it is a mistake to suppose that the choice lies between a privilege of complete secrecy on the one hand, and on the other hand, compulsory disclosure without restriction. It is possible, and sometimes desirable, that the claimant to the privilege should decline to produce documents or give evidence until he is ordered to do so by the court. Such a course is contemplated by statute and approved by the cases. Thus, s. 7 of the Bankers' Books Evidence Act, 1879, assumes that an application will be made to the court for an order for inspection of a banker's books, and in *R. v. St. Lawrence's Hospital*,[3] Lord GODDARD, C.J., approved the refusal of medical officers to disclose their communications with the Visitors to a hospital under the Mental Deficiency Acts without the order of the Court and, when such an order is made, it can be on such terms as, for example, that no use will be made of the information disclosed outside the particular proceedings before the court.[4] Non-compliance with the order would constitute a contempt of court, but it must be admitted that there are circumstances in which disclosure, even on the most stringent terms as to dissemination of the information, is abhorrent to the witness. He may not consider himself to be adequately protected by the discretion of the court simply because there are cases in which the question is both relevant and from the point of view of the party putting it, necessary.

(1) PRIEST AND PENITENT

The most obvious case for the creation of a new privilege is that of the Roman Catholic priest called upon to testify with regard to that which took place in the confessional. There is very little judicial authority on the subject, but such as there is is, like the opinion of all the text-writers, against the existence of any privilege according to English law. The only legal arguments that could be advanced in support of the priest's refusal to testify concerning statements in the confessional would be first, that the privilege must have existed at the time of the Reformation, and it has not been displaced by any statute or authoritative decision since that date; secondly, that disclosure would incriminate the priest by the canon law; thirdly that the privilege is implicitly recognised by the decision in *R. v. Hay*.[5] Sir JAMES STEPHEN appears to have answered the first point conclusively when he said:

> "I think the modern law of evidence is not so old as the Reformation, but has grown up by the practice of the Courts, and by decisions in the course of the last two centuries. It came into existence at a time when exceptions in favour

---

[1] *Re D. (Infants)*, [1970] 1 All E. R. 1088.
[2] *A.-G. v. Mulholland*, [1963] 2 Q. B. 477; at p. 489 and p. 492 per Lord DENNING, M. R., and DONOVAN, L. J. respectively.
[3] *R. v. St. Lawrence's Hospital Caterham Statutory Visitors, Ex parte Pritchard*, [1953] 2 All E. R. 766, at p. 772.
[4] See the order in *Chantrey Martin & Co. v. Martin (supra)*.
[5] (1860), 2 F. & F. 4.

of auricular confessions to Roman Catholic priests were not likely to be made. The general rule is that every person must testify to what he knows. An exception to the general rule has been established in regard to legal advisers, but there is nothing to show that it extends to clergymen, and it is usually so stated as not to include them." [1]

So far as the argument based on the possibility of self-incrimination is concerned, we have seen that it is doubtful whether at common law the privilege protects answers that would criminate the witness by any foreign system of law,[2] and it is still more doubtful whether it would be held to extend to answers prohibited by the canon law.

In *R. v. Hay*,[3] the prisoner was charged with larceny of a watch. A Roman Catholic priest had handed the watch to the police, and the priest was asked in Court from whom he had received the watch. He was compelled to answer this question. The judgment stressed the point that he was being asked about a fact as distinct from a communication,[4] and it is perhaps just arguable that the case impliedly recognises a privilege in the case of communications; but it can hardly displace the bulk of authority which, though inconclusive, is undoubtedly against the existence of the privilege.

Rule 219 of the American Law Institute's model code of evidence accords privilege to a "penitential communication", which is defined as:

"a confession of culpable conduct made secretly and in confidence by a penitent to a priest in the course of the discipline or practice of the church or religious denomination or organisation of which the witness is a member".

Were the problem to arise in an acute form in practice, most judges would probably sympathise with BEST, C.J., when he said "I, for one, will never compel a clergyman to disclose communications made to him by a prisoner; but if he chooses to disclose them I shall receive them in evidence".[5]

A privilege is conferred on penitential communications by statute in various parts of the Commonwealth, as well as by the American Model Code, Uniform and Federal Rules but, both the Law Reform Committee and the Criminal Law Revision Committee were opposed to any change in the English law.[6]

There may be circumstances in which a clergyman can invoke some recognised privilege or exemption, as when he assists in without-prejudice negotiations between estranged spouses—a matter that is discussed in s. 4, or when he is a prison chaplain and the Home Secretary prohibits him from testifying with regard to statements made to him by prisoners— a head of public policy that has, as yet, not been considered by the courts; but the mere fact that a clergyman is a marriage guidance counsellor and

---

[1] *Digest of the Law of Evidence* (12th edition), 220, where all the authorities are collected apart from the dictum in *Wheeler v. Le Marchant* (1881), 17 Ch. D. 675, at p. 681, which is also against the existence of the privilege.

[2] The matter is discussed by Nokes, *Professional Privilege*, 66 L. Q. R. 88 (1950).

[3] (1860), 2 F. & F. 4. The privilege is recognised in Eire as that of the priest (*Cook v. Carroll*, [1945] I. R. 515; see the discussion in 12 *Northern Ireland Legal Quarterly* 160 (1959)).

[4] Cf. *Brown v. Foster*, p. 255, *ante.*

[5] *Broad v. Pitt* (1828), 3 C. & P. 518 (*obiter*). A clergyman was obliged to disclose an admission of adultery made in conversation by a friend in *Normanshaw v. Normanshaw and Measham* (1893), 69 L. T. 468.

[6] 16th Report of the Law Reform Committee, paras. 46–7; 11th Report of the Criminal Law Revision Committee, paras. 272–5.

can only give evidence derived from meetings between the litigating spouses does not confer any privilege on him as distinct from the privilege enjoyed by the parties to without-prejudice negotiations.[1]

(2) PHYSICIAN AND PATIENT

There is more judicial authority on the subject of communications between doctors and their patients than there is on statements made to clergymen. It is uniformly against the existence of any privilege,[2] although BULLER, J., once said it was much to be regretted that legal professional privilege had not been extended to medical persons.[3] The problem is much more likely to arise in practice than that which relates to statements made to clergymen, for these are only likely to be relevant to litigation when they constitute admissions, and in many cases, no one will know whether they were made, whereas questions concerning medical treatment are both more likely to arise in a law suit, and more likely to be the subject of such knowledge as could warrant the calling of a doctor as a witness. Candour is certainly necessary for the proper exercise of the medical profession and the community's health is at least as important as the due administration of justice in an individual case, if not more so. Accordingly, if there is evidence that medical treatment is in any way hampered by the absence of some kind of medical professional privilege, there is every reason why it should be recognised. Rule 221 of the American Law Institute's code of evidence accords the privilege in civil actions and prosecutions for misdemeanour in the case of confidential communications reasonably necessary for the treatment in hand; rule 27 of the Uniform Rules is to the same effect; but rule 504 of the Federal Rules confines the privilege to communications with psychiatrists. This matter is also dealt with by statute in various parts of the Commonwealth, but both the Law Reform Committee and the Criminal Law Revision Committee were against any change in the English law.[4]

A doctor, like a clergyman, may be able to rely on some other head of privilege or exemption, such as that which relates to negotiations between estranged spouses and public policy which may, for instance, protect from disclosure communications with the Minister in connection with the National Health Service.[5]

SECTION 3. PRIVILEGES NOW SOLELY APPLICABLE TO CRIMINAL PROCEEDINGS
A. COMMUNICATIONS BETWEEN SPOUSES

Section 1 (d) of the Criminal Evidence Act, 1898, provides that

> "No husband shall be compellable to disclose any communication made to him by his wife during the marriage, and no wife shall be compellable to disclose any communication made to her by her husband during the marriage."

---

[1] *Pais v. Pais*, [1971] P. 119; [1970] 3 All E. R. 491.
[2] *Duchess of Kingston's Case* (1776), 20 State Trials 355; *R. v. Gibbons* (1823), 1 C. & P. 97; *Wheeler v. Le Marchant* (1881), 17 Ch. D. 675, at p. 681; *Garner v. Garner* (1920), 36 T. L. R. 196; *Hunter v. Mann*, [1974] 2 All E. R. 414.
[3] *Wilson v. Rastall* (1792), 4 Term Rep. 753, at p. 760.
[4] 16th Report of the Law Reform Committee, paras. 48–52; 11th Report of the Criminal Law Revision Committee, para. 276.
[5] 66 L. Q. R. 92.

From time to time it was suggested that there was a common law privilege attaching to marital communications which had only been partially superseded by statute, but the House of Lords decided that the privilege is entirely the creature of statute. In *Rumping* v. *Director of Public Prosecutions*,[1] a letter from the accused to his wife came into the possession of the police. It amounted to a confession of guilt of the murder with which he was charged, and it was held that the prosecution might rely on the letter.

The statutory wording only applies to communications made to the spouse by whom the privilege is claimed, and it can hardly be doubted that the Scots case of *Her Majesty's Advocate* v. *H. D.*[2] would have been decided in the same way by the English courts. The accused was charged with incest with his daughter, and his wife elected to give evidence for the prosecution. In spite of her husband's objection, it was held that she could disclose the contents of a relevant statement made by him to her because the statutory privilege was hers and she could waive it if she were minded to do so.

The wording of section 3 of the Evidence (Amendment) Act, 1853, repealed (except in relation to criminal proceedings) by section 16 (3) of the Civil Evidence Act, 1968, was identical with that of section 1 (d) of the Criminal Evidence Act, 1898, and it was restrictively interpreted in *Shenton* v. *Tyler*.[3] In that case it was held that the privilege only endures so long as the recipient of the communication is the husband or wife of the person making it. The result was that a widow was obliged to answer interrogatories concerning communications made to her by her late husband with regard to a secret trust alleged by the plaintiff; but the decision would have been the same if the defendant had been a divorced woman instead of a widow. If the decision applies to section 1 (d) of the Act of 1898, the words "husband" and "wife", when used in other parts of section 1 must be differently construed so as to include a divorced spouse testifying to matters occurring during the marriage so as to accommodate the decision in *R.* v. *Algar*[4] that *Monroe* v. *Twistleton*[5] still applies in criminal cases. It is not a particularly unusual thing for the same word to be construed in different senses in the course of the same statute, but this part of the decision in *Shenton* v. *Tyler* was neither approved nor disapproved by the House of Lords in *Rumping's Case*.

The Law Reform Committee considered that, if any privilege were to be retained in civil proceedings for marital communications, it should be that of the communicator, but they added "It is unrealistic to suppose that candour of communication between husband and wife is influenced to-day by section 3 of the Evidence (Amendment) Act, 1853, which, as we have pointed out, does not insure that marital confidences will be respected, or would be enhanced to-morrow by an amendment of the law on the lines indicated above (that the privilege should be that of the communicator)".[6] The Criminal Law Revision Committee agreed, and recommended the repeal of section 1 (d) of the Criminal Evidence Act, 1898.[7]

---

[1] [1964] A. C. 814; [1962] 3 All E. R. 256; affirming *Shenton* v. *Tyler*, [1939] Ch. 620; [1939] 1 All E. R. 827; on the point as to the non-existence of the common law privilege.
[2] 1953 S. C. (J.) 65.
[3] [1939] Ch. 620; [1939] 1 All E. R. 827.
[4] [1954] 1 Q. B. 279; [1953] 2 All E. R. 1381. See p. 159, *ante.*
[5] (1802), Peak Add. Cas. 219.
[6] 16th Report, para. 43.
[7] 11th Report, para. 173.

B. QUESTIONS CONCERNING MARITAL INTERCOURSE

Section 48 (1) of the Matrimonial Causes Act, 1973, provides that "The evidence of a husband or wife shall be admissible in any proceedings to prove that marital intercourse did or did not take place between them during any period." The provision originated in the Law Reform (Miscellaneous Provisions) Act, 1949, which abolished the rule in *Russell* v. *Russell*[1] under which spouses could not give evidence of non-access tending to bastardise a child born in wedlock. The 1949 Act created an entirely new privilege which was defined in the following words additional to those quoted from the Matrimonial Causes Act, 1973; "but a husband or wife shall not be compellable in any proceedings to give evidence of the matters aforesaid". The only justification for such a privilege is the not very convincing one of decency, and the words enacting it were repealed by section 16 (4) of the Civil Evidence Act, 1968, except in relation to criminal proceedings. The exception is preserved by the Act of 1973, although the Criminal Law Revision Committee recommended its abolition.[2] Perhaps there is room for an argument that, in spite of the reference to "any proceedings", criminal proceedings were not contemplated in an Act concerned with civil cases and now confined to matrimonial causes.

C. TITLE DEEDS

There was an old-established rule of evidence that a witness who was not a party could not be compelled to produce his title deeds or other documents relating to his title to any property.[3] POLLOCK, C.B., attributed the rule to the dogma that makes every man's house his castle and attaches such importance to property in land.[4] It appears that the theory was that someone who was rendered aware of a defect in the witness's title might bring proceedings from which the witness would otherwise be immune. The privilege was abolished for civil cases by section 16 (1) (b) of the Civil Evidence Act, 1968, and its abolition in criminal cases was recommended by the Criminal Law Revision Committee.[5]

SECTION 4. PRIVILEGES SOLELY APPLICABLE TO CIVIL PROCEEDINGS

A. COMMUNICATIONS WITH PATENT AGENTS

Under the Patents Act, 1949, proceedings of a contentious nature may take place before the Comptroller of Patents with a right of appeal to the Patents Appeal Tribunal. Patent agents frequently conduct such proceedings and they are then in the same position as a solicitor appearing for his client in the County Court. The Law Reform Committee therefore recommended that communications made for the purpose of pending or contemplated proceedings in the Patent Office or the Patents Appeal Tribunal should be entitled to privilege if made between the client, or his agents, and his patent agent, or between his patent agent and third parties, or between the client, or his agents, and third parties, for the purpose of

---

[1] [1924] A. C. 687.
[2] 11th Report, para. 173.
[3] *Pickering* v. *Noyes* (1823), 1 B. & C. 262.
[4] *Adams* v. *Lloyd* (1858), 3 H. & N. 351, at p. 363.
[5] 11th Report, para. 173.

obtaining information to be put before the client's patent agent.[1] Effect was given to this recommendation by section 15 of the Civil Evidence Act, 1968, which is expressly confined to communications made for the purpose of any pending or contemplated proceedings under the Patents Act, 1949, before the Comptroller or the Patents Appeal Tribunal.

B. STATEMENTS MADE WITHOUT PREJUDICE

As part of an attempt to settle a dispute, the parties frequently make statements "without prejudice". When this is done, the contents of the statement cannot be put in evidence without the consent of both parties, the case being one of joint privilege. The statements often relate to the offer of a compromise, and, were it not for the privilege, they would constitute significant items of evidence on the ground that they were admissions. Obviously it is in the public interest that disputes should be settled and litigation reduced to a minimum, so the policy of the law is in favour of enlarging the cloak under which negotiations may be conducted without prejudice. This policy is carried out by means of a rigorous insistence on the absence of any magic in the form of words used by the parties, everything being made to depend upon their intention, but there are a few points of detail that emerge from the cases. After they have been mentioned, something must be said about without-prejudice negotiations between estranged spouses—a matter which has come to the fore of recent years, the relation of the privilege to public policy and its limits.

(1) MISCELLANEOUS POINTS OF DETAIL

It was soon settled that a letter was privileged when, although it was not headed "without prejudice", it was stated to be without prejudice to the writer's rights.[2] The fact that the first of a series of letters is headed "without prejudice" may mean that the privilege attaches to the rest of the series.[3] If, at an interview held without prejudice between the parties' solicitors, it is agreed that further information shall be obtained from a third person, the privilege may attach to his report.[4] The fact that the second of a series of payments was received without prejudice to the claimant's rights may support an inference that the first payment was received under a similar agreement.[5] The courts have further encouraged without-prejudice negotiations by refusing to take them into account when considering questions of costs,[6] and the solicitors for the parties may claim privilege for the statements made in letters written on their clients' behalf in proceedings in which they are sued personally;[7] but the statement in respect of which privilege is claimed must have some bearing on negotiations for a settlement.[8]

---

[1] 16th Report, para. 26.
[2] *Cory* v. *Bretton* (1830), 4 C. & P. 462.
[3] *Paddock* v. *Forrester* (1842), 3 Man. & G. 903.
[4] *Rabin* v. *Mendoza & Co.*, [1954] 1 All E. R. 247.
[5] *Oliver* v. *Nautilus Steam Shipping Co.*, [1903] 2 K. B. 639.
[6] *Walker* v. *Wilsher* (1889), 23 Q. B. D. 335, applied to arbitrations in *Stotesbury* v. *Turner*, [1943] K. B. 370.
[7] *La Roche* v. *Armstrong*, [1922] 1 K. B. 485.
[8] *Field* v. *Commissioners of Railways for New South Wales* (1957), 99 C. L. R. 285, where the authorities are reviewed.

(2) WITHOUT-PREJUDICE NEGOTIATIONS BETWEEN ESTRANGED SPOUSES

If a solicitor is consulted by both husband and wife, professional privilege may attach to statements made to him by either of them so that he may not disclose them in subsequent matrimonial proceedings without the consent of the makers.[1] The ordinary law concerning without-prejudice statements applies to negotiations between the parties personally, or between their solicitors, which take place with a view to compromising a matrimonial cause; but some recent cases have been concerned with statements made to a mediator and the question arises as to whether he can decline to give evidence concerning them without the consent of the parties. The answer is in the affirmative, and although this would probably be the case with all negotiations carried on through a mediator, the promotion of marital harmony is an additional reason in favour of the promotion of the fullest possible privilege when the dispute is between husband and wife. A reconciliation between estranged spouses is not the same thing as the compromise of a disputed claim.

In *McTaggart* v. *McTaggart*,[2] a probation officer was obliged to give evidence concerning that which had passed at an interview between the parties at which he had been present. The spouses each gave evidence about this interview, and the Court of Appeal accordingly held that such privilege as attached to their statements to the probation officer had been waived, but the Court had no doubt that the statements were privileged although the privilege was that of the parties. In *Mole* v. *Mole*[3] it was decided that the privilege existed when only one of the parties had enlisted the services of a probation officer, so that he could not give evidence about a letter written to him by the other party without that person's consent. It was emphasised that a similar privilege would apply when one or other of the parties approached a doctor, clergyman or marriage guidance counsellor with regard to his or her matrimonial differences, and there was said to be a tacit understanding that negotiations were to be without prejudice in such cases. In *Henley* v. *Henley*[4] the initiative in endeavouring to effect a reconciliation was taken by a clergyman, a friend of the parties, and it was held that the privilege attached to statements made to him.

In *Bostock* v. *Bostock*[5] it was held that a solicitor could be obliged to give evidence about an interview which took place between the parties to divorce proceedings at his office, although one of the parties objected to his doing so. The ground of the decision was that the interview was not expressly stated to be without prejudice, but, even if this is good law so far as without-prejudice negotiations with regard to an ordinary dispute are concerned, it is most unlikely that the case will be followed in the divorce court.[6]

In *Theodoropoulas* v. *Theodoropoulas*,[7] it was held that, where spouses were endeavouring to effect a reconciliation in the presence of a third person,

---

[1] *Harris* v. *Harris*, [1931] P. 10.
[2] [1949] P. 94; [1948] 2 All E. R. 754.
[3] [1951] P. 21; [1950] 2 All E. R. 328; see also *Pais* v. *Pais*, [1971] P. 119; [1970] 3 All E. R. 491.
[4] [1955] P. 202; [1955] 1 All E. R. 590. [5] [1950] P. 154; [1950] 1 All E. R. 25.
[6] *Pool* v. *Pool*, [1951] P. 470; [1951] 2 All E. R. 563, is against *Bostock* v. *Bostock* and the latter case was doubted by the Court of Appeal in *Mole* v. *Mole*.
[7] [1964] P. 311; [1963] 2 All E. R. 772.

neither one of the parties, nor the third person, could give evidence of the terms of the conversation without the consent of the other party.[1]

(3) WITHOUT–PREJUDICE NEGOTIATIONS AND PUBLIC POLICY

Third parties may normally prove privileged communications, although secondary evidence of matters excluded by public policy is inadmissible. The last mentioned case therefore suggests that without-prejudice negotiations could equally well be treated under the head of public policy. This is especially true of the decisions concerning negotiations between estranged spouses where the element of public policy is most pronounced. Nonetheless, privilege, unlike public policy may always be waived, and it may well be the case that without-prejudice communications can be proved in proceedings between third parties. So far as the reconciliation cases are concerned, it is often suggested that the privilege should be that of the mediator, at any rate when he is a marriage guidance officer. Should this ever come to be law, there would be even more to be said for dealing with the matter under the head of public policy.[2]

No privilege attaches in affiliation proceedings to a statement made by the respondent to a case worker acting for an adoption society.[3] It has been held in Alberta that no privilege attaches to a statement made by the respondent in affiliation proceedings to a welfare officer who was making inquiries on behalf of the applicant. The matrimonial cases were distinguished on the score of public policy, the welfare officer not being a conciliator.[4]

In *Broome* v. *Broome*,[5] however, where the mediator was a representative of the Soldiers', Sailors' and Airmen's Families Association, the Secretary of State for War contemplated a claim to the effect that evidence of the negotiations could not be given on the score of public policy. Although he clearly had the doctrine of *McTaggart* v. *McTaggart* and *Mole* v. *Mole* in mind, his claim was one of a far more extensive nature and reference will be made to it in the next chapter.

(4) LIMITS OF THE PRIVILEGE

Once negotiations have been completed as the result of without-prejudice interviews or letters, a binding contract has been brought into existence and this may be proved by means of the without-prejudice statements.[6] The fact that without-prejudice letters were written and the dates borne by them, may sometimes be taken into account by the court, as where there is an allegation of laches,[7] but this does not involve a reference to the

---

[1] It is sometimes said that this decision may impede the establishment of a case of desertion on the grounds of the refusal of an offer to return, but the offer could be repeated more formally and without the without-prejudice cloak.

[2] The Law Reform Committee was against the creation of a statutory privilege for court welfare officers, and marriage guidance counsellors (16th Report, paras. 39–40).

[3] *R.* v. *Nottingham Justices, ex parte Bostock*, [1970] 2 All E. R. 641.

[4] *Re Child Welfare Act, Brysh* v. *Davidson* (1963), 42 D. L. R. (2d) 673. See also *Constable* v. *Constable*, [1964] S. A. S. R. 68 (husband's admission of adultery to children's welfare officer not privileged because officer was not conciliator).

[5] [1955] P. 190; [1955] 1 All E. R. 201.

[6] *Tomlin* v. *Standard Telephones & Cables, Ltd.*, [1969] 3 All E. R. 201.

[7] *Per* LINDLEY, L.J., in *Walker* v. *Wilsher* (1889), 23 Q. B. D. 335, at p. 338.

contents of the letters. Privilege does not extend to statements of fact made in the course of without-prejudice negotiations if such statements have no reference to the dispute between the parties, as where one of them casually admits that a document is in his handwriting.[1] It has likewise been held that a statement in a letter headed "without prejudice" to the effect that the writer was unable to pay his debts as they fell due could be proved as an act of bankruptcy in bankruptcy proceedings,[2] and a letter containing a threat contrary to the patent legislation was said to be nonetheless an infringement of that legislation because it was headed "without prejudice".[3] These words prevent the utilisation of the documents on which they appear for the purpose of drawing inferences from the fact that a compromise was contemplated, they do not have the effect of preventing acts of bankruptcy nor can they alter the nature of an illegal threat.

---

[1] *Waldridge* v. *Kennison* (1794), 1 Esp. 143.
[2] *Re Daintrey, Ex parte Holt*, [1893] 2 Q. B. 116.
[3] *Kurtz & Co.* v. *Spence & Sons* (1887), 58 L. T. 438. A libel is nonetheless a libel because it is contained in a letter headed "without prejudice".

CHAPTER XII

PUBLIC POLICY

Relevant evidence must be excluded on the ground of public policy when it concerns certain matters of state interest and when it relates to miscellaneous matters connected with previous litigation. These subjects are discussed in the first two sections of this chapter. Evidence that has been illegally obtained—a matter considered in section 3—is not generally discussed under the head of public policy. The English authorities are mainly concerned with facts discovered in consequence of inadmissible confessions, and we shall see that one of the reasons for excluding evidence of this nature is the risk that improper police methods might be encouraged if it were to be admitted too readily. There is nothing in the nature of a fully developed exclusionary rule under this head, but, if one is ever evolved, it might well be based on the public policy of discouraging a resort to illegality in order to obtain relevant evidence.

This head of exclusion of relevant evidence differs from privilege in two respects; first, privilege can be waived, whereas, with the exception of some of the matters discussed in section 2, an objection on the score of public policy must be taken by the judge if it is not raised by the parties of the Crown;[1] secondly, because, though secondary evidence may be given of privileged statements and documents, this is not so when the primary evidence is excluded by public policy.[2]

Far and away the most important aspect of the latter is that which is discussed in section 1, and, before referring to matters of detail, it would be well to emphasise the devastating effect which the exclusion of evidence at the instance of the head of a government department can have on the substantive rights of litigants. It may render it totally impossible for them to rely on matters which would otherwise have constituted an unanswerable cause of action or a complete defence. An example is provided by *Hennessy* v. *Wright*.[3] That was a libel action brought against the proprietor of a

---

[1] "The withholding of documents on the ground that their publication would be contrary to the public interest is not properly to be regarded as a branch of the law of privilege connected with discovery. 'Crown privilege' is for this reason not a happy expression. Privilege, in relation to discovery, is for the protection of the litigant and could be waived by him, but the rule that the interest of the state must not be put in jeopardy by producing documents which would injure it is a principle to be observed in administering justice, quite unconnected with the interests or claims of the particular parties in litigation, and, indeed, is a rule on which the judge should, if necessary, insist even though no objection is taken at all" (*per* Lord SIMON in *Duncan* v. *Cammell Laird & Co., Ltd.*, [1942] A. C. 624, at pp. 641–2; see also *Rogers* v. *Secretary of State for the Home Department*, [1973] A. C. 388; [1972] 2 All E. R. 1057; and *Anderson* v. *Hamilton* (1816), 2 Brod. & Bing. 156n.).

[2] *Cooke* v. *Maxwell* (1817), 2 Stark. 183, *per* BAYLEY, J. "If the document cannot, on principles of public policy be read in evidence, the effect will be the same as if it was not in evidence, and you may prove not the contents of the instrument." "In my opinion, if it is contrary to public interest to produce the original documents, it must equally be contrary to public interest to produce copies which the maker of the document has kept for his own information" (LYNSKEY, J., in *Moss* v. *Chesham U.D.C.*, unreported (January 17, 1945), cited in (1955) C. L. J. 62. His Lordship's ruling applied to all forms of secondary evidence of the document).

[3] (1888), 21 Q. B. D. 509.

newspaper in respect of a statement imputing that the plaintiff, the governor of a colony, had sent home garbled reports to the Colonial Secretary, and the defendant was, in effect, prevented from setting up the defence of justification. The Colonial Secretary would not produce the originals of the reports, the court would not order discovery of copies that were in the possession of the plaintiff, and, even if witnesses who could depose to the contents of the reports had been available, their evidence would have been inadmissible. The words used by FIELD, J., when dismissing the application for discovery are memorable.

> "First, the publication of a state document may involve danger to the nation. If the confidential communications made by servants of the Crown to each other, by superiors to inferiors, or by inferiors to superiors, in the discharge of their duty to the Crown were liable to be made public in a court of justice at the instance of any suitor who thought proper to say '*fiat justitia ruat caelum*', an order for discovery might involve the country in war. Secondly, the publication of a state document may be injurious to servants of the Crown as individuals. There would be an end of all freedom in their official communications, if they knew that any suitor could legally insist that any official communication, of no matter how secret a character, should be produced openly in a court of justice."

SECTION 1. MATTERS OF STATE INTEREST [1]

The objection that a particular item of evidence must be excluded because its reception would be contrary to state interest may be taken by the party against whom the evidence is tendered or the judge, but it is usually taken by, or at the instance of, the head of a government department. The matters that call for consideration are the scope of the rule, the method by which the validity of the objection to the adduction of the evidence is to be determined and the principles which should govern such determination.

A. STATEMENT AND SCOPE OF THE RULE

The rule can be simply stated as follows—relevant evidence must be excluded if its reception would be contrary to state interest; but "state interest" is an ominously vague expression and it is necessary to turn to the decided cases in order to ascertain the extent to which this objection to the reception of relevant evidence has been taken. Broadly speaking, the decisions fall under two heads—those in which evidence has been excluded because its disclosure would be injurious to national security (an expression which may be taken to include national defence and good diplomatic relations), and those in which evidence has been excluded because its reception would be injurious to some other national interest.[2] The first group of decisions has not excited much comment, but some of the cases included in the second may be thought to indicate an excessive concern for unnecessary secrecy. Police matters are dealt with separately for the sake of convenience. It may well be the case that the exclusionary

---

[1] See articles by Professor Street, *State Secrets—A Comparative Study*, 14 M. L. R. 121 (1951), and Sir Jocelyn SIMON (now Lord SIMON OF GLAISDALE), *Evidence Excluded by Considerations of State Interest*, C. L. J. (1955), 62.

[2] Decisions such as *Plunkett* v. *Cobbett* (1804), 5 Esp. 136, under which statements of that which was said, as distinct from the name of the speaker, in Parliament are inadmissible, have been left out of the ensuing discussions because they belong to constitutional law.

rule does not apply in criminal proceeedings but it will also be convenient to deal separately with these.

(1) NATIONAL SECURITY

In *Asiatic Petroleum Co., Ltd.* v. *Anglo-Persian Oil Co., Ltd.*,[1] the defendants, acting under the direction of the Board of Admiralty, refused to produce a letter to their agent on the ground that it contained information concerning the government's plans with regard to one of the Middle Eastern campaigns of the First World War. The information had of course been given to the defendants by the Board of Admiralty under the seal of the strictest secrecy, but, as SWINFEN-EADY, L.J., observed:[2]

> "The foundation of the rule is that the information cannot be disclosed without injury to the public interests, and not that the documents are confidential or official, which alone is no reason for their non-production: the general public interest is paramount to the interests of the suitor."

The defendant's objection was upheld, and a similar principle was successfully invoked in *Duncan* v. *Cammell Laird & Co., Ltd.*,[3] where the defendants to a claim for damages for negligence in relation to the construction of a submarine were directed by the Board of Admiralty to object to the production of numerous documents in their possession in their capacity as government contractors. The structure of our submarines is clearly a matter that affects our national security, and ought to be kept secret, especially when, as was the case when *Duncan* v. *Cammell Laird & Co., Ltd.* was decided, the country is at war.

The judgment shows that the production of a document may be withheld in the public interest either on account of its contents, or else because it belongs to a class which, on grounds of public policy, must as a class be withheld from production (e.g. cabinet minutes). This latter ground of objection is usually raised when some other public interest than that of national security is at stake, but the case in which reports of military inquiries,[4] communications of the commander-in-chief of our forces abroad with the government,[5] or reports by a high commissioner to his government[6] have been held to be exempt from production may be included under the head of national security for they relate, in a broad sense, to the defence of the nation and good diplomatic relations with other states.[7]

In some instances, the substantive law of defamation concerning the privileged occasions on which these communications were published would produce the same result as that which is brought about by the rule of evidence under consideration, and both branches of the law are stressed in some of the judgments. For example, *Chatterton* v. *Secretary of State for India*[8] was a libel action founded on a dispatch from the Commander-in-Chief in India to the Indian Government, and the decision of the Court of Appeal in favour of the defendant was based both on the ground that the

---

[1] [1916] 1 K. B. 822. [2] At p. 830.
[3] [1942] A. C. 624, [1942] 1 All E. R. 587.
[4] *Home* v. *Bentick* (1820), 2 Brod. & Bing. 130; *Beatson* v. *Skene* (1860), 5 H. & N. 838.
[5] *Chatterton* v. *Secretary of State for India in Council*, [1895] 2 Q. B. 189.
[6] *Isaacs (M.) & Sons, Ltd.* v. *Cook*, [1925] 2 K. B. 391.
[7] *R.* v. *Brixton Prison Governor, Ex P. Soblens* [1963] 2 Q. B. 243; [1962] 3 All E. R. 641.
[8] *Chatterton* v. *Secretary of State for India in Council*, [1895] 2 Q. B. 189.

communication was the subject of absolute privilege under the law of defamation, and on the fact that the document must be excluded from evidence as an act of state.

(2) OTHER NATIONAL INTERESTS

Many other national interests than that of security have been protected by the rule under consideration. The Inland Revenue have successfully objected to the production of a company's balance sheets at the hearing of a misfeasance summons against one of its directors;[1] the Minister of Transport successfully objected to the production of a report of a railway accident made to him under various statutory provisions at the hearing of an action for negligence against a railway company;[2] the Home Office have successfully objected to the production of reports made by doctors and police officers concerning the mental condition of a prisoner awaiting trial and his assault on the plaintiff, a fellow prisoner, who was claiming damages from the Office;[3] and the Minister of War successfully objected to the production of a soldier's medical sheets at the hearing of a divorce case.[4]

The judge at one of these trials [5] confessed to an uneasy feeling that justice might not have been done because the material before him was not complete, and he said that he had something more than an uneasy feeling that, whether justice had been done or not, it certainly would not appear to have been done; but this did not prevent the Crown from making an even bolder claim to have evidence excluded than any of those which have been mentioned so far in *Broome* v. *Broome*.[6] That was a divorce case in which the respondent was a soldier who had been serving in Hong Kong, where he was joined by his wife. When differences arose between the parties, the good offices of the representatives of the Soldiers', Sailors' and Airmen's Families Association were invoked. In due course, all the parties returned to England, and the wife issued a *subpoena ad testificandum* directed to the representative of the Association and a *subpoena duces tecum* addressed to the Secretary of State for War relating to documents concerning attempts to reconcile the petitioner and respondent that had been made by the S.S.A.F.A. The Minister objected to producing the documents and his objection was upheld; he also sought to have the *subpoena* directed to the S.S.A.F.A. representative set aside, but the judge declined to do this for procedural reasons which will be considered shortly. The head of public interest on which the Minister

---

[1] *Re Joseph Hargreaves, Ltd.*, [1900] 1 Ch. 347. The balance sheets were in the possession of the Inland Revenue Authorities for the purposes of tax assessment and the objection to production was founded on the desirability of secrecy. See also *Hughes* v. *Vargas* (1893), 9 T. L. R. 551, and contrast *Honeychurch* v. *Honeychurch*, [1943] S. A. S. R. 31 where a number of English authorities are discussed.

[2] *Ankin* v. *London and North Eastern Rail. Co.*, [1930] 1 K. B. 527.

[3] *Ellis* v. *The Home Office*, [1953] 2 Q. B. 135; [1953] 2 All E. R. 149.

[4] *Anthony* v. *Anthony* (1919), 35 T. L. R. 559. This is a difficult case, first, because it is hard to see how the statements in the medical sheets could be admissible evidence of their truth on account of the rule against hearsay (see *per* MACNAGHTEN, J., in *Spigelman* v. *Hocken* (1933), 150 L. T. 256, at p. 260), secondly, because it was conceded that the doctor could give evidence of his treatment of the respondent, but this is contrary to principle (*ibid.*). Cf. *Gain* v. *Gain*, [1962] 1 All E. R. 63.

[5] DEVLIN, J., in *Ellis* v. *The Home Office*, reported on appeal, [1953] 2 Q. B. 135; [1953] 2 All E. R. 149.

[6] [1955] P. 190; [1955] 1 All E. R. 201. Such a claim would not be made now, C. L. J. (1957), 11. The case was distinguished in *Whitehall* v. *Whitehall*, 1957 S. L. T. 96.

relied was the maintenance of the morale of the armed forces. The Crown wished to ensure that attempts at reconciling estranged spouses undertaken by the S.S.A.F.A. should receive the same protection from disclosure as is accorded to the efforts of probation officers and others;[1] but we have seen that this is a matter of privilege which belongs to the parties and can be waived by them. As SACHS, J., observed:

> "One cannot help noting that the steps which would extend the heads of public interest from 'maintaining the morale of the forces' to 'maintaining general public morale' and thence to 'maintaining the faith of the public in specific institutions serving it' are neither very large nor unduly illogical." [2]

It may be doubted, however, whether any claim to exclude evidence that has ever been made goes further than that which succeeded in *West* v. *West*,[3] a slander action brought by a lady against her father-in-law in which the special damage alleged was the cessation of invitations to court functions, and the Lord Chamberlain successfully objected to disclosing communications received by him concerning the plaintiff.

It seems that there must be some connection between the claim to exclusion and the central government before it will be recognised by the courts. In *Blackpool Corporation* v. *Locker*,[4] for instance, where the validity of a notice requisitioning a house was in issue, the courts made short shrift of the corporation's claim to exclude their interdepartmental communications in the public interest.

No distinction is drawn between cases in which the Crown or a government department is a party to the proceedings, and those in which the parties are private citizens or corporations. The former class of case has, however, increased since the Crown Proceedings Act, 1947, came into force, and, although an order for discovery may be made against the Crown under s. 28 of that statute, this is expressly made subject to the doctrine of public policy which is now under consideration.

(3) POLICE MATTERS

In *Marks* v. *Beyfus*,[5] an action for an alleged conspiracy to prosecute maliciously, the plaintiff called the Director of Public Prosecutions and wished to ask the name of the person who gave the information leading to the prosecution for which the Director had been responsible. The Court of Appeal held that the prosecution was a public one, that, in such a case, the information sought by the plaintiff ought to be withheld, and the trial judge had rightly disallowed the question.[6] The ban on the disclosure of the name of the informant appears to be confined to "public prosecutions", but there is no modern authority on the implications of this term.

In practice, the police disclose the names of witnesses of road accidents to the solicitors for the plaintiff, but, in civil cases, statements by witnesses to the police are still regarded as the subject matter of Crown privilege,[7]

---

[1] Pp. 262, *ante.*
[2] [1955] P. 190, at p. 200; [1955] 1 All E. R. 201, at p. 206.
[3] (1911), 27 T. L. R. 189.
[4] [1948] 1 K. B. 349, at p. 379; [1948] 1 All E. R. 85, at p. 97.
[5] (1890), 25 Q. B. D. 494.
[6] The objection may be taken by the judge: *A.-G.* v. *Briant* (1846), 15 M. & W. 169.
[7] See Public Law, (1962), 203.

and the claim to protection from disclosure on the ground of public policy has been upheld in the case of reports from one police officer to another.[1]

In *Rogers* v. *Secretary of State for the Home Department*[2] the House of Lords held that witness summonses served respectively on the Secretary of the Gaming Board and the Chief Constable of Sussex requiring them to produce the original and a copy of a letter from the Deputy Chief Constable to the secretary concerning the advisability of granting licences under the Gaming Act to the appellant should be set aside. The letter was based on information supplied to the police in confidence and was treated as belonging to a class which ought not to be disclosed in the public interest. The appellant, who had somehow obtained a copy of the letter, wished to prosecute the Deputy Chief Constable for criminal libel; the decision might well have been different if he had been the accused in a criminal case for, to quote Lord SIMON OF GLAISDALE:

> "Sources of police information are a judicially recognised class of evidence excluded on the ground of public policy unless their production is required to establish innocence in a criminal trial."[3]

(4) CRIMINAL CASES

Reference has already been made to the doctrine that rules under which evidence is inadmissible on the ground of professional privilege or public interest must yield in situations in which the reception of the evidence might establish innocence at a criminal trial or at least enable the accused to resist an allegation of crime.[4] There is at least one reported case in which disclosure of the name of an informant has been ordered,[5] and, although there are also reported cases in which evidence which might have helped the accused has been excluded,[6] it is said not to be the practice nowadays for the Crown to claim to exclude evidence in a criminal case on the ground of state interest.[7]

If a Crown witness's evidence is contradictory of a statement made by him, the prosecution should show the statement to counsel for the defence so that he can cross-examine upon it, and orders to hand over such a statement have been made.[8]

---

[1] *Auten* v. *Rayner*, [1958] 3 All E. R. 566, one of several cases which may require reconsideration after *Conway* v. *Rimmer*, [1968] A. C. 910; [1968] 1 All E. R. 874.

[2] [1973] A. C. 388; [1972] 2 All E. R. 1057.

[3] At p. 407, citing *R.* v. *Hardy* (1794), St. Tr. 199, at p. 808 (a case in which, though EYRE, C.J., recognised in argument the possible necessity of disclosure in order to ascertain the truth, the tenor of the arguments was against disclosure); *Hennessy* v. *Wright* (1888), 21 Q.B.D. 509, at p. 519; and *Marks* v. *Beyfus* (1890), 25 Q. B. D. 494.

[4] P. 250, *ante*.

[5] *R.* v. *Richardson* (1863), 3 F. & F. 693; see also *Webb* v. *Catchlove* (1886), 3 T. L. R. 159.

[6] *R.* v. *Watson* (1817), 32 State Tr. 1; *R.* v. *Cobbett* (1831), 2 State Tr. N.S. 789; *R.* v. *O'Connor* (1846), 4 State Tr. N. S. 935; *A.-G.* v. *Briant* (1846), 15 L. J. Ex. 265. See an article by A. Waram, [1972] Crim L. R. 675. See also *A.-G.* v. *Simpson*, [1959] I. R. 105, discussed by Coutts in Journal of Criminal Law, 1961, p. 71.

[7] [1959] Crim. L. R. 10.

[8] *R.* v. *Clarke* (1930), 22 Cr. App. Rep. 58; *R.* v. *Hall* (1958), 43 Cr. App. Rep. 29. If the witness is not called, there is no obligation to hand over his statement (*R.* v. *Bryant* (1946), 31 Crim. App. Rep. 146), but the witness must be made available to the defence if it is known that he can give material evidence. See also *Baksh* v. *R.*, [1958] A. C. 167 and the conflicting views of Lord DENNING, M.R., and DIPLOCK, L.J., in *Dallison* v. *Caffery*, [1965] 1 Q. B. 348, at p. 369 and pp. 375–6 respectively.

B. THE METHOD BY WHICH THE VALIDITY OF A CLAIM TO EXCLUDE EVIDENCE UNDER THE RULE IS TO BE DETERMINED

Before the decision of the House of Lords in *Conway* v. *Rimmer*,[1] the question of the proper method of determining the validity of a claim to exclude evidence in a civil case on the ground that its reception would be contrary to the public interest was a vexed one. This was due to the absolute terms of Lord SIMON's reasons for the unanimous decision of the House of Lords in *Duncan* v. *Cammell Laird & Co., Ltd.*[2] Put in its simplest terms, the question is whether the Minister's decision that the evidence should be withheld is absolutely binding on the courts. The problem can arise in relation to oral evidence, but most of the cases are concerned with objections to the production of documents.

Lord SIMON's speech in *Duncan* v. *Cammell Laird & Co., Ltd.* laid it down that, whether the claim to exclude a document was founded on the needs of national defence, diplomatic relations or the proper functioning of the public service, and whether the objection to production relates to the contents of a particular document or to the fact that the document belongs to a particular class, the judge must accept the minister's decision to exclude the evidence. Lord SIMON said that the objection could be taken on affidavit at an application for discovery, and this might suffice at the trial, although the attendance of the minister could be required by the judge.

Although they were not in complete accord, the previous English judgments had suggested that the judge has a residual power to insist on production of the document and to overrule the minister's claim to exclude it if necessary.[3] Contrary to what Lord SIMON stated to be the case, the House of Lords subsequently decided that, according to Scots law, the judge may, as a last resort, examine the document which the minister objects to produce,[4] and this view was adopted in some Commonwealth jurisdictions before and after *Duncan's Case*.[5]

Duncan v. *Cammell Laird & Co., Ltd.* was of course followed in the lower English courts,[6] but not without protest occasioned by the apparent unimportance, from the point of view of the jeopardy to the public interest which would be caused by the disclosure, of the evidence which was withheld. Some concessions were announced by the Lord Chancellor in 1956 and 1962 when he specified certain cases in which evidence would not be withheld;[7] but the courts and legal profession continued to be uneasy about the claim to exclude evidence on the ground that its disclosure would interfere with the smooth functioning of the public service by

---

[1] [1968] A. C. 910; [1968] 1 All E. R. 874.

[2] [1942] A. C. 624; [1942] 1 All E. R. 587.

[3] *Beatson* v. *Skene*, (1860), 5 H. & N. 838; *Hennessy* v. *Wright* (1888), 21 Q. B. D. 509; *Asiatic Petroleum Co., Ltd.* v. *Anglo-Persian Oil Co., Ltd.*, [1916] 1 K. B. 822; *Ankin* v. *London and North Eastern Rail. Co.*, [1930] 1 K. B. 527; *Spigelman* v. *Hocken* (1933), 150 L. T. 256, and 50 T. L. R. 87 (there are material differences between the reports).

[4] *Glasgow Corporation* v. *Central Land Board*, [1956] S. C. (H. L.). 1.

[5] *Robinson* v. *South Australia State* (No. 2), [1931] A. C. 704; *Corbett* v. *Social Security Commissioner*, [1962] N. Z. L. R. 878; *Bruce* v. *Waldron*, [1963] V. R. 3.

[6] See, for example, *Ellis* v. *Home Office*, [1953] 2 Q. B. 135; [1953] 2 All E. R. 149; *Broome* v. *Broome*, [1955] P. 190; [1955] 1 All E. R. 201; and *Gain* v. *Gain*, [1962] 1 All E. R. 63.

[7] The Times, June 6th, 1956; Public Law 1962, p. 203.

inhibiting candour of communication between civil servants, and, in *Re Grosvenor Hotel London* (No. 2),[1] the Court of Appeal held that, in certain classes of case, the judge has a residual power to inspect documents to the disclosure of which the minister objects. However, the majority of another division of the same court held in *Conway* v. *Rimmer*[2] that they were bound by *Duncan* v. *Cammell Laird & Co., Ltd.* to disclaim any such power. The House of Lords held that they were right, but overruled their decision.

Conway v. *Rimmer*[3] was an action for malicious prosecution brought by a former police probationer, who had been charged and acquitted of theft, against his former superintendant who had caused the charge to be brought. Contrary to the wishes of both parties, the Home Secretary objected to the production of five reports mentioned in the defendant's list of documents. Four of those reports related to the plaintiff's conduct as a probationer, and the other was made to the Chief Constable for transmission to the Director of Public Prosecutions in connection with the charge of theft. The House of Lords ordered production of the documents for inspection by them, and, after inspection, they ordered production to the plaintiff. Technically it would be wrong to regard *Duncan* v. *Cammell Laird & Co., Ltd.* as overruled because every member of the House was of opinion that the actual decision (that documents relating to the structure of our submarines should not be produced) was right; but the condemnation of Lord Simon's inclusion of routine documents among those to which the minister's objection, provided it was in the right form, should be conclusive was unanimous.

The present law is embodied in the following quotation from the speech of Lord Morris of Borth-y-Gest:

> "In my view, it should now be made clear that whenever an objection is made to the production of a relevant document it is for the court to decide whether to uphold the objection. The inherent power of the court must include a power to ask for a clarification or amplification of an objection to production, though the court will be careful not to impose a requirement which could only be met by divulging the very matters to which the objection related. The power of the court must also include a power to examine documents privately—a power which, I think, in practice should be sparingly exercised, but one which could operate as a safeguard to the executive in cases where a court is inclined to make an order for production where an objection is being pressed. I see no difference in principle between the consideration which should govern what have been called the contents cases and the class cases."[4]

Although there is no difference in principle between contents and class cases it was conceded that, if a minister swears or certifies that disclosure of a particular document would be contrary to the public interest, it is extremely unlikely that any court would wish to take the matter any further. It was also conceded in their Lordships' speeches that no court would order production of documents of certain classes such as cabinet minutes, communications with ambassadors abroad, and some communica-

---

[1] [1965] Ch. 1210; [1964] 3 All E. R. 354. See also *Merricks* v. *Nott-Bower*, [1965] 1 Q. B. 57; [1964] 1 All E. R. 717, and *Wednesbury Corporation* v. *Minister of Housing and Local Government*, [1965] 1 All E. R. 186.

[2] [1967] 2 All E. R. 1260.

[3] [1968] A. C. 910; [1968] 1 All E. R. 874; for comment see 84 L. Q. R. 172; 26 C. L. J. 173; 32 M. L. R. 142; 46 Can. Bar Rev. 452.

[4] At p. 971.

tions between heads of departments. These are cases, and there are no doubt others, in which the executive is better equipped to assess the public interest than the courts, but, in the case of most routine documents, the court should balance the public interest in the administration of justice, which calls for the production of all relevant documents, against the public interest in the nondisclosure of evidence which the minister thinks ought not to be disclosed.

The House of Lords made short shrift of the argument that the promotion of candour of communication between civil servants might of itself justify nondisclosure.

> "It is strange that civil servants alone are supposed to be unable to be candid in their statements made in the course of duty without the protection of an absolute privilege denied to their other fellow subjects."[1]

It was said that the minister should have a right of appeal, but the precise method of providing for this was not specified. Another matter which may have to be more fully worked out in the future is the appropriate procedure to be followed when the objection on the score of public interest is made in respect of oral evidence.[2] *Conway* v. *Rimmer* does not appear to add anything significant to the law with regard to criminal cases but, subject to the comparatively minor points which have just been mentioned, the position with regard to civil proceedings has been greatly clarified.

C. PRINCIPLES WHICH SHOULD GOVERN THE DETERMINATION

It is difficult to add anything to the statement that it is the duty of the court, in arriving at a decision on the question whether evidence should be withheld, to balance the public interest in the administration of justice against whatever public interest is likely to be injured by the disclosure of the evidence; but reference may be made to three decisions of the House of Lords since *Conway* v. *Rimmer*.[3] Each of them shows that, although, in itself, confidentiality is neither a ground of privilege nor a justification for withholding evidence in the public interest, it may have an important bearing on the latter issue.

In *Rogers* v. *Secretary of State for Home Department*,[4] the objections of the Home Secretary and the Gaming Board to the production of the original and a copy of a letter from the Deputy Chief Constable of Sussex to the Board was upheld. The letter concerned the suitability of the appellant to be a licensee under the Gaming Act, 1968. It was written in confidence, and, what was more important, very probably contained information given to the Brighton police against a promise of confidentiality. The case not being one in which production of the letter was required to resist a criminal charge, the ordinary protection accorded to certain types of information supplied to the police applied.[5]

---

[1] At p. 967, *per* Lord HODSON.
[2] See *Broome* v. *Broome*, [1955] P. 190, at p. 198.
[3] For Commonwealth decisions since *Conway* v. *Rimmer* see *Pollock* v. *Pollock and Grey*, [1970] N. Z. L. R. 771 and *McFarlane* v. *Sharp*, [1972] N. Z. L. R. 64.
[4] [1973] A. C. 388; [1972] 2 All E. R. 1057.
[5] But see the article by Whitmore, [1972] Crim. L. R. 682.

In *Alfred Crompton Amusement Machines, Ltd* v. *Customs and Excise Commissioners*,[1] internal communications between the Commissioners and their staff and communications of the Commissioners with third parties all of which were brought into existence to enable the Commissioners to fulfil their statutory obligation of forming an opinion concerning the basis on which purchase tax should be payable by the company were held to be proper subjects of a claim to withhold them from production in the public interest. In favour of disclosure there was the possibility that the appellants might feel aggrieved if the arbitration claimed by them by way of challenge of the Commissioners' opinion should go against them; but the communications were confidential and they were made in order to assist in the performance of the Commissioners' statutory duty. The case was obviously on the borderline and perhaps there will be some who will disagree with the following observation of Lord CROSS OF CHELSEA:

> "In a case where the contentions for and against disclosure appear to be fairly evenly balanced the court should, I think, uphold a claim for privilege on the ground of public interest and trust to the head of the department concerned to do whatever he can to mitigate the ill effects of nondisclosure."[2]

Norwich Pharmacal Co., Ltd. v. *Customs and Excise Commissioners*[3] was less of a borderline case. The appellants were owners and licensees of a patent, and information concerning imports published by the Commissioners showed that some importations must have been made by persons infringing the patent. The appellants sought an order that the Commissioners should disclose the names of the importers of the goods which were the subject of the patent. Though of the opinion that the Commissioners had rightly refused to make disclosure without an order of the court, the House of Lords made the order. The most relevant consideration was that the persons whose names were to be disclosed were almost certainly wrongdoers.[4] Other relevant considerations were said to be the relations between the wrongdoers and the Commissioners, whether the information could be obtained from another source, and whether giving it would involve the Commissioners in trouble which could not be compensated by an order for costs.[5]

SECTION 2. MISCELLANEOUS MATTERS CONNECTED WITH PREVIOUS LITIGATION

The judges of the superior courts cannot be compelled to give evidence concerning cases tried by them, and more or less closely analogous rules exist concerning the evidence of arbitrators, jurors or barristers.

A. THE EVIDENCE OF JUDGES OF THE SUPERIOR COURTS

In *R.* v. *Gazard*[6] it was held that a chairman of quarter sessions ought not to be compelled to go before the grand jury in order to depose to that which a witness had said in a previous case tried by him. PATTESON, J.,

---

[1] [1973] 2 All E. R. 1169. [2] At p. 1185. [3] [1973] 2 All E. R. 943.
[4] The only innocent importers would have been re-importers.
[5] On the last two cases see a note by C. Tapper, 37 M. L. R. 92.
[6] (1838), 8 C. & P. 595.

said, "It would be dangerous to allow such an examination as the judges of England might be called upon to state what occurred before them in court." It has since been held that the judges of inferior courts can be compelled to do this,[1] but the remarks of PATTESON, J., suggest that a privilege based upon the dignity of their office is conferred on the judges of the superior courts, although it is impossible to say exactly how far the privilege extends because there are very few authorities on the subject as the judges do not appear to object to giving evidence, at least from the well of the court, concerning that which occurred in cases tried by them when they can assist subsequent litigation by doing so. In *Buccleuch (Duke)* v. *Metropolitan Board of Works*,[2] CLEASBY, B., said:

> "With respect to those who fill the office of judge it has been felt that there are grave objections to their conduct being made the subject of cross-examination and comment (to which hardly any limit could be put) in relation to proceedings before them; and, as everything which they can properly prove can be proved by others, the courts of law discountenance and I think I may say prevent them being examined."

This suggests that the rule may be one of public policy rather than privilege, but the matter is not one upon which it is possible to make a final pronouncement in the present state of the authorities.

B. THE EVIDENCE OF ARBITRATORS

So far as arbitrators are concerned, it is settled that they can be compelled to give evidence with regard to that which occurred during the arbitration, and to state what matters were included in the submission, but they must not be asked questions about the reasons for their award.[3] Such a limitation may be justified on the ground that the evidence would be irrelevant as the reasons for an award could only be material at the hearing of an application to have it set aside; but there is also the point that the award must be treated as final in the absence of any proceedings of this nature. The basis of exclusion is similar to that under which evidence of the state of mind of the maker of a document is generally inadmissible.

C. THE EVIDENCE OF JURORS

There is a settled rule that jurors may not give evidence of discussions that took place in the jury box or jury room concerning the cases in which they were acting. Even if they are all prepared to swear that they intended to return a verdict for a greater sum of damages than that which appeared on the record, no alteration can be made.[4] Hard as it is, the point made in the judgment that it is better for the plaintiff to suffer an inconvenience than that his application should be allowed is probably a sound one. If the statement of all the jurors concerning that which they intended would justify a variation of the verdict, what would happen if some, or a majority

---

[1] *R.* v. *Harvey* (1858), 8 Cox C. C. 99.

[2] (1872), L. R. 5 H. L. 418, at p. 433. A subpoena may be issued against a Magistrate's Clerk to bring and produce notes of proceedings before the Magistrates (*McKinley* v. *McKinley*, [1960] 1 All E. R. 476).

[3] *Buccleuch's Case* (*supra*), applied to a member of a medical board under the National Insurance (Industrial Injuries) Act, 1946, in *Ward* v. *Shell Mex and B.P., Ltd.*, [1951] 2 All E. R. 904.

[4] *Jackson* v. *Williamson* (1788), 2 Term Rep 281. See also *Nesbitt* v. *Parrett* (1902), 18 T. L. R. 510; and *R.* v. *Thompson*, [1962] 1 All E. R. 65.

of them, made such a statement? The exclusionary rule is confined to evidence of discussions concerning their verdict that took place between the jurors. Accordingly, in *Ellis* v. *Deheer*,[1] a new trial was ordered on the ground that some jurymen had not been present in court when their verdict was announced, and it is probable that the fact that one of the jurors did not understand English would be a good ground for setting aside their verdict. As Lord ATKIN observed, finality is a good thing, but justice is better.[2]

D. THE EVIDENCE OF ADVOCATES

We have already seen that there are obvious reasons why an advocate should not give evidence in a case in which he is acting, and it is not customary to compel him to testify in later litigation concerning such matters as the terms of a compromise of a previous suit, but the whole question is more dependent on professional etiquette than anything in the nature of an exclusionary rule of evidence, and nothing more need be said about it in a work of this nature.

SECTION 3. ILLEGALLY OBTAINED EVIDENCE [3]

Cast into its simplest terms, the problem with which this section is concerned is whether there is a rule under which relevant evidence must be excluded because it was obtained illegally, for example, by a crime, tort, breach of contract or an infringement of official regulations such as those which bind the police when carrying out investigations. So far as the present English law is concerned, the short answer is that confessions are only admissible in a criminal case if they are proved to have been voluntary, in the sense that they were not obtained by fear of prejudice or hope of advantage exercised or held out by any person in authority or by oppression; but, subject to this important qualification, there is no such rule as that which has been suggested. The cases which lead to this conclusion are few, and there has been no full examination of the principles at stake by an English court. Yet these principles are of the highest significance. On the one hand, there is the general rule that all relevant evidence is admissible, and the fact that it was obtained illegally is immaterial so far as the case before the court is concerned; in particular, the method by which incriminating evidence was obtained may be thought not to justify the release of a guilty man, although it may warrant punitive or remedial proceedings against those responsible for the illegality. On the other hand, there is the argument that the slightest encouragement of illegal methods of obtaining evidence, and, in particular, the barest toleration of improper police practice is a worse evil than the escape of an occasional criminal. To quote from an important judgment in a Scottish case:[4]

---

[1] [1922] 2 K. B. 113.

[2] *Ras Behari Lal* v. *The King-Emperor* (1933), 102 L. J. P. C. 144, disapproving in the Privy Council the decision of the Court of Criminal Appeal in *R.* v. *Thomas*, [1933] 2 K. B. 489. For evidence of statements by jurors to third parties see *R.* v. *Symes* (1914), 10 Cr App. Rep. 284; *R.* v. *Armstrong*, [1922] 2 K. B. 555; *R.* v. *Box*, [1964] 1 Q. B. 430; [1963] 3 All E. R. 240.

[3] Cowen and Carter, *Essays on the Law of Evidence*, essays 2 and 3; Gottlieb, *Confirmation by Subsequent Facts*, 72 L. Q. R. 209 (1956), Glanville Williams, *Evidence Obtained by Illegal Means*, Criminal Law Review (1955), 339, and Heydon, [1973] Crim. L. R. 603 and 690.

[4] Lord COOPER in *Lawrie* v. *Muir*, 1950 S. C. (J.) 19, at p. 26.

"The law must strive to reconcile two highly important interests which are liable to come into conflict—(a) the interest of the citizen to be protected from illegal or irregular invasions of his liberties by the authorities, and (b) the interest of the state to secure that evidence bearing upon the commission of a crime and necessary to enable justice to be done shall not be withheld from courts of law on any mere formal or technical ground. Neither of these objects can be insisted upon to the uttermost. The protection for the citizen is primarily protection for the innocent citizen against unwarranted, wrongful and perhaps high-handed interference, and the common sanction is an action for damages. The protection is not intended as a protection for the guilty citizen against the efforts of the public prosecutor to vindicate the law. On the other hand the interest of the state cannot be magnified to the point of causing all the safeguards for the protection of the citizen to vanish, and of offering a positive inducement to the authorities to proceed by irregular methods."

We shall see that the most recent Scots decisions have gone far towards providing for a compromise between the two conflicting interests by according a large measure of discretion to the trial judge. The conflicting interests have produced conflicting views in the United States. The impropriety of acquitting A., who is guilty, on account of the illegal conduct of B., was forcefully put by CARDOZO, J., when he said:

"A room is searched against the law, and the body of a murdered man is found. If the place of discovery may not be proved, the other circumstances may be insufficient to connect the defendant with the crime. The privacy of the home has been infringed, and the murderer goes free." [1]

The contrary view was forcefully put by HOLMES, J., when he said:

"We must consider the two objects of desire both of which we cannot have and make up our minds which to choose. It is desirable that crimes should be detected, and to that end too all available evidence should be used. It is desirable that the government should not itself foster and pay for other crimes, when they are the means by which the evidence is to be obtained. If it pays its officers for having got evidence by crime I do not see why it may not as well pay them for getting it in the same way, and I can attach no importance to protestations of disapproval if it knowingly accepts and pays and announces that in future it will pay for the fruits. We have to choose, and for my part I think it a less evil that some criminals should escape than that the government should play an ignoble part." [2]

The American authorities are mainly concerned with the provisions of the constitution of the United States, and anything in the nature of a detailed discussion is beyond the scope of this book; but it is relevant to point out that the American courts adhere fairly rigidly to the doctrine of the exclusion of the "fruits of the poisoned tree", and, by way of contrast with the English courts, they stress the disciplining of the police as the motivation of the exclusionary rule. To quote from the majority judgment in the leading case of *Mapp* v. *Ohio*,[3] ". . . the purpose of the exclusionary rule is to deter—to compel respect for the constitutional guarantees [against illegal searches] in the only effective available way—by removing the incentive to disregard it." The English cases that will now be briefly considered concern either the admissibility of facts discovered in consequence of inadmissible confessions, or else the admissibility of evidence

---

[1] *The People* v. *Defoe* (1926), 242 N. Y. 413.

[2] *Olmstead* v. *United States* (1928), 277 U. S. 438.

[3] (1961), 367 U. S. 656; the judgment was quoting from that in *Elkins* v. *U.S.* (1960), 364 U. S. 206, at p. 217. The underlying psychology is highly questionable. The "bent" police officer thinks that no point will be taken on his illegal methods of obtaining evidence or that, if it is, he will be able to lie himself out of trouble.

procured in consequence of some unlawful act such as illegal search. The distinction is necessitated by the rule prohibiting the reception of involuntary confessions.

A. FACTS DISCOVERED IN CONSEQUENCE OF INADMISSIBLE CONFESSIONS

Voluntary confessions are received under an exception to the rule against hearsay discussed in chapter XIX. No doubt they are admitted because it is inherently probable that they are true, and the reason usually given for their exclusion is that they may well be untrue;[1] this is a point to be borne in mind in considering the cases mentioned below.[2] The problem with which the ensuing cases are concerned is whether incriminating facts discovered in consequence of an inadmissible confession should be received, and, if so, can such parts of the confession as relate to those facts be admitted? or can it even be argued that the entire confession is rendered admissible by what Wigmore described as its "confirmation by subsequent facts"?[3] For example, A. is charged with stealing. In consequence of an improper inducement he says, "I stole the goods and you will find them under my bed". The goods are found under A.'s bed. Their presence there is a highly relevant fact; can it be proved, notwithstanding the circumstances in which the search was first suggested? A.'s knowledge of the whereabouts of the stolen goods is also a relevant fact, can this be proved by reference to the second part of his statement although it was improperly induced? Finally A.'s confession that he did in fact steal the goods is conclusive of his guilt and strikingly confirmed by the discovery of the property in the place specified by A.; does this justify the reception of his entire utterance?

In *R.* v. *Warickshall*,[4] a woman who was charged as an accessory after the fact to theft and as a receiver of stolen goods was improperly induced to make a confession in the course of which she said that the property in question was in her lodgings where it was in fact found. The court held that the exclusion of a confession "forced from the mind by the flattery of hope, or by the pressure of fear" was not based on any breach of public faith that might be involved in its reception, but was due to the fact that the confession comes in such a questionable shape, when it is to be considered as the evidence of guilt, that no credit ought to be given to it. But:

> "this principle respecting confessions has no application whatever as to the admission or rejection of facts, whether the knowledge of them be obtained in consequence of an extorted confession or whether it arises from any other source; for a fact, if it exist at all, must exist invariably in the same manner whether the confession from which it derives be in other respects true or false. Facts thus obtained, however, must be fully and satisfactorily proved without calling in the aid of any part of the confession from which they may have been derived."

---

[1] *R.* v. *Warickshall* (1783), 1 Leach 263; *R.* v. *Thomas* (1836), 7 C. & P. 345; *R.* v. *Garner* (1848), 1 Den. 329; *R.* v. *Scott* (1856), Dears. & B. 47; *R.* v. *Mansfield* (1881), 14 Cox C.C. 639.

[2] See articles by Andrews, [1963] Crim. L. R. 15 and 77.

[3] III *Wigmore*, para. 856.

[4] (1783), 1 Leach 263; *R.* v. *Mosey* (1784), 1 Leach 265 n.

Ever since the discovery of the stolen goods was allowed to be proved in this case, it has been regarded as settled that facts discovered in consequence of inadmissible confessions may be received in evidence under English law, and this was said to be so in the judgment of the Court of Criminal Appeal in *R. v. Barker*—a decision which is, as we shall see, hard to reconcile with *R. v. Warickshall*—but the mere proof of the facts without any reference to the confession will not always be of much assistance to the prosecution. If the accused says that he stole a purse and threw it into a field, proof that it was discovered in that field will not avail against him in the absence of some evidence of his knowledge of the whereabouts of the stolen property unless it happens to bear his finger prints. Accordingly it is hardly surprising that efforts have been made to prove at least that part of the confession which is confirmed by the discovery of the facts mentioned by the accused.

These efforts have been successful in at least two reported cases. In *R. v. Griffin*,[1] the prisoner made an inadmissible confession that he had stolen money from the prosecutor and later handed him a note stating that it was part of the property which he had taken. The majority of the judges held that the Crown could prove both the production of the money and the prisoner's statement with reference to it. In *R. v. Gould*,[2] someone who was charged with burglary made a statement to a policeman in circumstances which induced the prosecution, with the approval of the court, to decline to offer it in evidence; but the statement contained some allusion to a lantern, which was afterwards found in a particular place, and the policeman was asked whether, in consequence of something which the prisoner had said, he searched for it. TINDALL, C.J., and PARKE, B., were both of opinion that the words used by the prisoner with reference to the thing found ought to be given in evidence, and the policeman accordingly stated that the prisoner told him he had thrown it into a certain pond. The other parts of the statement were not given in evidence and, although the report is not a particularly full one, it seems to be fairly clear that the finding of the lantern would have been irrelevant to the prisoner's guilt in the absence of some evidence of his knowledge of its whereabouts.

In the course of the argument in *R. v. Garbett*,[3] it was even suggested that the discovery of property in consequence of an otherwise inadmissible confession of theft would justify the reception of the prisoner's statement in its entirety. There is something to be said for such a conclusion from the point of view of strict logic for, as Wigmore observed:

> "Confirmation in material points produces ample persuasion of the trustworthiness of the whole. It can hardly be supposed that at certain parts the possible fiction stopped and the truth began, and that by a marvellous coincidence the truthful parts are exactly those which a subsequent search (more or less controlled by chance) happened to confirm";[4]

but, in *R. v. Berriman*,[5] ERLE, J., reverted to the views expressed in *R. v. Warickshall* according to which no part of the confession is rendered admissible by the discovery of the facts to which it refers. A woman was charged with concealment of birth, and counsel for the prosecution wished to ask a witness whether, in consequence of an answer improperly elicited

---

[1] (1809), Russ. & Ry. 151.   [2] (1840), 9 C. & P. 364.
[3] (1847), 2 Car. & Kir. 474, at p. 490, *per* Lord DENMAN, C.J.
[4] III *Wigmore*, pp. 338–9.   [5] (1854), 6 Cox C. C. 388.

from the prisoner by the magistrate at her preliminary examination, search was made which resulted in the discovery of an infant's remains. ERLE, J., interjected:

> "No. Not in consequence of what she said. You may ask him what search was made, and what things were found, but under the circumstances I cannot allow the proceeding to be connected with the prisoner."

The most recent English decision on this somewhat perplexing topic is *R.* v. *Barker*.[1] An accountant had been convicted for conspiring with his client to defraud the Inland Revenue. He had had an interview with a tax inspector at which an extract from *Hansard* had been read to him. It indicated that, when a person voluntarily disclosed past tax frauds, criminal proceedings would not be instituted. The prisoner thereupon produced incriminating books and documents which were admitted in evidence at his trial. When quashing his conviction TUCKER, J., said:[2]

> "The court . . . does not desire to question that there may be cases in which evidence can be given of facts the existence of which has come to the knowledge of the police as the result of an inadmissible confession. But in the present case the promise or inducement which was implied in this extract from *Hansard* expressly related to the production of business books and records and the court is of opinion that if, as a result of a promise, inducement or threat, such books and documents are produced by the person or persons to whom the promise or inducement is held out, or the threat made, those documents stand on precisely the same footing as an oral or written confession which is brought into existence as the result of such promise, inducement or threat."

It has been said with much force that there is an obvious difference between a book containing fraudulent accounts and a confession of past fraudulent accounting; but the Court of Criminal Appeal certainly does appear to have treated the account books as a prepared confession rather than a fact. The court has a discretion to exclude evidence obtained by a trick which it considers to have been unfair. The difficulty about *R.* v. *Barker* is that it proceeded on the footing that the account books ought to have been excluded as a matter of law.

The only statement that can confidently be made on the basis of the English authorities is that facts discovered in consequence of inadmissible confessions may certainly be proved in evidence if their relevance can be established without resorting to any part of the confession, and the cases conflict so far as the admissibility of the part of the confession showing the accused's knowledge of those facts is concerned.[3]

The 11th Report of the Criminal Law Revision Committee recommended an express provision in the draft Bill annexed to it that the fact that evidence of a confession is inadmissible shall not affect the admissibility of any facts discovered as a result of the confession;[4] but, subject to the points men-

---

[1] [1941] 2 K. B. 381; [1941] 3 All E. R. 33. So far as its facts are concerned, the effect of this decision was overruled by s. 34 of the Finance Act, 1942, now Income Tax Act, 1952, s. 504.

[2] [1941] 2 K. B. 381, at pp. 384–385; [1941] 3 All E. R. 33, at pp. 36–37.

[3] It seems clear that in Scotland, no part of an inadmissible confession can be received however much it is confirmed (*Chalmers* v. *H.M. Advocate*, 1954 S. C. (J.) 66). The confirmed parts of the confession are admissible in Canada (*R.* v. *St. Lawrence*, [1949] O. R. 215; *R.* v. *Haase* (1964), 50 W. W. R. 321). *R.* v. *St. Lawrence* was approved by the Supreme Court of Canada in *R.* v. *Wray* (1970), 11 D. L. R. (3d) 673, in which evidence of the finding of a gun with the assistance of the accused after he had made an inadmissible confession was held to have been wrongly excluded. Subsequently discovered facts are admissible under the Indian Evidence Act, 1872, s. 27.

[4] Para. 68.

tioned below, the Committee was against providing for the admissibility of any part of the confession because this might involve the judge in expressing, or appearing to express, an opinion that the confession, or part of it, was true.

In addition to containing assertions of guilt, a confession may be of evidential value because it shows that the maker writes, speaks or expresses himself in a particular way and thus helps to identify him as the culprit. For example, in *R.* v. *Voisin*,[1] Voisin was convicted of the murder of a woman, part of whose body had been found in a parcel in which there was also a piece of paper with the words "blady belgiam". The accused had been asked by a police officer if he had any objection to writing down the two words "bloody Belgian" and had said "Not at all" and had written down "blady Belgiam". The accused appealed unsuccessfully against his conviction on the ground, among others, that this writing ought to have been rejected as he had not been cautioned before being asked to write the words down. There was no question of an inadmissible confession; but it seemed to the committee that, if the words had been written in an inadmissible confession, it would be right that they should be admissible for the purpose of showing that the accused writes, speaks or expresses himself in a particular way; clause 2 (5) (c) of the draft Bill provides accordingly. The committee did not recommend that any part of an inadmissible confession should be admissible because it showed knowledge of an incriminating fact, such as the whereabouts of a window in a burgled house, on the part of the accused.

In spite of the refusal by ERLE, J., in *R.* v. *Berriman*[2] to allow a question to be put whether a discovery was made in consequence of something said by the accused, the Criminal Law Revision Committee expressed the view that, in practice, it is common for the witness reporting discovery to say that he made it "as a result of something said by the accused". The majority thought it proper to allow this, although a minority dissented on the ground that it is wrong that the jury should be informed indirectly of something of which it is thought that the interests of justice require that they should not be informed directly.[3]

B. THE ADMISSIBILITY OF EVIDENCE PROCURED IN CONSEQUENCE OF ILLEGAL SEARCHES AND OTHER UNLAWFUL ACTS

Turning to the English authorities on the admissibility of evidence procured in consequence of an illegal search or other unlawful act, they are uniformly in favour of its reception although there are not many of them. In *Jones* v. *Owen*[4] a constable searched the appellant illegally and found a quantity of young salmon in his pocket. This evidence was held to be admissible on a charge of unlawful fishing, MELLOR, J., expressing the view that:

---

[1] [1918] 1 K. B. 531.
[2] (1854), 6 Cox C. C. 388.
[3] 11th Report, para. 69. The minority objection is analogous to the objection to the old practice of receiving evidence of the fact, but not the contents, of a complaint in a sexual case, see p. 213, *ante*.
[4] (1870), 34 J. P. 759.

"It would be a dangerous obstacle to the administration of justice if we were to hold, because evidence was obtained by illegal means, it could not be used against a party charged with an offence."

In *Elias* v. *Pasmore*,[1] HORRIDGE, J., concluded that the interests of the state must excuse the seizure of documents which seizure would otherwise be unlawful if it appears that such documents were evidence of a crime committed by anyone. The case was not directly concerned with the admissibility of illegally obtained evidence, but it is frequently cited in this context and was mentioned by Lord GODDARD, C.J., when giving the advice of the Judicial Committee of the Privy Council in *Kuruma, Son of Kaniu* v. *R.*,[2] an appeal from Kenya whose law on this subject may be taken to have been the same as that of England. The accused had been convicted of being in unlawful possession of ammunition which had been discovered in consequence of a search of his person by a police officer below the rank of those who were permitted to make such searches. Although they referred the case to the Colonial Secretary on other grounds, the Board were of opinion that the evidence had been rightly admitted. Their view was that, if evidence is relevant, it matters not how it was obtained, although they recognised that the judge always has a discretion to disallow evidence in a criminal case if the strict rules of admissibility would operate unfairly against the accused. A suggested instance in which the judge might exercise such discretion was a case in which a document had been obtained from the prisoner by a trick. Their lordships also made it plain that they were not qualifying the law with regard to the admissibility of confessions in any way whatsoever. The question when a trick is of such a nature as to require the exclusion of evidence obtained in consequence of it has not been considered by the courts.[3]

The English authorities on the admissibility of evidence obtained by some unlawful act other than an illegal search are even scantier, but they all bear out the view, so laconically expressed by CROMPTON, J., in *R.* v. *Leatham*,[4] when he said, "It matters not how you get it if you steal it even, it would be admissible in evidence." This dictum was cited in *Kuruma's Case*, and it will be recollected that *Calcraft* v. *Guest*,[5] the leading authority on the admissibility of secondary evidence of privileged documents was decided on a similar principle.

It may therefore be concluded that, under English law, illegally obtained evidence is admissible, provided it does not involve a reference to an inadmissible confession of guilt, and subject to the overall exclusionary discretion enjoyed by the judge at a criminal trial.[6]

Apart from the special question of the admissibility of confessions, the Canadian cases are almost uniformly in favour of the reception of evidence in spite of the fact that it was obtained illegally, the sole concern of the

---

[1] [1934] 2 K. B. 164. This case must now be read with *Ghani* v. *Jones*, [1970] 1 Q. B. 693; [1969] 3 All E. R. 1700.　　　　[2] [1955] A. C. 197; [1955] 1 All E. R. 236.
[3] It is not clear what type of trick was in the contemplation of the board. In *R.* v. *Derrington* (1826), 2 C. & P. 418, a letter obtained by the turnkey from the prisoner under a false promise that he would post it was admitted in evidence against him (cf. *R.* v. *Pamenter* (1872), 12 Cox C. C. 177, a case that may require reconsideration after *Rumping* v. *Director of Public Prosecutions*, [1964] A. C. at p. 814; [1962] 3 All E. R. 256).
[4] (1861), 8 Cox C. C. 498, at p. 503. See the same judge in *Phelps* v. *Prew* (1854), 3 E. & B. 430, at p. 441. See also *Stockfleth* v. *De Tastet* (1814), 4 Camp. 10. To the same effect is *Lord Ashburton* v. *Pape*, [1913] 2 Ch. 469, at p. 473.
[5] [1898] 1 Q. B. 759, p. 241, *ante*.
[6] See p. 29, *ante*, as to this discretion.

court being with its trustworthiness.[1] Recent Scots cases, on the other hand, lay great stress on the discretionary element. In at least two instances, convictions have been quashed on account of the reception of evidence obtained by means of illegal searches.[2] Although it may only be a question of degree, the difference from English law is striking, first because of the ease with which appellate courts hold that the judge ought to have exercised his discretion in favour of excluding the impugned evidence, and secondly because there are signs that the discretion may exist under Scots law in civil cases, while there has been no parallel development in English procedure. In the Scots divorce case of *Rattray* v. *Rattray*,[3] it was held that a letter from the wife to the co-defendant must be received although it had been stolen from the post office by the husband who had suffered criminal punishment on account of his conduct. Lord YOUNG dissented because he thought that the court was bound to take notice of the statute law enacting that the pursuer's conduct was a crime, and to reject as evidence anything obtained by a violation of the law. This case was followed in *Maccoll* v. *Maccoll*,[4] but the judge said that, had he been a member of the court in *Rattray* v. *Rattray* he would have dissented with Lord YOUNG and on the same grounds. Having regard to the English authorities that have been cited, it is difficult to escape the conclusion that the letter would have been admitted in a divorce suit in England. It is, however, impossible to give a more precise statement about the judicial reactions to illegally obtained evidence north and south of the Tweed than is involved in the assertion that the Scots judges have recently canvassed the court's discretion to a far greater extent than their English brethren. The Scots judgments in favour of quashing convictions because the evidence was obtained illegally stem from Lord AITCHISON's statement that "an irregularity in the obtaining of evidence does not *necessarily* make the evidence inadmissible".[5] Confessions apart, it seems that such an irregularity will only make the evidence inadmissible in England if the circumstances are more exceptional than any that have come before our courts so far.

By way of contrast to the broad approach to the exclusionary discretion adopted by the Scots courts reference may be made to the extremely narrow approach of the majority of the Supreme Court of Canada in *R.* v. *Wray*.[6] They would confine it to cases in which the evidence tendered was of slight probative value as contrasted with its prejudicial propensities. Perhaps it is difficult to improve upon the formulation of the basis of this aspect of the exclusionary discretion adopted by the Privy Council in *King* v. *R.*[7] where the Judicial Committee held that evidence obtained in consequence of an illegal search warrant had been rightly admitted. "This

---

[1] *A.-G. for Quebec* v. *Begin*, [1955] 5 D. L. R. 394. The earlier authorities are cited in Cowen and Carter, *op. cit.*, 93 *et seq.*

[2] *Lawrie* v. *Muir*, 1950 S. C. (J.) 19; *McGovern* v. *H.M. Advocate*, 1950 S. C. (J.) 33. In *H.M. Advocate* v. *Turnbull*, 1951 S. C. (J.) 96, the evidence was excluded by the judge. For a case in which the Scots courts would have been prepared to receive illegally obtained evidence because of the danger that the accused would destroy the evidence against him, see *Hay* v. *H.M. Advocate*, 1968 S. C. (J.) 40.

[3] (1897), 25 R. (Ct. of Sess.) 315.   [4] 1946 S. L. T. 312.

[5] *H.M. Advocate* v. *McGuigan*, 1936 S. C. (J.) 16, at p. 18.

[6] (1970), 11 D. L. R. (3d) 673, at pp. 689–90.

[7] [1969] 1 A. C. 304 at p. 319, *per* Lord HODSON; cf. *Mathewson* v. *Police*, [1969] N. Z. L. R. 218.

was not in their opinion a case in which evidence has been obtained by conduct of which the Crown ought not to take advantage. If they had thought otherwise they would have excluded the evidence even though tendered for the suppression of crime." The concept of conduct of which the Crown ought not to take advantage would no doubt be applied by the English courts, although it must be admitted that they have, to date, been very sparing in the exercise of their discretion to exclude illegally or improperly obtained evidence.[1]

C. EVIDENCE THAT IS NOT OBTAINED ILLEGALLY

The ratio decidendi of some of the cases is not that relevant evidence is admissible although it was obtained illegally, but that relevant evidence is admissible because it was not obtained illegally and there was no reason for exercising the court's exclusionary discretion against its reception. In *Callis* v. *Gunn*,[2] for instance, it was held that, although no one can be obliged to allow his finger-prints to be taken in the absence of a court order, the police were not acting illegally in requesting a suspect to allow his prints to be taken, even though they did not administer any caution.

In *R.* v. *Maqsud Ali, R.* v. *Ashiq Hussain*,[3] Pakistanis suspected of murder went voluntarily with police officers to a room in the Bradford town hall in which, unknown to them, there was a microphone connected with a tape-recorder in another room. They were left alone in the room and proceeded to have a conversation in which incriminating remarks were made. The Court of Criminal Appeal held that the trial judge had rightly admitted the tape-recording of the incriminating conversation in evidence. "The criminal does not act according to the Queensberry rules. The method of the informer and of the eavesdropper is commonly used in the detection of crime. The only difference here was that a mechanical device was the eavesdropper."[4]

In *R.* v. *Murphy*,[5] the Northern Irish Court of Criminal Appeal held that the accused had been rightly convicted by a court martial of disclosing information useful to an enemy when the disclosure had been made to police officers posing as members of a subversive organisation. Lord MACDERMOTT, C.J. said, "Detection by deception is a form of police procedure to be directed and used sparingly and with circumspection; but as a method it is as old as the constable in plain clothes and, regrettable though the fact may be, the the day has not yet come when it would be safe to say that law and order could always be enforced and the public safety protected without occasional resort to it."[6]

---

[1] For a rare instance see *R.* v. *Payne*, [1963] 1 All E. R. 848, where, however, there was strictly speaking no illegality. For exclusion in Australia see *R.* v. *Ireland* (1970), 44 A. L. J. R. 263, and *R.* v. *Demicoli*, [1971] Qd. R. 358.

[2] [1964] 1 Q. B. 495; [1963] 3 All E. R. 677; *Carr* v. *R.* (1973), 14 A. L. J. R. 562.

[3] [1965] 2 All E. R. 464. For evidence of tape-recordings generally see p. 12, *ante*. The jury were warned to be careful about the translation. For other cases in which eavesdropping was held not to render the evidence inadmissible, see *R.* v. *Stewart*, [1970] 1 All E. R. 689, and *R.* v. *Keeton* (1970), 54 Cr. App. Rep. 267.

[4] At p. 469, *per* MARSHALL, J.

[5] [1965] N. I. 138.

[6] At pp. 147–148. For English cases on agents provocateurs see *R.* v. *Mullins* (1848), 3 Cox C. C. 526; *R.* v. *Bickley* (1909), 2 Cr. App. Rep. 53; *Brannan* v. *Peek*, [1948] 1 K. B. 68; [1947] 2 All E. R. 572; *Snedden* v. *Stevenson*, [1967] 2 All E. R. 1277. In several instances, the evidence of *agents provocateurs* is held admissible *sub silentio*, see for example, *Browning* v. *J. W. H. Watson (Rochester), Ltd.*, [1953] 2 All E. R. 775.

D. CONCLUSION

In conclusion it is respectfully submitted that the remarks of CARDOZO, J., and HOLMES, J., which were cited at the outset of this discussion are both tendentious. So far as those of CARDOZO, J., are concerned, if a room is searched and a dead body is found in it, it would certainly be a terrible thing if the guilty occupant were allowed to go free on a charge of murder because the search was technically illegal; but there must be some limit to this doctrine. What if admission were gained to the room in consequence of a violent assault, or what if the whereabouts of the corpse were ascertained by means of prolonged torture of the accused? On the other hand, in spite of the contrary opinion of HOLMES, J., the government does not foster and pay for other crimes whenever illegally obtained evidence is admitted. It is a mistake to suppose that the choice lies between admitting the evidence and leaving the aggrieved party to pursue such civil or criminal remedies against the wrongdoer as may be available, or rejecting the evidence as a warning to officialdom that convictions cannot be obtained by illegal action. Such an approach assumes that the conduct of the police is exclusively influenced by the number of convictions obtained. It leaves out of account the all-important sanctions provided by the opinion of those who pursue the same occupation as the person by whom the evidence was illegally obtained. Is it to be supposed that when the Lord Chief Justice said, ''The sooner the Bristol police study, learn and abide by the Judges' Rules the better'',[1] the conduct of the police of Bristol was unaffected because his lordship admitted a confession obtained in consequence of a breach of those rules? There must be a discretionary power to exclude illegally obtained evidence, at any rate in criminal cases, for public opinion would not tolerate its reception if it were procured by torture, however much it was confirmed by such convincing matters as the subsequent voluntary admission of the accused, but, in spite of the great weight of opinion to the contrary, too much importance may be attached to the rejection of illegally obtained evidence as an incentive to good behaviour on the part of the police. Bad behaviour, it is felt, is prompted by the hope that it will not be brought to the notice of the court, not by the belief that evidence discovered in consequence of it will be received in any event.

---

[1] *R. v. Mills and Lemon*, [1947] K. B. 297, at p. 299; [1946] 2 All E. R. 776, at p. 777.

CHAPTER XIII

ESTOPPEL

When an estoppel binds a party to litigation, he is prevented from placing reliance on or denying the existence of certain facts. This justifies the treatment of estoppel as an exclusionary rule of evidence. So regarded, it is less rigorous than the rules governing the exclusion of evidence on the ground of public policy because estoppels only operate if they are pleaded, but, like the exclusion of evidence on that ground, and unlike the exclusion of evidence under the rule relating to similar facts discussed in the next chapter, estoppels operate without reference to the purpose for which reliance is placed on a particular fact. From the point of view of the party in whose favour they operate, estoppels could be regarded as something which renders proof of certain facts unnecessary; also it is possible to argue that estoppel is better regarded as a matter of pleading or substantive law, rather than a rule of evidence.

Estoppels are of three kinds—by record, by deed and by conduct. After each of them has been considered, reference will be made to the question of the right place for estoppel in a comprehensive exposition of the law.

SECTION 1. ESTOPPEL BY RECORD.[1]

The principles underlying estoppel by record are "*Interest rei publicae ut sit finis litium*"—it is for the common good that there should be an end to litigation, and "*Nemo debet bis vexari pro eadem causa*"—no one should be sued twice on the same ground. The practical consequence is that, generally speaking, the order of a court of competent jurisdiction[2] is conclusive. An application may be made to have it set aside if it was obtained by fraud, and fraud or collusion in the obtaining of a judgment may be proved by a stranger to the proceedings.[3] These matters belong to the law of procedure, but the conclusive effects of judgments on the whole world as well as the parties to civil litigation have some bearing on the law of evidence. After they have been considered, reference will be made to the somewhat specialised questions of estoppel by record in matrimonial causes and criminal cases.

---

[1] Spencer-Bower, *Res Judicata* (2nd edition, by Sir Alexander Turner); M. L. Friedland, *Double Jeopardy*. Letters patent may constitute estoppel by record between the Crown and the grantee (*Cropper* v. *Smith* (1884), 26 Ch. D. 700), but the only estoppel of this nature which is worth any discussion in a work of this sort is estoppel by a judgment or *res judicata*, because the doctrine applies to judgments which are not those of a Court of Record (see Lord GUEST in *Carl-Zeiss Stiftung* v. *Rayner and Keeler, Ltd.* (No. 2), [1967] 1 A. C. 853, at p. 933; [1966] 2 All E. R. 536, at p. 564).
[2] *R.* v. *Hutchings* (1881), 6 Q. B. D. 300, shows that there is no estoppel where the justices exceeded their jurisdiction by declaring that a road was a highway.
[3] *R.* v. *Duchess of Kingston* (1776), 20 State Tr. 355.

It is important to stress the point that we are at present concerned with the extent to which judgments constitute an estoppel and thus prevent any evidence from being given to contradict them. There is a wholly different problem of the extent to which they can be regarded as *prima facie* evidence of the facts upon which they were founded which is discussed in Chapter XVI. This distinction, together with that between the effect of a judgment on parties and strangers respectively, may be illustrated by a hypothetical case in which A. has obtained judgment for a thousand pounds damages against B. on account of the negligence of C., B.'s servant, acting in the course of his employment. If B. seeks to recover this sum from C., C. will be estopped from denying that a thousand pounds was the sum which B. was ordered to pay A. because the judgment is conclusive as to its terms, even against strangers to the proceedings to which it was pronounced; but at common law it was not even admissible as evidence that C. was, in fact, negligent. If, as would hardly be likely to be the case, the question of C.'s negligence were to be raised again in litigation between A. and B., B. would be estopped from denying it because, as between parties to the proceedings in which they were obtained, judgments are conclusive so far as their grounds, as well as their terms, are concerned.

A. CONCLUSIVE EFFECT OF JUDGMENTS ON THE WHOLE WORLD—JUDGMENTS *IN REM*

A judgment is conclusive as against all persons of the existence of the state of things which it actually effects when the existence of that state is in issue or relevant to the issue.[1] Obvious examples are provided by an action for malicious prosecution in which the record of the Criminal Court would be conclusive of the acquittal of the plaintiff,[2] or an action by a surety against the principal debtor in which a judgment obtained against the surety by the creditor would be conclusive of the fact that it was obtained and the amount for which it was pronounced.[3] These examples may seem somewhat trivial, but the conclusiveness of a judgment with regard to the state of things which it actually effects is of great importance if it is *in rem*.

A judgment *in rem* is:

"A judgment of a court of competent jurisdiction determining the status of a person or thing, or the disposition of a thing (as distinct from a particular interest in it of a party to the litigation)". [4]

Allen v. *Dundas* [5] is a simple illustration of the effect of such a judgment so far as the whole world is concerned. The defendant was indebted to P., and,

---

[1] Stephen, *Digest of the Law of Evidence* (12th edition), art. 41. This article was adopted by Lord GODDARD, C.J., in *Hollington* v. *Hewthorn & Co., Ltd.*, [1943] K. B. 587, at p. 596; [1943] 2 All E. R. 35, at p. 39.　　[2] *Purcell* v. *Macnamara* (1807), 9 East 157.
[3] *Re Kitchin, Ex parte Young* (1881), 17 Ch. D. 668, at p. 673.
[4] *Halsbury's Laws of England* (Hailsham Edition), vol. 13, 405, adopted in *Lazarus-Barlow* v. *Regent Estates Co., Ltd.*, [1949] 2 K. B. 465, at p. 475; [1949] 2 All E. R. 118, at p. 122, by the Master of the Rolls who added "such a judgment is conclusive evidence for and against all persons whether parties, privies or strangers, of the matters actually decided". The courts have not developed the statement made in *Hill* v. *Clifford*, [1907] 2 Ch. 236, at p. 244, that there are two kinds of judgment *in rem*, one of which is conclusive against all the world, and the other of which is not. An instance of the latter was said to be an inquisition in lunacy "which has always been allowed to be read in a subsequent suit between third parties, as evidence of the lunacy, though it is not conclusive, and may be traversed."
[5] (1789), 3 Term Rep. 125.

on P.'s death, X. obtained probate of what purported to be P.'s will. The
defendant paid X. the amount of P.'s debt, and, when the grant of representation was set aside in favour of the plaintiff because the will was a
forgery, it was held that the defendant was not liable to pay the debt over
again to the plaintiff. Everyone was bound to give credit to the probate (a
judgment *in rem*) until it was vacated, which means that the plaintiff was
estopped from denying X.'s executorship at the material time. Other examples of judgments *in rem* are provided by the condemnation of a ship
by a Prize Court which precludes everyone from denying the non-neutral
nature of the cargo,[1] a determination that a street is a highway,[2] and a decree
of nullity or divorce.[3] A decree of jactitation of marriage, on the other hand,
on ly establishes that the petitioner is not married to the respondent so far
as it appears to the court which enjoins him to remain silent on the matter.
Accordingly, the judges advised the House of Lords on the prosecution of
the Duchess of Kingston in 1776 for bigamously marrying the Duke in the
lifetime of her husband, the Earl of Bristol, that the Crown was not estopped
from asserting the validity of her marriage to the Earl by a jactitation
decree she had obtained in the Ecclesiastical Court before going through
the impugned marriage ceremony.[4]

B. EFFECT OF JUDGMENTS ON PARTIES TO CIVIL CASES

Whether a judgment is *in rem* within the meaning of the above definition
or *in personam*—a term which can be taken to comprise all judgments that
are not *in rem*, its effect on the parties and those claiming through them
is much wider than its effect in litigation between strangers. This is because
the rule is that parties and their privies [5] are estopped from denying not
merely the state of affairs established by the judgment, that A. has been
adjudged liable to B. in the sum of a thousand pounds, for example, or
that C. is divorced, but also the grounds upon which that judgment was
based, that A. broke a contract with B., or that C. committed adultery.

(1) CAUSE OF ACTION ESTOPPEL

Estoppel by record *inter partes,* or "estoppel per *rem judicatam*" as it is
usually called, is of two kinds. The first, now generally coming to be known
as "cause of action estoppel", is dependent on the merger of the cause of
action in the judgment. Although its bearing on the substantive law is of
great importance, this kind of estoppel does not call for detailed consideration here. Once it appears that the same cause of action was held to lie or
not to lie in a final judgment between the same parties, or their privies,
litigating in the same capacity, there is an end of the matter. "If one party
brings an action against another for a particular cause and judgment is
given on it, there is a strict rule of law that he cannot bring another action
against the same party for the same cause." [6]

---

[1] *Geyer* v. *Aguilar* (1798), 7 Term Rep 681.
[2] *Wakefield Corporation* v. *Cooke*, [1904] A. C. 31.
[3] *Salvesen* v. *The Administrator of Austrian Property*, [1927] A. C. 641.
[4] 20 *Howell's State Trials*, 537.
[5] The expression is a rough equivalent for those claiming through the original party.
Privies are said to be either "in estate"—lessor and lessee or vendor and purchaser, for
instance, "in blood"—ancestor and heir; or "in law" testator and executor or intestate
and administrator, for instance.
[6] Per Lord DENNING, M.R. in *Fidelitas Shipping Co., Ltd.* v. *V/O. Exportchleb*, [1966]
1 Q. B. 630, at p. 640; [1965] 2 All E. R. 4, at p. 8.

There has been a tendency to extend the idea underlying cause of action estoppel to claims which, though not the subject of formal adjudication, could have been brought forward as part of the cause of action in the proceedings which resulted in the judgment alleged to constitute an estoppel. In the frequently quoted words of WIGRAM, V.C., "where a given matter becomes the subject of litigation in, and of adjudication by, a court of competent jurisdiction, the court requires the parties to that litigation to bring forward their whole case, and will not (except under special circumstances) permit the same parties to open the same subject of litigation in respect of matter which might have been brought forward as part of the subject in contest, but which was not brought forward, only because they have, from negligence, inadvertence, or even accident, omitted part of their case. The plea of *res judicata* applies, except in special cases, not only to points upon which the court was actually required by the parties to form an opinion and pronounce a judgment, but to every point which properly belonged to the subject of litigation, and which the parties, exercising reasonable diligence, might have brought forward at the time."[1]   Obviously it is desirable to protect defendants from plaintiffs who unnecessarily split up their claims against them; but a rigid application of the words of WIGRAM, V.C. could work great hardship on defendants who let judgment go against them by default, and the statement has been held to have no application to those judgments, the rules of cause of action estoppel being very narrowly applied in such cases.[2]

An illustration of the extension of cause of action extoppel mentioned by WIGRAM, V.C., is provided by *Public Trustee* v. *Kenward*.[3]   The defendant and his deceased wife had carried on a farming business in partnership. He was one of the executors of his wife's will and an account was taken in administration proceedings of his indebtedness to his wife's estate.   He made various counterclaims in respect of sums due to him, but he never raised the point that land forming part of the estate had been a partnership asset.   It was held that he was estopped from doing so when the Public Trustee claimed payment of the amount certified to be due from the defendant to the estate.   In such a case the failure to make the claim can reasonably be treated as an admission of its invalidity, but such an assumption will not always be justified and the explanation is inapplicable to cases in which the failure to make the claim was due to accident or inadvertence.

(2) ISSUE ESTOPPEL

The second kind of estoppel by record *inter partes* is often called "issue estoppel"; it may be regarded as an extension of the first for, to quote Lord DENNING, M.R., "within one cause of action, there may be several issues raised which are necessary for the determination of the whole case.

---

[1] *Henderson* v. *Henderson* (1843), 3 Hare 100, at p. 114; the references to exceptions are as significant for the law of today as they were for that of 1843.

[2] *New Brunswick Rail. Co.* v. *British and French Trust Corporation, Ltd.*, [1939] A. C. 1; [1938] 4 All E. R. 747; *Kok Hoong* v. *Leong Cheong Kweng Mines, Ltd.*, [1964] A. C. 993; [1964] 1 All E. R. 300; there is no estoppel by record where an action is dismissed for want of prosecution (*Pople* v. *Evans*, [1969] 2 Ch. 255; [1968] 2 All E. R. 743) or where proceedings are withdrawn (*Owens* v. *Minoprio*, [1942] 1 K. B. 193; [1942] 1 All E. R. 30), but there could be an estoppel by conduct in such a case.   For bastardy proceedings see *Robinson* v. *Williams*, [1965] 1 Q. B. 89; [1964] 3 All E. R. 12. Lord DEVLIN was critical of WIGRAM, V.C. in *Connelly* v. *Director of Public Prosecutions*, [1964] A. C. 1254 at pp. 1356 *et seq.*

[3] [1967] 2 All E. R. 870.

The rule then is that, once an issue has been raised and distinctly determined between the parties, then, as a general rule, neither party can be allowed to fight that issue all over again." [1] Although Lord DENNING went on to use words suggesting that the principle mentioned by WIGRAM, V.C. in connection with cause of action estoppel might apply to issue estoppel, it may be better to regard the latter as restricted to issues actually determined in the former litigation for there may be many reasons why a litigant did not raise a particular issue, and it would be unjust to prevent him from raising it in later litigation. [2]

Issue estoppel is a branch of the law which is only gradually being developed by the courts. Some uncertainty is therefore discernible in the leading judgments which often speak in terms of "general rules". An important statement is that of DIPLOCK, L.J., in *Mills* v. *Cooper*: [3]

> "A party to civil proceedings is not entitled to make, as against the other party, an assertion, whether of fact or of the legal consequences of facts, the correctness of which is an essential element in his cause of action or defence, if the same assertion was an essential element in his previous cause of action or defence in previous civil proceedings between the same parties or their predecessors in title, and was found by a court of competent jurisdiction in such previous civil proceedings to be incorrect, unless further material which is relevant to the correctness or incorrectness of the assertion by that party in the previous proceedings has since become available to him."

The reference to the availability of further material as something which will prevent the estoppel from arising suggests a significant distinction between issue estoppel and cause of action estoppel, for the fact that fresh material was available could have no bearing on the latter, at least in its direct, as distinct from its extended form.

The general conditions for the establishment of an issue estoppel are the same as those governing cause of action estoppel. There must be a final judgment between the same parties, or their privies, litigating in the same capacity on the same issue, and the estoppel must be pleaded.

(i) Finality.—Matrimonial causes apart, a decision of an inferior court will operate as an estoppel in the High Court, but the decision must be one from which there could have been an appeal. [4] The mere fact that there was no appeal does not prevent a judgment from being final. Questions of finality have been raised mainly in relation to foreign judgments and they are fully dealt with in books on the conflict of laws. [5]

(ii) Identity of parties.—In *Townsend* v. *Bishop*, [6] the plaintiff was

---

[1] *Fidelitas Shipping Co., Ltd.* v. *V/O. Exportchleb*, [1966] 1 Q. B. 630, at p. 640; [1965] 2 All E. R. 4 at p. 8; see also the judgment of DIPLOCK, L.J. in the same case and in *Thoday* v. *Thoday*, [1964] P. 181; [1964] 1 All E. R. 341. For earlier statements see *R.* v. *Inhabitants of Hartington Middle Quarter* (1855), 4 E. & B. 780; *Hoystead* v. *Taxation Commissioner*, [1926] A. C. 155, at p. 170; *Blair* v. *Curran* (1939), 62 C. L. R. 464, at p. 531.

[2] *Carl Zeiss Stiftung* v. *Rayner and Keeler, Ltd.* (No. 2), [1967] 1 A. C. 853, at p. 916 and p. 947; [1966] 2 All E. R. 536, at p. 555 and p. 573 per Lords REID and UPJOHN respectively. Lords REID and UPJOHN criticise the distinction taken by DIPLOCK, L.J. in *Thoday* v. *Thoday*, [1964] P. 181 at p. 198; [1964] 1 All E. R. 341, between issue estoppel and fact estoppel. Accordingly no reference is made to the latter in the text.

[3] [1967] 2 Q. B. 459, at p. 468.

[4] *Concha* v. *Concha* (1886), 11 App. Cas. 541.

[5] A foreign judgment can operate as a cause of action estoppel although there is no merger. There is difficulty in applying issue estoppel in the case of foreign judgments because it is not always easy to ascertain what was argued and decided.

[6] [1939] 1 All E. R. 805. Cf. *Kinnersley* v. *Orpe*, (1780), 2 Doug. K. B. 517 and the comment in *Outram* v. *Morewood* (1803), 3 East 346, at p. 366.

injured in a collision with the defendant's lorry when he was driving his father's car. The plaintiff's father sued for damages to the car, when the defendant's plea that it was caused by the contributory negligence of the plaintiff who was acting as his father's agent succeeded. It was held that the plaintiff was not estopped from denying his contributory negligence in an action in which he claimed damages for personal injuries. This was simply because the parties to the two actions were different.

If allowance is made for the notion of privity under which one party may be estopped because the person through whom he derives his right would be estopped, the question of identity of parties is not usually likely to cause trouble; but the unusual case of *Carl Zeiss Stiftung* v. *Rayner and Keeler, Ltd.* (No. 2),[1] shows that the requirements of identity and privity are narrowly construed by the English courts. In a previous action brought in the West German courts it had been held that the plaintiffs, a body known as the Council of Gera had no right to represent the Stiftung. The Stiftung then brought an action in the English courts by an English firm of solicitors, and it was held by a majority of the House of Lords that, although the solicitors were instructed by the Council of Gera, no estoppel precluded either the solicitors or the Stiftung from alleging that the action was duly authorised because the parties to the two proceedings were not identical and because there was no privity between the Council of Gera and the solicitors. Representation of a common principal does not lead of itself to privity.[2]

(iii) **Same capacity.**—In *Marginson* v. *Blackburn Borough Council*,[3] the defendant's omnibus was involved in a collision with the plaintiff's car which was being driven by his wife as his agent. She was killed, the plaintiff sustained personal injuries and some houses were damaged as well as the omnibus. The owners of the houses recovered damages in an action brought against Mr. Marginson and the Borough Council on the footing that each of them was vicariously liable for negligent driving. Both drivers were held to have been equally to blame, and the Council failed in a claim against Mr. Marginson for damages to the omnibus because Mrs. Marginson and the Council's driver were equally to blame. Mr. Marginson subsequently claimed damages for his own injuries and also sued as his wife's personal representative under the Law Reform (Miscellaneous Provisions) Act 1934 and the Fatal Accidents Acts. The Court of Appeal held that Mr. Marginson's personal claim failed because he was estopped from denying the contributory negligence of his wife by the finding that she and the Council's driver were equally to blame for the damage to the omnibus and, under the substantive law as it then stood, contributory negligence was a complete bar to recovery. On the other hand, it was held that Mr. Marginson was not estopped from denying his wife's contributory negligence in relation to his claims as her personal representative because he made those claims in a different capacity.

(iv) **Same issues.**—A strict construction of the requirement concerning identity of parties and their capacity can be justified on the ground that no

---

[1] [1967] 1 A. C. 853; [1966] 2 All E. R. 536.
[2] Lord WILBERFORCE, unlike the other members of the House, tended to think that the only ground on which it could be held that there was no estoppel was that the West German judgment was not final. From a realistic point of view he thought the parties were the same (the Council of Gera) and the issues raised in the causes of action were the same (passing off). There is American authority in favour of this more flexible approach.
[3] [1939] 2 K. B. 426; [1939] 1 All E. R. 273.

one ought to be wholly precluded from arguing a point by a decision taken in proceedings at which he was not represented. It is open to question whether the requirement with regard to identity of issues should be applied so strictly for it is undesirable that there should be conflicting decisions on what is in substance the same issue of fact even though there is a technical ground for treating it as different from that which was the subject of earlier litigation.

Some cases favour a narrow and some a broad approach to this question. In *Hoystead* v. *Commissioner of Income Tax* [1] the Privy Council held that a taxing authority was estopped from making an assessment for the year 1920–21 by a previous judgment relating to the assessment for the year 1918–19. In *Society of Medical Officers of Health* v. *Hope* (*Valuation Officer*),[2] on the other hand, the House of Lords held that a local valuation officer was not estopped from assessing the Society's premises for rates by a decision on a previous year's assessment that the Society was exempt. The question in these cases was basically whether one year's assessment raises a different issue from another year's assessment although the same legal point is involved, and special rules may be applicable to tax cases.

There is, however, an analogous conflict between broad and narrow views of issue estoppel in cases of negligence. *Marginson* v. *Blackburn Borough Council* [3] favours a broad approach because Mr. Marginson was held to have been estopped from denying that his wife's contributory negligence was, under the law as it then stood, the sole cause of his personal injuries because she had been held guilty of negligence on the claim by the Council for damages to its omnibus; yet there is a technical difference between the issues of negligence and contributory negligence.[4]

A broad view was also taken in *Bell* v. *Holmes* [5] and *Wood* v. *Luscombe*.[6] In the first of these cases, there had been a collision between a taxi driven by Bell and a car driven by Holmes. A passenger in Holmes's car successfully sued both drivers for negligence and obtained judgment against each of them. As between the two defendants, Bell was held liable for five-sixths of the passenger's damages, Holmes for one-sixth. Bell then sued Holmes for damages for personal injuries negligently inflicted in the same collision. It was held that he was estopped from alleging that he was other than five-sixths to blame for the collision; yet Holmes's duty to Bell's passenger and the extent of his responsibility for its breach were in law different issues from his duty to Bell and the extent of his responsibility for its breach.

The situation in *Wood* v. *Luscombe* was the converse of that in *Bell* v. *Holmes*. Motorcycles driven by Wood junior and Luscombe were in collision, and Wood senior, Wood junior's pillion passenger, sustained personal injuries. Luscombe sued Wood junior for personal injuries which he had sustained in the collision, and the parties were held equally to blame. Wood senior then sued Luscombe and recovered judgment against him.

---

[1] [1926] A. C. 155, not followed in *Mohamed Falil Abdul Caffoor* (*Trustees of the Abdul Caffoor Trust*) v. *Commissioner of Income Tax Columbo*, [1961] A. C. 584; [1961] 2 All E. R. 436.

[2] [1960] A. C. 551; [1960] 1 All E. R. 317. Lord KEITH OF AVONHOLME also held (at p. 569) that an estoppel could not bind the rating officer as he was carrying out a statutory duty; this could hardly prevent a cause of action estoppel from arising. On the whole question of estoppel against statutes see an article by J. A. Andrews in 29 M. L. R. 1 (1966).

[3] *Supra.* The cases down to 1957 are discussed in an article by Street, 73 L. Q. R. 358.

[4] This argument would be much stronger after *Nance* v. *British Columbia Electric Rail. Co.*, [1951] A. C. 601; [1951] 2 All E. R. 448.

[5] [1956] 3 All E. R. 449.   [6] [1966] 1 Q. B. 169; [1964] 3 All E. R. 972.

Luscombe had brought Wood junior in as a third party, and the question was to what extent Wood junior was liable to contribute to the sum which Luscombe had been adjudged liable to pay to Wood senior. It was held that he was estopped from denying that he was liable to contribute to the extent of fifty per cent; yet the duty owed by Wood junior to Luscombe and the extent, by which his responsibility for its breach was reduced by Luscombe's contributory negligence were in law different issues from their respective duties to Wood senior and the extent, as between themselves, of their responsibility for its breach.

A narrow view of issue estoppel was taken in *Randolph* v. *Tuck*.[1] The plaintiff was a passenger in a car driven by Tuck, the first defendant, and that car collided with a car driven by Steale, the third defendant, in the course of his employment with the second defendants. In an action brought by Tuck against Steale, Tuck was held solely to blame for the collision. Randolph was, however, held entitled to judgment against all three defendants and, on the claim for contribution by the second and third defendants, it was held that Tuck was not estopped from denying his sole responsibility for the damages due to the plaintiff. The decision proceeded primarily on the basis that Steale's breach of duty to Tuck and Tuck's contributory negligence which were in issue in the first action were, in law, different issues from that of the responsibility of the first and third defendants as between themselves for the damages sustained by the plaintiff.

Apart from *Marginson* v. *Blackburn Borough Council*, a decision of the Court of Appeal the authority of which is impaired by the fact that it preceded both the Law Reform Contributory Negligence Act, 1945, and the establishment of the principle that the basis of contributory negligence is the breach of the plaintiff's duty towards himself, all the English cases are decisions at first instance. As it is permissible to have regard to the pleadings, evidence and arguments in each action,[2] there is much to be said for the broad approach as it prevents the existence of conflicting judgments on what are substantially identical issues of fact. If the pleadings, evidence or points taken in argument in the second action are different from those of the first, the court hearing the second action would not, it seems, be bound to hold that there is an estoppel. The basis of the decisions in *Bell* v. *Holmes* and *Wood* v. *Luscombe* was that there was an estoppel because, though the issues were technically different, the issues of fact, and the evidence to support them, would be identically the same.

Both a broad and a narrow approach is also adopted by the Australasian cases on negligence.[3] Although it must be admitted that the narrow view greatly preponderates, the attractions of the broader view are made manifest by the South Australian case of *Black* v. *Mount and Hancock*.[4] Black and Hunt were passengers in a car driven by Hancock. That car collided with a

---

[1] [1962] 1 Q. B. 175; [1961] 1 All E. R. 814; *Johnson* v. *Cartledge and Matthews*, [1939] 3 All E. R. 654; *Association of Franciscan Order of Friars Minor* v. *City of Kew*, [1967] V. R. 732.

[2] The County Court Judges' notes were consulted in *Marginson's* case and *Randolph* v. *Tuck*. See also *Jenkins* v. *Tileman (Overseas), Ltd.*, [1967] N. Z. L. R. 484.

[3] *Jackson* v. *Goldsmith* (1950), 81 C. L. R. 446; *Edwards* v. *Joyce*, [1954] V. L. R. 216; *Clyne* v. *Yardley*, [1959] N. Z. L. R. 617; *Hood* v. *Commonwealth of Australia*, [1968] V. R. 619; *Ramsay* v. *Pigram* (1968), 42 A. L. J. R. 89; *Craddock's Transport, Ltd.* v. *Stuart*, [1970] N. Z. L. R. 499.

[4] [1965] S. A. S. R. 167.

car driven by Mount, and both Mount and Hancock were held liable to Hunt for personal injuries sustained by him in consequence of the collision. As between Hancock and Mount, Hancock was held 85 per cent to blame for Hunt's injuries, Mount 15 per cent. Black then sued both drivers and was held entitled to judgment against each. It was also held that Hancock was estopped, as against Mount, from denying that he was 85 per cent to blame for the injuries sustained by Black. No doubt the duties owed by the drivers to each of the passengers were in law distinct, but the passengers were sitting in the same seat of Hancock's car, and it is difficult to dispute the force of the following remark of CHAMBERLAIN, J. in support of his view that there was an estoppel: "The duties of care of each driver owed to the two passengers, the breach of those duties and the extent of their responsibility for the damage depended on precisely identical facts in each case."[1]

Even when the issues are identical, differences in the onus of proof may sometimes prevent an estoppel from arising. For this, if for no other reason, it would probably be held that an acquittal on a criminal charge of assault would not estop the prosecutor, at common law, from suing in tort on the same facts.[2] A plaintiff might, however, be estopped from denying facts relied on by the defence as justification if he were to sue the Crown for damages for an assault by a police officer if those facts had been the subject of a criminal conviction for some such offence as drunkenness or using insulting words on the occasion in question.[3] In such a case the heavier burden borne by the prosecutor on a criminal charge could not possibly operate adversely to the plaintiff.

(3) PLEADING

In *Voogt* v. *Winch*[4] it was held that the party alleging the existence of an estoppel by record must plead the former judgment and, if he fails to do so, it is merely an item of evidence in his favour which must be considered by the jury. If, notwithstanding the prior judgment or verdict, they are prepared to decide in favour of the opposite party, there is no reason why they should not do so, although they will no doubt be disposed to act as the tribunal did on the former occasion. The rules of pleading are, of course, less exacting than used to be the case, but it is still generally maintained that all estoppels must be specially pleaded.[5] The rule that,

---

[1] At p. 170.

[2] *Kosanovic* v. *Savapuu*, [1962] V. L. R. 321. There does not appear to be English authority directly in point. In practice the matter is liable to be affected by various provisions of the Offences Against the Person Act, 1861, on which see an article by P. M. North in 29 M. L. R. 16.

[3] *Cameron* v. *James*, [1945] V. L. R. 113; *Stimac* v. *Nichol*, [1942] V. L. R. 66. Again there does not appear to be English authority directly in point. If the civil proceedings are against an individual who was not the prosecutor on a summary criminal charge, or against the Crown after summary criminal proceedings, technical points might be taken with regard to the identity of the parties, because the parties to a summary prosecution are not the same as the parties to a prosecution on indictment. See *Clout* v. *Hutchinson* (1950), 51 S. R. (N.S.W.) 32 and *R.* v. *Tween*, [1965] V. R. 687. For a case distinguishing between the issues on a criminal complaint and civil claim alleging a deficiency in funds owing to a servant's default see *Beeches Working Men's Club and Institute Trustees* v. *Scott*, [1969] 2 All E. R. 420.

[4] (1819), 2 B. & Ald. 662. An estoppel may be pleaded in a second action although the writ was issued before judgment in the first (*Morrison Rose and Partners* v. *Hillman*, [1961] 2 Q. B. 266; [1961] 2 All E. R. 891).

[5] Odgers, *Principles of Pleading and Practice*, 20th Edn., 203.

when a judgment is not pleaded, it may, nevertheless, be treated as evidence of the facts upon which it was based in later proceedings between the same parties is hard to reconcile on principle with the common law rule that the judgment is not admissible as evidence of these facts in proceedings between third parties, or between one party to the earlier litigation and a stranger; but we shall see in Chapter XVI that there is good reason for regarding the latter rule as the questionable one.

C. MATRIMONIAL CAUSES [1]

There are numerous authorities on estoppel by record in matrimonial causes which are not easy to reconcile at first sight; but the apparent conflict can be largely, if not entirely, resolved if it is borne in mind that, whereas the ordinary principles of estoppel apply as between the parties, the divorce court is in a unique position on account of its special inquisitorial duty. It is true that several of the old cases must be read in the light of the Divorce Law Reform Act, 1969, which abolished the bars to divorce, but section 1 (3) of the Matrimonial Causes Act, 1973 (which now embodies the Act of 1969) provided, as did the corresponding section of the older statutes, that, on a petition for divorce, it shall be the duty of the court to inquire, so far as it reasonably can, into the facts alleged by the petition and into any facts alleged by the respondent. It is therefore still true to say that estoppels bind the parties to a matrimonial cause, but they frequently do not bind the court.

The statement that estoppels bind the parties means that:

> "once an issue of a matrimonial offence has been litigated between the parties and decided by a competent court, neither party can claim as of right to reopen the issue and litigate it all over again if the other party objects. . . . But the divorce court has the right, and indeed the duty in a proper case, to reopen the issue or to allow either party to reopen it, despite the objection of the other party (that is what is meant by saying that estoppels do not bind the divorce court)."[2]

Thus, in *Harriman* v. *Harriman*,[3] where a wife who had obtained a separation order from the magistrates on the ground of her husband's

---

[1] The following are among the principal cases on this subject. *Finney* v. *Finney* (1868), L. R. 1 P. & D. 483; *Conradi* v. *Conradi, Worrall and Way* (1868), L. R. 1 P. & D. 514; *Butler* v. *Butler*, [1894] P. 25; *Wilkins* v. *Wilkins*, [1896] P. 108, not followed in *Hayward* v. *Hayward*, [1961] P. 152; [1961] 1 All E. R. 236; *Harriman* v. *Harriman*, [1909] P. 123; *Stokes* v. *Stokes*, [1911] P. 195; *Pratt* v. *Pratt* (1927), 137 L. T. 491; *Woodland* v. *Woodland*, [1928] P. 169, not followed in *Hayward* v. *Hayward*, [1961] P. 152; [1961] 1 All E. R. 236; *Chalmers* v. *Chalmers*, [1930] P. 154; *Kara* v. *Kara and Holman*, [1948] P. 287; [1948] 2 All E. R. 16; *Hudson* v. *Hudson*, [1948] P. 292; [1948] 1 All E. R. 773; *James* v. *James*, [1948] 1 All E. R. 214; *Winnan* v. *Winnan*, [1949] P. 174; [1948] 2 All E. R. 862; *Sanders* v. *Sanders*, [1952] 2 All E. R. 767; *Richards* v. *Richards*, [1953] P. 36; [1952] 2 All E. R. 904; *Foster* v. *Foster*, [1954] P. 67; [1953] 2 All E. R. 518; *Bright* v. *Bright*, [1954] P. 270; [1953] 2 All E. R. 939; *Cooper* v. *Cooper*, [1955] P. 168; [1954] 3 All E. R. 358; *Thompson* v. *Thompson*, [1957] P. 19; [1957] 1 All E. R. 161; *Nokes* v. *Nokes*, [1957] 2 All E. R. 535; *Bernard* v. *Bernard*, [1958] 3 All E. R. 475; *Bullock* v. *Bullock*, [1960] 2 All E. R. 307; *Hull* v. *Hull*, [1960] P. 118; [1960] 1 All E. R. 378; *Hayward* v. *Hayward*, [1961] P. 152; [1961] 1 All E. R. 236; *Warren* v. *Warren*, [1962] 3 All E. R. 1031; *Laws* v. *Laws*, [1963] 3 All E. R. 398; *Thoday* v. *Thoday*, [1964] P. 181; [1964] 1 All E. R. 341; *Field* v. *Field*, [1964] P. 336; [1964] 2 All E. R. 81; *F.* v. *F.* [1968] 2 All E. R. 946; *Razelos* v. *Razelos* (No. 2), [1970] 3 All E. R. 386n.; *Porter* v. *Porter*, [1971] P. 282; [1971] 2 All E. R. 1037.

[2] *Per* DENNING, L.J., in *Thompson* v. *Thompson*, [1957] P. 19, at p. 29.

[3] [1909] P. 123.

desertion petitioned for divorce on the grounds of adultery and desertion at a time when it was necessary for her to establish both of these matrimonial offences, Cozens-Hardy and Fletcher-Moulton, L.JJ., each stressed the point that, though the husband might be estopped from denying the desertion, the court was not bound by the findings of the magistrates.[1] Fletcher-Moulton, L.J., put the following case:

> "The production of a decree for a judicial separation on the ground of cruelty is not as a matter of law sufficient to make it the judicial duty of the court to accept as a fact that the respondent has been guilty of such cruelty; and if the circumstances under which the decree was obtained are such as to raise a doubt in the mind of the court as to whether the cruelty was in fact committed, it would be entitled and bound to require such additional evidence as should be sufficient to convince it of the fact. But, although this is so, the respect paid to a judicial determination of a fact between parties (which in civil actions is evidenced by its creating a binding estoppel) would, I should presume, in ordinary cases lead the court to consider the fact of the cruelty to be adequately established by the production of the decree."

These views have, in effect, received statutory force, for s. 4 of the Matrimonial Causes Act, 1973,[2] provides that the jurisdiction of the court in divorce is not excluded by the fact that the petitioner has been granted a judicial separation, or a magistrates' separation or maintenance order, upon the same or substantially the same facts as are proved on a petition for divorce; and that the court may treat the decree or order as sufficient proof of the adultery, desertion or other ground upon which it was granted, but shall not pronounce a decree of divorce without receiving evidence from the petitioner. Even in cases to which the statute does not apply, it seems that, whereas a court of summary jurisdiction is bound by the previous findings of the divorce court[3] or another court of summary jurisdiction,[4] the divorce court is not bound by the previous findings of a court of summary jurisdiction,[5] although it seems that the divorce court is bound by findings of the same court,[6] subject to the provisions of the Act of 1973 which have just been mentioned.

One reason why the jurisdiction in divorce and nullity must be exercised with great circumspection is that it is concerned with status. In *Hayward* v. *Hayward*,[7] a husband and wife both suspected that their marriage was bigamous when it was celebrated because the husband's first wife was still alive. The husband subsequently admitted liability in maintenance proceedings, and the consequential finding that he had neglected to to maintain his wife would, in the ordinary case, have been sufficient to estop him from denying the validity of his marriage. It was nevertheless held that there was no estoppel affecting either party in nullity proceedings based on the bigamous nature of the marriage.

---

[1] At p. 132 and p. 142, respectively.

[2] Re-enacting earlier provisions. On the evidential significance of an order of a court of summary jurisdiction, see *Fromhold* v. *Fromhold*, [1952] 1 T. L. R. 1522; and *Turner* v. *Turner*, [1961] 3 All E. R. 944.

[3] *James* v. *James*, [1948] 1 All E. R. 214.   [4] *Stokes* v. *Stokes*, [1911] P. 195.

[5] *Winnan* v. *Winnan*, [1949] P. 174; [1948] 2 All E. R. 862.

[6] *Finney* v. *Finney* (1868), L. R. 1 P. & D. 483.

[7] [1961] P. 152; [1961] 1 All E. R. 236, preferring *Miles* v. *Chilton* (1849), 1 Rob. Eccl. 684 and *Andrews* v. *Ross* (1888), 14 P. D. 15 to *Wilkins* v. *Wilkins*, [1896] P. 108 (in so far as this case was based on estoppel) and *Woodland* v. *Woodland*, [1928] P. 169. It was also held that there was no estoppel by conduct, *Bullock* v. *Bullock*, [1960] 2 All E. R. 307 not being followed on this point. But on the point of estoppel by record, see *Marriage by Estoppel* by Tolstoy, 84 L. Q. R. 245.

D. CRIMINAL CASES [1]

(1) AUTREFOIS ACQUIT AND AUTREFOIS CONVICT

In a criminal case, the equivalent to a plea of cause of action estoppel is a plea of autrefois acquit or autrefois convict. The most usual tests for determining the validity of such pleas are whether the accused had been previously acquitted or convicted of the same offence, or of a substantially similar offence, or whether he could have been convicted at the first trial of the offence with which he is charged at the second. The formulation and application of these tests has produced a great deal of case-law which need not be considered here.[2]

Quite apart from the possibility of their founding pleas of autrefois convict or autrefois acquit, previous convictions and acquittals can lead to estoppels as between the Crown and the accused in subsequent criminal proceedings. When a previous conviction of the accused is put to him in cross-examination or proved against him, he cannot deny his guilt of the offence for which he was convicted.[3] So far as previous acquittals are concerned, a striking example of their operation as an estoppel is provided by *Sambasivam* v. *Malaya Federation Public Prosecutor*.[4] The appellant had been charged with two offences, carrying a firearm and being in possession of ammunition. He was acquitted of the second, but a new trial was ordered with regard to the first. At the second trial, the prosecution relied on a statement of the appellant in which he said that he was both carrying a firearm and in possession of amunition. He was convicted of carrying a firearm, but the Privy Council advised that his conviction should be quashed because the assessors had not been told that the prosecution had to accept that the part of the statement dealing with the ammunition was untrue. Lord MACDERMOTT said: [5]

> "The effect of a verdict of acquittal pronounced by a competent court on a lawful charge and after a lawful trial is not completely stated by saying that the person acquitted cannot be tried again for the same offence. To that it must be added that the verdict is binding and conclusive in all subsequent proceedings between the parties to the adjudication. The maxim *res judicata pro veritate accipitur* is no less applicable to criminal than to civil proceedings."

In *Connelly* v. *Director of Public Prosecutions*,[6] a majority of the House of Lords held that, even when a plea of autrefois acquit or autrefois convict is not available, the court has, in appropriate circumstances, a discretion to stay a second trial if it considers that it would be unfair to the accused to allow it to proceed; this too is a matter which does not call for detailed discussion here.

---

[1] Morris and Howard, *Studies in Criminal Law*, ch. VII.

[2] See the speech of Lord MORRIS OF BORTH-Y-GEST in *Connelly* v. *Director of Public Prosecutions*, [1964] A. C. 1254; [1964] 2 All E. R. 401, and the judgments of BRAY, C.J. and WELLS, J., in *R.* v. *O'Loughlin, Ex parte Ralphs*, [1971] 1 S. A. S. R. 219.

[3] The view of the effect of convictions as between the Crown and the accused taken in this book is challenged in an interesting article by D. Lanham in [1970] Crim. L. R. 428. Mr. Lanham's contention is that the conviction is no more than *prima facie* evidence of guilt. The view taken in this book is the logical consequence of the civil cases on the effect of judgments *inter partes*, but it must be admitted that is until *R.* v. *Hogan* (p. 299 *post*) it was no more supported by direct authority than Mr. Lanham's view although it is the view taken in para. 99 of the 11th Report of the Criminal Law Revision Committee.

[4] [1950] A. C. 458.

[5] At p. 479.

[6] [1964] A. C. 1254; [1964] 2 All E. R. 401. Cf. *R.* v. *Osborn* (1971), 15 D. L. R. (3d) 85.

(2) ISSUE ESTOPPEL

There is some difficulty in treating a criminal trial as something that can give rise to an issue estoppel. This is due to the fact that there are no real equivalents to pleadings, special verdicts, reasoned judgments and judges' notes from which it can be determined what incidental points were decided by the jury or magistrates. This difficulty may be illustrated by *R.* v. *Ollis* and *Connelly* v. *Director of Public Prosecutions*.

In *R.* v. *Ollis* [1] the accused had been charged and acquitted of obtaining a cheque by false pretences from one Ramsay. He was subsequently charged with obtaining cheques from others by similar false pretences, and Ramsay gave the same evidence at the second trial as that which he had given at the first. Ollis was convicted and his conviction was affirmed by a majority of the Court for Crown Cases Reserved. That court was unanimously of opinion that the acquittal had no bearing on the admissibility of Ramsay's evidence. The jury might have acquitted on the first charge on a variety of grounds. They might have concluded that the pretences were not made as alleged, or that the accused had no intent to defraud, or that the pretences did not cause the prosecutor to part with his property.

In *Connelly* v. *Director of Public Prosecutions,* [2] Connelly and others were charged and convicted of murder in the course of armed robbery. At the trial, Connelly relied primarily on an alibi, but his counsel also submitted that, even if Connelly did participate in the robbery, he was not guilty of murder because he did not know that one of his co-accused had a loaded gun. Connelly's conviction was quashed by the Court of Criminal Appeal because the jury had not been properly directed with regard to his alibi. He was then indicted for and convicted of the robbery, and his ultimate appeal to the House of Lords was unsuccessful. There was no way of establishing any separate issue in his favour, either by looking at the verdict of the jury or by looking at the judgment of the Court of Criminal Appeal which reversed that verdict.

A majority of the House of Lords in Connelly's case recognised the possibility of the application of issue estoppel in a criminal case. [3] It therefore seems that, if someone charged with murder in the course of robbery relies on alibi alone, and the summing-up virtually tells the jury to consider nothing but the alibi, an acquittal of the murder would entitle him, as of right, to be acquitted of the robbery at a later trial for that offence. [4] It would however, be rash to make predictions about the operation of issue estoppel in English criminal law because there are few, if any, authorities although the subject is covered fairly extensively by authority in other parts of the Commonwealth, especially Australia. [5]

In *G. (An infant)* v. *Coltart,* [6] G., a domestic servant, was convicted of stealing goods from Mrs. T., her mistress. Her defence was that she

---

[1] [1900] 2 Q. B. 758; see also *R.* v. *Norton* (1910), 5 Cr. App. Rep. 197.

[2] [1964] A. C. 1254; [1964] 2 All E. R. 401.

[3] Only Lord Devlin was against the introduction of issue estoppel into English criminal law.

[4] In most cases, the charges of murder and robbery would now be joined.

[5] *R.* v. *Wilkes* (1948), 77 C. L. R. 511; *R.* v. *Clift,* [1952] S. R. (N.S.W.) 213; *Mraz* v. *R.* (No. 2) (1956), 96 C. L. R. 62; *Brown* v. *Robinson,* [1960] S. R. (N.S.W.) 297; *R.* v. *Flood,* [1956] Tas. S. R. 95. See also *R.* v. *Wright,* [1965] 2 O. R. 337 commented on in 43 Canadian Bar Review 664 and *R.* v. *Carlson,* [1970] 3 O. R. 213.

[6] [1967] 1 Q. B. 432; [1967] 2 All E. R. 271.

intended to return the goods to Mrs. T. In order to rebut this, the prosecution had adduced evidence that G. had taken goods from Mrs. D., a guest of Mrs. T., and not returned them although told that Mrs. D. was going to South Africa. G. had, however, been acquitted of stealing from Mrs. D. at the instance of the prosecution on the mistaken assumption that the absence of Mrs. D. in South Africa was fatal to their case. It was held that the conviction of stealing from Mrs. T. must be quashed because it was not open to the prosecution to invite the court to make an inference that G. was guilty of an offence of which she had been acquitted. The case is not decisive as to the existence of issue estoppel in English criminal law because nothing was in fact decided as between G. and Mrs. D., and no separation of specific issues was necessary. Like *Sambasivam* v. *Malaya Federation Public Prosecutor*,[1] *Coltart's Case* simply decided that the prosecution may not, in case B, rely on evidence which is only relevant on the assumption that the accused was guilty of the offence charged in case A of which he was acquitted. These decisions can be regarded as extensions of *autrefois acquit* as much as instances of issue estoppel.[2] What is alleged to have been wrongly challenged in the second case is the innocence of the accused in the first, not the decision of a specific issue. The difficulty of isolating an issue in a criminal case was stressed by Lord Parker, C.J., in *Mills* v. *Cooper*[3] and by Eveleigh, J., in *R.* v. *Maskell*,[4] but, in these cases, there was no issue estoppel for want of identity of issues and parties respectively.

In *R.* v. *Hogan*,[5] Lawson, J., held both that issue estoppel applies in criminal proceedings and that reliance may be placed upon the doctrine by the prosecution. At his first trial, Hogan had unsuccessfully pleaded self defence to a charge of causing grievous bodily harm with intent contrary to section 18 of the Offences Against the Person Act, 1861. His victim then died, and Hogan was charged with murder. He was held to be estopped from denying that he caused grievous bodily harm to the deceased without lawful excuse, and with intent to do so. The result was that only such questions as whether the grievous bodily harm committed by Hogan had caused the deceased's death, and whether there had been provocation (a point that is irrelevant to liability under section 18), could be treated as live issues; Hogan was nonetheless acquitted.

SECTION 2. ESTOPPEL BY DEED

"A party who executes a deed is estopped in a court of law from saying that the facts stated in the deed are not truly stated."[6] Accordingly, if a deed contained a receipt for the purchase of property, the vendor was estopped in a common law action on the deed, from alleging that part of the money had not been paid, provided the estoppel was duly pleaded.[7] Further examples of the operation of the same doctrine of common law

---

[1] [1950] A. C. 458.
[2] *Per* Lord Devlin in *Connelly* v. *Director of Public Prosecutions*, [1964] A. C. 1280, at p. 1341.
[3] [1967] 2 Q. B. 459; [1967] 2 All E. R. 100.
[4] (1970), 54 Cr. App. Rep. 429 (see the suggestion at p. 432, that the matter may be better dealt with by a liberal exercise of the discretion to stay).
[5] [1974] 2 All E. R. 142.
[6] *Baker* v. *Dewey* (1823), 1 B. & C. 704, at p. 707, *per* Bayley, J.
[7] *Potts* v. *Nixon* (1870), I. R. 5 C. L. 45.

are provided by decisions on priorities according to which someone who executed a conveyance on the footing that he was seised of the legal estate was estopped from denying this fact,[1] and by a case put by Lord KENYON in *Hayne* v. *Maltby.* [2]

> "Where an heir apparent, having only the hope of succession, conveys during the life of his ancestor an estate, which afterwards descends upon him, although nothing passes at that time, yet when the inheritance descends upon him, he is estopped to say that he had no interest at the time of the grant."

In *Bowman* v. *Taylor*,[3] the principle was applied to recitals in a deed so that the defendant, a licensee of patent rights, was estopped from denying that the plaintiff was the inventor as he had executed a deed of licence which recited that this was the case. The governing principle was said to be the same as that which underlies estoppel by statements contained in the body of the deed: "If a party has by his deed directly asserted a specific fact, it is impossible to say that he shall not be precluded from disputing that fact."[4] It seems, however, that the basis of estoppel by recitals, if not of the entire doctrine of estoppel by deed was formulated in a more satisfactory way in the later case of *Stroughill* v. *Buck*.[5] It was said that:

> "When a recital is intended to be a statement which all the parties to the deed have mutually agreed to admit as true, it is an estoppel upon all. But, when it is intended to be the statement of one party only, the estoppel is confined to that party, and the intention is to be gathered from construing the instrument."[6]

This was treated as the ground upon which *Bowman* v. *Taylor* ought to have been decided in *Greer* v. *Kettle* [7] where Lord MAUGHAM said:

> "Estoppel by deed is a rule of evidence founded on the principle that a solemn and unambiguous statement or engagement in a deed must be taken as binding between the parties and privies and therefore as not admitting any contradictory proof."[8]

Whatever may be the true modern basis of the doctrine of estoppel by deed, its scope is extremely limited under the present law.[9] In the first place, it only applies between parties to the deed and those claiming through them.[10] Secondly, it only applies in actions on the deed. In *Carpenter* v. *Buller*,[11] for instance, the defence to an action of trespass was that the defendant was seised of the land in question and he produced a deed, made between himself, the plaintiff and a third party, in which this was stated to be the case; but it was held that the plaintiff was not estopped from denying the defendant's seisin because the action was not brought on the deed which did not directly concern the land. Thirdly, the doctrine only applies to clear and unambiguous statements,[12] and finally it does not

---

[1] *Doe* d. *Levy* v. *Horne* (1842), 3 Q. B. 757.

[2] (1789), 3 Term Rep. 438, at p. 441; *Church of England Building Society* v. *Piskor*, [1954] Ch. 553; [1954] 2 All E. R. 85.

[3] (1834), 4 L. J. K. B. 58.   [4] Lord DENMAN, C.J.

[5] (1850), 14 Q. B. 781.   [6] PATTESON, J.

[7] [1938] A. C. 156; [1937] 4 All E. R. 396.   [8] At pp. 171 and 404, respectively.

[9] Formerly the deed might have been an instrument of proof. There can be no estoppel by deed against a party claiming rectification (*Wilson* v. *Wilson*, [1969] 3 All E. R. 945).

[10] It is uncertain whether there can be an estoppel by deed poll, see *Cropper* v. *Smith* (1884), 26 Ch. D. 700.

[11] (1841), 8 M. & W. 209. See also *Re Simpson, Ex parte Morgan* (1876), 2 Ch. D. 72.

[12] *Onward Building Society* v. *Smithson*, [1893] 1 Ch. 1; *District Bank* v. *Webb*, [1958] 1 All E. R. 126.

prevent a party from setting up a plea of illegality or fraud or from availing himself of any fact which would have given rise to a right to rescind the deed in equity. This last limitation is of great importance, for it means that matters, such as the receipt for the purchase price of property in the body of the deed, which would formerly have supported a plea of estoppel at common law will now, generally speaking, be of little avail.

If the modern basis of the doctrine is agreement, there is not much point in preserving a separate head of estoppel by deed, for estoppel by agreement can easily be brought under the rubric of estoppel by conduct.

SECTION 3. ESTOPPEL BY CONDUCT [1]

A. HISTORICAL

Although ideas of the sort had previously existed in equity, it was not until *Pickard* v. *Sears* [2] that the doctrine of estoppel by conduct was clearly stated in a common law court. Then it was said that:

> "Where one by his words or conduct wilfully causes another to believe in the existence of a certain state of things, and induces him to act on that belief, or to alter his own previous position, the former is concluded from averring against the latter a different state of things as existing at that time."

In *Freeman* v. *Cooke*,[3] the word "wilfully" in the above passage was treated as equivalent to "with the intention that the belief which is induced should be acted upon", and it was accordingly held that the assignee of a bankrupt was not estopped from proving the latter's ownership of goods sold by the sheriff, although the bankrupt had said that the goods belonged to his brother under the mistaken impression that the sheriff was about to levy execution against his property and not that of his brother. There was clearly no intention to induce the sheriff to seize the goods as the brother's property, and the bankrupt had prevaricated to such an extent that no reasonable man would have given credence to any of his statements. When delivering judgment in *Freeman* v. *Cooke*, PARKE, B., nonetheless added that:

> "If, whatever a man's real intention may be, he so conducts himself that a reasonable man would take the representation to be true, and believe that it was meant that he should act upon it, and did act upon it as true, the party making the representation would be equally precluded from contesting its truth; and conduct, by negligence or omission, when there is a duty cast upon a person, by usage of trade or otherwise, to disclose the truth, may often have the same effect. As, for instance, a retiring partner omitting to inform the customers of the fact, in the usual mode, that the continuing partners were no longer authorised to act as his agents, is bound by all contracts made by them with third persons on the faith of their being so authorised." [4]

These observations embody the main principles underlying estoppel by conduct,[5] and the subject may be considered in outline under the heads

---

[1] Ewart, *Estoppel*; Pickering, *Estoppel By Conduct*, 55 L. Q. R. 400 (1939); Spencer-Bower, *Estoppel by Representation* (2nd ed. by Sir Alexander Turner).

[2] (1837), 6 Ad. & El. 469.   [3] (1848), 2 Exch. 654.

[4] See now Partnership Act, 1890, s. 14 (1). Further statutory provisions stating the common law of estoppel by conduct are s. 54–55 of the Bills of Exchange Act, 1882.

[5] A good modern statement of the principles underlying this branch of the law is that of DIXON, J., as he then was, in *Grundt* v. *Great Boulder Proprietary Gold Mine, Ltd.* (1937), 59 C. L. R. 641, at p. 674: "The principle on which estoppel in *pais* is founded is that the law should not permit an unjust departure by a party from an assumption of fact which he has caused another party to adopt or accept for the purpose of their legal rela-

of estoppel by agreement, estoppel by representation and estoppel by negligence (an expression which has not escaped criticism)[1] although it must not be supposed that these divisions of the subject are mutually exclusive. When this has been done, some reference will be made to the limitations of estoppel by conduct.

B. ESTOPPEL BY AGREEMENT

It not infrequently happens that two people agree, expressly, or by necessary implication, that their legal relations shall be based on the assumption that a certain state of facts exists, and, when this has been done, the original parties to the agreement, as well as those claiming through them,[2] are sometimes said to be estopped from denying the existence of the assumed state of facts. The agreement may take the form of a contract supported by consideration, as where a party to an arbitration agreement who nominates an arbitrator is estopped from disputing the qualifications of his nominee by an implied term in the agreement,[3] and as we have seen an agreement may be inferred from the terms of a deed, but neither consideration nor a seal is essential to its efficacy as an estoppel. Acquiescence in a particular construction of a document may likewise lead to an estoppel by agreement,[4] and this is the basis of the rules that, generally speaking, a tenant is estopped from denying his landlord's title[5] (but only during the currency of the lease[6]), a bailee that of his bailor,[7] and a licensee that of his licensor.[8]

C. ESTOPPEL BY REPRESENTATION

The classic statement of the principle governing estoppel by representation is that of Spencer-Bower:[9]

"Where one person (the representor) has made a representation to another person (the representee) in words or by acts or conduct, or (being under a

---

tions." "He may be required to abide by the assumption because it formed the conventional basis upon which the parties entered into contractual or mutual relations such as bailment, or because he has exercised against the other party rights which would only exist if the assumption were correct, as in *Yorkshire Insurance Co.* v. *Craine*, [1922] 2 A. C. 541, or because knowing the mistake the other laboured under, he refrained from correcting him when it was his duty to do so; or because his imprudence where care was required of him was the proximate cause of the other party's adopting and acting upon the faith of the assumption; or because he directly made representations upon which the other founded the assumption. But, in each case, he is not bound to adhere to the assumption unless, as the result of adopting it as the basis of action or inaction, the other party will have placed himself in a position of material disadvantage if departure from the presumption be permitted." (*Per* DIXON, J., in *Thompson* v. *Palmer* (1933), 49 C. L. R. 500, at p. 547.) Estoppel by conduct used to be called estoppel in *pais* because it depended on facts to be found by a jury (the country) and not on matter of record or deed.

[1] Spencer-Bower, *Estoppel by Representation* (2nd edition), 69, and, in the context of *non est factum*, Lord PEARSON in *Saunders* v. *Anglia Building Society* (on appeal from *Gallie* v. *Lee*), [1971] A. C. 1004, at p. 1038; but see the article by Professor Julius Stone 88 L. Q. R. 190.

[2] *Taylor* v. *Needham* (1810), 2 Taunt. 278.

[3] *Oakland Metal Co., Ltd.* v. *Benaim (D.) & Co., Ltd.*, [1953] 2 Q. B. 261; [1953] 2 All E. R. 650.

[4] *Re Lart, Wilkinson* v. *Blades*, [1896] 2 Ch. 788.

[5] *Cooke* v. *Loxley* (1792), 5 Term Rep. 4; *Terunnanse* v. *Terunnanse*, [1968] A. C. 1086; [1968] 1 All E. R. 651.

[6] *Harrison* v. *Wells* [1967] 1 Q. B. 263; [1966] 3 All E. R. 524.

[7] *Gosling* v. *Birnie* (1831), 7 Bing. 339.

[8] *Crossley* v. *Dixon* (1863), 10 H. L. Cas. 293.

[9] *Estoppel by Representation* (2nd edition), 4–5, adopted by Sir Raymond EVERSHED, M.R., in *Hopgood* v. *Brown*, [1955] 1 All E. R. 550, at p. 559.

duty to the representee to speak or act) by silence or inaction, with the intention (actual or presumptive), and with the result,[1] of inducing the representee on the faith of such representation to alter his position to his detriment, the representor, in any litigation which may afterwards take place between him and the representee is estopped, as against the representee, from making, or attempting to establish by evidence, any averment substantially at variance with his former representation, if the representee, at the proper time, and in the proper manner, objects thereto."

The reference to presumptive intention is necessary because:

"If a man, whatever his real meaning may be, so conducts himself that a reasonable man would take his conduct to mean a certain representation of facts, and that it was a true representation, and that the latter was intended to act upon it in a particular way, and he with such belief does act in that way to his damage, the first is estopped from denying that the facts were as represented". [2]

There can, for instance, be little doubt that, if, on facts such as those of *Freeman* v. *Cooke*, the debtor had contented himself with one positive assertion to the effect that the goods were his brother's, his assignee would have been estopped from claiming them.[3] On the other hand, in *Carr* v. *London and North Western Rail. Co.*,[4] the defendant's agent told the plaintiff that the company held three consignments of goods to his order when only two had been received. The plaintiff purported to sell three consignments, and had to pay damages to the purchaser of one of them; but it was held that he could not recover these from the defendant. If an estoppel did operate against the company, it would have been liable in conversion through its servant's refusal to deliver the plaintiff's goods to his order but there was no estoppel because there was no evidence that the defendant's agent realised that the goods would be sold by the plaintiff. It was also held that there was no negligence, and that, if there was, it was not the immediate cause of the subsale; but it is not clear whether the court was using the word "negligence" in the sense of carelessness in the abstract, or that of a careless breach of duty towards a specific person.

A case in which the representation was by acts or conduct rather than words was one in which an employee was held to be estopped from denying his employment by the fact that he had given notice terminating it.[5]

A case in which there was a duty to speak or act within the meaning of Spencer Bower's statement was *Greenwood* v. *Martins Bank*[6] in which a husband's failure to disclose the fact that his wife had been forging his cheques was held to estop him from alleging this to be the case in an action to recover the amounts paid to his wife and debited to his account by his bank. Similarly, in *Oades* v. *Spafford*,[7] a landlord agreed to sell property on the footing that the tenant would be liable for dilapidations, and it was held that his failure to disclose a release from this liability estopped him from denying its existence. Cases of the same species are those in which a person acquiesces in the erection of buildings on his land with the

---

[1] *The Skarp*, [1935] P. 134; *Cremer* v. *General Carriers S.A.*, [1974] 1 All E. R. 1.
[2] *Carr* v. *London and North Western Rail. Co.* (1875), L. R. 10 C. P. 307, at p. 317, *per* BRETT, J.
[3] See *Westen* v. *Fairbridge*, [1923] 1 K. B. 667.   [4] (1875), L. R. 10 C. P. 307.
[5] *Smith* v. *Blandford Gee Cementation Co., Ltd.*, [1970] 3 All E. R. 154.
[6] [1933] A. C. 51, distinguished in *West Country Cleaners (Falmouth) Ltd.* v. *Saly*, [1966] 3 All E. R. 210.
[7] [1948] 2 K. B. 74; [1948] 1 All E. R. 607.

knowledge that the builder supposes that the land is his, for, in such circumstances, the landowner will be estopped from denying this fact.[1]

D. ESTOPPEL BY NEGLIGENCE

In all the examples of estoppel by conduct that have been given so far, the party in whose favour the estoppel operated was either the person with whom an agreement was concluded or someone claiming through him, or else he was the person to whom a representation was made by the party estopped, or someone claiming through such person. There is, however, a type of estoppel, often called estoppel by negligence, in which the party in whose favour it operates is the victim of the fraud of some third person facilitated by the careless breach of duty of the other party. An example is provided by *Coventry Shepherd & Co.* v. *Great Eastern Rail. Co.*[2] In that case the defendants carelessly issued two delivery orders relating to the same consignment of goods, thus enabling the person to whom they were issued to obtain an advance from the plaintiff, and the defendants were held to be estopped as against him from denying the fact that the goods mentioned in the order were held on behalf of the assignor. Someone who puts documents of this nature into circulation owes a duty to those into whose hands they may come, and it is the fact that the documents were the creation of the defendants which distinguishes this case in the letter, if not in the spirit, from *Mercantile Bank of India, Ltd.* v. *Central Bank of India, Ltd.*[3] Railway receipts relating to a quantity of goods were pledged with the Central Bank as security for an advance when they were returned to their owners to enable them to get possession of the goods. The receipts were then delivered to the Mercantile Bank as security for a further advance, and it was held that the Central Bank was not estopped from asserting the priority of its claim to the goods. One ground of the decision was that the conduct of the first bank was not the legal cause of the detriment sustained by the second, for there was a well-known local practice under which receipts were returned by pledgees to their owners to enable them to get possession of their goods, but the decision was also based on the ground that the first bank owed no duty to the second when returning the receipts to their owners. The first bank did not bring the documents into existence, but it is open to question whether this warrants an opposite conclusion from that which was reached in the *Coventry-Shepherd Case.* Where there is no contractual duty of care, breach of which gives rise to an estoppel,[4] it is difficult to extract a safe guiding principle from the authorities on estoppel by negligence.[5]

---

[1] *Ramsden* v. *Dyson* (1866), L. R. 1 H. L. 129; *A.-G. to Prince of Wales* v. *Collom*, [1916] 2 K. B. 193.

[2] (1883), 11 Q. B. D. 776.

[3] [1938] A. C. 287; [1938] 1 All E. R. 52.

[4] *London Joint Stock Bank* v. *Macmillan and Arthur*, [1918] A. C. 777; contrast *Scholfield* v. *Lord Londesborough*, [1896] A. C. 514.

[5] Compare the protection given to the innocent purchaser of shares by *Colonial Bank* v. *Cady and Williams* (1890), 15 App. Cas. 267 and *Fuller* v. *Glyn, Mills, Currie & Co.*, [1914] 2 K. B. 168, with the lack of protection accorded by the common law doctrine of estoppel to the innocent purchaser of goods in cases which are not covered by the Factors Act, 1889 (see, for example, *Farquharson Brothers & Co.* v. *King & Co.*, [1902] A. C. 325; *Central Newbury Car Auctions* v. *Unity Finance, Ltd.*, [1957] 1 Q. B. 37; [1956] 3 All E. R. 905 and *Newtons of Wembley, Ltd.* v. *Williams*, [1965] 1 Q. B. 560; [1964] 3 All E. R. 532). Note also the difficulty of reconciling *Mercantile Bank of India, Ltd.* v. *Central Bank of India, Ltd.*, [1938] A. C. 287; [1938] 1 All E. R. 52 with *Lloyds Bank* v.

It is possible that when the cases and underlying principles come to be authoritatively reviewed it will be found that the requirements of duty of care and proof of carelessness can be dispensed with. All that is necessary, it may be urged, is proof of intentional words, acts or conduct, which can reasonably be construed as a representation by the representor to the representee who need not be in direct relationship. To take a hypothetical case mentioned by Lord PEARSON,[1] a busy managing director signs "blind" a pile of documents handed to him by his secretary, disregarding the chance that an extraneous document may have been inserted. For such a man, such conduct may not amount to carelessness, yet he intends to sign whatever documents happen to be in the pile. It is difficult to escape the conclusion that he would be estopped from denying his liability on the fraudulently inserted document to anyone who reasonably took it to be his and acted upon it with detrimental consequences. Yet, *ex hypothesi*, he would not have been careless, and he could only be said to owe a duty to the person acting on his signature on the basis that anyone who intentionally signs documents, taking a chance on what they are, owes a duty to anyone into whose hands the documents may come. Lord PEARSON's example was, however, mentioned in a case concerned with the very special plea of *non est factum* which, very exceptionally, enables signatories of documents to escape liability, and it cannot be denied that quite a number of the older decisions on estoppel by conduct turn on the requirement of a specific duty of care.

E. LIMITS ON ESTOPPEL BY CONDUCT

There are a few well-defined rules which limit the operation of the doctrine of estoppel by conduct and it is convenient to collect them together at the end of our treatment of the entire topic.

(1) MUST RELATE TO EXISTING FACT

The first universal requirement is that the estoppel must concern an existing state of facts. This is fundamental to all the common law cases, and *Jorden* v. *Money* [2] conclusively established that there could be no common law estoppel founded on a statement of future intention.

(2) MUST BE UNAMBIGUOUS

The second requirement of an estoppel by conduct is that it should be unambiguous. One reason why there was no estoppel in *Freeman* v. *Cooke* was that the allegations of the debtor lacked this characteristic, and a more modern illustration is provided by *Canadian and Dominion Sugar Co., Ltd.* v. *Canadian National (West Indies) Steamships, Ltd.*,[3] in which a receipt

---

Bank of America, National Trust and Savings Assn., [1938] 2 K. B. 147; [1938] 2 All E. R. 63. See further *Eastern Distributors, Ltd.* v. *Goldring*, [1957] 2 Q. B. 600; [1957] 2 All E. R. 525; *Campbell Discount Co., Ltd.* v. *Gall*, [1961] 1 Q. B. 431; [1961] 2 All E. R. 104; *Muskham Finance, Ltd.* v. *Howard*, [1963] 1 Q. B. 904; [1963] 1 All E. R. 81; *Mercantile Credit Co., Ltd.* v. *Hamblin*, [1965] 2 Q. B. 242; [1964] 3 All E. R. 592.

[1] *Saunders* v. *Anglia Building Society*, [1971] A. C. 1004, at p. 1038.

[2] (1854), 5 H. L. Cas. 185. Although, to raise an estoppel, the statement must concern existing fact, the distinction between law and fact is no easier to draw in this context than others (see *De Tchihatchef* v. *Salerni Coupling, Ltd.*, [1932] 1 Ch. 330). Promissory estoppel is outside the scope of this book.

[3] [1947] A. C. 46; *Woodhouse A. C. Israel Cocoa, Ltd., S.A.* v. *Nigerian Produce Marketing Co., Ltd.*, [1972] A. C. 741; [1971] 1 All E. R. 665.

stating that cargo was in good order was held not to estop a purchaser from denying this fact because it referred to an ambiguous bill of lading.

(3) RESULT MUST BE LEGAL

Finally, an estoppel cannot be relied on if the result of giving effect to it would be something that is prohibited by the law. Accordingly, when a statutory undertaking mistakenly charged less for electricity than the amount specified in the relevant enactment, it was held that no estoppel covered the case although the recipients of the electricity had acted to their detriment.[1] Lord MAUGHAM's opinion was that "this conclusion must follow from the circumstances that an estoppel is only a rule of evidence which, in certain special circumstances, can be invoked by a party to an action".[2]

SECTION 4. THE PLACE OF ESTOPPEL IN THE LAW

These words raise the general question of the rubric under which estoppel should be treated in an exposition of the whole of the law. The majority of the judges appear to have shared Lord MAUGHAM's view that it is a rule of evidence, and the classic statement to this effect is that of BOWEN, L.J., who said:

> "Estoppel is only a rule of evidence; you cannot found an action upon estoppel. Estoppel is only important as being one step in the progress towards relief on the hypothesis that the defendant is estopped from denying the truth of something which he has said." [3]

On the other hand, Lord WRIGHT said, "Estoppel is often described as a rule of evidence as indeed it may be so described. But the whole concept is more accurately viewed as a substantive rule of law",[4] and a dictum of the same judge in an earlier case shows that he was of this opinion because estoppel "may have the effect of creating substantive rights as against the person estopped".[5] If a rule of substantive law is one which defines rights, something may have the effect of creating them against a particular party without itself being such a rule. Accordingly it will be convenient to consider estoppel as a rule of substantive law, as having the same effect as a rule of substantive law, as a rule of evidence, and, for the sake of completeness, as a rule of pleading, for this is how it may have been regarded by Sir James Stephen.[6]

---

[1] *Maritime Electric Co., Ltd.* v. *General Dairies, Ltd.*, [1937] A. C. 610; [1937] 1 All E. R. 748; *Roma Electric Light and Power Co., Ltd.* v. *Hair*, [1955] S. R. Q. 311.
[2] At pp. 620 and 753 respectively. See also *Re Companies' Acts, Ex parte Watson* (1888), 21 Q. B. D. 301; *Minister of Agriculture and Fisheries* v. *Matthews*, [1950] 1 K. B. 148; [1949] 2 All E. R. 724; *Southend-on-Sea Corporation* v. *Hodgson (Wickford), Ltd.*, [1962] 1 Q. B. 416; [1961] 2 All E. R. 46; *Hayward* v. *Hayward*, [1961] P. 152; [1961] 1 All E. R. 236; not following *Bullock* v. *Bullock*, [1960] 2 All E. R. 307. On the whole subject see an article by J. A. Andrews, 29 M. L. R. 1.
[3] *Low* v. *Bouverie*, [1891] 3 Ch. 82, at p. 105.
[4] *Canadian and Dominion Sugar Co., Ltd.* v. *Canadian National (West Indies) Steamships, Ltd.*, [1947] A. C. 46, at p. 56.
[5] *Mercantile Bank of India, Ltd.* v. *Central Bank of India, Ltd.*, [1938] A. C. 287, at p. 297; [1938] 1 All E. R. 52, at p. 57.
[6] *Digest of the Law of Evidence* (12th edition), 200, where, however, he was concerned with estoppel by record. He regarded estoppel in *pais* as a rule of evidence (*ibid.*, 217).

A. ESTOPPEL AS A RULE OF SUBSTANTIVE LAW

If promissory estoppel associated with the decision in *Central London Property Trust, Ltd.* v. *High Trees House, Ltd.*[1] is rightly so-called, estoppel must be treated as a rule of substantive law in at least one of its aspects. Provided the court comes to the conclusion that a promise was made with the requisite intention and acted upon, it will be treated as binding for certain purposes notwithstanding the absence of consideration. There is no question of the law preventing certain facts from being proved, and the rules of evidence do not enter into the matter at all.

B. ESTOPPEL AS HAVING THE EFFECT OF A RULE OF SUBSTANTIVE LAW

These rules sometimes have the same effect as rules of substantive law. To take an example which has nothing to do with estoppel, the prohibition on the disclosure of certain affairs of state in the course of litigation is one of the exclusionary rules of evidence discussed in Chapter XII, and it may have the effect of preventing one of the facts in issue from being proved as when a colonial governor claims damages for a libel in a newspaper article alleging that his reports to the colonial secretary were garbled. No evidence can be given of the contents of the reports,[2] so the proprietor of the newspaper cannot successfully plead justification. The practical effect could be stated by saying that, under the substantive law, justification cannot be pleaded as a defence to an action for libel founded on statements concerning the reports of colonial governors, but this would not alter the fact that the proposition, though formally concerned with substantive law, really expresses the consequences of a rule of evidence. An estoppel relating to a fact in issue may likewise be stated in terms of a rule of substantive law. It could be said that, when a wharfinger acknowledges that he holds goods on behalf of a particular person, title is conferred on that person for the purposes of an action of conversion,[3] but this would not alter the fact that the statement concerns the effect of a rule of evidence. Whenever a party is estopped from denying a fact in issue, estoppel may be said to have the effect of a rule of substantive law.

C. ESTOPPEL AS A RULE OF EVIDENCE

Its true character as a rule of evidence at once becomes apparent when it concerns a relevant fact. Suppose a man was claiming damages for libel against his former wife who had divorced him for adultery and alleged that he was grossly immoral. He would be estopped from denying any acts of adultery upon which the divorce decree might be founded, but this would simply mean that an exclusionary rule of evidence prevented him from establishing one relevant fact—his innocence of adultery; anything else that tended to disprove the defendant's allegations would be admissible.

D. ESTOPPEL AS A RULE OF PLEADING

The law of estoppel is something which must be borne in mind by the pleader, for failure to plead an estoppel may prevent a party from raising

---

[1] [1947] K. B. 130; [1956] 1 All E. R. 256, n.
[2] *Hennessy* v. *Wright* (1888), 21 Q. B. D. 509.
[3] Cf. *Gosling* v. *Birnie* (1831), 7 Bing. 339.

it at the trial, and the terms of the pleadings in a given case may affect the extent to which the judge's findings constitute an estoppel by record; but these considerations do not justify the treatment of estoppel as itself a rule of pleading any more than the Limitation Acts, can be said to be concerned with this subject because they have to be specially pleaded.

E. CONCLUSIONS

The conclusion would appear to be that estoppel is, in strict theory, an exclusionary rule of evidence for the most part, but it has the effect of a rule of substantive law with such frequency that it is practically convenient to treat of it in detail when the different branches of the substantive law are under consideration. For similar reasons, parts of the subject are best dealt with in connection with the law of pleading and procedure.

CHAPTER XIV

EVIDENCE OF DISPOSITION AND CHARACTER

Throughout this chapter the term "disposition" is employed to denote a tendency to act, think or feel in a particular way. There are four obvious methods by which it might be proved in a court of law. In the first place, evidence of conduct on as great a variety of occasions as possible might be adduced, for it is to be assumed that someone who frequently acts in a given manner has a disposition to do so. Secondly, previous convictions tend to establish disposition, provided they can be treated as conclusive or at least received as evidence of the facts upon which they were founded.[1] Thirdly, a witness could be asked for his estimation of the disposition of one of the parties and finally evidence might be given of that party's reputation—the general opinion of his disposition prevailing among those who know him best. When this last method is adopted, the evidence is often spoken of as "evidence of character", although the word "character" is frequently used to mean disposition and not reputation. In an ideal world the distinction would be unimportant, but, as things are, it is not unknown for persons of evil disposition to have a good reputation and *vice versa*.

The chapter is primarily concerned with proof of disposition, convictions and reputation as relevant facts. No special rules apply to cases in which they are among the facts in issue, as all three matters would be if justification were pleaded in an action for libel based on allegations that the plaintiff was a man of fraudulent propensity, a convicted criminal and reputed thief.

The reception of evidence of disposition as a fact relevant to the issue is attended by several dangers. When it is proved by reference to a person's conduct on other occasions than that into which the court is inquiring, numerous collateral issues are liable to be raised and the opposite party can sometimes legitimately complain that he has been taken by surprise by the adduction of evidence which he might have been able to counter, had he but known that it was going to be given. The risk of prejudice is even more important than either of these matters, for an inference may all too readily be drawn from the fact that someone has a particular disposition to the fact that he acted in accordance with it. This is most likely to occur when the disposition in question is a bad one. Accordingly there is a rule, discussed in section 1, under which evidence of the improper conduct of a party on occasions other than that into which the court is inquiring must be excluded if it is only relevant as pointing to the conclusion that such party had a particular disposition and thence directly to the finding that he acted in accordance with it, unless his disposition is highly relevant to an issue raised at the trial.[2] The improper conduct may, however, be relevant for a variety of other reasons. A man is indicted for stealing one part of a pound

---

[1] See n. 3, p. 297, *ante.*
[2] See Hoffman, *South African Law of Evidence* (2nd edition), 34. I wish to express my indebtedness to this author's treatment of similar fact evidence.

note which had previously been torn into several pieces. Proof that he stole the other parts would tend to show that he is a dishonest person who might well commit further thefts, but it would also provide a more specific and infinitely more powerful reason for finding him guilty of the offence charged as the possessor of parts of a pound note has a stronger motive for acquiring the rest of it than anyone else in the world. Subject to the discretionary powers of exclusion vested in the judge in criminal proceedings, evidence must be received if it is substantially relevant on some ground other than its tendency to lead to the conclusion that a person acted in accordance with a general disposition towards bad conduct, and this accounts for the complicated state of the case law discussed in section 1.[1] Previous convictions usually do no more than suggest a disposition towards wrongdoing, but they are sometimes relevant for other reasons or rendered admissible by statute as will appear in section 2. Section 3 is concerned with a variety of rules governing evidence of character—a subject that is greatly affected by the substantive law.

SECTION 1. EVIDENCE OF THE IMPROPER CONDUCT OF THE PARTIES ON OTHER OCCASIONS (OR SIMILAR FACT EVIDENCE)[2]

A. STATEMENT AND ILLUSTRATIONS OF THE RULE

(1) STATEMENT OF THE RULE

Evidence of the misconduct of a party on other occasions (including his possession of incriminating material) must not be given if the only reason why it is relevant is that it shows a disposition towards wrongdoing in general, or the commission of the particular crime or civil wrong with which such party is charged, unless such a disposition is of particular relevance to a matter in issue in the proceedings as it would be, for example, if it were a disposition to employ a technique resembling, in significant respects, that alleged to have been employed on the occasion in question.

If someone is accused of theft on the 1st of January, evidence that he obtained money by deception on the 31st of December must not be adduced if it is solely relevant as supporting an argument that the accused was the kind of person who might commit theft, and this would also be the case with regard to evidence that the accused committed theft on the 31st of December; but, if the argument can be rendered more specific, and made to support a suggestion that the accused is disposed towards a particular method, as opposed to a particular kind, of wrongdoing, evidence

---

[1] The example of the torn pound note is given in Cowen and Carter, *Essays On The Law of Evidence*, 134. The complexity of the subject is due to the so-called principle of multiple admissibility, discussed p. 18, *ante*.

[2] There is a large literature on this subject some of which, though still important, has undeniably dated; see Ernest Williams, *Evidence to Show Intent*, 23 L. Q. R. 28 (1907), and *Evidence of Other Offences*, 39 L. Q. R. 212 (1923); Stowe, *Evidence of Similar Facts*, 38 L. Q. R. 63 (1922). The most helpful discussions of the modern law are Cowen and Carter, *op. cit.*, essay 4, and Stone, *The Rule of Exclusion of Similar Fact Evidence (England)*, 46 H. L. R. 954 (1933), to each of which the writer is particularly indebted. A vivid account of comparatively recent developments is given by McHugh, *Similar Facts in Criminal Cases*, 22 Australian Law Journal 502 and 551 (1949).

of his misconduct on other occasions may become admissible. Proof of deception in December might well be allowed on a charge of a similar kind of deception in January.[1]

It should be emphasised that the rule is confined to *misconduct* on other occasions. Evidence tending to show good conduct of a party on other occasions is frequently excluded because it is insufficiently relevant having regard to the collateral issues it might raise, and evidence of conduct which is neither good nor bad may be rejected for similar reasons,[2] but it is not rendered inadmissible by the ease with which an argument from the conduct on other occasions to disposition and thence to conduct on the occasion under investigation might be accepted.

Generally speaking, the misconduct alleged to have taken place on other occasions will itself be a crime or civil wrong, but the rule is not restricted to such cases. If A. is accused of driving a motor vehicle while under the influence of drink, the fact that he was often intoxicated at private parties would, it is believed, be inadmissible if tendered in order to prove his inebriated condition on the occasion into which the court is inquiring; but intoxication in private is neither a crime nor a civil wrong. Suppose that B. is alleged to have obtained money by deception. The fact that he had frequently made preparations to obtain money by a wholly different kind of deception contained in unposted letters would surely be inadmissible as evidence of fraudulent intent; but acts of preparation not amounting in law to attempts are neither crimes nor civil wrongs. In the New Zealand case of *R. v. Horry*,[3] the accused was convicted of a common assault upon a girl by endeavouring to kiss her. She had replied to his advertisement concerning employment, and received a letter asking her to meet him at a particular place. The accused did not contest these facts, but denied that he was guilty of the assault. Two other women gave evidence that they had answered the same advertisement, and met the accused in the same place after being asked to do so by a similar letter. Each of them was deceived in the sense that she discovered that the advertisement was not genuine, but the accused did not make improper overtures to either of them. Their evidence could have been treated as inadmissible because it was irrelevant, but the Court of Appeal stressed its prejudicial character when ordering a new trial. In *R. v. Rodley*,[4] on the other hand, evidence which the judge had considered to be of some relevance as showing lustful disposition at the time of the alleged crime was held to be irrelevant by the Court of Criminal Appeal and no particular emphasis was placed upon its prejudicial nature. In that case, a conviction for housebreaking with intent to commit a rape was quashed on account of the wrongful reception of evidence that the accused came down the chimney of another house during the same night and had intercourse with one of its inmates with her consent. As we saw in Chapter I, relevance is a matter of degree, and different views may sometimes be taken on the question whether a certain item of evidence is sufficiently relevant to be admissible.

---

[1] *R. v. Adamson* (1911), 6 Cr. App. Rep. 205.

[2] *Holcombe* v. *Hewson* (1810), 2 Camp. 391; and *Hollingham* v. *Head* (1858), 4 C. B. N. S. 388.

[3] [1949] N. Z. L. R. 791.

[4] [1913] 3 K. B. 468. The previous misconduct in *R. v. Ball*, [1911] A. C. 47, was not criminal when it took place, and that proved in *R. v. Shellaker*, [1914] 1 K. B. 414, had ceased to be the subject of criminal proceedings at the trial owing to lapse of time.

This is one of the branches of the law of evidence in which STEPHEN's failure to distinguish between relevance and admissibility has been most influential on the language used by the judges.[1] In some of the judgments in which it is rejected, the evidence is said to be "irrelevant" when "inadmissible" might have been a more felicitous expression, but it is asking too much to demand perfect precision of language from judges when it can have no effect on the practical consequences of their decisions. The evidence is rejected however it may be described. In some cases the word "irrelevant" is plainly appropriate to describe the ground for excluding evidence of misconduct on other occasions. This is so when the evidence is thought to have inadequate probative value so far as such misconduct is concerned, for it is then *a fortiori* inadequate in relation to the allegation of misconduct which is being considered by the court.

(2) ILLUSTRATIONS OF THE RULE

(i) Cases in which evidence is excluded as being irrelevant to misconduct on other occasions.—*Harris* v. *Director of Public Prosecutions* was just such a case. A policeman had been convicted of larceny from premises in the Bradford market on the eighth count of an indictment charging him with similar thefts of money from the same premises between May and July. So far as this count was concerned, the evidence was that a burglar alarm had been placed on the premises without the knowledge of the appellant who was on duty in the market at the time. Immediately after it sounded, detectives who had been lying in wait ran to the market and saw the accused standing near the premises. He did not approach them immediately although they were persons with whom he was acquainted, but he did so after disappearing from sight for a short period during which he could have placed marked money that had been left on the premises in the bin where it was found. The only evidence on the other seven counts was that thefts which were in some respects similar occurred at times at which Harris might have been on duty in the vicinity of the market although this was not shown to have been the case. The conviction was affirmed by the Court of Criminal Appeal,[2] but quashed by the House of Lords because the summing-up had not made it plain that that which occurred on the earlier occasions was irrelevant to the question of the accused's guilt on the eighth count.

> "The fact that someone perpetrated the earlier thefts when the accused may have been somewhere in the market does not provide material confirmation of his identity as the thief on the last occasion."[3]

Irrelevant evidence is inadmissible although, in some instances, of which *Harris* v. *Director of Public Prosecutions* is not one, the fact that it was admitted can safely be ignored. Strictly speaking, therefore, *Harris* v. *Director of Public Prosecutions* is an illustration of a more general and far older rule than the one under consideration [4] although Lord SIMON's speech has an important bearing on this latter rule. On one view of the evidence, *Noor Mohamed* v. *R.*[5] is also an example of the older and more

---

[1] For the confusion of STEPHEN's terminology, see p. 25, *ante*.
[2] *R.* v. *Harris*, [1952] 1 K. B. 309.
[3] *Per* Lord SIMON, [1952] A. C. 694, at p. 711; [1952] 1 All E. R. 1044, at p. 1050.
[4] The distinction between the two doctrines was taken by BYRNE, J., in *R.* v. *Patel*, [1951] 2 All E. R. 29.
[5] [1949] A. C. 182; [1949] 1 All E. R. 365.

general requirement with regard to relevance. The appellant had been convicted of murdering A., the woman with whom he had been living. He was a goldsmith, lawfully possessed of cyanide for the purposes of his business, and A. certainly met her death through cyanide poisoning although there was no evidence that the poison had been administered by the accused. He was on bad terms with her, and there was a suggestion that she might have committed suicide. The Judicial Committee advised that the conviction should be quashed because the judge had wrongly admitted evidence designed to show that the accused had previously caused the death of his wife, Gooriah, with whom he had also been on bad terms, by tricking her into taking cyanide as a cure for toothache. Of this evidence, an Australian judge who read it as set out in detail in the appeal book said:

> "Were it not for the statement in the judgment that there was evidence from which it might be inferred that the appellant had persuaded Gooriah to take poison by a trick, I would, with respect, have thought that there was none."[1]

When speaking of *Noor Mohamed's Case*, Lord SIMON said:

> "The Board there took the view that the evidence as to the previous death of the accused's wife was not relevant to prove the charge against him of murdering another woman, and if it was not relevant it was at the same time highly prejudicial."[2]

In *Noor Mohamed's Case* itself, Lord DU PARCQ said of the evidence concerning Gooriah's death:

> "If an examination of it shows that it is impressive just because it appears to demonstrate, in the words of Lord HERSCHEL in *Makin's* case,[3] 'that the accused is a person likely from his criminal conduct or character to have committed the offence of which he is being charged', and if it is otherwise of no real substance, then it was certainly wrongly admitted."[4]

There is, therefore, some reason for treating *Noor Mohamed* v. *R.* as an illustration, not so much of the general principle of relevancy, as of the more specific rule under consideration—the evidence was relevant, but only because it suggested that the accused was likely to have poisoned A. because he had already shown a disposition to use poison by his dealings with Gooriah.

(ii) How the rule with regard to facts showing bad disposition works.—The strongest illustrations of this more specific rule are provided by appeals from convictions for obtaining money by false pretences. In *R.* v. *Fisher*,[5] the Court of Criminal Appeal quashed a conviction for obtaining a pony and cart by false pretences concerning the state of the accused's family and bank account because evidence had been wrongly admitted concerning the obtaining of provender by false pretences with regard to the

---

[1] OWEN, J., in *R.* v. *Fletcher*, [1953] S. R. N. S. W. 70, at p. 79.
[2] *Harris* v. *Director of Public Prosecutions*, [1952] A. C. 694, at p. 708; [1952] 1 All E. R 1044, at p. 1048. See also p. 711.
[3] *Makin* v. *A.-G. for New South Wales*, [1894] A. C. 57, the leading case, fully discussed later in this chapter.
[4] [1949] A. C. 182, at p. 192; [1949] 1 All. E. R. 365, at p. 370.
[5] [1910] 1 K. B. 149. See also *R.* v. *Holt* (1860), Bell C. C. 280; *R.* v. *Ellis*, [1910] 2 K. B. 746; *R.* v. *Baird* (1915), 11 Cr. App. Rep. 186 (obtaining credit by fraud); *R.* v. *Boothby* (1933), 24 Cr. App. Rep. 112; *R.* v. *Slender*, [1938] 2 All E. R. 387; *R.* v. *Hamilton*, [1939] 1 All E. R. 469.

state of the accused's business. CHANNEL, J., stated the law in the following terms:

> "The principle is that the prosecution are not allowed to prove that the prisoner has committed the offence with which he is charged by giving evidence that he is a person of bad character and one who is in the habit of committing crimes, for that is equivalent to asking the jury to say that because the prisoner has committed other offences he must therefore be guilty of the particular offence for which he is being tried. But if the evidence of other offences does go to prove that he did commit the offence charged it is admissible because it is relevant to the issue, and it is admissible not because but notwithstanding that it proves that the prisoner has committed another offence."[1]

The application of the principle sometimes has a rather mechanical appearance. In *R.* v. *Slender*,[2] for instance, a conviction for obtaining money by the false pretence that it was needed to enable the accused to spend the night in Cheltenham was quashed on account of the wrongful admission of evidence relating to a previous obtaining of money by the accused by means of the pretence that they had work elsewhere and required the money for the journey to that place. In order that evidence should be admissible as showing a disposition to perpetrate fraud by a particular method, there must be a virtually complete similarity in the pretences. It has been truly said that this requirement places a premium on versatility.[3]

On a charge of incest, evidence of intercourse with a relation other than the one mentioned in the charge will generally be inadmissible because it does no more than show incestuous propensity,[4] but evidence of intercourse on other occasions with the relation mentioned in the charge is admissible because it is highly relevant as showing a propensity to commit incest with a particular person.[5] Similar distinctions are applied on charges of adultery, unlawful carnal knowledge and indecent assault. There must always be a nexus between the offence charged and the offence alleged to have occurred on another occasion. The nexus need not necessarily consist in the existence of a guilty passion on the part of one person for another, for it may be proved by the method by which the offences were alleged to have been committed; but some nexus there must be, both in time and in the nature of the offences.[6]

R. v. *Brown, Smith, Woods and Flanagan* [7] is a case in which there was no adequate nexus. The accused were charged with and convicted of shopbreaking. Smith had pleaded guilty to a previous offence of shopbreaking, and evidence relating to that offence had been admitted. The convictions were quashed by the Court of Criminal Appeal because the evidence of his previous offence had been improperly received against Smith, and it was prejudicial to the other accused because they were proved to have been associated with Smith. It was argued that there was a sufficient nexus

---

[1] [1910] 1 K.B. at p. 152.   [2] [1938] 2 All E. R. 387.
[3] 54 L. Q. R. 335 (D. W. L.).   [4] *R.* v. *Flack*, [1969] 2 All E. R. 784.
[5] *R.* v. *Ball*, [1911] A. C. 47. The evidence was admitted to rebut innocent association by showing inclination as well as opportunity arising from the fact that a brother and sister occupied the same bedroom. It was conceded in argument that evidence of intercourse by the brother with another sister would have been inadmissible. Evidence of intercourse with others may always be admissible owing to the special facts of a particular case.
[6] *R.* v. *Coombes* (1960), 45 Cr. App. Rep. 36; *R.* v. *Wilson* (1973), 58 Cr. App. Rep. 169.
[7] (1963), 47 Cr. App. Rep. 205; *R.* v. *Macpherson*, *R.* v. *Resnick* [1964] 2 O. R. 101; *R.* v. *Blackledge*, [1965] V. R. 397.

between Smith's previous shopbreaking and that of which he had been convicted because it occurred only five days earlier and at a place only twenty miles distant, but the Court of Criminal Appeal held that these facts tended to negative rather establish a nexus. It was also argued that the fact that each shopbreaking took place in the lunch hour when the shopkeeper was away constituted a nexus, but this was held to be too common a feature of shopbreaking to have that effect.

> "Supposing that a person charged with housebreaking was found with a piece of celluloid in his possession, and supposing it was found that he had used celluloid as a means of gaining access to 100 houses on previous occasions, could it possibly be said that that fact was any reason why the 100 other offences should be used to establish the identity of the accused as the perpetrator of the offence charged? . . . Were the court to approve of what was done in this case, it would mean the annihilation of the fundamental rule, that criminal propensity as such can never be adduced in order to establish the guilt of a person of the offence charged."[1]

The very unusual case of *R. v. Straffen*[2] is one in which the nexus was provided by the suggestion of an abnormal propensity to commit murder in a particular way. Straffen was charged with the murder of a small girl named Linda Bowyer, committed during the comparatively short period between his escape from custody in Broadmoor and his recapture. The child had been strangled, her body had been left unconcealed on the roadside, and no attempt had been made to interfere with her sexually. The accused had been seen near the place where the body was found, but there were other passers-by who might have committed the crime. A year previously Straffen had confessed to killing two other small girls in similar circumstances, and he had been found unfit to plead when charged with their murder. The Court of Criminal Appeal held that evidence of the confession had been rightly admitted at his trial for the murder of Linda Bowyer—not for the purpose of showing that Straffen was a "professional strangler"—but in order to identify the murderer of Linda Bowyer as being the same individual as the person who had murdered the other two little girls in precisely the same way. To state possible reasons for admitting the confession of the other murders in ascending order of relevance, the previous conduct of the accused rendered it probable that he was the culprit on the occasion in question because it showed that he was (a) a criminal, (b) a murderer, (c) a strangler, and (d) someone given to strangling small girls in peculiar circumstances. The evidence was plainly too remote to be admissible for the first reason, its relevance on the second and third grounds could hardly be disputed, but there is the ever-present risk that juries will be so impressed by arguments of this nature that they will pay inadequate attention to matters which are favourable to the accused. Therefore the confession might have been excluded if it had merely gone to show that Straffen had been guilty of murder, even if his previous victim had been strangled. The evidence was so extremely relevant for the fourth reason that it had to be received, notwithstanding the risk that has been mentioned. In the words of Professor Stone:

> "There is a human paradox here which logical formulation cannot resolve. In a trial for an unpleasant crime, evidence must be excluded which indicates

---

[1] EDMUND DAVIES, J. at pp. 210–211.
[2] [1952] 2 Q. B. 911; [1952] 2 All E. R. 657.

that the prisoner is more likely than most men to have committed it, but evidence must be admitted which tends to show that no man but the prisoner, who is known to have done these things before, could have committed it. There is a point in the ascending scale of probability when it is so near to certainty, that it is absurd to shy at the admission of the prejudicial evidence."[1]

When delivering the judgment of the Court of Criminal Appeal in *Straffen's* case, SLADE, J., said:

"It is an abnormal propensity to murder young girls and to do so without any apparent motive, without any attempt at sexual interference, where they can be seen and where, presumably, their deaths would be detected."[2]

SLADE, J. thought that, if the question of identity arose in a case of housebreaking and it was possible to adduce evidence of some hallmark or other peculiarity in relation to earlier housebreakings which was also apparent in the case of the housebreaking charged, evidence that the accused committed the earlier crimes would be admissible on the same principle. The precise stage at which the evidence ceases to show a mere disposition to commit a crime or civil wrong, and begins to manifest a propensity to do these things in a particular way, is no doubt something that varies from case to case.[3] *R.* v. *Straffen* and the other cases which have been mentioned show that in a limited number of situations, evidence of disposition is received although it is solely relevant as suggesting that the disposition was acted upon on the occasion under investigation. The disposition must, however, be of particular relevance because it relates to the pattern, not merely the kind of misconduct with which the court is concerned.

Although further illustrations of the exclusion of evidence of a party's misconduct on other occasions are scattered throughout the reports,[4] its most important practical function is that it prevents the Crown from giving evidence of the accused's previous convictions, and this is supplemented by the statutory prohibition on cross-examining the prisoner on the subject under the guise of testing his credit which is considered in the next chapter. The accused would be estopped from denying that he was guilty of the offence for which he had been convicted,[5] but the fact that someone

---

[1] 46 Harvard Law Review, 983–984.

[2] [1952] 2 Q. B. 911, at p. 916; [1952] 2 All E. R. 657, at p. 662.

[3] It is also a matter on which different views on different facts can easily be taken by different judges. Would the facts that Straffen's earlier victims had been boys, or girls with whom he had interfered sexually, have rendered the evidence of his other crimes inadmissible? Many may think that, in the circumstances, the fact that Straffen had escaped from Broadmoor would have been admissible whatever the cause of his detention might have been. If only five or six people could have committed a homicide, and one of them had just escaped from Broadmoor, the relevance of that fact can scarcely be exaggerated.

[4] *R.* v. *Butler* (1846), 2 Car. & Kir. 221; *R.* v. *Oddy* (1851), 2 Den. 264; *R.* v. *Winslow* (1860), 8 Cox C. C. 397; *R.* v. *Barron* (1913), 9 Cr. App. Rep. 236; *Perkins* v. *Jeffery*, [1915] 2 K. B. 702 (so far as exposure to other women than the prosecutrix was concerned); *R.* v. *Taylor* (1923), 17 Cr. App. Rep. 109; *R.* v. *Ferrier* (1968), 112 Sol. Jo. 519; in *Maxwell* v. *Director of Public Prosecutions*, [1935] A. C. 309 at p. 317, Lord SANKEY, L.C., spoke of the rule as one of the most jealously guarded principles of our criminal law. Its exclusionary effect on a charge of criminal negligence is illustrated by *Akerele* v. *R.*, [1943] A. C. 255, at p. 261; [1943] 1 All E. R. 367, at p. 370. On the assumption that the charge was one of injecting too great a quantity of the proper mixture, and not an improperly mixed dose, evidence of the effect of a doctor's injections on other patients would be inadmissible, though it was held admissible on the footing that he had injected the patients in respect of whom the charge was made, and the other patients, with an improperly mixed dose.

[5] But see n. 3, p. 297, *ante*.

commits an offence without reference to the circumstances in which he did so would generally only show that he had a disposition towards crime in general, or the commission of a particular crime, so proof of a conviction cannot often take a case outside the ban of the rule.[1]

(3) Formulation of the Rule in *Makin* v. *A.-G.* for New South Wales

In *Makin* v. *A.G. for New South Wales*,[2] Lord Herschell, L.C., said:

"It is undoubtedly not competent for the prosecution to adduce evidence tending to show that the accused has been guilty of criminal acts other than those covered by the indictment, for the purpose of leading to the conclusion that the accused is a person likely from his criminal conduct or character to have committed the offence for which he is being tried. On the other hand the mere fact that the evidence adduced tends to show the commission of other crimes does not render it inadmissible if it be relevant to an issue before the jury; and it may be so relevant if it bears upon the question whether the acts alleged to constitute the crime charged in the indictment were designed or accidental, or to rebut a defence which would otherwise be open to the accused."

This statement has been repeated in most of the subsequent judgments on the subject to such an extent that it has come to be regarded as an exhaustive, if necessarily concise, statement of the law; but it has the serious defect of failing to bring out the point that the admissibility of evidence of misconduct to show disposition is largely dependent on the fact that there are degrees of relevance. The result has been a failure to realise that relevant evidence is excluded by the first sentence of the passage, while the relevance of evidence admitted in consequence of the second sentence is often due to the fact that "criminal acts other than those covered by the indictment lead to the conclusion that the accused is a person likely from his criminal conduct or character to have committed the offence for which he is being tried". The first failure has, it is hoped, been made good once and for all by the speech of Lord Simon of Glaisdale in *Director of Public Prosecutions* v. *Kilbourne*.[3] So far as the second failure is concerned, it is only necessary to reflect on the facts of *R.* v. *Straffen*[4] in order to realise that evidence which does no more than show a bad disposition is admissible. It is true that the disposition was one to act in a highly specific way, fully entitling Slade, J., to speak of it as an "abnormal propensity", but the evidence admitted in *Straffen's Case* was nonetheless within the proscription of Lord Herschell's first sentence, and it was admitted, not because it was relevant to some special issue before the jury, nor because it rebutted some special defence otherwise open to the accused, but simply because it was, when

---

[1] Further illustrations of the rule are provided by cases in which the jury has been discharged, or the Court of Criminal Appeal has held that the jury ought to have been discharged, because of an accidental disclosure of the accused's past (*R.* v. *McCraig* (1925), 10 Cr. App. Rep. 68; *R.* v. *Firth*, [1938] 3 All E. R. 783). Sometimes it has been found possible to apply the proviso now contained in s. 2 (1) of the Criminal Appeal Act, 1968, when the jury has not been discharged in such a case (*R.* v. *Featherstone*, [1942] 2 All E. R. 672; *R.* v. *Fripp* (1942), 29 Cr. App. Rep. 6).

[2] [1894] A. C. 57, at p. 65 (P. C.), approved in the House of Lords in *R.* v. *Ball*, [1911] A. C. 47; *Thompson* v. *R.*, [1918] A. C. 221 and *Harris* v. *Director of Public Prosecutions*, [1952] A. C. 694; [1952] 1 All E. R. 1044.

[3] "That what was declared to be inadmissible in the first sentence of this passage [Lord Herschell's statement] is nevertheless relevant, i.e. logically probative, can be seen from numerous studies of offences in which recidivists are matched against first offenders" ([1973] A. C. 729, at p. 757). See also *Lowery* v. *R.*, [1973] 3 All E. R. 662.

[4] P. 315, *ante*.

coupled with evidence of opportunity on Straffen's part, well nigh conclusive on the general issue of his guilt, a point which is in danger of being
obscured by saying that the evidence was admissible because it tended to
prove "identity". Though *Straffen's Case* is the most vivid of them, we
shall see that there are many other instances in which evidence of misconduct other than that charged has been admitted although it does no more
than show a disposition to act in a particular way.

Once it is realised that this branch of the law is dependent on the existence of degrees of relevance, it becomes easy to dispose of a question,
prompted by contrasted dicta, concerning the form of the rule stated by
Lord HERSCHELL. Was he stating a general exclusionary rule in his first
sentence, and recognising the existence of exceptions in the second? or was
he stating an absolute rule prohibiting the adduction of evidence of other
crimes for a particular purpose in his first sentence, and recognising that
the same evidence might be admissible for other purposes in the second?[1]
The question becomes otiose once it is seen to be whether Lord HERSCHELL's
first sentence contains a ban on evidence which is only relevant as showing
disposition, while the second sentence recognises that highly relevant
evidence having that effect and no more may be admissible, or whether
the second operates by way of exception to the first in cases in which the
evidence proves a highly relevant disposition. In either event attempts to
produce a closed list of cases to which the second sentence applies is
taboo.[2]

This is hardly surprising in view of the fact that Lord HERSCHELL's
second sentence allows for the reception of evidence of other crimes "to
rebut a defence which would otherwise be open to the accused". The
classic interpretation of these words is contained in Lord SUMNER's
speech in *Thompson* v. *R.*:[3] "The mere theory that a plea of not guilty
puts everything material in issue is not enough for this purpose. The
prosecution cannot credit the accused with fancy defences in order to rebut
them at the outset with some damning piece of prejudice." These
words were in their turn construed by HUMPHREYS, J., to mean that the
defence must actually have been raised by the accused before evidence of
his misconduct on other occasions can be admitted to rebut it,[4] and flatly
contradicted by Lord GODDARD, C.J., in *R.* v. *Sims*,[5] In *Harris* v. *Director
of Public Prosecutions*,[6] however, Lord SIMON made the point that it cannot
always be necessary for the prosecution to wait for a defence to be raised
otherwise a submission that there was no case to answer might succeed
although evidence was available which, unless its effect could be displaced,
clearly established guilt by admissible means, notwithstanding the fact that
it also showed that the accused was a man of criminal propensities. In *R.*
v. *Hall*[7] Lord GODDARD, C.J., conceded that regard must be had to the
defences open to the accused, and it may be assumed that evidence of a

---

[1] Contrast the dictum of KENNEDY, J., in *R.* v. *Bond*, [1906] 2 K. B. 389, at p. 398, with
that of Lord GODDARD, C.J., in *R.* v. *Sims*, [1946] K. B. 531, at p. 537.

[2] *Per* Lord SIMON in *Harris* v. *Director of Public Prosecutions*, [1952] A. C. 694, at p.
705.

[3] [1918] A. C. 221, at p. 231.

[4] *R.* v. *Cole* (1941), 165 L. T. 125.

[5] [1946] K. B. 531, at p. 539.

[6] [1952] A. C. 694, at p. 705; see also *Noor Mohamed* v. *R.*, [1949] A. C. 182, at p. 191
(*per* Lord DU PARCQ).

[7] [1952] 1 K. B. 302, at p. 307.

party's misconduct on other occasions is admissible if it tends to rebut a defence that can fairly be said to be open to him, provided always that the evidence is either relevant for some reason other than its tendency to establish wrongdoing by proof of disposition, or else because it shows a disposition which is of particular relevance in all the circumstances of the case.

Due regard must also be had to what may be described as the "state of the pleadings", for an admission may make all the difference. This is a truism so far as civil cases are concerned, but it is also valid with regard to criminal proceedings.

> "If in a charge of burglary it is relevant to prove that the accused was at a certain place on the day of the burglary, and it was proposed to prove that fact by evidence that he on that day committed another offence in the same town, admission of the fact that he was there on the day would make the proof unnecessary and it would be excluded."[1]

This remark of a New Zealand judge made as long ago as 1916 would surely be applicable to an English trial for burglary at the present day.

B. CASES IN WHICH EVIDENCE OF THE IMPROPER CONDUCT OF A PARTY ON OTHER OCCASIONS IS ADMISSIBLE

For the purposes of exposition the cases in which evidence of misconduct on other occasions has been held to be admissible must be divided into categories, and it is proposed to discuss them under two heads—those in which the evidence concerns incidents in the transaction under investigation or offences of a continuing nature, and those in which the alleged misconduct on other occasions rebuts a defence or explanation fairly attributable to the defendant or accused. When these two categories have been discussed, reference will be made to various miscellaneous points and to some statutory provisions.

As a matter of law it does not seem to make any difference whether the alleged misconduct occurred before or after the events under investigation;[2] nor, as a matter of strict law, does it seem to make any difference whether the evidence is given in-chief or elicited in cross-examination. The provisions of s. 1 (f) of the Criminal Evidence Act, 1898 (discussed in the next chapter), must be borne in mind in the case of the cross-examination of the accused, and, even if these are complied with, the court may disallow cross-examination on that which has not been the subject of evidence in-chief.

(1) Incidents in the Transaction Under Investigation and Offences of a Continuing Nature

(i) Incidents in the transaction under investigation.—In the cases about to be discussed, the evidence of misconduct other than that charged was admitted because it was relevant for some reason quite independent of its tendency to show a bad disposition.

If the case against the accused is that he stirred up racial hatred by

---

[1] *R. v. Rogans* (1916), 35 N. Z. L. R. 265, at p. 304 (*per* DENISTON, J.).
[2] See the article by D. W. Logan, *Evidence of Subsequent Acts* (1934), 50 L. Q. R. 386.

reference to his experiences in prison, witnesses may prove what he said although it may go to show that he had been guilty of other crimes.[1]

If someone charged with murder is alleged to have escaped from the scene of the crime in a stolen car, or if the proceeds of a robbery are found at the place where a later crime was committed,[2] evidence tending to show the theft of the car, or the perpetration of the robbery by the accused is admissible. It may prove that he has a criminal disposition, but it also connects him with the crime charged to the same extent as would have been the case if he had escaped in his own car or left his belongings at the scene of the alleged crime. Similarly, if the accused denies that he was in the neighbourhood in which the crime was committed, evidence that he committed another crime there shortly before or after the occurrence which forms the subject matter of the charge would be admissible because it is relevant in the same way as the making of a social call at a material time would be relevant.[3]

Further examples of cases in which the behaviour alleged against persons accused of crime has rendered their misconduct at other times admissible as an incident in the transaction under investigation, are provided by *R.* v. *Salisbury*[4] and *R.* v. *Cobden.*[5] In the first of these cases, a postman was charged with stealing a letter containing banknotes belonging to Cox. These notes had been inserted in another letter from which the original contents had been abstracted and were traced to the possession of the accused. It was held that evidence of his interception of this letter was admissible as something essential to the chain of facts necessary to establish the larceny of Cox's notes. In *R.* v. *Cobden*, A., B. and C. were charged with breaking into a railway booking-office and stealing property there. None of this property was found in C.'s possession, and it was held that evidence of thefts from other booking-offices on the same night might be given because, if it were proved that C. was in possession of property stolen from these other stations, that fact, together with the rest of the circumstances of the case, might be evidence that all three prisoners were engaged in each crime, and that C. had received his share of the booty from the other offices. BRAMWELL, B., said, "The events of that night relating to these burglaries are so intermixed that it is impossible to separate them."

If A. is charged with maliciously shooting at B., evidence that he had attacked B. earlier on the same day may be admissible on the ground that the attacks were all part of one transaction.[6] When a man was charged with rape of a child, once it was proved that he had threatened to injure her if she complained of his conduct, it was held that evidence of subsequent penetrations might be given on the ground that the threat gave them such a continuity with the first as to render them part of the same transaction.[7]

The cloak of the same transaction has been held to render admissible evidence of a series of takings on the same day from the same till by a shop

---

[1] *R.* v. *Malik*, [1968] 1 All E. R. 582n.
[2] See the case cited in *R.* v. *Whiley* (1804), 2 Leach 983, at p. 985, p. 18, *ante* and *R.* v. *O'Meally*, [1953] V. L. R. 30.
[3] *R.* v. *Ducsharm*, [1956] 1 D. L. R. 732. The jury may have to be directed with regard to the limited purpose for which the evidence can be used. See also *R.* v. *Ward*, [1963] Qd. R. 56 (accused's denial that he knew how to drive rendered driving offences admissible).
[4] (1831), 5 C. & P. 155.   [5] (1862), 3 F. & F. 833.
[6] *R.* v. *Voke* (1823), Russ. & Ry. 531; *O'Leary* v. *R.* (1946), 73 C. L. R. 402; *R.* v. *O'Malley*, [1964] Qd. R. 226.
[7] *R.* v. *Rearden* (1864), 4 F. & F. 76.

assistant,[1] the continuous extraction of gas from the same pipe,[2] and the removal of coal from a number of different seams by the same owner of adjoining mineral rights.[3] The purpose for which such evidence was received has varied from case to case. The only common feature is that the element of continuity gives the additional facts a relevance that they would not possess in its absence. *R. v. Ellis* [4] is a typical example. The prisoner was charged with stealing six marked shillings from the till of the prosecutrix by whom he was employed as a shopman. The evidence was that marked money was placed in the till, and the prosecutrix's son watched the prisoner go to it with money received from customers. On several occasions, Ellis was seen to withdraw his hand from the till with his fist clenched and move it in the direction of his waistcoat pocket. The contents of the till were examined by the prosecutrix's son from time to time, and, in each instance, they were found to be less than they should have been. On his arrest, the prisoner was in possession of a sum corresponding to the deficiency in the till, consisting of some unmarked money in addition to the six marked shillings. The evidence tending to show that he had stolen or embezzled the former in the course of gaining possession of the latter was admitted because:

> "It went to show the history of the till from the time when the marked money was put into it up to the time when it was found in the possession of the prisoner".

If a man were charged with stealing money from a till on the 1st of January, evidence that he stole money from the same till on the 1st, or even the 31st, of December, could, generally speaking, only serve the purpose of showing that it was probable that he was guilty of the crime charged because he had committed the same kind of crime before, and it would therefore be inadmissible; but the evidence tending to show how Ellis stole or embezzled the unmarked money also showed how he took the marked coins. "If crimes do so intermix the court must go through the details." [5]

The conception of the "same transaction" as a unifying element is essentially procedural. It seems to have originated in cases concerned with the question whether charges of two or more felonies could properly be joined in the same indictment, the idea being that this was permissible if they formed part of the same transaction. When applied to the law of evidence, the conception has the advantages and disadvantages of all title headings. It is a convenient description for a miscellaneous class of cases in which evidence is admissible on account of its connection in time, place or circumstance with the event under consideration; but it sometimes leads to a misplaced emphasis on the question whether the "same transaction" is involved, without due regard being had to the respects in which it is contended that the evidence is relevant. It will be necessary to refer again to the cases mentioned in the last two paragraphs when discussing the *res gestae* doctrine in chapter XX, for a common way of

---

[1] *R. v. Ellis* (1826), 6 B. & C. 145.
[2] *R. v. Firth* (1869), L. R. 1 C. C. R. 172.
[3] *R. v. Bleasdale* (1848), 2 Car. & Kir. 765. See also *R. v. Shepherd* (1868), L. R. 1 C. C. R. 118 and *R. v. Henwood* (1870), 11 Cox C. C. 526. The authorities are conveniently reviewed in *R. v. Flynn* (1955), 21 C. R. 1, at p. 5.
[4] (1826), 6 B. & C. 145.
[5] Lord ELLENBOROUGH in *R. v. Whiley* (1804), 2 Leach 983.

stating the reason why certain items of evidence are admissible, is to say that they are part of the *res gestae* in one of the senses in which this phrase is used.

In some cases evidence has been received and cross-examination permitted about a party's misconduct on other occasions because it tends to confirm testimony about matters that were to some extent collateral to the main issue. In *R. v. Chitson*,[1] a man was charged with unlawful intercourse with a girl under sixteen. The prosecutrix alleged that he told her about his similar behaviour with another girl, and it was held that he could be cross-examined on this subject. In *R. v. Kennaway*,[2] a solicitor was charged with forgery of a will. The main witnesses against him were accomplices who said that though Kennaway signed the will, he told them that he did not wish to be named as executor because he had done the same thing some eighteen years earlier, and he was anxious not to facilitate the discovery of his previous crime. The evidence was held to have been rightly admitted and the accused to have been properly cross-examined about that which occurred eighteen years earlier because the answers might corroborate the evidence of the accomplices. In *R. v. Lovegrove*,[3] a woman was convicted of manslaughter by performing an illegal operation on the prosecutor's wife. The prosecutor said that he had been given the accused's address by another woman who stated that the accused had performed an illegal operation on her. Lovegrove's defence was that the only time she had seen the prosecutor was when he called to inquire about accommodation, and it was held that Lovegrove had been properly cross-examined concerning the alleged operation upon the other woman.

If someone voluntarily confesses, not merely that he is guilty of the crime charged, but also that he has misconducted himself in some other way, evidence tending to confirm this latter part of his statement is admissible because it would be strange if it were true while the first part was false. In *R. v. Evans*[4] the accused was convicted of murdering his child. One of the items of evidence against him was a statement which he had made to the police to the effect that he had murdered his wife as well as his child and concealed their bodies in the same place. The Court of Criminal Appeal held that the entirety of this confession, which was repudiated by Evans at his trial, had been properly read to the jury because the wife's body was found near that of her child. The ground on which evidence of this nature is received may readily be appreciated, and it does not call for further consideration.

(ii) Offences of a continuing nature.—In certain cases the definition of the crime or civil wrong under investigation involves an element of continuity and can only be established by proof of that which occurred on other occasions. Thus, in *Brown v. Eastern and Midland Rail. Co.*,[5] the plaintiff contended that a heap of stones placed near the highway on the defendant's land constituted a public nuisance. It had frightened the

---

[1] [1909] 2 K. B. 945. The fact that the prosecutrix referred in-chief to what the accused told her about the other girl must now be regarded as crucial although it was not stressed in the judgment (see *Jones v. Director of Public Prosecutions*, [1962] A. C. 635; [1962] 1 All E. R. 569).

[2] [1917] 1 K. B. 25. The *ratio decidendi* of this case must also be considered in the light of *Jones v. Director of Public Prosecutions* (*supra*).

[3] [1920] 3 K. B. 643.

[4] [1950] 1 All E. R. 610.   [5] (1889), 22 Q.B.D. 391.

plaintiff's horse, and evidence that it had caused other horses to shy on the same day was held to have been rightly admitted. As STEPHEN, J., said:

> "When the question is whether a particular act is a public nuisance, it is difficult to see how it can be proved to be so except by showing cases in which it has interfered with public right."

The same principle applies to other offences of a continuing or cumulative nature, such as trading when insolvent or permitting a house to be used as a brothel.[1] Proof of crimes or civil wrongs on other occasions is rendered admissible by the definition of the offence charged, and it therefore has a relevancy quite distinct from its tendency to show that the defendant or accused is a person of bad disposition or someone who exercises inadequate control over his property.

(2) Rebutting a Defence or Explanation Fairly Attributable to the Defendant or Accused

In many, but by no means all, of the cases about to be discussed, the evidence of misconduct other than that charged was admitted because, although it did no more than show bad disposition, it was highly relevant. This enhanced relevance is most frequently due to the fact that the disposition proved by the other misconduct is one to act in accordance with a particular technique, resembling, in significant respects, that employed in the crime charged; but it may be due to other considerations such as its tendency to show a disposition to commit a sexual offence against a particular person ("guilty passion"), or its tendency to confirm in a striking way the testimony of a Crown witness. In the latter event, the disposition proved by the other misconduct need not always be a disposition to commit the crime charged in a particular way or with a particular person.

When the problems raised by the cases about to be discussed are under consideration, it is very important that due regard should be paid to the other evidence adduced, or about to be adduced, by the prosecution, for the degree of relevance of the evidence tending to show disposition may be greatly affected by the other evidence in the case. If brother and sister are charged with incest, proof of their former incestuous association does more than show a tendency to commit incest, for it indicates the existence of a guilty passion between the two accused. Nevertheless, it is unlikely that such evidence would be admitted if the only other evidence were that they lived in the same house and often went out together; but if there was evidence that they occupied the same bedroom, there is no doubt that evidence of their former association would be admitted to show that they committed incest in that room.[2]

Where the evidence of disposition tends to show technique there must be unusual features connecting the crime or civil wrong charged with the misconduct on other occasions.[3] It is impossible to be precise about

---

[1] *Ex parte Burnby*, [1901] 2 Q. B. 458; *R. v. Brady, R. v. Ram*, [1964] 3 All E. R. 616; *Dale v. Smith*, [1967] 2 All E. R. 1133.

[2] *R. v. Ball*, [1911] A. C. 47.

[3] "In all these cases the evidence may tend to show the accused to be of bad disposition but it also shows something more. The other acts have specific features connecting them with the crime charged, and are on that account admissible in evidence. A similar distinction exists in the case of articles found in the possession of the accused. If they have no connection with the crime except to show that the accused has a bad disposition, the evidence is not admissible; but if there are any circumstances in the crime tending to show

the degree of similarity required. The requirement of similarity enhances the relevance of the misconduct on other occasions because the greater the similarity, the greater the coincidence which must be supposed if the accused's defence or explanation is to be believed, for the major premise of most arguments in support of the admissibility of similar fact evidence is that coincidences are rare. They may occur, but the jury's attention should be drawn to the fact that a coincidence of some magnitude must be assumed if the defence or explanation is to be accepted.

Five of the principal grounds why evidence of misconduct on other occasions is highly relevant although it does no more than show disposition are that it tends to rebut a defence of accident or involuntary conduct, to rebut a plea of ignorance or mistake, to rebut an innocent explanation of a particular act or the possession of incriminating material, to negative false identification of the accused as the culprit or to rebut the defence of innocent association. These heads of admissibility are not mutually exclusive. They simply provide one among many other ways in which the leading cases may be grouped together.

(i) Rebutting defence of accident or involuntary conduct.—The ground on which evidence tending to show other crimes or civil wrongs is admitted to negative accident was succinctly stated by A. T. LAWRENCE, J., in *R. v. Bond*:[1] "That the same accident should repeatedly occur to the same person is unusual, especially so when it confers a benefit on him." The defence of accident may be raised in a variety of different situations according to whether it is contended that the conduct of the defendant or accused had no causal connection with the fact of which complaint is made, or that such fact was the unintended consequence of the conduct of the defendant or accused or that such conduct was not voluntary. There are reported decisions dealing with each of these situations, although it is the first that has been before the courts most frequently.

(a) The question of causal connection.—In *R. v. Geering*,[2] a woman who was responsible for the feeding of her household was charged with murdering her husband by giving him arsenic. POLLOCK, C.B., admitted evidence

---

a connection between it and the articles, the evidence is admissible; thus in a case of burglary evidence is admissible that housebreaking implements such as might have been used in the crime were found in the possession of the accused" (*per* Lord GODDARD, C.J., in *R. v. Sims*, [1946] K. B. 531, at p. 538). "It is perfectly clear that evidence of a previous offence is admissible to rebut a defence of accident and also to rebut a defence of innocent intent; but the offence which it is sought to adduce in evidence must be of a similar character. There is no clear authority as to how similar the offence must be to make it admissible; but there must be some nexus both in time and in the nature of the offence" (*per* Lord PARKER, C.J., in *R. v. Coombes* (1960), 45 Cr. App. Rep. 36, at p. 39). See also *per* A. T. LAWRENCE, J., in *R. v. Bond*, [1906] 2 K. B. 389, at p. 424. The requisite degree of similarity may well vary from case to case. To rebut a defence of innocent intent in the case of a charge of abortion, all that is required is that the accused should have performed previous abortions with drugs or instruments (*R. v. Starkie*, [1922] 2 K. B. 295); but something more than the identity of the offences may be required on issues of mistaken identification (*R. v. Blackledge*, [1965] V. R. 397).

[1] [1906] 2 K. B. 389, at pp. 420–1.

[2] (1849), 18 L. J. M. C. 215. See also *R. v. Garner* (1864), 3 F. & F. 681; *R. v. Cotton* (1873), 12 Cox C. C. 400; *R. v. Heeson* (1878), 14 Cox C. C. 40; *R. v. Flannagan and Higgins* (1884), 15 Cox C. C. 403. All these cases concerned charges of murder by poisoning and similar fact evidence was admitted on the principles stated in *R. v. Geering*. In *R. v. Winslow* (1860), 8 Cox C. C. 397, such evidence was rejected. It may be treated as irreconcilable with the other cases cited in this note (*Makin v. A.-G. for New South Wales*, [1894] A. C. 57, at p. 64) or it may be reconciled with the other cases on the ground that, in *R. v. Winslow*, there was no evidence rendering it probable that the accused administered poison to any of his victims (46 H. L. R. 969).

of the later deaths of the accused's sons from arsenical poisoning first, because it confirmed the evidence already given to the effect that the husband's death had been caused by arsenic and secondly because it would enable the jury to determine whether he took the poison accidentally. It would certainly have been a strange thing if a number of people whose food was prepared by the same woman had each taken arsenic accidentally over a comparatively short period.

In *Makin* v. *A.-G. for New South Wales*,[1] a husband and wife were charged with murdering a baby. Its body was found buried in their garden and they were proved to have agreed to adopt it in consideration of the payment of a small premium by its parents. The reason given by the Makins for this apparently generous conduct was that Mrs. Makin had lost a child of her own. Thus far, though the circumstances might be thought to have been somewhat suspicious, it is very doubtful whether there would have been sufficient material before the jury to negative the hypothesis that the child met its death through natural causes and the accused had done nothing more heinous than to bury it irregularly; but the prosecution was allowed to lead evidence that the bodies of other babies taken in for small premiums for the same alleged reason were found buried in the yards of houses occupied by the accused. The accused were convicted, and the Privy Council held that the evidence had been rightly admitted to rebut the suggestion that the child's death was accidental in the sense that it was not caused by the conduct of the Makins.

A substantially similar case is *R.* v. *Smith*[2] in which the appellant was charged with murdering Bessie Munday, a woman with whom he had gone through a ceremony of marriage and who had met her death in a bath after insuring her life in his favour. The circumstances in which the body was found were consistent with death through epilepsy— a hypothesis which Smith did much to foster, but it was rebutted by proof of the deaths of two other women with whom he had gone through ceremonies of marriage. They, too, were drowned in their baths in similar circumstances, and the accused stood to gain financially in consequence of their deaths. The Court of Criminal Appeal held that this evidence had been rightly admitted and affirmed the conviction.

In the above three cases, and particularly in the second and third, the admissibility of the evidence of the other crimes can be explained on the basis that it showed a disposition to commit murder by means of a particular technique or on the basis that proof of the other "accidents" tended to enhance the improbability of the accident alleged by the accused.[3] In the next case, the disputed evidence was relevant independently of its tendency to show a propensity; the major premise of the reasoning justifying its reception was *post hoc ergo propter hoc*.

In *Hales* v. *Kerr*[4] the defendant was a barber, and the plaintiff contended that he had contracted a disease in consequence of the practice adopted by

---

[1] [1894] A. C. 57.   [2] (1915), 11 Cr. App. Rep. 229.
[3] ". . . Poisonings and fires though often the result of accident do not in ordinary human experience recur in the same family circle or in the case of the same occupier. Accordingly evidence is allowed to prove the recurrence of such poisonings or such fires respectively without proof that the party concerned was more than "involved" in order to show the high degree of improbability attending the hypothesis that the poisoning or fire under particular scrutiny was an accident" (*per* EVATT, J., in *Martin* v. *Osborne* (1936), 55 C. L. R. 367, at p. 385).
[4] [1908] 2 K. B. 601.

him with regard to the cleansing and keeping of his razors. It was held that evidence might be given to the effect that another customer had contracted a similar disease shortly after he had been attended by the defendant. To quote from the judgment of CHANNELL, J.:

> "It is not legitimate to charge a man with an act of negligence on a day in October and to ask a jury to infer that he was negligent on that day because he was negligent on every day in September. . . . But when the issue is that the defendant pursues a course of conduct which is dangerous to his neighbours, it is legitimate to show that his conduct has been a source of danger on other occasions, and it is a legitimate inference that, having caused injury on those occasions, it has caused injury in the plaintiff's case also."[1]

(*b*) *Unintended consequences.*—The defence of accident may be tantamount to saying, "Although I caused the injuries of which complaint is made, I did not intend to do so". This may be a complete defence or it may amount to the contention that an allegation of intentional wrongdoing should be reduced to a charge based on negligence. *R.* v. *Mortimer*[2] was a case of this latter class. The accused was convicted of murdering a female cyclist by driving his car into her, and evidence that he had driven his car into other female cyclists on the previous day, and later on the same day was admitted to show that he intended to knock the deceased down. If he had done so accidentally, though while driving with a high degree of negligence, the verdict should have been one of manslaughter, but the Court of Criminal Appeal held that the evidence had been rightly admitted to show intention and accordingly affirmed the conviction. The evidence was highly relevant—because it showed a most unusual propensity.

(*c*) *Involuntary conduct.*—In *R.* v. *Harrison-Owen*,[3] the accused was charged with burglary and pleaded that, although he broke into a house and removed some property, he did so in a state of automatism. The trial judge directed counsel for the prosecution to put a number of previous convictions for housebreaking and larceny to the accused saying:

> "in view of this defence that has been raised—that there was no intention in the act from start to finish, and that his presence in the house was purely accidental".

The accused was convicted, but his conviction was quashed because the evidence relating to his past misconduct had been wrongly admitted. The ground of the decision was that the trial judge confused accident and intent, but this is a statement that needs to be enlarged. The previous convictions merely proved that the accused had been guilty of the offences with which he had been charged in the past.[4] They only went to show that the accused was a man of dishonest disposition and could have no further relevance, but, if they had all followed upon a defence similar to that raised by the accused, the facts upon which they were based coupled with a succession of pleas of this nature would have been extremely relevant as suggesting a strange coincidence—whenever the accused was found inside someone else's

---

[1] At pp. 604–5.
[2] (1936), 25 Cr. App. Rep. 150.   [3] [1951] 2 All E. R. 726.
[4] On the view taken in this book (n. 3, p. 297, *ante*) the accused was estopped from denying that he committed larceny, etc., but the convictions as such were no evidence of the circumstances in which the crimes were committed, although some help might possibly have been obtained from the indictment. In *R.* v. *Porter* (1935), 25 Cr. App. Rep. 59, the accused had been convicted in respect of the matters proved at the trial, but they were established again by witnesses and no allusion was made to the former conviction.

house, he said he went there in a state of automatism. On the whole, although the decision in *R. v. Harrison-Owen* may be justified on account of the fact that the evidence showed no more than a propensity to commit house-breaking without reference to the circumstances, it would be unwise to treat the case as a decision to the effect that similar fact evidence is never admissible to rebut an allegation that the conduct of the accused was involuntary. The decision in *R. v. Harrison-Owen* was doubted by Lord DENNING in *Bratty v. A.-G. for Northern Ireland*.[1]

(ii) Rebutting accused's plea of ignorance or mistake of fact.—If it is admitted or proved that a person acted in a particular way, the contention that he did so in consequence of a mistake or ignorance of fact may yet have to be rebutted before the case against him is established. Substantially similar conduct with practically identical results on other occasions is clearly of the utmost relevance in order to negative such a plea, and it has been received in evidence for this reason in a number of cases. The evidence is relevant independently of its tendency to show disposition, even though the disposition may be to commit a particular crime in a particular kind of way.

> " It is not conclusive, for a man may be many times under a similar mistake, or may many times be the dupe of another; but it is less likely that he should be so often, than once, and every circumstance which shows that he was not under a mistake on any one of these occasions strengthens the presumption that he was not on the last." [2]

This observation was made in a case in which the accused had been convicted of obtaining an advance from a pawnbroker by false pretences concerning the quality of a ring. His defence was that he did not know it was worthless, and the Court for Crown Cases Reserved held that evidence had been rightly received concerning the obtaining of advances by similar means from other pawnbrokers shortly before the occasion covered by the indictment. A principal's plea that he was unaware of the fraudulent practices of his agent may likewise be rebutted by proof of similar conduct of the agent on other occasions from which the principal invariably benefited,[3] and a plea that false statements concerning the financial position of a business were prompted by excessive optimism rather than an intent to defraud has been held to warrant the reception of evidence concerning the obtaining of subscriptions to a business with the same name by means of similar statements on an earlier occasion.[4] In fact it may safely be assumed that knowledge that a certain result is likely to follow from particular conduct may always be proved by reference to similar results that have followed from the same conduct of the same person on an earlier occasion.[5]

> "Suppose a charge against a man that he had attempted to procure abortion: the same medicine might be administered with that intent or without it. If it

---

[1] [1963] A. C. 386, at p. 410.
[2] *R. v. Francis* (1874), L. R. 2 C. C. R. 128, at p. 131, *per* COLERIDGE, J.; *R. v. Gregg* (1964), 49 W. W. R. 732.
[3] *Blake v. Albion Life Assurance Society* (1878), 4 C. P. D. 94, a case also decided on system, so far as the acts of the agent were concerned. On this aspect of the decision see also *Barnes v. Merrit & Co.* (1899), 15 T. L. R. 419, and *R. v. Boyle and Merchant*, [1914] 3 K. B. 339. *Blake v. Albion Life Insurance* was distinguished in *Larson v. Boyd* (1919), 46 D. L. R. 126.
[4] *R. v. Porter* (1935), 25 Cr. App. Rep. 59.
[5] *R. v. Cooper* (1849), 3 Cox C. C. 547.

could be proved that he had often given that medicine before, and that he knew that abortion had always followed, surely that would be evidence against him." [1]

(iii) Rebutting innocent explanation of a particular act or of the possession of incriminating material.—In many cases the major issue is whether a particular act which is admitted or proved was done for an innocent purpose or with guilty intent. The innocent purpose is often negatived by "evidence of system", frequently a synonym for evidence of a propensity to commit a particular crime by means of a particular technique. A similar question may arise with regard to the possession of incriminating material—is there an innocent explanation of the possession? If not, the possession of the incriminating material may be a significant item of circumstantial evidence, or unlawful possession may be the gist of the crime charged.

(a) System

"A system is not necessarily criminal: most men carry on business on a system, they may even be said to live on a system. Where, however, acts are of such a character that, taken alone, they may be innocent, but which result in benefit or reward to the actor and loss or suffering to the patient, repeated instances of such acts at least show that experience has fully informed the actor of all their elements and details, and it is only reasonable to infer that the act is designed and intentional, and its motive the benefit or reward to himself or the loss or suffering to some third person." [2]

In *R.* v. *Bond*, from which this quotation is taken, the accused had been convicted of using instruments with intent to procure the abortion of E. A. J. The trial judge admitted the evidence of G. S. T. that the accused had performed a similar operation upon her nine months previously, and, in the course of her examination-in-chief, she said that he told her that he had "put dozens of girls right". Both E. A. J. and G. S. T. were servants of the accused who had been pregnant by him, and the court held that the evidence had been rightly received. Bond was a doctor, and his defence was that the instruments had been used when examining E. A. J. for leucorrhoea. As the charge related to an attempt, no question of accident or mistake was involved, the sole issue being the intention with which the admitted acts of the accused were performed, and his statement concerning his behaviour towards other girls suggested that he was a practised abortionist. It was, of course, possible that he had acted with an innocent intent, but it would have been a strange coincidence if he had done so when operating on someone who was pregnant by him with the same instruments as those employed on another woman for the purpose of relieving himself of the burden of paternity. It is an abuse of language to say that an isolated act proves system, and some of the judges in *R.* v. *Bond* would not have admitted the evidence of G. S. T. had it not been for the allegation concerning the accused's admission of having performed similar operations on numerous previous occasions, but an isolated act may suffice to support an argument based on the rarity of coincidences. That is why other judges in *Bond's Case* would have admitted evidence concerning the accused's conduct to G. S. T. as tending to negative innocent intent towards E. A. J., even if the former's testimony had not referred to the admission of similar

---

[1] At p. 550.
[2] A. T. LAWRENCE, J., in *R.* v. *Bond*, [1906] 2 K. B. 389, at p. 420.

behaviour on other occasions. Evidence tending to show that the accused was a practised abortionist has also been admitted in order to negative innocent intent in the use of drugs or instruments when there was no such connection between the patients and the accused as that which existed in *Bond's Case.*[1]

Evidence of what is said to constitute system has frequently been admitted in support of an allegation of fraud. In *R. v. Rhodes,*[2] the accused was charged with obtaining eggs by means of an advertisement suggesting that "Norfolk Farm Dairies" to which it referred was a genuine business when this was not the case. Evidence that he had obtained eggs on two subsequent occasions by means of a similar advertisement was held to have been rightly admitted by the Court for Crown Cases Reserved because it went to show the nature of the accused's business, *i.e.*, the falsity of the pretence. In *R. v. Ollis,*[3] the prisoner was convicted of obtaining money by false pretences by means of bad cheques on June 24th, June 26th and July 6th. The Court for Crown Cases Reserved held that evidence had been rightly admitted concerning the obtaining of a cheque in exchange for another valueless cheque on July 5th. The accused had already been tried and acquitted on a charge relating to this latter cheque, but his bank account, which had not been operated for three years, only showed a credit balance of three and ninepence, and the majority of the court considered that the evidence went to show that he was engaged on a systematic course of fraudulent conduct.

Evidence of system may be given to support the argument that the purpose of a series of acts must have been the performance of some further act constituting the *actus reus* of the crime charged.[4] The argument is best expressed in the words of EVATT, J., in the Australian case of *Martin v. Osborne* :[5]

> "Where a question in issue is whether, on a particular occasion, the proved acts of a party were accompanied by the performance by such party of a further act, it is permissible to show that such party was, at or about the time in question, engaged in a special kind of business, line of conduct, or manner of living, according to the exigencies of which the proved acts would ordinarily be accompanied by the performance of the further act in issue so as to constitute a typical instance of the business, line of conduct, or manner of living in which the party was so engaged. Provided that the business, line of conduct, or manner of living is of such a character as to render it very highly improbable that on the occasion in question the performance by the party concerned of the further act in issue would not accompany his proved acts."

These remarks were made in a case in which the accused was charged with operating a commercial transport vehicle without a licence. Such a vehicle was defined as one in which passengers were carried for a reward. It was proved that the vehicle was driven by the accused at the material time, but

---

[1] *R. v. Palm* (1910), 4 Cr. App. Rep. 253; *R. v. Starkie,* [1922] 2 K. B. 295 (evidence of use of drugs admissible on charge involving use of instruments); *R v. Ross and McCarthy,* [1955] S.R. Q. 48; *R. v. Powell, Iremonger and Kinley,* [1957] N. Z. L. R. 1. Cf. *Brunet* v. *R.*, [1928] S. C. R. 375, and *R. v. Campbell* (1947), 2 C. R. 351.

[2] [1899] 1 Q. B. 77; *R. v. Hurren* (1962), 46 Cr. App. Rep. 323. Cf. *R. v. Sagar,* [1914] 3 K. B. 1112, showing that, if the accused can do so, he may produce receipts in such a case to show that he was carrying on a genuine business.

[3] [1900] 2 Q. B. 758; *R. v. Wyatt,* [1904] 1 K. B. 188.

[4] It used to be thought that similar fact evidence was never admissible to prove the *actus reus,* but such a view is untenable in the light of such cases as *R. v. Ball,* [1911] A. C. 47.

[5] (1936), 55 C. L. R. 367, at p. 402.

there was no direct evidence that he received a reward. He was carrying passengers on a journey from Ballarat to Melbourne, and he stopped at various places en route where passengers boarded and alighted from the vehicle. Evidence of similar journeys on the two days preceding that covered by the charge was held to have been rightly admitted, and the conviction of the accused was upheld. There does not appear to be an English decision which is precisely in point, but there can be little doubt that the principle underlying *Martin* v. *Osborne* represents English law.

(*b*) *Purpose of possession of incriminating material.*—In *R.* v. *Armstrong*,[1] a solicitor was charged with murdering his wife by arsenical poisoning, and his defence was that she had committed suicide. On arrest he was found to be in possession of a considerable quantity of arsenic which he said he had purchased and kept for the purpose of killing weeds. He was proved to have bought arsenic shortly before his wife's death, and evidence that he attempted to poison a man with arsenic some eight months later was held to have been rightly admitted by the trial judge because it suggested that the appellant was lying when he said that he had purchased the poison for an innocent purpose. This is a somewhat surprising decision so far as the admissibility of similar fact evidence is concerned, for the defence of accident was not raised. The accused's conduct would have been highly relevant to that defence, but the relevance of the evidence for the purpose for which it was admitted was not very great; *R.* v. *Armstrong* was however mentioned in the House of Lords without any suggestion of disapproval in *Harris* v. *Director of Public Prosecutions*.[2]

If a man is charged with fraudulently uttering a forged deed, and he relies on the absence of guilty knowledge, proof that he was in possession of other forged deeds would render his defence less credible.[3]

In *R.* v. *Hodges* [4] the accused was charged with being in possession of housebreaking implements by night without lawful excuse. He was found in possession of skeleton keys, one of which had been filed down. His defence was that he had the keys in order to get into his lodgings, and evidence that he had shown these keys, or substantially similar ones, to two witnesses with the suggestion that they should "do a job" together with the aid of the keys was held to have been rightly admitted. Its tendency to negative the defence of lawful possession was obvious.

(iv) Negativing false identification of the accused.—One of the minor difficulties with which anyone seeking to expound the decisions on the admissibility of evidence of disposition has to contend is the presence of catch-words in the judgments. Evidence negativing accident or mistake is often said to be "evidence of system", and evidence negativing mistake is often spoken of as "proof of guilty knowledge". These catch-words are harmless enough, but such phrases as "evidence of identity", "proof of identity" and the like, which are frequently used in relation to the cases about to be discussed are liable to be confusing unless it is appreciated that they mean different things according to whether there is direct testimonial

---

[1] [1922] 2 K. B. 555; *cf. Noor Mohamed* v. *R.*, [1949] A. C. 182; [1949] 1 All E. R. 365 (p. 312, *ante*), where the appellant used cyanide in the course of his trade as a goldsmith so that his possession of poison did not call for an explanation.

[2] [1952] A. C. 694; [1952] 1 All E. R. 1044.

[3] *R.* v. *Mason* (1914), 10 Cr. App. Rep. 169.

[4] (1957), 41 Cr. App. Rep. 218. The evidence was also said to be admissible on the ground that it showed that the keys were capable of use as housebreaking implements. See also *R.* v. *Hannam* (1963), 49 M. P. R. 262.

evidence of the accused's participation in the crime charged. If there is, evidence of other misconduct may be admissible to confirm the witness's testimony. If there is no testimonial evidence to the effect that the accused was the perpetrator of the crime charged, evidence of his other misconduct may, provided it is sufficiently relevant, be admissible as an item of circumstantial evidence pointing to the guilt of the accused. Whether the "evidence of identity" is admissible to confirm testimony or as circumstantial evidence of guilt, it may take the form of proof of the possession of incriminating material.

(*a*) *Evidence concerning testimonial identification.*—In *Thompson* v. *R.*,[1] a case with a chequered career, the accused was convicted of gross indecency with two boys. The acts on which complaint were made were alleged to have occurred on March 16th, and the person who committed them was alleged to have made a further appointment with the boys for the 19th. The police were informed in the meantime, and they kept watch with one of the boys at the rendezvous—a public lavatory. The boy pointed the accused out to the police and, from the first, the only defence raised was mistaken identity: "You have got the wrong man." It was held that, having regard to the special nature of the defence, evidence had been rightly admitted of the discovery of powder puffs on his person and indecent photographs in the accused's room. To quote from the speech of Lord FINLAY:[2]

> "The whole question is as to the identity of the person who came to the spot on the 19th with the person who committed the acts on the 16th. What was done on the 16th shows that the person who did it was a person with abnormal propensities of this kind. The possession of the articles tends to show that the person who came on the 19th, the prisoner, had abnormal propensities of the same kind. The criminal of the 16th and the prisoner had this feature in common, and it appears to me that the evidence which is objected to afforded some evidence tending to show the probability of the truth of the boy's story as to identity."

The principle of this decision has been applied to cases in which the evidence of misconduct on other occasions consisted of the testimony of witnesses for the prosecution instead of incriminating material found in the possession of the accused. In *R.* v. *Hall*,[3] the appellant was convicted of acts of gross indecency on different occasions with C., B. and R. So far as the latter was concerned, Hall's defence was that he had never seen R., and it was held that evidence of C. and B. concerning acts done to them by the accused in circumstances similar to those narrated by R. had been rightly admitted by the trial judge because:

> "It was for the jury to say whether R. was a liar or a witness of truth, and in deciding that question they were entitled to take into account the evidence given by C. and B".[4]

Similarly, in *R.* v. *Robinson*,[5] the accused was charged with two robberies each effected by means of a hold-up with the same motor car. He was identified by one of the victims of the second crime, and the Court of Criminal Appeal held that the trial judge had rightly told the jury that, in deciding whether to accept this witness's evidence, they could consider the

---

[1] [1918] A. C. 221.   [2] At pp. 225–6.

[3] [1952] 1 K. B. 302; [1952] 1 All E. R. 66.

[4] At pp. 308, 69, respectively, *per* Lord GODDARD, C.J.

[5] (1953), 37 Cr. App. Rep. 95. See also *R.* v. *Giovannone* (1960), 45 Cr. App. Rep. 31; *R.* v. *Adami*, [1959] S. A. S. R. 81.

evidence identifying the accused as the perpetrator of the first robbery provided they believed it. In the words of the trial judge:

> "If Robinson is not a guilty man, he is a singularly unfortunate man. He is identified by different people, or said to be identified by two entirely different people, in respect of two entirely different raids."

The ground of the admissibility of this type of evidence was succinctly stated by HALLETT, J., when delivering the judgment of the Court of Criminal Appeal:

> "If the jury are precluded by some rule of law from taking the view that something is a coincidence which is against all the probabilities if the accused person is innocent, then it would seem to be a doctrine of law which prevents a jury from using what looks like ordinary common sense." [1]

The same technique had been employed in each of the robberies with which Robinson was charged, and it seems that the crimes with which *R.* v. *Hall* was concerned had significant features in common. When reliance is placed by the prosecution upon similarity of technique it is sometimes said that the "hall-mark" principle is invoked. This principle was applied in *R.* v *Davis* and *R.* v. *Murphy*[2] to the confirmation of a witness's visual identification of the accused by evidence of his association with a gang who had employed a technique in a second robbery strikingly similar to that which had been employed by him and his co-accused in the first. The evidence of association was the fact that Murphy, who was not charged with the second robbery, had been travelling in a car with those who were charged shortly after the occurrence of that robbery. It would be interesting to know how far this extension of the hall-mark principle can be taken. If A. is visually identified as the perpetrator of a burglary in which an unusual technique was employed, would evidence that he had been seen a week later talking to B., a burglar known to employ the same technique, be admissible to confirm the identification of A.?

It is essential that the facts of a case should be such that a Crown witness's identification of the accused might have been mistaken in order that evidence of the accused's misconduct on other occasions should be admissible to confirm it. In *R.* v. *Chandor*,[3] for instance, a Croydon schoolmaster was charged with indecent assaults on three of his pupils, A., B. and C. A. alleged that the incident affecting him occurred in the lake district, and the defence to this count was that the meeting never took place. The accused admitted that he had been with B. and C. in Croydon at the material times, but denied the occurrence of the incidents to which they deposed. The trial judge directed the jury that they might consider the evidence of B. and C. when deciding on the count concerning A. and, because of this, the accused's conviction was quashed by the Court of Criminal Appeal:

> "Evidence that an offence was committed by the accused against B. at Croydon could not be any evidence that the accused met A. in the lake district and committed an offence there."[4]

Yet, had the accused not been a schoolmaster and the prosecutors his pupils, the evidence rejected might, at any rate if it contained allegations

---

[1] 37 Cr. App. Rep., at p. 106.   [2] (1971), 56 Cr. App. Rep. 249.
[3] [1959] 1 Q. B. 545; [1959] 1 All E. R. 702; for articles inspired by this case see (1959), C. L. J. 210, and 75 L. Q. R. 333. See Addendum, *ante*.   [4] *Per* Lord PARKER, C.J.

significantly similar to those made by A., have been admitted to negative a mistake on his part.

On charges of abortion, evidence that the accused had performed other abortions is admissible to rebut the defence that he performed the operation in respect of which he is charged with innocent intent, but it has been held in Canada that such evidence is inadmissible when the defence is that the accused had nothing to do with the prosecutrix on the occasion in question.[1] *R.* v. *Chandor* suggests that an English court would come to the same conclusion provided there was no question of mistaken identification.

The following remarks of Lord SUMNER in *Thompson* v. *R.*[2] account to a large extent for the chequered career of that case:

> "Persons who commit the offences now under consideration seek the habitual gratification of a particular perverted lust which not only takes them out of the class of ordinary men gone wrong, but stamps them with the hall-mark of a specialised and extraordinary class as much as if they carried on their bodies some physical peculiarity."

In *R.* v. *Sims*[3] these remarks were used to justify a very wide *ratio decidendi* according to which evidence of homosexual misconduct on the part of the accused is always admissible on a homosexual charge without any reference to its resemblance to that charged. We shall see that *R.* v. *Sims* must now be restricted to its narrower *ratio decidendi*, but, although they were not cited in the judgment, Lord SUMNER's words are about all that can be quoted by way of authority for the decision of the Court of Appeal in *R.* v. *King*.[4]

In that case convictions of homosexual offences against two boys were upheld in spite of the fact that the accused had been asked in cross-examination whether he was a homosexual, a question which received an affirmative reply. One set of incidents was alleged to have taken place in a public lavatory, and the accused's defence was that he was not there at the time. Viewed as a decision on the admissibility of evidence of criminal propensity to confirm testimonial identification, *R* v. *King* goes much further than *Thompson* v. *R.* for the fact that the complainants gave evidence of the appointment of the 19th March at a place which Thompson was approaching on that day was treated as crucial by some of the Law Lords, while the powder puffs found on Thompson's person were treated as articles commonly used in the course of the crimes under consideration; but, although, as we shall see, *R.* v. *King* has been relegated to the class of decisions on their very special facts so far as the defence of innocent association (raised with regard to a second set of incidents) is concerned, it does not appear to have been the subject of adverse judicial comment as a decision on evidence of identity.

It was said in *R.* v. *Morris*[5] however, that, if facts similar to those of *Thompson* v. *R.* were to occur to-day, a different conclusion might well be reached.

> "But if that is so, it is not because the law has changed since *Thompson* v. *R.*,

---

[1] *Brunet* v. *R.*, [1928] S. C. R. 161; *R.* v. *Campbell* (1947), 2 C. R. 351.
[2] [1918] A. C. 221, at p. 235.
[3] [1946] K. B. 531, at p. 540.
[4] [1967] 2 Q. B. 338; [1967] 1 All E. R. 379; for comments see 83 L. Q. R. 186, 30 M. L. R. 441 and [1967] Crim. L. R. 633.
[5] (1969), 54 Cr. App. Rep. 69, at p. 79.

but because public attitudes and public habits, particularly in regard to homosexuality, may themselves have changed meanwhile."

This presumably means that it is now more likely to be recognised that a man may possess himself of photographs of nude boys, and even of powder puffs, without being a practising pederast; were the facts of Thompson's case to recur with the difference that there was evidence that the accused had committed homosexual offences with other boys, it is difficult to believe that such evidence would not be admissible, even if there were no similarity of technique. The coincidence with regard to the disposition of the alleged criminal of the 16th and that of the man who appeared to be keeping the appointment said to have been made for the 19th would have been no less striking to-day than it was in 1918.

(*b*) *Circumstantial evidence of identity.*—Although witnesses testified to his presence, at the material time, near the place where the victim of the murder alleged to have been committed by the accused was found, *R. v. Morris* is best regarded as a case in which the evidence of identity was circumstantial. Morris was charged with the murder of D., a girl of 8, attempted abduction of A., a girl of 10, and indecent assault upon Y., a girl of 5. He pleaded guilty to the charge of indecent assault, photographs of Y. in indecent postures having been found in his house. He was convicted of the other two offences and his appeal was unsuccessful. The evidence on the murder charge was that D. had been enticed by the accused to get into his car and her dead body was found on a heath in circumstances making it plain that the girl had been sexually assaulted; the position of D.'s corpse resembled that of Y. in the photographs, and they were accordingly held admissible on the murder charge. The Court of Appeal also held that the circumstances of the attempted abduction of A. sufficiently resembled those of the alleged enticement of D. to render that evidence admissible on the murder charge as well.

The most striking reported instance of the application of the hall-mark principle to circumstantial evidence of identity is *R. v. Straffen*.[1] There was abundant evidence that the accused had the opportunity of committing the murder with which he was charged as he had been seen to pass near the place where the victim's body was found near the time at which she must have been strangled, but this was also true of others. The evidence of the earlier murders committed by Straffen served to identify him, rather than any of the others, as the perpetrator of the crime under investigation.

On the facts of a particular case, the evidence of propensity may be admissible although it can hardly be said to fall within the hall-mark principle. For example, it has been held in Ontario that, where it is plain that a murder was committed by a homosexual, evidence that the accused had engaged in homosexual acts is admissible,[2] and it is not unlikely that such evidence would be admitted in England.

(*c*) *Identification by possession of the instruments of crime.*—

"We do not think that evidence of the possession of tools for the commission of crime is admissible only when it appears that tools of that nature were used in carrying out the alleged crime; it is sufficient if such tools might have been so used."[3]

---

[1] [1952] 2 Q. B. 911; [1952] 2 All E. R. 657; p. 315, *ante*.
[2] *R. v. Glynn*, [1972] 1 O. R. 403.
[3] *Thompson v. R.*, (1968), 42 A. L. J. R. 16, at p. 17.

These remarks in a judgment of the High Court of Australia were made in a case in which a conviction of safe-breaking by means of explosives was quashed because evidence of the accused's possession of picklocks had been received at the trial. Both the *ratio decidendi* and the *obiter dictum* represent English law.

In *R. v. Taylor*[1] the principle ground on which a conviction for shop-breaking was quashed was that evidence of the finding of a jemmy in the accused's house had been wrongly admitted because the door of the shop did not bear the marks of such an instrument, and the accused contended that they had broken the door without criminal intent while indulging in a drunken escapade. On the same principle it has been said that, if entry by keys is proved, the finding of a jemmy will not be admissible, and, if the entry were by means of a jemmy, evidence ought not to be received of the finding of skeleton keys in the possession of the accused.[2]

Although the judgment of the Court of Criminal Appeal was marred by the fact that it followed the broad judgment of that Court in *R. v. Thompson*,[3] and not the narrow *ratio decidendi* of the House of Lords in *Thompson v. R.*,[4] *R. v. Twiss*[5] may be regarded as a case in which the evidence of possession of incriminating material was received because it was of the same nature as that alleged to have been used in the commission of the crime charged; it is simply another illustration of the application of the hall-mark principle. Twiss was convicted of gross indecency with a boy whose evidence was that he went to Twiss's lodgings where he was shown a number of indecent photographs after which the act of which complaint was made took place. The defence put all the facts in issue and the Court of Criminal Appeal held that indecent photographs found in the possession of the accused were admissible evidence against him although some of them were not alleged to have been used in the course of the crime charged.

In *R. v. Reading*[6] the Court of Appeal held that material of a kind used in the type of robbery with which the accused were charged together with articles which might have been the proceeds of that robbery had been rightly admitted by the trial judge. The main basis of the *ratio decidendi* was that the scene upon which the police came on the accused's premises tended to identify the accused as the perpetrators of the crime charged.

(v) Rebutting defence of innocent association.—The defence of innocent association may sometimes amount to nothing more than an assertion that, although the acts alleged against the party charged were performed by him, he lacked the requisite guilty intent. In such a case, the evidence suggesting that the guilty intent existed may be confirmed by a witness's statement tending to show its existence on a proximate occasion. In *R. v. Hall*,[7] for instance, the accused had contended that the acts of which C. and B. complained were part of the medical treatment which he was giving them, and it was held that the evidence of each accused was admissible on the counts concerning the other, for it would certainly be a

---

[1] (1923), 17 Cr. App. Rep. 109.
[2] *R. v. Manning* (1923), 17 Cr. App. Rep. 85, at p. 88.
[3] [1917] 2 K. B. 630.
[4] [1918] A. C. 221.
[5] [1918] 2 K. B. 853; cf. *R. v. Gillingham*, [1939] 4 All E. R. 122; and *O'Brien v. R.*, [1963] W. A. R. 70.
[6] [1966] 1 All E. R. 521.
[7] [1952] 1 K. B. 302; [1952] 1 All E. R. 66.

coincidence for two people to make the same mistake about the nature of the medical treatment they were receiving. Evidence of the discovery of incriminating material is also admissible to rebut a defence based on the absence of guilty intent in acts that are proved or admitted to have been performed by the accused.[1]

The defence of innocent association may also amount to an assertion that, although the opportunity of doing the acts complained of existed, advantage was not taken of that opportunity. It is to rebut this type of assertion that evidence of the existence of a guilty passion between two people mentioned in a charge of adultery or a sexual offence is invariably admitted.[2]

In *R. v. Sims*,[3] another case with a chequered career, the accused was charged with sodomy and gross indecency with four men, and it was held that the judge had rightly refused an application for separate trials because the evidence of each accuser was admissible on the counts concerning the others. Lord GODDARD, C.J., subsequently explained the decision on the following grounds:

> "The judge was right to try all the four cases together because the fact was that not one, but four men, who admittedly had gone to the prisoner's house to spend the evening on different occasions, all said exactly the same advances had been made to them by the prisoner, and that exactly the same acts had been committed on them, which tended to show that the association which the prisoner had with these men was a guilty one and not an innocent one. His defence was that he used to invite these young men to have a game of cards and to sit with him in his cottage. The answer that the prosecution made was that in every one of these cases, although the prisoner said that each young man came to him innocently, each young man alleged that the prisoner had committed offences on him. On these grounds the court held that the evidence was admissible."[4]

The above passage supports what may be described as the narrow view of the *ratio decidendi* of *R. v. Sims*. The similar fact evidence was admissible because there were specific features which made each accusation bear a striking resemblance to the others. The evidence showed, not merely that the accused was a homosexual, but also that he proceeded according to a particular technique; but, as we have seen, the judgment also cited the passage from Lord SUMNER's speech in *Thompson v. R.*[5] in which he

---

[1] *R. v. Cole* (1941), 165 L. T. 125.

[2] *Weatherley* v. *Weatherley* (1854), 1 Ecc. & Ad. 193; *Boddy* v. *Boddy and Grover* (1860), 30 L. J. P. & M. 23; *Wales* v. *Wales*, [1900] P. 63 (adultery). *R. v. Ball*, [1911] A. C. 47; *R. v. Stone* (1910), 6 Cr. App. Rep. 89; *R. v. Bloodworth* (1913), 9 Cr. App. Rep. 80; *R. v. Cooper* (1914), 10 Cr. App. Rep. 195 (incest). Though generally inadmissible, incest with persons other than those mentioned in the charge may be rendered admissible by some such special factor as a father's statement that he was in the habit of indulging in innocent horse-play with his female children: *R. v. Ratahujui*, [1947] N. Z. L. R. 581; *R. v. Hare*, [1952] N. Z. L. R. 588 (indecent assault); *R. v. Shellaker*, [1914] 1 K. B. 414; *R. v. Hewitt* (1925), 19 Cr. App. Rep. 64; *R. v. Marsh* (1949), 33 Cr. App. Rep. 185; *The People (A.-G)* v. *Dempsey*, [1961] I. R. 288 (unlawful carnal knowledge). Unlawful carnal knowledge of another girl may be admissible on the facts of a particular case, e.g. to confirm the prosecutrix's evidence concerning a statement made to her by the accused. *R. v. Chitson*, [1909] 2 K. B. 945; *R. v. Hartley*, [1941] 1 K. B. 5, followed after discussion and with a dissenting judgment in *R. v. Whitham*, [1962] S. R. Qd. 49 (homosexuality). See also *R. v. Young*, [1923] S. A. S. R. 35; *R. v. Thompson* (1954), 20 C. R. 410; *Evans v. F.*, [1964] S. A. S. R. 130 (indecent exposure).

[3] [1946] K. B. 531; [1946] 1 All E. R. 697.

[4] *R. v. Hall*, [1952] 1 K. B. 302, at pp. 305–306; [1952] 1 All E. R. 66, at p. 68.

[5] [1918] A. C. 221, at p. 235. Other circumstances of the chequered career of *R. v. Sims* were (1) the assertion in the judgment that evidence of other misconduct is admissible without regard to the defence raised by the accused (p. 318, *ante*); and (2) the suggestion

equated homosexual propensity with physical deformity. This was said to justify the reception of the evidence of each accused on the counts concerning the others in order to rebut the defence of innocent association, quite independently of the similarity of the facts to which each witness deposed. It can be said with a fair degree of confidence that this view no longer represents the law. It is true that it was held that the accused's bare acknowledgment of homosexual propensity was admissible to rebut the defence of innocent association raised by the accused in *R. v. King*[1] with regard to the second set of incidents with which he was charged; but the Court of Appeal spoke of the case as a very special one in *R. v. Horwood*.[2]

Horwood was charged with attempted gross indecency with a boy. The boy's case was that Horwood had taken him for a ride in his car to a wood where they had got out and where the attempt had taken place before he succeeded in making off. Horwood's case was that he got out of the car alone and went into the wood in order to urinate, returning to find that the boy had disappeared. When interviewing him, a police officer asked Horwood whether he was a homosexual and received the reply that he had been although he was cured. It was held that the trial judge ought not to have admitted evidence of the question and answer, and Horwood's conviction was quashed. *King's Case* was treated as a special one on account of the much greater intimacy of the alleged innocent association, King having admitted to meeting his accusers in a public lavatory, inviting them home to spend the night with him, and sleeping with one of them in his bed and the other on the floor of his room.

A further reason in favour of the view that the broad *ratio* of *R. v. Sims* no longer represents the law is provided by Lord HAILSHAM's treatment of the similar fact evidence admitted to rebut innocent association in *Director of Public Prosecutions v. Kilbourne*.[3]

> "With the exception of one incident, each accusation bears a resemblance to the other and shows not merely that he [Kilbourne] was a homosexual which would not have been enough to make the evidence admissible, but that he was one whose proclivities in that regard took a particular form."

In *R. v. Chandor*[4] it was argued that the evidence of A. and B. and A. and C. respectively might be admissible to rebut the defence of innocent association raised by the accused with regard to C. and B.; but the Court of Criminal Appeal did not decide this point. It was observed, however, that, in the case of schoolmaster and pupil, there may be nothing suspicious in the association which calls for an explanation. The account of the facts is too brief to indicate the significance of this remark.

Another broad statement in the judgment in *R. v. Sims* is the following:

> "The probative force of all the acts together is much greater than one alone; for, whereas the jury might think that one man might be telling an untruth, three or four are hardly likely to tell the same untruth unless they were con-

---

that the evidence of an accomplice falling within the third class mentioned in *Davies v. Director of Public Prosecutions*, [1954] A. C. 378; [1954] 1 All E. R. 507; could not corroborate another accomplice, though it might help the jury to ascertain the truth (p. 180, *ante*).

[1] [1967] 2 Q. B. 338; [1967] 1 All E. R. 349, p. 333, *ante*.
[2] [1970] 1 Q. B. 133; [1969] 3 All E. R. 1156.
[3] [1973] A. C. 729, at p. 751. See Addendum, *ante*.
[4] [1959] 1 Q. B. 545; [1959] 1 All E. R. 702; p. 332, *ante*.

spiring together. If there is nothing to suggest a conspiracy their evidence would seem to be overwhelming."[1]

In *R.* v. *Flack*[2] SALMON, L.J., speaking for the Court of Appeal, said that this passage did not represent the present law if it meant that, whenever a sexual offence was charged in respect of A., evidence of similar offences against B., C. and D. was admissible. In *Flack's Case* it was held that, on a charge of incest against a brother in respect of three sisters, the evidence of each sister was inadmissible on the counts concerning the others, the defence being a simple denial.

SALMON, L.J., doubted whether the passage from *R.* v. *Sims* was intended to bear the meaning suggested above. It gives rise to speculation concerning the right form of summing-up to a jury in a case containing many counts in which the evidence on each is admissible on the others.[3] The jury must be told to consider each count separately.[4] Although it may involve a departure from the global reasoning of the passage from *R.* v. *Sims* quoted above, which seems to have contemplated the jury taking the evidence on every count into consideration when considering the accused's guilt on any one, including the first, the course adopted by Lord GODDARD, C.J., in *R.* v. *Robinson*[5] has much to commend it. It will be recollected that that case was concerned with two hold-ups. Lord GODDARD said:

> "You will be entitled, only if you come to the conclusion that you ought to convict Robinson of the first hold-up, to use that fact as strengthening the case against Robinson with regard to the second hold-up. As I say, you must decide perfectly independently, but I advise you first, to consider the Lyons hold-up. If you are not satisfied with Mr. Gilbert's identification in the Lyons hold-up, I should think you certainly would not be satisfied with Mr. Wood's identification in the second hold-up. If you are convinced by Mr. Gilbert's evidence, then you may find that helps you to come to a conclusion as to whether or not Mr. Wood is right in his identification with regard to the second hold-up."

C. MISCELLANEOUS

Three further points that call for consideration are the position when the accused volunteers evidence of or asks questions about his misconduct on other occasions, the way in which the judge's discretion to exclude prejudicial evidence operates in conjunction with the rule we have been considering, and the question whether there is an exception to the rule in the case of evidence obtained in answer to cross-examination to credit.

(1) EVIDENCE OF MISCONDUCT ON OTHER OCCASIONS GIVEN BY THE ACCUSED

In the days before the accused was allowed to give evidence on his own behalf or, in the case of a charge of felony, to be represented by counsel, the court occasionally prevented him from tendering incriminating docu-

---

[1] [1946] K. B. 531, at p. 540; contrast Lord HEWART, C.J., in *R.* v. *Bailey*, [1924] 2 K. B. 300, at p. 305 where, however, his Lordship may have had the dangers of a conspiracy in mind.
[2] [1969] 2 All E. R. 784.
[3] See *R.* v. *Muling*, [1951] N. Z. L. R. 1022.
[4] *R.* v. *Bailey*, [1924] 2 K. B. 300.
[5] [1953] 2 All E. R. 334.

ments in his own interest.[1] It may have been a misguided desire to protect the accused from the revelation of his past misdeeds which led to the objection to a line of questioning of the prosecution witnesses which would almost certainly have established the innocence of Adolf Beck. Beck was prosecuted for false pretences on the assumption that he was the same man as one John Smith, and counsel for the prosecution successfully prevented Beck's counsel from questioning witnesses with a view to establishing that John Smith was in prison at the particular time. Had he been allowed to put these questions, it would then have been possible for Beck's counsel to have established that his client was abroad at the material time. Whatever may have been the cause of this unfortunate occurrence at the first trial of Beck, there can be little doubt that the accused may, at any rate when it is clear that he is fully cognisant of the danger he runs, give evidence of his own misconduct on other occasions or ask questions with regard to it without being in any way concerned with the rule which we have been discussing. The terms of the direction which the judge should then give to the jury must depend on the facts of the particular case.[2] In appropriate circumstances, it may also be assumed that the defendant in a civil case may give evidence of his misconduct without regard to the principles which have been considered in this chapter.

(2) Judicial Discretion

In order that evidence should be admissible on the principles we have been considering, it must be relevant for some reason other than its tendency to show bad disposition, or highly relevant if it does no more. As relevance is a matter of degree, a judge has a substantial discretion when determining whether evidence is admissible under the rule; but, even so, there may be cases in which it is impossible to say that the evidence in question lacks the requisite degree of relevance, and yet it might be unfair to admit it, having regard to its probative value as contrasted with its prejudicial propensity. *Perkins* v. *Jeffery*[3] may be regarded as just such a case. The accused was charged with indecent exposure to Miss T. in July. Evidence of similar conduct towards the same woman in the previous May was held to have been rightly received because the defence was that the police had arrested the wrong man; but it was also held that, until it became clear that a plea of innocent intent was to be raised, evidence of exposure to other women ought not to be received. Clearly it had probative value on the issue of identity and tended to confirm Miss T.'s testimony in every respect; but its primary relevance lay in its tendency to negative a suggestion that the exposure took place without any criminal intent.

In *R.* v. *Fitzpatrick*,[4] the accused was charged with an indecent assault and indecent exposure within the following quarter of an hour. An

---

[1] *R.* v. *Horn Tooke* (1794), 25 St. Tr. 1.
[2] It has been held, rather harshly perhaps, in Ontario that, if an accused gives evidence of his previous convictions to anticipate cross-examination thereon under s. 12 of the Canada Evidence Act, according to which he is liable to cross-examination like an ordinary witness, the judge can tell the jury that they may take the conviction into account on the issue of liability and not merely as going to credit (*R.* v. *St. Pierre*, [1973] 1 O. R. 718).
[3] [1915] 2 K. B. 702. *Cf. R.* v. *Solomons*, also showing the significance of the stage of the trial at which the evidence is tendered. 1959 (2) S.A. 352. For discretion generally in relation to evidence see Chapter I, section 6.
[4] [1962] 3 All E. R. 840; *R.* v. *Doughty* [1965] 1 All E. R. 560.

application for separate trials was refused because the judge considered that the evidence concerning each offence was admissible on the other charge. The ensuing convictions were quashed by the Court of Criminal Appeal because the judge had not applied his mind to the question whether the evidence ought to have been excluded in the exercise of his discretion. Had he concluded that the evidence ought to have been excluded he would very likely have made an order for separate trials. The question of the admissibility of the evidence as a matter of law was left open by the Court of Criminal Appeal, but, even if the evidence was admissible on the ground that it went to show that the accused was acting under the stress of a continuous incident of sexual excitement,[1] its prejudicial effect would have been far greater than its probative value.

(3) Cross-Examination as to Credit

The general rule prohibiting the adduction of evidence tending to show bad disposition for the sole purpose of proving that a party committed the crime or civil wrong into which the court is inquiring is difficult to apply to the use that can be made of answers given in cross-examination as to credit. In civil cases, a suitor who elects to give evidence is in the same position as an ordinary witness. If A. claims damages for deceit on the ground that B. knowingly misrepresented the value of some property, B. can be cross-examined about a totally different kind of false pretence made to someone else in the past. His denials will be final in the sense that A. cannot call evidence in rebuttal, but the jury is not obliged to accept them and he might be constrained to make a damning admission. B.'s past conduct may not be used to support an argument that he was fraudulent on the occasion in respect of which he is being sued because he was fraudulent in other ways at other times, but account may be taken of the fact that he was fraudulent in other ways at other times in deciding whether he is to be believed when he swears that he was not fraudulent on the occasion in respect of which he is being sued. The subtlety of this distinction is enough to raise the greatest doubts with regard to its validity, and the gravest doubts may legitimately be entertained with regard to its utility in proceedings with a jury. There is, however, high authority in support of such a contrast in a leading criminal case. The accused may be cross-examined as to his credit whenever he throws away the shield provided by s.1 (f) of the Criminal Evidence Act, 1898, and, when speaking about cross-examination concerning other crimes in *Maxwell* v. *Director of Public Prosecutions*,[2] Lord Sankey, L.C., said:

> "The question whether a man has been convicted, charged or acquitted, even if it goes to credibility, ought not to be admitted, if there is any risk of the jury being misled into thinking that it goes not to credibility but to the probability of his having committed the offence with which he is charged."

In *R.* v. *Samuel*,[3] the appellant was held to have been properly convicted of larceny by finding and retaining a camera bearing the name of its owner. He threw away his shield by putting his character in issue in referring to occasions on which he had taken steps to restore lost property to those

---

[1] Had the interval between the two alleged offences been very slight, the evidence might have been said to form part of the *res gestae*.

[2] [1935] A. C. 309, at p. 321. See the commentary by Professor Stone in 51 L. Q. R. 443.

[3] (1956), 40 Cr. App. Rep. 8.

entitled to it, and was accordingly cross-examined about his previous convictions for theft. When dealing with an argument that the jury should have been warned that the convictions merely concerned the credibility of the accused, Lord GODDARD, C.J., said:

> "It is very difficult to see how if it is permissable to cross-examine a prisoner with regard to convictions, for instance, if he is a thief, and he is cross-examined on previous convictions of larceny, the jury is not, in effect, being asked to say: 'The prisoner is just the sort of man who would commit these crimes and therefore it is highly probable that he did.' In theory, at any rate, what the jury is being asked to do is to reject the prisoner's evidence when he says: 'I always intended to hand back the camera to the police when I had a reasonable opportunity.' By putting questions to him the prosecution were in fact trying to destroy his credibility and to say to the jury: 'It is all very well the prisoner saying that, but you are not obliged to believe him; look at his convictions which show that he is not a person to be believed on his oath in these matters.'" [1]

From the practical point of view, it is best to regard the use that can be made of the answers of the party charged to cross-examination as to credit as an exception to the general rule that his misconduct on other occasions is inadmissible if it is only relevant because it shows that he has a disposition to commit crimes or civil wrongs. From the theoretical point of view, it can be maintained that the answers are relevant for a further reason because the jury is not asked to proceed directly from bad disposition to an inference of guilt, as the argument is from conduct on other occasions to untrustworthiness of testimony. [2] Answers given in cross-examination to credit such as admissions of previous convictions ought not, in theory, to be counted as affirmative evidence against the accused, at most they only entitle the jury to disregard his evidence in its entirety.

D. STATUTORY PROVISIONS

Various statutes abrogate the rule discussed in this section in the particular circumstances to which they apply. Three of the most important of these are s. 15 of the Prevention of Crimes Act, 1871, s. 1 (2) of the Official Secrets Act, 1911, and section 27 (3) of the Theft Act, 1968.

Section 15 of the Prevention of Crimes Act, 1871, refers to s. 4 of the Vagrancy Act, 1824, under which a suspected person or reputed thief may be treated as a rogue and vagabond if he frequents or loiters in any street or public place with intent to commit an arrestable offence. In order to prove this intent, the statute of 1871 provides that it shall not be necessary to show that the person suspected was guilty of any particular act or acts tending to show his purpose or intent, and he may be convicted if, from the circumstances of the case, and from his known character as proved to the justice of the peace or court before whom or which he is brought, it appears to such justice or court that his intent was to commit an arrestable offence. It has been said that this allows:

---

[1] At p. 12.

[2] DARLING, J., stressed the distinction in his summing-up in *R.* v. *Morrison* (1911), 6 Cr. App. Rep. 159. See the discussion by R. N. Gooderson, 11 C. L. J. 388. It may, of course, occasionally be desirable that the judge should disallow the cross-examination in the exercise of his discretion mentioned by Lord SANKEY in *Maxwell's Case* shortly before the passage quoted in the text. A summing-up stressing the point that the accused's previous convictions were only relevant to the credibility of his oath as contrasted with that of the prosecutor was approved in *R.* v. *Cook*, [1959] 2 Q. B. 340; [1959] 2 All E. R. 97. See also *Selvey* v. *Director of Public Prosecutions*, [1970] A. C. 304; [1968] 2 All E. R. 497.

"something to be given in evidence which would otherwise, according to the common law of England, not be admissible, that is, laying before the tribunal of fact evidence of the previous bad character of the accused person although he had not himself put his character in issue".[1]

In practice, the "known character" of the accused is generally proved by his previous convictions, but such other matters as his association with criminals, or his misconduct on other occasions, may be urged in support of the conclusion that he intended to commit an arrestable offence on the occasion into which the court is inquiring.[2]

Section 1 (1) of the Official Secrets Act, 1911 (as amended by the Official Secrets Act, 1920), punishes various forms of spying if the accused's purpose was prejudicial to the State. Section 1 (2) provides that it shall not be necessary to show that the accused person was guilty of any particular act tending to show a purpose prejudicial to the safety or interests of the State and, notwithstanding that no such act is proved against him, he may be convicted if, from the circumstances of the case, or his conduct, or his known character as proved, it appears that his purpose was a purpose prejudicial to the safety or interests of the State. The wording of this subsection shows even more clearly than does that of s. 15 of the Prevention of Crimes Act, 1871, that evidence of the accused's misconduct may be given although it is only relevant because it shows that he is the kind of man whose purpose in doing certain acts might be of the type proscribed by the statute.

Section 27 (3) of the Theft Act, 1968, reads as follows:

"Where a person is being proceeded against for handling stolen goods (but not for any offence other than handling stolen goods), then at any stage of the proceedings, if evidence has been given of his having or arranging to have in his possession the goods the subject of the charge, or of his undertaking or assisting in, or arranging to undertake or assist in, their retention, removal, disposal or realisation, the following evidence shall be admissible for the purpose of proving that he knew or believed the goods to be stolen goods:
    (a) evidence that he has had in his possession, or has undertaken or assisted in the retention, removal, disposal or realisation of, stolen goods from any theft taking place not earlier than twelve months before the offence charged; and
    (b) (provided that seven day's notice in writing has been given to him of the intention to prove the conviction) evidence that he has within the five years preceeding the date of the offence charged been convicted of theft or handling stolen goods."

The subsection re-enacts, with some significant differences,[3] section 43 (1) of the Larceny Act, 1916, which, in its turn, re-enacted section 19 of the Prevention of Crime Act, 1871. Section 19 abrogated the effect of the decision in *R.* v. *Oddy*.[4] In that case, the third count of the indictment charged the accused with knowingly receiving stolen cloth which was found in his possession shortly after the theft, and the trial judge admitted evidence of the fact that other cloth which had been stolen three months previously was also found in the accused's house. The Court for Crown Cases Reserved held that he ought not to have done so, as the evidence merely went to show that the accused was in the habit of receiving stolen

---

[1] *R.* v. *Harris*, [1951] 1 K. B. 107, at p. 113; [1950] 2 All E. R. 816, at p. 818.
[2] *Clark* v. *R.* (1884), 14 Q. B. D. 92, at p. 100.
[3] On which see the 8th Report of the Criminal Law Revision Committee (Cmnd. 2977, 1966), paras. 157-9.
[4] (1851), 2 Den. 264. If the facts were to recur the decision would still be the same because there were also counts for theft.

cloth. It would have been different if there had been some further connecting link between the two items of evidence. For example, if the cloth had been stolen by the same person the fact of the discovery of both pieces in the accused's house would have been relevant as suggesting the existence of some arrangement for its disposal between the thief and the receiver.[1] Proof of guilty knowledge is, however, a notoriously difficult matter, in a receiving case, and the statutory provisions may be regarded as supplementary to the case-law concerning the provisional presumption arising from the accused's possession of the property mentioned in the indictment shortly after the theft.[2] It was held under the Act of 1916 that the court has a discretion to exclude evidence which was technically admissible under the subsection,[3] and this would no doubt be held to be the case under the Act of 1968.

E. THE PROPOSALS OF THE CRIMINAL LAW REVISION COMMITTEE[4]

The Criminal Law Revision Committee recommended a statutory formulation of the present law, embodied in clauses 3 (1) and 3 (2) of the draft Bill annexed to its 11th Report. They read as follows:

(1) "Subject to the provisions of this section, in any [criminal] proceedings evidence of other conduct of the accused shall not be admissible for the purpose of proving the commission by him of the offence charged by reason only that the conduct in question tends to show in him a disposition to commit the kind of offence with which he is charged or a general disposition to commit crimes."

In this section "other conduct of the accused" means conduct of the accused other than the conduct in respect of which he is charged."

(2) "In any [criminal] proceedings evidence of other conduct of the accused tending to show in him a disposition to commit the kind of offence with which he is charged shall be admissible for the said purpose if the disposition which that conduct tends to show is, in the circumstances of the case, of particular relevance to a matter in issue in the proceedings, as in appropriate circumstances would be, for example—(a) a disposition to commit that kind of offence in a particular manner or according to a particular mode of operation resembling the manner or mode of operation alleged as regards the offence charged; or (b) a disposition to commit that kind of offence in respect of the person in respect of whom he is alleged to have committed the offence charged; or (c) a disposition to commit that kind of offence (even though not falling within paragraph (a) or (b) above) which tends to confirm the correctness of an identification of the accused by a witness for the prosecution."

Rule 404 (b) of the American Federal Rules reads as follows:

"Evidence of other crimes, wrongs, or acts is not admissible to prove the character of a person in order to show that he acted in conformity therewith. It may, however, be admissible for other purposes, such as proof of motive, opportunity, intent, preparation, plan, knowledge, identity, or absence of mistake or accident."

---

[1] *R. v. Dunn* (1826), 1 Mood. C. C. 146; *R. v. Mansfield* (1841), Car. & M. 140; *R. v. Powell* (1909), 3 Cr. App. Rep. 1. The common law admissibility has been unaffected by the statutes.
[2] P. 42, *ante*.
[3] *R. v. List*, [1965] 3 All E. R. 710; *R. v. Herron*, [1967] 1 Q. B. 107; [1966] 2 All E. R. 26.
[4] See 11th Report, paras. 70–101. The proposals are criticised by C. Tapper in 36 M. L. R. 56 and defended by Cross in [1973] Crim. L. R. 400.

It is submitted that the subclauses of the draft Bill set out above are to be preferred firstly because r. 404 (b) makes no allowance for cases, such as *R.* v. *Straffen* in which evidence of other crimes is admissible to prove the character of a person in order show that he acted in conformity therewith; secondly, because the use of the ambiguous word "identity" in the enumeration of the other purposes for which character evidence is admissible is tantamount, at any rate where the evidence of the *actus reus* is circumstantial as it was in *Straffen's Case*, to saying that "evidence of character may be admissible when it goes to show that the accused was guilty of the crime charged."

Clause 3 (3) of the draft Bill attached to the 11th Report of the Criminal Law Revision Committee reads as follows:

> "Where in any [criminal] proceedings evidence of any other conduct of the accused is admissible by virtue of subsection (2) above for the purpose of proving the commission by him of the offence charged, and the accused has in respect of that other conduct been convicted of an offence by or before any court in the United Kingdom or by a court-martial there or elsewhere, then, if evidence tending to establish the conduct in question is given by virtue of that subsection, evidence that he has been so convicted in respect of it shall be admissible for that purpose in addition to the evidence given by virtue of that subsection."

As there are very few reported cases in which similar fact evidence has been received where the accused had already been convicted of the offences proved by that evidence, this provision is of no great practical importance. On the view taken in this book,[1] it would not constitute a change in the law because the accused would be estopped from denying his guilt of the offences of which he had been convicted and, the facts upon which the conviction was based being proved under clause 3 (2), the convictions would do more than merely show disposition.

It is to be hoped that clauses 3 (1) and 3 (2), with or without clause 3 (3), will find their way on to the statute book some day because they are vastly preferable as a starting-point for judicial thought on this difficult subject than the statement of Lord HERSCHELL in *Makin* v. *A.-G. for New South Wales*[2] which is the customary starting-point at present.

The remaining proposals of the Criminal Law Revision Committee are highly controversial. The first is that, where the *actus reus* of the crime charged is admitted, evidence of the accused's misconduct on other occasions should be admissible to prove *mens rea* or negative lawful excuse although it only shows a disposition to commit the kind of offence charged.[3]

---

[1] N. 3, p. 297, *ante.*

[2] [1894] A. C. 57, p. 317, *ante.*

[3] "In any [criminal] proceedings where the conduct in respect of which the accused is charged is admitted in the course of those proceedings by or on behalf of the accused, evidence of other conduct of the accused tending to show in him a disposition to commit the kind of offence with which he is charged shall be admissible for any of the following purposes, namely—
  (a) to establish the existence in the accused of any state of mind (including recklessness) proof of which lies on the prosecution; or
  (b) to prove that the conduct in respect of which the accused is charged was not accidental or involuntary; or
  (c) to prove that there was no lawful justification or excuse for the conduct in respect of which the accused is charged,
nothwithstanding that the other conduct is relevant for that purpose by reason only that it tends to show in the accused a disposition to commit the kind of offence with which he is charged:
  provided that no evidence shall be admissible by virtue of this subsection for the purpose of proving negligence on the part of the accused."

It is further proposed that, where evidence is admissible under the above recommendation, the accused's conviction, if any, in respect of the misconduct should be admissible even though the misconduct is not proved by any other evidence.

From the theoretical point of view there is much to be said for these proposals. One way of stating the principle underlying the reception of evidence of disposition is to say that it depends on the extent to which credulity would be strained if, though guilty of the other misconduct, the accused were not guilty of the offence charged. There is liable to be a greater strain on credulity where the *actus reus* is admitted than where this is not the case. For example, if on facts such as those of *R.* v. *Fisher*,[1] the making of the false pretences charged is denied, it may well be right to insist on a very high degree of relevance and hence of similarity in the case of the other false pretences; but, where the false pretences are admitted, it does seem rather absurd to exclude other dissimilar false pretences on the issue of intent to defraud. If it were accepted that evidence of other misconduct should be admissible on the issue of *mens rea* if it shows a disposition to commit the kind of offence charged and no more, it would be logical to admit evidence of the accused's conviction in respect of the other misconduct for that by itself would prove the requisite disposition.

In spite of the undoubted theoretical merits of these recommendations, it must be admitted that they bear a somewhat academic appearance, that the admission of the accused's previous convictions is probably repulsive to English public opinion, that it might not always be easy to ascertain in practice when the *actus reus* was admitted, and the question of what constitutes the same kind of offence as the offence charged could give rise to difficulty. For these reasons it may well be thought unlikely that these suggested changes in the law will prove to be acceptable.

SECTION 2. THE PREVIOUS CONVICTIONS OF THE PARTIES

A. CIVIL CASES

A party's conviction on a particular occasion may always be proved if it is among the facts in issue in a civil case, as when a libel in which the conviction was alleged is justified; but the only situation in which convictions for misconduct on other occasions than that into which the court is inquiring are regularly admitted is that which arises when a party is cross-examined as to his credit. The fact that he has been convicted may be elicited in cross-examination or if denied, proved under s. 6 of the Criminal Procedure Act, 1865.

B. CRIMINAL CASES

In criminal proceedings a conviction of the accused may always be proved when it is a fact in issue, as would be the case on a plea of *autrefois convict*. The previous conviction may also be among the facts in issue because it is an essential ingredient of the offence charged, as it is in proceedings under s. 7 of the Prevention of Crimes Act, 1871. A person commits an offence

---

[1] [1910] 1 K. B. 149, p. 313, *ante.*

under that section if, after two previous convictions, and within seven years of the last, he either gets his living by dishonest means or refuses to give an address when charged with an offence or is found about to commit an offence or is found on premises without being able to give a good account of himself. No crime is committed in such a case unless the previous convictions are proved, and evidence of them may therefore be given at the same time as that relating to the other facts in issue.[1]

We have seen that, generally speaking, previous convictions may not be proved against the accused as facts relevant to the issue because, although he is estopped from denying their propriety, they amount to nothing more than evidence of disposition and can have no additional relevance in the absence of evidence concerning the facts on which they were founded.[2] It should, however, be noted that, in addition to the possibility of eliciting or proving a conviction in consequence of cross-examination under the Criminal Evidence Act, 1898, s. 15 of the Prevention of Crimes Act, 1871, s. 1 (2) of the Official Secrets Act, 1911, and s. 27 (3) of the Theft Act, 1968, allow proof of previous convictions in the circumstances to which they apply.[3] These circumstances have already been mentioned, and nothing more need be said about them.

Previous convictions may be proved after verdict, in order to guide the court on the question of sentence.[4]

SECTION 3. EVIDENCE OF CHARACTER [5]

It will be recollected that the last two of the four obvious methods by which a person's disposition may be proved consist of assertions of a more or less general nature made by witnesses. They could be asked to express their opinion concerning a party's disposition, or they could be asked to state the nature of his reputation. If they are asked about particular bad acts, the rules discussed in section 1 are brought into play, while questions about particular good acts, or acts which are neither good nor bad, may be disallowed on the score of their insufficient relevancy having regard to the collateral issues to which they might give rise. It will be convenient to begin by considering the admissibility of evidence concerning the character of the accused in criminal cases apart from the Criminal Evidence Act, 1898, because this statute forms the subject of the next chapter. Reference will then be made to the admissibility of evidence concerning the character of the parties to civil suits and the admissibility of evidence concerning the character of certain third parties in both civil and criminal proceedings.

---

[1] *R. v. Penfold*, [1902] 1 K. B. 547. Procedure under the section is discouraged when there is evidence of other offences for which the accused might be prosecuted (*R. v. Goodwin*, [1944] K. B. 518; [1944] 1 All E. R. 506; *R. v. Johnson*, [1945] K. B. 419; [1945] 2 All E. R. 105).

[2] P. 316, *ante*.

[3] A previous conviction may be proved to show that the accused was a "suspected person" (*R. v. Fairbairn*, [1949] 2 K. B. 690), although the police were unaware of it (*R. v. Clarke*, [1950] 1 K. B. 523; [1950] 1 All E. R. 546). A conditional discharge under the Criminal Justice Act, 1948, cannot be proved under s. 15 of the Prevention of Crimes Act (*R. v. Harris*, [1951] 1 K. B. 107; [1950] 2 All E. R. 816).

[4] As to proof of previous convictions generally see chapter XXII, *post*. After verdict previous convictions may be read by a police officer from a list.

[5] Some points which are still of interest are made in an article by Rowlands (11 L. Q. R. 20). "*Examination and Cross-Examination as to Character*" (1895).

A. EVIDENCE OF THE CHARACTER OF THE ACCUSED APART FROM THE CRIMINAL EVIDENCE ACT, 1898

It has been recognised since the middle of the eighteenth century that the accused may call witnesses to speak to his good character or cross-examine the witnesses for the prosecution with a view to inducing them to do so. The prosecution might call evidence in rebuttal, and it came to be settled that witnesses to character must not speak to specific acts of the prisoner. Down to 1865, when *R. v. Rowton* was decided by the Court for Crown Cases Reserved, it was not finally established that the witnesses must depose to the reputation of the accused, and not to their opinion of his disposition. After *Rowton's Case* has been discussed, some statutory provisions will be mentioned and reference must be made to the type of question that can be put to the character witnesses in cross-examination before the effect of evidence of this nature is considered. It should be emphasised at the outset that, subject to statutes, none of which is of great importance apart from the Criminal Evidence Act, 1898, the prosecution can only give evidence of the character of the accused if he raises the issue. A vivid reminder of this fact is provided by *R. v. Butterwasser*.[1] The appellant had been convicted of unlawful wounding by razor slashing. He did not give evidence on his own behalf and he neither called witnesses to his character nor cross-examined the witnesses for the prosecution on this subject. They were, however, minutely questioned concerning their own criminal records and evidence was thereafter given of the accused's previous convictions. The appeal was allowed because the last-mentioned evidence had been improperly received.

> "By attacking the witnesses for the prosecution and suggesting they are unreliable, he is not putting his character in issue; he is putting their character in issue." [2]

In the circumstances of the case, no other kind of evidence of the accused's character would have been admissible. If he had given evidence after cross-examining the Crown witnesses on their characters he would have exposed himself to questions about his past under the Criminal Evidence Act, 1898.

(1) R. v. ROWTON

In *R. v. Rowton*,[3] a schoolmaster was charged with indecent assault on a boy, and called witnesses to his character. The Crown called a witness to give evidence in rebuttal, and this witness was asked about the accused's character for decency and morality of conduct. The reply was in these terms:

> "I know nothing of the neighbourhood's opinion because I was only a boy at school when I knew him, but my own opinion, and the opinion of my brothers who were also pupils of his, is that his character is that of a man capable of the grossest indecency and the most flagrant immorality."

It was held that this answer was not admissible in evidence because the witness ought only to speak to the accused's reputation—a matter about which he plainly knew nothing. The court confirmed that rebutting

---

[1] [1948] 1 K. B. 4; [1947] 2 All E. R. 415.
[2] *Per* Lord GODDARD, C.J., at pp. 7, 416, respectively.
[3] (1865), Le. & Ca. 520.

evidence was admissible, but their decision on the form which evidence of character should take was criticised by Stephen because:

> "A witness may with perfect truth swear that a man, who to his knowledge has been a receiver of stolen goods for years, has an excellent character for honesty if he has the good luck to conceal his crimes from his neighbours." [1]

Plainly there is much force in this view, but as recently as 1947, the Lord Chief Justice stressed the need for the better observance of the principles of *R.* v. *Rowton*.[2] It may therefore be taken to be settled that, at common law, disposition must be proved by reputation, not specific acts or opinion.[3]

(2) Statutory Provisions

When the word "character" is used in a statute which is concerned with the admissibility of evidence, it may often be apt to cover both disposition and reputation. There is authority for this view so far as the Criminal Evidence Act, 1898, is concerned,[4] and some support on principle may be derived from the fact that the accused may give evidence of his character by means of his own testimony under that act. No one can make worthwhile observations on the subject of his own reputation which is nothing other than "that which people say about him when he is not there". When a party speaks to his character, it must be to his disposition as proved, in the majority of cases, by overt acts to which he refers.[5] In s. 15 of the Prevention of Crimes Act, 1871, and s. 1 (2) of the Official Secrets Act, 1911, the accused's "known character" may, presumably, be proved by reputation, specific acts and opinion as to disposition; but it may well be the case that "character" means reputation and nothing else in the Previous Conviction Act, 1836, and s. 116 of the Larceny Act, 1861.

(3) Cross-Examination of Character Witnesses

The answers given by witnesses in cross-examination on the subject of the accused's character may be contradicted by other evidence. Character witnesses may be cross-examined about their own credibility, the accused's reputation and their knowledge of it; but difficulties have arisen with regard to rumours concerning the accused's conduct, his previous convictions and the divisibility of his character.

(i) Rumours.—In *R.* v. *Wood and Parker*,[6] robbery was the crime charged and, the accused having called a witness to character, the question arose whether this witness might be cross-examined with regard to a rumour that the accused had committed another robbery. Questions on the subject were allowed because, "Character is made up of a number of small circumstances of which his being suspected is one".[7] This suggests that the rumour may be used as evidence of the accused's disposition, and not

---

[1] *Digest of the Law of Evidence* (12th edition), 201.
[2] *R.* v. *Butterwasser*, [1948] 1 K. B. 4; [1947] 2 All E. R. 415.
[3] In the Bill attached to the 11th Report of the Criminal Law Revision Committee "character" means both disposition and reputation (see para. 134 of the Report).
[4] *Stirland* v. *Director of Public Prosecutions*, [1944] A. C. 315, at p. 324; [1944] 2 All E. R. 13, at p. 17, *per* Lord Simon, L.C.; but see the speech of Lord Devlin in *Jones* v. *Director of Public Prosecutions*, [1962] A. C. 635; [1962] 1 All E. R. 569, and *Dingle* v. *Associated Newspapers Ltd.*, [1961] 2 Q. B. 162, at pp. 195 and 198, *per* Devlin, L.J.
[5] See *per* Lord Denning in *Plato Films Ltd.* v. *Speidel*, [1961] A. C. 1090, at p. 1143.
[6] (1841), 5 Jur. 225. See also *R.* v. *Hodgkiss* (1836), 7 C. & P. 298.
[7] *Per* Parke, B.

merely as something that may cast doubt upon the witness's knowledge of the accused's reputation, but there is no clear English authority on the subject.

(ii) Convictions.—When dealing with the position at common law, successive editions of *Archbold* have contained a statement to the following effect:

> "If the defendant himself endeavours to establish a good character, either by calling witnesses himself, cross-examining the witnesses for the prosecution, or by himself giving evidence to that effect, the prosecution is at liberty, in most cases, to prove his previous convictions."[1]

Although originally based on cases turning on special statutes[2] this passage was approved by a dictum in *R. v. Redd*,[3] and, in the absence of any judicial expression of doubt on the subject, it may be assumed that any character witness in any criminal proceedings may be asked about a previous conviction of the accused, and, as a matter of strict law, the accused's previous convictions may, it seems, be proved in rebuttal.

(iii) Divisibility of the accused's character.[4]—The question remains whether the witness can be asked about any former conviction, or whether it must be relevant to the character trait under consideration. ALDERSON, B., would have answered the question to the latter effect for, in *R. v. Shrimpton*,[5] a case of larceny, he said that, if the previous conviction had been for rape, the jury would have been told that it had nothing to do with the prisoner's character for honesty. In *R. v. Winfield*,[6] however, the Court of Criminal Appeal was clearly of opinion that the conviction about which the character witness is asked need not concern the subject-matter of the charge under investigation. Winfield had been convicted of an indecent assault upon a woman. He called a witness to speak to his good behaviour with ladies, and it seems that she was cross-examined about his previous conviction for an offence involving dishonesty.[7] Winfield's appeal was allowed because the jury had been inadequately directed with regard to corroboration, but HUMPHREYS, J., expressed approval of the cross-examination as:

> "There is no such thing known to our procedure as putting half a prisoner's character in issue and leaving out the other half".

This principle has been criticised because:

> "If a man is charged with forgery, cross-examination as to his convictions for cruelty to animals can have no purpose but prejudice".[8]

It is submitted that the criticism is well founded, although *Winfield's Case* appears to have been approved in the House of Lords in *Stirland* v. *Director of Public Prosecutions*.[9] This decision is primarily concerned with

---

[1] 38th edition, para. 558.

[2] *R. v. Gadbury* (1838), 8 C. & P. 676, and *R. v. Shrimpton* (1851), 2 Den. 319.

[3] [1923] 1 K. B. 104. Although the effect of the decision has since been overruled by s. 573 of the Canadian Criminal Code, *R. v. Triganzie* (1888), 15 O. R. 294 is against the admissibility of a conviction to rebut the evidence of a witness to character at common law.

[4] See R. N. Gooderson, "*Is a Prisoner's Character divisible?*", 11 C. L. J. 377, (1953). The writer is much indebted to this article.

[5] (1851), 2 Den. 319, at p. 322.   [6] [1939] 4 All E. R. 164.

[7] The headnote and statement of facts in 27 Cr. App. Rep. 139 suggests that this course was adopted, but the cross-examination may have been of Winfield himself in which case we shall see that different considerations apply.

[8] Nokes, *Introduction to Evidence* (4th edition), 140.

[9] [1944] A. C. 315; [1944] 2 All E. R. 13.

the construction of the Criminal Evidence Act, 1898, and, if Winfield was asked about his previous conviction under that Act, as may have been the case, the question would have been easier to justify on principle as a matter affecting the credibility of his own˙previous statement about his character.

(4) The Effect of Evidence of Character

From time to time suggestions have been made that evidence of character is irrelevant and is only received in criminal cases as a gesture of humanity.[1] It is, however, difficult to escape the logic of the following observation of PATTESON, J.:

> "I cannot in principle make any distinction between evidence of facts and evidence of character: the latter is equally laid before the jury as the former, as being relevant to the question of guilty or not guilty: the object of laying it before the jury is to induce them to believe, from the improbability that a person of good character should have conducted himself as alleged, that there is some mistake or misrepresentation in the evidence on the part of the prosecution, and it is strictly evidence in the case." [2]

In *R.* v. *Bellis,*[3] the Court of Criminal Appeal expressed the opinion that evidence of good character goes primarily to the credibility of the accused, but added that, a direction that evidence of character was to be taken into account as something rendering the commission of the crime by the accused less likely, was, if anything, more favourable to the accused than a direction that the jury should consider the evidence of character as something affecting the credibility of the accused. "If he (the trial judge) directed them that the appellant was more credible by reason of his good character, it would have followed from that that he was less likely to commit the offence." Evidence of character could be given in a case in which the accused did not give evidence on his own behalf; it must therefore be treated as something which affects liklihood of guilt as well as credibility if, indeed, there is any distinction, even in theory, in this particular context.

The jury must not be directed only to consider evidence of good character if in doubt for, if they are in doubt, they should acquit in any event.[4]

B. EVIDENCE OF THE CHARACTER OF THE PARTIES IN CIVIL CASES

In *A.-G.* v. *Bowman*[5] it was decided that the defendant to an information for keeping false weights could not call a witness to character as the proceedings were civil, and, although the defendant's character might be directly relevant to such questions as those concerned with the removal of trustees, there does not appear to be a reported civil case in which evidence of his reputation has been received. His bad acts can be proved against him subject to the limitations discussed in section 1, while proof by himself or

---

[1] *Per* LUSH, J., in *Hurst* v. *Evans,* [1917] 1 K. B. 352, at p. 357, and *per* DEVLIN, J., in *R.* v. *Miller,* [1952] 2 All E. R. 667.

[2] *R.* v. *Stannard* (1837), 7 C. & P. 673. Section 412 of the New South Wales Crimes Act expressly provides that evidence of character is always evidence on the question of guilt.

[3] [1966] 1 All E. R. 552. See also *R.* v. *Richardson* and *R.* v. *Longman,* [1969] 1 Q. B. 299; [1968] 2 All E. R. 761.

[4] *R.* v. *Brittle* (1965), 109 Sol. Jo. 1028; *R.* v. *Broadhurst, Meaney and Bliss Hill* (1918), 13 Cr. App. Rep. 125.

[5] (1791), 2 Bos. & P. 532, n.

his witnesses of his good acts on other occasions would presumably be allowed if it were ever sufficiently relevant. It has never been suggested that a witness might be asked his opinion of the defendant's disposition.

Both plaintiff and defendant are liable to cross-examination as to credit in their capacity as witnesses, and evidence of the plaintiff's character may be given whenever it is directly in issue as affecting liability or the measure of damages.

A plaintiff's character may be directly in issue on the question of liability in an action for defamation when justification is pleaded, and the question whether specific acts, rumours or reputation can be received will depend on the pleadings in the particular case.[1] The plaintiff's character is also relevant to the amount of damages recoverable by him in proceedings for defamation. In *Scott* v. *Sampson*,[2] it was decided that the evidence which might be adduced in mitigation of damages for defamation must be confined to the plaintiff's reputation and might not consist of rumours or testimony concerning specific acts. This case has now been approved by the House of Lords.[3] It is clear that the evidence of reputation must relate to the segment of the plaintiff's life to which the defamation relates, and some members of the House pointed to the difficulty of drawing a sharp distinction between evidence of specific acts and evidence of reputation. Although evidence of specific acts is not admissible to show that they were performed, it may be admissible to show that the plaintiff has the reputation of a man who is in the habit of performing such acts.[4] Such matters as rumours and specific acts may be put to the plaintiff in cross-examination as to credit, his answers are final in accordance with the general rule discussed in Chapter X, and the judge must endeavour to separate the issue of credibility from that concerning the quantum of damages when he sums the case up to the jury.[5]

In an action for defamation, the plaintiff's previous convictions for offences relevant to the alleged defamation may be proved in mitigation of damages as well as in cross-examination to credit.[6] "They are the raw material upon which bad reputation is built up—they have taken place in open court they are matters of public knowledge. They are acted on by people generally as the best guide to his reputation and standing." [7]

It is possible to imagine many other cases in which a plaintiff's character might be in issue.

C. EVIDENCE OF THE CHARACTER OF THIRD PARTIES

(1) CRIMINAL CASES

The prosecutor is not a party to criminal proceedings, and, except in so far as it may be elicited in cross examination, his character may generally

---

[1] *Maisel* v. *Financial Times* (1915), 84 L. J. K. B. 2145.
[2] (1882), 8 Q. B. D. 491.
[3] *Plato Films Ltd.* v. *Speidel*, [1961] A. C. 1090; [1961] 1 All E. R. 876. In that case there was a plea of justification and the decision turned on the propriety of the particulars in the defendant's defence. When justification is not pleaded, particulars of matters to be relied on in mitigation of damages must be furnished, otherwise the defendant may not give evidence of them without the leave of the judge (R. S. C. O. 82, r. 7). The plaintiff may be cross-examined on such matters, although no particulars have been furnished, but the cross-examination goes to credit, not to the diminution of damages.
[4] *Waters* v. *Sunday Pictorial Newspaper Ltd.*, [1961] 2 All E. R. 758.
[5] *Hobbs* v. *Tinling*, [1929] 2 K. B. 1.
[6] *Goody* v. *Odhams Press*, [1967] 1 Q. B. 333.
[7] Lord DENNING, M.R., at p. 340.

not be proved. Thus, in *R.* v. *Wood*,[1] it was alleged that a man who brought a charge of robbery had made indecent approaches to the prisoner, and it was held that he could not adduce evidence of his good general reputation for decency. In the case of a prosecution for rape, however, the accused may adduce evidence in-chief concerning the prosecutrix's bad reputation for chastity.[2] She may be cross-examined about her intercourse with other men and the accused. In the former,[3] but not the latter,[4] event, her answers must be treated as final; but she may be contradicted by other evidence if she denies that she is a prostitute or a woman who has demanded money after consensual intercourse.[5]

(2) Civil Cases

It is difficult to think of situations in which the character of a third party would be in issue, or relevant to the issue, in civil proceedings. If it were relevant, it could no doubt be proved as there are no special exclusionary rules that might be applicable.

---

[1] [1951] 2 All E. R. 112.
[2] *R.* v. *Clarke* (1817), 2 Stark. 241.
[3] *R.* v. *Holmes* (1871), L. R. 1 C. C. R. 334; *Stokes* v. *R.* (1960), 105 C. L. R. 279; *R.* v. *Thompson*, [1951] S. A. S. R. 135.
[4] *R.* v. *Riley* (1887), 18 Q. B. D. 481.
[5] *R.* v. *Bashir* and *R.* v. *Manzur*, [1969] 3 All E. R. 692; *R.* v. *Krausz* (1973), 57 Cr. App. Rep. 466.

CHAPTER XV

THE CRIMINAL EVIDENCE ACT, 1898

Section 2 of this chapter is mainly a gloss on the last one, for s. 1 (f) of the Criminal Evidence Act, 1898, defines the extent to which the accused may be cross-examined on the subject of his disposition and character; some points of a more general nature are discussed in section 1.

SECTION 1. THE GENERAL EFFECT OF THE ACT

We have already seen how s. 1 of the Act made the accused and his spouse competent witnesses for the defence in all criminal cases,[1] and the limited extent to which the accused's spouse is compellable as a witness on his behalf, or competent or compellable as a witness for the prosecution or a co-prisoner has likewise been considered.[2] The privilege conferred by the Act on the matrimonial communications of all witnesses in criminal proceedings,[3] the time at which the accused should give his evidence,[4] his right to make an unsworn statement[5] and the right of reply have all been mentioned previously.[6] Two further matters remain to be considered, first, the position of an accused who does not give evidence, and second, the position of one who does.

S. 1 (a) of the Act provides that the person charged can only be called as a witness on his own application. It is doubtful whether many people in 1898 would have favoured a provision under which the accused would have become a compellable witness in the sense that he would be liable to inprisonment for contempt if he refused to answer questions, and it is difficult to believe that their numbers have greatly increased in the meantime. Nevertheless, in any system under which the accused is neither incompetent to give evidence on his own behalf nor compellable to answer questions put to him by the prosecution or the judge, adverse inferences are liable to be drawn from his failure to go into the witness box. This danger would not exist if the tribunal of fact were unaware of the accused's right to give evidence if he chooses to do so, but from the coming into force of the Act of 1898 onwards, magistrates have not been in this state of ignorance, and it is improbable that every member of any jury is in such a state to-day. The Act of 1898 can thus be said to have confronted the accused with the choice of opting not to give evidence with the consequential risk that adverse inferences will be drawn, or going into the witness box and thus exposing himself to cross-examination which might cause him to incriminate himself. Reflections of this nature even led some lawyers to regard the Act as a retrograde step. After it had been in force for as long as 16 years Mr. Ernest Williams wrote:

"No sooner have we elaborated precautions for insuring the voluntary character of confessions than we strike a blow at the underlying principle, and

---

[1] Chapter VIII.   [2] *Ibid.* See Criminal Evidence Act, 1898, s. 4.
[3] S. 1 (d), p. 258, *ante.*   [4] Chapter VIII.
[5] S. 1 (h), p. 164, *ante.*   [6] S. 3, p. 199, *ante.*

substitute the moral compulsion of the witness box for the physical compulsion of the rack."[1]

No present day lawyer would seriously advocate the repeal without replacement of the 1898 Act, but it certainly raises problems concerning an accused who chooses not to testify.

The problem raised by the Act with regard to an accused who does choose to testify concerns the position of an accused with a criminal record. Is he to be liable to cross-examination to credit on his previous convictions and bad character like any other witness, or is he to be protected against such cross-examination and, if so, to what extent?

A. THE ACCUSED WHO DOES NOT GIVE EVIDENCE

If common sense were to be given free rein it would be proper, once an accused is a competent witness, to draw inferences from his failure to testify in certain circumstances. One obvious example would be a murder case in which the accused was proved to have been in the deceased's company shortly before his death; another would be a case of theft or handling in which the accused was found in possession of the stolen goods, and there are many others. But one of the objects of the law of evidence is to prevent common sense from having a free rein because there are cases in which to permit it might lead to an unjust result. The accused might refrain from testifying, not because he was guilty, but because he feared cross-examination on his record, wished to protect a friend or was afraid that he might be obliged to disclose some compromising information about his doings, such as the fact that he had spent the night with his mistress. One answer to the first point is to prohibit the cross-examination of the accused on his record unless he is sufficiently misguided to say that he has a good character, but we shall see that this is not to everybody's taste. So far as the other points are concerned, there are those who would rest content with Bentham's observation that "probabilities and not improbabilities constitute the true ground of legislative practice;"[2] but it would be idle to deny that there are those who take the points very seriously.

(1) POSSIBLE COURSES

In the case of a trial by jury, three courses were open to the framers of the legislation of 1898. The first would have been to prohibit any comment by the judge or prosecution on the accused's failure to testify; the second would have been simply to prohibit comment by the prosecution; and the third would have been to make an express provision that the judge could, if he thought fit, draw the jury's attention to such inferences as might properly be drawn from the accused's failure to testify. The first course was ultimately adopted by the legislature of New South Wales,[3] and a provision permitting comment either by the judge or the prosecution was held to be an infringement of the fifth amendment of the United States constitution in *Griffin* v. *California*[4] by rendering it costly for the accused to exercise his privilege not to be a witness against himself. The

---

[1] (1914), 30 L. Q. R. 297.
[2] *Works*, Bowring edition, v. 7, p. 27.
[3] Crimes Act, 1900, s. 407, overruling *Kops* v. *R., Ex parte Kops*, [1894] A. C. 650.
[4] 380 U. S. 609. (1965).

second course was in fact adopted in the legislation. The third course is recommended in the 11th Report of the Criminal Law Revision Committee.[1]

It is by no means clear that the first course would have been particularly advantageous to the accused. In the words of the dissenting judgment in *Griffin's* case,

> "How can it be said that the inferences drawn by a jury will be more detrimental to a defendant under the limiting and carefully controlling language of the instruction here involved than would result if the jury were left to roam at large with only its untutored instinct to guide it, to draw from the defendant's silence broad inferences of guilt." [2]

The answer of the majority was:

> "What the jury may infer, given no help from the court, is one thing. What it may infer when the court solemnises the silence of the accused into evidence against him is quite another." [3]

(2) JUDICIAL COMMENT

S. 1 (b) of the 1898 Act provides that the failure of any person charged with an offence to give evidence shall not be made the subject of any comment by the prosecution. The Act had not been in force for very long before the courts decided, on the principle *expressio unius est exclusio alterius*, that there was no ban on comment by the judge.[4] For some time it appears to have been thought that the decision when, and how, to comment were within the unfettered discretion of the judge,[5] but it is now clear that the discretion is subject to appellate control.[6] The reported decisions most certainly do not suggest any tendency on the part of English judges to "solemnise the silence of the accused into evidence against him."

In *R. v. Mutch*,[7] the Court of Appeal concluded that, in almost every case, the comment should take the form described by Lord PARKER, C.J., in *R. v. Bathhurst*.[8] Lord PARKER had said that the jury should be told, if the judge were minded to make any comment at all, that "the accused is not bound to give evidence, that he can sit back and see if the prosecution have proved their case, and that, while the jury have been deprived of the opportunity of hearing his story tested in cross-examination, the one thing they must not do is assume that he is guilty because he has not gone into the witness box." *Bathhurst's* case was one in which diminished responsibility was pleaded in answer to a murder charge, and the conviction was quashed because the judge had gone too far in commenting on the accused's failure to testify. It was recognised that the number of diminished responsibility cases in which any comment should be made must be small, but it was also pointed out that, when comment is proper, it must take a

---

[1] Para. 110 *et seq.*
[2] 380 U. S. 621.
[3] 380 U. S. 614.
[4] *R. v. Rhodes*, [1899] 1 Q. B. 77; on the same principle it has been held that comment on behalf of a co-accused is permissible (*R. v. Wickham, R. v. Ferrara and R. v. Bean* (1971), 55 Cr. App. Rep. 199.)
[5] *R. v. Voisin*, [1918] 1 K. B. 531, at p. 536.
[6] *Waugh v. R.*, [1950] A. C. 203.
[7] [1973] 1 All E. R. 178.
[8] [1968] 2 Q. B. 99; [1968] 1 All E. R. 1175.

different form in a case in which the burden of proof is borne by the accused.[1]

The conviction was also quashed in *R.* v. *Mutch,* a case of robbery in which the defence was a simple denial, because the trial judge had suggested that the jury might draw unfavourable inferences from the fact that the accused had not been called to suggest an innocent explanation of facts proved by the prosecution. The Court of Appeal recognised that there were such cases in which a direction might be proper, but these were cases in which the undisputed or clearly established facts involved the accused to such an extent as to call for an innocent explanation if there were one.[2]

In *R.* v. *Sparrow,*[3] the Court of Appeal recognised that the interests of justice called for a strong comment in a case in which someone charged as a joint principal in a murder case raised the plea that he was only guilty of manslaughter because he had agreed with his co-accused that the latter's gun should only be used to frighten, not to shoot at, anyone attempting to apprehend them and did not go into the witness box to support it. Even so, the Court, while applying the proviso to s. 2 (1) of the Criminal Appeal Act, 1968, had no doubt that the trial judge had erred in suggesting that it was essential for the accused to go into the witness box in order that such a plea should succeed.

All that can be said on the authorities is that the questions whether the judge should make any comment, and how far he should go in commenting, depend on the particular facts, and that it is essential for the judge to make two things plain to the jury, first, that the accused has a right not to testify,[4] second, that they must not assume that he is guilty because he does not do so. *R.* v. *Sparrow* also decides that the mere fact that the judicial comment on this failure occurs several times in the course of the summing-up does not render it improper.

(3) THE RECOMMENDATION OF THE CRIMINAL LAW REVISION COMMITTEE

Whilst there are no doubt many people who consider that the present English law represents the best solution of the problem of insuring that justice is done to an accused who chooses not to give evidence, it has two defects. The first is the comparatively minor one that it is too vague on the subject of the extent to which the judge can go when he is minded to comment; the second, and far more serious defect is that the law generates the myth that there is a distinction between conferring on a judge the power to comment on the failure of an accused to testify and permitting him to point out to a jury what inferences could, in all the circumstances, be properly drawn from that fact, while leaving it to them to decide whether such inferences should be drawn. Even the superficially mild reminder that the jury has been deprived of the opportunity of hearing the accused's story tested in cross-examination is an invitation to infer that he has so

---

[1] "He [the accused] is not bound to go into the witness box, no-one can force him to go into the witness box, but the burden is upon him, and if he does not, he runs the risk of not being able to prove his case."
[2] *R.* v. *Corrie and Watson* (1904), 68 J. P. 294; *R.* v. *Bernard* (1908), 1 Cr. App. Rep. 218.
[3] [1973] 2 All E. R. 129.
[4] *R.* v. *Davison,* [1972] 3 All E. R. 1121.

little confidence in his story that he is not prepared to be cross-examined upon it, unaccompanied by the observation that there may be other reasons for not wishing to be cross-examined. The provision in clause 5 (3) of the draft Bill attached to the 11th Report of the Criminal Law Revision Committee that the court[1] or jury, in determining whether the accused is guilty of the offence charged, may draw such inferences from his failure to testify as appear proper at least has the merit of remedying the two defects which have been mentioned.

Two objections, which may only amount to one, have been raised against the proposal. They are that it would violate the accused's "right to silence", and relieve the prosecution of the burden of proving the accused's guilt. The right to silence is a right not to be obliged to answer, or pressurised into answering, questions, and it is said that the proposal of the Criminal Law Revision Committee would increase the pressure on the accused to assume the obligation of answering questions by going into the witness box. It is also said that the burden of proving his innocence will be shifted to the accused if the court or jury is empowered to draw inferences from his failure to testify. These objections seem to be more appropriate to the granting by the Act of 1898 to the accused of the option to testify than to the proposal of the Criminal Law Revision Committee. Inferences are bound to be drawn from the accused's failure to give evidence, and to that extent the Act of 1898 lightened the prosecution's burden of proof. The real choice seems to be between the prohibition of comment by the judge as well as the prosecution and a provision of the kind proposed by the Criminal Law Revision Committee. A provision, such as that which exists in some Commonwealth jurisdictions, including Queensland, that comment may come from the prosecution as well as the judge, would merely tend to perpetuate the myth that there is a rational distinction between commenting on, and pointing to inferences that can be properly drawn from, the accused's failure to testify. Under the Committee's proposal, just as much as under the present law, it would be necessary for the judge to insist that a direct inference of guilt must never be drawn from this failure; it simply detracts from the weight of any special defence that the accused may raise and, in some, but by no means all, circumstances, adds to the weight of the prosecution's case.

Clause 5 (3) of the Criminal Law Revision Committee's draft Bill also provides that the accused's failure to give evidence may, on the basis of proper inferences, be treated as corroboration of evidence given on behalf of the prosecution. We have seen that, under the present law, the accused's failure to give evidence cannot be treated as corroboration,[2] but, if the failure is something which can detract from the weight of a defence or add to the weight of the prosecution's case, it is difficult to see why it should not corroborate. If, on facts such as those of *R.* v. *Sparrow*,[3] evidence to the effect that Sparrow had been heard to agree to the use of a gun by his co-accused to shoot anyone who attempted to apprehend them had been given by an accomplice, it is as difficult to see why he should not be corroborated by the accused's failure to testify as it is to see how, under the present law, the judge could sum up to the jury without sinking into

---

[1] I.e. a Magistrates' Court trying a case summarily.
[2] P. 186, *ante.*
[3] P. 356, *ante.*

gibberish. The accused's absence from the witness box would call for strong comment as something which the jury should bear in mind when considering the weight of the defence, but the judge would have to go on to say that, notwithstanding what he had said by way of comment, they must not treat the fact on which comment was made as corroborative of the accomplice's evidence.

B. THE ACCUSED WHO DOES GIVE EVIDENCE

In the words of Lord SANKEY:

> "When Parliament by the Act of 1898 effected a change in the general law and made the prisoner in every case a competent witness, it was in evident difficulty and it pursued the familiar English system of compromise."[1]

If the ordinary rules governing the examination and cross-examination of witnesses were to be applied to the accused without restriction or modification, he would have been unduly favoured in one respect and unduly prejudiced in another respect. He would have been unduly favoured because he might have claimed the privilege against self-incrimination on the ground that his answer to a question might show that he had committed the crime under investigation. This danger was met by proviso (e) to s. 1 of the Act under which he may be asked any question in cross-examination notwithstanding that it would tend to incriminate him as to the offence charged, and it has been held that the proviso applies when one prisoner confines his evidence to statements exculpating his co-accused.[2]

It was thought that the accused would have been unduly prejudiced if he had anything in the nature of a criminal record because he would have been exposed to cross-examination concerning his past misdeeds as a matter affecting his credibility. This danger was met by s. 1 (f) which is itself a compromise because cross-examination as to credit is neither wholly prohibited nor invariably permitted. Its principal effect is to provide the accused with a shield which is only thrown away if he gives evidence of his good character or casts imputations on the prosecutor or the witnesses for the prosecution. When the shield is thrown away, the accused is liable to be cross-examined on his criminal record and past misdeeds.

Although the accused who gives evidence is technically in the same position as any other witness, subject to the important exceptions made by s. 1 (e) and s. 1 (f) of the Act of 1898, it would be unrealistic to regard their positions as substantially similar from the practical point of view. We have already seen that it is difficult, in practice, to discriminate between the use to be made of the answers given by the accused in cross-examination to credit and cross-examination to the issue. The sanctions of the law of perjury may operate quite differently in the case of the accused from the way in which they apply to an ordinary witness. The latter is confronted with the choice of telling the truth or taking the risk of a prosecution for perjury. This risk is bound to appear in a somewhat different light if the choice is to take it or run the risk of conviction for the more serious offence charged.[3] Considerations of this nature have led the judges to be a great

---

[1] *Maxwell* v. *Director of Public Prosecutions*, [1935] A. C. 309, at p. 317.
[2] *R.* v. *Rowland*, [1910] 1 K. B. 458. S. 1 (e) is not expressly confined to cases in which the accused is giving evidence "on his own behalf", and the court would not read these words into the proviso.
[3] See 19 M. L. R. 704.

deal more solicitous about the propriety of the cross-examination of the accused than that of any other witness. No doubt they have a discretion to disallow questions in each case, but it is most often stressed in relation to the questioning of the prisoner under the Act of 1898.[1] Counsel for the prosecution is repeatedly admonished not to drive the accused into throwing his shield away.[2] Even if this was not, in any sense, the purpose of the cross-examination, it may be held to have been improper because the crucial question is its effect upon the minds of the jury, not the purpose with which it was administered.[3] A further safeguard is provided by the requirements that Crown counsel should obtain the approval of the judge before embarking on cross-examination under s. 1 (f).[4]

Section 1 (f) has, however, led to numerous difficulties so far as its construction is concerned, and it is now necessary to consider them.

SECTION 2. THE INTERPRETATION OF S. 1 (f) [5]

Section 1 (f) reads as follows:

> "A person charged and called as a witness in pursuance of this Act shall not be asked, and if asked shall not be required to answer, any question tending to show that he has committed or been convicted of or been charged with any offence other than that wherewith he is then charged, or is of bad character, unless—
>
> > (i) the proof that he has committed or been convicted of such other offence is admissible evidence to show that he is guilty of the offence wherewith he is then charged; or
> >
> > (ii) he has personally or by his advocate asked questions of the witnesses for the prosecution with a view to establish his own good character, or has given evidence of his good character, or the nature or conduct of the defence is such as to involve imputations on the character of the prosecutor or the witnesses for the prosecution; or
> >
> > (iii) he has given evidence against any other person charged with the same offence."

It will be observed that the section begins with a prohibition on four types of question—those tending to show previous charges, those tending to show previous offences, those tending to show previous convictions and those tending to show bad character. Reference is then made to the situations in which such questions are permitted. So far as sub-paragraphs (f) (ii) and (iii) are concerned, the situations must be brought into existence by the accused himself; he must either put his character in issue, or cast imputations on the witnesses for the prosecution or give evidence against someone charged with the same offence. No action on the part of the

---

[1] See especially *R. v. Baldwin* (1925), 18 Cr. App. Rep. 175.
[2] *R. v. Eidenow* (1932), 23 Cr. App. Rep. 145.
[3] *R. v. Ellis*, [1910] 2 K. B. 746; *R. v. Sugarman* (1935), 25 Cr. App. Rep. 109.
[4] *R. v. McLean* (1926), 19 Cr. App. Rep. 104. Appeals have been allowed on account of improper questioning by the judge (*R. v. Ratcliffe* (1919), 4 Cr. App. Rep. 95) and counsel for a co-prisoner (*R. v. Roberts*,[1936] 1 All E. R. 23) as well as counsel for the prosecution. Under s. 399 of the Crimes Act (Victoria), the judge's leave to cross-examine under the equivalent of s. 1 (f) (ii) must be obtained in the absence of the jury.
[5] The writer is much indebted to two articles by Professor Julius Stone, "*Cross-examination by the Prosecution at Common Law and under The Criminal Evidence Act, 1898*", 51 L. Q. R. 443 (1935), and "*Further Problems in the Interpretation of the Criminal Evidence Act, 1898, s. 1, proviso (f)*", 58 L. Q. R. 369 (1942). Section 1 (f) must be read subject to s. 16 (2) of the Children and Young Persons Act, 1963. Someone aged 21 or more cannot be asked about convictions before he was 14. See Addendum, *ante.*

accused is necessary to render questions admissible under s. 1 (f) (i), but the omission from this part of the proviso of any reference to the fact that the accused has been charged with another offence or is of bad character renders it difficult to reconcile some of the decisions with the strict words of the statute.

It will be convenient to begin by considering the construction of the prohibition and then to discuss the situations in which cross-examination is permitted under s. 1 (f).

A. THE PROHIBITION

Although the prohibition is absolute in its terms, it does not prevent questions concerning his record being put to the accused in-chief on the rare occasions when he wishes to testify on that subject. Such words as "shall not be asked" and "shall not be required to answer" are considered to be inapplicable to evidence which is tendered voluntarily in-chief.[1]

Problems have been raised with regard to the relation between the prohibition and proviso (e), the meaning of the words "tend to show", the meaning of the word "charged" and the relation of the prohibition to the permissions conferred by the rest of s. 1 (f). These problems were considered by the House of Lords in the leading cases of *Jones* v. *Director of Public Prosecutions*,[2] *Stirland* v. *Director of Public Prosecutions*[3] and *Maxwell* v. *Director of Public Prosecutions*.[4]

(1) THE RELATION OF PROVISO (e) TO PROVISO (f)

According to proviso (e) the accused may be asked any question in cross-examination notwithstanding that it would tend to criminate him as to the offence charged. Its relation to proviso (f) was not discussed before *Jones's* case, but the two main views on the subject expressed in *Jones's* case were discernible in the earlier authorities. They may be described as the "literal" and "broad" views respectively. According to the literal view, proviso (e) permits questions tending directly to criminate the accused as to the offence charged, while proviso (f) prohibits, subject to exceptions which must be construed literally, questions tending to incriminate the accused indirectly as well as those which simply go to his credit as a witness. This view is supported by *R.* v. *Cokar*[5] where cross-examination about a previous charge was held to have infringed the statute although it related to an issue concerning liability, as distinct from credibility. At his trial for breaking and entering with intent to steal, his defence was that he had entered the house in question for the sake of warmth and in order to have a sleep. In the course of his cross-examination, Cokar denied that he knew it was no offence to enter a house in order to go to sleep, and the trial judge allowed counsel for the prosecution to put questions concerning a previous charge of breaking and entering which had resulted in an acquittal. It was probable that the accused had learned, in connection with that charge that it is not an offence to enter a house in order to go to sleep.

---

[1] *Jones* v. *Director of Public Prosecutions*, [1962] A. C. 635, at p. 663; [1962] 1 All E. R. 569, at p. 575 *per* Lord REID.
[2] [1962] A. C. 635; [1962] 1 All E. R. 569.
[3] [1944] A. C. 315; [1944] 2 All E. R. 13.
[4] [1935] A. C. 309.
[5] [1960] 2 Q. B. 207; [1960] 2 All E. R. 175. The literal view is also supported by the tenor of Lord SANKEY's speech in *Maxwell's* case.

Cokar was convicted, and his conviction was quashed by the Court of Criminal Appeal on the ground that the question concerning the previous charge had been wrongly admitted. Section 1 (f) (ii) and (iii) did not apply to the case because Cokar had neither put his character in issue, nor cast imputations nor given evidence against a co-prisoner, while questions concerning charges resulting in anything other than a conviction were held to be outside the purview of s. 1 (f) (i) from which the word "charged" is omitted.

According to the broad view, proviso (e) permits questions which tend to criminate the accused as to the offence charged directly or indirectly, and, in cases to which none of the exceptions apply, the prohibition in proviso (f) relates solely to cross-examination to credit. This view is supported by *R. v. Chitson* [1] and *R. v. Kurasch*.[2] Chitson was charged with unlawful intercourse with a girl of fourteen. In the course of her evidence in chief, the prosecutrix stated that he had told her that he had done the same thing to another girl. There was no evidence whether this other girl was beneath or above the age of sixteen at the material time, but it was held by the Court of Criminal Appeal that the prisoner had been properly examined with regard to his relations with her because, although the questions did no doubt tend to show that he was of bad character, they also tended to incriminate him as to the offence charged; if he had had intercourse with the other girl, that fact would confirm the prosecutrix's statement with regard to what he told her. If the other girl had been under sixteen at the material time, the case would have come within s. 1 (f) (i) because evidence that Chitson had committed another offence would have been admissible in-chief [3] but, if the other girl was over sixteen at the material time, no offence would have been committed against her; nevertheless despite the omission of the words "bad character" from s. 1 (f) (i) the cross-examination was held to be permissible because it was relevant to an issue in the case. In *R. v. Kurasch*, the appellant was charged with a conspiracy to defraud by means of a mock auction. His defence was that he was merely the servant of the proprietress of the auction room, and a question suggesting that she was his mistress was held by the Court of Criminal Appeal to have been properly put to him in cross-examination simply because it was relevant to the issue. The accused had done nothing to throw his shield away under s. 1 (f) (ii) or (iii), and, as the question merely tended to show immorality as opposed to the commission or conviction of another offence, the case fell outside the literal words of s. 1 (f) (i).

(2) The Meaning of "Tending to Show"—Jones v. Director of Public Prosecutions

In *Jones* v. *Director of Public Prosecutions*[4] a majority of the House of Lords sanctioned a construction of s. 1 (f) which does much to reduce the practical effect of the difference between the two views concerning the

[1] [1909] 2 K. B. 945. See also *R. v. Kennaway*, [1917] 1 K. B. 25.
[2] [1915] 2 K. B. 749.
[3] Even then a sufficient foundation for the cross-examination should have been laid by the evidence in-chief; *cf.* the treatment of *R. v. Kennaway* by the majority of the House of Lords in *Jones* v. *Director of Public Prosecutions*.
[4] [1962] A. C. 635; [1962] 1 All E. R. 569. The text represents part of an article by the writer in 78 L. Q. R. 407.

relationship of provisos (e) and (f). Jones was charged with the murder of a Girl Guide. His defence was an uncorroborated alibi that he had been with a prostitute, and he deposed to the details of a conversation he had had with his wife on his return home. It was necessary for him to explain why, before setting up this alibi, he had endeavoured to establish another one which would have been corroborated. He did so by stating, in the course of his evidence in-chief, that he had previously been in trouble with the result that he was afraid that the police would not pay much attention to an uncorroborated alibi. The alibi which Jones ultimately set up bore a striking resemblance to the alibi which he had set up at an earlier trial leading to his conviction for the rape of another Girl Guide. He was cross-examined with regard to the resemblances between the two alibis and the conversations with his wife to which he deposed at each trial. Although the terms of the cross-examination did not actually show that he had committed another offence, it was common ground among the members of the House of Lords who heard the appeal that the questions suggested that he was a person of bad character who had previously been suspected of, if not charged with, a serious crime. Jones was convicted, and the propriety of the cross-examination was challenged in the Court of Criminal Appeal. That court held that proviso (f) had not been infringed because the words "tending to show" mean "make known to the jury", and the jury had already been made aware of the fact that the accused had previously been in trouble by means of his evidence in-chief.[1] Jones appealed to the House of Lords, and the House was unanimously in favour of dismissing the appeal. Lords SIMONDS, REID and MORRIS did so for the reason given by the Court of Criminal Appeal, but Lords DENNING and DEVLIN expressly disagreed with it. They were in favour of dismissing the appeal on the broader ground that the cross-examination was relevant to the issue of the prisoner's liability because it tended to disprove his alibi; a considerable strain was put on the credulity of the jury when they were asked to believe that identical alibis were true, and that identical conversations took place between Jones and his wife. Lords SIMONDS, REID and MORRIS were of course also of opinion that the cross-examination was relevant for this reason, but, in their view, that did not of itself suffice to render the questions admissible under the statute. Had Jones not alluded in-chief to his previous trouble, the majority would have allowed the appeal.[2]

The view that "tending to show" means "make known" or "reveal" to the jury for the first time goes a long way towards reducing the practical effect of the difference between the literal and broad views concerning the relation between provisos (e) and (f) of the Criminal Evidence Act, 1898, if it applies to cases in which the evidence tending to show bad character has been given by the prosecution. On facts such as those of *R. v. Chitson*,[3] for example, the cross-examination was proper according to the majority,

---

[1] *R. v. Jones*, [1962] A. C. 635; [1961] 3 All E. R. 668.

[2] Unless they would have been prepared to apply what is now the proviso to s. 2 (1) of the Criminal Appeal Act, 1968, and dismiss the appeal on the ground that there had been no miscarriage of justice.

[3] [1907] 2 K. B. 945. This case, and *R. v. Kennaway*, [1917] 1 K. B. 25 were expressly stated to have been rightly decided for the wrong reasons by Lord REID in *Jones* v. *Director of Public Prosecutions*, [1962] A. C. 635, at p. 665; cf. *per* Lord MORRIS, another member of the majority, at p. 685.

but not for the reason given by the Court of Criminal Appeal in *Chitson's* case. The majority of the House of Lords in *Jones's* case would have decided *R.* v. *Chitson* as it was decided because the prosecutrix had given evidence of the accused's statement with regard to the other girl, and thus made known to the jury, before the cross-examination of the accused, that he was alleged to be a man of bad character. Lords DEVLIN and DENNING would have decided *Chitson's* case as it was decided for the reason given by the Court of Criminal Appeal, namely, that the cross-examination was relevant to an issue in the case and did not merely go to credit.[1] There are, however, many situations in which cross-examination must be rejected according to the majority opinion in *Jones* v. *Director of Public Prosecutions* although it would be admissible according to the broad view. For example, the questions concerning the accused's relations with the proprietress of the auction room upheld by the Court of Criminal Appeal in *R.* v. *Kurasch*[2] would be condemned on the reasoning of the majority of the House of Lords in *Jones's* case because there had been no previous suggestion to the jury that the proprietress was the accused's mistress. On this view the question would have been prohibited by s. 1 (f) and not permitted by s. 1 (e), but the question was perfectly proper according to the opinions of Lord DENNING and Lord DEVLIN.

The majority view in *Jones's* case must be taken to represent the present English law. There is therefore no point in a detailed discussion of the merits of the two opinions. The minority view is difficult to reconcile with the wording of the Act of 1898, but the majority view may operate harshly because:

"It is one thing to confess to having been in trouble before. It is quite another thing to have it emphasised against you with devastating detail."[3]

There may also be cases in which it would be difficult, if not impossible, to expose a false alibi by reference to the fact that the accused was in prison or with his mistress at the material time because the alibi was raised for the first time after the case for the prosecution had been closed.[4]

(3) THE MEANING OF "CHARGED"—STIRLAND V. DIRECTOR OF PUBLIC PROSECUTIONS

In *Stirland* v. *Director of Public Prosecutions*[5] the House of Lords decided that the word "charged" as used in s. 1 (f) means "charged in court". Accordingly, when a prisoner accused of forgery put his character in issue and said that he had never been charged before it was reasonable to suppose that he was using the word in this sense, and the trial judge should have disallowed questions concerning the suspicions that had been entertained against the accused by one of his employers. Lord SIMON, L.C., con-

---

[1] The same treatment was accorded by the majority to *R.* v. *Kennaway*, [1917] 1 K. B. 25.

[2] [1915] 2 K. B. 749. *R.* v. *Kurasch* was not cited in argument in *Jones's* case, but it was mentioned in the speech of Lord DEVLIN.

[3] *Per* Lord DENNING in *Jones* v. *Director of Public Prosecutions*, [1962] A. C. 635, at p. 667; [1962] 1 All E. R. 569, at p. 577.

[4] See examples given by Lord DEVLIN in *Jones's* case, [1962] A. C. 635, at p. 695; [1962] 1 All E. R. 569, at p. 596.

[5] [1944] A. C. 315; [1944] 2 All E. R. 13. See also *R.* v. *Wadey* (1935), 25 Cr. App. Rep. 104; and *R.* v. *Nicoloudis* (1954), 38 Cr. App. Rep. 118.

cluded his speech with six propositions to some of which it will be necessary to refer later. The first summarises the effect of s. 1 (f). According to the second, the accused may be cross-examined as to any of the evidence he has given in chief, including statements concerning his good record, with a view to testing his veracity or accuracy or to showing that he is not to be believed on oath.[1] The accused had been questioned before leaving his previous employment and was presumably well aware of the suspicions. Accordingly, he could presumably have been cross-examined on the subject if he had said in-chief that he had never previously been suspected of an offence. Lord SIMON's fifth proposition was that it is no disproof of good character that a man has been suspected or accused of a previous crime. Such questions as "Were you suspected" or "Were you accused" are inadmissible because they are irrelevant to the issue of character and can only be asked if the accused has sworn expressly to the contrary. When he does this, he may be said to have adopted a particular method of putting his character in issue. According to the sixth proposition, the fact that a question put to the accused is irrelevant is no reason for quashing his conviction, though it should have been disallowed by the judge. If the question is not only irrelevant but is unfair to the accused as being likely to distract the jury from considering the real issues and so lead to a miscarriage of justice, it should be disallowed, and if not disallowed, is a ground on which an appeal against conviction may be based. As there had been no miscarriage of justice, *Stirland's* appeal was in fact dismissed.

(4) THE RELATION OF THE PROHIBITION TO THE PERMISSION CONFERRED BY THE REST OF S. 1 (f)—MAXWELL V. DIRECTOR OF PUBLIC PROSECUTIONS

When the accused has thrown away the shield provided by the first part of s. 1 (f), it would be wrong to suppose that he can always be asked questions tending to show that he has committed, been convicted of or charged with other offences or is of bad character, because such questions must be relevant either to the issue or else to the credibility of the accused. Accordingly, it was decided by the House of Lords in *Maxwell* v. *Director of Public Prosecutions* [2] that, although a doctor charged with manslaughter by means of an illegal operation gave evidence of his good character, he ought not to have been asked whether a similar charge of which he was acquitted had been made against him in the past. In the instant case, it was impossible to say that the fact that the prisoner had been acquitted on a previous charge was relevant, or that it tended to destroy his credibility as a witness, and the appeal was allowed. Lord SANKEY, L.C., recognised the possibility of circumstances in which the fact of a charge resulting in an acquittal might be elicited from the prisoner. Among the instances he mentioned was that of a man charged with an offence against the person who might be asked whether he had uttered threats against his victim because he was angry with him for having brought an unfounded charge. A further instance is suggested by the later case of *R.* v. *Waldman* [3] in

---

[1] There was a difference of opinion between Lords MORRIS and DEVLIN in *Jones's* case as to whether this proposition was solely addressed to cases in which the accused's shield had been thrown away (see [1962] A. C. 635, at p. 683 and 707; [1962] 1 All E. R. 569, at pp. 588 and 603).

[2] [1935] A. C. 309.

[3] (1934), 24 Cr. App. Rep. 204. *Maxwell's* case was in fact decided earlier in 1934 although it was not reported in the Appeal Cases until 1935.

which the Court of Criminal Appeal upheld a conviction for receiving stolen goods although the accused, who had put his character in issue, had been asked about a previous acquittal on an earlier charge of receiving. The court appears to have considered that *Maxwell's* case could be distinguished because the question was addressed to a character witness as well as to the accused, and because the question was linked with one concerning a previous conviction for receiving. The court also recognised the possibility that a previous acquittal of receiving might be relevant to the accused's guilty knowledge on a subsequent occasion because the previous investigation ought to have stimulated the most careful inquiries in the later transaction, and thus militate against the credibility of statements to the effect that the accused acquired goods cheaply without asking questions concerning their origin.

It should be emphasised that both *Maxwell* v. *Director of Public Prosecutions* and *R.* v. *Waldman* were concerned with situations in which the shield had been thrown away. When this is not the case, it is extremely doubtful whether the accused could be asked about a previous charge resulting in an acquittal owing to the restricted phraseology of s. 1 (f) (i).

B. THE INTERPRETATION OF s. 1 (f) (i)

Section 1 (f) (i) allows the accused to be questioned concerning other offences when proof that he has committed or been convicted of them is admissible to show that he is guilty of the offence charged. Although there is not much authority on the point, there can be little doubt that this part of proviso (f) permits cross-examination about previous convictions when they have been proved in-chief on the rare occasions on which such a course is permissible.[1] There can also be little doubt that, when similar fact evidence has been given in-chief, the accused may be cross-examined about the other offences mentioned in such evidence.[2] The exclusionary rule applies just as much to evidence elicited in cross-examination as to evidence in-chief.[3] Therefore questions suggesting that the accused has been convicted of or has committed other offences which have not been proved in-chief would normally be inadmissible, but, if they are relevant on the principles discussed in section 1 of the last chapter, they may be permissible under s. 1 (f) (i) although they do not relate to matters proved in-chief. In general they will, however, be inadmissible, because a proper foundation should have been laid for the cross-examination by means of the evidence in-chief.[4]

In *R.* v. *Cokar*,[5] the Court of Criminal Appeal was clearly of opinion that no question concerning a previous charge other than one which was merely a preliminary to an admissible question concerning a conviction could be put under s. 1 (f) (i) and, in *Jones* v. *Director of Public Prosecutions*,[6]

---

[1] P. 345, *ante.*
[2] *R.* v. *Chitson*, [1909] 2 K. B. 945; *R.* v. *Kennaway*, [1917] 1 K. B. 25 (these cases must now be read subject to the majority views in *Jones's* case). See also *R.* v. *Cokar*, [1960] 2 Q. B. 207, at p. 210.
[3] See *per* Lord DEVLIN in *Jones's* case, [1962] A. C. 635, at p. 701; [1962] 1 All E. R. at p. 593.
[4] *Per* Lord MORRIS in *Jones* v. *Director of Public Prosecutions*, [1962] A. C. 635 at p. 685; [1962] 1 All E. R. 569, at p. 589.
[5] [1960] 2 Q. B. 207, p. 360 *ante.*, [1960] 2 All E. R. 175.
[6] [1962] A. C. 635 [1962] 1 All E. R. 569

the majority would clearly not have allowed a question tending to show bad character if the bad character had not previously been revealed to the jury. It may therefore be taken to be settled English law that s. 1 (f) (i) must be construed literally, and no words justifying questions about charges or bad character can be read into it.

The Australian Courts have consistently favoured a broad interpretation of the prohibition and s. 1 (f) (i), and the basis of most of their decisions seems to be that the draftsman inadvertently omitted to mention questions showing bad character in the Australian equivalents to s. 1 (f) (i). To quote the most recent judgment of the High Court on the point:

> "In the case of the offence committed and of the conviction the draftsman saw that he was expressly prohibiting proof of a fact he definitely identified independently of its operation or of the harm of introducing it in evidence, whereas in the case of questions tending to show that the accused is of bad character he was dealing with a description of cross-examination going to credit which he thought of as *ex hypothesi* outside the field of relevancy."[1]

C. THE INTERPRETATION OF S. 1 (f) (ii)

It will be convenient to divide the discussion of s. 1 (f) (ii) into two main parts—cases in which the accused puts his character in issue, and those in which the nature or conduct of the defence involves imputations on the character of the prosecutor or one of his witnesses.

(1) CHARACTER IN ISSUE

In order that the first part of the second exception to the prohibition may be brought into play, the court must be satisfied that the accused:

> "has personally or by his advocate asked questions of the witnesses for the prosecution with a view to establish his own good character, or has given evidence of his good character".

The latter phrase is apt to cover a case in which the prisoner calls a witness to character but does not cross-examine on the subject or allude to it in his own evidence in-chief. The exception is not brought into play when a defence witness volunteers a statement concerning the character of the accused which he had not been asked to make;[2] nor is the exception brought into play by the accused's reference to one of his many previous convictions as a ground for fearing the police because it would be wrong to infer that the accused meant that the occasion of the conviction was the only occasion on which he had previously been in trouble.[3] It has been held that a general examination into the circumstances surrounding the alleged crime with

---

[1] *Attwood* v. *R.*, [1960] A. L. R. 321, at p. 325. See also *R.* v. *Baxter*, [1927] S. A. S. R. 321; *R.* v. *Lambert*, [1957] S. A. S. R. 341; *R.* v. *May*, [1959] V. L. R. 683. The view that s. 1 (f) and its equivalents does not prohibit questions tending to show bad character and (presumably) questions tending to show charges, can be reached in three ways; (a) that of Lord DENNING in *Jones's* case, according to which there may always be cross-examination on matters relevant to the issue, (b) that of Lord DEVLIN in *Jones's* case according to which "character" in s. 1 (f) means "reputation" so that questions about specific acts falling short of an offence are outside the prohibition, and (c) the way adopted by the High Court of Australia in *Attwood's* case according to which the questions are *casus omissus* and words may be read into s. 1 (f) (i) and its equivalents.

[2] *R.* v. *Redd*, [1923] 1 K. B. 104.

[3] *R.* v. *Thompson*, [1966] 1 All E. R. 505 following dicta of Oliver, J., in *R.* v. *Wattam* (1952), 36 Cr. App. Rep. 72 at p. 78.

a view to establishing innocence does not expose the accused to cross-examination under s. 1 (f). Thus, in *R. v. Ellis*,[1] a dealer was charged with obtaining cheques from a customer by false pretences concerning the cost price of antiques and he cross-examined the Crown witnesses about his conduct towards the alleged victim with a view to negativing any intent to defraud. The Court of Criminal Appeal held that he ought not to have been asked questions under s. 1 (f) (ii) as the cross-examination had not been conducted with a view to establishing good character. No doubt it had that tendency, but an assertion of innocence might equally well be said to be tantamount to giving evidence of character.

Generally speaking the accused's own evidence of his character takes the form of allusions to his innocent or praiseworthy past, and the decisions certainly do not indicate any great reluctance on the part of the courts to hold that he has put his character in issue by such a reference. A man's allegations concerning his regular attendance at mass,[2] his assertion that he had been earning an honest living for a considerable time,[3] and his affirmative answer to the question whether he is a married man with a family in regular work [4] have been treated as instances in which the shield provided by s. 1 (f) would be thrown away. There seems to be some doubt whether a reference to honourable discharge from the army would have this effect,[5] and similar uncertainty prevails with regard to the statement by a man charged with traffic offences that he disapproved of speeding.[6] In *R. v. Samuel*,[7] the Court of Criminal Appeal did not experience much difficulty in arriving at the conclusion that someone who was charged with larceny by finding put his character in issue when he gave evidence with regard to previous occasions on which he had returned lost property to its owner.

It is necessary to consider the meaning of "character" as used in s. 1 (f) in general and the first part of s. 1 (f) (ii) in particular, the purpose of cross-examination under the exception, and the question of the divisibility of the accused's character.

(i) **The meaning of character.**—We have seen that, in ordinary language, "character" may mean either the reputation or the disposition of the person about whom the inquiry is being made, and that, at common law, a character witness might only be asked about the reputation of the accused.[8] The word is used no less than four times in proviso (f) and, in *R. v. Dunkley*,[9] a case concerned with imputations against a witness for the prosecution, Lord HEWART, C.J., said:

> "It is not difficult to suppose that a formidable argument might have been raised on the phrasing of this statute, that the character which is spoken of is the character which is so well known in the vocabulary of the criminal law—namely, the general reputation of the person referred to; in other words that 'character' in that context and in every part of it, in the last part no less than in the first, in the third part no less than in the second, bears the meaning which the term 'character' was held to bear, for example, in the case of *R. v. Rowton*."[10]

---

[1] [1910] 2 K. B. 746.
[2] *R. v. Ferguson* (1909), 2 Cr. App. Rep. 250.
[3] *R. v. Baker* (1912), 7 Cr. App. Rep. 252.
[4] *R. v. Coulman* (1927), 20 Cr. App. Rep. 106, *per* SWIFT, J., in the course of the argument.
[5] *R. v. Parker* (1924), 18 Cr. App. Rep. 14.   [6] *R. v. Beecham*, [1921] 3 K. B. 464.
[7] (1956), 40 Cr. App. Rep. 8.   [8] P. 347, *ante*.
[9] [1927] 1 K. B. 323, at p. 329. See also *Malindi* v. *R.*, [1967] 1 A. C. 439; [1966] 3 All E. R. 285.   [10] (1865), Le. & Ca. 520.

Lord HEWART concluded that it was much too late in the day to consider such an argument because it could not prevail without the revision, and, to a great extent, the overthrow of a very long series of decisions. When speaking of the first part of s. 1 (f) (ii) in *Stirland* v. *Director of Public Prosecutions*,[1] Lord SIMON, L.C., said:

> "There is perhaps some vagueness in the use of the term 'good character' in this connection. Does it refer to the good reputation which a man may bear in his own circle, or does it refer to the man's real disposition as distinct from what his friends and neighbours may think of him?"

Lord SIMON was inclined to think that both conceptions were combined in s. 1 (f).

In *Jones* v. *Director of Public Prosecutions*,[2] Lord DENNING took Lord HEWART'S view that it is too late to argue that "character" as used in the Act of 1898 means "reputation" and nothing else, but Lord DEVLIN expressed the opinion that this was the meaning intended by the draftsman of the statute.[3] He also thought that the point was still open at the level of the House of Lords. The effect of such a construction would be revolutionary and difficult to apply. When the accused testifies to his own good character, he must almost inevitably speak of his own good past acts [4] and it would certainly upset past decisions if it were to be held that a man who swore that he had led a good clean life and gone to mass every Sunday had not "given evidence of his own good character". If, throughout the entirety of s. 1 (f) "character" were to mean "reputation", it would be difficult to construe that part of s. 1 (f) (ii) under which the accused loses his shield if the nature or conduct of his defence involves imputations on the "character of the prosecutor or the witnesses for the prosecution". It would then become possible to argue that someone who swore that a policeman had extracted a confession from him by violence was not casting imputations on the character of a witness for the prosecution.

It was just such an argument that was rejected by the House of Lords in *Selvey* v. *Director of Public Prosecutions*,[5] a case turning on the construction of the second part of s. 1 (f) (ii), in which someone accused of buggery alleged that the prosecutor had offered to go on the bed with him for a pound, told him that he had already gone on the bed for that sum with another man, and, because his offer was rejected, dumped indecent photographs in the accused's room out of pique. It may therefore now be taken to be settled law that "character" when used in the Act of 1898 means both disposition and reputation.

(ii) The purpose of cross-examination under the exception.—In *Maxwell* v. *Director of Public Prosecutions*,[6] Lord SANKEY, L.C., said that:

> "If the prisoner by himself or his witnesses seeks to give evidence of his own good character, for the purpose of showing that it is unlikely that he com-

---

[1] [1944] A. C. 315, at p. 324; [1944] 2 All E. R. 13, at p. 17.
[2] [1962] A. C. 635, at p. 671; [1962] 1 All E. R. 569, at p. 580.
[3] [1962] A. C. 635, at p. 699; [1962] 1 All E. R., at p. 604.
[4] See *per* Lord DENNING in *Plato Films* v. *Speidel*, [1961] A. C. 1090, at p. 1143. "The plaintiff cannot speak as to his own character and reputation because he does not know what other people think of him, or at any rate he cannot give evidence as to what they think of him." Lord DEVLIN considers that the word "character" means "reputation" throughout the law of evidence (see *Dingle* v. *Associated Newspapers*, [1961] 2 Q. B. 162, at pp. 195 and 198; see also *Fridman*, The Solicitor's Quarterly, Vol. 1, p. 211 (1962)).
[5] [1970] A. C. 304; [1968] 2 All E. R. 497.
[6] [1935] A. C. 309, at p. 319.

mitted the offence charged, he raises by way of defence an issue as to his good character so that he may fairly be cross-examined on that issue just as any witness called by him to prove his good character may be cross-examined to show the contrary."

In so far as it is possible to distinguish cross-examination of the accused designed to establish the probability of his guilt from that which is concerned with the credibility of his testimony, *R. v. Samuel* and the above passage from Lord SANKEY's speech in *Maxwell's Case* show that cross-examination under the early part of s. 1 (f) (ii) may be directed to the first of these purposes. Our previous discussion of *R. v. Samuel* [1] has shown that, from the practical point of view, the distinction is liable to be a distinction without a difference, and there is no doubt that cross-examination is permissible under this part of s. 1 (f) (ii) when its main object is to induce the jury to believe that the accused's oath is not to be trusted. Thus, in *R. v. Wood*,[2] a man, charged with indecent assault upon a girl, put his character in issue and was held by the Court of Criminal Appeal to have been properly cross-examined concerning a conviction for an indecent assault upon another girl, which assault took place after that for which he was being tried. It was said that the chronological order of events did not render the conviction any less admissible as evidence tending to show that the accused was not of good character "at the time of the second trial",[3] and clearly this could only mean that the conviction was regarded by the court as relevant to the credibility of the accused's testimony.

In *R. v. Richardson* and *R. v. Longman*[4] Edmund DAVIES, L.J., speaking for the Court of Appeal, said:

"In our view, evidence of character, when properly admitted, goes to the credit of the witness concerned, whether the evidence disclosed good character or bad character, if the accused calls evidence of good character, and is shown by cross-examination to have a bad character, the jury may give this fact such weight as they think fit when assessing the general credibility of the accused."

These observations were made in the course of the refutation of the over-sophisticated argument that, evidence of convictions having been volunteered by one of the accused in anticipation of the cross-examination he had invited by casting imputations on the character of Crown witnesses, the jury should have been directed that the evidence merely showed the accused to be of bad character and did not go to his general credibility.

(iii) The divisibility of the character of the accused.—When the prisoner urges that he ought to be believed when he swears that he was innocent of a sexual crime because he has a good character for sexual morality, it certainly does tend to refute his contention to show that he was convicted of an indecent assault; but it is open to question whether a conviction for theft has the same effect. This raises the issue of the propriety of a dictum in *R. v. Winfield* on the assumption that the accused was cross-examined about his character. According to this dictum, "there is no such thing known to our procedure as putting half a prisoner's character in issue and leaving out the other half".[5] It will be recollected that Winfield was

---

[1] P.367, *ante*.
[2] [1920] 2 K. B. 179.   [3] At p. 182, *per* Lord READING, C. J.
[4] [1969] 1 Q. B. 299, at p. 311.
[5] (1939), 27 Cr. App. Rep. 139. *Winfield's Case* is discussed from the point of view of the Criminal Evidence Act, 1898, by R. N. Gooderson in 11 C. L. J. 386 *et seq*. The case is considered p. 349, *ante*, from the point of view of the cross-examination of a character witness at common law.

convicted of indecent assault upon a woman and that he called a witness to speak of his good behaviour with ladies. He had previously been convicted of larceny, and it is not clear whether this conviction was put to his character witness, in which case the matter fell to be determined by the common law principles that have already been discussed, or whether the cross-examination concerning the conviction was of Winfield himself under s. 1 (f) (ii) of the Act of 1898. In either event, the Court of Criminal Appeal appears to have approved of the cross-examination, although their observations on the subject were *obiter dicta* because the conviction was quashed on account of the inadequacy of the direction to the jury on the subject of corroboration. So far as the cross-examination of the prisoner was concerned, it ought not to have been used by the jury as a direct means of establishing his guilt, because it was only relevant on the very doubtful footing that a thief is more likely to commit an indecent assault than an honest man. Its relevance to the credibility of the prisoner's testimony is not much greater, although there is a little more force in the argument that a convicted thief is more likely to lie than others. Viewed as a matter affecting credibility, however, Winfield's cross-examination can be justified on the footing that having put his character in issue, he forfeited his right to be treated, as regards cross-examination, otherwise than as an ordinary witness, and an ordinary witness may be cross-examined about a conviction for any offence with a view to shaking his credibility. The law on this subject may not be beyond reproach, but it is the outcome of the view that cross-examination about a conviction for any offence is permissible under s. 6 of the Criminal Procedure Act, 1865,[1] and has nothing to do with the Criminal Evidence Act, 1898. Lord Simon's third proposition in *Stirland's* case[2] was:

> "An accused who 'puts his character in issue' must be regarded as putting the whole of his past record in issue. He cannot assert his good conduct in certain respects without exposing himself to inquiry about the rest of his record so far as this tends to disprove a claim to good character."

R. v. Winfield was cited, and it remains to be seen whether this will be held tantamount to House of Lords approval of the course that was adopted in that case.

(2) Imputations on the Character of the Prosecutor or his Witness[3]

Turning to the second part of s. 1 (f) (ii)—cases in which "the nature or conduct of the defence is such as to involve imputations on the character of the prosecutor or the witnesses for the prosecution", there are several decisons favourable to the accused in which the statutory words have been given their natural meaning. Thus, an attack upon the conduct of a magistrate or police officer not called as a witness for the Crown,[4] and a suggestion by someone accused of murder that the deceased had made indecent approaches to him,[5] have been held to fall outside the proviso so that they did not warrant cross-examination under it; but a strictly literal construc-

---

[1] P. 235, *ante.* See also *R. v. Morris* (1959), 43 Cr. App. Rep. 206 (cross-examination on conviction for dishonesty permitted by imputation of immorality against prosecution witnesses on charge of incest).

[2] [1944] A. C. 315, at p. 324; [1944] 2 All E. R. 13, at p. 18.

[3] See articles in Criminal Law Review (1961), pp. 142 and 213, and 29 M. L. R. 492.

[4] *R. v. Westfall* (1912), 7 Cr. App. Rep. 176.

[5] *R. v. Biggin*, [1920] 1 K. B. 213. Cases are conceivable in which the prosecutor would not be called as a witness, and imputations on his character would nonetheless expose the accused to cross-examination under the Act.

tion of s. 1 (f) (ii) would be unfavourable to the accused because it would mean that, in many cases, a plea of not guilty coupled with an assertion of innocence in the witness box would render the accused liable to cross-examination on his criminal record, on account of the tacit suggestion that the prosecutor or one of his witnesses had been guilty of perjury. The avoidance of such a conclusion has led to an uneasy conflict of authority palliated by an extensive exercise of the court's discretion. Although it would seldom be necessary to go behind *Selvey* v. *Director of Public Prosecutions,*[1] the authorities will be briefly reviewed before the rationale of the later part of s. 1 (f) (ii) and the purpose of the cross-examination which it permits are considered.

(i) Imputations.— In *R.* v. *Rouse,*[2] the accused's statement from the witness box that the prosecutor was a liar was held not to be sufficient to deprive him of his statutory protection.

> "Either the answer amounted to no more than a plea of not guilty put in forcible language such as would not be unnatural in a person in the defendant's rank in life, or it had nothing to do with the conduct of the defence."[3]

The judgment of the Court for Crown Cases Reserved was said to be confined to the special facts of the case, and this may account for the comparative ease with which the Court of Criminal Appeal concluded that an assertion by the accused that the prosecutor was such a horrible liar that his brother would not speak to him warranted cross-examination under s. 1 (f) (ii).[4]

When the veracity of the prosecutor or his witness is not challenged, the statute has often been construed favourably to the accused. He has, for example, been allowed to allege with impunity that a witness for the prosecution failed to hand over the proceeds of a cheque which he had been asked to cash.[5] It would, however, be too much to expect complete consistency, so it is pointless to inquire why someone who is charged with receiving throws away his shield if he casts aspersions on the morality of the prosecutrix,[6] while an allegation that the prosecutor is an habitual drunkard by someone charged with robbery does not have this effect.[7] A suggestion that a confession was obtained by threats or bribes,[8] that successive remands were obtained by the police to enable them to fabricate evidence,[9] and that a confession was dictated by one police officer to another [10] does mean that the conduct of the defence involves imputations

---

[1] [1970] A. C. 304; [1968] 2 All E. R. 497.

[2] [1904] 1 K. B. 184; *R.* v. *Grout* (1909), 3 Cr. App. Rep. 64; *R.* v. *Stratton* (1909), 3 Cr. App. Rep. 255; *R.* v. *Parker* (1924), 18 Cr. App. Rep. 14; *R.* v. *Manley* (1962), 46 Cr. App. Rep. 235.

[3] *Per* Lord ALVERSTONE, C.J., [1904] 1 K.B., at p. 189. For similar statements see *R.* v. *Jones* (1923), 17 Cr. App. Rep. 117, at p. 119; *R.* v. *Clark*, [1955] 2 Q. B. 469, at p. 478 and *R.* v. *Cook*, [1959] 2 Q. B. 340, at p. 345.

[4] *R.* v. *Rappolt* (1911), 6 Cr. App. Rep. 156.

[5] *R.* v. *Eidenow* (1932), 23 Cr. App. Rep. 145; *R.* v. *Morgan* (1910), 5 Cr. App. Rep. 157.

[6] *R.* v. *Jenkins* (1945), 31 Cr. App. Rep. 1. See also *R.* v. *Jones* (1909), 3 Cr. App. Rep. 67; *R.* v. *Morris* (1959), 43 Cr. App. Rep. 206.

[7] *R.* v. *Westfall* (1912), 7 Cr. App. Rep. 176. See Addendum, *ante*.

[8] *R.* v. *Wright* (1910), 5 Cr. App. Rep. 131. In *Selvey* v. *Director of Public Prosecutions*, [1970] A. C. 304, at p. 335, Lord DILHORNE considered this decision to be irreconcilable with *R.* v. *Westfall, supra*.

[9] *R.* v. *Jones* (1923), 17 Cr. App. Rep. 117.

[10] *R.* v. *Clark*, [1955] 2 Q. B. 469; [1955] 3 All E. R. 29. See also the cases in which allegations that a Crown witness was acting out of malice, in revenge or to shield himself have been held to warrant cross-examination under the proviso. *R.* v. *Roberts (otherwise*

on the character of the prosecutor or his witness. Lord HEWART, C.J., once said that a clear line is drawn between words which are an emphatic denial of the Crown's evidence, and words which attack the character or conduct of the witness; but the imprecise nature of this distinction was immediately emphasised when he added:

> "It was one thing for appellant to deny that he had made the confession; but it is another thing to say that the whole thing was an elaborate and deliberate concoction on the part of the inspector."[1]

(ii) **Reading words into s. 1 (f) (ii).**—Closely akin to the question of what does or does not amount to an "imputation" is the question whether it can be said that the accused is only exposed to cross-examination concerning his record when the nature or conduct of the defence is such as to involve "unnecessary" or "unjustifiable" imputations upon the character of the prosecutor or the witnesses for the prosecution. If the answer is in the negative, the prisoner who alleges that it was not he, but a Crown witness, who committed the crime charged, that the prosecutrix who asserts his guilt of rape was a consenting party to acts of immorality or that the man he assaulted was the aggressor will be unable to develop his defence without throwing his shield away. After an early tendency to answer the question in the affirmative,[2] an emphatic negative was the reply of a full Court of Criminal Appeal in *R. v. Hudson,*[3] a prosecution for larceny to which the defence was that the crime had been committed by a Crown witness.

Soon after *Hudson's* case, however, it came to be recognised that the court has a discretion to prohibit cross-examination under s. 1 (f) (ii) although it is permissible as matter of law.[4] In *R. v. Turner*[5] the Court of Criminal Appeal decided, on the strength of the preponderance of earlier authority, that allegations by someone accused of rape that the prosecutrix had not merely consented to intercourse but had also been guilty of gross indecency as a preliminary, did not, as a matter of law, deprive him of his shield, the case being one in which "some limitation must be placed on the words of the section since to decide otherwise would be to do grave injustice never intended by Parliament." With this exception, the difficulties mentioned in the last paragraph have been met, in so far as they have been met at all,[6] by the exercise of the court's discretion; but *R. v. Flynn,*[7] a case in which the defence to a charge of robbery was that the money obtained by the accused from the prosecutor was "hush money" voluntarily paid in consideration of the accused's silence with regard to homosexual advances, was of some help to an accused with a record because the Court

---

Spalding) (1920), 15 Cr. App. Rep. 65; *R. v. McLean* (1926), 19 Cr. App. Rep. 104; *R. v. Dunkley*, [1927] 1 K. B. 323.

[1] *R. v. Jones* (1923), 17 Cr. App. Rep. 117, at p. 120, see also *R. v. Levy* (1966), 50 Cr. App. Rep. 238.

[2] *R. v. Bridgwater*, [1905] 1 K. B. 131; *R. v. Preston*, [1909] 1 K. B. 568.

[3] [1912] 2 K. B. 464. Decisions to the same effect are *R. v. Cohen* (1914), 10 Cr. App. Rep 91; *R. v. Jenkins* (1945), 31 Cr. App. Rep. 1, and *R. v. Sargvon* (1967), 51 Cr. App. Rep. 394. See also *Kerwood v. R.* (1944), 69 C. L. R. 561; *Dawson v. R.* (1961), 106 C. L. R. 1.

[4] *R. v. Watson* (1913), 8 Cr. App. Rep. 249; *R. v. Cook*, [1959] 2 Q. B. 340; [1959] 2 All E. R. 97.

[5] [1944] K. B. 463; [1944] 1 All E. R. 599.

[6] See *R. v. Brown*, (1960) 44 Cr. App. Rep. 181, for a case of self defence in which they were hardly met.

[7] [1963] 1 Q. B. 729; [1961] 3 All E. R. 58.

of Criminal Appeal laid down a general rule according to which the discretion should be exercised in his favour when the nature of the defence necessarily involves imputations on the character of the prosecutor or his witnesses.

The facts of *Selvey* v. *Director of Public Prosecutions*[1] are given on p. 368. The case is primarily of importance because the authorities on the second half of s. 1 (f) (ii) were reviewed by the House of Lords. According to Lord DILHORNE they establish the following propositions:[2]

1. The words of the Statute must be given their ordinary natural meaning;
2. the section permits cross-examination of the accused as to character both when imputations on the character of the prosecutor and his witnesses are cast to show their unreliability as witnesses independently of the evidence given by them and also when the casting of imputations is necessary to enable the accused to establish his defence;
3. in rape cases the accused can allege consent without placing himself in peril of cross-examination;
4. if what is said amounts in reality to no more than a denial of the charge, expressed, it may be, in emphatic language, it should not be regarded as coming within the section.

The rape cases may either be treated as *sui generis*[3] or else explained on the ground that the defence of consent is nothing more than a denial by the accused that the prosecution has established one of the essential ingredients of the charge;[4] there is certainly no disposition on the part of the courts to extend the scope of these decisions

(iii) The discretion of the court and the duty to warn.—In *Selvey's* case the House of Lords confirmed, after full argument, the existence of a judicial discretion to prohibit cross-examination in spite of the fact that it is permitted as a matter of law by the terms of s 1 (f) (ii); but the House denied the existence of a general rule that the discretion should be exercised in favour of the accused when the proper development of his defence necessitates the casting of imputations on the prosecutor or his witnesses. Selvey's conviction was accordingly affirmed. The fact that the existence of the discretion was not recognised in the early days of the Criminal Evidence Act is a matter to be borne in mind when the early decisions are under consideration; it is possible that some of them should now be treated as cases in which there was an imputation although the judge would have been justified in prohibiting cross-examination in the exercise of his discretion, had he known that he possessed such a thing. Even now, in cases in which the judge does not apply his mind to the question of discretion, the the Court of Appeal may exercise its own discretion.[5] It may also uphold the judge's decision to allow cross-examination on a different ground from that upon which he relied.[6]

In *R.* v. *Cook*,[7] the Court of Criminal Appeal stressed the importance of giving some sort of warning to the defence that it was going too far. It was said that it has always been the practice for prosecuting counsel to indicate

---

[1] [1970] A. C. 304.   [2] At p. 339.
[3] *R.* v. *Cook*, [1959] 2 Q. B. 340, at p. 347.
[4] *R.* v. *Turner*, [1944] K. B. 463, at p. 469.
[5] *R.* v. *Cook*, [1959] 2 Q. B. 340; [1959] 2 All E. R. 97.
[6] *R.* v. *Clark*, [1955] 2 Q. B. 469, at p. 473.   [7] *Supra.*

in advance that he is going to claim his rights, or for the judge to give the defence a caution. This is especially needful when the prisoner is unrepresented.[1]

(iv) The rationale of the second half of s. 1 (f) (ii).

The rationale of this part of s. 1 (f) (ii) was stated in the following passage in a judgment of CHANNELL, J.:

> "If the defence is so conducted, or the nature of the defence is such, as to involve the proposition that the jury ought not to believe the prosecutor or one of the witnesses for the prosecution upon the ground that his conduct—not his evidence in the case, but his conduct outside the evidence given by him—makes him an unreliable witness, then the jury ought also to know the character of the prisoner who either gives that evidence or makes that charge, and it then becomes admissible to cross-examine the prisoner about his antecedents and character with the view of showing that he has such a bad character that the jury ought not to rely upon his evidence."[2]

In other words, it is a case of tit for tat.

(v) Purpose of the cross-examination allowed by s. 1 (f) (ii).

From this it follows that the purpose of the cross-examination permitted by this part of the Criminal Evidence Act, 1898, is to discredit the accused —a fact that was stressed by DARLING, J., in his summing up in *R. v. Morrison.* The accused was charged with murder by violence, and his counsel cross-examined one of the witnesses for the prosecution on the question whether she kept a brothel. Morrison was accordingly cross-examined in his turn with regard to his previous convictions for larceny and burglary. DARLING, J., told the jury that:

> "the only use to be made of these previous convictions is to show that when you have to rely upon his (the prisoner's) word as contradicting something stated by somebody else, or something which is not corroborated, you have not the word of a person who has done nothing wrong. . . . You have only the word of a man whose past career has been what you know it to have been."[3]

---

[1] For the appropriate procedure at a summary trial see *R. v. Weston-Super-Mare Justices, Ex parte Townsend,* [1968] 3 All E. R. 225n.

[2] *R. v. Preston,* [1909] 1 K. B. 568, at p. 575. See also *per* SINGLETON, J., in *R. v. Jenkins* (1945), 31 Cr. App. Rep. 1, at pp. 14–15, "It is only fair that the jury should have material to enable them to determine whether to believe the accused or the prosecution". See Addendum, *ante.*

[3] Cited from "*Notable British Trials*" in 11 C. L. J. at p. 388. The direction appears to have been approved by the Court of Criminal Appeal (*R. v. Morrison* (1911), 6 Cr. App. Rep. 159, at p. 169). In *R. v. Cook,* [1959] 2 Q. B. 340; [1959] 2 All E. R. 97 the trial judge told the jury he was sure that they would not be prejudiced by the fact that the accused admitted to having been convicted of criminal offences. Later he said this: "when allegations are made against police officers, or indeed any other witnesses for the prosecution, you should consider who is the person who is making them, and for that purpose you are entitled to take into consideration that he admits he is a convicted criminal. If you understand what I mean by that, it does not make it any more likely that he committed this crime, but it may mean that it is more unlikely that the allegations made against the police officers are true than if they were made by a person of good character." In the Court of Criminal Appeal this was said to have been a proper direction on the limited effect of the appellant's bad character. In *R. v. Brown* (1960), 44 Cr. App. Rep. 181, the trial judge said to the jury: "You will not allow your knowledge of his past to weigh your judgment of the evidence given in this case. It is relevant only in your consideration of the suggestion that it was Wright who was the aggressor on this occasion." This was the only live issue for the jury, and the case illustrates how it is often impossible to draw a distinction between utilising the results of cross-examination under the Act of 1898 to discredit the accused and utilising them to demonstrate the probability of the accused's guilt. The author is indebted to the Registrar of the Court of Criminal Appeal for having allowed him to see the papers in *R. v. Cook* and *R. v. Brown.* The above extracts do not appear in the reports of these cases. In *R. v. Vickers,* [1972] Crim. L. R. 101, a conviction was quashed because the judge did not direct the jury that the accused's previous convictions only went to his credit.

It is, however, very doubtful whether warnings of this nature prevent the prejudicial character of the accused's record from exercising a disproportionately strong influence on the jury. This part of s. 1 (f) (ii) is liable to place counsel for the defence in a somewhat embarrassing position. Assuming that the prosecution has, as it should,[1] informed him of his client's record and of the known records of witnesses for the prosecution,[2] he cannot cross-examine the witness without exposing the accused to retaliation in kind. On the other hand, failure to attack the witness's credibility may lead the jury to treat unreliable evidence as though it were trustworthy. This difficulty could be countered by a practice under which counsel for the Crown informs the court of such matters as the previous convictions of his witness, but there is no general rule to that effect.[3]

D. THE INTERPRETATION OF S. 1 (f) (iii)

The rationale underlying s. 1 (f) (iii) according to which the prisoner may be cross-examined about his past misconduct if "he has given evidence against any other person charged with the same offence" is, presumably, that he is in the same position as a witness for the prosecution so far as the co-accused is concerned, and nothing must be done to impair the right of a person charged to discredit his accusers. Accordingly it has been held that the court has no discretion to refuse leave to a co-accused to cross-examine under s. 1 (f) (iii) if it considers that the subsection applies to the case, although the court would have a discretion to refuse such leave if the application under the subsection were made by the prosecution.[4]

It is not necessary that there should have been any hostile intent in order that a person should have been held to have "given evidence against" his co-accused; the important point is, not the state of mind of the witness, but the likely effect of his testimony. It is enough if the evidence would have to be included in any summary of the evidence in the case which, if accepted, would warrant the conviction of the other person charged with the same offence;[5] the subsection applies whether the accused's evidence supports the prosecution's case against his co-accused in a material respect or undermines the defence of that co-accused.[6]

The words "any other person charged with the same offence" must be given their ordinary meaning. Accordingly, although successive possessions of the same forged bank notes are the "same offence" within the meaning of s. 1 (f) (iii),[7] it was held in *R. v. Roberts*[8] that someone charged with fraudulent conversion who had given evidence against his

---

[1] *Practice Direction*, [1966] 2 All E. R. 928.

[2] *Cf. R. v. Collister and R. v. Warhurst* (1955), 39 Cr. App. Rep. 100.

[3] *R. v. Carey and R. v. Williams* (1968), 52 Cr. App. Rep. 305.

[4] *Murdoch v. Taylor*, [1965] A. C. 574; [1965] 1 All E. R. 406; see an article by I. G. Carvell, 1965 Cr. L. R. 419; earlier authorities on the same point are *R. v. Ellis*, [1961] 2 All E. R. 928; *R. v. Stannard*, [1965] 2 Q. B. 1; [1964] 1 All E. R. 34; *R. v. McGuirk* (1964), 48 Cr. App. Rep. 75; *R. v. Riebold*, [1965] 1 All E. R. 653. In Tasmania there may be a discretion (*Hill v. R.*, [1953] Tas. S. R. 54). For cross-examination by co-accused generally see p. 227, *ante*.

[5] Lord MORRIS in *Murdoch v. Taylor*, [1965] A. C. 574 at p. 585, [1965] 1 All E. R. 406 at p. 416.

[6] per Lord DONOVAN in *Murdoch v. Taylor*, [1965] A. C. 574 at p. 592.

[7] *R. v. Russell*, [1971] 1 Q. B. 151; [1970] 3 All E. R. 924.

[8] [1936] 1 All E. R. 23.

co-accused, charged with having obtained the money alleged to have been fraudulently converted by false pretences, ought not to have been cross-examined on his previous convictions by his co-accused.

In *R. v. Lovett*,[1] Lovett was charged with stealing a television set and G., his co-accused, was charged with handling it. Lovett cast serious imputations on a witness for the prosecution and gave evidence against G. G.'s counsel immediately cross-examined Lovett on his previous convictions; he was convicted and G. acquitted. On Lovett's appeal against conviction the Court of Appeal held that cross-examination under s. 1 (f) (iii) was improper because the two accused were not charged with the same offence but, as counsel for the prosecution had intended to seek leave to cross-examine under s. 1 (f) (ii), the Court of Appeal exercised the discretion which the trial judge would have had and dismissed the appeal. On the authority of *R. v. Seigley*,[2] the Court expressed the view that the prosecution may, subject to the discretion of the judge to prohibit such a course, cross-examine under s. 1 (f) (iii); the Court also took the view that, subject again to the judge's discretion, cross-examination of an accused by his co-accused was permitted by s. 1 (f) (ii).

Of course the prosecution could not have been allowed to cross-examine under s. 1 (f) (iii) on the facts of *R. v. Lovett*, and it is only in very exceptional circumstances that an application for leave to cross-examine under that subsection would be likely to succeed; a possible instance would be a case in which two persons jointly charged with the same offence each gave evidence against the other, but, because they both had criminal records, neither cross-examined the other under s. 1 (f) (iii). The Court of Appeal could have exercised its discretion under s. 1 (f) (ii) in favour of G.[3] but did not consider it right to do so; an example of a case in which such a course might be proper would be one in which A., charged with stealing, swears that he was acting under the duress of his co-accused B., charged with handling, and of C., a witness for the prosecution. A judge could well take the view that, while there was every reason why his discretion under s. 1 (f) (ii) should be exercised against the prosecution, it should be exercised in favour of B.

We have seen that, even when an accused has not given evidence against his co-accused, the latter has a right to cross-examine him,[4] but unless he gives evidence against someone jointly charged with the same offence, he would not normally be liable to cross-examination by his co-accused on his criminal record and bad character. One of two accused who cross-examines a witness for the prosecution with a view to establishing that the other was the culprit by, for example, asking whether the alleged frauds did not stop while that other was in prison, does not, merely by doing so, expose himself to cross-examination under s. 1 (f).[5] When such a course is likely to be adopted, it is a matter for judicial discretion whether separate trials should be ordered.[6]

---

[1] [1973] 1 All E. R. 744.
[2] (1911), 6 Cr. App. Rep. 106.
[3] This assumes that no procedural point can be taken with regard to the exercise of the discretion in favour of someone who is not a party to the appeal.
[4] *R. v. Hilton*, [1972] 1 Q. B. 421; [1971] 3 All E. R. 541.
[5] *R. v. Miller*, [1952] 2 All E. R. 667; presumably the co-accused could be cross-examined on this point under s. 1 (f) (i).
[6] But see *R. v. Hoggins*, [1967] 3 All E. R. 334.

E. THE PROPOSALS OF THE CRIMINAL LAW REVISION COMMITTEE[1]

The Criminal Law Revision Committee recommended a compromise with regard to the cross-examination of the accused similar in principle to that adopted by s. 1 (e) and s. 1 (f) of the Act of 1898; but there are important differences of detail mentioned below. The relevant provisions are set out in clauses 6, 7 and 15 of the draft Bill annexed to the 11th Report. The word "character" is abandoned in favour of "reputation", "disposition" and, where appropriate, "credibility". The following are the principal recommendations.

(*i*) There should continue to be a general prohibition on questions "tending to reveal to the court or jury" the fact that the accused has committed, been charged with, convicted or acquitted, of any offence other than that charged, or that he is generally or in a particular respect a person of bad disposition or reputation. The words in inverted commas indicate an approval of the majority view in *Jones* v. *Director of Public Prosecutions*,[2] so far as the construction of the phrase "tending to show" is concerned.

(*ii*) The general prohibition should not apply to questions concerning facts admissible to prove the commission of the offence charged by the accused. Such matters are in the main dealt with by clause 3, the first two subclauses of which are intended to be a statement of the present law with regard to similar fact evidence;[3] but the recommended provision also avoids difficulties such as those occasioned by the restriction of s. 1 (f) (i) of the 1898 Act to questions tending to show that the accused has committed or been convicted of other offences. If the recommendation were adopted, *R.* v. *Cokar*[4] would be overruled and *R.* v. *Kurash*,[5] a decision which is wholly inexplicable on the majority view in *Jones* v. *Director of Public Prosecutions*,[6] would become explicable. In fact the Committee expressly approves the minority view in *Jones's* case concerning the relation of s. 1 (e) to s. 1 (f) (i) of the 1898 Act.

(*iii*) The effect of the first half of s. 1 (f) (ii) dealing with evidence of character is preserved, as is the rule concerning the indivisibility of the accused's character laid down in *R.* v. *Winfield*,[7] a decision of the Committee which some may well regret.

(*iv*) The Committee does, however, propose an important modification of the second half of s. 1 (f) (ii) of the 1898 Act. This is that the general prohibition on questions concerning misconduct other than that charged should only be lifted if the main purpose of the imputations was to raise an issue as to the credibility of one of the witnesses for the prosecution. Imputations necessary for the proper development of the defence could, if the recommendation were accepted, be made by the accused without running the risk of cross-examination on his past misdeeds. *Selvey* v.

---

[1] 11th Report, paras. 114–136; for criticism, see C. Tapper, 36 M. L. R. 167 (1973), and for a general discussion of the problem of the accused with a criminal record see Cross in 6 Sydney Law Review 173 (1969).
[2] [1962] A. C. 635; [1961] 3 All E. R. 668.
[3] P. 343, *ante*.
[4] [1960] 2 Q. B. 207; [1960] 2 All E. R. 175, p. 360, *ante*.
[5] [1915] 2 K. B. 749, p. 363, *ante*.
[6] [1962] A. C. 635; [1961] 3 All E. R. 668
[7] [1939] 4 All E. R. 164.

Director of Public Prosecutions would be overruled.[1]   The recommendation was a majority one for some members of the Committee favoured the retention of the existing law, while others favoured a provision more adverse to the accused, namely that he should, subject to the discretion of the judge, be liable to cross-examination to credit like any other witness without regard to the nature of his defence, and yet other members of the Committee favoured a provision according to which the accused should only lose his shield if he sets up his good character or gives evidence against a co-accused.   There are precedents for and against every solution of this thorny problem which has so far been proposed.   The accused is treated like an ordinary witness in Canada, where the judge must, if he does not exercise his discretion against the cross-examination of the accused on his record, instruct the jury not to regard the cross-examination as relevant to the accused's guilt.[2]   The solution proposed by the majority of the Committee is that of the American Model Code and Uniform Rules, as well as of the Ghana Criminal Procedure Code;[3] while the Israeli Criminal Procedure Law[4] only allows an accused who testifies to be cross-examined about his previous convictions if he gives or adduces evidence of character. The main argument in favour of the present English law is that it prevents an accused who testifies, for example, to the effect that he was recovering stolen property from the prosecutor and not robbing him, from masquerading as a consistently law abiding citizen when he has a number of previous convictions;[5] but it may nevertheless inhibit the development of a genuine defence.   The proposal of the majority of the Criminal Law Revision Committee would lessen this danger, but it would still make it possible for Crown witnesses with numerous previous convictions to go free from cross-examination on the subject simply on account of the fact, quite irrelevant to their credibility, that the accused also has previous convictions.   The Israeli Law thus has much to commend it, but it is doubtful whether any change in the present law going further than the proposal of the majority of the Criminal Law Revision Committee would be acceptable to the bulk of English practitioners.

(*v*) The Committee recommends that the accused should lose his shield if he gives evidence against any person "jointly charged with him in the same proceedings".   This is broader than the present law under which the shield is only lost if the accused gives evidence against someone "jointly charged with the same offence".   If the recommendation were adopted, *R.* v. *Roberts*[6] and *R.* v. *Lovett*[7] would be overruled.

(*vi*) when dealing with the privilege against self-incrimination, the Committee recommends a provision similar to s. 1 (e) of the Act of 1898 under which the accused cannot refuse to answer a question or produce a document or thing on the ground that to do so would tend to prove him guilty of the offence charged, but it proceeds to recommend a provision

---

[1] P. 368, *ante.*   Other decisions that would suffer this fate are *R.* v. *Hudson*, [1912] 2 K. B. 464, *R.* v. *Clark*, [1955] 2 Q. B. 469; [1955] 3 All E. R. 29, *R.* v. *Cook*, [1959] 2 Q. B. 340; [1959] 2 All E. R. 97 and *R.* v. *Brown* (1960), 44 Cr. App. Rep. 181.

[2] *Colpitts* v. *R.* (1966), 52 D. L. R. (2d) 416.

[3] Model Code, r. 106 (3), Uniform Rules, r. 21, and Ghana Criminal Procedure Code, 1960 s. 129 (5) (c).

[4] 5725 of 1965, s. 146.

[5] See, for example, *R.* v. *Sargvon* (1967), 51 Cr. App. Rep. 394.

[6] [1936] 1 All E. R. 23, p. 375, *ante.*

[7] [1973] 1 All E. R. 744, p. 376, *ante.*

to which there is no counterpart in the Act of 1898. The proposal is that the accused cannot refuse to answer a question relevant to an issue on the ground that it would criminate him or his spouse as to other offences, although he may refuse to answer questions on this ground if they only go to his credibility. To take two hypothetical cases on which the Committee considers the law to be unclear, A., charged with shoplifting, swears in-chief that he was not in the shop in question at the material time; he is asked in cross-examination where he was and objects to answering the question because his answer would tend to show that he was shoplifting in another shop. B., charged with theft, casts imputations on a witness for the prosecution and objects to answering a question in cross-examination as to whether he has made false tax returns. So far as the second case is concerned, the answer as to the present law may perhaps be found in the second part of s. 1 (f) (ii) of the Act of 1898, although there is no authority and the structure of s. 1 (f) may not be considered apt to override the privilege against self-incrimination. There is also no authority on the first example, but the English courts might follow r. 25 (g) of the American Uniform Rules, supported as it is by a preponderance of United States authority, and hold that the accused has waived his privilege against answering the question by opting to give evidence; it is very doubtful whether it could be held that the question comes within the general prohibition in s. 1 (f).[1]

---

[1] On the whole of the above paragraph see 11th Report of the Criminal Law Revision Committee, paras. 169–72.

CHAPTER XVI

EVIDENCE OF OPINION AND JUDICIAL FINDINGS AS EVIDENCE OF THE FACTS UPON WHICH THEY WERE BASED

The two main topics of this chapter are connected by the fact that the rule in *Hollington* v. *Hewthorn & Co., Ltd.* [1] (now largely abrogated in the case of civil proceedings), under which judicial findings are inadmissible as evidence of the facts found, is an instance of the application of the rule excluding evidence of opinion which is considered in section 1. This latter rule has come to be of far greater importance in the law of the United States than it is in that of this country. As long ago as 1898, Thayer said, "the quantity of decisions on the subject is most unreasonably swollen"[2] and he was speaking of the position in America. In 1940, Wigmore felt able to assert that, so far as the United States was concerned, the rule "had done more than any other one rule of procedure to reduce our litigation towards a state of legalised gambling".[3] In England, the reported decisions on the subject are comparatively few, and it is difficult to believe that the exclusionary rule gives rise to much trouble in practice. An explanation of this difference is offered in the following passage from an important book review:[4]

> "At the outset of the nineteenth century, the English writers, with the English love of conciseness, had laid down the general proposition that 'a witness must state facts not opinions'. In this country, the bench and bar were not misled by this statement. STARKIE, for instance, showed its limitations in practice (3rd edition, 1842, p. 173): 'It has been said that a witness must not be examined in-chief as to his belief or persuasion, but only as to his knowledge of the fact. . . . But, with respect to persuasion or belief as founded on facts within the actual knowledge of the witness, the position is not true.' In other words, we have never felt any hesitation, on this side of the Atlantic, in admitting statements by witnesses which are a compendious mode of summarising a sequence of inferences, based upon perceived facts."

Although the bulk of transatlantic case law on the subject may be due to an over-rigid adherence to the proposition that witnesses must state facts, not opinions, the English practitioner's gain has, to some extent, been the English writer's loss, for the mass of material has obliged lawyers and judges in the United States to subject the rule to deeper scrutiny than it has received in this country, and much reliance is placed on their work in section 1.

---

[1] [1943] K. B. 587; [1943] 2 All E. R. 35.
[2] *Preliminary Treatise on Evidence at Common Law*, 525.
[3] VII *Wigmore*, p. 27.
[4] P. A. Landon, reviewing King and Pillinger's *Opinion Evidence in Illinois* in 60 L. Q. R. 201.

SECTION 1.—EVIDENCE OF OPINION [1]

A. STATEMENT AND ILLUSTRATIONS OF THE EXCLUSIONARY RULE

(1) STATEMENT OF THE RULE

A witness may not give his opinion on matters which the court considers call for the special skill or knowledge of an expert unless he is an expert in such matters, and he may not give his opinion on other matters if the facts upon which it is based can be stated without reference to it in a manner equally conducive to the ascertainment of the truth. [2]

In the law of evidence "opinion" means any inference from observed facts, and the law on the subject derives from the general rule that witnesses must speak only to that which was directly observed by them. The treatment of evidence of opinion by English law is based on the assumption that it is possible to draw a sharp distinction between inferences and the facts on which they are based. The drawing of inferences is said to be the function of the judge or jury, while it is the business of a witness to state facts. But the law recognises that, so far as matters calling for special knowledge or skill are concerned, judges and jurors are not necessarily properly equipped to draw the right inferences from facts stated by witnesses. A witness is therefore allowed to state his opinion with regard to such matters provided he is expert in them.

Although the distinction between fact and inference is clear enough up to a point, there are borderline cases. The statement that a car was being driven on the left side of the road is plainly one of fact, while the assertion that a particular piece of driving was negligent is equally clearly a matter of inference from observed facts. Statements concerning speed, temperature, or the identity of persons, things and handwriting are, however, indissolubly composed of fact and inference. The law makes allowance for these borderline cases by permitting witnesses to state their opinion with regard to matters not calling for special knowledge whenever it would be virtually impossible for them to separate their inferences from the facts on which those inferences are based.

There are thus two broad spheres of evidence of opinion. The first concerns matters calling for specialised skill or knowledge. In this sphere the only questions are whether the subject of inquiry does raise issues calling for expertise and whether the witness is a qualified expert. The rule of evidence is only exclusionary in the sense that the testimony of non-experts is excluded on matters calling for a specialist. In the other sphere of evidence of opinion, such evidence will be excluded if the subject is one with regard to which fact and inference can conveniently be kept separate.

In so far as it is possible for them to do so, the courts set themselves against receiving evidence from any witness as to the very matter which the judge or jury has to decide. This is because litigants are entitled to have their disputes settled by a judge, with or without a jury, and not by the statement of witnesses. If witnesses are too readily allowed to give

---

[1] In the following pages much use has been made of material in VII *Wigmore*, ch. 67; Maguire, *Evidence, Common Sense and Common Law*, pp. 24–31, and Cowen and Carter, *Essays on the Law of Evidence*, essay 5.

[2] See *Sherrard* v. *Jacob*, [1965] N. I. 151, at pp. 157–8 *per* Lord MACDERMOTT.

their opinion concerning an ultimate issue, there is a serious danger that the jury will be unduly influenced:

> "If a cardinal of the Roman Catholic church is testifying before a jury mainly composed of Catholics, and states that, in his opinion, the defendant was driving negligently, it can hardly be supposed that the verdict would be other than for the plaintiff."[1]

This is an extreme case, but the reception of evidence of opinion on this kind of question is always liable to prevent a jury from troubling to make up its own mind. Even when they are receiving expert evidence, it has generally been the practice of the judges to prevent a witness from stating his opinion on an ultimate issue, such as the reasonableness of a covenant in restraint of trade,[2] the validity of a patent, or the construction of a document. "The admission of the opinion of eminent experts upon the issues leads to the balancing of opinions and tends to shift responsibility from the bench or the jury to the witness box."[3] The exclusion of opinion evidence on the ultimate issue can easily become something of a fetish, and we shall see that the law is relaxed for civil proceedings by s. 3 of the Civil Evidence Act, 1972.

(2) ILLUSTRATION OF THE EXCLUSIONARY EFFECT OF THE RULE

(i) **Non-expert opinion on matters calling for expertise.**—In so far as it is exclusionary, two classes of case are contemplated in the formulation of the rule at the beginning of this section, and it is hardly surprising that there should be but few reported decisions falling within the first class. A litigant would normally have to be in desperate straits before he thought of calling a witness who was not expert on the matter in question to give his opinion on a subject involving special skill or knowledge. This may have been the position of counsel for the defence in *R.* v. *Loake*[4] when he applied to the Court of Criminal Appeal for leave to call fresh evidence in support of the accused's plea of insanity. Among the witnesses he wished to call were a friend of the accused who saw him three days before the crime was committed and formed the opinion that he was insane, together with a magistrate who had come to a similar conclusion after visiting the prisoner in his cell. The court disposed of the application so far as these witnesses were concerned by saying that the friend's evidence was clearly inadmissible, and the magistrate was not an expert. Non-experts may be asked to state whether they consider a person with whom they are well acquainted to be sane, but this has been said to be no more than a "compendious mode of ascertaining the result of the actual observation of the witness, from acts done, as to the habits and demeanour" of such person.[5] There was no suggestion that either of the proposed witnesses in *Loake's Case* were at all intimately acquainted with the accused.

(ii) **Cases not calling for expertise.**—In *R.* v. *Chard*[6] the Court of Appeal held that the trial judge had rightly excluded medical evidence concerning the intention at the material time of someone charged with

---

[1] 60 L. Q. R. 202.   [2] *Haynes* v. *Doman*, [1899] 2 Ch. 13.
[3] *Joseph Crosfield & Sons, Ltd.* v. *Technichemical Laboratories, Ltd.*, (1913), 29 T. L. R. 378, at p. 379.
[4] (1911), 7 Cr. App. Rep. 71.
[5] Per PARKE, B., in *Wright* v. *Doe* d. *Tatham* (1838), 4 Bing. N. C. 489, at pp. 543–4. Cf. *R.* v. *Davies*, [1962] 3 All E. R. 97.
[6] (1971), 56 Cr. App. Rep. 268.

murder where there was no question of his being insane or suffering from diminished responsibility. A judge and jury are as competent as a psychiatrist to form an opinion about the past intention of a normal man. On similar grounds it has been held that expert evidence is inadmissible to explain the ordinary meaning of words such as "obscene or indecent"[1] or "calculated to deprave or corrupt"[2] when used in a modern general act of parliament.[3]

In *Ramadge* v. *Ryan*[4] a doctor claimed damages for a libel contained in an article in *The Lancet* in which it was said that another doctor had honourably and faithfully discharged his duty to his medical brethren by declining to act with the plaintiff who had associated himself with a quack. The doctor was not allowed to call a surgeon to say whether he would meet the plaintiff in professional consultation, or whether the other doctor had honourably discharged his duty to his profession because no reference was made to the rules of medical etiquette, and, though witnesses skilled in any art or science may be called to say what, in their judgment, would be the result of certain facts submitted to their consideration, they ought not to give an opinion on things with which a jury may be supposed to be equally well acquainted. No doubt the details of medical etiquette have been elaborated since *Ramadge* v. *Ryan* was decided, and the questions might be held admissible to-day, if a suitable foundation could be laid for them, but this does not affect the validity of the doctrine that an expert may not give a deliberate opinion on matters which do not call for expertise. This doctrine was again vividly illustrated in the Canadian case of *R.* v. *Kusmack.*[5] The accused was charged with murder by cutting his victim's throat, and his defence was that she had a knife in her hand when he seized her wrists, hitting her arm, with the result that the knife accidentally struck her throat. One of the grounds on which a new trial was ordered was that a doctor who had been called to give expert evidence concerning the cause of death had referred to some wounds on the deceased's hands, saying that he thought they were inflicted when she was protecting her throat from attack. In the word of PORTER, J.:

> "The subject on which the witness is testifying must be one upon which competency to form an opinion can only be acquired by a course of special study or experience. It is upon such a subject and such a subject only that the testimony is admissible."[6]

The doctor's observations about the wounds on the hands were purely conjectural, they were not made in consequence of his medical skill, and they were likely to confuse the jury. In fact they were the very kind of observation which illustrates the need for a rule excluding certain types of opinion evidence.

---

[1] *R.* v. *Stamford*, [1972] 2 Q. B. 391; [1972] 2 All E. R. 427.

[2] *R.* v. *Anderson*, [1972] 1 Q. B. 304; [1971] 3 All E. R. 1152.

[3] *Marquis of Camden* v. *Inland Revenue Commissioners*, [1914] 1 K. B. 641, at p. 650.

[4] (1832), 9 Bing. 333; contrast *Greville* v. *Chapman* (1844), 5 Q. B. 731, where the rules of a racing association were put in and the question whether a party's conduct was dishonourable was allowed.

[5] (1955), 20 C. R. 365.

[6] At p. 376. This was only one of the grounds on which a new trial was ordered, and the decision was confirmed on appeal without reference to it.

B. EXPERT EVIDENCE [1]

The courts have been accustomed to act on the opinion of experts from early times. As long ago as 1553 SAUNDERS, J., said:

> "If matters arise in our law which concern other sciences or faculties we commonly apply for the aid of that science or faculty which it concerns. This is a commendable thing in our law. For thereby it appears that we do not dismiss all other sciences but our own, but we approve of them and encourage them as things worthy of commendation." [2]

The learned judge's assertion was amply borne out by copious citations, but the early expert was often a member of the jury, and there was no question of his opinion being disregarded by that body. Expert witnesses began to play their modern role in the eighteenth century. In *Folkes* v *Chadd* [3] Mr. Smeaton, the famous engineer, was allowed to testify concerning his opinion whether an embankment had caused the silting of a harbour.

> "Mr. Smeaton understands the construction of harbours, the causes of their destruction, and how remedied. In matters of science no other witnesses can be called. . . . Handwriting is proved every day by opinion; and for false evidence on such questions a man may be indicted for perjury." [4]

In *Beckwith* v. *Sydebotham*, [5] Lord ELLENBOROUGH allowed shipwrights to testify concerning the seaworthiness of a ship. He said that, where there was a matter of skill or science to be decided, the jury might be assisted by the opinion of those peculiarly acquainted with it in their professions or pursuits; as the truth of the facts stated in them was not certainly known, their opinion might not go for much; but still it was admissible evidence. In cross-examination, they might be asked what they would think on the state of facts contended for by the other side. His Lordship was referring to a difficulty that is encountered in the reception of all kinds of expert evidence. In the vast majority of cases, the witnesses will not have perceived the occurrences with which the case is concerned. In *Beckwith* v. *Sydebotham* for instance, the shipwrights had not examined the ship whose seaworthiness was in issue, therefore their opinion had to be based on assumed facts. It is for the court to determine which party's version of the occurrences in issue is to be accepted. Accordingly, every effort must be made not to call upon the expert to give an opinion on the veracity of the ordinary witnesses in the case, or the validity of any inference concerning the existence of a disputed fact. This can only be done by framing a series of hypothetical questions—a procedure which, however necessary it may be, certainly complicates the issues in a particular case.

The facts upon which an expert's opinion is based must be proved by admissible evidence. If he observed them, he may testify to their existence, but, when the facts in question are dependent on ordinary human powers of perception, the expert may be contradicted by a lay witness, as when a police officer and a doctor give different accounts of the behaviour of someone accused of drunken driving when he was being questioned at a police station.[6] A doctor may not state what a patient told him about past symptoms

---

[1] See "*Expert Evidence*", by Hammelmann, 10 M. L. R. 32 (1947), and Learned Hand "*Historical and Practical Considerations regarding Expert Testimony*", 15 H. L. R. 40 (1901).
[2] *Buckley* v. *Rice-Thomas* (1554), 1 Plowd. 118, at p. 124.
[3] (1782), 3 Doug. K. B. 157.   [4] *Per* Lord MANSFIELD.
[5] (1807), 1 Camp. 116.   [6] *Sutton* v. *Prenter*, [1963] Qd. R. 401.

as evidence of the existence of those symptoms because that would infringe the rule against hearsay, but he may give evidence of what the patient told him in order to explain the grounds on which he came to a conclusion with regard to the patient's condition.[1] A valuer may express his opinion concerning the appropriate rent for particular premises even though he has not got first hand knowledge of comparable rents, but he may not give evidence about comparable rents of which he has not got personal knowledge.[2]

The functions of expert witnesses were succinctly stated by Lord President COOPER in *Davie* v. *Edinburgh Magistrates*[3] when he said:

> "Their duty is to furnish the judge or jury with the necessary scientific criteria for testing the accuracy of their conclusions, so as to enable the judge or jury to form their own independent judgment by the application of these criteria to the facts proved in evidence."

The Court of Session repudiated the suggestion that the judge or jury is bound to adopt the views of an expert, even if they should be uncontradicted, because, "The parties have invoked the decision of a judicial tribunal and not an oracular pronouncement by an expert".[4] This case reaffirmed the view that an expert might adopt statements made in scientific works as part of his testimony, and portions of such works might be put to him in cross-examination. To this extent they may be used as evidence in the case, but the judge is not entitled to form an opinion on the basis of other parts of the book.[5]

No useful purpose would be served by an endeavour to enumerate the matters which have been treated by the courts as requiring a sufficient degree of specialised knowledge to render expert evidence admissible.[6] They include medical and scientific questions, the meaning of technical terms, questions of commercial practice or market value, the provisions of a foreign system of law and the identity of a person's handwriting—a subject which is discussed in Chapter XXI. If the court comes to the conclusion that the subject of investigation does not require a sufficient degree of specialised knowledge to call for the testimony of an expert, evidence of opinion will generally be excluded.[7]

It is for the judge to determine whether the witness has undergone such a course of special study or experience as will render him expert in a particular subject, and it is not necessary for the expertise to have been acquired professionally. In *R.* v. *Silverlock*,[8] for example, the Court for Crown Cases Reserved considered that a solicitor might be treated as an expert in handwriting even if he had acquired his knowledge as an amateur. Most of the

---

[1] *Ramsay* v. *Watson* (1961), 108 C. L. R. 642; *Leis* v. *Gardner*, [1965] Qd. R. 181; *Leonard* v. *British Colombia Hydro and Power Authority* (1965), 49 D. L. R. (2d) 422.

[2] *English Exporters (London), Ltd.* v. *Eldonwall, Ltd.*, [1973] Ch. 415; [1973] 1 All E. R. 726.

[3] [1953] S. C. 34, at p. 40.

[4] [1953] S. C. 34, at p. 40   [5] *Collier* v. *Simpson* (1831), 5 C. & P. 73.

[6] For a comparatively recent example see *Re Pinion, Westminster Bank, Ltd.* v. *Pinion*, [1965] Ch. at p. 98; [1964] 1 All E. R. 891. See also *Scottish Shire Line, Ltd.* v. *London and Provincial Marine and General Insurance Co., Ltd.*, [1912] 3 K. B. 51 at p. 70 and *Carter* v. *Boehm* (1776), 3 Burr. 1905.

[7] *United States Shipping Board* v. *The St. Albans*, [1931] A. C. 632; *Clarke* v. *Ryan*, (1960), 103 C. L. R. 486. See also *Transport Publishing Co. Pty., Ltd.* v. *Literature Board of Review* (1957), 99 C. L. R. 111; *Harradine* v. *Commissioner for Railways*, [1962] S. R. (N. S. W.) 205; *Habessis* v. *Australian Iron and Steel Ltd.*, [1962] S. R. (N. S. W.) 126.

[8] [1894] 2 Q. B. 766; *R.* v. *Bunnis* (1964), 50 W. W. R. 422. *Cf. Clarke* v. *Ryan* (*supra*).

reported cases on the subject of a witness's skill are concerned with evidence of foreign law, a matter discussed in Chapter XXII. Specialisation is a matter of degree. It is not necessary for a doctor to have specialised in studies concerned with the rate at which the blood destroys alcohol before he can give evidence on such a subject based on analysts' tables,[1] and a stenographer who has familiarised herself with the contents of a tape recording may be treated as a temporary expert;[2] but experience in driving does not make a bombardier an expert on the subject of the capabilities of someone charged with drunken driving,[3] nor does a police officer's experience in investigating traffic accidents make him an expert for the purpose of reconstructing a particular motor accident.[4]

Although the expert witness has not escaped criticism,[5] he is probably the best means, compatible with the adversary system, of furnishing the judge and jury with information on matters calling for expertise. In their 17th Report the Law Reform Committee considered, but did not recommend, an extension to civil proceedings generally of the Admiralty practice under which the judge sits with assessors, or the adoption of a regular practice of appointing experts by the court; but the report contains a number of recommendations designed to reduce controversy on matters of expertise and increase the usefulness of expert testimony. These recommendations are embodied in R.S.C. Ord. 38, rr. 34–41 made in accordance with the provisions of s. 2 of the Civil Evidence Act, 1972.[6] The broad effect of these rules is that parties to civil litigation will be prevented from calling experts unless they have applied to the court for leave to do so, and the court may order disclosure of the experts' reports to the opposite party. The range of controversy will thus be defined and, as s. 1 of the Act of 1972 enables hearsay evidence of opinion to be given, it is possible to dispense with the actual calling of the expert in noncontroversial cases.

C. CASES IN WHICH NON-EXPERT OPINION IS ADMISSIBLE

When, in the words of an American judge,[7] "the facts from which a witness received an impression were too evanescent in their nature to be recollected, or too complicated to be separately and distinctly narrated", a witness may state his opinion or impression. He was better equipped than the jury to form it, and it is impossible for him to convey an adequate idea of the premises on which he acted to the jury.

"Unless opinions, estimates and inferences which men in their daily lives reach without conscious ratiocination as a result of what they have perceived with their physical senses were treated in the law of evidence as if they were mere statements of fact, witnesses would find themselves unable to communicate to the judge an accurate impression of the events they were seeking to describe."[8]

There is nothing in the nature of a closed list of cases in which non-

---

[1] *R. v. Somers*, [1963] 3 All E. R. 808.
[2] *Hopes and Lavery* v. *H.M. Advocate*, 1960 S. C. (J.) 104.
[3] *R. v. Davies*, [1962] 3 All E. R. 97.   [4] *Nickisson* v. *R.*, [1963] W. A. R. 114.
[5] See the observations of Lord CAMPBELL at the hearing of the *Tracey Peerage* (1843), 10 Cl. & Fin. 154, at p. 177, of JESSEL, M.R., in *Plimpton* v. *Spiller* (1877), 6 Ch. D. 412, and of Lord TOMLIN in *British Celanese, Ltd.* v. *Courtaulds, Ltd.*, (1935), 152 L. T. 537, at p. 543.
[6] R. S. C. Amendment 1974.
[7] GIBSON, J., cited in VII *Wigmore*, p. 12.
[8] 17th Report of the Law Reform Committee, para. 3.

expert opinion evidence is admissible. Typical instances are provided by questions concerning age,[1] speed,[2] weather, handwriting and identity in general. Proof of handwriting is discussed in Chapter XXI, but a word may be said here about the question of identification.

When a witness says, "that is the man I saw the other day", pointing to someone in court, or, "that is the man whose wedding I attended", pointing to a figure in a photograph,[3] or, "that is a copy of a picture of which I have seen the original",[4] there is clearly a sense in which it is true to say that he is expressing an opinion. He is not simply narrating what he has perceived in the past; but the perception on which his statements are founded cannot be conveyed to the jury in the same way that the premises for or against an inference of negligence can be narrated. In *Fryer* v. *Gathercole*[5] in order to prove the publication of a libellous pamphlet to friends of a female witness she was allowed to swear that she received a pamphlet from the defendant, lent it to friends in succession and put her name on it when it was ultimately returned to her. She said that she believed the pamphlet returned by the last borrower to be identical with that received from the defendant, but she could not swear to this fact because it was possible that another pamphlet had been substituted for the original. POLLOCK, C.B., disposed of an objection to the effect that her evidence was mere opinion by saying:

> "There are many cases of identification where the law would be rendered ridiculous if positive certainty were required from witnesses",

and PARKE, B., said in the course of the argument:

> "In the identification of person you compare in your mind the man you have seen with the man you see at the trial. The same rule belongs to every species of identification."

Every fact on which the identification is based cannot be satisfactorily given in evidence.

In some cases a non-expert witness has been allowed to give evidence of opinion on a subject on which expert testimony would have been admissible. Acquaintances of a person whose sanity is in issue may be asked whether they consider him sane, but this is not so much a demand for an opinion as a "compendious mode of ascertaining the result of the actual observation of the witness". Did the witness observe any action by the accused characteristically associated with persons of dubious sanity? Similarly, in *R.* v. *Davies*,[6] the Courts Martial Appeal Court held that on a charge of drunken driving, a non-medical witness might state that he formed the impression that the accused had been drinking but it was said that he must state the facts on which that impression was based, and it was also held that the witness ought not to have been allowed to add that he believed the accused to be unfit to drive, although an expert could have testified to this effect.

In *R.* v. *Beckett*,[7] the accused was charged with maliciously damaging a

---

[1] *R.* v. *Cox*, [1898] 1 Q. B. 179. [2] Road Traffic Regulation Act, 1967, s. 78A.
[3] *R.* v. *Tolson* (1864), 4 F. & F. 103.
[4] *Lucas* v. *Williams & Sons*, [1892] 2 Q. B. 113. [5] (1849), 13 Jur. 542.
[6] [1962] 3 All E. R. 97. See also *Sherrard* v. *Jacob*, [1965] N. I. 151; *R.* v. *German*, [1947] 4 D. L. R. 68; *Burrows* v. *Hanlin*, [1930] S. A. S. R. 54; *R.* v. *McKimmie*, [1957] V. L. R. 93; *R.* v. *Spooner*, [1957] V. L. R. 540; *R.* v. *Kelly*, [1958] V. L. R. 412; *Attorney-General (Rudely)* v. *James Kenny* (1960), 94 I. L. T. R. 185 (77 L. Q. R. 166); *Blackie* v. *Police*, [1966] N. Z. L. R. 910.
[7] (1913), 8 Cr. App. Rep. 204.

plate glass window worth more than five pounds. The fact that the window was worth more than five pounds was an essential ingredient of the offence, and it was held to have been proved by the statement of an assistant superintendent of the post office who swore that the window was worth more than five pounds. In cross-examination it became clear that his evidence was largely based on hearsay, but the Court of Criminal Appeal upheld the conviction on the footing that the case was proved by the witness's statement of his personal opinion as to the value of the window. The basis of the admissibility of this evidence was not considered by the court, and the decision is perhaps open to question on the ground that it raises insoluble problems of degree. Is it confined to non-expert opinion concerning the value of commonplace objects? If so, what are commonplace objects? Does it only apply where the witness opines that the value of an article exceeds a specified sum by a considerable amount? If so, what is a considerable amount? But *R.* v. *Beckett* was cited in a South Australian case in which it was said that the Court may always act on non-expert opinion as to value when no specialised knowledge is required.[1]

D. ULTIMATE ISSUES

(1) EXPERT WITNESSES

The common law rule that an expert witness may not be asked the question which the court has to decide is supported by civil cases,[2] but several criminal cases suggest that it is being eroded, and it is only necessary to consider criminal cases because s. 3 (1) of the Civil Evidence Act, 1972, expressly provides for the admissibility of an expert's opinion on a matter in issue in civil proceedings.[3]

In *R.* v. *Mason*[4] the defence to a charge of murder was that the deceased had committed suicide, and a doctor who had heard the evidence was asked whether it was his opinion that the fatal wound had been inflicted by someone other than the deceased. The Court of Criminal Appeal held that his answer was admissible as an opinion based upon an assumed state of facts and, in *R.* v. *Holmes*,[5] the same court decided that a doctor called in support of the accused's plea of insanity might be asked in cross-examination whether the prisoner's conduct after the crime indicated that he knew the nature of his act and that it was wrong, although these are of course the very points which determine the applicability of the M'Naghten rules. A doctor who has examined a motorist charged with

---

[1] *Wise* v. *Musolino*, [1936] S. A. S. R. 447. In some cases judicial notice may be taken that the value of an object exceeds the specified sum or evidence of its purchase price might suffice.

[2] See, for example, *Sills* v. *Brown* (1840), 9 C. and P. 601; *Rich* v. *Pierpont* (1862), 3 F. and F. 35; *North Cheshire Brewery* v. *Manchester Brewery Co.*, [1899] A. C. 83, at p. 85; *Haynes* v. *Doman*, [1899] 2 Ch. 13, at p. 24; *British Celanese, Ltd.* v. *Courtaulds, Ltd.* (1935), 152 L. T. 537, at p. 543.

[3] Clause 43 of the draft Bill attached to the 11th Report of the Criminal Law Revision Committee contains provisions identical to those of s. 3 of the Civil Evidence Act, 1972, with the addition of a subclause (43 (4): "Nothing in this section shall be taken to affect any rule of law as to the topics on which expert evidence is or is not admissible") to make it clear that expert evidence would continue to be inadmissible on the issue of obscenity, as distinct from the defence of public good, in prosecutions under the Obscene Publications Act, 1959 (see 11th Report, para. 269).

[4] (1911), 7 Cr. App. Rep. 67.

[5] [1953] 2 All E. R. 324; *Bleta* v. *R.*, [1964] S. C. R. 561.

drunken driving may likewise state whether, in his opinion, the accused was so drunk as not to have proper control of his car.[1]

In *Director of Public Prosecutions* v. *A. and B. C. Chewing Gum, Ltd.*[2] it was held that a child psychiatrist's evidence about the effect which "battle cards" sold with packets of bubble gum would have on children of various ages from five upwards ought to have been admitted on the issue, in a prosecution under the Obscene Publications Act, 1959, whether the cards were likely to deprave and corrupt the children. In the ordinary case jurors and magistrates are as capable as anyone else of judging the likely effects of a publication[3] but, where children are concerned, "any jury and any Justices need all the help they can get." Lord PARKER, C.J., pointed out that the psychiatrist was not, strictly speaking, being asked the very question which the court had to decide, but he said of the prohibition on questions on the ultimate issue:

> "I cannot help feeling that with the advance of science more and more inroads have been made into the old common law principles. Those who practise in the criminal courts see every day cases of experts being called on the question of diminished responsibility, although technically the final question 'Do you think he was suffering from diminished responsibility?' is strictly inadmissible, it is allowed time and time again without any objection."[4]

The common law rule, if there can still be said to be such a thing, is based on the undesirability of allowing the expert to become involved in the decision-making process, although it is difficult to believe that a properly directed jury would allow its functions to be usurped by an expert's answer to the question it had to decide. However that may be, the application of the rule sometimes amounts to nothing more than a play upon words. For instance, in one of the early medical negligence cases, it was held that a doctor who had been in court throughout the proceedings might not be asked whether he thought that the defendant was guilty of any want of skill, although he might be asked whether anything he had heard suggested improper conduct on the part of the defendant.[5] The tendency to disregard the rule is apparent in the Privy Council as well as in the English criminal courts. In *Lowery* v. *R.*[6], Lowery and King were convicted of the murder of a girl of fifteen. They each admitted that they were present at the killing but alleged that it was done by the other. It was held on Lowery's appeal that the Victorian trial judge had acted properly in allowing King to call a clinical psychiatrist who had interviewed both accused to swear that King was immature and emotionally shallow and that Lowery was the aggressive personality, more likely than King to have committed the crime. Evidence of a very similar nature was held inadmissible by the Supreme Court of Canada[7] because it came too near to answering the question the jury had to decide, but the Judicial Committee did not even refer to the ultimate issue rule.

---

[1] *R.* v. *Davies*, [1962] 3 All E. R. 97.
[2] [1968] 1 Q. B. 159; [1967] 2 All E. R. 504.
[3] *R.* v. *Calder and Boyars, Ltd.*, [1969] 1 Q. B. 151; [1968] 3 All E. R. 644; *R.* v. *Anderson*, [1972] 1 Q. B. 304; [1971] 3 All E. R. 1152.
[4] At p. 164.
[5] *Rich* v. *Pierpont* (1862), 4 F. & F. 35.
[6] [1974] A. C. 85; [1973] 3 All E. R. 662.
[7] *Lupien* v. *R.* (1970), 9 D. L. R. (3d) 1.

(2) NON-EXPERT WITNESSES

The existence of a particular issue may necessitate the reception of evidence which is not that of an expert and yet is nothing short of a witness's opinion concerning an ultimate issue in the case.   In *Mansell* v. *Clements*[1] the question on a claim for commission was whether a third party bought a house from the defendant through the intervention of the plaintiff, an estate agent.   The judge put the following question to the purchaser: "Would you, if you had not gone to the plaintiff's office and got the card, have purchased the house?"   The answer was "I think not." On appeal it was held that a verdict in favour of the plaintiff could have been justified without reference to the question and answer, but the judge was a member of the appellate court and he maintained his view concerning the propriety of the question.

Subject to the exceptional type of situation which has just been mentioned, it would seem that, if non-expert opinion is in reality evidence of fact given *ex necessitate* in the form of evidence of opinion, there should be no question of its inadmissibility because it deals with ultimate issues. This is borne out by the form of s. 3 (2) of the Civil Evidence Act, 1972, which suggests that no change in the law was intended.

> "It is hereby declared that where a person is called as a witness in any civil proceedings, a statement of opinion by him on a relevant matter [2] on which he is not qualified to give expert evidence, if made as a way of conveying relevant facts personally perceived by him, is admissible as evidence of what he perceived."

So far as criminal cases are concerned, the decisions on drunken driving indicate a difference of approach between the English and Northern Irish courts on the one hand, and the courts of Eire on the other.

In all these cases there are two questions although they may be phrased in different ways.   1. Had the accused taken drink? 2. Was he unfit to drive through drink? Factual evidence may be available with regard to the first, but we approach the realm of opinion evidence when someone who did not see the accused take drink deposes to his impression that the accused had done so. The second question can only be answered by opinion evidence.

We have seen that, in *R.* v. *Davies*,[3] the Court of Criminal Appeal allowed a non-expert who had not seen the accused take drink to answer the first question in terms of his impression, but not the second; there is no doubt that an expert, a doctor who had examined the accused, for example, would have been allowed to give his opinion with regard to both questions. The Court of Criminal Appeal allowed the non-expert to give his opinion on the first question because it was a compendious mode of stating the facts on which the opinion was based, the fact that the accused had a lurching gait and slurred speech etc. The objection to the witness answering the second question was stated to be that it involved the very point the court had to decide. In Eire, a non-expert has been allowed to give his opinion on both questions, on the first because the question whether a man was under the influence of drink is, like questions concerning identity, a question which cannot be adequately answered by enumerating observed facts, the second

---

[1] (1874), L. R. 9 C. P. 139.
[2] "In this section 'relevant matter' includes an issue in the proceedings in question" (s. 3 (3)).
[3] [1962] 3 All E. R. 97. For a full citation of authorities see n. 6, p. 387, *ante*.

because it did not differ in this respect from the first.[1] In the Divisional Court of Northern Ireland, Lord MACDERMOTT would have followed the Irish practice, but the majority preferred the English.[2] According to Lord MACDERMOTT, "As in the case of the inference that a person is under the influence of drink, the inference that the same person was incapable of having proper control may depend on the whole picture, on the conjoint effect of numerous facts and circumstances which lead to a sound conclusion but cannot be faithfully or completely reproduced in evidence."[3] The majority view was based on the courts' unwillingness to allow any witness to depose to ultimate issues, and it treated the first question as a compendious method of ascertaining observed facts.

E. REASONS FOR THE EXCLUSION OF CERTAIN KINDS OF EVIDENCE OF OPINION

There seem to be two main and two subsidiary reasons for the exclusion of those kinds of evidence of opinion that fall within the rule stated at the beginning of this section. The two main reasons are founded on the general principle that evidence of opinion is excluded when its reception would not assist, and might even mislead, the court. In the first place it is said that opinion evidence is irrelevant,[4] and this is largely true of non-expert opinion on a subject requiring expertise as well as opinion evidence concerning the ordinary meaning of common-place words, although some writers prefer to say that the evidence is insufficiently relevant to be admissible.[5] Secondly, it is said that the reception of opinion evidence would usurp the functions of the jury. This seems to be another way of stating the view that in many cases the jury would be tempted blindly to accept a witness's opinion, and that, in some cases, the witness might indicate what factual evidence he accepted or rejected—a most undesirable thing for him to do. The latter danger can be avoided, at the price of some elaboration, by the use of hypothetical questions requiring the witness to assume the existence of certain facts; but the first danger cannot be eliminated so easily. It is particularly apparent when a witness is asked for his views concerning one of the ultimate issues in the case, and accounts for the lengths to which the courts have gone in discouraging direct questions with regard to these matters.

The two subsidiary reasons for the rejection of certain kinds of evidence of opinion are the fact that a witness who merely speaks to his opinion cannot be prosecuted for perjury, and the danger that the reception of such evidence might indirectly evade other exclusionary rules. The first reason is of some antiquity,[6] but, although Lord MANSFIELD had it in mind when he said, in *Folkes* v. *Chadd*,[7] that Mr. Smeaton could have been prosecuted if he had wilfully given false testimony, no great stress is placed upon it at the present day. As a matter of substantive law, the precise extent of the pro-

---

[1] *A.G. (Rudely)* v. *James Kenny* (1960), 94 I. L. T. R. 185.
[2] *Sherrard* v. *Jacob*, [1965] N. I. 151.
[3] At p. 163.
[4] GODDARD, L.J., in *Hollington* v. *Hewthorn & Co., Ltd.*, [1943] K. B. at p. 595; [1943] 2 All E. R. at p. 40.
[5] Cowen and Carter, *Essays on the Law of Evidence*, 169.
[6] *Adams* v. *Canon* (1621), 1 Dyer 53b.   [7] P. 384, *ante*.

position is debatable. There is more force in the second reason, but it has not been stressed by the judges. The exclusionary rules most likely to be indirectly infringed by the reception of opinion evidence are those according to which irrelevant matter and hearsay are inadmissible. A witness can always be cross-examined on the grounds for his opinion, and, if these appear to be irrelevant the evidence can be ignored. The relationship of the opinion rule to the rule against hearsay calls for separate consideration.

F. THE RULE AGAINST HEARSAY AND EVIDENCE OF OPINION

The rule with regard to evidence of opinion originated in the same doctrine as that to which the rule against hearsay can be traced—every witness must be able to say that he had seen or heard that to which he deposes. He must have been an "*oyant*" and "*voyant*",[1] but the two rules, are now quite distinct although the same item of evidence may occasionally call for a consideration of both of them. For example, A. is prepared to swear that he heard B., who witnessed a collision between cars driven by C. and D., say, some time after the event, that it was due to the negligence of D. A.'s evidence would clearly infringe the rule against hearsay if tendered to prove D.'s negligence on his prosecution for careless driving, because a statement other than one made by a person while giving oral evidence would be tendered as evidence of the truth of that which was stated. The evidence would also be inadmissible because B.'s assertion was a statement of opinion of a kind that could not have been received if proffered by B. himself from the witness box. If A. had been at hand at the time of the collision, and he had heard B. make some exclamation concerning the negligent manner in which D. was driving, it is possible that he would be allowed to relate the statement as evidence of D.'s negligence, although B. was not called as a witness.[2] This is because there may be an exception to the rule against hearsay covering exclamations concerning an event made contemporaneously with its occurrence. So far as the opinion rule is concerned, B.'s opinion was spontaneous, or impulsive, as it was not the result of deliberation on his part; accordingly A.'s evidence as to what B. said would probably be admissible.

The leading case on evidence calling for a consideration of both the hearsay and the opinion rules is *Wright* v. *Doe* d. *Tatham*[3] which was elaborately argued on three occasions between 1830 and 1838. The sanity of a deceased testator named Marsden was in issue, and those who contended that he was sane when he executed his will tendered three letters written to him by acquaintances at the time. The writers of these letters had since died, and it was contended that the documents ought to be received (a) because they concerned business matters and showed that their authors regarded the addressee as sane, and (b) because Marsden displayed his sanity in the manner in which he acted on the letters. They were rejected in the Court of King's Bench, the judges in the Exchequer

---

[1] Thayer, *Preliminary Treatise on Evidence at Common Law*, 523–4.
[2] See *per* POLLOCK, C.B., in *Milne* v. *Leisler* (1862), 7 H. & N. 786, at p. 796.
[3] (1838), 4 Bing. N. C. 489. An analogous case is *Backhouse* v. *Jones* (1839), 9 L. J. C. P. 99, where the statements were oral.

Chamber were evenly divided and a majority of the judges advised the House of Lords that the letters were inadmissible. The judgment of the King's Bench was accordingly affirmed. The second ground upon which it was contended that the letters should be received was of no particular moment as it raised a question of fact. Evidence of the conduct of the testator is always admissible in such a case provided it is relevant, but the majority view was that there was no sufficient proof that Marsden had acted on the letters so as to indicate a rational appreciation of their contents. The first ground upon which it was contended that the evidence was admissible raised problems in connection with the rule against hearsay and the reception of opinion which have never since been so fully examined. The letters indicated that the writers treated Marsden as sane, therefore they were equivalent to an assertion of that fact, therefore they infringed the rule against hearsay, and the majority of the judgments proceeded on this footing. If the writers of the letters had been called as witnesses they could have been asked for their views concerning the testator's sanity. However, it does not follow that a layman's opinion on such an issue is admissible because the question is, as we have seen, merely "a compendious mode of ascertaining the result of the actual observation of the witness, from acts done, as to the habits and demeanour of the deceased". Accordingly it is arguable that the letters had to be rejected both because their reception would have infringed the rule against hearsay and also because they were mere statements of opinion on a matter with regard to which an ordinary witness's opinion, unsupported by details concerning his observations, would have been inadmissible. This seems to have been the view of the majority of the judges, although it was only PARKE, B., who gave much consideration to this aspect of the case. *Wright* v. *Doe* d. *Tatham* has been discussed at this stage because the exclusion at common law of convictions as evidence of the facts on which they were founded, when those facts are in issue, in subsequent civil proceedings springs from a combination of the hearsay rule with the rule rejecting certain types of opinion evidence.

SECTION 2.—JUDICIAL FINDINGS AS EVIDENCE OF THE FACTS UPON WHICH THEY WERE BASED [1]

In order to appreciate the problem with which this section is mainly concerned, it is necessary to refer to two distinctions mentioned in Chapter XIII—the distinction between a judgment and the facts upon which it was founded and the distinction between evidence and estoppel. Every judgment is conclusive as to the state of things it actually effects. If the question whether A. is a convicted criminal should be in issue, A.'s conviction for crime is conclusive, even if he is a stranger to the proceedings in which the issue arises. No judgment is conclusive against all the world as to the facts which must have been proved before it could be pronounced. If A. has been convicted of stealing a motor car, he is not precluded from denying his guilt in an action for conversion brought against him by the owner of the car,

---

[1] The common law is fully discussed in Cowen and Carter, *Essays on the Law of Evidence*, Essay 6. There are valuable notes on *Hollington* v. *Hewthorn & Co., Ltd.* in 59 L. Q. R. 299 and 21 Canadian Bar Review 653. Reference may also be made to Coutts, "*The Effect of a Criminal Judgment on a Civil Action*", 18 M. L. R. 331, (1955), and V *Wigmore*, para. 1671 (a).

and the insurer of the car would not be precluded from denying it was stolen should this fact be relevant in proceedings brought against him by the assured. Parties and their privies are, however, estopped from denying the facts on which a judgment was founded when the same question is raised in subsequent proceedings between them. A convicted thief would be unable to deny his guilt if that matter should be raised at his trial for another offence.[1] The problem with which this section is primarily concerned is whether and to what extent a judgment can be treated as evidence of the facts upon which it was founded when the proceedings in which this question is raised are between a party and a stranger, or two strangers? If A. is convicted of murder or robbery and he sues B. for libel in describing him as a murderer or robber, would the conviction be admissible evidence in support of pleas of justification on B.'s part? If H. obtains a divorce from W., on the ground of adultery with C., can Mrs. C. reply on the decree nisi as evidence at the hearing of her petition for divorce alleging C.'s adultery with W.? Before *Hollington* v. *Hewthorn and Co., Ltd.*[2] was decided there was authority for an affirmative answer to each of these questions, but the bulk of the earlier case law favoured a negative response.[3]

In *Hollington* v. *Hewthorn & Co., Ltd.*[4] the conviction of one of the defendants of careless driving was held to be inadmissible as evidence of his negligence in proceedings for damages on that ground against him and his employer. The main reason for the decision was that the conviction merely proved that another court, acting on evidence which was unknown to the tribunal trying the civil proceedings, was of opinion that the defendant was guilty of careless driving. The reception of the conviction as evidence of negligence would have infringed the hearsay as well as the opinion rule because it would have been treated as the equivalent of an assertion of negligence by a non-witness; but these points are indefensible technicalities.[5]

> "Rationalise it how one will, the decision in this case offends one's sense of justice. The defendant driver had been found guilty of careless driving by a court of competent jurisdiction. The onus of proof of culpability in criminal cases is higher than in civil; the degree of carelessness required to sustain a conviction of careless driving is, if anything, greater than that required to sustain a civil action for negligence. Yet the fact that the defendant driver

---

[1] But see n. 3, p. 297, *ante*.

[2] [1943] K. B. 587; [1943] 2 All E. R. 35.

[3] For an affirmative answer in the murder case see the judgment of Sir Samuel Evans, P. in *In the Estate of Crippen*, [1911] P. 108, at p. 115; for an affirmative answer in the divorce case see *Partington* v. *Partington and Atkinson*, [1925] P. 34. The following were the principle authorities: *R.* v. *Warden of the Fleet* (1698), 12 Mod. Rep. 337, at p. 339; *Gibson* v. *MacCarty* (1736), Cas. temp. Hard. 311; *Smith* v. *Rummens* (1807), 1 Camp. 9; *Blakemore* v. *Glamorganshire Canal Co.* (1835), 2 Cr. M. & R. 133; *March* v. *March* (1858), 2 Sw. & Tr. 49; *Leyman* v. *Latimer* (1878), 3 Ex. D. 352; *Yates* v. *Kyffin-Taylor and Wark*, [1899] W. N. 141. The majority of Commonwealth decisions both before and after *Hollington* v. *Hewthorn Co., Ltd.* seem to be in accord with the English case law, see for example *Shaw* v. *Glen Falls Insurance Co.*, [1938] 1 D. L. R. 502; *La Fonciere Cie d'Assurance de France* v. *Perras*, [1943] 2 D. L. R. 129; *MacFarlane Produce, Ltd.* v. *Canadian General Insurance Co.* (1965), 51 D. L. R. (2d) 646; *Re Maritime Asphalt Products* (1966), 52 D. L. R. (2d) 8; *R.* v. *Seery* (1914), 19 C. L. R. 15; but there are several contrary rulings, e.g., *Christie* v. *Christie*, [1922] W. L. D. 109, and *W.* v. *W.*, [1941] S. A. S. R. 144; *Jorgenson* v. *News Media (Auckland), Ltd.*, [1969] N. Z. L. R. 961.

[4] [1943] K. B. 587; [1943] 2 All E. R. 35.

[5] The *Hollington* v. *Hewthorn & Co., Ltd.* rule originated in the days when interested witnesses, parties and their spouses were incompetent in civil proceedings and may have been based on the possibility that the conviction would have been obtained by evidence which was inadmissible in the subsequent civil proceedings.

had been convicted of careless driving at the time and place of the accident was held not to amount to even *prima facie* evidence of his negligent driving at that time and place.

It is not easy to escape the implication in the Rule in *Hollington* v. *Hewthorn* that, in the estimation of lawyers, a conviction by a criminal court is as likely to be wrong as right." [1]

The *ratio decidendi* of *Hollington* v. *Hewthorn & Co., Ltd.* extends to findings in earlier civil proceedings in which the parties were not the same, and it has been overruled so far as previous findings of adultery and paternity, as well as criminal convictions, are concerned by ss. 11–13 of the Civil Evidence Act, 1968. After these sections have been considered, reference will be made to the position in criminal proceedings, and to other findings.

A. THE CIVIL EVIDENCE ACT, 1968, ss. 11–13

(1) Previous Convictions in Subsequent Civil Proceedings

S. 11 (1) of the Civil Evidence Act, 1968, provides that:

"In any civil proceedings the fact that a person has been convicted of an offence by or before any court in the United Kingdom or by a court martial there or elsewhere shall . . . be admissible in evidence for the purpose of proving, where to do so is relevant to any issue in those proceedings, that he committed that offence . . . but no conviction other than a subsisting one [2] shall be admissible in evidence by virtue of this section."

S. 11 (2) provides that:

"In any civil proceedings in which by virtue of this section a person is proved to have been convicted of an offence by or before any court in the United Kingdom or by a court martial there or elsewhere (a) he shall be taken to have committed that offence unless the contrary is proved; and (b) without prejudice to the reception of any other admissible evidence for the purpose of identifying the facts upon which the conviction was based, the contents of any document which is admissible as evidence of the conviction and the contents of the information, complaint, indictment or charge sheet on which the person in question was convicted shall be admissible in evidence for that purpose."

R.S.C. O. 18, r. 7 (a) requires a party to an action tried with pleadings who intends to rely on s. 11 to state that intention in his pleading, to give particulars of the conviction and to indicate the issue to which it is relevant. On facts such as those of *Hollington* v. *Hewthorn & Co., Ltd.*, once the conviction has been proved, and the negligence in respect of which the driver was convicted identified, the court will be bound to find in favour of the plaintiff unless the driver or his employer disproves negligence on the balance of probabilities. [3]

Various observations have been made about the weight to be attached to the conviction in the subsequent civil proceedings in which it is proved. In *Wauchope* v. *Mordecai*[4] the Court of Appeal did not suggest that the burden cast on the convicted defendant was a specially heavy one. In *Taylor* v. *Taylor*,[5] on the other hand, it was said that the verdict of the jury finding the respondent to divorce proceedings guilty of incest was

---

[1] 15th Report of the Law Reform Committee, para. 3.
[2] See *Re Raphael, Raphael* v. *D'antin*, [1973] 3 All E. R. 19. A conviction subject to appeal is subsisting but the civil court has power to adjourn the case pending the appeal.
[3] *Stupple* v. *Royal Insurance Co., Ltd.*, [1971] 1 Q. B. 50; [1970] 3 All E. R. 230.
[4] [1970] 1 All E. R. 417.   [5] [1970] 2 All E. R. 609.

entitled to great weight, while Lord DENNING, M.R., and BUCKLEY, L.J., took different views on this subject in *Stupple* v. *Royal Insurance Co., Ltd.*[1] In that case the plaintiff had been convicted of robbery from a bank which had been indemnified by the defendants. A sum of money found in the plaintiff's possession was paid over to the defendants under the Police (Property) Act, 1897. The plaintiff claimed this sum and the defendants counterclaimed for the balance of their indemnity. The Court of Appeal upheld the judgment for the defendants. Lord DENNING said:

> "I think that the conviction does not merely shift the burden of proof. It is a weighty piece of evidence of itself. For instance, if a man is convicted of careless driving on the evidence of a witness, but that witness dies before the civil action is heard (as in *Hollington* v. *Hewthorn & Co., Ltd.*) then the conviction itself tells in the scale in the civil action. It speaks as clearly as the witness would have done, had he lived. It does not merely reverse the burden of proof. If that was all it did, the defendant might well give his own evidence, negativing want of care and say: 'I have discharged the burden. I have given my evidence and it has not been contradicted.' In answer to the defendant's evidence the plaintiff can say: 'But your evidence is contradicted by the conviction.'"[2]

BUCKLEY, L.J., said:

> "In my judgment, proof of conviction under this section gives rise to the statutory presumption laid down in s. 11 (2) (a) which, like any other presumption, will give way to evidence establishing the contrary on the balance of probability without itself affording any evidential weight to be taken into account in determining whether that onus has been discharged."[3]

It is submitted that the approach of BUCKLEY, L.J., is to be preferred. The assessment of the weight of the conviction would be an impossibly difficult task. As BUCKLEY, L.J., pointed out, the propriety of the conviction is irrelevant in the civil action, the plaintiff would not discharge the onus cast upon him by s. 11 (2) (a) by proving that every witness who had given evidence against him at the criminal trial was guilty of perjury. He has to adduce sufficient evidence to satisfy the civil court that he was not negligent and, in spite of Lord DENNING's suggestion to the contrary, his own testimony without more will generally not suffice.[4]

As the conviction constitutes the basic **fact** of a presumption, it should be capable of corroborating other evidence where corroboration is required; it is stated by s. 11 (1) to be "admissible in evidence for the purpose of proving that [the accused] committed the offence". In *Mash* v. *Darley*[5] a Divisional Court treated the respondent's conviction of unlawful intercourse with the applicant as corroboration of her evidence in affiliation proceedings. The decision could hardly have stood with *Hollington* v. *Hewthorn & Co., Ltd.*, but it may well have been resuscitated by the 1968 Act.

As long as convictions are not conclusive evidence of the guilt of the person convicted, it is possible for him to obtain a retrial of the issues raised

---

[1] [1971] 1 Q. B. 50; [1970] 3 All E. R. 230. See the note by Zuckerman in 87 L. Q. R. 21 (1971).
[2] At p. 72. If available, the transcript or proof of evidence of the deceased witness in the criminal case would be admissible under the Civil Evidence Act, 1968.
[3] At p. 76.
[4] *Ludgate* v. *Lovett*, [1969] 2 All E. R. 1275 (negligent bailee); see also 15th Report of the Law Reform Committee, para. 25.
[5] [1914] 1 K. B. 1, affirmed on other grounds, [1914] 3 K. B. 1226.

in the criminal proceedings in a subsequent civil action by suing anyone implying that he was guilty of the offence for defamation. Even if the civil action were decided in his favour, the validity of the conviction would of course be unaffected. The Law Reform Committee took the view that, as a matter of substantive law, no-one ought to be at risk of incurring civil liability for stating that another was guilty of an offence of which he had been convicted; and conversely, no-one ought to be entitled, without incurring civil liability, to state that another person was guilty of an offence of which he had been acquitted.[1] The Committee therefore recommended that, in defamation actions, where the statement complained of alleges that the plaintiff has been guilty of a criminal offence, proof that he has been convicted of that offence should be conclusive evidence of his guilt, and proof that he was acquitted should be conclusive evidence of his innocence. The first, but not the second, of these recommendations was accepted. S. 13 (1) of the Civil Evidence Act, 1968 provides that:

> "In an action for libel or slander in which the question whether a person did or did not commit a criminal offence is relevant to an issue arising in the action, proof that, at the time when the issue falls to be determined, that person stands convicted of that offence shall be conclusive evidence that he committed that offence."[2]

(2) Findings of Adultery and Paternity

S. 12 (1) of the Civil Evidence Act, 1968, provides that:

> "In any civil proceedings—(a) the fact that a person has been found guilty of adultery in any matrimonial proceedings; and (b) the fact that a person has been adjudged to be the father of a child in affiliation proceedings before any court in the United Kingdom, shall . . . be admissible in evidence for the purpose of proving, where to do so is relevant to any issue in those civil proceedings, that he committed the adultery to which the finding relates or, as the case may be, is (or was) the father of that child . . ."

S. 12 (2) provides that:

> "In any civil proceedings in which by virtue of this section a person is proved to have been found guilty of adultery as mentioned in subsection (1) (a) above, or to have been adjudged to be the father of a child as mentioned in subsection (1) (b) above,—(a) he shall be taken to have committed the adultery to which the finding relates, or, as the case may be, to be (or have been) the father of that child, unless the contrary is proved on the balance of probabilities[3]. . . ."

"Matrimonial proceedings" means, for the purposes of s. 12, "Any matrimonial cause in the High Court or a County Court in England or Wales, or in the High Court in Northern Ireland, any consistorial action in Scotland, or any appeal arising out of such cause or action."[4] Therefore, if A. sues B. for a libel stating that he committed adultery on a particular occasion, the fact that he was found guilty of adultery in maintenance proceedings brought against him by Mrs. A. in a Magistrates' Court would be

---

[1] 15th Report of the Law Reform Committee, paras. 26–33.
[2] On facts such as those of *Goody* v. *Odhams Press, Ltd.*, [1967] 1 Q. B. 333; [1966] 3 All E. R. 369 in which one of those convicted of the great train robbery of 1963 claimed damages for a libel stating that he was guilty of the offence, the statement of claim, if it said no more, would be struck out.
[3] *Sutton* v. *Sutton*, [1969] 3 All E. R. 1348, at p. 1352.
[4] S. 12 (5).

inadmissible evidence in support of B.'s plea of justification. The inquisitorial duty of the High and County Courts in matrimonial causes may be thought sufficient to justify singling out the findings of those courts for special treatment; but the only justification for this treatment of affiliation proceedings is the requirement of corroboration in cases in which the mother gives evidence. To many it may seem curious that a finding of paternity by lay magistrates should cast the onus of disproving it on those seeking to deny it in subsequent civil proceedings, while a finding of negligence in a civil action in the High Court should not even be admissible as *prima facie* evidence of negligence in subsequent civil proceedings between different parties.

B. PREVIOUS CONVICTIONS IN CRIMINAL CASES

Although there is very little authority on the point, it seems that the principal of *Hollington* v. *Hewthorn & Co., Ltd.* applies to criminal cases. As between the Crown and the accused, the latter's previous conviction estops him from denying his guilt of the offence for which he was convicted,[1] but the conviction of a third party is inadmissible as evidence of the facts on which it was based. For example, the conviction of a principal is inadmissible as evidence of the commission of the main crime at the trial of an accessory,[2] and the conviction of the thief is inadmissible as evidence that the goods received were stolen at the trial of the handler.[3] One of the oldest justifications of the principal we have been considering applies in such cases for it would be possible for the principal or thief to have been convicted on evidence which is inadmissible against the accessory or handler, evidence of their spouses, for instance, but it is doubtful whether this warrants the retention of the principle even in criminal cases, and the 11th Report of the Criminal Law Revision Committee recommends the adoption of a clause for criminal proceedings similar to s. 11 of the Civil Evidence Act, 1968.[4]

C. ACQUITTALS

So far as the previous acquittal of a party is concerned, it may, of course, be proved when it is a fact in issue as would be the case in an action for malicious prosecution, but there are a variety of reasons why it should not be admitted as evidence of innocence in subsequent civil proceedings. Chief amongst these is the fact that the standard of proof is different, so that an acquittal only means that the case against the accused has not been proved beyond reasonable doubt. In *Packer* v. *Clayton*[5] there are some observations of AVORY, J., in a Divisional Court to the effect that, in affiliation proceedings, the acquittal of the respondent on a charge of a sexual offence against the complainant was something that could have been taken into account by the justices as showing that the girl's evidence did not convince the jury, but it is doubtful whether this could be said to be so after *Hollington* v. *Hewthorn & Co., Ltd.*

---

[1] But see n. 3, p. 297, *ante.*
[2] *R.* v. *Xaki*, 1950 (4) S. A. 332.
[3] *R.* v. *Turner* (1832), 1 Mood. C. C. 347; *R.* v. *Lee*, 1952 (2) S. A. 67; see also *Taylor* v. *Wilson* (1911), 76 J. P. 69 and *R.* v. *Hassan*, [1970] 1 Q. B. 423, at p. 426.
[4] Paras. 217–9.
[5] (1932), 97 J. P. 14; the opposite view was taken in *O'Donnell* v. *Hegarty*, [1941] I. R. 538. See further *Helsham* v. *Blackwood* (1851), 11 C. B. 111; *Helton* v. *Allen* (1940), 63 C. L. R. 691; *Re Emele*, [1941] 4 D. L. R. 197; *Lingor* v. *Lingor*, [1955] 1 D. L. R. 719.

D. OTHER FINDINGS

(1) JUDICIAL FINDINGS

Hollington v. *Hewthorn & Co., Ltd.* could probably be cited as authority for the proposition that all judicial findings are inadmissible as evidence of the facts found in subsequent proceedings which are not between the same parties or their privies. From this it follows that judicial findings in cases falling outside ss. 11–13 of the Civil Evidence Act, 1968, are still, subject to other statutory provisions,[1] no evidence of the facts found. The inadmissibility of the magistrates' finding of adultery mentioned above is one example; another would be an action for damages for negligence brought by a passenger injured in a bus accident, a finding of negligence in an earlier action brought by another passenger in respect of the same accident would be inadmissible

(2) INQUISITIONS

To quote Phipson's *Law of Evidence*,[2]

> "Inquisitions, surveys, assessments, reports and returns are admissible, but not generally conclusive, in proof of their contents when made under public authority, and in relation to matters of public interest or concern."

This common law exception to the combined operation of the hearsay and opinion rules covers a heterogeneous mass of cases ranging from extracts from Domesday book to a return by a bishop to a writ from the Exchequer directing him to ascertain the vacancies and advowsons in his diocese.[3] It was once thought that the verdict of a coroner's jury could be received under this head as evidence of the cause of a death, but it is now settled that that is not the case owing partly to the essentially preliminary nature of the inquiry, and partly to the unlikelihood of the coroner's attention being drawn to some points that might be of interest in the proceedings in which it was sought to adduce his return.[4] It is, however, settled that the old inquisitions and former master's orders in lunacy are admissible, though not conclusive, evidence of the unsoundness of mind of the person to whom they refer.[5] In *Hill* v. *Clifford*[6] the Court of Appeal adopted this analogy with regard to a finding of the General Medical Council that a dentist had been guilty of professional misconduct. The majority of the Court was prepared to treat it as evidence in subsequent proceedings for the dissolution of the dentist's partnership. *Hill* v. *Clifford* was not cited in *Hollington* v. *Hewthorn & Co., Ltd.*, but the cases can perhaps be distinguished because, being charged with the duty of inquiry, the General Medical Council fulfils a different function from that of a judge.

The combined operation of the hearsay and opinion rules would appear to exclude the fact that someone got a first in law on the issue whether he

---

[1] For example, under the Medical Act, 1956, s. 33 (2) the General Medical Council must treat a finding of fact in matrimonial proceedings as conclusive.

[2] 11th edition, p. 477.

[3] *Irish Society* v. *Bishop of Derry* (1846), 12 Cl. & Fin. 641.

[4] *Bird* v. *Keep*, [1918] 2 K. B. 692; *Calmenson* v. *Merchants Warehousing Co., Ltd.* (1921), 90 L. J. P. C. 134; *Barnett* v. *Cohen*, [1921] 2 K. B. 461.

[5] *Faulder* v. *Silk* (1811), 3 Camp. 126; *Harvey* v. *R.*, [1901] A. C. 601.

[6] [1907] 2 Ch. 236.

was a competent academic lawyer in, for example, a libel action. The absurdity of this result may lead some to doubt the soundness of the principles enunciated by Parke B. in *Wright* v. *Doe d. Tatham*,[1] a subject to which it will be necessary to refer again in the next chapter.

---

[1] P. 393, *ante*.

CHAPTER XVII

THE RULE AGAINST HEARSAY

The rule against hearsay applies to oral as well as written statements and, presumably, to signs or gestures.[1] The rule has already been formulated, and reference has been made to the distinction between hearsay and original evidence.[2] These matters must now be considered in greater detail.

A. STATEMENT AND ILLUSTRATIONS OF THE RULE

(1) STATEMENT

According to the rule against hearsay as formulated in chapter I, a statement other than one made by a person while giving oral evidence in the proceedings is inadmissible as evidence of any fact stated. This formulation conflates two common law rules, the rule that the previous statements of the witness who is testifying are inadmissible as evidence of the facts stated (sometimes spoken of as the "rule against narrative", or the "rule against self-corroboration"), and the rule that statements by persons other than the witness who is testifying are inadmissible as evidence of the facts stated (the rule against hearsay in the strict sense.)

At common law there is only one clear exception to the first rule, an informal admission proved by the party who made it. There are many common law exceptions to the rule against hearsay in the strict sense. If A. proves that B., the defendant in a running-down action, admitted to him that he was not keeping a proper look-out, A.'s evidence of what was said is admissible against B. under an exception to the rule against hearsay in the strict sense; but if B. admits in the course of his evidence that he told A. that he was not keeping a proper look-out, reliance may be placed by the plaintiff on the previous statement of the defendant as evidence of the facts stated.[3]

In chapter X we saw that, at common law, the previous consistent statements of witnesses are usually inadmissible as evidence of consistency though inconsistent statements might be proved, not as evidence of the facts stated, but in order to cast doubt on the witness's testimony. We

---

[1] *Chandra Sekera* v. *R.*, [1937] A. C. 220; [1936] 3 All E. R. 865, where the admissibility of signs made by a dying woman is considered.

[2] P. 6, *ante*. Useful monographs are *The Law of Hearsay Evidence*, by J. B. C. Tregarthen (1915), and *The Hearsay Rule*, by R. W. Baker (1950). Much use has also been made of articles by Professor Morgan in 48 H. L. R. 1138, and 62, *ibid.*, 177, as well as of Morgan, *Some Problems of Proof Under the Anglo-American System of Litigation*, 106 *et seq.* Several of the points made in this and the succeeding chapter were made by the writer in more or less the same form in *The Scope of the Rule against Hearsay*, 72 L. Q. R. 91 (1956), *What should be done about the Rule against Hearsay*, [1965] Crim. L. R. 68 and the *Periphery of Hearsay*, 7 Melbourne L. R. 1 (1969). The whole subject of hearsay and the reform of the law is fully described by D. Harding and others in 45 Australian L. J. 531 (1971).

[3] The exception of the admission has been described as the only "clear" one because of the possibility that previous statements of witnesses received as part of the *res gestae* are received as evidence of the facts stated.

also saw that previous consistent statements might be proved by way of exception to the general exclusionary rule in the case of complaints of sexual offences, statements forming part of the *res gestae*, statements rebutting a suggestion that the witness's testimony was a recent invention and sundry statements of the accused. In these cases the witness's previous statements are not, strictly speaking, received as evidence of the facts stated, and they are therefore not received under exceptions to the rule against hearsay.

This chapter is primarily concerned with the rule against hearsay in the strict sense. It has never been fully formulated judicially, but all the authorities concur in the view that:

> "Evidence of a statement made to a witness by a person who is not himself called as a witness may or may not be hearsay. It is hearsay and inadmissible when the object of the evidence is to establish the truth of what is contained in the statement. It is not hearsay and is admissible when it is proposed to establish by the evidence, not the truth of the statement, but the fact that it was made."[1]

This crucial distinction was overlooked by the trial judge in the case from which the above extract from the advice of the Judicial Committee of the Privy Council is taken. The appellant was charged with being in possession of firearms without lawful excuse and his defence was that he was acting under duress in consequence of threats uttered by Malayan terrorists. The judge would not allow the accused to state what had been said by the terrorists and the Judicial Committee advised that the conviction should be quashed because the reported statements were tendered as original evidence and ought to have been received as such.[2]

The rule against hearsay applies just as much to evidence elicited in cross-examination as to evidence in-chief. A deceased workman's statements to his widow on returning home after an accident have been held inadmissible at common law as evidence of its cause on a number of occasions.[3] If a widow narrates in cross-examination what her deceased husband told her about the cause of his injuries or illness, her statement is no more admissible as evidence of that fact than it would have been if made in-chief.[4]

(2) ILLUSTRATIONS

In *R.* v. *Gibson*[5] a conviction for unlawful wounding was quashed because the prosecutor had been allowed to narrate a statement which he heard an unidentified woman make immediately after a stone had been thrown at him. The statement was "The man who threw the stone went in there", and the maker of the statement pointed to the prisoner's house.

In *Sparks* v. *R.*,[6] an appeal from Bermuda, the accused, a white man,

---

[1] *Subramaniam* v. *Public Prosecutor*, [1956] 1 W. L. R. 965, at p. 969.

[2] For a similar oversight by a trial judge see *R.* v. *Willis*, [1960] 1 All E. R. 331.

[3] *Gilbey* v. *Great Western Rail. Co.* (1910), 102 L. T. 202; see also *Amys* v. *Barton*, [1912] 1 K. B. 40.

[4] *Beare* v. *Garrod* (1915), 113 L. T. 673; see p. 226, *ante*.

[5] (1887) 18 Q. B. D. 537. Were the facts to recur it is possible that, in the light of *Ratten* v. *R.*, [1972] A. C. 388; [1971] 3 All E. R. 801, the statement would be received as part of the *res gestae*.

[6] [1964] A. C. 964; [1964] 1 All E. R. 727. The statement was rejected as part of the *res gestae* because not sufficiently proximate in time. The child's statement would continue to be inadmissible on these facts even if the hearsay recommendation of the 11th Report of the Criminal Law Revision Committee were adopted (see para. 250).

was charged with an indecent assault on a girl between three and four years old. About an hour and a half after the event, the child told her mother that a coloured boy did it. The child did not give evidence and the Judicial Committee held that the trial judge had rightly rejected the evidence of what the child said to her mother, although the accused's appeal against conviction was allowed on other grounds. No point was made with regard to the fact that the child would have been incompetent to testify if she had been called, and it appears that the decision would have been the same, if the victim had not testified, whatever her age.

In *R. v. McLean*[1] the accused was charged with a robbery in which a car was used. There was evidence that, shortly before the robbery, the accused hired a car with the registration number BKB 138D. The victim was unable to identify the accused, but deposed to the fact that he took the number of the car used in the robbery and dictated it to a police officer, although he had no recollection of the number. The officer swore that he wrote the number down accurately and produced a piece of paper with BKB 138D written on it. The accused was convicted and his conviction was quashed by the Court of Appeal because there was no admissible evidence of the number of the car used in the robbery. Although there was the victim's sworn evidence that he dictated what he perceived, coupled with the police officer's sworn evidence that he wrote down what was dictated, the only purpose of the officer's narration of what was dictated was to prove the registration number of the car used in the robbery, a fact of which he had no personal knowledge and of which the victim had no recollection.[2]

One of the stock illustrations of the breadth of the hearsay rule is provided by some old English cases in which it was held that a witness cannot give admissible evidence of the place or date of his birth.[3] In more modern times, the fact that a witness cannot testify to his own age without infringing the rule against hearsay has been stressed by the South African and Australasian courts.[4] Generally speaking, the infringement does not give rise to any problems because age can be proved under a well recognised exception to the hearsay rule according to which statements in birth certificates are admissible evidence of the facts stated, but we shall see that the process of identifying the person named in the certificate as the person whose age is in question frequently involves the reception of hearsay evidence.

In *R. v. Saunders*[5] a conviction for conspiracy to defraud was quashed on account of the reception of a police witness's answers to the following ques-

---

[1] (1967), 52 Cr. App. Rep. 80. See also *Grew v. Cubitt*, [1951] 2 T. L. R. 305; *Jones v. Metcalfe*, [1967] 3 All E. R. 205, and *S. v. Tuge*, [1966] 4 S. A. 565. The facts in all these cases were less favourable to the reception of the evidence except that, in the third, the court contrived to apply the *res gestae* doctrine, but *Bradpiece v. South British Insurance Co.*, [1966] 2 S. A. 629 is inconsistent with *McLean's* case.

[2] Had the victim seen or checked what he dictated, he could have refreshed his memory with the assistance of the piece of paper; but the English courts do not allow a witness to refresh his memory with a document which he dictated while the events were fresh in his mind but did not check (*R. v. Mills* and *R. v. Rose*, [1962] 3 All E. R. 298); cf. *R. v. O'Linn*, [1960] 1 S. A., 545.

[3] *R. v. Erith (Inhabitants)* (1807), 8 East 539; *R. v. Rishworth (Inhabitants)* (1842), 2 Q. B. 476; *R. v. Day* (1841), 9 C. & P. 722.

[4] *R. v. Corris*, [1931] T. P. D. 471; *R. v. Young*, [1923] S. A. S. R. 35; *Carlton and United Breweries, Ltd. v. Cassin*, [1956] V. L. R. 186; *Smith v. Police*, [1969] N. Z. L. R. 856.

[5] [1899] 1 Q. B. 490; *Buckley v. Inland Revenue Commissioners*, [1962] N. Z. L. R. 29; cf. *R. v. Wilkins* (1849), 4 Cox C. C. 92.

tions: "Did you make inquiries as to whether any trade had been done by the prisoners?" and "Did you, as a result of such inquiries, find that any had been done?" The answer to the first was in the affirmative, while the second met with a negative response. Although the matter is not fully discussed in the report, the rule against hearsay was infringed because the court was asked to act on assertions made to the witness by third persons with regard to the prisoners' business, and these third persons should have been called as witnesses.

Cases of this nature serve as a reminder of the impropriety of devices mentioned by DEVLIN, L.J., to make that which is in reality hearsay evidence look as if it were nothing of the sort. The first "consists in not asking what was said in a conversation or written in a document but in asking what the conversation or document was about; it is apparently thought that what would be hearsay if fully expressed is permissible if decently veiled. The other device is to ask by means of "yes" or "no" questions what was done (just answer yes or no. Did you go to see counsel? Do not tell us what he said but as a result of it did you do something? What did you do?) This device is commonly defended on the ground that counsel is asking only about what was done and not about what was said. But in truth what was done is relevant only because from it there can be inferred something about what was said."[1]

In *Myers* v. *Director of Public Prosecutions*,[2] the accused was charged with conspiracy and receiving stolen cars. The case against him was that he purchased wrecked cars with their log books, and disguised stolen cars so as to make them conform with the log books of the wrecked cars. It was alleged that the accused then sold the cars as renovated wrecks. The prosecution called the owners of the stolen cars to identify them as those sold by the accused. The prosecution also called an officer in charge of the records of the manufacturers of the stolen cars to produce microfilms of the cards filled in by workmen showing the numbers cast into cylinder blocks on the stolen cars, and these numbers coincided with those on the cylinder blocks in the cars sold by the accused. The trial judge admitted the evidence of the officer in charge of records and the schedule of microfilms produced by him, the cards filled in by the workmen having been destroyed after being filmed. The accused was convicted and unsuccessfully appealed to the Court of Criminal Appeal on the ground that the manufacturers' records were inadmissible to prove that the numbers cast into the cylinder blocks on the stolen cars were as stated. The Court of Criminal Appeal dismissed the appeal on the ground that the rule against hearsay had not been infringed because the probative value of the records did not depend on the credit to be given to the unidentified workmen, but on the circumstances in which the records were maintained and the inherent probability that they were correct. The court considered that the records were, in the circumstances, the best means of checking the direct evidence of identification given by the owners of the stolen cars. Myers appealed to the House of Lords. His appeal was dismissed because the House was unanimously of opinion that, even if the records had been wrongly admitted

---

[1] *Glinski* v. *MacIver*, [1962] A. C. 726, at pp. 780, 781; [1962] 1 All E. R. 696, at p. 723.
[2] [1965] A. C. 1001; [1964] 2 All E. R. 881, followed in *R.* v. *Van Vreden* (1973), 57 Cr. App. Rep. 818 and *R.* v. *Porter* (1964), 48 D. L. R. (2d.) 277. *Potts* v. *Miller* (1940), 64 C. L. R. 282 was not cited.

in evidence, there had been no substantial miscarriage of justice. But a majority considered that the records ought not to have been admitted because "the entries on the cards were assertions by the unidentifiable men who made them that they had entered numbers which they had seen on the cars".[1] The majority was not prepared to countenance the creation of a novel exception to the hearsay rule to cover the case.

The actual decision in *Myers* v. *Director of Public Prosecutions* has been overruled by the Criminal Evidence Act, 1965; but that statute is only concerned with the admissibility of trade or business records, and *Myers's* case still obliges the courts to come to odd conclusions such as that a car's log book is not admissible evidence of the engine number,[2] or that a statement concerning the place of manufacture inscribed on goods is inadmissible as evidence of that fact.[3]

The decision in *Myers's* case also gives rise to serious doubts concerning the correctness of the decision of the Court of Criminal Appeal in *R.* v. *Rice*.[4] In that case it was held that the fact that a used air ticket bore the name of a particular person was admissible evidence that a person of that name travelled on the flight mentioned on the ticket. Winn, J., said "The relevance of that ticket in logic and its legal admissibility as a piece of real evidence both stem from the same root, viz. the balance of probability recognised by common sense and common knowledge that an air ticket which has been used on a flight and which has a name upon it has more probably than not been used by a man of that name . . ."[5] It was said that the ticket did not "speak its contents", but it is difficult to draw a distinction between a thing which does speak its contents, and a thing which, though it does not speak its contents, yet warrants an inference that those contents are true. The ticket was admitted as a piece of real evidence, but it is valueless unless regard is had to the inscription on the ticket and the inscription on the ticket is only of probative value if it warrants the inference that a statement was made by or on behalf of an intending traveller that a person of a certain name would be travelling. This may serve to distinguish the case of the used air ticket from the hypothetical examples of an article of female apparel or a club tie left on a plane. It would be possible to hold these items admissible as evidence that a woman, or a member of the club, was among the travellers without upholding the decision in *R.* v. *Rice*.[6] It must be confessed, however, that, if that case was wrongly decided, a court would be driven to such absurd conclusions as that a handkerchief bearing a name, or a passport are not evidence that a person of the name they bore travelled on the plane on which they were found.

In spite of the absence of English authority on the point, the rule against

---

[1] At p. 1022 *per* Lord Reid.

[2] *R.* v. *Sealby*, [1965] 1 All E. R. 701.

[3] *Patel* v. *Customs Comptroller*, [1966] A. C. 356; [1965] 3 All E. R. 593; *cf. State* v. *Lincey and Watson Pty., Ltd.*, [1965] 2 S. A. 502. See also *Miller* v. *Howe*, [1969] 3 All E. R. 451 (description on box may on facts be description of goods inside and not hearsay).

[4] [1963] 1 Q. B. 857; [1963] 1 All E. R. 832. Lord Pearce approved this decision in *Myers's* case, but he was not one of the majority. Another case which is hard to support after *Myers's* case is *Edwards* v. *Brookes (Milk), Ltd.*, [1963] 3 All E. R. 62.

[5] *Ibid.* at p. 871.

[6] *Cf.* 7 Melbourne Law Review 10 (1969). I now find it less difficult to escape the conclusion that, after *Myers's* case, a postmark is inadmissible evidence of the place of posting than I did (7 Melbourne Law Review 3). The matter is one of which the court would take judicial notice.

hearsay would, subject to exceptions, presumably prevent the production of a record as evidence of the non-existence of a fact, although this is a matter concerning which much may depend on the evidence before the court as to the practice with regard to the compilation of the record. If it were sought to establish that A. was not employed by B., the production of a list of B.'s employees, not containing A.'s name, would infringe the hearsay rule just as much as that rule would be infringed by the production of such a list containing A.'s name as evidence that A. was employed by B.

In *S.* v. *Becker*[1] it was necessary for the prosecution to prove that named persons to whom the accused purported to have made payments were either fictitious, or at any rate not employed by a particular department. An accountant was called to swear that he knew that it was the practice of the department for a file relating to each employee to be prepared, that he had searched for files and found none relating to persons of the names in question. The Cape Provincial Division held this evidence to be admissible, treating the case as indistinguishable from one in which it was sought to establish that A.B. was not on board a particular ship by giving evidence of a practice according to which every member of the ship's company had to wear a cap with his name sewn into it and to place it in a particular cupboard at a particular hour, together with evidence of a fruitless search for a cap with the name A.B. in it at the appropriate time and place. In these cases the evidence is circumstantial, turning on the probability that a particular practice was followed, not partly circumstantial and partly testimonial, requiring the court to infer at some stage that someone said or wrote something and then to assume that what was said or written was true. The distinction is, however, a very fine one. A list of employees is obviously intended by its author to convey information, and it is subject to one of the risks of all hearsay evidence, the possible inaccuracy of someone who is not before the court and liable to cross-examination; but the person responsible for preparing the files with which *S.* v. *Becker* was concerned might also have been inaccurate.[2] For English lawyers the answer, since the rejection by the House of Lords of the reasoning of the Court of Appeal in *Myers's* case, seems to be that it makes no difference if items of circumstantial evidence are subject to the same dangers in the way of human fallibility, or the same guarantees of trustworthiness, as hearsay statements; the crucial question is simply whether the court is being asked to act on such a statement.

(3) IMPLIED ASSERTIONS

It is now necessary to consider whether the hearsay rule has been extended to implied assertions. These are of two kinds, statements which were not intended by their maker to be assertive of the fact they are tendered to prove, and non-verbal conduct not intended to be assertive of the fact it is tendered to prove. An example of the first kind of implied assertion would be provided by a case in which efforts are made to establish X.'s presence at a particular place by calling a witness to swear that he heard someone say "Hello X." at that place. An example of the second kind of implied assertion would

---

[1] [1968] 1 S. A. 18.

[2] It may well be the better view that *S.* v. *Becker* was wrongly decided and the case is distinguishable from the hypothetical example of the caps (see Hoffman, *South African Law of Evidence* (2nd edition, p. 92, n. 15).

be provided by a case in which it is sought to show that X. was dead at a particular time by calling a witness to swear that he saw a doctor cause X.'s body to be placed on a mortuary van after examining him at that time.[1] In the first case the words "Hello X.", and in the second the conduct of the doctor, are respectively tendered as the equivalent of the express statement "X. is here" and "X. is dead". In each instance, the express statement would be inadmissible as evidence of the facts stated if narrated by someone other than its maker.

The main dangers against which the hearsay rule provides are the possible insincerity and inaccuracy of the maker of the reported statement. He may have been deliberately lying, or his powers of observation, memory or narration may have been defective. These dangers are considerably reduced by the sanctions of the oath and cross-examination to which testimony is subject but each of which is usually lacking in the case of hearsay assertions. These dangers are not nearly so marked in the case of implied as opposed to express assertions. People do not say "Hello X." in order to deceive passers-by into thinking that X. is there, and doctors do not place bodies on mortuary vans unless they have good reason to believe the bodies to be corpses.

The American Uniform and Federal Rules therefore confine the rule against hearsay to express assertions[2] and the late editor of Kenny's *Outlines of Criminal Law* is evidently of opinion that they represent English law. When speaking of *R. v. Gibson*[3] he said "If the woman had been heard to say as a man approached her 'Hello Mr. Gibson, where are you going?' it would clearly have been permissible for the witness to have repeated this remark just as he could have deposed that he heard the woman scream or shout 'shame' or run away."[4] There are, however, at least two authorities based on English law which suggest that the rule against hearsay has been extended to implied assertions. The authorities are *Teper* v. *R.* and *Wright* v. *Doe* d. *Tatham*.

In *Teper* v. *R.*[5] the appellant had been convicted of arson of a shop at which he carried on business. The only evidence to contradict his alibi was that of a policeman who swore that, in approaching the shop some twenty-five minutes after the conflagration began, he heard a woman in the crowd of spectators exclaim to a passing motorist who bore some resemblance to the accused, "Your place burning and you going away from the fire." The Judicial Committee advised that the conviction should be quashed because the above evidence ought not to have been admitted. The simplest explanation of this case is that the reception of the evidence infringed the rule against hearsay. Although the woman did not intend to tell anyone that

---

[1] In *the Estate of Loucks*, 160 Cal. 551. See also *Thomson* v. *Manhattan Railway*, 42 N.Y. Sup. 896 cited in *Baker* at p. 6 rejecting the fact that a physician treated a patient for a disease as evidence that the patient was suffering from it. For an Australian example see *Holloway* v. *Macfeeters* (1956), 94 C. L. R. 470 rejecting the fact that an unidentified motorist did not stop after an accident as evidence of the motorist's negligence in an action against the representative of the motor insurance fund. For a South African example see *State* v. *van Niekerk*, [1965] 1 S. A. 729.

[2] For criticism of this policy see Finman, *Implied Assertions as Hearsay*, 14 Stanford Law Review 682 (1962). See also *Implied Assertions and the Scope of the Hearsay Rule*, 9 Melbourne L. R. 268 (1973); I must plead guilty to the charge made against me in this article of having changed my mind more than once on the subject of implied assertions, but I am quite unashamed.

[3] P. 402, *ante.*

[4] 19th edition p. 500.

[5] [1952] A. C. 480; [1952] 2 All E. R. 447. The statement was rejected as part of the *res gestae.*

Teper was present, she did intend to tell Teper that she recognised him and was surprised by his conduct. The Crown relied on her statement as equivalent to an assertion of Teper's presence, and the danger of injustice flowing from an inaccuracy of her powers of observation was present to a most noticeable degree.

In *Wright* v. *Doe* d. *Tatham*[1] letters to a testator whose sanity was in issue were tendered as evidence of the writer's opinion that he was sane—the equivalent of an assertion that, in the writer's experience, the testator has always acted as a sane man—and the letters were rejected as a result of the combined operation of the rules relating to hearsay and evidence of opinion. However the arguments in favour of the reception of the letters might be phrased, there was no escaping the fact that the court was being asked to place its faith in the opportunities and powers of observation of persons who were neither on oath nor subject to cross-examination. Further instances in which evidence would have to be excluded on similar grounds were mentioned by PARKE, B. They included "the conduct of a physician who permitted a will to be executed by a sick testator; the conduct of a deceased captain on a question of seaworthiness, who after examining every part of the vessel embarked in it with his family, . . . these when deliberately considered, are with reference to the matter in issue in each case, mere instances of hearsay evidence, mere statements, not on oath, but implied in or vouched by the actual conduct of persons by whose acts the litigant parties are not to be bound".[2]

Those who maintain that the rule against hearsay does not extend to implied assertions could argue that, in the instances mentioned in the last paragraph, the evidence is excluded because it is liable to lead to too many side issues.[3] How thorough was the seacaptain's survey? Was he competent to conduct it? etc. They could cite authority to show that, where the danger of side issues is absent, the courts act on implied assertions.

In *Stobart* v. *Dryden* [4] the plaintiff proved the due execution of a mortgage deed on which he was suing by calling someone to verify the handwriting of the deceased attesting witness. The witness's confession of having altered the deed was held to be inadmissible hearsay.[5] One of the unsuccessful arguments for its admissibility was that, as the plaintiff used the declaration of the subscribing witness, evidenced by his signature, to prove the execution, the defendant might use any declaration of the same witness to disprove it. The answer given by PARKE, B., was "that evidence of the handwriting in the attestation is not used as a declaration by the witness, but to show the fact that he put his hand in that place and manner, in which in the ordinary course of business he would have done, if he had actually seen the deed executed. A statement of the attesting witness by parol, or written on any other document than that offered to be proved, would be inadmissible. The proof of actual attestation of the witness is, therefore, not the proof of a declaration but of a fact."

In *Lloyd* v. *Powell Duffryn Steam Coal Co., Ltd.*[6] a woman claimed work-

---

[1] (1837), 7 Ad. & El. 313. See also *Backhouse* v. *Jones* (1839), 6 Bing. N. C. 65; *Gresham Hotel Co.* v. *Manning* (1867), I. R. 1 C. L. 125.
[2] 7 Ad. & El. 387–8.   [3] P. 20, *ante*.
[4] (1836) 1 M. & W. 615.
[5] It could now be received under the Civil Evidence Act, 1968.
[6] [1914] A. C. 733; followed in *Nash* v. *Railways Commissioner*, [1963] S. R. (N. S. W.) 357.

men's compensation on behalf of her illegitimate child, who she alleged, was the posthumous son of a deceased employee of the defendants. As there was no doubt that the deceased was killed in the course of his employment, the claim succeeded if it could be proved that the child was the workman's son and that the workman would have supported him. After giving evidence of intercourse with the deceased and no one else, the woman deposed to a conversation in which he promised to marry her on being informed of her pregnancy. Two other witnesses gave evidence of conversations occurring shortly afterwards in which the deceased told them of what the woman had said and intimated that he intended to marry her. In the Court of Appeal it was sought to uphold the County Court Judge's decision to admit the evidence of what the deceased had said on the ground that it was the equivalent of an assertion that he was the father of the child and therefore admissible under the exception to the hearsay rule relating to declarations by deceased persons against their pecuniary or proprietary interest; but the court rejected this argument because one of the conditions of the admissibility of such declarations had not been satisfied as the workman had not got personal knowledge of his paternity of the child. Accordingly it was held that the evidence ought not to have been received.[1] The House of Lords allowed the appeal mainly on the ground that "To treat statements made by the deceased as statements made by a deceased person against his pecuniary interest, and therefore, though hearsay, proof of the facts stated, is wholly to mistake their true character and significance. This significance consists in the improbability that any man would make these statements, true or false, unless he believed himself to be the father of the child of whom Alice Lloyd was pregnant."[2] The deceased had treated Alice Lloyd as his fianceé, and there is a considerable body of authority to the effect that treatment is admissible evidence of relationship.[3]

Enough has been said to show that, on the present state of the authorities more than one view can justifiably be taken on the question whether the hearsay rule extends to implied assertions. The following submission must therefore be regarded as highly tentative. The submission is that the rule only applies to statements intended by their makers to be assertive, but statements of the form "Hello X." in the context of one person addressing another, are intended to be assertive by the maker. They express, not merely greeting, but also recognition, and they are therefore just as much hearsay statements when tendered as evidence of the presence of the addressee as the utterance with which *Teper* v. *R.*[4] was concerned. On the other hand, non-verbal conduct not intended to be assertive falls outside the ban of the hearsay rule even when, as in the instances mentioned by PARKE, B., in *Wright* v. *Doe d. Tatham*,[5] the conduct is only relevant because it points to the fact that the agent entertains a particular belief, such as the seaworthiness of the ship he has just inspected. At no stage in the reasoning justifying its admissibility is the court asked to assume that

---

[1] See [1913] 2 K. B. 130. The statements were also rejected because the contract to marry was not against interest, and they only conceded a contingent liability

[2] [1914] A. C. 741 *per* Lord ATKINSON.

[3] *Goodwright* d. *Stevens* v. *Moss* (1777), 2 Cowp. 591; *Morris* v. *Davies* (1837), 5 Cl. and Fin. 163; *Dysart Peerage Case* (1881), 6 App. Cas. 489; *The Aylesford Peerage Case* (1885), 11 App. Cas. 1; *Burnaby* v. *Baillie* (1889), 42 Ch. D. 282; *Re Jenion, Jenion* v. *Wynne,* [1952] Ch. 454; [1952] 1 All E. R. 1228; *B.* v. *A. G.,* [1965] P. 278; [1965] 1 All E. R. 62.

[4] [1952] A. C. 480; [1952] 2 All E. R. 447.

[5] P. 408, *ante*.

something said by one person to another was true. The fact that the belief was acted upon in the instances mentioned by PARKE, B., adds to the probative value of the evidence because, in general, deeds speak louder than words; but this does not mean that the evidence should never be excluded because it is irrelevant, or too remotely relevant. This is a perfectly sound explanation of the actual decision in *Wright* v. *Doe d. Tatham.*

B. STATEMENTS RECEIVED AS ORIGINAL EVIDENCE

Evidence is said to be "original" when a witness narrates another person's statement for some purpose other than that of inducing the court to accept it as true. Examples of this kind of evidence are given in the following paragraphs.

(1) STATEMENTS AS FACTS IN ISSUE

(i) Miscellaneous.—In several classes of case the question before the court is whether certain words were spoken or written, not whether they were true or false. Obvious instances are provided by actions for defamation and intimidation. To take two further examples, if it is alleged that persons in charge of a ship which had foundered were negligent because they failed to take precautions concerning the lighting of the wreck, the fact that the harbour master assured them that the wreck would be lighted negatives negligence, and no regard need be had to the question whether he intended to implement his undertaking.[1] Similarly, when duress *per minas* is raised as a defence to a criminal charge, the crucial question is whether the threats were uttered in circumstances in which the person against whom they were made would think that they would be carried out, and the intentions of those who made the threats are only of secondary significance.[2]

In some cases, there is no question of the applicability of the rule against hearsay because the statement tendered in evidence was not intended to be assertive, and there is no question of its being relied on as an implied assertion. Words are often the equivalent of acts which must be proved if in issue or relevant to the issue. "One asks another to attest a document, or to advance a sum of money, those are not merely words, but acts."[3] The speaking of such words may always be proved by a witness who heard them if they are relevant or in issue and they may conveniently be described as "operative" words.

(ii) Operative words.—There is a number of cases in which it is difficult, if not impossible, to say whether the assertion of an intention is received as a fact in issue or as proof of such a fact—the existence of the intention—under an exception to the rule against hearsay. If A. says to B., "I offer to sell you my horse for a hundred pounds", his words are presumably operative in their nature, for he will be bound by his offer if a reasonable man in B.'s position would have believed that A. intended to be bound. The same is doubtless true of statements by a debtor or his repre-

---

[1] *The Douglas* (1882), 7 P. D. 151.   [2] *Subramaniam* v. *Public Prosecutor* (p. 402, *ante*).
[3] *Per* ERLE, J., in *Shilling* v. *Accidental Death Insurance Co.* (1858), 1 F. & F. 116, at p. 120; *R.* v. *Chapman*, [1969] 2 Q. B. 436; [1969] 2 All E. R. 321 (doctor's consent to patient's having breath test not hearsay).

sentative concerning the purpose for which a payment is made,[1] and it is probable that, when A. delivers a chattel to B. stating that he is making a gift, his words are received as original evidence on account of their operative nature and not as a hearsay assertion concerning the purpose of the act they accompany. The answer to problems of this nature depends on the substantive law—is the speaker bound by the construction which would be placed on his words by a reasonable man—an objective test, or is his subjective intention the dominant consideration? No doubt the answer varies in relation to different branches of the law, and according to whether the acts of the speaker are unilateral, such as the making of a will,[2] or bilateral, such as the conclusion of a contract. When the test is objective a witness' narration of the speaker's words is received as original evidence and when the test is subjective the evidence can only be received under an exception to the rule against hearsay.

Re Wright, Hegan v. *Bloor*,[3] illustrates the difficulty that arises in determining whether a statement is received as original evidence or under an exception to the rule against hearsay. A testatrix who executed a power of appointment in 1917 wrote a letter to the appointee in 1911 saying that she regarded herself as bound by a bargain made with his father concerning the exercise of the power. When deciding that the appointment was a fraud on the power, P. O. LAWRENCE, J., said:

> "in principle the court ought to set aside such an appointment if it is satisfied that the appointor made the appointment *under the belief that he was bound by a corrupt bargain*, or even without any evidence as to his belief, if the appointor *states* that he had made such a bargain and that he intends to carry it out, and then makes an appointment in accordance with it."[4]

On the first hypothesis the letter was received under what is probably best regarded as an exception to the hearsay rule as evidence of the testatrix's state of mind in 1911—a state which might be presumed to have continued until 1917; but the letter constituted original evidence on the second hypothesis.

A series of Australasian decisions concerning the admissibility of evidence on charges of using premises for unlawful betting gives rise to a similar problem. If the police raid the premises and answer a number of phone calls from speakers who place bets but are not called as witnesses, are the police allowed to narrate what was said over the phone because the speakers' words were operative, or because of the application of an exception to the hearsay rule under which statements accompanying the act of phoning are admissible to show why it was done.[5] The authorities do not supply a clear answer to questions of this nature because it can hardly ever be of any practical importance so far as the law of evidence is concerned. If the evidence is admissible, the question whether it is original or hearsay

---

[1] *Walters* v. *Lewis* (1836), 7 C. & P. 344. "The question is not merely whether a particular sum was paid, but whether a payment was made for a particular purpose, and you cannot prove the purpose without letting in evidence of what was said when the money was handed over" (COLERIDGE, J.).

[2] In *Lister* v. *Smith* (1863), 3 Sw. & Tr. 282, a testator's statements negativing testamentary intent when he executed a codicil were allowed to be proved by a witness. In some situations proof of the speaker's real intention may be prevented by an estoppel.

[3] [1920] 1 Ch. 108.   [4] At. p. 119, italics supplied.

[5] *Davidson* v. *Quirke*, [1923] N. Z. L. R. 552; *Marsson* v. *O'Sullivan*, [1951] S. A. S. R. 224; *McGregor* v. *Stokes*, [1952] V. L. R. 347; *Marshall* v. *Watts*, [1953] Tas. S. R. 1; *Gorman* v. *Newton*, [1958] S. R. Qd. 169. Evidence of this nature would not, of course, suffice for a conviction if it stood alone.

could only be raised in the most exceptional circumstances. It is truly said that the evidence is only relevant if it is assumed that the unknown callers believed the premises in question to be a betting-shop, but they were acting on their beliefs and it is arguable that the phone calls were no more hearsay statements than letters stating that the enclosed cheques were sent in payment of betting accounts, or even the appearance outside premises alleged to contain a gymnasium of a number of persons in gym tunics.

(2) Statements as Facts Relevant to the Issue

(i) Miscellaneous.—True or false, an assertive statement may be a relevant fact in a great variety of circumstances. If it becomes material to know what a testator believed to be the contents of the will he was executing,[1] whether someone alleging fraud was misled,[2] or the nature of a husband's belief concerning the destination of his wife on leaving him,[3] evidence of what was said to them may be crucial, and the court is not concerned with the truth of the words used. Statements made to or about someone charged with murder may be all-important on the question of motive.[4] In proceedings for malicious prosecution or false imprisonment, statements made to the defendant by a third party concerning the criminal conduct of the plaintiff may be received on several issues, such as the reasonableness of the defendant's conduct and the quantum of damages, although they would infringe the rule against hearsay if tendered to prove the truth of that which they asserted.[5] A conversation between the thief and a receiver may be admissible to account for the receiver's statements to the police, though inadmissible as evidence of the truth of what was stated.[6]

Statements made by a person, as well as those made to him, may likewise be received as relevant facts on the footing that the truth or falsity of their contents is immaterial. They may not be assertive at all, as when the fact that a woman was heard to demand money is tendered in evidence on a charge of rape.[7] They may be assertive of some preposterous fact, as when a man's statement to the effect that he is observing pink elephants is tendered on the issue of his sanity or they may be demonstrably false, as in *A.-G.* v. *Good*,[8] where a wife's untrue statement that her husband was away from home was received on the issue whether he intended to defraud his creditors. Garrow, B., said:

> "The doubt on the present occasion has originated in calling that hearsay evidence which has no approximation to it. The answer is received as a distinct fact in itself, to be compared and combined with other facts; . . . Suppose an unreasonable time had intervened between the demand of entrance and the opening of the door . . . is not that a circumstance to be inquired into with a view to the fact under investigation. . . ."

---

[1] *Doe* d. *Small* v. *Allen* (1799), 8 Term Rep. 147 (statement to testator that second will duplicate of first admissible on issue of validity of second).

[2] *Gray* v. *New Augarita Porcupine Mines, Ltd.*, [1952] 3 D. L. R. 1 (statement by one company director to another admissible as suggesting that it was of such a nature that it could not mislead).

[3] *Hoare* v. *Allen* (1801), 3 Esp. 276 (wife's statement to husband that she was going to her uncle admissible to rebut suggestion that husband had connived at her leaving him in order to go to the defendant).

[4] *R.* v. *Edmunds* (1833), 6 C. & P. 164.

[5] *Perkins* v. *Vaughan* (1842), 4 Man. & G. 988.

[6] *R.* v. *Willis*, [1960] 1 All E. R. 331.

[7] *R.* v. *Guttridge* (1840), 9 C. & P. 471.　　　　　　[8] (1825), M'Cle. & Yo. 286.

(ii) Statements accompanying a relevant act or event.—We have seen that, in the case of a gift, a statement accompanying an act may be proved because it consists of operative words, not because it establishes its truth. An assertive statement may also be proved as a relevant fact on account of the manner in which it qualifies an accompanying act, and not in order to establish the truth of the assertion. Thus, in *Hayslep* v. *Gymer*,[1] a man asked his deceased father's housekeeper, who had delivered some of her late master's belongings to him, whether she had any more of the deceased's property, whereupon she handed over some bank notes remarking that she had received them as a gift from the deceased. This statement was held to be admissible because it qualified the act of handing over the notes which might otherwise have been construed as an admission by the housekeeper that she had no right to them. The statement could not have been received as evidence of the alleged gift, because no exception to the rule against hearsay applied to the case; nor would it have constituted a relevant fact independently of its truth if considered apart from the act it accompanied.

Whether they are true or false, operative or assertive, statements may be received because they constitute part of a relevant event, as when the cries of a large crowd caused to assemble by someone charged with treason by levying war, riot or unlawful assembly, are proved by onlookers.[2] The crucial question is the effect of the exclamations on others, and the intentions of the crowd are only of secondary significance.

(iii) Statements indicative of treatment.—In *Re Jenion, Jenion* v. *Wynne*,[3] a mother's statements to the effect that a number of her children, born during her marriage, were illegitimate, were admitted as evidence of that fact under the exception to the rule against hearsay relating to pedigree declarations by deceased members of a family mentioned in chapter XVIII. The Court of Appeal also held that a bare assertion that the children were his, made by the putative father to friends was admissible as original evidence, although MORRIS, L.J., was of opinion that:

> "Evidence of a bare and isolated declaration not linked with evidence of conduct and action gives no guidance to the truth if no heed be paid to the declaration itself."[4]

The other members of the court recognised that the probative value of the man's statement when treated as original evidence was insignificant, for the most that could be inferred from the mere fact that it was made was that there had been nothing in the demeanour of the alleged putative father to contradict the other evidence concerning the status of the children. This certainly involves a nice distinction. If A.'s deceased mother says he was illegitimate, her statement is admissible as evidence of its truth. If a man (since deceased) admits paternity of A., his statement is not admissible evidence of its truth, but the fact that it was made is nonetheless relevant because it does not contradict, and therefore confirms the truth of, the mother's statement. No use could be made of the fact that the putative father's statement showed that he believed himself to be

---

[1] (1834), 1 Ad. & El. 162.
[2] *R.* v. *Gordon (Lord)* (1781), 21 State Tr. 485. See also *Wilson* v. *R.* (1970), 44 A. L. J. R. 221 (statements in quarrels between husband and wife admissible to show terms on which they were living and not hearsay).
[3] [1952] Ch. 454; [1952] 1 All E. R. 1228.
[4] [1952] Ch. 454, at p. 484; [1952] 1 All E. R. 1228, at p. 1245.

the father of the children whose legitimacy was in issue because it could only have probative value if it was true and thus treated as equivalent to an assertion of paternity tendered as proof of that fact—a course which the Court of Appeal recognised to be prohibited by the rule against hearsay.

(iv) Implied assertions as original evidence of mental or bodily state.—We saw that, in *Lloyd* v. *Powell Duffryn Steam Coal Co. Ltd.*,[1] implied assertions appear to have been treated as original evidence of a person's state of mind. The same is probably true of behaviour which is used to prove the existence of a contemporaneous physical state or sensation. This appears to have been treated as original evidence in *Manchester Brewery* v. *Coombs*,[2] where, on the question whether the plaintiff had supplied a publican with good beer, the fact that the publican's customers left the beer they had ordered after tasting it was allowed to be proved. FARWELL, J., said a judge could not help drawing an inference from such evidence, and only allowed accompanying statements to be proved in-chief because cross-examining counsel would have been forced to ask questions concerning them in the hope of rebutting the inference suggested by the non-verbal behaviour of the customers.[3]

(v) Ancient documents

In *Malcolmson* v. *O'Dea*,[4] an assembly book of 1679 containing fishing leases granted by a predecessor in title of the plaintiff was held to be admissible evidence of the lessor's enjoyment of the fishing rights when the leases were granted. WILLES, J., said:

> "The proof of ancient possession is always attended with difficulty. Time has removed the witnesses who could speak to acts of ownership of their own personal knowledge, and resort must necessarily be had to written evidence. In some cases written statements of title are admitted even when they amount to mere assertions as in the case of a right affecting the public generally;[5] but the entry now under consideration is admissible according to a rule equally applicable to a fishery in a private pond as to one in a public navigable river. The rule is that ancient documents coming out of proper custody, and purporting on the face of them to show exercise of ownership, such as a lease or a licence, may be given in evidence without proof of possession or payment of rent under them as being in themselves acts of ownership and proof of possession."

It is of course possible to argue that, if acts which were not primarily intended to be assertive can be treated as hearsay, evidence of this nature is really received under an exception to the hearsay rule because the execu-

---

[1] [1914] A. C. 733; p. 408, *ante*.

[2] (1901), 82 L. T. 347. In *Tilk* v. *Parsons* (1825), 2 C. & P. 201 (see also *Ashley* v. *Harrison* (1793), 1 Esp. 48) the reasons given by customers for refusing to buy goods were held inadmissible. Clearly they are inadmissible if their only relevance is to show that they were valid, for that would be to admit hearsay evidence of the condition of the goods, and the consumer must be called to prove this; but on certain facts, the reasons might themselves be relevant; to the question, for example, whether the goods were rejected in consequence of rumours spread by the defendant to a libel action, and the reasons given by customers should then be admissible (*International Tobacco S.A. Ltd.* v. *United Tobacco Company South Ltd.*, [1953] 3 S. A. 879).

[3] The reasons might have been inadmissible in-chief because they contained assertions about the condition rather than the effect of the beer, or they might have been considered superfluous if concerned solely with the effect (*Saxlehner* v. *Appollinaris Co.*, [1897] 1 Ch. 893, at p. 900).

[4] (1863), 10 H. L. C. 593; *Bristow* v. *Cormican* (1878), 3 A. C. 641; *Neill* v. *Duke of Devonshire* (1882), 8 App. Cas. 135.

[5] They are then admissible under an exception to the rule against hearsay discussed in the next chapter.

tion of the lease is treated as an implied assertion of the lessor's right to grant it, and the payment of the rent is regarded as an admission of this fact. Such an approach would, however, be subject to the objection that, at no point in the reasoning leading to the admissibility of the evidence is the court asked to assume that anything said by anybody was true, and, as we saw in chapter I, it is possible to treat evidence of this nature as circumstantial proof of the ownership or possession of those who executed the documents.

> "The law permits ancient documents, either with or without proof of ancient payment of rent, to be given as evidence from which the jury may properly draw an inference that there was such possession. For in the ordinary course of things men do not make leases unless they act on them, and lessees do not, in general, pay rent unless they are in possession, so that the ancient payment of rent adds weight to the ancient indenture." [1]

C. RATIONALE OF THE RULE

Various justifications have been put forward by the judges for the existence of the rule against hearsay; they all relate to the rule in its strict sense. Although the reasons are very differently expressed, they generally each amount to an assertion that reported statements are untrustworthy evidence of the facts stated. To quote Lord NORMAND: "The rule against the admission of hearsay evidence is fundamental. It is not the best evidence and it is not delivered on oath. The truthfulness and accuracy of the person whose words are spoken by another witness cannot be tested by cross-examination and the light which his demeanour would throw on his testimony is lost." [2]

Hearsay may or may not be the best evidence of the fact stated according to whether the maker of the statement is available as a witness; but the rule under which it is excluded seems to have little historical connection with the best evidence rule. [3] The absence of an oath was given as a reason for the rejection of hearsay in the *Berkeley Peerage Case*, [4] but it had already been decided that the rule excluded statements which were on oath. [5] "Examinations upon oath, except in the excepted cases, are of no avail unless they are made in a cause or proceeding depending upon the parties to be affected by them, and where each has an opportunity of cross-examining the witness; otherwise it is *res inter alios acta*, and not to be received." [6] The absence of an opportunity to cross-examine the maker of the statement is, however, the best all-embracing reason that can be given for the rule.

A further reason is the danger that hearsay evidence may be concocted, but this is simply one aspect of the great pathological dread of manufactured evidence which beset English lawyers of the late eighteenth and early

---

[1] *Per* Lord BLACKBURN in *Bristow* v. *Cormican* (1878), 3 App. Cas. 641, at p. 668. It is, however, difficult to escape the conclusion that the hearsay rule was infringed in *Blandy-Jenkins* v. *Earl of Dunraven*, [1899] 2 Ch. 121, where an ancient compromise was used as proof of the bringing of the action comprised and an admission by the other party to it.

[2] *Teper* v. *R.*, [1952] A. C. 480, at p. 486; [1952] 2 All E. R. 447, at p. 449.

[3] Thayer, *Preliminary Treatise on Evidence at Common Law* 498.

[4] (1811), 4 Camp. 401, at pp. 414–5.

[5] *R.* v. *Eriswell (Inhabitants)* (1790), 3 Term Rep. 707.

[6] *Per* Lord KENYON.

nineteenth centuries. It is certainly possible to point to cases in which evidence of indisputable reliability has been excluded under the hearsay rule. [1]

It is sometimes said that hearsay is excluded because it is irrelevant. This is no doubt an outcome of Stephen's use of the word "relevant" as a synonym for admissible. Relevancy is not an appropriate notion for expressing the connection between the fact that a statement was made and the truth or falsity of the statement unless regard be had to the circumstances in which it was made; much hearsay which is very probably true on account of those circumstances is excluded, and even the Court of Criminal Appeal was misled into giving irrelevancy and not the infraction of the hearsay rule as the ground for rejecting such evidence. [2]

The fear that the jury would attach undue weight to hearsay is frequently said to be the ground of exclusion. This is both a doubtful proposition of fact and an historical rationalisation. In point of fact, it is difficult to believe that a jury would have much difficulty in realising that hearsay often lacks the cogency of testimony. So far as history is concerned, Professor Morgan of Harvard has shown that "While distrust of the jury had nothing to do with the origin of the hearsay rule, it has exerted a strong influence in preventing or delaying its liberalisation." [3] It is only in the nineteenth century that distrust of the jury is mentioned in the cases. Earlier judgments justified the exclusion of hearsay by reference to the absence of an oath or the absence of cross-examination.

Lastly it is said that hearsay is excluded because of the danger of inaccuracy through repetition. In the case of oral hearsay, there is no doubt a risk that, if A. is allowed to narrate what B. told him C. had said, the precise terms of C.'s original statement, or even its exact purport, will not be before the court; but no such risks are inherent in written hearsay and yet it is generally subject to the same common law ban as oral hearsay.

Some of the reasons mentioned above are wholly inapplicable to the ban on the proof of previous statements of witnesses as evidence of the facts stated, and others only apply in an attenuated form.

A previous consistent statement will usually be irrelevant because it adds nothing to the witness's testimony, but it may be the best evidence, as when it was made soon after an event which occurred a long time ago. It is true that such a statement will not normally have been made upon oath, but the witness swears in court that what he said on a former occasion is true, and he is liable to cross-examination. All that can be said against the reception of the statement so far as this latter possibility is concerned is that there was no chance of cross-examination on the statement when it was made, and the principal virtue of cross-examination "is in its immediate application of the testing process. Its strokes fall while the iron is hot." [4] The danger that a previous consistent statement will have been concocted is really only present in the case of a party witness, and it is a possibility of which the least instructed juror would be well aware.

The objections to the reception of prior inconsistent statements as evidence of the facts stated are that the statements were not made on oath and the witness swears that they are untrue. The court and jury will

---

[1] For two striking examples see *Stobart* v. *Dryden* (1836), 1 M. & W. 615 and *Myers* v. *Director of Public Prosecutions*, [1965] A. C. at p. 1009; [1964] 2 All E. R. 881.

[2] *R.* v. *Gordon*, *R.* v. *Spencer* (1958), 42 Cr. App. Rep. 177.

[3] *Some Problems of Proof Under the Anglo-American System of Litigation*, 117.

[4] Morgan, *op. cit.*, 131.

generally be well advised to ignore both the statement and the testimony, but, in rare cases, such as those in which the witness has been "got at" since he made the statement, there may be excellent reasons for accepting it as true.

D. THE REQUIREMENT OF PERSONAL KNOWLEDGE.— HEARSAY UPON HEARSAY

It might be thought that the danger of inaccuracies creeping in when hearsay is passed from mouth to mouth, or even from hand to hand, would warrant the total exclusion of hearsay as evidence of the truth of what was heard in all cases in which the maker of the statement heard by the witness, or the author of the document produced to the court, lacked personal knowledge of the facts stated. The adoption of such a course would, however, lead to the exclusion of valuable evidence in at least three types of case. In the first place, evidence of reputation, or of tradition and repute, indirectly involves the repetition of statements when the makers may well not have had personal knowledge of the facts stated. Evidence of reputation is, as we have seen, the standard method of proving character, and we shall see that questions of pedigree or of public rights can often only be proved by tradition and repute. Secondly, the courts sometimes accept evidence of belief, as when an affidavit states that the deponent is informed and verily believes that certain facts exist, or when an admission is received, although the person making it cannot be said to have had more than a belief in the truth of that which is admitted. Finally, many records are compiled by people who have got no personal knowledge of the facts recorded. In a number of cases, those who supply the information recorded to the compiler have not got personal knowledge. In many firms, A. may be under a duty to inform B. of the results of his stocktaking or of the numbers on the cylinder blocks put into an engine, B. may be under a duty to record such information and pass it on, together with further information to C., and so on. Intermediate records may be destroyed, and the compiler of the ultimate record may know nothing of the facts recorded; in some cases the persons supplying him with information will also lack such knowledge, yet the record will be a good deal more reliable than direct testimony.

Subject to cases such as those which have just been mentioned in which a rigid insistence on the requirement of personal knowledge in the maker of the statement would entail great inconvenience and the rejection of much valuable evidence, the unreliability of hearsay upon hearsay was thought by the Law Reform and Criminal Law Revision Committees to justify the continued prohibition of its reception, notwithstanding their recommendations that first hand hearsay statements (i.e. those made in a document or proved by the person who heard them made), should, subject to safeguards, be admissible. It is undoubtedly possible to give striking examples in which the adoption of this course will exclude highly significant evidence,[1] but a line has to be drawn somewhere and there is much to be said for drawing it at the point at which it ceases to be possible for the

---

[1] "A. and B., aged sisters, are both lying ill when they hear that their acquaintance X. has been arrested on a serious charge. A. realises that she saw X. board a train at a place and time which were inconsistent with his guilt, and she tells this to B. just before dying. B. communicates it to C., the parson, just before she too dies. The information chimes exactly with X.'s alibi defence at the trial" (Glanville Williams, [1973] Crim. L. R. 139).

court to know anything of the reliability, not merely of the maker of the statement, but also of the person to whom it was made.

E. EXCEPTIONS TO THE RULE AGAINST HEARSAY

Although there is only one clear common law exception to the rule prohibiting proof of the previous statements of witnesses as evidence of the facts stated (the informal admission proved by its maker), ample amends for the scantiness are made by the number and uncertainty of the common law exceptions to the hearsay rule in the strict sense. In addition to admissions and confessions proved by someone other than the party making them, there are the six well recognised exceptions of statements in public documents and statements by deceased persons made—against interest, in the course of duty, concerning the cause of death in homicide cases by the deceased when *in extremis*, concerning matters of pedigree and public or general rights;[1] but we shall see in chapter XIX that there are some less well defined exceptions. Furthermore, at least four types of statement often said to form part of the *res gestae*, discussed in chapter XX, are admissible as evidence of the facts stated. All the common law exceptions are, thanks to the Civil Evidence Act, 1968, discussed in the next chapter, confined to criminal cases. Perhaps it is essential that, owing to the peculiar positions of the accused and the police, the law governing the reception of hearsay statements in criminal cases should differ from that governing their reception in civil cases; but, even if the recommendations of the Criminal Law Revision Committee should be thought to go too far towards assimilation, there is certainly a need for statutory rationalisation of the law relating to hearsay evidence in criminal proceedings. This is all the more necessary since the House of Lords, in striking contrast with what the Supreme Court of Canada has subsequently done,[2] has, by a majority, set itself against the creation of new exceptions to the hearsay rule by the courts on the ground that the rationalisation of this branch of the law is best left to the legislature.[3]

The number of statutory exceptions to the rule is quite a large one, but most of them do not call for discussion in this book. There are notable exceptions in the case of the Criminal Evidence Act, 1965, discussed in chapter XIX, and the Civil Evidence Act, 1968, the discussion of which forms the major part of the next chapter. A few words may be added about the background and nature of this latter statute.

The Evidence Act, 1938, was the first general major inroad into the common law of hearsay evidence.[4] It was confined to civil proceedings and only applied to documentary hearsay. It also contained some unnecessary restrictions on the admissibility of this latter class of evidence, but, generally speaking, it rendered documentary hearsay admissible,

---

[1] The hearsay exception relating to declarations by testators concerning the contents of their wills (see *Sugden* v. *Lord St. Leonards* (1876), 1 P. D. 154) is abolished by the Civil Evidence Act, 1968.

[2] *Ares* v. *Venner* (1971), 14 D. L. R. (3d) 4.

[3] *Myers* v. *Director of Public Prosecutions*, [1965] A. C. 1001; contrast the attitude of the Court of Appeal in *Sugden* v. *Lord St. Leonards*, *supra*. A brief reference is made to the recommendations of the Criminal Law Revision Committee in chapter XIX.

[4] Lord Maugham was responsible for piloting the Act through Parliament, and he discussed the subject in an article in 17 Canadian Bar Review 469. There are now corresponding statutes in many parts of the Commonwealth.

provided the maker of the document was called as a witness or was unavailable for specified reasons such as his death or illness. The Civil Evidence Act, 1968, provides for the admissibility of oral as well as documentary hearsay and, in the case of the latter, it abolishes the irksome restrictions of the 1938 Act. It attaches several important conditions to the admissibility of hearsay statements, such as the calling of the maker as a witness or the existence of specified reasons for not doing so, and the notification to adverse parties of the intention to tender the statement in evidence.

It is customary to include statements admissible under the Evidence Act, 1938, in lists of exceptions to the rule against hearsay, and it was no doubt correct to do so as long as oral hearsay was generally inadmissible; but now that the 1938 Act has, in effect, been extended to oral hearsay by the 1968 Act, a revision of thought may be called for and it will certainly become necessary if ever the recommendations of the Criminal Law Revision Committee on the subject of hearsay are adopted. Speaking generally, the effect of those proposals is to apply the Act of 1968 to criminal cases. No doubt there would continue to be a sense in which the hearsay rule still existed, the statement of someone available, but not called as a witness would, for example, continue to be inadmissible,[1] and no doubt reference would have to be made to the hearsay rule when explaining parts of the legislation, but the emphasis would be quite different. The rule against hearsay would have ceased to be one of the major exclusionary rules of evidence. The books of the future would talk, not about exceptions to the hearsay rule, but about the conditions on which the previous statements of witnesses and the statements of non-witnesses are admissible as evidence of the facts stated. The Act of 1968 is best regarded as a statute prescribing such conditions. Although the point is one of semantics, rather than creating a huge exception to it, the Act can be said to have abolished the rule against hearsay as known hitherto in civil cases.

Unfortunately it is necessary to mention a complication beyond that occasioned by the great difference between the civil and criminal law concerning the admissibility of hearsay statements: this is that the common law exceptions to the hearsay rule and the Evidence Act, 1938, still apply to civil proceedings in magistrates' courts. The Lord Chancellor has power to apply the 1968 Act to such proceedings, but, at the time of writing (April 1974), he has not exercised it. The procedure contemplated by the Act of 1968 is not easily adaptable to magisterial cases, and the Law Reform Committee took the view that it might be better to apply whatever procedure was recommended by the Criminal Law Revision Committee.[2]

It is easy for an academic lawyer to become impatient with complications such as that which has just been mentioned, but he would do well to take heed of the following extract from para. 49 of the 13th Report of the Law Reform Committee:

> "We recognise the desirability of applying the same rules of evidence in civil cases irrespective of the court in which they are litigated; but rules of evidence are not an end in themselves and are justified only in so far as they assist the court by which they are applied to reach a just determination in the matter upon which it has to adjudicate."

---

[1] Subject to a discretion to admit it in civil cases.

[2] 13th Report, paras. 48–52.

Nonetheless readers interested in magisterial proceedings in civil cases must be warned that this book does not contain a full account of the relevant law of evidence.

Subject to the above caveat, it is now proposed to consider in successive chapters the admissibility of hearsay statements in civil proceedings, and the admissibility of statements (other than those forming part of the *res gestae*) in criminal proceedings; statements admitted as part of the *res gestae* are then dealt with in a separate chapter because they are received sometimes as original evidence and sometimes as evidence of the facts stated.

CHAPTER XVIII

HEARSAY STATEMENTS IN CIVIL PROCEEDINGS[1]

A hearsay statement was defined in chapter I as a statement other than one made by a person while giving oral evidence in the proceedings tendered as evidence of the facts stated. In consequence of the abolition of the common law exceptions to the hearsay rule by s. 1 (1) of the Civil Evidence Act 1968,[2] a hearsay statement is only admissible in civil proceedings by agreement or where provision is made for its reception by a statute or a rule of court. A number of statutes and rules makes such provision, but the only ones calling for treatment in this book are Part I of the Civil Evidence Act, 1968, and the Rules of the Supreme Court made under powers conferred by s. 8 of the Act.[3]

The objects of Part I of the 1968 Act are: to ensure that all first hand hearsay statements are admissible, provided prescribed conditions are fulfilled; to allow second hand hearsay statements to be received if contained in records, and in a few other cases; to give the court an inclusionary discretion but, except when the maker of the statement is called as a witness, or when the statement was made in earlier proceedings, no exclusionary discretion; and to prevent the party against whom the statement is tendered from being taken by surprise by its adduction at the trial.

By a "first hand" hearsay statement is meant a statement made by A. and proved either by the production of the document in which A. made it, or by the oral evidence of a witness who heard or otherwise perceived[4] the making of the statement by A. If a witness swears that A. told him that B. had said something, or if a document asserts that the author was told something, by another person, or that the author is repeating what he read in another document, the hearsay statement proved by the witness or narrated by the author of the documents is "second hand."

Ss. 2 and 3 of the Act deal with the admissibility of first hand hearsay statements, ss. 4 and 5 deal with the admissibility of statements contained in records, while s. 9 preserves some common law rules but converts them into statutory provisions by rendering them admissible by virtue of the section. The objects of Part I of the Act are to a large extent carried out

---

[1] Until Part I of the Civil Evidence Act is extended to magistrates' courts, the admissibility of hearsay evidence in civil proceedings in those courts will continue to be governed by the common law exceptions to the hearsay rule and the Evidence Act, 1938. The latter is dealt with in Chapter XX of the third edition of this book. The only important decision since its publication is *Dass* v. *Masih*, [1968] 2 All E. R. 226, in which a majority of the Court of Appeal said (obiter) that statements of opinion are admissible under s. 1.

[2] "In any civil proceedings a statement other than one made by a person while giving oral evidence in those proceedings shall be admissible as evidence of any fact [or matter] stated therein to the extent that it is so admissible by virtue of any provision of this part of this Act or by virtue of any other statutory provision or by agreement of the parties, but not otherwise." (The words in square brackets are necessitated by s. 1 of the Civil Evidence Act, 1972, which extends the 1968 Act, Part I, to statements of opinion.

[3] There are corresponding provisions in the Matrimonial Causes Rules and the County Court Rules.

[4] E.g. a statement made in gestures.

by R.S.C., O. 38, rr. 21–33. Part I has, subject to the necessary modifications, been extended to statements of opinion, other than those contained in computerised records admissible under s. 5 of the 1968 Act, by s. 1 of the Civil Evidence Act, 1972, and R. S. C. O. 38, r. 34 applies the earlier Rules to such statements, subject to such modifications as the court may direct, or the circumstances of the case require.[1]

SECTION 1. STATEMENTS ADMISSIBLE UNDER SS. 2 AND 3 OF THE CIVIL EVIDENCE ACT, 1968

S. 2 (1) of the Civil Evidence Act, 1968, reads:

> "In any civil proceedings a statement made, whether orally or in a document or otherwise, by any person, whether called as a witness in those proceedings or not, shall, subject to this section and to rules of court, be admissible as evidence of any fact [or matter][2] stated therein of which direct oral evidence by him would be admissible."

The rest of s. 2 and the rules of court call for a distinction between the cases falling within the two rules conflated in the formulation of the rule against hearsay adopted in this book and s. 1 (1) of the Civil Evidence Act, 1968,[3] the case in which the maker of the statement is called as a witness and that in which he is not called.

A. THE PREVIOUS STATEMENTS OF WITNESSES

(1) STATEMENTS ADMISSIBLE UNDER S. 2

The previous statement of a witness, consistent or inconsistent with his testimony, is admissible under s. 2 of the Act on two conditions, first, that the party calling the witness should have notified all other parties within the prescribed time before the trial[4] of his desire to give the statement in evidence, and second, that the trial judge should give leave for the statement to be given in evidence.

(i) **Notice.**—One of the objects of the notice procedure for which provision is made by O. 38, rr. 21–6 is to prevent surprise; another is to provide an incentive for parties upon whom a notice is served to agree to the reception of a hearsay statement without the necessity of calling the maker. It is unlikely that a party who has a witness available to prove a crucially important fact would not want to call him, but that party must nonetheless serve all other parties with notice of his desire to give a statement of that witness in evidence, if such be his desire, and the object of the requirement is to prevent him from taking his adversaries by surprise. Parties to litigation are seldom in complete accord on the question what is or is not an important fact; provision is therefore made by O. 38, r. 26 for the service of a counter-notice requiring the person named in the original notice

---

[1] O. 38, r. 36 and r. 41 apply to cases in which a party wishes to give in evidence the report of an expert whom he alleges cannot, or should not, be called as a witness.

[2] Added in consequence of s. 1 (1) of the Civil Evidence Act, 1972.

[3] The subsection is set out in n. 2, p. 421, *ante*. "We have chosen as our first topic 'the hearsay rule', in which we include not only the strict hearsay rule ('what the soldier said is not evidence') but also what is sometimes mis-called the rule against narrative ('what the witness himself said outside the witness box is not evidence.)" (13th Report of the Law Reform Committee, para. 5.)

[4] See O. 38, r. 21.

as the maker of the statement to be called as a witness. If that person is available as a witness, and he is not called, after receipt of a counter-notice by the party who served the original notice, the statement will, subject to the discretion of the court to rule otherwise, be inadmissible in evidence. An incentive not to serve a counter-notice without good cause is provided by O. 38, r. 32 under which, if it appears to the court that it was unreasonable to require the maker of the statement to be called, the costs of the preparation of the counter-notice may be disallowed and the party serving it may also be required to pay costs occasioned by it.

(ii) **Leave.**—S. 2 (2) of the Civil Evidence Act, 1968, reads in part as follows:

> "Where in any civil proceedings a party desiring to give a statement in evidence by virtue of this section has called or intends to call as a witness in the proceedings the person by whom the statement was made, the statement—
>
> (a) shall not be given in evidence by virtue of this section on behalf of that party without the leave of the court; and
> (b) without prejudice to paragraph (a) above, shall not be given in evidence by virtue of this section on behalf of that party before the conclusion of the examination-in-chief of the person by whom it was made . . ."

To a large extent this subsection embodies the reaction of the Law Reform Committee to what was thought to be a lax practice which prevailed, or might have prevailed, under the Evidence Act, 1938. A party could call a witness, ask him to verify his proof of evidence and put it in as of right, thus avoiding any examination-in-chief.

> "Examination-in-chief by question and answer without leading questions on matters in dispute plays an important part in our system of eliciting the truth under the adversary system. As every judge and advocate knows, witnesses often fail to 'come up to their proofs' in examination-in-chief—and this is one of the commonest ways in which truth will out." [1]

There are three exceptions to the prohibition of the reception of the witness's previous statements before the conclusion of his examination-in-chief. In the first place, the court may allow the statement to be proved by an earlier witness, and might do so, for instance, where a party to a running down action intended to call someone who had made a statement soon after the accident to a police officer who gives his evidence first and wishes to be released. Secondly, the court may allow a witness to narrate his previous statement in the course of his examination-in-chief on the ground that to prevent him from doing so would adversely affect the intelligibility of his evidence. For instance the most natural way for a witness to give his evidence may involve his stating what he said to his wife on a particular occasion, and perhaps also what she said to him; interruptions inspired by the rule against hearsay have, it is believed, been too frequent in the past. These exceptions are contained in s. 2 (2) of the 1968 Act. The third is the result of O. 38, r. 43, relating to reports of experts. When an expert is called as a witness in accordance with the procedure outlined on p. 386, his report may be given in evidence at the beginning of his examination-in-chief or at any other time directed by the court. Such a provision is desirable because the examination-in-chief of an expert as to opinion is quite different from the examination-in-chief of the ordinary

---

[1] 13th Report of the Law Reform Committee, para. 32.

witness as to fact; it may often take the form of a request to enlarge upon the report.

(iii) **Discretion.**—Under O. 38, r. 29 (1), the court has a discretion to admit a statement, if it thinks it just to do so, although no notice of desire to give the statement in evidence has been served. In *Morris* v. *Stratford-on-Avon U.D.C.*[1] the plaintiff had been struck, five years before the trial, by a lorry driven by an employee of the defendants who gave evidence for them. His evidence was inconsistent and confused, and, although no notice concerning a previous statement had been served on the plaintiff, the judge allowed the defendants to adduce a proof of evidence which a driver had given to a representative of their insurers some nine months after the accident. The judge's decision was upheld by the Court of Appeal. The Court did not think it mattered whether the case was regarded as one in which there was one discretion or two, the discretion under O. 38, r. 29, to waive the failure to give notice, and the discretion to grant leave to give the notice in evidence under s. 2 (2). The defendants had no particular reason to suppose that their driver would give confused evidence, and the Court of Appeal took the view that it would perhaps be unfortunate if the Civil Evidence Act were to be so interpreted that a party's advisers would feel it necessary to advise that notice should be served if ever there were the remotest possibility that leave to give that statement in evidence would have to be sought. At the same time, the Court recognised that failure to give the prescribed notice was a serious matter, that that notice should always be given when it was thought that an application for leave to give a statement in evidence would be made at the trial, and that justice to the opposite party might sometimes require an adjournment if the prescribed notice were not served.

(2) Statements Admissible under s. 3

There are no requirements concerning the service of a notice or the necessity of obtaining the leave of the court before the previous statement of a witness becomes admissible under s. 3 of the Civil Evidence Act, 1968. It is only necessary to set the section out and to indicate in footnotes the pages in this book at which the statements mentioned in the section have been discussed and the precise extent to which it changes the law.

S. 3 reads as follows:

(1) "Where in any civil proceedings—

(a) a previous inconsistent or contradictory statement made by a person called as a witness in those proceedings is proved by virtue of sections 3, 4 and 5 of the Criminal Procedure Act, 1865;[2] or

(b) a previous statement made by a person called as aforesaid is proved for the purpose of rebutting a suggestion that his evidence has been fabricated,[3] that statement shall by virtue of this subsection be admissible as evidence of any fact [or matter][4] stated therein of which direct oral evidence by him would be admissible."

---

[1] [1973] 3 All E. R. 263.

[2] For s. 3 (hostile witnesses) see p. 221, *ante*; for ss. 4–5, see pp. 228–9, *ante*; the law is changed because previous inconsistent statements are made admissible as evidence of the facts stated, although it does not follow that they will often be acted on as such.

[3] P. 216, *ante*. The law is changed because at common law the previous statement is only admissible to rebut fabrication, not as evidence of the facts stated; but it is doubtful whether the change is more than nominal.

[4] Civil Evidence Act, 1972, s. 1 (1).

(2) "Nothing in this Act shall affect any of the rules of law relating to the circumstances in which, where a person called as a witness in any civil proceedings is cross-examined on a document used by him to refresh his memory, that document may be made evidence in those proceedings; and where a document or any part of a document is received in evidence in any such proceedings by virtue of any such rule of law, any statement made in that document or part by the person using the document to refresh his memory shall by virtue of this subsection be admissible as evidence of any fact [or matter] stated therein, of which direct oral evidence by him would be admissible."[1]

B. THE PREVIOUS STATEMENTS OF NON-WITNESSES

The oral or written statement of someone who is not called as a witness is admissible as of right as evidence of any fact stated of which he could have given direct oral evidence[2] under s. 2 (1) of the Civil Evidence Act, 1968, if (i) the statement is proved in accordance with the terms of s. 2 (3); (ii) one of the reasons for not calling the maker as a witness mentioned in O. 38, r. 25, exists; and (iii) the appropriate notice has been served on all other parties to the proceedings by the party wishing to give the statement in evidence. The Court has a discretion to admit the statement although the second and third of the above requirements have not been met if it thinks it just to do so, and the Act contains guide-lines about the weight to be attached to the statement if admitted, as well as rules concerning the admissibility of evidence impugning the credibility of the maker. These requirements, guide-lines and rules may be described as the "main provisions"; after they have been considered, some special cases will be mentioned.

There is a further situation in which the statement of a non-witness is admissible under s. 2, namely, that in which a party desiring to give in evidence a statement of an available witness has served the appropriate notice on all other parties and has not been served with a counter-notice requiring the maker of the statement to be called. The party serving the notice has an option whether to call the maker of the statement as a witness, and if he opts against calling him, the court has no discretion to exclude the statement, although, if the maker is called, the statement will only be admissible with the leave of the court in accordance with the provisions of s. 2 (2) set out on p. 423.

(1) THE MAIN PROVISIONS

(i) Proof in accordance with s. 2 (3).—S. 2 (3) of the Civil Evidence Act, 1968, reads in part as follows:

"Where in any civil proceedings a statement which was made otherwise than in a document is admissible by virtue of this section, no evidence other than direct oral evidence by the person who made the statement or any person who heard or otherwise perceived it being made, shall be admissible for the purpose of proving it . . ."

The object of this provision is to ensure that only first hand hearsay statements are admissible under s. 2 (1). B. may prove what he heard A. say, but C. may not prove what B. told him A. said. A.'s written statement that he saw X. hit Y. is clearly admissible as evidence of that fact, and B.'s

---

[1] P. 202, *ante*. It is open to question whether the provision for the reception of the statement as evidence of the facts stated alters the common law.
[2] *Re Koscot Interplanetary (U.K.), Ltd., Re Koscot A.G.,* [1972] 3 All E. R. 829.

written statement that A. had told him that he saw X. hit Y. is equally clearly inadmissible as evidence of the assault; it is A.'s statement that has evidential significance on this point, and it is not "made" by A., but repeated by B., in a document. The latter term is very broadly defined by s. 10 (1) as including in addition to a document in writing, a map, plan, photograph, disc, tape, film or microfilm. "Statement" includes "any representation of fact [or expression of opinion][1] whether made by words or otherwise." We shall see that this could give rise to problems concerning the admissibility of implied assertions under s. 2, but, for the time being, it is only necessary to refer to a few problems which could be raised in exceptional circumstances, by the concept of a "statement made in a document."

The obvious instance of such a statement has already been given, A.'s written assertion that he saw X. hit Y.; but what if A. were to dictate the words "I saw X. hit Y." to B? It is to be assumed that, if B. duly wrote the statement down and A. checked the writing, any court would hold, on the ordinary principles of agency, that A. had made a statement in a document. Doubt begins to creep in if it is assumed that A. dictated the statement to B. but did not check what B. wrote. To cope with this possibility, the Criminal Law Revision Committee recommended the following subclause:

> "Where a person makes an oral statement to or in the hearing of another person who, acting at the instance of the maker of the statement, reduces it (or the substance of it) into writing at the time or reasonably soon afterwards, thereby producing a corresponding statement in a document, the statement in the document shall be treated . . . as having been made in the document by the maker of the oral statement not only where he has, but also where he has not, signified his acceptance of it as his."[2]

The courts may well reach the same conclusion on the construction of s. 2 (3) of the 1968 Act without the aid of any such subclause.

If B. were to eavesdrop on a conversation in which A. told C. that he saw X. hit Y., A.'s statement could be proved by B.; but, if B. were to write the statement down, it is hard to believe that any court would hold that A.'s statement was made in a document. Doubt again begins to creep in if one assumes that A.'s statement to C. was recorded on a concealed tape recorder of which A. was unaware.

If A. writes a letter to B. stating that he saw X. hit Y., and the letter cannot be found after due search, its contents could be proved under s. 2 (3) by a letter written by B. to C. in which B. narrated the substance of what A. had written to him, and this process might, in theory, be continued. However remote the letter ultimately placed before the court was from that written by A. to B., it is A.'s statement made in that lost letter which is the statement "made in a document" and received as evidence that X. hit Y. But the fact that statements made in documents may, on proof of due search for other documents narrating them, be admissible as evidence of the contents of those documents does mean that second, third or fourth hand "written" hearsay could be received under the Act. S. 6 (1) provides for the proof of statements contained in documents by the production of the

---

[1] Civil Evidence Act, 1972, s. 1 (1).

[2] Clause 31 (6) of the draft Bill, see paras. 254–5 of the 11th Report. The draft Bill contains provisions as to hearsay substantially similar to those of the Civil Evidence Act, 1968.

original or a copy of the document, authenticated in such manner as the court may approve; but, in the case put at the beginning of this paragraph, it is assumed that there is no copy of A.'s letter to B., the only evidence of its contents being the statements of its substance in the successive letters from B. to C., C. to D. etc.

(ii) Reasons for not calling the maker.—The following are the reasons, mentioned in s. 8 of the Act and incorporated in O. 38, r. 25, for not calling the maker of the statement as a witness: that he is dead, or beyond the seas, or unfit by reason of his bodily or mental condition to attend as a witness,[1] or that, despite the exercise of reasonable diligence, it has not been possible to identify or find him, or that he cannot reasonably be expected to have any recollection of matters relevant to the accuracy [or reliability][2] of the statement.

(iii) Notice.—The notice to be served by the party desiring to give the statement in evidence must specify the reasons upon which he relies for not calling the maker, and the party upon whom the notice is served may only serve a counter-notice if he contends that the maker of the statement can, or should, be called. In that event, the court may, on the application of any party, decide these questions.[3]

(iv) Discretion.—Under O. 38, r. 29, the court has a broad inclusionary discretion to admit a statement although no notice of desire to tender it in evidence was served, although a counter-notice requiring the maker to be called has not been complied with, and although no reason for not calling the maker exists. In *Ford* v. *Lewis*[4] the plaintiff, a girl of five at the time, was struck by a van driven by the defendant who was in a mental hospital at the time of the trial. Although no notice had been served in respect of either statement, the trial judge admitted a statement made by the defendant at some time during the period of nearly ten years which elapsed between the accident and the trial, and hospital notes[5] suggesting that the plaintiff's father, who had been with her at the time of the accident, was drunk. The reason given by the defendant's counsel for not serving the notices was that he was afraid that the plaintiff's witnesses might "trim" their evidence to meet the defendant's statement. A new trial was ordered on the plaintiff's appeal against judgment for the defendant because it could not be right to exercise the discretion conferred by O. 38, r. 29, in favour of someone who had deliberately flouted the rules.

(v) Weight and credibility.—S. 6 (3) enjoins the court, when estimating the weight to be attached to a statement to have regard to the questions whether it was made contemporaneously with the events to which it refers, and whether the maker had any incentive to conceal or misrepresent facts.

S. 7 provides that, when the maker of the statement is not called as a witness, any evidence which would, had he been called, have been admissible for the purpose of destroying his credibility, may be adduced; but evidence may not be given on matters as to which the maker's denials in cross-examination to credit would have been final. This simply means that evidence may be given of bias, previous convictions, bad reputation

---

[1] These facts may be proved by medical certificate, s. 8 (5).
[2] Civil Evidence Act, 1972, s. 1 (1).
[3] O. 38, r. 27.
[4] [1971] 2 All E. R. 983
[5] Admissible under s. 4 of the 1968 Act.

for veracity, mental or physical condition tending to show unreliability and, subject to notice by the person tendering the statement,[1] inconsistent statements.[2]

(2) Special Cases

(i) Statements in former proceedings.—The proviso to s. 2 (3) of the Civil Evidence Act, 1968, reads

> "Provided that if the statement in question was made by a person while giving oral evidence in some other legal proceedings (whether civil or criminal), it may be proved in any manner authorised by the court."

Accordingly O. 38, r. 28, enables any party, upon whom notice of intention to give in evidence a statement made in former proceedings has been served, to apply to the court for directions as to whether, and, if so, upon what conditions, the party desiring to give the statement in evidence will be permitted to do so, and as to the manner in which the statement and any other evidence given in the former proceedings should be proved.

Special provision had to be made for such a case because the party desiring to give the statement in evidence might otherwise simply prove a portion of the testimony of a witness in former proceedings, leaving out unfavourable passages; or the witness may have been disbelieved or contradicted by other evidence. All these matters may be dealt with on the application for directions.

Two further points may be mentioned. In the first place, this is the one instance in which the court has a discretion to exclude the statement of someone not called as a witness under s. 2, even though notice of desire to give it in evidence has been duly served; the statement of a witness who had been thoroughly discredited in the former proceedings would be a case in point. Secondly, if, as will usually happen, the court directs that the statement, and possibly much other evidence given in the former proceedings, be proved by a transcript of those proceedings, secondhand hearsay will be received at the trial for the testimony of the witnesses in the former proceedings will be proved by the hearsay statement of the shorthand writer, assuming of course that he is not called as a witness.

(ii) Co-defendants or co-plaintiffs.—A party's informal admissions are admissible evidence against him at common law, and the common law on this subject is preserved by s. 9 of the Act. Admissions are therefore fully discussed below; but, to quote para. 30 of the 13th Report of the Law Reform Committee,

> "One of the most striking effects of the rule against hearsay in its present form is that the out-of-court statement is inadmissible evidence against the other, even though the statement seriously inculpates the maker and is, for that reason, very probably true. The commonest example is the divorce case in which the respondent's admission of adultery with the co-respondent is no evidence against the co-respondent."

Not the least of the merits of the Civil Evidence Act, 1968, is that it puts an end to this absurdity. If A. and B. are co-defendants, and A. has made a statement implicating B., the plaintiff may (whether or not the statement also implicates A.) serve notice on A. and B. of his desire to give the statement in evidence; B. can then serve a counter-notice requiring the plain-

---

[1] O. 38, r. 31.   [2] For details see p. 232, *ante.*

tiff to call A. as a witness. It is, however, undesirable that a party should be obliged to call one of his opponents as his witness. In the case which has just been put, this problem might have been solved by means of the general discretion of the court under O. 38, r. 29 (1), to admit the statement even though A. was not called by the plaintiff; but O. 38, r. 29 (2), expressly states that the court may exercise its discretion if a refusal to do so might oblige the party desiring to give the statement in evidence to call an opposite party. If, in the example which has just been given, A. were to give evidence, the plaintiff could put his statement to him in cross-examination, but if, as would be most likely, the court were prepared to exercise its discretion, the statement could form part of the plaintiff's case against B. If it also implicated A., it would be admissible against him by virtue of s. 9, and there would accordingly be no point in his serving a counter-notice requiring the plaintiff to call him as a witness.[1]

Everything said above applies to cases in which one of two plaintiffs has made a statement implicating the other.

(iii) Statements by servants or agents of a party.—A further absurd result of the common law avoided by the Act of 1968 was that, if the servant or agent of a party had made a statement adverse to that party's case, it often happened that the statement could not be proved against that party, even if made in relation to a transaction in relation to which the maker was vicariously liable. For example, if a lorry driver were to admit that he had not been keeping a proper look out when, in the course of his employment, he ran A. down, A. could not rely on the statement as evidence against the driver's employer; he can do so now thanks to s. 2 of the 1968 Act, but B. can serve him with a counter-notice requiring him to call the driver. To quote again from the 13th Report of the Law Reform Committee,

> "Although not 'hostile' in the technical sense, such a witness might be unfavourably disposed towards the party who was forced to examine him in-chief and favourably disposed towards his cross-examiner."[2]

This is another matter which could have been dealt with under the general discretion conferred upon the court by O. 38, r. 29 (1), but O. 38, r. 29 (2), expressly states that the court may exercise its power to allow a statement to be given in evidence under s. 2 although the maker is not called, when its refusal to do so might oblige the party desiring to give the statement in evidence to call the servant or agent of the opposite party. In the example given above, there would of course be no objection to B. calling his driver if minded to do so.

(iv) Probate actions.—It sometimes happens that a party to a probate action wishes to prove statements made by the deceased as evidence of the facts stated. Indeed, he may wish to prove the deceased's account of the contents of his lost will. There would be no point in serving the opposite party with notice of desire to give the statements of the deceased in evidence because the opposite party would be unable to contest the death of the deceased. Accordingly O. 38, r. 21 (3), provides that no notice need be served in such a case.

The above reference to the deceased's account of the contents of his lost will provokes a general question with regard to the construction of

---

[1] Civil Evidence Act, 1968, s. 9 (5).   [2] Para. 31.

s. 2 (1) of the Civil Evidence Act, 1968. It renders a statement admissible "as evidence of any fact [or matter]¹ of which direct oral evidence by [the maker] would be admissible." It is clear that the reference to direct oral evidence by the maker is to the direct oral evidence he could have given in the proceedings had he been called, and, at any rate for the pedant, this raises problems in relation to cases in which the death of the maker of the statement is a prerequisite of the action in which the statement is tendered in evidence. The concept of the deceased giving direct oral evidence in an action for probate of his own will is not an easy one, and there is the same difficulty with regard to a will construction summons or a claim under the Fatal Accidents Acts in respect of the death of the maker of the statement. It is to be hoped that the courts will avoid the apparent impasse by holding that the 1968 Act requires them to imagine a probate action, will construction summons or claim under the Fatal Accidents Acts at the hearing of which the deceased miraculously appears to give evidence.

(v) **Undefended divorces.**—The object of the notice of desire to give a statement in evidence under s. 2 is to enable the opposite party to consider whether he wishes the maker of the statement to be called as a witness if available, to consider the validity of any reason given for not calling the maker and generally to make inquiries concerning the circumstances in which the statement was made. There is therefore no point in serving such a notice in undefended proceedings and the Matrimonial Causes Rules accordingly provide that the notice need not be served in undefended divorce cases.

(vi) **Implied assertions.**—As we have seen, "statement", for the purposes of the Civil Evidence Act, 1968, includes "any representation of fact [or expression of opinion],² whether made in words or otherwise." Does this include implied assertions?³ If it is desired to prove that A. was in a particular place at a particular time, can a witness prove, as a statement to be admitted under s. 2, that he heard someone, not called as a witness, say "Hello A." at that place and time? If it is desired to prove that a workman was not wearing protective spats, can a witness prove that he heard the workman's mate (since deceased) exclaim "What, no spats"? It is submitted that statements of this sort do imply representations of fact, the recognition, and hence the presence, of A., and the absence of spats, but the application of the Act to statements not intended to convey information is perhaps not as clear as it might have been. Accordingly the draft Bill attached to the 11th Report of the Criminal Law Revision Committee contains a subclause under which "a protest, greeting or other verbal utterance may be treated as stating any fact which the utterance implies."⁴ The Act of 1968 may well be so construed even in the absence of such a subclause. If it is not so construed, "Hello A." etc. will have to be treated as circumstantial evidence because hearsay statements are no longer admissible at common law in civil cases. The admissibility of these utterances as evidence of the presence of A. etc. will then depend upon the view taken by the court of their relevancy in all the circumstances. Their exclusion from the 1968 Act would mean that the party against whom they are tendered will not have an opportunity of checking the nature of the utterance, the credibility of its maker and other relevant

---

¹ Civil Evidence Act, 1972, s. 1 (1).   ² Civil Evidence Act, 1972, s. 1 (1).
³ P. 406, *ante.*   ⁴ Clause 41 (3).

matters. It is not difficult to imagine cases in which this would be regrettable.

The Act certainly does not extend to non-verbal conduct which was not intended to be assertive, such as that of the deceased sea captain mentioned by PARKE, B. in *Wright d. Doe* v. *Tatham*.[1]

SECTION 2. RECORDS ADMISSIBLE UNDER SS. 4 AND 5 OF THE CIVIL EVIDENCE ACT, 1968

There is no definition of a "record"[2] in the Civil Evidence Act, 1968; all that is required is that there should be a document containing information supplied to its maker directly or indirectly by one or more persons. A police officer takes a statement from a bystander who witnessed an accident; the officer's notebook would presumably be held to constitute a record. The foreman of a factory collects information from a number of workmen concerning work done by them. In due course the information is passed on to the officer in charge of records; the resultant compilation is a record although it is not a full reproduction of anyone's written or oral statement.

A. RECORDS ADMISSIBLE UNDER S. 4

(1) STATEMENTS ADMISSIBLE BOTH AS STATEMENTS UNDER S. 2 AND AS RECORDS UNDER S. 4

S. 4 (1) of the Civil Evidence Act, 1968 reads:

"Without prejudice to s. 5 of this Act [dealing with computerised records], in any civil proceedings a statement contained in a document shall, subject to this section and to rules of court, be admissible as evidence of any fact stated therein of which direct oral evidence would be admissible, if the document is, or forms part of, a record compiled by a person acting under a duty from information which was supplied by a person (whether acting under a duty or not) who had, or may reasonably be supposed to have had, personal knowledge of the matters dealt with in that information and which, if not supplied by that person to the compiler of the record directly, was supplied by him to the compiler of the record indirectly through one or more intermediaries each acting under a duty."

The main purpose of the subsection is to provide for the reception of hearsay statements which are not first hand, i.e. they are neither made in a document, nor proved by the direct oral evidence of the maker, nor proved by a witness who heard or otherwise perceived them being made. Many first hand hearsay statements are, however, admissible both as a statement under s. 2 and as a statement contained in a record under s. 4. The bystander's statement recorded in the police officer's notebook mentioned above is one obvious instance. The officer could prove the statement under s. 2 as someone who heard it being made, refreshing his memory from his notebook; or he could produce the latter as a record compiled by someone acting under a duty from information supplied by someone with personal knowledge of the matters dealt with in the information.

The overlap between s. 2 and s. 4 is of little practical importance because (agreement apart) the person who originally supplied the information from which a record admissible under s. 4 is compiled must either be called as a

---

[1] P. 408, *ante*.
[2] For some discussion see *Re Koscot Interplanetary (U.K.), Ltd., Re Koscot A.G.*, [1972] 3 All E. R. 829.

witness, or be unavailable for the reasons specified in O. 38, r. 25, i.e. because he is dead, beyond the seas, unfit, untraceable, or someone who cannot reasonably be expected to have any recollection of the matters dealt with in the information. These are the same reasons as those governing the admissibility of statements under s. 2 when the maker is not called. There are similar rules governing the notice which must be served on opposite parties by someone who wants to give in evidence a record admissible by virtue of s. 4, and the counter-notice which may be served.[1] These rules correspond with those governing admissibility of statements under s. 2, and everything said with regard to the admissibility of first hand hearsay (as a statement) applies to its admissibility (as a record) under s. 4. The supplier of the information is to all intents and purposes in the same position as the maker of a statement admissible under s. 2. If he is called as a witness, the record cannot be given in evidence without the leave of the court, and generally not before the conclusion of his examination-in-chief.[2] It seems, however, that where there is a choice between s. 2 and s. 4, it is better to tender the statement under the latter, thus bringing the record (the police officer's notebook, for example) directly before the court instead of treating it as a document which must be produced to the court as one used to refresh memory.

It has been said that a transcript of a witness's evidence in former proceedings is admissible both as a statement under s. 2 and as a record under s. 4;[3] it has even been suggested that a transcript of the judge's summing-up in a criminal case is admissible in subsequent civil proceedings as a record under s. 4,[4] although it is perhaps open to question whether the judge "supplies" information to the shorthand writer even if, contrary to the view taken with regard to the Evidence Act, 1938,[5] the witness supplies information to the shorthand writer.

(2) Statements Contained in Records Admissible under s. 4 Alone

As an example of a recorded statement admissible under s. 4 alone we may take the case of a lorry driver who informs a fellow servant that he delivered a load at X; the fellow servant makes a note of this fact and passes the note on to another servant who destroys it after entering the delivery in a book. This process can be continued for any length without affecting the admissibility of the ultimate record, provided the compiler and all the intermediaries were acting under a duty.

It is important to bear in mind that the original supplier of the information need not act under a duty. Hospital records are only one of many sets of records compiled from inquiries in relation to which the original source of information, the patient, can hardly be said to have been acting under a duty to supply it.

The existence of a duty to pass the information on and to compile the record reduces the chance of erroneous repetition which is the great weakness of hearsay upon hearsay. S. 4 (3) reads:

"Any reference in this section to a person acting under a duty includes a reference to a person acting in the course of any trade, business, profession

---

[1] R. S. C., O. 38, r. 21, r. 23 and r. 26.
[2] Civil Evidence Act, 1968, s. 4 (2).
[3] *Taylor* v. *Taylor*, [1970] 2 All E. R. 609.   [4] *Ibid.*
[5] *Barkway* v. *South Wales Transport Co., Ltd.*, [1949] 1 K. B. 54; [1948] 2 All E. R. 460.

or other occupation in which he is engaged or employed or for the purpose of any paid or unpaid office held by him."

It is not clear how far this provision is from being exhaustive. If, after an accident, A., a police officer acting under a duty, records a statement by B., who did not see the accident, that C. told him that one of the drivers was driving without lights, and it proves to be impossible to trace C., is the record admissible? The answer turns upon the question whether B. could be said to have been acting under a duty to pass the information on to A. Is a mere social duty, or the moral duty of citizens to help the police, sufficient?

Although the original supplier of the information need not have been acting under a duty, he must have had personal knowledge of the matters dealt with in the information, or have been someone who may reasonably be supposed to have had such knowledge. This is something which will often have to be inferred from the nature of the record and all the circumstances of the case. In *Knight* v. *David*,[1] for example, the plaintiff in an action concerning title to land tendered in evidence a map and apportionment survey made under the Tithe Act, 1836. It was held that these documents were admissible under s. 4 [2] because a living person could have testified to the facts that the machinery prescribed by the Tithe Act had been used and that a certain person was entered as proprietor. The fact that the commissioners had acted on information supplied by people with personal knowledge of the matters upon which they gave information was inferred.

Everything said in section 1 with regard to the credibility of the maker of the statement when he is not called as a witness applies to the original supplier of the information from which a record admissible under s. 4 is compiled; but evidence on this subject is not likely to be forthcoming in the case of a record of any antiquity.

B. RECORDS ADMISSIBLE UNDER S. 5 OF THE CIVIL EVIDENCE ACT, 1968: COMPUTERISED RECORDS [3]

S. 5 (1) of the Civil Evidence Act, 1968, reads:

"In any civil proceedings a statement contained in a document produced by a computer shall, subject to rules of court, be admissible as evidence of any fact stated therein of which direct oral evidence would be admissible, if it is shown that the conditions mentioned in subsection (2) below are satisfied in relation to the statement and computer in question."

The broad definition of "document" in s. 10 as inclusive of any disc, tape, soundtrack or other device in which sounds or other data (not being visual images) are embodied so as to be capable of being reproduced therefrom, is well adapted to computerised records. Also included are any film, negative, tape or other device in which visual images are embodied so as to be capable of being reproduced therefrom. Under s. 5 (6) "computer" means "any device for storing and processing information." This has been said to be "incredibly wide. A tape-recorder or a filing cabinet would ap--

---

[1] [1971] 3 All E. R. 1066.
[2] Although the judge preferred to rest his decision on the common law, preserved by s. 9, a section to which no express reference was made.
[3] I am heavily indebted to chapter 2 of *Computers and the Law* by Colin Tapper. The reference to the South Australian statute is also due to Mr. Tapper.

parently be included."[1]   But the comment may not make adequate allowance for the fact that the device has to be for processing as well as storing information.

The conditions mentioned in s. 5 (2) and elaborated in the following subsections are complicated; they can only be set out in the barest outline. The key to their comprehension lies in the substitution for the requirements of s. 4 of personal knowledge on the part of the supplier of the information and duty on the part of the intermediaries of the requirement of the regular operation of the computer system resulting in the document tendered in evidence. The conditions are that the document should have been produced by the computer during a period of regular use to store or process information for the purpose of any activities regularly carried on; that over that period the computer was regularly supplied with information of the kind contained in the statement tendered in evidence; that the computer was operating properly throughout the period; and that the information contained in the statement reproduces or is derived from information supplied to the computer in the ordinary course of those activities. A commentator on these conditions has said, "It is suggested that the whole turgid repetition could be abridged by making the sole condition of admissibility that the computer should have been operating properly at all material times."[2]

A provision of the South Australia Evidence Act, inserted in 1972, simply requires the court to be satisfied that the data from which the output is produced by the computer is systematically prepared upon the basis of information that would normally be acceptable in a court of law as evidence of the statements or representations contained in or constituted by the output. In addition to its simplicity, the advantage of the South Australian provision is that it gives the court more control than does s. 5 of the 1968 Act over the reliability of the information fed into the computer. A further merit of the South Australian provision is its adoption of computer language. "Data" takes the place of "information", and "output" takes the place of "statement."

To revert to the English Act, s. 5 (4) provides for the certification by the appropriate person of compliance with the conditions mentioned in s. 5 (2) as evidence of the matters stated, and R. S. C., O. 38, r. 24 requires the notice of desire to give in evidence a statement under s. 5 to contain particulars of the persons who occupied a responsible position in relation to the management of the computer and the supply of information to it. The party upon whom such notice is served may, by counter-notice, require these persons to be called as witnesses with the result that he will have an opportunity of cross-examining them.

SECTION 3. STATEMENTS AND RECORDS ADMISSIBLE UNDER S. 9 OF THE CIVIL EVIDENCE ACT, 1968

S. 9 in effect preserves some common law exceptions to the hearsay rule, but it formally converts them into statutory provisions by providing that statements admissible under them shall be admissible by virtue of s. 9. This course was necessitated partly by the fact that secondhand hearsay is admissible under these exceptions in cases falling outside s. 4 and s. 5,

---

[1] Tapper, *op. cit.*, 30.   [2] Tapper, *op. cit.*, 29.

and partly by the inappropriateness of the notice procedure to such cases. The effect of s. 9 (5) is that statements admissible under the section may be proved at the trial although no preliminary notices have been served. S. 9 (2) specifies four common law rules under which evidence is admissible by virtue of s. 9 (1); s. 9 (4) specifies three common law rules under which a statement tending to establish reputation or family tradition is received, and, where such evidence cannot, by service of the appropriate notice, be rendered admissible by virtue of s. 2 or s. 4, it is made admissible by virtue of s. 9 (3) (a).

A. STATEMENTS AND RECORDS ADMISSIBLE BY VIRTUE OF S. 9 (1)

The following are the rules admissible by virtue of s. 9 (1):

"Any rule of law—

    (a) whereby in any civil proceedings an admission adverse to a party to the proceedings, whether made by that party or by another person, may be given in evidence against that party for the purpose of proving any fact stated in the admission;

    (b) whereby in any civil proceedings published works dealing with matters of a public nature (for example, histories, scientific works, dictionaries and maps) are admissible as evidence of facts of a public nature stated therein;

    (c) whereby in any civil proceedings public documents (for example, public registers, and returns made under public authority with respect to matters of public interest) are admissible as evidence of facts stated therein;

    (d) whereby in any civil proceedings records (for example, the records of certain courts, treaties, Crown grants, pardons and commissions) are admissible as evidence of facts stated therein." [1]

Admissions are included because they may involve proof of secondhand hearsay as when someone not called as a witness admits that a child was his, and the statement could not be proved under s. 2 because of s. 2 (3), or under s. 4, because it is not contained in a record. Furthermore the application of the notice procedure to an admission could result in a party's being obliged to call his opponent, who has no need for protection against surprise in respect of his own admissions. As the case-law on the subject is quite extensive, admissions are dealt with in a separate section (section 5, below).

There is no need to deal at length with the second of the above rules. It is not difficult to think of historical facts which could only be proved in a contemporary court of law by recourse to the works mentioned and Lord HALSBURY was merely stating the dictates of common sense when he said "Where it is important to ascertain ancient facts of a public nature, the law does permit historical works to be referred to." [2] It was in accordance with those dictates that the report of the engineer responsible for the construction of the Thames tunnel in 1844 was admitted in 1904 as evidence of the nature of the soil above it in *East London Rail. Co.* v. *Thames Conservators,* [3] the report having been accepted by engineers ever since it was made; but it is regrettably true that a high degree of technicality has been allowed to creep into this branch of the law. In the case of old maps,

---

[1] S. 9 (2).
[2] *Read* v. *Bishop of Lincoln*, [1892] A. C. 644, at p. 653.   [3] 90 L. T. 347.

for instance, great stress is laid on the existence of a public duty on the part of those who prepared them[1] and, in *Fowke* v. *Berington*,[2] Habbington's *Survey of Worcestershire* was excluded on the issue whether a church was the old parish church.   The book was tendered as evidence of the condition of the church when Habbington saw it in the seventeenth century and, because there was no reference to public repute, the court treated this fact as one which was not of a public nature.   The exclusion of evidence of such obvious relevance has been the subject of judicial regret,[3] but the conversion of the common law rule into a statutory provision cannot of itself effect any change in this regard.[4]

Statements in public documents constitute a vast heterogeneous mass of exceptions to the hearsay rule which are examined in section 6 of this chapter.

The fourth rule specified in s. 9 (2) does not call for comment.

B. EVIDENCE OF REPUTATION ADMISSIBLE BY VIRTUE OF S. 9 (3) (a)

S. 9 (3) (a) provides that, in any civil proceedings, a statement which tends to establish reputation or family tradition with respect to any matter and which, if the Act had not been passed, would have been admissible in evidence by virtue of the common law rules mentioned in s. 9 (4) shall be admissible by virtue of s. 9 (3) (a), in so far as it is not capable of being rendered admissible under s. 2 or s. 4.

The following are the rules mentioned in s. 9 (4):

> "Any rule of law—
>
>> (a) whereby in any civil proceedings evidence of a person's reputation is admissible for the purpose of establishing his good or bad character;
>> (b) whereby in any civil proceedings involving a question of pedigree, or the existence of a marriage is in issue, evidence of reputation or family tradition is admissible for the purpose of proving or disproving pedigree or the existence of the marriage as the case may be;
>> (c) whereby in any civil proceedings evidence of reputation or family tradition is admissible for the purpose of proving or disproving the existence of any public or general right or of identifying any person or thing."

Taylor contended that evidence of reputation had nothing to do with the hearsay rule—the immediate object of inquiry being "the concurrence of many voices which raises a presumption that the fact in which they concur is true."[5]   Hearsay statements are nontheless hearsay statements because there are many of them, but it is important to distinguish, as Taylor does, between the establishment of reputation and the use made of it when established.   Reputation is established by a witness's evidence concerning the sayings and doings of a plurality of people.   Accordingly it has been said that a witness may not narrate a single person's statement of either the fact reputed or reputation unless it is the pedigree declaration of a member of the family with regard to a genealogical issue.[6]   There is

---

[1] Contrast *A.-G.* v. *Horner* (*No.* 2), [1913] 2 Ch. 140 with *A.-G.* v. *Antrobus*, [1905]
2 Ch. 188 where, however, the duty was statutory.
[2] [1914] 2 Ch. 308.   [3] *A.-G.* v. *Horner* (*No.* 2), *supra*.
[4] Civil Evidence Act, 1968, s. 9 (6).
[5] *Law of Evidence* (12th Edition), 367.
[6] *Shedden* v. *A.-G.* (1860), 30 L. J. P. M. & A. 217.

therefore no question of an infringement of the rule against hearsay so far as the establishment of reputation is concerned, but that rule is infringed whenever reputation is tendered as evidence of the facts reputed. If a witness deposes to the existence of a tradition concerning the existence of a public right prevailing in the community, or the neighbourhood's treatment of a couple as man and wife, he is recounting the express or implied assertions of a number of other people in order to establish the truth of that which was asserted.

The above distinction is taken in s. 9 (3) (b) of the Civil Evidence Act, 1968. The subsection provides that a statement which tends to establish reputation or family tradition under the rules mentioned in s. 9 (4) shall be admissible as evidence of the matters reputed or handed down, whether tendered under s. 2 or s. 4, or by virtue of s. 9 (3) (a); but, if the subsection had stopped there, it would have been difficult to tender reputation as evidence of the matters reputed under s. 2 or s. 4. As reputation is a multiplicity of statements, how could the notice procedure be applied? How could it be made clear whether the statements were first or second hand hearsay? To meet such difficulties s. 9 (3) (b) provides that, for the purposes of Part I of the Act, reputation shall be treated as a fact and not as a statement, or multiplicity of statements.

The result is that there will be many cases in which statements proving reputation can be given in evidence under s. 2 or s. 4 as tending to establish the facts reputed. For example, if A. deceased told B. that, according to the tradition prevailing in the locality of X., Y. land was common land, or that, according to the tradition prevailing in the A. family, his grandmother was illegitimate, these statements of fact could be proved by B. as evidence that Y. was common land, or that A.'s grandmother was illegitimate, under s. 2 of the 1968 Act. Very often, however, evidence of this nature will be in the form of a statement by A. deceased to B. that sundry deceased elders of X. had told him that Y. was common land, and s. 9 (3) was enacted to meet such cases.

Nothing need be said about evidence of character, but reference must be made to the matters of pedigree and public or general rights mentioned in s. 9 (4) because, at common law, they are the subject of technical requirements some of which will very probably be held to have survived the Act.

(1) Pedigree

At common law there is an exception to the hearsay rule under which the oral or written declarations of deceased persons, or declarations to be inferred from family conduct, are, subject to the conditions of admissibility mentioned below, admissible as evidence of pedigree. The evidence often takes the form of direct assertions of fact, as in the old leading case of *Goodright d. Stevens* v. *Moss*[1] where the question was whether a child was the legitimate offspring of its parents (since deceased), and Lord MANSFIELD admitted the parents' declarations, proved by the persons to whom they were made, to the effect that the child was born before their marriage. Such declarations would now, like any other first hand hearsay statement, be admissible under s. 2 of the 1968 Act. Lord MANSFIELD said that tradi-

---

[1] (1777), 2 Cowp. 591; *Murray* v. *Milner* (1879), 12 Ch. D. 845; *Re Turner, Glenister* v. *Harding* (1885), 29 Ch. D. 985.

tion is sufficient in point of pedigree, and referred to the treatment of a child as illegitimate (a matter which is best regarded as original evidence), an entry in a family bible, an inscription on a tombstone and a pedigree hung up in the family mansion. Without undue strain of language, the inscription on the tombstone could be proved under s. 2 of the Act as a statement made in a document by someone who cannot be identified or found. Whether the entry in the family bible or the hanging pedigree would be admissible under s. 2 would depend on the form of the statement to be given in evidence, but, and this is particularly true of the hanging pedigree, they might well have to be tendered as evidence of family tradition under s. 9 because second or third hand hearsay would be involved. Lord ELDON said that the tradition must prevail among persons having such a connection with the person to whom it relates that it is natural and likely, from their domestic habits and connections, that they are speaking the truth and could not be mistaken;[1] but this is a matter of weight rather than admissibility, although it is clear that, in order to be admissible, the tradition must be family tradition, and not, for example, that prevailing among the neighbours.

The common law conditions of admissibility of pedigree statements or, to employ the more usual word "declarations" are:

(i) that the declarant should have been dead;

(ii) that the declarations should relate to a question of pedigree, i.e. have a genealogical purpose;[2]

(iii) that the declarant should have been a blood relation, or the spouse of a blood relation, of the person whose pedigree is in issue;[3] and

(iv) that the declaration should have been made before the dispute in which it is tendered had arisen.[4]

All these conditions are now irrelevant so far as declarations of fact, as distinct from reputation, are concerned, provided they can be rendered admissible under s. 2. For example, the issue being A.'s legitimacy, A.'s mother writes to B. from America to say that she has heard of the dispute and may as well state the truth, viz. that she never married A.'s deceased father; the mother's statement is admissible under s. 2 as one made in a document by a person who is overseas. If the issue is whether the defendant to an action for breach of contract is an infant, an affidavit sworn by his deceased father in relation to another case is admissible, although the question is not one of pedigree.[5] If the issue is which of the twins C. and D. is the elder, the statement of a deceased nurse that she was present at the birth and marked C.'s foot as that of the first born may be proved under s. 2 by the person to whom it was made.[6]

---

[1] *Whitelocke* v. *Baker* (1807), 13 Ves. 510 at p. 514.

[2] *Haines* v. *Guthrie* (1884), 13 Q. B. D. 818; cf. *Hood* v. *Beauchamp* (1836), 2 Sim. 26 and *Shields* v. *Boucher* (1847), 1 De. G. & Sm. 40.

[3] *Johnson* v. *Lawson* (1824), 2 Bing. 86; *Shrewsbury Peerage Case* (1858), 7 H. L. C. 1, at p. 23; *Berkeley Peerage Case* (1811), 4 Camp. 401; on problems of legitimacy and legitimation see *Hitchins* v. *Eardley* (1871), L. R. 2 P. & D. 248; *Re Jenion, Jenion* v. *Wynne*, [1952] Ch. 454; [1952] 1 All E. R. 1228; *Re Perton, Pearson* v. *A.-G.* (1885), 53 L. T. 707; *Re Davy*, [1935] P. 1, followed in *Battle* v. *A.-G.*, [1949] P. 358. See also *Monkton* v. *A.-G.* (1831), 2 Ruff. & M. 147 and *B.* v. *A.-G.*, [1965] P. 278; [1965] 1 All E. R. 62.

[4] *Berkeley Peerage Case, supra.*

[5] Cf. *Haines* v. *Guthrie, supra.*

[6] Cf. *Johnson* v. *Lawson, supra.*

It is therefore only in a very restricted sense that s. 9 can be said to have preserved this common law exception to the hearsay rule. A statement tending to establish family reputation or tradition which would, but for the Act, have been admissible for the purpose of proving pedigree is only admissible by virtue of s. 9 if the common law conditions of admissibility are satisfied. Accordingly, if A.'s deceased father told him that his deceased father had often said that, according to family tradition, his grandfather only had one child, A. may prove these statements under s. 9, although they would be inadmissible as hearsay upon hearsay under s. 2; but if A.'s father had made these statements to B. a stranger, B. could not prove them under s. 8, and they would still be inadmissible under s. 2. On the other hand, if C. could prove that D., a deceased retainer of the X. family, had told him that, according to the family tradition X.'s grandfather was illegitimate, it seems that, although the statement would be inadmissible by virtue of s. 9, because inadmissible at common law as it was not the statement of a blood relation, the statement may be proved under s. 2, since s. 9 (3) (b) permits reputation to be treated as a question of fact if given in evidence under Part I.

Nothing need be said about evidence of reputation to establish the existence of a marriage where no question of pedigree is involved for this simply refers to the proof of a marriage by proof of the basiç fact of the presumption mentioned on p. 122. What must be proved is general reputation among neighbours etc., and there is no question of the survival of any common law restrictions concerning the persons by whose statements it may be proved, and the issues on which it is permissible to establish a marriage in this way.

(2) Public or General Rights

At common law an oral or written declaration by a deceased person concerning the reputed existence of a public or general right is admissible as evidence of the existence of such right provided the declaration was made before the dispute in which it is tendered had arisen, and, in the case of a statement concerning the reputed existence of a general right, provided the declarant had competent knowledge.

A public right is one affecting the entire population, such as a claim to tolls on a public highway,[1] a right of ferry,[2] or the right to treat part of a river bank as a public landing place.[3] Declarations by deceased persons tending to prove or disprove the existence of such rights are admissible at common law, and evidence of this nature is received on cognate questions such as the boundaries between counties and parishes,[4] and the question whether a road is public or private.[5]

A general right is one that affects a class of persons such as the inhabitants of a particular district, the tenants of a manor, or the owners of certain plots of land. Examples are rights of common,[6] the rights of corporations[7] and a custom of mining in a particular district.[8] The distinction from public

---

[1] *Brett* v. *Beales* (1830), 10 B. & C. 508.
[2] *Pim* v. *Curell* (1840), 6 M. & W. 234.
[3] *Drinkwater* v. *Porter* (1835), 7 C. & P. 181.
[4] *Brisco* v. *Lomax* (1838), 8 Ad. & El. 198; *Evans* v. *Rees* (1839), 10 Ad. & El. 151.
[5] *R.* v. *Bliss* (1837), 2 Nev. & P. K. B. 464.
[6] *Evans* v. *Merthyr Tydfil U.D.C.*, [1899] 1 Ch. 241.
[7] *Davies* v. *Morgan* (1831), 1 Cr. & J. 587.
[8] *Crease* v. *Barrett* (1835), 1 Cr. M. & R. 919.

rights is not precise and only important, if important at all, because it has been said that no evidence of competent knowledge of the subject-matter of the reputed right on the part of the declarant is necessary when the right is public because, "in a matter in which all are concerned, reputation from anyone appears to be receivable; but of course it would be almost worthless unless it came from persons who were shown to have some means of knowledge as by living in the neighbourhood, or frequently using the road in dispute." If, however, the alleged right is a general one, such as a mining right under certain land, "hearsay from any person wholly unconnected with the place in which the mines are found, would not only be of no value, but probably altogether inadmissible."[1]

A far more crucial distinction is that between public or general rights on the one hand and private rights on the other hand, for the latter cannot be proved by evidence of reputation.[2] But here again the distinction is none too precise, all that can be said is that a public or general right must be enjoyed by the claimant as a member of the public or as a member of some clearly defined class. Evidence of reputation is admissible when private and public rights coincide, as when the boundaries between two estates are coterminous with those between two hamlets.[3]

The common law conditions of admissibility of hearsay statements concerning reputed public or general rights are:

(i) the death of the declarant;
(ii) that the declaration should have been made before the dispute in which it is tendered;[4] and
(iii) that the declaration should concern the reputed existence of the right as opposed to a particular fact from which the existence of the right may be inferred.[5]

This last requirement marks a great distinction between the admissibility of pedigree declarations and the admissibility of declarations concerning public or general rights. In the case of each the declarant must be dead, and the statement must have been made before the dispute arose; but, whereas proof of reputation is only one way of establishing pedigree by hearsay at common law, it is the only way of doing so in the case of public or general rights.

All the above conditions must be fulfilled if evidence of the reputed existence of such rights is to be admissible by virtue of s. 9 of the Civil Evidence Act, 1968; but is this true of a statement which can, by virtue of s. 9 (3) (b) be treated as a statement of fact and thereby rendered admissible

---

[1] *Crease* v. *Barrett, supra;* see also *Rogers* v. *Wood* (1831), 2 B. & Ad. 245. Even in the case of a general right, the declarant need not be proved to have been resident in the neighbourhood (*Duke of Newcastle* v. *Broxtowe Hundred* (1832), 4 B. & Ad. 273.

[2] *R.* v. *Antrobus* (1835), 2 Ad. & El. 788; *Talbot* v. *Lewis* (1834), 1 Cr. M. & R. 495; *Lord Dunraven* v. *Llewellyn* (1850), 15 Q. D. 791 (see *Evans* v. *Merthyr Tydfil U.D.C.,* [1899] 1 Ch. 241, for the limits of this decision); *White* v. *Taylor,* [1969] 1 Ch. 150; [1967] 3 All E. R. 349.

[3] *Thomas* v. *Jenkins* (1837), 6 Ad. & El. 525.

[4] *Berkeley Peerage Case* (1811), 4 Camp. 401; the fact that the declaration was made to provide against future controversy does not affect its admissibility, nor does the existence of a general motive to misrepresent (*Moseley* v. *Davies* (1822), 11 Price 162) but see the judgment of JOYCE, J., in *Brocklebank* v. *Thompson,* [1903] 2 Ch. 344 where, however, the remarks about interested persons were *obiter.*

[5] *R.* v. *Lordsmere* (*Inhabitants*) (1886), 16 Cox, C.C. 65 (conviction for non-repair evidence road public.)

by virtue of s. 2? For example, if A., formerly the oldest inhabitant of a village, were to write from America, after a dispute had arisen concerning rights of common, stating that, according to the tradition which had prevailed in the village community, those rights were only enjoyed by the occupiers of certain lands, could A.'s statement be received under s. 2 as one made in a document by someone who is overseas? It is submitted that the answer is in the affirmative because the exclusion of statements made after a dispute has arisen is a common law restriction on the reception of hearsay under a particular exception to the hearsay rule and it has suffered the same fate as other restrictions on the admissibility of hearsay evidence at common law. Evidence of reputation is second hand hearsay and this would be inadmissible under s. 2 were it not for s. 9 (3) (b), but that subsection authorises the treatment of reputation as a matter of fact for the purposes of all of Part I of the 1968 Act.

A further, and possibly more difficult, question relates to the effect of the Act on the third common law condition of admissibility, that the declaration should concern the reputed existence of the right as opposed to a particular fact from which it might be inferred. In the past this has produced decisions of breathtaking absurdity. For example, in *Mercer* v. *Denne*,[1] the issue was whether the fishermen of Walmer had a customary right of immemorial antiquity to dry their nets on part of the foreshore. In support of the contention that the custom would not have existed throughout the relevant period, a survey, depositions and old maps were produced. They showed that the sea had run over the portion of foreshore in respect of which the customary right was claimed, but they were rejected because they amounted to statements of particular facts and had nothing to do with the reputed existence of the custom. Is the condition of admissibility under consideration simply a common law restriction on the reception of hearsay under an exception to the general rule excluding such evidence, or is it an independent rule, which can equally well be described as one of evidence or substantive law, which has survived the virtual abolition of the hearsay rule in civil cases? Perhaps it would be rash to predict the courts' answer to this question, but it is to be hoped that *Mercer* v. *Denne* and the congerie of similar decisions have not survived the Civil Evidence Act, 1968. The survey, depositions and old maps appear to have been documents in which statements were made by persons who could, if living, have given direct oral evidence with regard to the condition of the foreshore.

Whatever view may ultimately be taken by the courts on the matters mentioned above, some of the absurd results of past decisions will be avoided for the future, so far as rights of way are concerned, on account of the provisions of the Highways Act, 1959, s. 35.[2] The section provides that any map, plan or history of a locality is admissible to show whether a way has or has not been dedicated as a highway, or the date when such dedication took place. Such weight is to be given to the above documents as the court considers justified by the circumstances, including the antiquity of the document, the status of the person by whom it was made, its

---

[1] [1905] 2 Ch. 538; see also *R.* v. *Bliss* (1837), 7 Ad. & El. 550; *R.* v. *Berger*, [1894] 1 Q. B. 823; and *A.-G.* v. *Horner* (*No. 2*), [1913] 2 Ch. 140.
[2] Re-enacting the Rights of Way Act, 1932. See also National Parks Access to the Countryside Act, 1949.

purpose, and the custody in which it was kept or from which it was produced.

SECTION 4. CRITICISMS AND COMPARISONS

Since admissions and statements in public documents, discussed in the next two sections, are admissible in civil proceedings by virtue of s. 9 of the Civil Evidence Act, 1968, it is arguable that anything in the nature of a general appraisal of that Act should be deferred until they have been discussed; but, although it may well prove to be a permanent measure, s. 9 is so obviously meant to be a temporary provision, pending the codification of the law of evidence, that this seems to be the best place for a brief assessment of the merits of the 1968 Act.

It would be hard to maintain that the Act provides a perfect solution to the hearsay problem, but it is submitted that the solution it does provide is the best that has appeared to date. After some criticisms have been considered, an attempt will be made to justify the above submission by reference to the United States Federal Rules. It must be confessed, however, that it would be unwise to set too much store by a solution to the hearsay problem which only applies to civil cases; the great merit of the American solutions is that they also apply to criminal proceedings.

A. CRITICISMS

Reference has already been made to what are little more than points of drafting on which it would be possible to improve. These include the desirability of some clarification of the concept of a statement "made in a document",[1] the difficulty of applying s. 2 literally to cases, such as probate actions, will construction summonses and claims under the Fatal Accidents Acts, in which the death of the testator or victim of the tort whose statement a party might wish to tender as evidence of a fact of which "direct oral evidence by [the maker] would be admissible", is a condition precedent to the bringing of the action,[2] and the need for some clarification with regard to implied assertions.[3] The criticisms of s. 5, which deals with computerised records, are more than a matter of drafting, and it does seem that some clarification is called for, not to mention the simplification on the lines of the South Australian statute.[4] The merits of the virtual exclusion of secondhand hearsay, other than that contained in records, are also something more than a mere matter of drafting. Many people no doubt consider the policy of the Act to be sound in this regard, but there are also those who would argue for an unrestricted reception of hearsay evidence.[5]

A criticism which has not yet been mentioned concerns the somewhat elaborate notice procedure. The point is frequently made that parties are not always so advanced in their preparations for trial as to be able to give notice within the prescribed time (usually 21 days before the hearing). It certainly does seem somewhat superfluous to require notice of desire to give a statement in evidence in cases in which the maker is to be called as a witness, the leave of the court for the reception of the statement being

---

[1] P. 426, *ante.*   [2] P. 429, *ante.*   [3] P. 430, *ante.*
[4] P. 434, *ante.*   [5] P. 417, *ante.*

required in any event; but this point can be met by a generous exercise of the court's discretion such as that which occurred in *Morris* v. *Stratford-on-Avon U.D.C.*[1] When the maker of the statement is not to be called as a witness, the argument in favour of an obligation to give notice of desire to give the statement in evidence, if it is to be admissible as of right, is far stronger; but even here, when the statement is contained in a record, a case can be made out for a more relaxed rule. We shall see that, under the Criminal Evidence Act, 1965, trade and business records are admissible in criminal cases without any requirement of notice. As we have seen,[2] many statements admissible under s. 2 of the 1968 Act are also admissible as records under s. 4. If records were to be exempt from the notice procedure contemplated by the 1968 Act, the term might have to be restrictively defined.

B. THE FEDERAL RULES[3]

There are four possible solutions to the hearsay problem. The first is to assume that, generally speaking, all is well with the present law, leaving it to the courts to make such modifications as the occasion demands; but, as we have seen, such a solution could only be adopted in England if it were assumed that no modifications will be called for, because the House of Lords has, by a majority, set itself against the creation of further common law exceptions to the hearsay rule.[4] The second is to rationalise the existing exceptions by legislation, and to create new ones by the same means. This course has been adopted in the United States. It has much to commend it, notably continuity with the common law; but it does tend to produce a most unwieldy list of exceptions. There are no less than 31 in the Uniform Rules, and, though the arrangement is more logical and has more regard to practical convenience, we shall see that there are in effect as many in the Federal Rules. The third possible solution is that adopted by the Civil Evidence Act, 1968, the partial abolition of the rule permitting, subject to safeguards, first hand hearsay statements to be proved in all cases in which the maker is unavailable, by permitting, subject to the discretion of the court, all such statements to be proved when the maker is called, and by allowing for the reception of a fairly wide class of second hand hearsay statements. The fourth solution is that of total abolition: hearsay, however remote, would, in theory, be admissible without restriction. Nothing more need be said about this solution, although its adoption would bring English procedure into line with that of western Europe where, so far as is known, the theoretically unrestricted admissibility of hearsay causes no great difficulty.

After giving a definition of hearsay like that adopted in this book,[5] R. 801 of the Federal Rules provides that certain statements are not to be treated as hearsay. These are the previous inconsistent statements of witnesses, previous consistent statements rebutting fabrication or proving identification soon after the perception of the person identified, and a

---

[1] P. 424, *ante.*   [2] P. 431, *ante.*

[3] The following comments are based on the version published in 34 L. Ed. (2d) No. 5 (January 5th, 1973).

[4] *Myers* v. *Director of Public Prosecutions*, [1965] A. C. 1002; [1964] 1 All E. R. 877.

[5] " 'Hearsay' is a statement, other than one made by the declarant while testifying at the trial or hearing, offered in evidence to prove the truth of the matter asserted."

party's admissions. A general ban on the reception of hearsay is then followed by two groups of exceptions. The first group comprises situations in which hearsay statements are admissible although the maker is available. It includes statements made for the purpose of medical diagnosis or treatment, and the number of situations in this group is no less than 23. Hearsay statements included in the second group are admissible only if the maker is unavailable. There are five of them, one being "a statement . . . which narrates, describes, or explains an event or condition recently perceived by the declarant, made in good faith, not in contemplation of pending or anticipated litigation in which he was interested, and while his recollection was clear." Each group of exceptions concludes with "a statement not specifically covered by any of the foregoing exceptions but having comparable circumstantial guarantees of trustworthiness," an interesting provision leaving the development of the law to the courts.

It does scant justice to a carefully thought out set of rules to point to two situations where, it is submitted, the statements ought to be admissible, and yet they are not admissible; but such situations are almost bound to arise whenever the hearsay problem is dealt with by a general prohibition followed by a number of specific exceptions, instead of being followed by a general permission with qualifications. The situations in question are first, that which arose in *Morris* v. *Stratford-on-Avon U.D.C.*[1] in which a witness unexpectedly gave confused and inconsistent evidence, and second, the case in which the maker of the statement has not perceived the event described in it recently. Someone age 20 tells his friend that he vividly remembers how, on his 16th birthday, his father hit his mother. It is absurd not to allow the friend to prove this statement as evidence of the assault if the maker is not available.

Finally, it should be stressed that the Federal Rules are in some respects much laxer than the Civil Evidence Act with regard to the admissibility of hearsay. Statements made for the purpose of medical diagnosis by someone who is available as a witness ought never to be admissible as of right unless he is called. It is just the kind of case where "truth will out" in cross-examination if it has not already come out in the examination-in-chief.

SECTION 5. ADMISSIONS

Statements adverse to the maker's case are received as proof of the truth of their contents in civil and criminal proceedings. When made to a person in authority over a criminal prosecution, they are subject to special conditions of admissibility on account of the requirement that they must have been voluntary, and they are spoken of as confessions. When disserving statements are made by a party to civil litigation, or, in a criminal case, by the accused to someone who is not in authority, they are said to be admissions and must be distinguished from the formal admissions which may be made for the purposes of particular proceedings and were discussed in Chapter VII. Formal admissions bind the party by whom they were made, but the informal admissions we are about to consider may always be contradicted or explained away by their maker[2] when it is for the tribunal of

---

[1] P. 431, *ante*; or the witness may have become senile since he made the statement as in *Harvey* v. *Smith-Wood*, [1964] 2 Q. B. 171; [1963] 2 All E. R. 127, a decision on the Evidence Act, 1938.
[2] See, for example, *Smith* v. *Smith*, [1957] 2 All E. R. 397.

fact to determine the weight to be attached to them. They may constitute the sole, though sufficient evidence in support of a civil judgment,[1] or even a conviction of crime.[2]

This section is confined to admissions. As we have seen, they are admissible in civil cases by virtue of s. 9 (1) of the Civil Evidence Act, 1968. In that context, an admission "includes any representation of fact whether made in words or otherwise,[3] so long as it is adverse to the party against whom it is tendered and made by him or someone in privity with him. Conduct which was not intended to amount to a representation may constitute circumstantial evidence against the agent because it warrants an inference of consciousness of guilt or the weakness of a party's case, as when he suborns witnesses,[4] or remains silent when a denial of things said against him could reasonably have been expected.[5]

When considering the following account of the common law, the reader should bear in mind the possibility that, although a statement does not qualify for reception as a common law admission by virtue of s. 9 (1), it may yet be possible to give it in evidence under s. 2 or s. 4 of the 1968 Act. This would of course entail notice of desire to do so, with the possibility of a counter-notice which might require the opposite party to be called as a witness, but there will always be the further possibility of the court's exercising its discretion either to admit the statement although no notice has been served, or to dispense with compliance with the counter-notice. From the point of view of the party wishing to give it in evidence, the advantage of a statement's coming within the category of admissions is that it can be given in evidence as of right without the necessity of going through the notice procedure.

Admissions by words may be made in any form and any circumstances. In *R. v. Simons*,[6] for instance, it was proposed, on a charge of arson, to call a witness to prove what the prisoner said to his wife on leaving the magistrate's room after committal, and ALDERSON, B., allowed the witness to be called because "What a person is overheard saying to his wife, or even saying to himself, is evidence".

A verbal admission may be proved although it concerns the contents of a document which is not produced in circumstances in which secondary evidence would be inadmissible. In *Slatterie* v. *Pooley*,[7] the plaintiff sued on a covenant indemnifying him against debts set out in the schedule to a deed which was inadmissible for want of a proper stamp. An oral admission by the defendant that a certain debt was included in the schedule was received because, according to PARKE, B.:

"The reason why such parol statements are admissible, without notice to produce, or accounting for the absence of the written instrument, is that they are not open to the same objection which belongs to parol evidence from other

---

[1] *M'Kewen* v. *Cotching* (1857), 27 L. J. Ex. 41.
[2] *R. v. Sullivan* (1887), 16 Cox C. C. 347, an Irish case in which the English authorities are reviewed; *McKay* v. *R.* (1936), 54 C. L. R. 1.
[3] Civil Evidence Act, 1968, s. 9 (2).
[4] *Moriarty* v. *London Chatham and Dover Rail. Co.* (1870), L. R. 5 Q. B. 314; *R. v. Watt* (1905), 20 Cox C. C. 852.
[5] *Bessela* v. *Stern* (1877), 2 C. P. D. 265; cf. *Wiedemann* v. *Walpole*, [1891] 2 Q. B. 534; and, for an example in a criminal case, see *R. v. Watt* (1905), 20 Cox C. C. 852.
[6] (1834), 6 C. & P. 540; Cf. *Rumping* v. *Director of Public Prosecutions*, [1962] 3 All E. R. 256; *R. v. Foll* (1957), 25 C. R. 69 (tape recording). An infant's admissions are evidence against him (*Alderman* v. *Alderman & Dunn*, [1958] 1 All E. R. 391).
[7] (1840), 6 M. & W. 664.

sources, where the written evidence might have been produced; but such evidence is excluded from the presumption of its untruth, arising from the very nature of the case, where better evidence is withheld; whereas what a party himself admits to be true, may reasonably be presumed to be so."

The decision has been criticised because it flouts the best evidence rule and ignores the danger of inaccuracy attendant on the repetition of an admission,[1] but the foregoing quotation seems to provide an adequate answer to the first point, and ample allowance was made by PARKE, B., for the second when he added "the weight and value of such testimony is quite another question".

The fact that an admission was made under threats or in consequence of other pressures may greatly affect its weight, but does not appear to render it inadmissible. Thus it has been held in British Columbia that, in an action on an insurance policy, an admission of arson may be proved against the plaintiff although it was made in circumstances in which it would have been inadmissible as a confession on a criminal charge.[2] It should be borne in mind, however, that the rules of evidence may be waived by the parties to civil cases, and this may mean that an admission made pursuant to an agreement not to use it in evidence would be inadmissible.

A. CONDITIONS OF ADMISSIBILITY

An admission being any statement, express or implied, oral or written, which is adverse to a party's case, the only conditions of admissibility, when the statement emanates from the party himself concern the capacity in which he is acting and the reception of the entirety of the statement; there is also the question whether he must have had personal knowledge of the facts stated. When these matters have been considered, it will be necessary to say something about cases in which the statement does not directly emanate from the party himself. These cases give rise to problems relating to statements made in the presence of the parties, documents found in the possession of the parties and vicarious admissions.

(1) CAPACITY OF THE PARTY

If someone sues or is sued in a personal capacity, admissions made by him when acting in a representative capacity, as when he was litigating as guardian of an infant,[3] my be proved against him; but, when he is litigating in a representative capacity, admissions that would affect him in his personal capacity may not be proved against him. Thus, in *Legge* v. *Edmonds*,[4] a mother had made statements which could have been received as evidence of her adultery if she had been sued personally, and it was held that they were inadmissible in proceedings brought against her as administratrix of her late husband's estate in which proceedings the legitimacy of her child was in issue. The common law rule was justified by the broader principle that persons other than the maker of an admission ought not to be bound

---

[1] *Lawless* v. *Queale* (1845), 8 I. L. R. 382; Taylor's *Law of Evidence* (12th edition), vol. i, 286.

[2] *Jogender Singh, Bains* v. *Yorkshire Insurance Co., Ltd.* (1936), 38 D. L. R. (2d.) 417.

[3] *Beasley* v. *McGrath* (1804), 2 Sch. & Lef. 31; *Stanton* v. *Percival* (1855), 5 H. L. Cas. 257.

[4] (1855), 25 L. J. Ch. 125, at p. 141.

by it. Granted that this is a valid principle, it would clearly be improper to allow those represented by the maker of an admission to be affected by it, at any rate when it did not concern a matter in which his and their interest was identical; but the justification was no different from the justification of the hearsay rule on the ground that the statement could not be contradicted or questioned by the other party when it was made, and it could now be rendered admissible under s. 2 of the 1968 Act.

(2) Reception of Entire Statement

When a statement contains items favourable to a party's case in addition to the admission, the party relying on the latter cannot prevent the other items from being proved. Accordingly, the debit side of an account may be tendered as an admission against one party, but this will mean that the credit side may be treated as evidence against his adversary.[1] The self-serving nature of the parts of a statement that are favourable to the maker of an admission will no doubt affect their weight but there seems to be no reason why they should not be treated as evidence of the truth of that which they assert.[2]

(3) The Question of Personal Knowledge

In *Customs Comptroller* v. *Western Electric Co.*[3] the Judicial Committee held that an admission that goods were manufactured in the United States based solely on the markings to that effect on the goods was of no more value than the markings themselves which were inadmissible hearsay. "If a man admits something of which he knows nothing it is of no real evidential value."[4] It would be wrong to infer from this that personal knowledge of the facts admitted is a condition of admissibility. A witness has been allowed to narrate a party's statement of his own age as evidence of that fact[5] although it is not a matter of which the party could be said to have had personal knowledge. Even a party's assertion that he believes what his agent told him to be true may constitute evidence against him.[6] It seems that admissions which are not based on personal knowledge are technically admissible, although they may often have to be treated as devoid of evidential value. There must, however, be some evidence of belief in, or acceptance of, the fact admitted.[7]

B. STATEMENTS IN THE PRESENCE OF A PARTY

A statement made in the presence of a party is admissible evidence of its truth to the extent that it is expressly or impliedly admitted by the party's words or conduct. This principle is easy to state, and it is only necessary to refer to cases such as *Bessela* v. *Stern*[8] in which the defendant's

---

[1] *Harrison* v. *Turner* (1847), 10 Q. B. 482.
[2] *Smith* v. *Blandy* (1825), Ry. & M. 257, at p. 259.
[3] [1966] A. C. 367; [1965] 3 All E. R. 599.
[4] *Per* Lord HODSON at p. 601.
[5] *R.* v. *Turner*, [1910] 1 K. B. 346, at p. 362; see also *R.* v. *Jones* (1933), 24 Cr. App. Rep. 55.
[6] *Lustre Hosiery, Ltd.* v. *York* (1936), 54 C. L. R. 134.
[7] *Roe d. Lord Trimlestown* v. *Kemmis* (1843), 9 Cl. & Fin. 749; *Bulley* v. *Bulley* (1884), 9 Ch. Ap. 739.
[8] (1877), 2 C. P. D. 265.

offer of money to the plaintiff to enable her to go away was treated as an admission of her allegation that he had always promised to marry her. The statement is not evidence of the truth of its contents; it is only admissible as an introduction to the conduct of the party against whom it is tendered. That conduct may be evidence of an admission or acceptance of the statement, or it may be relevant for some such other reason as the fact that it amounted to a denial of the truth of the statement which was subsequently admitted; the case is one of conditional admissibility.[1] Almost all the authorities are criminal cases and, for this reason, they are discussed in the next chapter.[2]

C. DOCUMENTS IN THE POSSESSION OR CONTROL OF A PARTY

The fact that documents were found in the possession of a party may be proved for a variety of purposes. So far as the present inquiry is concerned, the only question is the extent to which they may be received as evidence against the party of the truth of their contents. On principle, a strong case should be necessary for the reception of the document for such a purpose, and this may account for the paucity of authority on the subject. Such as there is certainly warrants Professor Baker's conclusion that it is difficult to prove an admission against a party by his mere possession of the documents of a third person.[3] If it is clear that a party had access to and control over the contents of a document, they may be proved against him as evidence of their truth. In *Alderson* v. *Clay*,[4] for instance, the books of a society of which the defendant was a member were received as evidence that a purchase of goods was duly authorised with the result that he was liable to the vendor. Perhaps it is on the ground that he exercises some control over their contents that affidavits by a third person used by a party to legal proceedings may be tendered as evidence against him in subsequent proceedings,[5] but this may be treated as a vicarious admission.

D. VICARIOUS ADMISSIONS[6]

Admissions by those in privity with a party to litigation may be given in evidence against him. The phrase "in privity" as used here is not a technical term. It includes predecessors in title, referees, all manner of agents and sundry other miscellaneous cases. The statements received under these heads were generally against the interest of the declarants when they were made, and no doubt they would have been covered by another of the common law exceptions to the hearsay rule relating to declarations against interest discussed in the next chapter had this not come to be restricted in two important respects—the requirement that the maker of the statement must be dead when it is tendered, and the rule that the statement must have been against his pecuniary or proprietary interest when made. As things are, it must be frankly recognised that

---

[1] P. 24, *ante.*

[2] *R.* v. *Christie*, [1914] A. C. 545 is the leading case. For an example of the application of the principle in a civil case, see *Chantler* v. *Bromley* (1921), 14 B. W. C. C. 14. ⵊ

[3] Baker, The Hearsay Rule, 43.   [4] (1816), 1 Stark. 405.

[5] *Brickell* v. *Hulse* (1837), 7 Ad. & El. 454; *Richards* v. *Morgan* (1863), 4 B. & S. 641. *Saunders* v. *Saunders*, [1965] P. 499 (retention of letter from third party evidence of retainer's state of mind, but not of truth of contents).

[6] Hanbury, *Principles of Agency*, Chapter 10; Fridman, *The Law of Agency*, Chapter 20; Morgan, *The Rationale of Vicarious Admissions*, 42 H. L. R. 461.

there is no single rational basis for the reception of vicarious admissions as the subject is one in relation to which it is difficult to distinguish rules of substantive law from rules of evidence.

It will be convenient to begin by mentioning two important cases in which there is no privity between the maker of the statement and the party against whom it is tendered, so that it cannot be received as a vicarious admission. After this has been done, the standard examples of such admissions will be mentioned.

(1) CASES IN WHICH THER IS NO PRIVITY

(i) **Co-defendants, etc.**—The out-of-court admission of a co-defendant, co-plaintiff or co-accused is not admissible evidence against his fellow party to the litigation by virtue of the mere fact that they are joint parties or said to be jointly involved in a particular transaction. This principle applies in all cases, but is most vividly illustrated by its application to divorce proceedings where, as we saw when discussing the principle of multiple admissibility in Chapter I, the result was that in a divorce case there might be a finding that A. committed adultery with B. on account of A.'s extra-judicial admission, although there was no finding that B. committed adultery with A. because the admission came within the rule against hearsay and outside any exception to it so far as B. was concerned.[1]

Wigmore characterised the conclusion as "perfectly logical, but also perfectly and absurdly artificial".[2] A.'s statement could now be rendered admissible against B. under s. 2 of the Civil Evidence Act, 1968, by the service of the appropriate notice by the petitioner.[3]

(ii) **Party and witness in former proceedings.**—We have seen that affidavits of third persons used by a party in former proceedings may be received as evidence against him in subsequent litigation. The authorities on this subject were said to be in an uncertain and unsatisfactory condition by ATKIN, L.J., in *British Thomson-Houston Co., Ltd.* v. *British Insulated and Helsby Cables, Ltd.*[4] In that case the majority of the Court of Appeal decided that a transcript of the oral testimony of a witness, called by the plaintiffs in former proceedings, could not be tendered in evidence against them in the litigation before the court merely because the testimony was that of a witness upon whose evidence reliance had previously been placed by the plaintiffs. ATKIN, L.J., conceded that, in different circumstances, the transcript might have been admissible as evidence of the plaintiff's knowledge of a particular fact, or, had this been the case, on the footing that the witness was the plaintiffs' agent in the transaction to which he deposed.[5] The decision in the *British Thomson-Houston* case may in due course be applied to affidavits, but, until this is done, the authorities on the latter subject necessitate the treatment of a third person's affidavit used by a party in previous proceedings as a species of admission so far as subsequent litigation is concerned. The point is somewhat academic since, in both cases, resort will now normally be had to the provisions of the Civil Evidence Act, 1968, concerning the admissibility of statements

---

[1] *Morton* v. *Morton, Daly and McNaught,* [1937] P. 151; [1937] 2 All E. R. 470; *Rutherford* v. *Richardson,* [1923] A. C. 1.
[2] IV Wigmore, p. 117.
[3] P. 428, *ante*; for undefended divorces see *Practice Direction,* [1973] 3 All E. R. 180.
[4] [1924] 2 Ch. 160, at p. 168.
[5] At p. 170.

made in former proceedings,[1] although the point might become less academic if the court were minded to exercise its exclusionary discretion in the case of the affidavit.

(2) PREDECESSORS IN TITLE

The statement of a predecessor in title of a party to the litigation in which it is tendered is admissible evidence against him provided it relates to the title and was made when the maker had the interest qualified by the statement.[2] This rule appears to be the outcome of the substantive law under which no better title is acquired than that which was enjoyed by the predecessor. The limitations on the rule should be noted. The successor is not, as such, bound by his predecessor's admissions which do not concern the title, nor is he affected by a statement of a predecessor who had parted with his interest in the property when it was made.

(3) REFEREES

Statements made by someone to whom a party has referred others for information may be proved against him as admissions concerning the subject-matter of the reference. In *Williams* v. *Innes*,[3] the defendants were executors of a deceased's estate. They referred the plaintiff to one Ross for information concerning the assets, and it was held that that which Ross said could be proved against the defendants for:

> "If a man refers another upon any particular business to a third person, he is bound by what this third person says or does concerning it, as much as if that had been said or done by himself".

Similarly, if a defendant claims to retain goods on behalf of a named person, that person's statements become admissible evidence for the plaintiff in conversion.[4]

(4) AGENTS

(i) Agents' admissions in general.—Statements made by an agent within the scope of his authority to third persons during the continuance of the agency may be received as admissions against his principal in litigation to which the latter is a party. So far as the reception of admissions is concerned, the scope of authority is a strictly limited conception. It is sometimes said that the agent must be authorised to make the admission, but that is a confusing statement for admissions are often received although no one was expressly or impliedly authorised to make them. A better way of putting the matter is to say that the admission must have been made by the agent as part of a conversation or other communication which he was authorised to have with a third party. The authority to have such conversations or make such communications is frequently not co-terminous with an authority to act on behalf of the principal[5]—a point which has an important bearing on the limited extent to which a servant's admissions

---

[1] P. 428, *ante.*
[2] *Woolway* v. *Rowe* (1834), 1 Ad. & El. 114; *Falcon* v. *Famous Players Film Co., Ltd.,* [1926] 2 K. B. 474.
[3] (1808), 1 Camp. 364; *Daniel* v. *Pitt* (1806), 1 Camp. at p. 369; *R.* v. *Mallory* (1884), 13 Q. B. D. 33.
[4] *Harrison* v. *Vallance* (1822), 1 Bing. 45.
[5] See *Scott* v. *Fernhill Stud Poultry Farm Pty., Ltd.,* [1963] V. R. 12 holding a company not bound by a director's admissions.

concerning acts done by him in the course of his employment may as such be proved against his master.

In *Kirkstall Brewery Co.* v. *Furness Rail. Co.*,[1] the plaintiff claimed damages for the loss of a parcel, and it was held that a statement made by the defendants' stationmaster to a policeman suggesting that the goods had been stolen by a servant of the defendants could be proved against them. In *Great Western Rail. Co.* v. *Willis*,[2] on the other hand, the plaintiff claimed damages for the defendants' failure to deliver cattle promptly, and it was held that a statement made by a night inspector to the plaintiff suggesting that the beasts had been forgotten was inadmissible as evidence against the defendants. The conversation with which the last-mentioned case was concerned took place a week after delivery was due, but it seems that the real distinction between the two cases lies in the different circumstances in which the statements were made, as well, perhaps, as the larger scope of the stationmaster's authority. He was authorised to put the police in motion, and this necessarily included authority to draw attention to suspects, even if they should happen to be the company's servants, but the night inspector had no authority to answer inquiries of the kind that the plaintiff was making.

The statement of the agent which is tendered as an admission must, on the preponderance of authority, have been made to a third person, not to the principal. Thus, in *Re Devala Provident Gold Mining Co., Ltd.*,[3] a shareholder claimed to have his name removed from the company's register on the ground of misrepresentation in the prospectus, and it was held that a report made by the chairman to a meeting of the company could not be received against the company as an admission of the falsity of the prospectus. FRY, J., said that though the chairman was the agent of the company, the statement was not made in a transaction between the company and a third party, and, in his view, "When an agent is making a confidential report to his principal, the report is not admissible evidence in favour of a third party". The fact that the applicant was a shareholder in the company was held to make no difference.

The existence of the agency must be proved before the agent's admissions can be received against the principal.[4] The alleged agent's own statement of this fact would be inadmissible hearsay at common law (though admissible under s. 2 of the Civil Evidence Act, 1968), but it was held in *Edwards* v. *Brookes (Milk), Ltd.*[5] that if, in response to a request to see the depot manager, someone comes forward at a company's place of business and has a conversation with the inquirer, there is evidence from which an agency may be inferred. It is open to question whether this amounts to anything more than admitting hearsay because it is inherently reliable, a

---

[1] (1874), L. R. 9 Q. B. 468; *Fraser Henleins Pty. Ltd.* v. *Cody* (1944), 70 C. L. R. 100; *Lewis* v. *Crafter*, [1942] S. A. S. R. 30.

[2] (1865), 18 C. B. N. S. 748. Assuming that the statement was one of fact or, what is most unlikely, opinion, of which the maker could have given direct oral evidence, it could now be received under s. 2 of the Civil Evidence Act, 1968.

[3] (1883), 22 Ch. D. 593; *The Solway* (1885), 10 P. D. 137 is to the contrary, but it was criticised as being against previous English authority in *Swan* v. *Miller, Son and Torrance, Ltd.*, [1919] 1 I. R. 151, at pp. 176 and 185. It should be noted, however, that agents' reports could be rendered admissible under s. 2 of the Civil Evidence Act, 1968. See also *Warner* v. *Women's Hospital*, [1954] V. L. R. 410.

[4] *Wagstaff* v. *Wilson* (1832), 4 B. & Ald. 339; *R.* v. *Downer* (1880), 14 Cox C. C. 486; *Maxwell* v. *Inland Revenue Commissioners*, [1959] N. Z. L. R. 708.

[5] [1963] 3 All E. R. 62. Cf. *G. (A.)* v. *G. (T.)*, [1970] 2 Q. B. 643; [1970] 3 All E. R. 546.

course which is inconsistent with the speeches of the majority in *Myers* v. *Director of Public Prosecutions*.[1]

The statement tendered as an admission must have been made by the agent during the continuance of his agency. In *Peto* v. *Hague*,[2] an action for penalties for selling coal in short measure, the defendant's manager was said to have made certain statements to a witness, and they were held to be admissible because they related to a sale which was about to take place; but Lord ELLENBOROUGH said:

> "What he might have said respecting a former sale made by the defendant, or on another occasion, would not be evidence to affect his master."

Relatively few agents have authority to speak about past transactions, and, once an agent's employment as such has ceased altogether, he can have no authority to do so.

It seems that the same rules concerning the requirement of personal knowledge apply in the case of admissions by agents as in that of admissions by parties, but this is subject to the proviso that an agent, such as a solicitor, who is instructed to pass on information need not accept it in any way, and yet his statement may be evidence against his principal.[3]

It is now proposed to indicate very briefly how the foregoing principles are applied in the case of the specific agencies of employment and partnership.

(ii) Master and servant.—A direct result of the requirement that the making of the admission must be within the scope of the agent's authority if it is to be received against the principal is that a servant's admission is usually inadmissible in cases in which it is sought to make his master vicariously liable in tort. So far as this branch of the law of evidence is concerned, servants are treated as agents, and, so far as the course of employment is concerned, authority to do acts is far wider than authority to speak about them. In *Burr* v. *Ware R.D.C.*[4] the Court of Appeal would not allow an interrogatory against the defendants about admissions of negligence made by one of their drivers at an inquest. The proceedings arose out of a fatal accident alleged to have been caused by the driver's negligence, but the interrogatory was disallowed because, though the driving was in the course of employment, the admissions would not be evidence against the employer. Such an admission may be brought before the Court by the simple device of making the driver a defendant but, in theory at least, the admission will still only be evidence against him. Wigmore said "this rule as now universally administered makes a laughing stock of court methods";[5] it is just as well that the servant's statement can

---

[1] [1965] A. C. 1009; [1964] 2 All E. R. 881.

[2] (1804), 5 Esp. 134; *The Prinses Juliana, Esbjerg (Owners)* v. *Prinses Juliana (Owners)*, [1936] P. 139; [1936] 1 All E. R. 685. Such statements could be rendered admissible under the Civil Evidence Act, 1968.

[3] P. 447, *supra*. The *Actaeon* (1853), 1 Ecc. & Ad. 176.

[4] [1939] 2 All E. R. 688; 55 L. Q. R. 490; *Johnson* v. *Lindsay* (1889), 53 J. P. 599; *Price Yards Ltd.* v. *Tiveron Transport Co. Ltd. and Barbe* (1958), 11 D. L. R. (2d) 669. A ship owner is bound by the captain's informal admissions, but not those of the crew, though these may be received as part of the *res gestae*. A statement in the engineer's logbook has been received against a ship owner (*The Earl of Dumfries* (1885), 10 P. D. 31). In *Bruff* v. *Great Northern Rail. Co.* (1858), 1 F. & F. 344, it was held that a secretary's admission could not be admitted as proof of the receipt of a letter by a company. *Burr* v. *Ware R.D.C.* was not followed in *Botes* v. *Van Deventer*, [1966] 3 S. A. 182.

[5] IV Wigmore, para. 1078, n. 2.

now be rendered admissible against his master under s. 2 of the Civil Evidence Act, 1968.[1]

(iii) **Partners.**—An admission made by a partner concerning partnership affairs in the ordinary course of business is evidence against the firm. This common law principle is now embodied in s. 15 of the Partnership Act, 1890. Admissions by one of several people jointly interested in any contract or property are evidence against the others provided they were made during the existence of the interest.[2]

(5) MISCELLANEOUS CASES

The list of miscellaneous agencies could be indefinitely prolonged, but, in the main, it will be found that the question of the reception of vicarious admissions depends on the substantive law. This is certainly the case so far as admissions by one of several trustees or executors are concerned, and the same is true of the solicitor's authority to bind his client.

(i) **Admissions by a deceased.**—A case which cannot be regarded as one of agency but which ought, nevertheless, to be noted in a discussion of vicarious admissions, is the decision in *Marks* v. *Portsmouth Corporation*[3] that the defendant to an action under the Fatal Accidents Acts could rely on an admission by the deceased may also be justified by a reference to the substantive law. The admission suggested contributory negligence which was then a complete defence to proceedings under the Acts. Such a statement would, however, be equally admissible today as affecting damages. In *Marks's Case*, there was no claim under the Law Reform Act, 1934, but a relevant admission by the deceased would surely be received in such an action which is brought in his right. In fact there is less room for argument about the admissibility of the deceased's statement in such a case than in that of the action under the Fatal Accidents Acts because the decision in *Marks* v. *Portsmouth Corporation* is difficult to reconcile with the principle that those Acts confer an entirely new action on the dependents.[4]

(ii) **Conspirators.**—The admissions of one conspirator are receivable against the other if they relate to an act done in furtherance of the conspiracy, but not otherwise. The rule is based on implied agency but, because its practical importance in criminal cases is far greater than in civil cases, it is discussed in the next chapter.

(iii) **Husband and wife.**—Further enumeration of the examples of vicarious admissions would be out of place, but it may be added that the admissions of one spouse are not, as such, received against the other, although an agency may be held to exist on the particular facts,[5] or one spouse may have rendered the other's statement admissible evidence against himself or herself by inviting a third party to treat the other as a referee.[6]

---

[1] P. 429, *ante*.   [2] *Jaggers* v. *Binnings* (1815), 1 Stark. 64.
[3] (1937), 157 L. T. 261.
[4] *The Vera Cruz* (1884), 10 App. Cas. 59, at p. 70. It was for this reason that *Marks* v. *Portsmouth Corporation* was questioned and not followed in *Evans* v. *Hartigan*, [1941] S. R. N. S. W. 179. Those who have doubts about *Mark's* case could render the statement admissible under s. 2 of the Civil Evidence Act, 1968 (see also the doubt raised, unnecessarily it is hoped, on p. 429, *ante*).
[5] *Clifford* v. *Burton* (1823), 1 Bing. 199. See also *G. (A.)* v. *G. (T.)*, [1970] 2 Q. B. 643; [1970] 3 All E. R. (parent and child).
[6] *R.* v. *Mallory* (1884), 13 Q. B. D. 33.

SECTION 6. STATEMENTS IN PUBLIC DOCUMENTS

A. STATEMENT AND ILLUSTRATIONS OF THE EXCEPTION TO THE HEARSAY RULE

(i) STATEMENT OF THE EXCEPTION

In civil and criminal cases statements in public documents are generally admissible evidence of the truth of their contents. In criminal cases they are admissible by virtue of the common law and a heterogeneous mass of statutes. In civil cases, when they were admissible at common law, they are admissible by virtue of s. 9 (1) of the Civil Evidence Act, 1968; in some cases in which they were not admissible at common law they may be admissible, subject to compliance with the notice procedure, under s. 2 or s. 4 of the Act. If admissible in a civil case under some other statute, as many documents are, there is no question of their being rendered admissible under s. 2 or s. 4 of the 1968 Act for R. S. C., O. 38, r. 21 (2) states that the notice procedure shall not apply "in relation to any statement which is admissible as evidence of any fact stated therein by virtue not only of the said sections 2, 4 and 5 [of the Civil Evidence Act, 1968] but by virtue also of any other statutory provision." All that is required is that the conditions of admissibility laid down in the other statute should be complied with; usually there are none and the document is admissible in evidence on production of the original (or where permitted a copy) to the court.

The most succinct formulation of this exception to the hearsay rule is that of PHILLIMORE, J., in *Wilton & Co.* v. *Phillips*:[1]

> "A public document coming from the proper place or a certified copy of it is sufficient proof of every particular stated in it."

In *Re Stollery, Weir* v. *Treasury Solicitor*,[2] SCRUTTON, L.J., expressed the opinion that this was simply a restatement of the law laid down in the leading cases of *Irish Society* v. *Bishop of Derry*[3] and *Sturla* v. *Freccia*.[4] Some limit must, however, be placed upon the generality of PHILLIMORE, J.'s, statement, in view of the explanation of *Bird* v. *Keep*[5] adopted in *Re Stollery, Weir* v. *Treasury Solicitor*. In *Bird* v. *Keep* it was held that a death certificate was inadmissible evidence of the cause of death mentioned therein on information supplied by a coroner.[6] This conclusion was technically *obiter dictum* because the Court of Appeal considered that the cause of death was sufficiently proved by other evidence, but it was justified in *Re Stollery* on the ground that, as the registrar of births, deaths and marriages is bound by statute to record the verdict of a coroner's jury, and as that verdict was inadmissible evidence of the facts on which it was based, it would be absurd to treat the registrar's certificate as any proof of this particular fact. Such a certificate does, however, constitute evidence of the date, as well as the fact of the birth, marriage or death recorded,[7]

---

[1] (1903), 19 T. L. R. 390.   [2] [1926] Ch. 284, at p. 318.   [3] (1846), 12 Cl. & Fin. 641.
[4] (1880), 5 App. Cas. 623, H. L.   [5] [1918] 2 K. B. 692.
[6] *Bird* v. *Keep* was followed in *Chapman* v. *Amos* (1959), 18 D. L. R. (2d) 140.
[7] *Wilton & Co.* v. *Phillips (supra)*; *In the Estate of Goodrich, Payne* v. *Bennett*, [1904] P. 138; *Brierley* v. *Brierley and Williams*, [1918] P. 257. Now that hearsay statements of opinion are admissible under the Civil Evidence Act, 1968 (Civil Evidence Act, 1972, s. 1), a doctor's statement of the cause of death would be admissible under s. 4.

and, as was decided by the Court of Appeal in *Re Stollery*, a birth certificate may constitute a link in the evidence relating to the marriage of the parents of the child whose birth is recorded. A birth certificate is likewise evidence of the paternity of the person named therein as father.[1]

(2) ILLUSTRATIONS OF THE EXCEPTION

(i) **Registers.**—The admissibility of certificates of birth, marriage and death is now governed by statute; but, so far as the registers themselves are concerned, Lord BLACKBURN pointed out that:

> "In many cases, entries in the parish register of births, marriages and deaths, and other entries of that kind, before there were any statutes relating to them, were admissible, for they were 'public' then, because the common law of England making it an express duty to keep the register, made it a public document in that sense kept by a public officer for the purpose of a register, and that made it admissible".[2]

In *Lyell* v. *Kennedy*,[3] Lord SELBORNE said:

> "Foreign registers of baptisms and marriages or certified extracts from them are receivable in evidence in the courts of this country as to those matters which are properly and regularly recorded in them when it sufficiently appears (in the words of Mr. Hubbock's learned work on evidence) that they 'have been kept under the sanction of public authority and are recognised by the tribunals of the country' (*i.e.* of the country where they are kept) 'as authentic records'."

To this day, therefore, the contents of certain foreign registers are treated as proof of the facts stated by virtue of the common law. On the principle discussed by Lord BLACKBURN, an entry in a vestry book has been received as evidence of the election of a parish officer,[4] a statement in the logbook of one of the King's ships was evidence at common law of the time of sailing,[5] and entries in coastguards' books have facilitated proof of the state of the weather.[6] For similar reasons, entries in books kept by universities may be received to prove the granting of degrees,[7] and the public books of a corporation might be received at common law as evidence of matters of public interest stated in them,[8] although this subject is now mainly governed by statute.

(ii) **Returns.**—We have already seen that inquisitions, assessments, surveys, reports and returns are admissible in proof of the truth of their contents when made under public authority and in relation to matters of public interest or concern.[9] The leading authority is *Irish Society* v. *Bishop of Derry*[10] in which case the bishop's return to a writ from the exchequer stating the vacancies and advowsons in his diocese was received as evidence of these matters because it consisted of statements made by a public officer in discharge of a public duty. On similar principles, inquisitions and surveys of manors belonging to the Crown or the duchies of Cornwall

---

[1] *Jackson* v. *Jackson and Pavan*, [1960] 3 All E. R. 621. See also *Carlton and United Breweries, Ltd.* v. *Cassin*, [1956] V. L. R. 186 (statement of age on marriage certificate evidence of that fact).
[2] *Sturla* v. *Freccia* (1880), 5 App. Cas. 623, at p. 644.
[3] (1889), 14 App. Cas. 437, at pp. 448–9.
[4] *R.* v. *Martin* (1809), 2 Camp. 100. [5] *D'Israeli* v. *Jowett* (1795), 1 Esp. 427.
[6] *The Catherina Maria* (1866), L. R. 1 A. & E. 53.
[7] *Collins* v. *Carnegie* (1834), 1 Ad. & El. 695.
[8] *Shrewsbury (Warden, etc. of Mercers, etc.)* v. *Hart* (1823), 1 C. & P. 113.
[9] P. 399, *ante.*
[10] (1846), 12 Cl. & Fin. 641; *Tanenbaum* v. *Helpvic Ltd.*, [1960] 22 D. L. R. (2d) 333 following *Gyfford* v. *Woodgate* (1806), 11 East 297.

and Lancaster have been admitted to show the manorial customs and boundaries specified therein.[1] Land tax assessments and poor rate books have likewise been received as evidence of the ownership and occupation of land to which they related.[2] In *A.-G.* v. *Antrobus*,[3] tithe maps were received as evidence of the non-existence of certain rights of way when they were prepared because they were prepared after a public inquiry. Perhaps it is not going too far to regard a public statute as the outcome of a parliamentary inquiry. However that may be, recitals in such statutes are evidence of the facts stated [4] as are the contents of parliamentary journals and government gazettes so far as they relate to acts of state.[5]

(iii) Certificates.—Registers and returns are made pursuant to a public duty for the public benefit in circumstances in which there is usually some public check on their accuracy, and it was no doubt the absence of one or more of these guarantees of reliability that accounted for the reluctance of the common law to admit the mere certificate of a fact as evidence of that fact's existence.[6] The stock exception was the notary's certificate when treated as evidence of the due protest of a bill of exchange,[7] and there may have been others,[8] but the reception of certificates as evidence of the facts stated has been authorised by numerous statutes.

(3) RATIONALE OF THE EXCEPTION

(i) Necessity.—The object of many of these statutes is to obviate the necessity of calling an official to produce a register or return for which he is responsible, and it is sometimes said to be a principal justification for this exception to the hearsay rule that an enormous amount of public time would be wasted if it did not exist. It seems, however, that there is some confusion of thought in regarding this as a principal justification for the exception. No one would wish to deny the merits of any rule of law designed to prevent the waste of public time involved in calling a public official for the sole purpose of producing a document, but the waste of time which may have been caused by the necessity of adopting this procedure in the past was due to the rule requiring the production of an original document when reliance is to be placed on its contents, rather than the rule against hearsay. In nine cases out of ten this latter rule would be infringed when the original register or return was produced to prove its contents, because it is only when the official has personally observed some matter to which his report relates that the reception of hearsay evidence can be avoided. There is, of course, a necessity for the reception of such evidence in many of the cases in which public documents have been received to prove the truth of their contents; but this arises from the impossibility of procuring better evidence, and it is quite unconnected with the question of saving time.

---

[1] *Duke of Beaufort* v. *Smith* (1849), 4 Exch. 450.

[2] *Doe* d. *Strode* v. *Seaton* (1834), 2 Ad. & El. 171; *Smith* v. *Andrews*, [1891] 2 Ch. 678 (poor rate books).   [3] [1905] 2 Ch. 188.   [4] *R.* v. *Sutton* (1816), 4 M. & S. 532.

[5] *R.* v. *Holt* (1793), 5 Term Rep. 436, followed in *Walt Disney Productions, Ltd.* v. *H. John Edwards Publishing Co. (Pty.), Ltd.* (1955), 55 S. R. N. S. W. 162. The *London Gazette* is made evidence of a variety of matters by statute.

[6] *Omichund* v. *Barker* (1745), Willes 538, at pp. 549–50.

[7] *Brain* v. *Preece* (1843), 11 M. & W. 773, at p. 775.

[8] When, in *Krajina* v. *Tass Agency*, [1949] 2 All E. R. 274, the court accepted the certificate of the Soviet ambassador that Tass was a department of the Soviet state, was it receiving hearsay evidence or taking judicial notice?

(ii) Reliability.—In *Irish Society* v. *Derry*, the bishop was an interested party in the sense that some of the advowsons belonged to him, but, in the opinion of PARKE, B., this did not affect the reliability of the return to the extent of rendering it inadmissible. He said:

> "In public documents, made for the information of the Crown, or all the King's subjects who may require the information they contain, the entry by a public officer is presumed to be true when it is made, and it is for that reason receivable in all cases, whether the officer or his successor may be concerned in such cases or not."

PARKE, B., might have added "and whether the entry consists of hearsay upon hearsay or not", for second or third hand hearsay is undoubtedly received under this particular exception. It is evidence of belief on the part of the person making the entry.

Public duties are usually carried out, and failure to do so is often likely to be detected. The presumption mentioned by PARKE, B., is probably justified by the facts.

B. CONDITIONS OF ADMISSIBILITY—THE NATURE OF A PUBLIC DOCUMENT

It is clear from the above illustrations that there are several different kinds of public document. Different conditions of admissibility may apply to the different kinds of document when the somewhat heterogeneous exception to the hearsay rule now under consideration is invoked. As most of these conditions are common to most of the documents, it will be convenient to consider them under the head of the definition of a public document before referring to the different categories of public documents.

(1) THE DEFINITION OF A PUBLIC DOCUMENT

In *Sturla* v. *Freccia*,[1] the report of a committee appointed by the Genoese government on the fitness of a candidate for the post of consul which contained a statement of his age was rejected as evidence of that fact. The grounds on which the House of Lords held that the evidence should be rejected were that the report was not made under a strict duty to inquire into all the circumstances it recorded, it was not concerned with a public matter, it was not intended to be retained, and it was not meant for public inspection. A word must be said about each of these matters which may be treated as the usual prerequisites of a document's admissibility as a public document although the last appears in the forefront of Lord BLACKBURN's description which has been quoted on a number of subsequent occasions. He said he understood:

> "a public document to mean a document that is made for the purpose of the public making use of it, and being able to refer to it. It is meant to be where there is a judicial or quasi-judicial duty to inquire, as might be said to be the case with the bishops acting under the writs issued by the Crown".[2]

(i) Public duty to inquire and record.—In the case of returns, special stress is laid upon the duty to inquire, while the duty to record is more to the fore in the case of registers and certificates. It has, however, been

---

[1] (1880), 5 App. Cas. 623, H. L.
[2] At pp. 643–4.

said that, even in the latter case, the admissibility of a register depends on the public duty of the person compiling it to make an entry after satisfying himself of the truth of the statement.[1] The duty must be imposed on a public official in that capacity. Surveys made under private authority have been held to be inadmissible, although they were kept in a public office,[2] and baptismal registers kept by nonconformists or Quakers were inadmissible as evidence of the facts stated at common law.[3] Even if a duty to report to a public authority is imposed upon an official by statute, his report will not constitute proof of the truth of its contents if made solely in order to provide a check upon himself.[4]

(ii) Public matter.—It was recognised in *Sturla* v. *Freccia* that a matter may be public although it is not the concern of the entire community. Accordingly, the court rolls of a manor have been received as evidence of a custom,[5] but entries in a corporation's books were sometimes rejected at common law because they did not concern a public matter.[6] It is, however, doubtful whether this is something with regard to which any high degree of precision can be achieved.

(iii) Retention.—If a document is brought into existence for a temporary purpose it cannot be received under this head. Thus, in *Heyne* v. *Fischel & Co.*,[7] it was held that records compiled by the post office showing the times at which telegrams were received were inadmissible as there was no intention that they should be retained for public inspection, and Crown surveys were rejected on account of their temporary purpose in *Mercer* v. *Denne*.[8]

(iv) Public Inspection.—The possibility that the public may refer to the document undoubtedly enhances the credibility of its contents; but the decision in *Lilley* v. *Pettit*[9] which turned on this requirement may be thought to justify Professor Baker's comment that:

> "Accessibility of the public to documents should never have been raised from the status of an additional reason for admitting official records to that of a condition of admissibility".[10]

Lilley v. *Pettit* was a case in which a woman was prosecuted for making a false statement with regard to the paternity of her child in entering it as that of her husband. The prosecution tendered in evidence the regimental records of the army unit in which her husband had been serving abroad at all material times, but the Divisional Court held them to be inadmissible because they were not kept for the use and information of the public who

---

[1] Per ERLE, J., in *Doe* d. *France* v. *Andrews* (1850), 15 Q. B. 756.

[2] *Daniel* v. *Wilkin* (1852), 7 Exch. 429. The surveys might well be admissible under s. 4 of the Civil Evidence Act, 1968.

[3] *Re Woodward, Kenway* v. *Kidd*, [1913] 1 Ch. 392. In so far as they are not admissible by virtue of some other statute they would now be admissible under the Civil Evidence Act, 1968 (in *the Estate of H.*, [1949] V. L. R. 197).

[4] *Merrick* v. *Wakley* (1838), 8 Ad. & El. 170.

[5] *Heath* v. *Deane*, [1905] 2 Ch. 86.

[6] *Hill* v. *Manchester and Salford Waterworks Co.* (1833), 5 B. & Ad. 866.

[7] (1913), 30 T. L. R. 190.

[8] [1905] 2 Ch. 538; see also *White* v. *Taylor*, [1969] 1 Ch. 150; [1967] 3 All E. R. 349. There is no requirement of permanence for the admissibility of statements contained in records under s. 4 of the Civil Evidence Act, 1968.

[9] [1946] K. B. 401; [1946] 1 All E. R. 593. Cf. *Andrews* v. *Cordiner*, [1947] K. B. 655; [1947] 1 All E. R. 777 an affiliation case in which regimental records were admitted under the Evidence Act, 1938, as they would be under the Act of 1968.

[10] Baker, *The Hearsay Rule*, 137.

had not got access to them. Accordingly the prosecution failed. The result is no doubt surprising, but the principle on which it was reached was already deeply embedded in our law,[1] and has since been adopted by the Privy Council.[2]

(2) THE DIFFERENT CATEGORIES OF PUBLIC DOCUMENTS

The distinction between registers, returns and certificates taken in the foregoing illustrations of the exception is that of Wigmore.[3] Apart from its convenience from the point of view of exposition, it may have practical significance because the general conditions of admissibility which have just been enumerated undoubtedly undergo some modification when applied to different species of public document. In the case of registers, it may be fatal to the reception of the entry to prove that it was not made promptly[4] or in accordance with the prevailing practice relating to the keeping of the register.[5] Any excess of jurisdiction would be fatal to some types of return.[6] There would, however, be no point in endeavouring to lay down hard-and-fast rules, inferred from the cases, concerning the further conditions of admissibility which may have to be satisfied in the case of certain public documents, for each decision is highly dependent on its specific facts.

---

[1] See, for example, *A.-G.* v. *Horner (No. 2)* (p. 441, *ante*).

[2] *Thrasyvoulos Ioannou* v. *Papa Christoforos Demetriou*, [1952] A. C. 84; [1952] 1 All E. R. 179; see also *R.* v. *Kaipiainen* (1954), 17 C. R. 388.

[3] V Wigmore, para. 631 *et seq.*

[4] *Doe* d. *Warren* v. *Bray* (1828), 8 B. & C. 813.

[5] *Fox* v. *Bearblock* (1881), 17 Ch.D. 429; *Doe* d. *Davies* v. *Gatacre* (1838), 8 C. & P. 578.

[6] *Evans* v. *Taylor* (1838), 7 Ad. & El. 617.

CHAPTER XIX

HEARSAY STATEMENTS (OTHER THAN THOSE FORMING PART OF THE *RES GESTAE*) IN CRIMINAL CASES

In criminal cases hearsay statements are admissible by virtue of the common law as well as a variety of statutes. Reference is made to the statutory provisions of general interest in section 4 of this chapter. The common law is considered in the first three sections and again at the beginning of the next chapter. Some of the previous chapter is also relevant to the reception of hearsay in criminal proceedings. In view of the somewhat scattered nature of the discussion, the outcome of the fact that the law of evidence has been reformed in civil, but not in criminal, cases, it will be convenient to give a list of the principal common law exceptions to the hearsay rule applicable to criminal cases.

They are:

(1) statements in public documents;
(2) statements by deceased persons—against interest, in the course of duty, as to the cause of their deaths in homicide cases, as to pedigree, and as to public or general rights;
(3) admissions and confessions;
(4) statements in former proceedings;
(5) statements accompanying and explaining a relevant act;
(6) spontaneous statements relating to an event in issue;
(7) statements concerning the maker's state of mind or emotion; and
(8) statements concerning the maker's physical condition.

In the case of statements in public documents, the common law has been heavily supplemented by statute, and the subject has already been discussed in section 6 of the last chapter. Statements falling under heads (5)–(8) above are discussed at the beginning of the next chapter. Statements of deceased persons, admissions and confessions, and statements in former proceedings are the subjects of the first three sections of this chapter, some further miscellaneous points with regard to hearsay evidence also being mentioned in section 3.

SECTION 1. STATEMENTS OF DECEASED PERSONS

Statements as to pedigree and statements concerning public or general rights were discussed in the last chapter;[1] having regard to the restricted nature of the issues on which they are admissible, the number of criminal cases to which the law governing the reception of such statements is relevant at the present day is small. In practice, the number of criminal cases to which the law governing the admissibility of declarations against interest and in the course of duty is relevant may not be much larger; but these

---

[1] P. 437, *ante.*

declarations are admissible on every possible issue, although the conditions of their admissibility have a circumscribing effect. The conditions were evolved in civil cases and in a milieu which has little relevance to the principles on which hearsay should be admissible in contemporary criminal proceedings; but, in spite of the rather unrealistic nature of the process, there seems to be no alternative to giving an account of these two common law exceptions to the hearsay rule commensurate in detail with the rest of this book. The law governing the admissibility of dying declarations in homicide cases is no less anti-deluvian than that governing the admissibility of declarations against interest and in the course of duty. As a minimal step in law reform, the statements of all deceased persons on every relevant matter should be made admissible in all criminal cases.

A. DECLARATIONS AGAINST INTEREST

(1) Statement and Illustrations of the Exception

(i) Statement

In criminal cases the oral or written declaration by a deceased person of a fact which he knew to be against his pecuniary or proprietary interest when the declaration was made, is admissible as evidence of that fact and of all collateral matters mentioned in the declaration provided the declarant had personal knowledge of such fact and matters. Although practically all the authorities mentioned under this head and head B are civil, they govern criminal cases. Practically all the statements received or rejected under these common law exceptions to the hearsay rule would be admissible in civil proceedings under the Civil Evidence Act, 1968.

(ii) Illustrations

(*a*) *Statements against pecuniary interest.* The simplest instance of a declaration against pecuniary interest would be a bare acknowledgement of indebtedness. The acknowledgement must be "bare" in the sense that it is unilateral, for, if it is contained in a statement concerning an executory contract concluded by the declarant, the statement is not regarded as one that was against his interest when it was made. Thus, in *R. v. Inhabitants of Worth*,[1] an entry in a deceased farmer's book relating to a contract of service was held inadmissible as evidence of the hiring because the agreement was for the mutual benefit of the parties and the employer would only have been liable for salary if the services were duly rendered. A declaration by a deceased workman to the effect that he had promised to marry the mother of the child on whose behalf workmen's compensation was claimed was held to be inadmissible as evidence of the promise by the Court of Appeal in *Ward* v. *H. S. Pitt & Co.* which was reported together with *Lloyd* v. *Powell Duffryn Steam Coal Co.*[2]

A further simple illustration of a declaration against pecuniary interest is provided by *Gleadow* v. *Atkin*,[3] where an acknowledgement that the principal monies due under a bond were trust monies was received under this head. A statement by someone who has been duly constituted a trustee concerning the terms of the trust will not, generally speaking, amount to a declaration against interest, because he has nothing to lose personally by

---

[1] (1843), 4 Q. B. 132; cf. *Bagot's Executor and Trustee Co. Ltd.* v. *Fudge*, [1949] S. A. S. R. 297; *Conley* v. *Conley* (1968), 70 D. L. R. (2d) 352.
[2] [1913] 2 K. B. 130, C. A.   [3] (1833), 1 Cr. & M. 410.

the declaration. Accordingly, in *Re Gardner's Will Trusts, Boucher* v. *Horn*,[1] where a man had been mentioned as a trustee in his wife's will, his signed statement concerning the terms of a secret charitable trust she had communicated to him was held to be inadmissible after his death as evidence of those terms.

A statement acknowledging the receipt of money on behalf of a third person is plainly admissible under this head. Some of the earliest examples of this exception to the hearsay rule are, in fact, provided by entries in vicars' tithe books and statements contained in the books of bailiffs and stewards concerning money received on behalf of their employers.[2] In *Middleton* v. *Melton*,[3] a receipt in a private book kept by a deceased collector of taxes was admitted as evidence of a payment of tax although the person who made the payment was alive and could have been called as a witness. The exception is also brought into play by a receipt given by the deceased on his own behalf, for it is evidence of the release of the debtor and accordingly contrary to the creditor's interest. In the old leading case of *Higham* v. *Ridgway*,[4] an entry made by a deceased male midwife stating that he had delivered a woman of a child on a certain day and referring to the payment of his charges was received as evidence of the date of the child's birth. In the words of Lord ELLENBOROUGH, C.J.:

> "If this entry had been produced when the party was making a claim for his attendance, it would have been evidence against him that his claim was satisfied."

Lord ELLENBOROUGH added that:

> "It is idle to say that the word 'paid' only shall be admissible in evidence, without the context, which explains to what it refers."

He was, of course, speaking of the admissibility of the collateral statement concerning the date of the child's birth, and it will be necessary to refer to this aspect of the case later. On the preponderance of authority, if payment of a statute-barred debt is acknowledged, the receipt does not amount to a declaration against pecuniary interest because the payment revives the debtor's liability, and even if the entirety of a statute-barred debt were discharged, the receipt could hardly be said to be against the creditor's interest because it does not provide evidence of a release from an antecedent legal liability.[5]

(*b*) *Statements against proprietary interest.*—So far as declarations against proprietary interest are concerned, possession is *prima facie* evidence of ownership. A statement by the possessor to the effect that he is not the owner will therefore amount to a declaration against interest. The remarks of a tenant naming the person from whom he rented certain houses may accordingly be received as evidence of the fact that the reversion was vested

---

[1] [1936] 3 All E. R. 938.
[2] *Short* v. *Lee* (1821), 2 Jac. & W. 464, at p. 478.
[3] (1829), 10 B. & C. 317.
[4] (1808), 10 East 109.
[5] *Newbould* v. *Smith* (1885), 29 Ch. D. 882; *Briggs* v. *Wilson* (1854), 5 De G. M. & G. 12; cf. *Bradley* v. *James* (1853), 13 C. B. 822. The conflict was left unresolved by the Court of Appeal in *Coward* v. *Motors Insurers' Bureau*, [1962] 1 All. E. R. 531. Perhaps it is arguable that, after this case, a release from a moral obligation to pay money is against interest. The receipt for a payment within the limitation period would be against interest on the principle of *Higham* v. *Ridgway*.

in that person,[1] of the amount of the rent [2] and of the fact that it was paid,[3] provided, of course, that these last two matters were mentioned in the statement. It has even been held that, where a man was found to be felling timber, his declaration that someone else was the proprietor of the estate was admissible evidence as to who was the owner [4]—a conclusion which prompted Tregarthen to remark that:

> "Surely the law never appeared decked with a more luxuriant pair of ears than when it enunciated this judgment. The same train of reasoning would admit the bawdry of a tramp under a hedge on the presumption that he was lord of the manor."[5]

(*c*) *No derogation from superior title.*—The principle underlying the cases mentioned in the last paragraph is subject to the qualification that a tenant may not derogate from his landlord's title. This qualification was the basis of the decision in *Papendick* v. *Bridgwater* [6] where the plaintiff claimed a right of common appurtenant to a farm, and the statement of a deceased tenant of the farm negativing the existence of such a right was rejected as evidence for the defendant. Wigmore criticised this decision on the ground that it confuses the rule of evidence concerning the admissibility of declarations against interest with the substantive law that a tenant cannot dispute his landlord's title; [7] but this is surely a case in which the substantive law is rightly reinforced by a qualification of the logical implications of a rule of evidence. There is much to be said for COLERIDGE, J.'s observation that nothing would lead to greater inconvenience than that the landlord should be ousted of his rights by loose declarations of his tenants. *Papendick* v. *Bridgwater* was distinguished in *Blandy-Jenkins* v. *Dunraven (Earl)*[8] where the fact that the tenant of a predecessor in title of the defendant paid money under a compromise of an action of trespass brought by one of the plaintiff's predecessors in title was received as a declaration against interest. The bringing of the action showed that the plaintiff's predecessor performed acts of ownership and the compromise was not tendered as a denial of the title of the landlord of the other party.

(iii) Rationale of the exception

In *Ward* v. *Pitt (H. S.)* & *Co.*,[9] HAMILTON, L.J., recognised, as many others had done before,[10] that it is on the guarantee of truth, based on a man's conscious statement of a fact (even if it be to his own hindrance), that the whole theory of admissibility depends. He added that this seems sordid and unconvincing because "Men lie for so many reasons and some for no reason at all and some tell the truth without thinking or even in spite of thinking about their pockets"; but he concluded that it is too late to question the piece of eighteenth-century philosophy on which the exception is based, and it is difficult to dissent from either the observations on the rationale or the conclusions with regard to it.

---

[1] *Peaceable* d. *Uncle* v. *Watson* (1811), 4 Taunt. 16.
[2] *R.* v. *Birmingham Overseers* (1861), 1 B. & S. 763.
[3] *R.* v. *Exeter Guardians* (1869), L. R. 4 Q. B. 341.
[4] *Doe* d. *Stansbury* v. *Arkwright* (1833), 5 C. & P. 575.
[5] Tregarthen, *The Law of Hearsay Evidence*, 105.
[6] (1855), 5 E. & B. 166; *Crease* v. *Barrett* (1835), 1 Cr. M. & R. 919; *Scholes* v. *Chadwick* (1843), 2 Mood. & R. 507.
[7] V Wigmore, p. 279.   [8] [1899] 2 Ch. 121, C. A.
[9] [1913] 2 K. B. 130, at p. 138, C. A.
[10] See Baker, *The Hearsay Rule*, 66–7, for examples.

(2) CONDITIONS OF ADMISSIBILITY

(i) Death of declarant.—Although declarations against interest, made by a person still living at the time of the suit appear to have been received as evidence of their truth in two early cases,[1] *Stephen* v. *Gwenap* [2] conclusively established that the death of the declarant is a prerequisite of admissibility under this head. The defendant to an action on a loan wished to prove that he had made some payments on account to an agent for the plaintiff, and he proposed to produce the books of the agent who had absconded, but he was not allowed to do so because there was no evidence that the agent was dead.

(ii) Statement must be against the pecuniary or proprietary interest of the declarant when it was made.—There are three matters to be considered in connection with the requirement that the statement must have been against the interest of the declarant when it was made— the nature of the interest, the necessity of the statements being presently, not merely contingently, against interest, and the question whether it is sufficient that the statement should have been *prima facie* contrary to the interest of the declarant although it might have been to his advantage in certain circumstances.

(a) The nature of the interest.—The House of Lords is generally thought to have decided in the *Sussex Peerage Case*[3] that a declaration by a deceased person is not admissible as evidence of its truth on the ground that it exposed him to a criminal, as opposed to a pecuniary or proprietary, liability. It was held that a declaration by a deceased clergyman concerning a marriage at which he had officiated was inadmissible as evidence of the marriage although the celebrant was liable to criminal punishment under the Royal Marriage Act, 1772. Lord BROUGHAM said:

> "The rule as understood now is that the only declarations of deceased persons receivable in evidence are those made against the proprietary or pecuniary interest of the maker";

but Professor Baker has pointed out that Lord CAMPBELL was also of opinion that, even if declarations exposing the declarant to criminal liability were admissible, the statement with which the House was concerned would still have been inadmissible as there was no evidence that the clergyman was aware of the dangers to which he was exposing himself by his statement. The marriage was celebrated abroad and he might have believed that the statutory prohibition did not extend to it. Professor Baker asks whether it is not possible that, in a more definite case, where it was obvious that the declarant must have known what the consequences of his statement would be, the statement might be received. It is doubtful whether this course could be adopted by any court lower than the House of Lords, but few would disagree with Professor Baker's conclusion that

---

[1] *Walker* v. *Broadstock* (1795), 1 Esp. 458; *Doe* d. *Hindly* v. *Rickarby* (1803), 5 Esp. 4.

[2] (1831), 1 Mood. & R. 120. At common law, the declarant's death must be proved like other preliminary facts upon which the admissibility of evidence depends unless death can be presumed (*Doe* d. *Earl of Ashburnham* v. *Michael* (1851), 17 Q. B. 276).

[3] (1844), 11 Cl. & Fin. 85, H. L. Lord BROUGHAM seems to have been repelled by the idea that, if A. made an extrajudicial statement incriminating himself and B., the statement would, on the argument he was seeking to refute, be admissible against B. in criminal proceedings brought after A.'s death (pp. 110–11). But this result could easily follow under the present law, as when A. acknowledges his liability to repay money embezzled by himself and B.

there is a crying need for reform if the law is too firmly established to allow for an affirmative answer to his question.[1]

In *Re Perton, Pearson* v. *A.-G.*,[2] CHITTY, J., was prepared to receive a deceased's statement that he was illegitimate as evidence of that fact on the ground that the statement was against interest, and, although the judge mentioned the social stigma attaching to illegitimacy, he appears to have based his conclusion on the fact that the statement might have affected the proprietary rights of the deceased in an adverse manner.

There is no conclusive authority on the extent to which an acknowledgement of a tortious liability will suffice. On principle, there seems to be no reason why such an acknowledgement as that A. has assaulted B. should not amount to a statement against A.'s pecuniary interest, but, in some cases, the form of the declaration may give rise to difficulty. "I was negligent" might be excluded as a statement of opinion when a statement of fact is essential.[3] It has, however, been held in Canada,[4] that a statement by an injured passenger (since deceased) that a motorist had driven well on the occasion of an accident was admissible as tending to exempt the motorist from liability to the passenger.

In *Coward* v. *Motor Insurers' Bureau*,[5] the Court of Appeal held that the acknowledgment of a moral obligation to pay money was against the pecuniary interest of its maker. Oral declarations by the deceased suggesting the existence of an arrangement to pay for lifts to work were held to be admissible although they did not amount to the acknowledgment of a legal debt; but it has been contended with some force that the decision represents an extension of the old law.[6]

It is possible that a statement in answer to enquiries which might lead to liability as co-respondent in divorce proceedings is against interest in this context.[7]

(b) *Statement must be presently against interest.*—Granted that the interest must be pecuniary or proprietary:

> "The rule is that an admission which is against the interest of the person who makes it, at the time when he makes it, is admissible; not that an admission which may or may not turn out at some subsequent time to have been against his interest is admissible".[8]

Accordingly it was decided in the case from which this remark is taken that the acknowledgment of a debt by a bankrupt in his statement of affairs could not be regarded as against interest merely because he might subsequently have assets out of which the debt could be paid. In *Massey* v. *Allen*,[9] the entry by a stockbroker in his day-book that he had purchased certain shares on behalf of a client was held not to amount to a declaration against interest although it would have affected the stockbroker adversely

---

[1] Baker, *The Hearsay Rule*, 70.

[2] (1885), 53 L. T. 707. This is a difficult case because of the vague terms of the judgment. The judge did not consider the requirement that the statement should be against the declarant's present interest when made.

[3] The first condition mentioned by HAMILTON, L. J., in *Ward* v. *Pitt*, [1913] 2 K. B. 130, at p. 137 could be cited in support of this view.

[4] *Watt* v. *Miller*, [1950] 3 D. L. R. 709; but see *R.* v. *Schwarz*, [1923] S. A. S. R. 347.

[5] [1963] 1 Q. B. 259; [1962] 1 All E. R. 531.

[6] Professor Nokes in 25 M. L. R. 458.

[7] *B.* v. *A.-G.*, [1965] P. 278; [1965] 1 All E. R. 62.

[8] BRETT, M.R., in *Re Tollemache, Ex parte Edwards* (1884), 14 Q. B. D. 415–16.

[9] (1879), 13 Ch. D. 558.

if the shares had increased in value. The requirement that the declaration must have been against interest when made is, in fact, the basis of the rule that any reference to a contract by one party while it is still executory so far as the other is concerned is insufficient to bring the exception under consideration into play; but the principle applies in many other situations. Thus, in *Smith* v. *Blakey*,[1] it was the duty of the plaintiffs' confidential clerk (since deceased) to keep them advised of all business transacted at their branch office in Liverpool. He wrote them a letter stating that he had received three cases of shoes from the defendant, giving details of the terms on which they were received, and it was held that the letter was inadmissible as evidence of these terms because the possibility that the clerk would have been liable if the cases had been lost was too remote to render the letter a statement against his pecuniary or proprietary interest.

The goods were received at the plaintiffs' office, so the decision does not conflict with those in which an entry charging the entrant with the receipt of money on behalf of a third person has been proved under this head.

(c) *Statement must simply be* prima facie *against interest when made.*—In *Smith* v. *Blakey*, BLACKBURN, J., said:

> "No doubt when entries are against the pecuniary interest of the person making them, and *never could be made available for the person himself*, there is such a probability of their truth that such statements have been admitted after the death of the person making them, as evidence against third persons, not merely of the precise fact which is against interest, but of all matters involved in or knit up with the statement."

The words in italics have been approved in dicta in other cases,[2] but they are unduly rigorous, for there can be very few declarations which never could be made available for the declarant, and there are several decisions which can only be supported on the footing that it is sufficient if "the entry *prima facie* and in its natural meaning, standing alone, was against interest"[3] In *Re Adams, Benton* v. *Powell*,[4] the question was whether a woman's will was in existence at the time of her death, and a statement by her husband (since deceased) that he had destroyed the original after his wife's death and referring to its terms was received in evidence because he was in possession of real property and hence, presumptively, its owner. This property formed part of his wife's estate, and the will gave him a life interest in it. Accordingly, when all the facts were investigated, the husband's reference to the will was not one that never could be made available for him as, without it, he would have had no rights in relation to the property, but, on principles which have already been illustrated, the statement that he had been given a life interest was, *prima facie* and standing alone, against his interest. It is therefore submitted that this is all that is required under the present law.[5]

(iii) Declarant must have known statement to be against his interest.—In *Tucker* v. *Oldbury Urban Council*,[6] a claim for workmen's

---

[1] (1867), L. R. 2 Q. B. 326.

[2] *Ward* v. (*H. S.*) *Pitt & Co.*, [1913] 2 K. B. 130, at p. 137.

[3] The test propounded by JESSEL, M.R., in *Taylor* v. *Witham* (1876), 3 Ch. D. 605, at p. 607.

[4] [1922] P. 240; see also *Sly* v. *Sly* (1877), 2 P. D. 91.

[5] This was the view of GREER, J., in *Republica de Guatemala* v. *Nunez* (1926), 42 T. L. R. 625, at p. 628.

[6] [1912] 2 K. B. 317. The statement was also excluded as an admission binding on the claimant because she was suing in her own right and not that of the deceased.

compensation was made on behalf of the dependents of a deceased workman, and the Court of Appeal held that statements made by him to the effect that the injury to his thumb which caused his death was due to a whitlow were inadmissible as declarations against interest.

> "Such declarations are admitted on the ground that declarations made by persons against their own interest are extremely unlikely to be false. It followed therefore that to support the admissibility it must be shown that the statement was to the knowledge of the deceased contrary to his interest." [1]

This was said to be an essential prerequisite of admissibility in *Ward* v. *Pitt* (*H. S.*) *& Co.*,[2] and, on principle, its soundness is beyond dispute; but there are several cases in which it is difficult to believe that the condition was fulfilled.[3] It is doubtful whether many laymen know that possession is *prima facie* evidence of ownership, so it is hard to believe that those who are in possession and credit themselves with a qualified title know that they are making declarations against their interest. This point was put most forcefully by an American writer when he said:

> "By applying a rule of thumb test as to when a statement is against pecuniary or proprietary interest, and devising ingenious theories of interest, courts have admitted statements which the declarants could not conceivably have believed against their interest. . . . To support an English case we are required to believe that the life tenant of enclosed land was aware of a presumption that open pieces of waste land by the side of the highway belonged to the owner of the adjoining enclosed land between which and the highway the pieces lie; and this in spite of the fact that the life tenant came into possession of his estate two years after the waste land itself had been enclosed and was in the possession of another." [4]

In short, the technicality of this branch of the law prevents the application of sound principle in all but the simplest cases. The requirement as to the declarant's knowledge that the statement was against his interest may be advanced as a ground for rejecting evidence in a novel case, but it would be idle to pretend that the requirement has been considered frequently in the past.

(iv) Personal knowledge of facts stated.—The authorities conflict on the question whether the declarant must have had personal knowledge of the facts stated in order that his declaration should be admissible evidence of their existence, and the opinion of text writers is also divided.[5] In *Crease* v. *Barrett*,[6] a deceased clerk's entry of the payments made in respect of the workings of a particular mine for which he took responsibility of a lessee of the mineral rights was admitted in order to show that payments were made to the lessee in respect of that mine; for the clerk in fact had no knowledge that the ore for which he received payment had been raised from the mine in question. This is a decision to the effect that personal knowledge of the facts stated is unnecessary, but the preponderance of authority favours the opposite conclusion.

---

[1] FLETCHER-MOULTON, L.J., at p. 321. [2] [1913] 2 K. B. 130, at p. 137.
[3] *R.* v. *Exeter Guardians* (*supra*); *Taylor* v. *Witham* (*supra*).
[4] Jefferson in 58 H. L. R. 15 and pp. 18–19. The entire article repays careful study by those who are still seriously concerned with this exception to the hearsay rule. The English case is *Gery* v. *Redman* (1875), 1 Q. B. D. 161.
[5] See Baker, *The Hearsay Rule*, 73–5.
[6] (1835), 1 Cr. M. & R. 919; *Percival* v. *Nanson* (1851), 7 Exch. 1 is to the same effect, but it is not so clear that there was, in fact, absence of personal knowledge on the part of the declarant.

Crease v. *Barrett* involves the reception of hearsay upon hearsay under this head, for the clerk was told that the ore in respect of which payment was entered by him had been raised from the mine in question, and hearsay upon hearsay was also received in *Re Perton, Pearson* v. *A.-G.*,[1] where the deceased's declaration of his own illegitimacy was admitted, for no one can have personal knowledge of his illegitimacy; but, in *Roe* d. *Lord Trimlestown* v. *Kemmis*,[2] the *Sussex Peerage Case*[3] and *Sturla* v. *Freccia*,[4] the need for personal knowledge was stressed in the House of Lords, and, in *Lloyd* v. *Powell Duffryn Steam Coal Co.*,[5] in the Court of Appeal where this requirement formed part of the *ratio decidendi* as the deceased's statement that he was the father of the claimant did not satisfy the condition that "the fact stated is one of which he has peculiar knowledge or direct personal knowledge to the exclusion of hearsay". It is therefore submitted that this condition is part of the present law, although it must be stressed that there is quite a strong body of opinion to the contrary.

(3) COLLATERAL MATTERS

More often than not, a statement against interest is tendered to prove some fact other than that which it was against the declarant's interest to state. In *Higham* v. *Ridgway*, for instance, the receipt was not tendered in order to prove that the midwife's charges were paid, but so as to establish the date on which the child was delivered. The doctrine of this case has frequently been followed, although PARKE, B., appears to have thought that the authorities had gone too far.[6] In *Taylor* v. *Witham*,[7] a receipt for payment on account of twenty pounds against a debt for two thousand pounds mentioned in the same entry enabled the debt to be proved, and the only question so far as the present law is concerned is whether any rule governing the extent of this doctrine can be stated. When an account containing receipts and disbursements is produced, the question seems to be whether the statements on the one side and the other are so blended together that the one cannot be read without the other,[8] but it is impossible to go beyond this as everything depends on the facts of the particular case. This is shown by the use of necessarily vague expressions to the effect that a declaration against interest renders admissible "all that formed an essential part of it", or "closely connected and related matters", and no useful purpose would be served by an attempt to give further illustrations of their meaning.

---

[1] (1885), 53 L. T. 707 (*supra*).

[2] (1843), 9 Cl. & Fin. 749, at p. 780.

[3] (1844), 11 Cl. & Fin. 85, at p. 112.

[4] (1880), 5 App. Cas. 623, at pp. 632–3. "Declarations made against interest involve as a necessary element that the subject matter of the declaration must have been within the direct personal knowledge of the person making the declaration" (Lord SELBORNE).

[5] [1913] 2 K. B. 130. For the facts, and the grounds on which the House of Lords allowed an appeal, see p. 409, *ante*.

[6] *Davies* v. *Humphreys* (1840), 6 M. & W. 153, at p. 166.

[7] (1876), 3 Ch. D. 605. Some of the other cases in which the principle of *Higham* v. *Ridgway* has been applied are *Webster* v. *Webster* (1858), 1 F. & F. 401; *In the Goods of Thomas* (1871), 41 L. J. P. & M. 32; *Sly* v. *Sly* (*supra*); *Hudson and Humphrey* v. *Swiftsure (Owners), The Swiftsure* (1900), 82 L. T. 389; *Re Adams, Benton* v. *Powell* (*supra*); *Homes* v. *Newman*, [1931] 2 Ch. 112.

[8] *Doe* d. *Kinglake* v. *Beviss* (1849), 7 C. B. 456.

B. DECLARATIONS IN THE COURSE OF DUTY

(1) STATEMENT AND ILLUSTRATIONS OF THE EXCEPTION

(i) Statement.—In criminal cases the oral or written statement of a deceased person made in pursuance of a duty to record or report his acts is admissible evidence of the truth of such contents of the statement as it was his duty to record or report, provided the record or report was made roughly contemporaneously with the doing of the act, and provided the declarant had no motive to misrepresent the facts.

(ii) Illustrations.—In *Price* v. *Earl of Torrington,*[1] an action for the price of beer sold and delivered, entries which a deceased drayman employed by the plaintiff had made, or caused to be made, in the plaintiff's books were received as evidence of the delivery of the beer. In *Pritt* v. *Fairclough,*[2] a copy of a letter made by a deceased clerk in pursuance of his duty to his employer was received as evidence of the contents of the original. In *Mellor* v. *Walmesley,*[3] entries made by a deceased surveyor in his field book were received as evidence of the high-water mark on the seashore. The surveyor had been employed by the local authority to make a survey in connection with a proposed drainage scheme and the grounds on which the field book was admitted were stated by ROMER, L.J., to be that:

> "it was his duty to make measurements. He could not make a plan without taking measurements and he could not discharge his duty without making these entries".

(iii) Rationale of the exception.—The grounds of the exception appear to be that, in many cases, it would be impossible to obtain other evidence of a servant's acts after his death, and, in most cases, the likelihood of detection if errors were made together with the sanction of dismissal if the duty were unfulfilled afford some guarantee of the trustworthiness of the statement.

(2) CONDITIONS OF ADMISSIBILITY

The conditions of admissibility are that the declarant should be dead, he must have been under a duty to do an act and record or report it, the act must have been performed, the statement must have been made roughly contemporaneously with it and the declarant must have had no motive to misrepresent the facts.

(i) Death of declarant.—Nothing need be said with regard to the first of these requirements.

(ii) Duty to act and record or report.—So far as the second is concerned, a specific duty must have been owed by the declarant to another person and it must have related to the acts of the declarant.

(a) Specific duty to another.—In *Smith* v. *Blakey*[4] the plaintiffs' confidential clerk was under a general duty to report what took place at their Liverpool office, but he owed no particular duty with regard to the receipt of the shoes and the report of the transaction to his principals. In the words of BLACKBURN, J.:

---

[1] (1703), 1 Salk. 285. [2] (1812), 3 Camp. 305. [3] [1905] 2 Ch. 164, C. A.
[4] (1867), L. R. 2 Q. B. 326 p 466, *ante*; *R.* v. *O'Neally,* [1952] V. L. R. 499.

"The duty must be to do the very thing to which the entry relates and then to make a report or record of it."

In *Mercer* v. *Denne*,[1] a report alluding to damage by the sea to the walls of Walmer castle was excluded because there was no evidence concerning the instructions which had been given to the surveyor who made it in 1816.

In *R.* v. *Inhabitants of Worth*[2] and *Massey* v. *Allen*,[3] attempts were made to prove the employer's entry of a contract of hiring, and the broker's entry of a purchase of shares as declarations in the course of duty; but the attempts failed because, in each case, the duty, such as it was, was purely self-serving. An entry by a deceased doctor concerning his patient's disease was excluded on similar grounds in *Mills* v. *Mills*,[4] although it was recognised that the case would have been different if the doctor had been under a statutory duty to make the entry, and, had he practised in partnership, he might have owed a duty to his partner to make notes of all his cases. A similar strict view of the law was taken in *Simon* v. *Simon, Hogarth, Preston and Shaw*,[5] where a deceased doctor's report concerning the physical condition of the intervener in a divorce case was held to be inadmissible. Though in the possession of the intervener's solicitors, the report had not been made for the purposes of the divorce proceedings, and BUCKNILL, J., said that he could not see that the doctor had any duty to record the result of his examination. In *Rawlins* v. *Rickards*,[6] a deceased solicitor's entry of an attendance at which a deed was executed was received as evidence of execution. The decision is, however, out of accord with those that have previously been mentioned in this paragraph, and its validity has since been doubted.[7]

Entries by a solicitor's clerk may, of course, be received under the exception to the hearsay rule which is now being considered on account of the duty owed to his employer, and, in some cases, the duty to record may have been owed by the solicitor to his client. This is probably the best way of accounting for the decision in *Doe* d. *Patteshall* v. *Turford*[8] where one of the partners in a firm of solicitors served a notice to quit, and his indorsement of service was received as evidence of that fact after his death.

(b) *Duty must relate to acts of declarant.*—When speaking of the reception of declarations in the course of duty, Sir ROBERT PHILLIMORE said:

"Entries in a document made by a deceased person can only be admitted where it is clearly shown that the entries relate to an act or acts done by the deceased person and not by third parties."[9]

Accordingly, one of the reasons why he rejected entries made in a ship's logbook by a deceased mate was the fact that it concerned the navigation of another ship. In *Brain* v. *Preece*,[10] it was the duty of workmen to give

---

[1] [1905] 2 Ch. 538, C. A.
[2] (1843), 4 Q. B. 132 (p. 461, *ante*).
[3] (1879), 13 Ch. D. 558 (p. 469, *ante*).
[4] (1920), 36 T. L. R. 772. See also *Dawson* v. *Dawson and Heppenstall* (1905), 22 T. L. R. 52, excluding a statement by a deceased doctor to a patient concerning the nature of her illness. *Cf. Palter Cap Co.* v. *Great West Life Assurance Co.*, [1936] 2 D. L. R. 304, where a consultant owed a duty to a general practitioner.
[5] [1936] P. 17.   [6] (1860), 28 Beav. 370.
[7] *Hope* v. *Hope*, [1893] W. N. 20; *Eckroyd* v. *Coulthard* (1897), 32 L. Jo. 161.
[8] (1832), 3 B. & Ad. 890. The explanation was given in *R.* v. *Worth* (*Inhabitants*) (1843), 4 Q. B. 132, at p. 139.
[9] *The Henry Coxon* (1878), 3 P. D. 156.
[10] (1843), 11 M. & W. 773.

an account of coal delivered by them to a foreman (since deceased), and the foreman, in his turn, caused entries to be made concerning the deliveries. These entries were held to be inadmissible as the foreman had not got personal knowledge, and the recording process was one step less direct than that employed in *Price* v. *Torrington.*

(iii) Act must have been performed.—In *Rowlands* v. *De Vecchi,*[1] an office book containing a record of letters to be posted and kept by a clerk who had since died was rejected as evidence that a particular letter copied in the book had been posted. It seems, therefore, that the exception only covers records of acts done by the deceased, not records of acts to be done by him.

(iv) Contemporaneity.—It is impossible to lay down a precise rule with regard to the requisite degree of contemporaneity between the doing of the act and the production of the report. In *Price* v. *Torrington,* the entry was made in the evening of acts performed in the daytime and it was received, but, in *The Henry Coxon,*[2] entries concerning a collision at sea made in a ship's logbook two days after the event were rejected. All that can be said with certainty is that:

"The measure of contemporaneousness is not that period of time within which it is consistent with his duty to his employer that the party making the entry might wait to make his record".[3]

In the case from which this remark is taken, a report prepared a month after a survey was made was rejected although the surveyor had been prevented from preparing it by illness. It seems, therefore, that the standard of contemporaneity under this head is strict, and this is doubtless due to the fact that the probative value of the record is increased by its promptness.

(v) Absence of motive to misrepresent.—A further ground for the rejection of the entries in *The Henry Coxon* was that the mate had every reason to misrepresent the part played in the collision by his ship. Although the authority is somewhat scanty, it may therefore be assumed that the absence of a motive to misrepresent is one of the conditions precedent to the reception of declarations in the course of duty to prove the truth of that which they assert.

(3) Contrast with Declarations Against Interest

The most important respect in which the law relating to declarations in the course of duty as an exception to the hearsay rule differs from that governing declarations against interest is that the former, unlike the latter, can never be received as evidence of collateral facts. This was decided in *Chambers* v. *Bernasconi*[4] where the certificate of an officer whose duty it was to record the day and hour of an arrest was rejected as evidence of the place at which it occurred although this was stated in the certificate and the officer had died before the trial. Further respects in which the rules governing the two exceptions differ are the absence of any requirement as to contemporaneity and motive to misrepresent as conditions

---

[1] (1882), 1 Cab. & El. 10; cf. *R.* v. *Buckley* (1873), 13 Cox, C. C. 293.
[2] (1878), 3 P. D. 156.
[3] *Re Djambi (Sumatra) Rubber Estates, Ltd.* (1912), 107 L. T. 631, C. A., at p. 634, *per* HAMILTON, L.J.
[4] (1834), 1 Cr. M. & R. 347.

precedent to the reception of declarations against interest.[1] If, contrary to the submission that has already been made, personal knowledge of the declarant should be held to be unnecessary when a statement against his interest is received as evidence of its truth, yet another difference between the two exceptions to the hearsay rule that have so far been considered in this chapter will have been brought to light.

BLACKBURN, J., once accounted for the exclusion of collateral matter in the case of declarations in the course of duty by reference to the need for contemporaneity which went, in his view, to the essence of admissibility.[2] It seems that he would also have been prepared to justify the distinction on the ground that collateral facts are, so to speak, outside the purview of the duty to record; but there is probably no rational basis for any of the distinctions mentioned in the last paragraph.

C. DYING DECLARATIONS

(1) STATEMENT AND ILLUSTRATIONS OF THE EXCEPTION

(i) Statement.—The oral or written declaration of a deceased person is admissible evidence of the cause of his death at a trial for his murder or manslaughter provided he was under a settled hopeless expectation of death when the statement was made and provided he would have been a competent witness if called to give evidence at that time.

(ii) Illustrations.—In *R*. v. *Woodcock*,[3] a man was charged with the murder of his wife, and her statement concerning the cause of her injuries given on oath to a magistrate was received in evidence against the accused for, although the deceased said nothing of her impending death, the court was satisfied that she must have known she was on the point of dying. EYRE, C.B., said:

> "The principle on which this species of evidence is admitted is, that they are declarations made in extremity, when the party is at the point of death, and when every hope of this world is gone; when every motive to falsehood is silenced, and the mind is induced by the most powerful considerations to speak the truth; a situation so solemn and so awful is considered by law as creating an obligation equal to that which is imposed by a positive oath administered in a court of justice."

In *R*. v. *Mosley*,[4] the deceased did not die until eleven days after he made a statement implicating the accused, but he constantly said he was sure he would not get better in spite of encouragement from his surgeon who did not regard the case as hopeless. The judges were unanimously of opinion that the declarations had been properly received in evidence. In *R*. v. *Errington*,[5] on the other hand, similar declarations were excluded because the deceased did no more than say that he regarded himself as in great danger. In *R*. v. *Scaife*,[6] the deceased's statement that the accused would not have struck him in the absence of provocation was received as evidence favourable to the accused.

---

[1] The judgment of JESSEL, M.R., in *Taylor* v. *Witham* (1876), 3 Ch. D. 605, at p. 607, suggests that a motive to misrepresent goes to weight rather than admissibility in the case of declarations against interest, and no case seems to require strict contemporaneity before such statements can be received.   [2] *Smith* v. *Blakey* (1867), L. R. 2 Q. B. 326, at p. 333.

[3] (1789), 1 Leach 500.   [4] (1825), 1 Mood. C. C. 97.

[5] (1838), 2 Lew. C. C. 148.   [6] (1836), 2 Lew. C. C. 150.

(iii) Rationale of the exception.—The passage from the judgment of EYRE, C.B., in *R. v. Woodcock* is the classic statement of the rationale of this exception to the hearsay rule. The theory is that no one would wish to die with a lie on his lips. The exception has been held to have no application in a community such as the natives of Papua and New Guinea where the next life is believed to be spent in comfort on a neighbouring island and there is no sanction against lying when at the point of death.[1]

(2) CONDITIONS OF ADMISSIBILITY

The conditions on which dying declarations are admitted in evidence are the death of the declarant, that the trial should be for his murder or manslaughter, that his statement should relate to the cause of his death, that he should have been under a settled hopeless expectation of death and that he could have been a competent witness.

(i) Death of declarant.—Nothing need be said with regard to the first of these conditions.

(ii) Trial for murder or manslaughter.—The second is the outcome of restrictions placed at the beginning of the nineteenth century on what bade fair to become a general principle under which dying declarations might be received.[2] In *R. v. Mead*[3] the accused was charged with perjury. He obtained an order for a new trial and shot the deceased before it took place. A dying declaration made by the deceased concerning the transaction out of which the prosecution for perjury arose was rejected, ABBOTT, C.J., saying that dying declarations are only admissible where the death of the deceased is the subject of the charge, and the circumstances of the death are the subject of the declaration. This case really settled the law, but, as late as 1860, an unsuccessful attempt was made to obtain the reception of a woman's dying declaration on a charge against the accused of procuring her abortion.[4]

(iii) Statement must relate to cause of declarant's death.—The words of ABBOTT, C.J., indicate that the declaration is only admissible in so far as it relates to the cause of the deceased's death, and this is borne out by observations in *R. v. Murton*.[5] *R. v. Baker*[6] is to the contrary, for a statement made by a cook shortly before her death from poison believed to have come from a cake, to the effect that she had put nothing wrong in the cake was admitted on the trial of another servant for murdering the master of the house who had also eaten some of the cake. It is doubtful whether the case has much bearing on the law relating to dying declarations, for COLTMAN, J., took refuge in the language of *res gesta* by treating the two deaths as part of the same transaction. Perhaps the cook's remark is best regarded as a statement accompanying and concerning a relevant event—the death of the master of the house.

(iv) Declarant's settled hopeless expectation of death.—In the *Sussex Peerage Case*[7] Lord DENMAN said:

---

[1] *R. v. Madobi* (1963), 6 F. L. R. 1.
[2] See *Wright* d. *Clymer* v. *Littler* (1761), 3 Burr. 1244.   [3] (1824), 2 B. & C. 605.
[4] *R. v. Hind* (1860), 8 Cox C. C. 300. There is no authority on causing death by dangerous driving or abetting suicide.
[5] (1862), 3 F. & F. 492, at p. 494; *R. v. Buck*, [1941] 1 D. L. R. 302. Questions of remoteness of causation and the admissibility of deceased's statements of opinion could arise but have not been discussed in the English cases.
[6] (1837), 2 Mood. & R. 53.
[7] (1844), 11 Cl. & Fin. 85, at p. 112.

"With regard to declarations made by persons *in extremis,* supposing all necessary matters concurred, such as actual danger, death following, and a full apprehension at the time of the danger of death, such declarations can be received."

This suggests that the danger of death and the apprehension of it are to be treated separately, but the cases are all concerned with the second, and, in the absence of any authority, there is no point in speculating on the course that would be adopted with regard to a statement made by someone who believed himself to be dying when this was not the case although death in fact followed shortly after the making of the statement.

A number of judgments insist on the necessity of proving the apprehension of a speedy end on the part of the declarant. The words "settled hopeless expectation" come from the judgment of WILLES, J., in *R.* v. *Peel.*[1] They were approved by the Court of Criminal Appeal in *R.* v. *Perry,*[2] where the suggestion that there must be a settled hopeless expectation of *immediate* death was criticised.[3] We have already seen that, in *R.* v. *Mosley,* the death did not occur until eleven days after the statement. In one case, the interval was as much as three weeks.[4] It is immaterial that the deceased should have entertained hopes of recovery after the statement was made, so long as he or she had abandoned all hope of life when it was made.[5] The absolute necessity of compliance with this latter requirement was vividly illustrated by *R.* v. *Jenkins.*[6] This was a murder case in which the deceased made a statement implicating the accused. The statement was written down by a magistrate's clerk who included the words that it was made "with no hope of my recovery", and read it over to the deceased. Before signing the statement she caused it to be amended so as to read "with no present hope of my recovery", and it was held that the statement could not be received in evidence on account of the suggestion that the deceased entertained a faint hope of recovery. The express declaration of the deceased is treated as the best proof of settled hopeless expectation of death. But other considerations may also be taken into account, such as his having talked about the devolution of his property, the fact that he took leave of his family and the fact that he made arrangements about his funeral.[7] The courts have, however, been extremely reluctant to infer knowledge on the part of the deceased of his or her impending death from the surrounding circumstances. In *R.* v. *Morgan,*[8] for instance, the deceased's head was all but cut off, but DENMAN, J., held that he could not admit the dying declaration for this reason alone and the prosecution proceeded without it.

(v) **Competence of declarant.**—In *R.* v. *Pike,*[9] the statement of a child

---

[1] (1860), 2 F. & F. 21.   [2] [1909] 2 K. B. 697, C. C. A.
[3] The suggestion comes from the judgment of LUSH, J., in *R.* v. *Osman* (1881), 15 Cox C. C. 1. It was queried by CHARLES, J., in *R.* v. *Gloster* (1888), 16 Cox C. C. 471.
[4] *R.* v. *Bernadotti* (1869), 11 Cox C. C. 316.
[5] *R.* v. *Hubbard* (1881), 14 Cox C. C. 565; *R.* v. *Austin* (1912), 8 Cr. App. Rep. 27.
[6] (1869), L. R. 1 C. C. R. 187.
[7] *R.* v. *Spilsbury* (1835), 7 C. & P. 187, at p. 190.
[8] (1875), 14 Cox C. C. 337; *R.* v. *Cleary* (1862), 2 F. & F. 850; *R.* v. *Bedingfield* (1879) 14 Cox C. C. 341; *R.* v. *Rogers,* [1950] S. A. S. R. 102.
[9] (1829), 3 C. & P. 598. In *R.* v. *Perkins* (1840), 9 C. & P. 395, the declaration of a child of ten was received, he having been questioned about his belief whether he would be punished for lying. In *R.* v. *Austin (supra)* the point was raised in argument that the deceased would, if she had lived, have been an accomplice of the accused. Nothing was said in the judgment about the need for a direction concerning the desirability of corroboration, but presumably such a direction would now be given. In *R.* v. *Drummond* (1784),

of four made shortly before its death was rejected at the trial of the accused for the child's murder. According to PARKE, B.:

> "It is quite impossible that she, however precocious her mind, could have had that idea of a future state which is necessary to make such a declaration admissible."

This suggests that PARKE, B., would have excluded the dying declaration of an atheist, although it is doubtful whether the court would embark on the necessary inquiries. Now that the old restrictions on the competency of witnesses have been abolished, it is difficult to think of cases other than those of young children in which a dying declaration would have to be excluded on account of the incompetency of the declarant. No doubt the principle of *R.* v. *Pike* would apply to the statement of a lunatic. It will be recollected that, in *R.* v. *Woodcock*, the deceased was the accused's wife, but, in cases of violence, the accused's spouse is a competent witness for the prosecution, and it is hard to imagine a case of murder or manslaughter which would not come within this category.[1]

(iv) Hearsay upon hearsay.—No doubt if A., an adult under a settled hopeless expectation of death who has since died of gun-shot wounds, were to tell B. that X. had caused those wounds, and B. were to pass that information on to C., C. would not be allowed to prove B.'s statement as evidence that X. killed A.; but what if A. and B. had both been shot and mortally wounded by the same person? If, just before he died, A. were to tell B. that he had seen that X. was their assailant, and B. in his turn, just before he died, were to say to C.: "A. told me that he saw that it was X. who did it", could B.'s hearsay statement concerning the cause of his death be proved by C.? It is hardly surprising that there is no authority, but the example is sometimes cited by those who contend that, if and when the common law of hearsay in criminal cases comes to be reformed, it should be borne in mind that secondhand hearsay may be very relevant. A.'s statement to B. as to the cause of his death comes within an exception to the hearsay rule as does B.'s statement to C. as to the cause of his death; for this reason the latter would be admissible under r. 805 of the Federal Rules.[2]

SECTION 2. ADMISSIONS AND CONFESSIONS

A. ADMISSIONS

An outline of the common law with regard to informal admissions was given in section 5 of the last chapter. It applies to criminal as well as to civil cases. *R.* v. *Simons*,[3] the case of an admission by a husband to his wife overheard by a third party, is in fact one of the stock examples of in-

---

[1] Leach 337, the dying declaration of a convict was excluded, but the case is no longer authoritative, so far as its particular facts are concerned, after the abolition of the incompetency of convicted witnesses.

[1] If a doctor were prosecuted for manslaughter in consequence of an illegal operation performed by him on his wife with her consent would her dying declaration be admissible against him? The fifth condition of admissibility may be stated too widely in the text although it is so stated by other writers on the law of evidence.

[2] "Hearsay included within hearsay is not excluded under the hearsay rule if each part of the combined statements conforms with an exception to the hearsay rule provided in these Rules."

[3] P. 445, *ante.*

formal verbal admissions, just as *R.* v. *Watt*,[1] where the accused attempted to suborn witnesses, is one of the stock examples of admission by conduct. The inadmissibility of the extra-judicial statement of one of two co-accused as evidence against the other is a further stock instance in which there is no such privity as to allow for the reception of a statement as a vicarious admission. Quite a lot of the law with regard to these admissions is, in practice, confined to civil cases; but an accused may be bound by the adverse statements of his referee,[2] and the reception of evidence of the acts and statements of one of several people alleged to have been acting in concert against the other is a fairly common occurrence in criminal cases which will be discussed shortly.

When an admission is made to a person having some control over a criminal prosecution ("a person in authority"), its admissibility is subject to special rules turning on the requirement of voluntariness, and they are discussed later in this section.

The prosecutor ought in justice to be bound by his or her informal admissions as much as the accused, but a technical difficulty could be raised owing to the fact that he is not a party to the proceedings. If he gives evidence, his admissions can be put to him in cross-examination and, if necessary, proved against him as a statement inconsistent with his testimony but, as we have seen,[3] such a statement is not, in the case of a non-party witness, evidence of the facts stated. Technicalities of this sort were very properly ignored by the Court of Criminal Appeal in *R.* v. *Phillips*[4] but there is room for discussion concerning the scope of that decision. After this point has been considered, reference will be made to the details of the law governing the admissibility of statements made in the presence of the parties, and of statements by co-conspirators, two matters which were deferred in section 5 of the last chapter owing to their peculiar importance in criminal proceedings.

(1) R. v. PHILLIPS

In *R.* v. *Phillips*[5] a father was charged with incest with one of his daughters, who gave evidence against him together with her sister. In cross-examination the girls denied that they have ever been "schooled" by their mother, or that she told them what to say in previous proceedings taken against their father. The accused wished to call two women to swear that the daughters had made statements to that effect, but the judge would not allow him to do so, on the ground that the cross-examination merely went to the girls' credit so that their denials were final. The accused was convicted, but the conviction was quashed because the Court of Criminal Appeal considered that he should have been allowed to call the women as their evidence went to the foundations of his defence. In other words, it was considered that, if the women had been called, their evidence of what the children said to them would have tended to prove that the children had knowingly given false testimony under the influence of their mother. The justice of such a decision cannot be denied, but the hearsay nature of the evidence which the Court of Criminal Appeal regarded as admissible is equally indisputable.

---

[1] (1905), 20 Cox C. C. 852.   [2] *R.* v. *Mallory* (1884), 13 Q. B. D. 33.
[3] P. 228, *ante.*   [4] (1936), 26 Cr. App. Rep. 17.   [5] *Supra.*

Would the decision have been the same if the women could only have proved that the sister had been schooled by her mother? Should the mother be regarded as the prosecutrix? If so, does the decision mean that, in any case in which the accused can call witnesses to prove that a prosecution witness has admitted to having been suborned in some way, or can induce such a witness to make the admission in cross-examination, the admission constitutes affirmative evidence for the defence? If the accused can call a witness to swear that the prosecutor said that he knew that the accused was not guilty, should he be allowed to do so? The answer to all these questions certainly ought to be in the affirmative, although the judgment in *Phillips's* case may be an unsafe basis for an assumption that an affirmative answer would be given in every case. This is because the hearsay point was not considered.

(2) STATEMENTS IN THE PRESENCE OF A PARTY

We saw in the last chapter[1] that statements made in the presence of a party are admissible as an introduction to that party's reaction to them which may or may not prove to be relevant.

It is now necessary to consider practical difficulties arising from the fact that the words or conduct of the party in whose presence the statement was made may be ambiguous, and the question whether they amount to an admission of the truth of the statement must be left to the jury. Under the present law, a doctrine of conditional admissibility is applied to statements made in the presence of a party—they may be proved, but it may become necessary to disregard them. This is the result of the decision of the House of Lords in *R. v. Christie*[2] in 1914. It will be convenient to consider the authorities down to that date, the result of *R. v. Christie* and some practical difficulties which still make themselves felt from time to time.

(i) The cases before 1914

Two tendencies were discernible in the cases decided before 1914. In the first place, some of the older authorities seemed to favour a purely mechanistic approach by admitting the statement once it was proved to have been made in the presence or hearing of a party without pausing to consider the purpose for which it was received.[3] The second and more rational solution required the judge to decide whether there was evidence, in the shape of words or conduct on the part of the party in whose presence the statement was made, which would justify the jury in inferring that its truth was admitted. On this second view, the judge's decision constituted a preliminary finding of fact affecting the admissibility of evidence, and it had to be made before the statement could be narrated to the jury. Thus, in *R. v. Norton*,[4] a conviction for an offence against a

---

[1] P. 447, *ante.*

[2] [1914] A. C. 545. *R. v. Christie* was anticipated by *R. v. Grills* (1910), 11 C. L. R. 400. For conditional admissibility see p. 24, *ante*. *Christie's Case* is also important on secondary evidence of identification (p. 50, *ante*), the impossibility of self-corroboration (p. 207, *ante*), complaints (p. 209, *ante*), and *res gesta*. The boy's statement was not admissible under the latter head because of the interval of time intervening between the assault and the remarks; but this type of reasoning may require reconsideration after *Ratten* v. *R.*, [1972] A. C. 388; [1971] 3 All E. R. 801.

[3] *Neile* v. *Jakle* (1849), 3 Car. & Kir. 709; *R.* v. *Cox* (1858), 1 F. & F. 90. See also the argument of counsel in *R.* v. *Smith* (1897), 18 Cox C. C. 470.

[4] [1910] 2 K. B. 496.

young girl was quashed because there was, in the opinion of the Court of Criminal Appeal, no evidence that the accused had admitted the truth of the girl's allegation that he was the culprit made in response to a question put by him in the presence of witnesses. The court observed that, at trials on indictment, there would generally be no difficulty in deciding whether there was evidence, fit to be submitted to the jury, that the accused admitted the whole or part of a statement made in his presence, for his answer appears on the depositions, and the chance that the evidence with regard to it may be different at the trial is small enough to be disregarded. PICKFORD, J., added that there did not seem to be any practical difficulty where evidence of the answer did not appear in this way, for:

> "The fact of a statement having been made in the prisoner's presence may be given in evidence, but not the contents, and the question asked what the prisoner said or did on such a statement being made. If his answer, given either by word or conduct, be such as to be evidence from which an acknowledgement may be inferred, then the contents of the statement may be given and the question of admission or not in fact left to the jury; if it be not evidence from which such an acknowledgement may be inferred, then the contents of the statement should be excluded." [1]

(ii) R. v. Christie

In *R.* v. *Christie* the House of Lords held that the requirement that the judge should, in the first instance, determine whether there was evidence from which an admission of a statement made in a party's presence could be inferred, was not a rule of law, although it constituted a salutary rule of practice, which ought to be followed in most criminal cases. Christie had been convicted of an indecent assault on a small boy who gave his evidence unsworn, describing the assault, and identifying the accused as his assailant, but saying nothing about having identified him soon after the event. The boy's mother and a constable then gave evidence that, shortly after the offence was alleged to have been committed, the boy went up to Christie saying, "That is the man", and described the assault, to which the reply was, "I am innocent". On the authority of *R.* v. *Norton*, the Court of Criminal Appeal quashed the conviction, because the evidence of the mother and constable had been wrongly admitted as Christie had denied the truth of the boy's statement. The House of Lords dismissed the Crown's appeal because the trial judge had misdirected the jury on the question of corroboration, but laid down that there is no fixed rule of law that statements made in the presence of a party cannot be received in evidence until a foundation has been laid for their admission by proof of facts from which, in the opinion of the presiding judge, a jury might reasonably draw the inference that the accused had so accepted the statements as to make them in whole or in part his own. As Lord MOULTON observed, the fact that the allegations contained in the statement were denied by the accused cannot be conclusive in all cases, for his denial of a violent assault might be distinctly relevant, as a fact affecting his credibility, if he pleaded self-defence at his trial. From the strictly legal point of view, therefore, the correct procedure is for the prosecutor to give or call evidence of the making and contents of the statement in the first instance, leaving the presiding judge to tell the jury to disregard the statement alto-

---

[1] At p. 500.

gether if there is no evidence that the accused acknowledged its truth by words or conduct, or if it is not relevant to the state of mind or conduct of the accused for some other reason. Strictly, it is always for the jury, and not the judge, to determine whether to accept the accused's denial of the truth of a statement made in his presence, but, so far as criminal proceedings are concerned, it was recognised in *R. v. Christie* that, in most cases in which the truth of the statement was denied, the judge has a discretion to exclude the evidence because the effect on the minds of the jury of the accused being repeatedly and publicly charged to his face with the crime might seriously prejudice the fairness of his trial.

(iii) Practical difficulties

(a) *Direction to the jury.*—As PICKFORD, J., was at pains to show in *R. v. Norton*, statements made in the presence of a party are not, in themselves, evidence of the facts stated.

> "They are admissible only as introductory to or explanatory of the answer given to them by the person in whose presence they are made."[1]

The decision that, as a matter of law, they are conditionally admissible has given rise to some practical difficulties in criminal cases. The Court of Criminal Appeal found it necessary to insist on the importance of emphasising the point made by PICKFORD, J.,[2] and it is hard to believe that a jury can always rid itself of the impression made by the statement, however carefully they may be directed by the trial judge.

(b) *Co-accused's statement.*—This is particularly likely to be the case when two people are under arrest for the same crime, and one of them is informed of a statement implicating him which has been made by the other. The maker of the statement could not be called as a witness for the prosecution if tried together with the person implicated by it; but, to quote Lord GODDARD, C.J., when speaking of a state of affairs which existed when *R. v. Christie* was decided:

> "There used to be a practice by which the police would give evidence before the jury to the following effect: 'I saw the prisoner. I told him that John Smith had been arrested and had said "Yes, I was there and he (the prisoner) was with me"'. Then the prisoner made a statement and said, perhaps, that he was not there at all, but that was a means of getting before the jury the statement of John Smith."[3]

This practice is, in effect, condemned by rule 5 of the Judges' Rules which provides that, if a police officer wishes to draw the attention of someone charged with an offence to a statement by someone else charged with the same offence, he should hand him a copy without saying or doing anything to invite a reply. If someone who has thus received a copy of his co-accused's statement desires to make a reply, the usual caution should be administered, after which it would be perfectly proper to receive what he said in evidence. The Judges' Rules consist of recommendations drawn up by the judges at the request of the Home Secretary. The current rules

---

[1] [1910] 2 K. B. at p. 501. See *R. v. Thomas*, [1970] V. R. 674. holding that if there is a *voir dire*, the judge must simply rule on the question whether there is *prima facie* evidence of relevance.
[2] *R. v. Curnock* (1914), 111 L. T. 816; *R. v. Altshuler* (1915), 11 Cr. App. Rep. 243; *R. v. Pilley* (1922), 16 Cr. App. Rep. 138; *R. v. Adams* (1923), 17 Cr. App. Rep. 77.
[3] *R. v. Mills and Lemon*, [1947] K. B. 297, at p. 299; [1946] 2 All E. R. 776, at p. 777.

were published in 1964. They are intended to guide the police when interviewing suspects, and do not have the force of law. Accordingly, if the reply made by a prisoner to whom his co-accused's statement has been improperly read is intelligible without reference to the statement, it may be received in evidence against him as a confession, otherwise it will probably be excluded.[1]

(*c*) *Nature of the reply.*—Another practical difficulty which may be occasioned by the procedure of proving the contents of a statement made in the presence of an accused person without reference, in the first instance, to his reply, may be caused by the nature of the latter. In *Turner* v. *Underwood*,[2] for instance, the accused was charged with infringement of a bye-law by indecent behaviour in a railway train. When the complaint was narrated to him by a railway police sergeant, the accused said, "I have done time for this before". This was not a case in which previous convictions could have been proved in-chief, but it was held that there is no rule of law that what a prisoner says in relation to the charge is not evidence against him, even if it relates to his past record. Accordingly it was decided that evidence of the narration of the complaint and the accused's reply was properly received as the reply amounted to an admission of a deliberate act of indecency; but Lord GODDARD, C.J., added that:

"It is the practice as a rule in cases which are tried before juries that where the court knows there is something said by a man in his statement which admits a previous conviction, or shows other matter reflecting on his character, the court sees that that is not read out to the jury." [3]

(*d*) *The danger of the mechanical approach.*—When qualified by discretionary practices and the Judges' Rules, the law concerning the admissibility of statements made in the presence of a party may work well enough; but there is always a danger of a reversion to the old mechanical practice of allowing such statements to go to the jury without a reference to the evidential purpose served by them on the facts of the particular case. In *R.* v. *Black*,[4] for instance, the Court of Criminal Appeal held that the absence of comment from the accused, who was charged with poisoning his wife, on her statements to him concerning her symptoms after taking medicine which he had procured was evidence from which the jury might draw inferences. It is not suggested that this view was incorrect, but one could have wished for a more detailed consideration of the kind of inference that could be drawn—the probative value of the evidence. As long as due regard is had to this in every case, it cannot be said that there is anything seriously amiss with the law laid down in *R.* v. *Christie*. The logic of that decision is hard to escape, but it has to be applied with caution.

In the day to day administration of justice, the question whether the prisoner was present when a statement was made is undoubtedly a convenient test of admissibility, but it is open to question whether the bald assertion that all statements made in the presence of the accused are admissible can be accepted, even if it is recognised that the admissibility may only be conditional. To take the facts of a Queensland case,[5] if a man

---

[1] *R.* v. *Mills and Lemon* (*supra*); *R.* v. *Gardner and Hancox* (1915), 11 Cr. App. Rep. 265.
[2] [1948] 2 K. B. 284; [1948] 1 All E. R. 859.
[3] At pp. 286, 860, respectively.   [4] (1922), 16 Cr. App. Rep. 118.
[5] *Mahoney* v. *Fielding*, [1959] S. R. Qd. 479, following *Barnett* v. *McGregor*, [1959] S. R. Qd. 296. See also *R.* v. *Bailey*, [1956] S. A. S. R. 153; *Thatcher* v. *Charles* (1961), 104 C. L. R. 57; *R.* v. *Lindsay*, [1963] Qd. R. 386; *Woon* v. *R.* (1964), 109 C.L.R. 529; and *R.* v. *Spring*, [1958] N. Z. L. R. 468.

is arrested on a charge of drunken driving and his friends shout advice to him to refuse medical examination and insist on the presence of his own doctor in order to procure as much delay as possible so that he may have time to sober up, the evidence should surely be rejected from the outset in the absence of something showing that the accused accepted his friends' views that it was necessary for him to do as suggested.

(3) CONSPIRATORS

We saw in the last chapter[1] that the admissions of one conspirator are receivable against the other if they relate to an act done in furtherance of the conspiracy, but not otherwise. For example, in *R.* v. *Blake and Tye*,[2] the accused were charged with a conspiracy to pass goods through the customs without paying duty. Tye had made entries incriminating Blake as well as himself in two books. In one case the entry was a necessary part of the fraud, in the other case it was solely for the purposes of record and for Tye's convenience. It was held that the first entry was admissible against Blake as something tending to the advancement of the common object, but the second merely constituted evidence against Tye because it was concerned with the disposal of the plunder.

In determining whether there is such a common purpose as to render the acts and extra-judicial statements done or made by one party in furtherance of the common purpose evidence against the others, the judge may have regard to these matters, although their admissibility is in issue, as well as to other evidence.[3] This doctrine is obviously liable to produce circularity in argument.

> "Since what A. says in B.'s absence cannot be evidence against B. of the truth of what was said unless A. was B.'s agent to say those things, how can one prove that A. was B.'s agent to say them by showing what A. said?"[4]

The answer is that the agency may be proved partly by what A. said in the absence of B., and partly by other evidence of common purpose. It makes no difference which is adduced first, but A.'s statements will have to be excluded if it transpires that there is no other evidence of common purpose; it is another instance of conditional admissibility.[5]

The rule under consideration is not confined to cases of conspiracy as it is based on implied agency, and would apply, for example, to charges of aiding and abetting, even though the secondary party was not charged; but it is in relation to conspiracy trials that the rule may operate most oppressively. If there is a series of counts charging separate offences and a concluding count for conspiracy, evidence may be admissible against all the accused on the last count, although it would not be admissible against more than one of them on any of the separate counts.[6] The evidence often takes the form of directions given and acts done by the other parties which can take a much broader form when there is a conspiracy charge than when the charge relates to one specific transaction.

---

[1] P. 453, *ante.*
[2] (1844), 6 Q. B. 126; see also *R.* v. *Hardy* (1794) 24 State Tr. 1065; *R.* v. *Hunt* (1820), 3 B. and Ald. 566; *R.* v. *Whitaker*, [1914] 3 K. B. 1283.
[3] *R.* v. *Associated Northern Collieries* (1910), 11 C. L. R. 738.
[4] *R.* v. *Mayet*, [1957] 1 S. A. 492, at p. 494.
[5] *R.* v. *Sotsha*, [1965] 1 S. A. 259; *R.* v. *Victor*, [1965] 1 S. A. 249; *Tripodi* v. *R.* (1961), 104 C. L. R. 1.
[6] *R.* v. *Griffiths*, [1966] 1 Q. B. 589; [1965] 2 All E. R. 448.

B. CONFESSIONS[1]

(1) Statement and Illustrations of the Exception

(i) Statement.—A confession of crime is only admissible against the party making it if it was voluntary, i.e. provided it was not made in consequence of an improper inducement or threat of a temporal nature held out or made by a person in authority, or by oppression.[2] In this context, the expression "confession of crime" includes any inculpatory statement as well as a full admission of guilt.[3] There is no English authority on the question whether an apparently exculpatory statement can be relied on by the prosecution even though it was not made voluntarily. For example, if someone charged with murder says, when interrogated by the police in circumstances which would have rendered his ensuing confession inadmissible, that he last saw the deceased sleeping peacefully in his bed, but pleads self defence at his trial, can the prosecution discredit him by proving the statement in-chief or cross-examination? The Supreme Court of Canada has answered this question in the negative holding, by a majority, after a conflict of authority in Canada and the United States, that the prosecution cannot make use of any statement which was not given by the accused voluntarily.[4]

The above requirements concerning the admissibility of confessions are confined to cases in which the statement is tendered on behalf of the prosecution. In all other cases, the method by which the statement was obtained affects its weight rather than its admissibility.

> "What a person having knowledge about the matter in issue says of it is itself relevant to the issue as evidence against him. That he made the statement under circumstances of hope, fear, interest or otherwise strictly goes only to its weight. In an action of tort evidence of this kind could not be excluded when tendered against a tortfeasor, though a jury might well be told as prudent men to think little of it."[5]

A plea of guilty is a species of confession, although questions concerning its voluntariness are seldom raised. If leave to withdraw such a plea is granted, the fact that it was made is legally admissible evidence against the accused at his trial, although the judge has a discretion to exclude it if, for

---

[1] For the function of judge and jury with regard to confessions, see p. 61, *ante*; and see chapter XII, section 3, for the discovery of facts in consequence of inadmissible confessions.

[2] Principle E, in the introduction to the Judges' Rules of 1964 reads: "It is a fundamental condition of the admissibility in evidence against any person, equally of any oral answer given by that person to a question put by a police officer and of any statement made by that person, that it shall have been voluntary, in the sense that it has not been obtained from him by fear of prejudice or hope of advantage exercised or held out by a person in authority, or by oppression." This was said to represent the law in *Customs and Excise Commissioners* v. *Harz and Power*, [1967] 1 A. C. 760, at p. 818, and *R.* v. *Prager*, [1972] 1 All E. R. 1114 at p. 1119. See also *Callis* v. *Gunn*, [1964] 1 Q. B. 495, at p. 501.

[3] *Customs and Excise Commissioners* v. *Harz and Power*, [1967] 1 A. C. 760, at p. 818.

[4] *Piché* v. *R.* (1970), 11 D. L. R. (3d) 709. In England the accused may not be cross-examined on an inadmissible confession (*R.* v. *Treacey*, [1944] 2 All E. R. 229).

[5] *Per* Lord SUMNER in *Ibrahim* v. *R.*, [1914] A. C. 599, at p. 610. It is doubtful whether WINN, L.J., meant anything different when he said in *R.* v. *Richards*, [1967] 1 All E. R. 829 at p. 830: "This sphere of inducement is quite separate from the sphere in which persons not in authority make promises or threats which are alleged subsequently to have induced a statement or confession. In that latter sphere the question is always, what was in fact the effect of the inducement? Did it go so far as to deprive the person to whom it was made of free will and choice whether or not he would make a statement as he did?" (See also *R.* v. *Northam* (1967), 52 Cr. App. Rep. 97.)

example, someone who was ignorant of the law pleaded guilty to handling and alleges that he did not know the goods were stolen.[1]

Even though an out-of-court confession was voluntary within the principle stated at the beginning of this discussion, the judge has a discretion to reject it if he considers that it was obtained in circumstances which would render its reception unfair to the accused. The Judges' Rules of 1964 are expressly stated to be subject to the principle under which confessions are inadmissible as a matter of law if they are not voluntary. Confessions obtained in breach of the Judges' Rules are liable to be rejected at the judge's discretion. When considering the admissibility of a confession, it is therefore necessary to bear in mind first, the possibility that it may be inadmissible as a matter of law because it was not voluntary, secondly, the possibility that it may have been obtained by a breach of the Judges' Rules and therefore, though voluntary, liable to be rejected at the judge's discretion, thirdly, that it is liable to rejection at discretion because it was obtained in some other circumstances which would render its reception unfair to the accused. At the moment we are concerned with admissibility as a matter of law.

(ii) Illustrations.—The conditions of admissibility were held to have been satisfied in the leading case of *R. v. Baldry*.[2] A constable told the prisoner that he need not say anything to incriminate himself but what he did say would be taken down and used as evidence against him. It was held that the prisoner's confession was admissible. Today it may seem almost incredible that a conclusion of this nature should have to be embodied in elaborate judgments, but the previous decisions had displayed a solicitude for the interests of the accused which, however much it may have been justified by the harsh criminal procedure of the time, can, in retrospect, only be described as "liberalism run wild".[3] In the words of PARKE, B., in *Baldry's Case*:

> "In order to render a confession admissible in evidence it must be perfectly voluntary; and there is no doubt that any inducement in the nature of a promise or of a threat held out by a person in authority vitiates a confession. The decisions to that effect have gone a long way. . . . I think there has been too much tenderness towards prisoners in this matter. . . . Justice and common sense have too frequently been sacrificed at the shrine of mercy."

In *R. v. Jarvis*,[4] the accused's employer was investigating the defalcations of his employees with the aid of the police and said, "I should advise you that, to any question that may be put to you, you will answer truthfully, so that if you have committed a fault you may not add to it by stating what is untrue". The ensuing confession was held to be admissible, but only after KELLY, C.B., had said that the words "you had better tell the truth" had acquired a sort of technical meaning importing either a threat or a benefit, and WILLES, J., had asserted that his decision would have been different if they had been used. This was on account of old cases;[5] now that the accused can give evidence of their effect upon him, undue importance must not be placed on words. As much may depend on the cir-

---

[1] *R. v. Rimmer*, [1972] 1 All E. R. 604; see also *R. v. McGregor*, [1968] 1 Q. B. 371; [1967] 2 All E. R. 267 (accused's partial admission at trial in which jury disagreed admissible against him in his subsequent trial.)

[2] (1852), 2 Den. 430.

[3] Baker, *The Hearsay Rule*, 54. [4] (1867), L. R. 1 C. C. R. 96.

[5] *R. v. Enoch* (1833), 5 C. & P. 539; *R. v. Hearn* (1841), Car. & M. 109; *R. v. Garner* (1848), 1 Den. 329, at p. 331; *R. v. Baldry* (1852), 2 Den. at p. 442.

cumstances as on the terms of the inducement,[1] and it is arguable whether the statement by a policeman or prosecutor to a suspect that he had better tell the truth would necessarily vitiate a confession today, although there does not seem to be a reported case in which a confession has been received after the statement had been used without some such qualification as "Be a good girl and speak the truth"[2] or "You had better as good boys tell the truth".[3]

In *R.* v. *Richards*[4] it was held that the words of a police officer to a prevaricating suspect: "I think it would be better if you made a statement telling me exactly what happened" were capable of amounting to an inducement.

In *R.* v. *Cleary*[5] the accused's father said to the accused in the presence of police officers who were making inquiries concerning a capital murder "Put your cards on the table, tell them the lot, if you did not hit him they can not hang you." The Court of Criminal Appeal held that, in the circumstances, the words were capable of constituting an inducement and quashed the conviction which followed on the reception of a statement made by the accused after his father's exhortation.

In *Sparks* v. *R.*[6] a confession of guilt of an indecent assault was held to have been wrongly received because it might have been made in consequence of suggestions by the Bermudan police that, if the accused made a statement, he might be tried by a military court and his family would thereby be spared the embarrassment of publicity.

In *R.* v. *Northam*[7] a man on bail awaiting trial on charges of housebreaking was questioned by a police officer about another case of housebreaking and confessed to having played a minor part in it. Before confessing he had asked the officer whether it would be possible for the other offence to be taken into consideration at his forthcoming trial and the officer said that the police would have no objection. In the end he was tried separately for the other offence and convicted of it. Somewhat reluctantly, the Court of Appeal quashed the conviction.

> "It is not the magnitude, it is not the cogency to the reasonable man or to persons with such knowledge as is possessed by lawyers and others which is the proper criterion. It is what the average, normal, possibly quite unreasonable person in the position of the appellant at the time might have thought was likely to result to his advantage from the suggestion agreed to by the police officer."[8]

In *R.* v. *Smith*[9] a soldier had been stabbed in a fight and, immediately after the episode, a regimental sergeant major put his men on parade, saying that he would keep them there until he learnt who had been involved in

---

[1] *R.* v. *Priestley* (1966) 50 Cr. App. Rep. 183.

[2] *R.* v. *Stanton* (1911), 6 Cr. App. Rep. 198.

[3] *R.* v. *Reeve and Hancock* (1872), L. R. 1 C. C. R. 362.

[4] [1967] 1 All E. R. 829. Some of the decisions of this period are affected by judges' reluctance to hold a trial within the trial and the outdated view that the jury had to be instructed on voluntariness (p. 62, *ante*).

[5] (1963), 48 Cr. App. Rep. 116. See also *R.* v. *Moore* (1972), 56 Cr. App. Rep. 373. The consistency of *R.* v. *Cleary* with *R.* v. *Priestley* (*supra*) was questioned in *R.* v. *Richards* (*supra*).

[6] [1964] A. C. 964; [1964] 1 All E. R. 727. See also *R.* v. *Williams* (1968), 52 Cr. App. Rep. 439.

[7] (1967), 52 Cr. App. Rep. 97, followed in *R.* v. *Zaveckas*, [1970] 1 All E. R. 413.

[8] *Per* WINN, L.J., at p. 104.

[9] [1959] 2 Q. B. 35; [1959] 2 All E. R. 193.

the fighting. A confession which appears to have been made very shortly afterwards by the accused was held to be inadmissible, although it was recognised that what the regimental sergeant major did was a useful course of action to enable further inquiries to be made.

(iii) Rationale of the present law.—As ERLE, J., said in *R. v. Baldry*, "When a confession is well proved it is the best evidence that can be produced." In other words, the grounds for receiving a confession are identical with those on which an admission is received—if made freely, it is very probably true. A more difficult question relates to the reason why the courts still require such stringent conditions to be satisfied before receiving a confession.

Undoubtedly the possibility that a confession which was not voluntary would be untrue has been and still is[1] uppermost in the mind of the judges. But cases such as *R. v. Cleary, R. v. Richards* and *R. v. Northam* to which reference has just been made render it hard to treat the danger of unreliability as the sole ground of exclusion at the present day. Allowance must also be made for the dislike shared by English lawyers and laymen alike of the spectacle of a man being made, or put under what he might consider to be pressure to incriminate himself. There is also the desirability of doing everything possible to discourage improper police methods.[2] It is true that the law is not altogether logical for evidence obtained in consequence of an inadmissible confession is admissible as a matter of law, but this is a sphere in which compromise appears to be inevitable. As long as it is thought desirable to render confessions obtained by certain means inadmissible as a matter of law, there will always be cases in which the infringement of the legal rule was a venial one. *R. v. Smith* is an example. In such a case, it would be the thin end of the wedge to admit the confession, but to reject evidence obtained in consequence of the confession would be over scrupulous. Where the infringement of the legal rule is serious, the evidence obtained in consequence of it could be rejected at the discretion of the judge.

(2) CONDITIONS OF ADMISSIBILITY

(i) The burden of proof

The legal burden of proving that a confession was voluntary rests on the prosecution. This was settled by the Court for Crown Cases Reserved in *R. v. Thompson.*[3] Before receiving a confession of embezzlement, the chairman of the defrauded company told the accused's brother that it would be right for the accused to make a clean breast of it. There was no evidence that this remark had in fact been communicated to the accused, but the prosecution was unable to prove that such a communication had not taken place, and the confession was accordingly rejected. CAVE, J., said in each case the trial judge has to ask, "Is it proved affirmatively[4] that the con-

---

[1] *R. v. Ovenell*, [1969] 1 Q. B. 17, at p. 23, *per* BLAIN, J.

[2] Cowen and Carter, Essays in the Law of Evidence 42–51; see also *R. v. Thomas* (1836), 7 C. & P. 345 and *R. v. Garner* (1848), 1 Den. 329, at p. 331 which lay behind what is now **s. 149** of the Victoria Evidence Act, 1958, making likelihood of untruth the test of admissibility. See also s. 20 of the New Zealand Evidence Act, 1908, to the same effect.

[3] [1893] 2 Q. B. 12; *R. v. Batty*, [1963] V. R. 451; *R. v. Bodsworth*, [1968] 2 N. S. W. R. 132. The onus of showing that there is a case for the exercise of the discretion has been held to be on the accused in Victoria (*R. v. Smith*, [1964] V. R. 95).

[4] The standard is proof beyond reasonable doubt. *R. v. Sartori, Gavin and Phillips*, [1961] Crim. L. R. 397, p. 65, *ante*.

fession was free and voluntary—that is, was it preceded by any inducement to make a statement held out by a person in authority?" It is accordingly necessary to consider who is a "person in authority" and what is an "inducement" (including a threat) and, as the current exclusionary rule requires, what is meant by "oppression".

(ii) Person in authority

On principle the answer to the first question is anyone whom the prisoner might reasonably suppose to be capable of influencing the course of the prosecution, and there is nothing in the decided cases to suggest that this in incorrect. No one has sought to deny that a magistrate, constable or prosecutor is in authority. In *R.* v. *Upchurch*,[1] it was unsuccessfully contended that the prosecutor's wife was not in that position. A servant was charged with arson of his employer's house and the employer's wife's exhortation to confess because it might save the prisoner's neck led to the rejection of the confession. On the question whether an employer is, as such, in authority, PARKE, B., said in *R.* v. *Moore*:[2]

> "It is only when the offence concerns the master or mistress that their holding out the threat or promise renders the confession inadmissible."

Accordingly, he ruled that a maidservant's confession of murder of her child was admissible, though induced by her mistress. If the charge were one of theft from the employer, the latter would clearly be in authority. The wife of a constable, the prison chaplain and a doctor[3] are not in authority, but a gaoler and, with more certainty, the prosecutor's solicitor would come within this category, as does the owner of stolen goods although it may now be impossible for him to stultify a prosecution, or prevent one from being instituted.[4]

If an improper inducement is held out by someone not in authority in the presence of someone in authority the ensuing confession will be inadmissible unless the person in authority disassociates himself from the inducement.[5]

At one time there was some authority for the view that the improper inducement or threat must relate to the prosecution in order to render a confession made in consequence of it inadmissible;[6] but the House of Lords decided that this was not the law in *Customs and Excise Commissioners* v. *Harz and Power*.[7] The House held that, on a prosecution under the Purchase Tax Acts, a confession ought to have been excluded as having been made, not in consequence of any threat relating to the particular charge, but on account of a threat to prosecute for failure to answer questions at an interrogation which the customs officers to whom the confession was made were not authorised to conduct.

It is arguable that, with the disappearance of the requirement that the

---

[1] (1836), 1 Mood. C. C. 465.   [2] (1852), 2 Den. 522.
[3] *R.* v. *Gibbons* (1823), 1 C. & P. 97; *Re Eftoda* (1963), 37 D. L. R. (2d.) 269 (insurance adjuster not in authority).
[4] *R.* v. *Wilson and R.* v. *Marshall-Graham*, [1967] 2 Q. B. 406; [1967] 1 All E. R. 797.
[5] *R.* v. *Cleary* (1963), 48 Cr. App. Rep. 116.
[6] *R.* v. *Lloyd* (1834), 6 C. & P. 393; *R.* v. *Joyce*, [1957] 3 All E. R. 623. The actual decision in *Joyce's* case is still law, the account of the facts of *Lloyd's* case, where the statement was made in consequence of a promise that the accused would be allowed to see his wife, is too scanty to say whether it would now be followed; such a promise might be a very powerful inducement, if, for instance, the wife were dying.
[7] [1967] 1 A. C. 760.

inducement must relate to the prosecution, the requirement that it should come from someone in authority should also go; but the argument was rejected by the judicial committee in *Deokinanan* v. *R.*,[1] a case in which the confession was made to a friend of the accused who was in a nearby lockup. The Judicial Committee was, however, plainly sceptical about the merits of the rule that a confession is only inadmissible if the threat or inducement comes from a person in authority,[2] and the Criminal Law Revision Committee recommended its abolition.[3]

(iii) Absence of inducement or threat

Anything suggesting that the outcome of a confession might be some beneficial result in connection with the prosecution will render it inadmissible. Everything depends on the circumstances but some of the expressions which have been held to have an exclusionary effect are, "Tell me where the things are and I will be favourable to you",[4] "If you don't tell me you may get yourself into trouble and it will be worse for you",[5] and "I only want my money, if you give me that you may go the devil".[6] On the other hand, mere moral exhortation, even if not of the kind of which the Court approves,[7] will not render a confession inadmissible. "Be sure to tell the truth",[8] and "Don't run your soul into more sin, but tell the truth"[9] have been treated as innocuous. A suggestion of the possibility of a pardon, even if it is only conveyed by a placard,[10] will vitiate a confession, but the mere fact that the accused, without any external stimulation, considers that he would be pardoned if he confesses, does not affect the admissibility of his statement.[11]

The use or threat of violence would prevent a confession from being voluntary,[12] but *R.* v. *Smith*[13] shows that threats of a far gentler nature will also have this effect.

It is not every temporal inducement or threat that is improper. For instance, if the interrogation in *Commissioners of Customs and Excise* v. *Harz and Power* had taken a proper form, the ensuing statements of the accused would probably have been admissible against them although made in consequence of threats of prosecution for failure to answer and therefore not voluntary.

A confession is nonetheless admissible because made without a caution having been administered after a police officer had told the accused that he

---

[1] [1969] 1 A. C. 20; [1968] 2 All E. R. 346.
[2] "If the ground on which confessions induced by promises held out by persons in authority are held to be inadmissible is that they may not be true, then it may be that there is a similar risk that in some circumstances the confession may not be true if induced by a promise held out by a person not in authority, for instance if such a person offers a bribe in return for confession." (*per* Lord DILHORNE.)
[3] 11th Report, para. 58.
[4] *R.* v. *Thompson* (1783), 1 Leach 291.
[5] *R.* v. *Coley* (1868), 10 Cox C. C. 536.   [6] *R.* v. *Jones* (1809), Russ. & Ry. 152.
[7] *R.* v. *Wild* (1835), 1 Mood. C. C. 452. ("I hope you will tell me the truth in the presence of the Almighty.") *R.* v. *Gillham* (1828), 1 Mood. C.C. 186.
[8] *R.* v. *Court* (1836), 7 C. & P. 486; but see *The People (A.-G.)* v. *Flynn*, [1963] I. R. 255.
[9] *R.* v. *Sleeman* (1853), 6 Cox C. C. 245.
[10] *R.* v. *Blackburn* (1853), 6 Cox C. C. 333.
[11] *R.* v. *Godinho* (1911), 7 Cr. App. Rep. 12.
[12] *R.* v. *Fennell* (1881), 7 Q. B. D. 147; at p. 151; *R.* v. *Parratt* (1831), 4 C. & P. 570; *R.* v. *Luckhurst* (1853), 6 Cox C. C. 233. See also the references to "oppression" in *Callis* v. *Gunn* (*supra*) and in principle (e) in the Judges' Rules.
[13] [1959] 2 Q. B. 35; [1959] 2 All E. R. 193.

needed to take a statement and the accused had accompanied him to the police station. The fact that the accused probably thought that he was obliged to go to the station is immaterial.[1]

(iv) Duration of the inducement

On the facts of a particular case, an improper inducement may be held to have become ineffective through lapse of time or because of some intervening cause. In the Irish case of *R. v. Doherty*,[2] a constable told a prisoner in the morning that it would be better to tell the truth, and a confession made the same evening to another constable after a proper caution was held to be inadmissible. The Court of Criminal Appeal has said that the principle to be deduced from the cases is really this:

> "That if the threat or promise under whichthe first statement was made still persists when the second statement is made, then it is inadmissible. Only if the time limit between the two statements, the circumstances existing at the time and the caution are such that it can be said that the original threat or inducement has been dissipated can the second statement be admitted as a voluntary statement."[3]

(v) Oppression.—In *Callis v. Gunn*[4] Lord PARKER, C.J., said with reference to statements made by accused persons to the police that it was:

> "a fundamental principle of law that no answer to a question and no statement is admissible unless it is shown by the prosecution not to have been obtained in an oppressive manner and to have been voluntary in the sense that it has not been obtained by threats or inducements."

In *R. v. Prager*,[5] a case in which the confession of an airman on charges of espionage made after a prolonged, though interrupted, interrogation was held not to have resulted from oppression, the Court of Appeal adopted a statement made by SACHS, J., in *R. v. Priestley*:[6]

> "Whether or not there is oppression in an individual case depends upon many elements. . . . They include such things as the length of time of any individual period of questioning, whether the accused person had been given proper refreshment or not, and the characteristics of the person who makes the statement. What may be oppressive as regards a child, an invalid or an old man or somebody inexperienced in the ways of this world may turn out not to be oppressive when one finds that the accused person is of a tough character and an experienced man of the world."

The Court also relied on the following quotation from an address given by Lord MACDERMOT to the Bentham Club in 1968:

> "Questioning which by its nature, duration or other attendant circumstances (including the fact of custody) excites hopes (such as the hope of release) or fears, or so affects the mind of the suspect that his will crumbles and he speaks when otherwise he would have remained silent."

Anything which indicates that, when considering the admissibility of a

---

[1] *R. v. Joyce*, [1957] 3 All E. R. 623.
[2] (1874), 13 Cox C. C. 23; *R. v. Cooper* (1833), 5 C. & P. 535; cf. *R. v. Bate* (1871), 11 Cox C. C. 686.
[3] *R. v. Smith*, [1959] 2 Q. B. 35, at p. 41; followed on this point in *The People (A.-G.) v. Galvin*, [1964] I. R. 325.
[4] [1964] 1 Q. B. 495, at p. 501.
[5] [1972] 1 All E. R. 1114 at p. 1119.
[6] See the note in 51 Cr. App. Rep. 1.

confession, the court should have regard to all the circumstances, including the type of person who makes it, is to be welcomed, but it is to be hoped that a literal interpretation of Lord MACDERMOT's words will be avoided. If the rare case of a contrite man who makes a more or less spontaneous confession is excluded, every confession that was ever made was probably made in consequence of questioning but for which the maker would have stayed silent. It may well be essential to provide that confessions obtained by means other than improper threats and inducements should be inadmissible, but it is necessary to recognise that "oppression" is an indefinite and highly relative term.

(vi) **Whole statement must be received.**—If the prosecution relies on a confession, the whole statement becomes admissible and the accused may rely upon such self-serving portions of the statement as there may be, although they may not be accorded as much weight as the inculpatory parts.

> "What a prisoner says is not evidence unless the prosecutor chooses to make it so, by using it as part of his case against the prisoner; however if the prosecutor makes the prisoner's declaration evidence, it then becomes evidence for the prisoner as well as against him." [1]

(vii) **The proposals of the Criminal Law Revision Committee.**— The Criminal Law Revision Committee recommends the retention of the rule that a confession obtained by oppressive treatment of the accused should be inadmissible; but, so far as confessions obtained in consequence of threats or inducements are concerned, the Committee recommends that they should only be inadmissible if the threat or inducement was "of a sort likely, in the circumstances existing at the time, to render unreliable any confession which might be made by the accused in consequence thereof." [2] Three members of the Committee were in favour of the abolition of all restrictions on the admissibility of confessions, leaving it in every case to the tribunal of fact to decide what, if any, weight should be attached to the accused's statement having regard to the method by which it was obtained. [3] The Committee made no recommendation concerning the admissibility of confessions by persons whose state of mind was disturbed at the material time.

(viii) **The accused's state of mind**

A good deal of Commonwealth authority [4] supports the view that a confession will be inadmissible if obtained at a time when the accused's mind was so unbalanced as to render it wholly unsafe to act upon it. If one of the reasons for excluding confessions is the danger that they may be untrustworthy, it would be in accordance with principle to exclude a con-

---

[1] *R. v. Higgins* (1829), 3 C. & P. 603, at p. 604; see also *R. v. McGregor*, [1968] 1 Q. B. 371; [1967] 2 All E. R. 267.

[2] 11th Report, para. 65; see Victoria Evidence Act, 1958, s. 149 and New Zealand Evidence Act, 1908, s. 20.

[3] In *R. v. Baldry* (1852), 2 Den. 430, at pp. 445–7, PARKE, B., and Lord CAMPBELL seem to have thought that it might have been better if the law had adopted this course.

[4] *R. v. Lai Ping* (1904), 8 C. C. C. 467; *R. v. White* (1908), 18 O. L. R. 640; *R. v. Booher*, [1928] 4 D. L. R. 795; *R. v. Washer* (1948), 92 Can. C. C. 218; *R. v. Burnett*, [1944] V. L. R. 115; *Sinclair v. R.* (1947), 73 C. L. R. 316; *R. v. Starecki*, [1960] V. L. R. 141; *Jackson v. R.* (1962), 36 A. L. J. R. 198 (a decision of the High Court of Australia to the effect that evidence of the accused's mental state when the confession was made is admissible at the trial as well as on the *voir dire*; *cf. R. v. Murray*, [1951] 1 K. B. 391; [1950] 2 All E. R. 925; p. 62, *ante*); *R. v. Williams*, [1959] N. Z. L. R. 502.

fession made by someone whose mental state was such as to render his utterances completely unreliable. It is, however, difficult to formulate a governing principle, and it is probable that, in England, the matter will be treated as one of judicial discretion.[1] In Australia, the appropriate analogy has been said to be that of the competency of a witness whose sanity is challenged,[2] but confessions have been excluded when they emanate from someone whose sanity is beyond question, but who was, at the material time, labouring under the stress of a recent fainting fit,[3] or an attempted suicide.[4] Perhaps it is impossible to better the statement of a New Zealand Court which said:

> "In broad terms any circumstance which robs a confession of the quality described by the word voluntary will render the confession inadmissible."[5]

The Commonwealth authorities differ on the question of the onus of proof when the voluntariness of a confession having regard to the accused's state of mind is put in issue.[6]

(3) QUESTIONING SUSPECTS[7]

Quite apart from the question whether a statement is rendered inadmissible by the fact that it was the outcome of an inducement held out by a person in authority the courts are opposed to anything in the nature of a cross-examination of suspects by the police, particularly when the suspects are in custody. It stands to reason that, before there has been an arrest, a considerable amount of questioning must be permitted and answers encouraged, though they cannot be compelled, for, if this were not so, a great deal of crime would go undetected.[8] The attitude of the law and the reasons for it were summed up in the following words uttered by CHANNELL, J., in 1905 :[9]

> "You are entitled to ask questions for your information, as to whether you will charge the man, but the moment you have decided to charge him and practically get him into custody, then, in as much as a judge even can't ask a question or a magistrate, it is ridiculous to suppose that a policeman can."

(i) **The Judges' Rules.**—Since these words were uttered the matter has been clarified by the Judges' Rules, but it must be repeated that, provided they are voluntary within the principles which have just been discussed,

---

[1] *R. v. Stewart* (1972), 56 Cr. App. Rep. 272. The only earlier English cases of any relevance seem to be *R. v. Spilsbury* (1835), 7 C. & P. 187 and *R. v. Treacy*, [1944] 2 All E. R. 229.

[2] Judgment of DIXON, J., in *Sinclair* v. *R.* (supra).

[3] *R. v. Burnett* (supra).   [4] *R. v. Williams* (supra).   [5] *Ibid.*

[6] According to *R. v. Booher* (supra) the onus is on the Crown, but the judgment in *Sinclair* v. *R.* (supra) suggests that the onus is on the accused; see especially 73 C. L. R. 340.

[7] See *The Interrogation of Suspects*, by R. N. Gooderson, 48 Canadian Bar Review, 270 (1970).

[8] Investigations under the Official Secrets Acts are in a special category because there is a duty to answer.

[9] *R. v. Knight and Thayre* (1905), 20 Cox 711; *R. v. Best*, [1909] 1 K. B. 692; *R. v. Liebling* (1909), 2 Cr. App. Rep. 314; *R. v. Booth and Jones* (1910), 5 Cr. App. Rep. 177; *R. v. Winkel* (1911), 76 J. P. 191; *Ibrahim* v. *R.*, [1914] A. C. 599; *R. v. Crowe and Myerscough* (1917), 81 J. P. 288; *R. v. Voisin*, [1918] 1 K. B. 531; *R. v. Cook* (1918), 34 T. L. R. 515; *R. v. Booker* (1924), 18 Cr. App. Rep. 47; *R. v. Brown and Bruce* (1931),23 Cr. App. Rep. 56; *R. v. Bass*, [1953] 1 Q. B. 680; [1953] 1 All E. R. 1064; *R. v. Smith*, [1961] 3 All E. R. 972.

statements obtained in breach of the Rules are not inadmissible as a matter of law although they may be rejected in the judge's discretion; moreover the judge has a discretion to reject confessions which were obtained unfairly, even though they were voluntary and obtained without a breach of the Rules.

Rule I permits police questioning of anyone, whether a suspect or not, even if he is in custody, provided he has not been charged with or informed that he may be prosecuted for the offence[1] concerning which the questions are put. This permits the questioning of someone in custody on one charge about some other offence,[2] although questioning on a "holding charge" has been disapproved in Rhodesia.[3]

Rule II requires a caution to be given as soon as a police officer has evidence[4] which would afford reasonable grounds for suspecting that the person interrogated has committed an offence. Rule III requires a further caution when that person is charged[5] or informed that he may be prosecuted,[6] and provides that it is only in exceptional circumstances that questions may be put after the occurrence of these events. When such questions are put, a further caution must be administered.

Rule IV provides for the taking down of statements, Rule V is concerned with the case of two persons charged with the same offence and has already been mentioned,[7] while Rule VI provides that persons other than police officers charged with the duty of investigating offences or charging offenders shall, so far as may be practicable, comply with the Rules.[8]

(ii) **Comment on silence.**—From time to time the Court of Appeal (Criminal Division) and its predecessor (the Court of Criminal Appeal) have allowed appeals on the ground that the trial judge went too far when commenting in his summing-up on the accused's silence when charged.[9] The upshot of these decisions seems to be that, although the accused's silence may be treated as something which has a bearing on the weight of his evidence, it is not something which can support an inference that the story told by him in court is untrue; still less can it amount to corroboration of the evidence given against him.

---

[1] There is no guidance on the meaning of the word "offence" in the rules. It is hard to believe that they are regularly followed on inquiries concerning parking offences.

[2] *R.* v. *Buchan*, [1964] 1 All E. R. 502.

[3] *R.* v. *Sambo*, [1965] 1 S. A. 640.

[4] I.e. information which can be put before a court (*R.* v. *Osborne and Virtue*, [1973] Q. B. 678; [1973] 1 All E. R. 649).

[5] "Charged" as used in the Rules means formally charged, and not the informal charge given on arrest on suspicion (*R.* v. *Brackenbury*, [1965] 1 All E. R. 960; *R.* v. *Collier*, *R.* v. *Stenning*, [1965] 3 All E. R. 136).

[6] These words apply to the decision to issue a summons against someone not under arrest (*R.* v. *Collier*, *R.* v. *Stenning*, *supra*).

[7] P. 479, *supra*.

[8] *R.* v. *Nicholls* (1967), 51 Cr. App. Rep. 233 (storekeeper not professional investigator within Rule VI).

[9] *R.* v. *Tate*, [1908] 2 K. B. 680; *R.* v. *Feigenbaum*, [1919] 1 K. B. 431 (a case which is unlikely to be followed in view of *R.* v. *Keeling*, [1942] 1 All E. R. 507 and *Hall* v. *R.*, [1970] 1 All E. R. 322); *R.* v. *Whitehead*, [1929] 1 K. B. 99; *R.* v. *Charavanmuttu* (1930), 22 Cr. App. Rep. 1; *R.* v. *Parker*, [1933] 1 K. B. 850; *R.* v. *Naylor*, [1933] 1 K. B. 685; *R.* v. *Littleboy*, [1934] 2 K. B. 408; *R.* v. *Tune* (1944), 29 Cr. App. Rep. 162; *R.* v. *Lecky*, [1944] K. B. 80; 60 L. Q. R. 33 and 130; *Lecky's* case was followed in *R.* v. *Twist*, [1954] V. L. R. 121 where it was pointed out that the case had been applied in *R.* v. *Haddy*, [1944] K. B. 442; [1944] 1 All E. R. 319 (as reported in 170 L. T. 406); *R.* v. *Gerard*, [1948] 1 All E. R. 205 (64 L. Q. R. 176); *R.* v. *Davis* (1959), 43 Cr. App. Rep. 215; *R.* v. *Hoare*, [1966] 2 All E. R. 846; *R.* v. *Ryan* (1966), 50 Cr. App. Rep. 144; *R.* v. *Sullivan* (1966), 51 Cr. App. Rep. 102.

> "It is one thing to make an observation with regard to the force of an alibi, and to say that it is unfortunate that the defence was not set up at an earlier date so as to afford the opportunity of its being tested; it is another thing to employ that nondisclosure as evidence against an accused person and as corroborating the evidence of an accomplice."[1]

Since these words were spoken s. 11 of the Criminal Justice Act 1967 has made special provision with regard to notice of alibis in the case of trials on indictment,[2] and it has been held that the judge should not comment on the accused's failure to mention an alibi on arrest.[3]

The distinction taken in the above quotation has, however, also been taken in the case of other defences. Thus, in *R. v. Ryan*,[4] the accused, who was practically caught in the act of taking his employer's goods from a railway waggon, only raised the defence that he had been tidying things up at his trial. In the course of holding that the judge's comment on this fact fell on the right side of the line, Melford STEVENSON, J., speaking for the Court of Appeal, said:

> "It is we think clear ... that it is wrong to say to a jury 'because the accused exercised what is undoubtedly his right, the privilege of remaining silent, you may draw an inference of guilt'; it is quite a different matter to say 'this accused, as he is entitled to do, has not advanced at any earlier stage the explanation that has been offered to you to-day; you, the jury, may take that into account when you are assessing the weight which you think it right to attribute to the explanation.' "[5]

It is difficult not to have some sympathy with SALMON, L.J., when, in *R. v. Sullivan*,[6] a case in which the judge's comment was held to have gone too far, he said:

> "the line dividing what may be said and what may not be said is a very fine one, and it is perhaps doubtful whether in a case like the present it would be even perceptible to the members of an ordinary jury."

The distinction between treating the accused's pre-trial silence as something which may support an inference of guilt and as something which may reduce the weight of a defence is, like the analogous distinction between treating the accused's failure to give evidence as the basis of an inference of guilt and as a proper subject of comment,[7] a difficult one. Of course the jury must be told that the accused has a perfect right to remain silent and that they must on no account draw a direct inference of guilt from the fact that he exercised it. Furthermore, the circumstances of a particular case may be such that it would be wrong to infer guilt indirectly from the belatedness of the defence, but common sense suggests that there may also be occasions on which a legitimate line of reasoning would be that the belatedness of the defence shows that it is bogus, and that the absence of a credible answer to the prosecution's case warrants an inference that the case is unanswerable. Yet it is tolerably clear that, under the present law, a direction which canvassed the possibility of such reasoning, even though clearly stating that the decision whether to employ it was for the jury, would be upset. Some of the decisions naturally stress the fact that it would be unsafe to draw any inferences from the accused's silence after

---

[1] *Per* Lord HEWART, C.J., in *R. v. Littleboy*, [1934] 2 K. B. 408, at p. 413.
[2] P. 36, *ante*.   [3] *R. v. Lewis* (1973), 57 Cr. App. Rep. 860.
[4] (1966), 50 Cr. App. Rep. 144.   [5] At p. 148.
[6] (1966), 51 Cr. App. Rep. 102, at p. 105.   [7] P. 355, *ante*.

he has been cautioned in accordance with the Judges' Rules, but "the caution merely serves to remind the accused of a right which he already possesses at common law."[1] As things stand, the most prudent course, although it amounts to an abnegation of the customary role of the judge at a jury trial, may be thought to be for him to make no comment on the accused's pre-trial silence, and this is what the Court of Appeal has advised so far as silence after caution is concerned.[2]

(iii) **Proposals of the Criminal Law Revision Committee.**[3]—The Criminal Law Revision Committee recommended that failure by an accused on being interrogated by someone charged with the duty of investigating an offence, or on being charged with or informed that he may be prosecuted for the offence, to mention any fact on which he subsequently relies in his defence, may, provided the fact is one he could reasonably be expected to have mentioned, be the basis of such inferences as appear proper by the court or jury in determining whether there is a case to answer, or whether he is guilty of the offence; the Committee also proposed that the failure should be capable of amounting to corroboration of the evidence against the accused when it was required. The number of occasions on which it would be proper to draw the inferences at committal proceedings or even on a submission of no case would probably be rare, but there is no doubt that a substantial proportion of the cases in which judicial comment on silence has been held improper would have been decided differently if the recommendation had been in force.

The caution mentioned in the Judges' Rules would obviously be incompatible with the recommendation for it would be unsafe to draw inferences from a person's failure to mention facts after being told that he need not say anything. Accordingly there is a further recommendation that the Judges' Rules should be abolished, to be replaced by administrative directions which should contain provisions requiring police officers, when charging a suspect or informing him that he may be prosecuted, to hand him a notice explaining the effect of the new provisions concerning his silence.

The entire proposal has been the subject of considerable criticism and, although much of that criticism ignored the fact that only proper inferences may be drawn, some of it was well grounded. As is so often the case when the justification of rules of evidence is under consideration, the question is whether there is good reason for not allowing common sense to have a free rein. There can be little doubt that the recommendation is based on common sense and that the distinctions drawn in the cases are not; but it is argued with much force that the dangers of an abuse of power by the police would be increased if the recommendation were adopted. The dangers are that an ignorant and unwary suspect might be bullied into making admissions, from which he would now be restrained by the caution, before he had had an opportunity of calmly reflecting on his position and consulting his lawyer, and that, in some cases, the prosecution might "trim" their evidence to meet the defence.

Partial answers to the above points are that the adoption of the recommendation would mean that it would no longer be possible for a solicitor,

---

[1] Lord DIPLOCK in *Hall* v. *R.*, [1971] All E. R. 322 at p. 324.
[2] *R.* v. *Lewis* (1973), 57 Cr. App. Rep. 860.
[3] 11th Report, paras. 28–52; for comment see Zuckerman in 36 M. L. R. 509 (1973).

when allowed to see the suspect,[1] to advise him to say nothing, and that the recommendation should not be adopted until provision is made for the tape-recording of police interrogations. This was proposed by a minority of the Committee. There can be little doubt that the suggestion under consideration would be far more sympathetically received if all those concerned could be certain of what took place when the accused was interviewed and charged by the police; but there is undeniably a difficulty of which adequate account may not be taken by those who propose that a lawyer should be present throughout the entire interrogation of a suspect, or that the whole interrogation should be tape-recorded. The difficulty is that the questioning may well be concerned with subjects, such as the part played in various crimes by persons not under arrest, which ought not to be made public. Indeed it may be necessary to accept the fact that a certain amount of bargaining for information of that sort at police interrogations is inevitable. The question of tape-recording these interrogations is at present under review by the Home Office.

(iv) Developments in the United States and the right to silence. —The Criminal Law Revision Committee's recommendation to place what amounts to a measure of compulsion on a suspect had been preceded by converse developments in the United States. In *Miranda* v. *Arizona*[2] the Supreme Court ruled that, before interrogating a suspect the police must inform him of his right to say nothing, to consult counsel, and, should he be indigent, to be provided with counsel. It must also be made clear that the suspect continues to have these rights throughout the interrogation.

> "The current practice of incomunicado interrogation is at odds with one of our nation's most cherished principles—that the individual may not be compelled to incriminate himself. Unless adequate protective devices are employed to dispel the compulsion inherent in custodial surroundings, no statement obtained from the defendant can truly be the product of his free choice."[3]

The fifth amendment provides that no-one shall be compelled to be a witness against himself, and the effect of the American cases is to fuse the witness's privilege against self-incrimination with the rule that confessions are inadmissible unless they were made voluntarily into what has come to be thought of as a constitutional right to silence.

It is argued that proposals such as those of the Criminal Law Revision Committee with regard to belated defences tend, like the proposals of the same body permitting inferences to be drawn from the accused's failure to testify,[4] to violate that right by pressurising suspects to answer police questions. It would be a mistake to minimise the force of this argument, but it must not be forgotten that the real issue concerns the extent to which such proposals enhance the risk of an abuse of police powers for, whether or not a statute so provides, courts and juries will in fact continue

---

[1] The Judges' Rules are subject to the principle (c) "that every person at every stage of an investigation should be able to communicate and consult privately with a solicitor. This is so even if he is in custody provided that in such a case no unreasonable delay or hindrance is caused to the processes of investigation or the administration of justice by his doing so."

[2] 384 U.S. 436, 1965, enlarging on *Escobedo* v. *Illinois*, 378 U. S. 478, 1964, and extended in *Orozco* v. *Texas*, 394 U. S. 324, 1968; but see the retreat from Miranda in *Harris* v. *New York*, 401 U. S. 222, 1971.

[3] WARREN, C.J., at p. 457.   [4] P. 356, *ante.*

to apply their common sense and, in proper cases alone it is to be hoped, draw inferences from the fact that a particular defence was only raised late in the day.   The present law inhibiting a judge from giving a proper direction on the subject is something that requires justification; whether it is justified is a question which turns on the behaviour of the police.

SECTION 3. MISCELLANEOUS COMMON LAW EXCEPTIONS TO THE HEARSAY RULE

After dealing with testimony in former proceedings, it is proposed to say a little about evidence through interpreters and evidence of age because they both seem to involve exceptions to the hearsay rule at certain points.

A. TESTIMONY IN FORMER PROCEEDINGS

A number of statutes provides for the reception of depositions and statements of fact at subsequent stages of a criminal trial,[1] and it has been held at common law that the trial court may read a deposition taken at a coroner's inquisition when the deponent committed suicide after the inquest.[2]   The statutes providing for the reception at the trial proper of depositions taken at committal proceedings when the deponent has died or is ill are to a large extent enactments of the common law.[3]

In *R. v. Hall*[4] the jury had disagreed at the first trial.   At his second trial the accused wished to put in evidence the deposition and a transcript of the evidence of a Crown witness who had died between the two trials.   He wished to do this because the witness had been unsatisfactory in some respects.   The trial judge admitted the deposition, but rejected the transcript and the Court of Appeal allowed the accused's appeal because, although he had a discretion to exclude it, the judge should have admitted the transcript.   The decision turned on the common law and it seems that the conditions of admissibility of testimony in former proceedings are that the evidence should have been for or against the same accused, in relation to substantially the same facts, by a witness unable to attend the trial through death or illness but not, it seems, absence from the jurisdiction.[5]

It is sometimes said that evidence of this nature, whether it was originally given at an earlier stage of the same trial or in separate proceedings, is not received under an exception to the hearsay rule.   This is because the evidence was given on oath and was subject to cross-examination.   It is true that the evidence has been said to be of "as high a nature, and as direct and immediate as *viva voce* testimony,"[6] but the court is deprived of the opportunity of first hand experience of the witness's demeanour, and much of the force of cross-examination is lost if it does not take place before the tribunal which has to accept or reject the evidence.   At any rate, there is no doubt that the reception of the evidence infringes the hearsay

---

[1] E.g. Criminal Justice Act, 1925, s. 13;   Criminal Law Amendment Act, 1867, s. 6; Magistrates' Courts Act, 1952, s. 41;   Children and Young Persons Act, 1933, s. 43; Children and Young Persons Act, 1963, s. 27.

[2] *R. v. Cowle* (1907), 71 J. P. 152.

[3] *R. v. Beeston* (1854), Dears. C. C. 405 at p. 511 and p. 514.

[4] [1973] 1 Q. B. 496;   [1973] 1 All E. R. 1.   See also *R. v. McGregor*, [1968] 1 Q. B. 371; [1967] 2 All E. R. 267.

[5] *R. v. Scaife* (1851), 17 Q. B. 238, at p. 243.

[6] *Wright* v. *Doe* d. *Tatham* (1834), 1 Ad. & El. 3, at p. 22.

rule as formulated in this book; it must therefore be accounted for on the basis that it constitutes a common law exception to that rule which has to a large extent been taken over by statute.

B. EVIDENCE THROUGH INTERPRETERS

An accused who cannot understand English properly has a right to an interpreter.[1] There is also the possibility that it will be necessary for a witness to give evidence through an interpreter. In neither of these cases is there any hearsay problem. The interpreter testifies to what the witness says in court, and the witness, or accused, testifies to what he observed or did out of court. Two different people are testifying to two different things, and in neither case can it be said that the statement of someone other than a person who is giving oral evidence in the proceedings is tendered as evidence of the facts stated.

It sometimes happens, however, that a suspect is interviewed by the police with the assistance of an interpreter. If the police officer is ignorant of the suspect's language, the hearsay rule is infringed when the interpreter is not called, for the officer narrates to the court what the interpreter told him that the suspect said, and the court is asked to treat the interpreter's narrated statement as evidence of the words used by the suspect. The right course is to call the interpreter and allow him to refresh his memory with the aid of his notes.[2] He will then inform the court of the meaning of the words which he heard the suspect use and, where appropriate, the court can receive those words as an admission on the part of the suspect.

If the procedure contemplated in the administrative directions attached to the Judges' Rules is followed, the suspect's statement to the interpreter will have been written down in the foreign language and signed by the suspect; the interpreter will also have made an official translation of the statement. All that will be necessary at the trial is that the suspect's signature should be verified, unless admitted, and that the translation should be proved to be authentic, if that too is not admitted. The hearsay rule will be infringed by the reception of the statement as evidence of the facts stated, though the exception relating to confessions will be brought into play, but the reception of the translation as evidence of what the suspect signed will not infringe the hearsay rule because that fact will be proved by the witness called to authenticate the translation who will usually be the interpreter.

In territories such as Papua and New Guinea native interpreters are employed, and they often completely forget what took place and, being illiterate, have no notes with which to refresh their memories. In those cases the courts can only receive the police officer's evidence of what the interpreter told him the suspect said under an exception to the rule against hearsay.[3] Devices to disguise this fact by treating the interpreter as the agent of the suspect, or holding that there are not in reality two conversations, the one between the police officer and the interpreter and the other

---

[1] *R. v. Lee Kun*, [1916] 1 K. B. 337. The court has a discretion to allow a party to have an interpreter in a civil case (*In the Estate of Fuld, (No. 2) Hartley* v. *Fuld*, [1965] P. 405; [1965] 2 All E. R. 657.

[2] *R. v. Attard* (1959), 43 Cr. App. Rep. 90.

[3] *Gaio* v. *R.* (1961), 104 C. L. R. 419; *R. v. Kores* (1970), 15 C. R. N. S. 107; 7 Melbourne Law Review 3–5.

between the interpreter and the suspect, but one only, between the suspect and the officer, are, to say the least, unrealistic.

C. EVIDENCE OF AGE

As we saw in chapter XVII, one of the stock illustrations of the breadth of the hearsay rule is provided by cases in which it has been held that a witness cannot give admissible evidence of the date of his birth, and the same decision has been reached with regard to the witness's place of birth. Generally speaking, these cases give rise to no problem because age can be proved under a variety of well recognised exceptions to the hearsay rule (notably that relating to statements in public documents), by appearance, or by the recollection of past events by the person whose age is in question. It seems, however, that hearsay is allowed to creep in, where no recognised exception to the rule under which it is prohibited applies on account of the different methods of proving the identity of a person named in a birth certificate that have been permitted by the courts in civil and criminal cases. Let us assume that A.'s age is to be proved by production of a certificate referring to the birth of someone named A. Clearly it will be necessary for the court to be satisfied that the A. mentioned in the certificate is the same person as the A. whose age is to be proved, and the courts have admitted hearsay evidence on this point without stating that they are doing so.

In *R.* v. *Weaver*,[1] it was that of the child's grandmother who, though present at its birth, was not present at the registration; in *Wilton & Co.* v. *Phillips*[2] the evidence was that of a brother of the person whose age was in issue, and he does not appear to have been present either at the birth or registration; in *Re Bulley's Settlement*,[3] there was only an affidavit sworn by the claimant to a fund stating that he had reached his majority, and in *R.* v. *Bellis*,[4] the clerk to a board of guardians simply deposed to the result of inquiries which he had previously made about the age of the prosecutrix. In each of these cases the court acted on statements which must necessarily have been based on information supplied to the makers by third parties. It is submitted that this kind of evidence of age should be expressly treated as received under an exception to the hearsay rule.

SECTION 4. STATUTORY EXCEPTIONS TO THE HEARSAY RULE

There is a large number of statutory provisions under which hearsay statements are admissible in criminal cases. Most of them are of limited application. For example, under s. 27 (4) of the Theft Act, 1968, in proceedings for the theft of goods in transmission (whether by post or otherwise) or for handling goods stolen by such a theft, a statutory declaration by the sender or recipient that the goods were dispatched or received is admissible as evidence of those facts and of the condition of the goods, provided due notice is given to the accused and he does not require the maker of the declaration to be called. There are, however, only two provisions which are of general application in the sense that they are neither confined to proof of particular facts nor solely concerned with particular proceed-

---

[1] (1873), L. R. 2 C. C. R. 85.
[3] [1886] W. N. 80.
[2] (1903), 19 T. L. R. 390.
[4] (1911), 6 Cr. App. Rep. 283.

ings; these are the Criminal Evidence Act, 1965, and s. 9 of the Criminal Justice Act, 1967.

A. THE CRIMINAL EVIDENCE ACT, 1965

The Criminal Evidence Act, 1965, was passed in consequence of the decision of the House of Lords in *Myers* v. *Director of Public Prosecutions*[1] according to which, in a criminal case,[2] motor manufacturers' records were inadmissible as evidence of the numbers on cylinder blocks placed in the engines of cars by workmen.

S. 1 (1) provides as follows:

"In any criminal proceedings where direct oral evidence of a fact would be admissible, any statement contained in a document and tending to establish that fact shall, on production of the document, be admissible as evidence of that fact if—

(a) the document is or forms part of a record relating to any trade or business and compiled in the course of that trade or business, from information supplied (whether directly or indirectly) by persons who have or may reasonably be supposed to have, personal knowledge of the matters dealt with in the information they supply; and

(b) the person who supplied the information recorded in the statement in question is dead, or beyond the seas, or unfit by reason of his bodily or mental condition to attend as a witness,[3] or cannot with reasonable diligence be identified or found, or cannot reasonably be expected (having regard to the time which has elapsed since he supplied the information and to all the circumstances) to have any recollection of the matters dealt with in the information he supplied."

The 1965 Act is more liberal than s. 4 of the Civil Evidence Act, 1968, in that, where the information is passed from one person to another, there is no requirement that the intermediaries should, any more than the compiler of the record, have been acting under a duty; but the requirement that the record should have been compiled in the course of a trade or business will usually mean that the compiler at least will have been acting under a duty. The Act of 1965 is also more liberal than the 1968 Act, s. 4, in that there is no requirement of the service of a notice in order to render a record admissible. The 1965 Act is, however, narrower than s. 4 of the 1968 Act in that it is confined to trade or business records.

S. 1 (4) defines "business" as inclusive of "any public transport, public utility or similar undertaking carried on by a local authority and the activities of the post office." In *R.* v. *Gwilliam*[4] it was held that, even if a consignment note were a record, a point left open by the Court of Appeal, the Home Office Supply and Transport Store was not a trade or business. It is almost certainly still true to say that a soldier's regimental records are still inadmissible as evidence of the fact that he was abroad at a particular time.

As is the case with the 1968 Act, the 1965 Act does not contain a definition of a record, but a "document" is defined to include any device by which information is recorded or stored. This is apt to include discs and

---

[1] [1965] A. C. 1001; [1964] 1 All E. R. 877.
[2] Even at the time of the decision they would have been admissible in a civil case under the Evidence Act, 1938.
[3] The court may act on a medical certificate (s. 1 (2)).
[4] [1968] 3 All E. R. 821.
[5] Cf. *Lilley* v. *Pettit*, [1946] K. B. 401; [1946] 1 All E. R. 593.

tape-recordings. It has been pointed out that no special definition is required to cover a computer's print-out and it has been said that "This statute is simple, straightforward and sufficient to provide a satisfactory framework for the reception of computerised records in evidence in the area to which it relates;"[1] this is by way of contrast with s. 5 of the Civil Evidence Act, 1968.

B. CRIMINAL JUSTICE ACT, 1967, S. 9

Provided the conditions specified in s. 9 of the Criminal Justice Act, 1967, are fulfilled, agreed statements of facts may be admitted in evidence at any criminal trial to the same extent and with the same effect as oral evidence.[2] The principal conditions are that the statement should be signed and contain a declaration of the maker's knowledge that it was made subject to penalties in the event of its being used in evidence if the maker knew it to be false or did not care whether it was true, that a copy should have been served on the opposite party, and that no notice of objection should have been received from that party within seven days. It is also possible for the parties to agree to the reception of such a statement at or before the trial, although the provisions with regard to service of a copy of the statement and non-receipt within seven days of notice of objection have not been fulfilled.

SECTION 5. PROPOSALS OF THE CRIMINAL LAW REVISION COMMITTEE[3]

One of the aims of the Criminal Law Revision Committee was to follow the scheme of the Civil Evidence Act, 1968, as far as the differences between civil and criminal proceedings allow. Whether and to what extent this is a desirable aim are of course arguable points. It can be plausibly contended that the consequences of wrongful convictions and, though to a lesser degree, of wrongful acquittals, are so grave that the possible risk of an increase in the chances of incurring them by broadening the bases of the reception of hearsay evidence ought not to be taken. On the other hand, it can be contended with equal plausibility that the risks in question are greater under the present law than they would be under a system which provided for a more liberal reception of hearsay. Presumably we shall never know whether the acquittal and conviction were respectively justified in fact in *R.* v. *Gibson*[4] and *R.* v. *Thomson.*[5] In the first case, on a charge of unlawful wounding, the statement of an unidentified bystander that the man who threw the stone went into the house in which the accused was found was excluded, and in the second, a case of manslaughter, the deceased's statements that she intended to abort herself and had done so were likewise excluded. All that we can say with certainty is that, as decisions on the law of evidence, they were grossly unjust.

The Criminal Law Revision Committee recommended the adoption in criminal cases of more or less precise equivalents to s. 4 and s. 5 of the Civil Evidence Act, 1968, dealing respectively with ordinary and compu-

---

[1] Tapper, *Computers and the Law*, 27.
[2] *Ellis* v. *Jones*, [1973] 2 All E. R. 893.
[3] 11th Report, paras. 228–65. For comment and criticism, see Glanville Williams, [1973] Crim. L. Rev. 76 and 139.
[4] (1887), 18 Q. B. D. 537.   [5] [1912] 3 K. B. 19.

terised records, and the proposal has not been criticised, although the change in the law would not be cataclysmic because, subject to its restriction to trade or business records, the Criminal Evidence Act, 1965, deals adequately and simply with these matters. The Committee also recommends provisions substantially similar to those of the 1968 Act for the admissibility of the previous statements of witnesses. It is hard to justify a distinction in this regard between civil and criminal proceedings. All that can be said is that, in the case of previous inconsistent statements, it is more risky to receive them as evidence of the facts stated in criminal proceedings because there is more chance that the original statement will have been taken by an over-enthusiastic taker of statements, a police officer or a defence solicitor; but it is not everybody who will find this a very convincing point.

In the case of the hearsay statements of non-witnesses, the Committee recommends that there should be the same exclusion of secondhand hearsay as in the Civil Evidence Act, 1968.[1] With regard to first hand hearsay statements the Committee recommends the safeguards that, at a trial on indictment, the statement should be inadmissible without the leave of the court unless notice of intention to give it in evidence has been duly served, and that, at any trial, no statement should be admissible if made after the accused has been charged, summoned, or informed that he may be prosecuted, when the maker is abroad, unidentifiable or untraceable. The object of this last provision is to guard against the manufacture of evidence by means of a statement made by someone who "conveniently" disappears before the trial. The mere possibility of the reception in a criminal case of the statement of someone who cannot be identified has been regarded with horror by some critics, although *R.* v. *Gibson*[2] should serve as a reminder that such evidence can be very cogent. The fact that the statement would be inadmissible if made after charge should greatly restrict the dangers inherent in the reception of this kind of evidence; but, if the doctrine of the *res gestae*, discussed in the next chapter, is liberally applied, it might be better to restrict the admissibility of hearsay statements in criminal cases to those of persons who are either called as witnesses, dead, ill, abroad, or, though identifiable, untraceable.

Even so, this seems to be the right place to enter a protest against criticisms of a liberalising change in the law of hearsay which seem to apply the test of whether it would be safe to convict on such evidence alone. There are of course few, if any, cases in which this would be so, whether the law under consideration is the present or something different, but the hearsay statement may be of considerable significance when taken together with other evidence. Although it is legal to do so, and occasionally done, it cannot be often that it is safe to convict on the direct oral evidence of one witness.

Two hearsay problems peculiar to criminal proceedings are presented by the law concerning the competence and compellability of witnesses. The accused's spouse would be a competent witness for the prosecution in all cases if the proposals of the Criminal Law Revision Committee on the subject were adopted, but only exceptionally would he or she be a compellable witness for the prosecution. If the spouse were unable or un-

---

[1] For hypothetical cases in which the exclusion of secondhand hearsay could work hardship, see p. 417, n. 1, *ante* and p. 475, *ante*.   [2] P. 402, *ante*.

willing to testify, should the prosecution be allowed to give his or her state-ment in evidence? The accused is not a competent witness for the prose-cution, and he may opt not to give evidence for the defence. If he has made an admissible confession, that may be proved against him both under the present law and under the Committee's recommendations; but, if the confession implicates a co-accused, or if, without incriminating himself, an accused who does not give evidence has made a statement incriminating his co-accused, should the prosecution be allowed to give it in evidence?

The answer of the majority of the Committee to the first question was that the statement of the accused's spouse should only be given in evidence if he or she testifies for the prosecution or is, or would if living, have been compellable to do so. The argument in favour of the majority recom-mendation is that, to provide otherwise would tend to circumvent the law concerning the compellability of the accused's spouse; but there is a strong counter-argument based on the fact that the reason why the ac-cused's spouse is not made a compellable witness for the prosecution in most cases is the public's dislike of the spectacle of an unwilling husband or wife being compelled to incriminate his or her spouse; that argument loses its force when the spouse has already freely made a statement in-criminating his or her consort.

The Committee's answer to the second question was that, if an accused made a statement incriminating himself and his co-accused, the statement should be admissible against each, even though its maker does not give evidence.[1] This recommendation has been severely criticised; but it is hard to escape the conclusion that its adoption would at least constitute an improvement on the present English law. There are three possibilities in the situation under consideration. If A. and B. are being tried together, A.'s statement incriminating himself and B. could, as the Committee recommends, be admissible as evidence against each accused; it could, in accordance with current English law, be admissible against A. but not against B.; or it could, in accordance with the views of the United States Supreme court,[2] be inadmissible against either. It is submitted that the only acceptable solutions are the first or third. The objection to the se-cond is that the judge has to call upon the jury to perform an impossible feat, namely, to treat the statement as evidence against A., but not against B., "a recommendation to the jury of a mental gymnastic which is beyond, not only their powers, but anybody else's".[3] Hearsay, like most other evidence, ought to be admissible for all purposes or none.[4]

---

[1] The statement would likewise be admissible under the committee's proposals even though it did not incriminate the maker.

[2] *Bruton* v. *U. S.*, 391 U. S. 123, 1968.

[3] *Nash* v. *U. S.*, 54 F. (2d) 1006, at 1007, *per* LEARNED HAND, J.

[4] But in *R.* v. *Buggy* (1961), 45 Cr. App. Rep. 298, the Court of Criminal Appeal held that the fact that one accused had made a statement incriminating the other was not a ground for ordering separate trials.

CHAPTER XX

THE DOCTRINE OF *RES GESTAE*[1]

Unlike most of the principles of the law of evidence, the doctrine of the *res gestae* is inclusionary. Under it evidence may be received although it infringes the rule against hearsay, the opinion rule or the rule which generally prohibits evidence of bad disposition on the part of one of the parties, and there may be other exclusionary rules which are mitigated by the operation of the doctrine. Its inclusionary effect accounts for the fact that it is discussed after all the common law exclusionary rules other than those relating to documentary evidence have been considered.

We have seen that the assertion that an item of evidence forms part of the *res gestae* roughly means that it is relevant on account of its contemporaneity with the matters under investigation.[2] It is part of the story. An endeavour is now to be made to ascertain the extent to which the categories of admissibility under this head can be precisely stated. It will be convenient to begin by considering four exceptions to the hearsay rule (now only applicable to criminal cases) which are associated with the doctrine of *res gestae*.

A. FOUR EXCEPTIONS TO THE HEARSAY RULE ASSOCIATED WITH THE DOCTRINE OF *RES GESTAE* IN CRIMINAL CASES

These are statements accompanying and explaining a relevant act, spontaneous statements relating to an event in issue, a person's statements concerning his contemporaneous state of mind or emotion, and a person's statements concerning his contemporaneous physical sensation. A fair amount of reference to civil cases is inevitable, but it is important to bear in mind that the statements in question must, if they are to be received as evidence of the facts stated, be rendered admissible under the Civil Evidence Act, 1968. When this is done, the only question, so far as admissibility is concerned, will be the relevancy of the statement; would it have been admissible if contained in the direct oral evidence of the maker? Such special conditions of admissibility as the common law may attach to the statements (a matter on which there is uncertainty at several points) have ceased to apply in civil cases owing to the abolition of all common law exceptions to the hearsay rule.

At one time it was customary for distinguished writers, and even the most eminent judges,[3] to assert, apparently without qualification, that statements received as part of the *res gestae* are never received under an

---

[1] Four useful articles on this difficult subject are Morgan, *A Suggested Classification of Utterances admissible as Res Gestae*, 31 Yale Law Journal, 229 (1922); Stone, *Res Gestae Reagitatae*, 55 L. Q. R. 66 (1939); Nokes, *Res Gestae as Hearsay*, 70 L. Q. R. 370 (1954); and Gooderson, *Res Gestae in Criminal Cases*, C. L. J. (1956), 199; *ibid.* (1957), 55.

[2] P. 37, *ante*.

[3] *Per* Lord ATKINSON in *R. v. Christie*, [1914] A. C. 545, at p. 553.

exception to the hearsay rule; but the facts of the numerous cases cited by the writers are such as to render the contention quite untenable,[1] and, so far from the assertion being repeated by eminent judges, Lord REID once urged, in the course of the argument, that the question of *res gestae* could only arise if a statement were received as a hearsay statement.[2] His Lordship was of course concerned with the facts of the particular appeal; statements received as original evidence have, in the past, been said to constitute part of the *res gestae* on a number of occasions.

(1) STATEMENTS ACCOMPANYING AND EXPLAINING RELEVANT ACTS

(i) Statement and illustrations of the exception.—More than a hundred years ago, PARKE, B., spoke of "proof of the quality and intention of acts by declarations accompanying them" as an exception to the rule against hearsay that has been recognised from very early times on the ground of necessity or convenience.[3] The existence of this exception has not always been recognised by legal writers, but it is vouched for by numerous decisions. The rule was stated by GROVE, J., to be that:

> "Though you cannot give in evidence a declaration *per se*, yet when there is an act accompanied by a statement which is so mixed up with it as to become part of the *res gestae*, evidence of such a statement may be given".[4]

This does not indicate the purpose for which the evidence may be tendered, but there is a number of cases in which a statement was plainly received in order to establish the truth of its contents. This exception to the hearsay rule may be justified on the score of necessity because "the proper person to explain and justify a voluntary act is the man who acted",[5] as well as on the ground that the fact that the statement was made contemporaneously with the act enhances the probability that it was true.

It has repeatedly been held that, if a bankrupt goes or remains abroad, his intention in doing so can be proved by his declarations which may be oral or written.[6] In the words of Lord DENMAN:

> "The principle of admission is, that the declarations are *pars rei gestae*, and therefore it has been contended that they must be contemporaneous with it; but this has been decided not to be necessary, and on good grounds, for the nature and strength of the connection with the act are the material things to be looked to; and although concurrence of time cannot but be always material evidence to show the connection, yet it is by no means essential. . . . The substantive act proved *aliunde* is the departure from home, that is equivocal: the declaration made during the continuance of the act shows the intention with which it was done."[7]

---

[1] It is sufficient to refer to *R. v. Foster* (1834), 6 C. & P. 325, a case of manslaughter by reckless driving in which the deceased's statement made shortly after the collision was admitted "as the best possible testimony that, under the circumstances, can be adduced to show what it was that knocked the deceased down."

[2] *Ratten v. R.*, [1972] A. C. 378, at p. 381.

[3] *Wright v. Doe* d. *Tatham* (1837), 7 Ad. & El. 313, at p. 384.

[4] *Howe v. Malkin* (1878), 40 L. T. 196.

[5] *Per* Lord NORMAND in *O'Hara v. Central S.M.T. Co.*, [1941] S. C. 363, at p. 376.

[6] *Rawson v. Haigh* (1824), 2 Bing. 99; *Bateman v. Bailey* (1794), 5 Term Rep. 512; *Robson v. Kemp* (1802), 4 Esp. 233; *Rouch v. Great Western Rail. Co.* (1841), 1 Q. B. 51. These cases should be distinguished from *Ridley v. Gyde* (1832), 9 Bing. 349, and *Smith v. Cramer* (1835), 1 Bing. N. C. 585, where the debtor's statements were received as original evidence.

[7] *Rouch v. Great Western Rail. Co.* (1841), 1 Q. B., at p. 62.

In *Skinner & Co.* v. *Shew & Co.*[1] the question was whether a third party had been induced to break off contractual negotiations with the plaintiff by the defendant's threat of legal proceedings, and the court allowed the whole of a letter from the third party to the plaintiff to be read, because it both constituted the act of repudiation and contained the third party's reasons for discontinuing the negotiations. The statement of the latter, which was not that of a witness who was testifying, was thus admitted as evidence that it was the defendant's threat which caused the breakdown of the negotiations; but it is important to note the limited purpose for which declarations accompanying an act may be proved at common law. They are evidence of the actor's intention in acting, or his reasons for doing so, but they are not admissible to prove the existence of any fact mentioned in the statement of those reasons. For instance, in *Skinner & Co.* v. *Shew & Co.*, the letter from the third party to the plaintiff was not received as evidence of the fact that the defendant had made the threats it mentioned—a matter which was adequately proved by a letter from the defendant to the third party.

It is generally considered that this point was overlooked in *R.* v. *Edwards*[2] where, on a charge of murder, evidence that the deceased, the accused's wife, deposited an axe and a carving knife with a neighbour, saying that she felt safer with them out of the way, was received, apparently in order to prove previous threats by the accused.

(ii) Conditions of admissibility.—It seems that there are also three conditions with which the statements must comply before they can be received under this head—they must relate to the act, they must be roughly contemporaneous with it and they must be made by the actor. Before these conditions are considered, it should be stressed that the act which the statements accompany must itself be in issue or relevant to the issue. The point was pithily put by COLTMAN, J., when he said he was not aware:

> "of any case where the act done is in its nature irrelevant to the issue and where the declaration is *per se* inadmissible in which it has been held that the union of the two has rendered them admissible".[3]

The statement is, so to speak, parasitic on the act with regard to its admissibility. Unless the act can be shown to be at least of some possible relevance, without reference to the statement, the latter may not be proved as evidence of the truth of its contents.

(*a*) *Statement must relate to the act it accompanies.*—In *R.* v. *Bliss*[4] the limits of a certain road were in issue, and it was sought to prove a statement by a deceased owner of adjacent land who, when planting a tree, said that he was doing so on the boundary of his estate. This evidence was rejected because the declaration had no connection with the act done, and the doing of the act could not make such a declaration evidence.

(*b*) *Contemporaneity.*—The *raison d'être* of this exception to the hearsay rule is that the statement throws light on the nature of a relevant act because of its proximity to it, and, in the absence of such proximity, the statement would lack connection with the act and become a mere hearsay assertion

---

[1] [1894] 2 Ch. 581; *re Workmen's Compensation Acts, Cullen* v. *Clarke*, [1963] I. R. 368.　　　　[2] (1872), 12 Cox C. C. 230.

[3] *Wright* v. *Doe* d. *Tatham* (1837), 7 Ad. & El., at p. 361.

[4] (1837), 7 Ad. & El. 550.

about it. This distinction was taken by Lord DENMAN in *Peacock* v. *Harris* [1]
when he said, "A contemporaneous declaration may be admissible as part
of the transaction, but an action done cannot be varied or qualified by
insulated declarations". Contemporaneity is a matter of degree, and no
useful purpose would be served by an elaborate citation of authority.

   (c) *Statement must be by the actor.*—In *Howe* v. *Malkin*,[2] it was sought to
prove a statement concerning the boundaries of property made by the
plaintiff's father contemporaneously with the performance of some work
on the land by builders, and the evidence was rejected as it did not come
within the exception to the hearsay rule now under consideration because
the declaration was by one person, and the accompanying act was that of
another. It has been said that the admissibility of statements accompanying
acts is by no means so strictly confined because it is everyday practice in
criminal cases to receive the declarations of the victim as well as the
assailant, while in cases of conspiracy, riot and the like, declarations of all
concerned in the common object, although not defendants are admissible.[3]
It seems, however, that, so far as the first of these points is concerned, the
declarations of the victim are received under the next exception to the hearsay
rule to be discussed, while, so far as the second point is concerned the
declarations of rioters are usually received as original evidence,[4] and those
of conspirators as admissions by agents.[5]

(2) SPONTANEOUS STATEMENTS RELATING TO AN EVENT IN ISSUE MADE BY PARTICIPANTS OR OBSERVERS

(i) Statement and illustrations of the exception.—In *Thompson* v. *Trevanion*,[6] a civil action for an assault upon the plaintiff's wife, HOLT, C. J.:

> "allowed that that which the wife said immediately upon the hurt received
> and before that she had time to devise or contrive anything for her own
> advantage, might be given in evidence".

The report does not contain any information concerning the nature of the
statements or the purpose for which they were tendered, but the element
of spontaneity has ever since been insisted upon as a condition of admissibility under this head of the *res gestae* doctrine. In *Tustin* v. *Arnold & Sons*,[7]
a written statement made by the driver of a vehicle immediately after it
had been involved in a collision was held to be inadmissible against his
employer as part of the *res gestae* because it lacked the requisite degree of
spontaneity.

> "In such a case, words, even spoken words, do not become part of the *res
> gestae* unless they are made at the time and are the natural consequence of
> the collision, words which spring out of the fact of the collision inevitably,
> and are at any rate spontaneous."[8]

Although there does not appear to be any authority on the point, it would
be a mistake to treat this case as a decision to the effect that statements
contained in a document can never be received under this head of the *res
gestae* doctrine. For example, if A., charged with murder by poisoning,
were proved to have sent the deceased some tablets, it may well be that a
letter proved to have been written by the deceased to A. immediately

---

[1] (1836), 5 Ad. & El. 449.   [2] (1878), 40 L. T. 196.
[3] Phipson's *Law of Evidence* (11th edition), 83.
[4] *R.* v. *Gordon (Lord)* (1781), 21 State Tr. 485.   [5] P. 481, *ante.*
[6] (1693), Skin. 402.   [7] (1915), 84 L. J. K. B. 2214.   [8] BAILHACHE, J.

after taking some of the pills stating that they had caused him excruciating pain would be held to be admissible.[1]

Before Lord WILBERFORCE's important review of the authorities in *Ratten* v. *R.*,[2] the law concerning the admissibility of statements under this exception to the hearsay rule was in danger of becoming enmeshed in conceptualism of the worst type. Great stress was placed on the need for contemporaneity of the statement with the event,[3] but, what was far more serious, much attention was devoted to the question whether the words could be said to form part of the transaction or event with all the attendant insoluble problems of when the transaction or event began and ended. An illustration is provided by *R.* v. *Bedingfield*,[4] the most famous English decision on the subject. The accused was charged with murder by cutting a woman's throat and his defence was that she committed suicide. The deceased came out of the room in which the prisoner was subsequently found. Her throat was cut and she immediately cried "See what Bedingfield has done to me." She was evidently seeking assistance, but died before it could be given. COCKBURN, C.J., would not allow her statement to be proved because "it was something stated by her after it was all over, whatever it was, and after the act was completed." He had, however, previously observed that "anything uttered by the deceased at the time the act was being done would be admissible as, for instance, if she had been heard to say something as 'Don't, Harry'."[5] The statement of the deceased was excluded on somewhat similar facts in the Australian case of *Brown* v. *R.*[6] because the deceased had been walking away from the place where he had been shot (either accidentally or, as the prosecution alleged, deliberately) not to avoid a repetition of the attack, but in order to remedy its effects. The words were characterised as remarks "not naturally and spontaneously emanating from or growing out of the main transaction, but arising out of an independent and additional transaction."

The only English criminal case which supports the exception to the hearsay rule under consideration, when the maker of the statement is not called as a witness, is *R.* v. *Foster*.[7] On a charge of manslaughter, the deceased's statement, made very soon after he had been run down in a road accident, was received as evidence of how he came to be knocked down. There is even some commonwealth authority suggesting that the exception is non-existent.[8]

---

[1] Reference is sometimes made to *R.* v. *Podmore* (1930), 22 Cr. App. Rep. 36, but the documents found on the seat of the car in which the deceased's dead body was discovered were admitted as circumstantial evidence of a business association, discreditable to the accused, between him and the deceased.

[2] [1972] A. C. 378; [1971] 3 All E. R. 801.

[3] *Poriotis* v. *Australian Iron and Steel Co.*, *Ltd.* (1963), S. R. N. S. W. 991 where, however, as in some other Australian and Canadian cases, a large measure of discretion in this matter was accorded to the trial judge.

[4] (1879), 14 Cox C. C. 341. The words were held to be inadmissible as a dying declaration because it was not clear that the deceased was under a settled hopeless expectation of death. The decision was attacked by Taylor in a letter to the Times, and Cockburn replied in no unmeasured terms in 15 L. J. 5; see also Thayer, *Legal Essays*, 20–7. *R.* v. *Bedingfield* was approved in Canada in *R.* v. *Gilbert* (1907), 12 Can. Crim. Cas. 127.

[5] Cockburn would, it seems from his article, have admitted the statement if the woman had been pursued by the accused.   [6] (1913), 17 C. L. R. 570.

[7] (1834), 6 C. & P. 325; see also the Irish case of *R.* v. *Lunny* (1855), 6 Cox C. C. 477. For civil cases see "*The Schwalbe*" (1861), 4 L. T. 160 and *Davies* v. *Fortior*, *Ltd.*, [1952] 1 All E. R. 1359. For cases in which the maker of the statement was called see *R.* v. *Fowkes*, p. 216, *ante* and *R.* v. *Roberts*, p. 207, *ante*.

[8] *Adelaide Chemical and Fertiliser Co.* v. *Carlisle* (1939), 64 C. L. R. 514, at p. 531; *R.* v. *Leland*, [1951] O. R. 12.

R. v. Bedingfield and *R. v. Foster* were both cited in the speeches of the House of Lords in *R. v. Christie*,[1] but this should not be taken to mean that the decisions are any more or any less reconcilable than any other brace of cases in which the same principle has been applied to substantially the same facts with different results. This was certainly the view of Lord WILBERFORCE in *Ratten v. R.*,[2] when he described *Bedingfield's Case* as a decision "more useful as a focus for discussion than for a decision on the facts." Ratten was charged with and convicted of murdering his wife by shooting her. His defence was that the gun went off accidentally while he was cleaning it. There was evidence that the deceased was alive and apparently well at about 1.12 p.m. and the accused said that, after he had phoned for an ambulance, the police phoned him about 1.20. The prosecution called a telephone girl who swore that, about 1.15 a woman with an hysterical voice had phoned from the accused's house asking for the police, and that, the speaker having rung off, she spoke to the police who, in their turn had phoned the accused. The Judicial Committee held that the telephone girl's evidence had been rightly received; on one view the evidence was not hearsay for the phone call was relevant as contradicting the accused's statement that his call for the ambulance was the only one going out of the house between 1.12 and 1.20, by which time Mrs. Ratten was indubitably dead; the girl's evidence also went on to show that there was a frightened woman in the house and, on the facts, there was no doubt that that woman was the deceased. The Judicial Committee also accepted the Crown's contention that the girl's evidence was admissible on the ground that the conversation to which she deposed was a hearsay statement by the deceased forming part of the *res gestae*, and amounting to an assertion by the deceased that she was frightened by something her husband was doing or saying. Speaking of the criteria for receiving hearsay statements under this head of the *res gestae* doctrine, Lord WILBERFORCE said:[3]

> "The test should not be the uncertain one whether the making of the statement should be regarded as part of the event or transaction, this may often be difficult to show. But if the drama leading up to the climax has commenced and assumed such intensity and pressure that the utterance can safely be regarded as a true reflection of what was unravelling, or actually happened, it ought to be received."

Lord WILBERFORCE also said that the authorities

> "show that there is ample support for the principle that hearsay evidence may be admitted if the statement providing it is made in such conditions (always being those of proximate but not exact contemporaneity) of involvement or pressure to exclude the possibility of concoction or distortion to the advantage of the maker or the disadvantage of the accused."

When speaking of *R. v. Bedingfield*, Lord WILBERFORCE said:

> "there could hardly be a case where the words uttered carried more clearly the marks of spontaneity and intense involvement";.

It may therefore be assumed with some confidence that, were similar facts to recur, the decision would be different.

(ii) Conditions of admissibility.—It is doubtful whether it is possible

---

[1] [1914] A. C. 545, at p. 556 and p. 566.
[2] [1972] A. C., at p. 390.
[3] [1972] A. C. 378, at p. 389.

to be more precise with regard to the conditions of admissibility of hearsay statements under this head of the *res gestae* than to say that they must be spontaneous utterances made shortly before, during or soon after an event in issue, by observers of or participants in that event, and concerning it. It must be confessed that even this rough statement is more the result of inference from, rather than of statements in, the authorities. The authorities do, however, require a reference to two further questions. Must the statement concern the event in issue "directly"? Must there be other evidence of the event than the statement itself in order to render the latter admissible?

(*a*) *Directness.*—The first question is prompted by Lord NORMAND's treatment of *R.* v. *Gibson*[1] in *Teper* v. *R.*[2] Teper was charged with arson, and the Judicial Committee held that the trial judge should have rejected a police officer's evidence of the remark of an unidentified bystander made to a passing motorist, said by the officer to resemble the accused, expressing surprise at the fact that he was going away from the vicinity of his burning shop, such evidence having been tendered in rebuttal of the defence of alibi. There was every reason why the statement should have been excluded. It was of dubious contemporaneity, having been made some twenty-five minutes after the fire began; and there was no evidence that it was made by someone who witnessed the earlier stages of the conflagration. Furthermore, it did not relate to the commission of the alleged crime at all; but Lord NORMAND said:

> "For identification purposes in a criminal trial the event with which the words sought to be proved must be so connected as to form part of the *res gestae*, is the commission of the crime itself, the throwing of the stone, the striking of the blow, the setting fire to the building or whatever the criminal act may be."

The allusion to the throwing of the stone is a reference to *R.* v. *Gibson*, a case of unlawful wounding in which it was conceded on appeal that the prosecutor's evidence that he heard a woman, who was not called as a witness, say, immediately after he had been struck by a stone, "The man who threw the stone went in there" ought to have been rejected, although the accused was found in the house to which the woman had pointed. Lord NORMAND agreed that these words were closely connected in time and place with the assault.

> "But they were not directly connected with that event itself. They were not words spontaneously forced on the woman by the sight of the assault, but were prompted by the sight of a man quitting the scene of the assault and they were spoken with the purpose of helping to bring him to justice."

This reasoning is as pedantic as that by which it is sometimes sought to support *R.* v. *Bedingfield*[3] namely, that there were two transactions in that case, the assault, and the quest for assistance; the requirement that the statement should have directly concerned the event may be valid when the question is whether the statement can be treated as the equivalent of an act of identification, but it would still seem unduly technical to say that the

---

[1] (1887), 18 Q. B. D. 537.
[2] [1952] A. C. 480, at p. 487. Reference may also be made to Lord NORMAND's judgment in *O'Hara* v. *Central S. M. T. Co.*, 1941 S. C. 363.
[3] P. 506, *ante.* See also *Brown* v. *R.*, p. 506, *ante.*

remark with which *Gibson's Case* was concerned did not "directly" concern the throwing of the stone.[1]

It is difficult, if not impossible, to apply the requirement that the statement should "directly" concern the event to cases in which it was made shortly before the occurrence of the event. Nevertheless the requirement is included in clause 37 of the draft Bill attached to the 11th Report of the Criminal Law Revision Committee which reads as follows:

> "In any [criminal] proceedings a statement made by a person otherwise than in a document shall be admissible as evidence of any fact stated therein if—
>
> > (a) it directly concerns an event in issue in those proceedings which took place in the presence, sight or hearing of that person, and
> > (b) it was made by him as an immediate reaction to that event . . ."

(b) Other evidence.—As Lord WILBERFORCE pointed out in *Ratten* v. *R.*,[2] if it were not the case that there must be other evidence than that contained in the statement of the maker's association with the event, the statement would be lifting itself in to the area of admissibility; but he did not regard this as something which prohibited any reference to the statement on the question of admissibility. In *Ratten's Case* the other evidence may be said to have consisted of the accused's admission that the deceased met her death at his hands albeit, on his account of the facts, accidentally. In the South African case of *R.* v. *Taylor*,[3] where, on a charge of culpable homicide, witnesses near to the room in which the deceased was killed heard her exclaim "John, don't hit me any more or you will kill me", a serious question of admissibility might have arisen had they not also heard the sounds of a scuffle.

(iii) Rationale and utility.—As developed in the United States, the justification of this exception to the hearsay rule is the probability of the truth of the statement which is said to be guaranteed to some extent by the fact that the event to which it related was an exciting one.[4] The theory may be said to be that there are certain occurrences which will shake the truth out of the most consummate liar. After *Ratten* v. *R.*, a similar justification may come to be recognised in this country; but the psychology underlying the assumption has been questioned,[5] and it is open to question whether special provision should be made in a code of evidence for the reception of hearsay statements of the kind we have been considering. Were those responsible for the Civil Evidence Act, 1968, right in not including a special clause relating to such statements? Were the members of the Criminal Law Revision Committee right to include such a clause? So far as the first question is concerned, the statements in all the cases we have been considering could have been rendered admissible in civil proceedings by virtue of the Civil Evidence Act, 1968; but a statement by a young child cannot be made admissible under the 1968 Act and it can be argued that a special *res gestae* clause is desirable to cater for such a case.

---

[1] *Gibson's Case* will require reconsideration in the light of Lord WILBERFORCE's approval ([1972] A. C. 378, at p. 391) of *People* v. *De Simone* (1919), 121 N. E. 761.

[2] [1972] A. C. 378, at p. 391.

[3] [1961] 3 S. A. 614. For other South African cases in which the statements seem to have been treated as original evidence, see *R.* v. *Le Roux* (1897), 14 S. C. 424, *R.* v. *De Lew*, [1927] N. P. D. 276, and *R.* v. *Nichols*, [1931] N. P. D. 550.

[4] VI *Wigmore*, ch. 59.

[5] 28 Columbia Law Review 432.

For example, in civil proceedings on facts such as those of *Sparks* v. *R.*,[1] in which the child victim of an assault told her mother that the assailant was coloured, the child's hearsay statement would be inadmissible even if it could be brought within the *res gestae* principle at common law. It is, however, very doubtful whether it is necessary to have a special clause to cater for this remote contingency.

There is rather more justification for such a clause in the case of criminal proceedings because, in addition to the incompetency of young children, there are the facts that the accused's spouse is only compellable for the prosecution in cases of violence committed by the accused against his or her spouse, and the co-accused is not a compellable witness for the accused, and not even competent for the prosecution. Nonetheless, it may well be thought unnecessary to complicate an evidence code with special clauses to cover comparatively remote contingencies.[2]

(3) Statements Concerning the Maker's Contemporaneous State of Mind or Emotion

(i) Statement and illustrations of the exception.—A person's declarations of his contemporaneous state of mind or emotion are admissible as evidence of the existence of such state of mind or emotion.

In *Thomas* v. *Connell*[3] it was held on appeal that a bankrupt's statement that he knew he was insolvent was admissible to prove his knowledge of that fact at the time when he made a payment to the defendant. The statement was of course no evidence of the insolvency, and this point was emphasised by PARKE, B., when he said:

> "If a fact be proved *aliunde*, it is clear that a particular person's knowledge of that fact may be proved by his declaration . . . and under the impression that such evidence was admissible after proof of the fact to which it related, I postponed the reception of such declaration in a cause of *Craven* v. *Halliley* tried by me at York until after the fact was proved."

A person's declarations may likewise be proved in order to show his belief that defamatory statements referred to a particular individual,[4] his political opinions,[5] his affection for his spouse,[6] his dislike of his child,[7] and his fear of some burglars which prevented him from reporting their conduct to the police.[8]

(ii) The requirement of contemporaneity.—The only condition precedent to the admissibility of statements under this head is that they should relate to the maker's contemporaneous state of mind or emotion. The cases show that, as in the situations which have been previously discussed, contemporaneity is a question of degree. In *R.* v. *Vincent, Frost and Edwards*[9] the question was whether a public meeting caused alarm, and a

---

[1] [1964] A. C. 964; [1964] 1 All E. R. 727. The statement was made about an hour and a half after the assault. Were the facts to recur in criminal proceedings, it is just possible that the statement could be held admissible as part of the *res gestae* in view of the new approach in *Ratten* v. *R.*, [1972] A. C. 378; [1971] 3 All E. R. 801.
[2] But see 11th Report of the Criminal Law Revision Committee, para. 261.
[3] (1838), 4 M. & W. 267.
[4] *Du Bost* v. *Beresford* (1810), 2 Camp. 511; *Cook* v. *Ward* (1830), 4 Moo. & P. 99; *Jozwiak* v. *Sadek*, [1954] 1 All E. R. 3.
[5] *R.* v. *Tooke* (1794), 25 St. Tr. 344, at p. 390.
[6] *Trelawney* v. *Coleman* (1817), 1 B. & Ald. 90; *Willis* v. *Bernard* (1832), 8 Bing. 376.
[7] *R.* v. *Hagan* (1873), 12 Cox C. C. 357.
[8] *R.* v. *Gandfield* (1846), 2 Cox C. C. 43.
[9] (1840), 9 C. & P. 275.

policeman was allowed to swear that a number of bystanders had told him that the assembly frightened them. Although the report is silent on the point, the complaints must in some sense have referred to the past feelings of the complainants. In *R*. v. *Kay*,[1] on the other hand, where the question was whether a woman was aware, at the time of her marriage, that she had been falsely described in the banns, her mother's evidence that the woman said, after the marriage, that she knew of the false description before it took place, was held to be inadmissible.

(iii) Limited purpose for which declarations of contemporaneous state of mind or emotion may be received.—It is, of course, essential that the state of mind or emotion of the maker of a statement received under the exception to the hearsay rule which we are now considering should be in issue or relevant to the issue, and the statement must not be treated as evidence of any other fact to which it may refer. *Thomas* v. *Connell* shows that a man's assertion of knowledge of a fact is not always admissible evidence of that fact's existence. The converse proposition, that a statement of a fact's existence is not always admissible evidence of the maker's knowledge of it is illustrated by *R*. v. *Gunnell*.[2] The question was whether Gunnell had disclosed his misappropriation of certain monies before his public examination in bankruptcy. Marshall gave evidence that, before the examination, Andrews told him that Gunnell was guilty of the misappropriation, and it was held that this evidence ought to have been rejected. COLERIDGE, J., stressed the point that that which Andrews said to Marshall was no evidence of the misappropriation, but doubted whether it could be said that hearsay evidence is never admissible to prove knowledge of a fact. STEPHEN, J., said that the question was whether the fact that a man says a thing happened is evidence that he knew it happened. He added:

> "The simple assertion of any man, 'I know that A.B. committed murder', is not to be taken as evidence that he did know that A.B. committed murder. Here the evidence of Marshall that Andrews said that Gunnell told him something is put forward to prove that Andrews knew that Gunnell had done a certain thing, and I say that that cannot be done according to the laws of evidence."

The correctness of this decision seems to be beyond dispute because the question was whether Gunnell disclosed his malfeasances to Andrews before the examination, and Marshall's testimony that Andrews told him that Gunnell had done so, infringed the rule against hearsay, but the statement that the assertion of the existence of a fact is never evidence that the person making the assertion knew of its existence, would be far too wide. Everything depends on the purpose for which the evidence is tendered. Y.'s testimony concerning X.'s assertion that he knew that A.B. committed murder would be inadmissible to show that X. saw A.B. commit the crime, or was told that A.B. had committed it; but the testimony would be admissible to prove that X. believed A.B. to be a murderer, should that fact be in issue. Anything in the nature of an argument from a statement of knowledge or belief to the existence of the fact said to be known or believed would, of course, infringe the rule against hearsay.

(iv) Isolated declarations of intention.—The reception of isolated declarations of intention that are not roughly contemporaneous with a relevant act about which they were made gives rise to problems concerning the relevancy of the intention when proved rather than the admissibility

---

[1] (1887), 16 Cox C. C. 292.   [2] (1886), 16 Cox C. C. 154.

of the declarations to establish its existence. In *Sugden* v. *St. Leonards* (*Lord*)[1] MELLISH, L.J., said:

> "wherever it is material to prove the state of a person's mind, or what was passing in it, and what were his intentions, there you may prove what he said, because that is the only means by which you can find out what his intentions were".

The concluding words are a slight exaggeration, because a person's state of mind at a given time may be proved by his direct testimony in court, and by circumstantial evidence based on his conduct as well as by other people's declarations concerning his contemporaneous statements; but the correctness of the main part of the above passage is beyond dispute.

Granted that a man's intention may be proved by repetition of his words, problems of relevancy are generally raised first, when it is sought to infer the existence of the intention at an earlier or later time than that at which the words were spoken, and secondly, when it is sought to establish that the declared intention to do an act was subsequently carried out.

(*a*) *Prospectant or retrospectant continuance of intention.*—In *Robson* v. *Kemp*[2] Lord ELLENBOROUGH said, "If the declarations of the bankrupt had been made before his act (a fraudulent assignment) they may show with what intention it was done", and in *Re Fletcher, Reading* v. *Fletcher*,[3] COZENS-HARDY, M.R., said, "It is common practice, particularly in criminal cases, to prove intention at a particular time by words and acts at a subsequent date". A.'s declaration of intention on January 1st is received as testimonial evidence of that fact under an exception to the rule against hearsay, and the existence of the intention is then treated as an item of circumstantial evidence to prove the continuance of the intention up to 1st February, or its antecedent existence on December 1st. Obviously a point will be reached at which A.'s intention on January 1st is so remote as to be irrelevant to the question of his intention at another time, and, equally clearly, it is impossible to lay down hard-and-fast rules to determine when that point will be reached.

The danger that evidence may be concocted is something that must be borne in mind when the admissibility of the parties' declarations of intention is considered for it is on account of this danger that self-serving statements of the parties are generally rejected at common law. Illustrations of the rejection of such statements have already been given in Chapter X when the general prohibition on the proof of a witness's prior consistent statements was discussed. A party's self-serving statements are, generally speaking, equally inadmissible at common law when he is not called as a witness. This is well illustrated by the exclusion of the accused's self-serving declarations of intention in criminal cases decided before he was allowed to give evidence on his own behalf.

In *R.* v. *Petcherini*,[4] it was held that a priest charged with blasphemously burning the scriptures could not call witnesses to prove statements made by him in sermons before the occasion in respect of which he was prosecuted. He contended that he had said that only immoral books should be destroyed and CRAMPTON, J., said:

---

[1] (1876), 1 P. D. 154, at p. 251.   [2] (1802), 4 Esp. 233.
[3] [1917] 1 Ch. 339, at p. 342.
[4] (1855), 7 Cox C. C. 79. See also the statement of EYRE, C. J. in *R.* v. *Hardy* (1794), 24 State Tr. 1065, at p. 1093 quoted p. 2, *ante.*

"Declarations made two or three days, or even a week, previous to the transaction in question cannot be evidence, otherwise it would be easy for a man to lay grounds for escaping the consequences of his wrongful acts by making such declarations."

(*b*) *Previous declarations of intention as evidence of the performance of a subsequent act.*[1]—The question remains whether A's declaration on January 1st that he intends to do a certain act on the same day or later is admissible to prove that the act was done. The English authorities on this subject are scanty and inconclusive. In *Sugden* v. *St. Leonards (Lord),*[2] the testator's pre-testamentary declarations of his intention to benefit his daughter by his will were received as evidence that the last will he executed contained a legacy in her favour. The will was not forthcoming at the testator's death but there was other evidence of its contents. MELLISH, L.J., said:

"the declarations of the testator of what he intended to put into his will are obviously evidence which corroborates the other testimony as to what is contained in the will. But to my mind they do not themselves prove what were the contents of the will, they only corroborate the other evidence that has been given of the contents, because it is more probable that the testator has than that he has not made a particular devise, when he has told a person previously that he intended to make it, inasmuch as it shows that he had it in his mind to make such a will at the time he made that declaration."[3]

Such loosely worded statements were responsible for the fallacy, refuted in Lord REID's speech in *Myers* v. *Director of Public Prosecutions,*[4] that there is a category of evidence which, though otherwise inadmissible, is admissible for the purpose of corroboration; of course hearsay statements can seldom suffice alone, but it would be wrong to suppose that declarations of intention can never suffice to prove the contents of a lost will however short a time before the execution of the will the declarations were made, and however fully they were expressed. In *Johnson* v. *Lyford,*[5] a copy of a lost will was admitted to probate on proof that the testator spent a considerable time writing in the presence of A., handed him an envelope saying that it contained a copy of the will he had just prepared, and he was going to execute it at a certain publishers' office in the evening. There was evidence that the testator did execute a will that evening at the office mentioned by him, but there was no other evidence of the contents of the will. However, the cases dealing with the reception of pre-testamentary declarations of intention as evidence of the contents of lost wills may belong to a special category. In all of them the will was shown to have been duly executed, and as the testator's prior declarations were received in order to establish the contents of the original they may be said to have been concerned with the nature of an act, the performance of which was not in dispute, rather than with proof that a particular act was performed.

---

[1] See *State of Mind to Prove an Act*, 38 Yale Law Journal 283 by Hutchings and Slessinger.
[2] (1876), 1 P. D. 154.
[3] At p. 251. MELLISH, L. J.'s dissent was confined to the post-testamentary declarations.
[4] [1965] A. C. 1001; [1964] 2 All E. R. 881.
[5] (1868), L. R. 1 P. & D. 546. This could equally well be treated as a case turning on the reception of a statement accompanying an act. "It would often be impracticable to judge of the nature and quality of acts done, if the statement of the person doing them, immediately preceding or accompanying those acts were excluded from view." (At pp. 547–8.)

There is no support for the proposition that pre-testamentary statements of intention can be used to prove due execution.

The other authorities on the admissibility of declarations of intention as evidence of the subsequent performance of the act said to have been intended are in conflict. In *R.* v. *Buckley,*[1] the question was whether the accused was the man who murdered a police officer on a certain night, and LUSH, J., admitted a statement by the deceased to his superior in the morning in which he said he intended to go in search of the accused after dark. In *R.* v. *Wainwright,*[2] on the other hand, the prosecution sought to call a witness to say that the girl with whose murder the accused was charged told her on leaving her house that she was going to the accused's premises and COCKBURN, C.J., rejected the evidence on the ground that "it was only a statement of intention which might or might not have been carried out".

In *R.* v. *Thomson,*[3] an appeal against conviction for abortion on a woman who had died before trial, it was held that her statement of intention to perform the operation herself had been rightly excluded as evidence for the defence together with her later assertions that she had procured her own miscarriage. The reception of these later assertions as testimonial evidence of their truth would have infringed the rule against hearsay, and no attempt appears to have been made to discriminate between the two items of evidence. All that can be added to this meagre list of authorities are civil cases in which, without argument on the question of admissibility, statements by deceased workmen to the effect that they were going on deck to get some air[4] or leaving a room in order to relieve nature[5] have been received as evidence that they were taking the air or relieving nature when they met with an accident.

Attention has been focused on the problem we are considering in the United States by the decision in *Mutual Life Insurance Co.* v. *Hillmon.*[6] The question was whether a body found in Colorado was that of Hillmon or Walters, and letters from Walters stating that he would shortly be leaving for Colorado with Hillmon were received because they made it probable both that he did go on the projected journey and that he went with Hillmon. As the insurance company contended that Hillmon had murdered Walters, the reception of the letters for the second of these two purposes is particularly striking. It is one thing to argue that A. did an act because he previously said that he would do so. Surely it is another thing to argue that A. met B. because A. said that he intended to do so. A wittness would not be allowed to prove A.'s assertion that B. had agreed to meet him for the purpose of establishing that agreement, and Walters's letters only tended to show that he went to Colorado with Hillmon if it is assumed that Hillmon consented to go with Walters. The evidence in *R.* v. *Buckley* and *R.* v. *Wainwright* appears to have been tendered in order to show that the deceased met the accused, and is therefore open to objections similar to those which have just been raised with regard to the *Hillmon Case*.

In *R.* v. *Thomson*, on the other hand, no other person was involved in the

---

[1] (1873), 13 Cox C.C. 293. The statement can hardly have been received as a declaration in the course of duty, first because there was no evidence of the existence of the duty, and secondly, because it related to a future act (cf. *Rowlands* v. *De Vecchi* (1882), Cab. & El. 10).

[2] (1875), 13 Cox C. C. 171; *R.* v. *Pook* (1871), 13 Cox C.C., 172.   [3] [1912] 3 K. B. 19.
[4] *Marshall* v. *Wild Rose (Owners)*, [1910] A. C. 486.
[5] *Tracey* v. *Kelly* (1930), W. C. & Ins. Rep. 214.   [6] (1892), 145 U.S. 285.

act said to have been intended by the declarant and the existence of an intention to operate on herself was sufficiently relevant to be admissible. The rejection of the deceased's statements of intention can only be explained on the ground that, as her later assertions that she had in fact operated were inadmissible hearsay, it would have been absurd to admit the earlier declarations to serve the same purpose as the later inadmissible statements. So far as the cases of statements by workmen on leaving rooms are concerned, they can either be explained as instances of the reception of declarations to prove the performance of the act intended on ordinary principles of relevancy, or else they can be treated as cases in which contemporaneous statements concerning the purpose of an act (leaving the room) were received.

(4) Statements of Contemporaneous Physical Sensation

(i) Statement and illustrations of the exception.—A person's statements concerning his contemporaneous physical sensation are admissible evidence of that fact. In *Gilbey* v. *Great Western Rail. Co.*,[1] Cozens-Hardy, M.R., entertained no doubt that:

> "Statements made by a workman to his wife of his sensations at the time, about the pains in his side or head, or what not,—whether the statements were made by groans, or by actions, or were verbal statements,—would be admissible to prove those sensations".

The Master of the Rolls also held that the workman's assertion of the cause of his condition was inadmissible at common law, and his view of the law on both points is supported by a long line of authority.[2] For example, as long ago as 1846 it was said:

> "If a man says to his surgeon, 'I have a pain in the head', or 'in such a part of my body', that is evidence, but if he says to the surgeon 'I have a wound', and was to add 'I met John Thomas who had a sword and ran me through the body with it', that would be no evidence against John Thomas."[3]

The long line of authority on the admissibility of statements of contemporaneous physical sensation can hardly be said to have been shaken by the judgment of the Court of Criminal Appeal in *R.* v. *Black*,[4] but the court's hesitancy to admit evidence under this head is, at first sight, a little surprising. The accused had been convicted of murdering his wife by arsenical poisoning, and statements made by the deceased concerning her bodily symptoms after taking medicine procured by the accused were proved at the trial by the persons to whom they were made. When dismissing the appeal Avory, J., said:

> "If it had appeared that these were statements made behind the back of the appellant, it would have required grave consideration whether they could have been admitted, but the court is satisfied that they were made in his presence in such circumstances as to require some comment or answer from him, and that the absence of any such comment was evidence from which the jury might draw an inference."

We saw in the last chapter that statements made in the presence of a

---

[1] (1910), 102 L. T. 202.
[2] *Aveson* v. *Kinnaird (Lord)* (1805), 6 East 188; *R.* v. *Johnson* (1847), 2 Car. & Kir. 354; *R.* v. *Conde* (1867), 10 Cox C. C. 547; *R.* v. *Gloster* (1888), 16 Cox C. C. 471.
[3] *R.* v. *Nicholas* (1846), 2 Car. & Kir. 246, at p. 248, *per* Pollock, C.B.
[4] (1922), 16 Cr. App. Rep. 118.

party can be proved as something that may render his conduct in the face of them relevant, although the judge must tell the jury to ignore them if there is no evidence of such conduct. In view of the words used by AVORY, J., it can only be assumed that the requisite evidence was present in *R*. v. *Black*.

(ii) The requirement of contemporaneity.—It seems that the difficulty experienced by the Court of Criminal Appeal in deciding on the admissibility of the deceased's statements concerning her symptoms was that the statements related to past symptoms. In the course of the argument, SALTER, J., said:

> "Surely 'contemporaneous' cannot be confined to feelings experienced at the actual moment when the patient is speaking. It must include such a statement as 'Yesterday I had a pain after meals'."

This is a matter upon which it is impossible to lay down anything in the nature of a rule. At a trial for murder by means of an illegal operation in *R*. v. *Gloster*,[1] CHARLES, J., insisted that questions to a witness with regard to the deceased's statements about her symptoms must be confined to her contemporaneous symptoms, and added that nothing in the nature of a narrative is admissible as to who caused them or how they were caused. In *Aveson* v. *Kinnaird*,[2] usually regarded as among the earliest cases in which a deceased person's statements of bodily symptoms were received as evidence of their existence, utterances by a woman whose life had recently been insured by her husband made to a friend who found her in bed during the day, were received, not merely to prove the existence of the symptoms but also, it seems, to establish their previous existence when the deceased had been examined by a doctor some ten days earlier.

B. STATEMENTS FORMING PART OF THE *RES GESTAE* RECEIVED AS ORIGINAL EVIDENCE

Statements received as original evidence are frequently said to form part of the *res gestae*. The making of such statements may be in issue or relevant to the issue. When the question is whether operative words were used, they are often said to be part of the *res gestae*, and this is also the case with regard to reported statements received as matter affecting the credibility or weight of other evidence. It must be borne in mind that statements which can, in appropriate cases, be received under the four exceptions to the hearsay rule which have just been discussed may, in other cases, constitute original evidence.[3] A statement accompanying a relevant act may owe its significance to its falsity rather than its truth,[4] a statement made contemporaneously with a relevant event may have a significance which is quite unconnected with its truth or falsity, as when the fact that someone who was assaulted screamed, "You're throttling me", is admitted to explain why people rushed to his assistance; a statement of affection may owe its significance to the circumstances in which it was made, as when terms of

---

[1] (1888), 16 Cox C. C. 471.

[2] (1805), 6 East 188. In *Tickle* v. *Tickle*, [1968] 2 All E. R. 154, what the doctor said to the patient was held admissible as original evidence relevant to the latter's belief concerning his health. See also *Ramsay* v. *Watson* (1961), 108 C. L. R. 642.

[3] See *per* Lord BLACKBURN in the *Dysart Peerage Case* (1881), 6 App. Cas. 489, at p. 502; *Re Jenion*, [1952] Ch. 454, so far as the declaration of the putative father was concerned.

[4] *A.-G.* v. *Good* (1825), M'Cle. & Yo. 286; *Ridley* v. *Gyde* (1832), 9 Bing, 349.

endearment used by a co-respondent to the respondent are proved in a divorce case (the sincerity of the utterance being beside the point), and statements of contemporaneous physical sensation may have probative value as something said in the presence of a party.[1] In every case the vital question is neither the nature of the statement, nor the circumstances in which it was made, nor the best manner of describing it, but the purpose for which it is tendered in evidence.

C. EVIDENCE OF OPINION RECEIVED AS PART OF THE *RES GESTAE*

It seems that in certain cases evidence which would infringe both the rule against hearsay and the opinion rule may be received as part of the *res gestae* although it would be excluded if it consisted of statements made at a time which was at all remote from the events to which they relate. The typical example is provided by the reception of a bystander's statements alleging negligence on the part of one of the drivers involved in a motor accident,[2] for we have seen that a witness may not state his deliberate opinion on the matter. Although there is no authority on the point, it is possible that, if the bystander was called as a witness, he could narrate his own statements made contemporaneously with the occurrences to which he was deposing. It is also possible that, on a trial for murder by poisoning, the deceased's statement immediately after he had eaten an apple to the effect that it had poisoned him would be received although some such statement as, " I believe something in the apple I ate two days ago to be the cause of my present suffering", would be excluded.[3]

D. FACTS RECEIVED AS PART OF THE *RES GESTAE*

We have seen that facts are sometimes allowed to be proved on the footing that they form part of the *res gestae*. In this context too the phrase seems merely to denote relevance on account of contemporaneity.[4] We saw, however, in Chapter XIV, that it had a further implication in that evidence of facts forming part of the same transaction as that under inquiry may be received notwithstanding the general rule that evidence must be excluded if it does no more than show that someone is disposed to commit crimes or civil wrongs in general, or even crimes or civil wrongs of the kind into which the court is inquiring. Contemporaneity, continuity or the fact that a number of incidents are closely connected with each other gives the evidence an added relevance which renders it admissible in spite of its prejudicial tendencies.

E. *RES GESTAE* AND OTHER EXCLUSIONARY RULES

We have already seen that the doctrine of *res gestae* renders admissible the prior consistent statements of witnesses in spite of the common law prohibition on the proof of such statements in order to confirm present testimony. To gain sufficient weight to be admissible as part of the *res gestae*

---

[1] *R.* v. *Black (supra)*.

[2] As contemplated by POLLOCK, C.B., in *Milne* v. *Leisler (supra)*.

[3] Cf. *Chapdelaine* v. *R.*, [1935] S. C. R. 53.

[4] *R.* v. *Moore*, p. 37, *ante*; cf. *R.* v. *Hill* (1908), 1 Cr. App. Rep. 158, where, however, the basis on which the evidence was held to be admissible is obscure.

under this head, the statement must have formed part of the transaction to which the witness is deposing as in *Milne* v. *Leisler*;[1] alternatively it must have accompanied the act or event about which the witness is speaking.[2] The doctrine of *res gestae* may sometimes serve to qualify the rule that a witness's prior inconsistent statements are not evidence of the facts stated unless the witness happens to be a party, in which case his previous statement may constitute an admission. Suppose, for example, that, at the trial of Fowkes, the son had said that he had never identified the culprit as the Butcher. The son's statements on the occasion under investigation might have been proved by the policeman as affirmative evidence that it was was the Butcher who fired the shot, and not merely as something casting doubt on the son's testimony.[3]

Although there is no English authority on the subject, it is possible that an otherwise inadmissible confession would be rendered admissible by the *res gestae* doctrine. Suppose, for example, that a policeman were to chase a suspect from the scene of a murder and that, when he caught up with the suspect, the policeman were to say "If you don't tell me who killed the deceased I will kill you". If the suspect were to reply "I did", this spontaneous admission might be received, although it would plainly be inadmissible if made long after the event at a police station in response to such a threat as that which has been suggested.[4]

---

[1] (1862), 7 H. & N. 786; p. 215, *ante.*
[2] *R.* v. *Fowkes,* cited in Stephen's Digest of the Law of Evidence (12th edition), art. 3.
[3] The example is taken from R. M. Gooderson, C.L.J. (1957), at p. 70.
[4] This example is also taken from R. M. Gooderson in C.L.J. (1957), at p. 67.

CHAPTER XXI

DOCUMENTARY EVIDENCE

If a litigant wishes to rely upon the provisions of a document, he must render the court conversant with its terms. To this end it is generally incumbent upon him to produce the original, but he is dispensed from doing so in the circumstances mentioned in section 1. In many cases the court will require to be satisfied that the document was duly executed before admitting it in evidence, and these are discussed in section 2. Finally, difficult problems may arise with regard to the extent to which extrinsic evidence is admissible when it relates to the terms of a transaction embodied in a document, or the meaning of the words used in a written instrument. The principal rules are mentioned in section 3.

SECTION 1. PROOF OF THE CONTENTS OF A DOCUMENT

A. THE GENERAL RULE

(1) Statement and Illustrations of the General Rule

(i) Statement.—A party relying on the words used in a document for any purpose other than that of identifying it must, as a general rule, adduce primary evidence of its contents. This is often spoken of as the most important survival of the best evidence rule, although it antedates that rule by several centuries. The typical example of primary evidence in this context is the original document, but there are others which will be mentioned after the rule has been illustrated. The rule is subject to important exceptions of which the most notable relates to public documents, the contents of which may be proved by the production of a copy.

(ii) Illustrations.—The simplest illustration of the rule is provided by a case in which a party wishes to put his correspondence with his adversary in evidence. He will normally have the originals of letters received from his adversary, but he will be unable to prove the contents of his replies by the production of copies unless the case has been brought within one of the exceptions to the general rule by service of a notice to produce.[1] Other obvious illustrations are afforded by cases in which a party wishes to rely upon the terms of any document of which he merely has a copy or a more or less perfect recollection; but the rule may be brought into play in circumstances in which the possibility of its application is considerably less obvious. In *Macdonnell* v. *Evans*,[2] a witness for the plaintiff was asked in cross-examination whether a letter of his which was produced

---

[1] In civil cases this will be deemed to have taken place by virtue of the exchange of lists of documents (O. 27, r. 4 (3)) and the requirement of proof by the original may be waived by agreeing a bundle of correspondence.
[2] (1852), 11 C. B. 930; *Potts* v. *Miller* (1940), 64 C. L. R. 282; *Lakeman* v. *Finlay*, [1959] S. R. (N. S. W.) 5.

was written in reply to a letter charging him with forgery. The last-mentioned letter was not produced, and the question was disallowed because it assumed that there was a document in existence which should have been proved by production of the original. Similarly, in *Augustien* v. *Challis*,[1] the plaintiff alleged that the defendant, a sheriff, had negligently caused a *fi. fa.* to be withdrawn. The defendant sought to justify his conduct on the ground that rent was due to the debtor's landlord whose claim had priority to that of the plaintiff. The defendant called the landlord who testified to the fact that rent was due to him, but admitted that it was payable under a lease. This document was not produced, and the landlord's evidence was thus rendered inadmissible because, "The moment it appears that there is a lease, you cannot speak about its contents without producing it".[2] The lease had to be consulted in order to determine the amount of rent, if any, due to the landlord.

It is important to remember that the rule has its limitations. In the first place, it only applies to cases in which direct reliance is placed on the words used in a document. In *R.* v. *Holy Trinity, Kingston-upon-Hull (Inhabitants)*[3] it was held that the fact that a pauper was a tenant in a particular parish could be proved without reference to the original lease, as could the value of the premises. Relationships such as those of landlord and tenant, or partnership,[4] may be created by a document, but they can be proved by other evidence, such as the payment of rent or a witness's assertion that someone is his partner.

In the second place, the rule does not prevent reference being made to the terms of a document for the purpose of identifying it. A distinction must be drawn between referring to the contents of a document as marks of identification and as a means of communicating ideas.

> "For the purpose of identifying anything, whether it be a writing or anything else, proof may be given to show what it is; and therefore, in an action of trover for a promissory note, the contents of the promissory note may be stated verbally by a witness; the reason is, that the evidence is not of the contents as evidence, but for the purpose of identification."[5]

Finally, and *a fortiori*, if the bare fact of the existence of a document is in issue, it may be proved without recourse to the original, but the rule applies the moment reliance is placed upon the contents of the document. In *R.* v. *Elworthy*,[6] for instance, a solicitor was charged with perjury in having wilfully denied on oath that a draft of a statutory declaration had been prepared. No notice to produce the draft was given, but the Court for Crown Cases Reserved considered that this would not have excluded parol evidence of the existence of the draft and its possession by the accused. But the prosecution went further, and gave evidence of alterations in the draft in order to show that the accused's denial was wilful and, for this reason, the conviction was quashed. It was not a case in which it could be said that the indictment gave notice to the prisoner that he would be required to produce a particular document as, for instance, on a prosecution for forgery.

---

[1] (1847), 1 Exch. 279, see also *Twyman* v. *Knowles* (1853), 13 C. B. 222.
[2] *Per* PARKE, B., at p. 280.　　　　　　　　[3] (1827), 7 B. & C. 611.
[4] *Alderson* v. *Clay* (1816), 1 Stark. 405.
[5] *Boyle* v. *Wiseman* (1855), 11 Exch. 360, at p. 367, *per* MARTIN, B., citing *Whitehead* v. *Scott* (1830), 1 Mood & R. 2. See also *Commissioner of Railways for New South Wales* v. *Young* (1962), 35 A. L. J. R. 416.　　　　　　　　[6] (1867), L. R. 1 C.C. R. 103.

(2) TYPES OF PRIMARY EVIDENCE OF THE CONTENTS OF A DOCUMENT

(i) The original.—The primary evidence *par excellence* of the contents of a document is the original. Generally speaking there can be no great difficulty in determining which of several documents is the original; but it is sometimes necessary to have regard to the purpose for which or the party against whom the contents are tendered in evidence. In the case of a telegram, if the contents are tendered in evidence against the sender, the original is the message handed in at the post office;[1] so far as the receiver is concerned, there are many cases in which the original will be the written message received by him. A counterpart lease, executed only by the lessee, is the original so far as he and those claiming under him are concerned,[2] although the other part is the original as against the lessor. If duplicates of a deed are executed by all the parties to it, each duplicate is an original,[3] and, when this is so, each of them must be accounted for before secondary evidence of the contents of the deed becomes admissible.[4] An unsigned carbon copy of a letter, or one produced by means of a duplicating machine,[5] is not the original when the contents of the signed top copy are in issue. Similarly, if the question concerns the contents of a town planning notice served on a third person, the notice so served is the only original,[6] but there are cases where, as between the parties to the proceedings, the copy of a bill or invoice may, in effect be treated as a duplicate original because it is unnecessary for the person producing it to account for the original.[7] There are also cases in which any number of printed copies of a document may be treated as originals where, for example, the question concerns the contents of a placard and not the terms of the author's manuscript.[8]

(ii) Copy of document requiring enrolment.—There are certain private documents which must be filed in a court or other public office and, when they are thus filed, the copy issued by the court or other office may be treated as the original. Once again, everything turns on the purpose for which the contents of the document are tendered in evidence. The probate is, for instance, conclusive evidence of the words of the will in respect of which the grant was made and, for this purpose, it constitutes primary evidence, but, on questions of construction, the court may examine the original. Thus, in *Re Battie-Wrightson*,[9] the probate of the will of a testatrix who had an account at seven banks stated that she bequeathed the balance of her account "at the said bank" to a named person. There was no indication which bank account was intended, but the original will contained an erasure referring to a specific bank in the clause preceding the bequest which the court was thus enabled to construe. The probate had not superseded the document executed by the testatrix for all purposes.

---

[1] *R.* v. *Regan* (1887), 16 Cox C. C. 203.
[2] *Roe* d. *West* v. *Davis* (1806), 7 East 363.
[3] *Forbes* v. *Samuel*, [1913] 3 K. B. 706.
[4] *Alivon* v. *Furnival* (1834), 1 Cr. M. & R. 277.
[5] *Nodin* v. *Murray* (1812), 3 Camp. 228, N. P.; cf. *Durston* v. *Mercuri*, [1969] V. R. 507 (signed carbon may in some circumstances be the original).
[6] *Andrews* v. *Wirral Rural Council*, [1916] 1 K. B. 863.
[7] *Philipson* v. *Chase* (1809), 2 Camp. 110, as explained in *Andrews* v. *Wirral Rural Council (supra)*; *Colling* v. *Treweek* (1827), 6 B. & C. 394; *Buckley* v. *MacKen*, [1961] N. Z. L. R. 46.
[8] *R.* v. *Watson* (1817), 2 Stark. 116.
[9] *Re Battie-Wrightson, Cecil* v. *Battie-Wrightson*, [1920] 2 Ch. 330.

(iii) Admission of a party.—We have already seen that it was decided in *Slatterie* v. *Pooley*,[1] that the informal admission by one party to litigation constitutes primary evidence against him of the contents of a document. His opponent is thus dispensed from the necessity of producing the original or showing that the case comes within one of the exceptions to the rule requiring this to be done. The mere fact that the contents of a deed are recited in a later deed produced by one of the parties does not dispense with the necessity of producing the original of the earlier document if his opponent wishes to rely on other parts of it.[2]

(3) Types of Secondary Evidence of the Contents of a Document

Reference may be made to the different kinds of secondary evidence that can be given of the contents of a document before the circumstances in which such evidence is admissible by way of exception to the general rule are considered. Secondary evidence may take the form of all manner of different types of copy, including those proved by testimony to have been checked against the original which are known as "examined copies",[3] those bearing a certificate of their accuracy called "certified copies", "office copies", examined in the court office in which they are filed, and "government printer's copies" which are employed to prove the contents of certain other kinds of public documents such as statutes, treaties and royal proclamations. Other public documents are proved by examined or certified copies, and these kinds of secondary evidence, as well as that of less formal copies, are also employed in the case of private documents. These may also be proved by the oral evidence of persons able to recollect their contents.

As a general rule there are no degrees of secondary evidence,[4] so oral evidence of the contents of a document may be adduced without accounting for the absence of any copies that may be in existence, and there are no preferences as between the different kinds of copy. This is because the best evidence rule only prohibits the adduction of evidence which, by its very nature discloses the existence of a better means of proof. The production of a copy of a deed shows that the original is, or was, in existence, and this is also the case when a witness deposes to the contents of a writing which is not before the court; but a copy does not show that others were made, and oral evidence of the contents of the document does not suggest the existence of any but the original. The proposition that there are no degrees of secondary evidence is, however, of merely general application. In the case of many public documents, oral evidence of their contents would only be received if copies were unavailable, and the contents of a will that had been admitted to probate could never be proved by oral testimony as long as the original or probate was in existence.

There is authority for the view that the copy of a copy is inadmissible,[5] but there is also authority on the other side,[6] and there seems to be no reason why the copy of a copy should not be received in evidence provided

---

[1] (1840), 6 M. & W. 664 (p. 445, *ante*); *Price* v. *Woodhouse* (1849), 3 Exch. 616.
[2] *Gillett* v. *Abbott* (1838), 7 Ad. & El. 783.
[3] As to photographs of the *locus in quo* see *Hindson* v. *Ashby*, [1896] 2 Ch. 1, at p. 21.
[4] *Doe d. Gilbert* v. *Ross* (1840), 7 M. & W. 102.
[5] *Everingham* v. *Roundell* (1838), 2 Mood. & R. 138.
[6] *Lafone* v. *Griffin* (1909), 25 T. L. R. 308.

the witness producing it, or some other witness, makes it clear that the copy produced is a true copy of the first copy and that that copy was, in its turn, a true copy of the original. In *R.* v. *Collins* [1] it was necessary for the prosecution to prove that the accused knew that his bank account was inoperative. The prosecution called an assistant bank manager who produced a copy of the unsigned carbon copy of a letter sent by his colleague to the accused informing him that his account was closed. The accused had been called upon to produce this letter and, as he had not done so, secondary evidence was admissible. But the Court of Criminal Appeal held that the letter had not been properly proved by the bank manager because he did not swear that the copy produced was a true copy of the carbon or that the carbon was a true copy of the original apart from the signature. Had the bank manager testified to these matters, it seems that the court would have considered the letter to have been properly proved by his evidence.

B. EXCEPTIONS TO THE GENERAL RULE

Mention must be made of six exceptions to the general rule—cases in which the contents of a document may be proved by secondary evidence. These occur when the original is in the possession or control of the opponent of the party wishing to rely on the document and the opponent fails to produce it after receipt of a notice requiring him to do so; when the document is in the possession of a stranger who lawfully refuses to produce it after service of a *subpoena duces tecum*; when the original cannot be found after due search; when, though it is known to be in existence, the production of the original is, for practical purposes, impossible; when the production of the original would be highly inconvenient owing to the public nature of the document, or because it is an entry in a banker's book. This list of exceptions is not exhaustive, but it covers the important instances in which secondary evidence of the contents of a document may be adduced.

(1) OPPONENT'S FAILURE TO PRODUCE DOCUMENT AFTER NOTICE

(i) **Nature and purpose of notice to produce.**—A notice to produce informs the party upon whom it is served that he is required to produce the documents specified therein at the trial to which the notice relates. The notice does not compel production of the documents in question, but the fact that it has been served provides a foundation for the reception of secondary evidence. If a party wishes to compel his opponent to produce documents, the proper course is for him to serve the opponent with a *subpoena duces tecum* and this will be adopted when the party is not in a position to adduce satisfactory secondary evidence, or when an issue turns on the form of the original as when handwriting is material. [2] Notice to produce is not served in order to give the opponent notice that the docu-

---

[1] (1960), 44 Cr. App. Rep. 170; see the helpful case note by Hudson, 24 M. L. R. 178. The appellant's landlady testified to having communicated the contents of the letter to him when he was in hospital, and the court accordingly applied what is now the proviso to s. 2 of the Criminal Appeal Act, 1968.

[2] The accused should not be served with a *subpoena duces tecum* in a criminal case. The service of a notice to produce is unobjectionable because the accused need not comply with it.

ments mentioned in it will be used by the other party, and thus to enable the opponent to prepare counter-evidence, but so as to exclude the objection that all reasonable steps have not been taken to procure the original document. Accordingly, when the original is in court, notice to produce may be served during the trial.[1] The party serving the notice must put the documents it mentions in evidence if required to do so by the opponent upon whom the notice was served. The notice cannot be employed as a means of gaining inspection of documents without using them if they turn out to be unfavourable.[2] The party served with a notice to produce cannot rely upon the original of a document it mentions if secondary evidence of the contents of the document has been given in consequence of non-compliance with the notice.[3]

In civil cases, the parties exchange lists of documents after the close of the pleadings, and, under R.S.C., O. 27, r. 4 (3):

> "a party to a cause or matter by whom a list of documents is served on any other party . . . shall be deemed to have been served by that other party with a notice requiring him to produce at the trial of the cause or matter such of the documents specified in the list as are in his possession, custody or power."

(ii) **When service of notice is excused.**—In certain circumstances, service of notice to produce is excused, and a party may adduce secondary evidence of the contents of a document if the original is not produced by his opponent. The most important case in which this is so is when the document in question is itself a notice,[4] whether it be a notice to produce, notice of dishonour of a bill of exchange or notice by the prosecution of intention to rely on the accused's previous convictions. Another case in which there is no need to serve notice to produce is when the nature of the proceedings is such as to inform a party that he is required to produce the originals of certain documents at the trial. Obvious instances are provided by prosecutions for the theft of a document [5] or driving a motor vehicle without being adequately insured.[6] Service of notice to produce is also excused when possession of the document is admitted [7] or admitted to have been lost [8] by the opponent.

(2) Stranger's Lawful Refusal to Produce Document

When the original of a document is in the possession of a stranger to the litigation, the proper course for the party desiring to prove the contents

---

If he does not do so, he cannot be ordered to produce the original on account of the privilege against self-incrimination (*Trust Houses, Ltd.* v. *Postlethwaite* (1944), 109 J. P. 12); but the privilege does not apply to answers to questions when the accused is giving evidence and he may then perhaps be ordered to produce documents in his control (*R.* v. *Adams*, [1965] V. R. 563).

[1] *Dwyer* v. *Collins* (1852), 7 Exch. 639.

[2] *Wharam* v. *Routledge* (1805), 5 Esp. 235, N. P. *Quaere* whether this will apply to cases coming within O. 27, r. 4 (3).

[3] *Doe d. Thompson* v. *Hodgson* (1840), 12 Ad. & El. 135.

[4] *R.* v. *Turner*, [1910] 1 K. B. 346; *Practice Note* in [1950] 1 All E. R. 37; cf. *Andrews* v. *Wirral Rural Council*, [1916] 1 K. B. 863 showing that a subpoena is necessary in order to obtain production of a notice served on a stranger to the litigation.

[5] *R.* v. *Aickles* (1784), 1 Leach 294.

[6] *Machin* v. *Ash* (1950), 49 L. G. R. 87; *Bracegirdle* v. *Apted* (1951), 49 L. G. R. 790. In these cases secondary evidence was received of the accused's certificate of insurance.

[7] *Dwyer* v. *Collins* (1852), 7 Exch. 639.

[8] *R.* v. *Haworth* (1830), 4 C. & P. 254.

of the document is to serve the stranger with a *subpoena duces tecum*. The stranger may, however, be able to establish a claim to privilege in respect of the document when secondary evidence of its contents becomes admissible.[1]

The governing principle is the same as that which covers the next two exceptions to the general rule that are mentioned—it is impossible to compel production of the document, and it will apply in cases in which the person in possession of the original is beyond the jurisdiction of the court; but the principle does not apply when a stranger served with a *subpoena duces tecum* wrongfully refuses to produce the document,[2] for in such a case he may be made liable for any damage caused by his disobedience to the subpoena, and he may even be imprisoned for non-compliance with its terms.

(3) Lost Document

When the original of a document cannot be found after due search, its contents may be proved by secondary evidence. The requirement as to due search will be satisfied in different ways according to the differing circumstances of each case.[3] A party may adduce secondary evidence of the contents of a document if his opponent admits to having lost it or if a stranger served with a *subpoena duces tecum* does likewise. The contents of a lost will may be proved by secondary evidence to the same extent as those of any other lost document.[4]

(4) Production of Original Impossible

The production of the original of a document may be physically impossible in which case secondary evidence of its contents is admissible. It has been said that inscriptions on tombstones and walls are proved by copies every day.[5] Secondary evidence is likewise admissible when the production of the original is legally prohibited by, for example, a foreign court with custody of it,[6] or a law requiring it to remain affixed to the walls of a particular place such as a factory.[7]

(5) Public Documents

In *Mortimer* v. *M'Callan*,[8] it was held to be unnecessary to cause the originals of the books of the Bank of England to be produced. Alderson, B., said that if they were not removable on the ground of public inconvenience, that was upon the same footing in point of principle as in the case of that which is not removable by the physical nature of the thing itself.[9] At

---

[1] *Mills* v. *Oddy* (1834), 6 C. & P. 728, N. P. Secondary evidence is also admissible if the opponent obtained possession from someone served with a *subpoena duces tecum* (*Leeds* v. *Cook* (1803), 4 Esp. 256).

[2] *R.* v. *Inhabitants of Llanfaethly* (1853), 2 E. & B. 940.

[3] *Brewster* v. *Sewell* (1820), 3 B. & Ald. 296.

[4] *Sugden* v. *St. Leonards (Lord)* (1876), 1 P. D. 154.

[5] *Per* Alderson, B., in *Mortimer* v. *M'Callan* (1840), 6 M. & W. 58. Some kinds of inscriptions, *e.g.* those on banners, may be treated as equivalent to public speeches rather than writings, in which case the banners do not have to be produced (*R.* v. *Hunt* (1820), 3 B. & Ald. 566; for criticisms of the vague judgments in this case see 65 L. Q. R. 65.)

[6] *Alivon* v. *Furnival* (1834), 1 Cr. M. & R. 277.

[7] *Owner* v. *Bee Hive Spinning Co., Ltd.*, [1914] 1 K. B. 105.

[8] (1840), 6 M. & W. 58.

[9] See also *per* Pollock, C.B., in *Sayer* v. *Glossop* (1848), 2 Exch. 409, at p. 441: "If in point of law you cannot compel a party who has the custody of a document to produce

common law, the contents of numerous public documents [1] could be proved by copies of various kinds on account of the inconvenience that would have been occasioned by production of the originals. The mode of proving public documents is now governed by a host of statutes [2] and, in a work of this nature, it is only possible to mention a few that are of more or less general application.

Private Acts of Parliament are, where necessary, proved by the production of a Queen's Printer's or Stationery Office copy.[3] Royal proclamations may be proved by production of a Queen's Printer's copy or of the Gazette containing them, or of a copy certified to be correct by the appropriate official.[4] Orders in Council and Statutory Instruments are proved in the same way.[5] Journals of either House of Parliament are proved by production of a Queen's Printer's copy.[6]

Byelaws are proved under s. 252 of the Local Government Act, 1933, by the production of a printed copy endorsed with a certificate purporting to be signed by the clerk to the local authority containing details concerning the making and confirming of the byelaw and certifying that the document is a true copy.

Proclamations, treaties and other acts of state of any foreign state or British colony may be proved either by examined copy or by a copy authenticated with the seal of the foreign state or British colony.[7]

English state records, preserved in the Public Record Office, and letters patent are proved by sealed and certified copies.[8]

Finally, two more general provisions may be noted: the effect of s. 1 of the Evidence Act, 1845 is that when a statute permits a document to be proved by certified or sealed copy, it is unnecessary to prove certification or sealing, the mere production of the certified or sealed copy sufficing; under s. 14 of the Evidence Act, 1851, whenever any book or other document is of such a public nature as to be admissible in evidence on production from proper custody and no statute exists which renders its contents provable by means of a copy, it may be proved by certified or examined copy. The upshot of these two provisions, together with those of numerous special statutes, is that a very large number of copy documents may be put in evidence on mere production to the court, without there

---

it, there is the same reason for admitting other evidence of its contents as if its production were physically impossible."

[1] See p. 457, *ante*, for a definition of a public document.

[2] See *Wills on Evidence* (3rd edition), App. A.

[3] Evidence Act, 1845, s. 3; Documentary Evidence Act, 1882, equating Stationery Office copies with those of the Queen's Printer or Government Printer referred to in other statutes. Under s. 21 of the Interpretation Act, 1889, judicial notice is taken of all Acts of Parliament passed since 1850, unless there is an express provision to the contrary. Generally speaking, therefore, it is unnecessary to produce any particular copy of a modern statute.

[4] Evidence Act, 1845, s. 3; Documentary Evidence Act, 1868, s. 2.

[5] *R. v. Clarke*, [1969] 2 Q. B. 91; [1969] 1 All E. R. 924. Cases sometimes have to be adjourned so as to give a party an opportunity of producing a Stationery Office Copy. The Courts vary in their attitude towards insistence on the proper proof of statutory instruments and orders in Council, sometimes describing it as the imprescriptible right of a litigant to have it properly proved and, on other occasions, describing the insistence on proper proof as a technical triviality (see *Duffin* v. *Markham* (1918), 88 L. J. K. B. 581, and *Tyrrell* v. *Cole* (1918), 120 L. T. 156.) Cf. *Snell* v. *Unity Finance Ltd.*, [1964] 2 Q. B. 203; [1963] 3 All E. R. 50, suggesting judicial notice may be taken of all statutory instruments.

[6] Evidence Act, 1845, s. 3.

[7] Evidence Act, 1851, s. 7.

[8] Public Record Office Act, 1838, ss. 11–13; Patent's Act, 1949, s. 7.

being any question of accounting for the original or proving the accuracy of the copy.

(6) BANKERS' BOOKS

At common law, bankers' books, other than those of the Bank of England, are private documents; but the inconvenience which would have been occasioned by the necessity of producing the originals as and when required for the purposes of any litigation have been avoided by the Bankers' Books Evidence Act, 1879. Provided that the book is one of the ordinary ones of the bank, the entry was made in the ordinary course of business, the book is in the custody of the bank, and the copy has been examined against the original (all of which matters can be proved by the affidavit or the testimony of an officer of the bank),[1] a copy of an entry in a banker's book shall, in all legal proceedings be received as *prima facie* evidence of such entry, and of the matters, transactions and accounts therein recorded.[2] Under s. 7 any party to a legal proceeding can apply for an order that he be at liberty to inspect and take copies of any entries in a banker's book for the purpose of such proceeding. The section, like the rest of the Act, applies to civil and criminal cases alike, and the respondent cannot object to the making of an order on the ground that it will violate his privilege against self-incrimination; but an order is a serious interference with the liberty of the subject, and should only be made after careful consideration.[3]

SECTION 2. PROOF OF THE EXECUTION OF PRIVATE DOCUMENTS

The statutes which enable the contents of public documents to be proved by means of copies also dispense with the necessity of proving that the documents have been properly executed. In the case of a public document, therefore, the mere production of the appropriate copy will suffice to put it in evidence, but something more than production is required in the case of a private document. The court will require to be satisfied by evidence that it was duly executed, unless it is more than twenty years old and comes from the proper custody, in which event there is a presumption of formal validity. The due execution of a private document is proved by showing that it was signed by the person by whom it purports to have been signed and, when attestation is necessary, that it was attested. Accordingly, proof of handwriting and attestation will be discussed before various presumptions applicable to documents are considered.[4] The section concludes with a brief reference to the Stamp Acts.

---

[1] Ss. 4–5.

[2] S. 3. The section creates an exception to the hearsay rule as to the transactions to which the entry relates (*Harding* v. *Williams* (1830), 14 Ch. D. 197, questioned in argument in *Arnott* v. *Hayes* (1887), 56 L. J. Ch. 844, at p. 847, but see *Myers* v. *Director of Public Prosecutions*, [1965] A. C. 1009, at p. 1028 and p. 1033).

[3] *Williams* v. *Summerfield*, [1972] 2 Q. B. 513; [1972] 2 All E. R. 1334. In *Re Bankers' Books Evidence Act* (1879), *R.* v. *Bono* (1913), 29 T. L. R. 635, it was said that, in civil cases, the order should only be made when the material was of a kind of which discovery would have to be given, but, literally construed, this would exclude incriminating material.

[4] In civil cases, the due execution of a document is frequently the subject of a formal admission for the purposes of a particular trial and such an admission is deemed to have taken place under and subject to the provisions of O. 27, rr. 1 and 2. Proof of due execution is dispensed with when the document is in the possession of the opponent who refuses to

A. PROOF OF HANDWRITING

There are three types of evidence of handwriting which call for discussion—testimonial evidence, opinion and comparison.

(1) TESTIMONIAL EVIDENCE

The testimonial evidence may take one of the following forms: the testimony of the person whose handwriting is to be proved; his admissible hearsay statement; the testimony of someone who saw the document executed (whether he be an attesting witness or a bystander); and an admissible hearsay statement of someone other than the person whose handwriting is in question. Nothing need be said with regard to any of these forms of testimonial evidence except that it is usually unnecessary, in the first instance, for a witness to the signature to do more than swear that he saw someone sign in a particular name. The name will, in itself, be sufficient evidence of the identity of the signatory with the person whose handwriting is to be proved,[1] unless there are circumstances calling for investigation, or unless, perhaps, the name is a very common one.[2]

(2) OPINION

Witnesses who have not seen the document in question written or signed may depose to their opinion that the writing is that of a particular person. Such opinion may be based upon the witness's acquaintance with the handwriting of the person in question through having seen him write on former occasions. It makes no difference whether these occasions were many or few, and whether the signature was merely that of the signatory's surname without the addition of the Christian names appearing on the document before the court,[3] although these matters will affect the weight of the evidence.

It is unnecessary that the witness who thus deposes to his opinion should have seen the person whose writing is in question write at all, for it will be sufficient if he has received documents purporting to be written or signed by him,[4] and the capacity in which he has done so is immaterial, although this may affect the weight of the evidence.

> "The clerk who constantly read the letters, the broker who was ever consulted upon them, is as competent to judge whether another signature is that of the writer of the letters, as the merchant to whom they were addressed. The servant who has habitually carried letters addressed by me to others has an opportunity of obtaining a knowledge of my writing though he never saw me write or received a letter from me." [5]

There must, however, have been a sufficient opportunity for the witness to acquire such knowledge of the handwriting in question as to make it worthwhile receiving his evidence.[6]

---

produce it on notice (*Cooke* v. *Tanswell* (1818), 8 Taunt. 450; *Poole* v. *Warren* (1838), 8 Ad. & El. 582). This is also the case when the opponent produces the document but claims an interest under it (*Pearce* v. *Hooper* (1810), 3 Taunt. 60). The due execution of a document might be formally admitted in a criminal case under s. 10 of the Criminal Justice Act, 1967.

[1] *Roden* v. *Ryde* (1843), 4 Q. B. 626.   [2] *Jones* v. *Jones* (1841), 9 M. & W. 75.
[3] *Lewis* v. *Sapio* (1827), Mood. & M. 39, N. P.
[4] *Harrington* v. *Fry* (1824), 1 C. & P. 289.
[5] *Doe* d. *Mudd* v. *Suckermore* (1837), 5 Ad. & El. 703, at p. 750, *per* Lord DENMAN, C.J.
[6] *R.* v. *O'Brien* (1911), 7 Cr. App. Rep. 29; *Pitre* v. *R.*, [1933] 1 D. L. R. 417 (sight of two letters and two postcards insufficient).

(3) COMPARISON

There is a general sense in which it is true to say that:

> "All evidence of handwriting, except where the witness sees the document written, is in its nature comparison. It is the belief which a witness entertains on comparing the writing in question with an exemplar in his mind derived from some previous knowledge." [1]

but handwriting may also be proved by comparison in a more specific sense of the word. A document which is proved to have been signed or written by the person whose handwriting is in issue is first produced, and this is compared with the writing which is being considered by the court. On the basis of such a comparison, an expert in these matters may give evidence.[2] Strictly speaking an expert in handwriting should not be asked to say "definitely that a particular writing is to be assigned to a particular person. His function is to point out similarities between two specimens of handwriting or differences, and leave the court to draw their own conclusion".[3]

Although the evidence may be thought to be of less weight, an opinion with regard to the handwriting of the two documents may be given by a witness who is not an expert, or the document may be submitted to the court in order that the handwriting on each of them may be compared.[4] The document which is thus submitted to the jury for comparison with the one in dispute need not be relevant to the issues in the case in any other way,[5] and, if he gives evidence, the person whose handwriting is under consideration may be asked to write in court so that his writing may be compared with that on the document in question.[6]

Conclusions based on comparison of handwriting by those who are not experts must obviously be treated with considerable caution, and there are several instances in which the Court of Criminal Appeal has quashed a conviction after examining two specimens of handwriting which had been submitted to the jury at the trial.[7] It is wrong for a judge to invite the jury to make a comparison without the guidance of an expert although, where they have to be allowed to consider exhibits, he cannot do more than warn them of the risks of a comparison.[8] It has been held that a policeman who induced a prisoner to write while under arrest in order that his handwriting might be compared with that on a threatening letter which he was alleged to have written, was a biased witness and that his evidence of opinion based on a comparison ought not to have been submitted to the jury,[9] and, in *R.* v. *Harvey*,[10] it was said that the jury ought not to act on a comparison of the handwriting in books found in the possession of the prisoner with that on a document alleged to have been forged by him. These decisions may have turned on their special facts, for it appears

---

[1] *Ibid.*, at p. 739, *per* PATTESON, J.
[2] *R.* v. *Silverlock*, [1894] 2 Q. B. 766.
[3] *Wakeford* v. *Bishop of Lincoln* (1921), as reported in 90 L. J. P. C. 174.
[4] Criminal Procedure Act, 1865, s. 8, applying to civil and criminal cases.
[5] *Birch* v. *Ridgway* (1858), 1 F. & F. 270, N. P.; *R.* v. *Adami* [1959] S. A. S. R. 81.
[6] *Cobbett* v. *Kilminster* (1865), 4 F. & F. 490, N. P.
[7] *R.* v. *Smith* (1909), 2 Cr. App. Rep. 86; *R.* v. *Rickard* (1918), 13 Cr. App. Rep. 140.
[8] *R.* v. *O'Sullivan*, [1969] 2 All E. R. 237; *R.* v. *Tilley*, [1961] 1 All E. R. 406; *R.* v. *Smith* (1968), 52 Cr. App. Rep. 648.
[9] *R.* v. *Crouch* (1850), 4 Cox C. C. 163. Perhaps this case is best regarded as turning on an analogy with those in which the answers to questions improperly put by policemen to prisoners in custody were rejected.   [10] (1869), 11 Cox C. C. 546.

to have been ruled in a later case that evidence by a policeman that he had seen the accused write for his own purposes pending trial was admissible.[1]

In spite of the variety of the methods by which handwriting may be proved, there might be great difficulty in employing them to authenticate handwriting of any antiquity, and that is why the presumption of due execution to which reference will be made shortly is of the utmost utility.

B. PROOF OF ATTESTATION

For historical reasons to be mentioned at the end of the discussion, it is convenient to deal separately with proof of the attestation of wills and other documents required by law to be attested.

(1) WILLS

If it becomes necessary to prove the due execution of a will, it is essential to call one of the attesting witnesses if any are available. Before other evidence is admissible, it must be shown that all the attesting witnesses are dead, insane, beyond the jurisdiction or that none of them can be traced. This requirement holds good even if the execution can be proved by those who saw it though they were not attesting witnesses, but the witness is treated as if he had been called by the court so he may be cross-examined by the party seeking to prove execution,[2] professional privilege cannot be claimed in respect of his previous statements to solicitors concerning execution,[3] and any other evidence may be given if he denies execution or refuses to testify.[4]

If none of the attesting witnesses can be called for the reasons indicated in the previous paragraph, steps must be taken to prove the handwriting of at least one of them. This constitutes secondary evidence of attestation.

If evidence of handwriting is unobtainable, evidence of those who saw the will executed, or any other evidence from which an inference of due execution can be drawn becomes admissible, but it seems that every effort must first be made to prove the handwriting of one of the attesting witnesses.[5] If a will is proved to have been in existence after the testator's death, a copy may be admitted to probate on proof that the original was signed by the testator and bore the signature of two attesting witnesses, although the person giving this evidence is unable to recollect their names.[6] It should perhaps be added that, when probate is sought in common form, the rigorous requirements as to proof of due execution to which reference has just been made do not apply.

(2) OTHER DOCUMENTS REQUIRED BY LAW TO BE ATTESTED

In the case of the comparatively few documents, other than wills, to the validity of which attestation is essential, it may be proved by the testimony

---

[1] *R. v. McCartney and Hansen* (1928), 20 Cr. App. Rep. 179, C. C. A. For further cases turning on the proof of handwriting see *Lucas v. Williams & Sons*, [1892] 2 Q. B. 113, and *R. v. Hope* (1955), 39 Cr. App. Rep. 33. See also *R. v. Day*, [1940] 1 All E. R. 402.

[2] *Oakes v. Uzzell*, [1932] P. 19; *Re Webster, Webster v. Webster* (1974), *Times*, 8th June (general cross-examination permissible).

[3] *In the Estate of Fuld* (No. 2) *Hartley v. Fuld*, [1965] P. 405; [1965] 2 All E. R. 657.

[4] *Bowman v. Hodgson* (1867), L. R. 1 P. & D. 362; *In the Goods of Ovens* (1892), 29 L.R. Ir. 451; *Re Vere-Wardale, Vere-Wardale v. Johnson*, [1949] P. 395; [1949] 2 All E. R. 250.

[5] *Clarke v. Clarke* (1879), 5 L. R. Ir. 47.

[6] *In the Estate of Phibbs*, [1917] P. 93; *Re Webb, Smith v. Johnston*, [1964] 2 All E. R. 91.

of one of the subscribing witnesses, but it is unnecessary to call any of them if the person wishing to prove due execution does not desire to do so. He may content himself with proving the handwriting of an attesting witness, and, if he is unable to do this, he may have recourse to other evidence.

(3) HISTORY OF THE PRESENT LAW

The rule that one of the subscribing witnesses of an attested document must be called unless they were all unavailable used to apply to all attested documents, whether attestation was required by law or not. Lord ELLEN-BOROUGH said that the rule was "as fixed, formal, and universal as any that can be stated in a court of justice".[1] It probably originated in the ancient requirement that the witness to a deed should, where possible, be summoned to sit with the jury in the days when that body was composed of witnesses rather than triers of fact. In more modern times, the rule was justified on the ground that the parties to a document must be taken to have agreed that the document should not be given in evidence unless the attesting witness was called when possible,[2] but, by virtue of s. 7 of the Criminal Procedure Act, 1865 (which applies to civil and criminal cases), instruments to the validity of which attestation is not necessary may be proved as if there had been no attesting witnesses thereto, and s. 3 of the Evidence Act, 1938, provides that in any proceedings, civil or criminal, an instrument to the validity of which attestation is requisite may, instead of being proved by an attesting witness, be proved in the manner in which it might be proved if no attesting witness were alive. The only exception is the case of testamentary documents to which the section is expressly stated to be inapplicable. Section 7 of the Criminal Procedure Act, 1865, and s. 3 of the Evidence Act, 1938, are the authorities for the foregoing treatment of the proof of attestation.

C. PRESUMPTIONS RELATING TO DOCUMENTS

Attestation, like handwriting, would not be easily proved in the case of a document of any antiquity, but practical difficulties are, in the main, obviated by the presumption of due execution that attaches to a document proved or purporting to be not less than twenty years old, provided it is produced from proper custody. "Proper custody" is that which was reasonable and natural under the circumstances of the particular case. Expired leases may be expected to be in the custody of either lessor or lessee and those claiming under them, a family Bible may properly be in the custody of any member of the family. Proper custody in this context does not mean the most appropriate custody possible. Papers relating to a bishopric have been held to come from proper custody when found among the family papers of a deceased bishop and not, as they should have been, in the possession of the bishop for the time being;[3] but, in the absence of further explanation, the parish clerk's house is not a place of proper custody for the parish registers.[4] The other basic fact of the presumption—

---

[1] *R.* v. *Harringworth (Inhabitants)* (1815), 4 M. & S. 350. See Stephen's *Digest of the Law of Evidence* (12th edition), n. XIII.
[2] *Whyman* v. *Garth* (1853), 8 Exch. 803, *per* POLLOCK, C.B.
[3] *Meath (Bp.)* v. *Winchester (Marquess)* (1836), 3 Bing. N. C. 183.
[4] *Doe* d. *Arundel (Lord)* v. *Fowler* (1850), 14 Q. B. 700.

the age of the document—is prescribed by s. 4 of the Evidence Act, 1938, for criminal and civil cases. At common law the period was thirty years.

Several other useful presumptions relating to documents may be mentioned. A document is presumed to have been executed on the date it bears;[1] alterations in a deed are presumed to have been made before execution, otherwise the entire deed might be avoided, but alterations in a will are presumed to have been made after execution because they would not invalidate the entire testament.[2] It is sometimes said that there is a presumption that a deed, even when less than twenty years old, was duly sealed, but this is not a presumption which is at all clearly established by the authorities.[3]

D. THE STAMP ACT

In civil proceedings, stamp objections are taken by the court and cannot be waived by the parties.[4] If the original of a document is lost, or not produced after notice, it is presumed to have been duly stamped. If a document is shown to have been unstamped at a particular time, the ordinary provisional presumption of continuance applies, and there is evidence on which the court may find that the document was never properly stamped, but there is at least one case where language is used which suggests that the court must find that a lost document was duly stamped when the question is left doubtful by the evidence.[5]

SECTION 3. THE ADMISSIBILITY OF EXTRINSIC EVIDENCE AFFECTING THE CONTENTS OF A DOCUMENT

Having dealt with what may be called the "exclusiveness" of a document as evidence of its terms, it is now necessary to consider its conclusiveness. The general effect of the rule considered in Section 1 was that the contents of a document may only be proved by production of the original. The major problems with which this section is concerned are first, whether, once a transaction has been embodied in a document, evidence may be given of terms other than those it mentions, and, second, the extent to which evidence may be given of the meaning of the terms used in the document. In each instance, the problem is one of the admissibility of "extrinsic evidence", an expression which means any evidence other than the document the contents of which are under consideration. It is often said to be "parol evidence", and no doubt this is because it usually takes the form of oral testimony, but it may consist of other documents.

---

[1] *Anderson* v. *Weston* (1840), 6 Bing. N. C. 296.
[2] *Doe* d. *Tatum* v. *Catomore* (1851), 16 Q. B. 745.
[3] *Re Sandilands* (1871), L. R. 6 C. P. 411; *National Provincial Bank of England* v. *Jackson* (1886), 33 Ch. D. 1, at pp. 11 and 14; *Re Balkis Consolidated Co., Ltd.* (1888), 58 L. T. 300.
[4] *Bowker* v. *Williamson* (1889), 5 T. L. R. 382. Unstamped documents may be proved in criminal proceedings.
[5] *Closmadeuc* v. *Carrel* (1856), 18 C.B. 36.

A. THE CONCLUSIVENESS OF A DOCUMENT AS EVIDENCE OF THE TERMS OF THE TRANSACTION IT EMBODIES

(1) STATEMENT AND ILLUSTRATIONS OF THE RULE

(i) Statement

Extrinsic evidence is generally inadmissible when it would, if accepted, have the effect of adding to, varying or contradicting the terms of a judicial record, a transaction required by law to be in writing, or a document constituting a valid and effective contract or other transaction. Most judicial statements of the rule are concerned with its application to contracts, and one of the best known is that of Lord MORRIS who regarded it as indisputable that:

"Parol testimony cannot be received to contradict, vary, add to or subtract from the terms of a written contract or the terms in which the parties have deliberately agreed to record any part of their contract".[1]

Another well known statement is that of Lord DENMAN when he said:

"If there be a contract which has been reduced into writing, verbal evidence is not allowed to be given of what passed between the parties, either before the written instrument was made, or during the time that it was in a state of preparation, so as to add to or subtract from, or in any manner to vary or qualify the written contract."[2]

Statements of this nature are best regarded as statements of the effect of the substantive law of merger which is now based on the presumed intention of the parties.[3] If the court is satisfied that they effectively agreed to be bound by a written instrument, they are bound by its terms though unacquainted with them,[4] and though one of the parties believes that something said in the course of the negotiations is still binding. In such circumstances, it would be pointless to admit extrinsic evidence with regard to those negotiations because it is irrelevant. It is for the same reason that evidence that one of the parties to a written agreement did not intend to be contractually bound is inadmissible.[5] Evidence of antecedent negotiations is relevant and admissible if they retain their contractual effect or legal significance after the writing has been brought into existence. Such evidence is always admissible if tendered to establish the existence of a contract collateral to the writing, or the conclusion of a contract which is partly oral and partly in writing. Evidence of antecedent negotiations is likewise admissible when it is relevant owing to such provisions of the substantive law as the requirement of what is now s. 14 (3) of the Sale of Goods Act, 1893, that the buyer should make known to the seller that he relies on his skill and judgment.[6]

---

[1] *Bank of Australasia* v. *Palmer*, [1897] A. C. 540, at p. 545.

[2] *Goss* v. *Lord Nugent* (1833), 5 B. & Ad. 58.

[3] The law of merger originated in deeds and the rules of pleading, but it had come to apply to written contracts as part of the substantive law by the eighteenth century; compare Bacon's Maxims (reg. 25) with Viner's Abridgement (contract g. 18); contrast *Countess of Rutland's Case* (1604), 5 Co. Rep. 25 B. with *Meres* v. *Ansell* (1771), 3 Wils. 275. See also Salmond, *The Superiority of Written Evidence*, 6 L. Q. R. 75 (1890), and Wigmore, *A Brief History of the Parol Evidence Rule*, 4 Columbia Law Review 33–7 (1904). For modern developments, see Wedderburn in [1959] C. L. J. 58.

[4] *Parker* v. *South Eastern Rail. Co.* (1877), 2 C. P. D. 416, at p. 421.

[5] *Smith* v. *Mansi*, [1962] 3 All E. R. 857.

[6] *Gillespie Bros. & Co.* v. *Cheney Eggar & Co.*, [1896] 2 Q. B. 59; *Manchester Liners Ltd.* v. *Rea Ltd.*, [1922] 2 A. C. 74, at p. 85; *The Preload Company of Canada Ltd.* v. *The City of Regina* (1958), 13 D. L. R. (2d) 305.

(ii) Illustrations

(a) *Judicial records.*—Once it has been drawn up, the order of a court is conclusive evidence of that which was directed by the judge. Steps may be taken to have clerical errors corrected, and there may be an appeal; but, in any other proceedings, extrinsic evidence of the terms of the decision would be irrelevant.

(b) *Transactions required by law to be in writing.*—Even when a transaction is required by law to be in writing, extrinsic evidence is admissible in aid of the interpretation of the document, but that does not constitute an infringement of the rule under consideration. Additional or different terms may not be proved by extrinsic evidence. In *Re Huxtable*,[1] a testator bequeathed four thousand pounds to C. "for charitable purposes agreed between us". It was held that, though evidence was admissible to show what purposes had been agreed, it was not permissible to adduce evidence tending to show that only the income of the bequest was to be devoted to these purposes. That would have contradicted the will, whereas proof of the agreed purposes did not have this effect. In *Re Rees*,[2] a testator left part of his estate "to my trustees absolutely, they well knowing my wishes concerning the same". The Court of Appeal affirmed the judge's decision, reached without resort to extrinsic evidence, that, as a matter of construction, the estate was given on trust, and accordingly evidence showing that, in the events which had happened, the testator intended his trustees to take it beneficially was inadmissible because it would contradict the terms of the will as construed by the court.

(c) *Written contracts.*—In *Angell* v. *Duke*,[3] the defendant agreed in writing to let a house to the plaintiff together with the furniture therein. The plaintiff tendered evidence that, before the execution of the writing, the defendant had orally agreed to send in additional furniture, but it was held that such evidence was inadmissible because, having once executed the writing, without making the terms of the alleged parol agreement part of it, the plaintiff could not afterwards set up that agreement. It would have contradicted the restriction of the written document to furniture already in the house. In *Newman* v. *Gatti*,[4] an actress signed an agreement to understudy a named principal who left the employment of the defendant during the currency of the agreement. It was held that the actress could not give evidence of an oral undertaking that she should have the right to take the place of the principal because there was no evidence that this was to be a term of the contract. The Court of Appeal recognised that in some cases a collateral verbal contract for which the consideration was the entering into the principal contract might be proved, or it could happen that, after the written contract had been drawn up, the parties realised that it did not deal with a situation which might arise, and agreed to provide for that event; but the mere fact that a promise made during the negotiations preceding a written agreement is believed to be binding by the promisee when he signs the document does not prevent the doctrine of merger from operating.

---

[1] *Re Huxtable, Huxtable* v. *Crawford*, [1902] 2 Ch. 793.
[2] *Re Rees, Williams* v. *Hopkins*, [1950] Ch. 204; [1949] 2 All E. R. 1003.
[3] (1875), 32 L. T. 320, but see [1959] C. L. J. 65–6. *Kaplan* v. *Andrews*, [1955] 4 D. L. R. 553.
[4] (1907), 24 T. L. R. 18; see also *Grimston* v. *Cuningham*, [1894] 1 Q. B. 125 and *Aetna Factors Corporation Ltd.* v. *Breau* (1957), 10 D. L. R. (2d) 100.

The distinction between an addition, a variation and a contradiction has not been discussed by the courts. With the possible exception of *Angell* v. *Duke* the cases mentioned in the last paragraph were treated primarily as ones in which an effort was made to give extrinsic evidence of additional terms. A case which was treated as one of attempted variation is *Re Sutro (L.) & Co. and Heilbut, Symons & Co.*[1] A written contract having provided for the sale of rubber to be shipped to New York, evidence of a practice under which the goods were dispatched by rail for part of the journey was held to be inadmissible. The admissibility of evidence of a variation of a written contract which has once been concluded is plainly dependent on the substantive law. If, having regard to the rules of consideration, the variation is effective, and if, having regard to statutory provisions such as s. 40 of the Law of Property Act, 1925, it is enforceable, evidence of its terms will be received. When these conditions do not apply, such evidence will be irrelevant.

> "After the agreement has been reduced into writing, it is competent to the parties, at any time before breach of it, by a new contract not in writing, either altogether to waive, dissolve, or annul the former agreement, or in any manner to add to, or subtract from, or vary or qualify the terms of it, and thus to make a new contract, which is to be proved, partly by the written agreement, and partly by the subsequent verbal terms engrafted upon what will thus be left of the written agreement."[2]

These words were spoken in a case in which the plaintiff had agreed in writing to sell a number of lots of land to the defendant and tendered evidence of a subsequent oral agreement discharging him from the duty of making a good title to one of the lots. The evidence was held to be inadmissible on account of the Statute of Frauds, 1677;[3] but the court was clearly of opinion that evidence of the subsequent contractual variation or discharge of a written agreement is admissible in the ordinary case.[4]

Decisions which primarily turned on the question whether extrinsic evidence could be received of terms contradicting those of a written agreement are *Henderson* v. *Arthur*[5] and *Evans* v. *Roe*.[6] In the first case, a lease having been executed under which rent was payable in advance, the lessee was not allowed to give evidence of a prior undertaking by the lessor to accept rent in arrears. In the second case, evidence of a contemporaneous oral agreement that a written contract of service from week to week was to last for a year was rejected. To the same effect are cases in which, when a person has signed an agreement as "owner",[7] or "proprietor",[8] evidence that he was acting as agent for an undisclosed principal has been held to be inadmissible, as contradicting the unambiguous statement in the agreement.[9]

---

[1] [1917] 2 K. B. 348.

[2] *Goss* v. *Lord Nugent* (1833), 5 B. & Ad. 58, *per* Lord DENMAN, C.J.

[3] See now s. 40 of the Law of Property Act, 1925.

[4] A parol discharge as distinct from a variation was held effective in a case coming within s. 4 of the Sale of Goods Act, 1893 (now repealed), in *Morris* v. *Baron & Co.*, [1918] A. C. 1.

[5] [1907] 1 K. B. 10; see also *Goldfoot* v. *Welch*, [1914] 1 Ch. 213.

[6] (1872), L. R. 7 C. P. 138.   [7] *Humble* v. *Hunter* (1848), 12 Q. B. 310.

[8] *Formby Bros.* v. *Formby* (1910), 102 L. T. 116. This case, and *Humble* v. *Hunter*, were said to be no longer law by SCOTT, L.J., in *Epps* v. *Rothnie*, [1945] K. B. 562, at p. 565; [1946] 1 All E. R. 146, at p. 147 (*sed quaere*). The cases are discussed below. *Humble* v. *Hunter* was held to be good law in *Murphy* v. *Rae*, [1967] N. Z. L. R. 103.

[9] See the converse case of *Universal Steam Navigation Co.* v. *J. McKelvie & Co.*, [1923] A. C. 492 and contrast *Automobile Renault Canada Ltd.* v. *Maritime Import Autos, Ltd. and Kyley* (1962), 31 D. L. R. (2d) 592.

(2) Exceptions to and Cases Falling Outside the Rule

The case of a subsequent variation or discharge of a written agreement to which reference has already been made may be treated as an exception to the rule under consideration. Transactions required by law to be in writing may be discharged or varied by a parol contract, subject, in the case of a variation, to the requirements of the relevant statutes such as s. 40 of the Law of Property Act, 1925.[1] Evidence tending to establish such a contract may be regarded as evidence varying or contradicting the terms of the original document. The same can be said of evidence varying or discharging a contract embodied in a document when writing is not a necessary condition of its validity or enforcibility. The cases about to be considered can be regarded as exceptions to the rule or as falling outside it according to taste.

(i) **Public registers.**—Oral evidence has been received and accepted although it had the effect of establishing a different tonnage of a ship than that mentioned on the register of ships [2] and a different proprietorship of a taxicab than that shown on the register of hackney carriages.[3] No reasons were given for the first of these decisions. In the second case, the judgments of the Court of Appeal were exclusively concerned with the construction of the relevant statutes. The upshot seems to be that, subject to the terms of the statute under which it is kept, the contents of a public register are not conclusive. Extrinsic evidence affecting their truth is therefore admissible.

(ii) **Cases concerning the validity or effectiveness of a written contract or other document.**—Extrinsic evidence is admissible to show that a written contract or any other document is void for mistake,[4] or illegality,[5] or for non-compliance with the provisions of a statute,[3] or voidable on account of a fraudulent or innocent misrepresentation.[7] It is also permissible to prove by extrinsic evidence that a deed or written contract, unconditional on its face, was delivered as an escrow or signed subject to a condition precedent to its effectiveness as in *Pym* v. *Campbell*,[8] where the defendants agreed in writing to buy an invention from the plaintiff, subject to the oral stipulation that the transaction was conditional on the approval of the invention by the defendants' engineer. Extrinsic evidence was received concerning this stipulation and the fact that the invention had not been approved. Such evidence is also admissible to negative the implication of a warranty,[9] or to raise an equitable defence.[10] The rule

---

[1] *Morris* v. *Baron & Co., supra.*
[2] *The Recepta* (1889), 14 P. D. 131.   [3] *Kemp* v. *Elisha*, [1918] 1 K. B. 228.
[4] *Henkel* v. *Royal Exchange Assurance Co.* (1749), 1 Ves. Sen. 317; *Wake* v. *Harrop* (1861), 7 Jur. N. S. 710; *Cowen* v. *Trufitt Bros., Ltd.*, [1899] 2 Ch. 309; *Roe* v. *Naylor* (1918), 87 L. J. K. B. 958, at p. 968 (*non est factum*); *Craddock Brothers* v. *Hunt*, [1923] 2 Ch. 136, C. A.; *U.S.A.* v. *Motor Trucks ,Ltd.*, [1924] A. C. 196.
[5] *Collins* v. *Blantern* (1767), 2 Wils. 341.
[6] *Campbell Discount Co., Ltd.* v. *Gall*, [1961] 1 Q. B. 431; [1961] 2 All E. R. 104.
[7] *Dobell* v. *Stevens* (1825), 3 B. & C. 623.
[8] (1856), 6 E. & B. 370; *Wallis* v. *Littell* (1861), 11 C. B. N. S. 369; *Lindley* v. *Lacey* (1864), 17 C. B. N. S. 578; *Davis* v. *Jones* (1856), 17 C. B. 625; *Pattle* v. *Hornibrook*, [1897] 1 Ch. 25, distinguished in *Smith* v. *Mansi*, [1962] 3 All E. R. 857. See also *Frontier Finance, Ltd.* v. *Hynes and Niagara Sewing Machine Co.* (1956), 10 D. L. R. (2d) 206. *In Re Tait*, [1957] V. L. R. 405, instructions for a will were admitted to show that a revocation clause was conditioned on the insertion of other clauses inadvertently omitted.
[9] *Burges* v. *Wickham* (1863), 3 B. & S. 669.
[10] *Martin* v. *Pyecroft* (1852), 2 De G. M. & G. 785, followed in *Scott* v. *Bradley*, [1971] 1 Ch. 850; [1971] 1 All E. R. 583; *Wake* v. *Harrop* (1861), 1 H. & C. 202.

under consideration can hardly be said to be infringed in any of the cases mentioned in this paragraph because it only applies to valid and effective transactions.

(iii) **Consideration.**—The absence of consideration invalidates a simple contract in writing, and this may always be proved by extrinsic evidence. The fact that a bill of exchange contains the words "for value received" does not render evidence that it was an accommodation bill inadmissible in cases where that fact is relevant. When a deed contains no reference to consideration, or mentions a nominal consideration, extrinsic evidence concerning a real consideration has been held to be admissible. Thus, in *Turner* v. *Forwood*,[1] the plaintiff entered into an agreement under seal with a company and a director in which he assigned a debt due to him from the company for a thousand and fifteen pounds to the director in consideration of ten shillings, and it was held that oral evidence might be given of an antecedent agreement by the director to pay in full for the debt. The principle underlying such decisions appears to be that, as no consideration need, in general, be expressed in a deed in order that it should be effective, the parties may often be taken to have intended that their arrangements should be carried out, partly by a contract under seal, and partly by parol. As a matter of conveyancing practice, it became usual to insert a nominal consideration in many deeds in order to avoid the implication of a use, so it was reasonable to infer that, so far as the intention of the parties was concerned, these cases were the same as those in which no consideration was inserted in a deed. There is no authority dealing with the admissibility of extrinsic evidence to vary a real consideration stated in a deed. In *Turner* v. *Forwood*, Lord GODDARD, C.J., was not prepared to say that the principle applied by him was confined to cases in which a nominal consideration was expressed in a deed; but, if the principle is extended, the question as to what undertakings are to be treated as part of the consideration would give rise to difficulty.

(iv) **The real nature of the transaction.**—When it is relevant, having regard to the principles of common law and equity involved, extrinsic evidence may be given of the real nature of any transaction, whether it is recorded in a document in pursuance of legal requirements or at the instance of the parties. Thus evidence has been received to show that an apparent sale was really a mortgage,[2] and a secret trust could never be established without recourse to extrinsic means of proof.

(v) **Capacity of parties.**[3]—We have seen that, if someone signs a document as "owner" or "proprietor", extrinsic evidence of agency is inadmissible. This may be on the principle that only one person can comply with such descriptions, so the evidence would inevitably contradict the document. Extrinsic evidence of agency has been received in the case of such other forms of signature as "charterer",[4] "tenant"[5] and "landlord".[6] It is possible, however, that the true basis of the decisions excluding the ex-

---

[1] [1951] 1 All E. R. 746, C. A.; *Clifford* v. *Turrell* (1845), 1 Y. & C. Ch. Cas. 138 (*affirmed*, 14 L. J. Ch. 390); *Frith* v. *Frith*, [1906] A. C. 254.
[2] *Re Marlborough (Duke), Davis* v. *Whitehead*, [1894] 2 Ch. 133.
[3] For the admissibility of extrinsic evidence to show who was purchaser and who vendor, see *Newell* v. *Radford* (1867), L. R. 3 C. P. 52.
[4] *Drughorn (Fred), Ltd.* v. *Rederiaktiebolaget Transatlantic*, [1919] A. C. 203.
[5] *Danziger* v. *Thompson*, [1944] K. B. 654; [1944] 2 All E. R. 151.
[6] *Epps* v. *Rothnie*, [1945] K. B. 562; [1946] 1 All E. R. 146.

trinsic evidence was that it was a term of the contracts with which the court was dealing that the signatory should have been owner or proprietor. They were treated with reserve by Lord SHAW and said to be no longer law by SCOTT, L.J.[1] Extrinsic evidence has been received of the fact that the successive indorsers of a bill of exchange were co-sureties,[2] and, in *Young* v. *Schuler*,[3] where it was not clear whether the defendant had signed a guarantee as agent for a company or with the intention of making himself personally liable, evidence was received of his contemporaneous declaration to the latter effect. It might have been treated as an admission, but it seems to have been received on the principle, to be discussed later, under which declarations of intention are admissible in cases of equivocation.

(vi) Collateral undertakings, contracts partly oral and partly in writing or subject to usage.—We have seen that the Court of Appeal recognised in *Newman* v. *Gatti*,[4] that a collateral oral contract might be proved when it was concluded in consideration of the execution of a written contract. In *De Lassalle* v. *Guildford*,[5] for instance, the plaintiff made it plain to his landlord, the defendant, that he would not execute a lease unless the defendant gave a warranty concerning the healthy condition of the drains. Such warranty was given verbally, and the lease was duly executed. The lease did not refer to the state of the drains, but it was held that this fact did not prevent the adduction of oral evidence concerning the warranty.

A court may likewise come to the conclusion that the parties intended their contract to be partly oral and partly in writing, in which case the oral parts may be proved by parol testimony. In *Harris* v. *Rickett*,[6] the defendant was allowed to prove that a written agreement for a loan was accompanied by an oral stipulation that a bill of sale would be given. The plaintiff contended that the effect of this evidence was to add to or vary the writing but POLLOCK, C.B., said that:

> "the rule relied on by the plaintiff only applies when the parties to an agreement reduce it to writing and agree or intend that that writing should be their agreement".

A further example of the use of extrinsic evidence is provided by cases in which one party has been allowed to establish a trade usage provided it is not inconsistent with the writing.[7]

> "In all contracts, as to the subject-matter of which known usages prevail, parties are found to proceed with the tacit assumption of these usages; they

---

[1] In *Drughorn's Case* and *Epps* v. *Rothnie* respectively; but see *Murphy* v. *Rae*, [1967] N. Z. L. R. 103.

[2] *Macdonald* v. *Whitfield* (1883), 8 App. Cas. 733.   [3] (1883), 11 Q. B. D. 651.

[4] (1907), 24 T. L. R. 18, C. A., see also *Bristol Tramways, etc., Carriage Co.* v. *Fiat Motors*, [1910] 2 K. B. 831, at p. 838; and *Heilbut, Symons & Co.* v. *Buckleton*, [1913] A. C. 30, at p. 47.

[5] [1901] 2 K. B. 215; *Morgan* v. *Griffith* (1871), L. R. 6 Exch. 70; *Erskine* v. *Adeane* (1873), 8 Ch. App. 756; *City and Westminster Properties (1934), Ltd.* v. *Mudd*, [1959] Ch. 129; [1958] 3 All E. R. 733. The distinction between this last case and *Angell* v. *Duke* is that in *Angell* v. *Duke* the lessee did not insist on the provision of further furniture being part of the consideration for his executing the lease. Cf. *Couchman* v. *Hill*, [1947] K. B. 554; [1947] 1 All E. R. 103.

[6] (1859), 4 H. & N. 1.

[7] The distinction between usages which add to and contradict a document is difficult. Contrast *Brown* v. *Byrne* (1854), 3 E. & B. 703 with *Krall* v. *Burnett* (1887), 25 W. R. 305.

commonly reduce into writing the special particulars of their agreement but omit to specify these known usages, which are included, however, as of course, by mutual understanding: evidence therefore of such incidents is receivable. The contract in truth is partly express and in writing, partly implied or understood and unwritten." [1]

(vii) Memoranda.—In some cases, after an oral contract has been concluded, a memorandum relating to the whole or part of the transaction is prepared by one of the parties and handed to the other. The document may then be treated as a mere memorandum, and, as it has no contractual effect, additional matter may be proved. Whether the writing is to be treated thus, or whether it will be held to be, not a memorandum, but a contractual document, depends on the intention of the parties, which must, in the absence of direct evidence, be ascertained by means of the inferences which a reasonable man would draw from the terms of the document and the surrounding circumstances. In *Allen* v. *Pink*,[2] the plaintiff bought a horse from the defendant who handed him a receipt for the purchase price, and it was held that this did not preclude the plaintiff from proving an oral warranty of the fitness of the animal. Lord ABINGER, C.B., concluded that the paper appeared to have been meant merely as a memorandum of the transaction, or an informal receipt for the money, not as containing the terms of the contract itself. This case may be contrasted with *Hutton* v. *Watling* [3] in which a document providing for the sale of a business by the defendant to the plaintiff and containing an option to purchase the land on which the business was carried on was treated as contractual by the Court of Appeal with the result that the defendant's evidence, in an action for specific performance of the option, that no option was given was held to be inadmissible. The court treated the matter as one of construction, adding that:

"The true construction of a document means no more than that the court puts upon it the true meaning, being the meaning which the other party, to whom the document was handed or who is relying upon it, would put upon it as an ordinary intelligent person construing the words in a proper way in the light of the relevant circumstances." [4]

The cases on collateral contracts, contracts partly oral and partly in writing, contracts subject to usage and memoranda raise the question whether, at least in its application to contracts, what is often called the parol evidence rule is anything more than an empty tautology.[5] If the law is simply that extrinsic evidence is inadmissible when the parties intended that a document should contain their entire contract, extrinsic evidence is naturally inadmissible because it is irrelevant. Cases like *Hutton* v. *Watling* show that the rule is not a tautology because the parties are bound by the terms of a document if a reasonable man would have considered the document to

---

[1] *Per* COLERIDGE, J., in *Brown* v. *Byrne* (1854), 3 E. & B. 703.

[2] (1838), 4 M. & W. 140; as between the parties a bill of lading is a memorandum, *Ardennes S.S.* (*Cargo Owners*) v. *Ardennes S.S.* (*Owners*), [1951] 1 K. B. 55; [1950] 2 All E. R. 517; cf. *Leduc* v. *Ward* (1888), 20 Q. B. D. 475, turning on the point that the bill is conclusive evidence of the terms of the shipment as between shipowner and indorsee under the Bills of Lading Act, 1855. Another case in which a post-contractual document was treated as a memorandum is *Bank of Australasia* v. *Palmer*, [1897] A. C. 540.

[3] [1948] Ch. 398; [1948] 1 All E. R. 803; *Stuart* v. *Dundon*, [1963] S. A. S. R. 134.

[4] *Per* Lord GREENE, M.R., at pp. 403, 805, respectively.

[5] See the discussion of this point by G. H. Treitel in *The Law of Contract*, (3rd edition), p. 158.

be a contractual one. This is so even if one of them thought that the contract contained additional terms not mentioned in the document or that a clearly expressed term to which he had agreed bore a special meaning.[1]

(viii) **Proceedings between strangers.**—There is little doubt that, in proceedings between strangers to transactions required by law to be in writing, the circumstances in which extrinsic evidence is admissible are the same as those in which such evidence is admissible in proceedings between the parties to the document; but there is some authority for the view that extrinsic evidence is always admissible when the document merely embodies a transaction to the validity of which the writing is not essential even if it has the effect of varying, adding to, or contradicting the terms of the writing. In *R.* v. *Inhabitants of Cheadle* [2] the parish was allowed to call a pauper whose settlement was in issue to swear that a deed of conveyance to which he was a party was, contrary to its express terms, unsupported by consideration. In *R.* v. *Adamson*,[3] the accused was charged with obtaining money by false pretences as a premium payable under a deed of partnership executed by the prosecutor. It was held that the prosecutor could give evidence of a different consideration for the payment of the premium than that stated in the deed. Stephen treated these cases as authorities for a general exception to the rule prohibiting extrinsic evidence adding to, varying or contradicting the terms of a document,[4] but this rule certainly applies in some cases in which one of the parties to the proceedings was not a party to the writing. In *Mercantile Bank of Sydney* v. *Taylor*,[5] for instance, the bank was not allowed to adduce evidence of an oral agreement between themselves and one of several sureties, of whom the defendant was another, that the guaranteed debt should not be included in a release from liability given by them. The evidence received in *R.* v. *Inhabitants of Cheadle* would now be admissible in proceedings between parties to the deed [6] and *R.* v. *Adamson* may simply indicate that the rule does not apply in criminal proceedings. The authorities are too scanty to be a convenient subject for any generalisation.[7]

B. EXTRINSIC EVIDENCE IN AID OF INTERPRETATION [8]

It has been said that:

"The admission of extrinsic circumstances to govern the construction of a written instrument is in all cases an exception to the general rule of law which excludes everything *dehors* the instrument." [9]

---

[1] See the speech of Lord DENNING in *London County Council* v. *Henry Boot & Sons, Ltd.*, [1959] 3 All E. R. 636, at p. 641. The parties may be bound by terms to which they have agreed although they both think the terms have a different meaning from that ultimately placed on them by the court.

[2] (1832), 3 B. & Ad. 833. Contrast the operation of the rule that a document is exclusive evidence of its terms as illustrated by *Augustien* v. *Challis* (1847), 1 Exch. 279.

[3] (1843), 2 Mood. C. C. 286, C. C. R.

[4] *Digest of the Law of Evidence* (12th ed.), art. 99.   [5] [1893] A. C. 317.

[6] See *Frith* v. *Frith*, [1906] A. C. 254.

[7] It has been held in South Africa that the rule does not apply between strangers (*Davies* v. *Brooklands Car Sales* 1956, (1) S. A. 745).

[8] The classic work is Wigram's *Extrinsic Evidence in Aid of the Interpretation of Wills.* This should be supplemented by Thayer *op cit.*, ch. 10 and appendix C. by Vaughan Hawkins; Holmes, *The Theory of Legal Interpretation*, 12 H. L. R. 417; Phipson, *Extrinsic Evidence in Aid of Interpretation*, 20 L. Q. R. 245; and IX WIGMORE, para. 2458 *et seq.*, to which the author is heavily indebted. In the ensuing account the words "interpretation" and "construction" are treated as synonymous.

[9] *Per* Sir T. PLUMER, M.R., in *Colpoys* v. *Colpoys* (1822), Jac. 451.

But statements of this nature must be read with caution, for it would be impossible to interpret most documents if some extrinsic matter were not allowed to be proved. If a testator bequeaths "my piano to my son John", evidence must perforce be received to show that there were in existence at his death a chattel and a person corresponding to these descriptions. In the words of JAMES, L.J.:

> "You must always, of course, have evidence who are the persons mentioned, and you must also have evidence of what are the things bequeathed." [1]

The main problem in relation to the construction of a will is the extent to which it is permissible to go beyond these matters in cases of disputed interpretation, and a similar problem arises with regard to the construction of other documents—if there is a doubt concerning the persons or things to which the document refers, is it permissible to consider the surrounding circumstances and the extrinsic declarations of the parties in order to resolve the doubt, or must the document be held void for uncertainty? In some cases there may be no alternative to the adoption of the latter course. If a testator leaves his estate to "Lady   ", or to "One or other of my daughters Joan and Jane", even if it is proved that he was acquainted with women of title, or the father of daughters named Joan and Jane respectively, no further evidence might be forthcoming, in which case there would hardly be a rational alternative to holding that he died intestate. There is, however, an infinite variety of degrees of doubt concerning the certainty with which a document may be interpreted. At the one extreme there are the cases of complete uncertainty to which reference has just been made, at the other there is the case of virtually complete certainty as where a man leaves everything to "my only son John", and it is proved that he had but one son and that son's name is John.

The extent to which a document may be treated as conclusive as to the meaning of its terms is thus a question of degree. It can hardly ever be completely so, because some extrinsic evidence must be received, but the nature of such evidence, and the purposes for which it may be used in a case in which the meaning of a document is disputed, depends on the standard of interpretation by which the litigation must be decided.

(1) STANDARDS OF INTERPRETATION

Wigmore [2] spoke of four possible standards—the popular, the local, the common and the individual. The popular standard refers to the ordinary meaning of words; the local standard refers to possible variations of the popular within a particular community, trade or religious sect; the common standard covers the sense in which the words were understood by both parties to a contract, while the individual standard is that of one party to a transaction and is, in general, only relevant in cases of will construction. Subject to the need to resort to extrinsic evidence in order to ascertain the persons and things covered by the words used, the application of the popular standard is a matter of exegesis aided by judicial notice rather than evidence; judicial notice may be taken of some local or trade usages, but these are matters which usually have to be proved; the application of the common and individual standard calls, in the absence of anything in

---

[1] *Sherratt* v. *Mountford* (1873), 8 Ch. App. 928, at p. 929.
[2] Paras. 2458 and 2460.

the nature of a formal admission, for extrinsic evidence which can be either circumstantial or testimonial. Assuming that no exclusionary rules apply, the fact that the parties to a contract have a common objective may warrant an inference concerning the meaning they attached to certain clauses, just as the speech habits of a testator may justify a particular construction of the words used by him. The meaning of the contracting parties and the testator could also, subject to exclusionary rules, be proved in the one case by their direct oral evidence and, in either case, by their hearsay statements.

According to Wigmore, the application of each of the above standards should be, and to a large extent is, provisional. This means that extrinsic evidence in aid of interpretation may take a variety of forms and be adduced for a number of different purposes varying with the facts of the particular case; but Wigmore did not deny the existence of restrictions on its admissibility. Such restrictions may, as a matter of law, rule out one or more of the standards which have just been mentioned.

In the first place there is, as we shall see, a general rule (subject to very limited exceptions) excluding the statements of intention of the testator or contracting parties as evidence of the sense in which words were used by them in the will or written contract under consideration. The precise basis of that rule and the effect, if any, upon it of the Civil Evidence Act, 1968, are matters which will be discussed later.

Secondly, the individual standard must always be inapplicable when the court is concerned with the construction, as opposed to the existence, avoidance or rectification of a contract.

> "The words used may, and often do, represent a formula which means different things to each side, yet be accepted because that is the only way to get agreement and in the hope that disputes will not arise. The only course there can be is to try to ascertain the natural meaning." [1]

But the most important of all the restrictions on the application of any standard of interpretation but the popular is the survival or, assuming it has not survived, the influence, of what may be called the "plain meaning" rule. According to this rule, if the words of a document apply exactly to a particular person or thing in their ordinary natural sense, extrinsic evidence cannot be received to displace it. In other words, if the document contains names or descriptive phrases which are wholly appropriate when the popular standard of interpretation is applied, resort cannot be had, in the case of a contract, to the common standard, and, in the case of a will, to the individual standard.

> "Suppose . . . a testator left a legacy to his son John, and suppose he had a son John who had been living away from him, and there was another person named John living with him who was not his son but whom he called his son, in such a case would any evidence be admitted that his son John was not the person intended to be benefited. How can the fact of a testator being in the habit of calling a person his son who is not his son be evidence of surrounding circumstances? It is really evidence of the intention of the testator." [2]

(2) The Principal Rules of Interpretation

The following brief account of the principal rules of interpretation is designed to illustrate the principles according to which extrinsic evidence is

---

[1] *Per* Lord Wilberforce in *Prenn* v. *Simmonds*, [1971] 3 All E. R. 237, at p. 241.
[2] *Per* Kay, L.J., in *Re Fish, Ingham* v. *Rayner*, [1894] 2 Ch. 83, at p. 86.

received in aid of interpretation. Most of the illustrations are taken from cases of will construction, and, for this reason, it will be convenient to begin by setting out the seven propositions on which Wigram's Extrinsic Evidence in Aid of the Interpretation of Wills is based. Although they were formulated as long ago as 1831, they are the starting point of modern discussions such as that contained in the 19th Report of the Law Reform Committee to which reference is made at the end of this chapter.

(i) Wigram's propositions.—

(1) "A testator is always presumed to use the words in which he expresses himself according to their strict and primary acceptation, unless from the context of the will it appear that he has used them in a different sense, in which case the sense in which he thus appears to have used them will be the sense in which they are to be construed."

(2) "Where there is nothing in the context of a will from which it is apparent that a testator has used the words in which he has expressed himself in any other than their strict and primary sense, and where his words so interpreted are sensible with reference to extrinsic circumstances, it is an inflexible rule of construction that the words of the will shall be interpreted in their strict and primary sense, and in no other, although they may be capable of some popular or secondary interpretation, and although the most conclusive evidence of intention to use them in such popular or secondary sense be tendered."

(3) "Where there is nothing in the context of a will from which it is apparent that a testator has used the words in which he has expressed himself in any other than their strict and primary sense, but his words, so interpreted, are insensible with reference to extrinsic circumstances, a court of law may look into the extrinsic circumstances of the case to see whether the meaning of the words be sensible in any popular or secondary sense of which, with reference to these circumstances, they are capable."

(4) Where the characters in which a will is written are difficult to be deciphered or the language of the will is not understood by the court, the evidence of persons skilled in deciphering writing, or who understand the language in which the will is written, is admissible to declare what the characters are, or inform the court of the proper meaning of the words."

(5) "For the purpose of determining the object of a testator's bounty, or the subject of disposition, or the quantity of interest intended to be given by his will, a court may inquire into every material fact relating to the person who claims to be interested under the will, and to the property which is claimed as the subject of disposition, and to the circumstances of the testator and his family and affairs, for the purpose of enabling the court to identify the person or thing intended by the testator, or to determine the quantity of interest he has given by his will. The same (it is conceived) is true of every other disputed point respecting which it can be shown that a knowledge of extrinsic facts can, in any way, be made ancillary to the right interpretation of a testator's words."

(6) "Where the words of a will, aided by evidence of the material facts of the case, are insufficient to determine the testator's meaning, no evidence will be admissible to prove what the testator intended, and the will (except in certain special cases) will be void for uncertainty."

(7) "Notwithstanding the rule of law which makes a will void for uncertainty where the words, aided by evidence of the material facts of the case, are insufficient to determine the testator's meaning, courts of law in certain special cases admit extrinsic evidence of intention to make certain the person or thing intended where the description in the will is insufficient for the purpose. These cases may be thus defined:—Where the object of a testator's bounty, or the subject of disposition (i.e. the person or thing intended), is described in terms which are applicable indifferently to more than one person or thing, evidence is admissible to prove which of the persons or things so described was intended by the testator."

These propositions and the rules governing the admissibility of extrinsic evidence in aid of interpretation generally will now be illustrated by referring to the inadmissibility of extrinsic evidence to make a document, the admissibility, whenever necessary, of such evidence to translate the terms of a document or to prove the existence of the persons and things to which the document refers, the inadmissibility of extrinsic evidence to displace a sensible *prima facie* meaning as thus ascertained, the admissibility of circumstantial extrinsic evidence of the author's intended meaning in cases of uncertainty, the admissibility, in addition to such evidence, of the author's declarations of intention in the exceptional cases of equivocation and the rebuttal of certain presumptions.

(ii) The inadmissibility of extrinsic evidence to make a document.—Extrinsic evidence is inadmissible to show what words the author of the document intended to insert in total blanks therein, or what he meant by expressions which are too vague to be acted upon without resort to his declarations of intention that are not contained in the document or documents under consideration.

This rule is both a last resort and a minimal requirement. It is a last resort because the courts will only rely upon it as a ground for rejecting extrinsic evidence after all the other possible reasons for receiving such evidence have been examined and found to be inapplicable to the case in hand. The rule is a minimal requirement because it insists that the document must contain words of its author which are capable of being interpreted. He must not have reserved a power of completing it by his own utterances. Eyre, C.B., seems to have had this aspect of the rule in mind when he said:

> "All latitude of construction must submit to this restriction, namely, that the words may bear the sense which, by construction, is put upon them. If we step beyond this line, we no longer construe men's deeds, but make deeds for them." [1]

In *Baylis* v. *Attorney-General*,[2] Lord Hardwicke refused to admit extrinsic evidence of the intention of a testator with regard to a complete blank in his will, and, in *Hunt* v. *Hort*,[3] Lord Thurlow treated a bequest to "Lady   " as equivalent to a total blank so that the name intended by the testator could not be supplied by parol evidence. Partial blanks or imperfect descriptions may, however, be made good by circumstantial evidence of the intention of the author of the document. The identity of Mrs. G   ,[4] or   Price [5] mentioned in a will may be proved by evidence of the testator's acquaintanceship with someone to whom he was in the habit of referring as "Mrs. G   ", or with a Mr. Price of whose Christian name he was unaware.

In *Clayton* v. *Lord Nugent*,[6] a will contained bequests to the children of K., L. and M. A key to these initials in a document made after the will was held to be inadmissible. Had the key been in existence at the date of the will and clearly incorporated therein, it would have been admissible, and evidence that the testator was in the habit of referring to certain people as K., L. and M. might also have been received if this had been the case, but the reception of the key would have amounted to an acknowledgement of

---

[1] *Gibson* v. *Minet* (1791), 1 Hy. Bl. at p. 615.
[3] (1791), 3 Bro. C. C. 311.
[5] *Price* v. *Page* (1799), 4 Ves. 680.

[2] (1741), 2 Atk. 239.
[4] *Abbot* v. *Massie* (1796), 3 Ves. 148.
[6] (1844), 13 M. & W. 200.

the testator's right to reserve a power of testamentary disposition by means of a non-testamentary document.

(iii) The admissibility of extrinsic evidence to translate a document.—Extrinsic evidence is admissible to translate the terms of a document into words comprehensible by the court, to prove a custom or usage with reference to which the document is alleged to have been executed and to explain the meaning of common words which appear, from the context of the document itself, to have been used in a special sense.

In *Clayton* v. *Lord Nugent*, ALDERSON, B., said:

> "The case of a will written in cipher is quite different; because words on paper are but the means by which a person expresses his meaning and short-hand is, in this respect, like longhand, and equally admits of interpretation."

In *Goblet* v. *Beechey* [1] when construing the will of a sculptor the trial judge admitted evidence concerning the meaning of a bequest of "all the marble in the yard, the tools in the shop, bankers, mod tools and carving".

In *Smith* v. *Wilson* [2] where "a thousand rabbits" was held to mean "twelve hundred rabbits", Lord TENTERDEN, C.J., said:

> "I think that where in a deed, or in a declaration, or other pleading, a term is used to which an Act of Parliament has given a definite meaning, the use of the term will be governed by the meaning given by the Act of Parliament. There is no Act of Parliament which provides that an hundred rabbits shall consist of five score to the hundred.
> Then we must suppose that the parties to this deed used the word 'thousand' with reference to the subject-matter according to the meaning which it received in that part of the country. I cannot say, then, that evidence to show what was the acceptation of the term 'thousand' with reference to this subject-matter ought not to have been received at all."

In *Shore* v. *Wilson*,[3] a question arose concerning the effect of a deed conferring benefits on "poor and godly preachers of Christ's holy gospel". In their commonly accepted meaning, these words would have been too vague to be effective, but evidence was admitted to show that, in 1704, when the deed was executed, there existed a religious party by whom the phrase was used, and of which the lady who executed the deed was a member.

(iv) The admissibility of extrinsic evidence to prove the existence of persons and things mentioned in the document.—Extrinsic evidence is always admissible to prove the existence of persons and things to whom or to which the words of the document can reasonably be applied.

In the words of Lord ABINGER:

> "To understand the meaning of any writer, we must first be appraised of the persons and circumstances that are the subject of his allusions or statements; . . . All the facts and circumstances therefore respecting persons or property to which the will relates, are undoubtedly legitimate, and often necessary evidence, to enable us to understand the meaning and application of his words."

Reference has already been made to this manifestly essential rule which is embodied in Wigram's 5th proposition, and it is unnecessary to say anything more about it. The best evidence of the resort that is regularly made to it in practice is provided by the affidavit in support of the ordinary

---

[1] (1831), 2 Russ. & M. 624, L. C. On appeal the view was expressed that the evidence ought not to have been received but this seems to have been due to the special facts of the case—the question whether a gift of models by a former will was revoked.

[2] (1832), 3 B. & Ad. 728.   [3] (1842), 9 Cl. & Fin. 355.

originating summons raising a question of will construction. The affidavit contains information concerning the testator's affairs and estate without which it would be impossible for the judge to embark on his task of interpretation.

(v) The inadmissibility of extrinsic evidence to displace a sensible legal or commonly accepted meaning.—If words with a recognised legal or commonly accepted meaning can be sensibly applied to one person or thing, extrinsic evidence is generally inadmissible to show that the author of the document intended them to refer to some other person or thing.

The operative word in this, the plain meaning rule as here formulated, is "generally". There can be no doubt that the courts are, in the main, less inclined to insist on a strictly literal interpretation than they were in former days; but relics of this approach are to be found in some modern cases with the result that the law is difficult to state. Perhaps the best statement of the general position under the modern law is that of BLACKBURN, J., in delivering the opinion of the Exchequer Chamber in *Allgood v. Blake*.[1]

> "The general rule, we believe, is undisputed that, in trying to get at the intention of the testator, we are to take the whole of the will, construe it altogether, and give the words their natural meaning, unless, when applied to the subject-matter which the testator presumably had in his mind, they produce an inconsistency with other parts of the will, or an absurdity or inconvenience so great as to convince the court that the words could not have been used in their proper signification. . . . To one mind it may appear that an effect produced by construing the words literally is so inconsistent with the rest of the will, or produces an absurdity or inconvenience so great as to justify the court in putting on them another signification, which to that mind seems a not improper signification of the words, while to another mind the effect produced may appear not so inconsistent, absurd, or inconvenient as to justify putting any other signification on the words than their proper one, and the proposed signification may appear a violent construction. . . . We apprehend that no precise line can be drawn, but that the court must in each case apply the admitted rules to the case in hand; not deviating from the literal sense of the words without sufficient reason, or more than is justified; yet not adhering slavishly to them, when to do so would obviously defeat the intention which may be collected from the whole will."

In the case of written contracts, extrinsic evidence is likewise inadmissible to displace a well recognised meaning attaching to the words used.[2] Such evidence is admissible in the case of ambiguity and where the parties have contracted with reference to a particular practice or standard.[3] The fact that a particular construction might lead to practical difficulties cannot be proved by extrinsic evidence,[4] and it seems that the fact that one of the parties attached a special meaning to a particular clause to the knowledge of the other party cannot be proved by reference to their previous correspondence. Once it is plain that the parties have agreed to be bound by an unambiguous document, its construction is a matter for the court.[5]

---

[1] (1873), L. R. 8 Exch. 160.

[2] *Bank of New Zealand v. Simpson*, [1900] A. C. 182, at p. 189. Extrinsic evidence was held to have been rightly admitted on the facts.

[3] The type of repair customary in a given locality can be proved in litigation on a repairing covenant in a lease: *Burges v. Wickham* (1863), 3 B. & S. 669, at p. 698. See also *Mulvena v. Kelman*, [1965] N. Z. L. R. 656.

[4] *Gold v. Patman and Fotheringham, Ltd.*, [1958] 2 All E. R. 497.

[5] *London County Council v. Henry Boot & Sons, Ltd.*, [1959] 3 All E. R. 636, at p. 641. Reference should also be made to this case in the Court of Appeal [1959] 1 All E. R. 77, and to the case-note on the decision of the Court of Appeal in 75 L. Q. R. 149. See also

The fact that certain expressions have been interpreted again and again by the courts has led to a few absolute rules of construction the effect of which is to exclude extrinsic evidence of the intention of the author of the document. Let it once be shown that there are persons or things to whom or to which the words could apply, and evidence of a contrary intention, however great its weight may be, becomes inadmissible because it is irrelevant. A typical instance is provided by the exclusion, in the case of dispositions made before s. 15 of the Family Law Reform Act, 1969, came into force, of evidence showing an intention to benefit illegitimate at the expense of legitimate relations, when such intention was not manifested on the face of the document under consideration. After this rule has been examined, reference will be made to *Higgins* v. *Dawson*[1] as a comparatively modern instance of a literal interpretation which resulted in the exclusion of circumstantial evidence of the intention of the author of a document containing terms which have a generally accepted meaning, though not a specifically legal one.

(*a*) *Former preference for legitimate relationship.*—At common law there is a strict general rule under which illegitimates are excluded when words of relationship are used. To quote MALINS, V.C.:

> "Where you have a bequest of property to a class of persons, children, nephews, or nieces, or any class you like—'I give to my children', 'I give to my nephews and nieces', or 'I give to my brothers and sisters', and you find in the class designated legitimate members—you never can admit illegitimate children to share with them." [2]

The Vice-Chancellor was accordingly constrained to ignore facts in the case before him which strongly suggested that a testator had intended illegitimates to share in a gift to his brother's children of whom some were legitimate and others illegitimate. In *Re Fish*,[3] a testator bequeathed the residue of his estate to his niece E. W. He had no nieces, but his wife had two great nieces both of whom were named E. W. The misdescription would not have prevented the E. W. intended by the testator from benefiting under his will, and, as there were two of them, extrinsic evidence of such intention (which might have included the testator's declarations, as the case was one of equivocation) would have been admissible. There was a considerable body of evidence showing that the testator intended one of the two E. W.s to benefit, and he had always alluded to her as his "niece"; but she was illegitimate, so the evidence was held to be inadmissible and the other E. W. who was legitimate received the residue.

There are two exceptions to the general rule stated in the last paragraph. In the first place, the evidence of extrinsic circumstances concerning the family in question may show that it is impossible for legitimate children, born or to be born after the execution of the document under

---

James Miller & Partners, Ltd. v. *Whitworth Street Estates (Manchester), Ltd.*, [1970] 1 All E. R. 796 (subsequent conduct of parties irrelevant to construction), and *Prenn* v. *Simmonds*, [1971] 3 All E. R. 237 (evidence should be restricted to the factual background known to the parties at or before the date of the contract).

[1] [1902] A.C. 1.

[2] *Ellis* v. *Houstoun* (1878), 10 Ch. D. 236, at 241; *Hill* v. *Crook* (1873), L. R. 6 H. L. 265; *Dorin* v. *Dorin* (1875), L. R. 7 H. L. 568; *Re Pearce, Alliance Assurance Co., Ltd.* v. *Francis*, [1914] 1 Ch. 254. But see an article by J. H. C. Morris in 82 L. Q. R. 196, and *Sydall* v. *Castings, Ltd.*, [1967] 1 Q. B. 302; [1966] 3 All E. R. 770.

[3] *Re Fish, Ingham* v. *Rayner*, [1894] 2 Ch. 83.

consideration,[1] to have been intended to benefit, as where a testator makes a bequest to the children of his deceased daughter and it is proved that he knew that she never had a legitimate child. Secondly, the grantor may have "supplied his own dictionary" as the phrase goes.[2] He may have impliedly indicated an intention on the face of the document that illegitimates were intended to benefit from the gift. He may do this by referring to a child's mother and father as "husband" and "wife" when he knows that the marriage was void; he then means "to term the offspring of that so-called marriage the children according to that nomenclature".[3] The first exception does not affect the admissibility of extrinsic evidence of intention; in the case of the second, once the court decides to act on the dictionary principle, extrinsic evidence of intention may become admissible in order to resolve a conflict between the possible beneficiaries.[4]

The former preference for legitimates is something which will have to be borne in mind in relation to will construction for some time to come, but, in any disposition made after the coming into force of s. 15 of the Family Law Reform Act, 1969, any reference to the child or children of any person shall, unless the contrary intention appears, be construed as, or as including, a reference to any illegitimate child of that person. Any reference to a person or persons related in some other manner to any person shall, unless the contrary intention appears, be construed as or as including a reference to any person who would be so related if he, or some other person through whom the relationship is deduced, had been born legitimate.

(b) *Higgins* v. *Dawson*.—In *Higgins* v. *Dawson*,[5] the question was whether pecuniary legacies were payable out of the entire residuary estate of a testator or only out of such estate after two sums due to the deceased on mortgages had been deducted. The testator had bequeathed "all the residue and remainder" of these sums to named persons after "payment of my debts, funeral and testamentary expenses". In favour of the contention that the sums due on mortgage should be liable to bear their portion of the legacies, it was sought to adduce evidence that, when he made his will, the testator's estate apart from these sums, was insufficient to meet the legacies so that he must have intended to charge them on the mortgage debts. It was held that the evidence was inadmissible because the language used by the testator clearly meant that the residue of the sums due on mortgage was to be calculated without deducting anything in respect of the legacies.

(c) *The plain meaning rule to-day*.—As a comparatively recent decision of the House of Lords *Higgins* v. *Dawson* must count as the highwater mark of the application of the plain meaning rule under the modern law.

---

[1] In *Dorin* v. *Dorin* (*supra*) a gift to children was held to refer to legitimate children hereafter to be born with the result that illegitimate children were excluded.

[2] See Wigram's 1st proposition.

[3] *Per* Lord CAIRNS in *Hill* v. *Crook* (*supra*); *Re Wohlgemuth, Public Trustee* v. *Wohlgemuth*, [1949] Ch. 12; [1948] 2 All E.R. 882; *Re Fletcher, Barclays Bank, Ltd.* v. *Ewing*, [1949] Ch. 473; [1949[1 All E. R. 732.

[4] *In the Goods of Ashton*, [1892] P. 83.

[5] [1902] A. C. 1. This case was distinguished in *Re Bell, Bell* v. *Bell*, [1964] N. Z. L. R. 912 where evidence of the value of assets was received on the issue of the testator's intention to exercise a special power of appointment. The New Zealand Court of Appeal considered this course to be warranted by *Re Knight, Re Wynn, Midland Bank Executor and Trustee Co., Ltd.* v. *Parker*, [1957] Ch. 441; [1957] 2 All E. R. 252, and did not follow *Re Huddleston, Bruno* v. *Eyston*, [1894] 3 Ch. 595.

There are undoubtedly some striking illustrations from the past. In *Del Mare* v. *Rebello*,[1] a gift to the children of the testator's two sisters, Reyne and Estrella, was taken literally even though, some 28 years before the will was made, Reyne had adopted the name in religion of Maria Hieronyma on becoming a professed nun, and the testator had a third sister named Rebecca who, like Estrella, had children; evidence that he intended to benefit them was excluded. In *Doe* d. *Chichester* v. *Oxenden*,[2] "My estate of Ashton" was held to mean estates locally situate at Ashton, in spite of clear evidence that the testator and his steward constantly referred to the "Ashton estate" as including other lands. It is, however, of some significance that, when the point was last before them, the House of Lords seemed to regard the plain meaning rule as nothing more than a strong presumption. In *The National Society for the Prevention of Cruelty to Children* v. *The Scottish National Society for the Prevention of Cruelty to Children*[3] a testator who had lived all his life in Scotland and become interested in the Scottish Society shortly before his death gave a legacy to the National Society which only operated from London. The House held that there was insufficient evidence to support the claim of the Scottish Society; but Lord LOREBURN said, "The accurate use of a name in a will creates a strong presumption against any rival who is not the possessor of the name mentioned in the will." "What a man has said ought to be acted upon unless it is clearly proved that he meant something different from what he said."[4] This is plain common sense, but it leads one to doubt whether the rule stated in Wigram's second proposition set out on p. 543 is really "inflexible."

In the case of contractual documents there is certainly no inflexible rule; not only is extrinsic evidence admissible to resolve an ambiguity or uncertainty, as in the case of wills, but it is also admissible to raise one and then solve it, as where the terms of a conversation were admitted to show that "your wool" mentioned in the defendant's agent's written offer to buy wool included a quantity of wool purchased by the plaintiff from other farms.[5]

(vi) **The admissibility of extrinsic circumstantial evidence of the author's intended meaning.**—In cases of uncertainty due to misdescription, incomplete description or equivocation, extrinsic circumstantial evidence of the author's intended meaning is admissible. Such evidence may, *inter alia*, concern the author's relations with other people, his habits of speech and the names by which he referred to persons and things.

TINDAL, C.J., stated the law with regard to misdescriptions and incomplete descriptions when he spoke of a class of case:

> "in which the description contained in the will of the thing intended to be devised or of the person who is intended to take, is true in part, but not true in every particular. As where an estate is devised called A., and is described as in the occupation of B., and it is found, that though there is an estate called A., yet the whole is not in B.'s occupation; or where an estate is devised to a person whose surname or Christian name is mistaken; or whose descrip-

---

[1] (1792), 1 Ves. 412.
[2] (1810), 3 Taunt. 417, affirmed (1816), 4 Dow. 65; see also *Doe* d. *Westlake* v. *Westlake* (1820), 4 B. and Ald. 57.
[3] [1915] A. C. 207. See also *Re Meyers, London Life Association* v. *St. George's Hospital*, [1951] Ch. 534, at p. 541, and *Henderson* v. *Henderson*, [1905] 1 I. R. 353.
[4] At p. 212.
[5] *Macdonald* v. *Longbottom* (1860), 1 E. & E. 987 at p. 989, *per* BYLES, J.

tion is imperfect or inaccurate; . . . parol evidence is admissible to show what estate was intended to pass, and who was the devisee intended to take, provided there is sufficient indication of intention appearing on the face of the will to justify the application of the evidence." [1]

Reference has already been made to cases in which extrinsic evidence was admitted to cure various incomplete descriptions or misdescriptions. [2] In a work of this nature, it is only necessary to give details of *Doe* d. *Hiscocks* v. *Hiscocks* [3] and *Charter* v. *Charter*. [4]

In the first of these cases, land was devised to John Hiscocks the eldest son of John Hiscocks. John Hiscocks had two sons, Simon, the eldest, and John, his second son, who, however, was his eldest son by a second marriage. It was held that this fact, and a number of other circumstances pointing to an intention that the second son should benefit were admissible in evidence; but it was also held that the testator's declarations of intention were inadmissible. [5]

In *Charter* v. *Charter*, a testator gave the residue of his estate "to my son Forster Charter" and made him his executor. The testator had had a son named Forster, but the boy was dead when the will was made. Of the two sons who survived the testator, one was named William Forster Charter, the other Charles Charter. Probate was granted to W. F. Charter, but his brother's application to have it revoked and replaced by a grant in his favour succeeded before Lord PENZANCE whose order survived an appeal to the House of Lords which was evenly divided. Lord PENZANCE admitted evidence to the effect that the testator was on bad terms with William Forster Charter who lived away from home, that Charles lived with his father and mother (a significant fact because the will contemplated that the executor and widow would reside together), and that the deceased had made declarations of his intention to benefit Charles. All the members of the House of Lords who heard the appeal held that these declarations had been improperly admitted, but Lord CAIRNS and Lord SELBORNE considered that the rest of the evidence was sufficient to support the decision of Lord PENZANCE.

There is an equivocation in a document when its language applies equally well to more objects than one. It is not so much a case of misdescription as of an inadequate discrimination. A gift to "my son" is clear enough if the donor only has one son, but it is equivocal if he has more than one. To quote again from TINDAL, C.J., who, when talking of wills said there was a class of case:

> "where the description of the thing devised, or of the devisee, is clear upon the face of the will; but upon the death of the testator it is found that there are more than one estate or subject-matter of devise, or more than one person whose description follows out and fills the words used in the will. As where the testator devises his manor of Dale, and at his death it is found that he had two manors of that name, South Dale and North Dale; or where a man devises to his son John, and he has two sons of that name. In each of these cases respectively parol evidence is admissible to show which manor was intended to pass, and which son was intended to take."

---

[1] *Miller* v. *Travers* (1832), 8 Bing. 244, at p. 248.
[2] *Kell* v. *Charmer* (*supra*); *Abbot* v. *Massie* (*supra*); *Price* v. *Page* (*supra*).
[3] (1839), 5 M. & W. 363.   [4] (1874), L. R. 7 H. L. 364.
[5] Although it is too late to question this part of the decision it seems to be inconsistent with some passages in the judgment in *Miller* v. *Travers, supra*.

Equivocations, unlike misdescriptions, or incomplete descriptions, may be corrected by the author's declarations of intention, an expression which includes letters, drafts and instructions.

From the point of view of the admissibility of extrinsic evidence, the distinction between misdescriptions and imperfect descriptions on the one hand, and equivocations on the other hand, is more important than that which is still sometimes stressed [1] between patent and latent ambiguities. The word "ambiguity" is sometimes used in a loose sense to cover all kinds of inaccuracy, and sometimes in the stricter sense of equivocation. The distinction between patent and latent ambiguities is due to a mis-application of one of Bacon's maxims according to which "*ambiguitas* is never holpen by averment".[2] This was at one time taken to mean that extrinsic evidence is never admissible to resolve a patent ambiguity, i.e. one appearing on the face of the instrument, although such evidence might be admissible to resolve a latent ambiguity, i.e. one revealed by inquiry outside the instrument. If, in this context, "ambiguity" is used in a broad sense, it is possible to point to any number of cases in which extrinsic circum-stantial evidence has been admitted to resolve a patent ambiguity. Instances have already been given in the cases in which extrinsic evidence was admitted to fill in partial blanks in the description of beneficiaries under a will,[3] and as strong an example as any is provided by *Summers v. Moor-house* [4] in which it was held permissible to prove that a voting paper was the signatory's when it began "I the undersigned Francis Milthorp", and was signed "Francis Lee Sellars", the clerk having handed the wrong paper to Mr. Sellars. If ambiguity is used in the sense of equivocation, it may, it seems, be resolved by extrinsic evidence, even though it is patent, although examples of a patent equivocation may not be common in practice. Thus, if a legacy is left to "one of the children of A. by her late husband B.", there can hardly be any doubt that evidence would be admissible that, to the testator's knowledge, A. had but one child by B. The only circum-stances in which extrinsic evidence is inadmissible to explain a patent ambiguity in the loose sense is when it is prohibited or rendered un-necessary by some rule of law such as that which prevents the reception of extrinsic evidence to fill in total blanks, or s. 9 (2) of the Bills of Exchange Act, 1882, under which the words prevail over the figures in the event of their conflicting with regard to the sum payable under a bill of exchange.

(vii) The admissibility of the author's extrinsic declarations of intention.—The author's declarations of intention made orally or in documents other than that which is under construction are admissible (a) in cases of equivocation, and (b) to rebut certain equitable presumptions. The general exclusion of the author's extrinsic declarations of the meaning he intended his words to bear has been illustrated by a number of cases

---

[1] *Re Alexander's Will Trusts*, [1948] 2 All E. R. 111.

[2] *A Collection of some Principall Rules and Maximes of the Common Lawes of England* (1630), 91. The rule was originally one of pleading. It was wrongly treated as a rule of evidence by an eighteenth-century writer, Anon., *The Theory of Evidence*, (1761); see Thayer, *Preliminary Treatise on Evidence at Common Law*, 471–473. The admissibility of extrinsic evidence to resolve a patent ambiguity was recognised in *Colpoys v. Colpoys* (1822), Jac. 451.

[3] See for example *Price v. Page* (*supra*). Another strong case is *In the Goods of De Rosaz* (1877), 2 P. D. 66.

[4] (1884), 13 Q. B. D. 388.

to which reference has already been made, notably *Doe* d. *Hiscocks* v. *Hiscocks* and *Charter* v. *Charter*.

(a) *Equivocation.*—In *Doe* d. *Gord* v. *Needs*,[1] land was devised to "George Gord, the son of Gord", and extrinsic evidence showed that there were two persons answering that description. Evidence was admitted of the testator's declarations of intention indicating which of the two he meant to benefit. In the words of PARKE, B.:

> "There is no blank before the name of Gord the father, which might have occasioned a doubt whether the devisor had finally fixed on any certain person in his mind.[2]   The devisor has clearly selected a particular individual as the devisee. . . . The evidence of the declarations of the testator has not the effect of varying the instrument in any way whatever; it only enables the court to reject one of the subjects, or objects, to which the description in the will applies; and to determine which of the two the devisor understood to be signified by the description which he used in the will."

In *Re Hubbuck*,[3] the testatrix appointed "my granddaughter   " to be executrix and legatee under her will. Three of her granddaughters were living when she made her will and when she died. One of them was named Polly and evidence was received of statements made by the deceased to a friend to the effect that she wished to leave everything to Polly to whom a grant of probate was accordingly made. This is a very strong case for at least two reasons. First, its effect is to recognise something like a limited power on the part of the testatrix to vary the terms of her will by parol; secondly, it raises doubts concerning the wisdom of allowing the admissibility of certain types of evidence to turn on the distinction between a misdescription and an equivocation. In *Charter* v. *Charter* [4] Lord PENZANCE admitted the deceased's declarations of intention on the footing that the word "Forster" in the expression "my son Forster Charter" could, in effect, be treated as surplusage, with the result that there was an equivocation. All the members of the House of Lords disagreed with this approach which would, indeed, have warranted the reception of the declarations that were rejected in *Doe* d. *Hiscocks* v. *Hiscocks*; but it is difficult to give any rational justification for the rejection of the deceased's declarations in *Charter* v. *Charter* and *Doe* v. *Hiscocks* and their reception in *Doe* v. *Needs* and *Re Hubbuck*.

It seems that the insistence, in this context, on the distinction between a misdescription and an equivocation is largely due to historical considerations. In the words of Thayer:[5]

> "For centuries there had arisen certain familiar questions of ambiguity. In matters of record, in specialities, and in other writings, there had often been occasion to deal with the problem of a name or description equally fitting two or more persons, places, or things."

In such cases it had been recognised, long before the nineteenth century,

---

[1] (1836), 2 M. & W. 129.

[2] In that case the gift would have been void for uncertainty.

[3] *In the Estate of Hubbuck*, [1905] P. 129. As the will seems to have contained a blank, it might have been argued that the testatrix had not finally made up her mind. For further cases on equivocation see *Young* v. *Schuler* (p. 538, *ante*) and *Re Battie-Wrightson* (p. 521, *ante*).

[4] *Supra*. It has been held that there is an equivocation where the name used fits two people subject to a common false description (*Henderson* v. *Henderson*, [1905] 1 Ir. R. 353), and where the name is that of one person and a second, subject to a reversal of Christian names (*Bennett* v. *Marshall* (1856), 2 K. & J. 740.)

[5] *Op. cit.*, p. 417.

that extrinsic evidence of intention was admissible, and no distinction seems to have been taken between circumstantial evidence and direct declarations by the author of the document under consideration. During the nineteenth century, extrinsic evidence came to be received in cases of misdescription or incomplete description, but it was open to the courts to do, what they could not do in the case of equivocations, namely, to admit circumstantial evidence and reject direct declarations. This is what they did, although it is doubtful whether the consequences of their action have proved beneficial.[1]

Although declarations of the author's intention are excluded in cases of misdescription, statements are sometimes received as evidence of habit and this can give rise to subtle distinctions. Thus, in *Re Ofner*,[2] a testator bequeathed a hundred pounds "to my grand nephew Robert Ofner". He had no grand nephew of that name, but he had one named Richard Ofner, the brother of Alfred Ofner who was named in the will. It was held that instructions given by the deceased to his solicitor to the effect that he wished to give a legacy of a hundred pounds to Robert the brother of Alfred Ofner, were admissible, not as evidence of intention, but in order to show that the testator was in the habit of referring to the brother of Alfred as Robert. Richard Ofner was accordingly held to be entitled to the legacy. FARWELL, L.J., said:

> "In construing a will the court has to ascertain, not what the testator actually intended, as distinguished from what his words have expressed, but what is the meaning of the words he has used."

FARWELL, L.J., added that the instructions could not have been treated as of especial weight because of the nature of the document as that would be using them as evidence of intention as distinct from evidence of the meaning which it was legitimate to infer that the name Robert Ofner bore in the mouth of the testator. If there had been evidence that the deceased had also referred to the brother of Alfred as Richard the instructions could only have been admitted as showing that, before he made his will, there was at least one instance in which he had spoken of Alfred's brother as Robert.

(*b*) *Rebutting certain equitable presumptions.*—There are certain equitable presumptions, such as that against double portions, according to which a contrary intention to that which appears on the face of a document is to be presumed. Thus, if a will and codicil give legacies of the same amount for the same motive, it is presumed that they were intended to be substitutional and not cumulative. These presumptions may be rebutted by proof, *inter alia*, of the declarations of intention of the author of the document.[3] Stephen stated a general rule that:

> "If the document is of such a nature that the court will presume that it was

---

[1] The view that one course or the other should be followed both in the case of misdescription and in that of equivocation was taken by Stephen (*Digest*, note XV).

[2] *Re Ofner, Samuel* v. *Ofner*, [1909] 1 Ch. 60. For another case on will construction involving a subtle distinction between receiving a statement as evidence of intention and receiving it as evidence of some other fact see *Re Feather, Harrison* v. *Tapsell*, [1945] Ch. 343; [1945] 1 All E. R. 552. These cases were distinguished in *Paykel* v. *Guardian Trust & Executors Co. of New Zealand, Ltd.*, [1963] N.Z.L.R. 168 where the declarations of intention were also rejected on the issue of intention to exercise a general power of appointment.

[3] *Hurst* v. *Beech* (1820), 5 Mad. 351.

executed with any other than its apparent intention, evidence may be given
to show that it was in fact executed with its apparent intention."[1]

He did not discriminate between cases in which the evidence consists of
declarations and those in which it is circumstantial; nor did he indicate
whether declarations of intention must, if they are to be admissible, be
made substantially contemporaneously with the execution of the document.
Stephen cannot be criticised for these omissions, because the distinctions
have not been taken by the courts in this context.

(3) The Impact of the Civil Evidence Act, 1968

The courts will probably hold that the effect of the Civil Evidence Act,
1968, on the law governing the admissibility of the testator's declarations
of intention in aid of interpretation is minimal; but there are arguments
suggesting a contrary possibility which must be briefly noted. S. 1 (1) of
the Act reads as follows:

> "In any civil proceedings a statement other than one made by a person while
> giving oral evidence in those proceedings shall be admissible as evidence of
> any fact stated therein to the extent that it is so admissible by virtue of any
> provision of this part of this Act or by virtue of any other statutory provision
> or by agreement of the parties, but not otherwise."

This means that, for a statement such as one contained in a letter from the
testator to his solicitor expressing a wish to make provision in his will for
his nephew John Smith to be admissible, it must be rendered admissible by
virtue of Part 1 of the Act. As this result can be achieved by serving notice
of desire to give the statement in evidence,[2] the impact of the Act would
certainly be minimal if there were no more to be said; but difficulties
can be raised once the purpose for which the testator's letter is tendered in
evidence as a hearsay statement comes to be considered.

Let us begin by assuming that the testator had two nephews named
John Smith. The letter would undoubtedly have been admissible to
resolve the equivocation before the Act came into force. It can be received
under the Act "as evidence of any fact stated therein of which direct oral
evidence by [the testator] would have been admissible." This means that
we have to imagine the testator giving evidence at the hearing of a summons
for the construction of his own will; the notion is a curious one, but the
hope has already been expressed that the courts will find it possible to
handle it in such a way as to render the testator's statements admissible as
hearsay statements.[3] If they do so, the letter indicating a wish to benefit
the John Smith named therein will be admissible.[4]

Now let us assume that the testator had been obliged to draft and execute
his will before his solicitor could act on his instructions and that the will
gave a legacy to "my nephew John Smithers." If the testator had nephews
named John Smith and John Smithson respectively, but none named
Smithers, the letter would have been inadmissible in support of John

---

[1] Digest, art. 98 (9).

[2] R. S. C., O. 38, r. 21. There is an exemption from the requirement of notice in the
case of statements by the testator in a probate action, but not in that of a will construction
summons.

[3] P. 430, *ante*.

[4] It may be assumed that the John Smith mentioned in the letter was identified by, say,
an address, not mentioned in the will.

Smith's claim before the 1968 Act came into force; but, if it is possible to imagine a testator giving direct oral evidence in proceedings concerned with the construction of his will in order to render the letter admissible in the case put in the last paragraph, why should that possibility not suffice for the purpose of the present case? It is surmised that the answer given by the courts will be that the reasons why declarations of intention were generally inadmissible in aid of interpretation before the 1968 Act came into force was the rule that extrinsic evidence is inadmissible to contradict the terms of a document[1] and this rule has not been affected by the Act; accordingly the letter would be inadmissible in support of John Smith's claim against John Smithson. The rule prohibiting the contradiction of the terms of a document by extrinsic evidence would not be infringed in the case put in the last paragraph because the will would not be contradicted by the letter. It must be confessed, however, that the above reasoning is by no means beyond criticism. In the first place, although the will would not be contradicted by the letter in the case put in the last paragraph, the letter would, in effect, constitute an addition to it; secondly, it is not clear why extrinsic circumstantial evidence of intention should be admissible to contradict a will, although extrinsic testimonial evidence is only admissible to resolve an equivocation; finally there is little if any authority in support of the reasoning.[2]

(4) The 19th Report of the Law Reform Committee

In its 19th Report the Law Reform Committee recommends the extension of the equitable doctrine of rectification to wills.[3] With regard to the admissibility of extrinsic evidence in aid of interpretation the report recommends that all extrinsic evidence should be admissible except "direct evidence of the testator's dispositive intention." If this recommendation were adopted, the evidence rejected in *Doe* d. *Chichester* v. *Oxenden*[4] and *Higgins* v. *Dawson*[5] would be admissible. Another case in which extrinsic circumstantial evidence would be admissible would be one in which the question is whether the testator intended to exercise a special power of appointment. "Evidence of the extent of his property as compared with the extent of the bequests made would be admissible to show an intention to exercise the power."[6] All the members of the Committee were in favour of retaining the present rule under which the testator's statements of intention are admissible to resolve an equivocation in the narrow sense in which the term has been used in this book,[7] but a minority went much further and recommended the reception of such evidence in aid of interpretation in all cases. The difference between the majority and minority on this point turned largely on their views concerning the extent of the danger that the evidence in question might be manufactured. Fear of this danger which was mentioned in Chapter I seems to be just as influential to-day as it has been in the past.

---

[1] IX *Wigmore*, para. 2471.

[2] Passages might be cited from the judgment of TINDALL, C.J., in *Miller* v. *Travers* (1832), 8 Bing. 244, but that was a case in which the court was asked to receive evidence of the testator's instructions in order that words omitted by the draftsman might be read into his will.

[3] At present there is power to omit words from the probate, but not to add them.

[4] P. 549, *ante*.   [5] P. 548, *ante*.   [6] 19th Report, para. 52.

[7] The Report sometimes uses the word in a broader sense.

CHAPTER XXII

PROOF OF FREQUENTLY RECURRING MATTERS

There is a sense in which this chapter is redundant, for almost every point made in it can be found elsewhere in this book. The collection under one head of the different ways in which evidence may be given of certain matters which frequently have to be proved in litigation may, however, be of some use to the student, if not to the practitioner. The proof of handwriting and certain kinds of document, both private and public was considered in the last chapter as well as the important provisions of the Bankers' Books Evidence Act, 1879. It is now proposed to consider the proof of foreign law, birth, death, age, marriage and legitimacy, judgments, convictions and other orders of the court, and various other miscellaneous matters. Reference will from time to time be made to judicial notice and presumptions, although it is not customary to describe them as means of proof.The possibility of a fact being admitted formally or informally should be borne in mind when the following paragraphs are being read.

A. FOREIGN LAW [1]

We saw in Chapter III that, so far as the English Courts are concerned, foreign law is a question of fact which, since 1920, has to be decided by the judge. We also saw in Chapter III that, in this context, "foreign law" comprises the law of Scotland, the law of the British Dominions and Colonies and, to some extent, the laws of Eire and Northern Ireland as well as the law of a foreign country in the strict sense of the term.

The general rule is that foreign law must be proved by an expert witness who will, in a disputed or complicated case, give his evidence on oath in the ordinary way. In simple routine cases it is not uncommon for the evidence to be by affidavit, or resort might be had to the Civil Evidence Act, 1968.[2] The effect of the general rule is that foreign law cannot usually be the subject of judicial notice,[3] or, at common law, inferred from previous English decisions on the same subject.[4] Before s. 4 (2)–(5) of the Civil Evidence Act, 1972, came into force it had to be proved afresh by an expert in each case. There are, however, certain cases in which foreign law is the subject of judicial notice or something taken to have been established by a previous English case, and there are also some special statutory provisions governing the proof of foreign law. These matters will be con-

---

[1] For a much fuller discussion and citation of authority see Dicey and Morris's *Conflict of Laws*, 9th Ed., chap. 37.

[2] *Markes* v. *Markes*, (1955) 106 L. Jo. 75 (a decision on the Evidence Act, 1938); *Kirsch* v. *Kirsch*, [1958] S. A. S. R. 258.

[3] *Brenan and Galen's Case* (1847), 10 Q. B. 492, at p. 498.

[4] *M'Cormick* v. *Garnett* (1854), 23 L. J. Ch. 777.

sidered before reference is made to the question of the qualification of the expert when testifying in cases to which the general rule applies.

The burden of proof rests on the party asserting that foreign law differs from English law. This is frequently expressed, rather infelicitously, by saying that there is a presumption that foreign and English law are the same.

(1) JUDICIAL NOTICE AND PREVIOUS DECISIONS

We saw in Chapter VII that judicial notice may be taken of notorious facts, and, in some exceptional cases, the English courts have treated certain items of foreign law as matters of notoriety. The most famous instance is provided by *Saxby* v. *Fulton* [1] in which judical notice was taken of the fact that roulette is legal in Monte Carlo. Judicial notice might also be taken of the common law of Northern Ireland,[2] and the House of Lords will take judicial notice of Scots law.[3] Under the Maintenance Orders Act, 1950, s. 22 (2), judicial notice must be taken of the law with regard to maintenance orders in every part of the United Kingdom. It also seems to be settled that once a statute passed in a British possession is properly before an English court, that court may construe the statute with the result that a body of case law on the subject may be created.[4] The principal Statute is the Evidence (Colonial Statutes) Act, 1907, which is confined to British possessions, and it is not clear how far the English courts will construe foreign legislation without the guidance of an expert witness. There are cases in which the English courts appear to have done this, and their decisions are then, presumably, binding on other courts within the limits of the doctrine of precedent.[5]

S. 4 (2) of the Civil Evidence Act, 1972, permits the reception as evidence of foreign law of any previous determination by an English court of the point in question, provided it is reported in citable form,[6] and provided notice of intention to rely upon it has been given to the other parties to the proceedings.[7] The foreign law is to be taken to be in accordance with the determination unless the contrary is proved. It makes no difference whether the point was determined in civil or criminal proceedings, but foreign law may only be proved in this way in civil proceedings.[8]

---

[1] [1909] 2 K. B. 208; see also *Re Turner, Heyding* v. *Hinchliff*, [1906] W. N. 27.

[2] *Re Nesbitt* (1844), 14 L. J. M. C. 30, at p. 33. See *Irish Law in English Courts*, by G. D. Nokes, International and Comparative Law Quarterly (1960), p. 564.

[3] This is on account of the House's appellate jurisdiction in civil cases. It is doubtful whether the House of Lords would take judicial notice of Scots criminal law, should the question ever arise. The House would take judicial notice of the law of Northern Ireland.

[4] *Re Sebba, Lloyds Bank, Ltd.* v. *Hutson*, [1959] Ch. 166; [1958] 3 All E. R. 393, following *Re Goetze, National Provincial Bank, Ltd.* v. *Mond*, [1953] Ch. 96; [1953] 1 All E. R. 76. See also 22 M. L. R. 317; 24 *ibid.* 312. In *Mahadervan* v. *Mahadervan*, [1964] P. 233, at p. 240; [1962] 3 All E. R. 1108, at p. 1113, it was said that an English court can construe a written foreign law once it is in evidence. Most of the decisions on this matter relate to countries to which the Evidence (Colonial Statutes) Act, 1907, applies, although, in several instances, no reference is actually made to the Statute. See also *Shariff* v. *Azad*, [1966] 3 All E. R. 785.

[5] In *Re Cohn*, [1945] Ch. 5, the English court appears to have construed a provision in the German Civil Code with expert evidence, and presumably its decision on the point constitutes a precedent.

[6] I.e. in a report which could, if the question had been one of English law, have been cited as authority in any court in England or Wales.

[7] See R. S. C., O. 38, r. (7).

[8] There is a corresponding provision in the draft Bill attached to the 11th Report of the Criminal Law Revision Committee.

(2) OTHER STATUTORY PROVISIONS

Under the Evidence (Colonial Statutes) Act, 1907,[1] copies of Acts, Ordinances and Statutes passed by or under the authority of the legislature of any British possession shall be received in evidence by all courts of justice in the United Kingdom if purporting to be printed by the Government Printer [2] without any proof given that the copies were so printed. The term "British possession" means any part of Her Majesty's dominions exclusive of the United Kingdom.[3] It is clear that this statute enables an English court to receive a statute or subordinate legislation of a British possession in evidence on the mere production of a Government Printer's copy, but the Act of 1907 would not be much use if this were all that it has achieved, and it has been held in a number of cases that the English courts may construe the statute, acting on its provisions as so construed without anything in the nature of expert evidence.[4]

Two other statutes relevant to the proof of foreign law are the British Law Ascertainment Act, 1859, and the Foreign Law Ascertainment Act, 1861. The first applies to all parts of Her Majesty's dominions, and the second may be extended to any foreign country by convention. The effect of each Act is that an English court may state a case for the opinion of another appropriate British or foreign court. The opinion, when obtained, becomes evidence of the relevant foreign law.

Although the Evidence (Foreign, Dominion and Colonial Documents) Act, 1933, does not, strictly speaking, relate to the proof of foreign law, it contains useful provisions which should never be forgotten in cases involving a foreign element. Put very briefly, its effect is that Orders in Council may be made with regard to the proof, by authenticated copy, of extracts from public registers in the foreign country or dominion to which the order applies. The certificate is not merely evidence of the contents of the register, but also evidence of the facts stated. The statute is therefore of great utility in connection with the proof of births, deaths and marriages occurring abroad. In the case of a marriage, it will generally dispense with the necessity of calling an expert in the relevant foreign law in order to swear that the certificate would be accepted as evidence of the marriage in question in the courts of the foreign country. A number of Orders in Council have been made under the Act.

(3) EXPERT WITNESS

When a case falls within the general rule requiring proof of foreign law by an expert, the witness must be properly qualified. There has never been any doubt that a judge or practitioner in the jurisdiction whose law is in question is properly qualified,[5] but it is not altogether clear how far beyond this the English courts will go. In *Bristow* v. *Sequeville*,[6] a jurist consult, adviser to the Prussian consulate in London who had studied law in Leipzig and knew that the Code Napoleon was in force in Saxony was not

---

[1] See also the Colonial Laws Validity Act, 1865, s. 6.
[2] I.e., the Government Printer of the possession.
[3] *Quaere* whether this statute still applies to all Commonwealth countries.
[4] See the numerous cases cited in *Jasiewicz* v. *Jasiewicz*, [1962] 3 All E. R. 1017.
[5] *Baron De Bode's Case* (1845), 8 Q. B. 208.
[6] (1850), 5 Exch. 275.

allowed to give evidence concerning the Code. Language was used suggesting that it is essential to call a practitioner in every case, but other authorities show considerably laxer tendencies. Persons who have been held sufficiently qualified include a former, as opposed to a present, practitioner in the jurisdiction in question,[1] someone who was qualified to practice in that jurisdiction although he had never done so,[2] a Governor-General,[3] an embassy official,[4] and the reader in Roman Dutch law to the Council of Legal Education.[5] It has even been held that a merchant without legal qualification might testify concerning a branch of foreign law of which he had acquired knowledge in the course of his professional life, although this decision has not been followed throughout the Commonwealth.[6] S. 4 (1) of the Civil Evidence Act, 1972, finally disposes of *Bristow* v. *Sequeville* so far as civil proceedings are concerned by declaring that a person suitably qualified on account of knowledge or experience is competent to give evidence of foreign law irrespective of whether he has acted or is qualified to act as a legal practitioner in the country in question.[7]

The decision whether the proposed witness is properly qualified is made by the judge as a condition precedent to the admissibility of his evidence. In coming to a conclusion on a question of foreign law, the English courts may consider foreign statutes and decisions referred to by the expert witness, and, in the event of a conflict of expert testimony, the English judge must resolve it.[8]

B. BIRTH, AGE, DEATH, MARRIAGE AND LEGITIMACY

(1) BIRTH

There are four methods of proving birth. Far and away the most usual at the present day is the production of a certified copy of an entry in the register of births which may be received as evidence of the facts stated under the exception to the rule against hearsay relating to statements in public documents.[9] The court will require some evidence identifying the person whose birth is in question with the person referred to in the birth certificate. This might take the form of a direct statement by the person in question if he were testifying to the date or place of birth, though the evidence is at best hearsay and at worst pure guesswork. It could also be pro-

---

[1] *Re Duke of Wellington*, [1947] Ch. 506, at p. 514–515.
[2] *Barford* v. *Barford and McLeod*, [1918] P. 140. The cases conflict on the question whether an English barrister who has acquired his knowledge of foreign law in practice before the Privy Council is suitably qualified (*Cartwright* v. *Cartwright and Anderson* (1878), 26 W. R. 684; *Wilson* v. *Wilson*, [1903] P. 157).
[3] *Cooper-King* v. *Cooper-King*, [1900] P. 65.
[4] *In the Goods of Dost Aly Khan* (1889), 6 P. D. 6.
[5] *Brailey* v. *Rhodesia Consolidated, Ltd.*, [1910] 2 Ch. 95.
[6] *Vander Donckt* v. *Thellusson* (1849), 8 C. B. 812. The decision was said to be out of date, on account of the fewer facilities for obtaining the evidence which existed in 1849, in *Direct Winters Transport* v. *Duplante Canada Ltd.* (1962), 32 D. L. R. (2d) 268, but see *Ajami* v. *Customs Comptroller*, [1954] 1 W. L. R. 1405.
[7] There is a corresponding provision in the draft Bill attached to the 11th Report of the Criminal Law Revision Committee.
[8] See for example *Re Duke of Wellington*, [1947] Ch. 506.
[9] Births and Deaths Registration Act, 1953, s. 34. See Chapter XVIII, section 6; as to certified extracts from foreign registers, see the Evidence (Foreign Dominion and Colonial Documents) Act, 1933 and as to births on board ship the Merchant Shipping (Returns of Births and Deaths) Regulations, 1972, made under s. 75 of the Merchant Shipping Act, 1970.

vided by someone who was present at the birth, or by the informant to the Registrar; but, more often than not, the evidence of identity will be supplied by an affidavit in which the deponent, usually a member of the family of the person whose birth is in question will depose to his or her belief that that person is or was the same person as the one referred to in the exhibited birth certificate. The testimony of someone present at the birth to that fact, its place or date is a second and separate method of proving these matters. They may also be proved, in civil proceedings, by statements admissible by virtue of the Civil Evidence Act, 1968, and, in criminal proceedings, under exceptions to the hearsay rule relating to the declarations of deceased persons.[1]

(2) Age

There are four ways in which a person's age can be proved; two of them depend on direct evidence and two on the exceptions to the hearsay rule relating respectively to statements in public documents and declarations of deceased persons.

(i) Direct evidence.—A person's age may be proved by direct evidence (a) by the testimony of those present at his birth and (b) by inferences from his appearance which are permitted in special cases by certain statutes.[2] In the nature of things, it is not often that resort can be made to the first of these methods, and, in many instances, its use would, to some extent, involve reliance on hearsay. For example, A.'s grandmother was present at his birth, and she sees a child whom she believes to be A. once a quarter for the next ten years, after which she testifies to A.'s age in court. It cannot be said that she knows that A. is the child at whose birth she was present exclusively by means of her own observation. Even the mother's evidence of the child's age might well be based on hearsay evidence of identity at the earliest stages of the child's life. The court is authorised to act on inspection with regard to questions of age by several statutes, but, quite apart from these provisions the general effect of which is to make the result of the inspection *prima facie* proof of age, such result would, presumably, be evidence of age in every case.[3] It would be a kind of real evidence, though, in many instances, it would not be sufficient for the court to act on it without more.

(ii) Hearsay.—Probably the most usual way of proving age is the production of a birth certificate as evidence of the date of the birth specified therein under the exception to the hearsay rule relating to statements in public documents.[4] Evidence of the identity of the person whose age is in question with the person named in the certificate will be required.

In criminal cases age may be proved by declarations by deceased persons against interest or in the course of duty, and, when a genealogical issue is involved, by the pedigree declaration of a deceased relation. In these cases too, it may be necessary to find some evidence identifying the person referred to in the statement with the person whose age is in issue.

---

[1] Chapter XIX, section 1.

[2] Children and Young Persons Act, 1933, s. 99; Criminal Justice Act, 1948, s. 80 (3); Magistrates' Courts Act, 1952, s. 126 (5); Sexual Offences Act, 1956, s. 12 (3), s. 15 (5) and s. 28 (5).

[3] *Wallworth* v. *Balmer*, [1965] 3 All E. R. 721.

[4] See the Births and Deaths Registration Act, 1953, s. 34, and, as to foreign registers, the Evidence (Foreign, Dominion and Colonial Documents) Act, 1933. See also Merchant Shipping (Returns of Births and Deaths) Regulations, 1972.

(3) DEATH

There are six heads under which a person's death may be proved. It is not necessary to refer to any of them in detail because those that require discussion have already been discussed. The first and most usual way to prove death is to rely on a death certificate coupled with some evidence identifying the person named therein with the person whose death is in question.[1] Secondly, in a criminal case, reliance may be placed on the declaration of a deceased person made against interest or in the course of duty or, when a genealogical question is in issue, the pedigree declaration of a deceased relation. Evidence of identity may also be necessary in these cases. Thirdly, death may be proved by statements admissible under the Civil Evidence Act, 1968. Fourthly, reliance may be placed on the presumption of death discussed in Chapter VI. Even where the presumption is inapplicable, the court may feel warranted in inferring death from a protracted period of absence the length of which will vary according to the facts of each case. The fifth and sixth methods of proving death are to rely either on the evidence of someone who was present at its occurrence, or else on the evidence of someone who, though not present at its occurrence, was able to identify the corpse as that of the person whose death is in issue.

(4) MARRIAGE

When a marriage is in issue or relevant to the issue, the first thing that has to be proved is the celebration of a marriage ceremony. In certain cases, discussed in Chapter VI, this may be presumed from proof of cohabitation and repute. Subject to this further possibility, the person seeking to prove a marriage ceremony may rely on the same methods as those discussed in connection with the proof of birth. Evidence may be adduced from someone who was present at the wedding[2] and this is the method of proof almost invariably adopted in matrimonial cases.[3] Declarations that a couple were married may be received, in criminal cases, under exceptions to the hearsay rule relating to the statements of deceased persons as being against interest, or in the course of duty, or as to pedigree in cases involving a genealogical issue; and, in civil cases, under the Civil Evidence Act, 1968. The third and most usual method consists in the production of a marriage certificate coupled with evidence identifying the persons mentioned in the certificate with those whose marriage is to be proved. When they are available, such evidence will generally be supplied by the parties to the marriage. Whenever a certificate is available, the courts require it to be produced in addition to receiving the evidence of the parties as to the ceremony.

The second thing to be proved by someone who is seeking to establish a marriage is that the ceremony constituted a formally valid marriage. Generally speaking, it will have to be shown that a form recognised by the law of the place of celebration was adopted, but there are exceptions in the case of marriages celebrated abroad.[4] If the ceremony took place in England or Wales, the certificate is evidence of the marriage to which it relates,[5] but,

---

[1] Section 34 of the Births and Deaths Registration Act, 1953; Merchant Shipping (Returns of Births and Deaths) Regulations, 1972.
[2] This includes a party to the marriage.
[3] Statements may be received under the Civil Evidence Act, 1968.
[4] For details see Dicey and Morris's *Conflict of Laws* (9th edition), pp. 249 *et seq.*
[5] Marriage Act, 1949, s. 65.

in other cases, it will be necessary to produce expert evidence by a witness or by affidavit of formal validity according to the local law. This could be a costly requirement, and there are accordingly eight exceptions, the last two of which will no doubt supersede the others. These exceptions relate first to marriages celebrated in Scotland and Northern Ireland, certificates of which are recognised by the English courts as evidence of the facts stated under various statutory provisions.[1] Secondly, if the marriage took place in a British possession under a statute proved by virtue of the provisions of the Evidence (Colonial Statutes) Act, 1907, it is not the practice of the courts to require expert evidence of the validity of the marriage according to the local law, although such evidence may be required if there is any doubt whether the statute in question is still in force.[2] Thirdly, if the marriage took place in a country to which the Evidence (Foreign, Dominion and Colonial Documents) Act, 1933, has been applied by Order in Council, a certificate produced under that Act is evidence of the marriage to which it refers, and the English courts will require no further evidence of the formal validity of the marriage, although they will of course require the usual evidence of identity. A further exception to the requirement of proof of formal validity according to the local law is provided by the Foreign Marriage Act, 1892. All that is required is evidence that a marriage celebrated under that statute complied with its requirements. The fifth and sixth exceptions relate to marriages celebrated abroad according to the rites of the Church of England and it is unnecessary to go into details in a work of this nature.[3]

In spite of the numerous exceptions to the requirement of proof of formal validity under the local law, the general rule remained and it was often necessary to procure the attendance of an expert witness, or to obtain leave to read an affidavit by him to the effect that the certificate of the marriage would be recognised in the courts of the country in question. It was, for instance, held to be necessary in the case of an Irish marriage,[4] even in an undefended divorce, as neither the Evidence (Colonial Statutes) Act, nor the Evidence (Foreign, Dominion and Colonial Documents) Act, applied to Eire.

It is because of such possibilities that the seventh and eighth exceptions to the requirement of proof by testimony or affidavit of the legal validity of a foreign marriage are of great importance. Under r. 40 (1) of the Matrimonial Rules, 1973, the celebration and validity of a marriage which took place outside England and Wales may be proved, in any matrimonial proceedings in which the existence and validity of the marriage is not disputed, by the evidence of one of the parties and the production of the foreign marriage certificate or a certified copy of an entry in a foreign register of marriages. In other cases in which the existence and validity of

---

[1] Registration of Births, Deaths and Marriages (Scotland) Act, 1854: *Drew* v. *Drew*, [1912] P. 175 (Scotland); Evidence Act, 1851: *Whitton* v. *Whitton*, [1900] P. 178 (Eire before 1921, and Northern Ireland).

[2] The authorities are comprehensively reviewed in *Jasiewicz* v. *Jasiewicz*, [1962] 3 All E. R. 1017.

[3] Marriages celebrated according to the rites of the Church of England in the Channel Islands are recognised on production of certificate with evidence of identification because they are in the diocese of Winchester (*Pritchard* v. *Pritchard* (1920), 37 T. L. R. 104). According to *Ward* v. *Dey* (1846), 1 Rob. Eccl. 759, marriages celebrated according to the rites of the Church of England in any British Possession may be recognised on production of certificate with evidence of identity, but it is not clear how far this doctrine extends today.

[4] *Todd* v. *Todd*, [1961] 2 All E. R. 881.

the marriage is not disputed, reliance may be placed on the evidence of one of the parties, and the production of such a certificate or certified copy as a statement or record admissible by virtue of the Civil Evidence Act, 1968. Before this Act came into force, it was becoming increasingly common for the courts to accept a foreign marriage certificate as evidence of the validity of the marriage under the Evidence Act, 1938,[1] and it could be given in evidence, even without the evidence of one of the parties under the Act of 1968, as *prima facie* evidence both of the celebration of the marriage and of its validity according to the relevant foreign law.

Once the celebration of a formally valid marriage ceremony has been proved or presumed, there is, as we saw in Chapter VI, a presumption of essential validity which can be relied on in all cases. It is therefore unnecessary in the first instance, for anyone concerned with the proof of a marriage to concern himself with proof of such matters as capacity to marry or the reality of the consent of the parties.

(5) LEGITIMACY

In order to establish a child's legitimacy, reliance may be placed on the presumption of legitimacy discussed in Chapter VI. For this purpose it is simply necessary to prove that the child was born or conceived during its mother's marriage to her husband, after which it is incumbent on those denying legitimacy to prove illegitimacy.[2] Legitimacy may also be proved, in criminal cases, under exceptions to the rule against hearsay, notably that relating to pedigree declarations by deceased persons; and, in civil cases, by statements admissible under the Civil Evidence Act, 1968. It might also be proved by a statement in a public document, for the statements as to paternity in a birth certificate are evidence of their truth. Finally, reliance might be placed on a declaration of legitimacy which is a judgment *in rem* and therefore binding on the whole world.

C. JUDGMENTS AND CONVICTIONS

If the proof of judgments and convictions were not exhaustively covered by statutory provisions, it would be necessary to produce the actual record of the court and to call evidence identifying the relevant parties with the person mentioned in the record. The different statutory provisions may be summarised under the heads of civil and criminal cases.

(1) CIVIL CASES

A judgment of the House of Lords may be proved by production of the journal of the House. Judgments of the Court of Appeal and High Court may be proved by production of an office copy made in the central office or district registry.[3] Judgments of the County Court may be proved by a certified copy of the entry in the registrar's book.[4] Judgments of the magistrates in civil matters are also proved by the production of a certified extract from the court book.[5] There are special statutory provisions

---

[1] *Henaff* v. *Henaff*, [1966] 1 W. L. R. 598.
[2] See p. 118, *ante*, as to the standard of proof.
[3] R. S. C., O. 38, r. 10; Judicature Act, 1925, s. 85.
[4] County Courts Act, 1959, s. 26.
[5] Magistrates' Courts Rules, 1968, rr. 54 and 56.

relating to proceedings in bankruptcy.[1] Foreign or colonial judgments may be proved by production of an examined copy[2] or a copy sealed with the seal of the court under the provisions of s. 7 of the Evidence Act, 1851. In all the above cases, production of the relevant document will usually be sufficient to establish its authenticity because the court will take judicial notice of the seal or certificate attached to the document, but oral evidence may be required to identify the parties to the judgment with the person whose rights the court is considering, or those through whom such persons claim. Evidence of this nature is, however, often rendered unnecessary by some kind of formal admission.

(2) Criminal Cases

There are several redundant statutory provisions relating to the proof of convictions in criminal cases, and it will be convenient to deal separately with convictions on indictment, convictions before a Magistrates' Court, and convictions for traffic offences.

(i) Proceedings on indictment.—Under s. 13 of the Evidence Act, 1851, a certified extract of the court record signed by the clerk or other officer having custody of the court's records is sufficient evidence in any proceedings of an acquittal or conviction of an indictable offence. The certificate must be to the effect that "the paper produced is a copy of the record of the indictment, trial, conviction, and judgment or acquittal, as the case may be, omitting the formal parts", and it therefore seems that it would be inept to attempt to prove the result of a summary trial, even for an indictable offence under this section.

Under s. 6 of the Criminal Procedure Act, 1865, if a witness does not admit a conviction put to him in cross-examination, it may be proved by a certificate containing the substance and effect only (omitting the formal parts) of the indictment and conviction purporting to be signed by the clerk of the court or other officer having the custody of its records or their deputies.

Under s. 18 of the Prevention of Crimes Act, 1871, any previous conviction may be proved in any proceedings against any person by producing a record or extract defined, in the case of an indictable offence, as consisting of a certificate containing the substance and effect of the indictment and conviction, and purporting to be signed by the clerk or other officer with custody of the records or their deputies.

Section 39 of the Criminal Justice Act, 1948, provides for proof of previous convictions in any criminal proceedings by reference to finger-prints.[3] There must be evidence of the conviction, and evidence that the finger-prints of the person convicted are the same as those of the person against whom it is sought to prove the conviction. This evidence may take the form of three certificates. First there is a certificate of conviction signed by or on behalf of the Commissioner of Metropolitan Police exhibiting copies of finger-prints and stating that they are the finger-prints of the

---

[1] Bankruptcy Act, 1914, ss. 137 (2), 139 and 148 (2).

[2] An examined copy is one examined against the original. As evidence of the examination is usually necessary, proof by examined copy is rare.

[3] Under s. 23 (2) evidence that a person has previously been sentenced to corrective training or preventive detention shall, for the purposes of the section be evidence of the convictions and sentences which render him liable to that sentence.

person who was convicted. Secondly, there is a certificate signed by or on behalf of the governor of the prison or remand centre where the person against whom it is sought to prove the conviction was detained in connection with any criminal proceedings; this certificate states that the exhibited finger-prints were taken from the person in question while he was detained. Finally, there is another certificate signed by or on behalf of the Commissioner of Metropolitan Police stating that the finger-prints exhibited to the two previous certificates are identical.

A conviction or acquittal may be proved incidentally in the course of a prosecution for perjury by the means mentioned in s. 14 of the Perjury Act, 1911. This section is aimed primarily at a simple method of proving the fact of the former trial at which it is alleged that the perjury was committed. Under the section, the fact of a former trial on indictment may be proved by certificate of its substance and effect signed by the clerk to the court or other officer having the custody of its records or their deputies.

Having regard to the different object of the section, there is no redundancy between s. 14 of the Perjury Act and the other sections mentioned. Section 6 of the Act of 1865 is confined to proof of previous convictions against witnesses denying them in cross-examination, but, so far as convictions on indictment are concerned, there appears to be a complete overlap between the provisions of s. 13 of the Evidence Act, 1851 and the Prevention of Crimes Act, 1871, s. 18. As the certificates by means of which the convictions are proved are identical, the overlap cannot be said to do much harm. Section 39 of the Criminal Justice Act, 1948, is confined to criminal proceedings and is in practice likely to be confined to proof of convictions against an accused person. It will be observed that, in order to prove an acquittal on indictment it is necessary to rely on the provisions of s. 13 of the Evidence Act, 1851. Although no further proof than the production of the appropriate certificate is required of the matters certified, it will usually be necessary to prove the identity of the person mentioned in the certificate with the person against whom it is sought to prove the conviction when the procedure contemplated by the Acts of 1851 and 1871 is adopted. This is frequently provided by the evidence of a constable or warder who was present in court at the time of the conviction.

(ii) Result of summary trial.—A conviction after a summary trial may be proved under s. 18 of the Prevention of Crimes Act, 1871. The record of such conviction consists of a copy signed by any justice having jurisdiction over the offence in respect of which the conviction was made, or by the proper officer of the court making the conviction or by the clerk or officer of the court to which such conviction has been returned.

The procedure contemplated by s. 39 of the Criminal Justice Act, 1948, is applicable to summary cases.

Under rule 56 of the Magistrates' Courts Rules, 1968, the register of a Magistrates' Court or an extract certified by the clerk shall be admissible in any legal proceedings as evidence of the proceedings of the court entered in the register. It is by this means that acquittals on a summary trial must usually be proved [1] and that convictions can be proved although there is a redundancy with the provisions of the Act of 1871. Evidence of identity will of course also be required.

---

[1] See also the Offences Against the Person Act, 1861, s. 44.

Section 6 of the Act of 1865 is confined to convictions for arrestable offences or misdemeanours; there might therefore be room for an argument that there is no statutory authority for a question in cross-examination about a conviction for a summary offence. Such a question would, however, probably be admissible at common law. The problem of proving the result of a summary trial if a witness denies a conviction in cross-examination, does not appear to have troubled the courts, but the wording of the Act of 1865 suggests that s. 6 could not be relied on as authority warranting the proof of a summary conviction in rebuttal.[1]

(iii) Traffic Offences.—Under s. 101 (1) of the Road Traffic Act, 1972, the indorsement of a licence is *prima facie* evidence of a conviction. This provision is in addition to the other statutory provisions dealing with the proof of previous convictions which have just been mentioned; but its object is to enable justices to determine sentence and it does not supersede the other methods of proving convictions at the trial.[2]

D. MISCELLANEOUS

It would obviously be possible to protract a chapter of this sort indefinitely, but proof of most other frequently recurring points are dependent on special statutory provisions such as those of the Companies Act, 1948, and the Bankruptcy Act, 1914. Having dealt with a number of special statutory provisions under the head of convictions in criminal cases, it will be convenient to conclude with the proof of custom and ownership, two matters which are dependent on widely differing branches of the common law of evidence.

(1) CUSTOM AND USAGE

There are four ways in which the existence of a custom or usage may be proved. They constitute direct, circumstantial and hearsay evidence. The first method consists of the testimony of a witness who deposes, from his personal knowledge to the actual existence of the custom or usage. He states that he is well aware of the fact that lessees in a given locality have been in the habit of removing "way-going" crops, that is crops sown by the tenant before the termination of his lease,[3] or of any other custom or usage. The evidence may be based on the observation of many instances, and it may sometimes be based on reputation or hearsay. A second method of proving custom which also comes into the category of direct evidence is for a witness to testify to particular instances of its exercise. He refers to cases in which he or someone observed by him exercised the custom, but he does not generalise on the subject. The third way of proving a custom or usage depends on circumstantial evidence. It consists of evidence of a comparable custom in other localities similar to the one in question, or a comparable usage in other trades similar to the one in question. Finally, what is probably the most typical way of proving a custom is to rely on the

---

[1] The Criminal Law Revision Committee recommend the repeal, so far as they relate to criminal proceedings, of s. 13 of the Evidence Act, 1851, s. 6 of the Criminal Procedure Act, 1865, and s. 18 of the Prevention of Crimes Act, 1871, coupled with their replacement by a clause under which convictions may be proved by certificates signed by the clerk to the appropriate court and evidence of identity.

[2] *Stone* v. *Bastick*, [1965] 3 All E. R. 713 also requiring a certificate of disqualification from driving to refer only to the offence in respect of which the disqualification was imposed.

[3] *Cf. Wigglesworth* v. *Dallison* (1789), 1 Doug. K. B. 201.

declaration of a deceased person concerning public or general rights,[1] admissible, in criminal proceedings, under a common law exception to the hearsay rule and, in civil cases, under the Civil Evidence Act, 1968.

(2) OWNERSHIP

There are also four main ways in which ownership of real or personal property may be proved. The first consists of production of the documents of title which must, of course, be duly authenticated in the sense that their due execution must be proved unless they are produced from proper custody in circumstances giving rise to the presumption in favour of due execution in the case of documents more than twenty years old. Possession is *prima facie* evidence of ownership, and a second way in which ownership may be proved is by proof of possession of the property in question. In the case of real estate, proof of possession of connected property in circumstances rendering it probable that the owner of such connected property would, in addition, be the owner of the property in question may rank as a third means of proving ownership. Finally ownership may be proved by admissible hearsay statements.

---

[1] P. 439, *ante.*

INDEX

A

ABDUCTION,
competence of wife as witness, 148

ACCIDENT,
evidence of previous occurrences, 324
police, disclosure of statements to, 269

ACCOMPLICE,
agent provocateur, whether, 177
corroboration, adultery, in case of, 181,
    183
    by another, 179
    necessity for, 171, 174 *et
    seq.*
    what amounts to, 178
meaning of, 175
sexual offence, in relation to, 177, 181
warning as to evidence of, 174 *et seq.*
wife of, evidence of, 180

ACCUSED,
burden of proof borne by, 77–78
caution, of, 491
character of, evidence of, 18, 346–352.
    And see CHARACTER
co-accused evidence by, 375–776.
    meaning, 374
comment on failure to give evidence, 42,
    46, 355–356.
confession by, 31, 276, 482–495. *And
    see* CONFESSION
cross-examination as to—
    character, 359 *et seq.*
    convictions, 29, 237, 365. *And see* PRE-
    VIOUS CONVICTION
    credit, 340–341, 358, 374
    misconduct on other occasions, evi-
    dence of, 29, 338–339. *And see*
    CHARACTER
    other offences, 359
evidence, called by, 199
failure to give evidence, 42–46, 353 *et seq.*
    493–495
imputations as to prosecutor or witness,
    370–375, 376
previous acquittal, evidence as to, 364
previous convictions, 365 *et seq. And
    see* PREVIOUS CONVICTIONS
questioning by police, 491
right to reply, by, 199
silence when charged, 189, 491
statement in presence of, 24, 29, 447–
    448, 477
spouse as witness, 147, 148, 154 *et seq.*
    And see SPOUSE
testify, failure to, by, 42–46, 353 *et seq.,*
    493–495
unsworn statement from dock by, 146, 164

ACCUSED—*continued.*
witness as—
    competence of, 146, 151, 353
    for co-prisoner, 153
        defence, 146, 151
        prosecution, 146, 151
    general principles regarding, 358–359
    interpretation of statutory provisions,
        359 *et seq.*
    question tending to incriminate, 358
    unfair question, effect of, 364

ACQUITTAL,
estoppel by, 297
evidence, as, 398
previous, question as to, 364
proof of, 565

ACT OF PARLIAMENT,
Commonwealth, of, proof of, 557, 558
judicial notice of, 139
private, proof of, 526

ADMISSIBILITY OF EVIDENCE,
absence of jury during argument, 59
admission, 444 *et seq.*, 477 *et seq. And
    see* ADMISSION
affidavit, by, 196. *And see* AFFIDAVIT
air-ticket, and, 405
ancient document, 13, 414–415
appeal as to, 70
best evidence rule, 14
character of accused, 346–351 *And see*
    CHARACTER
circumstantial evidence, 14
complaint. *See* COMPLAINT
conditional admission, 24
conduct on other occasions, 18, 29
confession, 61, 482 *et seq. And see*
    CONFESSION
copy of document, 14, 60. *And see* COPY
declaration of intention, 35, 410 *et seq.*
    And see INTENTION
declarations. *See* DECLARATION
deposition, 197. *And see* DEPOSITION
dying declaration, 472–475 *And see*
    DYING DECLARATION
expert, 384 *et seq. And see* EXPERT
    EVIDENCE
facts affecting, 23, 58
    disclosed by inadmissible confes-
        sion, 278
general rule as to, 16
    right, 439–441
grounds of exclusion—
    danger of manufactured evidence, 22
    irrelevance, 18, 19, 22, 24
    multiplicity of issues, 20
    public policy, 265 *et seq. And see*
        AFFAIRS OF STATE ; PUBLIC POLICY

C

CAPACITY,
circumstantial evidence, as, 36
party to document, evidence as to, 537–
538
testamentary, 77, 83, 110

CELIBACY,
presumption as to, on death, 128

CERTIFICATE,
age, as evidence of, 560
birth, as evidence of, 456, 558–560
conviction, of, 564–566
death, as evidence of, 456, 558, 561
foreign register, as to, 558
marriage, as evidence of, 456, 558, 561–
563
paternity, as evidence of, 563

CHARACTER,
accused, of, evidence of, 18, 346–351
And see ACCUSED
bad, relevance of previous convictions,
317
defamation, in relation to, 351
defendant, of, in civil proceedings, 350–
351
disposition—
as part of, 368
meaning of, 309
particular method of crime, to, 313
reputation as proof of, 347
evidence of—
admissibility of, 18, 317
authorised by statute, 342, 345
civil cases, 350–351, 436–442
conduct on other occasions, 18, 310 *et
seq.*
criminal record of accused, 317
effect of, 350
excluded as irrelevant, 18, 312
general principles, 309
given against co-prisoner, 375
hall-mark principle, 332, 334
illustrations, 312
previous unrelated offence, 369–370
showing bad disposition, 313–317
good, evidence of, rebuttal of, 347 *et seq.*
relevance of previous
conviction, 345
homosexual propensity, 333, 337
imputations on, 370–375
incriminating material, possession of, 328
330, 335
loitering with intent, in relation to, 341
meaning of, 309, 346, 368
method of crime, evidence of, 310, 313,
332
previous acquittal, evidence as to, 364
conviction. *See* PREVIOUS CON-
VICTION
previous misconduct, evidence of—
accident, to disprove, 324–327
accused, given by, 338–339
alibi, to negative, 330–332
classification of cases, 324
continuing offences, 322–323

CHARACTER—*continued.*
previous misconduct, evidence of—
continued.
conviction, cross-examination of witness, 348, 350
evidence of, 316, 317
nature of offence, 369–370
crime of particular nature, 313–317
cross-examination as to credit, 340–341
homosexual acts, 333–337
identity, to prove, 330–332
ignorance, to rebut defence of, 327
innocent association, to rebut, 335–336
intention, to establish, 329
judge's discretion to exclude, 339–
340
mistake of fact, to rebut, 327
part of transaction in question, 319–
322
possession of incriminating material,
330
proof of coincidence, 324
system, 328–330
public nuisance, act involving, 323
rebuttal of defence, in, 318, 323–327,
349
repetitive or continuing nature, 323
res gestae, part of, 321–322
sexual acts, 314, 322, 332–333, 339
prosecutor, of, evidence of, 351, 370–375
reputation—
as part of, 367–368
evidence of, in civil cases, 350–351,
436–442
criminal cases, 347–350
pedigree, 437–439
public right, 439–442
rumour, cross-examination as to, 348
seduction, relevance in relation to, 352
spying, in relation to, 342
third parties, of, 351–352

CHILD. *See* INFANT

CIRCUMSTANTIAL EVIDENCE,
best evidence, rule as to, 14
corpus delicti proved by, 48
course of business as, 32
degrees of cogency of, 26
failure to furnish explanation, 42–46
habit, arising from, 34
identity, of, 51–52
knowledge or capacity as, 36
marriage, of, 51
meaning of, 8–9
motive or plan as, 34–35
opportunity, existence of, as, 36
res gestae as, 37
standards of comparison as, 37–39
subsequent facts as, 39

CIVIL PROCEEDINGS,
criminal proceedings compared with, 3–
4, 418 *et seq.*
hearsay rules. *See* HEARSAY

CLERGYMAN,
communication to, privilege, 256–258
marriage guidance counsellor, 257

DOCUMENT—*continued.*
computerised, 433–434
confidential, court's power to examine, 271
conclusiveness of—
 judicial records, 534
 rule as to, 533
 written contract, 534, 536
construction of, functions of judge and jury, 56
contract distinguished from memorandum, 539
copy of. *See* COPY
cross-examination, referred to in, 229,230
custom's officer's notes, 204
date of execution of, 532
definition of, 433
delivery of, proof of, 33
extrinsic evidence as to—
 admissible for identification, 520
 author's declarations of intention, 541
 blanks, completion of, 544
 capacity of parties, 537–538
 Civil Evidence Act, 1968, . . . 554–555
 collateral undertaking, 538
 consideration, 537
 contents of, 532
 contractual, 549
 equivocation, 542–543
 exception to hearsay rule. *See* HEARSAY
 existence of persons and things, 545
 general rule, 533, 540–554
 illegitimate children, intention to benefit, 547, 548
 inadmissible to make document, 544
  vary ordinary meaning, 546
 Law Reform Committee recommendations, 555
 meaning of words, normal, 546–547
 misdescription, to correct, 542, 549–551
 mistake, fraud and illegality, 536
 nature of transaction, 537
 proceedings between strangers, 540
 public register, 536
 rebutting certain presumptions, 553
 standards of interpretation, 541–542
 translation of terms, 545
 wills, 548, 549
foreign, proof of, 558
judicial notice of, 139, 140–141
logbook, 204
meaning of, 498
notice to admit, 140
official, judicial notice of, 139
parol evidence rule, 533, 539
party, in possession of, as admission, 448
policeman's notebook, 217
privileged, 249–251
private, production in Court, 163
produced by unsworn witness, 166
production contrary to public interest, 267 *et seq. And see* AFFAIRS OF STATE
 of, in Court, right to use as evidence, 229
proof of contents—
 admission by party, 522
 exclusion of oral evidence, 533

DOCUMENT—*continued.*
proof of contents—*continued.*
 extrinsic evidence as to, 533
 general rule, 519
 hearsay, 426
 illustrations, 519–520
 original, production of, 521
 secondary evidence, 522
proof of execution—
 attestation, 530
 handwriting, 528–530. *And see* HANDWRITING
 judicial notice, 139
 necessity to call witness, 530–531
 presumption as to, 139, 531–532
 when required, 527
proper custody, meaning of, 531
public, 435, 454 *et seq. And see* PUBLIC DOCUMENT
refreshing memory from, 204–207
 civil cases, 207, 425
secondary evidence of, 522–523. *And see* COPY
self-corroboration, 208
stamp duty on, 532–533
statement in, as evidence, *See* STATEMENT
unsworn witness, produced by, 166

DOCUMENTARY EVIDENCE,
meaning of, 13–14

DOMICILE,
change of, standard of proof, 104

DRUNKEN DRIVING,
English and Irish law differ on, 390–391
opinion evidence and, 390–391

DYING DECLARATION,
admission as evidence, 214, 472
Australian view on, 65
competence of declarant, 475
English view on, 65
expectation of death, 470–471
 judge's decision, 61
illustrations, 472
rationale of principle, 473
relative to cause of death, 473
trial for murder or manslaughter, 473
voir dire, and, 65

E

EQUITABLE PRESUMPTION,
evidence to rebut, 553–554

ESTOPPEL,
acquittal or conviction, by, 297
agreement, by, 302
ambiguity, prevented by, 305–306
burden of proof, effect on, 294
conduct, by, doctrine of, 301
 duty of case, 305
 limits on, 305–306
criminal cases, in relation to, 297–299
deed, by, 299–301
identity of issues, 291–294
issue, 289–294, 298–299

F

FACT IN ISSUE,
meaning of, 4
right of jury to determine, 69
statement as, 410–412
where identical with preliminary fact, 60–
61

FACTUM PROBANDUM,
meaning of, 8

FACTUM PROBANS,
meaning of, 8

FAIRNESS,
civil cases, 30–31
criminal trial, at, 29–30
judicial discretion as to, 29–30

FILM,
use of, as evidence, 13, 16

FINGERPRINTS,
admissibility of, as evidence, rules
governing, 46
evidence of identity by, 564
judicial discretion relating to, 46
Magistrates Court, power to order, 46

FOREIGN LAW,
determination of, function of judge, 57
expert evidence as to, 368, 558–559
judicial notice of, 557
proof of, 556–559
question tending to incriminate witness
under, 246
validity of marriage under, 562

FRAUD,
document voidable for, 536
evidence of previous, 329
judgment, effect on, 286

G

GENERAL RIGHT, 439–441. *And see*
PUBLIC RIGHT

GIFT,
statement accompanying, evidence of,
411, 413

H

HABIT,
presumption arising from, 34

HANDWRITING,
comparison as evidence of, 39, 529
expert evidence of, 240, 385, 529
non-expert opinion as to, 528–529
testimonial evidence of, 528

HEARSAY,
admissibility, 421 *et seq.* 449
admission as, 408, 428, 435, 445, 451,
475–481. *And see* ADMISSION

HEARSAY—*continued.*
age, proof by, 560
agent, 429, 451
agreed statement of facts, 499
bad reputation for veracity, evidence of,
based on, 238
civil proceedings, in, 421 *et seq.*
co-defendant, 428
computerised records, 433–434
confession, 482–495. *And see* CONFES-
SION
criminal proceedings, in, 460 *et seq.*
criticisms of rule, 442–444
divorce, undefended, 430
exceptions, 421
first hand, 221, 422–431
former proceedings, statements in, 428
general right, 439–441
implied assertions, 430
judicial discretion, 421, 423, 424, 425,
427
leave, 423–424
magistrates' courts, 419
meaning of, 6–8
notice, 422–423, 425, 427
operative words, 410–412
oral, 419
original evidence distinguished from 7
meaning of, 410
pedigree, 437–439
previous statement of—
non-witness, 425–431
witness, 422–425
probate actions, 429
proof of evidence, 425–427
public right, 439–442
records, in, 421, 431–442
relevant, admission of, 25
reputation, evidence, of, 436–442
res inter alios acta in relation to, 53, 415
rule against—
attestation as evidence of execution,
530
compared with evidence of opinion,
385, 392
exceptions to—
admission, 444 *et seq.*, 475 *et seq.*
And see ADMISSION
age, evidence of, 497
ancient document, 414–415
confession, 482 *et seq. And see*
CONFESSION
declaration against interest, 418,
461 *et seq. And see*
STATEMENT
as to public right, 418
And see STATEMENT
in course of duty, 469 *et
seq. And see* STATE-
MENT
of intention, 510 *et seq.*
And see INTENTION
dying declaration, 7, 64, 418, 472
et seq.
And see DYING DECLARATION
handwriting, proof of, 528
hearsay upon hearsay, 417, 457, 475

M

MAGISTRATE,
civil proceedings and, 68
criminal proceedings and, 68
death of, use of depositions after, 201
deposition taken by, use at trial, 198,
And see DEPOSITION
proof of judgment of, 564
submission of no case to, 68

MALICIOUS PROSECUTION,
reasonableness of proceedings, 57–58

MANOR,
court rolls as evidence, 458

MANSLAUGHTER,
dying declaration as evidence at trial,
472, 473. *And see* DYING DECLARA-
TION

MARITAL PRIVILEGE,
communications between spouses, 258–
259
marital intercourse, 260

MARRIAGE,
abroad, proof of, 57, 558, 562
certificate of, as evidence, 455, 562
deathbed, 121
evidence as to intercourse during, 116
forcible, 148
foreign, legality of, 562
formal validity, 120–121
presumption of—
cohabitation, arising from, 119, 122–
124
essential validity, 119, 121–122
formal validity, 104, 110, 113, 119–121
repute, arising from, 119, 122–124
when raised, 119
proof of, 51, 57, 561–563
ship, on, proof of, 562

MASTER AND SERVANT,
admission by servant, 452
confession of servant induced by master,
486

MATRIMONIAL CAUSES,
Act of 1973, 130–131
adultery, corroboration of admission of,
181, 183–184
Blyth v. *Blyth*, taken as authority on,
103–104
corroboration, absence of, rules governing, in, 183–184
dissolution of marriage, death presumed,
130
proof as a preponderance of probability,
on, 103–104
standard of proof in, 100–104
without prejudice negotiations between
spouses, 262–263

MEDICAL PRACTITIONER, *See*
DOCTOR

MENTAL DEFICIENCY. *See* INSANITY

MERCANTILE CUSTOM,
judicial notice of, 138

MICROFILMS,
evidence, as, 404

MILITARY COURT,
accused tried by, 484

MINISTER,
objection by, to producing document,
271 *et seq. And see* AFFAIRS OF
STATE

MISCONDUCT,
judicial discretion, prejudicial evidence
relating to, 31
other occasions, on, evidence of, 310 *et
seq. And see* CHARACTER

MISTAKE,
document void for, 536
negatived by proof of system, 327

MOTIVE,
circumstantial evidence, as, 34
system as evidence of, 328–330

MURDER,
dying declaration as evidence at trial,
472, 473. *And see* DYING DE-
CLARATION

N

NATIONAL SECURITY,
exclusion of evidence on ground of, 267–
268
minister's decision as to excluding evidence, 272

NEGATIVE AVERMENT,
obligation to prove, 83, 88
statutory proviso, in relation to, 89–90

NEGLIGENCE,
comparison as evidence of, 37
estoppel by, 304–305
operation of, in claim based on,
291
evidence of previous conduct to disprove,
327
opinion of witness as to, 389
presumption of, 43–44, 131–134
proof of in general, 134

NEW TRIAL,
application for, 71

NO CASE,
submission of, civil cases, 67
criminal cases, 67–68

NORTHERN IRELAND,
proof of law of, 556, 557
marriage in, 562

NOT GUILTY,
plea of, effect of, in criminal cases, 5

NOTICE,
to admit document, 140
fact, 140

WITNESS—*continued.*

person interested in proceedings as, 145–146

previous conviction of, informing Court, 375

question as to, 235, 349. *And see* PRE-VIOUS CON-VICTION

statement, of, evidence of, 7, 226–238. *And see* PRE-VIOUS STATEMENT

privilege. *See* PRIVILEGE OF WITNESS

probation officer as, 262

WITNESS—*continued.*

producing document not on oath, 166

prohibition on impeaching party's own, 220

refreshing memory, 202–207, 425

self-incrimination, protection against, 242–248. *And see* PRIVILEGE OF WITNESS

sovereign as, 162–163

spouse as, 147–149, 154–162 *And see* SPOUSE

subornation of, 235–236, 446

unfavourable, 220 *et seq. And see* UN-FAVOURABLE WITNESS

untraceable, 427

PRINTED IN GREAT BRITAIN BY OFFSET LITHOGRAPHY BY
BILLING AND SONS LTD., GUILDFORD AND LONDON